READING ROOM

Click inside a map of the United States or the entire world to access your choice of local, national, or international business news.

D1517150

National News

International News

SELF-ASSESSMENT TEST

Select from a number of popular self-assessment questionnaires. These instruments will enable users to evaluate and learn about their own interests and skills while receiving broad guidance and practical advice.

BUY ONLINE

Go to the Harcourt online store to purchase Study Guides, e-books, videos, and more.

ONLINE QUIZZING

Prepare for your next big exam using online quizzes that contain true/false and multiple-choice questions for each chapter in the text.

Look to the inside back cover for additional online resources for instructors

Contemporary Business

Tenth Edition

Contemporary Business

Tenth Edition

Louis E. Boone
University of South Alabama

David L. Kurtz
University of Arkansas

SOUTH-WESTERN ™
THOMSON LEARNING

Australia • Canada • Mexico • Singapore • Spain
United Kingdom • United States

SOUTH-WESTERN

★

™

THOMSON LEARNING

Contemporary Business, 10e

Louis E. Boone and David L. Kurtz

Publisher:
Mike Roche

Acquisitions Editor:
Tracy Morse

Market Strategist:
Beverly Dunn

Developmental Editor:
Kerri Jones

Project Editor:
Andrea Archer

Manufacturing Coordinator:
Diane Lohman

Compositor:
GAC Indianapolis

Printer:
RR Donnelley, Willard

ISBN: 0-03-033226-5

To the 3.2 million students around the globe who began their business careers
using *Contemporary Business* in their classes, making it the most widely used
business text in history,
and
To the memory of
Helen H. Boone
C. Reed Kurtz
James F. Kurtz

PREFACE

Welcome to *Contemporary Business*—a detailed road map to the twists, turns, chills, and spills of the modern marketplace. Today's students will soon be in the driver's seat to their own careers, setting their own paces, mapping their own courses. But there's a lot of new ground to cover between here and there. So buckle up. *Contemporary Business* puts students in the driver's seat now, giving them practice negotiating real-world business bumps, hills, and thrills. It's a ride students won't soon forget. It's a ride that will put them well on their way to real-world business adventure.

The 21st century business world is bursting with opportunity—and changes and challenges and new rules and innovations and. . . .The list is endless. Suffice it to say business has reached a new level of energy and excitement. So has *Contemporary Business*.

The new tenth edition of *Contemporary Business* mirrors today's dynamic business world like no text before it, giving readers an up-close and personal experience grappling with real business issues — so close they can almost hear the roars of Wall Street, feel the intense rivalry among leaner and keener competitors, smell the global possibilities, see technology revolutionizing business practice, and taste the satisfaction of an entrepreneurial triumph. *Contemporary Business, 10/e,* truly captures the spirit of business in action—and you won't miss a beat.

The latest edition integrates technology into every aspect of the text and package. Its practical approach enables students to immediately begin applying business concepts to their personal lives. A real-world emphasis offers students valuable insight into real business at work.

Modern-day business practice is nothing less than exhilarating. And no one harnesses the thrill of business in action like *Contemporary Business, 10/e.*

TEAM EFFORTS

One of the factors that makes *Contemporary Business, 10/e,* so unique is the vast amount of input that was invested into this new edition. First, there's personal experience. As educators, we daily encounter the needs and struggles of students as well as instructors. In addition, as we work through each revision of our text, we value feedback from past users of our books and reviewers of our manuscripts.

Now, for the tenth edition, we've expanded our "revision team" even further.

Contemporary Business, 10/e, is the beneficiary of an extensive research and review effort. In a massive marketing research initiative, we commissioned hundreds of surveys and conducted numerous focus groups involving instructors (users of *Contemporary Business* as well as competing texts), course coordinators, and department heads from across the country. We had one simple goal in mind: determine precisely what students and instructors wanted in their introduction to business text.

To everyone who participated in this effort, we—along with instructors and students worldwide—offer heartfelt thanks. As you can see, your involvement truly has made *Contemporary Business* a better book.

ACTIONS SPEAK LOUDER THAN WORDS

As with every edition of *Contemporary Business,* we take instructor and student feedback seriously. Very seriously! In fact, the results of our surveys and focus group studies can be found directly in the pages of the tenth edition, where we put your best ideas into action:

- **MORE SUCCINCT!** The tenth edition is a full chapter shorter than the ninth edition.
- **EARLY COVERAGE!** "Jump-Starting Your Business Career" has been moved to the front of the textbook. It offers practical insight to help students prepare for a successful business career.
- **NEW!** "A Guide to Your Personal Finances"—a separate module shrink-wrapped with each new book—demonstrates how the text's coverage of business financial decisions also applies to personal finance. A valuable resource students can reference for years to come, the module includes worksheets and exercises that help students plan their personal finances and gain experience in the stock market.
- **EXPANDED!** Our thoroughly revamped support package includes a Test Bank developed by the authors, an all-new PowerPoint CD-ROM created for instructors, and a new Student Companion CD packaged with every text.

KEY FEATURES

Like the editions before it, *Contemporary Business*, *10/e,* is packed with innovation, scoring a perfect "ten" with its lively features:

- **E-EXCELLENT!** Picking up where the ninth edition left off, *Contemporary Business*, *10/e,* has an even stronger technology emphasis. In-depth, practical coverage of technology begins early and is thoroughly integrated throughout the entire text and package. The book's major themes include technology and e-business.
- **NEW!** Chapter 7, "Electronic Commerce: The Internet and Online Business," gets students up to speed fast in the quick-paced, high-powered e-business arena.
- **EXPANDED!** Chapter 17, "Using Technology to Manage Information," focuses on internal information management issues, covering such emerging business technology options as application service providers, intranets, decision support systems, and protection from computer crime. It also discusses the problems that led to the demise of hundreds of dot.com high flyers during the early years of the 21st century and the success of traditional brick-and-mortar firms as they added online presence.
- **NEW!** Two "Clicks and Mortar" boxes in every chapter give insight into the practices of e-companies along with the workings of traditional brick-and-mortar firms.
- **NEW!** "Business Hits and Misses" boxes detail the experiences of actual businesses that have hit the mark, as well as those who have dropped the ball.
- **EXPANDED!** Introduced early and integrated throughout, the text's underlying entrepreneurial theme encourages students to look at issues from the perspective of business owners. Part II, "Starting and Growing Your Business," gives students practical insight into the most critical stages of business ownership and explores the high failure rate of new businesses and strategies for success.

In addition to the many innovations, *Contemporary Business* also includes the most popular features from prior editions—all completely revised and updated for the technologically advanced tenth edition:

- "Nothing but Net" end-of-chapter application exercises plug students into the Internet, sharpening their surfing skills and linking them to additional resources.

- Chapter-opening vignettes spotlight companies to which students can easily relate, such as Nantucket Nectars, Patagonia, and Razorfish, for example.

- Continuing to lead the market in its emphasis on ethics and social responsibility, the tenth edition introduces the topics within the first few pages of the text and then covers them in depth in Chapter 2, "Achieving Business Success by Demonstrating Ethical Behavior and Social Responsibility."

- The "Solving an Ethical Controversy" boxes featured in each chapter will incite lively classroom debate with their candid look at controversial issues.

- International coverage begins early and is integrated throughout, giving the text a truly global perspective. Two entire chapters are devoted to global business issues: Chapter 3, "Economic Challenges Facing Global and Domestic Business," and Chapter 4, "Competing in Global Markets."

- An entire chapter is devoted to teams and effective communication, reflecting the increasing emphasis in the workplace. Chapter 10, "Improving Performance through Empowerment, Teamwork, and Communication," spotlights motivation, employee empowerment, work teams, special-purpose problem-solving teams, cross-functional teams, team development, conflict resolution, oral and written communication, verbal and nonverbal communication, and communication technology.

- Quality, customer value, and relationship management discussions begin in Chapter 1 and are integrated throughout as the text illustrates how total quality management can be applied throughout the organization, how to use quality and customer satisfaction to create added value, along with the importance of employee involvement, empowerment, training, and teamwork to achieve world-class quality and—ultimately—customer satisfaction.

NEW CONTENT

Completely current, *Contemporary Business, 10/e,* includes the most up-to-date information available on issues important to 21st century businesspeople. Every example is new. The text is as up-to-the-minute as 21st century publishing will allow—and the frequently updated Boone and Kurtz Web site picks up where printed material leaves off, bringing instructors and students late-breaking news and updates to text materials.

- Deregulation and the California Power Crisis
- Reducing Drug Prices to Third-World AIDS Sufferers
- Do You Have What It Takes to Be an Entrepreneur?
- How Dot.coms Turned into Dot.com Bombs
- Ford/Firestone Recall Crisis
- Earthquake in Seattle
- What Should Sponsors Do When Tragedy Strikes? (NASCAR and the death of Dale Earnhardt)
- AOL/Time Warner Merger
- Development of Wireless Communications

- Measuring Web Surfers
- The Growing Shortage of Workers in the U.S.
- Why So Many Immigrants Become Entrepreneurs
- Free Trade, the World Trade Organization, and the Seattle Riots
- Taxing Internet Transactions
- Where the Federal Budget Surplus Came from—and What to Do with It

PEDAGOGICAL FEATURES

Premier Pedagogy

Setting the standard with each new edition, Boone and Kurtz continue to emphasize more outcome-based and skill-oriented pedagogical features.

- Under Pressure: Ford and Firestone Face Recall Crisis (Chapter 2)
- Can Coke Go Local in Europe? (Chapter 4)
- Organized Labor and the Global Economy (Chapter 11)

- 7-Eleven Gives Convenience Stores a New Meaning (Chapter 4)
- WeddingChannel.com Wants You to Say "I Do" (Chapter 6)
- Williams-Sonoma Cooks Up Relationship Marketing on the Web (Chapter 13)

- Napster and MP3 Aren't Music to Everyone's Ears (Chapter 2)
- Going Global Isn't So Easy for Internet Companies (Chapter 4)
- E-tailers Learn the Value of the Question, "May I Help You?" (Chapter 9)

RESOURCE PACKAGE

Innovations in the *Contemporary Business* resource package remain unrivaled. The tenth edition includes our most comprehensive collection of resource materials to date.

Inspired by feedback from previous users and participants in our recent research, the package gives instructors faster, easier access to a vast array of teaching tools, and it equips students with a wealth of hands-on, interactive, exciting learning resources. It truly offers something for every learning and teaching style.

20 ALL NEW! Videos

Professionally written and produced, this completely new video package was custom created especially for *Contemporary Business, 10/e.* Filmed during 2000–2001, the videos provide intriguing, relevant, and current real-world insight into the modern marketplace.

Tied directly to chapter concepts, the videos highlight how real-world organizations struggle with the challenges of 21st century business. Each video is supported by a written case with application questions. The videos feature the following organizations:

- Chapter 1: The Geek Squad
- Chapter 2: Equal Exchange
- Chapter 3: Burton Snowboards
- Chapter 4: L.A. Eyeworks
- Chapter 5: Corey and Co.
- Chapter 6: Annie's Homegrown
- Chapter 7: Terra Lycos
- Chapter 8: SAS Institute
- Chapter 9: Merrill Lynch
- Chapter 10: Dunkin' Donuts
- Chapter 11: Writer's Guild of America
- Chapter 12: *Vibe* Magazine
- Chapter 13: WBRU Radio Station
- Chapter 14: Stride Rite
- Chapter 15: Ipswich Shellfish
- Chapter 16: Oxygen Media
- Chapter 17: IBM
- Chapter 18: Uno Restaurant
- Chapter 19: Tweeter Home Entertainment
- Chapter 20: Morgan Stanley

Videos are available in traditional format, as well as digital format on CD-ROMs for instructors who want to incorporate them into an online Web course.

NEW! Four-Part Continuing Student-Oriented Video Case

This unique four-part series featuring The Geek Squad is an excellent review of topics covered in four of the parts in the text as it challenges students to apply text concepts to real-world issues. The Geek Squad demonstrates the concepts of entrepreneurship, management and leadership, marketing strategy, and finance as they relate to the success of a small computer fix-it shop.

NEW! FUBU Video

This all-new, custom-produced video gives students the inside track to today's entrepreneurs succeeding in a competitive marketplace. The video details the story of FUBU, the young African American entrepreneurs whose modest beginnings include making clothing in their homes before skyrocketing to the top of the fashion trade. The video proves that entrepreneurship is one career path in which age doesn't matter—and the sky's the limit if you find the right niche, product, audience, strategy, and so on.

This high-energy video is included with the Continuing Case Video that is available kitted with the text. In addition, the Media Instructor's Manual includes a summary of the video, as well as worksheets that instructors can assign to their students.

:C NEW! *Contemporary Business* Cue Cat Ready

Developed by Digital:Convergence™, this new technology connects to any home computer and, with the sweep of a bar code, gives students instant access to supporting Web sites and online quizzing. Linked to key conceptual topics discussed in the text, these cues are included in a booklet created specifically for *Contemporary Business*. The booklet is available with the text.

EXPANDED! Boone and Kurtz Web site

Completely revamped, our robust site delivers sundry resources right to students' and instructors' fingertips. Many of our improvements were based on suggestions directly from students and instructors. This interactive site gives students hands-on experience applying the Internet as a business tool, as well as helps them develop important life skills.

Updated regularly, the *Contemporary Business* Web site is a reservoir of information (enough that it could be used as the foundation for a distance-learning course). Just a few of the exciting features follow:

- **NEW! Monthly e-newsletters** supply instructors with late-breaking examples to use with the text.

- **NEW! "Gimme an A" Testing Service** gives instructors and students access (through the Harcourt Web site) to a database that enables them to create quizzes or be quizzed based on the topic they choose. The database of questions is so big that students can take multiple quizzes on one topic and never take the same quiz.

- **NEW! Student Online quizzing** feature includes multiple-choice and true/false questions that are specific to *Contemporary Business* chapter content, and scoring is interactive.

- **NEW! Class Act Instructor course management system** is available for qualified adopters and incorporates several features into one database, including Syllabus Generator, Gradebook, Class Messaging, and Quizzing functions. Instructors can select the features they want to import into their current systems or opt to use the entire class management system. For example, the quizzing feature can be manipulated and a computerized test bank imported, enabling instructors to create their own online quizzes and tests.

- **NEW! Instructor ancillaries** are posted on the Web site (password protected) for those who want to download any of the package in electronic form.

- **UPDATED!** The easy-to-navigate *Business Topics* site connects users to topic-specific publication links, trends and forecasts, data, company profiles, general articles, tools, exercises, and much more. Each topic site links instructors to teaching resources, bibliographies of articles related to text material, ideas on incorporating the Internet into the classroom, and more.

- **NEW!** This informative site offers students tips on in-the-office etiquette as well as international conduct and how to adapt to different customs.

- The *Reading Room* links users to business journals, daily newspapers, magazines, and marketing publications across the country and around the world.

- **NEW!** Professors are invited to visit the *Bulletin Board* to share ideas and suggestions about the exciting world of *Contemporary Business*.

- The **Web-Based Stock Market Game** helps students develop investment skills, teaching them how to access financial resources so they can make educated financial decisions. Students compete with classmates to achieve the greatest gain in stock value.

Stock Market Game

NEW! *Contemporary Business* e-Book

Trading printed pages for electronic ones, the e-book offers an electronic version of the entire text. With amazing clarity, the e-book allows users to view electronically in single- or double-page layouts, zoom in and out, add bookmarks, highlight, annotate, search text, and more. Available in both IBM compatible and Mac versions.

Instructor's Resource Manual

Renowned for its comprehensive, user-friendly innovations, the *Contemporary Business Instructor's Resource Manual (IRM)* has been expanded. Offering support for first-time instructors, longtime instructors, and everyone in between, each chapter is packed with a wealth of helpful resources, including the following:

- Changes from the previous edition
- Suggested class schedules
- Annotated learning goals
- Lecture outlines
- Answers to "Clicks and Mortar" questions
- Answers to "Business Hits and Misses" questions
- Answers to "Solving an Ethical Controversy" questions
- Answers to review questions
- Answers to critical-thinking questions
- "Nothing but Net" Teaching Notes
- Answers to video case questions
- Supplemental cases
- Team-building exercises
- Experiential exercises

- Projects
- Guest speaker suggestions
- Term paper suggestions
- Tips for teaching a distance-learning course

The *IRM* is available in printed and electronic formats.

ALL NEW! Instructor's PowerPoint CD-ROM Presentation Software

Created by Milton Pressley of the University of New Orleans, this powerful but easy-to-use multimedia presentation tool energizes classroom lectures—and students. It includes virtually all of the illustrations, tables, and charts from the text, along with television commercials and such supplementary material as additional print ads and experiential exercises. Organized by chapter, all the text's major definitions, topics, and concepts are outlined along with completely new material from outside sources.

Instructors can use this CD-ROM as is, or they can custom design their own multimedia classroom presentations by deleting (or hiding) unwanted slides and/or altering existing slides. Those whose presentation computers are connected to the Web can even link to specially selected Web sites by clicking on the WWW icon featured on many of the slides.

ALL NEW! Student Companion CD-ROM

Free with every textbook, this media-rich CD-ROM is a student version of the PowerPoint Presentation. It outlines key concepts, incorporates study questions and additional Web exercises into each chapter, reinforces figures and tables from the text, provides links to Web sites and Web exercises, uses additional print ads and television commercials to further illustrate text discussions, and includes the entire glossary from the text.

A unique "Technology and Teamwork Exercises in Contemporary Business" module provides practical tips and a variety of Web exercises to help students sharpen their navigation skills. The module focuses on the fast-paced advances in technology and their impact on business in the 21st century, giving students practice applying chapter concepts to real-world experiences.

ALL NEW! Media Instructor's Manual

Videos, Web materials, and our PowerPoint Presentation capabilities give instructors a plethora of options for lively, media-rich lectures and classroom presentations. And this comprehensive resource, the *Media Instructor's Manual (MediaIM)*, helps them pull it all together with ease. For example, for each chapter video and continuing video case, the *Media IM* includes teaching objectives, lists of chapter concepts spotlighted in the videos, outlines of the videos, answers to in-text video case questions, answers to the questions included at the end of each video, experiential exercises, and multiple-choice questions. It also includes lecture notes and exercises to accompany the FUBU video.

All NEW! Transparency Acetates with Teaching Notes

More than 200 new full-color overhead transparency acetates illustrate key concepts discussed throughout text—including text figures, ads, and tables—along with a host of ads not included in the book. A complete set of teaching notes is integrated into the detailed lecture outlines and included for the acetates.

COMPLETELY REVISED! Test Bank

We wrote the book on *Contemporary Business*—and the *Test Bank*. In our focus group studies, instructors made the case for a *Test Bank* developed by the textbook authors. We deliver with our revised and updated *Test Bank* of over 4,000 questions, each one keyed to a chapter learning goal, text page number, and type of question (knowledge or application). Questions include multiple choice, true/false, and a short essay for each learning goal. Mini-cases with multiple-choice questions and critical-thinking questions emphasize the importance of the concepts presented in each chapter. Questions vary in level of difficulty, giving instructors a wide variety from which to choose.

Computerized Test Bank

This new and improved version of EXAMaster works with the latest version of Windows and Windows NT operating systems. The CD-ROMs include online testing capabilities, a grade book, and much more.

Available in IBM compatible format (or Macintosh version upon request), the computerized version of the printed test bank enables instructors to preview and edit test questions, as well as add their own questions. The tests and answer keys also can be printed in "scrambled" formats.

Study Guide

An invaluable tool for helping students master business concepts, the *Study Guide* includes chapter outlines, experiential exercises, self-quizzes, cases, short-answer questions, and crossword puzzles for each chapter. Solutions appear at the end of the guide.

ALL NEW! Personal Finance Module

"A Guide to Your Personal Finances" will be shrink-wrapped with each copy of the textbook, equipping students with personal finance tools they can immediately apply to their own lives. The module's worksheets help students plan their personal finances, providing a relevant resource they can reference for years to come. Details on the Stock Market Game is also included.

Optional Modules

Offering additional insight into key business topics, several short modules are available separately or packaged with the text, giving instructors additional flexibility in customizing their introduction to business course:

- **Business Plan and Entrepreneurship Module:** The Internet continues to fuel the red-hot entrepreneurial sector, but as in any industry, promising dot.coms can quickly become dot.bombs—especially without a detailed business plan. And failed ventures are commonplace in every industry. But this insightful reference supplies aspiring entrepreneurs with a toolbox of business resources, helping them plan for success.

- **Performance Module:** In the real world, the bottom line is performance. Employees, managers, top-level executives, entire companies—every aspect of the firm is evaluated on performance. This unique module takes an in-depth look at performance issues, providing insightful material to reinforce class discussions.

- **Hispanic American Module:** Reflecting the increasing number of U.S. Hispanic-owned companies as well as burgeoning opportunities with Mexico-based operations, this module includes frequently used Spanish business terms, highlights contributions from Hispanic American business owners and executives, features leadership success stories, discusses the impact of NAFTA and GATT, and explores current opportunities for Hispanic American businesses, employment trends, and demographics.

- **African American Module:** Mirroring a more diverse marketplace and the increasingly powerful African American segment, this module explores opportunities for African Americans in the 21st century business environment, analyzes employment trends and demographics, features African American business role models and leaders, details entrepreneurial success stories, highlights black history, and spotlights contributions by African Americans as they relate to U.S. business. This module was extensively reviewed by leading African American academic and business leaders.

- **Quality Module:** Instead of a narrow conception of quality as affecting only production processes, *Contemporary Business* illustrates how total quality management can be applied throughout the entire organization. Employee involvement, empowerment, training, and teamwork are vital to achieve world-class quality—which promotes customer satisfaction.

- **Diversity Assessment:** Future (and current) business leaders must be well-versed in cultural diversity issues. Providing additional coverage for instructors who want to further emphasize cultural diversity, this module spotlights key issues in the diverse 21st century marketplace.

Discovering Your Business Career CD-ROM

Through this interactive multimedia program, students explore business career options like accounting, corporate financial management, information systems, risk management/insurance, retail bank management, sales, store operations, and many more. Full of practical insight, the CD-ROM walks students through the entire career-search process, from assessing their compatibility with different careers and determining the depth of their interest to effectively implementing a job search strategy.

The CD-ROM also includes Eric Sandburg's landmark career-planning software, which is based on the work of John Crystal, the major contributor to *What Color Is Your Parachute?* by Richard N. Bolles. This widely popular program guides students through all stages of the career-development process, from assessing professional skills to creating résumés and cover letters.

ACKNOWLEDGMENTS

No doubt, the tenth is our best edition of *Contemporary Business* to date. As we've said before, it's nothing short of a group effort. Many, many people offered suggestions and contributions to make this market leader even stronger. Every contribution made a difference.

Thanks again to all those colleagues who participated in our 16 focus groups or completed the survey upon which the focus groups were based. The focus group participants included the following:

Kenneth Anderson
Mott Community College

Donald B. Armstrong
Mesa College

Nathaniel Barber
Winthrop University

Alan Bardwick
Community College of Aurora

Keith Batman
Cayuga Community College

Daniel Biddlecom
Erie Community College/North Campus

Joseph Billingere
Oxnard College

Larry Blenke
Sacramento City College

Paula E. Bobrowski
SUNY Oswego

Charlane Bomrad Held
Onandaga Community College

Brenda Bradford
Missouri Baptist College

Barney Carlson
Yuba College

Maria Carmen Guerrero-Caldero
Oxnard College

Bonnie Chavez
Santa Barbara City College

Felipe Chia
Harrisburg Area Community College

Marie Comstock
Allan Hancock College

Rachna Condos
American River College

Ronald C. Cooley
South Suburban College

Suzanne Counte
Jefferson College

Pam Crader
Jefferson College

Dana D'Angelo
Drexel University

Dean Danielson
San Joaquin College

David DeCook
Arapahoe Community College

Richard L. Drury
Northern Virginia Area Community College/Annandale

Linda Durkin
Delaware County Community College

Lance J. Edwards
Otero Junior College

William Ewald
Concordia University

Carol Fasso
Jamestown Community College

Jan Feldbauer
Austin Community College

Sandie Ferriter
Harford Community College

Steven H. Floyd
Manatee Community College

Nancy M. Fortunato
Bryant and Stratton

John G. Foster Jr.
Montgomery College/Rockville

William D. Foster
Fontbonne College

Arlen Gastineau
Valencia Community College/West Campus

Bob Googins
Shasta Community College

Robert Gora
Catawba Valley Community College

Gary Greene
Manatee Community College

Blaine Greenfield
Bucks County Community College

Michael Hamberger
Northern Virginia Area Community College/Annandale

Neal Hannon
Bryant College

Chuck Henry
Coastline Community College

Thomas Herbek
Monroe Community College

Joseph Ho
College of Alameda

Alice J. Holt
Benedict College

Kathy Irwin
Catawba Valley Community College

Ralph Jagodka
Mount San Antonio College

Chris Jelepis
Drexel University

Don Kelley
Francis Marion University

B.L. Koblin
Pasadena City College

Carl Kovelowski
Mercer Community College

Ken Lafave
Mount San Jacinto College

Rita Lambrecht
Northeastern Junior College

Bruce Leppine
Delta College

Jim Locke
Northern Virginia Area Community College/Annandale

Kathleen J. Lorencz
Oakland County Community College

John Mack
Salem State College

Paul Martin
Aims College

Lori Martynowicz
Bryant and Stratton

Michael Matukonis
SUNY Oneonta

Virginia Mayes
Montgomery College/Germantown

Joseph E. McAloon
Fitchburg State College

Michael McLane
University of Texas, San Antonio

Ina Midkiff
Austin Community College

Rebecca Mihelcic
Howard Community College

Richard Miller
Harford Community College

Joseph Mislivec
Central Michigan University

Kimberly K. Montney
Kellogg Community College

Gail Moran
Harper College

Kenneth R. Nail
Pasco-Hernando Community College

Joe Newton
Buffalo State College

Janet Nichols
Northeastern University

Frank Nickels
Pasco-Hernando Community College

Sharon Nickels
St. Petersburg Junior College

Nnamdi L. Osakwe
Livingstone College

Tibor Osztreicher
Baltimore City Community College

George Otto
Truman College

Thomas Paczkowski
Cayuga Community College

Jack Partlow
Northern Virginia Area Community College/Annandale

Jeff Penley
Catawba Valley Community College

Robert Pollero
Anne Arundel Community College

Alton J. Purdy
Solano Community College

Surat P. Puri
Barber Scottia College

Angela Rabatin
Prince George's Community College

Linda Reynolds
Sacramento City College

Brenda Rhodes
Northeastern Junior College

Merle Rhodes
Morgan Community College

Pollis Robertson
Kellogg Community College

Robert Ross
Drexel University

Benjamin Sackmary
Buffalo State College

Nick Sarantakes
Austin Community College

Lewis Schlossinger
Community College of Aurora

Leon J. Singleton
Santa Monica College

Jeff Slater
North Shore Community College

Candy Smith
Folsom Lake College

Solomon A. Solomon
Community College of Rhode Island

R. Southall
Laney College

Bill Syversten
Fresno City College

Thomas Szezurek
Delaware County Community College

Daryl Taylor
Pasadena City College

John H. Teter
St. Petersburg Junior College

Gary Thomas
Anne Arundel Community College

Michael Thomas
Henry Ford Community College

Frank Titlow
St. Petersburg Junior College

Ariah Ullman
SUNY Binghamton

Sal Veas
Santa Monica College

Steven Wade
Santa Clara University

Dennis Wahler
San Jacinto Evergreen Community College District

Timothy Weaver
Moorpark College

Richard Wertz
Concordia University

Darcelle D. White
Eastern Michigan University

Jean G. Wicks
Bornie State University

Dave Wiley
Anne Arundel Community College

Richard J. Williams
Santa Clara University

Marth Zennis
Jamestown Community College

Earlier reviewers of *Contemporary Business* include:

Alison Adderly-Pitman
Brevard Community College

David Alexander
Angelo State University

Charles Armstrong
Kansas City Kansas Community College

James Leon Barton, Jr.
Auburn University

Robb Bay
Community College of Southern Nevada

Charles Beem
Bucks County Community College

Carol Bibly
Triton College

Steven E. Bradley
Austin Community College

Willie Caldwell
Houston Community College

Eugene J. Calvasina
Auburn University

Gerald Calvasina
Auburn University

Richard Calvasina
Auburn University

Rowland Chidomere
Winston-Salem State University

Robert Cox
Salt Lake Community College

Norman B. Cregger
Central Michigan University

Kathy Daruty
Los Angeles Pierce College

Jodson Faurer
Metropolitan State College at Denver

Blane Franckowiak
Tarrant County Community College

Edward Friese
Okaloosa—Walton Community College

Milton Glisson
North Carolina AT&T State University

Don Gordon
Illinois Central College

Stephen W. Griffin
Tarrant County Community College

Annette L. Halpin
Beaver College

Doug Hearth
University of Arkansas

Douglas Heeter
Ferris State University

Paul Hegele
Elgin Community College

Tom Heslin
Indiana University, Bloomington

Nathan Himelstein
Essex County College

Ava Honan
Auburn University

Vince Howe
University of North Carolina, Wilmington

Eva M. Hyatt
Appalachian State University

Gloria M. Jackson
San Antonio College

Steven R. Jennings
Highland Community College

Geraldine Jolly
Barton College

Dave Jones
La Salle University

Bill Kindsfather
Tarrant County Community College

Charles C. Kitzmiller
Indian River Community College

Kenneth Lacho
University of New Orleans

Fay D. Lamphear
San Antonio College

Paul Londrigan
Mott Community College

Thomas Lloyd
Westmoreland County Community College

James McKee
Champlain College

Linda S. Munilla
Georgia Southern University

George Otto
Truman College

Alton Parish
Tarrant County Community College

William E. Rice
California State University, Fresno

Martin St. John
Westmoreland County Community College

Eric Sandburg
Career Design Software

Catherine A. Sanders
San Antonio College

Gene Schneider
Austin Community College

Joan Sepic-Mizis
St. Louis Community College at Florissant Valley

Raymond Shea
Monroe Community College

Nora Jo Sherman
Houston Community College

E. George Stook
Anne Arundel Community College

James B. Stull
San Jose State University

Roland Tollefson
Anne Arundel Community College

Sheb True
Loyola Marymount University

Robert Ulbrich
Parkland College

W. J. Walters
Central Piedmont Community College

Tom Wiener
Iowa Central Community College

David Wiley
Anne Arundel Community College

Joyce Wood
Northern Virginia Community College

Gregory Worosz
Schoolcraft College

The authors are sincerely grateful to our editorial assistants Karen Hill, Phyllis Crittenden, and Mikhelle Taylor. Their efforts on our behalf are most appreciated.

The authors would also like to recognize the team of professors and individuals who participated in making the *Contemporary Business* supplements an outstanding and innovative package:

Gemmi Allen
Mountain View College

Kathy Daruty
Los Angeles Pierce College

Barbara Gorski
University of St. Thomas

Douglas Hearth
University of Arkansas

Douglas Peterson
Indiana State University

Milton Pressley
The University of New Orleans

Eric Sandburg
Career Design Software

Amit Shah
Frostburg State University

Finally, the tenth edition would never have become a reality without our publisher's editorial, production, and marketing team. Tracy Morse, Bev Dunn, Kerri Jones, Andrea Archer, Barb Lange, Emily Friel, Melissa Morgan, and Lisa Kelley did a wonderful job. Thanks so much.

Gene Boone

Dave Kurtz

Louis E. Boone and David L. Kurtz, co-authors of *Contemporary Business, Tenth Edition.* Five million plus college students have read the 44 books written by Gene Boone and Dave Kurtz. Many of these titles have appeared in multiple editions. The books have also been translated into Spanish, Chinese, French, Italian, and Portuguese.

Professors Boone and Kurtz started writing college textbooks shortly after they received their doctorates at the University of Arkansas. In addition to their writing careers, Gene and Dave have remained active classroom teachers for over 30 years. In fact, Gene Boone introduced and coordinated the introduction to business courses at his school. He later set up and led his school's sports marketing and management program. Together Gene and Dave have taught at seven major institutions in the United States as well as in the United Kingdom, Greece, and Australia.

The authors of your textbook have been widely recognized by their peers. Both have been appointed to endowed professorships. Gene was selected as his school's outstanding instructor. His co-author, Dave, has an honorary doctorate in pedagogy; has been named educator of the year by a professional association; and has been picked as his college's best student advisor.

Both authors have extensive business experience. Together or separately, they have owned and operated a sporting goods franchise; apple orchards; a small publishing house; and apartment complexes and vacation rental properties. Despite being active entrepreneurs, your authors have also consulted with various firms and presented training programs and industry conferences. In addition, Dave has testified as a marketing expert in various federal and state courts.

Both of Gene and Dave's major texts—*Contemporary Business* and *Contemporary Marketing*—are the market leaders in their respective fields. Your text, *Contemporary Business,* was honored by receiving the first William Holmes McGuffey Award for Textbook Excellence and Longevity in 1994. Five years later, Boone and Kurtz's *Contemporary Marketing* won an unprecedented second McGuffey Award. Today, the works of Gene Boone and Dave Kurtz continue to be the industry's benchmarks in the publication of business textbooks.

BRIEF CONTENTS

CONTENTS

PART II STARTING AND GROWING YOUR BUSINESS 165

PART III MANAGEMENT: EMPOWERING PEOPLE TO ACHIEVE BUSINESS OBJECTIVES 283

PART VI   MANAGING FINANCIAL RESOURCES   677

Jump-Starting Your Business Career

First things first. As the authors of your text, we'd like to begin by congratulating you. You chose a fine college. You picked an excellent instructor. And you have just enrolled in the single most important course on campus.

So how did you win all these compliments simply by signing up for this course? First, your decision reveals a personal interest in business—from your own personal experiences; those of one or more of your parents, or a close friend; and simply from observing successful businesspeople and deciding that a career in business meets your numerous objectives of achieving success, wealth, and the respect of others who knew you would go far if given the opportunity. But you have no intention of waiting for opportunity to wander down your street. No, you are taking the bull by the horns, and seizing opportunity by the throat to achieve your dreams (fuzzy though they might be at this point in your academic career).

And, you ask, why is this course such a good one? Within the time frame of a few months, you will be introduced to how business operates and why many business graduates choose to start their own businesses rather than work for others, and you'll get real insights about the various functional areas in a successful business and the professionals who build careers in each function. You'll also learn more about career opportunities, areas in which such opportunities are greatest, typical salaries, and the jobs that best match your personal strengths and interests. You will also learn about how businesses can—and do—tackle many of our society's more pressing human and social responsibility obligations, in a sustained effort to make the 21st century a more human and more humane world.

Selecting a career may be the most important decision you will ever make. That's why *Contemporary Business* begins by discussing the best way to approach career decisions and how to prepare for an *entry-level job*—your first permanent employment after leaving school. We then look at a range of business careers and discuss employment opportunities in fields that are related to each major part of the text.

In making your personal career plans, you need to become aware of employment projections and trends. According to the Bureau of Labor Statistics, the number of new jobs in every major occupational category will grow during this first decade of the 21st century. In addition, the supply of qualified people ages 25 to 34 to fill these positions will fall by almost four million men and women by 2010. These trends translate into exciting opportunities for those entering the workforce. As Alan Reynolds, director of economic research at the Hudson Institute, comments, "Young Americans will be in a strong position to enjoy rapid increases in real incomes over the next two decades."

Education will improve your prospects of finding and keeping the right job. In addition, with more education, you are likely to earn more and to meet educational requirements often needed for advancement to more responsible and higher-paying positions. Last year, the average full-time employee 18 or older with no high school diploma earned just over $16,000. Recent Census Bureau statistics reveal that the

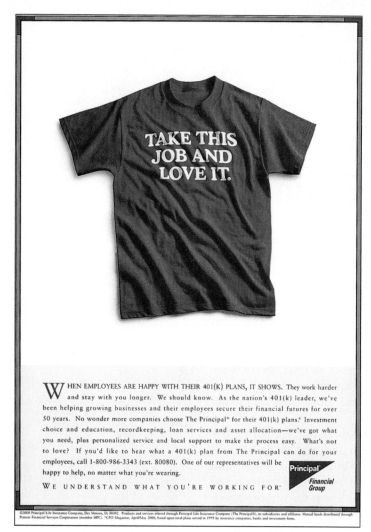

An ideal job is one that makes you want to get out of bed each morning—anxious to begin the day working at something you enjoy and that you get rewarded handsomely for performing at your typically superior level. This message from The Principal Financial Group focuses on the role of employee retirement programs in enhancing worker satisfaction.

average employee with a bachelor's degree earns $40,000-plus annually—two and a half times the pay of the high school dropout. Those with associates degrees earn roughly double the dropout's salary. Back in 1979, only 47 percent of the nation's best-paid employees (those in the top 10 percent income bracket) had college degrees; today seven out of ten do.

In addition to taking classes, try to gain related experience, either through a job or participation in campus organizations. Cooperative education programs, internships, or work–study programs can also give you hands-on experience while you pursue your education. These work experiences will often set you apart from other job-seekers in the eyes of recruiters.

INTERNSHIPS—INVALUABLE COMPONENT OF A BUSINESS EDUCATION

Many business students complete one—or even two—internships prior to completing their academic careers. These experiences are especially recommended for students with little or no practical business experience, and they add greatly to practical experiences that can enhance a job applicant's résumé. Although actor–comedian Bill Cosby once defined the word *intern* as "French for slave," most students use glowing terms to describe the value of their workplace experience.

Internships have been described as a critical link in bridging the theory–practice educational gap. They help to carry students between the academic present and the professional future. They provide an opportunity for students to learn how classroom theory is applied in real-world business environments.

In addition, internships can serve as critical networking and job hunting tools. In some instances, they lead to future employment opportunities, allowing students to demonstrate technical proficiency while providing cost-effective employee training for the company.

An excellent source of information about the nation's outstanding internships can be found at your local bookstore—*America's Top 100 Internships* by Oldman and Hamadeh. New editions are published annually by Villard Books in New York.

SELF-ASSESSMENT FOR CAREER DEVELOPMENT

You are going to spend a lot of time during your life working, so why not find a job that you enjoy? To choose the line of work that suits you best, you must first understand yourself. Self-assessment is often both a difficult and emotionally painful experience, since it involves answering some tough, frequently personal questions. Remember, however, it does pay off by helping you find a career that will be enjoyable, meaningful, and rewarding.

Not surprisingly, each of us has slightly different work-related values compared with those of our friends and family members. Table 1 lists the results of a recent study that asked U.S. employees to rank the aspects of a job that were most important to them. Most people ranked as most important the chance to do something

Table 1   **Most Important Aspects of a Job**

Aspect of Job	Importance	Satisfaction at Current Job
Chances to do something that makes you feel good about yourself	1	8
Chances to accomplish something worthwhile	2	6
Chances to learn new things	3	10
Opportunity to develop your skills and abilities	4	12
Amount of freedom you have on your job	5	2
Chances you have to do things you do best	6	11
Resources you have to do your job	7	9
Respect you receive from coworkers	8	3
Amount of information you get about your job performance	9	17
Your chances for taking part in making decisions	10	14
Amount of job security you have	11	5
Amount of pay you get	12	16
Way you are treated by coworkers	13	4
Friendliness of coworkers	14	1
Amount of praise you get for a job well done	15	15
Amount of benefits you get	16	7
Chances for promotion	17	18
Physical surroundings of your job	18	13

Note: Data from a systematic random sample drawn from 23,008 questionnaires.

THEY SAID IT

"When you reach my age and you find yourself eating light bulbs for a living, you know you've made some bad career moves along the way."

MATT HELY (B.1954)
ON HIS LIFE AS A CIRCUS PERFORMER

that made them feel good about themselves; other valued job characteristics included the chance to accomplish something worthwhile and the opportunity to learn. These respondents ranked the physical environment of a job and its promotional opportunities among the least important aspects.

Take a moment to rank the job factors listed in Table 1 as they affect your own job satisfaction. Which are most important to you? Which are least important? Be honest with yourself and rank these aspects according to how you really feel, as opposed to how other people might rank them. You can use this self-assessment exercise as a starting point for exploring careers that best meet the needs you identify as most important.

The number of resources offering help in choosing your planning is staggering. They include school libraries, career guidance and placement offices, counseling centers, and online job search services. You may also wish to talk with graduates from your school who are working in fields that interest you.

As another option, you might arrange an *informational interview,* a session with a company representative designed to gather more information about a firm or an occupation, rather than to apply for a job. If you are interested in a particular firm, for example, perhaps you could arrange an informational interview with someone who works there to find out what it is really like. If you are curious about working in a certain job area but are not completely sure it is for you, arrange an informational interview with someone who does that job. Find out what it really involves.

JOB SEARCH GUIDELINES

Once you have narrowed your choice of career possibilities to two or three that seem right for you, get your job search under way. Since the characteristics that made these career choices attractive to you are also likely to catch the attention of other job-seekers, you must expect competition. The best first step is to locate available positions that interest you; then be resourceful! Your success depends on gathering as much information as possible. Register at your school's placement office. Establish a placement or credentials file, including letters of recommendation and supporting personal information. Most placement offices send out periodic lists of new job vacancies, so be sure to get your name and address on the mailing list—and include your e-mail address. Become familiar with the process by which your placement office allocates limited interview slots with attractive employers.

Preparing Job Placement Materials

Most placement or credential files include the following information:

1. Letters of recommendation from people who know you—instructors, employers, and others
2. Transcripts of academic work to date
3. A personal data form to report factual information
4. A statement of career goals

The placement office will provide special forms to help you to develop your placement file. Complete these forms neatly and accurately, since employers are extremely interested in your ability to communicate in writing. Keep a copy of the final file for later use in preparing similar information for other employment sources. Check back with the placement office to make sure your file is in order, and update it whenever necessary to reflect additional academic accomplishments and added work experiences.

Letters of reference are very important. Secure recommendations selectively, and try to include a business instructor in your list of references. Always ask people personally if they will write a letter of recommendation for you. Be prepared to give them brief outlines of your academic preparation along with information concerning your job preferences and career objectives. This will help them prepare letters and may enable them to respond quickly. Remember, however, that these people are usually busy. Allow them enough time—at least a couple of weeks—to prepare their reference letters; then follow up on missing ones.

The HotJobs.com site is well organized and lets users cut and paste their résumés.

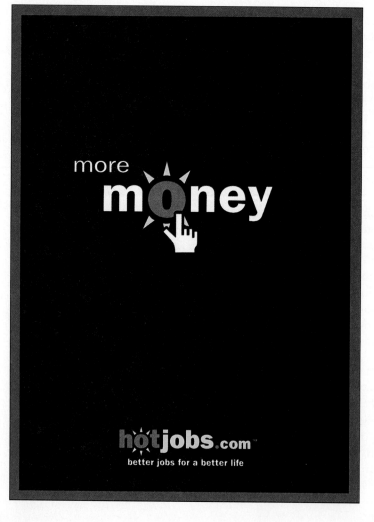

Finding Employment through the Internet

The Internet is playing an increasingly important role for both employers and job seekers. Companies of all sizes are posting their job opportunities on the Web, both on their own sites and on specialized job sites, such as The Monster Board (www.monster.com) and CareerMosaic (www.careermosaic.com). The largest job sites may receive hundreds of thousands of visits each day.

Despite the vast databases and fancy tools of the big career sites such as Monster.com, HotJobs.com, and Headhunter.net, savvy job seekers are beginning to find that their time is better spent zeroing in on niche boards with more focused listings. Telecommunications manager Ross Quam of San Diego turned to a niche site called Telecomcareers.net and discovered a handful of listings that seemed tailor-made for him. His résumé drew three offers within a week, one of which he accepted. He joined telecom company Qwest, earning $80,000 a year.[1]

An increasingly common component of company Web sites is to place an icon on their home page that visitors can click on to obtain information about current job openings at the firm. Recent Long Island University graduate Michelle Brown found her job opportunity while scanning the Enterprise Rent-A-Car Web site, looking to rent a car. "I saw a section for career opportunities, clicked on it, and couldn't get off." The site features profiles of three recent hires who tell of their rapid advancement at Enterprise, as well as a virtual "day-in-the-life" experience that follows a typical day at Enterprise. Her experience led Brown to apply—and secure—a job as a management trainee. After ten months, she was promoted to assistant manager.[2]

Newspapers, the source for traditional classified want ads, also post their ads on the Web. Job seekers can even visit sites that merge ads from many different newspapers into one searchable database, such as CareerPath (www.careerpath.com). Some sites go a step further and create separate sections for each career area. For example, entire sections may be devoted exclusively to accounting, marketing, and other business professions. Searches are narrowed according to geographic location, entry level, company name, job title, job description, and other categories.

Job seekers also connect with employers by posting their résumés on job sites. As an added service, many sites offer guidance in the preparation of a résumé. Employers search the résumé database for prospects with the right qualifications. One of today's most commonly used approaches is for an employer to list one or more *key-words* to select candidates for personal interviews—for example, "public relations," "network architecture," or "auditing"—and then browse the résumés that contain all the required keywords. Employers scan résumés into their human resources database, and then when a manager requests, say, ten candidates, the database is searched by keywords that have been specified as part of the request. Job seekers are responding to this computer screening of applicants by making sure that relevant keywords appear on their résumés.

Some job sites offer sections devoted exclusively to college students. College Grad Job Hunter (www.collegegrad.com) is a good example of a site focusing exclusively on entry-level opportunities. Job sites may list employers who are currently hiring, post internship opportunities, and provide general career resources covering areas such as salary information, interviewing, résumés, and financial aid. Web sites such as JobTrak (www.jobtrak.com) post job opportunities by employers seeking students from specific colleges and work in coordination with college placement offices.[3] *Career Magazine* (www.careermag.com) offers a wide range of career resources, as well as articles on job trends, work issues, and other topics.

The *Contemporary Business* Web site (www.contemporarybusiness.com) hosts a comprehensive job and career assistance section. The site is updated frequently to include the best job and career sites for identifying and landing the career you want, as well as current strategies for getting the best results from your Web-based career-search activities.

Finding Employment through Other Sources

The next step—identifying specific job openings—involves seeking out additional sources of information on available jobs, such as educational placement offices and private and public employment services.

Educational Placement Offices Your school's placement office is a good place to begin this search. If you have completed formal academic coursework at more than one college, check with placement offices at each institution about setting up a placement file. Some colleges have reciprocity agreements that permit students who have completed coursework at several schools to establish files with each school's placement office.

Private Employment Agencies Other useful sources to consider are private employment agencies. These firms often specialize in certain types of jobs, performing several services for both employers and job candidates that are not available elsewhere. For example, some private agencies interview, test, and screen job applicants.

A private employment agency usually charges the prospective employer a fee for finding a suitable employee. Other firms charge job seekers a fee for helping find them a job. Be sure that you understand the terms of any agreement you sign with a private employment agency.

State Employment Offices   For still another source of job leads, check the employment offices of your state government. However, in many states, these public agencies process unemployment compensation along with other related work. Because of the mix of duties, some people view state employment agencies as providing services for semiskilled or unskilled workers. These agencies do, however, list jobs in many professional categories.

Other Sources   A variety of additional sources can help you to identify job openings. Newspaper employment advertisements, especially Sunday editions of metropolitan newspapers, often prove to be rich sources of job leads. Trade journals or magazines may report this information. College instructors and administrators, community organizations, and family and friends can often provide job leads.

Another approach is to identify all the organizations where you think you might like to work. After checking the firms' Web sites for current job listings, mail a letter of inquiry and your résumé to those companies. If possible, direct your mailings to a specific person who has the authority to hire new employees. The letter should ask briefly about employment opportunities in a particular line of work. It should also ask for a personal interview.

Preparing a Résumé

Regardless of how you locate job openings, you must learn how to prepare and use a *résumé*, a written summary of your personal, educational, and professional achievements. The résumé is a very personal document covering your educational background, work experience, career preferences, major interests, and other personal information. It should also include such basic information as your home and e-mail addresses, as well as your telephone number.

Carefully review both your cover letter and résumé to make sure you avoid résumé blunders at this stage of the job search process. Here are three actual examples of what *not* to say to prospective employers:

- "Willing to relocate to a residence in an upscale neighborhood on the waterfront with easy access to mass transit."
- "My word-processing abilities are 50 words a minute, but when pushed I can increase my speed to 55 a minute."
- "I'm a hard worker, but don't do well with 'change' such as mergers, acquisitions, downsizings, relocations, and new phone systems."[4]

The primary purpose of the résumé is to highlight your qualifications for a job, usually on a single page. An attractive layout facilitates the employer's review of your qualifications. Figures 1, 2, and 3, illustrate traditional résumés in chronological, functional, and results-oriented formats.

Job seekers can prepare their résumés in several ways. Some use narrative sentences to explain job duties and career goals; others present information in outline form. A résumé to accompany a placement office credentials file can be quite short. Remember, too, to design it around your own needs and objectives.

Increasing numbers of organizations have moved to automated (paperless) résumé processing and applicant-tracking systems. As a result, if you write and design a technology-compatible résumé and cover letter, you'll enjoy an edge over an applicant whose résumé and cover letter can't be added to a database. Figure 4 lists tips for creating a "scanner friendly" résumé.

Here's the typical route that résumés and cover letters take at organizations using automated systems:

Cover letters and résumés are assigned a source code or a position code (connected to a particular job opening). They are scanned using optical character recognition (OCR). OCR converts graphic images into text. The information from the résumé/cover letter resides in a database until the organization purges it. (Sometimes the database also holds images of the résumé and cover letter.) Companies' purge policies vary.

Next, the computer uses artificial intelligence to read the recognized text and pulls out keywords from each section of the résumé. Typically, the computer looks for standard résumé sections (for example, "Work Experience" or "Education") so it's vital to stick to standard headings. After the computer has scanned the résumé and cover letter, it assigns one or more job categories to the applicant's record and builds a skills inventory from the information it has read. The more skills the computer finds on the résumé and cover letter, the better the chances that the résumé will be picked from the database when a relevant job opening occurs.

Those involved in the hiring process can query the database using criteria or keywords that they hope will find candidates whose skills and/or experiences fit the job opening. Résumés matching the job opening's criteria are typically forwarded electronically to the person with hiring authority, who then selects candidates for interviews.[5]

Beatrice Conner
4256 Pinebluff Lane
Cleveland, Ohio 44120
216–555–3296
bconner@aol.com

OBJECTIVE

Challenging office management position in a results-oriented company where my organizing people skills can be applied; leading to an operations management position.

WORK EXPERIENCE

ADM Distribution Enterprises, Cleveland, Ohio   **2000–Present**

Office Manager of leading regional soft-drink bottler. Coordinating all bookkeeping, correspondence, scheduling of 12-truck fleet to serve 300 customers, promotional mailings and personnel records, including payroll. Installing computerized systems.

Merriweather, Hicks & Bradshaw Attorneys, Columbus, Ohio   **1998–2000**

Office Supervisor and Executive Secretary for Douglas H. Bradshaw, Managing Partner. Supervising four clerical workers and two paraprofessionals, automating legal research and correspondence functions, improving filing and dictation systems, and assisting in coordinating outside services and relations with other firms and agencies. Promoted three times in 1 year from Secretary to Office Supervisor.

Conner & Sons Custom Coverings, Cleveland, Ohio   **1993–1998**

Secretary in father's upholstery and awning company. Performing all office functions over the years, running the office when the manager was on vacation.

EDUCATION

Mill Valley High School, Honors, Certificate   **1998**

McBundy Community College, Office Management, Automated Office Systems, **1999** Associate Degree

Telecom Systems, Word Processing Seminar Series, Certificate   **2000**

COMPUTER SKILLS

- Proficient with IBM-compatible computers and related software, including spreadsheets, graphics, desktop publishing, and word processing
- Packages: Excel, Lotus 1-2-3, Harvard Graphics, PowerPoint, Microsoft Word 6.0
- Familiar with Aldus Pagemaker and the Macintosh

PERSONAL

Member of various professional associations; avid reader; enjoy sports such as camping, cycling, scuba diving, skiing; enjoy volunteering in community projects.

FIGURE 1
Chronological Résumé

Learning More about Employment Opportunities

You should carefully study the various employment opportunities you have identified. Obviously, you will like some more than others, but you should consider a variety of factors when assessing each job possibility:

Timothy M. Richards
Two Seaside Drive
Los Angeles, CA 90026
213–555–7092
tmr@aol.com

OBJECTIVE
Joining a cohesive team effort in county government that has a positive impact on the quality of life in constituent communities, particularly in terms of traffic management and control.

PROFESSIONAL EXPERIENCE
Administration
Coordinating multilevel projects within fixed time frames and budget restrictions; maintaining smooth and frequent communications under adverse conditions of competing political party interference; sustaining loyalty throughout.

Planning
Preparing strategic, long-range, and intermediate-range plans using latest computer models; gaining participation and commitment of all key groups in planning processes; establishing reporting points and methods for all milestones in statewide political campaign; integrating planning for financial, strategic actions, capital items, and breaking issues on an ongoing basis.

Problem Solving
Writing position papers for contingencies and for direct appeal in state representative campaign; facilitating 50 discussion groups to reach consensus; contributing to strategy sessions on three campaigns; four months of coordinating community traffic-pattern hearings.

Leadership
Acting as a spokesperson with print and broadcast media and grassroots elements; establishing focus on common issues bringing differing factions together; setting standards and models for operating in various environments.

Traffic Management
Establishing computer-based modeling capability for 10,000 residents in a community traffic control project; assisting in implementing a three-tiered measuring system for tracking in-bound traffic volume in a high-risk neighborhood; submitting three proposals, now under consideration, for traffic reform in targeted communities.

WORK HISTORY
Whittier Community Traffic Study Project	**1999–Present**
Federal Traffic Studies Grant	**1999**
Part-time staff of four political campaigns	**1998–1999**
U. S. Navy Lieutenant	**1993–1998**

EDUCATION
UCLA mid-program, M.S. Communications	**Currently enrolled**
University of Oregon, B.S. Political Science	**1997**
Loma Linda Junior College, A.S. Journalism	**1995**

INTERNATIONAL EXPERIENCE
• Participated in an American Field Service (AFS) Exchange Program during senior year in high school (1992–1993). Attended classes and lived with a family for one month in Seville, Spain. Hosted Spanish "brother" for one month in the U.S.
• Traveled to France, England, Ireland, Switzerland, Germany, and Spain.

PERSONAL
Held various leadership positions in school and in community action groups. Special recognition for 5 years' work on city and college task forces. U.S. Navy Reservist.

FIGURE 2
Functional Résumé

1. Actual job responsibilities
2. Industry characteristics
3. Nature of the company
4. Geographic location
5. Salary and opportunities for advancement
6. How the job is likely to contribute to your long-run career objectives

Too many graduates consider only the most striking features of a job, perhaps its location or the salary offer. However, a comprehensive review of job openings should provide a balanced perspective of the overall employment opportunity, including both long-run and short-run factors.

Job Interviews

The first objective of your job search is obtaining an interview with a prospective employer. This interview demands considerable planning and preparation on your part. You want to enter the interview equipped with a good understanding of the company, its industry, and its competitors. Prepare yourself by researching the following essential information about the company:

1. How was the company founded?
2. What is its current position in the industry?
3. What is its financial status?
4. In which markets does it compete?
5. How is the firm organized?
6. Who are its competitors?
7. How many people does it employ?
8. Where are its production facilities and offices located?

This information is useful in several ways. First, it helps to give you a feeling of confidence during the interview. Second, it can keep you from making an unwise employment decision. Third, it can impress an interviewer, who may well try to determine how much you know about the company as a way of evaluating your interest level. A job applicant who fails to make the effort to obtain such information often risks elimination from future consideration.

But where do you find this company information? First, your school placement office or employment agency should have information on prospective employers.

Business instructors at your college may also provide tips. Your school or community library should have various references to help you investigate a firm, or you can write directly to the company. Many firms have informative Web sites, others publish career brochures. Finally, ask friends and relatives for input. They or someone they know may have had experience with the company.

Interviewers report two main reasons for poor performance in job interviews. Many job seekers fail due to ineffective communication, either because of inadequate preparation for their interviews or because they lack confidence. Remember that the interviewer will first determine whether you can communicate effectively. You should be specific in answering and asking questions, and you should clearly and positively express your concerns. The questions that interviewers ask most often include the following:

- "Why do you want this job?"
- "Where do you see yourself ten years from now?"
- "What are your strengths?"
- "What are your weaknesses?"
- "Why should I hire you?"

T. L. Chambers
3609 N.W. 57th Street
St. Louis, MO 63166
314–555–2394
tchambers@aol.com

OBJECTIVE

To apply my expertise as a construction supervisor to a management role in an organization seeking improvements in overall production, long-term employee relationships, and the ability to attract top talent from the construction field.

PROFESSIONAL EXPERIENCE

DAL Construction Company, St. Louis, Missouri   1998–Present
    Established automated, on-site recordkeeping system improving communications and morale between field and office, saving 400 work hours per year, and reducing the number of accounting errors by 20 percent. Developed a crew selected as "first choice crew" by most workers wanting transfers. Completed five housing projects ahead of deadline and under budget.

St. Louis County Housing Authority, St. Louis, Missouri   1996–1997
    Created friendly, productive atmosphere among workers enabling first on-time job completion in 4 years and one-half of usual materials waste. Initiated pilot materials delivery program with potential savings of 3.5 percent of yearly maintenance budget.

Jackson County Housing Authority, Kansas City, Missouri   1995
    Produced information pamphlet increasing applications for county housing by 22 percent. Introduced labor-management discussion techniques saving jobs and over $21,000 in lost time.

Carnegie Brothers Construction Company, West Palm Beach, Florida   1993–1994
    Introduced expediting methods saving 5 percent of overhead cost on all jobs and attracting a new $1.6 million client. Cut new-worker orientation time in half and on-site accidents by one-fourth through training and modeling desired behavior.

Payton, Durnbell & Associates Architects, Kansas City, Kansas   1992
    Developed and monitored productivity improvements saving 60 percent on information transfer costs for firm's 12 largest jobs.

EDUCATION
Central Missouri State University, Business   1995–1997

COMPUTER SKILLS
Familiar with Excel, Access, and Word for IBM compatibles.

PERSONAL
Highly self-motivated manager. Willing to relocate. Avid reader and writer.

FIGURE 3
Results-Oriented Résumé

It is important to know the name of the person (or persons) who will conduct the interview, what the interviewer's regular job responsibilities are, and who will make the final hiring decisions. Most people who conduct initial job interviews work in their firms' human resources divisions. These interviewers can make recommendations to line managers about which individuals to employ. Line managers who head the functional areas in which the applicant will be employed will get involved later in the hiring process. Some hiring decisions come from human resources personnel together with the immediate supervisor of the prospective employee. Most often, however, immediate supervisors make the decisions alone or in combination with input from senior employees from the department who will be colleagues of the newly hired person. Rarely does the human resources department have sole hiring authority.

In a typical format, the interviewer talks little during the interview. This type of *open-ended interview* forces you to talk about yourself and your goals. If you appear

1. Send originals; photocopies or faxed copies cause degraded text when scanned.

2. Use light-colored 8½" × 11" paper printed on one side only.

3. Do not use 11" × 17" paper folded to create pamphlet-like résumés.

4. Use popular sans serif fonts (e.g., Helvetica or Arial) in sizes from 10 to 14 points.

5. Avoid tabs.

6. Avoid graphics, shading, script fonts, italics, underlining, and boldfaced text.

7. Avoid horizontal and vertical lines.

8. Avoid parentheses and brackets.

9. Avoid compressed lines of text.

10. Use wide margins around the text.

11. Do not fold résumé when mailed.

12. Avoid dot matrix printers.

13. Avoid stapling the résumé.

FIGURE 4
Tips for Creating a "Scanner Friendly" Résumé

unorganized, the interviewer may eliminate you on that basis alone. When faced with this type of situation, be sure to express your thoughts clearly and keep the conversation on target. Talk for about ten minutes, then ask some specific questions of the interviewers. (Come prepared with questions to ask!) Listen carefully to the responses. Remember that if you prepare for a job interview, it will become a mutual exchange of information.

A successful first interview will probably lead to an invitation to come back for another interview. Sometimes this will include a request to take a battery of tests. Most students do very well on these tests because they have had plenty of practice in college!

It is not uncommon for applicants to receive a highly attractive job offer only after being rejected one or more times previously. Students at one Arizona school once pooled their rejection letters from would-be employers, reviewed them, and then voted on the company that had written the worst rejection letter. Here are excerpts from the five finalists:

- "After most careful consideration of your qualifications and background, we are unable to identify anything you can do for us . . ."
- "We're certain you could be more useful someplace else . . ."
- ". . . but we're sure you will find something you can do."
- "My conscience doesn't allow me to encourage you . . ."
- "Unfortunately, we have to be selective . . ."[6]

Employment Decisions

By this time, employers still considering you to be a viable job candidate know a lot about you from your placement file, résumé, and first interview. You should also know a lot about the company. The primary purpose of further interviews is to determine whether you can work effectively within the organization.

If you create a positive impression during your second or later interviews, you may be offered a job. Again, your decision to accept the offer should depend on how well the career opportunity matches your career objectives. Make the best entry-level job decision you can, and learn from it. Learn your job responsibilities as quickly and thoroughly as possible; then start looking for other ways to improve your performance and that of your employer.

THEY SAID IT

"The best career advice given to the young is, 'Find out what you like doing best and get someone to pay you for doing it.'"

KATHARINE WHITEHORN (B.1928)
BRITISH COLUMNIST

Nontraditional Students

At one time, colleges and universities served a market of mostly 18- to 22-year-olds. This was the primary age group that sought to break into the job market. A quick glance around your class is most likely enough to convince you that times have certainly changed.

More people are returning to school to complete academic programs, and more people who already have degrees are returning for more education. These sizable new groups of people enrolling in college classes today are often referred to as *nontraditional students.* Although the term covers any student who does not fit into the 18- to 22-year-old age group (the so-called traditional clients of higher education), it is actually inaccurate, since older students have become the norm on many campuses. In any case, nontraditional students have two other characteristics: they work, either full-time or part-time, and college is often only one of their daily responsibilities. Many are married, and many, regardless of current marital status, have children.

Most nontraditional students come from one of the following groups:

1. *Displaced homemakers* Full-time homemakers may return to school or join the workforce because of divorce or widowhood or for economic reasons.
2. *Military service veterans* Another major segment of nontraditional students enters school after discharge from the military.
3. *Technologically displaced workers* Someone who lost a job because of automation or industry cutbacks may return to school.
4. *Older, full-time employees* These workers may enter school to seek additional education to enhance career prospects or for personal satisfaction.

Challenges Faced by Nontraditional Students

Nontraditional students often face different challenges than do younger students. One is scheduling. Often, older students must juggle the responsibilities of work, school, and family. They may have to study at odd times: during meals, while commuting, or after putting the kids to bed. For another challenge, nontraditional students may be trying to change careers, so they must both learn skills in a different field and work toward breaking into that field with a new job.

Take heart, though. Nontraditional students also have a very important advantage: experience. Even experience in an unrelated field is a plus. Older students know how businesses operate. Often they have developed useful skills in human relations, management, budgeting, and communications. Also, through observing other people's mistakes and living through their own, they have often learned what not to do.

Like other students, nontraditional students need to access their accomplishments, skills, likes, and dislikes. The same exercises and resources suggested earlier can help both traditional and older students to assess their strengths and determine their career goals.

YOUR CAREER: A LONG-RANGE VIEW

Throughout your career, it is important to stay flexible and continue learning. Challenging new skills will be required of managers and other businesspeople during this first decade of the 21st century. Remain open to unexpected changes and opportunities that can help you learn and develop new skills. Remember . . . most people will have five or more different jobs during their lifetimes, so transferable skills are highly desirable for any career path.

The most important skill to learn may be just that: the ability to learn. Employers want workers who can collect and analyze both verbal and numerical information. Lew Shumaker, manager of college relations for duPont, emphasizes the importance of flexibility and the talent to function well in a culturally diverse workplace. "We are looking for graduates who have shown that they value those who are different from themselves," says Shumaker.

ADDITIONAL INFORMATION SOURCES

Business Careers on the Boone and Kurtz Web Site

A wealth of helpful career information is continually updated for business students using *Contemporary Business* at the following Web site: http//boone.swlearning.com.

Management Careers

Job and Career Information Sites

Introduction

The sites in this section will help you learn more about management careers and locate currently posted business job opportunities. Also, many sites include extensive career information and guidance, such as interviewing techniques and resume-writing. For example, see our description of College View Careers.

For job searches, most sites allow you to enter key words or phrases for the job titles or categories you seek. Some general advice:

1. When you enter a search word or phrase, try different conjugations of the word (ex. "manager" "management") or just enter the *root* of the word (ex. "manage" may cover "manager" or "management").

2. Each site has its own approach to defining your job search, so make it a habit to *review the help section or search tips* before you start looking for jobs.

3. Many sites allow you to search for jobs according to logical rules, using qualifiers such as "and" "or" "not" when entering keywords. If you place "and" between two or more words, only jobs which match *all* the keywords will be included. Inserting "or" between two or more words will yield jobs that contain *any* of the keywords. When you type the word "not" before a keyword, any job descriptions which include that word will be *excluded*.

The "Management Careers" section on the Web site enables you to learn more about business careers and to locate currently posted job opportunities. The site provides a vast number of career resources such as links to job sites, career guidance sites, newspaper job ads, and company information. It also provides ways for researching cities you might like to move to. Also, many links include extensive career information and guidance, such as interviewing techniques and tips for résumé writing.

Discovering Your Business Career—A Software Application

In addition to selecting *Contemporary Business* for classroom use, your instructor may have ordered a special CD-ROM with software to help you plan your career. In today's competitive job market, the most desirable and highest-paying jobs are likely to go to the most qualified candidates. Courses in business will prepare you for a number of entry-level positions. It is necessary for you to (1) recognize your own interests and abilities, (2) understand the general characteristics of the job you are seeking, and (3) know how your abilities can satisfy an employer's needs.

Discovering Your Business Career is a computer application that will help you determine which business careers most closely match your skills, experience, and interests. The software invites your input to questionnaires for each major business career track to aid you in determining how a job suits you. After you complete the questionnaire, the software generates an in-depth report assessing your compatibility with that track. The report also prints out a detailed profile of the career itself, its long-term opportunities, and its compensation levels. Once you have narrowed down your interests, you can begin engaging in the software's job search activities. They include guidelines for field research on careers, résumé preparation, letter writing, and preparation of telephone scripts. By matching your interests to the demands of a particular business career, you can then decide which elective courses will strengthen your marketability as a job candidate.

FINAL NOTE—THE AUTHORS' VIEW

DID YOU KNOW?

- *Nearly one of every ten new grads holds their first post-college job for less than a year, and one in four bails before the fifth anniversary.*

- *If you are adept at working with computers, you may want to examine career possibilities in America's fastest job-growth sector. Between now and 2008, job opportunities will at least double for computer support specialists, computer engineers, and systems analysts.*

- *Tomorrow's workers are much more likely to be senior citizens. Congress recently repealed a law that capped how much retirees could earn before forfeiting Social Security benefits—a move that is bringing thousands of people aged 65 and over back into the workforce.*

We believe that choosing a career is one of the most important decisions you will ever make. Choosing wisely and staying open to new opportunities will help make it a happy decision, too. Just imagine the satisfaction of getting paid to do something you enjoy!

Do not procrastinate or trust others to make this decision for you. Follow the steps outlined here and in other sources, and make your own decision. Your instructors, parents and other family members, friends, and advisors will offer to help in a multitude of ways, but in the end, it is your own decision.

We are confident that this textbook and its Web site will present a panorama of career options for you. Whatever you decide, be sure it is right for you. As the old saying goes, "You pass this way just once." Enjoy!

➤ Assignments

1. Prepare your own résumé following the procedures outlined earlier in this section. Ask your instructors, friends, relatives, and associates to critique it. What did you learn from this exercise?

2. Conduct an informational interview with someone in your community who is working in a profession that interests you. (Remember that this person is busy. Call first to request an appointment. The interview should take no more than 15 to 20 minutes. Come prepared with questions to ask.) Talk with your class about what you learned from the interview.

3. Discuss how you would answer each of the questions that interviewers most often ask.

4. Select a partner and take turns interviewing each other for a job in front of the class. (Use the interview questions mentioned earlier.) After completing the interviews, ask the class to give you feedback on how you looked and acted during your interview. Would they advise you to do or say anything differently?

5. Access the Career Center at the College View Web site:

   www.collegeview.com/careers

   Search the site to explore your interests, complete the assessments, learn about career training and internships, and other career information. Write a short summary of what you found and areas that interested you.

➤ Business Career Exercise

Résumés: Whether you are applying for a part-time or a full-time position, you need a well-prepared résumé.

Effective résumés communicate what you can offer a prospective employer, and the process of preparing a résumé helps you clarify your best assets.

This exercise will help you to do the following:

- Select the résumé format (chronological, functional, or results-oriented) that best represents your education, skills, and experience.
- Prepare both general résumés and custom résumés for specific employers.

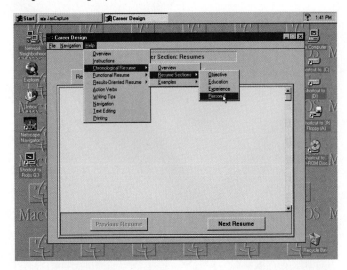

How to Locate the Exercise: Launch *Career Design* from the "Career Assistance" program group on the *Discovering Your Business Career* CD-ROM. Then select "Navigation" from the menu at the top of the screen, followed by "Career Sections" and then "Résumés."

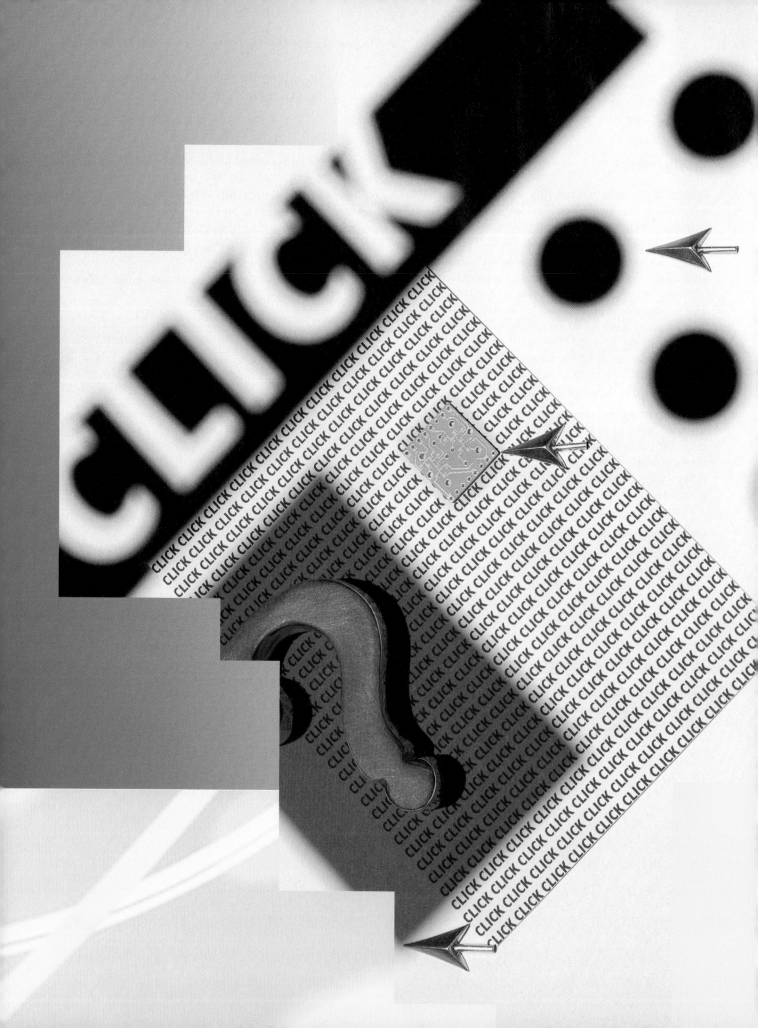

Business in a Global Environment

CHAPTER 1

Business: Blending People, Technology, and Ethical Behavior

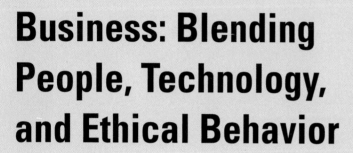

Learning Goals

1. Describe the private enterprise system and the roles played by individual businesses, competitors, and entrepreneurs within the system.

2. Explain how the historical development of the U.S. economy continues to influence contemporary business.

3. Outline the challenges and opportunities that businesses face in the relationship era.

4. Describe how technology is changing the way businesses operate and compete.

5. Relate the importance of quality and customer satisfaction to efforts to create value for customers.

6. Explain how individual businesses and entire nations compete in the global marketplace.

7. Describe how changes in the workforce are leading to a new employer–employee partnership.

8. Identify the skills that managers need to lead businesses in the new century.

9. Explain how ethics and social responsibility affect business decision making.

10. List four reasons for studying business.

Juicy Business: The Sweet Story of Nantucket Nectars

Picture two recent college grads trying to make a living without punching a time clock, wearing a jacket and tie, or sitting in front of a computer 12 hours a day. The guys are on a small powerboat, floating around Nantucket Harbor, off the coast of Massachusetts. They'll do anything customers ask them to—collect trash, do laundry, deliver morning muffins and newspapers. They even tow sailboats or disabled motorboats. Their boat, like their business, is called the Allserve. During the winter, there isn't much business—and not much to do. So the two guys, Tom First and Tom Scott, amuse themselves and their friends by cooking dinner for each other. One night First makes a fresh peach juice in his blender. Everyone loves the juice. First and Scott begin thinking, "Let's sell this off the boat next summer. We'll call it Nantucket Nectars."

Fifteen years later, Nantucket Nectars sells more than $50 million of juice each year. Ocean Spray bought half the company, but Scott and First still own the other half and serve as chief executive and chief operating officers, respectively. How did they get there? Both First and Scott admit that much of the journey has been one of trial and error. They knew nothing about bottling or distribution when they started, and they made a few mistakes. But they had a vision. They knew early on what they wanted—to make and sell the very best, freshest juice possible. They call themselves "the juice guys" because juice is their expertise; they quit collecting trash and doing laundry. They believe that quality differentiates Nantucket Nectars from its competitors. The company now offers five different lines of all-natural fruit juices, juice blends, iced teas, and lemonades. The pure juices are exactly that, with no added sugar. The juice blends, according to the company, have up to four times the amount of real fruit juice that major competitors have, and

they do not use sugary—and cheap—sweeteners such as high-fructose corn syrup. The teas and lemonade are flavored with real fruit juices, not artificial additives.

First and Scott also wanted to create value for their customers, so they sold their juices in larger bottles—12-ounce bottles for the pure juices, as opposed to 10 ounces, and 17.5-ounce bottles for the blends, as opposed to 16 ounces. Why? "It was what we wanted because that seemed to be how much you want to drink when you're thirsty," recalls Scott. "It's kind of big, frankly. We started making juice when we were 23, and when you're 23 you drink a lot." Though Scott says they no longer drink as much as they did when they were younger, they've stuck with the larger bottle size because people like it.

First and Scott represent the entrepreneurial spirit that is part of what makes the American economy hum. They had an idea, and they followed through with it. They stuck close to their vision, emphasized

quality, and created value for their customers. Now millions of people drink Pressed Apple Juice, Pineapple Orange Banana, and Authentic Lemonade every day.

And although you can't buy the juice online yet, the company Web site offers information about the products and places where you can buy them. The company has grown to more than 100 employees and has established itself in markets throughout the United States, Canada, Europe, Korea, and South and Central America. As you read *Contemporary Business* and learn more about business by completing this course, you'll encounter many entrepreneurs—some who still operate small companies and others whose start-up firms have grown into giant corporations. Who knows? By the time you finish this course—or graduate from college—you may have a business vision of your own.[1]

CHAPTER OVERVIEW

The first two years of the 21st century witnessed an event not seen in the U.S. in over a decade—an economic slowdown accompanied by a sharp drop in the stock market, the failure of a number of previous high-flying dot.com's, and unprecedented increases in gasoline, fuel oil, and natural gas prices. These events seemed even more unusual to Americans who had been riding high on a tremendous, decade-long wave of prosperity. The 1990s and early years of the 21st century saw a business expansion longer than any other in the nation's history. These good times brought major benefits to the lives of Americans:

- Of every 25 U.S. workers, 24 are employed, the highest level in over a quarter-century.

- To meet both domestic and overseas demand, total output of U.S. goods and services grew by 4 percent a year over the past decade—as much as the entire output of Germany. Economic growth continued, but at a lower rate of about 2 percent annually, during the recent slowdown.

- Although stock values are slightly lower than the unprecedented heights of 2000, their unprecedented rise over the last 5 years helped bring newfound wealth to the millions of people—about half of all U.S. families—who own shares of stock, either directly or through their retirement accounts.

- The prosperity of the past decade meant that plenty of income tax revenues were flowing into federal coffers. After decades of federal deficits, a significant event occurred. More money flowed into Washington than the government spent. The federal budget is continuing to operate at a surplus that is expected to surpass $2 trillion annually by 2010. Politicians are now debating about what to do with all of this money: reduce taxes, expand programs to protect the environment, improve education, provide prescription drug benefits to the elderly and low-income households of all ages, and/or begin paying off the national debt.

- High employment, low inflation, and moves to stimulate the economy by reducing borrowing costs have combined to boost consumer confidence. These moves are likely to increase home purchases and stimulate business investments in equipment aimed at increasing efficiency.[2]

Business growth opens doors of opportunity for those who are prepared to put ideas into action. John C. Diebel's idea was to put modern computing power into telescopes for amateur astronomers. An electrical engineer, Diebel grew tired of working at giant electronics companies, so he returned to his childhood passion of stargazing and started his own company, Meade Instruments, to build and sell telescopes. Inspired by Microsoft's legendary ability to bring computing software to the masses, Diebel had Meade's engineers adapt features of $15,000 telescopes to more affordable models. After two years, they created a telescope that sells for a few hundred dollars and includes a computerized attachment that lets users key in coordinates to direct the telescope to celestial objects. Before long, Meade's new telescope had captured more than half the market for telescopes sold to hobbyists. Diebel and his company also innovate in other product categories. They recently signed a deal to sell optical equipment for wireless communications, helping to propel Meade onto *Business Week*'s list of hot growth companies.[3] Not only do new companies put ideas into action, but trusted names like The Gap and Toys 'R' Us are seeking new ways to compete through online sales and global manufacturing. And companies that were once new—like Nantucket Nectars—have become strong competitors in their field.

In the new century, everyone is facing new challenges posed by the technological revolution, which is changing the rules of business. The combined power of telecommunications and computer technology is creating inexpensive, global networks that transfer voice messages, text, graphics, and data within seconds. These sophisticated technologies create new types of products, and they demand new approaches to marketing existing products. Technology is also speeding the rate of change in the business world, where new discoveries rapidly outdate inventions created just months before.

Promotional messages, like the one from Nextel shown in Figure 1.1, illustrate the impact of technology on people's daily lives. It has transformed the way we communicate and stay informed. As the picture and copy in the ad demonstrate, we can use cellular phones and the Internet to communicate from anywhere: A man received a text message on his cellular phone's screen, telling him the value of his stock had doubled. He used the same phone to send e-mail messages to his friends, canceling plans with them so he could celebrate with his wife. He also used the phone's two-way radio to ask his assistant to make dinner reservations, and he telephoned his wife to invite her to dinner. The advertising copy concludes, "Thanks to Nextel's new wireless Internet services, you have even more ways to keep you connected to the critical information you need to do business better and faster." This degree of flexibility in communicating was unimaginable just a few years ago.

Innovative technologies are also globalizing today's business world. Businesses can now easily manufacture, buy, and sell across national borders. You can order a Big Mac or a Coke almost anywhere in the world, and Japanese and Korean companies manufacture most of the consumer electronics products sold in the U.S. Mercedes Benz manufactures sport utility vehicles in Alabama, and many General Motors automobiles are assembled in Canada.

This rapidly changing business landscape compels businesspeople to react quickly to shifts in consumer tastes and other market dynamics. Success requires creativity, split-second decision making, and innovative vision. Whether you decide to start your own business, as John Diebel did, work for a small family-run business, or sign on with a large international corporation, your achievements will depend on your ability to keep pace with the constant changes in today's world.

Contemporary Business explores the strategies that allow companies to compete in today's interactive marketplace and the skills that you will need to turn ideas into action for your own career success. This chapter sets the stage for the entire text by defining *business* and revealing its role in society. The chapter's discussion illustrates how the private enterprise system encourages competition and innovation while preserving important individual freedoms. Later sections highlight the most important challenges and opportunities businesspeople have begun to face in the 21st century.

FIGURE 1.1
Technology: Transforming the Way People Communicate

WHAT IS BUSINESS?

What image comes to your mind when you hear the word *business*? Some people think of their jobs, others think of the merchants they patronize as consumers, and still others think of the millions of firms that make up the world's economy. This broad, all-inclusive term can be applied to many kinds of enterprises. Businesses provide the bulk of employment opportunities as well as the products that people enjoy.

Business consists of all profit-seeking activities and enterprises that provide goods and services necessary to an economic system. Some businesses produce tangible goods, such as automobiles, breakfast cereals, and computer chips; others provide services, such as insurance, Dixie Chicks and Eminem music concerts, car rentals, and lodging.

Business drives the economic pulse of a nation. It provides the means through which standards of living improve. The U.S. leads the world in national per capita output of goods and services.

At the heart of every business endeavor is an exchange between a buyer and seller. A buyer recognizes a need for a good or service and trades money with a seller to obtain that product. The seller participates in the process in hopes of gaining profits—a critical ingredient in accomplishing the goals necessary to maintain constant improvement in standards of living.

Profits represent rewards for businesspeople who take the risks involved in blending people, technology, and information to create and market want-satisfying goods and services. In contrast, accountants think of profits as the difference between a firm's revenues and the expenses it incurs in generating these revenues. More generally, however, profits serve as incentives for people to start companies, expand them, and provide consistently high-quality competitive goods and services.

Consider, for example, the role of profits among companies offering goods and services on the Internet. Few large firms saw the Internet as a business opportunity in its early years, but as customers began flocking to service providers like America Online and portals like Yahoo, online profitability began to look like a real possibility. Total 2001 revenues for Yahoo amounted to more than $1 billion, and the popular Internet portal continued its unbroken profitability streak by charging firms to advertise on its popular Web site. But numbers like that always seem to attract plenty of competition. A portal called iWon.com is trying to outdo Yahoo's information-for-free strategy by actually paying users to visit its site. Visitors to the iWon portal are entered into sweepstakes every time they use the site. The site's strategy is to attract huge numbers of visitors by awarding a $1 million prize every month and a $10 million prize every year. The number of visitors, in turn, is supposed to convince other companies to pay to advertise at the iWon Web site. Time will tell whether the strategy will be profitable. So far, companies are finding that profitability on the Internet is far from guaranteed, and many unprofitable Internet businesses have already shut down, including HomeWarehouse, Petstore.com, and Reel.com.[4] In the long run, even in cyberspace, profits are essential for business success.

Although the quest for profits is a central focus of business, businesspeople also recognize social and ethical responsibilities. To succeed in the long run, companies must deal responsibly with employees, customers, suppliers, competitors, government, and the general public.

Not-for-Profit Organizations

What characteristics link the National Football League, the U.S. Postal Service, the American Heart Association, and C-SPAN? For one, they are all classified as **not-for-profit organizations,** businesslike establishments that have primary objectives other than returning profits to their owners. These organizations play important roles in society by placing public service above profits. Not-for-profit organizations operate in both the private and public sectors. Private-sector not-for-profits include museums, libraries, business associations, charitable and religious organizations, and most colleges and universities. In addition, government agencies, political parties, and labor unions are classified as not-for-profit organizations.

A good example of a not-for-profit organization is New York's Metropolitan Museum of Art. Like profit-seeking businesses, the Met must generate funds to cover its operating costs. Revenues come from a number of sources, including individual donations, memberships, government grants, gift-shop sales, and special fund-raising drives. Such events provide added value to museum members and attract thousands of occasional and first-time visitors, who may become members. Not-for-profit organizations also rely on business activities ranging from human resource management to advertising. Figure 1.2 encourages corporations to support the Corporate Angel Network, a not-for-profit organization that provides free travel to people who need cancer treatment.

Not-for-profit organizations are a substantial part of the U.S. economy. More than one million not-for-profits currently operate in the U.S., not including tens of thousands of local, state, and federal government agencies. They control more than $1 trillion in assets and employ more people than the entire federal government and all 50 state governments combined. In addition, millions of volunteers work for them in un-paid positions. Not-for-profits secure funding from both private sources, including donations, and government sources. They are commonly exempt from federal, state, and local taxes.

Although they focus on goals other than generating profits, managers of not-for-profit organizations face many of the same challenges dealt with by executives who head profit-seeking businesses. A major challenge is obtaining the funding they need in order to provide their services. Public television and radio stations, for example, have become more creative in soliciting donations. In addition to the old standby of pledge drives urging viewers or listeners to send in $100 and receive a tote bag, compact disc (CD), or videocassette, public broadcasters try to build longer-term relationships with their members. In Boston, about 6 percent of the people who contribute to WGBH send in at least $300 a year. Of course, all of these big donors were once first-time members. The relationship building process begins with a thank-you note for the donation and a subscription to the station's monthly viewing guide. Midlevel and large contributors get special attention from the station. At the beginning of each programming season, they receive a letter describing specials to be aired that season, along with a direct phone number to WGBH's general manager, Jonathan C. Abbott. These donors are also invited to seminars, luncheons, program premieres, and other opportunities for face-to-face contact with the station's staff.

These events are designed to obtain feedback and cement member loyalty to the station. WGBH even applies research techniques, gathering data about viewers and dividing them into segments such as those who are parents of young children and those who pledged during a particular documentary. Invitations are targeted according to each group's likely interests. The station applies measurable criteria to its relationship building: The success of its events are evaluated in terms of participants' subsequent donations and other indicators of their involvement with the station. Such efforts have sustained WGBH's radio and television operations and helped it produce such popular

CANCER PATIENTS FLY FREE ON THE WINGS OF ANGELS.

Call the Corporate Angel Network, Inc., to learn how CAN may help you travel free for recognized cancer treatment. In comfort. In dignity. To find out how to become a corporate angel so that you may give a lift to a cancer patient at no cost to the corporation, please call today.

CAN
CORPORATE ANGEL NETWORK, INC.
tel. 914.328.1313 • www.corpangelnetwork.org

Corporate Angel Network, a not-for-profit organization, has flown more than 9,500 cancer patients through the generous cooperation and assistance of over 500 corporations.

FIGURE 1.2
The Corporate Angel Network: A Not-for-Profit Organization

What is a company's most prized possession? You might say its customers, its employees, or even its products. What about a not-for-profit organization's most prized possession? Your answer is likely to center on its reputation. Without an impeccable reputation, a not-for-profit organization cannot attract donors, members, or sponsors who keep it alive in order to further its mission—whether that is education, medical research, or preservation of the environment. So, not-for-profit organizations face many of the same challenges that commercial organizations face, including competition for funds required to survive and grow. In many cases, they have fewer resources to invest in marketing and updates in technology. But some not-for-profits are beginning to change their view of profits.

Recently, the College Board—which administered your SATs—launched a Web site designed to teach students how to do well on the tests. The site, at www.collegeboard.com, is a for-profit subsidiary, which can offer stock options and generate dividends for stockholders without harming the College Board's tax-free, not-for-profit status. Critics have been quick to give the new venture an *F*, claiming that this represents a conflict of interest. "If they can shift services to the for-profit that easily, why were they ever tax-free in the first place?" asks Andy Rosen, chief operating officer of one of the site's for-profit competitors, Kaplan Inc. College Board president Gaston Caperton argues that "we needed the capital and stock options to compete for the very best in the field."

In the field of health care, where former not-for-profits like Blue Cross, hospitals, and health maintenance organizations (HMOs) have actually dropped their not-for-profit, tax-free status, angry consumers want a refund for the tax breaks that these organizations enjoyed over the years. The American Medical Association has set up a Web site called Medem in conjunction with other medical societies, which links doctors and patients in a for-profit relationship. Currently, Medem is 80 percent owned by the medical societies, with the rest owned by investment funds, employees, and other investors. Medem's chief executive officer Edward J. Fotsch argues, "The advantages the societies bring to Medem are immeasurable." In other words, Medem's success may be partially due to the societies' reputations of integrity in the non-for-profit health care field. However, this initial success could backfire. As consumers begin to make the link between their health care providers

and profits, the reputations of these organizations may suffer. And the Internal Revenue Service may watch both the parent not-for-profit organizations and their for-profit subsidiaries more carefully than before to ensure that tax laws aren't being breached.

Trying to generate profits can also distract a not-for-profit organization from its primary mission. For instance, the Jane Goodall Institute spent months talking with investors about setting up an Internet portal based on the personality of Jane Goodall, the renowned researcher of chimpanzees. The organization didn't really need the extra money at the time, but a portal had the potential to generate tens of millions of dollars, so executive director Stewart Hudson went ahead with the project. Now, traditional donations have declined, and the Internet project has taken "attention away from other things, like our endowment drive," admits Hudson. The Institute may drop the portal project altogether.

No one would argue that not-for-profit organizations need the same cold cash to achieve their mission that companies need to be profitable and competitive. As these organizations look to the Internet for potential gain, they may need to find even more creative ways to harness technology for their benefit than their commercial counterparts do.

QUESTIONS FOR CRITICAL THINKING
1. Choose one of the organizations discussed and describe at least one way the group could use the Internet to attract members or donors without becoming profit oriented.
2. Do you think it is a good idea for not-for-profit organizations to look for legal ways to generate profits? Why or why not?

Sources: Diane Brady, "When Nonprofits Go after Profits," *Business Week*, June 26, 2000, pp. 173–174, 178; Gaston Caperton, "SAT Is 'Common Yardstick,'" *USA Today*'s Opinion Section, July 11, 2000, accessed at **www.collegeboard.com**; "College Board's New SAT Learning Center Is Only Online Source of Real SAT Questions for October Exams," College Board press release, October 11, 1999, accessed at **www.collegeboard.com**; "AMA, Six Other Physician Groups Launch Internet 'Supersite' with Health Information Patients Can Trust," American Medical Association press release, October 28, 1999, accessed at **www.ama-assn.org**.

programs as *Antiques Roadshow, Frontline,* and *This Old House* on television and public radio's *Prairie Home Companion* and *Car Talk*.[5]

As in the world of profit-seeking businesses, the new century is bringing changes to the not-for-profit sector. An aging and increasingly diverse population may require not-for-profits to find new ways of delivering services. Government funding is also declining, a trend that is forcing not-for-profit executives to develop new cost-cutting methods. Faced with increased competition for limited funding, not-for-profits also have to boost their effectiveness at marketing and fund-raising, a lesson that public broadcasting has already been applying. As the "Business Hits and Misses" box illustrates, some not-for-profits sell merchandise or have even set up profit-generating arms to provide goods and services that people are willing and able to pay for. The College Board, which prepares such standardized tests as the SAT, has made plans to offer test preparation assistance at a for-profit Web site, college-

Table 1.1	Factors of Production and Their Factor Payments

Factor of Production	Corresponding Factor Payment
Natural resources	Rent
Capital	Interest
Human resources	Wages
Entrepreneurship	Profit

board.com. The Metropolitan Museum of Art operates several stores as part of its not-for-profit operations. David E. McKinney, the museum's president, views the stores as a way to extend the organization's mission, not just bring in money.[6] These changes and others require leaders with strong business skills and experience. Consequently, many of the concepts discussed in this book apply to not-for-profit organizations as much as to profit-oriented firms.

Factors of Production

Capitalism, like other economic systems, requires certain inputs for effective operation. Economists use the term **factors of production** to refer to the four basic inputs: natural resources, capital, human resources, and entrepreneurship. Table 1.1 identifies each of these inputs and the type of payment received by firms and individuals who supply them.

Natural resources include all productive inputs that are useful in their natural states, including agricultural land, building sites, forests, and mineral deposits. For example, Willamette Industries operates a sawmill in Dallas, Oregon, a town southwest of Portland. The mill takes 2,500-pound second-growth logs from Oregon's hillsides and cuts them into boards.[7] Other companies use natural resources after they have been processed by companies like Willamette. Natural resources are the basic inputs required in any economic system.

Capital, another key resource, includes technology, tools, information, and physical facilities. *Technology* is a broad term that refers to such machinery and equipment as production lines, telecommunications, and basic inventions. Information, frequently improved by technological innovations, is another critical success factor, since both managers and operating employees require accurate, timely information for effective performance of their assigned tasks. Technology plays an important role in the success of many businesses. At the Willamette Industries sawmill, new technology lets the company produce the same amount of boards with 12 percent fewer trees. The mill uses lasers coupled with computers to scan logs and compute how to saw them so that they will yield the most profitable boards with the least waste. The computation takes into account each log's dimensions and the current prices for boards in varying sizes. Twelve pairs of computer-controlled saw blades then cut the log, swiveling to take into account its curvature. Additional laser sensors identify whether the resulting boards need finishing operations. Such advanced technology may seem surprising in a traditional industry like sawing lumber, but the company has no plans to stop there. In the future, the mill expects to apply x-ray and ultrasound technology to locate and account for inner defects such as rot and knots inside the logs.[8]

Money is necessary to acquire, maintain, and upgrade a firm's capital. Willamette's mill, for example, spends hundreds of thousands of dollars each year to upgrade its software and install new machines. A company's funds may come from investments by its owners, profits, or loans extended by others. Money then goes to work building factories; purchasing raw materials and

BUSINESS DIRECTORY

➤ **factors of production**   *basic inputs into the private enterprise system, including natural resources, human resources, capital, and entrepreneurship.*

component parts; and hiring, training, and compensating workers. People and firms that supply capital receive factor payments in the form of interest.

Human resources are also critical inputs in all economic systems. Human resources include anyone who works, from the chief executive officer (CEO) of a huge corporation to a self-employed auto mechanic. This category encompasses both the physical labor and the intellectual inputs contributed by workers. With the widespread use of computer technology, most companies now rely on their employees as a source of ideas and knowledge as well as physical effort. Ford Motor Co., which once pioneered the use of the assembly line, is now a leader in helping its people become sophisticated users of technology. In 2000 Ford announced that it would offer each of its employees a desktop computer, printer, and Internet access, all for just $5 a month. The strategy is aimed at assisting employees in becoming more computer literate and being able to apply computer technology on the job. It also enables them to communicate with one another and read company notices online, and perhaps will even inspire them to read what consumers are saying about Ford in Internet chat rooms and on Web sites. One industry observer praised Ford's initiative: "In a skills-short environment where it's hard to find people with the right knowledge, it's an amazing competitive edge."[9] This competitive edge is significant, because competitors cannot easily match another company's talented, motivated employees, the way it can buy the same computer system or purchase the same grade of natural resources.

Figure 1.3 emphasizes the importance of human resources to organizational goals and the need for employees to maintain and update their skills. An astronaut must be well equipped and trained to carry out a mission safely. In the ad, the Mony Group compares the training of its financial professionals to NASA's astronauts. Like NASA, the parent firm of Mutual of New York provides its people with "years of training, the best education," and "the latest technology" so that these experts can provide a valuable service to the firm's customers.

Entrepreneurship is the willingness to take risks to create and operate a business. An entrepreneur is someone who sees a potentially profitable opportunity and then devises a plan to achieve success in the marketplace and earn those profits. Some entrepreneurs, like John Diebel of Meade Instruments, set up new companies and ventures. Established firms benefit from entrepreneurship to revitalize them when market conditions change or new opportunities arise. At Microsoft, founder Bill Gates resumed the role of entrepreneur when he resigned as CEO a few years ago to focus on innovation and expansion possibilities.

To see how one firm utilizes the factors of production, consider Gene Cage's business, Papa Geno's Herb Farm, located in rural Roca, Nebraska. Its fragrant natural resources are not hard to identify: the soil and seedlings for dill, basil, lavender, and dozens of other herbs that Geno's sells to customers who place orders through its Web site and those of other online retailers who specialize in the worldwide sale of herbs. In addition to serving as major sources of customers for Geno's, some of these online merchants have also become sources of funds and technological capital: One large online retailer recently invested $1 million in Papa Geno's. It also assisted the herb grower by providing access to its information system and helped Papa Geno's in developing

FIGURE 1.3
Human Resources: Critical Factor of Production

sales forecasts. That way, it would be able to count on Papa Geno's as a reliable supplier. Herb entrepreneur Cage has embraced Internet technology and his alliances with online merchants because of their ability to bring him customers from around the globe and to fill orders at a lower cost than through traditional channels like catalogs. However, combining an old-fashioned business like raising herbs with modern technology presents a problem in the area of human resources. It is not easy to find people with expertise in both horticulture and the Internet and then convince them to move to a rural area like Roca. So Cage offers generous benefits and acts as a mentor to his 17 full-time employees. They are helping Cage grow his company faster than any herb. By 2004, Papa Geno's should be the largest U.S. nursery supplying fresh herbs directly to consumers.[10]

The next section looks at how the factors of production are allocated and used within the private enterprise system, the economic system in which U.S. businesses currently operate.

THE PRIVATE ENTERPRISE SYSTEM

No business operates in a vacuum. All operate within a larger economic system that determines how goods and services are produced, distributed, and consumed in a society. The type of economic system employed in a society also determines patterns of resource use. Some economic systems, such as communism, feature strict controls on business ownership, profits, and resources to accomplish government goals.

In the United States, businesses function within the **private enterprise system**, an economic system that rewards businesses for their ability to perceive and serve the needs and demands of consumers. A private enterprise system minimizes government interference in economic activity. Businesses that are adept at satisfying customers gain access to necessary factors of production and earn profits.

Another name for the private enterprise system is *capitalism*. Adam Smith, often identified as the father of capitalism, first described the concept in his book *The Wealth of Nations*, published in 1776. Smith believed that an economy is best regulated by the invisible hand of **competition**, the battle among businesses for consumer acceptance. Smith thought that competition among firms would lead to consumers receiving the best possible products and prices, because less efficient producers would gradually be driven from the marketplace.

This invisible hand concept is a basic premise of the private enterprise system. In the U.S., competition regulates economic life. To compete successfully, each firm must find a basis for **competitive differentiation**, the unique combination of organizational abilities and approaches that sets a company apart from competitors in the minds of consumers. Eyeglasses retailer Lenscrafters has differentiated itself from competitors through service. Customers get their new lenses in about an hour. By contrast, Wal-Mart uses so-called everyday low prices on brand name products to attract customers.

Businesses operating in a private enterprise system face a critical task of keeping up with changing marketplace conditions. Firms that fail to adjust to shifts in consumer preferences or ignore the actions of competitors leave themselves open to failure. For a success story, consider Levi Strauss. Decades ago, Levi's could sell jeans on the basis of consumers' love of the brand. But by the 1990s, consumers had moved on to other fashions, sales of jeans declined, and the San Francisco–based company had to shut down some of its factories. To resurrect itself, the firm turned to technology. Levi's started selling jeans through a process so old that it was radically new: measure customers and make jeans to fit their unique size and shape. Only instead of a tailor with a measuring tape, Levi's Personal Pair program invited women to be "digitized" in its Original Levi's Stores, and computers stored measurements in a database. The company produced jeans to match the measurements

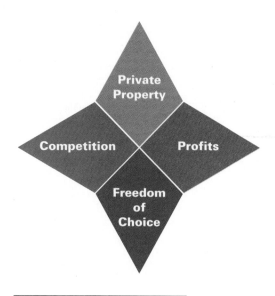

FIGURE 1.4
Basic Rights within a Private Enterprise System

and shipped them to customers for about $10 to $15 more than a pair of Levi's jeans would cost at the local retail store. Before long, Levi's was enjoying a high rate of repeat purchases and a low rate of product returns. Original Levi's Store shoppers are up to ten times as likely to make a purchase as is typical for shoppers, and many are so loyal they are willing to wait a couple of weeks for an appointment. Levi's has since expanded on its success. Through its Original Spin program, it offers customized jeans to men as well as women, and it has doubled the number of style options to encompass 1,500 variations.[11]

Throughout this book, our discussion focuses on the tools and methods that 21st century businesses apply to compete and differentiate their goods and services. "Clicks and Mortar" and "Business Hits and Misses" features demonstrate how individual businesspeople or companies have developed strategies for competitive differentiation. We also discuss many of the ways in which market changes will affect business and the private enterprise system in the years ahead. Chapter 3 focuses specifically on how businesses function within other economic systems.

Basic Rights within the Private Enterprise System

Certain rights critical to the operation of capitalism are available to citizens living in a private enterprise economy. As shown in Figure 1.4, these include the rights to private property, profits, freedom of choice, and competition.

The right to **private property** is the most basic freedom under the private enterprise system. Every participant enjoys the right to own, use, buy, sell, and bequeath most forms of property, including land, buildings, machinery, equipment, inventions, and various intangible kinds of property.

The private enterprise system also guarantees business owners the right to all profits (after taxes) earned by their activities. Although a business is not assured of earning a profit, its owner is legally and ethically entitled to any income it generates in excess of costs.

Freedom of choice means that a private enterprise system relies on the potential for citizens to choose their own employment, purchases, and investments. They can change jobs, negotiate wages, join labor unions, and choose among many different brands of goods and services. People living in the capitalist nations of North America, Europe, and other parts of the world are so accustomed to this freedom of choice that they sometimes forget its importance. A private enterprise economy maximizes individual human welfare and happiness by providing alternatives. Other economic systems sometimes limit freedom of choice in order to accomplish government goals, such as increasing industrial production.

The private enterprise system also permits fair competition by allowing the public to set rules for competitive activity. For this reason, the U.S. government has passed laws to prohibit "cutthroat" competition—excessively aggressive competitive practices designed to eliminate competition. It also has established ground rules that outlaw price discrimination, fraud in financial markets, and deceptive advertising and packaging.

The Entrepreneurship Alternative

One of the career options offered by capitalism is entrepreneurship. In fact, entrepreneurial spirit beats at the heart of private enterprise. An **entrepreneur** is a risk taker in the private enterprise system. Individuals who recognize marketplace opportunities are free to use their capital, time, and talents to pursue those opportunities for profit. The willingness of individuals to start new ventures drives economic growth and keeps pressure on existing companies to continue to satisfy customers. If no one were willing to take economic risks, the private enterprise system wouldn't exist.

By almost any measure, entrepreneurial spirit fuels growth in the U.S. economy. Of the businesses operating in the U.S. economy during the course of a year, about one in seven first started operating that year. These newly formed businesses are also the source of many of the nation's new jobs each year. Every year, they create more than one of every five new jobs in the economy. Most measures of entrepreneurship look at the smallest or youngest businesses, on the assumption that they are the enterprises in which entrepreneurship is most significant. These companies are a significant source of employment or self-employment. Out of the 19 million U.S. businesses currently in operation, 14 million are nonemployers, meaning people who are self-employed without any employees. Four out of every five U.S. employees currently work for a business with fewer than ten employees. Small companies also generate much of the nation's output of goods and services. In recent years, small businesses—those employing 500 or fewer people—have generated about half the nation's output, and three-quarters of the output in the service sector of the economy. Besides creating jobs and selling products, entrepreneurship provides the benefits of innovation. In contrast to more established firms, start-up companies tend to innovate most in fields of technology that are new and uncrowded, thereby making new kinds of products available to businesses and consumers.[12]

Entrepreneurs often find novel ways to use natural resources, technology, and other factors of production. Nathaniel Weiss found a creative application for technology: a package of hardware and software that translates music played on a guitar into sheet music. His product, called G-vox, became a hit among guitarists because it saved them the laborious process of transcribing the solos and songs they wrote. With publicity in guitar magazines, Weiss was able to sell G-vox in small music stores and through mail order. He then expanded on this success by developing G-vox products that work with other instruments and that not only transcribe music but also play the sounds of other instruments, so musicians can hear how they sound in an ensemble. These products are particularly useful for teaching. Weiss succeded because he not only had good product ideas but also worked with others to make his ideas a success. He negotiated a deal with Fender in which the guitar maker offered the G-vox guitar pickup—which sends information from the guitar to the belt-pack hardware—as an option on its guitars and distributed G-vox products to major guitar stores. When Weiss wanted to develop more products for the educational market, he teamed up with an educational publisher, McGraw-Hill. Thanks to Weiss's creativity and his ability to collaborate with others, G-vox Interactive Music has grown to 50 employees, and its size has been doubling every year.[13]

Entrepreneurship is also important to existing companies in a private enterprise system. Large firms often encourage entrepreneurial thinking, hoping to benefit from enhanced flexibility, improved innovation, and new market opportunities. At Hewlett-Packard (HP), restoring this kind of thinking was the mission of Carly Fiorino. When she took over as HP's CEO, Fiorino concluded that the company had grown so big that its emphasis on building consensus was slowing innovation to a crawl. She cut inefficiencies from the company's bloated structure and insisted that managers focus on a few areas where HP's future sales and profit potentials were strong. Fiorino considers these changes to be a return to the company's entrepreneurial roots: "We talk about 'The rules of the Garage' after the garage where Bill [Hewlett] and Dave [Packard] started. The rules were that bureaucracy and politics are ridiculous. Work quickly. Invent something significant."[14] Within the first year of Fiorino's leadership at HP, the company boasted a new structure and the launch of several innovations. These included a photo printer that prints directly from a digital camera, a printer capable of printing an entire book in five minutes or less, and software that can search the Internet to find products meeting a variety of buyer criteria and then arrange the purchase.

As the next section explains, entrepreneurs have played a vital role in the history of American business. They have helped to create new industries, developed successful new business methods, and improved U.S. standing in global competition.

Chapter 5 looks more closely at how individuals start their own business, and Chapter 6 returns to the subject of entrepreneurship.

SIX ERAS IN THE HISTORY OF BUSINESS

In the roughly four centuries since the first European settlements appeared on the North American continent, amazing changes have occurred in the size, focus, goals, and use of technology of U.S. businesses. As Table 1.2 indicates, U.S. business history is divided into six distinct time periods: (1) the colonial period, (2) the industrial revolution, (3) the age of industrial entrepreneurs, (4) the production era, (5) the marketing era, and (6) today's relationship era. The next sections describe how events in each of these time periods have influenced U.S. business practices.

The Colonial Period

Before the U.S. Declaration of Independence from Great Britain in 1776, colonial society emphasized rural and agricultural production. Colonial towns were small compared with European cities, and they functioned as marketplaces for farmers, craftspeople, doctors, bankers, and lawyers. The economic focus of the nation centered on rural areas, since prosperity depended on the output of farms and plantations. The success or failure of crops influenced every aspect of the economy.

Colonists depended on England for manufactured items as well as financial backing for their infant industries. Even after the Revolutionary War (1776–1783), the United States maintained close economic ties with England. British investors continued to provide much of the financing for developing the U.S. business system, and this financial influence continued well into the 19th century.

The Industrial Revolution

The industrial revolution began in England around 1750, moving business operations from an emphasis on independent, skilled workers who specialized in building products one by one to a factory system that mass-produced items by bringing together large numbers of semiskilled workers. The factories profited from the savings created by large-scale production, bolstered by increasing support from machines over time. As businesses grew, they could often purchase raw materials more cheaply in larger lots than before. Specialization of labor, limiting each worker to perform

Table 1.2 **Six Eras in Business History**

Era	Main Characteristics	Time Period
Colonial	Primarily agricultural	Prior to 1776
Industrial revolution	Mass production by semiskilled workers, aided by machines	1760–1830
Industrial entrepreneurs	Advances in technology and increased demand for manufactured goods, leading to enormous entrepreneurial opportunities	Late 1800s
Production	Emphasis on producing more goods faster, leading to production innovations like assembly lines	Prior to 1920s
Marketing	Consumer orientation, seeking to understand and satisfy needs and preferences of customer groups	Since 1950s
Relationship	Benefits derived from deep, links ongoing with individual customers, employees, suppliers, and other businesses	Began in 1990s

one or a few specific tasks in the production process, also improved production efficiency.

Influenced by these events in England, business in the U.S. began a time of rapid industrialization. Agriculture became mechanized, and factories sprang up in cities. During the mid-1800s, the pace of the revolution was increased as newly built railroad systems provided fast, economical transportation. In California, for example, the combination of railroad building and the gold rush fueled tremendous demand for construction.

The Age of the Industrial Entrepreneur

Building on the opportunities created by the industrial revolution, entrepreneurship increased in the U.S. during the late 19th century. In California in 1900, Arthur R. Wilson and several partners paid $10,000 in gold coins for a 27-acre parcel of granite-rich land. This natural resource was the basis for Granite Rock Co., which provided the material for roads and buildings in California's booming economy. During the early years, 15 Granite Rock employees worked ten-hour backbreaking shifts to knock the granite out of the quarry with sledgehammers and shovel it into railcars. Later on, new mining techniques would transform the firm's basic operations, but Wilson's entrepreneurial dream produced tons of the building blocks used in California's roads and buildings. [15]

Inventors created a virtually endless array of commercially useful products and new production methods. Many of them are famous today:

- Eli Whitney introduced the concept of interchangeable parts, an idea that would later facilitate mass production on a previously impossible scale.
- Robert McCormick designed a horse-drawn reaper that reduced the labor involved in harvesting wheat. His son, Cyrus McCormick, saw the commercial potential of the reaper and launched a business to build and sell the machine. By 1902, the company was producing 35 percent of the nation's farm machinery.
- Cornelius Vanderbilt (railroads), J. P. Morgan (banking), and Andrew Carnegie (steel), among others, took advantage of the enormous opportunities waiting for anyone willing to take the risk of starting a new business.
- Cleveland bookkeeper John D. Rockefeller saved and borrowed to finance his own dry goods trading business. The business thrived, and Rockefeller decided to go into oil refining. By age 31, he was well on his way to becoming one of the richest men in the world. The company he founded, the Standard Oil Company, is now a multibillion-dollar global business.[16]

The entrepreneurial spirit of this golden age in business did much to advance the U.S. business system and raise the overall standard of living of its citizens. That market transformation, in turn, created new demand for manufactured goods.

The Production Era

As demand for manufactured goods continued to increase during the early years of the 20th century, businesses focused even greater attention on the activities involved in producing those goods. Work became increasingly specialized, and huge, labor-intensive factories dominated U.S. business. Assembly lines, introduced by Henry Ford, became commonplace in major industries. Business owners turned over their responsibilities to a new class of managers trained in operating established companies. Their activities emphasized efforts to produce even more goods in quicker processes.

Granite Rock Co. kept pace with the changes. To offer high-quality granite in more than two basic sizes, in 1903 the granite supplier significantly improved the output of its quarries by investing in the latest technology: a steam-powered No. 3 McCully crusher. Not only did the machine produce better quality and more sizes, it increased output from 175 tons a *day* from manual labor to 20 tons an *hour*. A year later, a No. 5 McCully improved production speeds to 55 tons an hour. The company used technology to improve efficiency, and by freeing employees from grueling labor, it left them with energy to think about new ways to satisfy customers.[17]

During the production era, business focused attention on internal processes rather than external influences. Marketing was almost an afterthought, designed solely to distribute products generated by central company activities. Little attention was paid to consumer wants or needs. Instead, businesses tended to make decisions about what the market would get. For example, if you wanted to buy a Ford Model T automobile, you had no choice in color. Henry Ford's factories produced cars in only one color—black—because that decision simplified the manufacturing process.

The Marketing Era

The Great Depression of the early 1930s changed the shape of U.S. business yet again. As incomes nose-dived, businesses could no longer automatically count on selling everything they produced. Managers began to pay more attention to the markets for their goods and services, and sales and advertising took on new importance. During this period, *selling* was often synonymous with *marketing*.

Demand for all kinds of consumer goods exploded after World War II. After nearly five years of doing without new automobiles, appliances, and other items to contribute to the war effort, consumers were buying again. At the same time, however, competition also heated up. Soon businesses began to think of marketing as more than just selling; they envisioned a process of determining what consumers wanted and needed and then designing products to satisfy those needs. In short, they developed a **consumer orientation.**

Businesses throughout the U.S. formed marketing research units to analyze consumer desires before beginning actual production. Consumer choice skyrocketed. Today's automobiles no longer come just in black; instead, car buyers can choose from a wide range of colors and other accessories.

Businesses also discovered the need to distinguish their goods and services from those of competitors. **Branding,** the process of creating an identity in consumers' minds for a good, service, or company, is an important tool used by marketing-oriented companies. A **brand** can be a name, term, sign, symbol, design, or some combination that identifies the products of one firm and differentiates them from competitors' offerings.

One of the early masters of branding was Ray Kroc, who bought a small restaurant and built it into the enormous McDonald's restaurant chain. Kroc insisted that every one of his restaurants follow the same operating procedures and offer similar menu items, reinforcing the nationwide image of the growing restaurant franchise in consumer minds across the country. Today, the golden arches are among the best-known company symbols in the world.

The Granite Rock Co.—its name now compressed to Graniterock—also has joined the marketing era. Today, the company recognizes that customers want more than crushed stones; they also want timely access to materials. To serve this customer demand, Graniterock developed GraniteXpress, an automatic loading system that lets truck drivers pick up whatever a customer wants, at any time of day or night. Using a plastic smart card similar to an ATM card, a truck driver swipes it through a reader that determines what to load in the truck. The driver then pulls the truck under the loader, tugs a rope, and receives precisely the material ordered by the customer. Graniterock has since upgraded the technology, replacing the smart cards with radio-frequency tags that read orders without the driver having to stop and swipe a card. This focus on giving customers precisely what they want, when they want it, is a far cry from the two sizes of rocks pounded out with sledgehammers a century ago.[18]

The marketing era has had a tremendous effect on the way business is conducted today. Even the smallest business owners recognize the importance of understanding what customers want and the reasons why they buy.

The Relationship Era

Contemporary business is entering a new age. Unlike the industrial revolution, which was powered by manufacturing advances, this new era is driven by advances in information technology. Powerful computers, online connections, and other technologies are helping businesses to form deep, direct links with their customers, employees, suppliers, and other organizations. During this new era, the relationship era, business has begun to focus on developing and leveraging relationships for mutually beneficial returns. Graniterock invites customers to visit its Web site, not just to order products, but to calculate materials requirements, subscribe to its quarterly newsletter, and learn about its commitment to quality. The company has won prestigious awards for its quality processes and even offers seminars at its annual Quality Day. By interacting with Graniterock on its Web site, customers forge stronger ties than they would by simply viewing the occasional advertisement and calling to place orders for granite or ready-mix concrete.[19]

Business activities traditionally focused on increasing the number of exchanges, or transactions, between buyers and sellers with only limited attention to communications and little or no ongoing relationships between the parties. The goal was simply to entice as many customers as possible to buy at least once. Techniques like price discounts, coupons, and prizes in cereal boxes influence short-term purchase decisions. However, firms are realizing the limitations of this approach for long-term relationship building. Not only is it an expensive and inefficient way to do business, but it builds little protection against competitors, who can easily duplicate these moves and win away the firm's customers.

Businesses gain several advantages by developing ongoing connections with customers. Since it is much less expensive to serve existing customers than to find new ones, businesses that develop long-term customer relationships can reduce their overall costs. Long-term relationships with customers enable businesses to improve their understanding of what customers want and prefer from the company. As a result, businesses enhance their chances of sustaining real advantages through competitive differentiation.

Relationships have helped Dell Computer Corp. maintain a competitive edge as personal computers become less of an innovation and more of a commodity. The company developed its reputation for excellence by offering customized personal computers (PCs), sold over the telephone and delivered within days. Consumers and businesspeople alike can call Dell, specify the size of hard drive, modem speed, monitor dimensions, and so on, and the company builds the computer to order. Today customers can also place customized orders by clicking on options at the company's Web site. Dell further cements that relationship by including on-site service as part of the computer purchase.

For large and small business customers, Dell takes the relationship building further. When customers buy more than $50,000 worth of products from Dell each year, the company assigns an account manager to service the account, assisting the buyer in placing orders and solving any problems that might arise. The account managers get to know their customers and phone them with information about products that can help them improve their results. One of these small-business customers, Keith Dellova, a vice president at a brokerage firm called OnSite Trading, talks several times a week with his Dell account manager. Dellova says his Dell rep calls him with more ideas than "any of the other companies I do business with." Not surprisingly, he plans to place more orders with the company.

Dell uses high-tech as well as high-touch to stay close to its customers. Through its Web site, the company offers a service called Premier Page. Companies that set up a Premier Page can not only place orders there but also track order status and details of past purchases and arrange to have Dell install software on their computers, even their own customized programs. Customers can use their Premier page to connect to technical support instantly. Dell will even link its Web support into a customer's systemwide software. When a business buyer places an order with Dell, the customer's system then can calculate the impact on its budgets, inventories, and production planning. Intertwining the customer's and supplier's computer systems aids in reducing ordering costs as well as errors that might otherwise occur. Dell sales reps have more time to focus on learning about customers, and customers are hard-pressed to buy from any other supplier.[20]

Dell is just one of the thousands of both small and large businesses to discover that the relationship era is an age of connections. Connections—between not just businesses and customers, but also employers and employees, technology and manufacturing, and even separate companies—are fueling economic growth. The economies of countries around the world are also becoming increasingly interconnected, as businesses expand beyond their national boundaries. In this new global economy, techniques for managing networks of people, businesses, information, and technology are of paramount importance to business success.

Each new era in U.S. business history has forced managers to reexamine the tools and techniques they formerly used to compete. The relationship era is no different from the others. Tomorrow's managers will need creativity and vision to stay on top of rapidly changing technology and to manage complex relationships in the global business world of the fast-paced 21st century.

MANAGING THE TECHNOLOGY REVOLUTION

As the previous section discusses, the relationship era is driven by new technologies that are changing nearly every aspect of people's lives. To succeed in the 21st century, business leaders must understand how technology is changing the shape of not just business, but the world as a whole.

This insight can begin with a definition of **technology** as a business application of knowledge based on scientific discoveries, inventions, and innovations. In business, technology can streamline production, creating new opportunities for organizational efficiency. A factory may rely on automated machinery to produce finished products. In an office, computers may simplify the process of managing the information involved in running a business.

Technological breakthroughs such as supercomputers, laser surgery, and cars powered by electricity and natural gas result in new goods and services for consumers, improved customer service, reduced prices, and more comfortable working conditions. Technology can make products obsolete, just as contact lenses and laser surgery reduced the eyeglasses market, DVD made inroads on videocassette rentals, and CDs threaten to wipe out the cassette tape music market. It can also open up new business opportunities, as it has for UPS, detailed in the "Clicks and Mortar" box.

Changes in technology can also create whole new industries and new ways of doing business. By 2006, half of American workers are expected to be working in jobs that involve developing, maintaining, or using some form of information technology.[21] Technological innovations ranging from voice recognition and scanners to advanced fiber

Technology has revolutionized business—especially business communications. Williams Communications advertises its ability to assist businesses by providing high-tech services such as advanced business phone systems, superior data networking, call centers, network management, and even groundbreaking multimedia. These capabilities allow teams to work together as one.

UPS Keeps Trucking with Technology

Background. It's been almost a century since UPS drivers began delivering packages from Seattle department stores with a Model T Ford and a fleet of motorcycles. In fact, the company has driven through four of the country's six eras of business history: the age of industrial entrepreneurs, the production era, the marketing era, and the relationship era. For decades UPS adhered to a business model based on the production-era theories of Frederick W. Taylor, who focused on efficiency. Today, those recognizable brown-uniformed drivers—who deliver a total of nearly 12 million packages a day—are still trained to fasten their seatbelts with the left hand while sliding the key into the truck ignition with the right hand to save time. They carry their keys dangling from a pinky finger, walk briskly, load boxes evenly like a stack of bricks, and toot their horn when arriving at a delivery destination. Then there's the company's dress code: the uniform, no beards, undershirts in white or brown, black or brown polishable shoes with nonslip soles. And the list continues.

What Happened? In recent years, UPS has made some major changes. After a devastating drivers' strike in 1997, the company took a long hard look at itself and decided it was time for an update. The result? The brown uniforms are the same, but UPS has integrated high technology—including the Internet—throughout its organization. "The strike opened all the gates that we wanted to open in terms of developing more aggressive strategies," notes Joseph Guerrisi, a former UPS executive.

The Response. With an $11 billion investment in technology, UPS now has the capacity to track every movement of every shipped package within its system. This ability alone has repaired and reinforced its relationships with customers. UPS sales representatives can use a handheld computer to click into the UPS site, enter a tracking number, and find the goods their customers are waiting for. UPS drivers now carry a computerized clipboard called a DIAD, which contains an internal radio that simultaneously receives and sends delivery information. The moment a customer signs the electronic clipboard, the information is relayed throughout the UPS system. The DIAD can also transmit information about traffic jams and alternate routes for drivers. Through its logistics division, UPS dominates shipping from Internet retailers, even acting as a fulfillment center from its Louisville, Kentucky, warehouse for Nike.com.

But the biggest move of all is the company's use of technology to move into a delivery practice that had previously seemed obsolete to many marketers—a form of C.O.D., or collect on delivery. Under its pilot program involving an arrangement with Gateway, UPS began offering C.O.D. service for Gateway goods. UPS collected payment from customers on delivery and deposited the funds directly into Gateway's bank account. The program was so successful that UPS is looking for ways to expand it, such as to buyers and sellers involved in online auctions. But the larger implications could be in international trade, where UPS can pick up raw materials or parts in one country, pay for them there, and deliver them to a manufacturer in another country, where the manufacturer would pay UPS. This transaction not only provides cash to the supplier but also ensures safe and fast delivery of the goods to the manufacturer. The DIAD could ultimately receive, validate, and securely transmit credit card payments at the point of delivery—perhaps the ultimate form of C.O.D.

Today and Counting. The UPS technology network continues to grow through partnerships with companies like Oracle and IBM. Internet business customers like micronpc.com, MisterArt.com, and PlanetOutdoors.com have signed up for various UPS online tools to customize online services such as address validation, shipping options, and online tracking. Technology is now so pervasive at UPS that one business writer says, "UPS used to be a trucking company with technology. Now it's a technology company with trucks." Still, UPS hasn't forgotten its roots as a brick-and-mortar company. It hasn't changed the things that have worked for nearly a century: those big brown trucks, those pressed brown uniforms, those neatly stacked boxes and packages, those dark polished shoes. Such familiar images reassure people that the company remains conservative and reliable in an era of change. Which, after all, is what UPS is all about: getting the goods there on time.

QUESTIONS FOR CRITICAL THINKING
1. In what ways has UPS had to adapt from the production era to the relationship era of business?
2. UPS has made a major commitment to technology for the 21st century. Do you think this is a wise move? Why or why not?

Sources: UPS Web site, **www.ups.com,** accessed March 16, 2001; Kelly Barron, "Logistics in Brown," *Forbes Magazine,* January 10, 2000, pp. 78–83; Kelly Barron, "Addicting the Customer," *Forbes Magazine,* January 10, 2000, p. 83; "Out of the Box at UPS," *Business Week Online,* January 10, 2000, **www.businessweek.com.**

optics and online services are playing critical roles in advancing nations' standards of living as they begin the 21st century.

The Internet

Perhaps the most talked about technological innovation of the past decade is the Internet, a worldwide network of interconnected computers that, within limits, lets anyone with access to a PC or other computing

> **BUSINESS DIRECTORY**
> ➤ **Internet** *worldwide network of interconnected computers that, within limits, lets anyone with access to a personal computer send and receive images and data anywhere.*

device send and receive images and data anywhere. The roots of the Internet began when the U.S. Department of Defense created a secure military communications system in the late 1960s. Over time, other government and business computer networks were also created and interlinked. In 1986, the National Science Foundation facilitated comprehensive connections among many of these computer networks by dedicating five supercomputers that allowed all of the various networks to communicate with each other.

In 1993, Internet usage began to spread to individual users with the development of the **World Wide Web** *(or Web)*, an interlinked collection of graphically rich information sources within the larger Internet. The Web has opened new opportunities for organizations and individuals to communicate their messages to the world on Web sites, the data pages of the World Wide Web. Most Web sites offer interactive elements. A user simply clicks on a highlighted word or picture to receive information—text, photographs, charts, or even a song or movie clip. People access all this content from their office computer, home PC, or wherever they carry a Web-enabled mobile phone, which displays content on a small screen embedded in the handset. Since 51 percent of all U.S. households have at least one computer in their homes, not surprisingly, the majority of users connect to the Internet via a PC. By 2004, the vast majority of Internet users will hook up via telephones.[22]

Another Internet communications tool is electronic mail, commonly called **e-mail,** which is the electronic delivery of messages via Internet links. Using e-mail, individuals and businesses can instantly send messages and information around the globe. E-mail also allows documents, pictures, and spreadsheets to be sent almost anywhere in the world as attachments to messages. Such capabilities have helped make e-mail the most widely used Internet application.

What does the Internet mean to industry? For one thing, it represents a huge community of prospective customers. Hundreds of millions of people use the Internet, including a majority of U.S. households. As Figure 1.5 shows, the global Internet population is growing faster than that of the United States. Almost every country has Internet access, and more than one-tenth of the world's population is expected to be linked to the Internet by 2005.[23] Many of those people currently connected to the Internet are spending money online. Online sales currently exceed $200 billion a year, not including a few more billion dollars spent for online advertising.[24] Adding in revenues from companies that earn money from other Internet-related activities like selling hardware and software brings total Internet-related revenues above the $500 billion mark.[25] The Internet is also a major source of jobs. A recent study found that the number of Internet-related jobs had reached the 2.5 million mark— more than in the insurance industry and double the employment of the airline industry.[26]

The opportunities brought by the Internet are particularly significant for low-income developing nations. Even in countries where phone lines and computers are rare, people are accessing the Internet with mobile phones and at Internet cafes and public access centers sponsored by government and charitable organizations. At the I-Cafe in remote Ulan Bator, Mongolia, a newspaper reporter recently found students looking for scholarships to U.S. universities and a trader corresponding via e-mail with a partner in Russia. The trader, Tamir Hyadborjigin, uses the Internet to find and communicate with trading partners, including the Russian company, which supplies leather-processing equipment, and a California company from which he plans to import vitamins to sell in Mongolia. Besides negotiating purchases over the Web, Hyadborjigin plans to set up a Web site to sell leather products in other countries.[27]

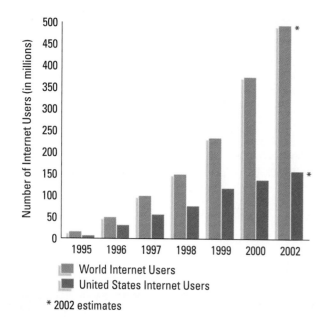

FIGURE 1.5
Growth of the Internet Population

Luster Group Succeeds by Building Relationships

Background. "You can't afford not to invest in technology today or you'll be left behind," warns Robert Luster, founder and head of the Luster Group, a nationwide construction management firm. Luster's company provides construction to large clients in both the private and government sectors, including AT&T, The Coca-Cola Company, and the U.S. Department of Justice. But technology is not enough unless it helps people communicate and build relationships—and relationships are the foundation of the Luster Group.

What Happened? In 1990, after working for the U.S. Department of Defense, Luster founded his company, Luster Construction Management, in San Francisco. He landed his first client even before he had time to build the staff needed to run the business. "I stuck my neck out and said I could have someone there the next day," he recalls. From that fast beginning, the work continued to roll in. Over the years, Luster set up separate organizations to focus on such phases of building design and construction as landscape architecture and general design services. These were ultimately combined in one coordinated group, Luster Group Inc. The company also developed its own Web site—one of the first in the industry—to provide direct contact with clients located throughout the U.S. and abroad. It also set up an intranet so that all employees in the now-nationwide organization could communicate with one another on projects.

The Response. As much as Luster's organization has grown, it is still a fairly small company by industry standards. But the company's founder is not fazed by that. In fact, he uses the moderate size of the Luster Group as an asset in developing relationships with clients. "[Some] clients say that my company is not a big house and therefore doesn't have all the skills needed in-house," he explains. "To counter that, I spend more time up front cultivating the relationships so the client is familiar with me and my company." Luster also forms alliances with other companies to market specific services to potential clients. Customers like this type of relationship building—they get personal attention to their specific needs that they couldn't get in a huge firm. And through this personal link with clients, Luster Group continues to grow.

Today and Counting. Luster plans to enhance his company's position as a full-service, highly professional organization by acquiring more firms that can supplement the Luster Group's operation. He is also adamant about building strong, positive relationships with the cities that surround San Francisco Bay. His sister Laura heads a division devoted to training and community development, which provides government-funded student internships and adult training. The company is also involved in such activities as workforce development, welfare-to-work, internships, and mentoring programs. "Many companies take money out of the community and don't give anything back," explains Luster. "I was trying to find a way to differentiate the Luster Group while breaking down barriers."

QUESTIONS FOR CRITICAL THINKING

1. In what ways can the Luster Group use the Web to differentiate itself from larger organizations by developing relationships with potential and existing clients?
2. Why is it important for an organization like the Luster Group to give back to its community?

Sources: "Luster Organization," company Web site, **www.luster.com**, accessed February 12, 2001; "Luster Opens Two New Branches," *American City Business Journals*, April 21, 1999, **www.bizjournals.com/sanfrancisco**; Gerda D. Gallop, "At the Top of Their Game," *Black Enterprise*, November 1998, pp. 116–117.

The Internet facilitates direct, interactive relationships between businesses and their customers. Instead of relying on intermediaries such as retailers, agents, and brokers to reach customers, businesses can now connect directly with the people who buy and use their products. This tool may dramatically change traditional business practices in some industries, as in the construction industry described in the "Clicks and Mortar" box. In 2001, people booked an estimated $5.3 billion in airline tickets at self-service Web sites like Travelocity and Expedia.[28] If travelers prefer to make their own reservations, what role will travel agents play? For travel agent Nancy Zebrick, the answer was to go online. After setting up a Web site, Zebrick generated so much volume that she shut her travel agency storefront to focus on services to her online clientele, later merging with 1travel.com, an online superstore for travel-related products.[29]

The Internet is also opening up new ways of interacting with customers, suppliers, and employees. Many firms have invested in **intranets,** closed network systems using Internet standards that allow for information sharing among employees, divisions, and geographically diverse locations. Other firms have created **extranets,** secure networks accessible from outside but only by trusted third parties such as familiar customers or suppliers.

The Internet's interactive capability also allows businesses to customize their products and communications for individual customers around the world. Catalog marketer Lands' End was the first business to use its Web site to let shoppers specify their physical characteristics that are then used to design three-dimensional models of themselves. They can try clothes from the Web site on the model and rotate the model 360 degrees to show how the clothes look on a person with those dimensions. The special software used by Lands' End has since been added to Web sites for Macy's and JCPenney. As the software's designer puts it, "It's exactly like meeting with a personal shopper."[30]

Chapter 7 details how companies are applying Internet technology to forge relationships with customers. Chapter 17 explains more about how businesses are using technology, including Internet resources, to manage information. Technology's role in various business functions is also a recurring theme throughout this book. Many of our "Clicks and Mortar" and "Business Hits and Misses" features report on firms' efforts to leverage technology for competitive advantage.

FROM TRANSACTION MANAGEMENT TO RELATIONSHIP MANAGEMENT

As business enters the 21st century, a significant change is taking place in the ways companies interact with customers. Since the industrial revolution, most businesses have concentrated on building and promoting products in hopes that enough customers would buy them to cover costs and earn acceptable profits, an approach called **transaction management.**

In the relationship era, however, businesses are starting to take a different, longer-term approach in their interactions with customers. These firms are seeking ways to actively nurture customer loyalty by carefully managing every interaction. They earn enormous paybacks for their efforts. A company that retains customers over the long haul reduces its advertising, sales, and account initiation costs. Since customer spending tends to accelerate over time, revenues also grow. Companies with long-term customers often can avoid the costly reliance on price discounts to attract new business, and they find that many new customers come from loyal customer referrals.

Increasingly, business focuses on **relationship management,** the collection of activities that build and maintain ongoing, mutually beneficial ties with customers and other parties. At its core, relationship management involves gathering knowledge of customer needs and preferences and applying that understanding to get as close to the customer as possible. Recently, General Electric (GE) has been applying Internet technology to maintaining customer relationships. In the GE Power Systems division, Web tools help customers get the best return on their GE products. GE's power-generating turbines cost millions of dollars and represent a significant investment for customers. Through an Internet link to GE, a turbine operator at one of GE's customers can use turbine optimizer software to compare the performance of a turbine with the same model operating in other locations throughout the world. The optimizer tells the operator what to do to improve the turbine's performance, detailing the financial benefits of making the change. It also lets the operator schedule a service call from GE to implement the change. In addition, customers of GE Power Systems can have the division set up a customized Web site to inform them about GE's turbines and other subjects of interest, as well as enable them to order products from equipment to services. With all this on the Web site, GE hopes customers will be reluctant to look elsewhere.

Other GE divisions are on the relationship management bandwagon. Polymerland, which handles plastics distribution, not only sells products online but helps customers decide when to order. Some big customers buy silos full of plastic nuggets, which they melt down to make products like cases for computers and cell phones. Polymerland installs sensors in its silos to measure when the amount of inventory falls below a given level. At that point, the system signals the customer to reorder.[31]

Celestica International, a Toronto-based company with operations in Mexico and elsewhere that makes electronics to order, also fosters close ties to customers. As a contract manufacturer, Celestica takes product designs from customers and figures out how to make it as efficiently as possible. Problems arise when the customers' designs do not account for the nuances of the production process. A major problem encountered by Celestica designers was design defects in more than 90 percent of customers' plans. Today, when a customer sends in an order, Celestica enters it into its computer, and specially designed software analyzes the design in terms of the information in the database, recommending changes that will improve the way the product is made. Customers go online to check and approve the recommendations. This fine-tuning enables Celestica to prevent most defects and fill orders faster and more economically.[32] By collaborating in product design, Celestica has moved its relationships with customers beyond buyer–seller interactions to a partnership in which customers have an important say in the company's activities.

Strategic Alliances and Partnerships

Businesses are also finding that they must form partnerships with other organizations to take full advantage of available opportunities. A **partnership** is an affiliation of two or more companies with the shared goal of assisting each other in the achievement of common goals. One such form of partnership between organizations is a **strategic alliance,** a partnership formed to create competitive advantage for the businesses involved.

Some of the most widely reported strategic alliances today involve partnerships between dot-com businesses—those formed to sell goods and services on the Internet—and traditional retailers that have experience selling to consumers through stores or catalogs. The traditional retailers contribute their expertise in buying the right amount of the right merchandise, as well as their knowledge of distribution— accepting orders and warehousing and transporting the goods. Often, they also provide a more familiar brand name. The dot-com businesses contribute their knowledge of the Internet, ability to provide the latest technology, and the fast pace of a start-up enterprise. For example, Petopia struggled to maintain market share against formidable competition from other online sellers of pet products. So it teamed up with brick-and-mortar superstore Petco. The two companies pool orders for merchandise and advertising so they can get better deals, and they share distribution resources to keep costs down. Petco stores provide information about the Petopia Web site, which is Petco's only online retailing presence. Through this strategic alliance, Petco gains a foothold in cyberspace, and Petopia gains access to the resources it needs for growth in a highly competitive environment.[33] Chapter 13 takes a closer look at other strategies that businesses are using to strengthen relationships with customers and other firms.

CREATING VALUE THROUGH QUALITY AND CUSTOMER SATISFACTION

Today's savvy consumers want the satisfaction of acquiring more than ordinary goods and services. Their demands extend beyond just low prices. Firms seeking to tighten bonds with customers must provide value to customers to earn their long-term loyalty.

Value is the customer's perception of the balance between the positive traits of a good or service and its price. Customers who think that they have received value— that is, positive benefits for a fair price—are likely to remain satisfied and continue their relationships with a firm. However, when customers perceive an inequitable balance between benefits and price, they become dissatisfied and start looking for opportunities outside their relationships with the business. Value is also an important way to differentiate goods and services from competing offerings. A firm that provides real value to customers often enjoys superior advantages and wider opportunities in the marketplace. A widespread myth is that being first to enter a market

SpaceWorks Web BusinessManager Suite software gives businesses the ability to improve interactions with their customers, and so enhance the quality and customer service at their Web sites. The software assists B2B companies with real-time ordering, inventory availability, order tracking, interactive marketing, and online billing and payment.

offers assurance of success. In fact, recent history shows examples of first movers losing out to companies that offered greater value. More people buy their personal computers from companies like Dell, which customize their offerings, than from industry pioneers like IBM. In the area of palm-top computers, PalmPilot was designed after the unsuccessful launch of the Apple Newton, enabling its creators to learn from Apple's mistakes. Similarly, although eToys was the first major online toy retailer, brick-and-mortar giant Toys 'R' Us took its time in creating a well-tested, user-friendly Web site and captured a significant part of the online toy market by offering shoppers the combination of a nearby retail outlet with the convenience of Internet shopping.[34]

Customers' value perceptions are often tied to **quality,** the degree of excellence or superiority of a firm's goods and services. Technically, *quality* refers to physical product traits, such as durability and performance reliability. However, quality also includes **customer satisfaction,** the ability of a good or service to meet or exceed buyer needs and expectations. In the realm of online shopping, quality includes not just the characteristics of the products sold but the ability of online sellers to protect credit card purchasers from theft or misuse of their card number and to deliver the products advertised within the promised time. One firm currently providing high-quality on-time delivery service is electronics seller Crutchfield.com. Its online catalog indicates which items are in stock. If a customer places an order, Crutchfield sends an e-mail message to indicate that the order was received, followed by another message when the product leaves the warehouse. In this way, Crutchfield goes beyond filling orders to providing customer satisfaction through communication.[35]

Technology wields a double-edged sword for customer satisfaction. On the one hand, using technology can give a business the ability to improve interactions with customers. On the other hand, technologies like online communications, computerized engineering, and satellite communications have led customers to expect more from firms with which they do business. Customers are no longer content to wait for replies to their questions or complaints. They expect instant responses and personalized attention to their needs. They now insist on products that can perform expanded functions with improved reliability. Firms that do not keep up with customer expectations lose customers to rivals that do.

Businesses in all industries face a common challenge of finding new ways to add value to customer interactions through increased customer satisfaction and quality. This statement introduces a recurring theme in this book—how businesses will compete in the relationship era. Chapter 12 discusses methods by which businesses create value for their customers through quality and customer satisfaction, and Chapter 13 discusses how businesses identify customer wants and build customer relationships.

COMPETING IN A GLOBAL MARKET

Businesses can no longer limit their sights to events and opportunities within their own national borders. The world's economies are developing increasing interdependence. To remain competitive, companies must continually search for both the most efficient manufacturing sites and the most lucrative markets for their products.

International trade is currently expanding at an annual rate of about 6 percent.[36] The United States is a major player in this global market: U.S. exports of merchandise account for more than 12 percent of the world's exports, and U.S. exports of commercial services represent more than 18 percent of the world's services exports.[37] Major trading partners—led by Canada, Mexico, Japan, and China—are shown in Figure 1.6. The ten nations listed there purchase 64 percent of all U.S. exports. In addition, they account for 70 percent of all goods imported to the United States.[38] Emerging economies in Latin America, eastern Europe, and Asia are presenting tremendous opportunities for trade. Rising standards of living in these countries have created increasing customer demand for the latest goods and services.

The prospects of succeeding in the global marketplace appeal to U.S. businesses, which can find huge markets outside North America. Of the world's 6 billion residents, just 5 percent reside in the United States. U.S. giants such as The Coca-Cola Company and Microsoft have proved that they can duplicate their domestic success abroad. As shown in Figure 1.7, of the world's top brands, measured in terms of their dollar value, most have their origins in the United States.

Going global was a significant growth opportunity for BCS Inc., which obtains and sells electronic scrap. BCS, based in Canoga Park, California, recycles scrap from electronics manufacturers, many of which have moved their operations to Mexico. BCS set up a division in Guadalajara, a center of electronics manufacturing. From that facility, the company sells materials to a variety of Asian customers, many of them in China. For globally oriented firms like BCS, foreign markets are both a source of material and a source of customers.[39]

Many U.S. businesses are also finding that imported goods made by foreign manufacturers can create new opportunities to satisfy the needs of domestic consumers. One of these businesses is Papa Geno's Herb Farm, described earlier in this chapter. Papa Geno's buys specialty herbs from the best suppliers, a strategy that sometimes requires a trip overseas. For example, the company buys lavender from a farmer in Provence, in southern France. Every year, two employees from Papa Geno's fly to France "with cash stuffed in their underwear" to sit down at the farmer's kitchen table, share a bottle of wine, and reach a deal with her.[40] For other companies, foreign suppliers are attractive because of their prices. An important reason the electronics industry is booming in Mexican cities like Guadalajara and Monterrey is that the costs of making circuit boards and assembling computers and electronic gadgets are much lower there. This trend provides a source of low-cost goods for U.S. consumers, as well as business opportunities for companies like BCS.

The U.S. is an attractive market for foreign competitors because of its size and high standard of living. Foreign companies like Matsushita, the Body Shop, and Sun Life of Canada operate production, distribution, service, and retail facilities here. Foreign ownership of U.S. companies has increased as well. MCA is a well-known firm with foreign parents. Foreign investment in the United States means additional competitive pressures for domestic firms.

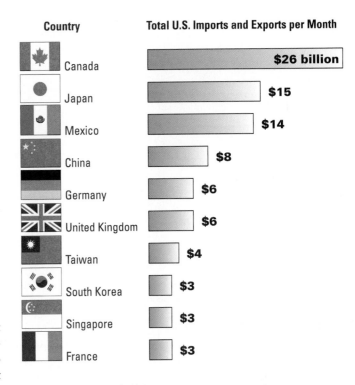

Country	Total U.S. Imports and Exports per Month
Canada	$26 billion
Japan	$15
Mexico	$14
China	$8
Germany	$6
United Kingdom	$6
Taiwan	$4
South Korea	$3
Singapore	$3
France	$3

FIGURE 1.6
Top Ten U.S. Trading Partners

Productivity: Key to Global Competitiveness

Global competitiveness requires nations, industries, and individual firms to work efficiently at producing goods and services. As discussed earlier, firms need a

BUSINESS DIRECTORY

➤ **customer satisfaction**   *ability of a good or service to meet or exceed buyer needs and expectations.*

Which of the following brands are U.S.-based? The answer is printed below the chart.

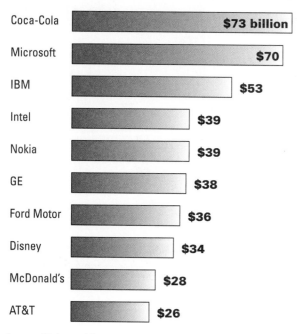

Coca-Cola	$73 billion
Microsoft	$70
IBM	$53
Intel	$39
Nokia	$39
GE	$38
Ford Motor	$36
Disney	$34
McDonald's	$28
AT&T	$26

Answer: Of the world's top ten brands, only Finland's Nokia is owned by a non-U.S. company.

FIGURE 1.7
Top Ten Brands Worldwide

number of inputs, or factors of production, to produce goods and services.

Productivity describes the relationship between the number of units produced and the number of human and other production inputs necessary to produce them. Productivity is, therefore, a ratio of output to input. When a constant amount of inputs generates increased outputs, an increase in productivity occurs.

Total productivity considers all inputs necessary to produce a specific amount of outputs. Stated in equation form, it can be written as follows:

$$\text{Total productivity} = \frac{\text{Output (goods or services produced)}}{\text{Input (human/natural resources, capital)}}$$

Many productivity ratios focus on only one of the inputs of the equation: labor productivity or output per labor-hour. An increase in labor productivity means that the same amount of work produces more goods and services than before.

Productivity is a widely recognized measure of a company's efficiency. In turn, the total productivity of a nation's businesses has become a measure of its economic strength and standard of living. Economists refer to this measure as a country's **gross domestic product (GDP)**—the sum of all goods and services produced within its boundaries. The GDP is based on the per capita output of a country—in other words, total national output divided by the number of citizens. The U.S. GDP is currently growing at an average rate of 3.9 percent a year. As Figure 1.8 shows, it remains the highest in the world.

Some economists argue that this measure doesn't necessarily prove that the United States is the most productive or competitive nation in the world. They point out that Americans actually work longer hours and take fewer vacations than do workers in other countries. If national output is calculated on the basis of production divided by the total number of hours worked in a nation, France and Germany would show higher productivity levels and several other European countries would be close to the United States. Even relatively young French and German workers receive annual vacations of five to six weeks, considerably longer than their counterparts in the United States. In short, if Europeans simply worked longer hours, Americans would lag behind in productivity.[41]

Even though the United States leads the world in GDP, continued economic growth in countries such as China, Germany, India, Singapore, South Korea, Taiwan, and Japan has aroused fears about the global competitiveness of the United States. Some suggest that U.S. managers focus too much on short-term goals and devote insufficient attention to developing long-range plans for worldwide competition. Plant closings, business failures, and employee layoffs are seen as signs of the need to invest more in long-term research, development, and innovation in order to remain competitive in the global market.

Nevertheless, steady productivity growth in the United States in the 1990s and the early years of the 21st century has bolstered confidence in the U.S. economy. Much of the credit goes to technology. During the past two decades, thousands of American companies invested heavily in information technology, and economists believe those investments are paying off in the first decade of the 21st century. Other countries that have made similar investments in technology also have been enjoying productivity gains, including Australia, Denmark, Finland, Ireland, and Norway. In these countries, information technology has enabled companies to innovate faster and maintain customer relationships and partnerships around the globe.[42] Chapter 4 examines these and other factors affecting global competitiveness, as well as the strategies employed by companies competing in the global market.

topie for Project

DEVELOPING AND SUSTAINING A WORLD-CLASS WORKFORCE

A skilled and knowledgeable workforce is an essential resource for keeping pace with the accelerating rate of change in today's business world. Employers need reliable workers to foster strong ties with customers and partners. They must build workforces capable of the productivity needed to compete in global markets. Business leaders are also beginning to realize that the brainpower of employees plays a vital role in a firm's ability to stay on top of new technologies and innovations.

A world-class workforce can be the foundation of a firm's competitive differentiation, providing important advantages over competing businesses. Building a world-class workforce is a difficult task, though, and it is made all the more complex by the changing characteristics of workers as well as the effects of recent business history.

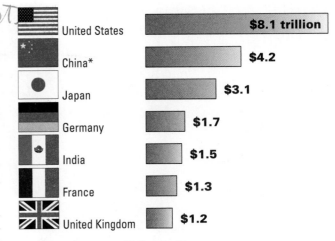

United States   **$8.1 trillion**
China*   **$4.2**
Japan   **$3.1**
Germany   **$1.7**
India   **$1.5**
France   **$1.3**
United Kingdom   **$1.2**

*Estimate; may overstate GDP by up to 25 percent.

FIGURE 1.8
Nations with the Highest Gross Domestic Product.

Preparing for Changes in the Workforce

In the coming decades, companies will face several trends that challenge their skills for managing and developing human resources: aging of the population, shrinking labor pool, growing diversity of the workforce, the changing nature of work, and increased mobility of workers.

Aging of the Population   Members of the baby boom generation, people born between 1946 and 1965, are nearing the peaks of their careers, and the oldest of them have begun to retire. Employers must therefore deal with issues arising from reliance on older workers, such as retirement, disability programs, retraining, and insurance benefits. By 2025, 62 million Americans will be senior citizens—nearly double today's number. As these elderly Americans leave the workforce, they will attract attention by businesspeople eager to earn profits by serving their needs. A similar trend is occurring on a global scale. The worldwide population of people 60 or older may exceed the population of children by 2050, for the first time on record.[43]

Retirement also creates human resource problems for thousands of businesses, because Generation Xers, people born between 1966 and 1976, represent only 21 percent of the population compared with nearly 42 percent for baby boomers who are beginning to leave the workforce. The result is a decline in the number of available adult workers. Companies are increasingly finding talent at the extremes of the age spectrum. Some are hiring tech-savvy teenagers to develop Web sites and program computers. The number of 16- to 19-year-olds employed by the computer industry quadrupled during a four-year period in the late 1990s. A notable example is Eric Lupton, a teenager who hasn't let his young age or his cerebral palsy stand in the way of a flourishing business. Lupton's satisfied customers include GM Fence, which has hired him to set up a Web site.[44] At the other end of the age spectrum, people are often staying on the job past the traditional retirement age of 65. Scott Bird works as a certified Microsoft trainer, even though he is in his 70s. Overall, the number of workers who are 65 or older increased more than 30 percent during the final decade of the 20th century.[45] Figure 1.9 shows an advertisement targeted to this group of workers, who have many contributions to make and dreams to fulfill.

Shrinking Labor Pool   During the final decades of the 20th century, cost cutters at many large companies eliminated jobs as a way to boost profits. Now managers face the opposite problem as the lowest unemployment rate in a quarter-century, coupled

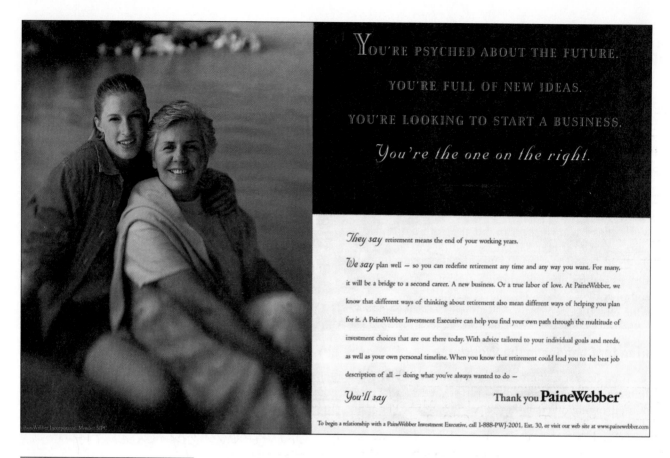

FIGURE 1.9
PaineWebber: Serving the Needs of an Aging Workforce

with the aging workforce, has led to a limited supply of skilled employees looking for jobs. More sophisticated technology has intensified the challenge by requiring that workers have more advanced skills. A recent U.S. Labor Department survey revealed that of job applicants who took tests administered by prospective employers, one applicant in five lacked the necessary math and reading skills.[46]

The challenge of a shrinking labor pool is especially great in developed nations, where the birthrate has shrunk to less than the rate of deaths. Particularly in Europe, the population of some countries is expected to decline over the first half of the century. The same forecasts predict continued growth in the U.S. population, because immigration more than makes up for the low birthrate. In the future, as in the past, immigrants will provide a significant share of the nation's labor and entrepreneurship to the United States as well as Canada, which has adopted a policy of permitting greater immigration.[47]

The challenge is very real for Julie K. Hilton, who operates six hotels in Panama City Beach, Florida. She once looked for employees at a local job fair. The 32 companies at the fair competed for the 30 job seekers who attended. Hilton has since established relationships with contractors who help her recruit immigrants from the Czech Republic.[48]

Increasingly Diverse Workforce. Reflecting these trends, the U.S. workforce is growing more diverse. Twenty years ago, ethnic minorities made up just 18 percent of the U.S. population. By 2005, members of these groups will represent 28 percent of the population, and by 2050, nearly 50 percent of Americans will belong to such ethnic groups as Hispanic Americans, African Americans, and Asian Americans. Persons of Hispanic and Asian descent represent the fastest-growing segments of the population. A recent U.S. Department of Labor report points out the potential advantages of this diversity:

We speak every language. We know every culture. And capitalizing on our diversity and immigration trends will position us to compete and win everywhere from the global marketplace to the corner market.

America's workforce of the future will include more people of color, older Americans, women, and people with disabilities. The availability of larger pools of workers creates the opportunity to maintain economic growth by tapping new human capital resources.[49]

To fulfill this promise, managers must be able to work effectively with diverse ethnic groups, cultures, and lifestyles to develop and retain a superior workforce for their company.

To benefit from diversity, executives of many companies develop explicit strategies to encourage and manage multiculturalism. Federal Express has established a Corporate Culture & Awareness department, which develops plans for promoting diversity. The department seeks diversity among not only employees, but customers and vendors as well. Even small companies can develop ways to encourage and work with diversity among their workforce, customers, and suppliers. Semifreddi's, an Emeryville, California, bakery specializing in gourmet bread, employs workers born in Cambodia, China, Laos, Mexico, Peru, Vietnam, and Yemen. The bakery's CEO, Tom Frainier, quickly realized that communicating with his multilingual workforce required more sophisticated measures than talking slowly. Once, for example, he announced that workers should not park on a particular side of the bakery, so that the space would be available for customers. But some employees thought he was asking them not to drive to work. The communication problems were even worse when Frainier tried to discuss more sophisticated matters, such as sharing information about the company's financial performance. So he began holding small meetings with groups of workers and providing translators at every meeting. He brings together people with similar abilities in speaking English, so that they feel less embarrassed to speak up. The extra effort to manage language differences provides Frainier with more feedback from his employees and better morale.[50]

FedEx has established a Corporate Culture & Awareness department that develops and manages the company's diversity and affirmative action efforts and also encourages programs to promote diversity among its employees, vendors, and customers. Ethnic minorities will make up 28 percent of the U.S. population by 2005, and capitalizing on this diversity will become even more essential in competing in the global marketplace.

The Changing Nature of Work   Not only is the U.S. workforce changing, but so is the very nature of work. Although the U.S. continues to lead the world in manufacturing, each year it depends less on the manufacturing sector as it continues to move toward an economy based on service industries. This change will lead U.S. employers to rely heavily on service workers with sharp knowledge skills as well as manufacturing and technological skills. New work lifestyles are also becoming common in business life. The number of telecommuters, who do their work at home for businesses located elsewhere, has grown. More than half of U.S. companies have a telecommuting program, and 8 percent of an average corporation's workforce telecommutes.[51] Other employers allow job flexibility so employees can meet family and personal needs along with job-related needs. Employers are also hiring growing numbers of temporary and part-time employees.

Another business tool for staffing flexibility is **outsourcing,** contracting with another business to perform tasks or functions previously handled by internal staff members. In addition to reducing the continuing costs of hiring and training new employees, outsourcing can make a firm more competitive. Businesses concentrate on the functions that provide competitive differentiation and delegate others that do not add to customer value, such as the details of developing information systems, providing employee benefits, or collecting late payments. Peter Hunt and Richard T. Takata relied heavily on outsourcing when they launched their online home improvement store, CornerHardware.com. Takata contributed deep knowledge of the hardware business, and Hunt was an expert in the financial aspects of running a company, but they needed someone to convert their business objectives into a sophisticated, user-friendly Web site. So CornerHardware.com turned to Xuma, a company specializing in the development of Web sites. The expertise of Xuma's programmers was essential because the company wanted a superior Web site that would offer images of tens of thousands of products, along with message boards, project instructions and tips, a glossary of hardware terms, a search engine, and real-time customer services; Xuma provided expertise, but using it also was economical because it could customize various Web site basics like databases and software for processing credit card information, rather than creating these elements from scratch. In addition, CornerHardware.com paid for the programmers only as long as it used their services; then Xuma's employees could move on to another customer's job. Perhaps most important, while Xuma's people were working late into the night getting CornerHardware.com online, Hunt and Takata were able to concentrate on financing and marketing the new business. By outsourcing Web site development, the company was able to launch the site within months of getting started.[52]

Increased Mobility of Workers   Employees are no longer likely to remain with a single company throughout their entire careers. With a strong demand for qualified employees, the nation's skilled workers are usually able to move quickly from one opportunity to another. Others choose nontraditional work arrangements such as self-employment and working for agencies that place temporary workers. Almost four-fifths of employers use some kind of nontraditional staffing, and temporary job agencies has experienced rapid growth during the past ten years. Kelly Services, a leader in the industry, places clerical workers, scientists, accountants, computer analysts, and lawyers in temporary positions in 19 countries.[53]

In a business environment where employees do not feel bound to a company for life, the employer's challenge is to retain talented people. This challenge is especially difficult when employers encounter people who interpret the tight job market to mean they can have whatever they want, regardless of the impact on the employer. Consider the following:

- On average, companies lose half of their employees within five years.
- A college graduate leaving school today will have nine jobs before reaching 32 years of age.
- Replacing a worker costs roughly half of that person's salary, in addition to the burden and stress put on colleagues and the organization as a whole.
- Although many firms calculate the direct cost of unwanted turnover, the indirect costs of loss of talent, customer satisfaction, work team morale, productivity, and quality are even more critical.[54]

Chapter 9 details various ways firms are using to motivate—and retain—employees.

The New Employer–Employee Partnership   To handle the challenges of a changing workforce and to gain competitive advantage by fully utilizing employee talents, many employers are trying to form new types of relationships with employees. They know that after the highly publicized layoffs of the past two decades, employees do not expect loyalty in the form of long-term employment. Consequently, employees do not expect that they should be loyal by spending their entire career at the same company. So employers are trying to build a new kind of relationship—among equals. They emphasize creating an employer–employee partnership that recognizes and encourages workers' important contributions to providing value and satisfying customers.

To forge the partnerships that support this new kind of commitment, employers emphasize listening to and respecting their employees. They share financial data and reward employees with company stock so that they participate in the firm's success. In addition, the new employer–employee partnership often includes the employer helping employees to develop their knowledge and skills so that they are more valuable to their current employer—and in the job market down the line.

Patio Enclosures, an Ohio company that builds and installs sunrooms, tries to build such partnerships. Demand for the company's work is strong, but few talented people are interested in construction work, and those who learn the trade often decide they can do better starting their own business. So Patio Enclosures offers employees a stock ownership plan and provides a full-scale training program. Its apprenticeship program trains installers and manufacturing employees and provides for pay increases as they learn new skills. Employees receive a booklet describing the criteria for each pay level. As they learn the necessary skills for a given level, the booklet is stamped. Executive vice president Jerry Fox says this program helps Patio Enclosures retain employees: "If an employee knows he's two or three jobs away from the next pay level, why would he want to jump to another place?"[55]

Reaping the Benefits of Diversity

As discussed previously, today's workers come from many different ethnic, lifestyle, and age groups. Enlightened business leaders recognize the gain they receive from encouraging all of their employees to contribute their unique perspectives, skills, and experiences.

Diversity, blending individuals of different genders, ethnic backgrounds, cultures, religions, ages, and physical and mental abilities, can enrich a firm's chances of success. Several studies have shown that diverse employee teams and workforces tend to perform tasks more effectively and develop better solutions to business problems than homogeneous employee groups. This difference is due in part to the varied perspectives and experiences that foster innovation and creativity in multicultural teams.

Since nearly every business serves a diverse group of customers, diversity in its workforce can improve management's understanding of customer needs and relationships with customer groups. Xerox's experience with diversity initiatives in the United States is preparing it to better serve international markets. The company's efforts in the United States have been aimed at recruiting and retaining people who reflect the diversity of the U.S. population. For its international diversity efforts, Xerox is focusing on increasing the representation of women among its employees. For example, in the United Kingdom, Xerox has a goal of hiring 40 percent more female sales representatives each year, with the expectation that many of these employees will be promoted into management positions. In support of that goal, the company holds workshops on equality and diversity and is developing mentoring programs. Xerox also provides training in cross-cultural issues. It expects that these programs will help Xerox better compete in Europe. As it continues to expand its diversity initiatives Xerox is positioning itself as a formidable competitor on a global scale. As one Xerox executive puts it, "Our customers stretch from China to the new democracies in Eastern Europe, from Africa to Latin America. A company that embraces diversity must better understand this diverse world."[56]

Also, practical managers know that attention to diversity issues can help them to avoid costly and damaging legal battles. Employee lawsuits alleging discrimination are now among the most common legal issues faced by employers. Losing a discrimination lawsuit can be very costly, yet in a recent survey, a majority of executives from racial and cultural minorities said they had seen discrimination in work assignments.[57]

Ethical and societal responsibility issues associated with diversity are discussed in more detail in the next chapter. Diversity and other issues related to human resource management are discussed further in Chapter 9.

WANTED: A NEW TYPE OF MANAGER

Once, managers were encouraged to be so-called organization men, wearing identical gray flannel suits and working in a world of strict rules and rigid hierarchies. Companies no longer recruit only the stereotypical male managers; they look for intelligent, highly motivated people with the ability to create and sustain a vision of how an organization can succeed. The 21st century manager must apply critical thinking skills and creativity to business challenges, steer change, and manage an increasingly diverse workforce.

Importance of Vision

An important managerial quality needed in the 21st century is **vision,** the ability to perceive marketplace needs and what an organization must do to satisfy them. For example, not many people imagine paper when they think of the information economy. Most people think of cell phones, laptop computers, and dot-com businesses. But not entrepreneur Norm Brodsky. Brodsky has found that the more information people create and gather with their computers, the more backup copies they print out. He already runs a successful records storage business, and on a tip from a supplier, he and two partners investigated a new line of work: secure document shredding. He quickly determined that destroying confidential records was a young and growing industry, with customers willing to pay a premium to maintain the security of their documents even as they are shredded. Some businesses drive a portable shredder directly to customers, and others collect documents in locked containers and shred all the customers' documents in bulk. By considering an unlikely source of business growth, Brodsky and his partners have launched what they expect to be a highly profitable company.[58]

The need for vision isn't limited to entrepreneurs. Steve Jobs is a true visionary in the personal computing industry. Jobs cofounded Apple Computer in the mid-1980s, revolutionizing the look and feel of computing with the Apple Macintosh. The Macintosh made computers friendly—not requiring users to memorize long strings of commands to perform work—and gave them a new tool, the mouse, for easy navigation. It also brought color to formerly dull desktop monitors. The company grew to become a powerful force in the industry. Then Jobs left Apple to pursue other interests; some failed and some succeeded. Without Jobs's creative spark, Apple floundered under its new management and increasingly bigger bureaucracy. At one point, there was speculation that the company would fold. So, Apple turned to its former leader for assistance in putting the company back on its feet. The result? Under Jobs's renewed direction, the company streamlined its organization and has refocused to produce sleek iMacs in rainbow colors and PowerMac G4s with their futuristic curved lines, clear plastic cases, and awesome power to handle video and graphics. More important, the company is back on track innovating and doing what it does best—fusing art and technology to make computing fun for customers.[59] Chapter 8 explains how vision and the ability to turn ideas into action affect a firm's chances of success as part of the discussion of strategic planning.

Importance of Critical Thinking and Creativity

Critical thinking and creativity are essential characteristics of the 21st century workforce. Today's businesspeople need to look at a wide variety of situations, draw connections between disparate information, and develop future-oriented solutions.

Critical thinking is the ability to analyze and assess information in order to pinpoint problems or opportunities. The critical thinking process includes activities like determining the authenticity, accuracy, and worth of information, knowledge, and arguments. It involves looking beneath the surface for deeper meaning and connections that can help to identify critical issues and solutions. To help you develop your critical thinking skills, questions intended to stimulate discussion follow every "Clicks and Mortar" and "Business Hits and Misses" story and each chapter.

Creativity is the capacity to develop novel solutions to perceived organizational problems. Although most people think of it in relation to artists, musicians, and inventors, that indicates a very limited definition. In business, *creativity* refers to the ability to see better and different ways of doing business. A computer engineer who solves a glitch in a software program is executing a creative act; so is a mail-room clerk who finds a way to speed delivery of the company's overnight packages.

In the highly competitive market for computer printers, even the most innovative manufacturers rely on creativity to devise novel ways to communicate with potential customers. Industry giant 3M uses the ad shown in Figure 1.10 to demonstrate the creativity of its new alternative to sandpaper, as well as the company's overall emphasis on innovating.

Fostering creativity in a large company like 3M can be difficult. When consulting for a company involved in the treatment of coronary artery disease, Clayton M. Christensen determined that over a 20-year period, none of the industry's major breakthroughs had been developed in its largest companies. Christensen studied a variety of industries and found the same pattern: Significant innovations tended to come from small companies. The same tendency seems to be true of the toy industry. Former Mattel president David Mauer says, "Once [the big companies] develop strong brands, it makes sense for them to keep extending those brands or to borrow from the movies. It's just less risky." Although this strategy keeps the big toy producers profitable, it makes the going more difficult for creative toy inventors—and for companies like Haystack Toys. Haystack's founders are looking for "needles in a haystack": fun, engaging toys unlike anything yet on the market. Haystack sponsors a contest called the Great American Toy Hunt, which judges hundreds of inventions and selects a few winners to receive funding for production and marketing. Both the concept of Haystack Toys and the ideas that its judges evaluate are products of creative thinking. And Haystack's potential for finding the next big hit is so attractive that industry giant Hasbro contacted the company about a possible alliance.[60]

Most people don't need to start a company like Haystack to foster creativity. Instead, some practice and mental exercise can cultivate the ability to think creatively. Here are some exercises and guidelines that foster creativity:

- In a group, brainstorm by listing ideas as they come to mind. Build on other people's ideas, but don't criticize them. Wait until later to evaluate and organize the ideas.

- Think about how to make familiar concepts unfamiliar. A glue that doesn't stick very well? That's the basis for 3M's popular Post-It notes.

- Plan ways to rearrange your thinking with simple questions like "What features can we leave out?" or by imagining what it feels like to be the customer.

FIGURE 1.10
Communicating 3M's Creativity

- Cultivate curiosity, openness, risk, and energy as you meet people and encounter new situations. View these encounters as opportunities to learn.
- Treat failures as additional opportunities to learn.
- Get regular physical exercise. When you work out, your brain releases endorphins, and these chemicals stimulate creative thinking.
- Pay attention to your dreams and daydreams. You might find that you already know the answer to a problem.[61]

At 3M, such behavior is encouraged by management. Not only does the company spend more than $11 billion a year on research and development, it directs employees to devote 15 percent of each workweek to daydreaming about inventions.[62] Creativity and critical thinking must go beyond generating new ideas, however. They must lead to action. In addition to creating an environment where employees can nurture ideas, managers must give them opportunities to take risks and try new solutions.

Ability to Steer Change

Today's managers must guide their employees and organizations through the changes brought about by technology, marketplace demands, and global competition. Managers must be skilled at recognizing employee strengths and motivating people to move toward common goals as members of a team. Throughout this book, real-world examples demonstrate how companies have initiated sweeping change initiatives. Most, if not all, have been led by managers comfortable with the tough decisions that today's fluctuating conditions require.

Factors that require organizational change can come from both external and internal sources; successful managers must be aware of both. External forces might include feedback from customers, developments in the international marketplace, economic trends, and new technologies. Internal factors might arise from new company goals, emerging employee needs, labor-union demands, or production problems.

At Yellow Corp., parent company of Yellow Freight truck lines, the pressure to change came from both external and internal forces. First, the federal government deregulated the trucking industry, forcing the company to compete hard for customers. Later, a Teamsters Union strike drove customers to nonunion competitors. Yellow tried to win them back with price cuts, but the strategy made the company unprofitable. When Maurice Myers took over as president, he determined that the company had to change to a more customer-driven strategy. A survey of the firm's customers revealed that their ideal transportation company would be capable of helping them operate more efficiently by offering services like just-in-time delivery and data sharing. Yellow responded by upgrading its information systems and developing a Web site that could meet customers' information needs. The changes were costly and required employees to shift their focus from internal concerns to customer wants and needs. But the effort was worthwhile. Yellow quickly began enjoying sales growth and profitability.[63]

The role played by change agents is examined in more detail in Chapter 6. Teamwork is a major topic in Chapter 10.

MANAGING ETHICS AND SOCIAL RESPONSIBILITY

In recent years, stories about misconduct by businesses and their employees have become all too common. Insurance regulators in Georgia and Florida ordered 28 companies to stop collecting higher premiums from African-American customers based solely on their race. A California firm avoided inspection of Mexican strawberries by smuggling them across the border, resulting in thousands of elementary school students being exposed to hepatitis. Former television personality Kathie Lee Gifford

SOLVING AN ETHICAL CONTROVERSY

You expect a certain amount of privacy in your own home. You don't have to answer the phone or the door if you don't want to, and there are laws prohibiting unwanted intrusions in both instances. But what about at the workplace, particularly now that the Internet allows employees access to a vast array of information and communication? And it works both ways, allowing outsiders access to employees. Fearing a lack of control over outgoing and incoming information, many employers have opted to monitor employees' Internet transmissions and activities with a variety of software that ranges in complexity from randomly searching for key words in transmissions to identifying every stroke at the keyboard.

Should employers have the right to monitor employees' use of computers at the workplace?

PRO

1. Companies need to be able to protect themselves from legal liability for the actions of employees, from corporate espionage, and from employee theft of information. The only way to do this is by monitoring Internet transmissions.
2. Employees who use the Internet for their own needs—shopping, personal e-mail, and game playing—during work hours are wasting company time and should be held accountable. A recent *Computerworld* survey revealed that employees often use the Internet to check sports scores, stock prices, and even job listings outside the organization during work time.
3. Employers who own or operate their own computer systems have a right to determine how these systems are used. Court decisions have consistently supported this argument.

CON

1. Computer databases, which track all kinds of employee activities, may contain personal or confidential information that could be harmful to employees. For instance, in a survey of *Fortune* 500 companies, 70 percent released confidential employee information to credit companies without informing the employee first. Some companies are now collecting genetic data on their employees, which could be misused.
2. Federal law already prohibits employers from covertly taping conversations or placing video cameras in locker rooms or changing rooms, so they should be prohibited from intruding on computer communications as well.
3. Employers must develop trust in their employees as part of the employer–employee relationship. Respecting their privacy is part of that relationship.

SUMMARY

As more and more employees gain access to computers and the Internet in the workplace, decisions about monitoring will evolve. Employers and employees alike benefit if the company sets clear policies regarding computer use, posts them and explains them to employees, and makes sure that employees understand the policies and the reasons behind them. Ideally, employees and employers should be able to develop and evaluate these policies together—so that they understand and trust each other over the course of their relationship.

Sources: Carol Pickering, "They're Watching You," *Business 2.0,* February 2000, pp. 135–136; Jessica Guynn, "Don't Expect Privacy at Work," *Mobile Register,* September 19, 1999, p. 3F; Del Jones, "Companies Grapple with Limiting Employee Abuse," *USA Today,* April 27, 1998, p. 1A.

---

issued a public apology after news stories revealed that a line of clothing carrying her name was manufactured using child labor. These and other cases demonstrate the importance of ethics and social responsibility in business.

Business ethics refers to the standards of conduct and moral values involving right and wrong actions arising in the work environment. Poor ethical standards can lead to public image problems, costly lawsuits, high levels of employee theft, and a host of other expensive problems. Ethical decision making can also foster trust, a vital element of strong relationships with customers, employees, and other organizations. It is particularly important for top executives to demonstrate ethical behavior, since employees often emulate their behavior. In addition, Internet technology has given rise to a whole new realm of ethics related to workers' rights to privacy, as described in the "Solving an Ethical Controversy" box.

Strong company and individual ethics are often the cornerstone of visionary companies. Drug manufacturer Johnson & Johnson has maintained a strong code of ethics for more than 50 years. These ethical standards form a framework for decision making throughout the company. When bottles of the firm's

BUSINESS DIRECTORY

➤ **business ethics** *standards of conduct and moral values involving right and wrong actions arising in the work environment.*

It's seen war. It's seen the passage of 185 years.
It's seen hopes and dreams.
And it's about to see better days.

It's the Star-Spangled Banner. The flag that inspired Francis Scott Key to pen our national anthem.
Now, thanks to Save America's Treasures – a joint effort of the White House Millennium Council and the
National Trust for Historic Preservation – and the major support of Polo Ralph Lauren and others,
it's making history again. This time, by undergoing a historic conservation and preservation treatment at the
Smithsonian's National Museum of American History. As we race into the next millennium, this symbol of
our land of opportunity can continue to inspire people for generations to come. To find out how you can help
preserve this and other American treasures, call toll free 1-877-TREASURE or visit
www.saveamericastreasures.org.

SAVE AMERICA'S TREASURES
NATIONAL TRUST FOR HISTORIC PRESERVATION

POLO RALPH LAUREN

FIGURE 1.11
Polo Ralph Lauren: Doing Well by Doing Good

best-seller Tylenol were found to have been laced with poison in the 1980s, executives did not hesitate to recall the product or deal openly with the media, because their actions were guided by deeply ingrained principles.

Working hand-in-hand with business ethics is **social responsibility**, a management philosophy that highlights the social and economic effects of managerial decisions. Businesses demonstrate their social responsibility in a variety of ways. Patagonia is widely known for its commitment to social responsibility. The company's objectives include treating employees well and supporting environmentalism. Its reputation for social responsibility has helped Patagonia establish a positive image in the minds of consumers.[64] Many companies demonstrate commitment to social responsibility. For example, as the Polo Ralph Lauren advertisement in Figure 1.11 explains, it is supporting the drive to restore the giant flag that inspired Francis Scott Key to write the U.S. national anthem. The ad not only tells about the effort and Polo Ralph Lauren's backing but also provides a phone number and Internet address that consumers can use to contribute their own support.

Chapter 2 explores business ethics, social responsibility, and the influence of business on society as a whole in detail. Each chapter also presents a feature highlighting a current ethical controversy in business.

WHY STUDY BUSINESS?

As business speeds into the 21st century, new technologies, population shifts, and shrinking global barriers are altering the world at a frantic pace. Businesspeople are catalysts for many of these changes, creating new opportunities for individuals who are prepared to take action. Studying contemporary business will help you to prepare for the future.

Throughout this book, you'll be exposed to the real-life stories of many businesspeople. You'll learn about the range of business careers available and the daily decisions, tasks, and challenges that they face. By the end of the course, you'll understand how marketing, accounting, and human resource management work together to provide competitive advantages for firms. This knowledge can help you to become a more capable employee and enhance your career potential.

Perhaps working for someone else isn't your dream. Like Peter Hunt and Richard Takata of CornerHardware.com, you may see yourself as an entrepreneur, building your own business and controlling your own future. Entrepreneurs are willing to take risks to create and operate a business. As earlier sections explain, entrepreneurship can bring tremendous rewards—and enormous risk. As you read each chapter, you will learn about successful and unsuccessful entrepreneurs. Those who succeeded can serve as valuable role models. Reading about the mistakes of other entrepreneurs can help you to avoid repeating these costly errors. In addition, Chapters 5 and 6 concentrate specifically on how to start your own business. The information in this book will lay the foundation for the practical skills you need to launch a successful venture.

Even if you do not plan on becoming a businessperson, your daily life will still be affected by business. Every time you shop at a supermarket, buy a car, or visit your bank, you interact with the business world. Each chapter examines the tools and tactics firms use to gain your business. Understanding these concepts will help you to make well-informed consumer choices, whether you are buying a new DVD player or stock in General Electric.

Finally, the business world has the resources and capabilities to solve—or create—many of the world's problems. This book discusses many examples of how organizations have shaped the world. The questions for ethical discussion in each chapter will help you understand the important influences of industry on society, government, and economics. Armed with this knowledge, you'll be prepared to help cure society's problems as they emerge during this new century.

WHAT'S AHEAD

The study of business is an exciting, rewarding field that covers an ever-changing global landscape. Now that this chapter has introduced some basic terms and issues in the business world of the 21st century, Chapter 2 takes a detailed look at the ethical and social responsibility issues facing contemporary business. Other chapters in Part I discuss how economics influences business and people's everyday lives. The final chapter in this part focuses on the challenges and opportunities faced by firms competing in global markets.

> **BUSINESS DIRECTORY**
>
> ➤ **social responsibility** *management philosophy that highlights the social and economic effects of managerial decisions.*

➤ Summary of Learning Goals

1. Describe the private enterprise system and the roles played by individual businesses, competitors, and entrepreneurs within the system.

The private enterprise system is an economic system that rewards firms based on how well they match and counter competitors' goods and services. Competition in the private enterprise system ensures success for firms that satisfy consumer demands. Entrepreneurs are the risk takers in the private enterprise system. If no one takes risks, no successful businesses emerge, and the private enterprise system will not function.

2. Explain how the historical development of the U.S. economy continues to influence contemporary business.

Contemporary business has benefited from the experiences and strengths of each era of business history. The production methods developed during the industrial revolution and the production era have helped U.S. businesses improve efficiency at producing goods. The emphasis on understanding and meeting consumer needs during the marketing era has given U.S. businesspeople insight into how to differentiate their goods and services in the global marketplace.

3. Outline the challenges and opportunities that businesses face in the relationship era.

Business in the 21st century is driven by relationships. Managers must find the best way to connect people, technology, and ethics in order to form strong partnerships with customers, employees, and other organizations. Opportunities include advances in technology and growth of global markets.

4. Describe how technology is changing the way businesses operate and compete.

Technology is the application of science and engineering to do practical work. New technologies are allowing businesses to provide new goods and services for consumers, improve customer service, lower prices, and enhance working conditions. However, technology is also changing the shape of some industries, sometimes creating entirely new industries. Technology also opens new questions about business ethics and social responsibility.

5. Relate the importance of quality and customer satisfaction to efforts to create value for customers.

Today's savvy consumers expect more than they received in the past. They are looking for goods and services with positive traits offered at fair prices, the essence of value. A customer's perception of value is tied to quality, the degree of excellence or superiority of a firm's goods and services. Quality also includes customer satisfaction, the ability of a good or service to meet or exceed buyer needs and expectations. If customers feel they have received value—that is, quality for a fair price—they are likely to remain satisfied and continue their relationships with a firm.

6. Explain how individual businesses and entire nations compete in the global marketplace.

Global competitiveness requires nations, industries, and companies to work efficiently at producing goods and services. *Productivity* describes the relationship between the number of units produced and the human and other production inputs needed to produce them. Productivity is a widely used measure of a company's efficiency. In turn, the total productivity of a nation's businesses has become a measure of its economic strength, standard of living, and ability to compete.

7. Describe how changes in the workforce are leading to a new employer–employee partnership.

Employers today face increasing diversity, an aging population, and the changing nature of work itself. These factors and others have led to shrinkage in the workforce, making it more difficult to find and keep the high-quality employees needed for successful competition. As a result, many businesses are striving to develop partnerships with their employees by recognizing and rewarding their contributions.

8. Identify the skills that managers need to lead businesses in the new century.

Because the workforce is changing, managers need to improve their abilities to coach, mentor, and nurture employees in order to avoid labor shortages and benefit from diversity. Managers in the new century need vision, the ability to perceive marketplace needs and how their firm can satisfy them. Critical thinking skills and creativity allow managers to pinpoint problems and opportunities and plan novel solutions. Finally, managers are dealing with rapid change, and they need skills to help steer their organizations through shifts in external and internal conditions.

9. Explain how ethics and social responsibility affect business decision making.

Business ethics are the standards of conduct and moral values involving right and wrong actions in the workplace. Businesses that set high ethical standards avoid public image problems, costly lawsuits, customer mistrust, and other expensive problems. They can also offer guidelines for executives and employees to apply in making decisions. Social responsibility is a management philosophy that highlights the social and economic effects of business decisions and actions. Socially responsible firms seek to give back to their communities, customers, and employees.

10. List four reasons for studying business.

Business influences nearly every aspect of society. An understanding of contemporary business provides an excellent foundation for building the skills and knowledge needed to handle the challenges and opportunities of the new millennium. Studying business will help you in at least four ways: (1) to learn about different business careers, (2) to assess the advantages and disadvantages of starting your own business, (3) to become a better-informed consumer and investor, and (4) to learn how business can contribute to solving many of the problems of society.

Business Terms You Need to Know

business 8
profits 8
factors of production 11
private enterprise system 13
competition 13

entrepreneur 14
Internet 21
customer satisfaction 26
business ethics 37
social responsibility 38

Other Important Business Terms

not-for-profit organizations 8
natural resources 11
capital 11
human resources 12
entrepreneurship 12
competitive differentiation 13

private property 14
consumer orientation 18
branding 18
brand 18
technology 20
World Wide Web 22

e-mail 22
intranet 23
extranet 23
transaction management 24
relationship management 24
partnership 25

strategic alliance 25

value 25

quality 26

productivity 28

gross domestic product (GDP) 28

outsourcing 31

diversity 33

vision 34

critical thinking 35

creativity 35

➤ Review Questions

1. In what ways are not-for-profit organizations a substantial part of the U.S. economy? What challenges will not-for-profits face in the next decade or two?

2. Identify and describe the four basic inputs that make up factors of production. Give a specific example of each.

3. What are the four rights that are critical to the operation of capitalism? Why would capitalism have difficulty functioning in a society that does not assure these rights for its citizens?

4. How is the relationship era different from the way business was conducted in each of the following historical periods listed? How is it similar?

    a. colonial era

    b. industrial revolution

    c. age of industrial entrepreneurs

    d. production era

    e. marketing era

5. Describe three ways the Internet has affected business in general.

6. What is the core of relationship management? How might a local phone company use relationship management to create value for its customers?

7. What is meant by the term *productivity*? How is the concept of GDP related to productivity?

8. What are some of the challenges that managers face in building a world-class work force in the 21st century?

9. Identify four qualities that the "new" managers of the 21st century must have. Why are these qualities important in a competitive business environment?

10. Define *business ethics* and *social responsibility*, and give a brief example of at least one company you know that practices each.

➤ Questions for Critical Thinking

1. The entrepreneurial spirit fuels growth in the U.S. economy. Choose a company that interests you—one you have worked for or dealt with as a customer—and read about the company in the library or visit its Web site. Learn as much as you can about the company's early history: Who founded it and why? Under what circumstances was the company founded? Is the founder still with the organization? Is the founder's original vision still embraced by the company? Why or why not? If not, in what ways has it changed?

2. Brands distinguish one company's goods or services from its competitors. As you probably know, we are surrounded by brands. In 30 seconds, brainstorm every brand you can think of. Do you use any of these products? Why or why not? How important is the brand to you?

3. The Internet has already begun to change many industries. Think of an industry you are familiar with that has changed—or will change—because of the Internet. Describe the changes. Do you think that the Internet has improved the industry's relationship with its customers? Why or why not?

4. Today, many organizations enter into strategic alliances to create a competitive advantage for the companies involved. Choose one of the following hypothetical alliances and write a memo describing how you think the alliance will benefit both organizations.

    a. Sears and Whirlpool

    b. Holiday Inn and American Airlines

    c. Disney World and Pizza Hut

    d. Columbia sportswear and American Ski Co.

5. Assume that to encourage creativity among its employees, Wal-Mart's head of store operations picks one product in which there is untapped potential and then challenges workers—from managers to clerks—to find ways to promote and sell more of it. This month's pick is duct tape. Suggest a plan for promoting and selling duct tape. What new uses might you suggest to encourage customers to buy more duct tape? How can you create more value for customers who purchase duct tape? What other products might you display the duct tape with? How would you display duct tape in the store to catch customers' attention? How can you attract new customers to use duct tape?

➤ Experiential Exercise

Background: In this chapter, you learn how employers are trying to form new types of relationships with employees. They are doing so in order to meet the challenges of a changing workforce and to gain a competitive advantage by fully using employee talents. Examples of this new employer–employee partnership include employers who

- Recognize and encourage workers' important contributions to providing value and satisfying customers
- Emphasize listening to and respecting their employees
- Share financial data and reward employees with stock in the company so that they can participate in the success of the firm
- Help employees develop their knowledge and skills so that they are more valuable to their current employer—and in the job market down the line

Directions: To get a better idea of how employers are building new relationships with their employees, locate examples of the new employer–employee partnership.

1. Prior to class, record *at least three employers* that practice any of the preceding examples of the new employer–employee partnership.

2. The information you record should include answers to the following questions:

- What is the source of your example (e.g., your personal work experience, that of a friend or relative, or an article you read in a newspaper or periodical)?
- What is the name of the organization?
- What are some specific examples of the employer–employee partnership? In other words, write more than "the employer emphasizes listening to and respecting employees." You should also include a specific example of *how* the organization goes about accomplishing it.

3. During class, form into teams of three or four students to share your findings. Select the two best examples from your group. Your team spokesperson will share the best examples with the rest of the class during the wrap-up portion of this exercise.

➤ Nothing but Net

1. Understanding Internet terminology. The Internet seems to have a language all its own. To help novice surfers better understand the Internet, several Web sites have glossaries of Internet terms. Visit the site listed here and define the following terms:

Bookmark

Cache

Cookie

HTML

Shopping bot

Spiders

www.lib.berkeley.edu/TeachingLib/Guides/Internet/FindInfo.htm

2. Becoming familiar with search engines. The Internet contains literally hundreds of thousands of different Web sites and billions of pages. Often finding what you want can be a lengthy and frustrating process. One tool to help you find what you're looking for is a search engine. Type in a word or a phrase and the search engines will find sites that match. Three of the most popular search engines are Alta Vista (**www.altavista.com**), Excite (**www.excite.com**), and Northern Lights (**www.northernlights.com**). Visit each site and, picking a key term from the chapter, use the search engine. Prepare a brief report on your experience. Which of the three search engines seemed to be most effective in locating the information you requested? Explain your preference in comparison with the other two search engines.

3. Finding information on a company. Virtually all companies today have Internet sites. On a company's Web site you can find information on its products or services, review recent financial statements, and learn about careers. Find and visit the Web sites of three of the companies listed in the chapter. From the standpoint of a prospective employee, what assumptions can you draw about the company from its Web site regarding job opportunities, employee benefits, and nearest company location to your current residence? Which of the three sites impressed you the most?

Note: Internet Web addresses change frequently. If you don't find the exact sites listed, you may need to access the organization's or company's home page and search from there.

The Geek Squad is exactly what it sounds like: a bunch of 30-something guys who wear clip-on ties and drive around in VW Beetles, retired ice cream trucks, and even an old police car repairing people's computers. And not always just *anyone's* computers—they have repaired computers for the Rolling Stones, Jonny Lang, and Ice Cube, along with a variety of restaurants, book distributors, travel agencies, and even the FBI. Company founder Robert Stephens doesn't refer to himself as CEO; instead, he prefers to be called Chief Inspector. He wears a chief's badge and calls his employees "special agents." However, it is unlikely that anyone would confuse Stephens's special agents with real FBI agents, unless the FBI dress code now includes "geek garb."

The Geek Squad is proud of their nerdy image. Squad members consider it part of the relationship they cultivate with customers. At a time when customer satisfaction with software support is the lowest it's been in ten years, the Geek Squad is cleaning up. They deliver value to their customers, offering on-site assistance 24 hours a day, seven days a week and fixing problems with different companies' conflicting software. The so-called agents know their stuff. They repair people's computer problems in record time, slap a bill on the customer's desk that says "Pay up, sucka," and leave the customer laughing—and happy. The Geek Squad's service costs a bit more, but customers aren't complaining. "We save time in the long run because we're down much less time," notes Kathee Flynn, a customer who owns a travel agency in Minneapolis, where the Geek Squad is headquartered.

The Geek Squad promises to respond to customers' crisis calls within seven minutes; the company also offers drop-off repair service for lesser charges; and it does not charge extra for house calls within twenty miles of the Twin Cities of Minneapolis and St. Paul. The Geek Squad also offers free drop-off services such as problem diagnosis, virus removal, and e-mail tech support, all guaranteed within 48 hours of when a customer drops off a machine. They handle both Windows and Mac programs, networking software, and programs on other high-tech appliances such as cell phones and digital assistants. All of this service adds up to quality, value, and customer satisfaction. Of his customers, Stephens says, "You wouldn't think rock stars use computers, but rock stars use laptops on the road, so actually they're the most finicky, demanding people. They're great practice for us." But working for finicky customers has its rewards: "We get the best concert tickets," boasts Stephens. "We get the best seats in every restaurant in town because we do everyone's computers."

The agents who work for the Geek Squad are vital to the company's success. "The techs are not really geeks, just cool people who love computers," says Stephens proudly. In other words, members of the Geek Squad not only relate to computers but also relate to other people, so they are adept at building relationships.

"I look for people with the right attitude and passion to pick up the knowledge they need," explains Stephens. A typical Geek Squad job description reads: "Impeccable verbal communication skills a must. General familiarity with PC systems, software and hardware necessary." Stephens's relationship with his employees is strong. Eric Kimmel, who worked for the Geek Squad as "director of intelligence" during his last two years of college decided to stay on after graduation because of Stephens, whom he refers to as "the best boss ever." How does Stephens manage to be the best boss? "Give people the opportunity to do a great job," he says. Stephens understands that his employees want to have fun at working hard. "We attract good people because we make computer repair glamorous," he explains.

Stephens started the Geek Squad while he was still in college, with a $200 investment. "I just saw my opportunity," he recalls. "While in college I was making extra money fixing computers, and I didn't see any other companies that were approaching the business in a unique, exciting way." Today Stephens has molded his technical knowledge and people skills into a business that is clearing several million dollars a year. Now he's expanding to Los Angeles. His goal is simple: "The complete and total global domination of the computer support business." He plans to accomplish this while wearing a clip-on tie.

QUESTIONS

1. What role do you see the Geek Squad playing in the private enterprise system?
2. Robert Stephens states that he saw an opportunity and took it. Look around your own environment. Can you identify a unique business opportunity for yourself? Describe it.
3. Identify ways in which technology could help the Geek Squad grow.
4. Access the company's Web site at **www.geeksquad.com.** Once competitors emerge, what steps could Robert Stephens take to continue to create value and build relationships with existing and new customers—both with the Web site and through other means?

Sources: Company Web site, **www.geeksquad.com,** accessed January 29, 2001; Bob Weinstein, "Geek Squad: Cool Tech Support," *Chicago Sun-Times,* November 19, 2000, **www.suntimes.com;** Bob Weinstein, "Company Builds on 'Geek' Image," *Chicago Sun-Times,* April 30, 2000, **www.suntimes.com;** Anni Layne, "Robert Stephens: Geek Squad Founder and Chief Inspector," *Fast Company,* [no month] 2000, **www.fastcompany.com;** Bridget McCrea, "Proudly Wearing the Clip-On Tie," *Office.com,* April 22, 1999, **www.office.com;** Jamie Allen, "Geek Squad Guide Offers Unique Computer Help," *CNN.com,* September 3, 1999, **www.cnn.com.**

Achieving Business Success by Demonstrating Ethical Behavior and Social Responsibility

Learning Goals

1. Explain the concepts of business ethics and social responsibility.

2. Describe the factors that influence business ethics.

3. List the stages in the development of ethical standards.

4. Identify common ethical dilemmas in the workplace.

5. Discuss how organizations shape ethical behavior.

6. Relate the ways government regulation affects business ethics and social responsibility.

7. Describe how businesses' social responsibility is measured.

8. Summarize the responsibilities of business to the general public, customers, and employees.

9. Explain why investors and the financial community are concerned with business ethics and social responsibility.

Patagonia Deserves a Pat on the Back

Decades ago, before being "green" was popular, Yvon Chouinard was climbing mountains. He didn't just climb them; he loved them. He loved the surrounding country, the water and air that fed it. Like many climbers of the era, he needed to make a living to support his passion, so he started a company called the Great Pacific Iron Works. The company manufactured and sold climbing gear based on Chouinard's own designs. Along the way, the company began developing a line of outdoor clothing. But handling two entirely different lines of goods—climbing gear and clothing—began to get complicated, so Chouinard sold off the hardware business to his employees and kept the clothing portion. The hardware company became Black Diamond, well known for reliable climbing gear. The "softwear" company became Patagonia. The rest is a story of golden fleece.

Nearly everyone in cold weather climates wears fleece, that soft, cozy fabric made of recycled plastic—and made popular by Patagonia. Because it's made of plastic, it does melt if you get too close to a campfire's flames, but stay away from fire and it should last forever. But those aren't necessarily the most important qualities of Patagonia's jackets, vests, and pants. Perhaps what's more important are the values of the firm's founder: Chouinard's unwavering belief in Patagonia's responsibility to consumers and to the environment. Since 1985, the firm has donated 10 percent of its annual profits to grassroots environmental groups. The company works constantly to reduce any pollution created in the manufacture of its goods, uses recycled polyester whenever possible, and now relies on organic cotton rather than conventional cotton, which is grown with pesticides. Company managers continually search for ways to reduce waste. Some items in the children's clothing line are made from scraps left over when the fabric has been cut for larger, adult-sized items. Patagonia even uses "processed chlorine-free post-consumer paper, tree-free paper, and soy-based inks whenever possible for printing our catalogs and other materials." Recently, the company held an international conference for its suppliers, including zipper makers and fabric processors, to look for ways

each company could change its processes to reduce environmental impact. Chouinard is an avid fisherman, so he also uses his firm's public relations clout to lead the fight to dismantle hydroelectric dams in regions where environmentalists have shown them to be destructive to such wildlife as spawning salmon.

None of these efforts is simple—or cheap. In fact, many of these practices cost the company more than if it operated conventionally. "To get organically grown cotton, I have to deal directly with the farmers," notes Chouinard, "and there's only one cotton crop a year. In some cases, I've had to cosign loans to keep them in business. When we started doing this, we lost about 20 percent of our sales. Now the stuff sells better than before, and I'll tell you why. A designer who begins with a bale of cotton takes his task seriously. He makes something more worthwhile."

Some people might call Chouinard an extremist, but others look to him as a leader in ethical and socially responsible business practices. He understands that if businesspeople don't save the planet, there won't be any planet on which to do business. "Businesspeople who focus on profits wind up in the hole," Chouinard warns. "For me, profit is what happens when you do everything else right. A good cast will catch a fish." Does his green approach work? Chouinard and his wife Malinda no longer have to live under the benches in their shop in order to save rent—the company reached $180 million in sales in a recent year, and he admits that he is rich. But he has never lost sight of what's right: the importance of a clear-running stream or the magnificence of the clean air on top of a mountain.[1]

CHAPTER OVERVIEW

As we discuss in Chapter 1, the underlying aim of most businesses is to serve customers at a profit. But most companies, like Patagonia, try to do more than that, looking for ways to give back to customers, society, and the environment. When does a company's self-interest conflict with society's and customers' well-being? And must the goal of seeking profits conflict with upholding high principles of right and wrong? In response to the second question, a growing number of businesses of all sizes are answering no.

CONCERN FOR ETHICAL AND SOCIETAL ISSUES

For years, 3M's highly profitable brand, Scotchgard, was used to protect against stains on furniture, carpets, and other products. Recently, the firm's management discovered that the product's main ingredient, which the body can convert to PFOS, is potentially dangerous. In 2000, 3M decided to discontinue production of Scotchgard. Even though the action affects sales, as well as 3M employees and customers, management decided that the risk to the environment and society was too great to take any other action.

An organization that wants to prosper over the long term cannot do so without considering business ethics, the standards of conduct and moral values governing actions and decisions in the work environment. Businesses also must take into account a wide range of social issues, including how a decision will affect the environment, employees, and customers. These issues are at the heart of *social responsibility*, the philosophies, policies, procedures, and actions directed toward the enhancement of society's welfare as a primary objective. In short, businesses must find the delicate balance between doing what is right and doing what is profitable.

For 3M Co., maintaining that balance has required the company to discontinue a widely used product in response to concerns about its safety. The product, Scotchgard fabric protector, seemed to be a godsend. Fabric coated with Scotchgard repels water and oils so effectively that it resists stains, so it is easy to keep clean. Besides coating carpets and furniture around the world, Scotchgard was used on candy wrappers and pet food packaging. The company believed the product's main ingredient—a form of fluorine called POSF, which the body converts to perfluorooctane sulfate, or PFOS—was harmless. However, in 1997 3M was testing a technology for analyzing blood samples and discovered traces of PFOS in samples from around the United States, even samples drawn from locations far from 3M factories.

So 3M commissioned research in which massive doses of PFOS were given to laboratory animals. The exposure resulted in death for the animals or their offspring. The company also sponsored research on the spread of PFOS in the environment, finding traces of the chemical as far away as the Pacific Ocean and the Baltic region of Eastern Europe. The enduring nature, widespread presence, and theoretical toxicity of PFOS generated concern among top-ranking 3M executives. By law, they could have waited for the EPA to act. Instead, they decided to discontinue sales of PFOS-related products, although they had been generating half a billion dollars' worth of annual revenues.[2]

In business, as in life, deciding what is right or wrong in a given situation does not always involve a clear-cut choice. Businesses have many responsibilities— to customers, to employees, to investors, and to society as a whole. Sometimes conflicts arise in trying to serve the needs of separate constituencies. At 3M, the decision to discontinue making PFOS-related products affects not only the firm's profits and the environment, but 3M's workers and customers as well. About 1,500 employees are involved in making the products in Alabama, Minnesota, and Belgium. Discontinuing the products places those jobs at risk, at least

Got a life?
Gotta ask for Scotchgard.™

Her dolly's thirsty and only juice will do. So don't leave the store without buying a carpet with genuine Scotchgard protection. Nothing protects better or lasts longer. No wonder Scotchgard products are used to take care of more carpet than any other brand. So whether you walk on it, sit on it or wear it, make sure to ask for Scotchgard protection.

There's protection. Then there's Scotchgard™ Protection.

© 3M 1999 "Scotchgard" is a trademark of 3M
For more information, visit our website: http://www.mmm.com

3M *Innovation*

over the short term. And one of the product lines, fire-fighting foams, is critical to society. So, the company is phasing out that product line more gradually than Scotchgard. In addition, 3M is working hard to develop alternative products that break down over time.

As Figure 2.1 indicates, four main forces shape business ethics and social responsibility: individual, organizational, legal, and societal forces. Rather than operating in a vacuum, each of the forces interacts with the other three, and the interactions powerfully affect both the strength and direction of each influence.

The ethical values of executives and individual employees at all levels can influence the decisions and actions a business takes. At 3M, the decision to discontinue production of Scotchguard involved the highest levels of management, with input from the company's scientists. When the scientists began reporting the results of animal tests, this information drew the attention of 3M's chief executive, who had them repeat the presentation to the company's top managers. Throughout your own business career, you will encounter many situations in which you will need to weigh right and wrong before making a decision or taking action. So, we begin our discussion of business ethics by focusing on individual ethics.

Business ethics are also shaped by the ethical climate within an organization. Codes of conduct and ethical standards play increasingly significant roles in businesses in which doing the right thing is both supported and applauded. At 3M, the decision to stop making Scotchgard was a matter of policy. In the words of 3M executive director Katherine E. Reed, "We believe that our responsibility for materials continues . . . into disposal. It's a concept we call life-cycle management."[3] This chapter demonstrates how a firm can create a framework to encourage—and even demand—high standards of ethical behavior and social responsibility from its employees.

It is clear, though, that not all companies successfully set and meet the ethical standards of firms such as 3M. To protect the public, federal, state, and local governments have enacted laws to regulate business practices. Many of these laws are examined in this chapter. The chapter also considers the complex question of just what business owes to society and how societal forces mold the actions of businesses. Finally, it examines the influence of business ethics and social responsibility on global business.

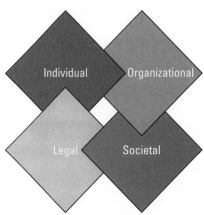

FIGURE 2.1
Forces Shaping Business Ethics and Social Responsibility

INDIVIDUAL BUSINESS ETHICS

In today's business environment, individuals can make the difference in ethical expectations and behavior. As executives, managers, and employees demonstrate their personal ethical principles—or lack of ethical principles— the expectations and actions of those who work for and with them can change.

What is the current status of individual business ethics in the United States? Although ethical behavior can be difficult to track or even define in all circumstances, evidence suggests that some individuals act unethically or illegally on the job. A recent poll of U.S. employees found that 30 percent knew of or suspected unethical behavior in their companies. In another poll, the main types of unethical behavior observed by employees were lying, withholding information, abusing or intimidating employees, inaccurately reporting the amount of time worked, and discrimination. Each year U.S. organizations lose more than $400 billion to fraud, or $9 per day per employee. The smallest companies typically experienced the highest-cost abuses of ethics.[4]

Technology seems to have expanded the range and impact of unethical behavior. For example, anyone with computer access to data has the potential to steal or manipulate the data or to shut down the system, even from a remote location. Often, the people who hack into a

BUSINESS DIRECTORY

➤ **business ethics**   *standards of business conduct and moral values.*

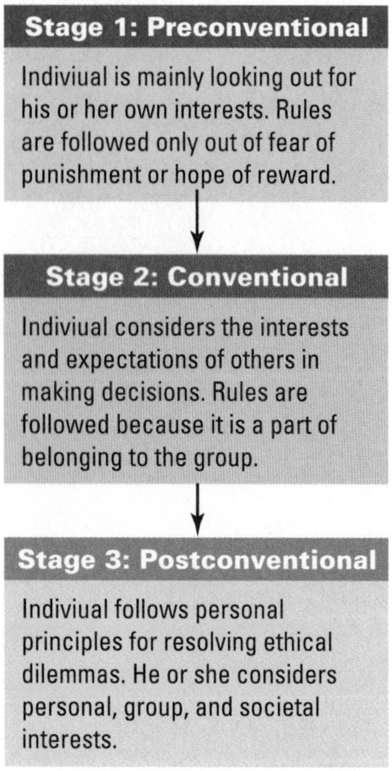

Stage 1: Preconventional

Indiviual is mainly looking out for his or her own interests. Rules are followed only out of fear of punishment or hope of reward.

Stage 2: Conventional

Indiviual considers the interests and expectations of others in making decisions. Rules are followed because it is a part of belonging to the group.

Stage 3: Postconventional

Indiviual follows personal principles for resolving ethical dilemmas. He or she considers personal, group, and societal interests.

FIGURE 2.2
Stages of Moral and Ethical Development

company's computers are employees, and some observers consider employee attacks to be the most expensive. Also, insiders are estimated to have committed two-thirds of the thefts of intellectual property, such as patented or copyrighted information.[5] Computer technology also helps people at one company attack another. Steven Cade, whose business, La Jolla Club Golf Co., specializes in child-sized golf clubs, recently admitted to using the Internet to spread deceptive messages about a much larger competitor, Callaway Golf Co. Cade admitted he used 27 screen names to post these messages.[6]

Nearly every employee, at every level, wrestles with ethical questions at some point or another. Some rationalize questionable behavior by saying, "Everybody's doing it." Others act unethically because they feel pressured on their jobs or have to meet performance quotas. Yet, some avoid unethical acts that don't mesh with their personal values and morals. To help you understand the differences in the ways individuals arrive at ethical choices, the next section focuses on how personal ethics and morals develop.

Development of Individual Ethics

Individuals typically develop ethical standards in the three stages shown in Figure 2.2: the preconventional, conventional, and postconventional stages. In the preconventional stage, individuals primarily consider their own needs and desires in making decisions. They obey external rules only because they are afraid of punishment or hope to receive rewards if they comply.

In the second stage, the conventional stage, individuals are aware of and act in response to their duty to others, including their obligations to their family members, coworkers, and organizations. The expectations of these groups influence how they choose between what is acceptable and unacceptable in certain situations. Self-interest, however, continues to play a role in decisions.

The postconventional stage, the final stage, represents the highest level of ethical and moral behavior. The individual is able to move beyond mere self-interest and duty and take the larger needs of society into account as well. He or she has developed personal ethical principles for determining what is right and can apply those principles in a wide variety of situations.

An individual's stage in moral and ethical development is determined by a huge number of factors. Experiences help to shape responses to different situations. A person's family, educational, cultural, and religious backgrounds can also play a role. Individuals can also have different styles of deciding ethical dilemmas, no matter what their stage of moral development.

To help you understand and prepare for the ethical dilemmas you may confront in your career, let's take a closer look at some of the factors involved in solving ethical questions on the job.

On-the-Job Ethical Dilemmas

In the fast-paced world of business, you will sometimes be called to weigh the ethics of decisions that can affect not just your own future but possibly the futures of your fellow workers, your company, and its customers. As already noted, it's not always easy to distinguish between what is right and wrong in many business situations, especially when the needs and concerns of various parties conflict.

Consider the situation faced by decision makers at pharmaceutical companies and the U.S. agency that regulates them, the Food and Drug Administration (FDA). They have to weigh the risks of releasing a new drug before thorough testing is complete against the benefits lost by not making a new drug available as soon as possible. One way FDA administrators have handled the dilemma is by setting standards that are relatively easy and quick to measure. A drug that lowers blood pressure or cholesterol levels receives approval on the assumption that it also reduces heart attacks and deaths. Once the FDA approves a drug, should the producers conduct follow-up

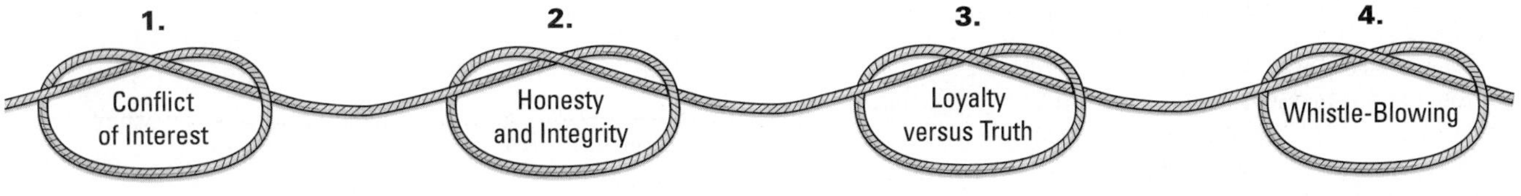

1.	2.	3.	4.
Conflict of Interest	Honesty and Integrity	Loyalty versus Truth	Whistle-Blowing

FIGURE 2.3
Common Business Ethical Challenges

tests? In some cases, the companies' decision makers are saying no. Although commonly prescribed drugs have been shown to reduce high blood pressure, the companies have not conducted regular follow-up studies to determine their impact on disease and death. Why? If every drug were tested for its ultimate effects on health, bringing a new medicine to market could take years longer, and the extra expense might make companies avoid developing some potentially beneficial products. In addition, ethics demands that researchers not withhold a treatment when one is available, so conducting follow-up tests can be difficult. So, decision makers at the FDA and drug companies must weigh practical economic and scientific constraints to make what are literally life-and-death decisions.[7]

As these examples illustrate, solving ethical dilemmas is not easy. In many cases, each possible decision can have unpleasant consequences and positive benefits that must be evaluated. The ethical dilemmas that confront managers of drug companies are just one example of many different types of ethical questions encountered in the workplace. Figure 2.3 identifies four of the most common ethical challenges that businesspeople face: conflict of interest, honesty and integrity, loyalty versus truth, and whistle-blowing.

Conflict of Interest   A conflict of interest exists when a businessperson is faced with a situation in which an action benefiting one person or group has the potential to harm another. Conflicts of interest may pose ethical challenges when they involve the businessperson's own interests and someone to whom he or she has a duty, or when they involve two parties to whom the businessperson has a duty. The "Clicks and Mortar" box discusses the conflicts of interest that entrepreneurial students and their faculty face with business start-ups on campus. Lawyers, business consultants, or advertising agencies would face a conflict of interest if they represented two competing companies: A strategy that would most benefit one of the client companies might harm the other client. Similarly, a real estate agent faces an ethical conflict if he or she represents both the buyer and seller in a transaction. In general, the buyer benefits from a low price, and the seller benefits from a high price. Handling the situation responsibly may be possible, but it would also be difficult. A conflict may also exist between someone's personal interests and those of an organization or its customers. An offer of gifts or bribes for special treatment creates a situation in which the buyer, but not necessarily his or her company, may benefit personally.

Ethical ways to handle conflicts of interest include (1) avoiding and (2) disclosing them. Some companies have policies against taking on clients who are competitors of existing clients. Most businesses and government agencies have written policies prohibiting employees from accepting gifts or specifying a maximum value of, say, $50. Or a member of a board of directors or committee might abstain from voting on a decision in which he or she has a personal interest. In other situations, people state their potential conflict of interest so that the people affected can decide whether they need to get information or help from another source.

Honesty and Integrity   Employers highly value honesty and integrity. An employee who is honest can be counted on to tell the truth. An employee with integrity goes beyond truthfulness. **Integrity** involves adhering to deeply felt ethical principles in business situations. It includes doing what you say you

BUSINESS DIRECTORY

➤ **conflict of interest**   *situation in which a business decision may be influenced by the potential for personal gain.*

Campus Dot.Coms: A New College Conflict?

Background. Maybe you know someone who has started a dot.com from a dorm room; maybe you've thought about it yourself. Bob Gibbons, a senior at Cornell University started BClick Network out of a house he shared with ten other people. Binoy Agarwal helped found OneWeb Solutions while he was a junior at the University of Tulsa. One study found that more than 60 percent of young people between the ages of 18 and 29 want to start their own business. Campus seems like the perfect place for such a venture. Students have access to state-of-the-art technology and even start-up funds from investors who come to campuses looking for the right dot.com to back. Some students no longer think they need diplomas for business careers. They're in a hurry. "It seems like suicide to wait until graduating," explains Bob Gibbons of BClick. "You have the resources of the university, and it's the ideal place to do it."

What Happened? The advantages of starting businesses in college have created some conflict-of-interest problems. Should students be allowed to use on-campus residences and their college or university computers in pursuit of personal commercial enterprise? Students welcome input from faculty advisers, but should the same faculty be allowed to invest in these companies or sit on their boards of directors? "The knowledge students are getting is very valuable and can be quickly applied to new businesses worth millions of dollars. That raises whole new issues as to the role that faculty should play," says Michael Rappa, a technology management professor at North Carolina State University.

The Response. Massachusetts Institute of Technology (MIT) recently issued explicit guidelines for faculty involvement in student businesses to avoid conflict of interest. Faculty members of the Wharton School at the University of Pennsylvania must get approval from the university before joining student firms. But many students and professors resist regulation because the reward can be so great. At MIT, a professor and doctoral student helped found Akamai Technologies, an Internet content delivery service, which raised $234 million in its initial public offering six months after opening. Students like to forge alliances with professors because it gives them credibility with investors. Notes David Schmittlein, deputy dean at Wharton, "It's an issue schools are going to have to deal with, because entrepreneurship is very important for students. More flexible rules for managing relationships with students and faculty are developing."

Today and Counting. What do these e-business entrepreneurs have to say about their college experience? "I don't think I've gotten as much out of college as I could have, but being a part of a company is a great educational experience in and of itself," says Chris Spencer, the founder and chief technology officer of Sentrisystems.com, which protects Web-based transactions. "You're tossed into the lion's den. You have to deal with the real world."

QUESTIONS FOR CRITICAL THINKING

1. Do you think campus-based Internet start-ups create a conflict of interest? Why or why not?
2. Write your own guidelines for the college or university you attend, outlining what you believe should be ethical behavior between a student entrepreneur and faculty or other school employees with regard to a business venture. Be sure to include the responsibilities of both sides.

Sources: Marla Dickerson, "A New Way of Doing Business," *Los Angeles Times,* accessed at **www.fasttrac.org.**, February 28, 2001, Sonya Colberg, "University of Tulsa Student Is Crazy about Business," *World's Own Service,* May 7, 2000, accessed from the OneWeb Solutions Web site, **www.onewebsolutions.com/article3.asp;** Stephanie Armour, "Net Firms Soar on Campus," *USA Today,* April 12, 2000, pp. 1B, 2B.

will do and accepting responsibility for mistakes. Behaving with honesty and integrity inspires trust, and as a result, it can help build long-term relationships with customers, employers, suppliers, and the public. Employees, in turn, want their managers and the company as a whole to treat them honestly and with integrity.

Unfortunately, violations of honesty and integrity are widespread. Some people misrepresent their academic credentials and previous work experience on their résumés or job applications. Others steal from their employers by taking home supplies or products without permission or by carrying out personal business during the time they are being paid to work. Many employees lie in order to protect themselves from punishment or to make their performance look better than it really is. Following the merger of CUC International and HFS to form a company called Cendant, managers from HFS discovered that the top managers at CUC had for years been reporting incorrect financial data about the company, claiming $500 million in profits that were purely fictional. CUC's former head, Walter Forbes, said he didn't know about the misbehavior and wasn't responsible for it. He resigned in exchange for a severance package worth $47.5 million. Others have challenged Forbes's statements of ignorance, and Cendant has taken Forbes to court in an attempt to force him to repay the entire amount.[8]

Loyalty Versus Truth Businesspeople expect their employees to be loyal and to act in the best interests of the company. When the truth about a company is not favorable, however, an ethical conflict can arise. Individuals may have to decide between loyalty to the company and truthfulness in business relationships. Individuals resolve such dilemmas in various ways. Some people place the highest value on loyalty, even at the expense of truth. Others avoid volunteering negative information but answer truthfully if someone asks them a specific question. People may emphasize truthfulness and actively disclose negative information, especially if the cost of silence is high, as in the case of operating a malfunctioning aircraft or selling tainted medicine. During the last decade, Texaco strongly defended itself against charges of racial discrimination. But a company executive secretly taped high-level meetings conducted to discuss the lawsuit, capturing on the tape a variety of damning statements of people using racial slurs and considering making evidence "disappear." The executive who taped the meetings then provided them to the *New York Times* and to the lawyers for the people suing Texaco.[9]

Whistle-Blowing   When an individual does encounter unethical or illegal actions at work, the person must decide what action to take. Sometimes it is possible to resolve the problem by working through channels within the organizations in order to correct the problem. If that fails, the person should weigh the potential damages to the greater public good. If the damage is significant, a person who places ethical standards above personal well-being may conclude that the only solution is to blow the whistle. Whistle-blowing is an employee's disclosure to the media or government authorities of illegal, immoral, or unethical practices of the organization. In recent years, several motion pictures, including *The Insider* (tobacco industry) and *Erin Brockovich* (ground-water contamination by power companies), contained plots centering on whistle-blowing. The Texaco manager who taped meetings and sent the tapes to the *New York Times* was engaging in this practice.

A whistle-blower must weigh a number of issues in deciding whether to come forward. Resolving an ethical problem within the organization is more loyal and can be more effective, assuming higher-level managers cooperate. A company that values ethics will try to correct a problem, and staying at a company that does not value ethics may not be worthwhile. In some cases, however, people resort to whistle-blowing because they believe the unethical behavior is causing significant damage that outweighs the risk that the company will retaliate against the whistle-blower. State and federal laws protect whistle-blowers in certain situations, such as reports of discrimination, but they may still experience dramatic retribution for their actions. That is probably why the executive who blew the whistle at Texaco chose to do so anonymously.

Obviously, whistle-blowing and other ethical issues arise relatively infrequently in firms with strong organizational climates of ethical behavior. The next section examines how a business can develop an environment that discourages unethical behavior among individuals.

HOW ORGANIZATIONS SHAPE ETHICAL CONDUCT

No individual makes decisions in a vacuum. Choices are strongly influenced by the standards of conduct established within the organizations where people work. Most ethical lapses in business reflect the values of the firms' corporate cultures.

As shown in Figure 2.4, development of a corporate culture to support business ethics happens on four levels: ethical awareness, ethical reasoning, ethical action, and ethical leadership. If any of these four factors is missing, the ethical climate in an organization will weaken.[10]

Ethical Awareness

The foundation of an ethical climate is ethical awareness. As we have already seen, ethical dilemmas occur frequently in the workplace. Employees, however, need

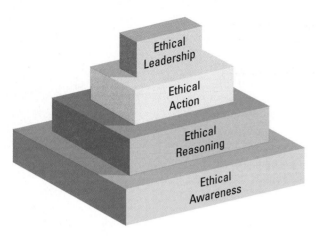

FIGURE 2.4
Structure of an Ethical Environment

help in identifying ethical problems when they occur. Workers also need guidance about how the firm expects them to respond.

One way for a firm to provide this support is to develop a code of conduct, a formal statement that defines how the organization expects and requires employees to resolve ethical questions. In a recent survey of employees, eight out of ten said their company had a written set of ethical standards.[11] At the most basic level, a code of conduct may simply specify ground rules for acceptable behavior, such as identifying the laws and regulations that employees must obey. Other companies, however, use their codes of conduct to identify key corporate values and provide frameworks that guide employees as they resolve moral and ethical dilemmas.

Canada-based Nortel Networks, an international telecommunications giant, uses a code of conduct to define its values and help employees put them into practice. The code of conduct defines seven core values that Nortel requires as the basis for becoming known as a company of integrity. The code also defines standards for conduct among employees and between employees and the company's shareholders, customers, suppliers, and communities. Employees are expected to treat one another with respect, including respect for individual and cultural differences, protect the company's assets, and fulfill whatever commitments they make. The code of conduct also states that each employee is responsible for behaving consistently with its standards and for reporting possible violations of the code. Nortel provides each employee with a copy of this code of conduct and also posts it on its Web site.[12]

Ethical Reasoning

Although a code of conduct can provide an overall framework, it cannot detail a solution for every ethical situation. Recall that some ethical questions do not have clear black-and-white answers, as in the situation described in the "Business Hits and Misses" box. Many ethical dilemmas involve gray areas that may require individuals to sort through several options and related consequences. Businesses must provide the tools employees need to evaluate these options and arrive at suitable decisions.

Many firms have instituted ethics training programs. More than 50 percent of the employees surveyed in one study reported that their companies provide training in the subject. Lockheed Martin Corp. has developed a training program in the form of interactive lessons that employees can access online. The sessions include cases performed by actors, plus tests in the form of multiple-choice questions. They cover a variety of business-related topics, from security to sexual harassment. The company also keeps tabs on which employees have completed which training sessions. In addition, Lockheed Martin uses a game called the Ethics Challenge, in which the players use cards and tokens to read about and resolve ethical quandaries based on real-life situations. The Experiential Exercise at the end of the chapter contains a small portion of the Ethics Challenge game. Everyone in the company, from hourly workers to the chairman, is required to play the Ethics Challenge once per year.[13] Although some observers debate whether ethics can actually be taught, this training can give employees an opportunity to practice applying ethical values to hypothetical situations as a prelude to applying the same standards to real-world situations.

Ethical Action

Codes of conduct and ethics training help employees to recognize and reason through ethical problems. However, firms must also provide structures and approaches that allow decisions to be turned into ethical actions. Texas Instruments gives its employees a reference card to help them make ethical decisions on the job. The card, the size of a standard business card, lists the following guidelines:

Napster and MP3 Aren't Music to Everyone's Ears

Nineteen-year-old Shawn Fanning thought he had a great idea: Offer free software to anyone who wanted it. The software allowed users to download music from their computers and send it to friends via the Internet. In other words, music buffs wouldn't have to actually buy their favorite tunes. But that meant recording artists, songwriters, and record labels wouldn't get their cuts. Shawn Fanning wasn't worried about the music industry. He went online with his site, called Napster.

Within a few months, 20 million users had downloaded half a billion songs, and the Recording Industry Association of America had filed suit against Napster in California, claiming that the company's "primary function is to enable and encourage copyright violations." Fanning insisted that his company was a "mere conduit" for music exchange; Napster itself did not sell or distribute any music. His supporters accused the music industry of being resistant to new technology, but many music artists, such as Hootie & the Blowfish and Alanis Morrissette, joined forces against Napster. "When our music is available online," they argued, "our rights should be respected." Ultimately, the San Francisco federal district court ruled against Napster, temporarily shutting the site down. But Fanning's attorney made the point that because of technology, this battle is not over. "If they were to shut [this type of company] down in America, it would move to Canada or somewhere else," he predicted. "There's a reason they call it the World Wide Web—it's literally worldwide."

In November 2000 Thomas Middlehoff, chairman and CEO of Bertelsmann, the world's third-largest media company, offered a deal to Napster. Although Middlehoff is still suing Napster along with the rest of the industry he is loaning Napster $50 million to develop technology and services designed to get users to pay for music rather than steal it. When and if Napster delivers, Bertelsmann will settle its copyright infringement and urge the other media companies to do the same. He wants to eventually turn Napster into a platform for downloading the whole spectrum of media products, including books, films, and magazines, from all companies.

Napster isn't the only online music site with problems. In 1997, Michael Robertson began promoting his new company, MP3, which offered a format for Internet music listening that made copying a breeze. The site's software allows users to listen to songs located in a "music locker" on the MP3's servers. Listeners must log on and stick compact discs into their PCs to prove that they already own the music. It took a while for the recording companies to pounce, but when they did, it was with a vengeance. They argued that the lockers had been set up illegally and sued MP3 for copyright infringe-ment. A federal judge agreed, temporarily shutting down the site. But MP3 reappeared. Robertson settled with BMG Entertainment and Warner Music, and talks with Universal, Sony, and EMI began. Robertson was looking for ways to work with the recording companies, not against them. The alliance was risky. It would probably cost MP3 $100 million in damages, and some of Robertson's 15 million customers would likely be turned off by it. But Robertson understood that he needed to change his tune for his company to survive: His new goal was to "become the cable TV network of the music business." In a major setback several months later, a federal judge ordered MP3 to pay $250 million in damages to Universal. The judge said that he wanted to send a strong message to companies like MP3 and Napster that "may have a misconception that, because their technology is novel, they are somehow immune from the ordinary applications of laws in the United States." Not surprisingly, Robertson vowed to appeal. "We believe that everyone should have the right to listen to the music they purchase, even if it's on the Internet," he said. A professor of intellectual property law at the University of California suggests that the music industry move away from such lawsuits and instead look toward new technology and ways to distribute digital music. "They can't just make digital music go away by suing everyone who's involved in it," he observes. "The demand is too great." There are a growing number of alternatives to Napster and MP3. Music fans are now able to download their favorite songs from file-sharing systems such as Splooge, Toadnode, and Swapoo.

QUESTIONS FOR CRITICAL THINKING

1. Do you think that the founders of Napster and MP3 behaved ethically? Why or why not? Identify any gray areas you perceive in the dilemmas faced by these companies. Try to come up with at least one possible solution to the extreme actions of either shutting these companies down or letting them operate without guidelines.

2. How does ethical leadership come into play at these two companies? How might it affect the future of each company?

Sources: Stephanie Stoughton, "Online Site Fined Millions for Music Use," *The Boston Globe*, September 7, 2000, pp. C1, C7; Adam Cohen, "Taps for Napster?" *Time*, July 31, 2000, pp. 34–35; Fred Vogelstein, "Record Labels' New Best Friend: MP3," *U.S. News & World Report*, July 3, 2000, pp. 36–45; Amy Kover, "Who's Afraid of This Kid?" *Fortune*, March 20, 2000, pp. 129–130; *The Wall Street Journal*, January 15, 2001, p. B1; Jack Ewing, "A New Net Powerhouse," *Business Week*, November 13, 2000, pp. 46–52.

- Does it comply with our values?
- If you do it, will you feel bad?
- How will it look in the newspaper?
- If you know it's wrong, don't do it!
- If you're not sure, ask.
- Keep asking until you get an answer.[14]

Goals set for the business as a whole and for individual departments and employees can affect ethical behavior. A firm whose managers set unrealistic goals for employee performance may find an increase in cheating, lying, and other misdeeds, as employees attempt to protect themselves. In today's Internet economy, the high value placed on speed can create a climate in which ethical behavior is sometimes challenged. Ethical decisions often require careful and quiet thought, and such thought seems to be nearly impossible in a business that is moving at warp speed.

Some companies encourage ethical action by providing support for employees faced with dilemmas. One common tool is an employee hotline, a telephone number that employees can call, often anonymously, for advice or to report unethical behavior they have witnessed. Nortel Networks, for example, operates a Business Ethics Advice Line. Employees from around the world can contact the advice line via phone or e-mail to ask for advice in applying the code of conduct in specific situations. Some companies also create ethics officers, individuals responsible for guiding employees through ethical minefields.

Ethical Leadership

Executives must not only talk about ethical behavior but also demonstrate it in their actions, especially in extreme or emergency situations, such as that faced by Ford and Firestone, described in the "Solving an Ethical Controversy" box. This principle requires employees to be personally committed to the company's core values and be willing to base their actions on them. Employees questioned about ethical leadership said they saw more ethical behavior in organizations where supervisors "set a good example of ethical business behavior." Among employees in companies where supervisors modeled such behavior, only 25 percent reported observing ethical misbehavior in the preceding year. That number was 72 percent among those who believed their supervisors did not set a good example. Employees in companies with ethical role models also reported higher levels of satisfaction.[15] Consistent with these findings, another large-scale study found that when employees think their employer's ethics program was designed primarily to protect upper management from being blamed for misconduct, the program actually promotes unethical behavior.[16]

However, ethical leadership should also go one step further and charge each employee at every level with the responsibility to be an ethical leader. Everyone should be aware of transgressions and be willing to defend the organization's standards. The Nortel Networks guidelines specifically communicate these responsibilities. The company tells employees, "You have a responsibility to ask questions when you have doubts about the ethical implications of any given situation or proposed course of action" and "You have a responsibility to report any concerns about business practices within the corporation that may violate this Code of Business Conduct."[17] As noted earlier, Nortel also provides employees with the tools for carrying out these responsibilities.

Bridgestone/Firestone recently recalled 6.5 million ATXk and Wilderness tires used on popular pickup trucks and SUVs, including the Ford Explorer shown here. The tire recall, due to defects that cause the tires to peel and shred, followed reports of over 200 deaths that were attributed to the problem.

Unfortunately, not all organizations are able to build this solid framework of business ethics. Because the damage from ethical misconduct can powerfully affect a firm's stakeholders—customers, investors, employees, and the public—pressure is exerted on businesses to act in acceptable ways. The next section examines the legal and governmental forces that are designed to safeguard society's interests when businesses fail at self-regulation.

CONTROLLING BUSINESS BEHAVIOR THROUGH GOVERNMENT REGULATION

Although few would disagree that businesses should act ethically and responsibly, it is clear that not all companies behave this way. When businesses fail to regulate their own actions, consumers and other businesses can suffer serious consequences. Because of this threat, federal, state, and local governments sometimes step in to regulate business activity. Governments pass laws limiting undesirable

SOLVING AN ETHICAL CONTROVERSY

For the leaders of Ford Motor Co. and Bridgestone/Firestone Inc., the summer of 2000 probably felt like facing a firestorm. The National Highway Traffic Safety Administration (NHTSA) had been investigating several models of Firestone tires after receiving nearly 800 complaints that the tires were defective, and it determined that more than 200 deaths had been caused by the tires peeling and shredding. The tires had been used on Ford's popular Explorer as well as other sport utility vehicles. Within hours of the release of the NHTSA report, a recall plan was announced. Yet the two companies' troubles were only beginning. At the very heart of the crisis lay the issue of ethical leadership. Although neither firm covered itself with glory as reports from around the globe surfaced that both companies had been aware of the problems as early as 1996, most media coverage gave the edge to Ford's handling of the situation, preferring to lay blame at Firestone's feet. But Firestone had its own way of dealing with the problem—its Japanese CEO resigned, and its new U.S. CEO took the helm to deal with the crisis.

Did Ford display greater ethical leadership than Firestone during the tire recall crisis?

PRO

1. Ford responded much more quickly to the problem than did Firestone. When Ford initially asked Firestone to recall the tires manufactured at its Venezuelan plant, the tiremaker declined.
2. Ford displayed much greater openness to the public about the tire disaster than did Firestone. Executives made themselves available to the media—including CEO Jac Nasser's televised statements.

3. Ford also made itself available to consumers, including establishing a hot line and Web site where consumers could ask questions and get information pertaining to their own situation.

CON

1. Bridgestone/Firestone demonstrated openness by allowing Ford to release confidential records of a computer analysis that used raw data from the tiremaker to determine which tire models were defective.
2. When it became apparent that the recall was going to take too long and more consumers would be at risk, Bridgestone/Firestone stepped up production at its Japanese plants to speed up the recall and the delivery of replacement tires.
3. Although Firestone announced its own tire replacement plan, Ford moved ahead by authorizing replacement with competitors' tires, which would be paid for by Bridgestone/Firestone. "Bottom line: Firestone will be paying to put people in other people's tires," said one Detroit tire wholesaler.

SUMMARY

Determining the degree of responsibility of participants in a complicated crisis, especially one that involves loss of lives, is itself a complicated process. In this case, confusion reigned for a long time. At the grassroots level, consumers couldn't get their tires replaced fast enough; and dealers often didn't even know which tires were on the recall list and which weren't. But each company had a golden opportunity to demonstrate ethical leadership, which, regardless of the outcome of the crisis, could only strengthen its relationship with consumers, consumer groups, and society in general.

Sources: "New Man, Same Agenda," ABCNews.com, October 11, 2000, abcnews.go.com; Irene M. Kunii and Dean Foust, "Crisis Management: 'They Just Don't Have a Clue How to Handle This,'" *Business Week*, September 18, 2000, p. 43; "NHTSA Investigating Failure of Firestone Brand Tires," Cnn.com, August 3, 2000, **www.cnn.com**; "A Nasty Turn for Ford," *Time*, January 15, 2001, p. 45.

actions or requiring desirable actions. They also may offer various incentives for socially desirable behavior. The Canadian government has a program called Reno$ense, which helps store managers set up displays for home improvement and energy-efficient products in a way that encourages shoppers to make their homes more environmentally friendly. The government makes the promotional materials available to stores at no charge.[18]

Many of the major federal laws affecting business are listed in Table 2.1. Legal protections for employee safety and equal employment opportunities are covered later in this chapter. Many of the laws that affect specific industries or individuals are described in other chapters. For example, legislation affecting international business operations is discussed in Chapter 4. Laws designed to assist small businesses are examined in Chapter 5. Laws related to formation and operation of labor unions are described in Chapter 11. Finally, legislation related to banking and the securities markets is discussed in Chapters 19 and 20.

The history of government regulation in the United States can be divided into three phases: regulation of competition, consumer protection, and deregulation. Because an understanding of the political and legal environment in which business decisions are made is closely linked to ethics and social responsibility, the following

Table 2.1 Major Federal Laws Affecting Business

Date	Law	Description
A. Laws to Maintain a Competitive Environment		
1890	Sherman Antitrust Act	Prohibits restraint of trade and monopolization; delineates a competitive marketing system as national policy.
1914	Clayton Act	Strengthens the Sherman Act by restricting such practices as price discrimination, exclusive dealing, tying contracts, and interlocking boards of directors where the effect "may be to substantially lessen competition or tend to create a monopoly."
1914	Federal Trade Commission Act	Prohibits unfair methods of competition; established the Federal Trade Commission, an administrative agency that investigates business practices and enforces the FTC Act.
1938	Wheeler-Lea Act	Amended the FTC Act to further outlaw unfair practices and give the FTC jurisdiction over false and misleading advertising.
1950	Celler-Kefauver Antimerger Act	Amended the Clayton Act to include major asset purchases that decrease competition in an industry.
B. Laws to Regulate Competition		
1936	Robinson-Patman Act	Prohibits price discrimination in sales to wholesalers, retailers, or other producers; prohibits selling at unreasonably low prices to eliminate competition.
1993	North American Free Trade Agreement (NAFTA)	International trade agreement between Canada, Mexico, and the United States designed to facilitate trade by removing tariffs and other trade barriers among the three nations.
C. Laws to Protect Consumers		
1906	Federal Food and Drug Act	Prohibits adulteration and misbranding of foods and drugs involved in interstate commerce; strengthened by the Food, Drug, and Cosmetic Act (1938) and the Kefauver-Harris Drug Amendment (1962).
1958	National Traffic and Safety Act	Provides for the creation of safety standards for automobiles and tires; strengthened by the Transportation Recall Enhancement, Accountability, and Documentation (TREAD) Act of 2000 to include stronger manufacturer reporting requirements, rollover testing, and penalties for misleading information on auto defects that cause death or injury.
1966	Fair Packaging and Labeling Act	Requires disclosure of product identification, name and address of manufacturer or distributor, and information on the quality of contents.
1967	Federal Cigarette Labeling and Advertising Act	Requires written health warnings on cigarette packages.
1968	Consumer Credit Protection Act	Truth-in-lending law requiring disclosure of annual interest rates on loans and credit purchases.
1970	Fair Credit Reporting Act	Gives individuals access to their credit records and allows them to change incorrect information.
1970	National Environmental Policy Act	Established the Environmental Protection Agency to deal with various types of pollution and organizations that create pollution.
1971	Public Health Cigarette Smoking Act	Prohibits tobacco advertising on radio and television. 1999 settlement between the tobacco industry and the state attorneys general resulted in a $246 billion settlement for use in covering health-care costs of smokers and to fund antismoking promotions in addition to further advertising restrictions.
1972	Consumer Product Safety Act	Created the Consumer Product Safety Commission with authority to specify safety standards for most products.
1975	Equal Credit Opportunity Act	Bans discrimination in lending practices based on sex, marital status, race, national origin, religion, age, or receipt of payments from public-assistance programs.
1990	Nutrition Labeling and Education Act	Requires food manufacturers and processors to provide detailed nutritional information on the labels of most foods.
1990	Children's Television Act	Limits the amount of advertising to be shown during children's television programs: up to 10.5 minutes per hour on weekends and 12.0 minutes per hour on weekdays.
1990	Americans with Disabilities Act (ADA)	Protects the rights of people with disabilities; makes discrimination against the disabled illegal in public accommodations, transportation, and telecommunications.
1999	Deceptive Mail Prevention and Enforcement Act	Requires that direct mail from sweepstakes operators clearly state that no purchase is necessary to win or to improve the chances of winning; prohibits such mailings from saying the recipient is a winner unless the person has won a prize.
D. Laws to Deregulate Specific Industries		
1978	Airline Deregulation Act	Permits commercial airlines to set fares and choose new routes.
1980	Motor Carrier Act and Staggers Rail Act	Significantly deregulates the trucking and railroad industries by permitting them to negotiate rates and services.
1996	Telecommunications Act	Significantly deregulates the telecommunications industry by removing barriers to competition in local and long-distance phone and cable television markets.

sections examine how each of these regulatory phases has shaped, and still influences, the business landscape.

Regulation of Competition

As Chapter 1 shows, competition is the cornerstone of a private enterprise economy. During the late 19th and early 20th centuries, however, government became concerned that power in many industries was too concentrated in the hands of small numbers of companies. These huge firms not only stifled competition, but also had little incentive to act ethically. In response, the federal government began to intervene to regulate competition and commercial activities.

Some industries, such as electric utilities, became regulated. Throughout most of this century, government regulations allowed only one power company in a given market. Regulators reasoned that the large capital investment required to construct electric transmission lines made this type of regulation appropriate. In a **regulated industry,** competition is either limited or eliminated, and close government control is substituted for free competition. In most cases, regulated industries are those closely tied to the public interest and for which competition would be wasteful or excessive.

The second form of government regulation, enactment of statutes, has led to both state and federal laws that affect competition and various commercial practices. More than a century ago, the federal government began to regulate competition with the Sherman Antitrust Act of 1890. This act prohibits any contract or conspiracy that tends toward restraint of trade. It also declares illegal any action that monopolizes or attempts to monopolize any part of commerce.

Another major federal law, the Clayton Act of 1914, forbids such trade restraints as tying contracts, interlocking directorates, and certain anticompetitive stock acquisitions. A tying contract requires the exclusive dealer for a manufacturer's products to carry other, perhaps unwanted products in inventory. In interlocking directorates, competing companies have identical or overlapping boards of directors. The Clayton Act also forbids any purchase of another company's stock that reduces competition.

Both the Sherman Act and the Clayton Act are enforced by the Antitrust Division of the U.S. Department of Justice. Violators are subject to not only criminal fines or imprisonment but also civil damage suits by competitors or other parties. In some cases, the government allows the accused firm to enter into a consent order, under which it agrees voluntarily to cease the conduct that the government alleges is inappropriate. The Celler-Kefauver Antimerger Act (1950) amended the Clayton Act to prohibit major asset purchases that decrease competition in an industry. For example, the Justice Department stopped the planned acquisition of Sprint by WorldCom, a deal that would have combined the second- and third-largest providers of long-distance phone service in the United States. The government acted out of concern that the acquisition would stifle competition in the long-distance and Internet marketplaces. Companies sometimes address such concerns by selling off parts of their business to preserve competition.[19]

The Federal Trade Commission Act of 1914 banned unfair competitive practices and set up the Federal Trade Commission (FTC) to administer various statutes that apply to business. The powers and investigative capacities of the FTC have grown rapidly over the years; today, it is the major federal regulatory and enforcement agency to oversee competitive practices. The FTC can sue violators or enter into consent orders with those that agree to cease questionable practices. The FTC recently won a case against Toys 'R' Us. The court found that Toys 'R' Us had entered into agreements with toy manufacturers so that each would limit the products it distributed to discount stores, knowing that the other companies would do the same. By coordinating these agreements among an industry's major competitors, Toys 'R' Us kept its advantage in selling low-price toys but violated the FTC Act.[20]

In recent years, FTC investigators have been examining the details of industry activities and proposed mergers to look for possible anticompetitive behavior, including long-term implications and the impact on specific groups of customers. When Arco and BP Amoco planned a merger, the agency found that the combined companies would monopolize oil production on Alaska's North Slope, enabling them to charge unfairly high prices to oil refineries on the West Coast.

During the Great Depression of the 1930s, other laws aimed at protecting competitors were enacted when independent merchants felt the need for legal protection against competition from larger chain stores. A major federal law enacted during this period, the Robinson-Patman Act, sought to protect smaller competitors against low prices charges by larger competitors in an attempt to force them out of business. This text covers many other specific business practices regulated by government in other sections and in Appendix B, "Business Law."

Consumer Protection

Although the objective of consumer protection underlies most business-oriented laws—including the Sherman Act and the Clayton Act—many of the major consumer-oriented laws have been enacted during the past 40 years. Federal and state legislation plays a major role in regulating product safety. The Consumer Product Safety Act of 1972 created a powerful regulatory agency called the Consumer Product Safety Commission (CPSC). The agency has the authority to ban products without court hearings, order recalls or redesigns of products, and inspect production facilities, and it can charge managers of negligent companies with criminal offenses. Other federal laws, such as the Poison Prevention Packaging Act of 1970, set guidelines for product labels of manufacturers in various industries. In addition, the dramatic rise in product liability lawsuits over the past two decades has pushed businesses in all industries to pay greater attention to customer safety issues.

Another area of consumer protection involves giving consumers full and accurate information. Laws such as the Fair Packaging and Labeling Act and the Consumer Credit Protection Act require that companies provide specific information about their products, from vitamins to auto loans. The FTC investigates complaints of fraudulent offers. Its Bureau of Consumer Protection offers consumers a toll-free phone number (1-877–FTC-HELP) and a form on its Web site (www.ftc.gov) where consumers can report fraudulent offers. Their reports go into a database that is available to law enforcement officials in the United States and Canada.[21] A later section takes a closer look at consumer protection issues in the context of businesses' social responsibilities to customers.

Deregulation

During the closing years of the 20th century, **deregulation,** the movement toward eliminating legal restraints on competition in various industries, began to significantly reshape the legal environment for many industries. Considerable controversy continues to surround the government's role in regulating business and the benefits of allowing industries to compete without intense government control.

During this phase, the federal government has worked to increase competition in a number of industries, including telecommunications, utilities, transportation, and banking, by discontinuing many regulations and permitting new firms to enter these markets and allowing existing businesses to expand their service offerings to new markets. The trend toward deregulation started in 1978 with the Airline Deregulation Act, which encouraged competition among airlines by allowing them to set their own rates and to add or abandon routes based on profitability.

Critics of deregulation often point out negative effects of the trend. Some say that deregulation may lead to increasing prices as competitors are eliminated. Others suggest that firms may sacrifice safety in the name of competition. All of these issues are legitimate concerns.

The latest industry undergoing deregulation is the electric utility industry. With 198 investor-owned utilities in the United States, it is also the largest industry to be deregulated so far. California became the first state to open electricity sales completely to free competition. Consumers and businesses can now choose to buy from several different electricity suppliers, and the suppliers can specialize in transmitting electricity to substations, distributing it to customers, or handling marketing and billing activities. Other state regulatory agencies are beginning to follow California's lead. Supporters claim that deregulation will slash the price of electricity and force companies to view their customers as more than a name on a bill. Critics say that savings are likely to be small and warn that not all suppliers will be equally reliable. Customers seem to be wary of deregulation. After California spent $90 million to advertise that consumers can choose their power company, 85 percent of consumers said they were aware of that choice, but only 1 percent had elected to change from their existing utility. And in 2000, when a prolonged heat wave combined with soaring prices of natural gas used to fuel most power-generating facilities, some California consumers saw their electricity bills spike 240 percent, which unleashed a backlash against utility deregulation.[22]

Government Regulation of Cyberspace

The Internet remains a frontier for regulation. Regulation of Web-based business is difficult, because the Internet is a borderless market. For it to function as a global marketplace, governments must work together to develop a stable economic and legal environment in which firms can operate freely, regardless of jurisdiction. Policies such as regulation of content, encryption (coding) of sensitive information, and protection of electronic payments cannot be decided separately by each country.

Reaching an internationally agreed-upon system for Internet communication and transactions will take years. In the meantime, governments, businesses, and Internet users are facing issues that require immediate attention. Particular areas of concern arise because the Internet makes it easy to spread information, regardless of its accuracy. As the number of Internet users grows, so too do the instances of online fraud. In 1999, ten times as many complaints were filed with the FTC as in 1997. Many come from people who try to buy online but never receive products they have paid for. Others overpay for items at online auctions because people post an item for sale and then use other aliases to post phony high-price bids. Some of them even use aliases to post flattering "reviews" of their own trustworthiness, further luring innocent buyers into the trap. The anonymity of the Internet also poses problems for sellers, because it provides a whole new set of tricks for buyers with stolen credit card numbers. As Internet usage and related problems continue to grow, the FTC has stepped up its policing of cyberspace. The agency has assigned 80 staff members to full-time duty on issues related to Internet commerce, including fraud.[23]

Consumers are becoming more concerned about guarding their privacy. In a recent survey, three out of every five Web users have decided to avoid using at least one financial Web site because of concern about how personal data would be used, and nearly two of every three have refused to give data to a financial Web site because they thought it was unnecessary or too personal. In this climate of consumer concern and lax industry self-regulation, the likelihood of consumer protection laws is growing.[24]

Congress has already tried to protect the privacy of children. The Children's Online Privacy Protection Act required Web sites to post privacy policies and collect verifiable consent from parents before they collect personally identifiable information from children under age 13 years. The law required that parents be able to review information about their children and delete it if they desired. But the law was attacked as a violation of the First Amendment right to free speech. In 2000, a federal appeals court ruled the law was unconstitutional, and the government

BUSINESS DIRECTORY

➤ **deregulation** *regulatory trend toward elimination of legal restraints on competition.*

is reviewing its options.[25] Chapter 7 looks more closely at the issues surrounding Internet commerce.

ACTING RESPONSIBLY TO SATISFY SOCIETY

A second major issue affecting business is the question of social responsibility. In a general sense, social responsibility is management's acceptance of the obligation to consider profit, consumer satisfaction, and societal well-being of equal value in evaluating the firm's performance. It is the recognition that business must be concerned with the qualitative dimensions of consumer, employee, and societal benefits as well as the quantitative measures of sales and profits, by which business performance is traditionally measured. Businesses may exercise social responsibility because such behavior is required by law, because it enhances the company's image, or because management believes it is the ethical course of action.

Historically, a company's social performance has been measured by its contribution to the overall economy and the employment opportunities it provides. Variables such as wage payments often serve to indicate social performance. Although profits and employment remain important, today many factors contribute to an assessment of a firm's social performance, including providing equal employment opportunities; respecting the cultural diversity of employees; responding to environmental concerns; providing a safe, healthy workplace; and producing safe, high-quality products.

A business is also judged by its interactions with the community. To demonstrate their social responsibility, many corporations highlight charitable contributions and community service in their annual reports and on their Web site. Among them:

- Anheuser-Busch collaborates with community groups to prevent alcohol abuse, drunk driving, and underage drinking. As Figure 2.5 shows, the company encourages sellers of alcoholic beverages to enforce laws against selling alcohol to minors. It also provides advertising and financial support for programs that educate parents and students about responsible drinking.[26]

  - Procter & Gamble contributes millions of dollars through the Procter & Gamble Fund, corporate contributions, product donations, individual facilities' gifts, and other types of giving. The company donates products to America's Second Harvest, a network of food banks. It donates to universities and research organizations patents that do not fit the company's strategic plans but may offer commercial potential, thereby providing revenue to the organizations that apply the patents.[27]

Some firms measure social performance by conducting **social audits,** formal procedures that identify and evaluate all company activities that relate to social issues such as conservation, employment practices, environmental protection, and philanthropy. The social audit informs management about how well the company is performing in these areas. Based on this information, management may take steps to revise current programs or develop new ones.

Outside groups may conduct their own evaluations of businesses. Various environmental, religious, and public interest groups have created standards of corporate performance. Reports on many of these evaluations are available to the general public. The Council on Economic Priorities produces publications such as

FIGURE 2.5
Anheuser-Busch: Encouraging Responsible Sales of Alcoholic Beverages

CHECK ID. AT THE VERY WORST YOU MIGHT
MAKE A 35-YEAR-OLD'S DAY.

"May I see your ID?" A simple phrase, but one of great importance. To help store owners like Lee, Anheuser-Busch designed a program called "Operation ID." It helps retailers spot fake IDs and verify valid ones. In the last 10 years, Anheuser-Busch and its distributors have given retailers nearly one million of these ID-checking tools to help stop sales to minors. It's people like Lee and programs like this that have helped reduce teenage drinking by 45% since 1982.

TEENAGE DRINKING DOWN 45%

WE ALL MAKE A DIFFERENCE.

Department of Health & Human Services, 1999.

Budweiser

www.beeresponsible.com

The Better World Investment Guide, which recommends basing investment decisions on companies' track records on various social issues, including environmental impact, nuclear weapons contracts, community outreach, and advancement of women and minorities. Other groups publicize their evaluations and include critiques of the social responsibility performance of firms. The Center for Science in the Public Interest evaluates the healthfulness of the food marketed to consumers.[28]

Many firms find that consumers evaluate their social track records in retail stores through their purchase decisions. Some consumer groups organize boycotts of companies they find to be socially irresponsible. In a **boycott,** consumers refuse to buy a company's goods or services. Mail Abuse Prevention System (MAPS) offers a new twist on the old-fashioned boycott: a service that blocks incoming mail from companies that it believes have sent spam. The company compiles the Real-Time Blackhole List, a list of reported spammers, and for those who subscribe, it deletes mail from those sources or returns it to the sender. Bouncing the messages back not only spares the receiver, it can also swamp the sender's Web site so that it effectively shuts down during the onslaught. Companies that place online marketing messages treat MAPS with kid gloves. MessageMedia, for example, says it has refused to work with clients who do not adhere to MAPS guidelines, because a misstep by one of its clients could land MessageMedia on the list.[29]

As Figure 2.6 shows, the social responsibilities of business can be classified according to its relationships to the general public, customers, employees, and investors and other members of the financial community. Many of these relationships extend beyond national borders.

FIGURE 2.6
Responsibilities of Business

Responsibilities to the General Public

The responsibilities of business to the general public include dealing with public health issues, protecting the environment, and developing the quality of the workforce. Additionally, many would argue that businesses have responsibilities to support charitable and social causes and organizations that work toward the greater public good. In other words, they should give back to the communities in which they earn profits. Such efforts are called *corporate philanthropy.* Figure 2.7 summarizes these four responsibilities, which are discussed in the sections that follow.

Public Health Issues   One of the most complex issues facing business as it addresses its ethical and social responsibilities to the general public revolves around public health. Central to this debate is the question of what businesses should do about products that are inherently dangerous, like tobacco, alcohol, and handguns. Tobacco products represent a major health risk, contributing to heart disease, stroke, and cancer among smokers. Families and coworkers of smokers share this danger as well, since their exposure to secondhand smoke increases their risks for cancer, asthma, and respiratory infections. Recently, courts have agreed with this assessment of smoking as a health risk, and tobacco companies have been assessed heavy fines to compensate for their actions. In 1998, Philip Morris and three other tobacco companies agreed to a $206 billion settlement with 46 states. Two years later, a Florida jury ordered the tobacco industry to pay $145 billion in punitive damages to Florida smokers who had developed illnesses associated with long-term smoking. Philip Morris, whose products represent one of every two cigarettes sold in the United States, was ordered to pay about half the entire amount. Faced with prospect of even more legal action, Philip Morris and other tobacco companies have spent tens of millions of dollars on socially responsible activities and causes, such as youth smoking prevention programs, food banks, and medical assistance in developing countries. But not everyone is buying the

FIGURE 2.7
**Business Responsibilities to
the General Public**

**Public Health
Issues**
AIDS
Smoking
Alcohol Abuse
Drug Abuse

**Corporate
Philanthropy**
Monetary Donations
  to Charitable and
  Social Organizations
Support for Employee
  Volunteer Efforts
Donations of Goods to
  Charitable and
  Social Organizations

**Protecting the
Enivironment**
Avoiding Pollution
Recycling
Green Marketing
Environmentally
  Friendly Technologies

**Developing the
Quality of the
Workforce**
On-the-Job Training
Education Benefits
Operating Where
  Jobs Are Needed
Valuing Diversity

sincerity of the tobacco industry's attempts at social responsibility. Even though Philip Morris ranks among the highest contributors to charitable events, it also ranks near the bottom in surveys of consumer attitudes toward individual businesses. "With their charitable donations, they're trying to divert attention away from the harm that they're doing," says Matt Myers, president of Campaign for Tobacco-Free Kids. "In essence, they're trying to buy forgiveness for the harm their product causes and their ongoing wrongful behaviors."[30]

Substance abuse, including alcohol abuse, is another serious public health problem worldwide. Motor vehicle accidents are a major killer, and drunk drivers cause many serious crashes. Alcohol abuse has also been linked to serious diseases such as cirrhosis of the liver. Other risks to public health and safety come from fatty foods, television violence, and motorcycles.

Of particular concern is the impact of such products on vulnerable groups. Alcohol ads appeal to teenagers. Absolut vodka ads have even become collector's items for many teens, raising concerns that the company is encouraging underage drinking. Many consumers view alcohol advertising, whether aimed at adults or young people, as socially irresponsible. Some brewers have tried to counter these views by sponsoring advertising campaigns that promote moderation.

Businesses also face challenges when dealing with the consequences of diseases like AIDS, which is especially dangerous because, on average, five years pass between a person's first exposure to HIV, the virus that causes AIDS, and actual development of the disease. During this period, people may not show any symptoms, and they probably don't even know they have the virus, but they are still carriers who can transmit the disease to others. This large pool of unknown carriers contributes greatly to the rapid spread of the disease.

The onslaught of AIDS has forced companies to educate their workers about how to deal with employees and customers who have the deadly disease. Health care for AIDS patients can be incredibly expensive, straining the ability of small companies to pay for health care coverage. Do companies have the right to test potential employees for the AIDS virus and avoid this expense? Some people believe that this screening would violate the rights of job applicants; others feel that a firm has a responsibility not to place AIDS patients in jobs where they could infect members of the general public. These are difficult questions. In resolving them, a business must balance the rights of individuals against the rights of society in general.

Protecting the Environment Businesses consume huge amounts of energy, which increases the use of fossil fuels like coal and oil for energy production. This activity introduces carbon dioxide and sulfur into the earth's atmosphere, substances that many scientists believe will result in dramatic climate changes during the 21st century. Meanwhile, the sulfur from fossil fuels combines with water vapor in the air to form sulfuric acid. The acid rain that results can kill fish and trees and pollute ground water. Wind can carry the sulfur around the entire globe. Sulfur from factories in the United States is damaging Canadian forests, and pollution from London smokestacks has been found in the forests and lakes of Scandinavia. Other production and manufacturing methods leave behind large quantities of waste materials that can further pollute the environment and fill already bulging landfills.

For many managers, finding ways to minimize the **pollution** and other environmental damage caused by their products or operating processes has become an important economic, legal, and social issue. The solution can be difficult. Ford Motor Co. recently issued a Corporate Citizenship Report in which it admitted that its sport utility vehicles (SUVs) are environmentally harmful as well as dangerous to automobile drivers involved in accidents with them. However, the vehicles are also highly profitable and any automaker without an SUV in its product line is rushing to add one. So while Ford is trying to develop more socially responsible products, it intends to continue making and selling SUVs.[31]

Despite Ford's experience, companies are finding they can be environmentally friendly and profitable, too. Over the past quarter century, 3M has reduced emissions of hazardous wastes, mainly by finding alternatives to toxic solvents. The changes have saved the company hundreds of millions of dollars. And the $3.1 million Dow Chemical has spent to reduce toxic emissions at its Midland, Michigan, plant actually result in savings of $5.4 million a year. These kinds of savings come from sources like greater efficiency, reduced operating costs, and less money spent on complying with regulations.[32] The logic of this approach is plain to Peter Senge, who chairs the Society for Organizational Learning. According to Senge, nature produces no waste—every creature's waste products provide food for something else—but in modern America, business uses 200 times each person's body weight to make products, and 99 percent of that weight eventually becomes waste.[33]

Another solution is **recycling**—reprocessing used materials for reuse. Recycling can sometimes provide much of the raw material that manufacturers need, thereby conserving the world's natural resources and reducing the need for landfills. Several industries are developing ways to use recycled materials. One innovative solution comes from Interface, which makes commercial carpeting. Rather than merely selling carpet for a business customer to throw away after it wears out, the company rents the carpet. When the customer is finished using it, Interface removes and replaces it; then it recycles the old carpet.[34]

ABSOLUT CITRON.

Even though Absolut runs its award-winning ads in magazines with adult (21 and older) readerships, it is virtually impossible to screen underage readers from such ads. This ad, which appeared in *Traditional Home*, was placed in a magazine whose readers are more likely to be 21 and older. However, thousands of underaged people are faithful readers of the publication.

BUSINESS DIRECTORY

➤ **recycling** *reprocessing of used materials for reuse.*

If a business says a product is...	The product or package must...
Biodegradable	break down and return to nature in a reasonably short period of time.
Recyclable	be entirely reusable as new materials in the manufacture or assenbly of a new product or package.
Refillable	be included in a system for the collection and return of the package for refill. If consumers have to find a way to refill it themselves, it is not *refillable.*
Ozone Safe/Ozone Friendly	must not contain any ozone-depleting ingredient.

FIGURE 2.8
FTC Guidelines for Environmental Claims in Green Marketing

Prius, Toyota's new hybrid vehicle, captures the energy produced during normal deceleration and converts it back into power. As the ad states, "When it sees red, it charges"— when you put on the brakes. The hybrid car drives away under electric power, saving fuel and gas money, and releases up to 90 percent fewer emissions.

Many consumers have more favorable impressions of environmentally conscious businesses; in fact, they often prefer to buy from such firms. To target these customers, companies often use **green marketing,** a marketing strategy that promotes environmentally safe products and production methods. McDonald's formed an Animals' Welfare Advisory Council, which brings together scientists and animal rights leaders to review the conditions of the animals raised to supply the restaurant chain. McDonald's now requires its egg suppliers to provide better living conditions for its chickens. The fast-food chain's requirements include increasing the amount of living space from 40 square inches to 72 square inches per chicken and abandoning the practice of withholding food for 5–14 days to increase egg production. Company spokesman Walt Riker told a newspaper reporter, "We are doing this because we feel the social responsibility to enhance animal welfare." Animal rights organizations applauded the move, while pointing out that the changes still leave chickens too little room to move around or spread their wings. Such efforts may be a practical one for a global company. The European Union is already beginning to require the changes that McDonald's announced, and the U.S. Department of Agriculture is considering similar measures. Still, by taking these actions, McDonald's is positioning itself as a company that cares about animal welfare.[35]

A business cannot simply claim that its goods or services are environmentally friendly. In 1992, the FTC issued guidelines for businesses to follow in making environmental claims. A firm must be able to prove that any environmental claim made about a good or service has been substantiated with reliable scientific evidence. In addition, as shown in Figure 2.8, the FTC has given specific directions about how various environmental terms may be used in advertising and marketing.

Environmental concerns can lead to new technologies. The Toyota Prius and Honda Insight automobiles combine high-efficiency gasoline engines with electric motors into a hybrid car that generates less pollution than a standard gasoline-powered automobile. Each company has launched the cars by producing a few thousand and limiting their distribution until sales results indicate consumer interest. Toyota began selling the Prius on its Web site only. With the huge increase in gasoline prices, consumers have expressed considerable interest in these hybrid cars, and other automakers have announced plans to develop their own models. Furthermore, automakers expect the demand for hybrid cars to exceed that for electric-only vehicles, because they recharge themselves, rather than requiring that the driver park them for a while to recharge the battery.[36]

Sometimes the new technologies themselves raise controversy. An example is **genetic engineering,** a type of biotechnology that involves altering crops or other living things by inserting genes that provide them with a desirable characteristic, such as nutritional value or resistance to pesticides. One of the most controversial of these genetically modified (GM) crops has been corn engineered to make Bacillus thuringiensis (Bt), a type of bacteria that acts as a natural insecticide. The potential value of such a crop is that it reduces the need for chemical pesticides. Critics warn that it could be an ecological disaster. If most corn makes Bt, caterpillars could become resistant to it, requiring *more* pesticide use in the long run. In addition, some research has suggested that exposure to the corn is deadly to monarch butterfly caterpillars. Critics also fear that introducing genes from one type of plant into another—for example, daffodil genes have been used to add beta-carotene to rice—may create products with hidden allergens that could trigger a dangerous allergic reaction in susceptible people.

Some consumers, especially in Europe, have resisted buying GM foods. Both U.S. and foreign farmers are uncertain whether to adopt the technology, because consumer resistance could make the crops worthless in the marketplace. Already, some food processors are willing to pay premium prices for food that has not been genetically engineered. Frito-Lay asked its corn suppliers to plant only unmodified seeds, and Wild Oats Market and Whole Foods Market are eliminating GM ingredients from their store brands. An agreement negotiated under the United Nations Convention on Biodiversity allows countries to ban imports of GM seeds, animals, and crops and to require labels on living GM goods, such as animals and whole grains, saying that they may contain GM organisms. Taco Bell recently recalled its taco shells distributed through supermarkets due to concerns about adverse consumer reactions when it discovered that GM corn had been used. Still, biotech food has become part of American agriculture. About one-third of the corn and almost half the soybeans currently grown in the United States have been genetically engineered to either include an insecticide or resist herbicides used to kill weeds around the crops. The companies that provide these technologies are hoping that sentiment will become more favorable when food producers begin offering products engineered to provide health benefits, such as eggs with reduced cholesterol.[37]

Developing the Quality of the Workforce   In the past, a nation's wealth has often been based on its money, production equipment, and natural resources. A country's true wealth, however, lies in its people. An educated, skilled workforce provides the intellectual know-how required to develop new technology, improve productivity, and compete in the global marketplace. It is becoming increasingly clear that in order to remain competitive, U.S. business must assume more responsibility for enhancing the quality of its workforce.

In developed economies like that of the United States, most new jobs require college-educated workers. Companies find it more economical to hire overseas workers for low-skilled tasks, because wages are lower in developing nations. With demand greatest for workers with advanced skills, the difference between the highest-paid and lowest-paid workers has been increasing. Among full-time workers in the United States, the top 10 percent earn an average of $1,200 per week, compared with just $275 for the average worker in the bottom 10 percent. Twenty years ago, a college graduate on average earned 38 percent more than someone with only a high school diploma, but today the college graduate earns 71 percent more.[38] Clearly, education is essential to the well-being of the workforce. Businesses must encourage students to stay in school, continue their education, and sharpen their skills. Companies must also encourage employees to learn new skills and remain competitive.

Organizations also face enormous responsibilities for helping women, members of various cultural groups, and those who are physically challenged to contribute fully to the economy. Failure to do so is not only a waste of more than half the nation's workforce but also devastating to a firm's public image. Socially responsible firms advertise and act on their commitment to a diverse workforce. They may post jobs on a Web site like HotJobs.com, which links with wemedia.com, a Web site serving the interests of people with disabilities. Figure 2.9 describes the partnership between HotJobs.com and wemedia.com, which gives people with disabilities access to the best jobs to pursue their potential.

I DON'T WANT YOUR PITY.
I WANT THE JOB.

Millions of talented people seek something more from life. And they're ready and able to earn it. That's why wemedia.com has teamed up with HotJobs.com to offer access to the best jobs for people with various disabilities. It's part of how wemedia.com serves the needs of the more than 54 million Americans with disabilities, enabling them to pursue their potential without compromise.

Cary Fields, President/CEO

we media.com

FIGURE 2.9
Wemedia.com and HotJobs.com:
Partnering to Encourage Hiring
People with Disabilities

Through a commitment to developing employee diversity, Texaco has successfully rebounded from a racial discrimination lawsuit. When information that the company's top managers had engaged in racist behavior became public, the company was embarrassed, and its stock price tumbled. Texaco quickly agreed to settle the lawsuit and crafted a plan to place more value on diversity among employees. Recruiting methods were revised to reach a more diverse pool of applicants, and scholarship programs were launched to develop talented minorities interested in key careers like the physical sciences and international business. The company set specific goals for hiring and promoting qualified minority employees, and to achieve those goals, it included women and minorities on human resource committees and established mentoring programs. Within three years, Texaco had increased its recruiting of minorities to more than four of every ten new hires, and its promotions of minorities accounted for one out of every five promotions.

Corporate Philanthropy   As Chapter 1 points out, not-for-profit organizations play an important role in society by serving the public good. They provide the human resources that enhance the quality of life in communities around the world. To fulfill this mission, many not-for-profit organizations rely on financial contributions from the business community. Firms respond by donating billions of dollars each year to not-for-profit organizations. This **corporate philanthropy** includes cash contributions, donations of equipment and products, and supporting the volunteer efforts of company employees. Recipients include cultural organizations, adopt-a-school programs, community development agencies, and housing and job training programs.

Corporate philanthropy can have many positive benefits beyond the purely altruistic rewards of giving, such as higher employee morale, enhanced image, and improved customer relationships. Procter & Gamble's donation of its unneeded patents to research programs provides motivation to the company's own research and development staff. They can see that their efforts will bear fruit, even if the patents do not directly benefit the company. In addition, by supporting research and educational institutions, P&G is helping to develop a future pool of researchers, some of whom may work for or with the company. In an effort to maximize the benefits of corporate giving in an era of downsizing, businesses have become more selective of the causes and charities they choose to support. Many seek to align their marketing efforts with their charitable giving. For example, many companies make contributions to the Olympics and create advertising that features the company's sponsorship. This is known as *cause related marketing*.

Another form of corporate philanthropy is volunteerism. In their roles as corporate citizens, thousands of businesses encourage their employees to contribute their efforts to projects as diverse as Habitat for Humanity, the United Way, and Red Cross blood drives. In addition to making tangible contributions to the well-being of fellow citizens, such programs generate considerable public support and goodwill for the companies and their employees. In some cases, the volunteer efforts occur mostly during off-hours for employees. In other instances, the firm permits its workforce to volunteer during regular working hours. Nortel Networks offers a combination of grants, use of company facilities, and limited time off work for volunteers in the locations where it has facilities, from Atlanta to Paris to Beijing. Community involvement for each city is coordinated by an employee who makes sure the efforts are in line with company guidelines.[39]

Responsibilities to Customers

Businesspeople share a social and ethical responsibility to treat their customers fairly and act in a manner that is not harmful to them. Consumer advocate and recent presidential candidate Ralph Nader first pioneered this idea in the late 1960s. Since then, **consumerism**—the public demand that a business consider the wants and needs of its customers in making decisions—has gained widespread acceptance. Consumerism is based on the belief that consumers have certain rights. The most frequently quoted statement of consumer rights was made by President John F. Kennedy in 1962. Figure 2.10 summarizes these consumer rights. Numerous state and federal laws have been implemented since then to protect these rights.

FIGURE 2.10
Consumer Rights as Proposed by President Kennedy

The Right to Be Safe   Contemporary businesspeople must recognize obligations, both moral and legal, to ensure the safe operation of their products. Consumers should feel assured that the goods and services they purchase will not cause injuries in normal use. **Product liability** refers to the responsibility of manufacturers for injuries and damages caused by their products. Products that lead to injuries, either directly or indirectly, can have disastrous consequences for their makers. The problems with the Bridgestone Firestone tires provide a dramatic example, as discussed in the "Solving an Ethical Controversy" box earlier.

Many companies put their products through rigorous testing to avoid safety problems. Still, testing alone cannot foresee every eventuality. Companies must try to consider all possibilities and provide adequate warning of potential dangers. When a product does pose a threat to customer safety, a responsible manufacturer responds quickly to either correct the problem or recall the dangerous product. For example, when consumers found bits of an aluminum soft-drink can in their Campbell's vegetable beef soup, the company recalled the product, publishing the product details so consumers could know whether their soup might have been affected. Campbell's then investigated and determined that a soft-drink can apparently had been embedded in a load of carrots or potatoes that went through a dicing machine. The company prints a toll-free telephone number on its soup cans, which helps consumers to report problems quickly when they arise, as well as to ask questions about products.[40]

The Right to Be Informed   Consumers should have access to enough education and product information to make responsible buying decisions. In their efforts to promote and sell their goods and services, companies can easily neglect consumers' right to be fully informed. False advertising is a violation of the Wheeler-Lea Act. In addition, the FTC and other federal and state agencies have established rules and regulations that govern advertising truthfulness. These rules prohibit businesses from making unsubstantiated claims about the performance or superiority of their goods or services. They also require businesses to avoid misleading consumers. Businesses that fail to comply face scrutiny from the FTC and consumer protection organizations. In one case, the FTC responded to complaints by filing charges against Star Publishing Group, which under the name National Consumer Services placed want ads promising as much as $800 per week for starting a home-based business. Consumers who called the toll-free number in the ad reached a recording selling a guide to start a business that the recording falsely implied would involve government work.

The FDA, which sets standards for advertising conducted by drug manufacturers, recently eased restrictions for prescription drug advertising on television. In print ads, drug makers are required to spell out potential side effects and the proper uses of prescription drugs. Because of the requirement to disclose this information,

Like a lullabye
for your sensitive baby.

When your baby is sensitive, your doctor may recommend a soy formula. Many moms choose Carnation Alsoy, from Nestlé, a company that understands feeding babies. Alsoy provides the vitamins, minerals and nutrients your baby needs all in a gentle soy protein formula. And Alsoy is priced to save you up to 20%. It's a formula you can count on to help you and your baby rest a little easier. To learn more about Nestlé Carnation Baby Formulas, call 1-800-456-6035 or visit us at www.verybestbaby.com. Remember, breastmilk is the ideal food for babies. Talk to your doctor about your feeding choices.

Bring out the very best in your baby.™

Nestlé, one of the world's leading baby food makers, promotes the safety of its Alsoy soy formula for babies allergic to milk. At the same time, it responsibly urges mothers to "Remember, breastmilk is the ideal food for babies. Talk to your doctor about your feeding choices." At its Web site, www.verybestbaby.com, parents can find safety information on such topics as "Baby Proofing Your Home," "Safety around the House," and "Baby and the Family Pet."

prescription drug television advertising was limited. Now, however, the FDA says drug ads on radio and television can directly promote a prescription drug's benefits if they provide a quick way for consumers to learn about side effects, such as displaying a toll-free number or Internet address. The FDA also monitors "dietary supplements," including vitamins and herbs. These products may make claims about their general effect on health but may not claim to cure a disease, unless the company has presented the FDA with research and received the agency's approval. For example, a product may say it helps the body maintain a healthy immune system, but not that it fights colds.

The responsibility of business to preserve consumers' right to be informed extends beyond avoiding misleading advertising. All communications with customers—from salespeople's comments to warranties and invoices—must be controlled to clearly and accurately inform customers. Most packaged-goods firms, personal computer makers, and other makers of products bought for personal use by consumers include toll-free customer service numbers on their product labels, so that consumers can get answers when they have questions about a product.

To protect their customers and avoid claims of insufficient disclosure, businesses often include warnings on products. As Figure 2.11 shows, sometimes these warnings go far beyond what a reasonable consumer would expect.

The Right to Choose   Consumers should have the right to choose which goods and services they need and want to purchase. Socially responsible firms attempt to preserve this right, even if they reduce their own sales and profits in the process. Other companies are not as ethical about protecting a consumer's right to choose, though. Some credit card companies have a policy of charging higher rates to customers who ask to close their accounts. FleetBoston Financial charges 26.99 percent on the remaining balances of consumers who have canceled their accounts. The company says the higher rate is fair, because customers who close their accounts are less likely to keep up with their payments.[41] Consumers do not always realize they can protect themselves by paying off the card before they cancel the account.

Since the long-distance telephone industry has been deregulated, some customers have also been the victims of fraud. Several unscrupulous long-distance carriers have duped customers into switching their service through an unsavory practice called *slamming*. The firms get customers to sign contest-entry forms that contain less-than-obvious wording saying they agree to be switched. In other cases, long-distance companies have switched customers without their consent after making telemarketing calls to them.

The Right to Be Heard   Consumers should be able to express legitimate complaints to appropriate parties. Many companies expend considerable effort to ensure full hearings for consumer complaints. The eBay auction Web site assists buyers and sellers who believe they were victimized in transactions conducted through the site. It deploys a 200-employee team to work with users and law enforcement agencies to combat fraud. The company provides all users with insurance coverage of up to $200 per transaction, with a $25 deductible. It operates a feedback forum, where it

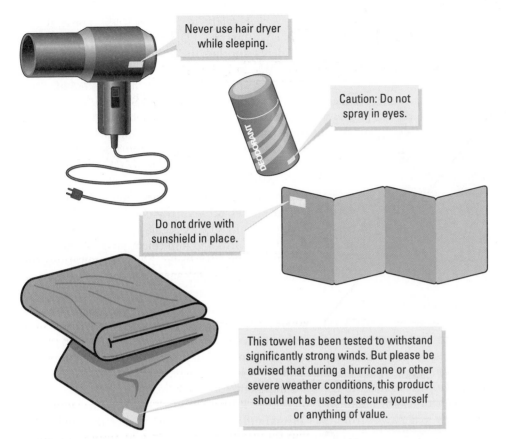

Never use hair dryer while sleeping.

Caution: Do not spray in eyes.

Do not drive with sunshield in place.

This towel has been tested to withstand significantly strong winds. But please be advised that during a hurricane or other severe weather conditions, this product should not be used to secure yourself or anything of value.

FIGURE 2.11
Wacky Warning Labels   The number of product liability lawsuits has skyrocketed. To protect themselves, businesses have become more careful about including warnings on products. However, some companies may go overboard, as demonstrated by these actual product warning labels.

encourages users to rate one another. The auction site operates a software program that tracks individuals' bidding performance, looking for patterns associated with fraudulent behavior. And when it receives complaints of fraud, eBay forwards them to the FTC. So, although eBay cannot prevent all instances of fraud, it does provide an environment in which buyers and sellers feel protected.[42]

Responsibilities to Employees

As Chapter 1 explains, one of the most important business resources is the organization's workforce. Companies that are able to attract skilled and knowledgeable employees are better able to meet the challenges of competing globally. In return, businesses have wide-ranging responsibilities to their employees, both here and abroad, as discussed in the "Clicks and Mortar" box. These include workplace safety, quality of life issues, avoiding discrimination, and preventing sexual harassment and sexism.

Workplace Safety   A century ago, few businesses paid much attention to the safety of their workers. In fact, most business owners viewed employees as mere cogs in the production process. Workers—many young children—toiled in frequently dangerous conditions. In 1911, 146 people, mostly young girls, died in a fire at the Triangle Shirtwaist Factory in New York City. Contributing to the massive loss of life were the sweatshop working conditions at the factory, including overcrowding, blocked exits, and a lack of fire escapes. The horrifying tragedy forced businesses to begin to recognize their responsibility for their workers' safety.

The safety and health of workers while on the job is now an important business responsibility. The Occupational Safety and Health Administration (OSHA) is the main federal regulatory force in setting workplace safety and health standards. These mandates range from broad guidelines on storing hazardous materials to specific

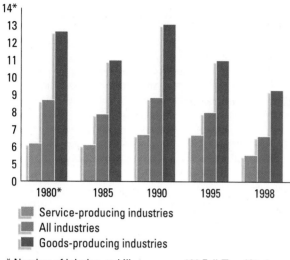

Service-producing industries
All industries
Goods-producing industries

* Number of Injuries and Illnesses per 100 Full-Time Workers

FIGURE 2.12
Rates of Workplace Injuries and Illnesses

standards for worker safety in industries like construction, manufacturing, and mining. OSHA tracks and investigates workplace accidents and has the authority to fine employers who are found liable for injuries and deaths that occur on the job. As Figure 2.12 shows, workplace injuries and illnesses declined during the 1980s and 1990s. Even though rates of injury and illness are lower in service industries than in goods-producing industries, the four industries with highest injury rates are all service providers: restaurants, hospitals, nursing homes, and retail stores. Most reports to OSHA involve injuries, most of which involve disorders arising from making the same motion over and over, such as carpal tunnel syndrome.[43]

Although businesses occasionally complain about having to comply with too many OSHA regulations, ultimately management must set standards and implement programs to ensure that workers are safe in the workplace. The Jewel supermarket chain shows employees training videos about safe practices. The videos teach about fire safety, germs transmitted in blood, and actions to take if the store is robbed. The store makes special efforts to protect teenage employees. They are expected to read and sign a statement that they will not use any machinery, including the elevator, lift equipment, or meat slicers. Use of power equipment is limited by law to employees 18 years of age or older, and those employees must undergo training before the store permits them to use the equipment. Laws also extend extra protection to teenage workers by limiting the number of hours they work and the number of trips they may make away from their primary place of employment each day. Protection of young workers is especially significant because almost one workplace injury in three involves employees with less than a year's experience.[44]

Quality of Life Issues   Balancing work and family is becoming harder for many employees. They find themselves squeezed between working long hours and handling child-care problems, caring for elderly parents, and solving other family crises. A "sandwich generation" of households, those caring for two generations—their children and their aging parents—has arisen. As the population ages, the share of American households providing informal care to a relative or friend age 50 years or older is expected to double—from one household in five in the mid-1990s to more than two in five in the early years of the 21st century. At the same time, as married women spend more time working outside the home, they have an average of 22 fewer hours per week to spend on family.[45] The employees juggling work with life's other demands aren't just working mothers. Childless couples, single people, and men all express frustration with the pressures of balancing work with family and personal needs.

Helping workers find solutions to these quality of life issues has become an important concern of many businesses, but finding answers isn't always easy. Some companies offer flexible work arrangements to support employees. Other firms offer benefits such as subsidized child care or on-site education and shopping to assist workers trying to balance work and family.

Another solution has been to offer **family leave** to employees who need to deal with family matters. Under the Family and Medical Leave Act of 1993, businesses with 50 or more employees must provide unpaid leave annually for any employee who wants time off for the birth or adoption of a child, to become a foster parent, or to care for a seriously ill relative or spouse. The law requires that employers grant up to 12 weeks of leave each year. This unpaid leave also applies to an employee who has a serious illness. Workers must meet certain eligibility requirements. Employers must continue to provide health benefits during the leave and guarantee that employees will return to equivalent jobs. The issue of who is entitled to health

The Gap Is Sew Responsible

Background. When you pull on your t-shirt and jeans in the morning, you probably don't think much about where they were made or who made them. But clothing companies such as the Gap, with suppliers located all over the world, have to think about it. Although the company does not own any factories overseas, it contracts with facilities in more than 50 countries, and it wants to maintain good working conditions in those factories. So the Gap has a written Code of Vendor Conduct and has a global network of employees to monitor factory compliance. The code covers areas such as discrimination, forced labor, child labor, wages and hours, working conditions, and housing. Monitoring teams visit the Gap's facilities every three months to conduct detailed safety inspections, review payroll records, and interview workers. The teams use diverse experts—attorneys, industrial safety experts, and representatives from human rights organizations. Before a factory can become part of the Gap operations, it must be inspected and evaluated. If the factory does not pass the review, it is rejected. If the factory does pass, its managers must sign a binding agreement to follow the Code of Conduct.

What Happened? Even with such an extensive program, the Gap has faced problems. In 1999, the organization was named, along with eighteen other companies, in a class-action lawsuit about working conditions in a factory in the Northern Marianas Islands. To complicate matters further, the Gap was accused of misleading consumers by placing "Made in the U.S.A." labels on clothing that was made in the Marianas Islands factory.

The Response. Since the Marianas Islands are actually a U.S. territory, the Gap is required by law to use the U.S.A. label for clothes manufactured there. So it wasn't trying to mislead the public. Several of the companies mentioned in the class-action suit did settle, but the Gap maintained its innocence and decided to defend itself in the lawsuit.

Today and Counting. Millions of Gap customers continue to make the Gap and its other units—Old Navy and Banana Republic—an American institution. In fact, Old Navy has become so popular that some Gap customers have shifted their alliance to the lower-priced, hipper Old Navy. But the Gap isn't about to fold its khakis anytime soon. "Whatever their [problems] are, I would be hesitant to bet against them," notes one industry analyst. "It's one of the few companies to endure for a generation. It's thrived, evolved, and led the industry."

QUESTIONS FOR CRITICAL THINKING

1. Access the Gap's Code of Vendor Conduct at its Web site (www.gapinc.com/about/global-manuf/code_overview/code.htm). The code covers many areas of responsibility to employees. What areas of responsibility to society in general might it also address?
2. The Gap has "thrived, evolved, and led the industry." Do you think that one of the reasons the company has endured is because of its attitude toward ethics and social responsibility? Why or why not?

Sources: "About Gap Inc." and "Code of Vendor Conduct," The Gap corporate Web site, **www.gapinc.com**, accessed January 23, 2001; The Gap Web site, **www.gap.com**, accessed January 23, 2001; Paul Sloan, "Is That Gordon Gekko at the Gap?" *U.S. News & World Report*, April 24, 2000, p. 46; Stacy Perman, "Mend That Gap," *Time*, February 14, 2000, pp. 60–62.

---

benefits can also create a dilemma as companies struggle to balance the needs of their employees against the staggering costs of health care.

The Family and Medical Leave Act gives employees the right to take time off, but because the leave is unpaid, many workers find that they cannot afford to use this right. Some states have considered addressing this problem by offering unemployment compensation to parents who take time off to care for a newly born or adopted child. The U.S. Labor Department recently issued a ruling authorizing states to experiment with this type of unemployment compensation as part of their unemployment insurance programs. States that elect to participate in this experiment can authorize partial wage replacement to parents who take approved leave. In contrast to the scope of the Family Medical and Leave Act, this benefit applies only to births or adoptions in states that elect to provide the benefits. Also, in states where it is available, the unemployment compensation would be available to employees at companies of any size, so long as they meet the state's eligibility requirements for unemployment compensation. The Labor Department plans to evaluate whether parents who receive the benefits are more likely to remain in the workforce over the long run.[46]

Ensuring Equal Opportunity on the Job   Businesspeople face many challenges managing an increasingly diverse workforce in the 21st century. By 2050, ethnic minorities and immigrants will make up nearly half of the U.S. workforce. Technological advances are expanding the ways people with physical disabilities can contribute in

| Table 2.2 | Laws Designed to Ensure Equal Opportunity |

Law	Key Provisions
Title VII of the Civil Rights Act of 1964 (as amended by the Equal Employment Opportunity Act of 1972)	Prohibits discrimination in hiring, promotion, compensation, training, or dismissal on the basis of race, color, religion, sex, or national origin.
Age Discrimination in Employment Act of 1968 (as amended)	Prohibits discrimination in employment against anyone aged 40 years or over in hiring, promotion, compensation, training, or dismissal.
Equal Pay Act of 1963	Requires equal pay for men and women working for the same firm in jobs that require equal skill, effort, and responsibility.
Vocational Rehabilitation Act of 1973	Requires government contractors and subcontractors to take affirmative action to employ and promote qualified disabled workers. Coverage now extends to all federal employees. Coverage has been broadened by the passage of similar laws in more than 20 states and, through court rulings, to include persons with communicable diseases, including AIDS.
Vietnam Era Veterans Readjustment Act of 1974	Requires government contractors and subcontractors to take affirmative action to employ and retain disabled veterans. Coverage now extends to all federal employees and has been broadened by the passage of similar laws in more than 20 states.
Pregnancy Discrimination Act of 1978	Requires employers to treat pregnant women and new mothers the same as other employees for all employment-related purposes, including receipt of benefits under company benefit programs.
Americans with Disabilities Act of 1990	Makes discrimination against the disabled illegal in public accommodations, transportation, and telecommunications; stiffens employer penalties for intentional discrimination on the basis of an employee's disability.
Civil Rights Act of 1991	Makes it easier for workers to sue their employers for alleged discrimination. Enables victims of sexual discrimination to collect punitive damages; includes employment decisions and on-the-job issues such as sexual harassment, unfair promotions, and unfair dismissal. The employer must prove that it did not engage in discrimination.
Family and Medical Leave Act of 1993	Requires all businesses with 50 or more employees to provide up to 12 weeks of unpaid leave annually to employees who have had a child or are adopting a child, or are becoming foster parents, who are caring for a seriously ill relative or spouse, or who are themselves seriously ill. Workers must meet certain eligibility requirements.

the workplace. Businesses also need to find ways to responsibly recruit and manage older workers and workers with varying lifestyles. In addition, beginning with Lotus Development Corp. in 1982, companies have begun to extend benefits equally to employees, regardless of sexual orientation. In particular, that means the company offers benefits like health insurance to unmarried domestic partners if it offers them to spouses of married couples. Companies that now offer these gender-neutral benefits include Boeing, Citigroup, Disney, General Mills, and Prudential.[47] This treatment reflects the view that all employee groups deserve the right to work in an environment that is nondiscriminatory.

To a great extent, efforts at managing diversity are regulated by law. The Civil Rights Act (1964) outlawed many kinds of discriminatory practices, and Title VII of the act specifically prohibits discrimination in employment. As shown in Table 2.2, other nondiscrimination laws include the Equal Pay Act (1963), the Age Discrimination in Employment Act (1967), the Equal Employment Opportunity Act (1972), the Pregnancy Discrimination Act (1978), the Civil Rights Act of 1991, and numerous executive orders. The Americans with Disabilities Act (1990) protects the rights of physically challenged people. The Vietnam Era Veterans Readjustment Act (1974) protects the employment of veterans of the Vietnam war.

Perhaps the next round of protection will extend to the level of genetics. As scientists make progress in decoding the human genome, some people worry that employers will discriminate based on genetic characteristics, such as a gene that predisposes a person to cancer or some other costly disease. In fact, the executive branch of the federal government is now prohibited from discriminating on the basis of genetic information. When he signed the order, former President Clinton stated that he hoped it would serve as a challenge to businesses and other government agencies to adopt similar policies.[48]

The **Equal Employment Opportunity Commission (EEOC)** was created to increase job opportunities for women and minorities and to help end discrimination based on race, color, religion, disability, gender, or national origin in any personnel action. To enforce fair-employment laws, it investigates charges of discrimination and harassment and files suit against violators. The EEOC can also help employers set up programs to increase job opportunities for women, minorities, people with disabilities, and persons in other protected categories.

Fair treatment of employees is more than a matter of complying with EEOC regulations, however. Like white male employees, women and people of color want opportunities to excel and rewards for excellence. They also want to be treated with respect. Yet in a survey of minority executives, nearly half said they had been the butt of a racial or cultural "joke" at work, and almost two-thirds said they had observed a racial double standard in the way jobs are assigned.[49] A minority employee who misses out on a plum assignment may miss out on the big raise that goes with it. As the employee's salary grows more slowly, managers may eventually begin to use the size of the salary as an indicator that the employee contributes less to the organization. Chapter 9 takes a closer look at diversity and employment discrimination issues as part of a discussion of human resource management.

Sexual Harassment and Sexism   Every employer has a responsibility to ensure that all workers are treated fairly and are safe from sexual harassment. Sexual harassment refers to unwelcome and inappropriate actions of a sexual nature in the workplace. It is a form of sex discrimination that violates the Civil Rights Act of 1964, which gives both men and women the right to file lawsuits for intentional sexual harassment. More than 15,000 sexual harassment complaints are filed with the EEOC each year, of which about 12 percent are filed by men. Thousands of other cases are either handled internally by companies or never reported.

Two types of sexual harassment exist. The first type occurs when an employee is pressured to comply with unwelcome advances and requests for sexual favors in return for job security, promotions, and raises. The second type results from a hostile work environment in which an employee feels hassled or degraded because of unwelcome flirting, lewd comments, or obscene jokes. The courts have ruled that allowing sexually oriented materials like pinup calendars and pornographic magazines at the workplace can create a hostile atmosphere that interferes with an employee's ability to do the job. Employers are also legally responsible to protect employees from sexual harassment from customers and clients. The EEOC's Web site informs employers and employees of criteria for identifying sexual harassment and how it should be handled in the workplace.

Preventing sexual harassment can be difficult because it involves regulating the conduct of individual employees. Ford Motor Co. unsuccessfully tried to end sexual harassment in Chicago-area factories over the course of several years. Beginning in 1994, female workers reported to the EEOC that they had been subjected to offensive language, name-calling, and unwanted touching by coworkers and supervisors. After a two-year investigation, the EEOC agreed and reached a settlement with Ford. Then a group of women in another Ford factory complained of similar mistreatment. Ford sent its head of manufacturing to the facility to announce zero tolerance of sexual harassment and detail the type of behavior that the company expected. The company fired 10 employees and took disciplinary actions against others. Nevertheless, a group of women complained that the problems continued, and the EEOC again supported their complaints, even finding that offensive materials had been posted in the building. After months of negotiations, Ford agreed to spend $7.5 million to compensate the victims and $10 million to train employees and managers in appropriate behavior. The company also agreed to triple the number of female supervisors in the factories and to make prevention of sexual harassment a requirement for granting raises and promotions to plant managers.

BUSINESS DIRECTORY

> **sexual harassment** *inappropriate actions of a sexual nature in the workplace.*

To avoid sexual harassment problems, many firms have established policies and employee education programs aimed at preventing such violations. An effective harassment prevention program should include the following measures:

- Issuing a specific policy statement prohibiting sexual harassment
- Developing a complaint procedure for employees to follow
- Creating a work atmosphere that encourages sexually harassed staffers to come forward
- Investigating and resolving complaints quickly, and taking disciplinary action against harassers

Unless all of these components are supported by top management, sexual harassment is difficult to eliminate.

Sexual harassment is often part of the broader problem of **sexism**—discrimination against members of either sex, but primarily affecting women. Some examples of sexism are blatant, as when a woman earns less than a male colleague in the same job or when a male employee gains a promotion over a better-qualified female. More subtle instances might be failure to introduce the only female in a work group to a client or giving women less important or less challenging work assignments.

One important sexism issue concerns equal pay for equal work. On average, U.S. women earn 77 cents for every dollar earned by men. In the course of a working lifetime, this disparity adds up to a gap of $420,000. This data actually represent a slight closing of the pay gap between men and women. As recently as 1979, women's earnings were only 63 percent of men's. The percentage of women who hold managerial and professional positions has grown to 49 percent, compared with 41 percent in 1983, but that trend has not necessarily reduced the pay gap. In many of these jobs, the difference between men's and women's pay is actually wider than average. Female doctors earn just 62 cents for every dollar earned by male doctors, and female financial managers earn 61 cents for every dollar earned by male financial planners. In general, women and men start with similar salaries, and the differences develop over time, with men typically paid more than women who have comparable experience.[50]

Responsibilities to Investors and the Financial Community

Although a fundamental goal of any business is to make a profit for its shareholders, investors and the financial community demand that businesses behave ethically as well as legally. When firms fail in this responsibility, thousands of investors and consumers can suffer. The Coca-Cola Company saw its share price tumble following problems with product safety and fair employment practices. In Belgium, 42 children were hospitalized when they complained of dizziness and nausea after drinking Coke. The company investigated, admitted the product didn't smell right, but insisted it would not cause illness. A public relations executive said, "[Coke] may make you feel sick, but it is not harmful." Only after the Belgian government ordered Coke products to be removed from stores did the company's chief executive visit Belgium to apologize. At headquarters, the social responsibility problems took the form of a lawsuit alleging racial discrimination. Although the company had a reputation for fostering diversity, it tarnished its image by making management changes that effectively demoted the company's top black executive, Carl Ware. Ware announced his retirement, and the company recovered from that public relations disaster only after its new chief executive, Douglas Daft, lured Ware back with an offer to run a new division. During these problems, the firm's stock price dropped 27 percent.[51]

State and federal government agencies are responsible for protecting investors from financial misdeeds. At the federal level, the Securities and Exchange Commission (SEC) investigates suspicions that publicly traded firms engaged in unethical or illegal behavior. For example, it investigates accusations that a business is using faulty accounting practices to inaccurately portray its financial resources and profits to investors. In 2000, the SEC adopted a rule requiring that publicly traded companies make announcements of major information to the general public, rather than first disclosing the information to selected major investors.[52] The agency also operates an Office of Internet Enforcement to target fraud in online trading and online sales of stock by unlicensed sellers. Chapter 19 discusses securities trading practices further.

Besides honesty, social responsibility to investors includes providing for highly qualified management talent to run the company successfully. Before listing a company on its exchange, the New York Stock Exchange requires that it have an audit committee that includes at least three independent directors, at least one of them having expertise in financial management. But the trend among dot-com businesses has so far been to limit the size of the board of directors and to include few outside directors (qualified persons who are not company employees). The justification is that this helps the company act faster. A recent study of 39 Internet companies revealed that their boards of directors are smaller, have fewer outside directors, and have smaller audit and compensation committees than non–dot-com firms of similar size. A typical board of directors of a dot-com might have two or three company managers, two members from venture capital firms that supplied the company's funding, and two directors from outside the company. So far, high stock prices for dot-com businesses have let managers remain confident that their boards have the necessary talent. However, as the market is weeding out all but the strongest Internet firms, many dot-com managers may wish they had brought more experienced people on board, and investors could be left poorer because of their failure to do so.[53]

WHAT'S AHEAD

The decisions and actions of businesspeople are often influenced by outside forces such as the legal environment and society's expectations about business responsibility. Firms also are affected by the economic environments in which they operate. The next chapter discusses the broad economic issues that influence businesses around the world. Our discussion will focus on how factors such as supply and demand, unemployment, inflation, and government monetary policies pose both challenges and opportunities for firms seeking to compete in the global marketplace.

➤ Summary of Learning Goals

1. Explain the concepts of business ethics and social responsibility.

Business ethics refers to the standards of conduct and moral values that govern actions and decisions in the workplace. Businesspeople must take a wide range of social issues into account when making decisions. Social responsibility refers to management's acceptance of the obligation to consider profit, consumer satisfaction, and societal well-being of equal value in evaluating the firm's performance.

2. Describe the factors that influence business ethics.

Among the many factors shaping individual ethics are personal experience, peer pressure, and organizational culture. Individual ethics are also influenced by family, cultural, and religious standards. Additionally, the culture of the organization where a person works can be a factor.

3. List the stages in the development of ethical standards.

In the preconventional stage, individuals primarily consider their own needs and desires in making decisions. They obey external rules only from fear of punishment or hope of reward. In the conventional stage, individuals are aware of and respond to their duty to others. Expectations of groups, as well as self-interest, influence behavior. In the final, postconventional stage, the individual can move beyond self-interest and duty to include consideration of the needs of society. A person in this stage can apply personal ethical principles in a variety of situations.

4. Identify common ethical dilemmas in the workplace.

Conflicts of interest exist when a businessperson is faced with a situation where an action benefiting one person has the potential to harm another, as when the person's own interests conflict with those of a customer. One type of behavior that generates a conflict of interest is bribery. Honesty and integrity are valued qualities that engender trust, but a person's immediate self-interest may seem to require violating these principles. Loyalty to one's employer sometimes conflicts with truthfulness. Whistle-blowing is a possible response to misconduct in the workplace, but the costs of blowing the whistle are high.

5. **Discuss how organizations shape ethical behavior.**

Employees are strongly influenced by the standards of conduct established and supported within the organizations where they work. Businesses can help shape ethical behavior by developing codes of conduct that define their expectations. Organizations can also use this training to develop employees' ethics awareness and reasoning. They can foster ethical action through decision-making tools, goals consistent with ethical behavior, and advice hotlines. Executives must also demonstrate ethical behavior in their decisions and actions in order to provide ethical leadership.

6. **Relate the ways government regulation affects business ethics and social responsibility.**

Because businesses sometimes fail to regulate their own actions, federal, state, and local governments may step in to regulate business activity. The federal government regulates competition and commercial activities. In a regulated industry, competition is either limited or eliminated, substituting close government control for free competition. Laws have also been enacted to protect against unfair competition and to protect consumers. Deregulation has significantly reshaped the legal environments in many industries in the last two decades. As unethical practices on the Internet have become a problem, the government has begun to regulate behavior in cyberspace, especially with regard to fraud and violations of privacy.

7. **Describe how businesses' social responsibility is measured.**

Today's businesses are expected to weigh their qualitative impact on consumers and society, in addition to their quantitative economic contributions such as sales, employment levels, and profits. One measure is their compliance with labor and consumer protection laws and their charitable contributions. Another measure some businesses take is to conduct social audits. Public-interest groups also create standards and measure companies' performance relative to those standards. Consumers may boycott groups that fall short of social standards.

8. **Summarize the responsibilities of business to the general public, customers, and employees.**

The responsibilities of business to the general public include protecting the public health and the environment, and developing the quality of the workforce. Additionally, many would argue that businesses have a social responsibility to support charitable and social causes in the communities in which they earn profits. Business also has a social and ethical responsibility to treat customers fairly and protect consumers upholding the rights to be safe, to be informed, to choose, and to be heard. Businesses have wide-ranging responsibilities to their workers. They should make sure that the workplace is safe, address quality of life issues, ensure equal opportunity, and prevent sexual harassment.

9. **Explain why investors and the financial community are concerned with business ethics and social responsibility.**

Investors and the financial community demand that businesses behave ethically as well as legally in handling their financial transactions. Businesses must be honest in reporting their profits and financial performance in order to avoid misleading investors. The Securities and Exchange Commission is the federal agency responsible for investigating suspicions that publicly traded firms have engaged in unethical or illegal financial behavior.

Business Terms You Need to Know

business ethics 46	deregulation 58
conflict of interest 49	social responsibility 60
whistle-blowing 51	recycling 63
code of conduct 52	corporate philanthropy 66
regulated industry 57	sexual harassment 73

Other Important Business Terms

integrity 49	social audit 60	boycott 61

➤ Review Questions

1. What do the terms *business ethics* and *social responsibility* mean? Cite an example of each. What are the four main forces that shape business ethics and social responsibility?

2. Identify and describe briefly the three stages in which individuals typically develop ethical standards. What are some of the factors that determine the stage of moral and ethical development an individual occupies at any given time?

3. What are the four most common ethical challenges that businesspeople face? Give a brief example of each.

4. What are the four levels of development of a corporate culture to support business ethics? Describe each briefly.

5. How do organizational goals affect ethical behavior? How might these goals interfere with ethical leadership? Give an example.

6. How does government regulate both competition and specific business practices? Describe specific regulations with which businesspeople should be familiar. What is deregulation? What are its advantages and disadvantages?

7. What basic consumer rights does the consumerism movement try to ensure? How has consumerism improved the contemporary business environment?

8. What is a cookie? How does it work? What are some of the pros and cons of using cookies in Internet businesses?

9. What are some of the major factors that contribute to the assessment of a company's social performance?

10. Identify the major benefits of corporate philanthropy.

➤ Questions for Critical Thinking

1. Write your own personal code of ethics, detailing your feelings about ethical challenges such as lying to protect an employer or coworker, favoring one client over another, misrepresenting credentials to an employer or client, and using the Internet for personal purposes while at work. What role will your personal ethics play in deciding your choice of career and acceptance of a job?

2. "Everybody exaggerates when it comes to selling products, and customers ought to take that with a grain of salt," said one advertising executive recently in response to a complaint filed by the Better Business Bureau about misleading advertising. "Don't we all have a brain, and can't we all think a little bit, too?" Do you agree with this statement? Why or why not?

3. Imagine that you work for a company that makes outdoor clothing, such as L.L. Bean, Timberland, or Patagonia. Write a memo describing at least four specific ways in which your company could practice corporate philanthropy.

4. Imagine that you are the human resources director for a company that is trying to establish and document its responsibilities to its employees. Choose one of the responsibilities described in the chapter—such as workplace safety—and write a memo describing specific steps your company will take to fulfill that responsibility.

5. Suppose that you own a small firm with 12 employees. One of them tells you in confidence that he has just learned that he is HIV positive, which may lead to AIDS. You know that health-care costs for AIDS patients can be disastrously high, and this expense could drastically raise the health insurance premiums that your other employees must pay. What are your responsibilities to this employee? To the rest of your staff? Explain.

➤ Experiential Exercise

Background: Lockheed Martin, with more than 147,000 employees worldwide and 2002 sales surpassing $25 billion, is one of the world's premier systems engineering and technology companies. Lockheed Martin has caught the attention of *The New York Times*, CNN, *The Washington Post,* and even *People Magazine* for its innovative ethics awareness training program featuring characters from the popular comic strip *Dilbert*. The *Dilbert* characters not only brand the program but also provide humor to break up the learning.

The Ethics Challenge is a highly interactive board game in which teams of employees compete by figuring out how to respond to realistic scenarios. Each scenario presents an ethical dilemma, along with a range of responses. As teams discuss the cases, they hear other people's opinions and experiences and gain firsthand experience in applying the company's ethical decision-making model.

Ethical Decision Making Model

1. Evaluate information
2. Consider how your decision might affect stakeholders (employees, customers, communities, shareholders, suppliers)
3. Consider what ethical values are relevant to the situation (honesty, integrity, respect, trust, responsibility, citizenship)
4. Determine the best course of action that takes into account relevant values and stakeholders' interests

Directions: Either work alone or as a member of a group to complete this exercise.

1. Use the Lockheed Martin's Ethical Decision Making Model to help you select the best option in the two case files following. In addition to answers designated A, B, C, and D, each case includes a Dogbert answer, which is worth zero points, since it usually is the worst thing you could possibly do. Some answers are better than others and will rate point values between 0 and 5.
2. After circling your answers for both case files, read the "Leader's Comments" section at the end of this exercise to find the rationale for each potential answer and find the points assigned to each response.

CASE FILE NUMBER: 29

Category: *Quality Assurance*
Target Audience: *Program/project managers*
Setting the Standard: *Integrity*

You are the manager of a program that is behind schedule, over budget, and of questionable quality. You feel you should stop the program, rethink it, and put all the proper processes in place to successfully complete delivery. Your boss has ordered you to pull out all stops and deliver the equipment. You feel quality is likely to suffer using this approach. You should:

Potential Answers:

A. Listen to your boss—put maximum pressure on the team to deliver.
B. Go to the company Ethics Officer and tell him about your boss's approach.
C. Go back to your boss and let him know you are not comfortable with his approach, because it may mean delivering a substandard product.
D. Organize a corrective-action team to identify ways to improve quality and still meet schedule.

Dogbert: Have a slogan about quality printed on coffee mugs.

CASE FILE NUMBER: 50

Category: *Use of Company Resources*
Target Audience: *All employees*
Setting the Standard: *Responsibility*

A coworker tells you that a supervisor has been using his recently hired administrative assistant to type his term papers for evening college courses that he is taking. The assistant is required to do the typing on the job at the expense of other job-related tasks. But she has not officially complained, except to the coworker, because she fears retribution from her supervisor if she does protest. Since you are not a supervisor, can you do anything to help in this situation?

Potential Answers:

A. Yes—tell the coworker that what she has described is a violation of the corporation's code of ethics and that she should report it to her manager; but don't get involved yourself.
B. No—this is only secondhand information; you are not affected by the supervisor's behavior; and it is not your job to interfere in the private matters of a supervisor. Do nothing, or you may become the target of retribution yourself.
C. Yes—immediately confirm the situation with the administrative assistant; then report the conduct directly to her supervisor's manager for further action.
D. Yes—take the information you have to the company Ethics Officer for further action.

Dogbert: **Yes,** suggest she submit his term papers as your department's contribution to the company newsletter.

Source: Lockheed Martin's *The Ethics Challenge*, All New 1998 Version.

➤ Nothing but Net

1. **Social responsibility of business.** Every year *Business Ethics* magazine compiles its list of the 100 best corporate citizens. Visit the magazine's Web site and read the profiles of a few of the companies from their list. Prepare a brief report outlining the criteria used by *Business Ethics* and why these companies made the list.

   www.business-ethics.com/afew.htm

2. **Protecting the environment.** Many companies are in the forefront of the environmental protection movement. Visit one company that you believe is committed to environmentally-friendly business practices. Write a report on that company's efforts. Some examples include:

   www.ford.com/default.asp?pageid=103

   www.johnsonandjohnson.com/who_is_jnj/

   www.patagonia.com/enviro

3. **Community involvement.** Part of being a good corporate citizen is being involved in the community. One example of community involvement is education. Two companies that are heavily involved in efforts to improve education are Dow Chemical and Microsoft (mainly through the Bill and Melinda Gates Foundation). Visit each company's Web site and make a list of what each company is trying to do to improve education. Overall, how effective do you believe firms can be at improving the quality of education?

www.dow.com/about/corp/social/social.htm (click on education)

www.gatesfoundations.org (or **www.microsoft.com/company**)

Note: Internet Web addresses change frequently. If you don't find the exact sites listed, you may need to access the organization's or company's home page and search from there.

When you sip your cup of morning coffee—whether it's in your dorm room or in the trendy coffee shop down the street—you probably don't think about where it came from. Even if you're familiar with the jargon—*arabica beans, varietals, dark roast*—and even if you can name the major coffee-producing countries, such as Costa Rica and Colombia, you probably aren't thinking about the people who grow the beans thousands of miles away. But, the coffee-growing business is so important in Central and South America that it provides many jobs for people who otherwise would be unemployed. When you buy a pound of gourmet coffee at $8 to $9 per pound, about 40 cents actually reaches the farmers who grew it. Where does the rest of the money go? To agents who offer the lowest possible price to buyers who then put their own brand labels on the coffee. The 20 million coffee farmers who are left in poverty call these middlemen "coyotes" because they prey on the poor.

Equal Exchange Inc., a gourmet coffee company founded in 1986 in Canton, Massachusetts, is working to change these unfair practices by engaging in its own ethically and socially responsible way of doing business. By adopting the concept of "fair trade," Equal Exchange buys coffee directly from the growers themselves, eliminating the middlemen. As a result, the growers gain as much as 50 cents more per pound. Because coffee is the leading source of foreign currency in Latin America, this arrangement is significant to the economy of the region. It is also significant to each individual coffee farmer. "We used to live in houses made of corn husks," recalls Don Miguel Sifontes, who operates a farm in El Salvador. "Now we have better work, better schools, homes of adobe, and a greater brotherhood of decision makers."

The concept of fair trade, first adopted in Europe about fifteen years ago, illustrates the idea that businesses are responsible and accountable to their employees, their customers, and the general public. Equal Exchange growers receive better prices under exclusive agreements with farming cooperatives, customers are guaranteed high-quality coffee at fair prices, and the general public in the growers' regions benefit from projects that the farm cooperatives have undertaken with the additional income they make. Such projects range from reforestation programs to building new schools. Equal Exchange follows a strict set of fair trade guidelines in its purchase of coffee:

- *Buy directly from small farmer cooperatives.* These cooperatives are owned and run by the farmers themselves. Each cooperative governs the even distribution of income and ser-

vices, such as education and healthcare. Buying direct means that profits go to the farmers rather than agents or other middlemen, reducing the need for growers to engage in more profitable activities, such as growing marijuana and other illegal endeavors, in order to survive.

- *Pay a fair price.* Equal Exchange pays a guaranteed minimum price for its coffee, regardless of how low the coffee market itself may drop. This price assures that farmers will be able to make a living wage during downturns. Of course, the price rises as the market rises.

- *Provide advance credit to growers.* Equal Exchange makes credit available to its farmers. Historically, credit was unavailable or offered only at extremely high rates, trapping farmers in debt. "When we sign a contract with producers, we pay up to 60 percent of the contract six months in advance," notes marketing manager Erbin Crowell. "If a hurricane hits, we share the risk." In fact, several years ago, a hurricane did hit—"Mitch" slammed into Nicaragua, causing deaths, injuries, and millions of dollars in damage. Equal Exchange worked with Lutheran World Relief to raise funds for residents who suffered because of the hurricane.

- *Encourage ecologically sustainable farming practices.* Equal Exchange helps growers use environmentally friendly farming methods, protecting both the local environment and consumers from toxic chemicals. In this way, the company demonstrates social responsibility not only to the health of workers and consumers but also to the local environment. The company pays a premium price for certified organic and shade-grown coffee, both of which are better for the environment.

Not surprisingly, Equal Exchange is also ethical in its conduct toward competitors. Recently, when specialty coffee giants Starbucks and Green Mountain announced that they were entering into fair trade agreements with farmers, Equal Exchange publicly congratulated them. "Believe it or not, we want more, not less competition," says Equal Exchange co-founder and co-executive director Rink Dickinson. "That's because we know these farmers and their struggles. They urgently need more importers to pay a just price. So we encourage our fellow roasters to expand on the modest fair trade programs they've announced so far." With this statement, Dickinson raised the bar of ethical standards in the coffee business—knowing that his company can clear it with ease.

QUESTIONS

1. At what stage of ethical development would you place Rink Dickinson and his colleagues? Why?
2. Suppose Dickinson discovered that one of Equal Exchange's co-operatives was engaging in unethical practices of its own, such as growing illegal products, selling coffee to competitors, or not paying fair wages to workers. What do you think he would do?
3. If you were to do a social audit of Equal Exchange, what company activities would you identify that relate to social issues? What activities or programs might you suggest to the company for an even better social audit?
4. Visit Equal Exchange's Web site at **www.equalexchange.com** to learn about the company. Then create an advertisement for Equal Exchange Coffee. What characteristics of the company do you think would appeal to consumers?

Sources: Equal Exchange Web site, **www.equalexchange.com,** accessed January 10, 2001; Marjorie Kelly, "Leading the Way to Fairer Trade Practices," *Business Ethics,* accessed at the inc.com Web site, **www.inc.com,** January 10, 2001; "Fair Trade Coffee Pioneers Welcome Competitors to Their Niche," company press release, September 21, 2000; Gina Imperato, "Let's Do Lunch!" *Fast Company,* April 2000, **http://pf.fastcompany.com.**

CHAPTER 3

Economic Challenges Facing Global and Domestic Business

Learning Goals

1. Distinguish between microeconomics and macroeconomics.

2. List each of the factors that collectively determine demand and those that determine supply.

3. Compare supply and demand curves and explain how they determine the equilibrium price for a product.

4. Contrast the three major types of economic systems.

5. Explain each of the four different types of market structures in a private enterprise system.

6. Identify the major factors that guide an economist's evaluation of a nation's economic performance.

7. Compare the two major tools used by a government to manage its economy.

8. Describe the major global economic challenges of the 21st century.

U.S. Sports Camps Scores Big Online

When the American economy is strong, consumers have more money to spend. That means more kids can pack their bags and head off to summer camp with their friends. And in the sports-crazed U.S., many of them sign up with one of the 500 sports programs managed by U.S. Sports Camps. For a week or two, kids can sleep away from mom and dad and work on forehand volleys, chip shots, slam dunks, backstrokes, and shots on soccer goals—whatever their hearts desire. Most camps are located on college campuses and run by college coaches, so the kids have the thrill of tasting what it's like to hit the big-time collegiate sports scene. The coaches hire their own on-site instructors, and U.S. Sports Camps handles the marketing and administration of the programs.

Summer camp is a seasonal event, which means that the demand—the number of customers who want the service—is not constant year-round. Most registration occurs between March and July, when families are making summer vacation plans, so U.S. Sports Camps builds up its customer service staff during those months. Since developing a successful Web site, however, the company has had to hire fewer extra staff members for those busy months because customers can register online whenever they please. "We've done 20 percent more business [this year] with 20 percent less staff because people are registering over the site," says CEO Charlie Hoeveler.

Hoeveler is always looking for ways to attract people to the Web site year-round, to keep them interested. U.S. Sports Camps has added extra features to the site such as sports-specific bulletin boards that provide

updated information to enthusiasts anytime of the year. Hoeveler is convinced that people who get interested during the off-season are more likely to sign up early. In

fact, the company starts accepting registrations in December for the following summer. Hoeveler explains, "I just send a message out to all 40 tennis camp coaches saying, 'I'm going to be on your tail to get confirmation of new dates and prices because we are going to update this Web site. We would like to get those early deposits.'" Coaches don't really mind the added pressure; they'd rather see their camps fill up, and they know that it's good exposure for their college programs.

Hoeveler has found other ways to increase demand for his camps: creating links

among the different sports on the Web site. After all, different children in the same family may be interested in different sports. So when a mom logs on to find a volleyball

camp for her daughter, she may see that there's a perfect golf camp for her son only a few miles away. She can gather information about both camps at the site and register there with a few keystrokes and mouse clicks. It's so easy to accomplish at the Web site, and she's happy not to have to make dozens of phone calls. "The cross-marketing opportunities are amazing," remarks Hoeveler. "More than one kid in a family often means more than one sport. With the site, we can capture all that business." That should add up to a big score for U.S. Sports Camps.[1]

CHAPTER OVERVIEW

U.S. Sports Camps shows how one company benefits from a strong economy and how managers can find creative ways to increase the number of customers attracted to a business, even during traditionally slow times. At any company, employees are a resource that the firm uses to produce its goods and services—in this case, summer camps. In return, employees gain wages, skills, and education that improve individuals' lives and raise the overall quality of the workforce.

Looking at the exchanges that companies and societies make as a whole, we are speaking of their **economic systems,** that is, the combination of policies and choices a nation makes to allocate resources among its citizens. Countries vary in the ways they allocate scarce resources.

Economics, the social science analyzing the choices made by people and governments in allocating scarce resources, affects each of us, since everyone is involved in producing, distributing, or simply consuming goods and services. In fact, your life is affected by economics every day. When you decide what goods to buy, what services to use, or what activities to fit into your schedule, you are making economic choices.

The choices you make often are international in scope. Consider, for example, someone who decides to buy a new piece of luggage. Along with such U.S. companies as Lands' End and Eddie Bauer, the person might consider buying from Louis Vuitton. If he or she buys the Louis Vuitton bag shown in Figure 3.1, this one person with a single purchase has become involved in international trade by choosing to buy from a French supplier. Businesses also make economic decisions when they choose how to use human and natural resources, invest in machinery and buildings, and form partnerships with other firms.

FIGURE 3.1
Making Economic Choices between Domestic and Imported Products

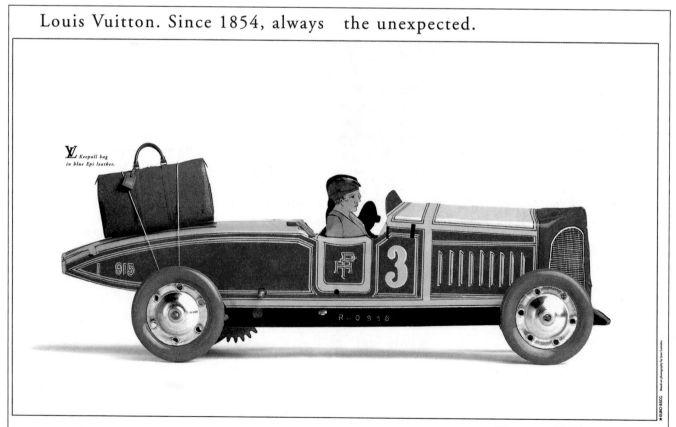

Louis Vuitton. Since 1854, always   the unexpected.

Keepall bag in blue Epi leather.

Available exclusively in Louis Vuitton shops and select department stores. For more information or the store nearest you, please call: 1-800-458-7927.

Louis Vuitton
The spirit of travel

Economists refer to the study of small economic units, such as individual consumers, families, and businesses, as **microeconomics.** On a broader level, government decisions about the operation of the country's economy also affect you, your job, and your financial future. When the U.S. Congress decided to adopt welfare reform in the mid-1990s, it emphasized providing incentives and training so that welfare recipients could obtain the qualifications necessary to find jobs. That policy affected the supply of labor and the demand for child-care services. The study of a country's overall economic issues is called **macroeconomics.** (*Macro* means large.) This discipline addresses such issues as how an economy maintains and allocates resources and how government policies affect people's standards of living. Chapter 1 describes the increasing interdependence of the world's nations and their economies. Reflecting that interdependence, macroeconomics examines not just the economic policies of individual nations, but the ways in which those individual policies affect the overall world economy. Microeconomics and macroeconomics are interrelated disciplines. Macroeconomic issues help to shape the decisions made every day by individuals, families, and businesses.

In this chapter we introduce economic theory and the economic challenges facing individuals, businesses, and governments in the global marketplace. We begin with the microeconomic concepts of supply and demand and their effect on the prices people pay for goods and services. Next, we explain the various types of economic systems, along with tools for comparing and evaluating their performance. Then we examine the ways in which governments seek to manage economies in order to create stable business environments in their countries. The final section in the chapter looks at some of the driving economic forces that are affecting people's lives at the beginning of the 21st century.

MICROECONOMICS: THE FORCES OF DEMAND AND SUPPLY

A good way to begin the study of economics is to look at the economic activities and choices of individuals and small economic units such as families and firms. These economic actions determine both the prices of goods and services and the amounts sold. Microeconomic information is vital for a business, because the survival of the business depends on selling enough of its products at prices high enough to cover expenses and earn profits. This information is also important to consumers, whose well-being may depend on the prices and availability of needed goods and services.

At the heart of every business endeavor is an exchange between a buyer and a seller. The buyer recognizes that he or she has a need or wants a particular good or service and is willing to pay a seller in order to obtain it. The seller wants to participate in the process because of the anticipated financial gains from selling the good or service. So the exchange process involves both demand and supply. **Demand** refers to the willingness and ability of buyers to purchase goods and services at different prices. The other side of the exchange process is **supply,** the willingness and ability of sellers to provide goods and services for sale at different prices. Understanding the factors that determine demand and supply, as well as how the two interact, can help you to understand many actions and decisions of individuals, businesses, and government. This section takes a closer look at these concepts.

Factors Driving Demand

For most people, economics amounts to a balance between their unlimited wants and limited financial means. Because of this dilemma, each person must make choices about how much money to save and how much to spend, as well as how to allocate spending among all the goods and services competing for

BUSINESS DIRECTORY

➤ **economics**   *social science that analyzes the choices made by people and governments in allocating scarce resources.*

➤ **demand**   *willingness and ability of buyers to purchase goods and services.*

➤ **supply**   *willingness and ability of sellers to provide goods and services for sale.*

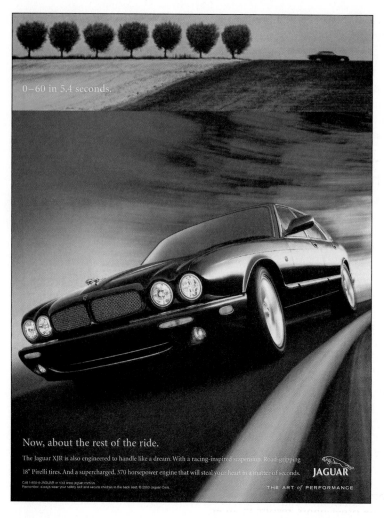

0–60 in 5.4 seconds.

Now, about the rest of the ride.

The Jaguar XJR is also engineered to handle like a dream. With a racing-inspired suspension. Road-gripping

18" Pirelli tires. And a supercharged, 370 horsepower engine that will steal your heart in a matter of seconds.

JAGUAR

Call 1-800-4-JAGUAR or Visit www.jaguar.com/us.
Remember: always wear your safety belt and secure children in the back seat. © 2000 Jaguar Cars.

THE ART *of* PERFORMANCE

FIGURE 3.2
Consumer Preferences, Incomes, and the Prices of Substitute Products Affect Demand for Automobiles

attention. This continuing effort to address unlimited wants with limited means caused one writer to refer to economics as "the dismal science."

Even though you may be convinced that the Jaguar in Figure 3.2 is the perfect answer to your automotive needs, a quick look at the required monthly payments may force you to compromise with a less expensive Suzuki Samurai. And, even if you can afford the monthly payments on the Jaguar, you may still select the more economical Samurai so that you can spend the money you save on new clothes, a white-water rafting trip, or a more expensive apartment with an extra bedroom. So, demand is driven by a number of factors that influence how people decide to spend their incomes.

As these examples demonstrate, price is one of the most important factors influencing demand. In general, as the price of a good or service goes up, people buy smaller amounts. In other words, as price rises, the quantity demanded declines. At lower prices, consumers are generally willing to buy more of a good. A **demand curve** is a graph of the amount of a product that buyers will purchase at different prices. Demand curves typically slope downward, meaning that lower and lower prices attract larger and larger purchases.

Over the years, a steep decline in prices for personal computers (PCs) has been matched by strong growth in demand. Even as computing power has increased, computer sellers have been able to cut prices from $1,642 in 1997 to less than $900 for an average PC—complete with a printer and audio speakers—today. Rebates from manufacturers and Internet service providers (ISPs) can push the cost even lower. As prices tumbled, more and more consumers and businesses have snapped up the machines. In the U.S. today, most businesses and the majority of households have PCs. Also, as ISPs cut the cost of Internet access to below zero—enticing users by giving away money while covering costs by selling advertising—the number of low-income Internet users has been growing at the rate of 50 percent a year.[2]

Gasoline provides another good example of how demand curves work. Figure 3.3 shows a possible demand curve for the total amount of gasoline that people will purchase at different prices. When gasoline is priced at $1.59 a gallon, drivers may fill up their tanks once or twice a week. At $2.09 a gallon, many of them may start economizing. They may make fewer trips, start carpooling, or ride buses to work. So the quantity of gasoline demanded at $2.09 a gallon is lower than the amount demanded at $1.59 a gallon. The opposite happens at $1.09 a gallon. Some drivers may decide to top off their tanks more often than they would at a higher price; they may also decide to take cross-country vacations or drive to school instead of taking the bus. As a result, more gasoline is sold at $1.09 a gallon than at $1.59 a gallon. These relationships were played out in real life: when gas prices soared in the Midwest, consumers didn't just complain—they cut back on their driving. In a poll of consumers, almost half said they had reduced the amount they drive.[3] And one woman told a *Time* magazine reporter that when gas prices in the Midwest rose above $2 a gallon, she left her Ford Econoline van in the garage and started using her husband's smaller Pontiac Grand Am or walked.[4]

Economists make a clear distinction between changes in the quantity demanded at various prices and changes in overall demand. A change in quantity demanded,

FIGURE 3.3
Demand Curve for Gasoline

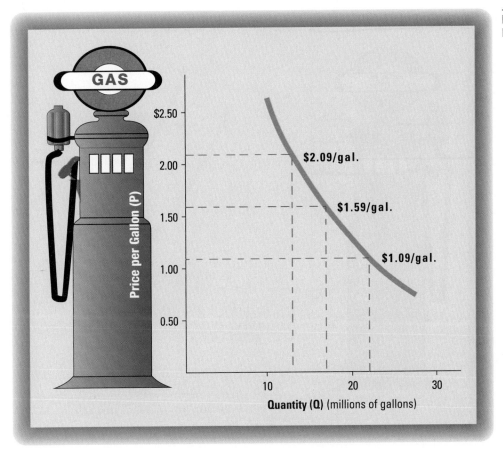

such as the change that occurs at different gasoline prices, is simply movement along the demand curve. A change in overall demand, on the other hand, results in an entirely new demand curve.

As Americans' incomes have risen, they have purchased gas-guzzling vehicles like sport-utility vehicles (SUVs). At the same time, in developing countries like India and China, consumers have been able to afford cars for the first time. These changes have increased the demand for gasoline at all prices. Figure 3.4 shows how the increased demand for gasoline worldwide has created a new demand curve. The new demand curve shifts to the right of the old demand curve, indicating that overall demand has increased at every price. A demand curve can also shift to the left when the demand for a good or service drops. However, the demand curve still has the same shape.

Although price is the underlying cause of movement along a demand curve, many factors can combine to determine the overall demand for a product—that is, the shape and position of the demand curve. These influences include customer preferences and incomes, the prices of substitute and complementary items, the number of buyers in a market, and the strength of their optimism regarding the future. Changes in any of these factors will produce a new demand curve.

Take a change in income as an example. As consumers have more money to spend, firms can sell more products at every price. This means the demand curve has shifted to the right. The price of complementary goods also can influence demand. If the price of gasoline remains high, we would expect the demand for SUVs to fall as some consumers switch to more fuel-efficient forms of transportation. Table 3.1 describes how a demand curve is likely to respond to each of these changes.

For a business to succeed, management must carefully monitor the factors that may affect demand for the goods and services it hopes to sell. In setting prices, firms often try to predict how the chosen levels will influence the amounts they sell. In recent years, The Coca-Cola Company has experimented with smart vending machines,

FIGURE 3.4
Shift in the Demand Curve for Gasoline

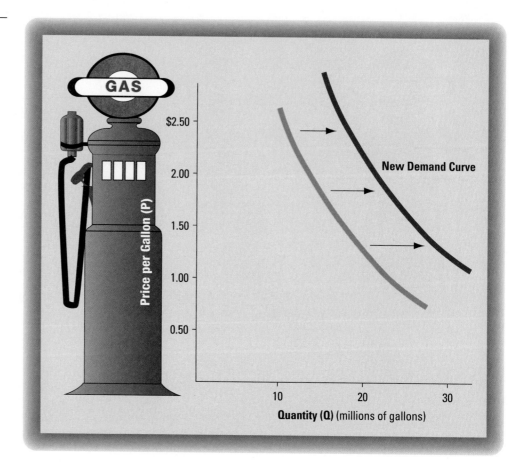

adjusting their prices to such variables as the weather. When it's hot outside, the machines could automatically raise the price. Or if the vending machine contains too many root beers and it's still five days until it's scheduled to be restocked, the machine could lower the price of root beer. Businesspeople also try to influence overall demand through advertising, sales calls, product enhancements, and other marketing techniques.

FACTORS DRIVING SUPPLY

Important economic factors also affect supply, the willingness and ability of firms to provide goods and services at different prices. Just as consumers must make choices about how to spend their incomes, businesses must also make decisions about how to use their resources in order to obtain the best profits.

Table 3.1   Expected Shifts in Demand Curves

Factor	Demand Curve Shifts	
	to the Right *if*:	to the Left *if*:
Customer preferences	increase	decrease
Number of buyers	increases	decreases
Buyers' incomes	increase	decrease
Prices of substitute goods	increase	decrease
Prices of complementary goods	decrease	increase
Future expectations become more	optimistic	pessimistic

FIGURE 3.5
Supply Curve for Gasoline

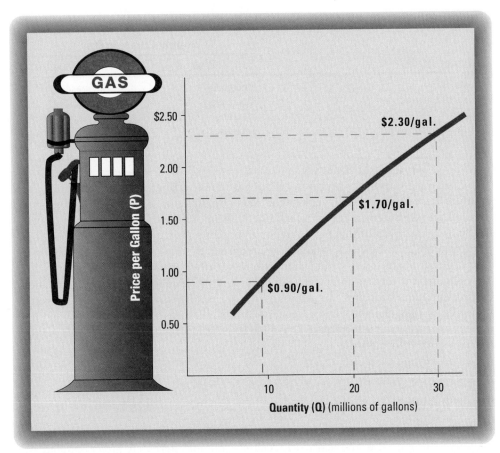

Obviously, sellers would prefer to command high rather than low prices for their goods or services. A **supply curve** graphically shows the relationship between different prices and the quantities that sellers will offer for sale, regardless of demand. Movement along the supply curve is the opposite of movement along the demand curve. So as price rises, the quantity sellers are willing to supply also rises. At progressively lower prices, the quantity supplied decreases. In Figure 3.5, a possible supply curve for gasoline shows that increasing prices for gasoline should bring increasing supplies to market, as oil companies are motivated by the possibility of earning growing profits.

Businesses require certain inputs to operate effectively in producing their goods and services. As we discuss in Chapter 1, these **factors of production** include natural resources, capital, human resources, and entrepreneurship. *Natural resources* include everything that is useful in its natural state, including land, building sites, forests, and mineral deposits. *Human resources* include the physical labor and intellectual inputs contributed by managers and operative employees. *Capital* refers to resources such as technology, tools, information, physical facilities, and financial capabilities. The fourth factor of production, *entrepreneurship*, is the willingness to take risks to create and operate a business.

Factors of production play a central role in determining the overall supply of goods and services. A change in the cost or availability of any of these inputs can shift the entire supply curve, either increasing or decreasing the amount available at every price. For example, if the cost of raw materials (natural resources) rises, producers may respond by lowering production levels, shifting the supply curve to the left. On the other hand, if an innovation in the production process allows them to turn out more products using less raw materials than before, the change reduces the overall cost of the finished products, shifting the supply curve to the right. Table 3.2 summarizes how changes in various factors can affect the supply curve.

Table 3.2 **Expected Shifts in Supply Curves**

| Factor | Supply Curve Shifts | |
	to the Right *if*:	to the Left *if*:
Costs of inputs	decrease	increase
Costs of technologies	decrease	increase
Taxes	decrease	increase
Number of suppliers	increases	decreases

A leftward shift in the supply curve for gasoline contributed to the price spike that buyers experienced a few years ago. The Organization of Petroleum Exporting Countries (OPEC) member nations limited the amount of crude oil they made available. With supplies of this key ingredient limited, its price soared above $35 a barrel, or more than twice the price of a year earlier. A series of accidents involving oil pipelines also interfered with the supply of oil, further driving up the cost. Other factors limited movement along the supply curve. In particular, oil refineries have been operating more efficiently by keeping inventories low, so they were unprepared to meet the strong demand that preceded the price hikes. Also, clean-air laws went into effect that required reformulated gasoline to be sold in the Midwest. These new requirements restricted the ingredients that could be used, although the result is cleaner-burning gasoline.[5]

How Demand and Supply Interact

Separate shifts in demand and supply have obvious effects on prices and the availability of products. In the real world, changes do not alternately affect demand and supply. Several factors often change at the same time—and they keep changing. Sometimes such simultaneous changes in multiple factors cause contradictory pressures on prices and quantities. In other cases, the final direction of prices and quantities reflects the factor that has changed the most.

Figure 3.6 shows the interaction of both supply and demand curves for gasoline on a single graph. Notice that the two curves intersect at *P*. The law of supply and demand states that prices (*P*) are set by the intersection of the supply and demand curves. The point where the two curves meet identifies the **equilibrium price**, the prevailing market price at which you can buy an item.

If the actual market price differs from the equilibrium price, people tend to make economic choices that restore the equilibrium level. When holiday shoppers set out to purchase the highly touted Sony Playstation2, they discovered that initial production of 500,000 of the $299 black boxes was simply not enough to match pent-up U.S. demand. International travelers began to look for the high-demand item in foreign cities. Others turned to eBay, only to discover that bidding had hit more than $500.

In the case of gasoline, the shortage of oil caused a price increase that angered consumers and drew the attention of regulators such as the Federal Trade Commission. Oil refiners responded to the above-equilibrium prices by stepping up exploration and production. In addition, a number of the OPEC nations, fearful that the high prices might harm the strong economies of oil-importing countries, increased export oil sales. The U.S. government also decided to increase supply by selling part of its strategic oil reserves.[6]

In other situations, suppliers react to market forces by increasing the price. When DaimlerChrysler introduced its highly successful PT Cruiser, the level of demand caught the company by surprise. Waiting time for delivery grew as orders outstripped the automaker's ability to produce the vehicles. Several dealers responded with a price increase. They began adding as much as $10,000 to the PT Cruiser's list price. Even the National Transportation Safety Board had to pay the $10,000

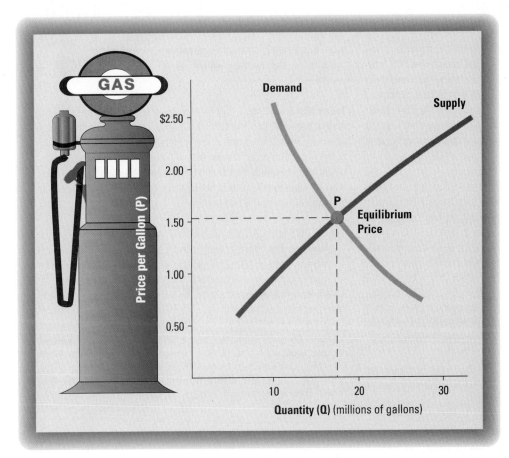

FIGURE 3.6
Law of Supply and Demand

markup when it purchased two models for crash testing. The law of supply and demand had arrived at a market-clearing price.[7]

As we point out earlier, the forces of demand and supply can be affected by a variety of factors. One important factor is the larger economic environment. The next section explains how macroeconomics and economic systems influence market forces and, ultimately, demand, supply, and prices.

MACROECONOMICS: ISSUES FOR THE ENTIRE ECONOMY

The political and economic choices made in recent years by North Korean leader Kim Jong Il have influenced the daily lives of North Koreans since the death of his father in 1994. In a country where a famine killed an estimated 2 million of the nation's 22 million people, the U.S. built goodwill in a formerly isolationist land by donating 1.5 million tons of grain. A telling event regarding globalization occurred during a visit to the North Korean capital of P'yŏngyang by then U.S. Secretary of State Madeleine Albright. Albright, learning that Kim was a basketball fan, presented him with a gift: a basketball signed by basketball Hall of Famer Michael Jordan.

Every country faces decisions about how to best use the four basic factors of production. Each nation's policies and choices help to determine its economic system. But the political, social, and legal environments differ in every country. So, no two countries have exactly the same economic system. In general, however, economic systems can be classified into three categories: private enterprise systems, planned economies, or combinations of the two, referred to as mixed economies. As business becomes an increasingly global undertaking, it is important to understand the primary features of the various economic systems operating around the world.

Ingram Micro Competes Online

Background. During the first years of Internet commerce, retailing experts predicted that distributors—the companies that move goods from one place to another for sale by stores—had only a limited amount of time left. The reasoning was that once e-commerce vendors gained strength, they'd order goods directly from manufacturers, rendering the traditional system of independent distributors obsolete. So, competition from suppliers and customers would simply squeeze them out.

What Happened? Ingram Micro, the largest distributor of computer hardware and software in the world, didn't buy this argument. To survive and remain competitive in a changing economy, Ingram decided to change the way it did business. It took its business online. And instead of focusing on bulk distribution—transporting large amounts of goods—Ingram restructured itself so that it could ship one unit directly to a customer, complete with a customized packing slip from the manufacturer or Internet retailer. In addition, Ingram worked to strengthen its relationship with retailers, setting up a Web site to share product descriptions and photos with entrepreneurs who wanted to create their own storefront on the Web.

The Response. Ingram's customers love the "new" company, because Ingram now creates greater value for them. In doing so, Ingram has actually strengthened its position in the industry rather than weakened it.

Today and Counting. Ingram's competition will increase as the idea of one-unit shipping takes hold. Distributors in industries such as books, music, toys, and office supplies have already latched on to the idea, and other distributors will surely follow. Ironically, Internet retailers may find themselves competing with distributors who are able to take orders online as well. By then, Ingram may be one step ahead of the competition.

QUESTIONS FOR CRITICAL THINKING

1. How has the Internet increased competition for businesses such as Ingram Micro? How has it made business more efficient?
2. What factors might influence the demand for Ingram's services in the next few years?

Sources: "Company Biography," Ingram Micro Web site, **www.ingrammicro.com**, accessed March 16, 2001; "Ingram Micro Celebrates $1 Billion Sales Milestone with Cisco," Ingram Micro press release, October 2, 2000; J. William Gurley, "Why Online Distributors—Once Written Off—May Thrive," *Fortune*, September 6, 1999, pp. 270, 272.

Capitalism: The Private Enterprise System and Competition

Most industrialized nations operate economies based on the **private enterprise system**, also known as *capitalism* or a *market economy*. A private enterprise system rewards businesses for meeting the needs and demands of consumers. Government tends to favor a hands-off attitude toward controlling business ownership, profits, and resource allocations. Instead, competition regulates economic life, creating opportunities and challenges that businesspeople must handle in order to succeed. The "Clicks and Mortar" box describes one business that moved online to remain competitive in a changing industry.

The relative competitiveness of a particular industry is an important consideration for every firm, because it determines the ease and cost of doing business within that industry. Four basic degrees of competition take shape in a private enterprise system: pure competition, monopolistic competition, oligopoly, and monopoly. Table 3.3 highlights the main differences between these types of competition.

Pure competition is a market structure, like that of small-scale agriculture, in which large numbers of buyers and sellers exchange homogeneous products, so no single participant has a significant influence on price. Instead, prices are set by the market itself as the forces of supply and demand interact. Firms can easily enter or leave a purely competitive market, because no single company dominates. Also, in pure competition, buyers see little difference between the goods and services offered by competitors.

Agriculture is probably the closest modern example of pure competition. The grain grown and sold by one farmer is virtually identical to that sold by others. As the weather affects the supply of wheat, soybeans, and cotton, the price for these commodities rises or falls according to the law of supply and demand. In a recent year, a hot, dry August damaged crops from midwestern and southern farms, so the price of soybeans rose about ten cents per bushel from the previous year. However, because the amount produced would still be a record soybean crop, the price

| Table 3.3 | **Types of Competition** | | | |

	Types of Competition			
Characteristics	**Pure Competition**	**Monopolistic Competition**	**Oligopoly**	**Monopoly**
Number of competitors	Many	Few to many	Few	No direct competition
Ease of entry into industry by new firms	Easy	Somewhat difficult	Difficult	Regulated by government
Similarity of goods or services offered by competing firms	Similar	Different	Similar or different	No directly competing products
Control over price by individual firms	None	Some	Some	Considerable in a pure monopoly; little in a regulated monopoly
Examples	Small-scale farmer in Kansas	Hallmark card shop	Boeing aircraft	Rawlings Sporting Goods, exclusive supplier of major-league baseballs

remained at about the level farmers could charge during the recession they experienced during the 1980s. Demand, of course, also plays a role in prices for commodities. Growing international demand for U.S. wheat has been strong enough to keep prices for that crop steady, even as production has increased.[8]

Monopolistic competition is a market structure, like that for retailing, in which large numbers of buyers and sellers exchange relatively well-differentiated (heterogeneous) products, so each participant has some control over price. Sellers can differentiate their products from competing offerings on the basis of price, quality, or other features. In an industry that features monopolistic competition, it is relatively easy for a firm to begin or stop selling a good or service. The success of one seller often attracts new competitors to such a market. Individual firms also have some control over how their individual goods and services are priced.

An example of monopolistic competition is the market for pet food. Consumers can choose from private-label (store brands) and brand-name products in bags, boxes, and cans. Producers of pet food and the stores that sell it have wide latitude in setting prices. Consumers can choose the store or brand with the lowest prices, or sellers can convince them that a more expensive offering is worth more because it offers better nutrition, more convenience, more information, or other benefits. In this crowded marketplace, over a dozen online pet suppliers have sprung up to compete with supermarkets, national pet store chains, and neighborhood pet stores. To attract customers in this competitive market, Petsmart has set prices at money-losing levels; it collects 62 cents for every dollar it spends on purchases and shipping. Petsmart hopes to survive long enough to build an online brand name and to see other Internet competitors fail. As this occurs, the company will survive by eventually paring its costs while also increasing sales in a less-competitive market. The approach appears to be working, as a number of competitors, such as Pets.com, have halted operations. In the meantime, consumers are enjoying the benefits of competition. In New York, Web designer Laura Medley says she checks several sites each week to compare prices of food and supplies for her dog and three cats. She permits pet stores to send her e-mail about products on sale, and she buys from whichever merchant is having a sale. Sometimes, she says, products she wants are given away free to lure customers.[9]

An **oligopoly** is a market situation in which relatively few sellers compete and high start-up costs form barriers to keep out new competitors. In some oligopolistic industries, such as paper and steel, competitors offer similar products. In others, such as aircraft and

BUSINESS DIRECTORY

➤ **private enterprise system** *economic system in which business success or failure depends on how well firms match and counter the offerings of competitors; also known as capitalism or a market economy.*

automobiles, they sell different models and features. The huge investment required to enter an oligopoly market tends to discourage new competitors. The limited number of sellers also enhances the control these firms exercise over price. Competing products in an oligopoly usually sell for very similar prices, because substantial price competition would reduce profits for all firms in the industry. So, a price cut by one firm in an oligopoly will typically be met by its competitors.

Consider the business of making linerboard, or paper for cardboard boxes. In this commodity-type industry, prices depend largely on supply and demand. If supply grows faster than a company can contain its expenses, the business can operate at a loss. Ireland-based Jefferson Smurfit Group, which had built itself into one of the largest makers of linerboard, faced this problem when its competitors Weyerhaeuser and Georgia-Pacific increased their capacity so fast that prices for the product plunged. In two years, earnings fell to one-third of earlier levels. But because Jefferson Smurfit was a giant company, it had the resources to compete. The Irish company merged its U.S. operations with Stone Container Corp., the largest U.S. producer of linerboard and then closed four of the company's factories, laying off 1,700 employees and reducing North America's supply of linerboard. These actions boosted the price of linerboard 30 percent—and Smurfit's earnings along with it. Justifying the changes, Michael Smurfit says, "We are trying to send a message to the industry. If you bring on new capacity, bring it on to meet demand. Don't destroy your own market." Competitors seem to have heard the message. Some have cut back their production of linerboard as well, and no competitor has announced plans to expand.[10]

The final type of market structure is a **monopoly**, in which a single seller dominates trade in a good or service for which buyers can find no close substitutes. A *pure monopoly* occurs when a firm possesses unique characteristics so important to competition in its industry that they serve as barriers to prevent entry by would-be competitors. Rawlings Sporting Goods has the entire market for major-league baseballs, thanks to a deal with professional baseball.[11] From the 1930s to the 1990s, De Beers enjoyed a near-monopoly in the market for diamonds, by virtue of owning or buying any rough diamonds it could throughout the world. The company at one time controlled 90 percent of the world's diamond supply. However, recent discoveries of diamond reserves outside De Beers's control, coupled with a promise to stop buying diamonds sold to raise money for armed conflicts in the African nations of Angola, Sierra Leone, and the Democratic Republic of Congo, have reduced the company's share of the market to 60 percent.[12]

Many firms create short-term monopolies when research breakthroughs permit them to receive exclusive patents on new products. In the pharmaceuticals industry, drug giants like Merck, Pfizer, and Pharmacia & Upjohn invest billions in research and development programs. When the research leads to successful new drugs, the companies can enjoy the benefits of their patent: the ability to set prices without fear of competitors undercutting them. Recently, the pharmaceutical industry has come under fire for the high prices of drugs in U.S. markets, as the "Solving an Ethical Controversy" box discusses.

Similarly, as the company that first developed synthetic turf, AstroTurf has three-quarters of the market for synthetic playing surfaces in North America. That prominent position erects barriers for competitors with new products, even though a survey of National Football League (NFL) players found that most believed AstroTurf was the source of more injuries than grass. During the 1990s, FieldTurf, a Montreal company, began to sell an alternative. Instead of AstroTurf's nylon fibers, FieldTurf has a blend of fibers in a carpet filled with layers of sand and ground-up rubber. User feedback indicates that it has the comfort and safety of grass at a much lower cost than either grass or AstroTurf. FieldTurf armed itself for competition with 37 patents, some pending, along with insurance in case it needed to defend those patents in court. With product demonstrations that include NFL veteran Steve Furness sliding on FieldTurf without getting burns, the company is beginning to land

SOLVING AN ETHICAL CONTROVERSY

You've got a runny nose and watery eyes; sometimes you feel as though you can hardly breathe. Like millions of other people around the world, you suffer from allergies. There are plenty of medications to treat your condition. The old-style antihistamines, such as Benadryl, are available without prescription in the U.S. They are effective but have sedative side effects, making people drowsy. The newer antihistamines such as Claritin, Allegra, and Zyrtec are available by prescription only. They are effective and do not make people sleepy. Because the older antihistamines are available over-the-counter, they are much cheaper than the newer ones. But suppose you have an allergy attack while you are in Canada. Did you know you can buy the very same Claritin at a lower price and without a prescription? A month's supply of Claritin costs about $62 in the U.S., not including the doctor's visit. A month's supply of Claritin in Canada—or most other industrialized countries—costs about $15. Schering-Plough, the manufacturer of Claritin, cited the drug's safety record in its overseas petition for nonprescription status for Claritin. In the U.S., the company says it "believes the prescription-only status for Claritin presents the best medical option available for allergy patients." Most of Schering-Plough's revenues from Claritin come from the U.S., where its prescription-only status shields it from price competition. Other countries haggle for price cuts with drug manufacturers. The Food and Drug Administration (FDA), which regulates the status of drugs, does not change the status of a prescription drug unless requested to do so by its manufacturer.

Should pharmaceutical companies be allowed to shield themselves from price competition in the U.S. via prescription-only status for their new drugs while at the same time selling them over-the-counter in other countries?

PRO

1. Drug companies invest millions of dollars in research and production of their drugs, and they need to recoup that investment in order to generate funds for further research. These expenditures explain the tremendous medical breakthroughs that have occurred during the past two decades.
2. In a free market, drug companies are allowed to charge whatever price they believe is appropriate and competitive for their goods.
3. Any new drug should remain in prescription-only status, regardless of price, for a designated amount of time to evaluate its performance among the general public.

CON

1. As soon as a newer, safer drug is available, the FDA should approve it for nonprescription status—for the good of the general public.
2. Price competition is good for the consumer, and drug manufacturers can sell more products when more medications are sold at a lower price.
3. Reducing the cost of some allergy drugs would cut costs for consumers and insurance companies, thereby lowering the skyrocketing cost of health care.

SUMMARY

Rob Seidman, vice president for pharmacy at Blue Cross of California, notes that "Claritin is one of the safest drugs in the world. The requirement to see a doctor has nothing to do with health and everything to do with marketing." Blue Cross has petitioned the FDA to change its policy regarding prescription drugs that are proven safe. And Congress has approved a bill allowing drugs exported overseas to be reimported to the U.S. at lower cost. It is unclear what the effects of such a change would be: lower costs for drugs in the U.S. or fewer exports to other countries.

Source: "Drug Imports Could Have a Cost," *Chicago Tribune,* October 1, 2000, section 1, p. 22; Dennis Cauchon, "Why Allergy Drugs Cost So Much," *USA Today,* April 12, 2000, pp. 1A, 4A; "New Study Suggests Government Price Controls for Pharmaceuticals Harm Patients, Don't Save Money," *PR Newswire,* April 29, 1999.

---

some contracts. If it succeeds, its patents could enable FieldTurf to end the temporary monopoly enjoyed by AstroTurf.

Because a monopoly market lacks the benefits of competition, the U.S. government regulates monopolies. Besides issuing patents and limiting their life, the government prohibits most pure monopolies through antitrust legislation such as the Sherman Act and the Clayton Act. As discussed in Chapter 2, the U.S. government has applied these laws against monopolistic behavior by Microsoft and by disallowing the proposed merger of Worldcom and Sprint. In other cases, the government permits certain monopolies in exchange for regulating their activities.

With *regulated monopolies*, a local, state, or federal government grants exclusive rights in a certain market to a single firm. Pricing decisions—particularly rate-increase requests—are subject to control by regulatory authorities such as state public service commissions. An example is the delivery of first-class mail, a monopoly held by the

United States Postal Service (USPS), formerly a government agency. When the USPS wants to increase the price of stamps, Congress must approve the change.

As we saw in Chapter 2, the government during the 1980s and 1990s has favored a trend away from regulated monopolies and toward *deregulation*. Regulated monopolies that have been deregulated include long-distance and local telephone service, cable television, cell phones, and electrical service. Deregulation of electric utilities began when California opened its market in 1998. Since then, it has occurred gradually, on a state-to-state basis, with about half the states on board. In those states, private companies can compete with utilities to sell electricity and natural gas. Amway, representing Columbia Energy Services, offers natural gas for sale to customers in Georgia and Ohio. Green Mountain Energy has signed up customers in California and Pennsylvania who are willing to pay extra in exchange for energy that the company says will be generated in environmentally friendly ways. However, utilities continue to deliver gas or electricity to users, as well as to provide maintenance.[13]

Planned Economies: Communism and Socialism

In a **planned economy,** government controls determine business ownership, profits, and resource allocation to accomplish government goals rather than those set by individual businesses. Two forms of planned economies are communism and socialism.

The writings of Karl Marx in the mid-1800s formed the basis of communist theory. Marx believed that private enterprise economies created unfair conditions and led to worker exploitation, because business owners controlled most of society's resources and reaped most of the economy's rewards. Instead, he suggested an economic system in which all property would be shared equally by the people of a community under the direction of a strong central government. **Communism** is an economic system in which private property is eliminated, goods are owned in common, and factors of production and production decisions are controlled by the state.

Marx believed that elimination of private ownership of property and businesses would ensure the emergence of a classless society that would benefit all. Each individual would contribute what he or she could, and resources would be distributed according to each person's needs. Under communism, the central government owns the means of production, and the people work for state-owned enterprises. The government determines what people can buy, because it dictates what is produced in the nation's factories and farms.

Many nations adopted communist economic systems during the 20th century in an effort to improve the quality of life for their citizens. In practice, however, communist governments often give people little or no freedom of choice in selecting jobs, purchases, or investments. Communist governments often make mistakes in planning the best uses of resources in order to compete in the growing global marketplace. Government-owned monopolies often suffer from inefficiency.

Consider the former Soviet Union, where large government bureaucracies controlled nearly every aspect of daily life. Shortages became chronic, because producers had little or no incentive to satisfy customers. The quality of goods and services also suffered for the same reason. When Mikhail Gorbachev was selected as the last prime minister of the dying Soviet Union, he took strides to improve the quality of Soviet-made products. Gorbachev authorized an exhibition of shoddy and defective goods produced by the Soviet workers, including a whole consignment of boots with high heels attached to the toes. Effectively shut out of trading in the global marketplace and caught up in a treasury-depleting arms race with the United States, the Soviet Union faced severe financial problems. Eventually these economic crises led to the collapse of Soviet communism and the breakup of the Soviet Union itself.

A second type of planned economy, **socialism,** is characterized by government ownership and operation of major industries. This system shares some common beliefs with communism, in that socialists assert that major industries are too important to a society to be left in private hands and that government-owned businesses can serve the public's interest better than can private firms. However, socialism also allows private ownership in industries considered less crucial to social welfare, like retail shops, restaurants, and certain types of manufacturing facilities.

What's Ahead for Communism? Many formerly communist nations have undergone dramatic changes in recent years. Some of the most exciting developments have occurred in the republics that formerly composed the Soviet Union. These new nations have restructured their economies by introducing Western-style private enterprise systems. By decentralizing economic planning and sweetening incentives for workers, they are slowly shifting to market-driven systems. These revolutionary changes inspired *Forbes*—a magazine that widely promotes capitalism—to proclaim in Figure 3.7, "All hail the final victory of capitalism."

Economic reforms in the former communist countries haven't always progressed smoothly. Although many have opened their arms to Western entrepreneurs and businesses, these investors have often encountered difficulties such as official corruption, crime, and the persistence of bloated bureaucracies. Reducing the power of government-operated monopolies has also proved a difficult challenge.

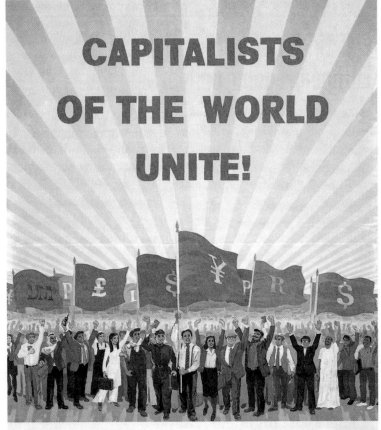

FIGURE 3.7
The Verdict from *Forbes*: Communism Gives Way to Capitalism

Today, communism remains firmly entrenched in just a few countries, like the People's Republic of China, Cuba, and North Korea. Even these staunchly communist countries, however, show signs of growing openness toward some of the benefits of private enterprise as possible solutions to their economic challenges. Since 1978, China has been shifting toward a more market-oriented economy. The national government has given local government and individual plant managers more say in business decisions and has permitted some small private businesses. In addition, households now have more control over agriculture, in contrast to the collectivized farms introduced with communism.

Another symbol of China's changing economic strategy accompanied the 1997 return of Hong Kong to Chinese rule. President Jiang Zemin's government has promised that Hong Kong's businesses will continue to operate in a private enterprise economic system. That decision has helped China to achieve the world's second-largest gross domestic product (GDP).[14]

Mixed Market Economies

In theory, private enterprise systems and planned economies adopt basically opposite approaches to operating economies. In practice, however, most countries implement **mixed market economies,** economic systems that display characteristics of both planned and market economies in varying degrees. In nations generally considered to have a private enterprise economy, government-owned firms frequently operate alongside private enterprises.

France has blended socialist and free enterprise policies for hundreds of years. The nation's banking, automobile, utility, aviation, steel, and railroad industries have traditionally been run as nationalized industries, controlled by the government. Meanwhile, a market economy flourishes in other industries. Over the past two decades, the French government has loosened its reins on state-owned companies, inviting both competition and private investment into industries previously operated as government monopolies.

The proportions of private and public enterprise can vary widely in mixed economies, and the mix frequently changes. Like France, dozens of countries have converted government-owned companies into privately held firms during the past two decades, in a trend known as **privatization**. Governments may privatize state-owned enterprises to raise funds and to improve their economies, believing that private corporations can manage and operate the businesses more cheaply and efficiently than government units can.

As the earth's growing population places greater demands on its water resources, some countries are privatizing their water supplies. The business of supplying water involves purifying it, distributing it, and handling wastewater. That worldwide business generates $400 billion annually, making it four-tenths the size of the oil industry—and it is expected to grow significantly over the next decade. The World Bank estimates that unless conditions change, about one person in three will be without clean water by 2025. When governments invite them, private industries are rising to the challenge. For example, France's Suez Lyonnaise des Eaux has upgraded the water supply in Buenos Aires. Under the agreement with the Buenos Aires government, Suez charges less for water and agreed to invest $3 billion to add water delivery to an additional 3 million mostly poor customers. To run the system more efficiently than the government did, Suez cut the workforce by half and replaced leaky pipes. By operating efficiently, it generates cash to upgrade the system. Suez also checked up on its major customers and found that many had been underpaying; it boosted revenues by making billing more accurate. Suez has followed up on its South American success by winning contracts in Atlanta, Casablanca, Jakarta, Manila, and other cities.[15]

Table 3.4 compares the three alternative economic systems on the basis of ownership and management of enterprises, rights to profits, employee rights, and worker incentives.

EVALUATING ECONOMIC PERFORMANCE

Ideally, an economic system should provide two important benefits for its citizens: a stable business environment and sustained growth. In a stable business environment, the overall supply of all goods and services is aligned with the overall demand for all goods and services. No wild fluctuations in price or availability complicate economic decisions. Consumers and businesses not only have access to ample supplies of desired products at affordable prices, but also have money to buy the items they demand.

Growth is another important economic goal. An ideal economy incorporates steady change directed toward continually expanding the amount of goods and services produced from the nation's resources. Growth leads to expanded job opportunities, improved wages, and a rising standard of living.

Flattening the Business Cycle

In reality, a nation's economy tends to flow through various stages of a business cycle: prosperity, recession, depression, and recovery. No true economic depressions have occurred in the United States since the 1930s, and most economists believe that

| Table 3.4 | Comparison of Alternative Economic Systems | | | |

System Features	Capitalism (Private Enterprise)	Planned Economies		
		Communism	**Socialism**	**Mixed Economy**
Ownership of enterprises	Businesses are owned privately, often by large numbers of people. Minimal government ownership leaves production in private hands.	The government owns the means of production with few exceptions, like small plots of land.	Basic industries are owned by the government, but private owners operate some small-scale enterprises.	A strong private sector blends with public enterprises. The private sector is larger than that under socialism.
Management of enterprises	Each enterprise is managed separately, either by its owners or by people who represent the owners, with minimal government interference.	Centralized management controls all state enterprises in line with 3- to 5-year plans. Planning now is being decentralized.	Significant government planning pervades socialist nations. State enterprises are managed directly by government bureaucrats.	Management of the private sector resembles that under capitalism. Professional managers are also common in state enterprises.
Rights to profits	Entrepreneurs and investors are entitled to all profits (minus taxes) that their firms earn. However, they are expected to operate in a socially responsible manner.	Profits are not acceptable under communism.	Only the private sector of a socialist economy generates profits.	Entrepreneurs and investors are entitled to private-sector profits, although they often must pay high taxes. State enterprises also typically are expected to break even or to provide financial returns to the government.
Rights of employees	The rights to choose one's occupation and to join a labor union have long been recognized.	Employee rights traditionally were limited in exchange for promised protection against unemployment.	Workers have the right to choose their occupations and to join labor unions. However, the government influences career decisions for many people.	Workers have the right of job choice and labor-union membership. Unions often become quite strong in these countries.
Worker incentives	Considerable incentives motivate people to perform at their highest levels.	Incentives are emerging in communist countries.	Incentives usually are limited in state enterprises but do motivate workers in the private sector.	Capitalist-style incentives operate in the private sector. More limited incentives influence public-sector activities.

society is capable of preventing future depressions through effective economic policies. Consequently, they expect a recession to give way to a period of economic recovery. Figure 3.8 shows the four stages of the business cycle.

Both business decisions and consumer buying patterns differ at each stage of the business cycle. In periods of economic *prosperity* such as that experienced in the U.S. during the past ten years, unemployment remains low, strong consumer confidence about the future leads to record purchases, and businesses expand to take advantage of marketplace opportunities. During *recessions*—cyclical economic contractions that last six months or longer—consumers frequently postpone major purchases and shift buying patterns toward basic, functional products carrying low prices. Businesses mirror these changes in the marketplace by slowing production, postponing

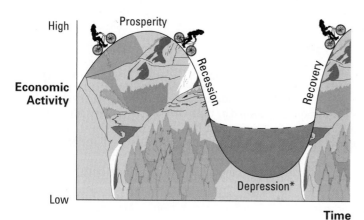

FIGURE 3.8
Four Stages of the Business Cycle
*Many economists believe that sufficient government tools are available to prevent the occurrence of a major depression. Thus, a recession would be followed by an economic recovery.

expansion plans, and reducing inventories. Should the economic slowdown continue in a downward spiral over an extended period of time, the economy falls into depression. Many Americans have grown up hearing stories from their grandparents who lived through the 1930s haunted by the specter of joblessness (a 25 percent unemployment rate at one point), idle factories, and despair about the future. However, some companies can actually manage to prosper during poor economic times, as discussed in the "Clicks and Mortar" box.

In the *recovery* stage of the business cycle, the economy emerges from recession and consumer spending picks up steam. Unemployment begins to decline, as business activity accelerates and firms seek additional workers to meet growing production demands. Gradually, the concerns of recession begin to disappear, and consumers start purchasing more discretionary items such as vacations, new automobiles, and other extravagances.

Economists observe several indicators to measure and evaluate how successfully an economic system provides both stability and growth. These variables include productivity as measured by GDP, rate of inflation or deflation, employment levels, and relative economic freedom.

Productivity and the Nation's Gross Domestic Product

An important concern for every economy is **productivity**, the relationship between the goods and services produced in a nation each year and the inputs needed to produce them. In general, as productivity rises, so does an economy's growth and the wealth of its citizens. In a recession, productivity stagnates or even declines.

As Chapter 1 explains, a commonly used measure of productivity is a country's **gross domestic product (GDP)**, the sum of all goods and services produced within a nation's boundaries each year. Economists calculate per capita GDP by summing the total output of all goods and services produced within a country and then dividing that output by the number of citizens. A country's GDP is an important indicator for measuring its business cycle, since a shrinking GDP indicates a recession. As the economy again begins to expand, GDP reflects this growth.

In the U.S., GDP is tracked by the Bureau of Economic Analysis (BEA), a division of the U.S. Department of Commerce. Current updates and historical data on the GDP are available at the BEA's Web site (www.bea.doc.gov).

Price-Level Changes

Another important indicator of an economy's stability is the general level of prices. For most of the 20th century, economic decision makers have concerned themselves with **inflation**, rising prices caused by a combination of excess consumer demand and increases in the costs of raw materials, component parts, human resources, and other factors of production. The first type is referred to as *demand-pull inflation*; the second type is called *cost-push inflation*. America's most severe inflationary period during the last half of the 20th century peaked in 1980, when general price levels jumped almost 14 percent in a single year.

In extreme cases, an economy may experience **hyperinflation**—an economic situation characterized by soaring prices. In 1993, for example, Ukrainian consumers suddenly saw the price of food, clothes, and housing soar 50 times what they had paid the previous year!

Inflation devalues money as persistent price increases reduce the amount of goods and services people can purchase with a given amount of money. This is bad news for people whose incomes do not keep up with inflation or who have most of their

Thai Union Frozen Products: Surviving in a Fishy Business

Background. Nearly 30 years ago, American seafood companies began looking for lower-cost canneries than those available at home, and Thai Union Frozen Products (TUF) was happy to fill that demand. With productive but cheap labor—about 60 cents an hour, as opposed to $4 an hour in American Samoa—TUF could supply American companies with all the canned and frozen fish they wanted, at a lower cost. In addition, owner Kraisorn Chansiri and his son Thiraphong developed a less expensive way to process smaller tuna, which were typically thrown away by American canneries. And the Chansiris avoided debt wherever possible.

What Happened? In the late 1990s, nearly every Asian country suffered a severe economic downturn. Thailand's currency, the baht, nearly sank under the debt of risky real estate deals, indebted finance companies, and overextended high-tech companies. The situation spelled doom to many Thai-based businesses, but not TUF. When the economic crisis came, TUF was already strong financially, with low supply costs and continued high demand.

The Response. At the height of the Asian recession, TUF reported a 51 percent increase in its net profits on sales that actually increased 36 percent over the previous year. How did this low-profile company in a decidedly unglamorous business manage not only to stay afloat but to prosper during a continent-wide recession? Although 96 percent of the company's revenues are in U.S. dollars,

from major importers like Chicken of the Sea, only 50 percent of its costs are. When the Thai baht tumbled, TUF's balance sheet remained relatively stable. In fact, as the economy leveled off, TUF's stock shares actually began to rise. "The crisis proved we had the right approach to our business," says Thiraphong Chansiri.

Today and Counting. With health-conscious U.S. consumers demanding more and more seafood, U.S. imports of canned tuna continue to grow by 15 percent a year. TUF is in a good position to be selling $1 billion of seafood within the next few years. "We are focused on being a low-cost producer," remarks Chansiri. As the company continues to prosper in very turbulent seas, Chansiri noted, "We can survive anything."

QUESTIONS FOR CRITICAL THINKING
1. What types of worldwide events might influence the demand for canned fish? The supply?
2. In what ways might Asia's economic recovery affect TUF?

Sources: "Company History," Thai Union Frozen Products Web site, **www.thaiuniongroup.com,** accessed March 15, 2001; Jervina Lao and Julian Gearing, "Bankok's Biggest Catch," *Asiaweek,* December 24, 1999, accessed at **www2.cnn.com**/ASIANOW/asiaweek/magazine; Justin Doebele, "The Big Tuna," *Forbes,* November 1, 1999, p. 386.

---

savings in investments paying a fixed rate of interest. Inflation can be good news to those whose income is rising, if they have debts at a fixed rate of interest. A home owner during inflationary times is paying off a fixed-rate mortgage with money that is worth less and less each year. Inflation helped a strong stock market to drive up the number of millionaires from 2 million in 1991 to over 7 million in just ten years. But, because of inflation, being a millionaire does not make a person as rich as it once did. In terms of buying power, $1 million today equals $173,000 four decades ago. Put another way, to live like a 1960s millionaire, you would need almost $6 million.[16]

When increased productivity keeps prices steady, it can have a major positive impact on an economy. In a low-inflation environment, businesses can make long-range plans without the constant worry of sudden inflationary shocks. Low interest rates encourage firms to invest in research and development and capital improvements, both of which are likely to produce productivity gains. Consumers can purchase growing stocks of goods and services with the same amount of money, and low interest rates encourage major acquisitions like new homes and autos.

Although falling prices, or deflation, might seem like a positive economic indicator, this is not necessarily true. A wave of consumer pessimism about the future might drive down demand and prices as people postpone purchases, increase savings, and restrict spending to wait out the expected crisis. Businesses would lose money on the lower-priced goods or be stuck with inventories they are unable to sell. These trends would likely prompt management decision makers to scale back production plans. The results could include layoffs, declines in the value of personal investments such as homes, and other symptoms of a recession.

In the U.S., the government tracks changes in price levels with the **Consumer Price Index (CPI),** which measures the monthly average change in prices of goods and services. The federal Bureau of Labor Statistics (BLS) calculates the CPI monthly

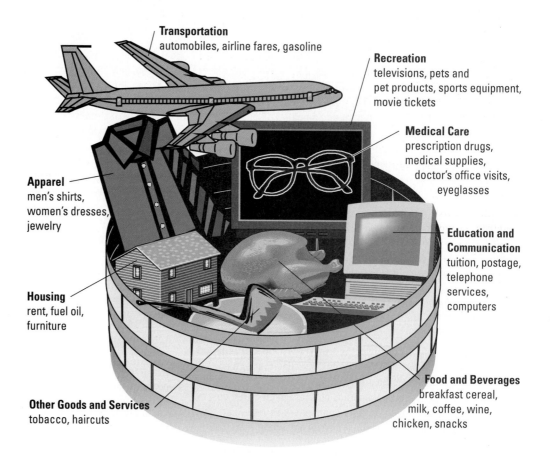

Transportation
automobiles, airline fares, gasoline

Recreation
televisions, pets and pet products, sports equipment, movie tickets

Apparel
men's shirts, women's dresses, jewelry

Medical Care
prescription drugs, medical supplies, doctor's office visits, eyeglasses

Education and Communication
tuition, postage, telephone services, computers

Housing
rent, fuel oil, furniture

Food and Beverages
breakfast cereal, milk, coffee, wine, chicken, snacks

Other Goods and Services
tobacco, haircuts

**FIGURE 3.9
What's in the Market Basket for the CPI?**

based on prices of a *market basket*—a compilation of the goods and services most commonly purchased by urban consumers. Figure 3.9 shows the categories included in the CPI market basket.[17] Each month, BLS representatives visit thousands of stores, service establishments, rental units, and doctors' offices all over the U.S. to price the multitude of items in the CPI market basket. They compile the data to create the CPI. So, the CPI provides a running measurement of changes in consumer prices.

The CPI is not a perfect measure of inflation. Critics complain that it may actually overstate inflation by not fully accounting for changes in the goods that people buy. If breakfast cereal gets more expensive, many consumers will switch to toast, and the amount they spend will not increase as fast as a simple measure of cereal's price would suggest. The CPI also does not directly measure the change in costs to businesses. A *Producer Price Index (PPI)* is another economic indicator used to track prices. In contrast to the CPI, a PPI looks at prices from the seller's perspective. The BLS computes three major categories of PPIs:

1. The PPI for *finished goods* measures the prices sellers obtained for items that will not undergo further processing, including goods sold to consumers and machinery sold to businesses.
2. The PPI for *intermediate goods* measures the prices sellers obtained for items that will require further processing, including ingredients for food products, components to be assembled into finished goods, and boxes for shipping items.
3. The PPI for *crude goods* measures the prices sellers obtained for raw materials to be used in making parts or finished goods.

Employment Levels

People need money in order to purchase the goods and services produced in an economy. Because most consumers earn that money by working, the number of people in a nation who currently have jobs is an important indicator of both overall stability and growth. People who are actively looking for work but unable to find jobs are counted in unemployment statistics.

Economists refer to a nation's **unemployment rate** as an indicator of its economic health. The unemployment rate is usually expressed as a percentage of the total workforce. The total labor force includes all people who are willing and available to work at the going market wage, whether they currently have jobs or are seeking work. The U.S. Department of Labor, which tracks unemployment rates, also includes so-called *discouraged workers* in the total labor force. These individuals want to work but have given up looking for jobs.

Unemployment can be grouped into the four categories shown in Figure 3.10: frictional, seasonal, cyclical, and structural unemployment. *Frictional unemployment* applies to members of the workforce who are temporarily not working but are looking for jobs. This pool of potential workers includes new graduates, people who have left jobs for any reason and are looking for others, and former workers who have decided to return to the labor force. *Seasonal unemployment* is the joblessness of workers in a seasonal industry. Construction workers and farm laborers typically must contend with bouts of seasonal unemployment when wintry conditions make work unavailable.

Cyclical unemployment includes people who are out of work because of a cyclical contraction in the economy. During periods of economic expansion, overall employment is likely to rise, but as growth slows and a recession begins, unemployment levels commonly rise. At such times, even workers with good job skills may face temporary unemployment.

Structural unemployment applies to people who remain unemployed for long periods of time, often with little hope of finding new jobs like their old ones. This situation may arise because these workers lack the necessary skills for available jobs or because the skills they have are no longer in demand. For instance, technological developments have increased the demand for people with computer-related skills but have created structural unemployment among many types of manual laborers.

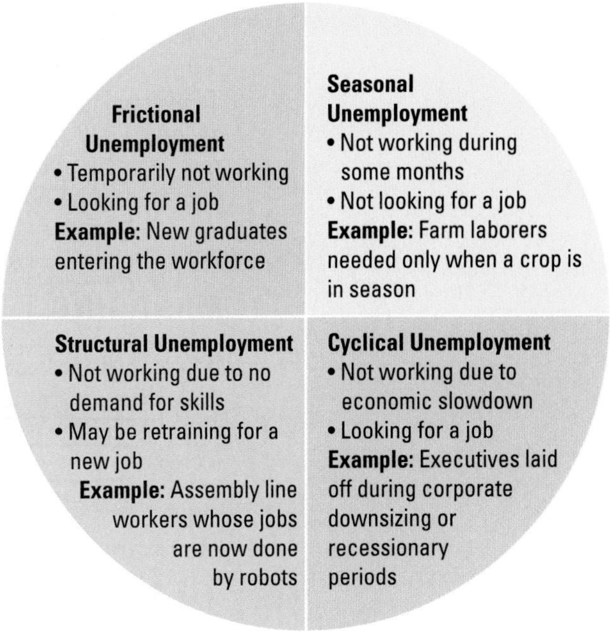

Frictional Unemployment
• Temporarily not working
• Looking for a job
Example: New graduates entering the workforce

Seasonal Unemployment
• Not working during some months
• Not looking for a job
Example: Farm laborers needed only when a crop is in season

Structural Unemployment
• Not working due to no demand for skills
• May be retraining for a new job
Example: Assembly line workers whose jobs are now done by robots

Cyclical Unemployment
• Not working due to economic slowdown
• Looking for a job
Example: Executives laid off during corporate downsizing or recessionary periods

FIGURE 3.10
Four Types of Unemployment

Relative Economic Freedom

Some economists have suggested another way to measure and compare the world's economies. They advocate looking at the *relative economic freedom* enjoyed in each country.

The Fraser Institute, a Canadian economic think tank, has developed a formula for measuring relative economic freedom by comparing 23 economic variables in categories such as property rights, government regulation, and restrictions on trade. In the most recent year of the study, Hong Kong and Singapore were tied for having the most economic freedom. The other countries in the top ten were, in order, New Zealand, the United States, the United Kingdom, Ireland, Canada, Australia, the Netherlands, Luxembourg, and Switzerland. In last place among the 123 nations ranked in the study was Myanmar. Other nations at the bottom of the list were the Democratic Republic of Congo, Sierra Leone, and Rwanda.

The findings suggest a positive relationship between a country's economic freedom and its economic prosperity. The countries that score in the top one-fifth in terms of economic freedom enjoyed an average GDP per person of over $18,000 and an average growth rate of 1.6 percent. Among countries in the bottom one-fifth, the average GDP per person was less than $1,700 and the economy was declining at a rate of 1.3 percent annually. In addition, average life expectancy is much longer in the top-ranked nations.[18]

MANAGING THE ECONOMY'S PERFORMANCE

Besides just measuring economic growth and evaluating stability, economists provide tools that governments use to manage their countries' economic performance. A national government can use both monetary policy and fiscal policy to fight inflation, increase employment levels, and encourage growth.

Monetary Policy

A common method of influencing economic activity is **monetary policy,** government action to increase or decrease the money supply and change banking requirements and interest rates to influence spending by altering bankers' willingness to make loans. An *expansionary monetary policy* increases the money supply in an effort to cut the cost of borrowing, which encourages business decision makers to make new investments, in turn stimulating employment and economic growth. By contrast, a *restrictive monetary policy* reduces the money supply to curb rising prices, over-expansion, and concerns about overly rapid economic growth.

In the U.S., the Federal Reserve System ("the Fed") is responsible for formulating and implementing the nation's monetary policy. It is headed by a chairperson (currently Alan Greenspan) and a Board of Governors, each of whom is appointed by the president. All national banks must be members of this system and keep some percentage of their checking and savings funds on deposit at the Fed.

The Fed's Board of Governors uses a number of tools to regulate the economy. By changing the required percentage of checking and savings accounts that banks must deposit with the Fed, the governors can expand or shrink funds available to lend. The Fed also lends money to member banks, which, in turn, make loans at higher interest rates to business and individual borrowers. By changing the interest rates charged to commercial banks, the Fed affects the interest rates charged to borrowers and, consequently, their willingness to borrow.

The Fed has a number of other monetary policy tools at its disposal. Each of these is described in detail in Chapter 19.

Fiscal Policy

Governments also influence economic activities through taxation and spending decisions. Through revenues and expenditures, the government implements **fiscal policy,** the second technique that officials use to control inflation, reduce unemployment, improve the general welfare of citizens, and encourage economic growth. Increased taxes may restrict economic activities, whereas lower taxes and increased government spending usually boost spending and profits, cut unemployment rates, and fuel economic expansion.

Each year the president proposes a budget for the federal government, a plan for how it will raise and spend money during the coming year, and presents it to Congress for approval. A typical federal budget proposal undergoes months of deliberation and many modifications before receiving approval. The major sources of federal revenues and categories of expenditures are shown in Figure 3.11.

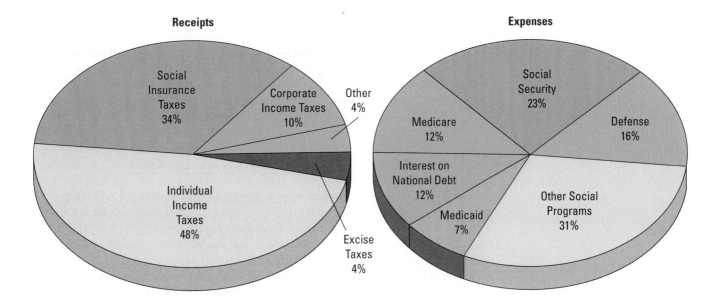

FIGURE 3.11
U.S. Federal Budget: Where the Money Comes From and Where It Goes

The federal budget includes a number of different spending categories, ranging from defense and social security to interest payments on the national debt. The decisions about what to include in the budget have a direct effect on various sectors of the economy. During a recession, the federal government may approve major spending on interstate highway repairs to improve transportation and increase employment in the construction industry. In the mid-1990s, the government launched a drive to connect public schools to the Internet. Supported by federal dollars, public schools spent $27 billion over five years. Such spending provided revenues for companies selling computer hardware and software and may have reduced the amount of money spent on books and staff.[19]

The primary sources of government funds to cover the costs of the annual budget are taxes, fees, and borrowing. Both the overall amount of these funds and their specific combination have major effects on the economic well-being of the nation. One way governments raise money is to impose taxes on sales and income. Increasing taxes reduce people's and businesses' incomes, leaving them with less money to spend. Such a move can reduce inflation, but overly high taxes can also slow economic growth. So, governments try to establish a level of taxation that enables them to provide the services that citizens want without slowing economic growth too severely.

In Mexico, President Vicente Fox promised strong government efforts to improve education and eliminate poverty. To fulfill these promises, Fox must improve his country's taxation system. Currently, one-third of Mexico's tax revenues come from the oil industry, so tax revenues swing up and down along with oil prices. Fox is considering measures to broaden the tax base, perhaps by eliminating loopholes that exempt many businesses and by lowering tax rates to encourage more citizens to file accurate tax returns. Such changes are badly needed, because the share of GDP Mexico collects as taxes is small by global standards.[20]

Taxes don't always generate enough funds to cover every spending project the government hopes to undertake. When the government spends more than the amount of money it raises through taxes, it creates a **budget deficit**. To cover the deficit, the U.S. government has borrowed money by selling Treasury bills, Treasury notes, and Treasury bonds to investors. All of this borrowing makes up the **national debt**. Currently, the U.S. national debt is about $5.6 trillion, or more than $20,000 for every U.S. citizen.[21] Even though the

BUSINESS DIRECTORY

➤ **monetary policy**   *government action to increase or decrease the money supply and change banking requirements and interest rates to influence bankers' willingness to make loans.*

➤ **fiscal policy**   *government spending and taxation decisions designed to control inflation, reduce unemployment, improve the general welfare of citizens, and encourage economic growth.*

➤ **budget deficit**   *funding shortfall that results when the government spends more than the amount of money it raises through taxes and fees.*

federal government spent more money than it received from taxes and fees during every year through the last three decades of the 20th century, over half of the nation's state governments are required by their constitutions to balance their annual budgets.

In recent decades, citizen groups and politicians have called for a halt to the long-time practice of borrowing to fund government spending in excess of its income. Instead, they advocate a **balanced budget**, in which the total revenues raised by taxes equal total proposed spending for the year. By 1998, the federal government accomplished a feat not experienced since 1969—a balanced budget. The government reached this goal through a combination of healthy income-tax receipts made possible by a prosperous, technology-driven economy and spending cuts in such areas as defense and welfare payments.

Achieving a balanced budget does not, however, erase the federal debt—it must be paid off. The Treasury Department in 2000 began paying down the debt at a rate averaging about $14 billion per month. Politicians continue to debate how fast the nation should use revenues to reduce its debt. For households, reducing or eliminating debt is usually beneficial. But for the federal government, the decision is more complex. When the government raises money by selling Treasury bills, it makes safe investments available to investors worldwide. If foreign investors cannot buy Treasury notes, they might turn to other countries, reducing the amount of money flowing into the United States. U.S. government debt has also been used as a basis for pricing more risky investments. If the government issues less debt, the interest rates it commands would be higher, raising the overall cost of debt to private borrowers. In addition, the government uses the funds from borrowing, at least in part, to invest in such publicly desirable services as education and scientific research. To the extent that the economy needs such public services, debt reduction may not always be the most beneficial use of government funds. However, others argue that paying down the national debt will free up more money to be invested by individuals and businesses.[22] For details about the current and past amounts of the national debt, see the Bureau of the Public Debt Web site (www.publicdebt.treas.gov).

The U.S. Economy: These Are the Good Old Days

During the 10-year period since 1991, the U.S. economy enjoyed the longest period of economic expansion in its history. Even though an economic downturn occurred during the final months of the Clinton Administration, GDP continued to increase, although at a lower annual rate of about 1 percent. Although Americans grew concerned about declines in the stock market averages and reports of reduction in consumer and business spending that meant falling profits for hundreds of firms, most people continue to believe that these *are* the good old days. Longer-term indicators continue to paint a very positive picture of sustained growth and relative economic stability.

Continuing Growth.   Despite the recent slow down, the U.S. GDP has been enjoying a strong cycle of growth since the latest expansion began over a decade ago. Fueling much of this growth is the continuing success of companies in health care, drugs, energy, and some high-tech industries. In addition, international trade, discussed in the next chapter, has helped to fuel demand for U.S. goods and investment in U.S. business. Corporate profits rose 14 percent in one year, signaling not only an increase in productivity but strong payoffs from investments in expansion programs. Investors have responded by pushing the U.S. stock market to historic highs. The Dow Jones stock index of major U.S. companies has tripled since the expansion began, and the Nasdaq's index of smaller companies, which includes many high-tech stocks, has risen fivefold.[23]

For individual businesses, economic growth opens new doors. Harvard Business School student Joseph Ngai and former consultant Jeffrey Kaplan took advantage of the Internet boom of the 1990s to launch Campus24, a service that offers online auctions to college students. The company serves a significant market, considering that a growing share of the population is going to college and that, by a recent estimate, college students spend over $90 billion every year on living expenses and entertainment. Also, this segment of the population spends plenty of time online. To earn revenues, Campus24 sells advertising and charges sellers a fee. The site quickly attracted the attention of CollegeClub.com, which offers voice mail, e-mail, and chat groups and wanted to add auctions. CollegeClub purchased Campus24 in exchange for stock in the auction business. Such transactions were possible because investors were optimistic about investments in the information economy.[24]

Keeping Inflation in Check   In recent years, both the CPI and PPI have reported little or no inflation in the U.S. economy. The CPI rose by 6 percent in 1990, but by the end of the decade CPI figures had dropped to 2 percent. Growth in the PPIs also shrank as the 21st century began. The PPI for finished goods was 3 percent, for intermediate goods it was less than half a percent, and the PPI for crude goods actually fell by almost 4 percent.[25] Given suggestions that the CPI may actually overstate inflation by not fully accounting for changes in the goods people buy, inflation experienced in the U.S. may have been close to zero.

Much of the credit for this modest inflation goes to greater productivity and to the Fed's monetary policy.[26] Productivity rose strongly during the past decade, as companies began to enjoy the fruits of their investments in information technology and automation.[27] In addition, the Fed has set interest rates to keep inflation under control. Immigration has also helped to moderate inflation in the United States by increasing the supply of workers and slowing wage increases.

Continuing Strong Employment   U.S. firms are employing more people than ever, with over 19 million new jobs created since the early 1990s. A million of those jobs are in high-technology industries, where wages are far outpacing growth in the cost of living.[28] In recent years, the national unemployment rate has remained around 4 percent.

But some U.S. companies and industries are still making structural changes to their employment practices. Layoffs during the last two years of the 20th century numbered over 670,000 workers a year, six times more than in 1989.[29] But although layoffs continue in the early years of the 21st century, a recent study revealed that workers who are laid off are almost twice as likely to get a new job within a month as they were in 1992.[30] One reason may be the greater number of jobs available through temporary-help agencies. As the number of such jobs has grown, some workers who might otherwise be looking for employment sign up to work as temps.[31] In addition, many companies are changing, rather than reducing, their employment. Elcotel closed a factory making pay phones and laid off the assemblers working there, but at the same time, it was hiring engineers and software developers to design pay-phone software. It couldn't transfer employees into these jobs, because the assemblers didn't have the necessary skills.[32]

If any part of the country is well acquainted with how technology can bring both volatility and opportunity, it must be California's Silicon Valley, where the boom in PCs gave way to a boom in Internet applications. Today, as investors become impatient with money-losing dot-coms, some Silicon Valley companies are shutting their doors even as others get started. Don McInnes decided to celebrate the beginning of the new century by launching a new career. He left his marketing job at a traditional software company to work for a financial services Web site. Within six months, the company had changed both its strategy and its management, and McInnes found himself back in the job market. He tried starting his own company, then the following April landed a job at a new firm called Brightware, which planned to raise money by selling stock. But dot-com stock prices were tumbling, and Brightware decided it had to cut costs. Again, McInnes was laid off. He posted his resume on the Internet, and before long 50 companies had contacted him. A month after he left

Experts are already calling the early years of the new century "the good old days," and with good reason. The U.S. economy is experiencing record strength, including a 30-year low in unemployment rates. The Internet has provided tremendous opportunities for entrepreneurs, a few of whom became multimillionaires overnight. But the millions aren't flowing equally among all demographic groups. Although the Internet has ushered in what some call "colorblind commerce," it seems that African Americans still lag behind in opportunity.

"There's that adjustment thing," explains Dwayne Walker, CEO of the Seattle-based Internet company ShopNow.com. He's describing the reaction he sometimes gets when he meets with investors and others in person, instead of over the Internet. "You can tell that they're thinking, 'He's black,'" he says. It's a vicious economic circle. Investors like doing business with people whom they already know, or have something in common with—say, a shared school, previous employer, or geographic region. They create networks this way, which remain intact as they get involved with start-ups. The trouble is, many of the graduate business schools are predominantly white; and many Internet start-ups are born in California's Silicon Valley, which is also predominantly white. The number of prominent African American executives in existing companies is still relatively small, which means there are fewer mentors and role models for young African American entrepreneurs. "People in technology are not prejudiced," says Frank Levy, a general partner at Wasabi Fund, which bankrolls Internet start-ups. "They're open and tolerant. But it's easiest to make money with people you know."

Where does that leave African American businesspeople like Walker who want a slice of the Internet pie? Walker, who headed up marketing for Microsoft's corporate operating system and database software business before founding ShopNow.com, which links 20,000 merchants with consumers, argues that although there are hurdles to clear, money speaks louder than skin color. "Ultimately, the green thing is bigger than the black thing," he quips. Jerry Johnson, an African American entrepreneur who runs the Small Business Exchange, which gathers and publishes data on opportunities for minorities, agrees. "The color issue is out of the picture. What determines whether people will do business has to do with what's on the Web site."

QUESTIONS FOR CRITICAL THINKING

1. In what ways could the economy benefit by creating opportunities for greater participation in e-commerce ventures by African Americans and other minorities?
2. What steps could existing Internet companies take to attract African American employees, mentor them, and encourage entrepreneurship?

Sources: Small Business Exchange Web site, **www.sbeinc.com,** accessed March 2, 2001; John D. McKinnon, "Unemployment Declined to a 30-Year-Low," *The Wall Street Journal,* February 7, 2000, pp. A2, A10; Doug Levy, "Colorblind Commerce?" *USA Today,* August 17, 1999, pp. 1B, 2B.

Brightware, McInnes had completed 15 interviews and was preparing to decide on his next marketing management job.[33] However, some segments of the population are just beginning to take advantage of opportunities in technology, as discussed in "Business Hits and Misses" box.

Growing Budget Surplus   The strong economy has also helped the federal government to accomplish its goal of balancing the budget. Three decades passed between the 1969 balanced budget and the budget surplus of 1999. Several factors contributed to this achievement. First, reductions in government spending helped slash the deficit by more than $400 billion over five years. The strong economy helped, too. As individual households and business earnings grow, they pay increasing tax bills.

Estimates for future budget surpluses vary widely because no one can be sure whether the government will continue taxing and spending at current rates. The Congressional Budget Office recently estimated that by 2010, the surplus could exceed $1.9 trillion. But the temptation to allocate budget surpluses to fund additional programs is great; if Congress votes to increase funding for Medicare and Social Security, and if it passes tax cuts, the surplus is expected to shrink to a few hundred billion dollars. Failing to continue spending cuts could bring the surplus down to zero.[34]

Can the Good Times Last Forever?   At present the U.S. economy retains much of its recent strength. But future prosperity is not guaranteed. Attempts by the Fed to curb inflation with interest rate hikes can discourage business borrowing and related growth. Also, as the high-tech industry becomes more mature, its growth is beginning to slow. Investors may react by refusing to bid up the stocks. This is an especially serious risk for Internet start-ups, which have encountered major problems recently in raising money through stock offerings. And if stock prices level off or dip, the impact will spread widely—to the employees who receive stocks as part of their earnings as well as the many households that have savings and retirement plans invested in the stock market. Also, buoyed by the expansion, Americans have been borrowing more and more, and bankruptcy filings have climbed, even without a recession.[35]

Another concern is renewed inflation. The low unemployment rate pressures employers to raise wages to attract and keep workers. In Steubenville, Ohio, a low jobless rate keeps Telespectrum Worldwide from operating at full capacity because it can't find enough people to fill all its telemarketing jobs. The company increased wage rates, gives raises for those who stay on the job beyond three months, and pays bonuses for bringing in new employees.[36] Pressures to increase wages, without corresponding growth in productivity, would cause profits to drop. Firms might respond by laying off workers. Business cutbacks and rising unemployment would slow overall economic growth. The final section of this chapter examines some other economic challenges that lie ahead.

GLOBAL ECONOMIC CHALLENGES OF THE 21ST CENTURY

Businesses face a number of important economic challenges in this new century. As the economies of countries around the globe become increasingly interconnected, governments and businesses must compete throughout the world. Although no one can predict the future, both governments and businesses will likely need to meet several challenges to maintain their global competitiveness. This section overviews four key challenges: the continuing shift toward a global information economy, the aging of the world's population, continuing emphasis on improving quality and customer service, and efforts to enhance the competitiveness of every country's workforce.

The Shift toward a Global Information Economy

The economic growth that began in the industrial revolution of the late 1700s was driven by manufacturing advances that enabled businesses to speed mass production of goods. But the economic growth of the 21st century is propelled by technological advances that enable businesses to use, manage, and control information more effectively. Since the 1970s, U.S. businesses have increased their purchases of information technology at a rate of 25 percent a year, spending about one-third or more of their total investments on this technology.[37] As they learn to establish processes that take advantage of the new technology, they are working smarter than before, using brains, not brawn, to push economic growth.

American companies are leading the information revolution. According to the Department of Commerce, by 2006 half of all American workers will hold jobs in information technology or in industries that "intensively utilize information technology, products, and services."[38] Computers enhance productivity in sectors from agriculture to manufacturing as companies figure out new applications. Mitec Controls has applied information technology to the old-fashioned business of conducting fire-safety inspections of buildings. The traditional approach was for inspectors to carry a paper checklist as they walked through buildings. At Mitec, employees now carry handheld computers equipped with bar-code scanners. They scan codes on equipment like sprinkler systems, fire extinguishers, and smoke detectors, and they type notes into the computer. They transmit the data electronically to the company's information network, where Mitec's software prepares reports. Customers can go online to download the results. Mitec saves money by using relatively inexpensive equipment and reducing the time to prepare reports. It also has created a new source of revenue: it licenses its technology to other inspectors.[39]

Investments in information technology have paid off for U.S. businesses by increasing their global competitiveness. Worker productivity is rising, customer service is improving, and production costs in many industries are shrinking or remaining constant. Some analysts believe that businesses have enjoyed the fruits of their investments in networked computers, and when those gains are no longer contributing as much to the expansion, the future holds more returns from investments in the Internet economy.[40] Companies are setting up Web sites to publish specifications and using Internet browser technology to search for the best prices. Healtheon WebMD is creating an online marketplace designed to bring together doctors, hospitals, patients, and insurance companies. This source of efficiency is only now becoming widespread. In the first four years of the millennium, the share of Internet transactions is expected to grow from half a percent to 10 percent of all business-to-business sales. One analyst summed up the advantages of using the Internet to improve marketplace efficiency this way: "There are literally trillions of dollars of efficiencies that will be wrung out of this economy."[41]

Even though the U.S. leads the world in information technology, other nations are quick to learn from the U.S. experience, and the information economy is becoming more global. Not only can information technology improve efficiency in operations, but it can also improve the speed of learning, so this development may spread faster than other worldwide trends. Businesses in Europe and Asia are investing hundreds of billions of dollars in information technology each year. Analysts expect that the number of Internet users in Asia and Western Europe will more than double during the first five years of this century. In India, the software industry is growing at a rate of more than 50 percent a year. Semiconductors—the "brains" inside a computer— are also a global growth industry. The real gains will come as companies begin to use these investments to improve productivity. Valeo, a French maker of automobile parts, invested $300 million in modern technology, including a Web site that lets the company accept bids from suppliers. The investments are essential for keeping accounts with big customers like Ford and General Motors.[42] In Japan, Askul, which supplies office products, lets companies order on the Internet and offers next-day delivery. Thanks to the improved efficiency of handling online orders, Askul has been able to double its sales without hiring more employees.[43]

As in the U.S., the big challenge worldwide is to find enough qualified human workers. However, the U.S. may be losing its edge in this regard. Indian universities, for example, graduate twice as many engineers each year as the U.S. does. And even at American universities, many of the students enrolled there come from overseas. The number of doctoral degrees in science and engineering has been growing, and two-thirds of that growth comes from foreign students.[44]

Effect of an Aging Population

As we see in Chapter 1, most nations are experiencing some graying of their populations. In the U.S., the median age has passed 35 years, and the baby boomers— people born between 1946 and 1965—make up the largest population group. These people will approach retirement age over the next two decades. By 2025 over 62 million Americans will be 65 or older—nearly double today's number.[45] Contributing to the aging of the population is the trend toward longer life spans. In the U.S., life expectancy at birth has grown over the past century, from 45 years for babies born at the beginning of the 20th century to more than 75 years for babies born this year. So, the trend toward a large elderly population is expected to continue. Longer life spans are a worldwide trend, with life expectancy in India growing from 50 to 60 years over the past three decades and in Mexico it is approaching the rates seen in the developed nations.[46]

An aging population increases the demand for health care, retirement benefits, and other support services. This trend could put budgetary pressure on governments, as they struggle to meet these changing demands. Expectations for government services are growing along with the elderly population. Since the mid-1980s, as hospitals have shortened patient stays, Medicare spending on home health care, skilled nursing homes, and rehabilitation care has skyrocketed. For people over 85, average spending for such services has grown almost tenfold in inflation-adjusted dollars. This increase has contributed to a doubling of Medicare spending per beneficiary since the 1980s.[47]

Employers also will have to deal with pressing issues due to the aging of their workforces: retirement, worker disabilities, and insurance. Baby boomers make up about half of the nation's workforce, and many are now in their mid-50s.[48] As they begin to retire, U.S. businesses will need to find ways to replace their skills in the workplace. Generation Xers, people born between 1966 and 1976, are a much smaller population group, so employers face the possibility of significant labor shortages early in the 21st century.

The aging of the workforce also provides some benefits to the economy. One is that employers have a pool of available—and experienced—workers, many of them willing and able to return to work on a part- or full-time basis. Another is that the relatively high age of the workforce helps to hold down unemployment rates because on average, older workers change jobs less often than their younger colleagues and spend less time looking for work.[49] In fact, the average U.S. worker holds about nine jobs between the ages of 18 and 34, holding over half those jobs by the age of 24.[50]

Demand for many goods and services will also change as the baby boomers age. Retired consumers will probably demand fewer large homes, SUVs, child-care services, and bank loans. They will, however, have a growing need for medical care, insurance, travel services, and retirement housing. Successful businesses will respond to these changing marketing opportunities.

Companies that currently offer goods and services geared toward the needs of young consumers aren't likely to disappear, of course, but they may need to adjust their strategies. They may shift their focuses toward overseas markets in search of continued growth opportunities. Many Asian countries have relatively large numbers of young consumers who could fill the gap left by the aging U.S. baby boom generation.

Although the U.S. population is aging and many people are retiring at younger ages from jobs they hold, a surprising number take full- or part-time positions with other firms or start their own businesses. This growing number of well-trained, experienced workers represents an important source of human resources.

Improving Quality and Customer Service

Companies hoping to compete in the global economy of the 21st century will have to continue improving product quality and customer service. Technology can help firms develop exciting new products or improve existing ones. Gallo is using technology to improve the quality of its premium Gallo of Sonoma line of wines. Among its rows of grapevines, the winery has installed poles mounted with solar panels and wind vanes. These mini-weather stations use radio signals to transmit up-to-the-minute data on wind patterns, temperature, and humidity levels. A computer analyzes the data and sends signals when conditions might require action. Employees can pinpoint the problems with a global positioning satellite system that identifies each area of the vineyard. Because Gallo can intervene quickly if vines are threatened, the quality of the grapes is higher, and consumers are willing to pay as much as $60 for a bottle of Gallo of Sonoma wine.[51]

Customer service is another important aspect of a competitive strategy that defines how a firm treats its customers. Businesses show that they value exceptional customer service when they create the easiest possible systems for customers to order and receive their products. They also design systems such as customer-service hot lines to resolve product-related customer complaints. Clothing retailer Lands' End has maintained its reputation for quality service by providing personal help for online shoppers. Customers can click on a button that lets them type messages to a Lands' End operator. When Julia Deputy wanted advice on choosing the right size of cargo pants for her daughter, she traded messages with an operator. Before long, Deputy had completed her $25 transaction and was delighted with the experience. Cameraworld recently added voice communications capability at its Web site so that visitors can talk to a customer service representative. One of every four persons who use the voice capability complete a purchase, whereas only 3 percent of the people who visit the site buy anything.[52]

Another firm that lets customers get immediate answers is 1-800-Flowers.com. The online florist offers three options for customers with questions. They can telephone the company, submit e-mail messages, or sign on to eQ&A Chat. Company representatives monitor questions as they come in to the chat site, and each rep handles about six sessions at a time. The representative reads a question and types in an answer; then while the recipient is reading the reply, the rep moves on to the next question. Handling inquiries in this way is more efficient than fielding phone calls, and it also makes customers happy because they don't have to leave the Internet to get a reply. According to Marc Noel, the supervisor for the chat operators at 1-800-Flowers.com, this kind of customer service is essential because people who buy flowers online expect the process to be finished in minutes. They don't want to wait around for someone to get back to them with details.[53]

Maintaining the Competitiveness of the Workforce

Success in contemporary business hinges on whether a company creates an environment that encourages employees to innovate and follow up on new ideas. Internal systems must then quickly move new ideas through product development and into the marketplace.

Successful innovation requires workers to be trained to use the company's technology effectively. Employees must have the skills to control, combine, and supervise work operations, and they must be motivated to provide the best-quality products and highest levels of customer service. Ericsson, Sweden's successful telecom equipment supplier, applies these lessons to its operations in Raleigh, North Carolina, where unemployment is below the national average. The company has expanded onsite training so that its employees can develop their skills in both engineering and management. The firm's staffing manager, Ken Dean, explains, "This expands the pool of people we can hire" as managers. Instead of looking outside the company for people with management backgrounds, it can develop them internally from its current workforce. Dean is also convinced that this policy makes Ericsson employees want to stay and take advantage of these development opportunities.[54]

The skills and education levels that businesses demand of their workforces are changing in the information economy. Effective workers must now be able to ask appropriate questions, define problems, combine information from many different sources, and deal with topics that stretch across disciplines and cultures. Companies are investing in training programs in order to develop the worker skills they need.

A well-trained and highly motivated workforce benefits the overall economy as well as individual businesses. Increasingly, education is becoming essential for high-paying jobs. College graduates not only earn more, but their much-demanded skills help to keep them employed. U.S. college graduates are half as likely to be unemployed as high school graduates.[55] In the U.S., education levels have grown over the past two decades. Among workers aged 25 to 54, only four in ten had high-school diplomas in 1950. By 2002, the number had grown to nine of every ten employees, and the share of workers with college degrees has risen from 7 percent to 29 percent.[56]

Recognizing the importance of developing the workforce, governments around the world often take the lead in this cause. In Ireland, economic success is largely tied to government investment in education and training. Among the world's countries, Ireland ranks second in terms of the share of national income spent on public education. In addition, the country has lowered barriers to foreign investment and promotes its business-friendly conditions, as the ad for Ireland's Industrial Development Agency shows in Figure 3.12. The combination of a well-educated workforce and friendly economic policies has lured companies such as Dell Computer, Microsoft, and Intel to Ireland's shores. Today the nation enjoys low unemployment, strong growth, and average income about the same as that of Britain.[57] In today's global marketplace, similar government initiatives may be required from other countries seeking to develop competitive workforces.

CREATING A LONG-TERM GLOBAL STRATEGY

No country is an economic island in today's global economy. Not only is an ever-increasing stream of goods and services crossing national borders, but many businesses have become true multinational firms, operating manufacturing plants and other facilities around the world. As global trade and investments grow, events in one nation can reverberate around the globe. For instance, recent forecasts of record sales by the U.S. computer industry were proven incorrect when a major earthquake in Taiwan interrupted the production of key components like computer chips and motherboards. Producers of PCs delayed the launch of new models and worried about maintaining expected profit levels. Buyers have grown accustomed to steady declines in computer prices, and computer makers had to rethink business strategies that had been based on a world of falling chip prices. The Taiwanese earthquake shook businesses across the ocean.[58]

Despite the risks of world trade, global expansion can offer huge opportunities to U.S. firms. With U.S. residents accounting for less than 1 in every 20 of the world's 6 billion people, growth-oriented American companies cannot afford to ignore the world market. U.S. businesses also benefit from the lower labor costs in other parts of the world, and some are finding successful niches importing goods made by foreign manufacturers. In addition, the huge purchasing power of the United States makes this market desirable for foreign companies. As we saw in the "Clicks and Mortar" box earlier, one of these is Thai Union Frozen Products, which sells frozen and canned seafood. The company keeps its canned-tuna business profitable by operating in Bangkok, where wages are low, and by using new technology for processing relatively small fish. It sells its exports to the United States under the name Chicken of the Sea, the second-biggest tuna brand after its U.S. competitor StarKist.[59] With strong competition from companies like Thai Union, the biggest challenge for U.S. businesses in the 21st century is to develop long-term strategies for global competitiveness that minimize risk while maximizing these opportunities.

FIGURE 3.12
Government Spending Aimed at Business Development in Ireland

WHAT'S AHEAD

Global competition is a key factor in today's economy. In Chapter 4 we focus on the global dimensions of business. We cover basic concepts of doing business internationally and examine how nations can position themselves to benefit from the global economy. Then we describe the specific methods used by individual businesses to expand beyond their national borders and compete successfully in the global marketplace.

➤ Summary of Learning Goals

1. Distinguish between microeconomics and macroeconomics.

Microeconomics is the study of economic behavior among individual consumers, families, and businesses whose collective behavior in the marketplace determines the quantity of goods and services demanded and supplied at different prices. By contrast, macroeconomics is the study of the broader economic picture and how an economic system maintains and allocates its resources; it focuses on how a government's monetary and fiscal policies affect the overall operation of an economic system.

2. List each of the factors that collectively determine demand and those that determine supply.

Demand is the willingness and ability of buyers to purchase goods and services at different prices. Factors that collectively determine overall demand for a good or service include customer preferences, the number of buyers and their incomes, the prices of substitute goods, the prices of complementary goods, and consumer expectations about the future. Supply sums up the willingness and ability of businesses to offer goods and services for sale at different prices. Overall supply is determined by the costs of inputs (natural resources, capital, human resources, and entrepreneurship), costs of technology resources, taxes, and the number of suppliers operating in the market.

3. Compare supply and demand curves and explain how they determine the equilibrium price for a product.

A demand curve is a graph showing the amount of a good or service buyers will purchase at different prices. Since buyers likely will demand increasing quantities of a good at progressively lower prices, demand curves usually slope downward as they move to the right. By contrast, a supply curve is a schedule of the amounts of a good or service that businesses will offer for sale at different prices. Since sellers will likely make progressively more goods and services available as prices rise, supply curves usually slope upward as they move to the right. The interaction of the supply and demand curves determines the equilibrium price, the price at which the quantity supplied by sellers is precisely equal to the quantity demanded.

4. Contrast the three major types of economic systems.

Each of the world's national economies can be classified as either a private enterprise economy, a planned economic system such as communism or socialism, or a mixed market economy. A private enterprise system is characterized by individuals and private businesses pursuing their own interests without undue governmental restriction; by private ownership of factors of production; by investment decisions made by private industry rather than by government decree; and by determination of prices, products, resource allocation, and profits through competition in a free market. In a planned economy, the government exerts stronger control over business ownership, profits, and resources in order to accomplish government—rather than individual—goals. Communism is an economic system without private property; goods are owned in common, and factors of production and production decisions are controlled by the state. Socialism, another type of planned economic system, is characterized by government ownership and operation of all major industries. The final type of economic system, a mixed market economy, blends government ownership and private enterprise, combining characteristics of both planned and market economies.

5. Explain each of the four different types of market structures in a private enterprise system.

Four basic models characterize competition in a private enterprise system: pure competition, monopolistic competition, oligopoly, and monopoly. Pure competition is a market structure, like that in small-scale agriculture, in which large numbers of buyers and sellers exchange homogeneous products, so no single participant has a significant influence on price. Monopolistic competition is a market structure, like that in retailing, in which large numbers of buyers and sellers exchange relatively well-differentiated (heterogeneous) products, so each participant has some control over price. Oligopolies are market situations, like those in the steel and airline industries, in which relatively few sellers compete and high start-up costs form barriers to keep out new competitors. The final market structure is a monopoly, in which only one seller dominates trade in a good or service, for which buyers can find no close substitutes. Privately-held local water utilities and firms that hold exclusive patent rights on significant product inventions are examples.

6. Identify the major factors that guide an economist's evaluation of a nation's economic performance.

Economists consider several economic indicators to measure and evaluate the success of an economic system in providing a stable business environment and sustained growth. A nation's productivity is evidence of its economic strength and competitiveness. Gross domestic product, the market value of all goods and services produced within a nation's boundaries each year, is a commonly used measure of productivity. Changes in general price levels—inflation, price stability, or deflation—are important indicators of an economy's general stability. The U.S. government measures price-level changes by the Consumer Price Index. A nation's unemployment rate is an indicator of both overall stability and growth. The unemployment rate shows the number of people actively seeking employment who are unable to find jobs as a percentage of the total labor force. A final factor is the relative economic freedom enjoyed by individuals and private businesses in a nation.

7. Compare the two major tools used by a government to manage its economy.

The various tools used by government officials to influence the economy can be categorized as elements of either monetary policy or fiscal policy. Monetary policy encompasses a government's efforts to control the size of the nation's money supply. Various methods of increasing or decreasing the overall money supply affect interest rates and therefore affect borrowing and investment decisions. By changing the size of the money supply, government can encourage growth or control inflation. Fiscal policy, the second government tool, involves decisions regarding government revenues and expenditures. Changes in government spending affect economic growth and employment levels in the private sector. However, government must also raise money, through either taxes or borrowing, to finance its expenditures. Since tax payments represent funds that might otherwise have been spent by individuals and businesses, any taxation changes also affect the overall economy.

8. Describe the major global economic challenges of the 21st century.

Twenty-first century business is being propelled by technological advances that enable firms to enhance the effectiveness of their use, management, and control of information. A highly trained workforce is an essential requirement for businesses in taking advantage of this change. A second important economic challenge involves dealing with the effects of an aging population. Both government and business must be prepared to accommodate changing demands in health care, social security, and other support services. Customer service and quality remain vital ingredients for competitive superiority in the global market. A final factor in gaining competitive advantage is a competitive workforce. Both government and business must formulate effective plans for developing the skills and knowledge of workers in the 21st century. Not only do goods and services move across national borders, but companies operate in many parts of the world. Despite the added risks, serving a global market offers many opportunities. Businesses can find more customers as well as lower costs by operating in other countries.

Business Terms You Need to Know

economics 84
demand 85
supply 85
private enterprise system 92
communism 96

socialism 96
mixed market economy 97
monetary policy 104
fiscal policy 104
budget deficit 105

Other Important Business Terms

economic systems 84
microeconomics 85
macroeconomics 85
demand curve 86
supply curve 89
factors of production 89
equilibrium price 90

pure competition 92
monopolistic competition 93
oligopoly 93
monopoly 94
planned economy 96
privatization 98
productivity 100

gross domestic product (GDP) 100
inflation 100
hyperinflation 100
Consumer Price Index (CPI) 101
unemployment rate 103
national debt 105
balanced budget 106

➤ Review Questions

1. Distinguish between macroeconomics and microeconomics. Give at least one example of issues addressed by each.

2. Draw supply and demand graphs that estimate what will happen to demand, supply, and the equilibrium price of pizza if these events occur:

   a. A widely reported medical report suggests that eating cheese supplies a significant amount of the calcium needed in one's daily diet.

   b. Consumer incomes decline.

   c. The price of flour decreases.

   d. The state imposes a new tax on restaurant meals.

   e. The biggest competitor leaves the area.

   f. The price of hamburgers increases.

3. In what ways do businesses try to influence overall demand? Specifically, what might the manufacturer of a new line of lightweight folding scooters do?

4. Identify and give examples of the four factors of production.

5. Identify and compare the three major types of economic systems. What is the current status of each of these systems in the today's world? What potential benefits does each system offer? What negatives are associated with each system?

6. Identify the four basic degrees of competition that appear in a private enterprise system. Which type of competition does each of the following businesses face?

   a. a 100-acre dairy farm in New England

   b. Burger King

   c. United Airlines

   d. the United States Postal Service

   e. Ford Motor Co.

   f. Oracle

7. What is the difference between recession and depression? By what variables do economists measure and evaluate how successfully an economic system provides both stability and growth?

8. In what ways do the Fed's Board of Governors regulate the economy? What are the primary sources of government funds to cover the costs of the annual budget?

9. Based on comments by experts reported in this chapter, how would you describe the condition of the U.S. economy today? What are some concerns for the future?

10. In the information economy, how are skills and education levels that businesses must demand of their workforces changing?

➤ Questions for Critical Thinking

1. Describe a situation in which you have had to make an economic choice in an attempt to balance your wants with limited means. What factors influenced your decision?

2. Think of one of your favorite American companies—your choice can be anything from a clothing manufacturer, to a dot-com, to a music retailer. Consider the fact that the firm you selected enjoys many freedoms in the private enterprise system. How would this company survive in a different economic system? How might the firm have to change?

3. Do you think that planned economies will survive well into the 21st century? Why or why not? What types of changes, if any, would you expect to see them making?

4. In the past, many proposals have been made for privatizing certain federal or state-run agencies such as Social Security, Medicare, and the USPS. Do you favor privatization of some of these agencies? Why or why not?

5. Consider your economic lifetime so far. What stages of the business cycle have you experienced? In what ways have these stages affected your life?

➤ Experiential Exercise

Directions: In this chapter, you learned that customer service is a crucial aspect of a business's competitive strategy. Complete the following steps to examine some of the customer service issues organizations and their customers deal with regularly:

1. Form discussion groups of three to five students.

2. Make a copy of the following table to record your responses. Look at the customer service issues listed in column 1 of the following table, and use your collective experiences as customers to identify examples of customer service problems in columns 2 and 3.

3. Conclude your discussion by filling in column 4 of the table. That column should contain recommendations for what the organizations could have done differently to improve their customer service.

Customer Service Issue	Example of a Negative Experience	Example of an Ineffective Method Being Used	Recommendation for Improving Customer Service Issue
1. Ordering goods or services			
2. Receiving goods or services			
3. Resolving good- or service-related customer complaints			
4. Getting good- or service-related questions answered			
5. Being asked for feedback on customer satisfaction issues through, for example, phone or mail surveys after a purchase			
6. Handling of any of these customer service issues at e-commerce Web sites, such as online banking, online stock trading, auction sites, online shopping, or online education			

Nothing but Net

1. **Gross domestic product.** As discussed in the chapter, GDP represents the total value of goods and services produced by a nation's economy. In the United States, the Bureau of Economic Analysis (BEA), which is part of the Department of Commerce, compiles statistics on U.S. GDP. Visit the Web site **www.bea.doc.gov/bea**, and click on "GDP and related data." Answer the following questions:

   a. What is the current level of GDP? By how much has GDP changed over the prior quarter?

   b. What is the difference between nominal GDP and real GDP?

   c. What are the four general components of GDP? Which one of the four is the largest? Which one grew the fastest? Which component grew the slowest?

2. **Consumer price index.** The CPI is the most widely followed measure of inflation. Go to the BLS Web site (http://stats.bls.gov/cpihome.htm) and click on "News Releases." Read the current CPI report. Prepare a report answering the following questions:

   a. What was the overall rate of inflation during the preceding month?

   b. Each item in the basket of goods and services has a weight. (The higher the weight, the greater its influence on the overall index.) What are the weights for housing, transportation, apparel, prescription drugs, and dairy products? Which of the five rose the fastest? Which rose the least?

3. **Electric utility deregulation.** Electric utilities are among the most heavily regulated companies in the United States. Several states—most notably California and Wisconsin—as well as the federal government have begun to experiment with the partial deregulation of the electric utility industry. Visit each of the following Web sites and prepare a brief report outlining the pros and cons of electric utility deregulation:

www.citizen.org/cmep/restructing/utilityderegulation1.htm

www.cato.org (search the site for articles concerning utility deregulation)

www.eei.org/issues (click on "regulation and competition")

Note: Internet Web addresses change frequently. If you don't find the exact sites listed, you may need to access the organization's home page and search from there.

Companies build demand for their goods and services in a variety of ways. Automaker Kia attracts buyers with current styling and low prices. Sony increases the demand for its Play Station games by limiting the supply, making the computer games harder to get—and more popular. A ski resort like New York's Lake Placid builds demand by hosting a variety of competitions and activities for tourists and athletes year round—from horse shows to figure skating tournaments. Jake Burton built demand by creating a sport.

Burton, founder and owner of Burton Snowboards, won't take credit for inventing snowboarding, which he says has actually been around since the 1920s. But when he was a teenager, Burton started sliding down hills on a wooden board with a rope attached to it called a "Snurfer." The Snurfer was primitive and didn't offer much control to the rider, but Burton was hooked. "From that time on, I felt like it could be a sport, but it wasn't a sport for the company that was manufacturing it. They were selling [the Snurfer] like it was a hula hoop or something," he recalls. Burton thought he could improve on the design—and the sport.

In 1977, Burton moved from New York to Vermont to start Burton Snowboards. "I was blindly optimistic," he says. In addition to all of the struggles associated with developing a new product, Burton had to build awareness of and interest in the new sport itself. "I became more concerned with hyping the sport to make sure it happened so that I was right," Burton recalls. One major hurdle was the fact that at that time, ski resorts didn't allow snowboarding on their slopes, so snowboarders had to climb hills, carrying their snowboards, in order to ride down. Burton knew he had to change that situation, or his sport—and company—would never get off the ground. He had to build demand not only among consumers but among the ski resorts that attracted those consumers, convincing them that snowboarders would eventually become an important market. He got his first break when Vermont's Stratton Mountain Resort agreed to allow snowboards on its slopes.

Gradually, interest in the sport and in Burton Snowboards spread. Then Burton began to get inquiries from European dealers and distributors, which opened up a whole new market for him. Fifteen years later, demand had increased so much that snowboarding debuted as an Olympic sport at the Nagano Winter Olympics in 1998—proof positive that the sport had arrived. Today, Burton Snowboards conducts business in more than thirty countries, with three thousand dealers worldwide.

Still, the company hasn't stopped looking for new ways to build demand by attracting new recruits to the sport. Recognizing that snowboarding has been taught and learned haphazardly—which worries adult riders and parents of young riders—Burton Snowboards has established a systematic method of teaching called the Learn-To-Ride (LTR) program. The program includes lessons taught by certified American Association of Snowboard Instructors, as well as specially manufactured Burton boards, boots, and bindings designed for beginners. Stowe Mountain Resort, in Stowe, Vermont, was one of the first resorts to host the LTR program. "For over a decade, Stowe has been the frontier for learning to snowboard," notes Jeff Wise, director of the Stowe Snowboard School. "Learning from the industry's leading professionals has been made even better with the addition of LTR equipment."

In addition, in 1995 Burton Snowboards started a nonprofit, after-school learning program for underprivileged and at-risk children in the Burlington, Vermont, area where the company is based. The program, called "Chill," has since expanded to Boston, Los Angeles, New York, and Seattle. "Chill" takes schoolchildren snowboarding once a week for seven weeks, providing everything they need, from equipment to lift passes to instruction. Why do this? "There are so many companies out there doing things for the environment, but we decided to address the people side of things," says Burton. "Chill" not only takes kids off the streets but puts them on the slopes—creating a whole new generation and economic class of snowboarders.

During the rush to grow businesses quickly, when it seemed that companies couldn't go public fast enough, Jake Burton says he'd rather not. He likes the control that ownership of the company gives him, and the flexibility. "I'm first and foremost a snowboarder," he says, "and I use the fact that I don't have to be [in my office] every day like I used to as an opportunity to get more immersed in the sport." Such enthusiastic words from a man who took a sport from its infancy to its debut at the Olympics—and brought a whole new category of athletes along for the ride.

QUESTIONS

1. In addition to the materials discussed in the case, what other factors might affect demand for Burton Snowboards?
2. What factors might affect supply of the snowboards?
3. What type of competition would you consider the snowboard industry to be at this time? Why? (Refer to Table 3.3, Types of Competition, in the chapter to help you support your answer.)
4. What challenges might Burton Snowboards face when doing business abroad?

Sources: Josh Reid, "Burton Snowboards Establishes Learn to Ride Program," **www.boarding.com,** accessed January 17, 2001; "Burton Snowboards Rides the 'Net at Breakneck Speed with NaviSite," *Business Wire,* January 16, 2001; "Burton Snowboards," *Fortune,* **www.fortune.com,** accessed November 21, 2000; "Stowe and Burton Snowboards Work to Make Riding Easy for Beginners," press release, September 6, 2000, **www.stowe.com;** Portland Helmich, "Chairman of the Board," *Business People Vermont,* August 2000, **www.vermontguides.com;** "Snowboard Maker Finds Ideal e-Commerce Solution with Windows DNA," *Microsoft Business,* June 12, 2000, **www.microsoft.com.**

CHAPTER 4

Competing in Global Markets

Learning Goals

1. Explain the importance of international business and the main reasons why nations trade.

2. Discuss the relationship of absolute and comparative advantage to international trade.

3. Describe how nations measure international trade and the significance of exchange rates.

4. Identify the major barriers that confront global businesses.

5. Explain how international trade organizations and economic communities reduce barriers to international trade.

6. Compare the different levels of involvement used by businesses when entering global markets.

7. Describe the types of international organizational structures available to businesses.

8. Distinguish between a global business strategy and a multidomestic business strategy.

MTV: At 20, It's the Coolest TV Channel around the World

A whole generation has grown up with MTV in the U.S. Now, a global generation of young people is growing up with their favorite MTV music and videos—in their own countries, in their own languages, with their own stars. From Russia to Australia to Brazil, people are tuning in. In the Philippines, MTV is the second most watched cable station. In Moscow's Red Square, 200,000 young people attend an MTV-sponsored concert. In a London suburb, 1,500 guests rock at an MTV-sponsored party.

MTV is international business—with a beat. There's a huge international market of young people out there who love music, and MTV is in the thick of it. Although now hugely successful, MTV's initial venture into foreign markets was hardly harmonious. First, the company tried piping in American programming—in English—throughout Europe. Viewers were interested in Michael Jackson but not much else that was American. Local competitors appeared, attracting both viewers and sponsors away from MTV. "We were going for the most shallow layer of what united viewers," admits CEO Tom Freston. "It didn't go over well." So MTV learned its lesson and began to pay more attention to the cultures and tastes of consumers in its foreign markets. A few years later, it launched five separate feeds to Europe, each designed to address the tastes of a particular region.

In providing custom-tailored programming, MTV increased the level of its involvement in different countries. Now local programming is routine in most MTV markets. "People root for the home team, culturally and musically," explains William Roedy, the London-based president of MTV's international networks. "Local repertoire is a worldwide trend. There are fewer global megastars." So, in India, where people love music from movie soundtracks, most of the MTV music comes from Hindi films. But any new MTV operation begins

with a foundation of MTV values and procedures. The company begins by sending trusted employees—known as expatriates—to the new country. "We start with expatri-

ates to do a gene transfer of a company culture and operating principles," says Freston. Gradually, management and programming shift to the local culture. Describing the process in India, Freston notes, "We want them to be inside the Indian's head."

Government regulations have hindered MTV's global expansion. Some governments are so protective of their own business interests that they prohibit any foreign competition. Instead, they produce local look-alikes who imitate MTV's style. Such regulations have inhibited MTV's attempts to start channels in Canada and South Africa. Although MTV has a popular channel in Italy, the federal government is reducing the number of licensed broadcasters it will allow. And in Japan, MTV must have a local partner in order to expand. Political events have an impact on MTV broadcasts, as well.

After U.S. warplanes accidentally bombed the Chinese Embassy in Kosovo, the Chinese government refused to air an MTV awards program produced specifically for the Asian market. Eventually, the MTV Mandarin Music Honors program was aired for 300 million Chinese households, in partnership with the government-owned Chinese station. MTV has also had to learn from its own mistakes, much as it did with its programming errors in Europe. In India, MTV initially included the country's flag in its local logo, which many Indians found disrespectful.

Despite missing a few notes, MTV executives know that the company has a product with worldwide appeal—music—and a nearly unlimited potential market. The company's goal for this market is simple. "We want MTV in every household," says Roedy. That's every household, in every town, in every country.[1]

CHAPTER OVERVIEW

Consider for a moment how many products you used today that came from outside the U.S. Maybe you drank Brazilian coffee with your breakfast, wore clothes manufactured in Honduras or Malaysia, drove to class in a German or Japanese car fueled by gasoline refined from Venezuelan crude oil, and watched a movie on a television set assembled in Mexico for a Japanese company like Sony. A fellow student in France may be wearing Levi's jeans, using a Gateway or Compaq computer, and drinking Coca-Cola.

Like Volkswagen, Levi Strauss, Gateway, Sony, and The Coca-Cola Company, most U.S. and foreign companies recognize the importance of international trade to their future success. As Chapter 1 explains, economic interdependence is increasing throughout the world as companies seek additional markets for their goods and services and the most cost-effective locations for production facilities. No longer can businesses rely only on sales in domestic markets. Today, foreign sales are essential to U.S. manufacturing, agricultural, and service firms as sources of new markets and profit opportunities. Foreign companies also frequently look to America when they seek out new markets.

Thousands of products cross national borders every day. The computers that U.S. manufacturers sell in France are **exports,** domestically produced goods and services sold in markets in other countries. **Imports** are foreign-made products purchased by domestic consumers. Together, U.S. exports and imports make up about one-fourth the U.S. gross domestic product (GDP). U.S. exports exceed $950 billion each year, and annual imports total $1.2 trillion. That total amount is nearly double the nation's imports and exports just a decade ago.[2]

For dot.com powerhouses like eBay and Amazon.com, global markets mean global revenues. In Europe, eBay has been generating sales of $87 million, eight times the amount brought in by its largest competitor, a British company called QXL, which operates in 11 countries. In the first nine months after opening its European site, eBay was capturing a larger audience than QXL's in both Germany and Britain. Amazon.com has purchased online booksellers in Germany and Britain. Its European sales are five times greater than those of its key European competitor, BOL.[3]

Transactions that cross national boundaries may expose a company to an additional set of environmental factors—new social and cultural practices, economic and political environments, and legal restrictions. Before venturing into world markets, companies must adapt their domestic business strategies and plans to accommodate these differences.

This chapter travels through the world of international business to see how both large and small companies approach globalization. First, we consider the reasons nations trade, the importance and characteristics of the global marketplace, and the ways nations measure international trade. Then we examine barriers to international trade that arise from cultural and environmental differences. To reduce these barriers, countries turn to organizations that promote international trade and multinational agreements designed to encourage trade. Finally, we look at the strategies firms implement for entering global markets and how they develop international business strategies.

WHY NATIONS TRADE

As domestic markets mature and sales growth slows, companies in every industry recognize the increasing importance of efforts to develop business in other countries. McDonald's opens restaurants in Latin America, Nike sells shoes in the Philippines, and Amazon.com lures book buyers with fast delivery in Germany. These are only a few of the thousands of American companies taking advantage of foreign interest in their goods and services. Likewise, the U.S. market, with the world's largest purchasing power, attracts thousands of foreign companies to American shores. Large populations, substantial resources, and rising standards of living are boosting the attractiveness of many countries as targets for U.S. exports.

International trade is vital to a nation and its businesses because it boosts economic growth by providing a market for its products and access to needed resources. Companies in nations that promote global trade can expand their markets, seek out growth opportunities in other nations, and make their production and distribution systems more efficient. They also reduce their dependence on the economies of their home nations.

International Sources of Factors of Production

Business decisions to operate abroad depend on the availability, price, and quality of labor, natural resources, capital, and entrepreneurship—the basic factors of production—in the foreign country. The key factors for participating in the information economy are skilled human resources and entrepreneurship. The relative openness of the U.S. to immigration has permitted it to attract thousands of needed engineers and scientists from other countries. In contrast, in 2002, demand for skilled workers in Western Europe exceeded supply by 20 percent.[4] With talented workers so critical, companies tend to set up shop near the workforce they want to hire. The ability to locate near nine different universities lured Hewlett-Packard and Nokia to Barcelona, where both operate research and development facilities.[5]

Other key factors in choosing overseas markets include favorable regulatory conditions and healthy business climates. Companies that thrive on innovation and speedy decisions look for business environments where regulations will not slow them down. The freedom of this kind of environment positions organizations to attract the best talent worldwide. Amid the technology boom in the United States, the Dallas-based Baylor Institute for Immunology Research hired French biologist Nicolas Taquet. Not only could the U.S. facility offer him double what he was earning in France, but outside the government-dominated French bureaucracy, Taquet can more readily get the materials he needs for his cancer research. Although he misses his native country, Taquet says, "I'm so motivated here that I work weekends and nights. That wasn't the case back home."[6]

Many U.S. businesses have found international opportunities because many countries actively recruit them as sources of entrepreneurship and capital. As Russia's Internet population grows, the country's businesspeople want to get involved in Internet commerce. Russian start-ups are looking for U.S. investors who will bring not only money but also management talent. The United States, in contrast, has not only people who pioneered Internet commerce but also an enormous demand for investing in high-tech enterprises both at home and abroad.

One Russian company looking for management talent as well as capital is Kaspersky Lab, which develops and markets antivirus software. The company's revenues have grown steadily, but it needs help in becoming competitive internationally. Its CEO, Natalya Kaspersky, is looking for a foreign partner to assist with funding to expand and guidance in building a strong international image. So, she is seeking management expertise along with capital. Kaspersky points out that Russia's limited experience with capitalism requires her to find help outside her country: "We have only ten years of business history—where could people [in Russia] get business experience?"[7]

Trading with other countries also allows a company to spread risk, because different nations may be at different stages of the business cycle or in different phases of development. If demand falls off in one nation, the company may still enjoy strong demand in other nations. As discussed in Chapter 3, the U.S. has been enjoying the fruits of past investments in information technology. European countries are several years behind in making such

---

BUSINESS DIRECTORY

➤ **exports** *domestically produced goods and services sold in other countries.*

➤ **imports** *foreign goods and services purchased by domestic customers.*

investments. However, it is likely that Europe will soon begin enjoying similar gains in productivity and wealth as a result of expanded investment. Asia, which has recently been recovering from a recession, has increased its technology investments and may follow Europe, even as growth in the U.S. economy slows.[8] Later sections of the chapter discuss how these elements affect businesses.

Size of the International Marketplace

In addition to pursuing the production factors of human and natural resources, entrepreneurship, and capital, companies are attracted to international business by the sheer size of the global marketplace. Only 1 in every 5 people of the world's 6 billion-plus population live in relatively well-developed countries. The remaining 5 billion live in less-developed countries. The share of the world's population in the less-developed countries will continue to increase over the coming years because of differences in birth rates. Of the 78 million babies born each year, 19 of every 20 are born in the less-developed nations.[9]

As developing nations expand their involvement in global business, the potential for reaching new groups of customers dramatically increases. Firms looking for new sales are inevitably attracted to giant markets like China and India, with populations of 1.2 billion and 1 billion each. However, people alone are not enough to create a market. Economic demand also requires purchasing power. As Table 4.1 shows, population size is no guarantee of economic prosperity. Only two of the ten most populous countries, the U.S. and Japan, appear on the list of those with the highest per capita GDP.

Even though people in the developing nations have lower per capita incomes than those in the highly developed economies of North America and Western Europe, their huge populations do represent lucrative markets. Even when the high-income segments of those populations amount only to small percentages of all households, their sheer numbers may still represent significant and growing markets. Although overall India is very poor, it has somewhere between 150 million and 200 million well-educated middle-class consumers. In recent years, the Indian government has opened the country to more foreign trade, making this market even more attractive to business. Two companies that have recently responded to the lure of this giant marketplace by building factories in India are Kellogg Co. and Wm. Wrigley Jr. At present, few Indians chew gum or eat breakfast cereal, but these companies are betting young Indians will be willing to learn some new habits.[10]

Many developing countries have posted high rates of annual GDP growth. Compared with the 4 percent growth of the long U.S. economic expansion, South Korea recently enjoyed GDP growth of over 10 percent. China's growth moved at a 7 per-

Table 4.1	**The World's Top Ten Nations Based on Population and Wealth**		
Country	**Population (in millions)**	**Country**	**Per Capita GDP (in U.S. dollars)**
China	1,247	Luxembourg	$33,700
India	1,001	United States	30,200
United States	282	Norway	27,400
Indonesia	216	Monaco	25,000
Brazil	172	Japan	24,500
Russia	146	United Arab Emirates	24,000
Pakistan	138	Switzerland	23,800
Bangladesh	127	Belgium	23,200
Japan	126	Denmark	23,200
Nigeria	104	Liechtenstein	23,000

In 20 years, Emerging Market GDP will grow from $8 trillion ▶ to $40 trillion

(creating a new middle class).

These people can't wait to get started.

They're busy creating infrastructures, airlines, cars, buildings with elevators, offices and homes with air conditioners — and a growing appetite for comfort, security, travel — now. That's why we're in emerging markets.

Not as outsiders, but as integral partners. Making the best contacts, finding the best ventures, building the best work force, taking the best competitive positions and starting the best kind of growth curve — long and steady.

Sure, there may be bumps. But there's only one direction these markets can go in the next two decades. Forward. And only one way to capitalize on it.

Be there first.

Otis   Carrier   Pratt & Whitney   Sikorsky   Hamilton Standard   UT Automotive   ☀ United Technologies

FIGURE 4.1
The United Technologies Vision: Emerging Markets Are Growing

cent pace after two years of expanding in the range of 10 percent annually.[11] India's GDP growth has recently ranged from 5 to 6 percent annually.[12] These markets represent opportunities for global businesses, even though their per capita incomes lag behind those in more developed countries. Dozens of international firms are currently establishing operations in these and other developing countries to position themselves to benefit from local sales driven by rising standards of living. As Figure 4.1 explains, United Technologies is one of those companies: As the overall GDP of the emerging markets quintuples from $8 trillion to $40 trillion, its people will be buying everything from buildings with elevators to homes with air conditioning. United Technologies wants to ensure that some of those purchases include its Otis elevators and Carrier air conditioners.

In South America, the biggest Internet market is Brazil. The number of Internet subscribers tripled during the first three years of the 21st century to more than 6 million. Many are lured online by offers of free connections that banks are providing their customers. With the huge potential market in Argentina, Brazil, and other South American countries, not even competition as fierce as free services are discouraging companies that want to compete by selling paid subscriptions for Internet access. The leading contenders are a Brazilian service called Universo Online (UOL) and a Spanish company called Terra Networks. They are competing directly with the banks by offering free services, to be paid for through advertising sales. In addition, America Online has partnered with Venezuela's Cisneros Group to provide a paid-subscription service called AOL Latin America. Although UOL has the initial edge, not only in terms of the biggest subscriber base but also in the most content created in Portuguese, Brazil's official language, AOL believes its Brazilian joint venture will eventually enjoy the premium slice of this huge market.[13]

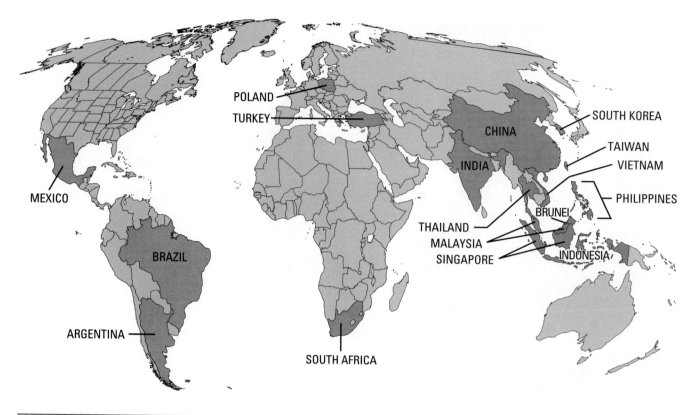

FIGURE 4.2
Major Emerging Markets for the 21st Century

Major World Markets

The major trading partners of U.S. firms include the country's northern and southern neighbors, Canada and Mexico. Other important global partners include Japan, China, Germany, and the United Kingdom. It is not a coincidence that these countries represent the world's major market regions: North America, Western Europe, the Pacific Rim, and Latin America. These regions encompass not only Germany, the United Kingdom, and Japan but also such emerging markets as India, Malaysia, and Vietnam. As Figure 4.2 shows, many of the world's most attractive emerging markets are located in Latin America and around the Pacific Rim.

North America With a combined population of over 400 million and a total GDP of $9.2 trillion, North America represents one of the world's most attractive markets. The U.S.—the single largest market in the world and the most stable economy—dominates North America's business environment. Although less than 1 person in 20 lives in the U.S., the country's $8 trillion GDP represents more than one-fourth of total world output.[14] Major U.S.-based corporations like Citicorp, General Electric, and Motorola maintain sizable investments both around the world and in North America.

Canada, our neighbor to the north, is far less densely populated but has achieved a similar level of economic development. Two-thirds of Canada's GDP is generated in the services sector, and three of every four Canadian workers are engaged in service occupations. The country's per capita GDP places Canada near the top ten nations in terms of its people's spending power. Canada's economy is fueled by trade with the U.S. Exports to the U.S. are equivalent to about one-third of Canada's GDP. In addition, three-quarters of the nation's imports come from the United States. U.S. business is also attracted by Canada's human resources. Many of Canada's professionals have moved to the U.S., lured by the availability of jobs with higher pay and lower tax rates.[15]

South of the border, Mexico is moving quickly from developing-nation to industrial-nation status, thanks largely to the North American Free Trade Agreement, discussed later in this chapter. Stretching 2,100 miles from the Pacific Ocean to the Gulf of Mexico, the U.S.-Mexican border is home to 1,500 **maquiladoras,** foreign-owned businesses that manufacture products for export from this duty-free zone. About 450,000 Mexicans work in *maquiladoras* serving the clothing and automotive industries. Another 300,000 assemble electronics products, and 50,000 more are engaged in service *maquiladoras*—handling tasks ranging from laundering uniforms to answering phones and processing data.

These job creations are drawing Mexicans to towns near the U.S. border, and these towns are growing into cities. Higher incomes and greater urbanization are changing the Mexican culture and landscape. Greater buying power—and immigrant managers—are providing a market for car rental offices, fast-food restaurants, hotels, and other businesses.

Western Europe   Together, the nations of Western Europe, particularly Germany, the United Kingdom, France, and Italy, make up a sophisticated and powerful industrial region with a combined GDP three-fourths as large as that of the U.S. Solidifying the importance of this market is the European Union (EU), a 15-nation economic community discussed later in the chapter. International companies with headquarters in this region include Royal Dutch Shell, Nestlé, DaimlerChrysler, and Glaxo Wellcome. Significant investments from around the world are flowing into European nations, as foreign companies locate manufacturing and distribution facilities across the continent. Over half of U.S. investments in foreign companies flow to Europe.[16]

Ireland is Europe's fastest-growing economy. With a combination of tax cuts and investments in education, the country has made itself attractive to over 500 high-tech foreign firms, including Dell, Pfizer, and Microsoft. Intel's largest non-U.S. facility is a wafer fabrication plant west of Dublin that turns out Pentium III microchips. Ireland never prospered in the industrial age; it has moved straight from an agricultural to an information economy. Ireland is currently Europe's leading exporter of software, with an economy so strong that the nation is not just an exporter of high-tech products—it is an importer of human resources.[17]

The Pacific Rim   The major nations of the large and growing region known as the Pacific Rim are Australia, China (including Hong Kong), Indonesia, Japan, Malaysia, the Philippines, Singapore, South Korea, and Taiwan. The industries that fuel Asian economies—electronics, automobiles, and banking—are strong competitors to U.S. firms. In addition, Asia's technology-driven markets, rapid urbanization, and its growing middle class make this region a significant market for U.S. goods and services. See the "Clicks and Mortar" box for a description of how one Japanese entrepreneur is using the Internet to increase his company's competitiveness.

Leading the new cycle of growth are Korea, China, Malaysia, Taiwan, Singapore, and Hong Kong. China, whose 1.2 billion inhabitants have traditionally been known as a leading source of labor in manufacturing low-priced goods like toy dolls and clothing, is today challenging both the U.S. and Japan with its capabilities for low-cost production of high-tech products. Its leading exports to the U.S. are electrical machinery, toys and sports equipment, footwear, other machinery, and furniture and bedding.[18] Foreign companies also have operations in China. Intel has a production facility in Shanghai and is planning a research center for Beijing.[19]

China's biggest investor is a tiny seaport on the country's southern edge. Hong Kong was a British colony until 1997, when it rejoined the People's Republic of China. Under British rule, the government barely involved itself in business affairs, and as a result, Hong Kong developed a booming entrepreneurial economy. The Chinese government promised to grant Hong Kong a high degree of autonomy as a capitalist economy for 50 years. The Hong Kong government has kept taxes and

7-Eleven Gives Convenience Stores a New Meaning

Background. Imagine cruising into your local 7-Eleven store for your favorite flavor Slurpee and a bag of chips. While sipping your drink, you can browse through a few Web sites at the Internet terminal and maybe order a book and a CD. You decide you need some cash, so you click into the ATM and retrieve a few bucks. A week later, you come back to the 7-Eleven to pick up the book and CD you ordered. Where is this happening, you say?

What Happened? This scenario has been taking place for several years in Japan, a country that has suffered from an economic slowdown as well sluggish entry into e-commerce. Toshifumi Suzuki, CEO of 7-Eleven Japan, which owns 72 percent of all 7-Elevens in the U.S., thinks the idea makes perfect sense. More importantly, so do Japanese consumers.

The Response. Ninety-three percent of Japanese consumers who order books from the Web site Esbooks while in a 7-Eleven store opt to pick up their orders at the store instead of having them delivered at home. "The Japanese would rather pick up their goods and pay for them at a *konbini* [convenience store]," says Morihiko Ida, head of equities research at Century Securities. "So that could boost sales." Suzuki isn't stopping there. He plans to install ATMs at his 8,200 Japanese stores—among the first ATMs in Japan—which will allow 24-hour banking as well as payment for online purchases.

It's not surprising that Suzuki is bringing his own version of e-commerce to the United States. Starting with 250 stores in Texas, in-store computers will offer bill payment, payroll check cashing,

money wiring, and ticket purchasing for entertainment events as well as travel. Next, Suzuki wants to convince online retailers to deliver products to the 7-Eleven distribution network so consumers can pick up their orders at the nearest store. Right now, the goods will have to be smaller items because 7-Eleven stores are small. And 7-Eleven employees will have to be trained to handle the systems. But they already restock empty shelves via handheld computer terminals. "Nobody else in the U.S. has that," notes James Keys, CEO of 7-Eleven U.S.

Today and Counting. So far, 7-Eleven Japan has managed to maintain steady growth in a sagging economy as well as attract once-reticent Japanese consumers to the Internet for their shopping. Who would have guessed that the maker of something as simple as a Slurpee might introduce e-commerce to a nation?

QUESTIONS FOR CRITICAL THINKING

1. Do you think Suzuki's ideas would be successful in the European Union? Why or why not?
2. As the Japanese economy recovers, how might 7-Eleven be affected?

Sources: Irene M. Kunii, "From Convenience Store to Online Behemoth?" *Business Week,* April 10, 2000, p. 64; Benjamin Fulford, "I Got It @ 7-Eleven," *Forbes,* April 3, 2000, pp. 53–54; Jim Rohwer, "Japan Goes Web Crazy," *Fortune,* February 7, 2000, pp. 115–118.

---

regulation at low levels compared with the rest of Asia, but it has increased government participation in the economy: Without soliciting bids, the government recently awarded land to a private developer to create facilities for high-tech businesses.[20]

Latin America During the 1990s, Latin American countries reduced government spending and encouraged investment. Privatization of port facilities, railways, telecommunications, mining, and energy attracted new industry. As a result, foreign investment in Latin America, particularly Brazil and Argentina, has grown, along with the goods and services available to consumers. Much of that investment came from the U.S. and Europe.[21]

However, cuts in government spending during the early years of this decade have taken their toll on people who relied on government services and jobs. Of the world's regions, Latin America has the largest gap between the incomes of the rich and poor.[22] Such trends have increased political instability, and investors have avoided such troubled countries as Colombia and Venezuela.

Despite such problems, Latin America is a big market for high-technology products. In particular, the Internet is providing new opportunities for Latin American businesses as Internet usage claims a growing share of the population.

With many Latin Americans living in poverty, governments and other agencies are trying to help their citizens gain access to Internet opportunities. In Peru, a nonprofit organization called the Peruvian Science Network (RCP) has helped to establish hundreds of public Internet centers and runs seminars to teach people about Internet businesses. @Altec Cyber Park, Latin America's first Internet host, stores hundreds of Web sites on its computer servers, so Latin Americans can link to local sites faster and at lower cost.

Besides providing the hardware and networks, businesses are finding opportunities in providing Internet-related services. Terra, shown in Figure 4.3, offers Web portals to Spanish-speaking customers in Spain and the U.S. as well as Latin America.

Absolute and Comparative Advantage

Few countries can produce all the goods and services their people need. For centuries, trading has been the way that countries can meet the demand. If a country can focus on producing what it does best, it can export surplus domestic output and buy foreign products that it lacks or cannot efficiently produce. The potential for foreign sales of a particular good or service depends largely on whether the country has an absolute advantage or comparative advantage.

A country has an *absolute advantage* in making a product for which it can maintain a monopoly or that it can produce at a lower cost than any competitor. For centuries, China enjoyed an absolute advantage in silk production. This luxurious fabric was woven from fibers recovered from silkworm cocoons, making it a prized raw material in high-quality clothing. Demand among Europeans for silk led to establishment of the famous *silk road,* a 5,000-mile link between Rome and the ancient Chinese capital city of Xian.

Absolute advantages are rare these days. But some countries manage to approximate absolute advantages in some products. Because many oil deposits are in the Middle East, these countries have a degree of control over oil supplies, which they sometimes manipulate to affect their income. Climate differences can give some nations or regions an advantage in growing certain plants. A rare, expensive herb called wasabi grows in valleys along Japan's mountain rivers. The Japanese use wasabi to make a hot green condiment for sushi. Because the absolute advantage of wasabi's rarity makes real wasabi so expensive, the version sold in most U.S. stores is a bland imitation concocted from horseradish and green food coloring. However, an American entrepreneur named Roy Carver III recently determined that his company, Pacific Farms, can grow the plant along Oregon's coast, where the microclimate resembles that of wasabi's natural habitat.[23]

A nation can develop a *comparative advantage* in a product if it can supply it more efficiently and at a lower price than it can supply other goods, compared with the outputs of other countries. China has long held a comparative advantage in producing toys and clothing due to very low labor costs. On the other hand, Japan has maintained a comparative advantage in producing electronics by preserving efficiency and technological expertise. By ensuring that its people are well educated, a nation can also develop a comparative advantage in providing skilled human resources.

Canon has recently adopted a strategy for research and development based on various nations' comparative advantage in engineering knowledge. Rather than basing all the company's research at its Tokyo headquarters, the company is planning to operate regional headquarters in Europe and the Americas, each focused on a different area of expertise. Engineers at Canon Research America in Palo Alto, California, concentrate on digital and networking technology. Engineers at Canon Research Center France focus on telecommunications. According to Canon's president, Fujio Mitarai, this is a departure from the past practice of making overseas research a

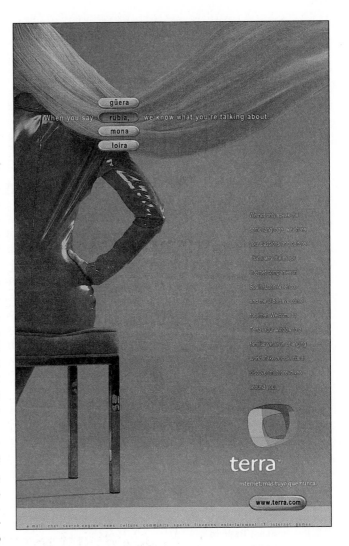

FIGURE 4.3
Terra: Web Portals for Latin America, Spain, and the United States

simple extension of Japanese activities: "From now on, we want to give birth to new value abroad. We want to make the best of the different kinds of expertise available in different countries."[24]

MEASURING TRADE BETWEEN NATIONS

Clearly, engaging in international trade provides tremendous competitive advantages to both the countries and individual companies involved. Any attempt to measure global business activity requires an understanding of the concepts of balance of trade and balance of payments. Another important factor is currency exchange rates for each country.

A nation's **balance of trade** is the difference between its exports and imports. If a country exports more than it imports, it achieves a positive balance of trade, called a *trade surplus*. If it imports more than it exports, it produces a negative balance of trade, called a *trade deficit*. The United States has run a trade deficit every year since 1976. Despite being the world's top exporter, the U.S. economy has an even greater appetite for foreign-made goods. At the beginning of the 21st century, the trade deficit set an all-time record high of $265 billion.[25]

As Figure 4.4 shows, U.S. exports have been growing, but imports have been growing faster. Because imports exceed exports, the trade balance shown in the shaded area is a deficit. This year, that deficit will surpass $1 trillion. Trade deficits with two countries—China and Japan—account for over half of this deficit.

A nation's balance of trade plays a central role in determining its **balance of payments**—the overall flow of money into or out of a country. Other factors also affect the balance of payments, including overseas loans and borrowing, international investments, profits from such investments, and foreign aid payments. Figure 4.5 illustrates the components of a country's balance of payments. To calculate a nation's balance of payments, subtract the monetary outflows from the monetary inflows. A

FIGURE 4.4
U.S. International Trade in Goods and Services

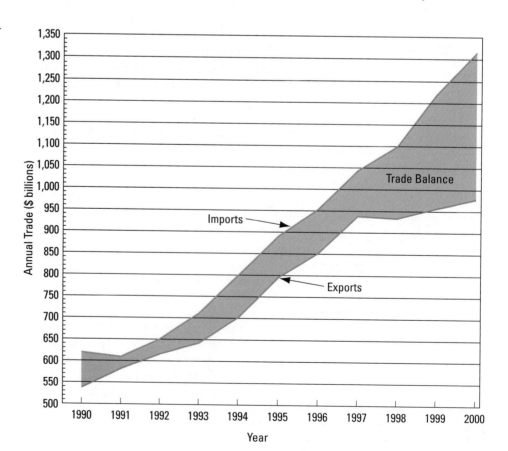

FIGURE 4.5
Components of the Balance of Payments

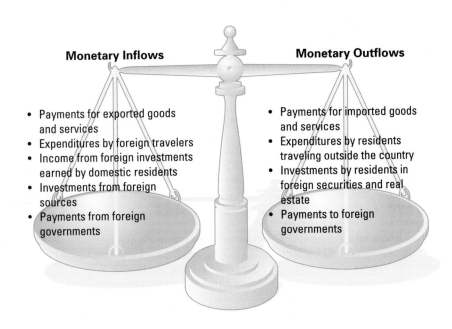

Monetary Inflows

- Payments for exported goods and services
- Expenditures by foreign travelers
- Income from foreign investments earned by domestic residents
- Investments from foreign sources
- Payments from foreign governments

Monetary Outflows

- Payments for imported goods and services
- Expenditures by residents traveling outside the country
- Investments by residents in foreign securities and real estate
- Payments to foreign governments

positive balance of payments, or a *balance of payments surplus*, means more money has moved into a country than out of it. A negative balance of payments, or *balance of payments deficit*, means more money has gone out of the country than enters it.

Major U.S. Exports and Imports

The United States, with combined exports and imports of over $2 trillion, leads the world in the international trade of goods and services. As listed in Table 4.2, the leading categories of goods exchanged by U.S. exporters and importers range from crops, including exports of wheat and soybeans and imports of coffee, to computers and electrical machinery. Strong U.S. demand for imported goods is partly a reflection of the nation's prosperity and diversity. In November 1999, for only the second time in the 20th century, the U.S. recorded a trade deficit in food and beverages. This deficit arose from the willingness of U.S. consumers to pay for imported fish, bananas, and coffee, as well as such treats as caviar and out-of-season fruits like strawberries in November or apples in May.[26]

Although the U.S. imports more goods than it exports, the opposite is true for services. U.S. exporters sell more than $270 billion in services annually. Much of that money comes from travel and tourism—money spent by foreign nationals visiting the United States. U.S. service exports also include business and technical services such as engineering, financial services, computing, legal services, and entertainment. Other services involve technologies developed by U.S. firms that earn royalties and licensing fees from users abroad. Many service exporters are well-known companies, including American Express, American Airlines, America Online, AT&T, Citibank, Walt Disney, Allstate Insurance, and Federal Express, as well as retailers such as Foot Locker, The Gap, Office Depot, Toys 'R' Us, and Costco.

As noted earlier in the chapter, businesses in many foreign countries want the expertise of U.S. financial and business professionals. In addition, entertainment is a major growth area for U.S. service exports. Disney, which already operates theme parks in France and Japan, is preparing to build a theme park on Hong Kong's Lantau Island. The company plans to invest $318 million to own a 43 percent share of the new Magic Kingdom plus three hotels. In addition, Disney will earn fees for managing the theme park, scheduled to open in 2005.[27]

To compete in a diverse global economy characterized by stiff competition for human talent, U.S. companies expanding abroad frequently require services in

BUSINESS DIRECTORY

► **balance of trade**   *difference between a nation's exports and imports.*
► **balance of payments**   *difference in money flows into or out of a country.*

Table 4.2	Top Ten U.S. Exports and Imports		
Exports		**Imports**	
Electrical machinery	$66 billion	Vehicles	$119 billion
Vehicles	$54 billion	Computers and office equipment	$77 billion
Agricultural products	$51 billion	Electrical machinery	$54 billion
Computers and office equipment	$41 billion	Clothing	$54 billion
Airplanes	$35 billion	Televisions, VCRs, and other consumer electronics	$42 billion
General industrial machinery	$30 billion	Crude oil	$37 billion
Power-generating machinery	$29 billion	Agricultural products	$36 billion
Specialized industrial machinery	$27 billion	General industrial machinery	$29 billion
Scientific instruments	$24 billion	Power-generating machinery	$28 billion
Televisions, VCRs, and other consumer electronics	$23 billion	Specialized industrial machinery	$23 billion

these markets. When El Sitio USA set up a network of Spanish-language Web sites, it hired a Brazilian agency, Denison, Sao Paulo, to develop its advertising campaign. The bilingual campaign features baseball hero Sammy Sosa with the slogan, "To lugar en Internet," which means "your home on the Internet."[28]

With annual imports exceeding $1 trillion, the U.S. is by far the world's leading importer. American tastes for foreign-made goods, which show up as huge trade deficits with the consumer-goods exporting nations of China and Japan, also extend to European products. Last year, the 15 EU countries shipped more than $200 billion of merchandise, including Audi cars, Roquefort cheese, and high-tech machinery, to U.S. buyers, which is more than a 10 percent increase over the previous year.[29]

Exchange Rates

A nation's **exchange rate** is the rate at which its currency can be exchanged for the currencies of other nations. Each currency's exchange rate is usually quoted in terms of another currency, such as the number of Mexican pesos needed to purchase one U.S. dollar. Table 4.3 compares the values of several currencies against the U.S. dollar. Besides exchange rates for the currencies of various nations, the table shows the exchange rate for the euro, the currency of the EU. European consumers and businesses can use the euro to pay bills by check, credit card, or bank transfer. Euro coins and notes are also used in most EU-member countries.

Currency values fluctuate, or "float," depending on the supply and demand for each currency in the international market. In this system of *floating exchange rates*, currency traders create a market for the world's currencies based on each country's relative trade and investment prospects. In theory, this market permits exchange rates to vary freely according to supply and demand. In practice, exchange rates do not float in total freedom. National governments often intervene in the currency markets to adjust the exchange rates of their own currencies. In recent years, the euro has fluctuated greatly in value, from a high of $1.19 to a low of about $.80.[30]

Nations influence exchange rates in other ways as well. They may form currency blocs by linking their exchange rates to each other. Many governments practice protectionist policies that seek to guard their economies against trade imbalances. For instance, national governments sometimes take deliberate action to devalue their currencies as a way to increase exports and stimulate foreign investment. **Devaluation** describes a fall in a currency's value relative to other currencies or to a fixed

Table 4.3 Foreign Exchange Rates for Selected Currencies

Country	Currency Unit	2001 Exchange Rate (per U.S. dollar)
Canada	Dollar	1.5
China	Renminbi	8.3
European Union	Euro	1.1
France	Franc	6.9
Germany	Mark	2.1
India	Rupee	45.9
Italy	Lira	2,058.5
Japan	Yen	118.1
Mexico	Peso	9.8
South Korea	Won	1,283.5
Switzerland	Franc	1.6
Thailand	Baht	42.6
United Kingdom	Pound	0.7

standard. In Brazil, a recent currency devaluation made investing in that country relatively cheap, so the devaluation was followed by a flood of foreign investment. Pillsbury bought Brazil's Brisco, which makes a local staple, *pao de queijo*, a cheese bread formed into rolls and served with morning coffee. Other foreign companies invested in Brazil's construction, tourism, banking, communications, and other industries.[31] In Germany, few people complained about the falling value of the euro. Manufacturing fuels the nation's economy, with exports making up one-fourth of its GDP. At a devalued euro, manufacturing equipment priced in euros looks like a good deal to customers with dollars or yen to exchange.[32]

Exchange rate changes can quickly create—or wipe out—a competitive advantage, so they are important factors in decisions about whether to invest abroad. When the euro's value plunged relative to the U.S. dollar, American exports to Europe brought home fewer dollars at the new exchange rate. In Europe, the declining value of the euro meant that a price of 10 euros was not worth as much, so companies were pressured to raise prices, potentially fueling inflation. At the same time, the falling euro made European vacations more affordable for American tourists, because their dollars were worth more relative to the euro. In contrast, European travelers found that their euros bought less in America at the new exchange rate.

For an individual business, the impact of the euro's devaluation depends on where that business buys its materials and where it sells its products. Tellabs generates one-fifth of its sales in Europe, so the falling euro cut into its sales. However, the company also manufactures in Europe, so the falling euro also reduced the cost of manufacturing, measured in dollars. Tellabs predicted that the decline of the euro would have no effect on company profits. Other companies with significant

BUSINESS DIRECTORY

➤ **exchange rate** value of one nation's currency relative to the currencies of other countries.

sales in Europe, including McDonald's and Wm. Wrigley Jr., complained that the declining euro was reducing their revenues.[33]

Currencies that owners can easily convert into other currencies are called *hard* currencies. Examples include the euro, the U.S. dollar, and the Japanese yen. The Russian ruble and many central European currencies are considered *soft* currencies, because they cannot be readily converted. Exporters trading with these countries often prefer to barter, accepting payment in oil, timber, or other commodities that they can resell for hard-currency payments.

BARRIERS TO INTERNATIONAL TRADE

All businesses encounter barriers in their operations, whether they sell only to local customers or trade in international markets. Countries such as Australia, Germany, and New Zealand regulate the hours and days retailers may be open. Germany recently forced Wal-Mart to raise its prices to be more in line with local competitors. The differences and difficulties are multiplied many times over for businesses with international operations. Besides complying with a variety of laws and exchanging currencies, international companies may also have to reformulate their products to accommodate different tastes in new locations. Frito-Lay exports cheeseless Chee-tos to Asia, and Domino's Pizza offers pickled ginger pizzas at its Indian fast-food restaurants.

In addition to social and cultural differences, companies engaged in international business also face economic barriers as well as legal and political ones. Some of the hurdles shown in Figure 4.6 are easily breached, but others require major changes in a company's business strategy. To successfully compete in global markets, companies and their managers must understand not only how these barriers affect international trade but also how to overcome them.

Social and Cultural Differences

The social and cultural differences among nations range from language and customs to educational background and religious holidays. Understanding and respecting these differences are critical in the process leading to international business success. Businesspeople with knowledge of host countries' cultures, languages, social values, and religious attitudes and practices are well equipped for the marketplace and the negotiating table. Acute sensitivity to such elements as local attitudes, forms of address and expectations regarding dress, body language, and timeliness also help them to win customers and achieve their business objectives. Without this knowledge, companies may discover that their goods and services will not appeal to customers in foreign countries.

Language English may be considered the main language of business, but for much of the world, it is not the primary language. More people speak Mandarin Chinese and Spanish than English. English is the third most spoken language in the world, followed by Bengali, Hindi, Portuguese, Russian, Japanese, and German.[34] It is not

FIGURE 4.6
Barriers to International Trade

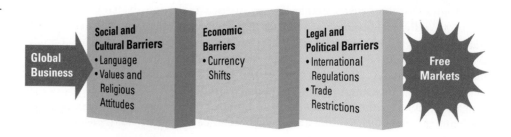

uncommon for students for whom English is not their first language to spend eight years of elementary and high school in English language classes. Understanding a business colleague's primary language may prove to be the difference between closing an international business transaction and losing the sale to someone else. Company representatives operating in foreign markets must not only choose correct and appropriate words but also translate words correctly to convey the intended meanings. Firms may also need to rename products or rewrite slogans for foreign markets.

Potential communication barriers include more than mistranslation. Companies may present messages through inappropriate media, overlook local customs and regulations, or ignore differences in taste. This sensitivity is especially critical in cyberspace. Web site developers must be aware that visitors to a site may come from anywhere in the world. Some icons that seem friendly to U.S. Internet users may shock people from other countries. A person making a high-five hand gesture would be insulting to people in Greece; ditto the index finger making a circle with the thumb in Brazil and a two-fingered peace sign with the back of the hand facing out in Great Britain. Even colors can pose problems. In the Middle East, people view green as a sacred color, so a green background on a Web page would be inappropriate there.[35]

Gift-giving traditions employ the language of symbolism. In China, for example, it is customary to give gifts at the lunar new year, but some types of gifts carry inappropriate meanings. For example, giving a clock is a bad idea, since the Chinese consider a clock to be a symbol of death.[36]

Values and Religious Attitudes   Even though today's world is shrinking in many ways, people in different countries do not necessarily share the same values or religious attitudes. Marked differences remain in workers' attitudes between traditionally capitalist countries and those adopting new capitalist systems and even among traditionally capitalist countries.

U.S. society places a higher value on business efficiency and low unemployment than European society, where employee benefits are more valued. The U.S. government does not regulate vacation time, and employees typically receive no paid vacation during their first year of employment, then two weeks' vacation, eventually working up to three or four weeks if they stay with the same employer for many years. In contrast, the EU mandates a minimum paid vacation of four weeks per year, and most Europeans get five or six weeks. Before Berlin bank employee Britta Niehoff left for a three-week bicycling trip, she told a newspaper reporter, "I am not like the Americans who believe the world would collapse if they were away from their workplace for more than two weeks. I work really hard, and for me real relaxation only starts after two weeks."[37] In these countries, a U.S. company that opens a manufacturing plant would not be able to hire any local employees without offering vacations in line with that nation's business practices.

U.S. culture values national unity with tolerance of regional differences. The U.S. is viewed as a national market with a single economy. European countries that are part of the 15-member EU are trying to create a similar marketplace. However, many resist the idea of being European citizens first and British, Danish, or Dutch citizens second. British consumers differ from Italians in important ways, and U.S. companies that fail to recognize this variation will run into problems with brand acceptance.

Religion plays an important role in every society, so businesspeople also must cultivate sensitivity to the dominant religions in countries where they operate. Understanding religious cycles and the timing of major holidays can help prevent embarrassing moments when scheduling meetings, trade shows, conferences, or events such as the dedication of a new manufacturing plant. People doing business in Saudi Arabia must take into account Islam's month-long observance of Ramadan, when work ends at noon. Friday is the Muslim Sabbath, so the Saudi workweek runs from Saturday through Thursday. Furthermore, Muslims abstain from alcohol and consider pork unclean, so gifts of pigskin or liquor would be offensive.

"Here, at our Multilingual Center, we put a strong accent on communications.

"As BellSouth service representatives, we answer billing and services questions from our non-English-speaking customers.

"We're from all over the world, but we all share the same goal—to go above and beyond to serve our customers' needs.

"And great things happen when we work together. We come up with new ideas...like our Spanish language telephone bill for our customers in Florida."

"We assist our customers in eight different languages."

Alexandra Angrand
Multilingual Center

BellSouth has many talented and dedicated people like Alexandra. We think they provide real service to our customers by helping them in new and creative ways.

BELLSOUTH®
Nobody knows a neighbor like a neighbor.℠

http://www.bellsouth.com

BellSouth, a data, voice, and video communications company serving the southeastern states of the U.S., recognizes the increased diversity of its marketplace. This diversity has been increased by substantial immigration during the past 40 years. BellSouth has responded to the needs of its customers by offering assistance in eight different languages. The company even offers telephone bills in Spanish for the large number of Spanish-speaking households in Florida.

Economic Differences

Business opportunities are flourishing in densely populated countries such as China and India, as local consumers eagerly buy Western products. Although such prospects might tempt American firms, managers must first consider the economic factors involved in doing business in these markets. A country's size, per capita income, and stage of economic development are among the economic factors to consider when evaluating it as a candidate for an international business venture.

Infrastructure   Along with other economic measures, businesses should consider a country's infrastructure. **Infrastructure** refers to basic systems of communication (television, radio, print media, telecommunications), transportation (roads and highways, railroads, airports), and energy facilities (power plants, gas and electric utilities). With widespread access to personal computers (PCs), the United States led the way in the use of Internet technology. However, many consumers in Western Europe, Japan, and Hong Kong own cellular phones. In Europe the rate of mobile-phone ownership exceeds that of the U.S. The availability of this technology makes these countries fertile soil for Internet businesses that adapt to wireless communication. Consumers in Hong Kong can use cell phones to place bids at the Cat-Street.com auction site. Mobile-phone subscribers in Finland can buy candy and soft drinks from vending machines or pay for car washes by pressing buttons on their phones.[38] Also, although North America has the greatest percentage of small businesses on the Internet, a larger share of German small businesses use the Internet to make purchases, and a larger share of British small businesses sell products online.[39]

Financial systems also provide a type of infrastructure for businesses. In the United States, buyers have widespread access to checks, credit cards, and debit cards, as well as electronic systems for processing these forms of payment. In many African countries, such as Ethiopia, no local business accepts credit cards, so travelers to the capital city Addis Ababa are warned to bring plenty of cash and traveler's checks. Lack of easy-to-use and affordable payment systems has slowed Internet commerce in Japan. Companies that issue credit cards discourage merchants with their terms—high fees for processing the cards, as well as burdensome paperwork and slow payment. When Echigo Meimon Shukai went online, the Japanese *sake* company arranged to accept payment by credit card. Credit card companies charged the firm 4 percent of each sale as a fee for processing payments, but they left plenty of work to Echigo. The company must add up its sales and fax the amounts to the credit-card companies. After that, Echigo must wait four weeks for payment. Not only that, but credit cards are expensive for Japanese consumers, so many of them don't even bother to get a card. They prefer to wire payments from a convenience store or post office. With these limits on the convenience of credit cards, it is no wonder that Japanese online consumers spend only 6 percent of the amount spent by U.S. online consumers.[40]

Currency Conversion and Shifts   Despite growing similarities in infrastructure, businesses crossing national borders encounter basic economic differences: national currencies. Although many countries buy and sell in U.S. dollars, firms may trade in the local currency—the Mexican peso, Indonesian rupee, Swiss franc, Japanese yen, and English pound.

Foreign currency fluctuations may present added problems for global businesses. As explained earlier in the chapter, the values of the world's major currencies fluctuate in relation to each other. Rapid and unexpected currency shifts can make pricing in local currencies difficult. Shifts in exchange rates can also influence the attractiveness of various business decisions. A devalued currency may make a nation less desirable as an export destination, because of reduced demand in that market. However, devaluation can make the nation desirable as an investment opportunity, because investments there will be a bargain in terms of the investor's currency.

Political and Legal Differences

Similar to social, cultural, and economic differences, legal and political differences in host countries can pose barriers to international trade. China limits the use of encryption on Web sites and restricts Internet companies that want to raise money on international stock exchanges. Mexico's Federal Competition Commission has strengthened enforcement of that country's antitrust laws. Among other decisions, it prevented The Coca-Cola Company from acquiring Cadbury Schweppes brands in Mexico, on the grounds that the acquisition would give the company a 70 percent share of the Mexican soft-drink market.[41] To compete in today's world marketplace, managers involved in international business must be well versed in legislation that affects their industries.

Some countries impose general trade restrictions. Others have established detailed rules that regulate how foreign companies can operate. The one consistency among all countries is the striking lack of consistent laws and regulations governing the conduct of business.

Political Climate   An important factor in any international business investment is the stability of the political climate. The political structures of many nations promote stability similar to that in the U.S. Other nations, such as Indonesia, Congo, and Bosnia, feature quite different—and frequently changing—structures. Host nations often pass laws designed to protect their own interests, often at the expense of foreign businesses.

In recent years, the political structures of Russia, Turkey, the former Yugoslavia, Hong Kong, and several central European countries (including the Czech Republic and Poland) have seen dramatic changes. Such political changes almost always bring changes in the legal environment. Hong Kong's new status as part of China is an example of an economy where political developments produced changes in the legal and cultural environments. Since the collapse of the Soviet Union, Russia has struggled to develop a new market structure and political processes. The current president, Vladimir V. Putin, has strengthened law enforcement to help legitimate businesses by cracking down on the organized-crime figures who have built business empires on a pattern of bribery and extortion.[42]

Legal Environment   When conducting business internationally, managers must be familiar with three dimensions of the legal environment: U.S. law, international regulations, and the laws of the countries where they plan to trade. Some laws protect the rights of foreign companies to compete in the United States. Others dictate actions allowed for U.S. companies doing business in foreign countries.

The *Foreign Corrupt Practices Act* forbids U.S. companies from bribing foreign officials, political candidates, or government representatives. This act prescribes fines and jail time for U.S. managers who are aware of illegal payoffs. Until recently, many countries, including France and Germany, not only accepted the practice of bribing foreign officials in countries where such practices were customary, but they allowed tax deductions for these expenses. In 1999, representatives of the U.S., France, Germany, and 31 other countries signed the Organization for Economic

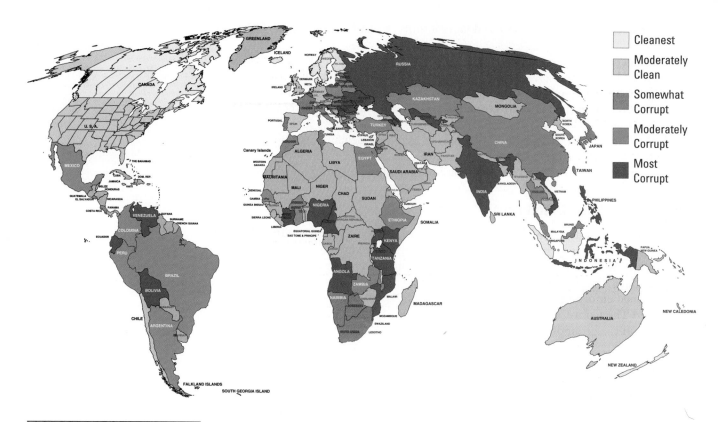

Cleanest

Moderately Clean

Somewhat Corrupt

Moderately Corrupt

Most Corrupt

FIGURE 4.7
Corruption in Business and Government

Cooperation and Development Anti-Bribery Convention. This international agreement makes offering or paying bribes a criminal offense and ends the deductibility of bribes.[43]

Still, corruption continues to be an international problem. Its pervasiveness, combined with U.S. prohibitions, creates a difficult obstacle for Americans who want to do business in many foreign countries. Chinese pay *huilu,* and Russians rely on *vzyatka.* In the Middle East, palms are greased with *baksheesh.* Figure 4.7 compares 53 countries based on surveys of perceived corruption. This Corruption Perceptions Index is computed by Transparency International, a Berlin-based international organization that rates the degree of corruption in 90 countries observed by businesspeople and the general public.[44]

The growth of online business with the unfolding information age has introduced new elements to the legal climate of international business. Ideas, patents, brand names, trademarks, copyrights, and other intellectual property are difficult to police, given the availability of information on the Internet. However, some countries are adopting laws to protect information obtained by electronic contacts. Malaysia imposes stiff fines and long jail terms on those convicted of illegally accessing computers and using information that passes through them.

International Regulations   To regulate international commerce, the United States and many other countries have ratified treaties and signed agreements that dictate the conduct of international business and protect some of its activities. The U.S. has entered into many *friendship, commerce, and navigation* treaties with other nations. Such treaties address many aspects of international business relations, including the right to conduct business in the treaty partner's domestic market. Other international business agreements involve product standards, patents, trademarks, reciprocal tax policies, export controls, international air travel, and international communications.

In 2000, Congress granted China full trade relations with the U.S. China agreed to lower trade barriers, including subsidies that held down the prices of food exports, restrictions on where foreign law firms can open offices, and taxes charged on imported goods. China also promised to halve these taxes, called *tariffs*, over the course of five years. The United States, in exchange, granted China equal access to U.S. markets enjoyed by most other countries.[45]

Many types of regulations affect the actions of managers doing business in international markets. Not only must worldwide producers and marketers maintain required minimum quality levels for all the countries in which they operate, but they must also comply with numerous specific local regulations. European countries impose hundreds of regulations affecting marketers. Britain prevents advertisers from encouraging children to engage in such unhealthy behavior as eating frequently throughout the day or replacing regular meals with candy and snack foods. Sweden also places limits on television and radio ads directed to children 12 years and under.[46] Germany and France allow publishers to set prices that retailers charge for their books. Because companies like Amazon.com adhere to the fixed prices, German customers looking for English-language books can get better prices by buying at the U.K. Web site, even with the extra shipping costs. German law prohibits most price discounts, so cheap last-minute air fares are illegal on German Web sites. Without the ability to lure flyers by offering special deals, few European airlines sell tickets online.[47]

A lack of international regulations or enforcement can generate its own set of problems. Software piracy offers an example. China is especially notorious for piracy. Illegally copied U.S. software as well as music and movies cost American firms billions of dollars in lost revenues. Others copy consumer goods ranging from shampoo to cigarettes. Joseph M. Johnson, president of Bestfoods Asia's Chinese operations, estimates that one-fourth of the Skippy peanut butter sold in China is actually counterfeited.

U.S. companies are alarmed about the lost sales and possible damage to their brands' reputation if consumers become disappointed or even sick after using inferior fakes. Anheuser-Busch encountered Chinese retailers stocking Budweiser beer before they had ever seen a company sales representative. The labels on the bottles looked legitimate, but a sip of the contents immediately gave away the fact that the beer was pirated. Trying to keep ahead of the Chinese pirates, the company started using labels on which special images appear only when the bottles are cold.

Types of Trade Restrictions

Trade restrictions such as taxes on imports and complicated administrative procedures create additional barriers to international business. They may limit consumer choices while increasing the costs of foreign-made products. Trade restrictions are also imposed to protect citizens' security, health, and jobs. A government may limit exports of strategic and defense-related goods to unfriendly countries to protect its security, ban imports of insecticide-contaminated farm products to protect health, and restrict imports to protect domestic jobs in the importing country.

Trade restrictions grow out of a country's legal structure, often in response to the political environment. Some restrictions are intended to punish or protest countries' political actions. The *Helms-Burton* Act, a controversial law enacted in 1996, imposes trade sanctions against Cuba and permits U.S. companies and citizens to sue foreign companies and their executives if they use assets expropriated from U.S. owners to do business in Cuba. It also denies U.S. visas to executives of firms facing lawsuits for violating the act.

Other restrictions are imposed to promote trade with certain countries. Still others protect countries from unfair competition. Table 4.4 summarizes major arguments for and against trade restrictions.

Regardless of the political reasons for trade restrictions, most take the form of tariffs. In addition to tariffs, governments impose a number of nontariff—or administrative—barriers. These include quotas, embargoes, and exchange controls.

Table 4.4 **Arguments for and against Trade Restrictions**

For	Against
Protect national defense and citizens' health	Raise prices for consumers
Protect new or weak industries	Restrict consumer choices
Protect against a practice called *dumping*, in which products are sold for less abroad than in the home market, competing unfairly with domestic goods	Cause retaliation by other countries, which limits export opportunities for businesses
Protect domestic jobs in the face of foreign competition	Result in loss of jobs from international business
Retaliate for another country's trade restrictions	Cause inefficient allocations of international resources

Tariffs Tariffs are taxes, surcharges, or duties on foreign products. Governments assess two types of tariffs—revenue and protective tariffs—both of which make imports more expensive for domestic buyers. Revenue tariffs generate income for the government. Upon returning home, U.S. leisure travelers who bring back goods are taxed 10 percent of the amount in excess of $400. This duty goes directly to the U.S. Treasury. The sole purpose of a protective tariff is to raise the retail price of imported products to match or exceed the prices of similar products manufactured in the home country. In other words, protective tariffs seek to level the playing field for local competitors.

Of course, tariffs create a disadvantage to companies that want to export to the countries imposing the tariffs. In addition, governments do not always see eye to eye on the reasons behind protective tariffs. The EU recently banned U.S. beef treated with growth hormones, on the grounds of health concerns. The U.S. government disputed these concerns and retaliated by imposing 100 percent tariffs on such European products as Roquefort cheese, Danish ham, Italian tomatoes, and German chocolate. These measures, which harmed both the European producers of these goods and the U.S. retailers that specialize in imported foods, were designed not so much to protect U.S. cheese, ham, tomato, and chocolate producers but to help beef producers by persuading Europe to change its policy. None of the U.S. tariffs applied to products produced in Britain, which did not support the EU ban on beef imports.[48]

Nontariff Barriers Nontariff, or administrative, trade barriers restrict imports in more subtle ways than tariffs. These measures may take such forms as quotas on imports, unnecessarily restrictive standards for imports, and export subsidies. Because many countries have recently substantially reduced tariffs or eliminated them entirely, they increasingly use nontariff barriers to boost exports and control flows of imported products.

Quotas limit the amounts of particular products that countries can import during specified time periods. Limits may be set as quantities, such as number of cars or bushels of wheat, or as values, such as dollars' worth of cigarettes. Governments regularly set quotas for agricultural products and sometimes for imported automobiles. The U.S. government has imposed about 1,000 quotas related to clothing imports from various countries. All of these quotas are scheduled to be lifted by 2005.

Quotas help to prevent **dumping**, a practice that developed during the 1970s. In one form of dumping, a company sells products abroad at prices below its cost of production. In another, a company exports a large quantity of a product at a lower price than the same product in the home market and drives down the price of the domestic product. Dumping benefits domestic consumers in the importing market, but it hurts domestic producers. It also allows companies to gain quick entry to foreign markets.

Charges of dumping are difficult to prove, but most countries have the authority to set quotas if they suspect it. In addition to establishing quotas, companies can protect themselves against dumping by requesting that their government impose an antidumping duty, thus offsetting the cost advantage of the foreign good.

More severe than a quota, an **embargo** imposes a total ban on importing a specified product or even a total halt to trading with a particular country. In addition to their punitive effects, embargoes can protect citizens' health, as was the intent of the European ban on beef from animals treated with hormones. Embargo durations can vary to accommodate changes in foreign policy. The U.S. government recently began to restore diplomatic relations with Iran and lifted its embargo on carpets, dried fruits, pistachios, and caviar imported from that country. However, the United States maintained an embargo on Iran's biggest export, oil. Pistachios represent Iran's third-largest export, but the United States may not resume its place as a major buyer of the nuts. Since the first sack of pistachio seeds was sent from Iran to California, the state has developed its own pistachio crop. California growers say they still have an advantage because of high duties imposed on imported pistachios during the 1980s when Iranian companies were accused of dumping the nuts on the U.S. market. U.S. growers also insist they have developed a superior product in the meantime.[49]

Another form of administrative trade restriction involves **exchange controls.** Imposed through a central bank or government agency, exchange controls affect both exporters and importers. Firms that gain foreign currencies through exporting are required to sell them to the central bank or another agency. Importers must buy foreign currencies to pay for their purchases from the same agency. The exchange control authority can then allocate, expand, or restrict foreign exchange to satisfy national policy goals.

REDUCING BARRIERS TO INTERNATIONAL TRADE

Although tariffs and administrative barriers still restrict trade, overall the world is moving toward free trade. Several types of organizations ease barriers to international trade, including groups that monitor trade policies and practices and institutions that offer monetary assistance. Another type of federation designed to ease trade barriers is the multinational economic community, such as the EU. This section looks at the roles these organizations play.

Organizations Promoting International Trade

For the 50 years of its existence, the **General Agreement on Tariffs and Trade (GATT),** an international trade accord, sponsored a series of negotiations, called *rounds*, that substantially reduced worldwide tariffs and other barriers. Major industrialized nations founded the multinational organization in 1947 to work toward reducing tariffs and relaxing import quotas. The last set of negotiations (the Uruguay Round) cut average tariffs by one-third, in excess of $700 billion, reduced farm subsidies, and improved protection for copyright and patent holders. In addition, international trading rules now apply to various service industries, with specific details yet to be resolved. Finally, the new agreement established the **World Trade Organization (WTO)** to succeed GATT. This new organization includes representatives from 135 countries, and others have applied to join. In 2000, the U.S. agreed to support China's membership in the WTO.

World Trade Organization   Since 1995, the WTO has monitored GATT agreements among the member nations, mediated disputes, and continued the effort to reduce trade barriers throughout the world. Unlike

BUSINESS DIRECTORY

> **tariff**   *tax imposed on imported goods.*

> **World Trade Organization (WTO)**   *135-member international institution that monitors GATT agreements and mediates international trade disputes.*

provisions in GATT, the WTO's decisions are binding on parties involved in disputes.

The WTO has grown more controversial in recent years as it issues decisions that have implications for working conditions and the environment in member nations. The United States lost a dispute in which Brazil and Venezuela said the U.S. government had set a higher standard for emissions from foreign gasoline than from domestic supplies. The WTO ruled that the U.S. standard must be the same for imports and domestic products, so standards were reduced for U.S. gasoline. Environmentalists were dismayed that the government's decision would lead to increased air pollution. Concerns have also been expressed that the WTO's focus on lowering trade barriers encourages businesses to keep costs down through practices that may increase pollution and human rights abuses. Particularly worrisome is the fact that the organization's member countries must agree on policies, and the 77 developing countries tend not to be eager to lose their low-cost advantage by enacting stricter labor and environmental laws. As M.G. Quibria of Manila's Asianic Development Bank points out, "There's an Asian consensus that human rights should not be linked to trade." Other critics fret that if well-funded U.S. giants like fast-food chains, entertainment companies, and Internet retailers operate free of constraints on their entry into foreign markets, they will wipe out smaller foreign businesses serving the distinct tastes and practices of other countries' cultures.

Trade unions in developed nations complain that the WTO's support of free trade makes it easier to export jobs to low-wage countries. According to the U.S. Department of Commerce, about a million U.S. jobs are lost each year as a result of imports or movement of work to other countries. They are not always minimum-wage jobs either. General Electric's Aircraft Engines division runs a global engineering project employing 300 engineers in Brazil, India, Mexico, and Turkey. Hiring engineers in these developing nations helps General Electric lower costs. Although free trade can also contribute to economic growth, creating new jobs, all these concerns about WTO policy have led to protest demonstrations—sometimes violent—beginning with the WTO meeting in Seattle a few years ago.[50]

World Bank   Shortly after the end of World War II, industrialized nations formed an organization to lend money to less-developed and developing countries. The **World Bank** primarily funds projects that build or expand nations' infrastructure such as transportation, education, and medical systems and facilities. The World Bank and other development banks provide the largest source of advice and assistance to developing nations. Often, in exchange for granting loans, the World Bank imposes requirements intended to build the economies of borrower nations.

The World Bank has come under fire for making loans with conditions that ultimately hurt the borrower nations. When developing nations are required to balance government budgets, they are sometimes forced to cut vital social programs. One World Bank official agrees that the critics are right in some situations: "Some of the conditions set were too harsh . . . and made tough economic conditions worse."[51] In addition, environmental and human rights activists maintain that the World Bank should consider the impact of its loans on the environment and the treatment of workers. Some observers believe that the organization is beginning to make progress in this regard.[52]

International Monetary Fund   Established a year after the World Bank, the **International Monetary Fund (IMF)** was created to promote trade through financial cooperation, and in the process, eliminate barriers. The IMF makes short-term loans to member nations that are unable to meet their budgetary expenses. It operates as a lender of last resort for troubled nations. In exchange for these emergency loans, IMF lenders frequently extract significant commitments from the borrowing nations to address the problems that led to the crises. These steps may include curtailing imports or even devaluing currency. Throughout its existence, the IMF has worked to prevent financial crises by warning the international business community when countries encounter problems meeting their financial obligations. Often, the IMF lends to countries to keep them from defaulting on prior debts and to prevent economic crises in particular countries from spreading to other nations. However, like the WTO and World Bank, the IMF has come under criticism. One criticism is that economic problems sometimes arise because banks and other businesses become insolvent, not because of government policies. IMF restrictions on government spending then don't address the real economic problems plaguing some troubled economies.[53] The IMF has responded to criticism by establishing an independent group to review its policies and recommend reforms.[54]

Another concern is that IMF lending has placed many poor nations in an impossible position. Some countries owe far more money than they can ever hope to repay, and the debt payments make it impossible for their governments to deliver desperately needed services to their citizens. The nations of sub-Saharan Africa are hard-pressed to deal with the ravages of AIDS, yet their debt exceeds their GDP and is three times as high as their total annual exports. Critics maintain that situations like these can only be improved by forgiving the debt. Canceling $45 million of Uganda's debt payments permitted that nation to cut school tuition and almost double the number of children enrolled in primary school. The arguments in favor of debt forgiveness are primarily humanitarian, but the major argument against it is that it will merely encourage nations to borrow with no intent to repay their loans.[55]

International Economic Communities

International economic communities reduce trade barriers and promote regional economic integration. In the simplest approach, countries may establish a *free-trade area* in which they trade freely among themselves without tariffs or trade restrictions. Each maintains its own tariffs for trade outside this area. A *customs union* sets up a free-trade area and specifies a uniform tariff structure for members' trade with nonmember nations. In a *common market*, or economic union, members go beyond a customs union and try to bring all of their trade rules into agreement. The EU is an example.

One example of a free-trade area is the **North American Free Trade Agreement (NAFTA)** enacted by the U.S., Canada, and Mexico. Other examples of regional trading blocs include the MERCOSUR customs union (joining Brazil, Argentina, Paraguay, Uruguay, Chile, and Bolivia), and the ten-country Association of South East Asian Nations (ASEAN). To ensure continuing success in meeting its goal of creating peace, stability, and prosperity, ASEAN holds annual meetings at which members review developments and give directives for meeting economic and political challenges. Figure 4.8 shows the size of these economic communities.

NAFTA

NAFTA became effective in 1994, creating the world's largest free-trade zone with the U.S., Canada, and Mexico. By eliminating all trade barriers and investment restrictions among the three nations over a 15-year period, NAFTA opens more doors for free trade. The agreement also eases regulations governing trade in services, such as banking, and establishes uniform legal requirements for protection of intellectual property. The three signatory countries can trade with one another without tariffs or other trade barriers, simplifying shipments of goods across the partners' borders. Standardized customs and uniform labeling regulations create economic efficiencies and smooth import and export procedures.

By eliminating trade barriers, NAFTA expands choices of products and suppliers for consumers. Domestic producers in the U.S., Canada, and Mexico have gained access to a larger market. Many items are

BUSINESS DIRECTORY

➤ **North American Free Trade Agreement (NAFTA)**   *1994 agreement among the U.S., Canada, and Mexico to break down tariffs and trade restrictions*

FIGURE 4.8
NAFTA, MERCOSUR, and ASEAN
Free-Trade Areas

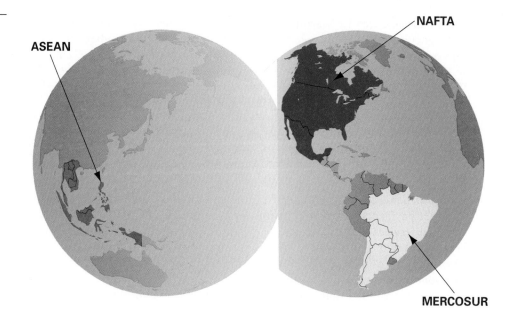

produced at lower per-unit costs than before NAFTA, because companies are able to plan for larger volumes of output.

Trade among the partners has increased steadily, with U.S. exports to Mexico growing at almost twice the rate of exports to other countries. Since NAFTA went into effect, Mexican exports grew from $52 billion to $137 billion, and foreign direct investment in Mexico doubled.[56] Critics blame NAFTA for causing more than 200,000 jobs to shift from the U.S. to Mexico. Especially hard hit were jobs in the apparel, electrical and electronic equipment, and transportation equipment industries. However, the Department of Commerce says trade with Canada and Mexico supports 2.6 million U.S. jobs and job loss is the result of changing technology, not international trade. Depending on their political agenda, observers are likewise split on whether NAFTA has helped or hurt the environment and labor conditions. Critics say producers have moved operations to Mexico to avoid stricter pollution controls and labor laws. Advocates of NAFTA argue that Mexico has improved conditions in order to trade with the U.S. and Canada.[57]

The growth of trade under NAFTA has encouraged the participants to pursue similar agreements with other countries. The Mexican government recently negotiated a NAFTA-style agreement with the EU.[58]

European Union

Perhaps the best-known example of a common market is the European Union (EU). The EU combines 15 countries, 350 million people, and a total GDP of $5 trillion to form a huge common market. Several central European countries and former Soviet republics have also applied for EU membership.

The EU's goals include promoting economic and social progress, introducing European citizenship as a complement to national citizenship, and giving the EU a significant role in international affairs. To achieve its goal of a borderless Europe, the EU is removing barriers to free trade among its members. This highly complex process involves standardizing business regulations and requirements, standardizing import duties and taxes, and eliminating customs checks, so that companies can transport goods from England to Italy as easily as from New York City to Boston.

Unifying standards and laws can contribute to economic growth. The EU established a common standard for mobile phones, called GSM. This standard enabled Nokia and Ericsson to develop a pan-European customer base for their cellular phones. Eventually, Nokia became the biggest seller of mobile communications devices worldwide.[59] But just as NAFTA sparked fears in the U.S. about free trade with Mexico, some people in Western Europe have worried that opening trade with countries like Poland, Hungary, and the Czech Republic will cause jobs to flow eastward to lower-wage economies.[60]

The EU also introduced the euro to replace currencies like the French franc and Italian lira. For the 11 member states that participated, potential benefits include eliminating the economic costs of exchanging one currency for another and simplifying price comparisons. Businesses and their customers have been able to make check and credit card transaction in euros since 1999, and euro notes and coins were introduced in 2002.

GOING GLOBAL

While expanding into overseas markets can increase profits and marketing opportunities, it also introduces new complexities to a firm's business operations. Before making the decision to go global, a company faces a number of key decisions, beginning with the following:

- Determining which foreign market(s) to enter
- Analyzing the expenditures required to enter a new market
- Deciding on the best way to organize the overseas operations

These issues vary in importance depending on the level of involvement a company chooses. Education and worker training in the host country would be much more important for a bank planning to open a foreign branch or an electronics manufacturer building an Asian factory than for a firm that is simply planning to export American-made products.

The choice of which markets to enter usually follows extensive research focusing on local demand for the firm's products, availability of needed resources, and ability of the local workforce to produce world-class quality. Other factors include existing and potential competition, tariff rates, currency stability, and investment barriers. A variety of government and other sources are available to facilitate this research process. A good starting place is the *CIA World Factbook,* which contains country-by-country information on geography, population, government, economy, and infrastructure.

U.S. Department of Commerce counselors at the agency's district offices offer a full range of international business advice, including computerized market data and names of business and government contacts in dozens of countries. As Table 4.5 shows, the Internet provides access to many resources for international trade information.

Levels of Involvement

After a firm has completed its research and decided to enter a foreign market, it can choose one or more of the entry strategies shown in Figure 4.9:

- Exporting or importing
- Entering into contractual agreements like franchising, licensing, and subcontracting deals
- Direct investment in the foreign market through acquisitions, joint ventures, or establishment of an overseas division

Although the company's risk increases with the level of its involvement, so does its overall control of all aspects of producing and selling its goods or services.

BUSINESS DIRECTORY

➤ **European Union (EU)**   *15-nation European economic alliance.*

Table 4.5 International Trade Research Resources on the Internet	
Web Site and Address	**General Description**
Asia, Inc. www.asia-inc.com	Business news in Asia, featuring articles on Asian countries from India to Japan
Europages www.europages.com	Directory of and links to Europe's top 150,000 companies in 25 European countries
Emerging Markets Directory www.emdirectory.com	Links to sites with information about the emerging markets of Asia, Latin America, Europe, Africa, and the Middle East
World Trade Organization www.wto.int	Details on the trade policies of various governments
CIA World Factbook www.odci.gov/cia/publications	Basic facts about the world's nations, from geography to economic conditions
STAT-USA www.stat-usa.gov	Extensive trade and economic data, information about trends, daily intelligence reports, and background data (access requires paid subscription to the service)
U.S. Commercial Service www.usatrade.gov	Information about Commerce Department counseling services, trade events, and U.S. export regulations
U.S. Business Advisor www.business.gov	One-stop access to a range of federal government information, services, and transactions
U.S. State Department travel.state.gov/travel_warnings.html	Listing of the State Department's latest travel warnings about conditions that may affect safety abroad, supplemented by a list of consulate addresses and country information

Companies frequently combine more than one of these strategies. Web portal Yahoo! used joint ventures with local firms to gain a quick presence in Japan, Britain, France, Germany, and South Korea. Only after developing experience as an international company has Yahoo! begun to engage in direct investment by creating foreign subsidiaries. Waiting to develop expertise before moving overseas is risky for online businesses, though, because Web sites are so easy for competitors to copy. Alando, an auction Web site based in Germany, looks remarkably like eBay. Rather than fight the company, eBay entered Germany by acquiring Alando.[61]

Importers and Exporters When a firm brings in goods produced abroad to sell domestically, it is an importer. Conversely, companies are exporters when they produce—or purchase—goods at home and sell them in overseas markets. An importing or exporting strategy provides the lowest level of international involvement, with the least risk and control.

Los Angeles Fiber Co., based in Vernon, California, sells fibers used to stuff cushions and pillows. Two of every five dollars of its annual sales are export sales. The company faces challenges when collecting payments from foreign customers, in part

FIGURE 4.9
Levels of Involvement in International Business

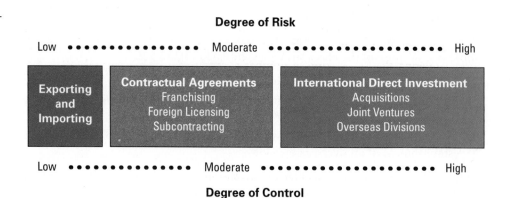

because foreign banks in many countries do not measure up to U.S. banking standards. The company has dealt with foreign banks that collect money from their customers, then take two to four weeks to move those funds into Los Angeles Fiber's bank account. Because of this delay, the firm's top managers have become experts in learning which banks they can rely on. Los Angeles Fiber encourages customers to open accounts with banks that meet its standards and has dropped customers that won't switch.[62]

Exports are frequently handled by special intermediaries called *export trading companies.* These firms search out competitively priced local merchandise and then resell it abroad at prices high enough to cover expenses and earn profits. When a retail chain like Dallas-based Pier One Imports wants to purchase West African products for its store shelves, it may contact an export trading company operating in a country such as Ghana. The local firm is responsible for monitoring quality, packaging the order for transatlantic shipment, arranging transportation, and handling the customs paperwork and other steps required to move the product from Ghana to the U.S.

Firms engage in exporting of two types: indirect and direct exporting. A company engages in *indirect exporting* when it manufactures a product, such as an electronic component, that becomes part of another product that is sold in foreign markets. The second method, *direct exporting,* occurs when a company seeks to sell its product in markets outside its own country. Often the first step for companies entering foreign markets, direct exporting is the most common form of international business. Firms that find success in exporting their products may then move on to other entry strategies.

In addition to reaching foreign markets by dealing with export trading companies, novice exporters may choose two other alternatives: export management companies and offset agreements. Rather than simply relying on an export trading company to assist in locating foreign products or foreign markets, an exporting firm may turn to an *export management company* for advice and expertise. These international specialists help the first-time exporter complete paperwork, make contacts with local buyers, and comply with local laws governing labeling, product safety, and performance testing. At the same time, the exporting firm retains much more control than would be possible with an export trading company.

An *offset agreement* matches a small business with a major international firm. It basically makes the small firm a subcontractor to the larger one. Such an entry strategy helps a new exporter by allowing it to share in the larger company's international expertise. The small firm also benefits in such important areas as international transaction documents and financing.

Countertrade A sizable share of international trade involves payments made in the form of local products, not currency. This system of international bartering agreements is called **countertrade.**

A common reason for resorting to international barter is inadequate access to needed foreign currency. To complete an international sales agreement, the seller may agree to accept part of the purchase cost in currency and the remainder in other merchandise. Since the seller may decide to locate a buyer for the bartered goods before completing the transaction, a number of international buyers and sellers frequently join together in a single agreement.

Countertrade may often be a firm's only opportunity to enter a particular market. Many developing countries simply cannot obtain enough credit or financial assistance to afford the imports that their people want. Countries with heavy debt burdens also resort to countertrade. Russian buyers, with their country's soft currency, may resort to trading local products ranging from crude oil to diamonds to vodka as payments for purchases from foreign companies unwilling to accept Russian rubles. Still other countries, such as China, may restrict imports. Under such circumstances countertrade may be the only practical way to win government approval to import needed products.

Contractual Agreements   Once a company, large or small, gains some experience in international sales, it may decide to enter into contractual agreements with local parties. These arrangements can include franchising, foreign licensing, and subcontracting.

Franchising   Common among U.S. companies, franchising can work well for companies seeking to expand into international markets, too. A **franchise,** as described in detail in Chapter 5, is a contractual agreement in which a wholesaler or retailer (the franchisee) gains the right to sell the franchisor's products under that company's brand name if it agrees to the related operating requirements. The franchisee can also receive marketing, management, and business services from the franchisor. While these arrangements are common among leading fast-food brands such as Pizza Hut, McDonald's, and KFC, other kinds of service providers also often look to franchising as an international marketplace option.

The Howard Johnson hotel chain is using franchising to expand into Europe. Its franchise agreement with a U.K. business called Premier Hotels calls for Premier to develop 40 hotels in Austria, Belgium, Germany, Luxembourg, the Netherlands, Portugal, Spain, and Switzerland. Premier already operates Howard Johnson hotels in Great Britain. Calling on the experience of a European firm makes sense, because chain hotels are relatively uncommon in Europe. At the same time, the franchising arrangement enables the hotels to tap into the Howard Johnson's reservation system, which also includes specialized management software.[63]

Foreign Licensing   In a **foreign licensing agreement,** one firm allows another to produce or sell its product, or use its trademark, patent, or manufacturing processes in a specific geographic area. In return, the firm gets a royalty or other compensation.

Licensing can be advantageous for a small manufacturer anxious to launch a well-known product overseas. Not only does it get a market-tested product from another market, but little or no investment is required to begin operating. The arrangement can also allow entry into a market otherwise closed to imports due to government restrictions.

Licensing a brand is a $26 billion industry today. General Motors (GM) started engaging in licensing almost by accident. The company had been spending millions of dollars a year on lawsuits against companies that were placing GM brands on clothing. Then the company realized that caps and T-shirts bearing the Corvette logo could be a source of profits, not a drain on the legal department. GM has since negotiated over 1,200 licensing agreements to place its brands on goods from cologne to clothing, generating over $1 billion a year in revenues.

Most licensed brands are American, but Europeans have been jumping on the licensing bandwagon. Jaguar has licenses for its name on eyeglass frames, footwear, and fragrances. Aston Martin has a licensing program with makers of model cars and a video game.[64]

Subcontracting   The third type of contractual agreement, **subcontracting,** involves hiring local companies to produce, distribute, or sell goods or services. This move allows a foreign firm to take advantage of the subcontractor's expertise in local culture, contacts, and regulations. Subcontracting works equally well for mail-order companies, which can farm out order fulfillment and customer service functions to local businesses. Manufacturers practice subcontracting to save money on import duties and labor costs, and businesses go this route to market products best sold by locals in a given country.

Many high-tech firms rely on subcontractors known as contract electronics manufacturers (CEMs). The CEMs specialize in producing items from PC components to cell phones according to the specifications of the companies that design and market those products. Businesses currently using CEMs include Hewlett-Packard, Cisco, IBM, and Motorola. Companies with names like Solectron, Celectica, and

Going Global Isn't So Easy for Internet Companies

It's a standard business concept: If you want to enter a foreign market, buy a foreign company. That way, you don't have to worry about finding workers who speak the language or figuring out what types of goods and services consumers want. Going global this way would seem to be even easier for Internet companies, just by their boundaryless nature. That's what executives at Amazon, eBay, and Yahoo! thought. Amazon bought two small online book-sellers—Bookpages in the United Kingdom and Telebuch in Germany. eBay acquired Alando.de, a German online auctioneer. Yahoo! followed a slightly different route by creating eight different country-specific Yahoo!s throughout Europe and is expanding into Asia.

Despite early and modest success, these three U.S. e-businesses are hardly dominating their European markets. Amazon was successful in circumventing German regulatory problems, and its two acquisitions now generate revenues of approximately $300 million a year. But there aren't really any more start-ups for it to buy in Europe; other European companies have already snapped them up. In the United Kingdom, British entrepreneur Timothy Jackson scooped eBay with his own online auction site, then quickly signed exclusive agreements in other European countries. eBay compounded its own problems by pricing items in U.S. dollars, which alienated many British customers. And although Yahoo! is Britain's number one portal, the French portal Wanadoo has many advantages, including being tied to the national telephone monopoly.

So far, these American Internet firms are not discouraged, and none has plans to pack its bags and head home. Fabiola Arredondo, managing director for Yahoo! Europe, believes that her company will duplicate its U.S. success in the long run. "Users who are comfortable with the Internet will be switching to Yahoo! more and more," she predicts. In fact, one reason Yahoo! has attained number-one status in Britain is because the national telephone company lost its monopoly. Should this occur in other countries, Yahoo! is ready to step in. But the American companies have a long way to go in foreign markets before their brand names carry the clout that they do at home. Acquiring local firms in foreign markets is the first step, not the last.

QUESTIONS FOR CRITICAL THINKING

1. In addition to acquiring local companies, what other steps can the American Internet companies take to increase their level of involvement in foreign markets?
2. In what ways can these companies create value for consumers in these markets?

Sources: Brian Bergstein, "Yahoo! Dumps Amazon," The Associated Press, September 19, 2000, **abcnews.go.com**; Chris Taylor, "All Boxed In," *Time*, September 4, 2000, **www.time.com**; "Yahoo! India Opens Today," Yahoo! press release, June 29, 2000, **docs.yahoo.com**; Katarzyna Moreno, "Global Pains," *Forbes*, March 20, 2000, pp. 286–288; John Schwartz, "EBay Greatly Expands Live Online Auction Bidding," *New York Times*, January 22, 2001, downloaded from **www.nytimes.com**, January 29, 2001.

Flextronics International not only assemble electronics but help with design, testing, and even product servicing. They are likely to operate more efficiently than the companies whose names are on the products because they invest in the latest software and manufacturing equipment and serve various customers. Flexible machinery and production tracking software enable companies like HMT Technology to track every detail of the manufacturing process, making immediate adjustments when problems arise or orders change. The company uses its technology to make disks for computers at a significantly lower cost than its Japanese competitors pay to make similar products.[65]

A key disadvantage of subcontracting is that companies cannot always control their subcontractors' business practices. As discussed in Chapter 2, several major U.S. companies have been embarrassed by reports that their subcontractors used child labor to manufacture clothing.

International Direct Investment   Investing directly in production and marketing operations in a foreign country is the ultimate level of global involvement. Over time, a firm may become experienced and successful at conducting business in other countries through exporting and contractual agreements. Its managers may then decide to establish manufacturing facilities in those countries, open branch offices, or buy ownership interests in local companies.

In an *acquisition*, a company purchases another existing firm in the host country. An acquisition permits a company to gain an international presence very quickly, as discussed in the "Business Hits and Misses" box. Wal-Mart enjoyed an 86 percent increase in foreign sales after it acquired ASDA, a British supermarket chain with annual revenues of $14 billion.[66] Looking the other way across the Atlantic, the French company Infogames Entertainment is using acquisitions to help it break into the

Background. Gaining a foothold in a global marketplace can be tricky. Some companies fold under the increased competition; others turn to global suppliers for a competitive solution. Sikorsky Aircraft Corp. is one of the latter. Sikorsky makes helicopters for commercial and military use. The firm's copters are often seen on search and rescue missions, disaster relief flights, and U.S. Army or National Guard operations. One product, the Sikorsky Helibus, represents a current trend by companies attempting to gain a competitive edge in the global marketplace: forming a joint ventures.

What Happened? Sikorsky doesn't hire international participants in the Helibus project merely as subcontractors to produce or assemble parts according to the firm's blueprints. Instead, each of Sikorsky's partners has the authority to design the components they build. The cabin is designed and built by Mitsubishi Heavy Industries, and the cockpit module is designed by Aerospace Industrial Development Corp., both Japanese firms. The fuselage comes from Gamesa in Spain, and the vertical fin travels from China's Jingdezhen Helicopter Group. The landing gear and fuel sponsors are manufactured by Embraer in Brazil. All of these parts arrive at Sikorsky's Connecticut facility, where they are assembled—along with Sikorsky-built components such as the transmission and rotor system.

The Response. How does this design process work? Each partner has the responsibility to make its own technology infrastructure improvements. "We [try] not to dictate too much to them," says a Sikorsky manager. In other words, each of the partners assumes a certain amount of risk and responsibility in getting the Helibus to the launchpad. As fragmented as it sounds, the system works because of technology. Three-dimensional electronic modeling helps far-flung designers work together to spot and correct potentially costly—and dangerous—design conflicts. In fact, as various versions of the Helibus model were sent to partners, they spotted over 1,300 conflicts in design—before any of the components was actually manufactured, saving Sikorsky untold millions. Designers and engineers communicate via e-mail and the Internet. These communications take place in English, which is considered the universal language of the aerospace industry. The 3-D modeling and Internet communication make it possible for smaller teams to operate efficiently.

Today and Counting. In speaking of the relationship that Sikorsky shares with its foreign suppliers, "this is a leading edge concept," says David Burdick, vice president of engineering applications at Gartner Group. "The . . . partners are true design collaborators rather than design fulfillers. They have the authority to originate design intent rather than just process it." Is the collaboration working? The company recently signed an extremely competitive contract worth an estimated $186 million with the Austrian Ministry of Defense, and its revenues climbed to a lofty $1.4 billion in a recent year.

QUESTIONS FOR CRITICAL THINKING

1. In what ways might Sikorsky seek to increase its level of involvement in the global market?
2. What barriers to trade might Sikorsky face if it tries to increase its level of involvement in a country like China?

Sources: "Sikorsky Aircraft Corporation: About Us," company Web site, **www.sikorsky.com,** accessed January 29, 2001; "Sikorsky Wins Austrian Contract," Reuters Online News, October 9, 2000; Frank Colucci, "Hatching the Helibus," *Executive Edge,* June/July 1999, pp. 28–34.

---

huge American market for video games. The company's first major success, a haunted-house adventure called Alone in the Dark, helped the company establish a positive reputation among video game developers, but it needed a way to get shelf space in U.S. stores. So Infogames bought Accolade, a San Jose publisher of video games. With that deal, Infogames got not only Accolade's games but also a distribution channel through video game stores and major chains like Toys 'R' Us and Wal-Mart.[67]

Joint ventures allow companies to share risks, costs, profits, and management responsibilities with one or more host country nationals, as described in the "Clicks and Mortar" box. Like many auto companies in recent years, General Motors has increased its global role by entering into joint ventures with competitors in other countries. It recently exchanged stock shares with Fiat Auto, giving the U.S. and Italian carmakers a stake in each other's success. In addition, the two companies jointly run their European and Latin American engine and transmission factories. The shared operations are expected to save them billions of dollars through greater efficiency. GM has also formed alliances with Suzuki Motor Corp., Isuzu Motors, and Fuji Heavy Industries, a combination that accounts for one of every four cars produced in the world.[68]

By setting up an *overseas division,* a company can conduct a significant amount of its business overseas. This strategy differs from that of a multinational company

Table 4.6   The World's Top Ten Multinationals

Rank and Company	Corporate Headquarters	Revenues (in billions)
1. General Motors Corp.	United States	$177
2. Wal-Mart Stores	United States	167
3. ExxonMobil	United States	164
4. Ford Motor Co.	United States	163
5. DaimlerChrysler	Germany	160
6. Mitsui	Japan	119
7. Mitsubishi	Japan	118
8. Toyota Motor	Japan	116
9. General Electric	United States	112
10. Itochu	Japan	109

in that a company with overseas divisions remains primarily a domestic organization with international operations. Gateway Computer, for instance, sells 10 percent of its products in Europe, the Middle East, and Africa. To serve these regions, the company operates a call center in Dublin, offering technical support and customer service. A call center in Ireland lets Gateway take advantage of low taxes, a skilled multilingual workforce, and Ireland's advanced telecommunications infrastructure. When Gateway set up the call center, it also got financial help from the Irish Development Authority. The call center also gives Gateway the advantage of being closer to its growing base of customers on the other side of the Atlantic.[69]

From Multinational Corporation to Global Business

A **multinational corporation (MNC)** is an organization with significant foreign operations. As Table 4.6 shows, firms headquartered in the U.S. and Japan dominate the list of the world's largest multinationals. Of the top 20 MNCs, the only exceptions to the U.S.-Japanese dominance are Germany's DaimlerChrysler, Royal Dutch/Shell (with headquarters divided between Britain and the Netherlands), France's AXA, Britain's BP Amoco, and Germany's Volkswagen.

Since the 1960s, when the first concerns surfaced about their influence on international business, MNCs have undergone a number of dramatic changes. For one, despite the continuing dominance of U.S. companies, America can no longer claim most of the top slots. Today's MNC is just as likely to be based in Japan (Sony, Nissan, and Matsushita, for example), with others based in Germany (DaimlerChrysler, Volkswagen) or Switzerland (Nestlé, Credit Suisse). Additionally, MNCs integrate capital, technologies, and even ideas from their various global operations. These operations no longer function as distant market outposts.

Many U.S. multinationals, including Nike and Wal-Mart, have expanded their overseas operations because they believe that domestic markets are peaking and foreign markets offer greater sales and profit potential. Other MNCs are making substantial investments in developing countries in part because these countries provide low-cost labor compared with the U.S. and Western Europe. In addition, many MNCs are locating high-tech facilities in countries with large numbers of technical-school graduates, such as India. But MNCs can experience difficulties in foreign markets, as the "Solving an Ethical Controversy" box discusses.

As MNCs contribute to a global economy, they reap the benefits of the global marketplace. Consumers in countries as geographically and culturally distant as Saudi Arabia and Canada shave with Gillette's razor blades, wash clothes with Procter & Gamble's Tide detergent, and use computers with Intel chips inside. Nike is crafting an international strategy aimed at both winning the marketing game

BUSINESS DIRECTORY

➤ **multinational corporation (MNC)** *firm with significant operations and marketing activities outside its home country.*

Goldman Sachs International provides financial infrastructure by financing developing businesses all over the world. In this ad from *The Economist* magazine, the company advertises its ability to provide support to make a big idea a success—wherever the company is located.

and enabling its international customers to win at the sports of their dreams. The company offers teens in Southeast Asia a line of footwear priced for households of limited means. Compared with the $50 to $150 shoes sold in the U.S., shoes in Nike's Play Series line are priced at the equivalent of about $25. The Play Series shoes are advertised to consumers in India, Indonesia, Malaysia, the Philippines, Singapore, and Thailand with the slogan "It's My Turn" beside images of national and international sports heroes. To help young people get their turn at sports, Nike has built Play Zone playgrounds with courts that can be used for games from basketball to badminton. The company has also donated equipment in rural areas. For Asian kids, some of whom play in bare feet, Nike is introducing the whole concept of wearing the right shoes for the game.[70]

Sources of Export Assistance

Regardless of the global business strategy that a company chooses, it may require export assistance. Companies can tap a variety of resources for this help. The U.S. Department of Commerce maintains a toll-free information hot line (1-800-USA-TRADE) that describes various federal export programs. The Web site of the Commerce Department's International Trade Administration (www.ita.doc.gov) also provides links to trade information, as well as Country Commercial Guides.

Companies can also seek advice from trade counselors at the Commerce Department's 68 district offices, who can offer information about exporting, computerized market data, and names of contacts in more than 60 countries. Some of these services are free; others are reasonably priced.

INTERNATIONAL ORGANIZATION STRUCTURES

The decision to go global must be followed by a series of additional decisions that specify the most appropriate organization structure for the expanded operation. The level of involvement in international business is a key factor in these decisions. Although a firm engaged in simple export activities may be best served by an export trading company, another company with extensive overseas sales may establish its own sales force for each country in which it operates. Figure 4.10 lists the alternative organization structures that are typical of global business firms.

Independent Agents

One method of entering international markets avoids the need to commit a major investment for developing and maintaining an overseas sales force: Using **independent agents.** These marketing intermediaries serve as independent sales forces in foreign markets, earning commissions on sales they book. They typically make sales calls on prospective customers, collect payments, and ensure customer satisfaction. Most cover limited geographic markets and hold down costs by representing multiple companies that produce related, noncompeting products.

Companies entering new foreign markets frequently rely on independent agents for several reasons:

- They understand their target markets, including customs and local environments.

- They represent minimal-risk entry alternatives for first-time exporters. If the firm is unhappy with an independent representative, it can terminate the relationship.

- Since most exporter–independent agent agreements specify compensation based on sales, they limit financial risks.

Exporters considering distributing through independent agents can secure names of local agents in various countries by contacting state export bureaus of the U.S. Department of Commerce. These agencies can also assist in developing sales agreements.

Licensing Agreements

As described earlier in the chapter, some firms try to increase revenues without making significant foreign investments by licensing their products, brand names, or production processes to other firms. Under this arrangement, the firm receiving the license has exclusive rights to use the production process or to manufacture and/or market the product in a specified market. In return, the firm granting the license typically receives an up-front fee plus an ongoing percentage of product sales.

Licensing agreements can be advantageous for companies seeking to enter foreign markets. License holders are usually large, well-known companies that depend on sales of the licensed products for their revenues. Because they invest more resources in the product than independent agents would, they often provide more effective representation in foreign markets. Also, licensing agreements are relatively inexpensive and easy to create. The license holder is familiar with the target market, and the exporting company can draw on its experience and expertise instead of spending money researching the market and culture.

Licensing agreements bring an important limitation, however: They usually specify long time periods. A company that wants to attract the best license holder in a market typically must grant exclusive rights to the product for five years or even longer. Firms may benefit from such time commitments if license holders provide effective support, but these contracts are difficult to terminate if the license holders prove to be ineffective partners.

Branch Offices

A branch office involves a different kind of commitment to foreign investment by a company. Instead of relying on a third party, the firm establishes its own overseas facility. In this way, it both improves its control and strengthens its presence in the host country. That was Trillium Digital Systems' objective when it opened a branch office in the United Kingdom. Trillium, which markets communications software, wanted to have people working in Europe to forge closer ties with its overseas customers and provide better support for its overseas sales representatives. A European office was a natural move for Los Angeles–based Trillium, because it has been selling globally from the start. The company's first customer was from France, and its second customer was from Japan. Trillium's hiring practices back up this level of commitment to multinational sales. Employees speak over two dozen different languages.[71]

FIGURE 4.10
Alternative Structures for International Organizations

Can Coke Go Local in Europe?

The Coca-Cola Company is living proof that being big doesn't necessarily mean being better when it comes to relationships in foreign markets. After several years of serious blunders, the dominant global soft-drink supplier is now trying to rebuild its relationships—and its reputation—in Europe. What went wrong? First, all decisions about advertising, products, and packaging were made at the company's Atlanta headquarters instead of carefully considering the values and tastes of each local market. Second, the company charged inappropriately high prices for Coke concentrate in foreign markets. Third, the firm alienated foreign government officials with its aggressive efforts to capture a bigger market share in their countries. Finally, the company reacted too slowly to a scare in Belgium in which cans of Coke were found to be contaminated with a sulfur compound. As a result, public trust crumbled, and Coca-Cola products were pulled from shelves in several European countries.

Does The Coca-Cola Company deserve a second chance to rebuild its relationship with European markets?

PRO

1. The Coca-Cola Company is making sincere efforts to right its previous wrongs in Europe. The company has hired local marketers, set up expanded communications offices, and is developing soft drinks—such as a pear-flavored drink in Turkey and a berry drink in Germany—geared toward local tastes.
2. The company has rehired Carl Ware, well-known for his previous work with local officials and community groups, as head of a global public affairs unit. In this move, "Coke will be able to

sense the economic, political, and social sensitivities" in its European markets. Ware might insist on buying more raw materials locally and increasing the firm's involvement with local affairs.
3. Executives say they have learned their lesson from the way the contamination scare was handled. "The crisis had taught us the need to get closer to local consumers," says Marc Mathieu, president of the new Benelux and France division.

CON

1. The company should not be let off the hook for the contamination problem. "When you have a recall for any consumer-product company, you are floating in very dangerous water," says beverage analyst George Thompson.
2. The company had no contingency plan in place for such a consumer crisis. Such an oversight is inexcusable in such a large corporation.
3. The Coca-Cola Company has misread the European marketplace in other ways, especially in its aggressive attempts to acquire European companies and bully its way through government regulations.

SUMMARY

The Coca-Cola Company's future in Europe is anything but certain. Although attempts have been made to rebuild its reputation, sales have been slow to respond. Wary consumers have been sipping other soft drinks. Carl Ware admits, "We've got work to do."

Sources: William Echikson and Dean Foust, "For Coke, Local Is It," *Business Week,* July 3, 2000, p. 122; Dean Foust, "Will Coke Go Better with Carl Ware?" *Business Week,* January 24, 2000, p. 138; Nick Pachetti, "Tempest in a Coke Can," *Worth,* October 1999, pp. 51–56; James L. Graff, "A Big Fizzle for Coca-Cola," *Time,* June 28, 1999, **www.time.com.**

To maintain a branch office in another country, a firm must develop an understanding of both the local market and its culture. This requirement demands a more extensive investment in time and experience than working with an independent agent or licensee. Many firms choose to combine branch offices and licensing agreements. The two strategies can complement each other, since license holders provide access to the local market, and the branch office can oversee the activities of the license holder.

Strategic Alliances

Similar to a joint venture, a **strategic alliance** is an international business strategy in which a company finds a partner in the country where it wants to do business. These partnerships can create competitive advantages in new markets by allowing the parties to combine resources and capital into new, jointly owned business ventures. Both the risks and profits are shared, firms maintain control over their international activities, and they benefit from the local market expertise of their partners. A number of countries, including Mexico and China, have laws that require foreign firms doing business in their countries to work through such alliances.

With a growing number of travelers shopping for their plane tickets online, airlines have been forming alliances to sell tickets. One of these efforts is a seven-company venture of airlines based in the Asia-Pacific region. The airlines, including Australia's Qantas, Cathay Pacific Airways, and Singapore Airlines, post schedules and ticket prices at a Web site where customers can make purchases. When travelers buy directly from the airlines, the airlines don't have to pay commissions to travel agents. For this reason, airlines are trying to set up their own sites, rather than depending on independent sites like Expedia and Travelocity to sell tickets. Qantas hopes to save millions of dollars by selling online.[72]

Direct Investment

Unlike strategic alliances, a firm makes a **direct investment** in a foreign market when it buys an existing company or establishes a factory, retail outlets, or other facilities there. Direct investment entails the most complete involvement in foreign trade, but it also brings the most risk. Companies that invest directly in other countries must consider a number of issues discussed in this chapter, including the cultural environments, political stability, labor markets, and currency stability they will likely encounter.

As Figure 4.11 shows, U.S. companies—the most active in international direct investments—allocated over half of their $980 billion in total direct investment to Europe. The U.S. market is also a popular investment location for foreign investors, which recently invested over $800 billion in projects ranging from factories to dot.com enterprises.

When Matsushita Electrical Industrial Co. wanted to participate in Silicon Valley's innovation, the Japanese MNC planned to build its own laboratory. However, it quickly learned that U.S. engineers preferred to start their own businesses and capitalize on the Internet boom. So Matsushita adopted an investment strategy. It set up a venture capital fund to invest in U.S. start-ups working on technologies of interest to Matsushita. The company hopes to benefit from America's innovative, individualistic culture by helping to finance its entrepreneurs. At the same time, Matsushita's investment reflects a change from a manufacturing-oriented business philosophy to one that takes chances on future technology.[73]

DEVELOPING A STRATEGY FOR INTERNATIONAL BUSINESS

In developing a framework within which to conduct international business, managers must first evaluate their corporate objectives, organizational strengths and weaknesses, and strategies for product development and marketing. They can choose to combine these elements in either a global strategy or a multidomestic strategy.

Global Business Strategies

A **global business** (or *standardization*) **strategy** specifies a standardized, worldwide product and marketing strategy. The firm sells the same product in essentially the same manner throughout the world. Many companies simply modify their domestic business strategies by translating promotional

MICRO-MANAGE.
MACRO-MINE.

A few minutes can mean a difference of thousands of tons in the mining business. But controlling the big picture, today, is often a matter of keystrokes. Komatsu, a world leader in mining hardware, created Komatsu Mining Systems (KMS) to tackle the software end. KMS enables mine operators to lower cost per ton at every step of production.

This total production partnership delivers the operational efficiencies of Modular Mining's DISPATCH® systems, monitoring and managing every aspect of mine operation in real time. Optimizing everything from dispatch and loading to monitoring equipment wear and setting maintenance schedules.

Every detail is backed by Komatsu's full range of mining equipment. Dump trucks, bulldozers and loaders that are world leaders in capacity, speed, reliability and, especially, size. Backed by Komatsu's on-site service, maintenance and local support anywhere in the world.

Not only is KMS optimizing mine productivity today, it's also laying the infrastructure for the potential gains of fully automated mines in the near future. Whether your business is mining, construction or demolition, Komatsu's expertise and equipment, hardware and software, will enhance your operational efficiency by the ton.

Head Office: 2-3-6 Akasaka, Minato-ku, Tokyo 107-8414 Japan Tel: 81-3-5561-2617 Fax: 81-3-3505-9662 www.komatsu.com   **KOMATSU**

Two world-class heavy-equipment multinationals are Tokyo-headquartered Komatsu and U.S.-based Caterpillar. Komatsu's mining-equipment product line includes dump trucks, bulldozers, and loaders. Its Komatsu Mining Systems subsidiary provides software to use in controlling mining operations. In addition to its machinery and equipment, the company offers product service support "backed by Komatsu's on-site service, maintenance, and local support anywhere in the world."

FIGURE 4.11
Destinations and Sources of Direct Investment Dollars

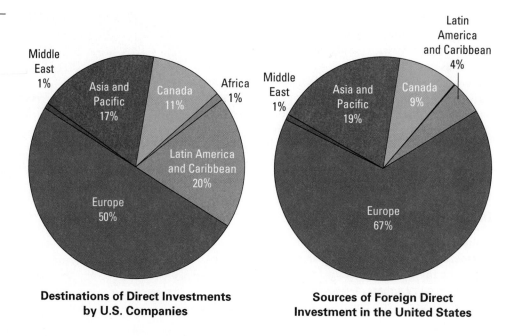

Destinations of Direct Investments by U.S. Companies

Sources of Foreign Direct Investment in the United States

brochures and product-use instructions into the languages of the host nations. Toyota adapts its marketing not only to international markets but to groups within nations. It is the biggest buyer of automobile advertising targeted to Hispanic Americans.[74]

Following its merger with Daimler Benz, Chrysler combined its international and U.S. sales and marketing divisions into a single global division. The objective of the change is to create and convey a single marketing message to its customers around the world, in support of global brands. DaimlerChrysler's first major test of the new global strategy was the launch of its PT Cruiser, a hybrid of a minivan and sport utility vehicle with 1930s-era styling. To prepare the advertising campaign, DaimlerChrysler's ad agency gathered ideas from offices in the different countries where the PT Cruiser would be sold. The only adaptations of the ads are translating the words into local languages and placing the steering wheel on the right in the United Kingdom, Australia, and Japan.[75]

A global marketing perspective can be appropriate for some goods and services and certain market segments that are common to many nations. The approach works for products with universal appeal, like Coca-Cola, and for luxury items like jewelry. Executives at Metabolife International are hoping that a global strategy will also work for its herbal remedies, as consumers change their views of health care. Americans are becoming more accustomed to the use of single herbs, but Chinese consumers have a vast and complex array of herbs, each combination designed for a specific symptom. Metabolife executives think the time may be right to introduce a product that will seem more sophisticated to Americans used to one-herb remedies, while simplifying the traditional complicated Chinese standards. Metabolife's line of remedies, under the brand Chinac, combines herbs targeted to particular ailments, such as colds, headache, or arthritis, but not to slight variations of symptoms in various forms of these ailments. Metabolife hopes that Americans and Chinese alike will appreciate the ease with which they can select the Chinac remedies.[76]

Multidomestic Business Strategies

Under a **multidomestic business** (or *adaptation*) **strategy,** the firm treats each national market in a different way. It develops products and marketing strategies that appeal to the customs, tastes, and buying habits of particular national markets. Companies that neglect the global nature of the Internet can unwittingly cause problems for potential customers by failing to adapt their strategy. Jo Van Samang, a marketing manager in Belgium, tried to order from a U.S.-based Internet company but failed when the site rejected his order because he did not fill in the "state" field on the order form. David Topping, marketing director for UpDate Marketing, a provider of marketing software, notes that European customers are less comfortable with online shopping than their U.S. counterparts. So Topping says a Web site that wants to attract European visitors should not simply assume they are ready to make a purchase. Topping recommends that Web sites be tailored to different comfort levels—perhaps offering lower-priced products on a site for Europeans so that they can build up comfort with online shopping or offering a list of places to buy products off line.[77]

Dell Computer tailors its Web sites to the needs of different regions. Of Dell's 80 Web sites, 34 have Internet business capabilities matched to the local country. Dell Japan offers an advanced form of its Premier Pages, customized for particular business customers. The Premier Pages for Dell Japan keep track of service needs and Dell's response, as well as providing news about Dell products. Sites are also customized to reflect differences in local languages and currencies. However, one thing is the same from region to region: Dell's commitment to service. This understanding of customers' needs—different languages but a common desire for good service—has helped Dell take the lead in selling computers online.[78]

When Maytag prepared to sell refrigerators and washing machines in China, it researched the ways it should adapt its marketing. The company thought it might bring its well-respected brand name to China, but consumer research indicated that the Chinese failed to recognize the Maytag name and also perceived American appliances as too big and bulky. In addition, Chinese consumers expected Japanese and European appliances to be more economical and innovative. Based on this information, Maytag decided to use the brand name Rongshida, after its Chinese partner, Hefei Rongshida. To offset the less favorable perceptions of American appliances, Rongshida's ads emphasize well-built appliances with valuable benefits of such features as hardworking washing machine parts and self-defrosting freezers.[79] As this example shows, learning about international customers is an important part of preparing for the global economy.

WHAT'S AHEAD

Examples in this chapter indicate that both large and small businesses are relying on world trade, not just major corporations. Chapter 5 examines the special advantages and challenges that small-business owners encounter. In addition, a critical decision facing any new business is the choice of the most appropriate form of business ownership. Chapter 5 also examines the major ownership structures—sole proprietorship, partnership, and corporation—and assesses the pros and cons of each. The chapter closes with a discussion of recent trends affecting business ownership, such as the growing impact of franchising and business consolidations through mergers and acquisitions.

> **BUSINESS DIRECTORY**

> **multidomestic business strategy** *developing and marketing products to serve different needs and tastes of separate national markets.*

> ## Summary of Learning Goals

1. **Explain the importance of international business and the main reasons why nations trade.**

   The U.S. is both the world's largest importer and the largest exporter, although less than 5 percent of the world's population lives within its borders. With the increasing globalization of the world's economies, the international marketplace offers tremendous opportunities for U.S. and foreign businesses to expand into new markets for their goods and services. Doing busness globally provides new sources of materials and labor. Trading with other countries also reduces a company's dependence on economic conditions in its home market. Countries that encourage international trade enjoy higher levels of economic activity, employment, and wages than those that restrict it. The major world markets are North America, Western Europe, the Pacific Rim, and Latin America. Emerging markets such as China and Brazil will become increasingly important to U.S. businesses over the next decade.

2. Discuss the relationship of absolute and comparative advantage to international trade.

Nations usually benefit if they specialize in producing certain goods or services. A country has an absolute advantage if it holds a monopoly or produces a good or service at a lower cost than other nations. It has a comparative advantage if it can supply a particular product more efficiently or at a lower cost than it can produce other items.

3. Describe how nations measure international trade and the significance of exchange rates.

Countries measure the level of international trade by comparing exports and imports and then calculating whether a trade surplus or a deficit exists. This is the balance of trade, which represents the difference between exports and imports. The term *balance of payments* refers to the overall flow of money into or out of a country, including overseas loans and borrowing, international investments, profits from such investments, and foreign aid. An exchange rate is the value of a nation's currency relative to the currency of another nation. Currency values typically fluctuate, or "float," relative to the supply and demand for specific currencies in the world market. When the value of the dollar falls compared with other currencies, the cost paid by foreign businesses and households for U.S. products declines, and demand for exports may rise. An increase in the value of the dollar raises the prices of U.S. products sold abroad, but it reduces the prices of foreign products sold in the United States.

4. Identify the major barriers that confront global businesses.

Businesses face several obstacles in the global marketplace. Companies must be sensitive to social and cultural differences, such as languages, values, and religions, when operating in other countries. Economic differences include standard of living variations and levels of infrastructure development. Legal and political barriers are among the most difficult to judge. Each country sets its own laws regulating business practices. Trade restrictions like tariffs and administrative barriers also present obstacles to international business.

5. Explain how international trade organizations and economic communities reduce barriers to international trade.

Many international organizations seek to promote international trade by reducing barriers. The list includes the World Trade Organization, World Bank, and In-

ternational Monetary Fund. Multinational economic communities create partnerships to remove barriers to flows of goods, capital, and people across the borders of member nations. Two major economic agreements are the North American Free Trade Agreement and the European Union.

6. Compare the different levels of involvement used by businesses when entering global markets.

Exporting and importing, the first level of involvement in international business, involves the lowest degree of both risk and control. Companies may rely on export trading or management companies to assist in distribution of their products. Contractual agreements such as franchising, foreign licensing, and subcontracting offer additional, flexible options. Franchising and licensing are especially appropriate for services. Companies may also choose local subcontractors to produce goods for local sales. International direct investment in production and marketing facilities provides the highest degree of control but also the greatest risk. Firms make direct investments by acquiring foreign companies or facilities, forming joint ventures with local firms, and setting up their own overseas divisions.

7. Describe the types of international organizational structures available to businesses.

Once a company's managers decide on the desired level of international involvement, they must choose the appropriate organizational structure for their overseas venture. An independent agent represents an exporter in a foreign market. A license holder typically makes a larger investment in the product than does an independent agent, and may be likely to provide better representation for the product. However, licensing arrangements require longer time commitments than working with independent agents. Branch offices are units of an international firm located in foreign countries. Strategic alliances are joint ventures with local companies that combine resources and capital to create competitive advantage.

8. Distinguish between a global business strategy and a multidomestic business strategy.

A company that adopts a global (or standardization) strategy develops a single, standardized product and marketing strategy for implementation throughout the world. The firm sells the same product in essentially the same manner in all countries in which it operates. Under a multidomestic (or adaptation) strategy, the firm develops a different treatment for each national market. It develops products and marketing strategies that appeal to the customs, tastes, and buying habits of particular national markets.

Business Terms You Need to Know

exports 122
imports 122
balance of trade 130
balance of payments 130
exchange rate 132
tariff 140

World Trade Organization (WTO) 141
North American Free Trade Agreement (NAFTA) 143
European Union (EU) 144
multinational corporation (MNC) 151
global business strategy 155
multidomestic business strategy 156

Other Important Business Terms

maquiladora 127
devaluation 132
infrastructure 136
quota 140
dumping 140
embargo 141
exchange control 141

General Agreement on Tariffs and
     Trade (GATT) 141
World Bank 142
International Monetary Fund (IMF) 142
countertrade 147
franchise 148

foreign licensing agreement 148
subcontracting 148
joint venture 150
independent agent 152
strategic alliance 154
direct investment 155

➤ Review Questions

1. How does a business go about deciding whether to trade with a foreign country? What are the key factors for participating in the information economy on a global basis?

2. According to Table 4.1, which country or countries represent attractive markets for foreign businesses? Why?

3. What is the difference between absolute advantage and comparative advantage? Give an example of each.

4. Can a nation have a favorable balance of trade and an unfavorable balance of payments? Why or why not?

5. Identify several potential barriers to communication when a company attempts to conduct business in another country. How might these be overcome?

6. Explain the concept of *infrastructure*. In what ways does the infrastructure of a foreign country affect a company's attempts to do business in that country?

7. Identify and describe briefly the three dimensions of the legal environment for global business.

8. What are the major nontariff restrictions affecting international business? Describe the difference between tariff and nontariff restrictions.

9. What is NAFTA? How does it work?

10. What are the key choices a company must make before making the final decision to go global?

➤ Questions for Critical Thinking

1. When Britain transferred Hong Kong to China in 1997, China agreed to grant Hong Kong a high degree of autonomy as a capitalist economy for 50 years. Do you think this agreement will hold up? Why or why not? Consider China's economy, population, infrastructure, and other factors in your answer.

2. The tremendous growth of online business has introduced new elements to the legal climate of international business. Ideas, patents, brand names, copyrights, and trademarks are difficult to monitor because of the boundaryless nature of the Internet. What steps could businesses take to protect their trademarks and brands in this environment? What steps might countries take? Do you think such steps should even be taken? Why or why not?

3. The WTO monitors GATT agreements, mediates disputes, and continues the effort to reduce trade barriers throughout the world. However, widespread concerns have been expressed that the WTO's focus on lowering trade barriers may encourage businesses to keep costs down through practices that may lead to pollution and human rights abuses. Others argue that human rights should not be linked to international business. Do you think that environmental and human rights issues should be linked to trade? Why or why not?

4. The IMF makes short-term loans to developing countries that may not be able to repay them. Do you agree that the IMF should forgive these debts in some cases? Why or why not?

5. Describe briefly the EU and its goals. What are the pros and cons of the EU? Do you predict that the EU alliance will hold up over the next 20 years? Why or why not?

➤ **Experiential Exercise**

Background: *Fortune* magazine has published "The *Fortune* Global 500," a statistical snapshot of the world's largest corporations, every year since 1990. This exercise is designed to (a) help you learn more about this important list, (b) see how much you already know about the biggest global businesses, and (c) learn some new things about global business.

Directions: Your instructor will direct you to either work alone or as a member of a group to answer these questions. Use the most recent edition of "The *Fortune* Global 500," which is published in *Fortune* magazine normally in late July or early August, or go to *Fortune*'s online version at **www.fortune.com/fortune/global500.**

1. On what is the Global 500 ranking based (for example, profits, number of employees, sales revenues)?
2. Among the world's ten largest corporations, list the countries represented with the number of companies from each country.
3. Identify the top-ranked company along with its Global 500 ranking and country for each industry classification listed in the following table:

Global 500 Rank	Industry Classification	Company	Country
	Food and Drug Stores		
	Industrial and Farm Equipment		
	Petroleum Refining		
	Utilities: Gas and Electric		
	Telecommunications		
	Pharmaceuticals		

4. _____ is the Global 500 company with the greatest assets.
5. _____ is the Global 500 company with the highest profits.
6. Each of the 500 corporations is identified by industry. In the following table, list the five top-ranked industries based on the number of companies in that industry that made the Global 500 list:

Rank	Industry Classification	Number of Companies
1		
2		
3		
4		
5		

7. In the following table, list the three industries with the fewest companies represented on the Global 500 list and list at least one company from each industry in column two:

Industry Classification	Company

8. In the following table, identify the top two employers in the world—the two companies employing more people than any other company:

Company	Industry	Employees	Country

9. Identify the two largest beverage companies in the world. Fill in their names and other information requested in the following table:

Global 500 Rank	Company	Sales Revenues

10. Which country has the greatest representation in the "Electronics, Electrical Equipment" industry classification? Which has the greatest representation in "Banks: Commercial and Savings"?

➤ **Nothing but Net**

1. **Going Global.** One of the most successful internationally focused companies is Finnish cell phone manufacturer Nokia. Visit the company's Web site and then list five interesting facts about Nokia.

   www.nokia.com/main.html

2. **World Trade Organization (WTO).** Visit the WTO Web site. Prepare an oral report for your class on the WTO's organizational structure and the services it provides to member nations. Address the question of how WTO membership is determined.

www.wto.org

3. **European Monetary Union (EMU).** The EMU has recently experienced some growing pains. In 2000, Danish voters rejected a proposal to switch from their national currency, the krone, to the euro, and the British remain steadfast in retaining the pound sterling as the official currency of the United Kingdom. Use your search engine to find the latest information and news related to the EMU. Prepare a brief report outlining the current status and some of the major issues facing the EMU. The following Web site provides a good starting point.

http://fullcoverage.yahoo.com/fc/world/European Monetary Union

Note: Internet Web addresses change frequently. If you don't find the exact sites listed, you may need to access the organization's home page and search from there.

"We've known each other forever," say Gai Gherardi and Barbara McReynolds, co-owners and designers of an internationally acclaimed eyeglass company. They've been business partners forever, too—at least since 1979 when they founded L.A. Eyeworks as their own personal cure for, as they put it, "creative frustration." The pair had worked together in an optical store during the late 1960s and enjoyed the business, but they were bored with the eyeglass styles available. They had plenty of autonomy as employees—they held poetry readings and political discussions at the shop while they sold glasses—but they wanted to do something on their own. "We were pushing to do something new," recalls McReynolds.

When they opened their first shop on Melrose Avenue in Los Angeles, nothing much was going on in the neighborhood. They chose the location for that reason—the street was not going to dictate who the shoppers at the new store would be. To stock the store, they carefully selected uncirculated old stock from existing eyeglass manufacturers and transformed them by tinting the lenses and dyeing and changing the frame surfaces. They gave their store a clean, streamlined design so it would feature the glasses themselves. "We were successful from the first day," recalls Gherardi.

Pretty soon, the team was doing what they really wanted to—creating their own designs. They found a manufacturer in France who was willing to produce the frames and began showing their goods at optics-oriented trade shows. Orders poured in from retail department stores like Bendel's, fashion retailers, and optical buyers. Then in 1986 they decided to try a trade show in Paris. Ironically, although the show was a success, no one from France bought the glasses. Instead, customers came from Germany and Holland. The following year, Gherardi and McReynolds took their goods to trade shows in Milan and again in Paris. Customers from Belgium, Scandinavia, and Italy seemed to understand and love what they were doing, and the French were catching on. So they began to think about setting up a distribution warehouse in Europe.

"We looked at the best countries to do business in," says McReynolds. In other words, they identified the countries that supported the type of business in which L.A. Eyeworks engages. They reviewed tax structures, currency exchange rates, and ease of transportation. They settled on an industrial/office park run specifically to support international commerce. Located in France just one mile from the Swiss border and a stone's throw from the Geneva airport, the L.A. Eyeworks European operations headquarters handles business for Europe and the Middle East.

"We opened bank accounts in the countries where we were doing business and learned everything about shipping costs, currencies, and so forth," note the duo. At the same time, Gherardi and McReynolds were learning the complexities of conducting business on a global scale. For instance, invoicing practices vary from country to country, and customer service representatives need to speak several languages. "Customers want to speak in their own language," observes McReynolds. These language differences could be potential barriers to a company trying to establish a presence in another region of the world, but McReynolds and Gherardi simply view it as a challenge.

Cultural differences come into play as well, and both partners emphasize that their company strives to accommodate those differences. "But we needed to go forward as an American company representing the culture of our company and not let that go by the wayside. That's a really tricky thing," they pointed out. It has been important for L.A. Eyeworks to maintain its edgy image because that image is part of what customers are buying. Eyeglass shoppers like L.A. Eyeworks's new, risky designs because they represent leading design and fashion innovation. "Customers are interested in the energy that comes out of L.A.," says McReynolds. "They want in on it—the stories, the art, the culture." People everywhere want to sport frames with names like Chops, Zipper, Sprawl, or Nifty.

But there are some places in the world where L.A. Eyeworks—the product and the image—just doesn't work. For instance, in India, the economy simply can't support high-priced luxury goods (L.A. Eyeworks glasses sell for $275 a pair and up). And India has created a closed-door policy on manufacturing by charging extremely high duties on imports. The government prefers to have goods manufactured and sold within the country's borders. In addition, there is little protection of licensing or trademark rights. So L.A. Eyeworks does not feel that right now India would be a successful market. On the other hand, L.A. Eyeworks glasses can be found in Germany, Switzerland, Italy, France, England, Australia, Japan, Singapore, Hong Kong, New Zealand, Canada, and eastern Europe—to name just a few places.

The company's famous slogan, "A face is like a work of art—it deserves a great frame," seems to be as universal as the celebrity appeal that comes along with stars like Jodie Foster, Matthew Lillard, Jennifer Tilly, and Elton John, who wear the glasses, and some of whom model them in advertisements. Belinda Carlisle did one of the company's first ads. But not every ad works in every country. Recently, the company decided to photograph a Chinese Olympic basketball player—who happened to be the tallest woman in China—for one of its advertisements, thinking that Chinese customers would be attracted to it. Instead, it fell flat with the Chinese, but the American audience loved it.

McReynolds and Gherardi continue to push the boundaries of eyeglass design and fashion. And although their company's success has grown way beyond their first shop on Melrose Avenue, it has not outgrown the goal of the first sign that hung in that store: "changing the face of L.A." Perhaps the sign might be edited a bit to read, "changing the face of the world."

QUESTIONS

1. Latin America is identified as one of the world's most attractive emerging market regions, yet L.A. Eyeworks currently has only a minor presence there. Do you think this would be a good market for L.A. Eyeworks to pursue more actively? Why or why not?
2. In addition to those discussed in the case, what other trade barriers might L.A. Eyeworks face in different countries?
3. How do you think the European Union might affect L.A. Eyeworks?
4. What types of strategic alliances might L.A. Eyeworks form in order to grow into new areas?

Sources: Company Web site, **www.laeyeworks.com,** accessed April 14, 2001; Deborah Martin, "Benefit Big on Spectacle," *San Antonio Express-News,* November 23, 2000, p. 1E; Anne-Marie Otey, "FashionDish LA Dish," *FashionDish,* July 7, 2000, **www.fashiondish.com;** "Shades," *Los Angeles Magazine,* December 1997 [no page]. Permission for this material must be applied for directly to L.A. Eyeworks.

Starting and Growing Your Business

CHAPTER 5

Options for Organizing Small and Large Businesses

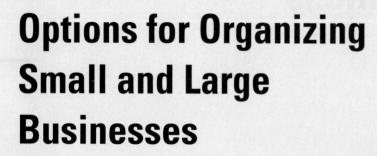

Learning Goals

1. Distinguish between small and large businesses, and identify the industries in which most small firms are established.

2. Discuss the economic and social contributions of small business.

3. Compare the advantages and disadvantages of small business.

4. Describe how the Small Business Administration assists small-business owners.

5. Explain how franchising can provide opportunities for both franchisors and franchisees.

6. Summarize the three basic forms of business ownership and the advantages and disadvantages of each form.

7. Identify the levels of corporate management.

8. Describe recent trends in mergers and acquisitions.

9. Differentiate among private ownership, public ownership, and collective ownership (cooperatives).

Ritz Foods: A Chip Off the Old Block

Just when you thought every kind of chip possible had been produced by now, a new one comes along. Only this chip isn't made from potatoes or corn or any other familiar vegetable. Instead, it comes from the tropical yuca plant. The yuca (pronounced *you'* ka), grows mainly in South America. And Gerald Ritthaler, a 70-year-old former executive with an adventurous spirit, is convinced that these crispy yuca chips are going to be the next rage. So he bought a farm in Venezuela, came up with a plan, began growing yuca plants, and formed a company called Ritz Foods.

Ritthaler doesn't fit the stereotype of today's small-business owner. He's near retirement age instead of 20-something, and his business isn't based on the Internet. But he has an entrepreneur's passion for his product and is convinced he's found a market niche he can fill: an all-natural, medium-priced snack food. Ritthaler can claim an all-natural label because his chips have no preservatives, no artificial color, and no cholesterol. In fact, he has extended the shelf life of the chips by using more expensive sunflower oil instead of preservatives. As for quality, yuca chips are thicker than regular potato chips, which makes them easier to dip, they absorb less oil than potato chips and so contain "40 percent less fat that regular potato chips," and many testers love the crunchy taste. With all this going for him, Ritthaler still refuses to price his chips—called Tropic's—high to compete against other gourmet brands. "I'd rather sell six bags at $2.98 than two at $3.79," he says.

Still, competition in the snack food business is fierce. Ritthaler is up against the giants, including Frito-Lay, the $10 billion king of the chip industry. Frito-Lay snack foods fill supermarket shelves as well as those of chains like Subway sandwiches, making it tough for Tropic's five flavors, no matter how good they are, to nibble away at Frito-Lay's retail shelf space. And larger ethnic food companies like Goya, which has a lock on big sales areas such as New York, are already producing plantain and yuca chips. But experts in the business believe that Ritthaler has a chance if he plays his chips

right. Michael Schall, president of Guiltless Gourmet and creator of the first baked tortilla chip, notes, "A one-product company with several flavors has got to stay highly

focused. You've got to know which retailers to call on." James Shufelt, president of the Snack Food Association, advises, "[Ritthaler] needs to define that segment of the population that is familiar with yuca. Once he locates those ethnic groups, he needs to find the outlets that are interested in what are essentially low-volume, attractively packaged products. Those outlets would give his products the best chance of survival."

Ritthaler's business plan has never included the fast-paced, initial public offering of stock and early cash-out that characterizes many of today's Internet start-ups. Instead, he believes that a vertically integrated company—one that literally grows needed raw materials, converts them into chips, and then sells the final product itself—is his best chance for being profitable in the long run. Ritthaler does not yet draw a salary for himself; his plan at this stage is

to plow all earnings back into the business—literally. "We were never expecting a quick return," says Bill McKee, a nonactive investment partner and long-time colleague in other ventures with Ritthaler. And although he says he would consider buyout offers, Ritthaler is more likely to grow his company by acquiring smaller U.S. companies whose products fit with those of Ritz Foods.

As you read this chapter, you'll learn how a variety of small companies got their start. Some have succeeded, and some have failed. Some have grown larger, and others have preferred simply to fill a small niche. Each contributes to the economy in important ways, and each begins with the owner's commitment to his or her idea. "I know it will sell," says Ritthaler with enthusiasm. "I wouldn't be this far if I didn't. I'll do a taste test with any potato chip in the United States. I'd be very surprised if I didn't win."[1]

CHAPTER OVERVIEW

If you have ever thought of operating your own business, you are not alone. In fact, on any given day in the United States, more people are trying to start new businesses than are getting married or having children. However, before entering the world of contemporary business, an entrepreneur needs to understand its framework.

Like Gerald Ritthaler of Ritz Foods, every business owner must choose the form of legal ownership that best meets the company's needs. Several variables affect the choice of the best way to organize your business:

- How easily can you set up this type of organization?
- How much financial liability can you afford to accept?
- What financial resources do you have?
- What strengths and weaknesses do you see in other businesses in the industry?
- What are your own strengths and weaknesses?

We begin this chapter by focusing on small-business ownership, including the advantages and disadvantages of small-business ventures. We also look at the services provided by the U.S. government's Small Business Administration (SBA). The role of women and minorities in small business is discussed in detail, as well as global opportunities for small-business owners. We then provide an overview of the three forms of private business ownership—sole proprietorships, partnerships, and corporations. Next, we explore the structures and operations typical of larger companies and review the trends in business with a fresh look at mergers, acquisitions, and multinational corporations. The chapter concludes with an explanation of public and collective ownership.

MOST BUSINESSES ARE SMALL BUSINESSES

Although many people associate the term *business* with international giants like ExxonMobil, Citigroup, Wal-Mart, and General Electric, nine out of ten firms with employees have fewer than 20 people on staff, and 98 percent have fewer than 100 employees. The vast majority of U.S. businesses have no payroll at all: over 14 million people in the United States are earning business income without any employees.[2] Almost half the sales in the United States are made by small businesses.[3]

Small business is also the launching pad for entrepreneurs from every sector of the diverse U.S. economy. One-third of the nation's 17 million small businesses are owned by women. Hispanic-owned businesses account for 4 percent of all U.S. businesses with fewer than 100 employees. African Americans own another 3.6 percent, and Asian Americans 3.5 percent.[4]

1/3 women owned

What Is a Small Business?

How do you distinguish a small business from a large one? Are sales the key indicator? What about market share or number of employees? The SBA, the federal agency most directly involved with this sector of the economy, considers a **small business** to be a firm that is independently owned and operated and is not dominant in its field. The SBA also considers annual sales and number of employees to identify small businesses for specific industries.

- Most manufacturing businesses are considered small if they employ fewer than 500 workers.
- To be considered small, wholesalers must employ no more than 100 workers.
- Most kinds of retailers and other services can generate up to $5 million in annual sales and still be considered a small business.

- An agricultural business is generally considered small if its sales are no more than $500,000 a year.[5]

The SBA has established size standards for specific industries. These standards, which range from $500,000 to $25 million in sales and from 100 to 1,500 for employees, are available at the SBA's "Size Standards" Web page, shown in Figure 5.1.

Since government agencies offer a number of benefits designed to help small businesses compete successfully with larger firms, operators of small businesses are interested in determining whether their company meets the standards for designation as a small business in their industry. If it qualifies, the company may be eligible for government loans or for government purchasing programs that encourage proposals from smaller suppliers.

SBA helped us with a place to hang our hats...

Tom Merritt and Mike Pereyo, Owners & Partners, oobe, inc.

U.S. Small Business Administration

And sweaters and jackets and shirts, too. Just four years ago, Mike and Tom had a dream to design clothing for people who love the outdoors as much as they do. So, they created a business for the outside, inside us all.

Their dream of owning and operating a successful business is now a reality. Getting started wasn't easy, but Mike and Tom found that the U.S. Small Business Administration was there with guidance and a loan when they needed it most.

Through its nationwide network, the SBA also offers equity capital, counseling and technical assistance on every aspect of small business management and federal government contracting assistance.

If your dream is to own or expand your small business, contact the SBA at 1-800-U ASK SBA or answerdesk@sba.gov. Who knows, the SBA could help you with a place to hang your hat, too.

The SBA does not endorse or imply agreement with any of the opinions, products and/or services expressed. All SBA programs are extended to the public on a nondiscriminatory basis.

FIGURE 5.1
Small-Business Services Provided by the SBA

Typical Small Business Ventures

For decades, small businesses have competed against some of the world's largest organizations as well as multitudes of other small companies. One of these fearless competitors is SoapWorks, started by Amilya Antonetti to sell hypoallergenic cleaning products. More experienced marketers ridiculed Antonetti's attempt to compete against such giants as Procter & Gamble and Clorox. However, her experience with her son's health problems, which were aggravated by chemicals in mainstream cleaning products, convinced her that a market existed for soaps and detergents with pure and simple ingredients. SoapWorks doesn't have much money for advertising, but the company buys time on the family-oriented California radio station KFAX, and the station invites Antonetti to answer questions and offer tips on its *Life Line* call-in program. SoapWorks also provides free samples to children's hospitals and women's shelters. Ultimately, though, the company's best sales tool consists of the customers who try the products and are delighted with the results. Some report that skin conditions clear up, and people who once had to let the house air out after they cleaned can stay inside on cleaning day. These customers have convinced store managers at such national chains as Albertson's and Safeway to carry the SoapWorks line.[6]

For centuries, most nonfarming small businesses have been concentrated in retailing and the service industries. As Figure 5.2 indicates, small businesses provide the majority of jobs in the construction, agricultural services, wholesale trade, services, and retail trade industries. Small service businesses can be as high-touch as a country inn or hair stylist, or as high-tech as Diamond Technology Partners. Diamond is the brainchild of three Chicago entrepreneurs, who recognized the importance of the Internet to business before most businesspeople even understood what it was. The three men founded Diamond to help companies figure out how they could apply Internet and related technologies to their business strategies. Their foresight attracted such major clients as General Motors, Goldman Sachs, and Sears. As Internet consulting becomes more widely available,

Industry

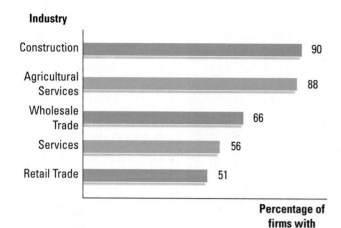

Construction	90
Agricultural Services	88
Wholesale Trade	66
Services	56
Retail Trade	51

Percentage of firms with fewer than 500 employees

FIGURE 5.2
Top Five Industries for Small Business

Diamond has expanded its services to remain competitive. The company now provides expertise in creating and managing the software needed to carry out an Internet-based strategy. Staying ahead of the technology curve has enabled Diamond to sparkle. Its rapid growth in sales and profits recently placed the company on *Business Week*'s list of Hot Growth Companies.[7]

Retailing is another important industry for today's small businessperson. General merchandising giants like Wal-Mart, Kmart, and Sears may be the best-known retailing firms, but small, privately owned retail stores far outnumber them. Small-business retailing includes stores that sell shoes, jewelry, office supplies and stationery, clothing, flowers, drugs, convenience foods, and thousands of other products. People wishing to form their own business have been attracted to retailing throughout history because of the ability to start a firm with limited funds, rent a store rather than build a custom facility, and use family members to staff the new business.

A successful retail example is Powell's Books, based in Portland, Oregon. In contrast to Amazon.com's well-known high-tech, stock-everything strategy, Powell's competes by specializing in used, sometimes hard-to-find books. Through its seven bookstores and its Web site (Powells.com), Powell's serves customers who like buying from the little guy (or woman) and who don't mind paying extra to find something special to read. Their different strategies permit the two competitors to benefit one another. Powell's buys returned books from Amazon at a discount and sells them as used. Amazon fills orders for out-of-print books through Powell's. The strategy will never make Powell's an industry leader, but that is just fine with the retailer's founder, Michael Powell. Of his Web site, Powell says, "I don't want the site to grow too fast; it would stress out my staff."[8]

Small business also plays a significant role in agriculture. Although most farm acreage is in the hands of large farms, the majority of farmers still operate small

Small business retailer Powell's Books specializes in used and hard-to-find books. It uses the Web to reach beyond the Pacific Northwest to a wider audience of readers who are looking for that special book not available through bookstore chains.

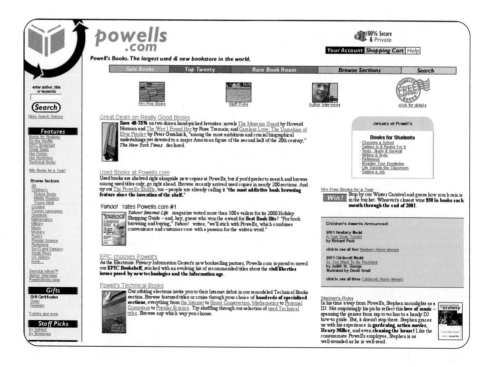

businesses. Most U.S. farms are owned by individual farmers or families, not partners or shareholders.[9] The family farm is a classic example of a small-business operation. It is independently owned and operated, with relatively few employees, relying instead on the labor of family members.

Almost half of small businesses in the United States are **home-based businesses**—firms operated from the residence of the business owner. During the period between 1960 and 1980, fewer people worked at home, largely because the number of farmers, as well as doctors and lawyers in solo practices, was declining. But since then, the number of people working at home has more than doubled. A major factor in this growth is the increased availability of personal computers (PCs) and such communications devices as fax machines, low-cost photocopiers, and electronic mail. With more recent advances in computer technology and widespread adoption of the Internet, the Census Bureau expects to find that the share of people working at home and the number of home-based businesses will grow even faster during the first decade of the 21st century.[10]

Operating a home-based business can help owners keep their costs low. Like over half of all African American–owned businesses without employees, the Crafty Sisters' Gift Boutique operates out of the homes of its owners. The two partners, Jayne Cain and Cassaundra Williams-Anderson, make a variety of Afrocentric crafts, including dolls, figurines, and jewelry, which they sell over the Internet. According to Cain, by forgoing a store, the Crafty Sisters are able to make a profit at a much lower level of sales—and at much lower prices for each item they sell.[11] Other benefits of a home-based business include greater flexibility and freedom from the time and expense of commuting. Drawbacks include isolation and less visibility to customers. Of course, if your customers visit you online, they don't care where your office is located.

Jayne Cain and Cassaundra Williams-Anderson boosted sales for their home-based Afrocentric crafts business, Crafty Sisters' Gift Boutique, with a Web site. "I love collecting figurines, but I couldn't find African-American ones anywhere. So I started making them," says Jayne Cain.

Like the Crafty Sisters' Gift Boutique, many small businesses are more competitive because of the Internet. By one estimate roughly 62 percent of small businesses have an online presence.[12] But the Internet does not automatically guarantee success, as discussed in the "Business Hits and Misses" box. Setting up a Web site can be relatively inexpensive and gives a business the potential to reach a huge marketplace. One such company is Salem Five Cents Savings Bank. The Massachusetts bank is tiny, with only nine branches, but it also has a significant presence on the Internet. It established that presence by acting quickly in the mid-1990s, when Internet banking was still an innovation. Salem Five hired programmers to set up a high-quality Web site and offered depositors low fees plus high interest rates on savings. Before long, the bank had attracted thousands of accounts. It was especially attractive to customers working on overseas assignments and looking for an easy way to handle financial matters. When bigger banks began to compete by adding Internet service, Salem Five changed its online name from salemfive.com to directbanking.com and honed its focus to New England, where the bank already had a good reputation to build on. It continues to innovate and has opened branches with automated-teller machines and Internet kiosks offering videoconferencing with bank representatives. High technology coupled with concern for customer service keeps Salem Five in business even as the biggest banks spend millions of dollars on advertising.[13]

American business history is filled with inspirational stories of great inventors who launched companies in barns, garages, warehouses, and attics. For young visionaries like Apple Computer founders Stephen Jobs and Steve Wozniak, the logical option for transforming their technical idea into a commercial reality was to begin work in a family garage. The impact of today's entrepreneurs, including home-based businesses, is discussed in more depth in Chapter 6.

It seemed like a great idea: use the Internet to bring together musicians who wanted to buy and sell used equipment. Fred Bramante, founder of Daddy's Junky Music, had already been in the retail music business for 25 years, selling everything from electric guitars to microprocessor-based keyboards, first at his shop in Connecticut and later in New Hampshire. He liked to stage live auctions at his shops, which were often successful. "My motto is, 'When things get cheap, the cheap get things,'" says Bramante. So it seemed like a natural transition to online auctions in 1997.

At first, the new site—called RockAuctions—offered a sparse 50 or 60 items per week. But within two years, several hundred customers were bidding on as many as 1,000 items each week. Bramante and Robert Timmins, the company's vice-president of e-commerce, thought they had a foolproof setup. Buyers wanting to bid on a guitar are required to register with a credit card number. When the auction closed, the winner's card would automatically be charged, and RockAuctions would ship the guitar. "One of the nice advantages to our system is that we don't have to chase a private party for payment like you have to do if you're selling on eBay or Amazon," explained Timmins. "Once an item is sold, we get paid immediately. Since we set the minimum bid, a single bid means a guaranteed sale."

The system sounded perfect. But less than a year later, Bramante merged RockAuction with Daddy's Used Gear By Mail, shutting down the online auction site. Customers interested in making purchases were referred to the Daddy's Web site, where they could view an online catalog and make purchases by phone or fax, not online. "Our [Web] pages are here to give you a much quicker way to see what we have in stock than by waiting for your monthly catalog," explains the site. "The used inventory list is updated daily Monday through Friday." The site also has an e-mail subscription list for notification of special deals, as well as the option to contact the company by e-mail.

Although the Internet helps many small businesses get going, it does have its pitfalls. "Behind all the magic of the Internet is a lot of hard work doing text entry, warehousing, and fulfillment," notes Timmins. And when it doesn't work—for whatever reason—smart entrepreneurs move on. Bramante's company continues to list over 10,000 items, many of which are covered by warranty. Daddy's Junky Music has been playing a funky tune for more than a quarter of a century, and with Bramante's good business sense, it's likely that his company will continue to make music for as long as he wants.

QUESTIONS FOR CRITICAL THINKING
1. What might be some reasons why RockAuction stopped using the online auction method of sales within three years of opening?
2. What advantages does Bramante have in operating a small business as it undergoes change? What might be some disadvantages?

Sources: "Info & FAQs," Used Gear By Mail Web site, **www.ugbm.com**, accessed January 8, 2001; Daddy's Junky Music Web site, **www.daddys.com**, accessed January 8, 2001; Leigh Buchanan, "The Best of the Small Business Web," *Inc. Technology* No. 4, 1999, pp. 63–64.

CONTRIBUTIONS OF SMALL BUSINESS TO THE ECONOMY

Small businesses form the core of the U.S. economy. Businesses with fewer than 500 employees generate 47 percent of total U.S. sales and over half the nation's gross domestic product. Ninety-nine of every 100 U.S. businesses are small businesses. In addition, small businesses employ 53 percent of the nation's private nonfarm workforce.[14]

Creating New Jobs

Small businesses make tremendous contributions to the U.S. economy and to society as a whole. One impressive contribution is the number of new jobs created each year by small businesses. Three of every four new jobs created over the past ten years were at small companies with fewer than 500 employees. A significant share of these jobs were created by the smallest companies—those with four or fewer employees. Small firms are dominant factors in many of the industries that have added the most jobs: engineering and management services, construction trade contractors, wholesale trade, amusement and recreation, social services, and restaurants.[15]

Even if you never plan to start your own business, you will probably work for a small business at some point in your career, especially early on. Not only do small firms employ over half of all U.S. employees, they are more likely than large firms to employ the youngest (and oldest) workers. In addition, as detailed in a later section of this chapter, small businesses offer significant opportunities to women and minorities.

Small businesses also contribute to the economy by hiring workers who traditionally have had difficulty finding jobs at larger firms. Compared with large companies, small businesses are more likely to hire former welfare recipients.[16] Driven in part by their limited budgets, small businesses may be more open to locating in economically depressed areas, where they contribute to rehabilitating neighborhoods and reducing unemployment. Envios, a service that wires money overseas for its customers, hires immigrants who have not yet mastered English. Since most of the firm's customers speak Spanish, the company is not strict about its requirement that employees be bilingual. Sometimes Envios finds highly talented Spanish-speaking employees, including doctors, lawyers, and accountants who have recently moved to the United States. These employees typically stay only until they polish their English and obtain licenses to work in their professions. Although they do not stay long, Envios benefits from their education and skill at serving other people. The employees and communities also benefit because these recent immigrants are able to earn incomes through this work during the time they are improving their knowledge of English.[17]

Creating New Industries

The small-business sector also gives entrepreneurs an outlet for developing their ideas and perhaps for creating entirely new industries. Many of today's successful high-tech firms—Microsoft, Cisco Systems, Yahoo!, and Dell Computer—began as small businesses.

The growth of such businesses not only provides new goods and services but also fuels local economies. The high-tech companies in California's Silicon Valley created a need for many support services. A company called iQuantic provides human resources consulting to Silicon Valley clients, and to be close at hand, it located in a former mattress factory in San Francisco. By locating in San Francisco's run-down Mission District, iQuantic brought money into that neighborhood.[18]

Another contribution of small business is its ability to provide needed services to the larger corporate community. The movement toward corporate downsizing that began in the early 1990s created a demand for other businesses to perform activities previously handled by company employees. Outsourcing such activities as security, employee benefits management, maintenance, and logistics created opportunities that were often filled by employees of small businesses.

Attracting New Industries

Community leaders realize the importance of small businesses to their cities, and successful revitalization programs have improved conditions in depressed areas by attracting new industries. A federal program called the New Markets Initiative has been proposed to target areas where more than 20 percent of residents live in poverty or where the median income is significantly below the statewide average. Businesses in those areas would be eligible for government-guaranteed loans, as well as tax incentives such as tax credits and exemption from paying tax on certain gains.[19]

Businesses need more than government incentives, however. They also need access to the necessary resources, including qualified workers, reasonably priced facilities, and strong markets. Other influences on location decisions include the availability of government funded worker-training programs, sources of financing, and positive attitudes shown by city officials and local community groups.

ADVANTAGES OF A SMALL BUSINESS

Small businesses are not simply smaller versions of large corporations. They differ greatly in forms of organization, market positions, staff capabilities, managerial styles, organizational structures, and financial resources. But these differences

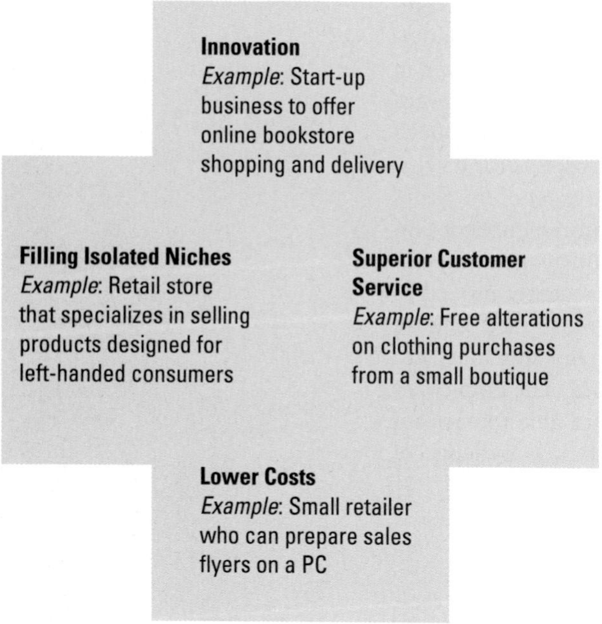

Innovation
Example: Start-up business to offer online bookstore shopping and delivery

Filling Isolated Niches
Example: Retail store that specializes in selling products designed for left-handed consumers

Superior Customer Service
Example: Free alterations on clothing purchases from a small boutique

Lower Costs
Example: Small retailer who can prepare sales flyers on a PC

FIGURE 5.3
Advantages of Small-Business Ownership

usually seem like strengths to small-business owners, who find many advantages in operating small businesses rather than working within large, powerful, multinational corporations. As Figure 5.3 indicates, the four most important advantages are innovation, superior customer service, lower costs, and opportunities to fill isolated niches.

Innovation

To compete effectively with giant corporations backed by massive resources, small firms often have to find new and creative ways of conducting business. In sharp contrast to such large traditional consulting firms as Accenture (formerly Andersen Consulting Group) is Second City Communications (SCC), an outgrowth of a popular improvisational comedy theater on Chicago's North Side. The company offers workshops and customized performances for corporate clients who hope that a dose of humor will stimulate creative thinking without undermining the company's values and leaders. In the words of SCC's cofounder Joe Keefe, the company was founded to "bring comedy where it is most desperately needed, which is in business." In one SCC sketch, an employee drones through a presentation without recognizing that the PowerPoint slides are becoming increasingly absurd and inciting a rebellion from the audience. The company treads the fine line between humor and ridicule so well that hundreds of companies have hired it to help employees look at themselves with a fresh perspective. Their patronage has generated such strong revenues that they help cover the costs of operating the original Second City Theater.[20]

Small businesses are often fertile ground in which to plant innovative ideas for new goods and services. As a chemist in the pharmaceutical industry, Thomas E. D'Ambra saw many exciting ideas neglected because his employer lacked the resources to pursue them. D'Ambra decided that a market existed for a company that would offer research services. D'Ambra's start-up business, Albany Molecular Research, focused on research and development for new drugs on a contract basis. Today, the company employs 200 chemists and tackles research projects for such industry giants as duPont Pharmaceuticals and Eli Lilly. With his customers facing a continued shortage of talented chemists, D'Ambra foresees a strong future for Albany Molecular.[21]

In a typical year, small firms will develop twice as many product innovations per employee as larger firms. They also obtain more patents per sales dollar than do larger businesses. The fact that small firms are a richer source of innovations is even more evident by the fact that large firms are more likely to patent their discoveries.[22] Key 20th-century innovations that were developed by small businesses include the airplane, the audiotape recorder, double-knit fabrics, the optical scanner, the PC, soft contact lenses, and the zipper.

Superior Customer Service

A small firm often can operate with greater flexibility than a large corporation, allowing it to tailor its product line and services to the needs of its customers. The Internet auction site eBay adapts its strategy according to demand. The company reviews how the site is used and adjusts its services accordingly. Recently, eBay noted that the number of small businesses purchasing goods on the site had grown faster than overall auction traffic and that purchases by small businesses tended to be larger than the average eBay purchase. Seeing this demand by small businesses, the company launched eBay Business Exchange, a service tailored to small businesses. A link to Business Exchange appears on eBay's home page, and the Business Exchange page lists items from trucks to computers that would be useful to small businesses.[23]

Low Costs

Small firms may be able to provide goods and services at prices that large firms cannot match. Small businesses usually minimize overhead costs—costs not directly related to providing specific goods and services—allowing them to earn profits on lower prices. Many small businesses avoid rent and utility expenses by operating out of the owners' homes. In addition, these firms often carry little or no inventory, further reducing total operating costs. The Crafty Sisters' Boutique, described earlier, is an example. The partners operate out of their homes to reduce their overhead expenses and keep prices low.

A typical small business sets up a lean organization with a small staff and few support personnel. The lower costs of maintaining a small permanent staff can provide a distinct advantage for a small business. Instead of hiring high-income attorneys and accountants as permanent staff members, small-business owner–managers typically hire these professionals when needed for special projects or as outside consultants. This approach typically helps to hold down payroll costs for the small business. When Covad Communications arranged to obtain millions of dollars in financing, it needed to set up payroll, benefits, and management systems in a hurry, before the money arrived. Covad hired Startup Resources, whose human resource experts, accountants, and information service consultants specialize in handling such business matters, while company founders concentrated on products and markets. Not only does Startup Resources save its clients weeks they might have spent investigating insurance plans and office layouts, but the company has established relationships with real estate agents, insurance companies, and others that help it get the job done efficiently.[24]

Another source of cost savings is the quantity and quality of work performed by the business owner. Entrepreneurs typically work long hours with no overtime or holiday pay. In addition, their family members may contribute services at little or no pay as bookkeepers, laborers, receptionists, production assistants, and delivery personnel.

Filling Isolated Market Niches

Large, growth-oriented businesses tend to focus on large segments of the overall market. The growth prospects of market niches are simply too limited and the expenses involved in serving them too great to justify the time and effort. Because high overhead costs force large firms to set minimum sizes for their target markets, small, underserved market niches have always attracted small businesses that are willing and able to serve them, as does Concierge Services for Students, described in the "Clicks and Mortar" box.

The founders of the HirePotential employment service determined that an unmet demand existed for an employment agency that specialized in placing as-yet-untapped segments of the workforce in jobs. Those workers include disabled and older workers, veterans, and welfare recipients. With highly qualified human resources already scarce and expected to become scarcer in the United States, HirePotential sees its role as helping employers expand their efforts at hiring diverse employees. As Sara Poticha, the firm's vice president, points out, "Corporations [don't] necessarily know how to integrate and really accommodate the untapped workforce." HirePotential steps in to assess its clients' work setting and technology, as well as human resource needs. It assesses the skills and needs of the job candidates in its database and helps place them in positions for which they are qualified. When

Steve and Sally Colby are the sole owners and employees at their innovative e-store OfftheDeepEnd.Com. Everything they sell is tacky, cheesy, silly. You'd go straight to their Web site to find household must-haves like flamingo lawn statues, a battery-operated fan shaped like a sumo wrestler, and plastic cockroaches. The Colbys are delighted that their innovative business attracts buyers who "do what they like and buy what they like." And there seems to be a lot of them out there—annual sales reached $200,000 recently.

Background. Small businesses—*really* small businesses—can fill isolated niches that large companies wouldn't even bother with. Imagine that you were a boarding school student from a foreign country here in the United States. Your parents are thousands of miles away, unable to help you out with the daily tasks of living in an unfamiliar country. That's where Concierge Services for Students comes in.

What Happened? Started by two Boston moms who had already raised several kids and sent them to boarding school, then hosted their kids' friends from foreign countries when the students couldn't travel home for vacations and holidays, Concierge Services provides a bit of parenting away from home. Tammy Kumin, Concierge's co-founder and the daughter of an Iranian business executive, knew what it was like to emigrate to a different country. Her partner Joan Alfond simply knew kids. They had an idea, recognized a market or need, and went to work.

The Response. A decade later, Concierge Services for Students has shopped for furniture and bedding for a student's dorm room, taken a Chilean boy shopping for prep school clothes and hockey gear, stocked two Muslim boys' dorm fridge with food for the religious holiday Ramadan, retrieved a runaway California girl and placed her safely on a plane home, and chaperoned a skiing trip to Maine. "They're a godsend," says the admissions chief for the Fay School in Boston, Lois Poirot. The dynamic duo had just found hotel rooms for four Fay School students from Taiwan who were stranded at a New York airport in a snowstorm. Kumin and Alfond, who between them speak five different languages, have also been seen cheering at soccer games and baking cookies for kids whose real moms are far away. "They [the students] really feel they have three mothers looking after them," explains Kumin.

Concierge Services' rates aren't exorbitant, either. Parents pay $400 per student for cards with an 800 number. Whatever Kumin, Alfond, and their two staffers can accomplish by phone from the office is done without extra charge. If they need to shop for or transport a child, the rate is $40 per hour. This fee is pocket change for many of the parents, who are sometimes royalty in other countries. "We've had many princes and princesses," notes Kumin. Some parents go all the way, paying Concierge Services $3,250 per year to be a legal guardian. Given the cost of boarding school, the guardianship is a bargain. It can really help when a student gets into a scrape—either legally or medically.

Today and Counting. The program has been so successful that some students continue with it when they enter college. So, in a way, the tiny market is expanding naturally. But a large market isn't what Kumin and Alfond are after. They like the fact that "their" kids want to stick around. "When you think it's all over, they're still there," says Alfond. She likes being a surrogate to 350 kids around New England. It's not such a large family, after all.

QUESTIONS FOR CRITICAL THINKING

1. How would Concierge Services' business be affected if Kumin and Alfond decided to expand outside the New England area?
2. How would Concierge Services' business change if the company decided to include local, American-born students as part of its clientele?
3. What steps might Concierge Services take to maintain its competitive edge if a competitor enters the market?

Sources: "About Us" and "Guardian Program," Concierge Services for Students' Web site, accessed January 8, 2001, **www.conciergeforstudents.net**; "An Admissions Guide for International Students," Admissions Quest Web site, accessed January 8, 2001, **www.admissionsquest.com**; Brigid McMenamin, "Rent-a-Mom," *Forbes*, February 21, 2000, p. 118.

Lori Akers became visually impaired as a result of diabetes, her employer didn't know how to accommodate a blind employee but feared that firing her would violate the Americans with Disabilities Act. Unsure what to do, the company let Akers sit idle. Frustrated, she turned to HirePotential, which helped her find a better job.[25]

In addition to filling smaller niches, certain types of businesses prefer to work with small organizations. Many service businesses illustrate this point. In a small medical practice or accounting firm, you are more likely to know who is providing the service you receive. Finally, economic and organizational factors may dictate that an industry consist primarily of small firms. Upscale restaurants and personal shopping services are typically small business operations, keeping the owners in close contact with their customers.

DISADVANTAGES OF A SMALL BUSINESS

Although small businesses bring a number of strengths to the competitive marketplace, they also have disadvantages in competing with larger, more established firms. A small business may find itself especially vulnerable during an economic downturn, since it may have accumulated fewer resources than its larger competitors to cushion a sales decline.

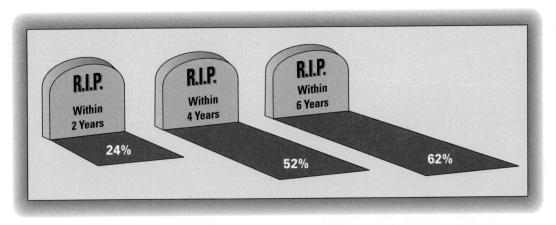

FIGURE 5.4
Rate of Business Failures

The primary disadvantages facing today's small businesses include management shortcomings, inadequate financing, and government regulations. These issues—quality and depth of management, availability of financing, and ability to wade through government rules and requirements—are so important that firms with major deficiencies in one or more areas may find themselves in bankruptcy proceedings. As Figure 5.4 shows, almost one new business in four will permanently close its doors within two years of opening them, and 62 percent will fail within the first six years of operation. Although highly motivated and well-trained business owner–managers can overcome these potential problems, they should thoroughly analyze whether one or more of these problems may threaten the business before deciding to launch the new company.

Management Shortcomings

Among the most common discoveries at a post mortem examination of a small-business failure is inadequate management. Business founders often possess great strengths in specific areas such as marketing or interpersonal relations, but they may suffer from hopeless deficiencies in others like finance or order fulfillment. Large firms recruit trained specialists to manage individual functions; small businesses frequently rely on small staffs who must be adept at a variety of skills.

An even worse result frequently occurs when people go into business with little, if any, business training. Some new businesses are begun almost entirely on the basis of what seems like a great idea for a new product. Managers assume that they will acquire needed business expertise on the job. All too often, the result is business bankruptcy.

If you are seriously contemplating starting a new business, heed a word of warning. Learn the basics of business *first*, and *second*, recognize your limitations. Although most small-business owners recognize the need to seek out the specialized skills of accountants and attorneys for financial and legal assistance, they often hesitate to turn to consultants and advisers for assistance in areas where they lack knowledge or experience, such as marketing.

Founders of new businesses frequently struggle with an ailment that might be called "the rose-colored-glasses syndrome." Filled with excitement about the potential of newly designed products, they may neglect important details like marketing research to determine whether potential customers share their excitement. Individuals considering launching a new business should first determine whether the proposed product meets the needs of a large enough market and whether they can convince the public of its superiority over competing offerings.

One of the most dramatic instances of inadequate management in recent years was the failure of Boo.com, an online fashion store. The company's founders were both experienced in setting up Internet businesses, having recently sold another Internet start-up, an online bookstore called Bokus, to try a bigger enterprise. They

By 1994, 13 Rubio's Restaurants located in southern California and owned by Ralph Rubio and his father, Ray, had reached $10 million in sales. But they wanted to move their restaurant chain beyond its family business roots and knew that additional management talent was needed. So they lured executives from Jack in the Box, Carl's Jr., and Taco Bell. By 2001, the company had crossed the $100 million mark. "I know the key to success is to surround myself with great people to free me to do what I do best [advertising and marketing]," says Ralph Rubio.

put together a five-page business plan and then headed for New York to look for financing. Impressed by the broad outlines of the plan and eager to become a leader in European dot.com financing, J. P. Morgan & Co. uncharacteristically agreed to provide start-up capital. J. P. Morgan's involvement then gave the Benetton and Moet-Hennessey Louis Vuitton fashion empires the confidence to invest as well.

With world-class investors and millions of dollars in the bank, Boo.com looked like a winner. The company opened offices in Munich, Paris, New York, and Amsterdam and poured money into a sophisticated Web site with 3-D graphics, a virtual changing room, and the ability to handle orders in seven languages and 18 currencies. They designed and redesigned the Web site's mascot, Miss Boo. Then the launch date was postponed after some major investors expressed concern that Boo's chief financial officer (CFO) lacked accounting skills and wasn't controlling the company's enormous expenses. Months after the original launch date, Boo.com finally opened for business. But instead of the much-anticipated flood of orders, the site received a flood of complaints. Compared with most major Internet connections, the site was very slow, and it wouldn't work at all with Macintosh computers. To jump-start online orders, the company began slashing prices. Within two months, sales had passed the $1 million mark, but expenses were at about $10 million. It was too late. Investors, watching in horror as the firm spent $10 million to generate $1 million in sales, were unwilling to pour more money into the venture, and the company had spent all its money. Boo.com laid off its staff and sold what was left of the company to fashionmall.com.[26]

Inadequate Financing

Another leading cause of small-business problems is inadequate financing. In too many instances, first-time entrepreneurs start new businesses assuming that their firms will generate enough funds from the first month's sales to finance continuing operations. Building a business takes time, though. Employees must be trained, equipment purchased, deposits paid for rent and utilities, and marketing dollars spent to inform potential customers about the new firm and its product offerings. Unless the owner has set aside enough funds to cover cash shortfalls during the first several months in which the business is becoming established, the venture may collapse at an early stage. Read the "Solving an Ethical Controversy" box for details about the battle for financing and competitiveness in the online pet store industry.

After surviving the cash crunch that often accompanies the first months of operation, a business must confront another major financial problem: uneven cash flows. For most small and large businesses, cash inflows and outflows do not display even patterns; instead, they fluctuate greatly at different times of the year. Small retail outlets generate much of their annual sales revenues during the December holiday period. Florists make most of their deliveries during three holidays: Valentine's Day, Easter, and Mother's Day. Large firms may build up sufficient cash reserves to weather periods of below-average sales, or they can turn to banks and other lenders for short-term loans; business start-ups often lack both cash balances and access to sources of additional funds.

With no track record and few assets to pledge as collateral, the owners of a small business usually discover that banks are highly reluctant to make business loans.

It's Dog-Eat-Dog in the Online Pet Supply Industry

It's a jungle out there. Someone got the idea that pet owners are busy, they buy the same products regularly—and pets can't drive to the pet supply store themselves. The Internet seemed like a natural way to bring goods and services to pet owners, and the online pet supply industry was born. A host of online start-ups launched their Web business almost at the same time. Start-ups with names like Pets.com, Petopia, PetPlanet.com, and Allpets.com began wrestling early for big-time financing. In the dogfight that has ensued, some questionable practices have come to light. Like many other Internet start-ups, these companies launched stock offerings when they had just barely begun to do business. Amazon.com, which acquired 40 percent of Pets.com, pressured investment banks to refuse to underwrite the offerings of competing online pet supply companies. Also, according to one competitor, the company was engaging in unfair pricing: "Pets.com [was] dumping product at way below cost. They should be slammed with an antitrust suit." In fact, several of the online pet store companies have been collecting 40 cents to 60 cents in sales for every dollar paid to suppliers and shippers. And other questionable practices have occurred: Petopia ran two promotions for products that it could not fulfill when customers responded to it.

Should questionable practices by start-up businesses be overlooked in the interest of their future success?

PRO

1. Since financing is so hard to come by, new businesses should be allowed to raise money as quickly and efficiently as they can, in any manner that works.
2. Every new business makes mistakes; those made by start-ups, particularly in an online competitive environment, should be overlooked in the interest of strengthening the industry as a whole.
3. Intense, no-holds-barred competition like that in the online pet supply industry will result in the strongest companies surviving, creating the greatest value for consumers.

CON

1. New businesses—and new industries—should be subject to the same ethical guidelines that existing businesses and industries are, in the interest of fair competition.
2. Cutthroat competition involving questionable practices does not create value for the consumer or contribute to the economy, and it should be discouraged.
3. No business wins in a price war. Competitors should actually try to support each other when an industry is new, in order to strengthen the industry as a whole.

SUMMARY

Executives for the online pet supply companies assert that their financial situations and competitive practices are legitimate. "We're building ahead of the curve," says Julie L. Wainwright, former chief executive for Pets.com, of her company's practice of selling product below cost. Pets.com and others are simply trying to grab their share of the market before it's too late. But while all of these competitors battled for customer awareness and buyer loyalty by offering below-cost prices, they encountered the inevitable problem of profitability. To their dismay, customers who might have saved $6 on a 20-pound bag of dog food, but ended up paying $7 for shipping, were unlikely to become the online pet stores' best friend. Also, dog food can be bought almost everywhere. The results were almost inevitable: By 2001, Pets.com and the other online operators had bit the dust. All that remains of the industry is Petsmart.com.

Sources: Jon Swartz, "Pet e-tailers Go to Dogs as Pets.com Rolls Over," *USA Today,* November 8, 2000, p. B1; Patricia Riedman, "Sock Puppet Joins Homeless," *Advertising Age,* November 13, 2000, p. 86; Arlene Weintraub and Robert D. Hof, "For Online Pet Stores, It's Dog-Eat-Dog," *Business Week,* March 6, 2000, pp. 78–79; Clare Saliba, "The End of Petopia," February 2, 2001, downloaded from **www.ecommercetimes.com,** February 6, 2001.

Small firms rely less on debt for financing than large businesses do, with less than half of small companies borrowing money at least once during the course of a year.[27] As Figure 5.5 shows, credit cards, despite their relatively high interest rates, are an important source of financing for small businesses. The heaviest users of credit cards for business financing are tiny firms with fewer than ten employees. In addition, as discussed in the next chapter, many entrepreneurs rely on personal loans as well as their own or their relatives' savings as sources of financing to start a business.

Software developer Jinny Crum-Jones raised plenty of money to get started but then didn't follow through on her original plans to generate revenues. Crum-Jones had developed software that used Internet technology to assist pharmaceutical companies in managing drug research. When she launched her company, Persimmon IT, in the late 1990s, investors were looking for Internet ventures to back, and Persimmon got money from Siemans, one of Germany's largest corporations. However, instead of bringing her original software to market, Crum-Jones decided to diversify

> ### THEY SAID IT
>
> *"Banks will lend you money if you can prove you don't need it."*
>
> MARK TWAIN (1835–1910)
> AMERICAN AUTHOR

FIGURE 5.5
Sources of Small-Business Financing

*Trade credit is purchasing goods or equipment from a supplier who finances the purchase by delaying the date of payment for those goods.
†A line of credit is an agreement between a bank and a borrower, indicating the maximum amount of credit the bank will extend to the borrower.
‡Total exceeds 100 percent because businesses typically use more than one source of financing.

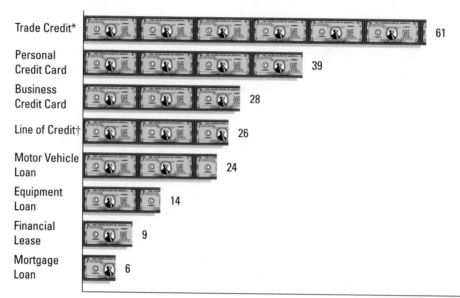

Source of Financing

Trade Credit* 61
Personal Credit Card 39
Business Credit Card 28
Line of Credit† 26
Motor Vehicle Loan 24
Equipment Loan 14
Financial Lease 9
Mortgage Loan 6

Percentage of Businesses Using Source‡

by simultaneously developing other software for a wider market. Despite spending $500,000 a month and quadrupling its employees, Persimmon moved too slowly. By the time it released its products, the company had spent all its money without generating any revenues. Eventually, Crum-Jones sold the rights to her software to two different companies and closed Persimmon.[28]

Inadequate financing can compound management shortcomings by making it more difficult for small businesses to attract and keep talented people. Typically, a big company can offer a more attractive benefits package and a higher salary. Steven Carter took a 60 percent pay cut to move from NBC to Internet start-up iVillage. In place of a high salary, the company offered him a riskier but potentially invaluable alternative: stock options, the right to buy stock in the firm at a below-current market price. The options could have made Carter rich if he and the company had succeeded as hoped. However, in less than a year, his career with iVillage was over—and without a job, Carter concluded he could not afford the $100,000 fee to exercise his options.[29]

With less money to spend on employees, successful small companies need to be more creative. Ronald Richey, who runs Precision Plastics, an injection-molding plant in Columbia City, Indiana, watched one-fifth of his employees quit each year. Lacking sufficient employees to operate the factory, he had to keep some of his machinery idle every week. Richey tried better communication and hiring temporary workers, but nothing worked. Then he thought of an innovative arrangement: if employees would work five six-hour shifts without lunch breaks, he would pay them 40 hours' wages each week for 30 hours of work. Two weeks into the new plan, turnover plummeted—and quality improved. Even with what is effectively a higher pay scale, Precision's profits have grown.[30]

Government Regulation

Small-business owners often complain bitterly of excessive government regulation and red tape. Paperwork costs alone account for billions of small-business dollars each year. A large company can better cope with requirements for forms and reports. These firms may decide that it makes economic sense to hire or contract with specialists in specific types of regulation, such as employment laws and workplace safety regulations. Small businesses often struggle to absorb the costs of government paperwork because of their more limited staff and budgets. Some small firms close down for this reason alone.

Recognizing the burden of regulation on small businesses, Congress sometimes exempts the smallest companies from certain regulations. Except for manufacturers, companies with ten or fewer employees are exempt from some data collection requirements of the Occupational Safety and Health Administration.[31] Most small-business owners comply with employment and other laws, believing that such compliance is ethically correct and fosters better employee relations than trying to determine which regulations don't apply to a small business. To help small businesses comply with employment laws, the U.S. Department of Labor provides forms and guidelines at its "eLaws Advisors" Web page. Employers can also file these forms online.

Taxes are another burdensome expense for a small business. In addition to local, state, and federal income taxes, employers must pay taxes covering workers' compensation insurance, social security payments, and unemployment benefits. Although large companies have similar expenses, they generally have more resources with which to cover them.

INCREASING THE LIKELIHOOD OF BUSINESS SUCCESS

In spite of these challenges, many small businesses do succeed. How can a prospective owner gain the numerous advantages of running a smaller firm while also overcoming the disadvantages? Most successful entrepreneurs believe that two recommendations are critical:

- Develop a business plan.
- Use the resources provided by such agencies as the SBA and local business incubators for information, advice, funding, and networking opportunities.

Creating a Business Plan

Perhaps the most important task an entrepreneur faces is creating a business plan. An effective business plan can mean the difference between a company that succeeds and one that fails. A **business plan** is a written document that provides an orderly statement of a company's goals, the methods by which it intends to achieve these goals, and the standards by which it will measure achievements.

Plans give the organization a sense of purpose. They provide guidance, influence, and leadership, as well as communicating ideas about goals and the means of achieving them to associates, employees, lenders, and others. In addition, they set standards against which achievements can be measured. Planning usually works best when the entire organization participates in the process. Planning can combine good ideas presented by employees and communicate information while making everyone feel a part of the team.

Although no one format best suits all situations, a good small-business plan will include a detailed time frame for achieving specific goals, projections of money flows (both income received by the business and funds disbursed to pay expenses), and units for measuring achievement (sales, profits, or changes in market share). A business plan should also cover the methods by which the firm will achieve specific goals, procedures it will follow, and values that define important standards for conduct. Perhaps most important, the plan should always be open to revision.

Before writing a business plan, a business owner should answer some questions:

- How would you explain your idea to a friend?

- What purpose does your business serve? How does your idea differ from those behind existing businesses?
- What is the state of the industry you are entering? Who will be your customers or clients?
- How will you market the firm's goods or services?
- How much will you charge?
- How will you finance your business?
- How will you measure your firm's success or failure at specific time intervals?
- What characteristics qualify you to run this business?

Give special attention to the name of your proposed business. Does the name reflect the firm's goals? Is it already registered by someone else? Does it convey any hidden meanings to other people? What does it mean phonetically in other languages? Is it offensive to any religious or ethnic groups? On a humorous note, *Inc.* magazine recently offered some tongue-in-cheek comments about some company names proposed in an entrepreneurship competition. To the *Inc.* editors, NuGoo.com sounded like a high-tech adhesive—it's supposed to be a financial Web site for Chinese users—and Indolis sounded like a place to go to do nothing online—it's supposed to be a site where businesses trade with one another. And if you want to find love at 888meet.com, you'll be sorry to hear that the site is planned as a system for managing teamwork in companies.[32]

Be sure to do adequate research. Trade journals are excellent sources of industry-related information. The Small Business Development Centers on many college campuses, the SBA in Washington, D.C., many local chambers of commerce, and your local library can also assist in this research. You may gain useful insights by talking to suppliers in the industry and to local licensing authorities. How many similar businesses have succeeded? How many have failed? Why? What risks are specific to your industry? What markups are typical in the industry's pricing structure? What are common levels of expenses and profit percentages? Another way to gather information is to shop the competition. When she was planning a day-care facility, Tonya Davis and her niece visited other day-care centers to compare costs of enrolling a child. Davis quickly learned that she had been planning to charge too little. Armed with that information, she met with an accountant at her city's chamber of commerce to compare how various prices would affect her profits.[33]

A business plan typically includes the following components:

Business Plan

Executive Summary

- An EXECUTIVE SUMMARY should answer the who, what, why, when, where, and how questions for the business in brief. Although the summary appears early in the plan, it probably should be the last element written.

Introduction

- An INTRODUCTION should give a general statement of the concept, purpose, and objectives of the proposed business, along with an overview of the industry. This element should include a brief description of the owner's education, experience, and training, with references to a résumé included later in the plan.

Marketing

- A MARKETING section should describe the firm's target market, its anticipated competitors, and plans for distribution, advertising, pricing, and locations of facilities. This section should cover the background of the industry and industry trends as well as the potential of the new venture. It should also point out any unique or distinctive features of the business, including industry cycles such as busy and slow seasons, and explain the reasons for choosing a particular start-up date.
- The MARKETING section should also cover equipment rental, leasing, or purchase costs, and the influences of traffic volume, neighboring businesses, demographics, parking,

accessibility, and visibility. Further discussion should review labor costs, utility access and rates, police and fire protection, zoning restrictions, and other government rules and regulations.

Financials

· The FINANCIAL section should detail an operating plan forecast, a plan for obtaining capital, and a description of plans for spending funds.
· The FINANCIAL section should also estimate assets and liabilities and analyze when the firm will reach the breakeven point—the level of sales at which revenues equal costs.

Résumés of Principals

· RÉSUMÉS OF THE PRINCIPALS of the business should be included in a plan written to obtain funding.

Within these sections, a business plan should cover some other topics. It should indicate whether the firm will be organized as a sole proprietorship, partnership, or corporation, and it should identify when it will need to hire employees. Other important facts are job descriptions for employees; the lines of authority in the business; a risk management plan, including detailed information on insurance; a list of suppliers with methods for assessing their reliability and competence; and a policy for extending credit to customers.

Since business plans are essential tools for securing outside funds, the financial section requires particular attention to detail. KnowledgeWorks, a developer of sophisticated databases, updated its business plan when it was preparing to incorporate. To appeal to bankers' conservative mind-set, chief executive officer (CEO) Gerald Whitson started with a conservative estimate of revenues, then cut about 10 percent off the top. With expenses, he inflated his estimate by 7 percent. That way, he assumed, if his company didn't perform up to expectations, it would still look good, and KnowledgeWorks would have a cushion that would allow it to keep any promises it made to lenders. With that approach, it was no surprise that KnowledgeWorks was able to negotiate a bank loan to help it expand as a corporation.[34]

If, like the KnowledgeWorks plan, a business plan becomes part of a request for financing, the lender will examine the owner's management skills and experience, the major risks associated with the enterprise, available collateral, and the firm's ability to repay the loan. Potential outside investors are more likely to evaluate its potential for profits and growth and place less emphasis on downside risks.

If certain assumptions underlie the body of the plan, tie them into the financial section. A plan for two outlets, for example, should provide cash-flow projections that show how the firm will cover the costs involved with each. Deal with both significant and insignificant variables. The bankers or investors who analyze a plan may not know whether your firm will spend $250 or $25,000 to install an exotic, high-tech part, but they will know that a telephone system for 50 people will cost more than $250 per month. Carelessness with seemingly insignificant variables can undercut credibility.

Itemize monthly expenses rather than simply projecting annual amounts. A firm with $100,000 in annual costs may not spend exactly $8,333 each month. Some expenses are paid monthly and some only once each year. An owner who must cover several large annual payments at the beginning of the year but failed to report this in the financial section of the firm's business plan will be running back to financiers during the first month to explain problems with the cash-flow projection—not a good way to start. In addition to cash flow, a business plan should project a detailed profit-and-loss statement. It must also state all assumptions it makes about the conditions under which the firm will operate.

The assembled plan should be neat and easy to use. It should include a table of contents so that readers can turn directly to the parts that most interest them. Also, the format should be attractive and professional.

Small Business Administration

Small businesses can also benefit from using the resources provided by the Small Business Administration (SBA). The SBA is the principal government agency concerned with helping small U.S. firms, and it is the advocate for small businesses within the federal government. Over 3,000 employees staff the SBA's Washington, D.C., headquarters and its regional and field offices. The primary operating functions of the SBA include providing financial assistance, aiding in government procurement matters, and providing management training and consulting.

Financial Assistance from the SBA   Contrary to popular belief, the SBA seldom provides direct business loans. Its major financing contributions are the guarantees it provides for small-business loans made by private lenders, including banks and other institutions. Direct SBA loans are available in only a few special situations, such as natural disaster recovery and energy conservation or development programs. Even in these special instances, a business applicant must contribute a portion of the proposed project's total cost in cash, home equity, or stocks in order to qualify.

The SBA also guarantees *MicroLoans* of less than $25,000 to start-ups and other very small firms. MicroLoans may be used to buy equipment or operate a business but not to buy real estate or pay off other loans. These loans are available from non-profit organizations located in most states. Other sources of MicroLoans include the federal Economic Development Administration, some state governments, and certain private lenders, such as credit unions and community development groups.

Small-business loans are also available through SBA-licensed organizations called **Small Business Investment Companies (SBICs).** These organizations use their own capital, supplemented with government debt, to invest in small businesses. Like banks, SBICs are profit-making enterprises, but they are likely to be more flexible than banks in their lending decisions. Well-known companies that used SBIC financing when they were start-ups include Apple Computer, Callaway Golf Co., AOL Time Warner, Federal Express, Intel, and Sun Microsystems.

Another financial resource underwritten by the SBA is the Angel Capital Electronic Network (ACE-Net), which matches entrepreneurs looking for start-up capital with potential investors willing to exchange their money and advice for partial ownership of the company. Entrepreneurs post information about their businesses on ACE-Net's Web site, where potential investors can review it. Interested parties contact the firms. The goal is to help businesses seeking smaller amounts of capital than those typically handled by venture capital firms.

Other Specialized Assistance   Although government purchases represent a sizable market, small companies have difficulty competing for this business with giant firms, which employ specialists to handle the volumes of paperwork involved in preparing proposals and completing bid applications. Today, many government procurement programs specifically set aside portions of these orders for small companies; an additional SBA role involves assisting small firms in securing these contracts. With **set-aside programs,** certain government contracts (or portions of those contracts) are restricted to small businesses. Every federal agency with buying authority must maintain an Office of Small and Disadvantaged Business Utilization to ensure that small businesses receive a reasonable portion of government procurement contracts. To help connect small businesses with government agencies, the SBA's Web site offers the Procurement Marketing & Access Network (PRO-Net&trade), which includes a search engine for finding business opportunities as well as a chance for small businesses to provide information about themselves.

In addition to help with financing and government procurement, the SBA delivers a variety of other services to small businesses. It provides information and advice through toll-free telephone numbers and its Web site. Through the Service Corps of Retired Executives, volunteers share business advice based on their years of experience. The SBA also offers hundreds of publications at little or no cost, and it

Table 5.1	**Programs and Services of the Small Business Administration**

A. Business Counseling and Training

Small Business Development Center (SBDC)
Over 1,000 SBDCs provide management and technical assistance to small businesses and would-be entrepreneurs. They are cooperative efforts among the SBA, the academic community, the private sector, and state and local governments.

Service Corps of Retired Executives (SCORE)
Nationwide, 12,400 SCORE volunteers in nearly 400 chapters and at www.score.org provide expert advice, based on years of firsthand experience and shared knowledge, on virtually every phase of business.

Business Information Center (BIC)
BICs offer small-business owners access to state-of-the-art computer hardware and software as well as counseling by SCORE volunteers.

SBA OnLine
This Internet bulletin board offers links to government services, SBA publications and data, calendars of events, online training, and special-interest groups at www.sbaonline.sba.gov.

Women's Network for Entrepreneurial Training (WNET); Veterans' Entrepreneurial Training (VET); and Office of Native American Affairs (ONAA)
These three programs provide in-depth entrepreneurial training for women, veterans, and Native Americans. Resources include workshops and mentoring programs.

B. Lending Programs

7(a) Loan Guaranty
The SBA guarantees loans of up to $750,000 made by participating lenders.

SBALowDoc and SBAExpress
These two programs speed up and simplify the process of obtaining guaranteed loans for $150,000 or less.

Small Business Investment Companies (SBICs)
The SBA licenses private firms (SBICs) to invest in small businesses, especially start-ups.

7(m) MicroLoan
The MicroLoan program provides short-term loans ranging from under $100 to $25,000 for small-scale financing purposes such as inventory, supplies, and working capital.

C. International Trade Assistance

U.S. Export Assistance Center (USEAC)
USEACs combine in single locations the trade-promotion and export-finance resources of the SBA, the U.S. Department of Commerce, and the Export-Import Bank of the United States.

D. Federal Government Procurement

Prime Contracting and Subcontracting
This program increases opportunities for small businesses in the federal acquisition process. It initiates small-business set-asides, identifies new small-business sources, and counsels small firms on how to do business with the federal government.

Procurement Marketing & Access Network (PRO-Net&trade)
This online service lets small businesses list their capabilities and search for procurement opportunities.

sponsors popular conferences and seminars. Table 5.1 summarizes several of the programs that the SBA currently offers to small-business owners.

Business Incubators

In recent years, local community agencies interested in encouraging business development have implemented a concept called a **business incubator** to provide low-cost, shared business facilities to small, start-up

BUSINESS DIRECTORY

➤ **Small Business Administration (SBA)** *federal agency that assists small businesses by providing management training and consulting, financial advice, and support in securing government contracts.*

➤ **business incubator** *organization that provides low-cost, shared facilities to small, start-up ventures.*

ventures. A typical incubator might section off space in an abandoned plant and rent it to various small firms. Tenants often share secretaries, WATS lines, copiers, and other business services. The objective is that, after a few months or years, the fledgling business will be ready to move out and operate on its own.

Hundreds of business incubator programs operate nationwide. About half are run by not-for-profit organizations including industrial development authorities. The remainder are divided between college- and university-sponsored incubators and business-run incubators.[35] These facilities offer management support services and valuable management advice from in-house mentors. Operating in an incubator gives entrepreneurs easy access to such basic needs as telephones and human resource experts. They also can trade ideas with one another. At an incubator called eHatchery, an online merchant called Simply Collectible couldn't figure out how to reduce its high shipping costs until its owners talked to the logistics expert at FigLeaves.com, another eHatchery start-up, and learned how to spend less on boxes. FigLeaves.com, which offers top-of-the-line underwear at its Web site, also got help with the site's design from eHatchery programmers.[36]

In the Internet sector, private, for-profit incubators like Internet Capital Group, Idealab, and CMGI set up shop to assist dot.com businesses in getting started in exchange for an ownership share in the company. They offered financing and managerial assistance acquired from working with dozens of other Web-based B2C and B2B firms. Idealab, for instance, has backed such start-ups as eToys, eMachines, and other high-tech businesses. When Internet stocks tumbled in the early years of the 21st century, incubators reacted by drastically reducing the number of start-ups they worked with as well as raising their criteria for adding new firms to their portfolio.[37]

Large Corporations Assisting Small Businesses

Corporate giants often devise special programs aimed at solving small-business problems. In doing so, they are not acting out of humanitarian interests. Instead, they recognize the size of the small-business market, its growth rate and buying power, and the financial rewards for firms that support small businesses. UPS has broadened its package delivery service to help small businesses with the details of filling orders and processing returns. Figure 5.6 describes how UPS might help a small-business founder who has a good idea for a product and Web site but lacks experience in other aspects of running a business.

Like the manager in Figure 5.6, many small businesses can use widely available tools to set up Web sites. However, not many have the expertise to troubleshoot problems with these sites. Jackie Monticup decided to expand her Virginia magic shop by going online. After learning how to design a Web site, she created a site named Magictricks.com. Before long, most of her sales were coming from online shoppers, but Monticup knew she was still missing out on lots of potential business. People would call the store to ask for help with the Web site, and a sizable percentage of people who got to the order page quit before completing a purchase. Monticup couldn't afford the rates charged by most computer consultants, so she

FIGURE 5.6
UPS: A Large Firm Providing Specialized Services for Small Businesses

visited a Web site called MyComputer.com, which offered more affordable rates for diagnosing and fixing common problems. After using software supplied by the Web site to track usage patterns of visitors to Magictricks.com, she discovered that many users were drawn to her Web page called Magic Library, which offered lots of information about magic but no information about ordering products. Monticup modified the site to highlight products for sale, and her sales improved. Besides tracking usage, MyComputer.com checks links to make sure they really take users to the named sites, and it lists the Web site with search engines. Its WatchDog service checks and rechecks the Web site to make sure it is widely accessible from around the world. Costs for these services start at $59 a year for checking links and about $20 a month to analyze site traffic and monitor downtime—prices that are within reach of most small businesses.[38]

Another way that small businesses get help from other companies is by forming an alliance to achieve mutual goals. When drugstore.com, the leading online pharmacy launched in February 1999, it quickly constructed a network of strategic partnerships, meeting a consumer demand at every point where consumers interact with their drugstore.

- At the corner drugstore—drugstore.com has an exclusive 10-year relationship with RiteAid, making it the online pharmacy for the chain's 3,800 stores.

- Through health insurance providers and pharmacy benefits managers (PBMs)—drugstore.com offers discounts and prescriptions to two of the top five insurance providers as well as two of the largest PBMs.

- On the Internet—drugstore.com is the exclusive Health and Beauty provider for the Internet's largest retailer, Amazon.com.

As a result, Amazon was able to offer health and beauty items to its more than 25 million customers without redirecting resources toward the expensive and complex effort of building a trusted online pharmacy. Because of the partnership, the drugstore.com management team was able to learn from the Amazon team's experience, and apply those lessons along the way. As Amazon CEO Jeff Bezos said in one interview, drugstore.com employees were "better prepared for their launch than we were by a factor of about a million."[39]

Playing with much bigger partners may involve risks for a small business, however. By giving away partial ownership in exchange for a partnership, a small company loses some of the control and potential rewards it might otherwise keep. In addition, the larger partner's objectives may not be as close a match as the small business's management had hoped. An alliance with Walt Disney Co. marked the beginning of the end for Toysmart.com. Toysmart's CEO, David Lord, had expected Disney's enormous resources to keep the online toy store afloat during the difficult early years. But after acquiring partial ownership in Toysmart, Disney decided to refocus on its more profitable Disney-branded products, and it became impatient with Toysmart's failure to earn a profit. Toysmart managers complained that Disney moved too slowly for an Internet business; months passed before Disney added a requested link on its site from an icon for books to the Toysmart site. In the end, Disney decided to stop funding Toysmart, and the site shut down.[40]

SMALL-BUSINESS OPPORTUNITIES FOR WOMEN AND MINORITIES

The thousands of new business start-ups each year include growing numbers of women-owned firms as well as new businesses launched by African Americans, Hispanics, and members of other minority groups. The numbers of women-owned and minority-owned businesses are growing much faster than the overall growth in U.S. businesses. The people who start these companies see small-business

Atkinson-Baker Inc.: Not Your Grandfather's Law Firm

Background. Women have been part of the legal profession for a long time. But Sheila Atkinson-Baker, who has been a professional court reporter for more than two decades, had an idea for coaxing her venerable colleagues into the Internet age: launching a court-reporter scheduling service from the Web. Why was this such a groundbreaking idea? "Lawyers tend to be set in the way they do things," says Atkinson-Baker.

What Happened? Court reporters are professionals who take notes during testimony—often depositions outside the courtroom—and type up the transcript. With $1,500, Atkinson-Baker set up her site in 1995 and began to lead her legal clients toward the Web. It wasn't easy at first: lawyers and computers didn't mesh. But when it became apparent that the Atkinson-Baker site could provide real value, they began to pay attention.

The Response. Since court schedules, attorney schedules, and the locations of plaintiffs, defendants, and witnesses tend to represent a maze, a service like Atkinson-Baker's, which hires and sends court reporters just about anywhere in the country to take depositions, can be a gift of time and convenience for everyone involved. Atkinson-Baker knows this. "Our company makes one promise to the legal world: one call to us and we'll do the rest," states the Web site, at www.depo.com. "We get the job done with a comprehensive dedication to meeting our client's demands at any time and in any location—across town or across the country. And always at competitive local rates."

While there may be other scheduling services, Atkinson-Baker's was the first to offer scheduling via the Web. Clients can fill out a deposition scheduling form right on the site and submit it. Atkinson-Baker will take care of the rest. In addition, the company offers real-time deposition technology, through which clients can retrieve complete data and transcripts on their cases through the Internet, which saves a great deal of time and expense for them—and for

Atkinson-Baker. Atkinson-Baker will set up a password-protected on-line calendar for clients, including past and future commitments, to which they can refer any time. Finally, the Web site offers a wide range of references for legal professionals, such as notification of federal rule changes and updated information on trial courts by state.

Today and Counting. To satisfy her lawyer clients, Atkinson-Baker needs to attract the best court reporters around the country. So her company's site includes information on professional development for court reporters, as well as opportunities for employment. Potential job candidates can learn the requirements necessary for becoming a court reporter, review the basic steps necessary to produce a transcript, or take a refresher on basic steno machine key groups. In one year, Atkinson-Baker hired 30 court reporters who had applied for jobs after referring to the career development information on the Web site. Today, the company boasts a staff of 80 and a stable of 800 court reporters located around the United States.

QUESTIONS FOR CRITICAL THINKING

1. Do you think that Sheila Atkinson-Baker could have achieved as much success if she had been an employee in a large firm? Why or why not?
2. In what ways does a small company like Atkinson-Baker's contribute to the economy?

Sources: "About Atkinson-Baker Court Reporters," Atkinson-Baker company Web site, **www.depo.com,** accessed January 8, 2001; "Top Innovators in Customer Service," The *Inc./*Cisco Growing with Technology Awards, June 2000, accessed at **www.inc.com**; Leigh Buchanan, "The Best of the Small Business Web," *Inc. Technology,* No. 4, 1999, p. 106.

ownership and operation as an attractive and lucrative alternative to working for someone else.

Women-Owned Businesses

In the United States today, more than 9 million women-owned firms provide jobs for almost 28 million people. Almost two of every five U.S. businesses are owned by women, compared with one-fourth to one-third of businesses worldwide.[41] About one of every eight of these businesses are owned by minority women.

Women, like men, have a variety of reasons for starting their own companies. Like Amilya Antonetti of SoapWorks, described earlier in the chapter, some are driven by an idea they believe can help others. Some have a unique business idea that they want to bring to life, as the "Clicks and Mortar" box describes. Others decide to strike out on their own when they lose their jobs or become frustrated with the bureaucracies in large companies. In other cases, women leave large corporations when they feel blocked from opportunities for advancement. Sometimes this occurs because they hit the so-called *glass ceiling*, discussed in Chapter 8. Because women are more likely than men to be the primary caregivers in their families, some may seek self-employment as a way to achieve flexible working hours so they can spend time with their families.

The fastest growth among women-owned firms is occurring in the construction, wholesale trade, transportation and communications, agribusiness, and manufacturing industries.[42] One woman who created a successful manufacturing business is Karen Alvarez of Dublin, California. She got her original product idea when she was grocery shopping with her children and one child fell from the shopping cart. To prevent such accidents, which occur to thousands of children every year, Alvarez developed the Baby Comfort Strap, a simple padded strap that parents use to buckle a small child to a cart or stroller. She consulted experienced retailers and manufacturers for help in developing packaging, pricing, and testing. When the Baby Comfort Strap proved to be a reliable seller, Alvarez began a successful strategy to generate publicity about the proneness of shopping carts to result in injuries to small children. This led to widespread concerns about the problem, concerns that helped her take the product nationwide.[43]

As the number of female small-business owners have grown, they have also been able to establish powerful support networks in a relatively short time. Many nationwide business assistance programs serve women exclusively. Among the programs offered by the SBA are the Women-Owned Business Procurement program, which teaches women how to market to the federal government; the Women's Network for Entrepreneurial Training, which matches experienced female entrepreneurs with women trying to get started; and dozens of Women's Business Centers, which offer training and counseling in operating a business. In addition, women can find encouragement, advice, and mentors by joining organizations like the National Foundation for Women Business Owners and Independent Means. The latter organization targets young women interested in starting a business.

Minority-Owned Businesses

Business ownership is also an important opportunity for America's racial and ethnic minorities. In recent years, the growth in the number of businesses owned by African Americans, Hispanics, and Asian Americans far outpaced the growth in the number of U.S. businesses overall. Figure 5.7 shows the percentages of minority ownership in major industries. The relatively strong presence of minorities in the services and retail industries is especially significant, because these industries contain the greatest number of businesses.

Hispanics are the nation's largest group of minority business owners, followed by Asian American and African American owners. The SBA attributes some of this pattern to the recent growth in immigrants from Latin America and Asia. Historically, large shares of immigrants to the United States have started businesses. Most African American business owners were born in the United States, compared with half of Hispanic owners and one-third of Asian-American owners. Even more growth lies ahead for Hispanic-owned businesses during this decade, especially as trade between the United States and Latin America increases under NAFTA. Also, businesses owned by Hispanics and Asian Americans are more likely to export than are U.S. businesses in general.[44]

Despite their progress, minority business owners still face some obstacles. Minority entrepreneurs tend to start businesses on a smaller scale and have more difficulty finding investors than other entrepreneurs. They rely less on

FIGURE 5.7
Types of Businesses Owned by Racial and Ethnic Minorities

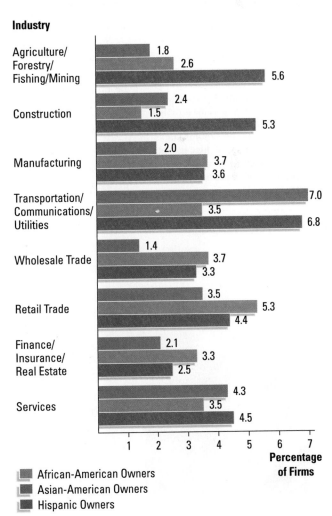

Industry

Agriculture/Forestry/Fishing/Mining	1.8 / 2.6 / 5.6
Construction	2.4 / 1.5 / 5.3
Manufacturing	2.0 / 3.7 / 3.6
Transportation/Communications/Utilities	7.0 / 3.5 / 6.8
Wholesale Trade	1.4 / 3.7 / 3.3
Retail Trade	3.5 / 5.3 / 4.4
Finance/Insurance/Real Estate	2.1 / 3.3 / 2.5
Services	4.3 / 3.5 / 4.5

Percentage of Firms

■ African-American Owners
■ Asian-American Owners
■ Hispanic Owners

bank credit than do other business owners, possibly because they have a harder time getting loans from banks. The difference is especially pronounced in the case of African-American entrepreneurs. Only 15 percent of black-owned businesses borrow from banks, less than half the rate for small businesses overall. Studies have found evidence that African American applicants from equally creditworthy companies are more likely to be denied loans than applicants of other races. So, black business owners have had to be creative in getting financing.[45]

The challenges of being a minority business owner are not limited to dealing with banks. In the realm of high-tech business, much of the investment capital is in the hands of networks of people who met one another at largely white universities. In spite of this disadvantage, the demand for talented people and the nature of online communication are creating opportunities for people like ShopNow's CEO Dwayne Walker. Walker, an African American whose company is an online shopping site with big-name brands, recognizes that others sometimes see a black high-tech CEO as something of a novelty, but he wisely recognizes that what is most important to his business associates is that his company does its job well.[46]

THE FRANCHISING ALTERNATIVE

A major factor in the growth of small business is a unique approach called franchising. **Franchising** is a contractual business arrangement between a manufacturer or another supplier and a dealer. The contract specifies the methods by which the dealer markets the good or service of the supplier. Franchises can involve both goods and services; some well-known franchises are McDonald's, Subway, Fantastic Sams, Mail Boxes Etc., Re/Max, and Blockbuster Video.

Starting a small, independent company can be a risky, time-consuming endeavor, but franchising can reduce the amount of time and effort needed to expand. The franchisor has already developed and tested the concept, and the brand may already be familiar to prospective customers.

The Franchising Sector

Franchising started just after the U.S. Civil War, when the Singer Co. decide to build its business by franchising retail sewing-machine outlets. The concept became increasingly popular after 1900 in the automobile industry. Automobile travel led to demand for local auto sales and service outlets as well as gasoline, oil, and tires. These manufacturers set up systems of franchised distributors to establish local retailers in each retail location—auto dealers, gas stations, tire stores, and auto-parts retailers. Soft-drink and lodging firms also set up their distribution systems through a network of local and regional franchises.

Today, the franchising concept continues its rapid growth. U.S. franchises generate sales of $1 trillion annually and employ over 8 million people. Areas in which strong growth is likely to continue include children's educational services, like Sylvan and Huntington Learning Centers, and carpet cleaners, maid services, and lawn-care specialists, which help time-starved but afflu-

Franchisor Fantastic Sams advertises its ability to give salon owners a significant advantage because its name is "instantly recognized by consumers." As a franchisor, the company will provide the systems for recruitment and retention, purchasing, education, and inventory, as well as advertising support and programs to attract customers. "Attract A Crowd" states the ad, by buying a franchise that is "the most recognizable and successful brand in the hair salon industry."

Attract A Crowd.
Join the most recognizable and successful brand in the hair salon industry.

Be part of a business that makes people feel good about themselves.

The Fantastic Sams brand gives our salon owners a significant advantage because it's instantly recognized by consumers. And since there's no haircare experience required, you can jump right in and get started. All the systems you need are here, including recruitment and retention, purchasing, education and inventory. Plus, you'll get strong advertising support and proven programs that attract customers.

GOTTA BE THE HAIR!

Fantastic Sams

Contact us today and find out how *you* can attract a crowd as a Fantastic Sams franchise owner. Individual, multi and master licenses available.

(800) 441-6588   Fax (714) 779-3422   www.fantasticsams.com

ent consumers take care of their homes. In addition, the aging of the population bodes well for businesses catering to older Americans. Home Instead Senior Care offers nonmedical services to seniors who need help with tasks like house cleaning and food preparation.[47] Compared with U.S. businesses in general, firms owned by African Americans and Asian-owned businesses are more likely to be franchises.[48]

Franchising is also popular overseas. In a recent six-month period, McDonald's opened more than 500 restaurants outside U.S. borders. The franchising giant now has outlets in more than 100 countries.[49]

Franchising Agreements

The two principals in a franchising agreement are the franchisee and the franchisor. The dealer is the *franchisee*, a small-business owner who contracts to sell the good or service of the supplier—the *franchisor*—in exchange for some payment (usually a flat fee plus royalties expressed as a percentage of sales by the franchisee). The franchisor typically provides building plans, site selection help, managerial and accounting systems, and other services to assist the franchisee. The franchisor also provides name recognition for the small-business owner who becomes a franchisee. This public image is created by their familiarity with the franchise in other geographic areas and by advertising campaigns, all or part of which is paid for by franchisee contributions.

The franchisee purchases both tangible and intangible assets from the franchisor. A franchisor may charge a management fee in addition to its initial franchise fee and a percentage of sales or profits. Another may require contributions to a promotional fund. Total costs can vary over a wide range. Start-up costs for a Bennigan's Grill & Tavern can run anywhere from $1 million to $2 million. By contrast, a Jazzercize franchise can cost $20,000 or less.[50]

Franchise agreements often provide for the franchisees to receive materials, equipment, and training from the franchisor. Charmain and Charles Smith bought a Fruitfull Frozen Fruit Bars franchise from Happy & Healthy Products for $28,000, financing much of the purchase price with an SBA-backed loan. Charmain, with a decade of experience in the food service business, runs the franchise. Her husband, who also has a full-time job as a corporate financial executive, provides accounting and other services. The basic agreement with Happy & Healthy Products provides the franchisees with ten freezers, two pallets of frozen fruit and yogurt bars, and a week of training, which covers sales and the company's products and equipment. The franchisee then sells the product to retailers to be stocked either in Fruitfull freezers or the retailer's own freezers. The Smiths' franchise has 43 such accounts in Georgia, including Kroger supermarkets, a chain of health clubs, and school cafeterias. The owners expect that before long, they will have 100 accounts with annual revenues of $75,000 to $100,000. Charles Smith admits that some executives would be reluctant to take on a job that involves driving a delivery truck, but, he counters, "It's a fun and flexible way to make money."[51]

Benefits and Problems of Franchising

As for any other business property, a franchise purchaser bears the responsibility for researching what he or she is buying. Poorly financed or poorly managed franchise systems offer opportunities no better than those in poorly financed or poorly managed independent businesses. Although franchises are more likely than independent businesses to succeed, many franchises do go out of business. The franchising concept does not eliminate the risks of a potential small-business investment; it merely adds alternatives.

Advantages of franchises include a prior performance record, a recognizable company name, a business model that has proven successful in other locations, a tested management program, and training. An existing franchise has posted a performance record on which the prospective buyer can base comparisons and judgments. Earlier results can indicate the likelihood of success in a proposed venture. In addition, a widely recognized name gives the franchisee a tremendous advantage; car dealers, for instance, know that their brand-name products will attract particular segments of the market. A tested management program usually allows the prospective franchisee to avoid worrying about setting up an accounting system, establishing quality control standards, or designing employment application forms. In addition, most franchisors offer valuable business training. McDonald's teaches the basics of operating a franchise at its Hamburger University in Oak Brook, Illinois. Franchise operators quickly learn to meet customer expectations by following strict guidelines for how many seconds to cook the french fries and what words to use when serving customers. By following the franchisor's standards and building on an existing brand name, franchise operators typically can generate profits faster than an independent business owner can.[52]

Shelton Jefferson benefited from franchising when he wanted to expand his company. On his own, he had built a computer networking business. His own knowledge and experience were enough to lead the company as it provided the necessary hardware and software for computer networks, but customers were asking for training as well. Because Jefferson lacked expertise in providing training, he bought a franchise from a computer education company called The Fourth R. The franchisor helped him build computer training into a $500,000 business.[53]

On the negative side, franchise fees and future payments can be a very expensive cost category. Like any business, a franchise may well be unprofitable in its first months and at times thereafter. Payments to the franchisor can add to the burden of keeping the business afloat until the owner begins to earn a profit.

Another potential drawback stems from the fact that the franchisee is linked to the reputation and management of the franchise. If customers are unhappy with their experience at another franchise unit, this dissatisfaction can harm the reputations of other franchisees in the same area. A strong, effective program of managerial control is essential to offset any bad impressions created by unsuccessful franchises. Before signing on with a franchisor, potential franchisees should carefully study its financial performance and reputation. Sources of information include the information provided by the franchisor, as well as state consumer protection agencies, the Better Business Bureau, and the Federal Trade Commission (FTC). The FTC's Web site includes advice for franchisees and reports of complaints against franchisors.[54] Potential franchisees also should study the franchise agreement carefully, to make sure they can succeed within the limitations of the agreement. In some instances, franchisors will decide to pursue additional sales by establishing new distribution outlets, outlets that may compete directly with established franchisees. Subway sandwiches generated considerable ill will among its franchised outlets when it began setting up operations in retail gas stations. An important question that should be answered in today's online business environment is this: does the franchisor retain the right to sell the same products online that the franchisee is trying to sell through a local outlet? Such online competition might be less of a problem for a Mexican food franchise than for a franchise that provides secretarial services.

Finally, some people are more suited to the demands of operating a franchise than others. Any person who is considering buying a franchise must think first about whether he or she has the right personality for the endeavor. Chapter 6 features an in-depth discussion of the basic characteristics that entrepreneurs should bring to their new endeavors.

SMALL BUSINESS GOES GLOBAL

As recently as five years ago, only about 3 percent of small U.S. businesses with employees were involved in exporting.[55] For a small business, it is daunting to confront the global challenges, including cultural, legal, and economic barriers, described in

Chapter 4. But even with this tiny percentage engaged in exporting, small businesses play a key role in international trade. Over 95 percent of U.S. exporters are businesses with fewer than 500 employees, and they sell over one of every four dollars worth of all U.S. exports. Small businesses with Asian or Hispanic owners are most likely to export.[56] Also, with electronic commerce and the Internet, a small business now can enter new markets almost as easily as getting a Web address and setting up a home page.

Role of the Internet in International Expansion

Some small businesses generate much of their annual revenue from overseas sales, and the global reach of the Internet forces online companies to recognize these international markets quickly. StarMedia, based in New York, set out to create Web portal sites in Spanish and Portuguese. Its original plan was to become a major site in Latin America. However, Spain's Telefonica Group also was attracted to the Latin American market, and StarMedia quickly realized it had a European competitor. So StarMedia decided to deliver its competitive strengths directly to Telefonica's front door by opening an office in Madrid to create and run a Spanish portal tailored to Spain's Internet users.[57]

Even if they don't maintain Web sites, companies hoping to sell their products in other countries can use the Internet as an important information resource. By surfing the Web, small-business owners can find leads on potential customers, gather information about overseas markets, and pinpoint government restrictions. Chapter 4 identifies the major trade and exporting resources available on the Internet, and Chapter 7 discusses in more detail how the Internet is contributing to the globalization of business.

Growth Strategies for Small Businesses

As the previous chapter discusses, licensing is a relatively simple way to enter a foreign market. Under a *licensing agreement,* one firm allows another to use its intellectual property in exchange for compensation in the form of royalties. Examples of intellectual property include trademarks, patents, copyrights, and technical know-how. For instance, a firm that has developed a new type of packaging might license the process to foreign companies.

Sometimes a small firm can achieve exporting success by teaming up with another organization that can provide services it cannot afford on its own. An *export management company* is a domestic firm that specializes in performing international marketing services as a commissioned representative or distributor for other companies. Another option for a small firm is to purchase needed goods and sell its products internationally through an *export trading company,* a general trading firm that plays varied roles in world commerce, including importing, exporting, countertrading, investing, and manufacturing.

ALTERNATIVES FOR ORGANIZING A BUSINESS

Whether small or large, every U.S. business fits one of three categories of legal ownership: sole proprietorships, partnerships, and corporations. As Figure 5.8 shows, sole proprietorships are the most common form of business ownership. However, the simple *number* of firms organized according to each model may overstate the importance of sole proprietorships and understate the role of corporations in generating revenues, producing and marketing goods and services, creating jobs, and paying taxes. After all, a corporate giant such as Wal-Mart, with annual sales of over $200 billion, has a huge impact on the nation's economy, exceeding the collective effect of thousands of small businesses organized as proprietorships.

FIGURE 5.8
Forms of Business Ownership

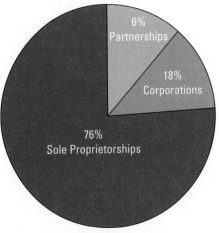

6%
Partnerships

18%
Corporations

76%
Sole Proprietorships

Table 5.2	**Comparing the Three Major Forms of Private Ownership**				
Form of Ownership	**Number of Owners**	**Liability**	**Advantages**	**Disadvantages**
Sole proprietorship	One owner	Unlimited personal liability for business debts	1. Owner retains all profits 2. Easy to form and dissolve 3. Owner has flexibility	1. Unlimited financial liability 2. Financing limitations 3. Management deficiencies 4. Lack of continuity
Partnership	Two or more owners	Personal assets of any operating partner at risk from business creditors	1. Easy to form 2. Can benefit from complementary management skills 3. Expanded financial capacity	1. Unlimited financial liability 2. Interpersonal conflicts 3. Lack of continuity 4. Difficult to dissolve
Corporation	Unlimited number of shareholders; up to 75 shareholders for S corporations	Limited	1. Limited financial liability 2. Specialized management skills 3. Expanded financial capacity 4. Economies of large-scale operations	1. Difficult and costly to form and dissolve 2. Tax disadvantages 3. Legal restrictions

Each form offers unique advantages and disadvantages, as outlined in Table 5.2. To overcome certain limitations of the traditional ownership structures, owners may also use three specialized organizational forms: S corporations, limited-liability partnerships, and limited-liability companies. Along with the basic forms, this section also briefly examines each of these alternatives.

Sole Proprietorships

The most common form of business ownership, the **sole proprietorship** is also the oldest and the simplest, because no legal distinction separates the sole proprietor's status as an individual from his or her status as a business owner. Although sole proprietorships are common in a variety of industries, they are concentrated primarily among small businesses such as repair shops, small retail outlets, and service providers, like painters, plumbers, and lawn-care operations.

Sole proprietorships offer advantages that other business entities cannot. For one, they are easy to form and dissolve. (Partnerships are also easy to form, but they are difficult to dissolve.) A sole proprietorship offers management flexibility for the owner along with the right to retain all profits, after payment of personal income taxes. Retention of all profits and responsibility for all losses give sole proprietors the incentive to maximize efficiency in their operations.

Minimal legal requirements simplify entering and exiting a sole proprietorship. Usually the owner must meet only a few legal requirements for starting one, including registering the business or trade name—to guarantee that two firms do not use the same name—and taking out any necessary licenses. Local governments require that certain kinds of licenses be obtained before opening restaurants, motels, retail stores, and many repair shops. Some occupational licenses require firms to carry specific types of insurance, such as liability coverage.

The ease of dissolving a sole proprietorship is an attractive feature for certain types of enterprises. This advantage is particularly important for temporary businesses set up to handle just a few transactions. For example, a part-time concert promoter could create a business to organize a single concert at a local arena.

Ownership flexibility is another advantage of a sole proprietorship. The owner can make management decisions without consulting others, take prompt action when needed, and keep trade secrets where appropriate. You've probably heard people say, "I like being my own boss." This flexibility leads many business owners to prefer the sole proprietorship organization form.

A disadvantage of the sole proprietorship form is the owner's financial liability for all debts of the business. Also, the business must operate with financial resources limited to the owner's personal funds and money that he or she can borrow. Such financing limitations can keep the business from expanding. Another disadvantage is that the owner must handle a wide range of management and operational tasks; as the firm grows, the owner may not be able to perform all duties with equal effectiveness. Finally, a sole proprietorship lacks long-term continuity, since death, bankruptcy, retirement, or a change in personal interests can terminate it.

These limitations can make potential customers nervous about buying major goods or services from a sole proprietorship. In cases in which they know the form of organization being used by their supplier, they may worry that the sole proprietor will not be around long enough or have the resources to fulfill the agreement. Douglas D. Troxel wanted to offer his services as a consultant on mainframe computers, but big companies wouldn't sign contracts with him because he was operating as a sole proprietorship in his independent consulting business. So Troxel formed a corporation, named Serena Software in honor of his children, Sergie and Athena. His corporation began to land bigger jobs, generating enough funds for Troxel to hire a CEO with marketing expertise. The new CEO, Richard A. Doerr, developed a marketing program with newer and more popular software applications, helping the company grow beyond $75 million in annual sales while Troxel kept customers happy by maintaining a close watch over product quality.[58]

Partnerships

Another option for organizing a business is to form a partnership. The Uniform Partnership Act, which regulates this ownership form in most states, defines a **partnership** as an association of two or more persons who operate a business as co-owners by voluntary legal agreement. The partnership was the traditional form of ownership for professionals offering services, such as physicians, lawyers, and dentists. Today, most of these service providers have switched to other organizational forms to limit personal liability.

Like sole proprietorships, partnerships are easy to form. The legal requirements consist of registering the business name and taking out the necessary licenses. Partnerships also offer expanded financial capabilities in cases where each partner invests money. They also usually increase access to borrowed funds compared with sole proprietorships. Another advantage is the opportunity for professionals to combine complementary skills and knowledge. In the earlier example of Charmain and Charles Smith's Fruitfull Frozen Fruit Bars franchise, the two franchise owners each contribute important skills. Charmain has experience as a manager in the food service business, and Charles has a financial background.

Like sole proprietorships, most partnerships have the disadvantage of unlimited financial liability. Each partner bears full responsibility for the debts of the firm, and each is legally liable for the actions of the other partners. Partners must pay the partnership's debts from their personal funds if it ceases operations and its debts exceed its assets. Breaking up a partnership is also a much harder undertaking than dissolving a sole proprietorship. Rather than simply withdrawing funds from the bank, the partner who wants out must find someone to buy his or her interest in the firm.

In many states, partners can minimize some of these risks by organizing as a *limited liability partnership.* In many respects, such a partnership resembles a general partnership, but laws limit the liability of the partners to the value of their investments in the company.

BUSINESS DIRECTORY

➤ **sole proprietorship**   *form of business ownership in which the company is owned and operated by one person.*

➤ **partnership**   *form of business ownership in which the company is operated by two or more people who are co-owners by voluntary legal agreement.*

The death of a partner also threatens the survival of a partnership. A new partnership must be formed, and the estate of the deceased is entitled to a share of the firm's value. To ease the financial strains of such events, business planners often recommend life insurance coverage for each partner, combined with a buy–sell agreement. The insurance proceeds can repay the deceased partner's heirs and allow the surviving partner to retain control of the business.

Partnerships are also vulnerable to personal conflicts. Personal disagreements may quickly escalate into business battles. Good communication is the key to resolving conflicts before they damage a partnership's chances for success or even destroy it.

Corporations

A **corporation** is a legal organization with assets and liabilities separate from those of its owner(s). Regular corporations are sometimes referred to as *C corporations* to distinguish them from other specialized types used by some firms. Although even the smallest business can choose the corporate form of organization, most people think of large companies when they hear the term *corporation*. In truth, many corporations are extremely large businesses.

Wal-Mart, whose annual worldwide sales have passed the $200 billion mark, recently passed long-time No. 1-ranked General Motors as the largest U.S.-based corporation in terms of sales. Third and fourth largest are ExxonMobil and GM's rival, Ford Motor Co. The list of the ten largest U.S. corporations contains four more manufacturers—General Electric, IBM, Philip Morris, and Boeing—as well as banking firm Citigroup and telecommunications provider AT&T. Each of the ten companies earns annual revenues over $50 billion. Wal-Mart generates sales of over $1 billion *every 36 hours!*[59]

The corporate ownership form offers considerable advantages. First, because a corporation acquires the status of a separate legal entity, its stockholders take only limited financial risk. If the firm fails, they lose only the money they have invested. Protection also applies to legal risk. When neurologist Christopher J. Newman blamed radiation from his Motorola cell phone for his brain tumor, he sued Motorola, not the company's owners. The limited risk of corporate ownership is clearly reflected in corporate names throughout the world. Whereas many U.S. and Canadian corporations include the *Inc.* designation in their names, British firms use the *Ltd.* abbreviation to identify their *limited* liability. In Australia, the abbreviation for *Proprietary Limited—Pty. Ltd.*—is frequently included in corporate names.

Corporations offer other advantages. They can draw on the specialized skills of many employees, unlike the typical sole proprietorship or partnership, for which managerial skills are usually confined to the abilities of their owners and a small number of employees. Corporations gain access to expanded financial capabilities based on the opportunity to offer direct outside investments such as stock sales.

The large-scale operation permitted by corporate ownership also brings several advantages. Employees can specialize in their most effective tasks. A large firm can generate internal financing for many projects by transferring money from one part of the corporation to another. Long manufacturing runs usually promote efficient production and allow the firm to charge highly competitive prices that attract customers.

One disadvantage for a corporation is the double taxation of corporate earnings. After a corporation pays federal, state, and local income taxes on its profits, its owners (stockholders) also pay personal taxes on any distributions of those profits they receive from the corporation in the form of stock dividends. Figure 5.9 shows how this process works.

Corporate ownership also involves some legal issues that sole proprietorships and partnerships do not encounter. The number of laws and regulations that affect corporations has increased dramatically in recent years.

To avoid double taxation of business income while achieving or retaining limited financial liability for their owners, a number of firms have implemented modified

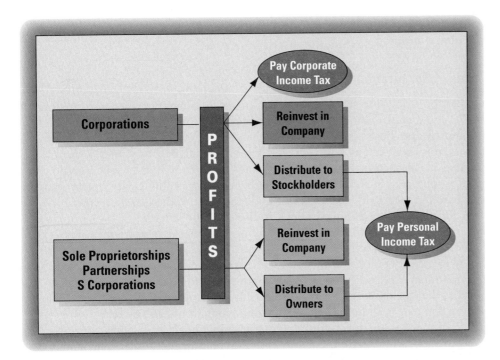

forms of the traditional corporate and partnership structures. Businesses that meet certain size requirements, including ownership by no more than 75 shareholders, may decide to organize as *S corporations,* also called *subchapter S corporations.* These firms can elect to pay federal income taxes as partnerships while retaining the liability limitations typical of corporations.

Business owners may also form **limited liability companies (LLCs)** to secure the corporate advantage of limited liability while avoiding the double taxation characteristic of corporations. An LLC is governed by an operating agreement that resembles a partnership agreement, except that it reduces each partner's liability for the actions of the other owners.

Changing Legal Structures to Meet Changing Needs

Before deciding on an appropriate legal form, someone planning to launch a new business must consider dozens of factors, such as these:

- Personal financial situations and the need for additional funds for the business start-up and continued operation
- Management skills and limitations
- Management styles and capabilities for working with partners and other members of top management
- Concerns about exposure to personal liability

Although the legal form of organization is a major decision, new business owners need not treat it as a permanent decision. Over time, changing conditions such as business growth may prompt the owner of a sole proprietorship or group of partners to switch to a more appropriate form.

ORGANIZING AND OPERATING A CORPORATION

One of the first decisions in forming a corporation is determining where to locate its headquarters and where it will do business. This section describes the various types of corporations and considers the options and procedures involved in incorporating a business.

Types of Corporations

Corporations fall into three categories: domestic, foreign, or alien corporations. A firm is considered a **domestic corporation** in the state where it is incorporated. When a company does business in states other than the one where it has filed incorporation papers, it is registered as a **foreign corporation** in each of those states. A firm incorporated in one nation that operates in another is known as an **alien corporation** where it operates. Some firms—particularly large corporations with operations scattered around the world—may operate under all three of these designations.

A fourth category of corporations is discussed in Chapter 4. *Multinational corporations* are firms with significant operations and marketing activities outside their home countries. Examples include General Electric, Siemens, and Mitsubishi in heavy electrical equipment and Timex, Seiko, and Swatch in watches. Electronics multinational Philips has set up headquarters for some of its product lines in the parts of the world known for their leadership in developing such products. The European company's audio business is based in Hong Kong, and operations for its digital set-top boxes are in California. Other multinationals are paying more attention to what they can learn from employees in different locales, rather than simply issuing directives from headquarters. Workers at ST Microelectronics' Malaysian factory dramatically reduced the time they needed to assemble certain microchips, and the company used the techniques developed in Malaysia to increase productivity of ST employees at its factory in Morocco.[60]

The Incorporation Process

Suppose that you decide to start a business, and you believe that the corporate form offers the best way to organize it. Where should you set up shop? How do you establish a corporate charter? The following sections discuss the procedures for creating a new corporation.

Where to Incorporate   Location is one of the most important considerations for any small-business owner. Although most small and medium-sized businesses are incorporated in the states where they do most of their business, a U.S. firm can actually incorporate in any state it chooses. The founders of large corporations, or of those that will do business nationwide, often compare the benefits provided in various states' laws to corporations in various industries.

The favorable legal climate in Delaware and the speed and simplicity of incorporating there has prompted a large number of major corporations to organize as Delaware corporations. Over half of the companies in *Fortune* magazine's list of the top 500 companies are incorporated there. This popularity has led to incorporations becoming a $400 million government-run industry in Delaware.[61]

The Corporate Charter   Each state mandates a specific procedure for incorporating a business. Most states require at least three *incorporators*—the individuals who create the corporation—which opens incorporation possibilities to small businesses. Another requirement demands that a new corporation adopt a name dissimilar from those of other businesses; most states require that the name must end with the words *Company, Corporation, Incorporated,* or *Limited* to show that the owners have limited liability. Figure 5.10 lists ten elements of the articles of incorporation that most states require for chartering a corporation.

The information provided in the articles of incorporation forms the basis on which a state grants a **corporate charter,** a legal document that formally establishes a corporation. After securing the charter, the owners prepare the company's bylaws, which describe the rules and procedures for its operation.

Corporate Management

Depending on its size, a corporation will have some or all of the ownership and management levels illustrated in Figure 5.11. At the top of the figure are **stockholders**. They acquire shares of stock in the corporation and so become part owners of it. Some companies, such as family businesses, are owned by relatively few stockholders, and the stock is generally unavailable to outsiders. In such a firm, known as a *closed corporation* or *closely held corporation*, the stockholders also control and manage all activities. In contrast, an *open corporation*, sometimes called a *publicly held corporation*, sells stock to the general public, establishing diversified ownership, and often leading to larger operations than those of a closed corporation.

Stock Ownership and Stockholder Rights

Publicly held corporations usually hold annual stockholders' meetings. During these meetings, managers report on corporate activities, and stockholders vote on any decisions that require their approval, including elections of officers.

Stockholders' role in the corporation depends on the class of stock they own. Shares are usually classified as common or preferred stock. Although owners of *preferred stock* have limited voting rights, they are entitled to receive dividends before common-stock holders. If the corporation was dissolved, they would have first claims on assets, once debtors were repaid. Owners of *common stock* have voting rights but only residual claims on the firm's assets, which means they are last to receive any income distributions (dividends). Since one share is typically worth only one vote, those holding a few shares generally have little influence on corporate management actions. The various types of common and preferred stock are described in detail in Chapter 20.

Board of Directors

Stockholders elect a **board of directors**—the governing body of a corporation. The board sets overall policy, authorizes major transactions involving the corporation, and hires the CEO. Most boards include both inside directors (corporate executives) and outside directors—people who are not employed by the organization. Sometimes, the corporation's top executive also chairs the board. Generally, outside directors are also stockholders.

Corporate Officers and Managers

The CEO and other members of top management, such as the chief operating officer (COO), chief information officer (CIO), and CFO, make most major corporate decisions. Managers at the next level down the hierarchy, middle management, handle the ongoing operational functions of the company. At the first tier of management, supervisory personnel coordinate day-to-day operations, assign specific tasks to employees, and often evaluate workers' job performance. The activities and responsibilities of managers at various levels in the organization are described in detail in Chapter 8.

Employee-Owned Corporations

Another alternative in creating a corporation is *employee ownership,* in which workers buy shares of stock in the company that employs them. The

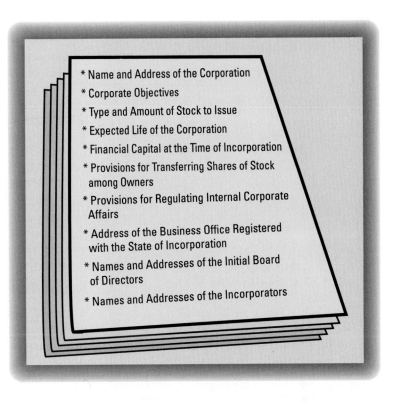

* Name and Address of the Corporation
* Corporate Objectives
* Type and Amount of Stock to Issue
* Expected Life of the Corporation
* Financial Capital at the Time of Incorporation
* Provisions for Transferring Shares of Stock among Owners
* Provisions for Regulating Internal Corporate Affairs
* Address of the Business Office Registered with the State of Incorporation
* Names and Addresses of the Initial Board of Directors
* Names and Addresses of the Incorporators

FIGURE 5.10
Traditional Articles of Incorporation

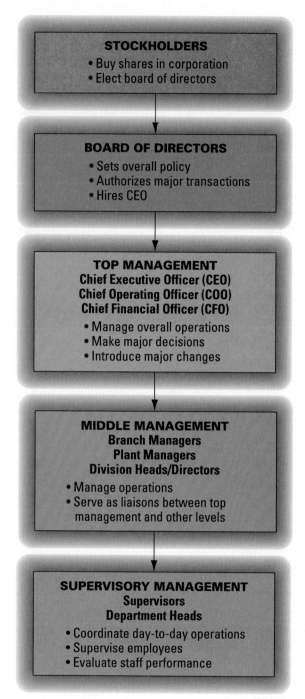

FIGURE 5.11
Levels of Management in a Corporation

corporate organization stays the same, but most stockholders are also employees.

The popularity of this form of corporation is growing. About 15 percent of the private-sector (nongovernment) workforce participates in a plan in which at least half a company's employees own stock in the company. Ten times as many employees had received stock options in 2000 as did just a decade earlier. Several trends are behind the growth in employee ownership. One is that employees have seen soaring stock prices and want to share in the wealth. Another is that managers want employees to care deeply about the company's success so that they will contribute their best effort. Since human resources are so essential to the success of a modern business, employers want to build their employees' commitment to the organization.[62] Employee-owned firms are discussed in more detail in Chapter 11.

Not-for-Profit Corporations

The same business concepts that apply to firms whose objectives include earning profits also apply to *not-for-profit corporations*—firms pursuing objectives other than returning profits to owners. About 1.5 million not-for-profits operate in the United States, including charitable groups, social welfare organizations, and religious congregations.[63] This sector includes museums, libraries, religious and human-service organizations, private secondary schools, health-care facilities, symphony orchestras, zoos, and thousands of other groups such as government agencies, political parties, and labor unions.

An example of a not-for-profit corporation is The Abbey Store. This organization sells products, not to accumulate wealth, but to enable its residents to continue in their chosen vocation of prayer and meditation. The abbey, located in Conyers, Georgia, recommends books on spiritual and religious matters. As shown in Figure 5.12, visitors to the abbey's Web site can place orders, which are handled through Amazon.com, which donates a portion of the sales dollars to the abbey.

Most states have laws that set out separate provisions dealing with the organization structures and operations of not-for-profit corporations. These organizations do not issue stock certificates, since they pay no dividends to owners, and ownership rarely changes. They are also exempt from paying income taxes.

WHEN BUSINESSES JOIN FORCES

Today's corporate world features many complex unions of companies, not always in the same industry or even in the same country. Many well-known firms have changed owners, become parts of other corporations, or split into smaller units. Current trends in corporate ownership include mergers and acquisitions and joint ventures.

Mergers and Acquisitions

In recent years, merger mania has hit U.S. corporations.[64] Petroleum giants became even larger due to such giant combinations as BP Amoco and ExxonMobil. Cereal-products giant Kellogg's purchased Keebler, whose well-known brands include

Cheez-It crackers and Famous Amos cookies. Growth was also the primary motivation behind the sale of Quaker Oats, maker of breakfast foods and GatorAde, to PepsiCo. The 9,000-plus mergers during a recent year were led by deals in the entertainment, banking, and broadcasting industries and involved price tags in the billions. Consider just a few:

- America Online (AOL), the world's largest Internet service provider, merged with Time Warner, the number-two U.S. cable company, in a deal with a $183 billion price tag.
- Bell Atlantic announced a $77 billion merger with GTE.
- CBS and Viacom arranged a $70 billion plan to merge.

In addition, smaller organizations are making mergers and acquisitions part of their growth strategy. A banking firm called Premier Bancshares completed nine acquisitions of community banks over four years, increasing its assets from $75 million to $2 billion over the period.[65] Figure 5.13 shows the recent dramatic rise in mergers and acquisitions.

The terms *merger* and *acquisition* are often used interchangeably, but their meanings differ. In a **merger,** two or more firms combine to form one company; in an **acquisition,** one firm purchases the property and assumes the obligations of another. Acquisitions also occur when one firm buys a division or subsidiary from another firm. Many mergers and acquisitions cross national borders, as managers attempt to enter new markets and improve global competitiveness for their companies. Recently, the annual worldwide value of acquisitions and mergers reached $3.4 trillion, led by Vodafone's announcement that the British provider of wireless service would acquire German telecommunications giant Mannesmann for a record-breaking $190 billion. Many of these combinations are driven by the desire to establish an international presence faster than a company can do by developing new products on its own or simply expanding to new markets.

Mergers can be classified as vertical, horizontal, or conglomerate. A **vertical merger** combines firms operating at different levels in the production and marketing process—the combination of a manufacturer and a large retailer, for instance. A vertical merger pursues one of two primary goals: (1) to ensure adequate flows of raw materials and supplies needed for a firm's products or (2) to increase distribution. Software giant Microsoft Corp. is well known for merging with small firms that have developed products with strong market potential. Large petroleum companies often try to reduce the uncertainty of their future petroleum supplies by acquiring successful oil and gas exploration firms.

One of the most-reported mergers in recent years, the linking up of AOL and Time Warner, was a kind of vertical merger. It served as a way to unite Time Warner's content—movie studios, television programming, cable television, music, and publishing—with AOL's "pipes"—its 25 million–subscriber Internet service. America Online benefits from having access

The Abbey Store is a quality religious goods and bookstore that is dedicated to excellence in selection, value, and service. Since 1946, our store has provided an ever-growing selection of Catholic products and has become a major source of income for our monastery.

Even as we expand our business into the mail order and Internet markets, all profits continue to support the Monastery of the Holy Spirit in Conyers, Georgia.

Blessings,
The Monks
Monastery of the Holy Spirit

The Abbey Store
Monastery of the Holy Spirit
2625 Hwy. 212 S.W. • Conyers, GA 30094-4044 • 800-592-5203 • Fax: 770-860-9343
Email: abbeystore@abbeystore.org

Web site design ©2000 Relevant Arts

FIGURE 5.12
Web Site for a Not-for-Profit Corporation

billions

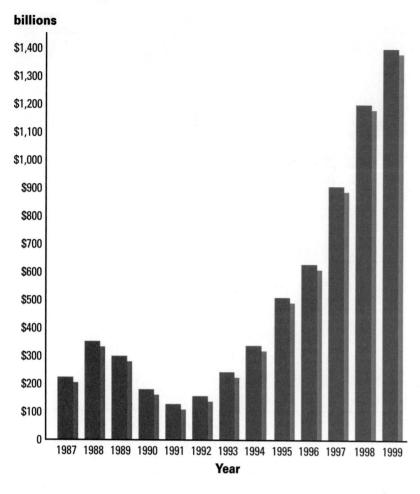

FIGURE 5.13
Spending on U.S. Mergers and Acquisitions

to more material to offer at its Web site, and Time Warner has access to a ready-made on-line audience.[66]

A **horizontal merger** joins firms in the same industry that wish to diversify, increase their customer bases, cut costs, or offer expanded product lines. A desire for combined financial resources prompted a horizontal merger between former competitors Webvan Group and HomeGrocer.com. The combined companies, which now operate under the Webvan name, sell groceries online and deliver them to consumers' homes. The companies had been serving different territories, mostly on the West Coast, so the merger gave them a larger market of customers than either had alone. Merging freed the two young companies from spending money to compete against one another as they expanded. Instead, Webvan can use its combined capital of over $600 million to maintain profitability while it establishes a national presence.[67]

A **conglomerate merger** combines unrelated firms. The most common reasons for a conglomerate merger are to diversify, spur sales growth, or spend a cash surplus that might otherwise make a firm a tempting target for a takeover effort. Conglomerate mergers may join firms in totally unrelated industries. A company well known for its conglomerate mergers is GE, which owns television broadcaster NBC and cable programmers CNBC and MSNBC (in a venture with Microsoft), along with its businesses such as appliances, aircraft engines, and industrial products. Experts debate whether conglomerate mergers are beneficial. The usual argument in favor of such mergers is that a company has management expertise it can use to succeed in a variety of industries. However, the stock of an acquiring company often falls in price when it makes an acquisition, suggesting that investors doubt the value of this strategy.

Joint Ventures—Specialized Partnerships

A **joint venture** is a partnership between companies formed for a specific undertaking. Sometimes, a company enters into a joint venture with a local firm or government, sharing the operation's costs, risks, management, and profits with its local partner. A joint venture also may enable companies to solve a mutual problem. Four U.S. pipeline companies entered into a joint venture to provide better service to the oil refineries that use their services. Their venture, called Transport4, created an online resource at which oil companies can schedule use of the pipelines and track the delivery of petroleum, which often must pass through more than one company's pipelines to reach its destination. Transport4 collects orders and schedules petroleum shipments through the four pipeline companies' systems. It frees customers from calling each company to negotiate and renegotiate schedules.[68] As discussed in the previous chapter, joint ventures also offer particularly attractive ways for small firms to conduct international business, since they bring substantial benefits from partners already operating inside the host countries.

PUBLIC AND COLLECTIVE OWNERSHIP

Most business organizations are owned privately by individuals or groups of people, but municipal, state, or national governments own some firms. In addition, groups of people collectively own some companies. Public ownership is common in many industries, both in the United States and abroad.

Public Ownership

One alternative to private ownership is some form of **public ownership,** in which a unit or agency of government owns and operates an organization. In the United States, local governments often own parking structures and water systems. The Pennsylvania Turnpike Authority operates a vital highway link across the Keystone State. The federal government operates Hoover Dam in Nevada to provide electricity over a large region.

Government-Owned Corporations

Sometimes, public ownership results when private investors are unwilling to invest in what they consider to be a high-risk project. This situation occurred with the rural electrification program of the 1930s, which significantly expanded utility lines in sparsely populated areas. At other times, public ownership has replaced private ownership of failed organizations. Certain functions, such as municipal water systems, are considered so important to the public welfare that government often implements public ownership to protect its citizens from problems. Finally, some nations have used public business ownership to foster competition by operating public companies as competitive business enterprises. In Bogota, Colombia, the government runs a television and radio network, Instituto Nacional de Radio & Television, that broadcasts both educational and commercial programs. Public ownership remains common abroad, despite a general trend toward privatization.

Customer-Owned Businesses: Cooperatives

Another alternative to traditional private business ownership is collective ownership of a production, storage, transportation, or marketing organization. Such collective ownership establishes an organization referred to as a **cooperative** (or co-op), whose owners join forces to collectively operate all or part of the functions in their industry.

Cooperatives allow small businesses to obtain quantity purchase discounts, reducing costs and enabling the co-op to pass on the savings to its members. Marketing and advertising expenses are shared among members, and the co-op's facilities can also serve as a distribution center.

Cooperatives are frequently found in small farming communities, but they also serve the needs of large growers of specific crops. For instance, Blue Diamond Growers is a cooperative that represents California almond growers. Retailers have also established co-ops. Ace Hardware is a cooperative of independently owned hardware stores. Financial co-ops, such as credit unions, offer members higher interest rates on deposits and lower interest rates on loans than other institutions could provide.

WHAT'S AHEAD

The next chapter shifts the book's focus to the driving forces behind new-business formation: entrepreneurs. It examines the differences between a small-business owner and an entrepreneur and identifies certain personality traits typical of entrepreneurs. The chapter also details the process of launching a new venture, including identifying opportunities, locating needed financing, and turning good ideas into successful businesses. Finally, the chapter explores a method for infusing the entrepreneurial spirit into established businesses—intrapreneurship.

➤ Summary of Learning Goals

1. Distinguish between small and large businesses, and identify the industries in which most small firms are established.

Small businesses can adopt many profiles, from part-time, home-based businesses to firms with several hundred employees. A small business is a firm that is independently owned and operated, is not dominant in its field, and meets industry-specific size standards for income or number of employees. Small businesses operate in every industry, but wholesale trade, agricultural services, and construction feature the highest proportions of small enterprises.

2. Discuss the economic and social contributions of small business.

Small businesses create most of the new jobs in the U.S. economy and employ the majority of U.S. workers. They provide valuable outlets for entrepreneurial activity and often contribute to creation of new industries or development of new business processes. Women and minorities find small-business ownership to be an attractive alternative to opportunities available to them in large firms. Small firms may also offer enhanced lifestyle flexibility and opportunities to gain personal satisfaction.

3. Compare the advantages and disadvantages of small business.

Small firms can often operate with greater flexibility than larger corporations can achieve. This flexibility allows smaller businesses to provide superior customer service, develop innovative products, and fill small market niches ignored by large firms. However, small businesses also must operate with fewer resources than large corporations can apply. As a result, they may suffer from financial limitations and management inadequacies. Taxes and government regulation can also impose excessive burdens on small businesses.

4. Describe how the Small Business Administration assists small-business owners.

The U.S. Small Business Administration helps small-business owners to obtain financing through a variety of programs that guarantee repayment of their bank loans. The SBA also assists women and minority business owners in obtaining government purchasing contracts. It offers training and information resources, so

business owners can improve their odds of success. Finally, the SBA advocates small-business interests within the federal government.

5. Explain how franchising can provide opportunities for both franchisors and franchisees.

A franchisor is a company that sells the rights to use its brand name, operating procedures, and other intellectual property to franchisees. Franchising helps business owners to expand their companies' operations with limited financial investments. Franchisees, the individuals who buy the right to operate a business using the franchisor's intellectual property, gain a proven business system, brand recognition, and training and other support from the franchisor.

6. Summarize the three basic forms of business ownership and the advantages and disadvantages of each form.

A sole proprietorship is owned and operated by one person. Although sole proprietorships are easy to set up and offer great operating flexibility, the owner remains personally liable for all of the firm's debts and legal settlements. In a partnership, two or more individuals agree to share responsibility for owning and running the business. Partnerships are relatively easy to set up, but they do not offer protection from liability. Also, partnerships may experience problems if a partner dies or when partners fail to communicate or establish effective working relationships. When a business is set up as a corporation, it becomes a separate legal entity. Individual owners receive shares of stock in the firm. Corporations protect owners from legal and financial liability, but double taxation reduces their revenues.

7. Identify the levels of corporate management.

Stockholders, or shareholders, own a corporation. In return for their financial investments, they receive shares of stock in the company. The number of stockholders in a firm can vary widely, depending on whether the firm is privately owned or it makes its stock available to the public. Shareholders elect the firm's board of directors, the individuals responsible for overall corporate management. The board has legal authority over the firm's policies. A company's officers are the top managers who oversee its operating decisions.

8. Describe recent trends in mergers and acquisitions.

The worldwide pace of mergers and acquisitions continues to grow. U.S. corporations are spending record amounts on mergers and acquisitions. These business combinations occur worldwide, and companies often merge with or acquire other companies to aid their operations across national boundaries. Vertical mergers help a firm to ensure access to adequate raw materials and supplies for production or to improve its distribution outlets. Horizontal mergers occur when firms in the same industry join in an attempt to diversify or offer expanded product lines. Conglomerate mergers combine unrelated firms, often as part of plans to spend cash surpluses that might otherwise make a firm a takeover target.

9. Differentiate among private ownership, public ownership, and collective ownership (cooperatives).

Managers or a group of major stockholders sometimes buy all of a firm's stock. The firm then becomes a privately owned company, and its stock is no longer publicly traded. Some firms allow workers to buy large blocks of stock, so the employees gain ownership stakes. Municipal, state, and national governments also own and operate some businesses. This public business ownership has declined, however, through a recent trend toward privatization of publicly run organizations. In a cooperative, individuals or companies band together to collectively operate all or part of an industry's functions. The cooperative's owners control its activities by electing a board of directors from their members. Cooperatives are usually set up to provide for collective ownership of a production, storage, transportation, or marketing organization that is important to an industry.

Business Terms You Need to Know

small business 168
business plan 181
Small Business Administration (SBA) 184
business incubator 185
franchising 190
sole proprietorship 194

partnership 195
corporation 196
stockholder 199
board of directors 199
merger 201
acquisition 201

Other Important Business Terms

home-based business 171
Small Business Investment Company (SBIC) 184
set-aside program 184
limited liability company (LLC) 197

domestic corporation 198
foreign corporation 198
alien corporation 198
corporate charter 198
vertical merger 201

horizontal merger 202
conglomerate merger 202
joint venture 202
public ownership 203
cooperative 203

➤ Review Questions

1. What is meant by the term *small business*? How do small businesses contribute to a nation's economy?

2. What are the advantages of a small business? What are the disadvantages?

3. What are the benefits of a good business plan? Identify the seven major components of a business plan.

4. What is the Small Business Administration? What does it do?

5. Why have Hispanic Americans become the nation's largest group of minority business owners? Why do economists predict that this growth of Hispanic-owned businesses will continue during the 21st century?

6. Describe a typical franchising agreement. What are the advantages and disadvantages of such an agreement?

7. What is a sole proprietorship? Why is this form of business ownership the most frequently used? What are its advantages and disadvantages?

8. What is a corporation? What are the advantages and disadvantages of corporate ownership?

9. Distinguish between a closed corporation and an open corporation.

10. In what ways are mergers and acquisitions different? What type of merger does each of the following scenarios describe?

   a. A television station in one region merges with a television station in another.

   b. A large juice manufacturer merges with an orchard company.

   c. An Internet company merges with a chain of department stores.

➤ Questions for Critical Thinking

1. Imagine that you are preparing to write a business plan for your own idea for a new company. First, choose one of the following ideas (or come up with one of your own):

   a. An Internet retailer for bicycles, skateboards, and scooters

   b. A shop that offers homemade, heat-and-serve meals

   c. An online magazine

   d. A firm that provides people to do household chores such as yard work and grocery shopping

   Next, answer the questions for business owners in the "Creating a Business Plan" section on pages 181–182. Once you have answered these questions, do you still think your business idea is viable? Why or why not?

2. Read the business page of your local or city newspaper, and choose a small business that has been profiled or written about in the paper. What do you think makes this business successful?

3. Propose an idea for a business incubator in an industry that interests you. Describe where the incubator would be located, how it would function, and what it is intended to accomplish.

4. What kind of company might Fresh Samantha, a maker of premium juice drinks in Maine, want to make an alliance with? Why? What precautions should Fresh Samantha take in entering into an alliance?

5. Do you think that consumers benefit from public ownership of such functions as municipal water systems and the postal service? Why or why not?

➤ Experiential Exercise

Background: Franchising has launched the careers of many successful small business owners. As the chapter states, "U.S. franchises generate sales of $1 trillion and employ over 8 million people." This exercise is designed to give you a closer look at the franchising experience.

Directions: Identify a successful franchise in your community. When choosing your company, you may wish to use a well-known national franchise such as one of those mentioned in the chapter (McDonald's, Subway, Fantastic Sams, Mail Boxes Etc., Re/Max, or Blockbuster Video) or you may choose one that is unique to your region of the country.

1. Contact the franchise owner of the establishment you selected, introduce yourself as a student from the college you attend, tell him or her that you have an assignment in your business class to interview a franchise owner. Explain that you have a list of five questions you'd like to ask and that you'd appreciate him or her scheduling a 15-minute appointment with you where you could meet in person or talk over the telephone to get the information required for this assignment.

2. Make sure you arrive a few minutes early for your scheduled appointment (or call at the appointed time), dress appropriately, and are prepared to conduct the interview in a professional and timely manner. At the conclusion of the interview, be sure to thank the franchise owner for his or her time and expertise.

3. Interview Questions:
   • How many years have you been in this franchise business? How many other franchise locations do you own?

   • Please tell me briefly about how you got into this particular franchise. For example, did you consider other franchise opportunities besides this one? What about this particular franchise appealed most to you?

   • What was the most challenging aspect of opening the firm?

   • To give me a better understanding of the requirements involved in franchising, please give me any terms or conditions you feel comfortable revealing regarding the franchising agreement between you and the franchisor.

   • What do you like best about being a franchise owner? What do you like least?

4. Submit a paper to your instructor in which you summarize the results of the franchisee's responses to the questions. Include any other interesting information you learned during your interview.

➤ Nothing but Net

1. Home-based businesses. Assume you're considering starting a small, home-based business. Select a business opportunity that you feel suits your interests and skills and could be operated from your home, dorm room, or apartment. Prepare a brief business plan. Then visit the following Web site. What are the ten rules for business success that are listed on the Web site? What are the top ten problems of working at home? Based on these lists, how would you modify your business plan?

www.powerhomebiz.com/index/feature.htm

2. **Franchising.** Several Web sites have been developed to help people evaluate the possibility of owning and operating a franchise. Visit the following site and prepare a written report describing the four types of franchising and the five steps to developing a successful franchise.

www.betheboss.com

3. **Small business statistics.** The U.S. Small Business Administration compiles and publishes extensive statistics on small business. One report, published each year, details small business lending activities. Visit the SBA Web site listed here and click on the most recent report on small business lending activity.

www.sba.gov/advo/stats/lending

After reviewing the data, answer the following questions:

a. What is a *micro-business loan*?

b. In total, how much money did U.S. banks lend to micro-businesses?

c. Which five U.S. banks made the most micro-business loans during the most recent year reported on the Web site?

d. Which states have the most micro-business-friendly banks?

Note: Internet Web addresses change frequently. If you do not find the exact sites listed, you may need to access the organization's or company's home page and search from there.

Thinking like a kid isn't necessarily the same as being a kid. When you're a kid, you don't have many options. You have to go to school. You have to do your chores. You have to wear certain clothes. No one wants to hear your opinion about anything. But when you're an adult who thinks like a kid—like Tom Corey, founding partner of Corey & Co.—everyone wants to listen. Many companies recognize the tremendous market for child-oriented goods and services, from television programs to toys. Tom Corey creates the images for these companies that attract kids like magnets.

From its three separate studios located in a renovated schoolhouse outside Boston, the partnership develops designs for specific markets. With roughly sixty employees, Corey's company can zero in on the needs of each client. At the Corey, McPherson, Nash studio, designers create Web sites and other media for larger companies such as Ernst & Young and Genetics. The second studio is Big Blue Dot, where designers come up with print, broadcast, and multimedia designs for and about kids. Hatmaker, the third studio, concentrates on the development of new television channels. Each "boutique" studio operates separately, yet they all work together when necessary.

Perhaps Corey & Co.'s most recognizable image is the logo for cable TV's Nickelodeon channel. "When [Nickelodeon] came to us, they were looking for a new on-air identity," recalls Annie Baumann, director of new business and marketing for the Big Blue Dot studio. "We started working with them by developing a logo and a statement called Nickelodeon's Rules and Tools." The document clarified Nickelodeon's mission and goals, which then helped the network establish its brand identity among viewers and advertisers. But the key to Big Blue Dot's success with the logo was its own mission, which "is to create great, unforgettable design for

kids. We really have a vested interest in producing outstanding work for kids," notes Baumann.

Quality is paramount at Corey & Co. "We definitely have standards about what types of projects we will and will not work on. It's not just about selling to kids; it's also about educating." To that end, Big Blue Dot recently teamed up with Children's Television Workshop and Nickelodeon to develop "Noggin," a Web site and digital channel for kids. The goal of Noggin is for kids to have a place to learn that's fun and free of pressure. Big Blue Dot was involved in the channel's development every step of the way, including coming up with the channel's slogan, "What sparks you?" The channel's programming is both challenging and entertaining. Corey & Co. manages to keep coming up with high-quality design by thinking like kids. "We like to say we constantly keep one finger on the pulse of kid trends," notes Baumann. Employees at Big Blue Dot attend child-oriented conferences and media events, as well as keep current by reviewing periodicals and other publications for kids. But perhaps more important, Big Blue Dot hires employees who "get" kids, people who have "a real commitment to understanding kids." Once a week, employees get together for lunch and ask each other the important questions, such as "How do families connect to the Web?" or "Do standardized tests make kids smarter?"

Corey & Co. is the quintessential small business for the new economy. Like many small businesses before it, the company fills a niche—or several niches with its different studios. It provides services to a broad spectrum of larger businesses. And yet, through the use of the Internet and its own innovations, Corey & Co. has been able to expand on design concepts to the point that it could be argued that the company has launched its own industry. It's an industry in which children and adults come together in a common goal of educating and entertaining through a vast network of new media, where innovation comes from within the four walls of an old, renovated schoolhouse.

QUESTIONS

1. What are some of the advantages to the way Corey & Co. is organized? What might be some of the disadvantages?
2. How might Corey & Co. change if it evolved from a partnership to a publicly held corporation?
3. What challenges might Corey & Co.'s designers face if the company was asked to create a logo and other visuals for a foreign television station?
4. Access the Corey & Co. Web sites—available as links through the main Web site at **www.corey.com**—and watch some of the programming on Noggin, if you have access to it, or access its Web site at **www.noggin.com.** What do you find appealing about the visual designs associated with the company's separate divisions? Is there anything you don't like? Write a brief review of the Web sites or channels.

Sources: Corey & Co. Web site, **www.corey.com,** accessed February 6, 2001; Big Blue Dot Web site, **www.bigblue.com,** accessed January 23, 2001; Michael McPherson, "Tom Corey Tribute," AIGA Boston, June 26, 2000, **www.boston.aiga.org;** Dave Avdoian, "The Children's Place," December 1999, **www.newenglandfilm.com;** Nichole Bernier, ed., "Style," *Boston Magazine,* [no date], **www.bostonmagazine.com,** accessed January 24, 2001.

CHAPTER 6

Starting Your Own Business: The Entrepreneurship Alternative

Learning Goals

1. Define the term *entrepreneur,* and distinguish among an entrepreneur, a small-business owner, and a manager.

2. Identify three different types of entrepreneurs.

3. Explain why people choose to become entrepreneurs.

4. Discuss conditions that encourage opportunities for entrepreneurs.

5. Describe the role of entrepreneurs in the economy.

6. Identify personality traits that typically characterize entrepreneurs.

7. Summarize the process of starting a new venture.

8. Explain how organizations promote intrapreneurship.

Mark Cuban: From One Playing Field to Another

Guess where the founder of Broadcast.com is? No, Mark Cuban is probably not in front of his computer. He's likely to be found either in the locker room or on the basketball court, cheering on his latest venture: the Dallas Mavericks of the National Basketball Association (NBA). How did Cuban get there? After Broadcast.com went public in a roaring success, it attracted the attention of Yahoo!, which later bought the company for $5.7 billion. So Mark Cuban—now one of the nation's youngest billionaires—had to find something else to do. He still wanted his own business, but in professional big-league sports, it's impossible to start your own team single-handedly. So he looked around for an existing team that might be available for purchase. Cuban's search was successful. For a cool $280 million he was able to buy a not-very-good basketball team for sale by Ross Perot Jr.

Although the Mavericks acquisition was considered a poor investment by many, Mark Cuban doesn't care what other people think. He's an entrepreneur. He likes risks and challenges. He likes being his own boss. He likes turning things around. Taking a mediocre team and turning it into a winning one is the kind of project he thrives on. He has no experience as a sports team owner, but that doesn't seem to matter. He's been ridiculed for making extravagant gestures toward his players, like buying the team plush towels and designer luggage. But he claims that he spends relatively little on these small items that people remember and appreciate. "Everything I do is about taking away excuses," says Cuban. "A player can't get enough sleep because he has a foam pillow. We upgrade hotels on the road." His colleagues have begun to see the method in Cuban's madness. "He will improve his franchise because of that enthusiasm," admits Indiana Pacers president Donnie Walsh. "It's good to have an owner come in with that excitement."

Cuban has frequently tripped over the rules of the court, stepping on more than a few toes: NBA executives worry that his enthusiasm and his financial outlays for room upgrades and other player benefits may up the ante throughout the league, and they

are naturally somewhat defensive. "The problem with Mark is, he might force us to go out and do the same things," notes Walsh. "But, in the meantime, my one comment to him is, 'I don't think there are any stupid people in this league.'" The NBA is a large organization that is resistant to change, but in Cuban's former Internet environment, change is necessary for survival. "In the NBA there's the feeling the industry's going strong, there's nothing to fear," says Cuban ominously. He worries that the NBA will not be ready to meet the business demands of a new environment, and he is well aware of current business failures by such prominent B2C dot.coms as Garden.com, ValueAmerica, and Living.com, which failed to adapt. Of course, he's got ideas—he wants to wire the new Dallas sports arena as an ultra-broadband environment, giving marketers access to tens of thousands of consumers and charging them fees for that access. He's got companies like IBM and Texas Instruments in

mind. But he would like this to be done at all NBA arenas—and it's been a hard sell in the NBA so far. "In the Internet, you make the rules. Here you spend your days and nights learning them," shrugs Cuban. So even though Cuban is his own boss, he still has to answer to the NBA—something he's not used to.

When Cuban bought the Mavericks, making money was not at the top of his list of goals for the organization. After all, he didn't need another billion in his bank account. He bought a house for $15 million because he had plenty of money, but he hasn't bothered to furnish it. He says that he just doesn't need furniture. He bought a jet because he wanted one. But he bought the Mavericks because they were his hometown team, they couldn't sell seats to their home games, and he wanted to turn them into winners. He may just do it. If not, he'll have a good time trying.[1]

CHAPTER OVERVIEW

Like millions of people, you'd probably love to start and run your own company. Perhaps you've spent time trying to come up with an idea for a business you could launch. If you've been bitten by the entrepreneurial bug, you're not alone. More than ever, people like Mark Cuban are choosing the path of entrepreneurship for their careers.

How do you become an entrepreneur? Experts advise that aspiring entrepreneurs should learn as much as possible about business by completing academic programs such as the one in which you are currently enrolled and by gaining practical experience by working part- and full-time for business employers. In addition, invaluable insights about the pleasures and pitfalls of entrepreneurship can be obtained by reading newspaper and magazine articles and biographies of successful entrepreneurs. These inputs will help aspiring entrepreneurs learn how these people handled the challenges of launching their businesses. Advice you need to launch and grow a new venture is all around. Some resources are listed in Table 6.1 to get you started.

Table 6.1 **Resources for Aspiring Entrepreneurs**

Magazines

Entrepreneur *Success* *Hispanic* *Inc.* *Nation's Business* *Black Enterprise*	All of these magazines offer articles about entrepreneurs' experiences, as well as business trends and advice on starting and running a business. Many offer additional information at their Web sites.

Web Sites

Allbusiness.com (www.allbusiness.com)	Advice on starting and running a business, free sample forms and contracts, discounts on products.
Center for Entrepreneurial Leadership (www.celcee.edu/)	A database of articles on entrepreneurship, plus links to informational materials and organizations.
Entrepreneur.com (www.entrepreneur.com)	Tips, articles, message boards, sample forms and contracts, and a link to HomeOfficeMag.com, an online magazine.
The Entrepreneurial Edge (http://edge.lowe.org)	Online publication of the Edward Lowe Foundation, which supports the foundation's mission of encouraging entrepreneurship by offering information on starting a business, plus stories of entrepreneurs.
The Entrepreneur's Mind (www.benlore.com/index.html)	Online magazine that gives real-life stories from successful entrepreneurs and advice from business experts.
EntreWorld (www.entreworld.org)	Information from the Kauffman Center for Entrepreneurial Leadership on starting, running, and growing a business, including first-person accounts from entrepreneurs.
Small Business Administration (www.sba.gov)	This government-run site provides information about starting a business, as well as SBA services for small-business owners.

Entrepreneurship Associations

Association of African-American Women Business Owners	P.O. Box 13858, Silver Spring, MD 20911–3858; 301–585–8051.
Association of Collegiate Entrepreneurs (chapters on many college campuses)	Wichita State University, Center for Entrepreneurship, 1845 Fairmount, Wichita, KS 67260–0147; 316–689–3000.
The Entrepreneurship Institute	3592 Corporate Drive, Suite 101, Columbus, OH 43231; 614–895–1153.
International Directory of Young Entrepreneurs	Boston, MA; 617–562–8616.
Young Entrepreneurs' Organization	1199 N. Fairfax St., Suite 200, Alexandria, VA 22314; 703–519–6700; www.yeo.org.

In this chapter we focus on pathways for entering the world of entrepreneurship, describing the increasingly important role that entrepreneurs play in the economy. The chapter explains why a growing number of people choose this way of participating in business. It discusses the characteristics that help entrepreneurs succeed and the ways they start new ventures. The chapter ends with a discussion of methods by which large companies try to incorporate the entrepreneurial spirit.

WHAT IS AN ENTREPRENEUR?

You learned in Chapter 1 that an **entrepreneur** is a risk taker in the private enterprise system, a person who seeks a profitable opportunity and takes the necessary risks to set up and operate a business. Many entrepreneurs start their businesses from scratch, but you don't have to launch your own company to be considered an entrepreneur. Consider Ray Kroc, founder of McDonald's. He started by buying a small hamburger shop and grew this small venture into a multibillion-dollar global business.

Entrepreneurs differ from many small-business owners. Although many small-business owners posess the same drive, creative energy, and desire to become big-business owners, others may be content to operate a business that provides a comfortable living. By contrast, the typical entrepreneur tries to make the business grow. Entrepreneurs combine their ideas and drive with money, employees, and other resources to create a business that fills a market need. That entrepreneurial role can make something significant out of a small beginning. In preparing its most recent listing of the 500 fastest-growing U.S. companies, *Inc.* magazine found that over half began operations with $20,000 or less in the bank. Yet after a few years, the typical *Inc.* 500 company had 64 employees on its payroll and was generating sales of over $10 million a year.[2]

Entrepreneurs also differ from managers. Managers are employees who direct the efforts of others to achieve an organization's goals. In the case of small start-up firms, owners may find it necessary to serve as owner–managers to implement their plans for the business and to offset human resource limitations at the fledgling company. Entrepreneurs may also perform a managerial role, but their overriding responsibility is to use the resources of their organizations—employees, money, equipment, and facilities—to accomplish their goals. Particularly in the start-up stage of a new venture, entrepreneurs pursue their ideas for business success and take the initiative to find and organize the resources they need to start and build their ventures. Bill Gates recognized his own entrepreneurial role at Microsoft when he resigned from the chief executive post of his now-giant enterprise to take on the new position of "chief software architect." The change enables Microsoft's new chief executive officer (CEO), Steve Ballmer, to focus on managing the company while Gates looks for new business opportunities. Also, Microsoft's growth has come not from Gates's talents as a programmer—most people agree that Microsoft's programs usually borrow existing ideas—but his savvy is in deploying resources to build a strong market for his products. The measure of Gates's success as an entrepreneur is the hugely profitable business he built by developing markets for operating systems and business software.[3]

On a smaller scale, Nicola Shirley has been dedicated to the success of her business, a Philadelphia restaurant called Jamaican Jerk Hut, which specializes in West Indian cooking. To get started, Shirley borrowed money from family and friends. As her restaurant became profitable, she patiently invested the earnings back into the business and was rewarded with steady growth. Her restaurant now has seven full-time employees and revenues of about $500,000. Shirley insists on top-quality employees and food because she wants the restaurant to grow and succeed over the long term. Beyond this, Shirley has a mission to educate people about the cuisine of her native Jamaica. She is writing a book about its food, and she makes

BUSINESS DIRECTORY

➤ **entrepreneur** *person who seeks a profitable opportunity and takes the necessary risks to set up and operate a business.*

Nicola Shirley relied on her Jamaican background and one of her talents to start and grow her business: West Indian cooking. Shirley built on the popularity of her restaurant, Jamaican Jerk Hut, to expand into a line of food products under the label JaHut. Because of her vision, hard work, and energy, Shirley can savor her success.

FIGURE 6.1
Categories of Entrepreneurs

Classic Entrepreneur
Person who sees a business opportunity and uses resources to tap the market

Entrepreneurs

Change Agent
Manager who tries to revitalize an established firm

Intrapreneur
Person who develops innovations within a large organization

appearances on cooking shows and at food expos. In addition, Shirley's company has begun to distribute a line of foods under the label JaHut. These plans and ambitions define Nicola Shirley as an entrepreneur.[4]

Studies of entrepreneurs have identified certain personality traits and behaviors common to them that differ from those required for managerial success. One of these traits is the willingness to assume the risks involved in starting a new venture. Some employees leave their jobs to start their own companies and become successful entrepreneurs. Others find that they lack the characteristics required to start and grow a business. Entrepreneurial characteristics are examined in detail in a later section of this chapter.

CATEGORIES OF ENTREPRENEURS

Entrepreneurs apply their talents in different situations. These differences give rise to a set of distinct categories of entrepreneurs. As Figure 6.1 shows, three basic categories exist: classic entrepreneurs, intrapreneurs, and change agents.[5]

Classic entrepreneurs identify business opportunities and allocate available resources to tap those markets. The story of Ari B. Horowitz exemplifies the actions of a classic entrepreneur. Horowitz declares that he is "in the business of building businesses." In the first decade after earning his college degree, he started or led the growth of five companies, most of them serving high-tech industries. Horowitz looks for markets that have large potential, then seeks an advantage through speed, relying on his drive and selling ability to quickly assemble the money and people needed to serve those markets. For example, Horowitz started Gray Peak, a consulting firm specializing in high-tech businesses. While he was still managing that company, he realized that the demands of hiring and managing skilled employees presented another business opportunity: providing that service to other companies. So Horowitz began Opus 360 Corp. to provide an online service called FreeAgent.com, which matches independent consultants with clients and lets businesses track employees' work on individual projects. At the time he started Opus 360, no company had yet established itself as the leader in automating management of professional services, and Horowitz saw that fact as an opportunity. With a track record of success, he has been able to attract major investors who want to back startups. Early in the game, Horowitz had accumulated far more capital for Opus 360 than his nearest competitor, and hundreds of consultants were using his site to look for job listings and benefits such as group health insurance.[6]

Intrapreneurs are entrepreneurially oriented people who seek to develop new products, ideas, and commercial ventures within large organizations. For example, 3M Co. continues to develop innovative products by encouraging intrapreneurship among its personnel. Some of 3M's most successful products began as inspirations of intrapreneurs. Art Frey invented the Post-It Note, and intrapreneurs Connie Hubbard and Raymond Heyer invented the Scotch-Brite Never Rust soap pad. Intrapreneurship will be discussed later in this chapter.

Change agents, also called *turnaround entrepreneurs,* are managers who seek to revitalize established firms to keep them competitive in today's marketplace. Elisabeth Robert played this role at Vermont Teddy Bear Co. In the early 1990s, the maker of furry bears in fancy costumes was enjoying fast growth, fueled by its Bear-Gram service, which delivers teddy bears nationwide. With millions of dollars pouring in, the company launched ambitious marketing plans including three stores, a variety of bear-branded goods from knapsacks to books, and sponsorship of a NASCAR driver. Before long, this unfocused activity was causing the company to lose money. Vermont Teddy Bear promoted Robert, then its chief financial officer (CFO), to CEO and asked her to straighten out the mess. Using her background in finance, she began a careful evaluation of where the money was coming from and where it was going. Not only were the Teddy Bear stores expensive to operate, they were generating only half the sales the company had expected. So Robert shut them down.

Then she asked the big question: "What business are we in?" Half the people who had been visiting the stores were buying bears to ship elsewhere, and they were spending over $70 per bear. Clearly, they wanted more than just a stuffed animal. Robert concluded they were buying a special gift that conveyed a message, much as a person does by sending a gift of flowers. She determined that the company needed a fundamental change in its marketing strategy. Now offering a higher-quality, tastefully packaged toy bear—one that Robert likes to call a "creative alternative to flowers"—Vermont Teddy Bear is again profitable.[7]

Although these categories of entrepreneurs involve different situations, they all offer the satisfaction of building a successful enterprise that provides jobs and meets a market need. Classic entrepreneur Nicola Shirley focuses building the size of her business and the reputation of her Jamaican cuisine, as well as maintaining "a quality restaurant around for the long haul."[8] Richard McNamara has combined similar ambitions with his talents as a change agent to build his company, Activar, by acquiring struggling manufacturing companies and making them viable. When he buys a company, he meets with each of its employees to see whether they are willing to contribute the necessary dedication to turning the company around. Often this means determining what the original founder can contribute; someone who launched a company based on a good product idea might contribute most at the head of the engineering department. McNamara admits that the hard decisions needed to convert a failing company to profitability are unappealing to some people, but "the satisfaction is great when you know that you made it where someone else failed."[9]

Elisabeth Robert brought new focus to her flagging company, Vermont Teddy Bear, as its change agent. Drawing on her finance background, the new CEO halted the company's expensive and unproductive marketing efforts, such as sponsoring a NASCAR driver and producing a vast array of additional products that didn't deliver sales—what she calls "teddy-bear crap." Vermont Teddy Bear is now back on track with its warm and fuzzy gift shipments—a creative alternative to flowers.

> **THEY SAID IT**
>
> *"Ignore the stock market, ignore the economy, and buy a business you understand."*
>
> WARREN BUFFETT (B.1932)
> CEO, BERKSHIRE HATHAWAY, AND
> ONE OF AMERICA'S RICHEST
> ENTREPRENEURS

REASONS TO CHOOSE ENTREPRENEURSHIP AS A CAREER PATH

If you want to start your own company someday, you have plenty of company. In one 12-month period, the National Foundation for Independent Business found that 5 million Americans had started businesses.[10] As Figure 6.2 illustrates, roughly one in ten U.S. adults under the age of 45 years is involved in starting a business with the expectation of owning at least part of it. A recent survey reported that about half of Americans expressed interest in starting a business.[11] This interest is especially strong among young adults. Three out of every ten people between the ages of 18 and 29 years want to run their own business.[12] Since the early 1980s, a heightened interest in entrepreneurial careers has been observed, spurred in part by publicity celebrating the successes of entrepreneurs like Steve Case

> **BUSINESS DIRECTORY**
>
> ► **classic entrepreneur** *person who identifies a business opportunity and allocates available resources to tap that market.*
>
> ► **intrapreneur** *entrepreneurially oriented person who develops innovations within the context of a large organization.*
>
> ► **change agent** *manager who tries to revitalize an established firm to keep it competitive.*

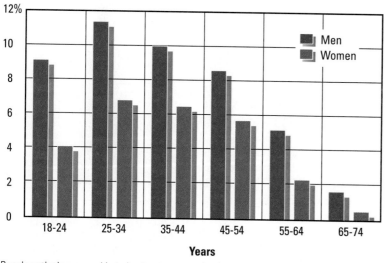

Years

People actively engaged in trying to start a new business and expecting to own all or part of the business.

FIGURE 6.2
U.S. Adults Currently Engaged in Starting a Business

of AOL Time Warner, Martha Stewart of the company bearing her name, and Bill Gates of Microsoft.

The popularity of entrepreneurship is evident on America's college campuses. In an era of prosperity and technological change, the lure of setting up a business is irresistible to many students. At the University of Pittsburgh, lecturer Robert Atkin says many of his students treat research projects as an invitation to plan a business, and some even try out their ideas. Comments Atkin, "There is a tremendous belief that they can do this that I didn't see ten years ago." With the fast pace of change in today's economy, instructors are hard-pressed to counsel students to wait until they have work experience. Babson College is among several colleges that have instead set up business incubators to help students start off with guidance.[13]

People choose to become entrepreneurs for many different reasons. Some are motivated by dissatisfaction with the organizational work world, citing desires to escape unreasonable bosses or insufficient rewards and recognition as motives to start their own firms. Other people start businesses because they believe their ideas represent opportunities to fulfill customer needs. Luis Espinoza founded a business to meet the unmet demand for Hispanic foods in his new home in northern Indiana. Espinoza had grown up in Texas, where his family enjoyed authentic Mexican foods. Although Espinoza found a significant, growing Hispanic community in Indiana, the local stores didn't know what products to offer these customers. One supermarket chain tried buying foods from a Texas distributor and stocked its shelves with items that appeal to Mexican tastes— in a neighborhood of Puerto Ricans, who prefer less spicy dishes. Espinoza knew he could do better. He learned about local tastes and set up Inca Quality Foods to provide canned goods and spices tailored to stores' local clientele. He convinced a Kroger's manager to let him set up a display; when sales increased, he landed a contract to service Kroger's stores in the area.[14]

As Figure 6.3 states, people become entrepreneurs for one or more of four major reasons: desire to be one's own boss, desire to succeed financially, desire to attain job security, and desire to improve one's quality of life. Each of these reasons is described in more detail in the following sections.

Being One's Own Boss

Self-management is the motivation that drives many entrepreneurs. Knowing this, advertisers are responding with portrayals of the American independent professional as an individual who has control over when, where, and how he or she works. Figure 6.4 illustrates the alluring image of this type of business founder. The advertiser, Guru.com, offers a Web site where such entrepreneurs can look for projects and find links to business-related goods and services.

Michael Kite served as change agent when he took over his father's company, Freeflow Products, which makes plastic parts. He led the unprofitable business into profitability by expanding its product line and finding new customers. Kite says being his own boss frees him from trying to satisfy the demands of those in authority. Without a boss looking over his shoulder, Kite feels better able to find the best solutions to problems.[15]

Mike Weagley realized he wanted to live up to higher standards than he could as an employee. Following his high school graduation, Weagley had worked his way up through jobs at a chain of car washes until he was managing the maintenance

FIGURE 6.3
Why People Become Entrepreneurs

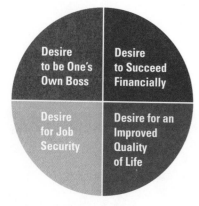

2 pm conference call

Go ahead and multitask.
As an independent professional, you're an expert in your field, and the master of your day - you're a guru. Whether you're a web developer, creative director or anything in between, you now have a home on the web. A gold mine of projects, resources like health insurance and tax tips, and a place to connect with other gurus just like you.

Power for the independent professional

FIGURE 6.4
Guru.com: Portraying an Entrepreneurial Icon

department. His employer was upgrading to new technology, and Weagley dedicated himself to remodeling facilities and installing computer systems. However, the company's top management cut back the budget for remodeling, and Weagley concluded that he could not provide an adequate quality level with the remaining money. He objected unsuccessfully, so he left to start his own business, Pro-Tech Welding and Fabrication. Weagley has grown the snowplow manufacturer into a $5.5 million business with a place on the *Inc.* 500. And he remains steadfast in his determination that short-term profits not override quality.[16]

Financial Success

Entrepreneurs are wealth creators. Many start their ventures with the specific goal of creating a profitable business and reaping its financial rewards. They believe they won't get rich by working for someone else. In recent years, the flood of money pouring into dot.coms encouraged the belief that starting a business—especially a high-tech business—is a reliable path to wealth. Self-employed Americans are four times as likely to accumulate a million dollars as those who work for someone else.[17] And the business press publishes plenty of stories about the more dramatic successes. In one such story, Daniel Dye and Mark Beckloff cashed in $8,000 from their 401(k) retirement savings to start a business that makes and sells gourmet dog treats. The company, called Three Dog Bakery, saw revenues soar from $8 million to $40 million in just two years.[18]

Although entrepreneurs often mention financial rewards as a motive for starting their businesses, the path to riches can be long and uncertain. Among the *Inc.* 500 CEOs, almost one-fourth took no compensation at all from their businesses during its first five years of operation. Eric J. Ruff is an example of an entrepreneur who struggled financially. When he started his software business, PowerQuest, his first long-term goal was modest: to be able to afford to "supersize" his order of french fries when he took his family to McDonald's, without worrying whether he could afford the price. Ruff was surprised to discover that reaching this goal took four years. However, when that day arrived, he felt proud.[19]

And what of those famous dot.coms that started in a garage or spare bedroom and grew to a valuation of tens of millions of dollars? David Birch's consulting firm, Cognetics, has a database of 10 million U.S. companies, but successes of this magnitude represent only a handful of those companies—not more than "one-tenth of one-tenth of 1 percent."[20] These companies make the news precisely because they are so unusual.

Job Security

Although the unemployment rate is low and the demand for skilled employees is high, many workers lack job security. As recently as 2001, each of these corporate giants downsized by eliminating thousands of jobs: AOL Time Warner, JCPenney, DaimlerChrysler, Lucent, and WorldCom. In the wake of that trend, a growing percentage of the American workforce decided to create their own job security by starting their own businesses. The U.S. Small Business Administration (SBA) has found that the majority of new jobs created have been in the smallest companies, with a significant share of those jobs coming from the creation of new companies.[21]

Although working for others may not guarantee job security, lack of security is also an issue for entrepreneurs. An entrepreneur's job depends, not on the decisions of employers, but on the decisions of customers and investors and on the cooperation and commitment of the entrepreneur's own employees. David Sun and John Tu, the founders of Kingston Technology, recognized this risk and incorporated it into their business philosophy. In the late 1980s they founded their company to provide memory upgrades for computers. It was a risky business, with heavy competition based on price, and Sun bet his partner a car that they would go out of business within a year. The partners crafted not only a focused business strategy but plans to provide for employees if Kingston should fail. Instead of fear for their jobs, the founders exude a focus on integrity. As Sun puts it, "Even if the whole industry [goes] out of business, if I can take care of my employees, then I have no shame on myself." Their concern for others carries over into their relationships with customers. Sun and Tu have a reputation for integrity, fulfilling promises even when swings in prices cut into their profits.

The founders' commitment to employees and customers helps Kingston Technology retain them even as the company moves quickly to act on new opportunities. Kingston now designs and makes memory, processor, and storage upgrades for a variety of computer types, along with packaging and testing microchips and helping customers manage their suppliers and supplies for these components. When Kingston reorganizes to move into new markets, employees are flexible because they trust Sun and Tu. With their support, Sun and Tu have built Kingston into a successful 2,000-employee, $1.5 billion company that has endured for more than a decade. So Tu won his bet with Sun, and he received a new Jaguar.[22]

Quality of Life

Entrepreneurship is an attractive career option for people seeking to improve their quality of life. Starting a business gives the founder some choice over when, where, and how to work. Roger Greene founded Ipswitch, a software company, with the ideal of moderation. His goal is moderate growth, and he encourages employees to take plenty of time

Concern for employees and customers has brought Kingston Technology through the tough, competitive high-tech market of computer memory, storage, and processor upgrades. The company's founders, David Sun and John Tu, recognized the critical importance of employee dedication and flexibility, so they built strong relationships based on integrity and trust. Customers have also noticed the company's quality and reliability.

off. In fact, each employee is expected to take at least five weeks off a year, a common employee benefit in many European firms but extremely unusual for a U.S. firm. Greene's attitude is, instead of working hard to earn enough money to enjoy life, "live life as it goes along and do neat things while you're working and enjoy every year of your life." To protect this value, Ipswitch has not raised money through a stock offering or from venture capitalists, because these outside investors would likely push management to achieve faster growth and profits. In addition, management avoids praising employees for working nights and weekends. In this environment, both Greene and his employees benefit from quality of work life, and employees know it. Ipswitch's employee turnover is about half the industry average.[23]

Despite the example of Ipswitch's Roger Greene, most entrepreneurs work long hours and at the whims of their customers. Adam Kanner, founder of an Internet business called Edu.com, says he typically works at least 90 hours a week. Much of that time, he is away from home looking for investors and customers.[24] As Heather Blease's technical support company, EnvisioNet, was making a transition from 3 to 1,500 employees, she was juggling business growth with the needs of her three children, all under the age of six years. She says it was painful to hear one son ask her, as she flew off to a fund-raising meeting, "Mommy, do you love your company more than me?" But Sandra Kurtzig, founder of ASK Group, says the payoff can sometimes come when children are older. One of her children, now grown, wants Kurtzig to join him in his own start-up, putting a whole new and gratifying look on the prospect of the empty nest.[25] Ironically, Kurtzig started ASK Group as a part-time occupation after leaving General Electric so that she could spend more time with her family.[26] For other entrepreneurs, the hard work and challenges are just part of the joy of entrepreneurship. Freeflow Products' Michael Kite, discussed earlier, considers entrepreneurship to be the opposite of boredom. As he puts it, "Just because I'm mellow [about being my own boss] doesn't mean I want to sit around all the time."[27]

THE ENVIRONMENT FOR ENTREPRENEURS

If you feel motivated to start your own company, conditions have never favored entrepreneurship more than they do today. For one improvement, the status of entrepreneurship as a career choice has been rising. The movement of entrepreneurship toward the business mainstream began in the early 1980s after Steve Jobs of Apple Computer and other high-tech entrepreneurs gained national attention by going public—that is, selling stock in their companies. Today's entrepreneurs are reaping the benefits of growing interest among investors, as discussed later in the chapter, and the applications made possible by new technology. Historian Ria David compares these times to the early years of the industrial revolution and the mystique of such industry titans as Carnegie, Rockefeller, and J. P. Morgan: "There's that same sense of boundless opportunity, that anyone can go out and make a fortune."[28] Along with that optimism comes respect for those who try, even if they fail. In Massachusetts, Dan Nevers is trying to launch a site to sell a line of toys, not an easy industry in which to build a successful company. In spite of obstacles, he is unafraid: "There's no longer a black mark to try to start a business and fail."[29] In addition to favorable public attitudes toward entrepreneurs and the growth in financing options, other factors that support and expand opportunities for entrepreneurs are identified in Figure 6.5: globalization, education, information technology, and demographic and economic trends. Each of these factors is discussed in the following section.

Globalization

The globalization of business, described in preceding chapters, has created many opportunities for entrepreneurs. Entrepreneurs are marketing their products abroad and hiring international talent. Among the fastest-growing small U.S. companies, almost two of every five have international sales.[30] One entrepreneur who sees

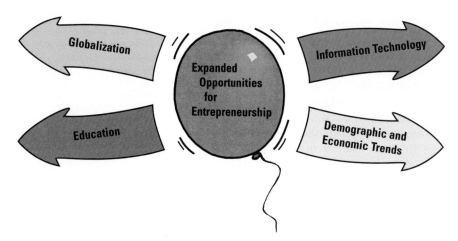

FIGURE 6.5
Factors Supporting and Expanding Opportunities for Entrepreneurship

international opportunities is Bettye Pierce Zoller, who used her experience in teaching English to form ZWL Publishing, which sells her audiobook, *Speaking Effective English*. When the U.S. and China reached the free-trade agreement, described in Chapter 4, Zoller was ready to tap this huge market's desire to learn English. Her plans include not simply selling the tapes but helping students through one-on-one instruction online, by mail, and in person.[31]

In a more unusual move, William Heinecke "exported" his own entrepreneurial talents by moving to Thailand, borrowing $1,200, and opening two businesses: an office-cleaning service and a public relations firm. Before long, he had money to get into a third line of work: the fast-food industry. He bought a Pizza Hut franchise, in spite of the common belief that Asian consumers wouldn't be interested in pizza because bread and cheese are not staples of the Asian diet. But Heinecke adapted toppings to Thai flavors, and before long his franchise was profitable and growing. Since then, Heinecke has opened more than 100 restaurants, including franchises with Mister Donut, Burger King, and Dairy Queen.[32]

Entrepreneurs are also forming business partnerships with foreign partners with similar business goals to expand their businesses around the globe. Thanks to the Internet, even teenagers are hooking up with foreign partners. For fun, Michael Furdyk set up a Web site to explain the workings of the Internet. From his home computer in Toronto, he met another teen, Michael Hayman, who lived in Australia, where he ran a site called MyDesktop.com, which offers help with the Windows computer operating system, as well as tips on computer games. Furdyk joined Hayman in the MyDesktop business, and they began attracting thousands of visitors each month. They hired Internet advertiser DoubleClick to sell advertising on the site. Eventually they added e-mail newsletters and began attracting a million visitors a month, as well as attention from an online publishing business called internet.com. That publisher bought MyDesktop for $1 million plus future payments based on the site's performance.[33]

Education

The past two decades have brought tremendous growth in the number of educational opportunities for would-be entrepreneurs. Today, hundreds of U.S. colleges offer classes in starting and managing a business, and many of them offer entrepreneurship curricula. Some of these schools, including Alfred University, University of St. Thomas, and Miami University of Ohio, are adding entrepreneurship courses to programs outside the usual business curriculum, on the assumption that people in other disciplines might eventually start a business. Alfred University offers a course on entrepreneurship and the arts to help artists make their work a viable means of support. A student with a rock band applied what he learned and wrote a business plan that has enabled the band to become profitable.[34]

Another way business schools are responding to the interest in entrepreneurship is by helping their students start businesses. Babson College has a program in which a few students are permitted to replace several of their usual classes with launching an actual business under coaching from an entrepreneur-turned-professor. Fordham University offers a class in which students interact with CEOs of high-tech start-ups.[35] For Shannon Scherer, a marketing student who set up a business to market her father's sculptures online, the advantages of starting a business at school are as obvious as the school's high-quality faculty and facilities.[36]

For today's college students, education in entrepreneurship often includes some friendly competition in the form of business plan contests. Among the most famous is the one sponsored by business incubator Garage.com. Its contest invites hundreds of teams of students to refine their plans and present them to a panel of Silicon Valley judges, in the hope of winning a grand prize of $150,000. At a recent Garage competition, the winning plan was for a company called Quicksilver Genomics, put together by a team of students from San Francisco. Their business plan calls for a company that will use Internet technology to speed up the discovery of new prescription drugs.[37]

Besides schools, many organizations have sprouted up in recent years to teach entrepreneurship to young people. The Center for Entrepreneurial Leadership offers training programs for learners from kindergarten through community college. The center's Entreprep summer program teaches high school juniors how to start and manage a company. Students in Free Enterprise is a national not-for-profit organization in which college students, working with faculty advisers, teach grade school and high school students and other community members the value of private enterprise and entrepreneurship. The Association of Collegiate Entrepreneurs has chapters on many college campuses in the U.S. and Canada.

Information Technology

The explosion in information technology (IT) has been one of the biggest boosts for entrepreneurs. As computer and communications technologies have merged, accompanied by dramatically falling costs, entrepreneurs have gained tools that help them compete with large companies. Information technology helps entrepreneurs work quickly and efficiently, provide attentive customer service, increase sales, and project professional images.

Advances in IT have also created demand for new products, and entrepreneurs have risen to the challenge. Some have started businesses that directly apply IT. The most widely reported examples are companies with Web sites that offer products and information online, such as GreenTree Nutrition, which founder Don Kendall Jr. hoped would attract buyers of dietary supplements by offering original articles, newsletters, and the option of customizing vitamin orders.[38] Other entrepreneurs start businesses to support high-tech companies. TechBooks started in 1988 to do technical publishing and has since generated millions of dollars in business by preparing Internet versions of large publishers' printed works. Entrepreneurs have started other successful businesses to provide consulting or staffing in IT. Companies that provide software or IT services are by far the largest industry represented in the *Inc.* 500 list of entrepreneurial successes.[39]

The Internet is a challenge as well as an opportunity for entrepreneurs. Customers can go online to check prices and buy from large or small companies anywhere in the world, so entrepreneurs need to find a distinctive advantage over big competitors. Bruce Roberts, who runs Leesburg Pharmacy in the Virginia town of the same name, sees his advantage as serving special needs. With a growing number of patients filling routine prescriptions at big drugstore chains and over the Internet, Roberts specializes in custom prescriptions, such as for hospice patients who need strong pain relief or for animals that resist taking medicine. Down the road from Roberts's pharmacy, the Potomac Gallery uses the Internet to expand its range of customers and products. The gallery sells some of its

IRIS is a software company that provides high-tech service for the real estate industry. In the photo are the company's "Fab Four Founders": Maggie Etheridge, Eddie Ureno, Dan Wooley, and Greg Robertson. They designed software that would do for real estate agents what browsers do for Web surfers. With more than 50,000 agents using its IRIS access program, the company was recently purchased by HomeSeekers.com, a publicly traded Multiple Listing Service, which wants to be a one-stop shop for real estate agents.

Background. If you decide to get married in the next two or three years, you'll probably head to the Web for some help. That's what Tim Gray and Raj Dhaka, founders of WeddingChannel.com, are banking on. They started their site for several reasons. First, they were looking for a business opportunity on the Web. Second, they had both recently been involved with wedding hassles—Gray had gotten married, and Dhaka had attended seven weddings in one summer. Third, they understood the demographics: nearly 2.4 million couples get married every year, at an average cost of about $19,000. In other words, Americans are willing to spend for the perfect wedding.

What Happened? Gray and Dhaka launched their site, WeddingChannel.com in 1997, and despite heavy competition, their site is number one for helping brides, grooms, and guests navigate wedding obstacles. The site does everything from helping the bride choose her gown to assisting the couple track guest responses, 24 hours a day, seven days a week. But the real coup for these entrepreneurs is their recent alliance with Federated Department Stores, parent company to shops like Bloomingdale's, Macy's, Burdines, Rich's, and Stern's. "For better or worse, women have to drag their intended into the store to see what the cups and saucers look like. I believe people will buy online, but I don't believe brides will register exclusively online," says CEO Donald Drapkin. Carol Ferrara, a research analyst with GartnerGroup agrees. "Chances are your grandmother will still go to Macy's to buy the gift." Also, it's easier for the couple to walk into a store to return or exchange gifts after the wedding.

The Response. Brides, grooms, and their friends and family seem to love the site—and its relationship with department stores. Brides and grooms can go to Macy's, browse through the china and household goods, then register online right there. Or they can do so at home. Other potential partners have taken notice, and *Brides* magazine recently made a deal with WeddingChannel.com as well. And although advertisers have been knocking at the site's door, WeddingChannel keeps its banner advertising to a minimum to avoid cluttering the site.

Today and Counting. WeddingChannel founders and CEO Drapkin like being ahead of the competition for now, but they continue to think about the future. "A new bride comes along every ten seconds," says Drapkin, and he wants them all to log on to his company's site. Some potential plans include live online bridal fashion shows as well as tracking customers through anniversaries and birth announcements. "Once I have you," jokes Drapkin, "unless you stop me, you are a demographic dream."

QUESTIONS FOR CRITICAL THINKING
1. Why is Drapkin's last statement significant?
2. Why is the link between WeddingChannel.com and its brick-and-mortar partners so important? Do you think it will continue to be important over the rest of this decade? Why or why not?

Sources: "Company Profile," the WeddingChannel.com, **www.weddingchannel.com,** accessed February 12, 2001; "Bloomingdale's and WeddingChannel.com Launch Online Partnership," company press release, *PR Newswire*, October 23, 2000; Catherine Fredman and Ann Graham, "Wedding Present," *Executive Edge*, Feb/March 2000, pp. 23–27.

lithographs at the Web site of Mill Pond Press, and owner Linda Callagy serves her clientele's interest in Civil War history by downloading information and prints about the era from the site of an art publisher, Hadley House.[40]

Demographic and Economic Trends

Demographic trends, such as the aging of the U.S. population and the growth of two-income families, create opportunities for entrepreneurs to market new goods and services. Entrepreneurs take advantage of such trends to offer everything from retirement homes to grocery delivery services.

One trend that is likely to continue over the next few decades is the competition for talented workers. As noted in the previous section, many fast-growing start-ups are addressing the challenge of recruiting workers by offering specialists on a contract basis. The federal government has launched a program called 21st Century Skills for 21st Century Jobs to provide funding for organizations to train workers in skills that are especially needed. Entrepreneurs will undoubtedly find opportunities to help provide this training.

The strong economy of the past decade has presented opportunities for entrepreneurs to offer products that consumers might do without in harder times, such as the luxury weddings described in the "Clicks and Mortar" box. Well-off Americans are increasingly willing to spend money on their pets, for example. Spending on pets rose throughout the 1990s, with no slowing in sight. A significant share of that money goes for veterinary care, including such formerly unheard-of procedures as CAT scans and chemotherapy for pets. Jay Bloom found that only one company offered insurance to help pet owners foot the bill, and its policies had many exclusions. So Bloom decided to provide an alternative: Pet Assure, a discount club that gives its members 25 percent off veterinary care expenses as well as discounts on other goods and services such as pet grooming. Veterinarians sign up in exchange for the expected increase in visits, plus a 50 percent share of annual membership fees. Other entrepreneurs have cashed in on pet owners' indulgences. Joyce Shulman founded Rover Group to sell "performance snacks" enhanced with such healthful ingredients as flaxseed and brewer's yeast. Sherri Morrelli started Good Dogma Co. to market aromatherapy products for dogs.[41]

Entrepreneurship Around the World

The growth in entrepreneurship is a worldwide phenomenon. The role of entrepreneurs is growing in most industrialized and newly industrialized nations and in the emerging free-market countries in eastern Europe. However, the level of entrepreneurship varies considerably, even among industrialized nations. In a study of ten countries, the U.S. had the highest level of entrepreneurship, with 1 out of 12 people involved in starting or expanding a business. In contrast, the level of entrepreneurial activity in Finland was just 1 out of 67 people.[42] Figure 6.6 compares the amount of entrepreneurial activity in the ten countries studied.

Entrepreneurs abroad struggle harder to start businesses than do their U.S. counterparts. Obstacles include government regulations, high taxes, and political attitudes that favor big business. In addition, cultural values in other countries do not always match the U.S. in the high value placed on seizing a business opportunity.

Davidi Gilo is a citizen from one country with a strong tradition of entrepreneurship: Israel. As digital processing boomed in the 1980s, Gilo founded DSP Group to produce microchips that convert analog signals like voice communication into digital messages used in consumer electronics such as answering machines. At the time, most consumer electronics companies were in Japan, so DSP Group immediately became an exporter. The situation became more complex in the 1990s, because answering machines were on the way out, to be replaced by popular cell phones. Gilo's company developed the microchips and software for this new technology, but selling these new products proved more difficult. Gilo moved to Tokyo to devote himself to building new customer relationships. He brought over five chip designers, assigning each to one of the company's major customers. Eventually, his patience was rewarded with $16 million in business with his Japanese customers. DSP's next step has been to expand into other countries by developing products that meet their standards for cellular communications. DSP now has an office in California, and one-fourth of its sales are to U.S. customers.[43]

FIGURE 6.6
Levels of Entrepreneurial Activity in Ten Countries

For young people well acquainted with the Internet, cyberculture may override differences in national culture. In Berlin, which has struggled to attract industrial business after the fall of the Berlin Wall, many Internet entrepreneurs have moved to vacant lofts and warehouses to set up businesses. People who are attracted to the revolutionary spirit of the Internet expansion also enjoy the spirit of change in Berlin, as the city adjusts to western-style economic freedom. By 2001, there were 400 Berlin start-ups involved in Internet business or advertising. They included auction site Alando.de, later acquired by eBay. Alando's founders chose Berlin for its freewheeling atmosphere. The city's atmosphere also lured dooyoo.de, which offers a guide to online shopping. Dooyoo.de founder Felix Frohn-Bernau says, "We were convinced that the culture we want in the office could only be found here in Berlin."[44]

THE INFLUENCE OF ENTREPRENEURS ON THE ECONOMY

From Thomas Edison's development of the phonograph to the birth of Apple Computer in Steve Jobs's garage, American entrepreneurs have given the world goods and services that have changed the way people live, work, and play. The list includes ballpoint pens, Netscape Navigator software, fiberglass skis, Velcro fasteners, the Yahoo! Internet directory, FedEx delivery service, and Big Mac hamburgers. As Figure 6.7 describes, entrepreneurs play a significant role in the economy by creating major innovations, increasing the number of jobs in the economy, and providing opportunities for women and minorities.

Innovation

Entrepreneurs create new products, build new industries, and bring new life to old industries. By one count, entrepreneurs are the force behind two-thirds of the inventions and 95 percent of major innovations made since World War II.[45] As Amar V. Bhidé, in his widely acclaimed book *The Origin and Evolution of New Businesses,* says, this innovation rarely takes place in major leaps but moves in small steps, as entrepreneurs try out small modifications of the status quo and abandon any ideas the market rejects.[46] For example, Netscape Navigator was not the first Web browser, but it was the first to be relatively easy to use. This ease of use translated into market acceptance, and the World Wide Web went from an obscure government-sponsored technology to a major link among individuals and businesses.

Some innovations are born of personal experiences. Chuck Templeton watched his wife make last-minute dinner reservations over the phone and thought there must be an easier way to find a table at a good restaurant. He drew an analogy to online reservations for airline tickets and came up with the idea for OpenTable.com. The service signs up restaurants and provides the hardware and software to link them to its Web site. Diners go to the Web site to look for available tables, searching by neighborhood or cuisine, or looking up restaurants by name. OpenTable.com indicates the times at which tables are available, and the hungry consumer clicks to select a preferred restaurant, table, and desired time.[47]

Other entrepreneurs identify better ways to serve business customers. Mini-Tankers was founded in Australia to provide superior service in the sale of diesel fuel. Construction firms and highway contractors sometimes work late into the evening, but if they run out of fuel at night, they can't buy from the major oil companies, which generally close in the evening. Not only is Mini-Tankers

FIGURE 6.7
Influence of Entrepreneurs on the Economy

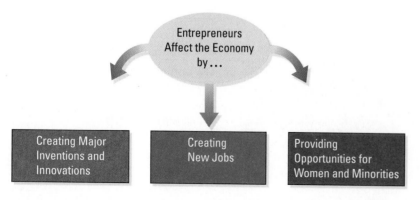

Entrepreneurs Affect the Economy by . . .

Creating Major Inventions and Innovations

Creating New Jobs

Providing Opportunities for Women and Minorities

open around the clock, but the company sends a truck right to the customer's site. In addition, each truck is equipped with a computer that generates a receipt containing information to help the customer analyze the efficiency of its diesel-burning machinery. This successful concept is now improving service in the U.S. market for diesel fuel, with Mini-Tankers' trucks operating in Seattle, Portland, Chicago, and St. Louis.[48]

Job Generation

Entrepreneurs are a vital source of new jobs. Research on job generation and entrepreneurial activity has found that fast-growing start-ups—about 3 percent of all firms—have become the principal job creators in the U.S. These companies, frequently called **gazelles,** created about two-thirds of the new jobs in the U.S. during a recent three-year period.[49] Rapid growth by start-ups is also expected to be a significant source of future job creation.

Entrepreneurial job creation typically involves a small number of employees per firm but is spread over many, many companies. Strategic Communications Group more than tripled in size during a recent 12-month period, growing from 10 to 35 employees. The marketing and public relations firm struggled until a banker advised founder Marc Hausman to hire a CEO. Hausman found a recently retired financial officer willing to work for his company part-time, freeing Hausman to develop many more client relationships. The new business enabled him to hire additional employees.[50]

Entrepreneurs sometimes see potential employees where established businesses overlook them. Frank Tucker started Tucker Technology to install and maintain telecommunications equipment, and he located in an economically disadvantaged area of Oakland, California. Driving to work, Tucker says, "I'd see all the human resources on the street corner. Clearly, they had no jobs to go to." Recognizing that much of his installation and maintenance work required only basic skills, Tucker began to hire local people, teach them the job, and pay them a substantial $23 an hour—fair compensation for the grimy working conditions. In this way, Tucker can compete in the quest for workers, and his community also benefits by attracting a new business and increasing local job opportunities.[51]

Diversity

Entrepreneurship offers excellent economic opportunities for women and minorities. As illustrated in Figure 6.8, today's entrepreneurial success stories have a colorful cast. This advertisement for Phoenix's investment advice states that the barriers to making money have fallen, and a new generation of entrepreneurs has "already made an indelible mark on American business."

The number of women- and minority-owned start-ups has grown tremendously in recent years. As noted in Chapter 5, the pace in growth of business start-ups is faster among Hispanics, African Americans, and Asian Americans than among the population at large, and much of that growth is among

FIGURE 6.8
Diversity of 21st-Century Entrepreneurs

recent immigrants. Also, women are the entrepreneurs behind almost half of the millions of business start-ups in the U.S.[52]

The range of businesses they operate defeats the usual stereotypes. Female entrepreneurs are engaged in service and manufacturing businesses ranging from Sheila Thompson's 70-employee manufacturer of wooden models of historic buildings and other collectibles to Ella D. Williams's systems engineering firm. Williams's company, Aegir Systems, also employs 70 people, including electrical engineers, computer scientists, and graphic designers.[53]

Realizing the value of both women- and minority-owned start-ups in creating jobs and promoting diversity, many large companies have developed diversity programs that help these entrepreneurs get start-up capital, subcontracts, and other assistance. Eastman Kodak, General Motors, JCPenney, Toyota, and United Airlines, are large firms that offer supplier diversity programs. Large companies frequently advertise in magazines like *Black Enterprise* and *Hispanic,* encouraging readers to contact their directors of supplier diversity for information about their diversity programs.

CHARACTERISTICS OF ENTREPRENEURS

The examples of entrepreneurship you've read so far may give the impression that people who strike out on their own are a different breed. In addition to having similar motivations, successful entrepreneurs are more likely than other people to have parents who were entrepreneurs. They also tend to have personality traits in common. Researchers have associated many personality traits with successful entrepreneurship. They report that entrepreneurs are more likely to be inquisitive, passionate, self-motivated, honest, courageous, flexible, intelligent, and reliable people. The eight traits summarized in Figure 6.9 are especially important for people who want to succeed as entrepreneurs.[54]

Vision

Entrepreneurs begin with a *vision*, an overall idea for how to make their business idea a success, and then they passionately pursue it. Bill Gates and Paul Allen launched Microsoft with the vision of a computer on every desk and in every home, all running Microsoft software. Their vision helped Microsoft to become the world's largest marketer of computer software. It guided the company and provided clear direction for employees as Microsoft grew, adapted, and prospered in an industry characterized by tremendous technological change.

At Amazon.com, vision has helped entrepreneur Jeff Bezos lead his employees through the turbulent birth of the Internet economy. Bezos's vision is of a "culture of customer obsession." When his company was just two years old, it faced its first major competition, as Barnes & Noble entered the Internet marketplace for books. People questioned whether Amazon could survive against an experienced book retailer. Bezos told Amazon employees that they should "wake up terrified every morning,

FIGURE 6.9
Characteristics of Entrepreneurs

Entrepreneurial Personality

Vision

High Energy Level

Need to Achieve

Self-Confidence and Optimism

Tolerance for Failure

Creativity

Tolerance for Ambiguity

Internal Locus of Control

but to be very precise what they were terrified of"—and that, he said, should be the company's customers, the people with whom the company had an important relationship. Bezos used his role as visionary to keep employees focused on what would enable the company to continue growing in a more competitive environment.[55]

High Energy Level

Entrepreneurs willingly work hard to realize their visions. Starting and building a company requires an enormous amount of hard work and long hours. Some entrepreneurs work full-time at their regular day jobs and spend weeknights and weekends launching their start-ups. Many devote 14-hour days seven days a week to their new ventures. In his ten-year study of entrepreneurs, author Amar Bhidé found that what distinguishes successful entrepreneurs from other business owners is that they "work harder, hustle for customers, and know that the opportunity may not last for more than six or eight months."[56]

A major reason why entrepreneurship demands hard work is that start-up companies typically have a small staff and struggle to raise enough capital. Under these resource constraints, the entrepreneur has to make up the difference. When two engineers started Gilat Satellite Networks to build satellite systems, they had to work extremely hard to compete with giant corporations like EchoStar and Hughes Network Systems. They offered to do whatever was necessary to tailor a system to the client's needs. Gilat's first customer was Rite Aid, the drugstore chain. The company won the contract by agreeing to adapt its satellite system in significant ways. The two founders and four other members of the project's development team put in many nights and evenings to fulfill their commitment. Cofounder Amiram Levinberg says simply, "In a high-tech start-up such as Gilat . . . it's a given that there will be some 12-hour days."[57]

The challenge for entrepreneurs is to balance the hard work with the rest, recreation, and family time that are so essential to good health and continued creativity. Tom Melaragno routinely worked 12-hour days when he started Compri Consulting, a firm that provides consulting and staffing for information technology projects. As Melaragno's company has grown, he has become more able to delegate work, freeing time for his wife and children, workouts at a local health club, and his rock band, Orphan Boy.[58]

Need to Achieve

Entrepreneurs work hard because they want to excel. Their strong competitive drive helps them to enjoy the challenge of reaching difficult goals and promotes dedication to personal success. Entrepreneurship expert Amar Bhidé says successful entrepreneurs have "an almost maniacal level of ambition. Not just ambition to make a comfortable living, to make a few million dollars, but someone who wants to leave a significant mark on the world."[59]

Maria de Lourdes Sobrino's dream was to find success in the U.S. A Mexican immigrant, Sobrino moved with her husband and daughter to Los Angeles, where she opened a travel business concentrating on travel between the U.S. and Mexico. But economic woes in Mexico ended demand for her services, and personal conflicts ended her marriage. Sobrino needed a new way to support herself, and an idea came to her: selling small cups of flavored gelatin, a common treat in Mexico that had not yet found its way to U.S. stores. Identifying stores that would take a chance on the new product required persistence. Store managers didn't understand the product, so

Heather Howitt is the high-energy CEO of Oregon Chai, an $11-million manufacturer and marketer of tea lattes. She balances motherhood and running the company, while squeezing in two-hour runs through a nearby Portland park. She maintains her work and life balance by delegating some tasks she had previously done herself: some management tasks, sales calls, and travel to trade shows.

THEY SAID IT

"Anyone who needs an alarm clock to wake up is not an entrepreneur."

REV. JESSE JACKSON (B.1941)
AMERICAN CIVIL RIGHTS LEADER

Sobrino honed the marketing strategy for her company, LuLu's Dessert Factory. She identified Latino communities and visited independent stores. Finally, one allowed her to leave gelatin cups, with payment contingent on sales. When Sobrino returned to her spartan office, a message was waiting for her: "Please come back, Señora. Your gelatins are sold." That was the turning point for LuLu's. When her product became popular in local stores, a food broker began to carry it, and Sobrino borrowed money to expand her facilities. Paying off the loans was difficult and took years, but today LuLu's is a $12 million company with 45 products offered in West Coast stores. Through hard work and determination, Sobrino is achieving her goals. She says, "I enjoy my company, customers, and my 100 employees so much now because I fought hard for them."[60]

Self-Confidence and Optimism

Entrepreneurs believe in their ability to succeed, and they instill their optimism in others. Often, their optimism resembles fearlessness in the face of difficult odds. Sean Rones, founder of a San Diego media firm called World Footprint, needed plenty of self-confidence to land the contract to sell all the outdoor advertising for dot.com businesses during the 2000 Sydney Olympics. How did a small U.S. firm get such exclusive rights? First Rones and his partner, Eric Davis, determined that the Olympics would be a great setting for advertising an Internet business. Rather than assuming that advertising rights surely must have been sold, Rones flew to Sydney in 1999. There, he pursued negotiations, undaunted by local media firms and other businesspeople hoping to scare him into giving up a share of World Footprint. Within a year, Rones had a contract for his company to sell ad space on billboards and on signs placed on buildings and in buses and taxis. Not altogether surprising for this bold entrepreneur, Rones has a dangerous hobby: bull riding in rodeos. Rones believes that contending with the risks of being thrown by a bull requires the same sort of concentration and persistence he displays in his entrepreneurial role: "When trying to market your company, you can't be intimidated by the levels of management and the people hiding behind their voice mails. You have to believe that this way of thinking will only lead to rewards."[61] Sometimes, though, overconfidence can blind an entrepreneur and jeopardize the business, as it did with Rocky Aoki in the "Solving an Ethical Controversy" box.

Anthony Triglione was optimistic that if he could find customers, he could execute his business idea, even with essentially no start-up capital. Triglione's idea came from his observations at trade shows. In his job selling exhibit space, he noticed that when people attended the shows, they tended not to move into certain corners of the room. Triglione thought they just needed something attention-getting to attract them, and an on-the-spot tournament with a golf simulator sounded like just the thing to draw their attention. He cold-called an association whose members produce trade shows and learned the happy news that the association was about to put on a trade show of its own. Triglione offered to provide his service at no charge in exchange for some free space in one of the hall's "dead zones." The association agreed, but Triglione didn't even have a golf simulator. He raised money from family members, bought a used simulator, and spent a few days figuring out how to use it. Visitors to the show loved Triglione's idea, and he has succeeded in building his company from an idea plus a lot of optimism into a $1.6 million business.[62]

Tolerance for Failure

Entrepreneurs view setbacks and failures as learning experiences. They're not easily discouraged or disappointed when things don't go as planned. For Robert Luster, a major setback involved making a transition from his role as army officer to civilian entrepreneur. His first construction management firm, Athena Management Engineers, failed after two years, as Luster got used to the subtleties of communication in

Does the Buck Stop at the Top for Unethical Acts?

Rocky H. Aoki gained his first taste of fame as an Olympic wrestler from Japan. When his wrestling career was over, he looked for something else to do. The son of a stage-show performer, he got a terrific business idea: provide entertainment to people while they are eating. But this business wasn't dinner theater, it was "eatertainment." He founded Benihana, a Japanese eatery where knife-juggling chefs and Japanese drummers continue to thrill guests 35 years after the first restaurant opened. Aoki constantly staged flashy events to attract attention for Benihana, and he came to symbolize his company to the public. But in 1998, Aoki pleaded guilty to charges that he illegally gained $346,000 in stock profits based on a tip from a company insider that then Apple Computer chairman John Sculley would be leaving the company. Although the news was clearly bad, Benihana executives hardly took notice. Aoki did offer to resign before he was indicted. "The lawyers told me it would be bad press" for the company, he says. "I didn't want to hurt Benihana." But although the company accepted his resignation, it kept him on at an annual $500,000 consulting fee, Aoki still owns 51 percent of Benihana, and the new executives never issued a press release or held a press conference. Benihana simply went back to business as its former leader faced jail time.

Should a company support its founder when he or she behaves unethically or illegally?

PRO
1. Without Aoki, there would be no Benihana, so Benihana should loyally stand behind its creator, whatever the consequences.

2. Aoki's illegal profits did not benefit Benihana, so the company itself should not get involved in the stock scandal in any way.
3. The company risks patrons' and investors' confidence if it makes public statements against its founder, so it should do as little as possible.

CON
1. Benihana should have been much more open about Aoki's problems. It risked its shareholder's money by not publicly severing ties with Aoki.
2. A company that is so closely tied to the entrepreneur who founded it needs to distance itself from unethical or illegal acts or suffer the consequences.
3. Trying to sweep unethical or illegal acts under the rug hurts businesses' image and credibility in the eye of the public.

SUMMARY
Benihana executives, including new chairman Joel Schwartz, chose the course of ignoring the crisis until it died down. Meanwhile, the company opened a new self-serve sushi bar with Aoki as consultant and began working with a licensee on a line of dressings and sauces. All the while, the company's stock price continued to rise and the knife jugglers continued to flash their blades.

Sources: "Executive Biographies: Rocky H. Aoki—Founder," Benihana Web site, **www.benihana.com,** accessed February 12, 2001; Luisa Kroll, "Business As Usual," *Forbes,* November 1, 1999, pp. 260–262; "Focus: Benihana, Inc.," *Restaurant Investor,* volume 10, number 25, May 1998, accessed at **www.savannahcorp.com/archive/May98.**

the private sector. He then formed Luster Construction Management and won his first client by promising he could have someone on site the next day. While he was waiting for a reply, Luster began screening candidates, so when the client called and asked Luster to start the next morning, he was ready. Today Luster's business is generating $10 million in sales and has over 100 employees.[63]

Creativity

Entrepreneurs typically conceive new ideas for goods and services, and they devise innovative ways to overcome difficult problems and situations. Kimberly Porrazzo turned a family problem into an entrepreneurship opportunity. When she became pregnant several years ago, she set about looking for a nanny so she would be able to return to her job. However, she was unimpressed with the nanny agencies in her area, and she couldn't find leads on her own. Porrazzo concluded that she had identified an unmet need for help in independently searching for a nanny. She developed a manual called *The Nanny Kit*, which she marketed at seminars she presented. When parents at the seminars asked her to consult with them, Porrazzo saw another business opportunity—providing personal consultations. But offering one-to-one service was so labor-intensive that Porrazzo looked for alternative ways to grow her business. She set up the Southern California Nanny Center Web site, which offers parents a database of nannies. This success led to an appearance on the *Today Show*

Background. Platform shoes are back. As with many fashion cycles, the young people who are wearing these shoes weren't even born the last time they were in fashion. And it seems as though one man is responsible for the trend: Steve Madden. Madden dropped out of college and got a job selling shoes in a Long Island shoe store, but he wanted to achieve more—and he wanted control over his career. So he decided to try a few of his own shoe designs. He sold them from store to store and began to get some takers. Then came the platforms.

What Happened? The entrepreneur says he got the idea when he noticed that a teenage girl in a shoe store had added her own platform to a pair of shoes he had designed. "I immediately stole the idea," admits the shoe designer. Madden figured he was on to something and began to add platforms to all of his designs—from casual loafers to leopard-print sandals.

The Response. Shoppers love the new shoes. High school girls clomp around in fat-soled canvas sneakers and country stars like the Dixie Chicks prance back and forth across the stage in glittery numbers. "His shoes go with everything," raves MTV video jockey Ananda Lewis, who owns at least 20 pairs. The shoes were so popular that the company tripped when it was unable to fulfill the demand from department stores and suffered from unexpected markdowns. Recognizing his limits as a financial person, Madden hired a financial specialist to handle these problems, and today the company is back on the right path.

Today and Counting. Currently, Madden sells his trendy shoes through 2,500 department stores and specialty shops, 45 of his own retail shops, and his Web site. The company is still small enough and flexible enough to react to changes in consumer tastes, and it can get a new shoe to the marketplace in 40 days, versus 180 days for larger companies. In fact, he can turn over his inventory eight times a year rather than the standard four times. Such quickness gives Madden an advantage over his competitors. However, Madden is not content to rest on the popularity of one fashion. He recently expanded his line to include snake print purses, shearling coats, and studded jeans. But he confesses that he worries about it, because he wants to achieve perfection. "I'm very nervous about it. I never think it's going to be good enough," he says. If he notices his young customers altering these items the way they altered his original shoes, he's likely to follow their example—and have another hit.

QUESTIONS FOR CRITICAL THINKING
1. Madden didn't revolutionize the shoe industry. But what creative improvements did he make that contributed to his success?
2. Does Madden seem to have a tolerance for ambiguity? Why or why not?

Sources: "FAQ's: Product Information," Steve Madden Ltd. Web site, **www.stevemadden.com,** accessed February 12, 2001; "Steve Madden, Ltd., Announces Record Third Quarter Results," *PR Newswire,* November 1, 2000; Kelly Barron, "Sole Man," *Forbes,* November 1, 1999.

and inquiries about similar databases for other parts of the country. At that point, Porrazzo needed a creative expansion plan. She combined her manual and her experience into a franchise business, which she markets as a part-time, home-based business. In this way, Southern California Nanny Center has become a fixture in other major cities as well.[64]

Entrepreneurs often achieve success by making creative improvements, rather than single-handedly revolutionizing an industry. Amar Bhidé's research identified a substantial amount of creativity among entrepreneurs "at the tactical level"—in other words, in the ways entrepreneurs built their businesses, more so than in the product itself.[65] Steve Madden, of Steve Madden Ltd. shoe fame, built a fashion empire by bringing back platform shoes, as described in the "Clicks and Mortar" box. Successful entrepreneurs tend to be creative in how they get attention from prospective investors or customers and in the ways they build trust in the absence of a proven track record. Sean Rones, founder of World Footprint, described earlier, landed an interview with *Entrepreneur's Start-Ups* magazine by dressing in full rodeo regalia and riding his horse to the magazine's offices.[66]

Tolerance for Ambiguity

Entrepreneurs take in stride the uncertainties associated with launching a venture. Dealing with unexpected events is the norm for most entrepreneurs. With limited funding, the typical entrepreneur cannot afford to stockpile resources to prepare for the future but must act quickly as orders come in. That was Seth Goldman's experience when he founded a company to market Honest Tea. He experimented with a variety of ingredients until he created a flavor he thought would taste good either hot or cold, then lined up an appointment with buyers at the Fresh Fields/Whole Foods chain of natural-foods grocers. He brewed his original flavor of Honest Tea in his home kitchen and took a thermos full of the tea to his appointment. The buyers were delighted and ordered 15,000 bottles. Now Goldman had a problem: he still needed a way to produce all that tea. Undaunted, he found help from an expert in the bottling industry. He arranged to have the tea produced at a factory in Buffalo. As demand for the tea grew and the company diversified into eight varieties of bottled tea plus tea bags, Goldman's company purchased part ownership of a bottling facility in New Kensington, Pennsylvania.[67]

Tolerance for ambiguity is different from the love of risk taking that many people associate with entrepreneurship. Successful entrepreneurship is a far cry from gambling, because entrepreneurs look for strategies that they believe have a good chance of success, and they quickly make adjustments when a strategy isn't working. Stanley Adelman has founded four companies, and he succeeds by investing small amounts of money to provide products for which a strong demand exists. Adelman's first business was Systems Strategies, a computer consulting company he started in the 1970s. He observed that little capital is needed to start a consulting firm: "You just go out there and sell services." Of course, even in the consulting business, success does require human talent coupled with entrepreneurial drive. Adelman had those resources, and he built a fast-growing enterprise. Then, while consulting with Citibank, he realized that the hardware systems he was developing for securities trading would interest other companies. His second business, Systems Strategies Equipment Corp., sold the hardware. Adelman's third business offered software built to customer specifications—a very safe venture, because the company was building something the customer had already asked for. In the mid-1980s, he sold all three companies, allowing him to start his fourth business, Aegis Software, another consulting firm that has enjoyed rapid growth.[68]

An important way entrepreneurs manage ambiguity is by keeping close to customers, so that they can adjust their offerings in keeping with customer desires. Sylvia Woods expanded from a Harlem restaurant into the packaged-foods business by listening to her customers. Patrons of Sylvia's Restaurant, famous for its soul food, loved her homemade barbecue sauce so much that they begged to buy some to take home. Around Christmastime, some would visit the restaurant with empty jars, asking to buy sauce for gifts. Even local firefighters showed up with gallon jugs and asked for sauce. Woods teamed up with her son Van and launched Queen of Soul Food, starting with bottles of barbecue sauce. They added other items that customers praised, including bottled hot sauce and canned vegetables.[69]

Internal Locus of Control

Entrepreneurs believe that they control their own fates, which means they have an internal locus of control. You won't find entrepreneurs gazing into a crystal ball or looking for a four-leaf clover—they take personal responsibility for the success or failure of their actions rather than believing in luck or fate. They neither make excuses for their shortcomings nor blame others for their setbacks and failures. Figure 6.10 appeals to this self-sufficiency by offering businesspeople a Web site at which they can check airfares, purchase their own e-tickets, and select their seats. The ad shows entrepreneur Stefanie Syman, cofounder of feedmag.com, as an icon of someone who takes control: she "edits her own e-zine" and "books her own e-tickets," and she is pictured, literally, on top of things.

Another entrepreneur who exhibits a strong internal locus of control is Ken Craig. He once managed a Jack in the Box fast-food outlet in Southern California and was preparing to purchase a franchise. But in the mid-1990s, some customers in Washington State became ill from eating Jack in the Box hamburgers contaminated by *E. coli* bacteria. Within days, as the news spread, business at Craig's restaurant

Stefanie Syman

co-founder feedmag.com

edits her own e-zine

books her own e-tickets

check fares • select seats • buy tickets • work smart • Northwest Airlines

nwa.com

FIGURE 6.10
An Entrepreneur with an Internal Locus of Control

plummeted to near zero. Craig hated his lack of control over events at a restaurant chain he did not own: "I wanted to be in a position where whatever happened was a result of my own actions." So instead of buying a franchise, Craig headed up his own business, Spenser Communications, building the telecommunications firm into a $4.3 million company.[70]

Some entrepreneurs have such a strong inner locus of control that they have trouble sharing control of the business when growth makes delegation necessary. Max Carey founded Corporate Resource Development to provide marketing-related consulting services. The company grew quickly under his leadership, but eventually Carey's efforts to control every detail and solve every problem created such an intimidating and frustrating atmosphere that it became difficult for the company to attract and keep the best people. In addition, Carey was physically exhausted. He eventually learned to moderate his desire for control by listening more carefully and reacting more slowly, which allowed him to tap the full potential of his employees. However, maintaining that less-controlling style is something that Carey says requires continual effort and self-monitoring.[71]

After reading this summary of typical personality traits, maybe you're wondering if you have what it takes to become an entrepreneur. Take the test in Figure 6.11 to find out. Your results may help you determine whether you would succeed in starting your own company.

STARTING A NEW VENTURE

The examples of entrepreneurs presented so far have introduced many ways to start a business. This section discusses the process of choosing an idea for a new venture and transforming the idea into a working business. Part of that process involves choosing a name, as discussed in the "Business Hits and Misses" box.

Selecting a Business Idea

In choosing an idea for your business, the two most important considerations are (1) finding something you love to do and are good at doing and (2) determining whether your idea can satisfy a need in the marketplace. People willingly work hard doing something they love, and the experience will bring personal fulfillment. The old adages "Do what makes you happy" and "To thine own self be true" are the best guidelines for deciding on a business idea.

Success also depends on customers, so would-be entrepreneurs must also be sure that the idea they choose has merit in the marketplace. The most successful entrepreneurs tend to operate in industries where a great deal of change is taking place and in which customers have difficulty pinpointing their precise needs. These industries, including advanced technology and consulting, allow entrepreneurs to capitalize on their strengths, such as creativity, hard work, and tolerance of ambiguity, to build customer relationships.[72] Nevertheless, examples of outstanding success occur in every industry, from glamorous high-tech companies like Cisco Systems to

ENTREPRENEUR POTENTIAL ASSESSMENT FORM

Answer each of the following questions:

Yes No

☐ ☑ 1. Are you a first-generation American?

☑ ☐ 2. Were you an honor student?

☐ ☐ 3. Did you enjoy group functions in school—clubs, team sports, even double dates?

☐ ☐ 4. As a youngster, did you frequently prefer to spend time alone?

☐ ☐ 5. As a child, did you have a paper route, a lemonade stand, or some other small enterprise?

☐ ☐ 6. Were you a stubborn child?

☐ ☐ 7. Were you a cautious youngster, the last in the neighborhood to try diving off the high board?

☐ ☐ 8. Do you worry about what others think of you?

☐ ☐ 9. Are you in a rut, tired of the same routine every day?

☐ ☐ 10. Would you be willing to invest your savings—and risk losing all you invested—to go it alone?

☐ ☐ 11. If your new business should fail, would you get to work immediately on another?

☐ ☐ 12. Are you an optimist?

Answers: 1. Yes = 1, No = −1; 2. Yes = −4, No = 4; 3. Yes = −1, No = 1; 4. Yes = 1, No = −1; 5. Yes = 2, No = −2; 6. Yes = 1, No = −1; 7. Yes = −4, No = 4 (if you were a very daring child, add another 4 points); 8. Yes = −1, No = 1; 9. Yes = 2, No = −2; 10. Yes = 2, No = −2; 11. Yes = 4, No = −4; 12. Yes = 2, No = −2.

Add up your total score. A score of 20 or more points indicates strong entrepreneurial tendencies. A score between 0 and 19 points suggests some possibility for success as an entrepreneur. A score between 0 and −10 indicates little chance of successful entrepreneurship. A score below −11 indicates someone who's not the entrepreneurial type.

discounters like Wal-Mart. According to one study, about 3 to 5 percent of the companies in any industry are growing exceptionally fast, so entrepreneurs do not need to limit their sights to industries characterized by rapid growth. The study advises entrepreneurs to be not only the best but also innovative and different.[73]

The following guidelines may help you to select an idea that represents a good entrepreneurial opportunity for you:

FIGURE 6.11
Think You Might Be a Good Entrepreneur?

For any entrepreneur, choosing a name for a new company is both exciting and frustrating. You want to select just the right set of words to convey what your company is about, what it does, whom you want to serve. For Internet entrepreneurs, however, the challenge is even greater. A single word or words must convey goods and services that consumers can't touch, hear, or smell. Not only that, the corresponding Internet address must be one that is not already owned by someone else. A Bob's Bike Shop might be operating in Seattle and another Bob's Bike Shop in Boston, but there can only be one bobsbikes.com. And while Bob in Seattle might decide to change the name of his shop to Cycle Madness by having a new sign painted and running some new ads in the local paper, it's much more difficult—and expensive—to change an Internet address once it has been established. Not surprisingly, there have already been some winners and losers in the e-commerce name game.

Several years ago, Andrew Busey started a Web business called ForMyHome.com, to sell bookshelves, beds, and other home furnishings. But the name just wasn't exciting, and he knew he had to invest in a change before he went online or his company could quickly go down the drain. He found it nearly impossible to come up with a short, punchy name on his own, so he hired a Web site design company to help him. And the hunt began. Even the design firm had trouble at first. "A lot [of their suggestions] were neat, but they were weird and obscure," recalled Busey. He rejected such ideas as Patina.com and Livespace.com. Finally, one name grabbed his attention: Living.com. It conveyed what his business was about, it was easy to remember, and it was easy to spell. It also was general enough to encompass Busey's ideas for future expansion from furniture to other areas of home life.

Ironically, Busey passed on another proposed name—Furniture.com—because he was afraid it would pigeonhole his business. Domain names, which are not free if they have been registered by someone else, can be expensive, and the businessperson who had registered that name wanted $1 million for it. Eventually, the name went to Andrew Brooks, CEO of a company based in Massachusetts that sold furniture online. Busey paid a comparatively cheap $160,000 for Living.com, which was owned by the California Association of Realtors. With all the competition, was the name scramble worth the effort and money? It seemed so at first, but both Living.com and Furniture.com failed within a few months following their initial launch. Even with solid names, customers did not flock to the Internet to buy furniture.

Some names frustrate consumers because it's impossible to tell at the outset what type of business the sites are in. Take Monster.com, which pairs up companies with job hunters. Without the millions of dollars the company has spent in advertising, no one would have known what the site was about. Now, it's a brand name that has been imprinted in people's minds. The same could be said for Tavolo Inc., whose address is www.tavolo.com. The company's name used to be Digital Chef Inc. Although it was descriptive, it was a dud when it came to inspiring aspiring cooks. The new name evokes the romance of Italian cooking (*tavolo* is Italian for *table*), and the site is visited often.

In the end, choosing a name for an Internet site is an enormously important business decision. Consider the choice of Andrew Raskin, who recently started an Internet company that helps other businesses "set up Web-based referral programs that reward site users for getting friends to visit, register, or make a purchase." After hiring several consultants to generate ideas, Raskin and his partner settled on a name: Gazooba Corp. In December 2000 Gazooba's new president and CEO decided to change the company's name to Qbiquity Corporation. The new name was chosen as a reflection of the customers who utilize their services, as well as the value of word-of-mouth advertising. Was it worth the initial cost of hiring consultants given the name change? Maybe Qbiquity is a better fit.

QUESTIONS FOR CRITICAL THINKING

1. Which name do you think better fits the word-of-mouth advertising company? Explain your answer.
2. In what ways might a company's name affect the type of financing it is able to acquire?

Sources: "Online Furniture Industry Experiences Shakeout," *Business Wire*, November 10, 2000; Andrew Raskin, "The Game of the Name," *Inc.*, February 2000, pp. 31–32; Nick Wingfield, "The Game of the Name," *The Wall Street Journal*, November 22, 1999, p. R14; "Gazooba Changes Name to Qbiquity," Qbiquity Web site **wwwqbiquity.com**, February 6, 2001.

- List your interests and abilities. Include your values and beliefs, your goals and dreams, things you like and dislike doing, and your job experiences.
- Make another list of the types of businesses that match your interests and abilities.
- Read newspapers and business and consumer magazines to learn about demographic and economic trends that identify future needs for products that no one yet offers.
- Carefully evaluate existing goods and services, looking for ways you can improve on them.
- Decide on a business that matches what you want and offers profit potential.
- Conduct marketing research to determine whether your business idea will attract enough customers to earn a profit.

- Learn as much as you can about the industry in which your new venture will operate, your merchandise or service, and your competitors. Read surveys that project growth in various industries.

Like Kimberly Porrazzo, whose Southern California Nanny Center was described earlier, many entrepreneurs start businesses to solve problems that they experienced either at work or in their personal lives. Others are more methodical in their search for business ideas. Cherrill Farnsworth actually studies government regulations to look for new business ideas. In the 1970s, she operated a bus franchise in Houston. After selling Suburban Transportation Co. to the City of Houston, Farnsworth evaluated her experience. She concluded that she had a talent for putting deals together, so she started and ran three different equipment-leasing businesses that profited from tax regulations, including investment tax credits. In the 1980s, Farnsworth identified an opportunity in a then-new medical technology, magnetic resonance imaging (MRI). Medicare did not yet reimburse hospitals for MRI scans, so hospitals didn't want to buy the equipment. Farnsworth launched a chain of centers providing MRI services. A decade later, she spotted another trend in medical care, a new interest in managed care. Building on her experience with the MRI centers, Farnsworth founded HealthHelp, which manages radiology services for HMOs and insurance companies. Farnsworth has built Houston-based HealthHelp into one of the nation's fastest-growing small businesses, with almost $15 million in sales. Says Farnsworth of her skill at identifying and developing opportunities, "I used to think that entrepreneurship was more an art than a science, that it was a gift of something. I don't believe that anymore."[74]

An entrepreneur's need for marketing research varies depending on the business idea, industry, and competitive conditions. An innovative idea with an unproven potential customer base may require more research than a proposal to improve an existing product. By contrast, Wayne and Marty Scott serve a tiny but reliable niche: clowns. The husband-and-wife team operates Clown Shoes & Props from their Florida home. They make shoes to order by adapting a few basic styles such as wingtips, Mary Janes, and sneakers. When customers call, the Scotts ask them to send in photos plus a description of the clown's character. For a clown called Cooker T, whose character is a chef, the Scotts decorated shoes with pairs of knives and forks cut from leather and crossed on top of the shoes. Other shoes might be adorned with squirting flowers or with flaps that represent mouths that open and close as the clown walks. Besides crafting these obvious features, the Scotts devote attention to the important task of making the shoes comfortable to wear. Inside each giant clown shoe is an inner shoe, which the Scotts fit by measuring the performer's feet or providing instructions for the performer to use. With their attention to detail, the Scotts have captured one-fifth of the U.S. market for custom clown shoes, including clowns from circus giant Ringling Bros. Barnum & Bailey.[75]

An inventor–entrepreneur will need to protect the rights to the invention by securing a patent for it. At its Web site (www.uspto.gov), the U.S. Patent and Trademark Office provides information about this process, along with forms for applying for a patent. Since 2000, inventors have been able to apply for a patent online at this Web site. Also, the "Counseling Literature" page at the Web site of the Boston-area Better Business Bureau (www.bosbbb.org) provides a link to basic information about applying for a patent and commercializing an invention. That article also lists names and addresses of organizations and other resources that can help you to turn an idea into a business.

Wayne and Marty Scott have built a business by clowning around. The couple crafts custom clown shoes to fit each clown's unique character. Shown here are samples they created for a recent Ringling Bros. circus tour.

Not all entrepreneurs need to launch an entirely new business, however. Aspiring entrepreneurs can choose from two other popular options: buying an existing business and buying a franchise.

Buying an Existing Business   Some entrepreneurs prefer to buy established businesses rather than assume the risks of starting new ones. Buying an existing business brings many advantages: employees are already in place, serve established customers, and deal with familiar suppliers; the good or service is known in the marketplace; and the necessary permits and licenses have already been secured. Getting financing for an existing business also is easier than it is for most start-ups. Some sellers may even help the buyers by providing financing and offering to serve as consultants.

To find businesses for sale, contact your local chamber of commerce as well as professionals such as lawyers, accountants, and insurance agents. It is important to analyze the performance of businesses under consideration. Most people want to buy a healthy business so that they can build on its success. Masoud M. Anwarzai bought Marathon Runner Courier Service with the help of an SBA-guaranteed loan. The lender, Heller Financial, not only was willing to approve the loan for the purchase but encouraged Anwarzai to borrow enough to establish a pool of working capital. Heller was impressed both with Anwarzai's own credit history and the business's solid finances.[76] In contrast, turnaround entrepreneurs enjoy the challenge of buying unprofitable firms and making enough improvement in their operations to let them begin to generate profits. Success with a turnaround strategy requires that the entrepreneur have definite and practical ideas about how to operate the business more profitably.

Buying a Franchise   Like buying an established business, a franchise offers a less risky way to begin a business than starting an entirely new firm. Yet franchising still involves risks. You must do your homework, carefully analyzing the franchisor's terms and capabilities for delivering the support it promises. Energetic preparation helps to ensure that your business will earn a profit and grow.

Although a franchisee must agree to follow the procedures mandated by the franchisor, entrepreneurs can still find ways to inject their creativity into their franchises and make them grow. A case in point is William Heinecke's Pizza Hut franchise in Thailand, described earlier in this chapter. Chapter 5 addresses business opportunities in franchising.

Creating a Business Plan

In the past, most entrepreneurs launched their ventures without creating formal business plans. Although planning is an integral part of managing in the world of business, entrepreneurs traditionally seize opportunities as they arise and change course as necessary. For Frieda Caplan, open-mindedness substituted for a formal business plan. In its early years in the 1960s, Caplan's wholesale produce business grew because she was willing to carry products for which her competitors saw no significant market. Caplan explains her success this way:

> When farmers came by and offered novelties like Jerusalem artichokes, which I renamed Sunchokes, and limes and papayas and mangoes, [my competitors] had no interest. They said, "Go see Frieda—she might be interested, because she handles odd things, like mushrooms."

With this strategy of open-mindedness, Caplan not only built sales of about $10 million a year, she attracted publicity and developed a national following. But Caplan realized that her approach had limitations. When her daughter Karen completed her management degree, Caplan hired her to provide more goal-oriented leadership. The elder Caplan calls this "the smartest business decision

Table 6.2	Online Resources for Preparing a Business Plan
Allbusiness.com www.allbusiness.com	The "Business Planning" page provides links to examples, templates, and tips for writing a plan.
American Express www.americanexpress.com	Click on the "Small Business" tab, then go to the "Information Resources" section to find information about business plans. A "Try It Yourself" page lets you create a plan for a start-up and then get feedback on your plan.
EntreWorld www.entreworld.org	The "Starting Your Business" section has links to information and resources for researching and writing a plan, as well as presenting it to lenders or investors.
Morebusiness.com www.morebusiness.com	To see a sample plan, select "Business & Marketing Plans" from the list of templates.

I've ever made." With Karen's vision and planning, Frieda was able to navigate its second phase of growth, to revenues of $35 million.[77]

Although the planning process for entrepreneurs differs from a major company's planning function, today's entrepreneurs are advised to construct business plans following the guidelines presented in Chapters 5 and 7. Careful planning helps the entrepreneur prepare enough resources and stay focused on key objectives, and it also provides an important tool for convincing potential investors and employees that the enterprise has the ingredients for success. Entrepreneurial business plans vary depending on the type of start-up, but the basic elements of such a plan—stating company goals, outlining sales and marketing strategies, and determining financial needs and sources of funds—apply to all types of ventures. The Internet also offers a variety of resources for creating business plans. Table 6.2 lists some of these online resources.

Finding Financing

A key issue in any business plan is financing. How much money will you need to start your business, and where will you get it? Requirements for **seed capital**—funds to launch a company—depend on the nature of your business and the type of facilities and equipment you need. Among the nation's fastest-growing small businesses, about two-thirds were started with $50,000 or less in seed capital, and over 40 percent began with $10,000 or less.[78]

Arnold Tompkins successfully started his consulting business by planning a solid financial foundation. The attorney spent two years planning his venture and saving money from his salary plus fees for speaking engagements that he lined up to build his name recognition. Once he had saved $25,000, Tompkins resigned from his job and started Tompkins Consulting, which specializes in management issues related to health and human services. The amount he saved was based on careful estimates of his business and personal expenses over several months until his consulting work began to bring in revenues.[79]

The vast majority of entrepreneurs rely on personal savings, advances on credit cards, and money from partners, family members, and friends to fund their start-ups. Ginny Ferguson and Denise Brown started *Bikes & Spikes,* a motorcycle magazine focusing on female enthusiasts, by tapping all the personal sources of credit they could think of: credit cards, stock holdings, retirement savings, and refinancing of Brown's house and both women's vehicles.[80] As Figure 6.12 illustrates, convincing others to invest in a new company can be difficult. However, new ventures with an attractive, well-thought-out business plan may be able to secure funds in two forms: debt financing and equity financing.

BUSINESS DIRECTORY

➤ **seed capital** *initial funding needed to launch a new venture.*

You're convinced that your business will succeed.

The problem is, you have to convince others.

NOTICE
You need a business plan. But you don't know how to write a business plan. Smartonline.com can help. With everything you need to write an executive summary. An operations plan. Sales and growth strategies. Easily. Convincingly. Because we show you how. And our technology lets you access and edit any of your documents, anywhere in the world. Even share them with people around the block or across the ocean. Proving that you no longer have to work hard. Just smart.

Small business answers from small business owners.

www.smartonline.com

FIGURE 6.12
Preparing to Convince Others to Invest in a Business

Debt Financing When entrepreneurs use **debt financing,** they borrow money that they must repay. Loans from banks, finance companies, credit card companies, and family and friends are all sources of debt financing. Although many entrepreneurs charge business expenses to personal credit cards because they are relatively easy to obtain, high interest rates make this source of funding expensive. Annual interest charges on a credit card can run as high as 20 percent, while rates for a home equity loan (borrowing against the value of a home) currently run as little as 8 percent. In exchange for a lower interest rate, borrowers with a home equity loan pledge the value of their home, so if the borrower does not repay the loan, he or she risks losing the home.

Still, credit card financing may be a viable option for entrepreneurs who expect to grow quickly and know that they can pay off their debt in a short time. Once the company has passed the start-up phase, entrepreneurs may continue to use credit cards for purchases they can pay off quickly. Herbert J. Mallet obtained an American Express card for his business, Broudy Printing. He uses the corporate card to buy paper and other supplies. Depending on the time of the month in which he purchases the supplies, this arrangement gives him up to 50 days before he has to pay the bill without incurring interest charges. Because the card enables Broudy Printing to pay its suppliers quickly, the company even gets a discount this way. But Mallet cautions entrepreneurs not to resort to a credit card unless they are sure they can pay on time: "If you don't have the cash flow to pay off your bills each month, and you get sucked into those [late-payment] penalties, you're going to wind up going down a dark, bleak road."[81]

Many banks turn down requests for loans to fund start-ups, fearful of the high risk such ventures entail. Only a small percentage of start-ups raise seed capital through bank loans, although some new firms can get SBA-backed loans, as discussed in Chapter 5. The challenge has historically been even greater for entrepreneurs who are women or ethnic minorities. As noted in Chapter 5, minority-owned businesses are less likely than white-owned businesses to have bank loans. Some, as in the previous example of consultant Arnold Tompkins, who is African American, simply wait to start their businesses until they can acquire enough capital without borrowing. Women, too, report that they have been taken less seriously than their male counterparts when they seek debt financing. Deborah Naybor had difficulty borrowing money for her land-surveying company. One bank approved her loan application for $70,000, but gave her 30 days to repay it.[82]

Similarly, Lisa Argiris was disappointed with her borrowing experiences as founder of International Musical Suppliers. She quickly secured a $50,000 line of credit to launch her mail-order musical instruments company, but the bank resisted when she wanted to borrow additional funds to expand her business into the more profitable realm of instrument rentals. After considerable frustration, Argiris concluded, "My bank was really just interested in supporting me because of my public-relations value to them—as a minority and female business owner—not because they really understood or believed in my business concept." She took her business elsewhere, eventually arranging $1 million in loans from Citigroup.[83]

Like Argiris, persistent women and minorities are finding loans, as lenders begin to appreciate their significance as business founders. Some institutions, including First Union Bank, Fleet Bank, and Wells Fargo Bank, have even begun to tailor offerings to female entrepreneurs. Also, as noted in the preceding chapter, the SBA has programs designed to help female and minority entrepreneurs get financing.

Applying for a bank loan requires careful preparation. Bank loan officers want to see a business plan and will evaluate the entrepreneur's credit history. Since a start-up has not yet established a business credit history, banks often base lending decisions on evaluations of entrepreneurs' personal credit histories. Banks are more willing to make loans to entrepreneurs who've been in business for a while, show a profit on rising revenues, and need funds to finance expansion. Some entrepreneurs have found that local community banks are more interested in their loan applications than the giant national banks are.

Equity Financing   To secure equity financing, entrepreneurs exchange a share of ownership in their company for money supplied by one or more investors. Entrepreneurs invest their own money along with funds supplied by other people and firms that become co-owners of the start-ups. An entrepreneur does not have to repay equity funds. Rather, the investors share in the success of the business. Sources of equity financing include family and friends, business partners, venture capital firms, and private investors.

Teaming up with a partner who has funds to invest may benefit an entrepreneur with a good idea and skills but no money. Investors may also have business experience, which they will be eager to share because the company's prosperity will benefit them.

Like borrowing, equity financing has its drawbacks. One is that investment partners may not agree on the future direction of the business and in the case of partnerships, if they cannot resolve disputes, one partner may have to buy out the other to keep operating. Bob Shay started Rightfit Sports to sell ski boots, and six years later, Lee Findell bought a 50 percent share of the company. The two built Rightfit into a 14-store, $9 million company, but later decided to dissolve the partnership. Rightfit's founder decided to sell Shay his share of the business, except for two Utah stores that were renamed Surefoot. Shay's decision to start over was successful and he built his new company into a rapid-growth, 24-store chain.[84]

Venture capitalists are business organizations or groups of private individuals that invest in new and growing firms. These investors expect to receive high

BUSINESS DIRECTORY

➤ **debt financing**   *borrowed funds that entrepreneurs must repay.*

➤ **equity financing**   *funds invested in new ventures in exchange for part ownership.*

➤ **venture capitalists**   *business firms or groups of individuals who invest in new and growing firms.*

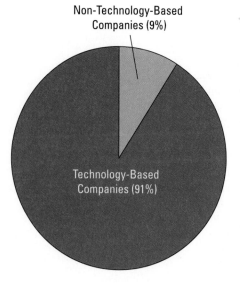

Non-Technology-Based Companies (9%)

Technology-Based Companies (91%)

FIGURE 6.13
Where Venture Capital Dollars Go

rates of return, typically more than 30 percent, within short time periods of five or fewer years. Consequently, they tend to concentrate their investments in firms in fast-growing industries such as technology and communications. As Figure 6.13 shows, 91 cents of every dollar of venture capital in recent years have been invested in technology-based companies. Prior to the widespread failures of dot.coms in the early years of the 21st century, a sizable portion of venture capital flowed into start-up Internet firms. Although venture capital firms have received a great deal of press coverage, the $36 billion they invest annually flow to a very limited number of businesses. Less than one-tenth of firms receiving funds from venture capitalists are start-ups, and most are high-tech companies.[85]

A larger source of investors in start-ups consists of angel investors. **Angel investors** are wealthy individuals willing to invest money directly in new ventures in return for equity stakes. They invest more capital in start-ups than do venture capitalists. In contrast to venture capitalists, angels focus primarily on new ventures. Many angel investors are themselves successful entrepreneurs who want to help aspiring business owners through the familiar difficulties of launching their businesses. Angel investors back a wide variety of new ventures. Some invest exclusively in certain industries, others invest only in start-ups with socially responsible missions, and still others prefer to back only women entrepreneurs.

Because most entrepreneurs have trouble finding wealthy private investors, angel networks form to match business angels with start-ups in need of capital. UniversityAngels.com links alumni interested in investing with students who have start-up ideas. WomenAngels.net targets female entrepreneurs. The SBA's Angel Capital Electronic Network (ACE-Net) provides online listings to connect would-be angels with small businesses seeking financing. Similar networks try to expand the old-boy network of venture capitalists to new investors and entrepreneurs as well. Venture capitalists that focus on women include the Women's Growth Capital Fund (www.wgcf) and Viridian Capital (www.viridiancapital.com).

As entrepreneurs start their businesses, they spend much of their time seeking and securing financing. Most company founders perform all the activities needed to operate their businesses because they don't have enough money to hire additional employees. The majority of entrepreneurs begin as sole proprietors working from their homes. After their initial start-up periods, however, entrepreneurs must make many management decisions as their companies begin to grow. They must establish legal entities, buy equipment, choose facilities and locations, assemble teams of employees, and ensure compliance with a host of government regulations. These challenges are discussed in other chapters throughout this book.

INTRAPRENEURSHIP

Large, established companies try to retain the entrepreneurial spirit by encouraging **intrapreneurship,** the process of promoting innovation within their organizational structures. Today's fast-changing business climate compels large firms to innovate continually to maintain their competitive advantages. Entrepreneurial environments created within companies such as 3M, Thermo Electron, Xerox, and Intuit can help these larger firms retain valuable employees who might otherwise leave their jobs to start their own businesses.

Large companies support entrepreneurial activity in varied ways. One leader in this area, 3M Corp., has established companywide policies and procedures that give employees personal freedom to explore new products and technologies. 3M allows its researchers to spend 15 percent of their time working on their own ideas without approval from management. The company's hiring process is designed to select innovative people. Using a personality profile of characteristics shared by its top creative scientists, 3M has crafted questions and scenarios that help company interviewers gauge the creative skills of job candidates. In addition to traditional product development, 3M implements two intrapreneurial approaches: skunkworks and pacing programs. A **skunkworks** project is initiated by an employee who conceives an idea and then recruits resources from within 3M to turn it into a commercial product. Pacing programs are company-initiated projects that focus on a few products and technologies in which 3M sees potential for rapid marketplace winners. The company provides financing, equipment, and people to support such pacing projects.

Intrapreneurship has succeeded at 3M largely because of the company's high value of innovation. According to consultant Gary Hamel, intrapreneurship requires these and other signs of management commitment. Companies that succeed with intrapreneurship give their intrapreneurs ready access to company resources like brands and talented employees. In addition, they should give their intrapreneurs wide latitude to carry out their ideas, once management has approved the overall strategy. Finally, says Hamel, intrapreneurial companies should be bold about adopting ideas from people both inside and outside the company.[86]

Intraneurship need not be limited to giant firms. Elite Information Systems, a Los Angeles–based marketer of billing software, let its chief technology officer, Mark Goldin, switch from his managerial position to the role of intrapreneur. Goldin was planning to leave Elite to start a company offering access to time and billing software over the Internet. However, Elite agreed to let him stay on the payroll and start his business as an operation within Elite. Because Elite lacked the resources of a giant like 3M, it required Goldin to obtain approval for his strategy within two months. Offsetting that challenge, the company contributed managerial talent as well as office space and money. When Goldin obtained approval for Elite.com, management supplied needed funding to get his enterprise going in less than half a year. This time line reflected the start-up's distinctive culture within Elite; normally, the company spends two years developing new software. Under severe time pressure, Goldin benefited from his knowledge of the company's human resources and customers, as well as the free rein management has allowed him outside of the time constraints. So far Goldin has succeeded in bringing Elite.com online; the next step facing him is to make the company-within-a-company profitable.[87]

Recognizing that entrepreneurial employees often leave to form their own start-ups, some companies actually encourage employees to take the plunge. The Walt Disney Co. is an icon of creativity, and many of its creative people leave to start businesses on their own. Among them is Jake Winebaum, formerly president of Walt Disney Magazine Publishing and intrapreneurial founder of Disney Online. While at Disney, he loved the climate of innovation in which he ran Disney.com, ABCNews.com, ESPN.com, and Go.com. He found the process of starting these operations inside Disney to be very similar to the process of starting a new company. In fact, the experience reminded him how much he loved being an entrepreneur, and he left to start a business incubator called eCompanies, with the goal of helping businesses move from ideas to operating businesses within a few months' time. Winebaum credits Disney with helping him learn how to identify business ideas with good potential.

WHAT'S AHEAD

The next chapter turns to a realm of business in which many entrepreneurs have been active during the past decade: electronic commerce, or business use of the Internet. The chapter describes the technology behind electronic commerce. It introduces the challenges and opportunities available to entrepreneurs and other businesspeople who want to communicate with and sell to customers on the Internet. Not many years ago,

---

BUSINESS DIRECTORY

➤ **angel investors**   *wealthy individuals who invest directly in a new venture in exchange for an ownership share.*

➤ **intrapreneurship**   *process of promoting innovation within the structure of an existing organization.*

Internet technology was a novelty except among high-tech firms and tech-savvy individuals. Today it is an integral factor in starting and growing a business.

➤ Summary of Learning Goals

1. Define the term *entrepreneur*, and distinguish among an entrepreneur, a small-business owner, and a manager.

Unlike many small-business owners, entrepreneurs typically own and run their businesses with the goal of building significant firms that create wealth and add jobs. Entrepreneurs are visionaries. They identify opportunities and take the initiative to gather the resources they need to start their businesses quickly. Both managers and entrepreneurs use the resources of their companies to achieve the goals of those organizations.

2. Identify three different types of entrepreneurs.

The three categories are classic entrepreneurs, intrapreneurs, and change agents. A classic entrepreneur identifies a business opportunity and allocates available resources to tap that market. An intrapreneur is an employee who develops a new idea or product within the context of an organizational position. A change agent is a manager who tries to revitalize an existing firm to make it a competitive success.

3. Explain why people choose to become entrepreneurs.

People choose this kind of career for many different reasons. Reasons most frequently cited include desires to be one's own boss, to achieve financial success, to gain job security, and to improve one's quality of life.

4. Discuss conditions that encourage opportunities for entrepreneurs.

A favorable public perception, the availability of financing, the falling cost and widespread availability of information technology, globalization, entrepreneurship education, and changing demographic and economic trends all contribute to a fertile environment for people to start new ventures.

5. Describe the role of entrepreneurs in the economy.

Entrepreneurs play a significant role in the economy as a major source of innovation and job creation. Entrepreneurship also provides many opportunities for women and minorities, who may encounter limits to their progress in established businesses.

6. Identify personality traits that typically characterize successful entrepreneurs.

Successful entrepreneurs share several typical traits, including vision, high energy level, need to achieve, self-confidence and optimism, tolerance for failure, creativity, tolerance for ambiguity, and internal locus of control.

7. Summarize the process of starting a new venture.

Entrepreneurs must select an idea for their business, develop a business plan, obtain financing, and organize the resources they need to operate their start-ups.

8. Explain how organizations promote intrapreneurship.

Organizations encourage entrepreneurial activity within the company in a variety of ways. Hiring practices, dedicated programs such as skunkworks, access to resources, and wide latitude to innovate encourage intrapreneurship within established firms.

Business Terms You Need to Know

entrepreneur 213
classic entrepreneur 214
intrapreneur 214
change agent 215
seed capital 237

debt financing 238
equity financing 239
venture capitalist 239
angel investor 240
intrapreneurship 240

Other Important Business Terms

gazelles 225

skunkworks 241

➤ Review Questions

1. What are the differences among entrepreneurs, small-business owners, and managers? What are the similarities?

2. Identify the three categories of entrepreneurs. How are they different from each other?

3. What are the four major reasons for becoming an entrepreneur?

4. How have globalization and information technology created new opportunities for entrepreneurs?

5. In what ways do entrepreneurs influence the overall economy?

6. Identify the eight characteristics that are attributed to successful entrepreneurs. Which trait or traits do you believe are the most important for success? Why?

7. What are the benefits and risks involved in buying an existing business or a franchise?

8. Why is creating a business plan an important step for an entrepreneur?

9. Describe the different types of financing that entrepreneurs may seek for their businesses. What are the risks and benefits involved with each?

10. What is intrapreneurship? How does it differ from entrepreneurship?

➤ Questions for Critical Thinking

1. Think of an entrepreneur whom you admire, or choose one from the following list: Bill Gates of Microsoft, Jeff Bezos of Amazon.com, Martha Stewart, or Oprah Winfrey of Harpo Productions. Explain why you admire this entrepreneur, including ways in which the person has contributed to his or her industry as well as the economy.

2. Current demographic and economic trends support entrepreneurs who are creating new businesses. One of these trends is the willingness of Americans to spend more money on certain goods and services. On your own or with a classmate, brainstorm a trend that may be a good idea for a new business. Write one or two paragraphs describing the trend and how it could be applied to a business.

3. Review the eight characteristics of successful entrepreneurs. Which characteristics do you possess? Do you think you would be a good entrepreneur? Why?

4. Think of an innovative product recently introduced by an existing company—a company that has used intrapreneurship. How does the new product fit within the scope of the company's existing products? Do some research in the library or on the Internet to see how successful the new idea is and how it was brought to life. Be ready to explain your findings.

5. Many entrepreneurs are motivated by working in an area they love. Think about something you love to do that you believe could be turned into a business. What aspect of the activity would actually be turned into a business? For example, if you love to play golf or shop at vintage clothing stores for 1970s-style attire, how would you shape this interest into a business?

➤ Experiential Exercise

Directions: *Black Enterprise, Entrepreneur,* and *Inc.* magazines are good sources for this research project on successful entrepreneurs. However, you may use any current periodical that contains features on how individuals have started their own businesses.

1. Locate an article published within the past 12 months that features an entrepreneur and the business he or she started.

2. Prepare a five-minute class presentation in which you summarize the selected article. Your presentation should include the information you consider most relevant and interesting. But, assuming the information is provided in the article, your talk should also answer the following questions:

   a. What was the source(s) of the entrepreneur's business idea?

   b. What aspects of a business plan appeared to be most important to this entrepreneur? Consider such areas as stating company goals, outlining sales and marketing strategies, or determining financial needs.

   c. How did the entrepreneur finance the new business?

   d. Did you find any information that might suggest that this entrepreneur possesses any of the eight characteristics of successful entrepreneurs?

i. Vision	v. Tolerance for failure
ii. High energy level	vi. Creativity
iii. Need to achieve	vii. Tolerance for ambiguity
iv. Self-confidence and optimism	viii. Internal locus of control

➤ Nothing but Net

1. **Entrepreneurship education.** Many colleges and universities have begun programs in entrepreneurship education. Recently, a comprehensive study examined the value of these programs. Information on the study can be found at the following Web sites. Review the

findings of the study and prepare a brief report summarizing its key findings.

www.bpa.arizona.edu/programs/berger

www.emkf.org

2. **Venture capital.** As noted in this chapter, venture capital is a major source of funding for start-up companies. The following Web site contains information on venture capital, including the criteria used by venture capitalists when making funding decisions and sources of venture capital. Visit the site and click on the section titled "Ask the Experts." Prepare an oral report to your class on the four guidelines for raising capital.

www.vcapital.com

3. **Starting a business.** Starting your own business requires certain personal skills and abilities. Visit the following Web site and take the test that measures how ready a person is to start his or her own business. Based on the results, do you think you're ready to start a business? Why or why not?

http://score.smalloffice.com/readiness_tests.shtml

Note: Internet Web addresses change frequently. If you do not find the exact sites listed, you may need to access the organization's or company's home page and search from there.

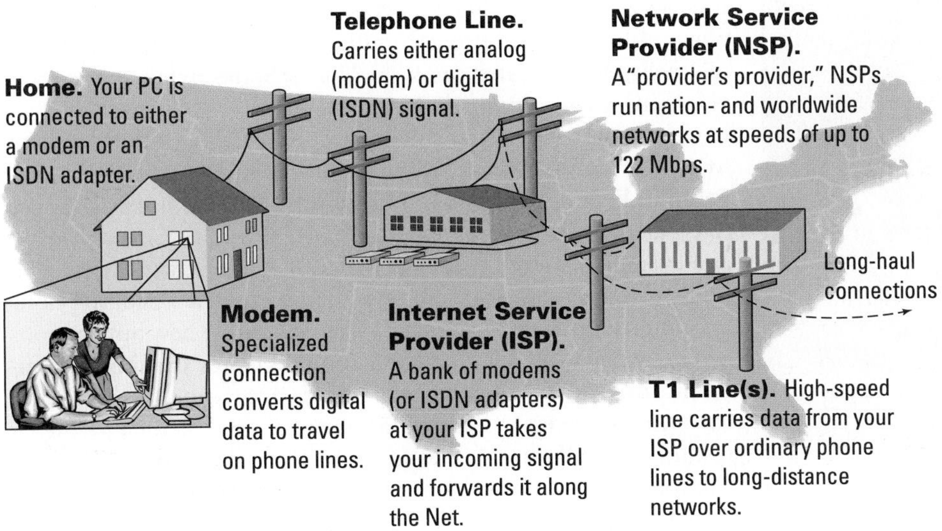

FIGURE 7.1
How Information Travels on the Internet

Home. Your PC is connected to either a modem or an ISDN adapter.

Telephone Line. Carries either analog (modem) or digital (ISDN) signal.

Network Service Provider (NSP). A "provider's provider," NSPs run nation- and worldwide networks at speeds of up to 122 Mbps.

Modem. Specialized connection converts digital data to travel on phone lines.

Internet Service Provider (ISP). A bank of modems (or ISDN adapters) at your ISP takes your incoming signal and forwards it along the Net.

Long-haul connections

T1 Line(s). High-speed line carries data from your ISP over ordinary phone lines to long-distance networks.

In addition, many types of companies are selling the hardware and software required for Internet use as well as providing support services. Telecommunications companies provide local and long-distance network transmission lines, and computer and electronics manufacturers supply resources that help to complete the Internet's infrastructure. Software developers create programs for a host of Internet applications such as multimedia transmissions and Web page design. Entertainment and media companies develop the content that Web surfers see, and service businesses offer Web site design and specialized software for electronic commerce. U.S. businesses spend an estimated $120 billion annually to develop or improve their presence on the Internet.[4] Also, many companies sell advertising on their Web pages to generate revenue.

How the Internet Works

The Internet is a remarkable system of cooperating networks. In seconds, you can send e-mail from Montana to Hong Kong, search the archives of European newspapers, plan your next vacation, gather product information, or buy a best-selling novel.

To understand how this complex system of networks operates, follow the journey of an e-mail message that you send to a friend in a different state. In the example shown in Figure 7.1, your message begins its Internet journey at your personal computer (PC), from which it travels through phone lines; modems convert digital data into analog form compatible with the phone lines. The data arrives at the modems of your **Internet service provider (ISP)**, an organization that provides access to the Internet through its own series of local networks. Thousands of ISPs offer local Internet access to North American cybernauts.

This process is similar but faster if your friend has newer broadband technology, such as a **digital subscriber line (DSL)**, a cable modem, or a satellite link to the Internet. With DSL, data travel over standard telephone lines between computers and telephone switching stations, but a DSL router or modem makes the data move at higher frequencies and much faster speeds. This technology permits voice and DSL transmissions to be transmitted simultaneously over the same phone line, and the Internet connection is continuous, so the user does not have to dial up for

BUSINESS DIRECTORY

➤ **Internet (or Net)** worldwide network of interconnected computers that lets anyone with access to a personal computer send and receive images and data anywhere.

➤ **World Wide Web (Web)** collection of resources on the Internet that offers easy access to text, graphics, sound, and other multimedia resources.

➤ **Web site** integrated document composed of electronic pages that integrate text, graphics, audio, and video elements, as well as hypertext links to other documents.

➤ **Internet service provider (ISP)** organization that provides access to the Internet, usually via the public telephone network.

THE BATMOBILE IS JET-POWERED. BULLETPROOF. FIREPROOF. AND REACHES SPEEDS OVER 300 MPH. COULD WE POSSIBLY IMPROVE ON IT?

YES.

NOW THE VEHICLE THAT HAS EVERYTHING HAS ONSTAR! IF BATMAN'S AIR BAG DEPLOYS, WE'LL RECEIVE A SIGNAL AND CHECK ON HIM. IF A VILLAIN STEALS THE BATMOBILE, WE'LL TRACK IT RIGHT AWAY AND NOTIFY THE POLICE. WE CAN EVEN SEND REMOTE SIGNALS TO UNLOCK HIS DOORS OR DIAGNOSE HIS ENGINE WHILE HE'S DRIVING. YOU CAN'T GET YOUR OWN BATMOBILE. BUT YOU CAN GET ONSTAR ON YOUR NEXT VEHICLE. TO FIND OUT HOW, CALL 1-888-ONSTAR-7 OR VISIT WWW.ONSTAR.COM.

OnStar
HOW CAN WE HELP YOU?

BATMAN AND ALL RELATED CHARACTERS, NAMES AND INDICIA ARE TRADEMARKS OF DC COMICS ©2000. ©2000 ONSTAR CORP. ALL RIGHTS RESERVED.

Using wireless technology, the OnStar vehicle communications system lets OnStar know if an air bag deploys or the vehicle is stolen. It can even send remote signals to unlock the car doors or diagnose an engine problem while the car is being driven.

Internet service. A cable connection uses the same line that supplies cable television programming. Satellite hookups have been relatively slow to catch on in the United States, where phone service is inexpensive and reliable. However, users in other countries have been faster to adopt satellite technology, which allows them to connect to the Internet from a cellular phone as well as a computer. In Finland, more than two-thirds of people use cell phones to connect to the Internet and look up information, send e-mail, and even make purchases.[5] But wireless technology is catching on in the U.S., as it offers faster downloading than a standard phone hookup can deliver. Wireless capabilities enable new applications of the Internet, such as General Motors' OnStar dashboard communications system, which lets drivers access the Internet from their cars. Drivers with OnStar can use the Internet to find a restaurant, make reservations, get driving directions, and even call for help if they have a flat tire along the way.[6]

What happens when the message reaches the recipient's ISP network? The answer to this question requires a basic understanding of client/server systems. The message you sent is stored with the ISP's **server,** a larger, special computer that holds information and then provides it to clients on request. A **client** is another computer or device that relies on the resources of one or more servers for help with its own processing. Traditionally, clients have been desktop PCs, but Internet users are increasingly connecting from various other devices, including laptop and palmtop computers, televisions, and cell phones. Servers efficiently distribute resources to a network of client computers as needed. When your friend wants to check his or her e-mail, the message travels back through phone, DSL, or cable lines or via wireless transmission to his or her modem.

The ISP functions as the intermediary for its customers. Monthly or hourly user fees cover the cost of equipment such as ISP modems, servers, related software, proprietary and leased networks, and in some cases original content. Some ISPs offer free services to consumers, but the trade-off for users is being forced to view large amounts of advertising posted on the site. Although many of them consider this barrage of ads more annoying than paying monthly subscription fees, the number of users of free ISP services continues to grow.

Who's on the Net?

Although the Internet was born in the United States, its users now live on every continent. At the beginning of the 21st century, 43 percent of Internet users were in the U.S., but the share of users from other countries is growing. By 2006, about three-quarters of the Internet user population will live outside the U.S.[7] As Figure 7.2 shows, of the world's 375 million Internet users, the four nations with the largest concentrations of Net users are located on three different continents: North America (United States), Asia (Japan), and Western Europe (Germany and the United Kingdom). South America, the fourth continent represented among the top ten, lists Brazil as the nation with the largest concentration located south of the equator.

Recent studies of U.S. Internet users reveal some major trends toward an increasingly diverse Net population:

- Although the Internet was once dominated by men, the gender gap has narrowed. Women now represent more than half of Internet users in the United States and a sizable share in other nations—more than a third in the United Kingdom and Germany and four in ten in Sweden.[8] Women were estimated to be 45 percent of the Internet's global population in 2001.[9]

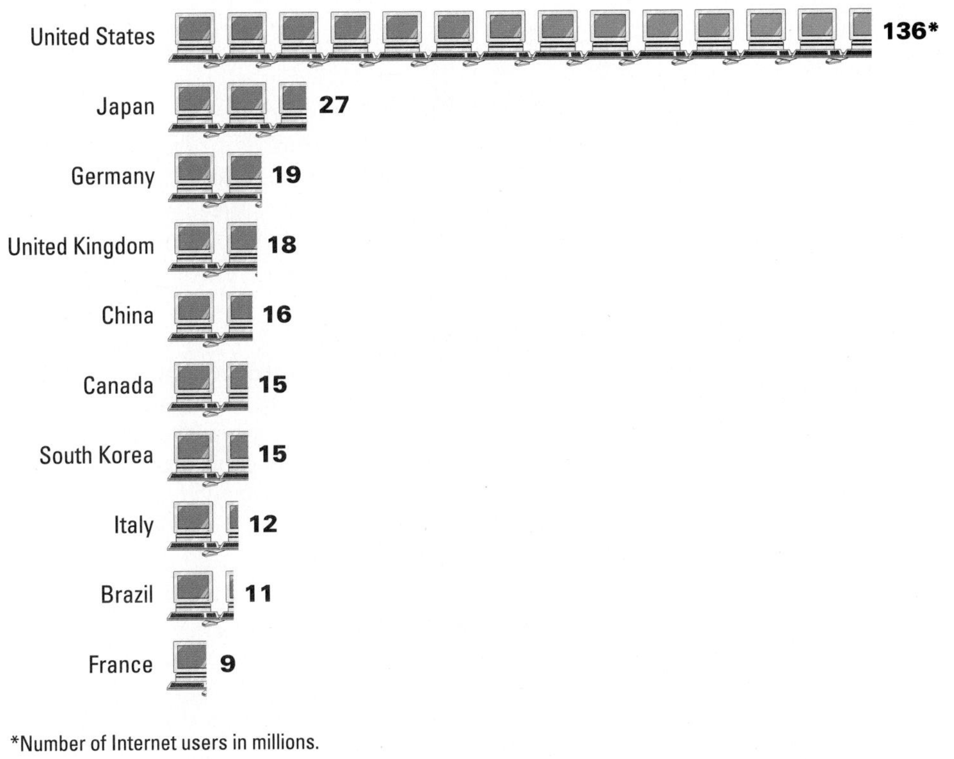

United States ▫▫▫▫▫▫▫▫▫▫▫▫▫▫▫ **136***

Japan ▫▫▫ **27**

Germany ▫▫ **19**

United Kingdom ▫▫ **18**

China ▫▫ **16**

Canada ▫▫ **15**

South Korea ▫▫ **15**

Italy ▫▫ **12**

Brazil ▫▫ **11**

France ▫ **9**

FIGURE 7.2
Top Ten Internet Users

*Number of Internet users in millions.

- The earliest users of the Internet were disproportionately white and Asian American, but black and Hispanic Americans are now obtaining Internet access at a faster rate.[10]
- The average age of users is rising. The fastest-growing share of the Internet population is adults 45 years of age and older, and this age group spends more time on the Internet than 18- to 24-year-olds.[11]
- Net users tend to be more affluent and to attain higher levels of education than the general population.[12]
- Time spent online is rising, taking away from television and newspapers, as well as time spent in stores and with family and friends.[13]

Just as the population of individuals using the Internet is becoming more like the overall population, so is the mix of businesses on the Internet. A Web site once set a company apart as "high-tech," but most large businesses have by now established an Internet presence. Today, two of every five U.S. small businesses have Web sites, and more than two-thirds of them are connected to the Internet. Small businesses owned by women and minorities use the Net most often.[14]

Using the Net's Four Functions

What do these "Netizens" do online? As Figure 7.3 shows, one or more of four primary functions are performed on the Web: communication, information gathering and sharing, entertainment, and business transactions (e-commerce).

Communication   Most people go online to communicate. For both households and businesses, the most popular application of the Internet in the U.S. is e-mail. In fact, e-mails now outnumber regular mail by ten to one. Its popularity is easy to understand: e-mail is simple to use, travels quickly, and can be read at the receiver's convenience. Also, longer documents can be sent as attachments to e-mail messages.

FIGURE 7.3
Four Functions of the Internet

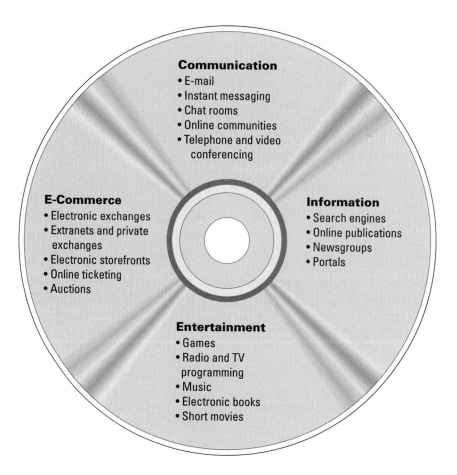

Communication
- E-mail
- Instant messaging
- Chat rooms
- Online communities
- Telephone and video conferencing

E-Commerce
- Electronic exchanges
- Extranets and private exchanges
- Electronic storefronts
- Online ticketing
- Auctions

Information
- Search engines
- Online publications
- Newsgroups
- Portals

Entertainment
- Games
- Radio and TV programming
- Music
- Electronic books
- Short movies

A more recent adaptation of e-mail is **instant messaging.** With this application, when someone sends a message, it is immediately displayed on the recipient's computer screen. As sender and recipient reply to one another, they can communicate in real time.

Another popular way to communicate online is through chat rooms. Chat rooms provide a forum in which a group of people can share messages. When someone sends a message, it is displayed for all to see. Users join chat sessions on topics that interest them. The resulting **online communities** are not only personally satisfying but an important force for businesses. Some companies participate in or even sponsor such communication. Playing Mantis has built a successful business manufacturing and selling car models and action figures from the 1960s. If you have older relatives who long for a model Corvette Stingray or The Phantom or Green Hornet action figures, you can send them to Playing Mantis to satisfy that need. In addition to manufacturing the toys, the company generates interest in them by participating in online chat rooms. Customer service manager Lisa Greco routinely participates in these discussions. In the mid-1990s, when online communication was still new, a Web site called Hobbytalk began sponsoring a bulletin board for collectors of Playing Mantis's line of Polar Lights models, later adding boards for other product lines. Greco routinely logs on to answer questions and announce new products. Over the years, regular visitors to the site have developed a sense of belonging to it—and a passion for Playing Mantis and its products. When Playing Mantis modernized its Web site, the launch was a mess, but high-tech members of this unofficial community patiently surfed the site and posted recommended fixes. Within days, the company got the site running properly. Greco and the other managers of Playing Mantis are convinced that this type of communication gives them an unbeatable edge—customers who feel like part of the company.[15]

Voice technology is now coming to the Web, and video-conferencing won't be far behind. Internet telephony allows users to use their computers to dial up and speak to friends and business associates alike. Voice messages are divided into segments called *packets*, which move over the transmission lines and are reassembled at the receiving end. Although the voice quality is currently not as good as regular telephone service and some packets can arrive out of sequence, the quality and reliability will improve in the future.

Businesses also use the Internet to communicate promotional messages. Marketers use the Web to build brand relationships and offer goods and services via e-mail, advertisements, sweepstakes, and more. Use of the Internet as a tool for marketing communications is discussed in Chapter 16.

Information   In a recent consumer survey, 82 percent of Web users said getting information was one of the reasons they use the Internet.[16] Internet users meet their need for information at commercial sites such as AskJeeves and Northern Light, which search for information on topics entered by the user. Or they may visit online publications such as the *Chicago Tribune*'s and *The Wall Street Journal*'s online editions. Government sites provide a wealth of free data in the public domain. **Newsgroups** provide a forum for participants to share information on selected topics. Another fast-growing area of the Internet consists of sites providing online educational services. John Chambers, chief executive officer (CEO) of Cisco Systems, recently wrote in a *New York Times* editorial, "Education over the Internet is going to be so big, it's going to make E-mail usage look like a rounding error." One-third of U.S. colleges now offer some sort of accredited degree online, and private investment in education-related Internet companies more than doubled every year throughout most of the 1990s. These companies include publishers, schools, and corporate training services.[17]

With such an enormous variety of possibilities, some of the most popular Web sites are **portals**, sites designed to be a user's starting place when entering the World Wide Web. The most widely visited Web sites are Yahoo! (www.yahoo.com), America Online (www.aol.com), and Microsoft Network (www.msn.com).[18] All of these sites serve as portals, offering links to search engines, weather reports, news, yellow pages, maps, and other popular types of information, as well as e-mail, chat rooms, and the ability to bookmark favorite sites in order to click to them directly in the future.

Many sites specialize in particular types of information. For example, Travelocity, Expedia, Lowest Fare, and a number of other sites search for airline flights that meet the user's criteria for date, city, and price. Visitors to the UPS Web site (www.ups.com) can check the delivery status of their packages. Other sites offer product reviews, maps and driving directions, stock prices, sports coverage, and much, much more.

Businesses turn to the Web to gather information about their rivals and to assess industry trends. Executives can visit competitors' Web sites to learn about new-product announcements and check financial reports. They can read trade and business publications online and visit the Web sites of their professional organizations. Business-oriented Web portals offer links useful to businesspeople. The CEO Express Web site offers links to business publications, industry statistics, travel services, search engines, and other sites that can help with a manager's work. Other companies, including

Jeeves.
Diligently serving
Louise since 1998.

Introducing Jeeves, the world's first Internet butler.

Just type a question in your own words and Jeeves promptly finds the answer.
How many calories am I burning? Where can I stay in Paris? How do I fix a flat tire?
Jeeves is asked millions of questions every day. What's yours?

Wanna know?   **Ask Jeeves**   Ask.com

The commercial Web site AskJeeves helps humanize online searches. Using the site is as simple as typing in a question you want answered. Want to know where to find the lyrics to your favorite song? Just type your question in at ASK.com and Mr. Jeeves will answer in a matter of seconds.

FIGURE 7.4
Web Page Sweepstakes Designed to Generate Customer Data

Yahoo!, Viador, and Microsoft, set up portals tailored to the individual needs of their business customers. These corporate portals combine a company's data with information from the Internet.

Companies can also use the interactive technology of the Internet to gather information about their customers. For example, some sites ask visitors for personal information through registration or sweepstakes entry forms. Figure 7.4 shows a sweepstakes site run by fastfreefun.com. To enter, visitors to this site provide their name, e-mail address, and other information. Sites that accept online orders gather the user-provided data, such as shipping addresses, along with purchase data. Even sites that do not ask for data can track the usage patterns of visitors to the site. With each type of data, marketers can adapt content, services, and advertising to their typical Web site users.

As an information source, the Internet is only as reliable as the individuals and companies who provide the information published there. Articles posted on Encyclopedia Britannica's Web site are likely to be more objective than Web sites put up by individuals to promote a particular viewpoint. Likewise, the ease of sending e-mail messages has markedly increased the speed with which people disseminate so-called urban legends, such as the story that the AIDS virus was on needles in gasoline pumps or flesh-eating viruses were found on banana peels. Because of the spread of misinformation, some practical cautions are essential for Web information gatherers:

- Know your source. Whenever you read information on the Web, make sure you have identified the provider of the information. Is it a reputable publication or news service, a known expert, or an organization or person with a position to promote? Recently, there has been a rash of attempts to manipulate stock prices by posting misinformation on investment sites. The rumor spreaders then try to cash in on the wild swings in stock prices—and they hurt other investors in the process.[19] The moral? Check the accuracy of information on the Web before acting on it.

- Investigate information by checking more than one source. The old saying "If it sounds too good to be true, it probably is" applies to the Internet just as it does in the rest of the world.

- Don't believe all the e-mail announcements forwarded to you, especially messages that urge you to "forward this to 20 friends." Check out the story at one of the Web sites that specialize in squelching false rumors and urban legends. These include the U.S. Department of Energy's Computer Incident Advisory Capability (CIAC), at ciac.llnl.gov, and About.com's Web pages titled "Virus Hoaxes" and "Urban Legends and Folklore." These sites are not only informative, but highly entertaining.

Entertainment Besides reading urban legends, Internet users are finding other entertainment online, including everything from concert Webcasts to online gaming. Some Internet users even participate in more than one form of entertainment at once. A study of children using the Internet found that 86 percent of teenage girls who go

With the Click of a Shutter, Camera World Becomes cameraworld.com

Background. Nearly 25 years ago, Korean-born businessman Jack Shin founded Camera World, a small retail shop for amateur photo buffs in downtown Portland, Oregon. When the business got going, he added a mail-order component that dovetailed easily with his retail operation. Shin assembled a simple order fulfillment and shipping infrastructure that was so efficient the company still uses it today, although the system was computerized in 1992.

From the beginning, Shin stuck to a few crucial principles. First, he refused to deal in "gray market" merchandise—goods not meant to be sold in the United States—which is so prevalent in the camera business. Instead, he developed solid relationships with executives from Fuji, Canon, Nikon, and others. Those relationships remain intact today. Second, he established the goal that mail-order customers would receive their merchandise within five days of ordering—no matter what. He also made returns simple and convenient. Third, he staffed the phones with a sales force made up of professional and qualified amateur photographers who could answer customer questions. As a result, Camera World developed a loyal following among camera manufacturers and consumers. "We make customers very happy, and they remember we give service, service, service. Repeat customers [are a] big part of our business," emphasizes Shin. Within a decade, Camera World was doing 70 percent of its business by mail order.

What Happened? Then markets and the world itself began to change, and Shin decided to sell out, with the help of Walt Mulvey, a retail-management expert who helped Shin ready the company for sale. Swedish-born businessman Alessandro Mina was looking for an opportunity and liked what he saw. "We saw this terrific sleeper and thought we could turn it into a full-fledged Net business," says Mina.

The Response. Mina and Mulvey took Camera World online. But they didn't take any shortcuts. "We made it a point to visit every supplier personally, take them out to dinner, and assure them that the business would continue," explains Mina. The suppliers went along. "At first we had some doubts about their ability to take over the business and move it to the Net, but they were able to build on the infrastructure to handle it," admits Eliott Peck, director and general manager for the camera division of Canon USA.

Today and Counting. In a 20,000-square-foot warehouse, workers scurry back and forth with order printouts and shipping boxes, filling orders in much the same way they always have. During the recent holiday shopping season, when many online companies failed to get their goods to customers, cameraworld.com fielded roughly 25,000 site visits a day, sold cameras at $600 apiece, and shipped 90 percent of its Internet orders within 24 hours. "We maintained heavy inventories to ship on time, and it all worked pretty well," says the company's new chief executive officer, Terry Strom. "But one thing's for sure: The Internet is raising the standard of performance for any retailer."

Recently updated, cameraworld.com's site is easy to use for both consumers and businesses. Cameraworld.com handles new and established commercial accounts as well as government accounts, in addition to all those shutterbugs who just want to take pictures of their vacations, family holidays, and pets. All customers get the same personalized treatment, which is why they keep coming back. Manufacturers remain loyal as well. On a scale of 1 to 10 among dealers, "I've always given them a 10," says Elliot Peck of Canon.

QUESTIONS FOR CRITICAL THINKING

1. Cameraworld.com has successfully used the Web to conduct transactions. What other ways might the company use the Internet to further strengthen its relationship with customers and suppliers?
2. Visit www.cameraworld.com and compare it with other sites you have visited. Is the site designed well? What are its strong points? If you detect any weak points, what improvements would you suggest?
3. Cameraworld.com is successful because of the strong infrastructure and relationship with suppliers and customers that it built before going online. Can you think of any other reasons why the company maintains success at e-commerce?

Sources: Company Web site, **www.cameraworld.com**, accessed February 6, 2001; Bronwyn Fryer, "When Something Clicks," *Inc. Technology* no 1, 2000, p. 62.; Robert Goldfield and Andy Giegerich, "Corillian, camerworld.com: Two Different Paths," *The Business Journal of Portland*, February 7, 2000, **www.bizjournals.com/portland**.

online listen to the radio at the same time. Other Web surfers manage to watch television while they are online. These mixed-media users, whom marketers call *telewebbers*, number an estimated 44 million in the U.S.[20]

Online providers of entertainment can offer competitive prices, speed, and boundless services. Games, radio programming, short movies, and music clips are available online, sometimes for free, with the costs borne by advertising on the Web site. And after decades of predictions that we will someday do most of our reading on computer screens, the technology finally seems to be in place. Products like the Rocket eBook allow users to download a book's contents from the Internet and read it on a handheld device that simulates a book. In 2000, Stephen King's novel *Riding the Bullet* became the first mass-market book published exclusively in electronic format. In the first day of the book's release, 400,000 copies were downloaded—or at least ordered, since the huge demand caused backups at booksellers' Web sites. That traffic may have indicated pent-up demand for high-tech publishing or perhaps the fact that the book was free on the first day it was offered.[21] Other titles have been published both in paper and electronically, including Mario Puzo's *Omerta* and Arthur Golden's *Memoirs of a Geisha*.

The availability of free content poses some ethical and business challenges, discussed later in the chapter. However, those issues are unlikely to chase entertainment off the Internet.

Business Transactions: E-Commerce   A newer application of Web technology, electronic business transactions, are growing at lightning speed. Customers can not only learn about companies and their products on the Internet but complete purchases. As discussed in Chapters 13 and 15, this gives the Web a key role in businesses' sales and distribution strategies. Organizations from multinational corporations to individual entrepreneurs have established a Web presence or have begun planning one. Today customers can go online to buy everything from toys and books to cars and business equipment. As growing numbers of companies sell their products on the Web, business success requires understanding the Web's advantages and its limitations and incorporating its use into a firm's overall business plans and strategies. The owners of Camera World built on its solid reputation when they took the business online, as the "Clicks and Mortar" box described.

A Web presence builds awareness of a company's products and brands, provides the means for one-on-one communication with customers, and can allow customers to place orders from anywhere in the world, at any time of day. At Ticketmaster's Web site, customers can purchase tickets to the upcoming Fiona Apple concert, printing them out on their own printer. They can also look up local entertainment listings and even sign up for an online dating service to find someone to invite to the concert.[22] These activities are the substance of *electronic commerce*, called *e-commerce* for short.

THE SCOPE OF ELECTRONIC COMMERCE

When a Silicon Valley giant like Oracle needs office furniture, its people naturally look online. They head for the Web site of a furniture company called CRI. By entering a password, they can view pages tailored to their purchase history, where they can see specifications, prices, and order forms. Not only does the site let customers place orders, but it allows them to plan office layouts by viewing, revising, and commenting on drawings. In addition, CRI plans to offer customers access to information about the status of their current orders and ways the company has resolved any past problems with their orders. So, the Web not only enables CRI and its customers to complete transactions, it also provides speedy, effective customer service.[23]

Like CRI and Oracle, companies around the world are discovering the advantages of **electronic commerce (e-commerce)**, marketing goods and services over the Internet by exchanging information between buyers and sellers, while in the process minimizing paperwork and simplifying payment procedures. As with other types of buyer–seller interaction, e-commerce involves a chain of events for customer and seller. It starts with product information; moves through the order, invoicing, and payment processes; and ends with customer service.

The first wave of e-commerce brought techniques such as charge-card approval systems, point-of-sale terminals, scanners, and even early Internet selling—all activities focused mainly on lowering sellers' costs. As more firms discover the benefits of e-commerce, and as the Internet offers progressively more affordable services for almost any business, power begins to shift toward buyers, who gain access to a wider range of vendors.

A number of innovations promote both business-to-business and business-to-consumer e-commerce. One is encryption systems, which enable users to gather credit card numbers and other personal data required for completing transactions while protecting the security of purchasers. Another is the growing use of broadband technologies, which enable users to download more data at much faster speeds. Broadband makes technologies such as video and audio streaming more enjoyable and thus more attractive to users. With such developments, the number of businesses participating in e-commerce is growing fast. More than half of U.S. companies today have sold products online, twice the number making such sales just four years ago.[24]

The growth of e-commerce has attracted an army of specialized software firms and other service suppliers that provide expertise for firms taking their first steps into this competitive arena. As Figure 7.5 describes, global computer giant IBM offers its business customers both software and services designed to build virtual stores that go far beyond traditional Web sites. Although IBM originally was known as a producer of mainframe computers, it now generates one-fourth of its revenue from sales related to e-commerce—75 percent of that from software, services, and related technology. The company has a huge staff of consultants working on jobs ranging from designing Web sites to converting huge databases from "legacy" (old mainframe) systems to Internet systems. IBM will even run e-commerce systems for companies that want to outsource this activity. The company also sells its own personal computers online and offers answers to technical questions on its Web site. It even trains employees over the Internet as well as in classrooms. As a result, IBM's Internet presence is both generating sales and slashing costs.[25]

FIGURE 7.5
IBM's Key Role in Electronic Commerce

Profiting from E-Commerce

Much of the hype about e-commerce centers on sales of goods and services over the World Wide Web, but online product sales represent only one of several ways to generate revenue online. For example, two e-commerce businesses called Ezgov.com and GovWorks.com are partnering with governments to set up Web sites at which citizens can interact with government agencies to register cars, pay taxes, look for government jobs, and participate in government auctions, among other activities. The companies generate revenues by charging users a fee for each transaction and selling advertising space on their sites.[26]

So far, however, only a minority of companies report profits from their Web sites. Of sites catering to business customers, 27 percent were reported to be profitable in their first year. In contrast, among the sites that have survived at least three years, 42 percent claim to be profitable.[27] Profitability among online retailers—companies selling to consumers rather than business customers—is most common among those that already had off-line customers, including catalog retailers like Lands' End and Hanover Direct, whose catalogs include Gump's, the Company Store, and International Male. Such businesses have an advantage because consumers are more familiar with them and are reminded of the Web sites every time they look at the companies' catalogs.[28]

As Figure 7.6 shows, the business potential of e-commerce involves more than sales transactions.

THEY SAID IT

"Within five years, the term 'Internet Company' won't mean anything, because everyone will be an Internet company. The Internet becomes a fundamental part of your business."

KIM POLESE (B.1962)
FOUNDER, MARIMBA, INC.

BUSINESS DIRECTORY

➤ **electronic commerce (e-commerce)** *process for online marketing of goods and services—including product information; ordering, invoicing, and payment processes; and customer service.*

FIGURE 7.6
Benefits of E-commerce

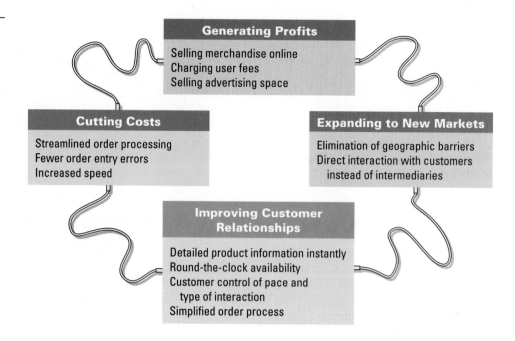

Companies also establish an Internet presence to expand beyond their geographic boundaries to reach new markets, cut costs, and improve customer relationships. Putting massive industrial catalogs on the Web, for example, saves publishing and postage costs. With a few keystrokes, customers can send orders and service requests directly from their computers to the seller's computer—cutting the need for inbound telemarketing personnel and other customer service representatives.

The two main types of e-commerce are transactions between businesses and transactions between businesses and customers. Both are offering new opportunities, but business-to-business e-commerce is taking the lead. Business-to-business transactions are fueling the growth of e-commerce and forging new relationships along the way.

Business-to-Business Transactions Lead the Way

One of the oldest applications of technology to business transactions is **electronic data interchange (EDI)**, computer-to-computer exchanges of invoices, purchase orders, price quotations, and other business documents between buyers and sellers. EDI requires compatible hardware and software systems to exchange data over a network. Use of EDI cuts paper flow, speeds the order cycle, and reduces errors. In addition, by receiving daily inventory status reports from vendors, companies can set production schedules to match demand.

Wal-Mart was one of the first major corporations to adopt EDI in the early 1990s. In fact, the retailer refused to do business with distributors and manufacturers that did not use compatible EDI standards. EDI is one of the major reasons Wal-Mart was able to operate with the efficiency that made it a market leader. It can buy just the products its customers want, just when it needs to restock its shelves, a system known as *quick response.*

From those early efforts to computerize business transactions, companies have taken the next technological leap—to the Internet—and are reaping rewards for doing so. **Business-to-business e-commerce,** known as **B2B,** is the use of the Internet for business transactions between organizations. One-fourth of all B2B transactions are expected to take place on the Internet in 2003, amounting to $2.8 trillion. This penetration of e-commerce is predicted to increase to more than 40 percent of B2B sales by 2005.[29] Those sales are spread out across many businesses. The number of U.S. businesses engaged in B2B e-commerce is expected to grow from 30 percent to more than 90 percent in one year.[30] Cisco Systems, Intel, and IBM are among the companies that generate billions of dollars in revenues online each year.

In addition to generating revenues from product sales, B2B e-commerce also provides detailed product descriptions whenever they are needed and slashes order-processing expenses. Business-to-business transactions, which typically involve more steps than consumer purchases, can be much more efficient on the Internet. Orders placed over the Internet typically contain fewer errors than handwritten ones, and when mistakes occur, the technology can quickly locate them. So, the Internet is an attractive option for business buying and selling. In some industries, relying on the Internet to make purchases can reduce costs by one-eighth.[31]

Initially, companies used their own Web sites to conduct isolated B2B transactions. Now the types of transactions and sites have become more varied. The principal forms of B2B e-commerce include electronic exchanges, extranets, and private exchanges.

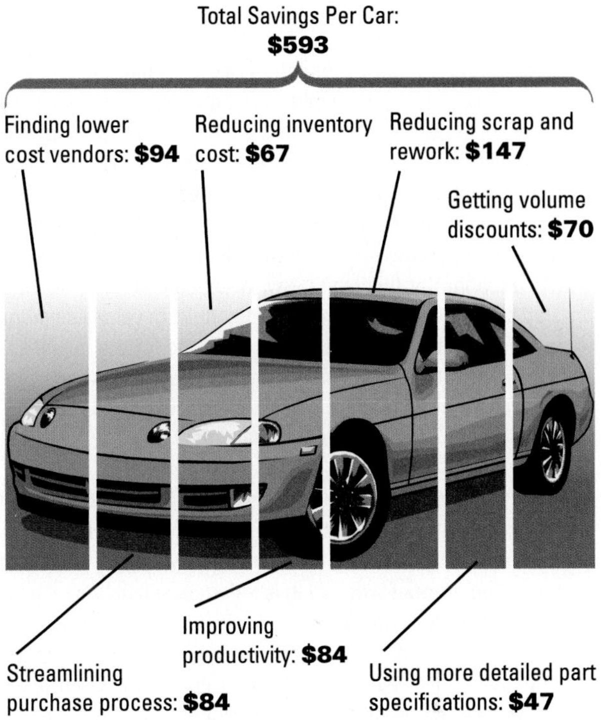
Total Savings Per Car:
$593
Finding lower cost vendors: **$94**
Reducing inventory cost: **$67**
Reducing scrap and rework: **$147**
Getting volume discounts: **$70**
Streamlining purchase process: **$84**
Improving productivity: **$84**
Using more detailed part specifications: **$47**

FIGURE 7.7
How Online Parts Exchanges Save Money for Automakers

Electronic Exchanges The earliest B2B e-commerce usually consisted of a company setting up a Web site and offering products to any buyer willing to make online purchases. More recently, businesses are buying and selling through **electronic exchanges**, Web-based marketplaces that cater to a specific industry's needs. General Motors, Ford, DaimlerChrysler, Renault, and Nissan are jointly investing in the start-up of an online parts exchange, called Covisint. Their plan, expanding on each company's earlier individual effort, is to create a global system through which each automaker can order all its parts and supplies. The contractors and subcontractors who participate can also buy from one another. The automakers hope that by posting planned design changes and actual production data on the system, they will encourage more efficient operations—for themselves and their suppliers. As Figure 7.7 shows, such savings can ultimately reduce the cost of a car by hundreds of dollars. The automakers also hope the system will bring auto manufacturers closer to building cars to meet individual orders, rather than trying to anticipate demand.[32] The "Clicks and Mortar" box explores another industry that has benefited from an electronic exchange, this time in the form of an auction.

The steel industry has also seen the advantages of electronic exchanges. At two Web sites, MetalSite.com and e-Steel.com, steel companies post data about product selection, availability, and prices. Steel buyers can visit the sites to look for the best deal and place orders. Steel makers benefit because they can find buyers for the excess inventory, and the buyers can find greater selection and better prices than they usually did when shopping by placing one phone call after another. LTV Corp., a U.S. steel-making giant, has used the Web site to unload tons of inventory, making the company more competitive with its foreign rivals. Francis P. Mangano, an LTV manager, says that without MetalSite, "we would have been selling roughly half of what we are selling now."[33]

Another example is the retail industry, which has set up the WorldWide Retail Exchange, in which nearly a dozen retailers, including Kmart, Safeway, and Britain's Marks & Spencer, conduct transactions with their suppliers. As with the automakers and steel industry, the retailers expect the exchange to help them reduce their overall cost of purchasing supplies and inventory and operate more efficiently. A notable holdout among exchange participants is Wal-Mart, the world's largest retailer. The firm's management believes that its participation in such a venture is more likely to benefit its competitors than to help Wal-Mart.[34]

BUSINESS DIRECTORY

➤ **business-to-business (B2B) e-commerce** *electronic business transactions between organizations using the Internet.*

FreeMarkets Brings the Gavel Down on Prices

Background. Picture a bunch of ordinary purchasers scattered around the country, hunched over their computers, linked to each other and to a home base via the Internet. At home base, which looks like the control room of the Starship Enterprise, more computers hum and whir while a huge video screen displays rapidly changing prices. Look more closely, and you'll see that the prices are actually falling. You've already figured out that this is an Internet auction. But this isn't eBay, where the prices rise as buyers slap bids on everything from antique dolls to yard-sale mugs. This is FreeMarkets, where suppliers compete for the business of organizational buyers who might be purchasing anything from gears to printed circuit boards used in manufacturing their goods. FreeMarkets was founder Glen Meakem's idea.

What Happened? While working at General Electric, Meakem proposed that the company set up a system whereby suppliers would compete for General Electric's orders in live, open, electronic auctions. The Internet was still in its infancy, and servers were yet to appear. Yet Meakem was so enthusiastic that he exclaimed, "This idea will transform the global economy!" General Electric declined to become involved. Although GE is now considered one of the most-admired corporations, it was slow to adopt Internet technology; in 1994, when Meakem made his proposal, it was considered a nonissue.

The Response. Meakem decided to strike out on his own, founding FreeMarkets. Meakem understood that manufacturers spend roughly one-third of every dollar in sales on parts; about $5 trillion a year globally goes toward the purchase of industrial parts. In addition, the purchase process is usually inefficient, involving huge amounts of time and paperwork. Meakem decided to cut through the red tape. He developed a system whereby suppliers promise to deliver parts on a standardized schedule, with identical payment terms and inventory arrangements. The only variable is price. FreeMarkets consults with buyers and screens suppliers

so that, by the time an auction takes place, each is familiar with the process and has the most information possible about issues such as quality ratings and manufacturing processes. The online auction itself takes less than half an hour. The price starts high and moves downward. On their own computer screens, sellers can see exactly how much their competitors have bid and how low they must drop to make the sale.

Today and Counting. So far, buyers and sellers love the system, and FreeMarkets claims a market cap of $7 billion. Giants like General Motors, United Technologies, Raytheon, Emerson Electric, and Quaker Oats, who thought they already knew how to play the parts-purchasing game, have found themselves saving another 15 percent on parts, materials, and services through FreeMarkets. "This FreeMarkets auction idea is revolutionizing procurement as we know it," says Kent Brittan, vice president of supply management of United Technologies. In fact, General Motors loves the system so much it has set up its own. Meakem isn't thrilled about the move, but it was bound to happen sooner or later. After all, imitation is the sincerest form of flattery.

QUESTIONS FOR CRITICAL THINKING
1. Think of an industry in which you think FreeMarkets might work well. Write a brief memo describing why you think your industry would benefit from online auctions.
2. As competition such as the General Motors program begins to appear, what steps can FreeMarkets take to stay ahead?

Sources: "What We Do," FreeMarkets Web site, **www.freemarkets.com**, accessed February 8, 2001; Larry Seben, "FreeMarkets Revenue Hits New Record," LocalBusiness.com—Pittsburgh, July 25, 2000, **www.localbusiness.com**; Shawn Tully, "The B2B Tool that Really Is Changing the World," *Fortune*, March 20, 2000, pp. 132-140; Geoffrey Colvin, "America's Most Admired Companies," *Fortune*, February 21, 2000, pp. 108-111.

Extranets and Private Exchanges Internet commerce also offers an efficient way for businesses to collaborate with suppliers, partners, and customers through **extranets**, secure networks used for e-commerce and accessible through the firm's Web site by external customers, suppliers, or other authorized users. Extranets go beyond ordering and fulfillment processes by giving selected outsiders access to internal information. As with other forms of e-commerce, extranets provide additional benefits such as enhanced relationships with business partners. Intelsat, which operates global communications satellites, has an extranet called Intelsat Business Network (IBN). The more than 2,300 users of IBN log on from 400 organizations to check the availability of satellite capacity, view satellite maps, download corporate documents, and participate in discussion groups. Users can personalize their IBN account so that it shows information about only the services they use.[35]

Security and access authorization remain critical issues, and most companies create virtual private networks that protect communications traveling over public communications media. These networks control who uses a company's resources and what users can access. Also, they cost considerably less than leasing dedicated lines.

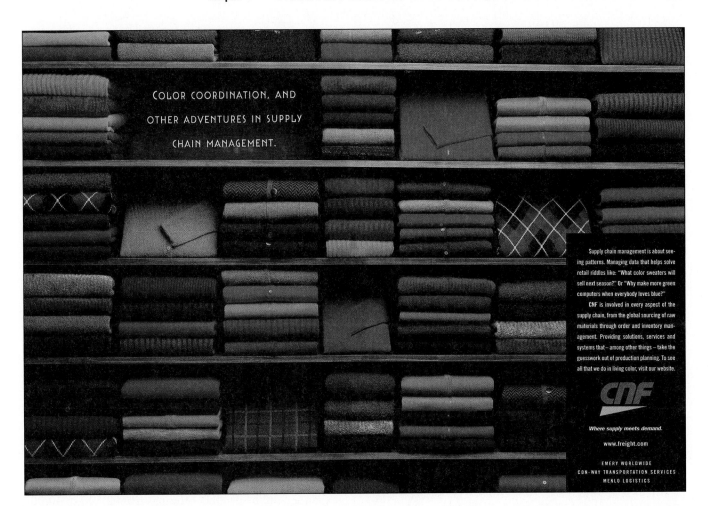

COLOR COORDINATION, AND OTHER ADVENTURES IN SUPPLY CHAIN MANAGEMENT.

Supply chain management is about seeing patterns. Managing data that helps solve retail riddles like: "What color sweaters will sell next season?" Or "Why make more green computers when everybody loves blue?"

CNF is involved in every aspect of the supply chain, from the global sourcing of raw materials through order and inventory management. Providing solutions, services and systems that — among other things — take the guesswork out of production planning. To see all that we do in living color, visit our website.

CNF

Where supply meets demand.

www.freight.com

EMERY WORLDWIDE
CON-WAY TRANSPORTATION SERVICES
MENLO LOGISTICS

FIGURE 7.8
Benefits from Allying with Distribution Partners

The next generation of extranets is the **private exchange,** a secure Web site at which a company and its suppliers share all types of data related to e-commerce, from product design through delivery of orders. A private exchange is more collaborative than a typical extranet, so this type of arrangement has sometimes been called "c-commerce."[36] The participants can use it to collaborate on product ideas, production scheduling, distribution, order tracking, and any other functions a business wants to include. Partners in a private exchange often form strategic alliances, similar to those described in Chapter 4. IBM has been creating a private exchange for its Personal Systems Group to use for product design, procurement, and logistics. The system permits IBM employees to identify qualified suppliers that can provide necessary components. The suppliers, in turn, can look up IBM's sales data and forecasts to manage their own inventory.[37] As Figure 7.8 shows, companies like CNF can participate in an exchange by providing services and data related to distributing goods.

Another variant of extranets is an *intranet,* which provides similar capabilities but limits users to an organization's employees. Intranets are discussed in Chapter 17.

Business-to-Consumer Transactions Gain Ground

One area of e-commerce that has consistently grabbed news headlines and attracted new fans is Internet shopping. Known as **business-to-consumer e-commerce,** or **B2C,** it involves selling directly to consumers over the Internet. Driven by convenience and improved

1. Books
2. CDs, DVDs, videos
3. Computer software
4. Travel-related services
5. Clothing/apparel

FIGURE 7.9
Top Five Products Purchased Online

Expedia.com is one of the successful new generations of B2C online travel services. In addition to offering discount rates, it supplies added value via simple-to-use and secure transactions and travel tips for each destination.

Four-star hotel: $400

Four-star hotel: $225

Introducing Expedia® Special Rates. Through direct negotiations with our hotel partners, we offer you exclusive prices on top quality hotels that beat standard rates by up to 70%. Plus you'll get all the other insights you need so you don't just book a trip, you book the right trip. Book the perfect flight. Reserve the right car. Easy and secure transactions, all at the right price. Backed by our 24-hour customer support.

Don't just travel. Travel Right:

You can also find us under Travel on msn!

security for transmitting credit-card numbers and other financial information, online retail sales, sometimes called *e-tailing*, have surpassed $30 billion and are climbing. Even with these increases, Internet retail sales are still a tiny fraction of the overall retail market. Only seven-tenths of one percent of all retail sales occur online.[38] In some product categories—computers, books, and audio and video recordings—online retailing has reached at least 10 percent of the market.[39] Figure 7.9 lists the top five products purchased online. Other popular online purchases include entertainment services, computer hardware, and specialty gift items.

A wide array of B2C e-commerce products are available. Industries such as investment and banking, online reservations and sales for travel and vacations, traditional retailing, and online auctions offer consumers a staggering array of products with just the click of a mouse. E-commerce has even invaded the staid world of legal services. At the Web site of eLawForum Corp., potential clients can describe their needs for legal work and invite bids from law firms. Assessing a lawyer's credentials and character online is difficult, so the approach might be too risky when the stakes are high. However, the cost-saving potential is attractive for someone looking to handle routine matters. For lawyers, eLawForum offers a way to attract new clients.[40]

Microsoft's Expedia online travel service represents another popular Internet business application. In addition to providing information and booking flights, hotel reservations, and auto rentals, the Web site supplies "insider" tips designed to resemble conversations with travelers who have recently visited the chosen destinations.

E-tailing and Electronic Storefronts Major retailers are staking their claims in cyberspace. Many have set up **electronic storefronts,** Web sites where they offer items for sale to consumers. Wal-Mart received such a positive response to the launch of its electronic storefront that it expanded online product offerings from 2,500 to 40,000 items. Macy's and Bloomingdale's department stores have put their bridal registry, personal shopping, and interior-decorating services online. In a recent month, the top 20 Web retailers, measured in terms of the number of buyers, included such well-known names as Amazon.com, Ticketmaster, Barnes and Noble, Sears, Staples, and JCPenney.[41] Generally, retailers provide an online catalog at which visitors click on items they want to buy. These items are placed in a file called an **electronic shopping cart.** When the shopper indicates that he or she wants to complete the transaction, the items in the electronic shopping cart are listed on the screen, along with the total amount due, so that the customer can review the whole order and make any changes desired before making a payment.

Online retail selling works best for nontechnical products like flowers, books, compact discs, and travel and financial services. Even the sale of somewhat technical items, such as personal computers, has proven enormously successful through the combination of low prices, user-friendly Web sites, and 24-hour customer support offered by firms like Dell Computer and Gateway. In general though, cybershoppers like familiar goods that they can safely purchase without touching or trying out first. Marketing research firm Jupiter Communications predicts that the fastest-growing categories of online sales to consumers will be groceries, housewares, toys and specialty gifts like gourmet food, music, apparel, and videos.[42]

Developing Safe Online Payment Systems In response to consumer concerns about the safety of sending credit card numbers over the Internet, companies have developed secure payment systems for e-commerce. The most common forms of online payment are electronic cash, electronic wallets, and smart cards. Netscape Communications is one of several organizations that encrypt any sensitive information to protect consumers. **Encryption** is the process of encoding data for security purposes. When such a system is active, users see a special icon that indicates that they are at a protected Web site.

To increase consumer security, a group of companies, including Visa, Master-Card, and various technology suppliers, banded together to create Secure Electronic Transaction (SET), an industrywide standard for secure Internet payment transactions. Buyers using SET register with a bank and pay for purchases with **electronic cash** from their accounts using digital certificates that verify their identities. Adopting a standard technology provides consistency among merchants, card companies, software developers, and financial institutions. CyberCash is one company that specializes in providing secure online payment systems by incorporating SET into its encryption system.

An electronic wallet is another online payment method. An **electronic wallet** is a computer data file at an e-commerce site's checkout counter that contains not only electronic cash but credit card information, owner identification, and address. With electronic wallets, customers do not have to retype personal information each time they make a purchase at that site. Consumers simply click on the electronic wallet after selecting items, and their credit card payment information, name and address, and preferred mailing method is transmitted instantly.

Besides using electronic cash or wallets, online consumers have other choices for making payments. **Smart cards**—plastic cards that store encrypted information on embedded computer chips rather than magnetic strips—are convenient and better protected, so they are among the most popular methods of Internet payment. A smart card "reader" attaches to a shopper's computer, where the card is swiped for payment. In addition to storing e-cash, smart cards can also store data from several credit card companies, a driver's license number, and even health information. Other companies, including PayPal, Billpoint, and eMoneyMail, are offering online transfers of cash. When directed by the user, these programs send payments from a bank or credit card account to the recipient's account.[43]

E-Commerce Challenges

As noted earlier, e-commerce has its problems and challenges. Consumers are concerned about protecting their privacy and being victimized by Internet fraud, frustrated with unreliable and hard-to-use Web sites, and annoyed over the inconveniences of scheduling deliveries and returning merchandise. Businesses are concerned about fair use of their trademarks and copyrights, potential conflicts with business partners, and difficulty in measuring the effectiveness of Internet-based promotion. In addition to these issues, governments are looking to e-commerce for increased sales tax revenue. Internet retailers and government officials are now locked in a debate over the collection of sales tax for online purchases, as discussed in the "Solving an Ethical Controversy" box. Figure 7.10 summarizes the roadblocks to e-commerce.

Internet Security and Privacy Online security poses a major roadblock to the acceptance of consumer e-commerce, because consumers worry that information about them will become available to others without their permission. Marketing research indicates that privacy is the top concern of Internet users.[44] As the earlier discussion of Internet payments explained, concern about the privacy of credit card

FIGURE 7.10
Roadblocks to E-Commerce

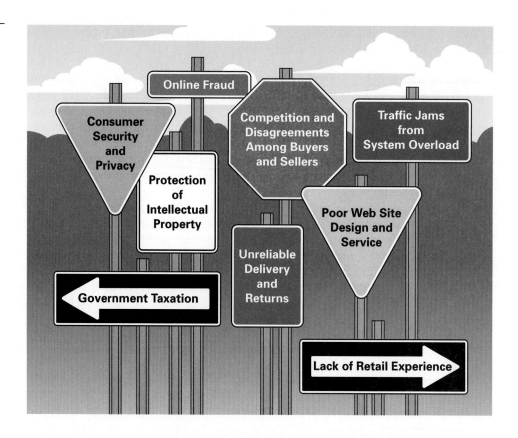

numbers has led to the use of secure payment systems. To add to those security systems, e-commerce sites require passwords as a form of authentication—that is, to determine that the person using the site is actually the one authorized to have access to the account. More recently, **electronic signatures** have become a way to enter into legal contracts such as home mortgages and insurance policies online. In 2001 a new federal law allows companies and individuals to use e-signatures.[45] With an e-signature, an individual obtains a kind of electronic identification and installs it in his or her Web browser. Signing the contract involves looking up and verifying the buyer's identity with this software.[46]

Thanks to cookies, the automatic data collection method introduced in Chapter 2, Web users leave electronic trails of personal information about their buying and viewing habits. The way that companies use cookies has the potential both to make visits to the Web site more convenient and to invade computer users' privacy. DoubleClick abandoned a plan to merge its data on Web use with a database of catalog orders, which would have given the company the ability to target online advertising to individual consumers based on their shopping habits.[47] Similarly, Amazon.com received such bad press over its plan to publicize customer shopping information by company or group, called Purchase Circles, that it now allows customers to request removal of their names. With a reported 23 million customers, Amazon's customer database is one of the largest online, and keeping its customers happy is critical to its success.[48]

Most consumers want assurances that any information they provide won't be sold to others without their permission. In response to these concerns, online merchants have been taking steps to protect consumer information. For example, many Internet companies have signed on with Internet privacy organizations like TRUSTe, shown in Figure 7.11. By displaying the TRUSTe logo on their Web sites, they indicate that they have promised to disclose how they collect personal data and what they do with the information. Prominently displaying a privacy policy is an effective way to build customers' trust.

E-Commerce and Taxes: Should They Meet?

If nothing is certain but death and taxes, then it was inevitable: lawmakers, traditional merchants, and Internet retailers are locked in a debate over whether Internet sales should be taxed. When Web-based retail sales began to take off, no one wanted to hamper its progress by slapping taxes on the activity. But now, state and local officials around the country—except in Alaska, Delaware, Montana, New Hampshire, and Oregon, which have no sales tax—are beginning to worry that their sales-tax base is slowly being eroded by increasing Internet retail transactions.

Should Internet sales be subject to tax?

PRO

1. Many states depend on sales taxes for revenues, and those revenues will decrease as shoppers increasingly turn to the Internet. States already lose some sales tax revenues to certain out-of-state mail-order and catalog sales. Failure to collect sales taxes will also ultimately hurt local brick-and-mortar businesses that are required to charge sales tax—and also pay property taxes—causing further erosion of the local tax base.
2. A tax break actually benefits consumers in upper income brackets, because they are the ones who can afford the computers as well as the goods and services offered on the Internet. Poorer consumers are thus stuck paying sales taxes when they shop at local businesses.
3. Several plans have been presented to calculate a simplified, streamlined sales tax so that it can be calculated and collected easily by both large and small Internet vendors.

CON

1. Collecting a sales tax will hamper the growth of e-commerce.
2. Introducing a sales tax will be extremely complicated, costing businesses more to implement than the actual taxes themselves.
3. Internet sales actually promote business activity elsewhere, for instance, increased shipping and other distribution functions, and so offset lost tax revenues.

SUMMARY

Internet retailers like the freedom that the current moratorium on taxes gives them. It provides them time to get sites up and running and, they hope, turn a profit. State and local officials, as well as brick-and-mortar businesses, fear that a continued ban on Internet sales tax will erode their own tax base and profitability. The issue has already gone before Congress more than once, and it will not go away anytime soon. The debates will continue over the need for breaks to allow new e-commerce sites to develop and the need for a level playing field for all businesses to compete.

Sources: Margret Johnston, "Legislators Debate Proposals for E-Commerce Taxes," *civic.com*, July 12, 2000, **www.cnn.com.technology**; David Hardesty, "Streamlined Sales Tax Project Moves Ahead," *E-Commerce Tax News*, July 9, 2000, **www.ecommercetax.com**; Mary Hillebrand, "U.S. Treasury Supports Internet Tax Ban," *E-Commerce Times*, June 6, 2000, **www.EcommerceTimes.com**; Howard Gleckman, "The Great Internet Tax Debate," *Business Week*, March 27, 2000, pp. 228–236; Howard Gleckman, "A First Step to Net Taxes," *Business Week*, September 20, 1999, p. 38; Ashlee Vance, "Trade Group Gives Technical Advice to Congress," CNN.com, downloaded from **www.cnn.com**, accessed February 6, 2001.

A policy is only as good as the company publishing it, though. Consumers have no assurances about what happens if a company is sold or goes out of business. Now-defunct Toysmart.com promised customers that it would never share their personal data with a third party. But when the company landed in bankruptcy court, it considered selling its database, one of its most valuable assets. And Amazon.com has told customers openly that if it or part of its business is purchased at some point, its database would be one of the transferred assets.[49] With these concerns, it is no wonder that some companies are profiting by selling software designed to protect privacy. For example, a program called Freedom enables the user to set up online identities, called "nyms." Online activity done under a nym uses encryption that makes the activity untraceable—even for law enforcement officials. Another package called PersonaValet allows users to determine which personal data to reveal when they visit Web sites that have installed software that works with PersonaValet.[50]

Such privacy features may become a necessary feature of Web sites if consumer concerns continue to grow. They also may become legally necessary. Already in the United States, the **Children's Online Privacy Protection Act (COPPA)** requires that Web sites targeting children younger than 13 years of age obtain "verifiable parental consent" before collecting any data that could be used to identify or contact individual users, including names and e-mail addresses.[51] Congress has also begun considering laws to protect the privacy of adult users.

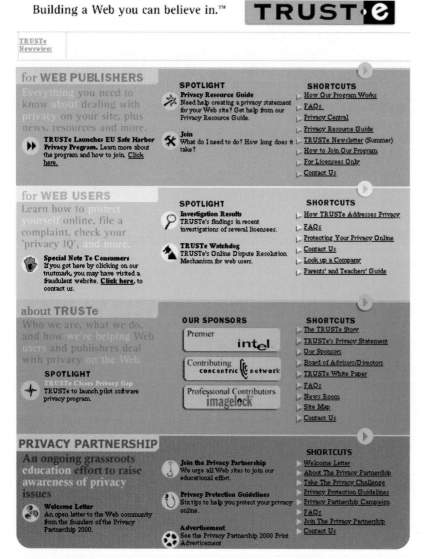

FIGURE 7.11
TRUSTe Organization Attempts to Build Customer Confidence Online

Security concerns are not limited to consumers. Employees are realizing that their employers can monitor their online behavior and e-mail messages at work. Some companies even specialize in helping employers use such information. Tacit Knowledge Systems builds a database from key terms in employees' e-mail. The primary objective is to help a company identify which employees have knowledge that they can contribute to the company—for example, knowledge about a particular competitor or type of product. Of course, many employees might be uncomfortable with their employer tracking what they write about. So, Tacit's software allows employees to decide which aspects of their personal profile they want to make public.[52]

Companies, too, are concerned about the privacy of their data, and with good reason. An employee of Legend Airlines recently discovered that an employee of American Airlines had logged into Legend's area of the Sabre scheduling and ticketing network. The American employee had correctly guessed the password of an acquaintance who worked at Sabre, using it to look up schedule information for Legend, and then failed to log off the system. The Legend employee discovered the intrusion a week later when the Sabre system wouldn't let the employee make scheduling changes because someone else— the American employee—was logged on. American insists that its employee was acting in good faith, and Sabre has since increased the security of its passwords.[53]

To prevent such intrusions, companies install combinations of hardware and software called firewalls to keep unauthorized Net users from tapping into private corporate data. A **firewall** is an electronic barrier between a company's internal network and the Internet that limits access into and out of the network. However, an impenetrable firewall is difficult to find. A determined and skilled hacker can often gain access. So, it is important for companies to test their Web sites and networks for vulnerabilities and provide backups of critical data in case an intruder breaches security measures.

Internet Fraud   Fraud is another barrier to e-commerce, and as more people go online, this crime is increasing. The Federal Bureau of Investigation and Department of Justice reported online auctions as the number-one source of fraud. They have logged more than 1,000 complaints a week and expect that rate to increase to 1,000 a day as the Internet Fraud Complaint Center becomes more widely used.[54] Auction fraud ranges from merchandise that does not match the description the bidder was given, such as fraudulent paintings, to products that were purchased but never delivered.

Investment scams are the second most common crime. Unreliable company information posted anonymously on the Web by disgruntled employees or predators who want to cash in on a stock's rise or fall are the most common "cybersmears." The misinformation can vary from untrue reports of problems with company products to character attacks on executives—anything to change the public's view of a company.[55] Law enforcement officials are gearing up to pursue online criminals, but untangling the layers of hidden online identities is proving difficult, though not impossible, to do. In the meantime, consumers and companies are being hurt by these fraudulent acts.

Traffic Jams Caused by System Overload   It sounded like a Web surfer's dream: the entire *Encyclopedia Britannica* available free online, for anyone with Internet access. Internet users anywhere could use that trusted source to look up articles on world history, art, or any other topic covered by that respected publication. But when the encyclopedia's content first became available, the reality was more like a nightmare. Users completely overloaded the Web site, and Encyclopedia Britannica's computers couldn't handle the traffic. The company went back to the drawing board and hired Akamai Technologies to handle content delivery through its own system of computers. A month later, the site relaunched successfully.[56] As Encyclopedia Britannica and Victoria's Secret—which suffered a similar traffic jam during the Webcast of a lingerie fashion show—have discovered, the Internet's increasing popularity has also increased the likelihood of delays and service outages, even as more users depend on their links. In addition, hackers can tie up a Web site with programs that flood it with inquiries. Whatever the cause of these traffic jams, they are costly in terms of lost business and frustrated customers.

Solutions to these problems are on the way. Internet service providers are adding capacity, and networking equipment manufacturers have recently introduced new technology capable of handling higher volumes of Internet traffic than older devices could manage. Many businesses also operate backup systems to ensure availability of Internet connections to customers. Companies like Akamai distribute content among thousands of computer servers, so that traffic to a Web site can be rerouted if it becomes too heavy.

Poor Web Site Design and Service   For e-commerce firms to attract customers—and keep them—companies must meet customer expectations. The biggest customer expectations are that they'll be able to find what they want without frustration and get questions answered. This obvious point has been a challenge on the digital frontier of cyberspace. Web sites are not always well designed and easy to use. In fact, two-thirds of Web shopping carts are abandoned before a customer places an order.[57] In other words, among the people who start selecting items to buy online, most of them change their minds before making a purchase. As Figure 7.12 suggests, some types of retailers have done much better than others in making online shopping a positive experience.

Surprisingly, many Web sites can receive e-mail but do not have a system for replying to the messages. Brightware, a provider of e-mail software, tested e-mail capabilities by sending a simple question—Who is your CEO and how do I contact him or her?—from a fictitious person to the biggest U.S. corporations at their e-mail addresses. The question was ignored by 62 percent of the companies, an increase from a similar test the year before. Among the companies that did reply, some took as long as two weeks. Commented Preston Dodd, an analyst with Jupiter Communications,

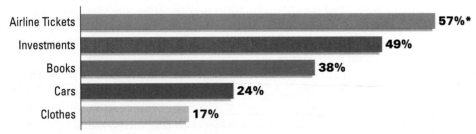

Airline Tickets	57%*
Investments	49%
Books	38%
Cars	24%
Clothes	17%

FIGURE 7.12
Five Products Consumers Would Prefer to Purchase Online

*Percentage of consumers preferring online shopping to traditional outlets.

"It's like giving somebody your phone number and they call for five days without getting an answer."[58]

Unreliable Delivery and Returns   Another challenge to successful e-commerce is merchandise delivery and returns. Retailers sometimes have trouble making deliveries to on-the-go consumers. And consumers don't want to wait for packages to be delivered. Also, if customers aren't satisfied with products, then they have to arrange for pickup or send packages back themselves. Several new companies are working to fill the need for reliable delivery and returns. PaxZone has established local businesses in the Chicago area that will receive shipments from retailers and arrange for returns from customers. The service is free to consumers, but the company charges a fee to the retailer, which benefits by not having to make repeated deliveries. An Arlington, Virginia, company called Brivo Systems has developed software that works with a "smart box" for home deliveries. Internet orders are given unique passwords, which the delivery person uses to gain access to the drop box.[59]

Lack of Retail Experience   "Pure-play" dot-coms—companies that started their lives online, without a history of traditional stores or catalogs—usually lack the expertise of running warehouses, customer service centers, and other aspects of selling to and satisfying customers. The 1999 Christmas season was the first big season of online retailing. Some 22 million consumers spent more than $5 billion on the Internet, but many of them were unimpressed with the experience. The ugly duckling of the season was the Toys 'R' Us Web site, which launched to great fanfare, then found it could not meet the demand. In mid-December, the company announced it could not guarantee delivery by Christmas Day, and dismayed parents around the country scrambled to find other sources of toys.[60] The "Business Hits and Misses" box describes some retailers' and shoppers' experiences with holiday e-tailing.

In contrast, Lands' End, which made its name as a service-oriented catalog retailer of classic clothing, has so far maintained its image online. As the company's Internet sales approach $100 million, its reliable distribution system has kept pace with the demand. Lands' End uses the same system for online sales as for its catalog orders.[61] Because of expertise in all parts of retailing, companies that combine their brick-and-mortar operations with e-commerce are gaining ground over those with little or no experience.

Competition and Disagreements Among Buyers and Sellers   Companies spend time and money to nurture relationships with their partners. But when a manufacturer uses the Internet to sell directly to customers, it can compete with its usual partners. Retailers often have their own Web sites, and they don't want their suppliers, the manufacturers, competing with them for sales. As e-commerce broadens its reach, producers must decide whether these relationships are more important than the potential of selling directly on the Web.

Mattel, well known for producing toys such as Barbie, Cabbage Patch dolls, and Matchbox cars, sells most of its products in toy stores and toy departments of other retailers, such as Wal-Mart. The company wants an Internet presence, but it would cut the retailers out of this important source of revenue if it sold toys online to consumers. Mattel cannot afford to lose the goodwill and purchasing power of giant retailers like Toys 'R' Us and Wal-Mart. So, the company sells only specialty products online, including pricey American Girl dolls, which were never sold in these stores, and software games.[62] In contrast, upscale toy retailers can sell Mattel products on the Internet competing with Mattel.

Pricing is another potential area of conflict. In their eagerness to establish themselves as Internet leaders, some companies have sold merchandise at unprofitable prices. This price slashing undercuts profits. American Leather sells custom leather furniture through upscale retailers, and each dealer serving a geographic area has an exclusive contract for the collections it offers in its area. But at least one dealer began

The Big Holiday Headache

A holiday season was supposed to be the time that Internet retailers did everything except actually slide down chimneys to deliver toys. According to different sources, online sales for the year hovered between $8 billion and $10 billion, more than double the year before. Brick-and-mortar retailers like JCPenney and Toys 'R' Us hung out their Web shingles, and Internet startups like etoys, CDNow, and SmarterKids.com, got ready to rake in the money. As executives of these companies went to sleep at night, more than visions of sugar plums danced in their heads.

As it turned out, 22 million shoppers did spend more than $5 billion between Thanksgiving and Christmas. But it wasn't without a struggle. And if the major glitches hadn't occurred, that number might have been much higher. It seemed that the Grinch was determined to steal Christmas from the Web.

Web sites proved to be poorly designed and difficult to use. Customer frustrations mounted. When one customer logged on to JCPenney.com simply to order pajamas for his grandchildren, he clicked the pj's into his electronic shopping cart and then spent an hour trying to delete unwanted items that appeared there. When he finally found his way back to the main menu to process his final order, he discovered that some of the items he wanted were out of stock. Disgusted at the waste of his time, he canceled the whole order. Gap.com offered hundreds of products online but lacked a way for consumers to search through them. Wal-Mart.com didn't allow first-time shoppers to drop anything into their shopping carts without going through a lengthy check-in process.

Then there's the issue of supply and demand. So many shoppers decided to try making holiday purchases online that many companies—like JCPenney—simply ran out of stock. Perhaps the most publicized—and disastrous—story was of toysrus.com, which began the season with fanfare and a huge ad campaign designed to attract shoppers to the site. But by December, it was clear that the toy retailer couldn't fill all its orders, and large numbers of frustrated parents and grandparents were left empty-handed. Some e-customers were so put off by the experience that they vowed never to shop on the Internet again. "I doubt I will ever shop again online for Christmas," says one. "It is not worth the wait, lies, ill-informed customer service reps, and the hassle and stress."

All of this stress translates to real numbers. Only 2 percent of consumers who visit an online store actually buy anything, whereas in the "real" shopping world, more than 50 percent of consumers who visit a brick-and-mortar mall make a purchase, says one. What can online retailers learn from this experience?

"Reality caught up with the hype," remarks Lise Buyer, an e-tailing analyst at Credit Suisse First Boston. Even Buyer had a bad online experience. She tried to order a television as a gift for her dad from Amazon.com, until she learned that the shipping charges would be $100. But companies seem to be making sincere efforts to win back customers. One solution is to turn to the experts: software developers who can fix the glitches on Web sites. Barnes & Noble is considering a new tool from Inxight Software to help customers browse through its enormous databases. Interactive Pictures offers software to hotels, real estate brokers, and even auto manufacturers that allows customers to experience goods and services online with more realistic three-dimensional pictures. PeopleSupport is helping companies improve their customer service by providing online service representatives for their Web sites.

Retailers who work out the kinks in the way they deliver goods and services to their customers likely will survive; those who don't, won't. Either way, it's a pretty safe bet that in holiday seasons to come, they will be better prepared for the holiday spirit of giving.

QUESTIONS FOR CRITICAL THINKING

1. In addition to making Web sites easier to navigate, what steps might online retailers take to be prepared for busy holiday seasons?
2. In addition to difficult Web sites and lack of inventory, what other problems might online retailers face? What might be some potential solutions to these problems?
3. Although the primary function of the sites discussed here is e-commerce, how might these companies expand their functions to attract more customers and develop long-term relationships with them?

Sources: Quentin Hardy, "The Last Etail," *Forbes,* February 7, 2000, p. 71; Katrina Brooker, "The Nightmare Before Christmas," *Fortune,* January 24, 2000, pp. 24–26; Luisa Kroll, "Happy Together," *Forbes,* January 10, 2000, pp. 156–157; Silvia Sansoni, "Santa Claws," *Forbes,* December 27, 1999, pp. 282–284; "About Inxight," Inxight Web site, **www.inxight.com,** accessed February 6, 2001.

offering American Leather furniture at a discount to customers outside its market area. Other dealers complained, so American Leather established a policy that dealers were not to advertise the company's products on the Internet. Instead, American Leather offered links to local dealers on its own Web site and made plans to allow buyers to order online, with the sale to be directed to the dealer serving the consumer's geographic area.[63]

Protection of Intellectual Property Along with privacy, intellectual property is difficult to protect on the Internet. Intellectual property is a trademark; invention; or literary, musical, artistic, photographic, or audiovisual work. The open sharing of information online can conflict with the desire of organizations to protect the use of their brand names, copyrights, logos, patents, and other intellectual property. Computer programmer David Simon recently tried to help his daughter watch her favorite cartoon series, *Pokémon*, by saving episodes on his family's home computer network. Her friends wanted to watch, too, so Simon posted them on a Web page for them to download. Eventually, he expanded the Web site to list television shows typed in from the newspaper TV listings, with instructions to click on Record and Play buttons to watch shows on demand. Thanks to a recommendation from a site called Netsurfer, Simon's site soon had tens of thousands of registered users, and would-be investors were contacting Simon. Then a dozen major entertainment companies, including AOL Time Warner and Walt Disney, sued Simon for illegally broadcasting their programming.[64] Their reaction is similar to that of recording companies when MP3 made downloading music files relatively easy and popular.

Even the choice of domain names can cause headaches for companies that have spent millions of dollars to develop a good reputation and widespread recognition. When the Internet was new and few companies understood the value of a Web presence, some individuals registered domain names that used companies' brand names, as well as the names of celebrities. When the companies got ready to go online, they were surprised to find that someone else had the right to use their name in cyberspace. At first, trade name owners had little recourse, but the legal environment has begun to change. The Anticybersquatting Consumer Protection Act imposes fines on people who in bad faith intend to profit from registering or using a domain name that is identical or similar to a company's trademark or an individual's name. The challenge for companies trying to protect their intellectual property is that the law requires them to show in court that the other party is using their name in bad faith in order to profit from it.[65]

Companies have used a variety of approaches to protect themselves in the freewheeling world of the Internet. When a dissatisfied customer set up a Web site at www.dunkindonuts.org to post complaints about the food at Dunkin' Donuts, the doughnut chain initially threatened to sue him for misusing its trademarks. Instead, it arranged to buy the site and use it as a tool for obtaining consumer opinions, which brought a constructive end to a difficult situation. Ford Motor Co. at first thought it had something wonderful when Robert Lane, a diehard fan of the Ford Mustang, set up sites to share information about his favorite automobile. The company even gave him a press pass so he could write news for his fellow Mustang lovers. Anonymous sources sent Lane confidential company documents, and he regularly destroyed them until he became dissatisfied with the company. Ford began asking Lane to modify his site but rebuffed his requests that it sponsor his site. Lane began publishing the proprietary documents, and Ford sued him for publishing its trade secrets. Before Lane shut down the site, he posted about 100 more Ford documents there.

Not every company has had such an alliance backfire. Lucasfilm worked with fan sites for *Phantom Menace* to build excitement before the release of that Star Wars episode. Fan sites also drove much of the success of another movie, *The Blair Witch Project*.[66] The winners in cyberspace have to figure out how to participate in an environment where the flow of information is not always within their control. When information can zip around the globe within seconds, an after-the-fact lawsuit is not much protection.

MANAGING A WEB SITE: DOING BUSINESS ON THE INTERNET

Business Web sites serve many purposes. They broaden customer bases, provide immediate accessibility to current catalogs, accept and process orders, and offer personalized customer service. As technology becomes increasingly easy to use, anyone with a computer equipped with a modem can open an Internet account and place a simple Web site on the Internet. How people or organizations use their sites to achieve their goals determines whether their sites will succeed. Figure 7.13 lists some key questions to consider in developing a Web site.

Developing Successful Web Sites

Tod Johnson, CEO of the Media Metrix marketing research firm, notes, "It's easy to build a bad Web site, harder to build a good one."[67] When judging Web sites, success means different things to different businesses. One firm might feel satisfied by maintaining a popular site that conveys company information or reinforces name recognition—just as a billboard or magazine ad does—without requiring any immediate sales activity. Web sites like those of *The New York Times* and *USA Today* draw many visitors who want the latest news, and Yahoo!, Netscape, C/Net, and ESPNSportsZone are successful because they attract millions of visitors. High-traffic sites like these add to their success by selling advertising space to other businesses.

- What is the purpose of the Web site?
- How can we attract repeat visitors?
- What external links should be established to draw visitors to the site?
- What internal links to databases and other corporate resources are needed?
- What should the domain name be?
- What should the site contain?
- How should it work?
- Who should put the site on the Net—company or Web host?
- How much money should be spent to set up and maintain the site?
- How current does information on the site need to be?

FIGURE 7.13
Questions to Consider in Developing a Web Site

Internet merchants need to attract customers who transact business on the spot. Some companies find success by hosting Web sites that offer some value-added service to create goodwill for potential customers. Organizations like the Mayo Clinic and accounting giant Ernst & Young provide useful information or links to related sites that people frequently visit. But to get people to stay at the site and complete a transaction, the site must also be secure, reliable, and easy to use.

Planning and Preparation   What is the company's goal for its Web site? Answering this question is the first and most important step in the Web site development process. As we saw in the opening vignette, for Charles Schwab, the primary objective was to sign up new customers. So, the discount broker's Web site designers put a link called "Open an Account" prominently in the upper left-hand corner of the home page. In addition, to reinforce Schwab's image as a respectable investment firm, the site uses a businesslike color scheme suggesting pinstripes.[68] Objectives for the Web site also determine the scope of the project. If the company's goal is to sell merchandise online, the site must incorporate a way for customers to place orders and ask questions about products, as well as links to the company's databases to track inventory and deliveries. As in this example, the plan includes not only the appearance of the Web site but also the company's behind-the-scenes resources for making the Web site deliver on its promises.

Other key decisions include whether to create and maintain a site in-house or to contract with outside experts. Some companies prefer to retain control over content and design by producing their own sites. However, since acquiring the expertise to develop Web sites can be very time-consuming, hiring specialists may prove a more cost-effective option. Major companies have such complex needs that specialists are essential, so companies such as Macromedia are enlisted to provide both software and consulting services to clients for their Web sites, as illustrated in Figure 7.14.

Naming the Web site is another important early step in the planning process. A domain name should reflect the company and its products and be easy to remember. For companies in the United States, the last part of the domain name identifies an affiliation category. Examples include .com for businesses, .org for organizations, .gov for government sites, and .edu for educational institutions. For companies outside the United States, the last part of the domain name identifies the country of origin, such as .ca for Canada and .jp for Japan. In addition to the existing dot-com, dot-gov, and dot-org addresses, seven new suffixes were approved and added to the Internet's naming system in late 2000. The new suffixes include .aero, .biz, .coop, .info, .museum, .name, and .pro. These suffixes were created to alleviate overcrowding in the .com domain and represent the first major addition of Internet addresses in more than a decade. With millions of dot-com names already registered, the search for a unique, memorable, and easily spelled name can be difficult.

FIGURE 7.14
Macromedia: E-Commerce
Web Site Developer

When Andrew Busey decided to create an e-commerce site for home furniture, he first thought of ForMyHome.com, which he was able to register, but it just wasn't catchy enough. So Busey and the design firm that was developing his site pondered the alternatives. Furniture.com was already taken, and its owner wanted $1 million for it. Eventually, they settled on Living.com. Not only is the name easy to spell, but the term is general enough to make sense if the site broadens its offerings beyond furniture. However, the California Association of Realtors had already registered the name. Busey negotiated the right to use the name in exchange for more than $100,000. The willingness of companies like Living.com to pay for the right to use a particular domain name reinforces the importance of this business asset. Living.com's competition appreciates the importance of domain names, too. Furniture.com has since registered three misspellings, Livng.com, Livign.com, and Lving.com, giving it the potential to capture customers with poor typing skills by setting up links to Furniture.com at those Web addresses.[69]

Content and Connections   Content is one of the most important factors in determining whether visitors return to a site. People obviously are more inclined to visit a site that provides material that interests them. Many e-commerce Web sites try to distinguish themselves by offering information or online communities along with a chance to buy. For example, Tavolo is an electronic storefront for gourmet cooking supplies, and it lures traffic to the site with weekly menu planners, printer-ready recipes, and features that convert menus between metric and U.S. measurement systems, adjust measurements for different numbers of servings, and create shopping lists for weekly menus.[70] Many sites offer links to other sites that may interest visitors. Hyperlinks to related Web sites increase exposure and traffic, but they can also take visitors away before they buy anything.

Standards for good content vary for every site, but available resources should be relevant to viewers, easy to access and understand, updated regularly, and written or displayed in a compelling, entertaining way. When the World Wide Web was a novelty, a page with a picture and a couple of paragraphs of text seemed entertaining. But such "brochureware" falls far short of meeting today's standards for interactivity, including the ability to accept customer data and orders, keep up-to-the-minute inventory data, and respond quickly to customer questions and complaints. Also, today's Internet users are less patient about figuring out how to make a site do what it promises. They won't wait ten minutes for a video clip to download or click through five different pages to complete a purchase. So, a good Web site looks simple and intuitive to its users, a quality the developers can guarantee only by testing a site on its intended audience.

After making content decisions and designing the site, the next step is connecting to the Internet by placing the required computer files on a server. Companies can have their own dedicated Web servers or contract to place their Web sites on servers at ISPs or other host companies. Most small businesses lack the necessary expertise to set up and run their own servers; they are better off outsourcing to meet their hosting and maintenance needs. They also need to draw business to their site. This usually requires a listing with the major search engines, like Yahoo!, Lycos, and Excite.

Costs and Maintenance

As with any technological investment, Web site costs are an important consideration. The highly variable cost of a Web site includes not only development expenses but also the cost of placing the site on a Web server, maintaining and updating it, and promoting it. A reasonably tech-savvy employee with off-the-shelf software can create a simple piece of brochureware for a few hundred dollars. A Web site that can handle e-commerce will cost at least $10,000 and perhaps millions. Creating it requires understanding of how to link the Web site to the company's other information systems.[71]

Although developing a commercial Web site with interactive features can cost tens of thousands of dollars, putting it online can cost as little as $20 a month for a spot on a **Web host**'s server such as America Online.[72] And Web hosts deliver a huge audience. In a typical week, 30 million people visit the AOL site and another 25 million log on to Yahoo!. Like so much new technology, the cost of putting a site on a server is falling. ISPs like America Online, CompuServe, and NetCom host many commercial sites for basic monthly charges depending on the number of Web pages. A number of e-commerce service providers are offering services for a few hundred dollars or even for free. Treadmill Doctor, which repairs treadmills, set up a Web site to answer common questions about that type of exercise equipment. The company used a template from Bigstep.com to create the site and pays Bigstep $14.95 plus $.20 per transaction to host the site. Bigstep allows the company to update the site at no charge.[73] Similarly, Hodge Products sells combination locks on its www.combolock.com site, created using template software from a service called Sitematic. To operate the site, Hodge pays just under $40 a month to Sitematic, which processes all the transactions and lets Hodge offer up to 20 different products on its site.[74] Some e-commerce service providers also take care of listing the site with search engines, usually for an additional fee.

In addition to installation and connection fees, managers must ensure that their company's Web site stays current over time. Visitors don't return to a site if they know the information never changes or that claims about inventory or product selection are not current. Consequently, updating design and content is another major expense. In addition, site maintenance should include running occasional searches to test that links to the company's Web site are still active.

Measuring Web Site Effectiveness

How does a company gauge the return from investing in a Web site? Measuring the effectiveness of a Web site is a tricky process, and a site's answer depends on the purpose that it serves. Figure 7.15 lists some measures of effectiveness. Profitability is relatively easy to measure in companies that generate revenues directly from online product orders, advertising, or subscription sales. However, a telephone order resulting from an ad on a Web site still shows the sale as a phone sale, not a Web site sale, even though the order originated at the site.

FIGURE 7.15
Measures of Web Site Effectiveness

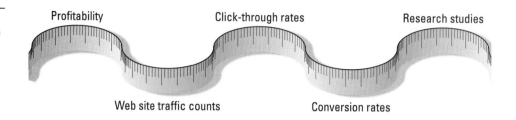

For many companies, revenue is not a major Web site objective. Only about 15 percent of large companies use their Web sites to generate revenue; the rest use them to showcase their products and to offer information about their organizations. For such companies, measures of success include increased brand awareness and brand loyalty, which presumably translate into greater profitability off-line.

Some standards guide efforts to collect and analyze traditional consumer purchase data, such as how many Ohio residents bought new Honda Accords the previous year, watched HBO's award-winning *The Sopranos,* or tried Burger King's new french fries. Still, the Internet presents several challenges for marketers. Although information sources are getting better, it is difficult to be sure how many people use the Internet, how often, and what they actually do online. Some Web pages display counters that measure the number of visits. However, the counters can't tell whether someone has spent time on the page or skipped over it on the way to another site, or whether that person is a first-time or repeat viewer.

Advertisers typically measure the success of their ads in terms of **click-through rates,** meaning the percentage of people presented with a banner ad who click on it, thereby linking to a Web site or a pop-up page of information related to the ad. Recently, the average click-through rate has been declining to about half of one percent of those viewing an ad. This rate is much lower than the 1.0 to 1.5 percent of responses to the average direct-mail advertisement. Low click-through rates have made Web advertising less attractive than it was when it was novel and people were clicking on just about anything online. Selling advertising has therefore become a less reliable source of e-commerce revenues.[75]

As e-commerce gains popularity, new models for measuring its effectiveness are being developed. A basic measurement is the **conversion rate,** the percentage of Web site visitors who make purchases. A conversion rate of 3 to 5 percent is average by today's standards.[76] A company can use its advertising cost, site traffic, and conversion rate data to find out the cost to win each customer. A company that spends $10,000 to attract 5,000 visitors to a Web site with a 4 percent conversion rate is obtaining 200 transactions, or .04 × 5,000. It spent $10,000 for those 200 transactions, so the advertising cost is $50 per transaction, meaning each of those customers cost $50 to acquire through the advertising campaign.

Among all categories of online advertisers, the average cost to get an online customer is $38. For Internet pure-plays, those only transacting business online, the cost is an astronomical $82, but the customer acquisition cost is just $11 per customer for retailers that also sell through stores or catalogs.[77] To be profitable, a site with an average conversion rate needs to generate a lot of revenue with each transaction—one reason many Internet start-ups have been having difficulty generating profits. So, e-commerce businesses are trying to boost their conversion rates by ensuring their sites download quickly, are easy to use, and deliver on their promises. At Net-Grocer, a low conversion rate meant that people were visiting the site but not buying anything. The Web site led off with a beautiful presentation of the company's mission statement, so visitors had to wait for it to download, then click through more pages before they could buy their groceries. The company shifted to an emphasis more characteristic of selling food—focus on the products coupled with coupons and fast links to make purchases. Soon the conversion rate had tripled, and the size of an average order grew as well.[78]

Besides measuring click-through and conversion rates, companies can study samples of consumers. Research firms such as PC-Meter and Relevant Knowledge recruit panels of computer users to track Internet site performance and evaluate Web activity; this service works in much the same way that ACNielsen monitors television audiences. The WebTrends service provides information on Web site visitors, including where they come from, what they see, and the number of "hits," or visits to the site, during different times of the day. Other surveys of Web users investigate their brand awareness and their attitudes toward Web sites and brands.

THE GLOBAL ENVIRONMENT OF E-COMMERCE

For many companies, future growth is directly linked to a global strategy that incorporates e-commerce. The United States leads the world in technology, communications infrastructure, and ownership of PCs and other consumer technology products, but Netizens live on every continent. Currently, 136 million Americans use the Internet, followed by 83 million in Europe, 69 million in the Asia-Pacific region, and millions more in South America, Africa, and the Middle East. Together, they spend well over $600 million online and are expected to spend ten times that amount in 2004.[79]

With so many users and so much buying power, the Internet creates an enormous pool of potential customers. Companies can market their goods and services internationally and locate distribution sources and trading partners. Customers can search for products at their convenience, browsing through online catalogs that always show current information. Brothers Sam and Shobit Gupta use the Internet as both a source of demand for their product and a way to work with customers. Their company, NetEcho, designs Web sites. Shobit Gupta supervises a team of designers in New Delhi, India, while Sam Gupta communicates with American clients from his home in Seattle. They start out with conference calls to learn about the culture of the company whose site they are designing. Then the programmers get to work. At the end of each workday, they post their work on the Internet for the client to review. Clients check the progress of the design and send feedback via e-mail, thus skirting the challenges of a 12-hour difference in time zones. Not only do clients get work comparable to that of U.S. design firms, they pay the much lower going rate for Indian programmers. NetEcho's satisfied clients include Technology Control Corp., which gave NetEcho the assignment to develop its Web site, then returned to the company when it was ready to expand the site.[80]

One practical implication of this global marketplace is the different languages that buyers and sellers speak. Reflecting the Internet's origins, more than half of users now communicate in English. However, the remainder use other languages, led by Japanese, German, Chinese, Spanish, and French.[81] As Figure 7.16 points out, Web site developers need to consider offering online information in more than one language. So far, however, three of every four Web pages are in English, slowing the adoption of the Internet in non-English-speaking countries.[82] Other international differences are important, too. Auction site eBay goofed in the United Kingdom by launching a site with prices given in U.S. dollars. After realizing that its British audience was offended, the company switched to local currency.[83]

E-commerce can heighten competition. In the virtual global marketplace, rivals can cross the oceans to enter your market. Many manufacturers use the Internet to search through online catalogs for the lowest-priced parts. No longer can local suppliers assume that they have locked up the business of neighboring firms. And U.S. firms cannot expect that their earlier experience with the Internet gives them an edge in foreign markets. Yahoo!, which has been in Europe longer than any other U.S.-based portal, operates eight country-specific versions. They represent 15 percent of Yahoo's total traffic, but

FIGURE 7.16
Importance of Considering the Internet's Global Population

Yahoo! enjoys the biggest slice of the market in the United Kingdom. In France, for example, the top portal is Wanadoo, which is the default portal of France's biggest Internet service provider, France Telecom.

Still, the Internet is a valuable way to expand a company's reach, especially for small businesses that would otherwise have difficulty finding customers overseas. Some customers are lured by the chance to save money compared with purchasing through other channels. David Butler, a retired sales manager in England, bought a Ford from a Belgian dealer and saved $5,000 off the price he would have paid at home. Inspired, he began shopping for a video camera from retailers based in the United States, where savings would far outweigh the costs of shipping and customs.[84]

WHAT'S AHEAD

The Internet is revolutionizing the way we communicate, obtain information, seek entertainment, and conduct business. It has created tremendous opportunities for B2B and B2C e-commerce. So far, B2B transactions are leading the way online. B2C e-commerce is undergoing a shakeout: Companies that combine expertise in traditional retailing with the new online technology have gained a firmer foothold in cyberspace.

In upcoming chapters, we look at other trends that are reshaping the business world of the 21st century: We explore the critical issues of how companies organize, lead, and manage their work processes; manage and motivate their employees; empower their employees through teamwork and enhanced communication; handle labor and workplace disputes; and create and produce world-class goods and services.

➤ Summary of Learning Goals

1. Discuss how the Internet provides new routes to business success.

The Internet, a worldwide network of interconnected computers, removes limitations of time and place so that transactions can occur 24 hours a day between people in different countries. It creates opportunities for companies that provide Internet infrastructure, access, and content, as well as for firms that use its resources in their business operations. The Internet offers a cost-effective way for managers to gather competitive intelligence; perform marketing research; showcase, sell, and in some cases distribute products; and offer customer service and technical support.

2. **Describe the increasing diversity of Internet users.**

From strictly a U.S. defense network, the Internet has grown to include users all over the world. The gender gap has also narrowed; women now represent roughly half of all Internet users. Ethnic and racial diversity is also increasing, with Asian Americans, African Americans, and Hispanic Americans going online in larger numbers. The average age of Internet users is also rising, reflecting the widespread acceptance of the Net.

3. **Summarize the Internet's four functions and provide examples of each.**

The Internet provides a means of communication through e-mail, instant messaging, and chat rooms. Internet telephony and videoconferencing are also being established online. The Net provides information services through search engines and portals, as well as online publications and newsgroups. Net entertainment is growing through online gaming, radio and television programming, electronic publishing, and music and movies. E-commerce, or online business transactions, make up the fourth function. E-commerce takes the form of electronic exchanges, extranets and private exchanges, electronic storefronts, online ticketing, and auctions.

4. **List the major forms of business-to-business e-commerce.**

Electronic data interchange was an early use of technology to conduct business transactions. E-commerce is the process of selling goods and services through Internet-based exchanges of data. It includes product information; ordering, invoicing, and payment processes; and customer service. In a B2B context, e-commerce uses Internet technology to conduct transactions between two organizations via electronic exchanges, extranets, and private exchanges.

5. **Name the major forms of business-to-consumer e-commerce.**

In a B2C context, e-commerce uses the Internet to connect companies directly with consumers. E-tailing and electronic storefronts are the major forms of online sales to consumers. Payment methods include electronic cash, electronic wallets, smart cards, and online transfers of cash.

6. **Describe some challenges associated with Internet selling.**

The growth of Internet retailing is currently limited by consumer security and privacy concerns, fraud, and system overload. In addition, poor Web site design and service, unreliability of delivery and returns, and lack of retail expertise can limit e-commerce success. The Internet can also generate conflict among buyers and sellers. Businesses also face challenges in protecting their intellectual property and proprietary data online.

7. **Describe how companies develop and manage successful Web sites.**

Businesses establish Web sites to expand their customer bases, increase consumer awareness of their products, improve customer communications, and provide customer service. Before designing a Web site, a company's decision makers must first determine what they want to achieve with the site. Other important decisions include who should create, host, and manage the site; how to promote it; and how much funding to allocate. Successful Web sites contain informative, up-to-date, and visually appealing content. Sites should also download quickly and be easy to use. Finally, management must develop ways of measuring how well a site accomplishes its objectives.

8. **Explain how global opportunities result from e-commerce.**

Technology allows companies to compete in the global market and workplace. Even the smallest firms can sell products and find new vendors in international markets. Through its own Web site, a company can immediately reach customers all over the world. Improved communications among employees in different locations create new ways of collaborating on projects.

Business Terms You Need to Know

Internet (Net) 248
World Wide Web (Web) 248
Web sites 248
Internet service provider (ISP) 249

electronic commerce
 (e-commerce) 256
business-to-business e-commerce
 (B2B) 258
extranets 260

business-to-consumer e-commerce
 (B2C) 261
click-through rates 274
conversion rate 274

Other Important Business Terms

domain name 248

digital subscriber line (DSL) 249

server 250

client 250

instant messaging 252

online community 252

newsgroup 253

portal 253

electronic data interchange (EDI) 258

electronic exchange 259

private exchange 259

electronic storefronts 262

electronic shopping cart 262

encryption 263

electronic cash 263

electronic wallets 263

smart cards 263

electronic signatures 264

Children's Online Privacy Protection Act (COPPA) 265

firewall 266

Web host 273

➤ Review Questions

1. Describe the path your e-mail takes in traveling from your computer to your friend's. How would this path differ if your friend has a DSL connection?

2. Using the statistics cited in this chapter, construct a profile of the "typical" Internet user.

3. What are the four primary functions performed on the Web? Describe a practical business application of each.

4. Suppose your supervisor asked you to use the Internet to find the best supplier of office furniture for the new site your company is moving to. Explain several precautionary measures you might take as you gather information on furniture companies.

5. Discuss the benefits that a small company might enjoy by establishing a Web presence.

6. Name several ways that companies generate revenue online.

7. What are the differences between B2B and B2C e-commerce?

8. Describe several of the challenges that both businesses and consumers face as they engage in e-commerce. Cite some potential solutions to these problems.

9. If you were to advise the CEO of a company that wants to develop a Web site, what steps would you recommend that the company take to build a successful site?

10. In what ways do companies measure the effectiveness or success of a Web site?

➤ Questions for Critical Thinking

1. Consider the following statement: "To remain competitive in the next decade, every business must have a Web site or at least be connected to the Internet." Do you agree or disagree? Why? If you disagree, name at least one type of business that you believe could succeed without the Internet.

2. More than 80 percent of Web users say that obtaining information is one of the reasons they use the Internet. How might an adventure travel company use this statistic to attract potential customers to its Web site?

3. Many businesses are banding together to form exchanges that serve large segments of an industry, such as the auto industry. However, Wal-Mart has decided not to follow this route. Do you think this is a wise decision for Wal-Mart? Why or why not?

4. Do you believe that companies should monitor employees' online behavior and e-mail messages at work? Why or why not? If so, discuss any boundaries you feel should be respected.

5. By setting up a Web site, companies can have instant access to a global marketplace. What are some advantages and disadvantages that a pure-play e-commerce company might encounter in setting up a Web site for global e-commerce? How would the advantages and disadvantages differ for a company with retail experience?

➤ Experiential Exercise

Background: The Internet is a powerful resource for businesses. As the chapter explains, about 30 percent of U.S. businesses are currently engaged in B2B e-commerce, with nearly 90 percent online by 2002.

Directions: Assume you work for Paula Brewer, a small-business owner who is interested in developing a B2B e-commerce site on the Web. Research the Internet to find resources for Brewer to use in developing the company's new B2B Web site. You may wish to use **www. geobiz2biz.com,** an online directory with links to more than 100 Web sites for a wide variety of information resources, including the following:

- Web-based business solutions
- B2B auctions
- Procurement services
- Sales force management

- Supplier information
- Publicity/advertising
- Business tools

Print out the home page for either GeoBiz2Biz.com or a similar site you found. Submit a three-page report to Brewer that includes the home page printout of the Web site you recommend to get her started in B2B e-commerce. In the remainder of your report, summarize five links on the Web site you selected that you think are most important for her to visit. For each of the five sites listed in your report, include (1) the reason why you recommend the link as particularly important and (2) any necessary explanations about the link that would be helpful to Brewer.

> ### Nothing but Net

1. **B2B.** As noted in the chapter, IBM offers extensive consulting services, software, and hardware for firms engaged in e-commerce. Assume you're an entrepreneur and you'd like to expand your presence in the B2B market. Visit the IBM e-commerce Web site at

   www.ibm.com/e-commerce

   Read about the services offered by IBM to B2B entrepreneurs. Prepare a brief oral report to your class summarizing these services and some of the case studies where IBM has assisted firms in their B2B activities.

2. **Rating e-commerce Web sites.** Gomez.com is one of the leading authorities on e-commerce. As such, Gomez.com rates various e-commerce companies. Go to the Gomez.com Web site at

   www.gomez.com

   Prepare a brief report in which you identify the following:

   a. The highest-rated airline Web site

   b. The highest-rated e-toy Web site

   c. The methods Gomez.com uses to rate e-commerce sites

3. **Internet retailing experience.** Assume the role of a consumer who wishes to purchase the latest best-selling novel over the Internet. The two leading online booksellers are

   www.amazon.com

   www.bn.com (Barnes and Noble)

   Visit both sites and learn enough about each site so you can describe them both to a friend, including which you'd recommend and why.

   Note: Internet Web addresses change frequently. If you do not find the exact sites listed, you may need to access the organization's or company's home page and search from there.

In a few short years, the Internet has revolutionized the way companies do business. Of course, there have been huge successes as well as painful failures among the companies that have embraced the Internet—particularly those that have relied on the Internet for their very survival. But overall, the Internet offers global opportunities for a variety of individuals and organizations. One of those is Lycos Inc.

Founded in 1995, Lycos Network was initially an Internet portal—an entryway much like its larger competitors Yahoo! and America Online. Within a few years, experts predicted that the company would capsize in the Web, swamped by its giant competitors. "We were in danger of being an afterthought in early 1998," recalls Lycos chief financial officer Edward Philip. But a series of changes has turned Lycos around. Today, according to industry watcher Media Matrix, the company's collection of sites is the fourth-largest destination for people using the Web. "We had less funding and were late to market, yet we beat the odds and have flourished," boasts CEO Bob Davis. The company also has a new name: Terra Lycos. More on that later.

Lycos saved itself largely through a series of alliances and acquisitions, along with the introduction of new tools and services that benefit both consumers and business customers. One service, the "Lycos Daily 50 Report," helps marketers follow emerging consumer trends by tracking the topics that typical users search the Internet for. The report is simply a list of the fifty most popular search terms of the past seven days. It removes company names, porn sites, and Internet utility terms such as "chat room" and comes up with the fifty most useful words and phrases. "Our goal is to create an up-to-date list of the people, places, and things that Internet users are interested in," explains Jonathan Levine, director of content development. "It's a great way for people to stay current. For marketers, this tool can be used to get an idea about emerging consumer trends." This is just one way that the Lycos site helps create opportunities for other businesses.

During the past few years, Lycos has allied with or acquired companies such as Tripod Inc. and HotBot. Lycos and Bell Canada created a new company called Sympatico-Lycos, which would provide Canadians with expanded Internet resources for the business-to-business market. In the fall of 2000, Lycos became the "exclusive community provider for the Olympic Games," hosting and managing all Olympic athlete chats, message boards, and fan clubs for the Sydney Olympics. McDonald's joined the party as a sponsor of the Lycos Olympic site, in exchange for featured advertising. "This is a powerful combination linking two global leaders in support of the Sydney Olympic Games, and we look forward to continuing to work with McDonald's to further leverage the strengths of both companies," stated Jeff Bennett, senior vice president of corporate development at Lycos. Later, Lycos Asia received a license from the Chinese government to operate one of China's first foreign-owned Web sites. Previously, foreign-owned Web companies could function only through partnerships with Chinese institutions that would exert control over operations.

While all of these alliances are potential opportunities, they also increased the complexity of the company—and the complexity of its problems. So, Lycos hired its first chief information officer, Tim Wright. "They were looking for someone with experience in acquisitions, someone who knew how to handle multiple staffs of skilled people and knew how to blend disparate pieces together," Wright explains. In other words, Wright's job was to figure out how to weave technology and people together in a way that allowed workers and managers in the acquired companies to continue to do what they do best. He also showed them how their relationship with Lycos could actually increase their business. "We let [acquired companies] know right away that we can help them by redirecting our traffic to their site and recirculating traffic back their way," says Wright.

But the biggest deal for Lycos was still to come. The company agreed to be acquired by Spanish Internet service provider Terra Networks in a stock swap that valued Lycos at around $12.5 billion, with the idea that the merger would begin to create a megaportal to the Internet that would dominate Europe and Latin America. Pep Valles, the founder of Terra, views the deal as the global opportunity of a lifetime. "Who hits first hits twice," he remarks, repeating an old Spanish saying. "On the Internet, who hits first hits ten times." He sounds a bit like the first Lycos television commercial, which brought Lycos to the attention of many American consumers. The ad featured a black lab retriever named Lycos who streaked back and forth from the edge of the world to his owner, finding anything that his owner asked for. "Go get it!" the voice of Lycos's owner commanded. And Lycos did.

QUESTIONS

1. Using information in the chapter, outline three ways that you think Terra Lycos could help other businesses create opportunities for themselves using the Internet.
2. What methods might Terra Lycos use to measure the effectiveness of the various Web sites of its affiliates and subsidiaries?
3. Identify three challenges that managers of Terra Networks and Lycos will likely face as they merge the two organizations.
4. Visit the Terra Lycos Web site at **www.lycos.com.** As a user, what do you think its strengths and weaknesses are?

Sources: Lycos Web site, **www.lycos.com,** accessed January 19, 2001; "Lycos and McDonald's Form Global Marketing Relationship," *Business Wire,* September 20, 2000; "Lycos to Host All Athlete Chats for Sydney 2000 Olympic Games, *Business Wire,* September 13, 2000; Ross Kerber, "Lycos Asia Wins License in China," *The Boston Globe,* September 11, 2000, **www.boston.com;** Daniel Helft, "Terra's Terror," *The Standard,* July 3, 2000, **www.thestandard.com;** Stewart Deck, "Free To Be," *CIO Magazine,* June 1, 2000, **www2.cio.com;** Betsy Schiffman and Amy Doan, "Lycos and Terra Networks: A Marriage Made in Spain, *Forbes,* May 16, 2000, **www.forbes.com;** Jon Swartz, "Bob Davis, Lycos' Savior," *Forbes,* March 30, 2000, **www.forbes.com;** "Lycos Tool Highlights Emerging Consumer Trends," *Forbes,* September 15, 1999, **www.forbes.com.**

Management: Empowering People to Achieve Business Objectives

CHAPTER 8

Management, Leadership, and the Internal Organization

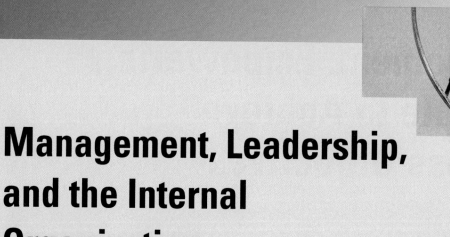

Learning Goals

1. Define *management* and the three types of skills necessary for managerial success.

2. Explain the role of vision in business success.

3. Summarize the major benefits of planning and distinguish among strategic planning, tactical planning, and operational planning.

4. Describe the strategic planning process.

5. Contrast the two major types of business decisions and list the steps in the decision-making process.

6. Define *leadership* and compare different leadership styles.

7. Discuss the meaning and importance of corporate culture.

8. Describe the purposes of an organization structure.

9. Explain the five major forms of departmentalization and the four main types of organization structures.

The next time you pick up a Nokia wireless phone, ask yourself this: how did a firm that began operating over 135 years ago as a lumber mill in the forests of Finland become the world's largest supplier of mobile phones? One major factor is leadership. Outstanding strategic planning is the second ingredient in the firm's success. These two factors are followed closely by an organization culture that promotes creative decision making at every level of the organization.

In the late 1960s, several Finnish companies merged—the Finnish Cable Works, the Finnish Rubber Works, and the Nokia forest products company. The company became a huge conglomerate manufacturing a wide range of products including paper, chemicals, and rubber. The Cable Works already made power transmission cables and phone lines, so there was a fairly natural progression into an electronics division centered on telecommunications.

Fast forward to the early 1990s, when Nokia had new telecommunications products to sell but was floundering. The company was streamlined to focus solely on telecommunications. A new chief executive officer (CEO) was also brought on board: Jorma Ollila, who has all the traits of an inspirational leader—empathy, self-awareness, and objectivity—but no special technical skills. Since then, Ollila and his team of top managers have turned the company around so that it now rakes in 70 percent of the profits earned in mobile-phone manufacturing. Nokia is now the world's leading mobile phone supplier, competing against the likes of Ericsson, Panasonic, and Siemens.

Nokia's strategy is to produce communications devices that are easy to use—so easy that more people will want to buy Nokia's products than will buy any other company's. Combining advanced technology and ease of use means that Nokia must keep developing better, more appealing, more innovative products. To do so, Ollila and his top managers delegate much of the company's planning and decision making to those who know how to bring the products to market. "The objective is to always have decisions made by the people who have the best knowledge," says Matti Alahuhta, one of Ollila's top managers. For instance, Tony Mitchell, a production manager at Nokia's phone factory in Texas, is a

middle manager. But he thoroughly understands the company's philosophy and enjoys the freedom of making decisions that will benefit production at his factory. "That's unique to Nokia—the freedom a group is allowed to take," he explains. "There are certain shared systems we keep as standard, but you're allowed to be creative." Each manager takes personal responsibility for the full scope of issues related to his or her job. Design head Frank Nuovo acts as a gatekeeper for the thousands of ideas that pour in from all over the company. "I'm responsible for the continuity—the face and soul of the product," he notes. "It has to go through me."

So, although employees have virtually free rein to make decisions, there is a controlling function at Nokia. Nuovo is in charge of design. Chief financial officer (CFO) Olli-Pekka Kallasvuo, who started with Nokia as an attorney, keeps order in finance. Pertti Korhonen, senior vice president of operations, logistics, and sourcing,

holds the reins for Nokia's phone manufacturing facilities around the world. All of these managers are part of Ollila's top management team.

What helps bind the company together? Nokia has a strong corporate culture. "It's the way the organization creates a meeting of minds among people," remarks Ollila. "How do you send a very strong signal that this is a meritocracy, and this is a place where you are allowed to have a bit of fun, to think unlike the norm, where you are allowed to make a mistake?" Somehow, the signal does comes through—loud and clear—both to employees and to the general public. According to the consulting firm Interbrand, Nokia has the eleventh most valuable brand. And it could move up the list as the cell phone continues to gain ground as an essential appliance in businesses and households. The company's mission says it all: to take "a leading, brand-recognized role in creating the mobile information society." Or to put it in Ollila's words, to "bring the Internet to everybody's pocket." Check your own pocket; if you don't have a Nokia phone there now, you might someday soon.[1]

CHAPTER OVERVIEW

The importance of effective managers like Jorma Ollila cannot be overstated. In any successful business such as Nokia, the skills of good managers are behind and drive that success. When companies fail, poor management usually is one of the leading causes. A firm's ability to survive, grow, and profit starts with its managers' ability to envision how a business can satisfy marketplace needs.

A management career brings challenges that appeal to many students in introductory business courses. When asked about their professional objectives, many students say, "I want to be a manager." You may think that the role of a manager is basically being the boss. But in today's business world, companies are looking for much more than bosses. They want managers who understand technology, can adapt quickly to change, skillfully motivate subordinates, and realize the importance of satisfying customers. These types of managers will continue to be in great demand because their performance strongly affects their firms' performance.

This chapter begins by examining how successful organizations use management to turn visions into reality. The chapter describes the levels of management, the skills that managers at all levels in the organization need, and the functions that managers perform. It tells how the first of these functions, planning, helps managers to meet the challenges of a rapidly changing business environment and to develop strategies that guide a company's future. The following sections of the chapter explore the types of decisions that managers make, the role of managers as leaders, and the importance of corporate culture. The chapter concludes by examining the second function of management—organizing.

WHAT IS MANAGEMENT?

Management is the process of achieving organizational objectives through people and other resources. The manager's job is to combine human and technical resources in the best way possible to achieve the company's goals. Managers are not involved directly in production; that is, they do not themselves produce finished products. Instead, they direct the efforts of others to accomplish goals.

Management principles and concepts apply to not-for-profit organizations as well as profit-seeking firms. The local library director, the head of the Salvation Army, and a Boy Scout troop leader all perform the managerial functions described later in this chapter. Managers preside over organizations as diverse as Columbus State Community College, the New York Stock Exchange, and the Starbucks coffee shop down the street.

The Management Hierarchy

A local fast-food restaurant such as McDonald's typically works through a very simple organization that consists of an owner/manager and an assistant manager. By contrast, large organizations develop more complex management structures. Ford Motor Company manages its activities through a chairperson of the board, 4 executive vice presidents, 5 group vice presidents, 28 vice presidents, and 7 staff officers, plus plant managers and supervisors. All of these people are managers, because they combine human and other resources to achieve company objectives. Their jobs differ, however, because they work at different levels of the organization.

A firm's management usually has three levels: top, middle, and supervisory management. These levels of management form a management hierarchy, as shown in Figure 8.1. The hierarchy is the traditional structure found in most organizations. Managers at each level perform different activities.

The highest level of management is top management. Top managers include such positions as CEO, CFO, and executive vice president. Top managers devote most of their time to developing long-range plans for their organizations. They make decisions such as whether to introduce new products, purchase other companies, or enter new geographic markets. Top managers set a direction for their organization and inspire the company's executives and employees to achieve their vision for the company's future. After defense contractors AlliedSignal and Honeywell merged, Michael R. Bonsignore took over as chief executive of the new company, which retained the name Honeywell. He set ambitious goals for sales growth of 8 to 10 percent, representing the best growth rate that either of the predecessor companies had achieved on its own. To achieve this goal, he had to inspire cooperation between employees from two formerly competing organizations with very different strengths. The old Honeywell had been known for its ability to work closely with customers, whereas AlliedSignal had a reputation for operating efficiency and tough quality standards. Bonsignore's challenge was to get employees to focus on shared goals and care equally about customer service and efficiency.[2] Besides such internal issues, top managers spend much of their time building good relationships between the company and the public. They do so by participating in activities involving governmental and community affairs.

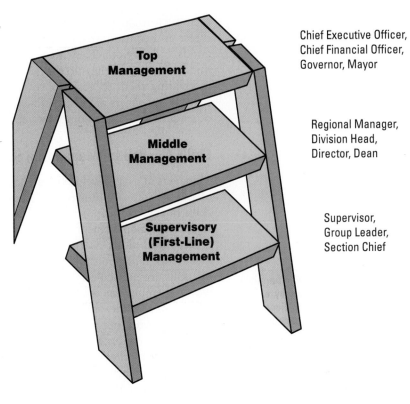

Chief Executive Officer, Chief Financial Officer, Governor, Mayor

Regional Manager, Division Head, Director, Dean

Supervisor, Group Leader, Section Chief

**FIGURE 8.1
The Management Hierarchy**

Women and minorities may encounter more difficulty than white males in advancing to top management positions. According to the U.S. Labor Department, women hold 8 million of the country's 18 million managerial positions, yet only 2.4 percent of top corporate positions are held by women. Part of the reason why few women have top management jobs is the so-called **glass ceiling,** an invisible barrier that resists the efforts of women in moving up the corporate hierarchy beyond a certain point. Top managers in many firms—including JCPenney, Colgate-Palmolive, and Dow Chemical—have established programs to help women break such barriers.

Middle management, the second tier in the management hierarchy, includes positions such as general managers, plant managers, division managers, and branch managers. Middle managers' attention focuses on specific operations, products, or customer groups within an organization. They are responsible for developing detailed plans and procedures to implement the firms' strategic plans. If top management decided to broaden the distribution of a product to a new region, a sales manager assigned to that region would be responsible for determining the number of salespeople assigned to that territory. If top management decided to institute a companywide total quality management program, a quality control manager in the customer service department might design a survey to gather feedback on customer satisfaction. For example, at Honeywell, middle managers are responsible for targeting the products and customers to be the source of the sales growth expected by CEO Bonsignore. To achieve more sales, the middle managers might budget money for product development, identify new uses for existing products, and improve the ways they train and motivate salespeople.

Supervisory management, or first-line management, includes positions such as supervisor, line manager, and group or team leader. These managers are directly responsible for assigning nonmanagerial employees to specific jobs and evaluating their performance every day. Managers at this first level of the hierarchy work in direct and continuing contact with the employees who produce and sell the firm's goods and services. They are responsible for implementing the plans developed by middle managers; they do this job by providing technical assistance to workers and motivating them to accomplish daily, weekly, and monthly goals. At Honeywell, first-line managers are responsible for production, sales, purchasing, accounting, and other activities of the company's employees.

Skills Needed for Managerial Success

Managers at every level in the management hierarchy must exercise three basic types of skills: technical, human, and conceptual skills. All managers must acquire these skills in varying proportions, although the importance of each type of skill changes at different management levels.

Technical skills are the manager's ability to understand and use techniques, knowledge, and tools and equipment of a specific discipline or department. Technical skills are particularly important for first-line managers, who frequently interact with the employees who carry out the tasks of their specialty. Technical skills lose relative importance at higher levels of the management hierarchy, but most top executives started out as technical experts. The résumé of a vice president of information systems probably lists experience as a computer analyst, and that of a vice president of marketing often shows a background in sales. At Microsoft, founder Bill Gates's experience in developing a personal computer (PC) operating system helps him understand the challenges and opportunities for new kinds of software. He has identified a need for an operating system that can power all kinds of devices that connect to the Internet and a goal of selling a handheld computer using such an operating system. But the specifics of developing and marketing this hardware and software are primarily the responsibility of lower-level managers and employees.

Human skills are interpersonal skills that enable a manager to work effectively with and through people. Human skills include the ability to communicate with, motivate, and lead employees to accomplish assigned activities. Managers need human skills to interact with people both inside and outside the organization. Bill Gates, Steve Ballmer, and the other executives of Microsoft must inspire their employees who are developing and launching the Pocket PC in a difficult business environment. Microsoft employees could become discouraged because the Pocket PC is the company's sixth attempt to launch a handheld computing device since its Pen for Windows device launched and flopped in 1990, and it faces stiff competition from the popular Palm computer.[3] Maintaining commitment, creativity, and cooperation in a fast-moving environment where other companies are competing for talent requires strong human skills. At the same time, Microsoft's top managers must convince investors that the strategy will work, as well as defend the company's public image in the face of its continuing antitrust legal case.

At all levels of management, human skills have become more crucial because of globalization and increased workplace diversity. Managers need to relate to people from cultures and ethnic backgrounds different from their own. Recognizing the growing emphasis on human skills, many firms offer training in areas such as diversity, communication, and conflict resolution. In Mountain

Burt Shavitz, a beekeeping hermit in Maine, and Roxanne Quimby, a 34-year-old waitress and divorced mother, started an improbable business based on beeswax—Burt's Bees. Roxanne relied on technical skills learned from living off the land and researching old farm journals to develop beeswax products such as candles, stove polish, and shoe polish. Business boomed, and Roxanne bought Burt's part of the business. Today, Roxanne successfully uses human and conceptual skills in managing the business. She expanded into cosmetics and pet products and moved the company to North Carolina, a cosmetics center. Customers such as Gardener's Eden, Smith & Hawkin, Smithsonian Museum Store, Zona, Bloomingdale's, and many health food stores have swarmed.

View, California, the Growth & Leadership Center (GLC) counsels Silicon Valley managers in developing their human skills. In the high-tech world, many of the middle and top managers are young people with plenty of technical savvy but without the wisdom of experience. The founder of GLC, psychologist Jean Hollands, sees managers who routinely intimidate, blame, or withhold information from employees. Companies send managers to Hollands because she is adept at pinpointing such flaws and helping managers see how that behavior inhibits their success and makes employees unhappy. Hollands claims that 85 percent of her clients are promoted after working with her, and that almost all of them get better performance reviews.[4]

Conceptual skills determine a manager's ability to see the organization as a unified whole and to understand how each part of the overall organization interacts with other parts. These skills involve an ability to see the big picture by acquiring, analyzing, and interpreting information. Conceptual skills are especially important for top-level managers, who must develop long-range plans for the future direction of their organization. At Microsoft, top management views the development of the Pocket PC as more than a new product. It is part of an overall mission, in Bill Gates's words, to give "people the power to do anything they want, anywhere they want, and on any device." The Pocket PC's operating system, Windows CE, is meant to be used in a variety of small devices, from television set-top boxes to gaming consoles, as well as for such business applications as gas pumps and production equipment.[5]

Special Skills for Overseas Managers

Many firms realize that growth requires expansion overseas. They may assign managers to their overseas operations and markets. In addition, companies that operate internationally may bring managers from various countries to the home office or may send managers from one country to work in another country where the company has a presence. The chief executives of three large U.S. businesses are from Australia: Jac Nasser at Ford Motor Company, Geoffrey Bible at Philip Morris, and Douglas Daft at The Coca-Cola Company. They bring a management style that is relatively open, egalitarian, and witty—a style that is attractive to U.S. businesses. When Nasser arrived in Detroit, he headed off rumors that he had installed a Jacuzzi in his office by inviting groups of employees to visit him at Ford's headquarters.[6]

Managers who accept assignments in international operations or foreign-based offices need special skills. They must learn local languages, cultural customs, and the practices and expectations of foreign business environments. Awareness of differences among cultures is an important human skill, whether managers choose to adopt different culture styles or carefully use their own style, knowing it may differ from employees' expectations. When Nissan formed an alliance with France's Renault, the French carmaker sent Carlos Ghosn of Brazil to Japan to make Nissan's operations more efficient. In his role as chief operating officer of Nissan, Ghosn determined that for the company to survive, it had to save money by shutting factories, cutting jobs, and simplifying ties to suppliers. Such moves are routine in the U.S. but virtually unheard of in Japan. Ghosn's position as a foreigner may enable him to take actions that would be unthinkable in a Japanese-born executive. However, the role of outsider is hardly pleasant. In one meeting, Ghosn urged managers to envision reductions of 25 to 30 percent. The managers laughed until Ghosn delivered the bad medicine: "No one in purchasing, engineering, or administration will receive a pay increase until they [show] what their contribution is to this [cost cutting]."[7] This blunt talk is counter to Japanese norms. So, using it was a calculated risk taken to shock people into action.

Even when managers have the technical and conceptual skills for foreign assignments, culture shock and the stress of unfamiliar environments pose difficult challenges. The prevalence of two-income families further complicates matters, since transferred managers' spouses may not find comparable work in their new homes. Even if a spouse does not work outside the home, family members often struggle

Herb Kelleher, Chairman of Southwest Airlines, uses his legendary management skills to motivate his employees. States Kelleher, "Who comes first, your employees, your shareholders, or your customers? My mother taught me that your employees come first. If you treat them well, then they treat the customers well, and that means your customers come back and your shareholders are happy." *Fortune* magazine ranks Southwest as one of the "100 Best Companies to Work For" and its pilots recently bought Kelleher this Harley, painted in company colors.

to adjust to living in a different culture. To increase success rates for overseas assignments, some firms implement methods for choosing and preparing managers for overseas assignments. Psychological testing can help select managers most suited to the challenges of working in different countries. Many firms provide training in local languages and cultures, find jobs for spouses, and pay for private international schools for children.

Managerial Functions

In the course of a typical day, managers spend time meeting and talking with people, reading, thinking and writing, and observing the workplace. As they perform these activities, managers are carrying out four basic functions: planning, organizing, directing, and controlling. Planning activities lay the groundwork, and the other functions are aimed at carrying out the plans.

Planning Planning is the process of anticipating future events and conditions and determining courses of action for achieving organizational objectives. In the earlier example of Nissan, Carlos Ghosn determined that profitability for the struggling car company required Nissan to begin operating more efficiently, so he established a target of cutting costs by 20 percent. Effective planning can help a business to crystallize its vision, described in the next section, as well as avoid costly mistakes and seize opportunities. Effective planning requires an evaluation of the business environment and a well-designed road map of the actions needed to lead a firm forward. In a later section of this chapter, we elaborate on the planning process.

Organizing Once plans have been developed, the next step in the management process typically is organizing—the means by which managers blend human and material resources through a formal structure of tasks and authority. This activity involves classifying and dividing work into manageable units by determining specific tasks necessary to accomplish organizational objectives, grouping tasks into a logical pattern or structure, and assigning them to specific positions and people. Managers also must staff the organization with competent employees capable of performing the necessary tasks and assigning authority and responsibility to these individuals. Often, as at Nissan, organizing involves studying a company's existing structure and determining whether to reorganize it so that the company can better meet its objectives. The organizing process is discussed in detail later in this chapter.

Directing Once plans have been formulated and an organization has been created and staffed, the management task focuses on **directing,** or guiding and motivating employees to accomplish organizational objectives. Directing includes explaining procedures, issuing orders, and seeing that mistakes are corrected. At Nissan, Ghosn adopted a straightforward approach to directing when he told managers that future pay increases depended on their success in cutting costs. Managers may also direct in other ways, such as getting employees to agree on how they will meet objectives and inspiring them to care about customer satisfaction or their contribution to the company.

The directing function is an especially important responsibility of supervisory managers. To fulfill their responsibilities to get things done through people, supervisors must be effective leaders. In addition, middle and top managers must be good leaders and motivators, and they must create an environment that fosters such leadership. A later section of this chapter discusses leadership, and Chapters 9 and 10 discuss motivating employees and improving performance.

Controlling   Controlling is the function of evaluating an organization's performance to determine whether it is accomplishing its objectives. The basic purpose of controlling is to assess the success of the planning function. The four basic steps in controlling are to establish performance standards, monitor actual performance, compare actual performance with established standards, and, if performance does not meet standards, determine why and take corrective action. Controlling provides feedback for future rounds of planning. At Nissan, controlling signaled the company's poor profits, which Nissan addressed with an objective to cut costs.

THE NEED FOR VISION

As Chapter 1 discusses, business success almost always begins with a vision, a perception of marketplace needs and the methods an organization can use to satisfy them. Vision serves as the target for a firm's actions, helping to direct the company toward opportunities and differentiating it from its competitors. Michael Dell's vision of selling custom-built computers directly to consumers helped distinguish Dell from hundreds of other computer industry start-ups. John Schnatter, founder of Papa John's Pizza, keeps his vision—and his menu—focused to satisfy his pizza-loving customers, as described in the "Clicks and Mortar" box.

Vision helps companies to unify the actions of far-flung divisions, keep customers satisfied, and sustain growth. As Earthlink Network grew from just two employees to become the second-largest Internet access provider in the United States, the company stayed focused on its vision. In the words of the company's founder, Sky Dayton, "We decided to focus on the access business—not to build networks, not to create browsers, not to develop content." Amid the frenzy of funding dot.com businesses, Earthlink turned down opportunities that were unrelated to its vision. This concentration kept the company from becoming distracted and wasting resources during a period of rapid growth.[8]

Vision must be focused and yet flexible enough to adapt to changes in the business environment. When PCs became commonplace, Microsoft had to abandon its now quaint-sounding vision of a PC on every desk and in every home. The company's new vision of enabling people to do whatever they want, wherever they want positions Microsoft to jump on technologies for palm-top computing, Internet on television, cell phone Internet hookups, and all the other new technologies in the works.

Another company with a flexible vision is World Wrestling Federation Entertainment (WWF). The key to WWF's vision is in its name: "We're all about entertainment," says Linda McMahon, the company's chief executive. The company has moved beyond the "sport" of professional wrestling to encompass many ways of presenting the stories of its wrestlers. Along with the *Smackdown!* show on cable television, WWF generates earnings from compact discs and videos of WWF music, a variety of merchandise from action figures to T-shirts, and autobiographies of WWF stars. Other possibilities for the future include new television shows, such as an action-adventure series and a late-night talk show featuring WWF wrestlers. The highly profitable company has enjoyed earnings growth of 188 percent in a recent three-year period.[9]

However, vision is only the first step along an organization's path to success. Although a clear picture of a firm's purpose is vitally important, turning a business idea into reality takes careful planning and action. The next sections take a closer look at the planning and implementation process.

BUSINESS DIRECTORY

> **planning**   *process of anticipating future events and conditions and determining courses of action for achieving organizational objectives.*

> **vision**   *perception of marketplace needs and methods an organization can use to satisfy them.*

Papa John's Pizza: The Ingredients for Success

Background. Who doesn't love pizza? John Schnatter, the 30-something founder of Papa John's Pizza, based in Louisville, Kentucky, is obsessed with it. He has been ever since he got his first job as a teenager at Rocky's Sub Pub and later began selling pizzas from his father's tavern. Even in that early start to his career, he showed promise: while he sold pizzas for his father, he turned around the tavern's business, which had been $64,000 in the hole.

What Happened? In 1985, Schnatter opened his first Papa John's shop, and by 1989 he had about 20 stores around Louisville. Taking his cue from the success of food enterprises like Kentucky Fried Chicken, in 1988 he expanded beyond the city limits. Today, with Schnatter still in charge, Papa John's operates more than 2,000 stores in 48 states, as well as eight international markets. Customers can even order their pizzas online. And although Papa John's has an 11 percent slice of the pizza market compared with Pizza Hut's 50 percent, the competition is paying attention.

Schnatter's success can most likely be attributed to two main ingredients: a clear, focused vision and effective leadership. When asked, he says he thinks about pizza 17 hours a day. Presumably during the other 7 hours, he's either asleep or spending time with his wife and three children. Papa John's sells only pizza—no sandwiches, pasta dishes, or appetizers. "People just want pizza. If I want pizza, I basically just call and order a pizza," says a restaurant industry analyst. So, Papa John's stays focused on one product that Schnatter thinks it can produce better than anyone else.

The Response. "At Papa John's we have a simple formula for success: Focus on one thing and try to do it better than anyone else," states the company's Web site. "By keeping the Papa John's menu simple, we are able to focus on the quality of our product by using only superior-quality ingredients." That focus caused Pizza Hut to object to the Papa John's advertising slogan, "Better Ingredients. Better Pizza." A federal court in Dallas ruled that Papa John's could no longer use the trademarked slogan because it could not sub-

stantiate the claim, but that ruling was later overturned by a court of appeals. Controversy over the slogan did not have an impact on Papa John's emphasis on high-quality or fresh ingredients, nor did it seem to affect consumers' perception of the company. Instead, the competition appears to be following in Papa John's footsteps. "I would say there is a greater focus today than there was eight or nine years ago on quality," admits Pizza Hut president Mike Rawlings. "But I'd think that's true about the food business in general."

Today and Counting. John Schnatter still seems to enjoy being in charge of his company, now serving as CEO. "I realized I loved running a business," he recalls about his earlier experiences. "I loved every bit of it. I had found my calling." As the company expands overseas, he is likely to remain a hands-on leader. He's been known to phone executives at three in the morning to fire questions at them. But the reason he does so is that he simply wants to serve customers the best pizza, anywhere in the world.

QUESTIONS FOR CRITICAL THINKING

1. As Papa John's expands to different countries, in what ways might John Schnatter have to change his leadership style?
2. Create a new slogan for Papa John's that reflects the company's focused vision. If possible, visit the company's Web site using "Papa John's Pizza" as a keyword on your computer to get some ideas for your slogan.

Sources: "Appeals Court Upholds 'Better Ingredients. Better Pizza.' Slogan," Papa John's press release, September 19, 2000; "The Papa John's Story," Papa John's Web site, **www.papajohns.com**, accessed April 8, 2001; Kirsten Haukebo, "Papa John's Dad Finds His Calling," *USA Today*, February 22, 2000, p. 3B; Kirsten Haukebo, "Sharing Hometown Spices Up Rivalry," *USA Today*, February 22, 2000, p. 3B.

IMPORTANCE OF PLANNING

When Roger A. Enrico took over the helm of PepsiCo, the company was losing market share under a continuing onslaught from its rival, The Coca-Cola Company, coupled with the drain of trying to run relatively unprofitable enterprises such as fast-food restaurants. Enrico decided the company needed a new plan. He determined that PepsiCo's plan for profitability would focus on its two strongest product lines: packaged foods with its Frito-Lay snacks and drinks including Pepsi-Cola soft drinks and Tropicana juices. The company would sell its fast-food operations and drop efforts to compete where management believed Pepsi's brands could not dominate the market. So, PepsiCo stopped warring with Coke in every part of the world and tried for a share of emerging markets where no soft drink yet dominated. In addition, the company focused on sales in grocery stores, where Pepsi's brands have performed well in the past.

The company demonstrated to stores that its brands together were the second-largest source of their sales, trailing only Kraft Foods. Also, snacks are more profit-

Table 8.1	**Types of Plans**	
Type	**Description**	**Example**
Strategic	Establish overall objectives; position the organization within its environment for time periods ranging from short term to long term	Time Warner's plans to strengthen its presence on the Internet by merging with America Online
Tactical	Implement activities and resource allocations, typically for short-term periods	PepsiCo's efforts to build sales in supermarkets by using displays that place its snacks and drinks side by side
Operational	Set quotas, standards, or schedules to implement tactical plans	A customer service department's requirement to handle grievances within 48 hours of receipt
Adaptive	Ensure flexibility for responding to changes in the business environment by developing scenarios to take advantage of potential opportunities or respond to foreseeable problems	Microsoft's development of an operating system for use in a variety of small computing devices that may become popular
Contingency	Prepare for emergencies	Electric utilities' preparation for responding to possible sudden surges in demand, as during a heat wave

able to sell than many other supermarket products. With that message, the company persuaded stores to collaborate with PepsiCo on displaying snack foods and drinks together, encouraging shoppers as a result to buy snacks with their drinks, and vice versa. By implementing this plan, the company has become significantly more profitable. Although its sales have fallen since it spun off its fast-food chains, its profits are higher than ever.[10] PepsiCo's experience underscores the importance of planning based on a realistic assessment of opportunities combined with a clear-sighted evaluation of company strengths and competitive threats.

A typical outcome of the planning process is the creation of a formal written document called a **business plan.** The business plan states the firm's objectives and specifies the activities and resources required to achieve them. It also includes details about the markets in which the firm plans to compete, its financial resources, and the competitive situation facing each of its products. Both new and existing companies create business plans, but these documents are particularly important for entrepreneurial ventures.

Types of Planning

Planning can be categorized by scope or breadth. Some plans are very broad and long range, focusing on key organizational objectives. Other types of plans specify how the organization will mobilize to achieve these objectives. Table 8.1 explains these basic types: strategic, tactical, operational, adaptive, and contingency planning. Each step in planning incorporates more specific information than the last. From the global mission statement to general objectives to specific plans, each phase must fit into a comprehensive planning framework. The framework also must include narrow, functional plans aimed at individual employees and work areas and relevant to individual tasks. These plans fit within the firm's overall planning framework, allowing it to reach objectives and achieve its mission.

Strategic Planning   The most far-reaching level of planning is **strategic planning**— the process of determining the primary objectives of an organization and then adopting courses of action and allocating resources to achieve those objectives. Strategic planning evaluates conditions through a wide-angle lens to determine the long-range goals of the organization. An example of strategic planning is the process through which PepsiCo planned to concentrate on snack foods and drinks in markets where it could achieve dominance. Management determined that the two product categories together gave the company strength for negotiating with the stores that are its customers—a strength PepsiCo calls "the power of one." To measure the

THEY SAID IT

"No plan can prevent a stupid person from doing the wrong thing in the wrong place at the wrong time—but a good plan should keep a concentration from forming."

CHARLES E. WILSON (1890–1961)
U.S. SECRETARY OF DEFENSE DURING THE EISENHOWER ADMINISTRATION

Can SAP Regain Its Strength?

Hasso Plattner is in a pickle. As CEO of the German-based SAP, the lumbering software giant, he is perceived by many as both the organization's leader for change *and* its greatest barrier to change. And SAP needs to change if it is going to survive. It is true that the $4.9 billion company has been the world leader in enterprise resource software systems, but with more and more of its customers getting into e-commerce, SAP has failed to keep up with the pace. The key feature of the Internet is speed—and SAP has been too slow in getting out the e-commerce products its customers want and need. So, when companies wanted to link their sales forces to the Web, they turned to Siebel Systems instead. When they wanted to tie together materials and parts suppliers, they found the technology at i2 Technologies.

SAP hasn't missed the boat entirely—the company was working on e-commerce technology for both of the products mentioned. The trouble is, the organization just couldn't get them to market fast enough. It seems that the holdup has come from the organization's heavily bureaucratic structure and Plattner's own insistence on reviewing every facet of every project. For instance, no advertisement can run on the company's new Web site, mySAP.com, without Plattner's stamp of approval on size, color, and even placement on the screen. "People have great ideas, but somehow down the line they're always getting stopped," notes Marc Elmhorst, CEO of Impress, a German organization that refits SAP programs for the Web. With Plattner's insistence on complete control as an autocratic leader, decisions are slowed tremendously, and managers have neither the freedom nor the authority to make decisions based on their own expertise. Meanwhile, competitors like Commerce One have been luring away SAP's once-loyal customers, including automaker DaimlerChrysler. SAP salespeople have been defecting to the competition as well, and the stock plunged 50 percent in one quarter. Until recently, Plattner seemed completely unaware of his own role in the company's decline. "I don't know what we're doing wrong," he admitted at an SAP users conference.

Weeks later, however, he appeared to have gotten the message. He vowed to turn the company around with some radical strategic planning. First is a strategic alliance with rival Commerce One, which will combine the strengths of the two organizations and emphasize building business-to-business markets on the Web. Second is an unprecedented move in the German business world: Plattner has convinced SAP's board of directors to offer stock options to more than more than 2,000 of the company's 22,000 employees. Third, Plattner is spinning off software development units into three divisions—new products, services, and support systems—that will operate independently of the cumbersome SAP bureaucracy. Fourth, he has laid down a plan for streamlining the product installation process. The result? A closer focus on customers and speed, speed, speed. "Our old projects took 18 months or two years. Internet speed means four weeks, six weeks," notes Wolfgang Kenna, CEO of SAP America.

To accomplish all of this, Plattner not only has to change an organization, he has to change himself—his own managerial style. No one can say which is more difficult, but he is determined to achieve both.

QUESTIONS FOR CRITICAL THINKING
1. How would you define the new primary objectives of SAP?
2. What do you think would be the best leadership style for accomplishing the kinds of change that Plattner envisions?

Sources: Erich Luening, "SAP, Commerce One to Build Utilities Online Exchange," **C/Net News.com,** August 9, 2000; Stephen Baker and Spencer E. Ante, "Can SAP Swim with the Swiftest?" *Business Week,* June 26, 2000, pp. 186–188; "SAP Revamps Software Development Unit," Bloomberg News, June 2, 2000, accessed at **C/Net News.com;** "Companies to Combine Cutting-Edge Software, World-Class Recruiting Services," SAP Press Release, February 12, 2001, accessed from SAP Web site, **www.sap.com/press/index.htm.**

success of this strategy, the company set goals in terms of its sales and profits. Companies sometimes need to adjust their strategies to remain competitive, as did SAP, described in the "Business Hits and Misses" box.

Tactical Planning Tactical planning involves implementing the activities specified by strategic plans. Tactical plans guide the current and near-term activities required to implement overall strategies. At PepsiCo, tactical plans included identifying the markets in which the company would concentrate and the products it would offer in each market. Tactical planning also included establishing the plan of demonstrating to stores that they could benefit by working with PepsiCo to sell more snacks and drinks. Although strategic and tactical plans apply to different time frames, both contribute to the achievement of organizational objectives.

Operational Planning Operational planning creates the detailed standards that guide implementation of tactical plans. This activity involves choosing specific work targets and assigning employees and teams to carry out plans. Unlike strategic planning, which focuses on the organization as a whole, operational planning deals with developing and implementing tactics in specific functional areas such as production,

FIGURE 8.2
Adaptive Planning for Flexible Business Needs

human resources, or marketing. Operational plans may state quotas, standards, or schedules. An operational plan at PepsiCo might include which store managers to visit, along with an objective for what displays to encourage the managers to set up, what sales increase should result, and how to follow up after the stores try the new displays.

Adaptive Planning   All planning, whether at the strategic, tactical, or operational level, needs to develop courses of action that are fluid and forward-looking enough to adapt to changes in the business environment. In Figure 8.2, Zurich Insurance Company offers custom-tailored policies that can be modified as a business's circumstances change. To succeed in the volatile business world, companies must emphasize focus and flexibility in their plans. In other words, they must practice **adaptive planning.** For David Wheeler and his company, InfoGlide, adaptive planning has meant spotting new business opportunities. Wheeler originally founded his company to market a database program that analyzes crime reports and other data to identify suspects. But, although police departments found it useful, not many public agencies could afford the program. So Wheeler adapted the program for a more profitable market segment—insurance companies, which analyzed customer claims and related data to spot patterns of suspected fraud. Then Wheeler saw that he could interpret the software's benefits more broadly as a way for companies to learn more about all their customers. He expanded his marketing efforts, offering companies the potential to learn about their best customers, not just those engaging in fraud. As management continually revisited its strategy, InfoGlide has grown from a start-up to a $100 million company.[11]

In emphasizing a focus for planning, managers identify and then build on the company's strongest capabilities. In the case of InfoGlide, this meant the product's ability to make sense of mountains of data, coupled with companies' desire to know about their customers. To emphasize flexibility in planning, managers must develop scenarios of potential future activities to prepare the firm to take full advantage of opportunities as they occur. An important way to do this is to notice when sales start flooding in from an unexpected source or for a supposedly minor product. Barry Sheehy of a Georgia management consulting firm called CPC Econometrics says a good opportunity for entering a new business usually does not spring from the company's central activities. Instead, "it usually comes as an opportunity on the periphery," as when InfoGlide's Wheeler considered the fraud-tracking elements of his law enforcement software.[12] Similarly, when PepsiCo implemented its "power of one" strategy, Frito-Lay products began generating more than 70 percent of the company's profits, though PepsiCo was founded as, and still bears the name of, a soft-drink company.[13]

Contingency Planning   Planning cannot always foresee every possibility. Threats such as terrorism, natural disasters, and rapid economic downturns can throw even the best-laid plans into chaos. To handle the possibility of business disruption from negative events like these, many firms use **contingency planning,** which allows a firm to resume operations as quickly and as smoothly as possible after a crisis while openly communicating with the public about what happened. This planning activity involves two components: business continuation and public communication. Many firms have developed management strategies to speed recovery from accidents such as airline crashes, factory fires, chemical leaks, product tampering, and product failure.

A contingency plan usually designates a chain of command for crisis management, assigning specific functions for particular managers and employees in an emergency. Contingency planning also involves training workers to respond to emergencies, improving communications systems, and recovering the use of technology such as computer records and telecommunications systems. Additionally, contingency plans look at issues of safety and accident prevention to minimize the risk of crises in the first place.

Another important aspect of contingency planning is setting up a system for communicating with the media and public during and after a crisis. When a crisis occurs, the firm involved must quickly tell the truth. Accepting responsibility, even at the cost of short-term profitability, is a critical gesture, since early honesty means so much in the court of public opinion. Ford CEO Jac Nasser took this lesson to heart. He spoke on television about the problem of tire blowouts on the company's popular Explorer sport utility vehicles. Even though he did not have all the details of the problem, he assured the public that his company would not rest until the cause was found. Such a crisis management plan must ensure that the firm faces the public and makes amends. These steps may range from simple product replacements, such as Ford's replacement of the problem Firestone tires, to payment of medical or monetary claims. Finally, the underlying cause of the problem must be determined and systems established to make certain that it does not recur. Hiring a highly regarded, independent research group to determine what caused the problem is recommended as a method of ensuring objectivity.

Planning at Different Organizational Levels

Although managers spend some time on planning virtually every day, the total time spent and the type of planning done differ according to the level of management. As Table 8.2 points out, members of top management, including a firm's board of directors and CEO, spend a great deal of time on long-range planning, while middle-level managers and supervisors focus on short-term, tactical planning. Employees at all levels can benefit themselves and their company by making plans to meet their own goals.

Table 8.2	**Planning at Different Management Levels**	
Primary Type of Planning	**Managerial Level**	**Examples**
Strategic	Top management	Organizational objectives, fundamental strategies, long-term plans
Tactical	Middle management	Quarterly and semiannual plans, departmental policies and procedures
Operational	Supervisory management	Daily and weekly plans, rules and procedures for each department
Adaptive	All levels	Ongoing, flexible plans; quick response to changes in the environment
Contingency	Primarily top management, but all levels contribute	Ongoing plans for actions and communications in an emergency

THE STRATEGIC PLANNING PROCESS

Strategic planning often makes the difference between an organization's success and failure. Strategic planning has formed the basis of many fundamental management decisions:

- PepsiCo's decision to get out of the fast-food business
- America Online and Time Warner's decision to merge
- Amazon.com's decision to sell toys, electronics, and other products beyond books and musical recordings

Successful strategic planners typically follow the six steps shown in Figure 8.3: defining a mission, assessing the organization's competitive position, setting organizational objectives, creating strategies for competitive differentiation, implementing the strategy, and evaluating the results and refining the plan.

Defining the Organization's Mission

In an earlier section, this chapter points out the importance of an underlying vision for an organization. The first step in strategic planning is to translate the firm's vision into a mission statement. A **mission statement** is a written explanation of an organization's business intentions and aims. It is an enduring statement of company purpose, highlighting the scope of operations, the market it seeks to serve, and the ways it will attempt to set itself apart from competitors. A mission statement guides the actions of people inside the firm and informs customers and other stakeholders of the company's underlying reason for existence. After creating the mission statement, a business should share it with employees, suppliers, partners, shareholders, and customers. Figure 8.4 shows a symbol of DoubleTree Hotels' mission statement. The company offers fresh-baked cookies to guests as a symbol of its mission to make them feel at home while traveling.

Earthlink Network's mission statement is to provide direct and inexpensive connections to the Internet "in every home and business." This statement is both ambitious in its definition of a market and specific in its definition of its product. It challenges employees to provide a service that Internet users will want, while keeping the company focused on its line of business. Sky Dayton, Earthlink's founder, says, "We believed in our vision so wholeheartedly that we rejected all other moves and deals that didn't come from that initial hunger. More important, we were able to compel others to join us."[14]

Although mission statements may seem simple, their development can be one of the most complex and difficult aspects of strategic planning. Completing these statements requires detailed consideration of company values and vision. Effective

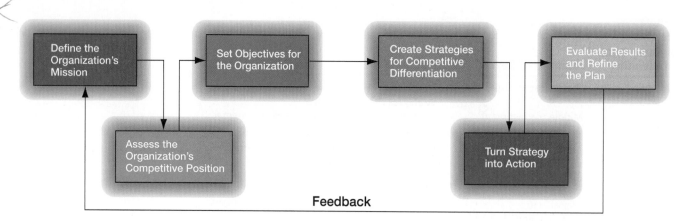

FIGURE 8.3
Steps in the Strategic Planning Process

FIGURE 8.4
A Symbol for a Mission Statement

mission statements indicate specific, achievable, inspiring principles. They avoid empty promises, ego stroking, and unrealistic statements.

Assessing Competitive Position

Once a mission statement has been created, the next step in the planning process is to assess the firm's current position in the marketplace. This phase also involves an examination of the factors that may help or hinder the organization in the future. Two frequently used tools in this phase of strategic planning are SWOT analysis and forecasts of future sales performance.

SWOT Analysis   A **SWOT analysis** is an organized method of assessing a company's internal strengths and weaknesses and its external opportunities and threats. SWOT is an acronym for *strengths, weaknesses, opportunities,* and *threats.* The basic premise of this review is that a critical internal and external study of reality should lead managers to select the appropriate strategy to accomplish their organization's objectives. SWOT analysis encourages a practical approach to planning based on a realistic view of a firm's situation and scenarios of likely future events and conditions. Household Finance Corporation capitalized on its strengths and opportunities when it developed computer software to increase the efficiency with which it could process loan applications, as described in the "Clicks and Mortar" box. The framework for a SWOT analysis appears in Figure 8.5.

To evaluate a firm's strengths and weaknesses, the planning team may examine each functional area such as human resources, finance, marketing, and information technology. Entrepreneurs may focus on the individual skills and experience they bring to a new business. Large firms may also examine strengths and weaknesses of individual divisions and geographic operations. Usually, planners attempt to look at strengths and weaknesses in relation to those of other firms in the industry.

For Starbucks, a key strength is consumers' positive image of the company's brand, which gets them to stand in line to pay several dollars for a cup of coffee. The company's strategic plans have included various

Background. Applying for a loan—to buy a car or a home or to do some remodeling—has always been a painful chore. You fill out endless forms, undergo complete scrutiny of your finances, then wait for days, weeks, or even longer for the bank or loan company to give you an answer. A couple of years ago, Household Finance Corporation (HFC) decided to find a way to change that. In an industry where the two major factors in remaining competitive are efficiency and customer knowledge and service, most financial organizations were failing at both simply because there wasn't a mechanism for selling the most financial services efficiently while avoiding making each customer feel about as special as a loan number.

What Happened? Household Finance went looking for a solution and found Vision. Vision is a software system that integrates all the steps of a loan application from beginning to end, connects to an intelligent loan assessment engine, and returns an answer in minutes. About six years ago, HFC's then head of consumer finance, Bob Elliot, predicted that speed would become an increasingly vital issue in the consumer loan industry. Ken Harvey, now HFC's chief information officer, began contemplating the possibilities. Previously, building such a system was just too big to consider with all the different banking regulations from state to state and detailed personal variables about each customer. But Harvey figured out a solution: something called object-oriented architecture for the system. To really do it right would cost the company about $83 million. But CEO Bill Aldinger recognized the opportunities that the new system would provide for his company and gave the project his approval. "I give Bill Aldinger credit," says Harvey. "He realized we could leverage our investment much better" with the costly component-based architecture that was necessary to build the system. "It took courage to make the investments that were counterintuitive in this industry," notes Patricia Wallington, a judge in the Enterprise Value Awards, which HFC received.

The Response. Household Finance capitalized on an opportunity, and the payback has already started to flow into the company.

HFC's branches can now sell 10 percent more loans in a period of time than they could before the implementation of Vision. In addition, the company's efficiency has improved radically—HFC has seen a 40 percent return on its investment within Vision's first few years of operation. And Vision's components grow "smarter" as they collect and process more data. The system is able to "take into consideration the potential lifetime value of the customer," claims Harvey. Meanwhile, HFC purchased Beneficial Corp, one of its largest competitors, now overseeing 1,400 branch offices in 46 states.

Today and Counting. HFC's strength—consumer finance—dovetailed perfectly with the opportunity to offer speed and personal service. Salespeople now report that they can spend more time with customers and potential customers because they are not overloaded with paperwork. There will be threats, as other financial organizations begin to build and implement their own systems. But HFC hopes to develop loyal customers early in the game. If loan approvals are quick and customer service is more personal and responsive than in the past, HFC has the opportunity to offer more financial products to its customers. The idea, after all, is to keep them coming back. So far, Vision seems to promise just that.

QUESTIONS FOR CRITICAL THINKING
1. In addition to the threat of competitors building similar systems, what other threats might HFC encounter in the next few years?
2. In what ways might Vision change the way HFC managers do their jobs?

Sources: "Our History," Household Finance Corp. Web site, **www.household.com,** accessed April 14, 2001; Derek Slater, "Loan Star," *CIO,* February 1, 2000, p. 106; Elaine M. Cummings, "In Search of Excellence," *CIO,* February 1, 2000, pp. 62–66.

ways to build on that strong brand loyalty by attaching it to new products and expanding into new markets. The expansion efforts have included a Starbucks Web portal, bottled Frappucino iced coffee, acquisitions of other coffee retailers, and the opening of Starbucks outlets in Europe, Asia, and the Middle East.[15]

SWOT analysis continues with an attempt to define the major opportunities and threats the firm is likely to face within the time frame of the plan. Possibilities include environmental factors such as market growth, regulatory changes, or increased competition. Starbucks saw an opportunity in the growth of the Internet and the interest in online shopping. It set up a Web portal designed to sell coffee, related accessories, gourmet foods, kitchenware, and even home furnishings. In addition, Starbucks's experience in Japan, where each outlet has average sales that top those in the U.S., suggested that overseas expansion presents a solid opportunity. A threat is that consumers may tire of their cappuccinos and lattes and switch to something else. The company has begun addressing that threat with the purchase of a gourmet tea company, Tazo.

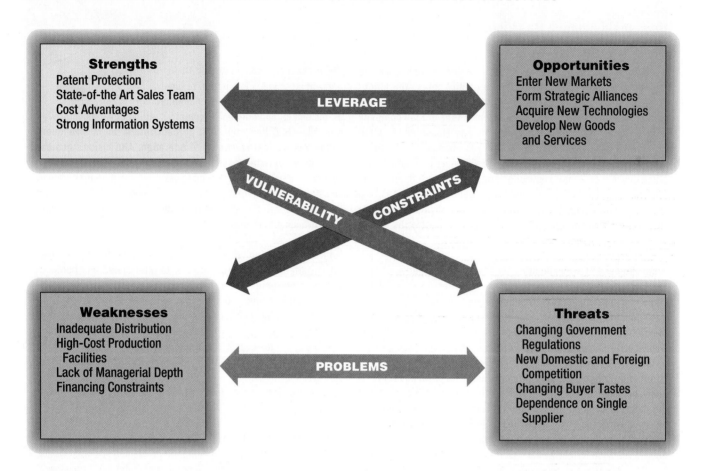

FIGURE 8.5
Elements of SWOT Analysis

Some aspects of Starbucks's strategy have succeeded better than others. The Web portal was initially disappointing. The brand was not strong enough to persuade consumers to visit Starbucks.com for furniture, and the company dropped the least successful offerings. However, Starbucks kept the site, with links to sources of music, cooking items, and wine. Starbucks is devoting more of its attention to its stores, where sales continue to be strong.[16]

If a firm's strengths and opportunities mesh successfully, as at the Starbucks retail stores, it gains competitive leverage in the marketplace. On the other hand, if internal weaknesses prevent a firm from overcoming external threats, as in the case of the Starbucks Web site, it may find itself facing insurmountable difficulties. A SWOT analysis is a useful tool in the strategic planning process because it forces management to look at factors both inside and outside the organization. SWOT analysis examines not only the current picture but also necessary current actions to prepare for likely future developments.

By preparing to address threats and weaknesses, a company can often overcome these potential problems. For example, when Paul Howley first learned about eBay's auction Web site, he was afraid that the ease of buying specialty goods online spelled doom for his company, called That's Entertainment, which runs two small stores packed with collectibles. The stores have prospered as places for collectors to visit repeatedly in their quest for just the right items to complete their collections of comic books and other entertainment memorabilia. Howley knew he couldn't compete head on with eBay, so he tried to join the Internet Age with a different strategy. By occasionally offering items at eBay's site, he found an opportunity within the threat: at eBay, That's Entertainment could sell items that appealed to buyers in other parts of the country or to only a select few collectors. For example, Howley quickly and profitably sold a bat autographed by St. Louis Cardinals great Stan Musial and a huge cat's head prop from a concert by Kiss. At the same time, to keep his regular customers coming in, Howley continues selling most items in his stores, where customers can enjoy meeting one another and browsing through the shelves.[17]

Forecasting   A second tool used to assess the firm's competitive position and a complement to SWOT analysis is forecasting, the process of estimating or predicting a company's future sales or income. Forecasts can focus on the short term (under one year), intermediate term (one to five years), or long term (over five years).

Qualitative forecasting methods are subjective techniques. The company might ask salespeople, managers, executives, or outside consultants to suggest probable levels of short-term sales. Some businesses also survey their customers about purchasing plans and develop forecasts based on the data collected. Because they rely on subjective assessments, qualitative forecasts are sometimes limited in their usefulness.

Quantitative forecasting uses historical data and mathematical models to predict how the firm will perform. A business may track sales performance over a period of time, look for ongoing trends, and forecast future growth or declines based on the identified trends. This method is called *trend analysis*.

Forecasts are important because they guide the planning process and support decision making. They can help managers pinpoint potential opportunities and threats that may interfere with the company's plans. On the other hand, they can become outdated and may require revisions due to environmental changes.

Saks Fifth Avenue stores support a socially responsible cause when they advertise that for four days they will donate a percentage of their sales to the "Fashion Targets Breast Cancer" campaign.

Setting Objectives for the Organization

After defining the company's mission and examining factors that may affect its ability to fulfill that mission, the next step in planning is to develop objectives for the organization. Objectives set guideposts by which managers define the organization's desired performance in such areas as profitability, customer service, and employee satisfaction. The mission statement delineates the company's goals in general terms, but objectives are more concrete statements. More and more businesses are setting explicit objectives for performance standards other than profitability. As public concern about environmental issues mounts, many firms find that operating in an environmentally responsible manner pays off in good relations with customers. Others channel some of their profits into socially responsible causes, such as funding educational programs and scholarships.

At Continental Airlines, objectives include satisfying customers. Each month, the Department of Transportation tracks such airline performance measures as customer satisfaction, on-time performance, and frequency of lost luggage. Several years ago, Continental ranked last in most of those measures, and late and canceled flights were costing the company $6 million a month. Continental's chief executive, Gordon Bethune, declared that if Continental could achieve a ranking among the top three in any month, the company would split the $6 million with employees, amounting to a $65 per employee bonus for the month. Employees began to collaborate on solutions to flight delays, and before long, they were earning the monthly bonuses. Continental also spent some of the savings on upgrading equipment, which helps the airline continue meeting its performance objectives.[18]

Creating Strategies for Competitive Differentiation

Developing a mission statement and setting objectives point a business toward a specific destination. To get there, however, the firm needs to map the strategies it will follow to compete with other companies pursuing similar missions and objectives. The underlying goal of strategy development is **competitive differentiation,** the unique combination of a company's abilities and approaches that place it ahead of competitors. Common sources of competitive differentiation include human resources, product innovation, technology, and financial management. Figure 8.6 shows how some firms have leveraged these sources of differentiation to their advantage.

Product innovation is a key part of the strategy at General Mills. In the slow-growth food industry, General Mills is succeeding by developing food products that support the busy, eat-on-the-go lifestyle of modern Americans. New products must meet a basic criterion: can consumers eat it one-handed? In other words, can consumers wolf down the product without utensils or much investment of time and effort? For example, Go-Gurt—kid-friendly yogurt in a squeezable plastic tube—has propelled General Mills to become the top seller of yogurt and inspired the company to launch an adult version called Expresse. The company also has developed versions of breakfast cereal shaped into bars containing a layer of milk solids, so they offer

FIGURE 8.6
Sources of Competitive Advantage

Source	Example
Human Resources	Central Parking Corp. only hires college graduates to manage the company's public parking lots. The managers help institute formal management systems, sell new customers, and improve customer satisfaction.
Product Innovation	Cosmetic manufacturer Hard Candy developed a line of nail polishes in unusual shades. The company relies on a continual stream of new, innovative product shades to compete with large manufacturers like Revlon.
Technology	Dell Computer Corporation continually rethinks its operations. It pioneered such ideas as building PCs to order, selling customized computers over the Internet, and using customized Web pages to interact with customers. By purchasing only the components it needs to fill orders, quickly assembling computers, and shipping products immediately, Dell keeps its costs well below competitors'.
Financial Management	Ross Stores Inc. purchases and sells end-of-season merchandise. Company buyers actively negotiate with manufacturers to get the lowest cost of goods. Tight controls on operating expenses also keep prices low. The savings translate into low prices for customers, a key advantage in the highly competitive retail market.

the same nutrients as a bowl of cereal and milk. In addition, the company has acquired Pillsbury and has big hopes for its dough division. Explains General Mills's CEO, Steve Sanger, "If you think about handheld foods, most of them are dough wrapped around something."[19]

Implementation: Turning Strategy into Action

Once the first four phases of the strategic planning process are complete, managers face even bigger challenges. They must begin to put strategy into action by identifying the specific methods and deploying the resources needed to implement the intended plans. In this stage, managers draw heavily on their human skills as they achieve objectives through the efforts of their employees.

Citadel Communications Corporation, a chain of radio stations in midsized markets, has a successful track record of implementing strategy. Citadel's strategy is to identify markets with relatively little competition—and relatively low prices for radio stations—coupled with a potential for growth. It acquires stations in these markets, looking especially for opportunities to create so-called flanking formats, in which two similar stations serve different groups of listeners. The company might set up two country stations for two different age groups. By staging joint promotions and using the same music director, the two stations can operate more profitably than either could on its own. To implement this strategy, Citadel sells stock and bonds to raise money and watches for signs of growth in midsized cities, such as announcements that a city plans to build an airport. Within a week after Citadel buys stations, CEO Larry R. Wilson and a team of managers visit the stations and meet the entire staff. They look for ways to consolidate the staffs in multistation deals, but each station maintains its own sales staff. In Wilson's experience, salespeople are most motivated if they represent only one station. Implementing this strategy has grown Citadel from two Tucson radio stations to a profitable chain of over 200 stations sprinkled around the U.S.[20]

Monitoring and Adapting Strategic Plans

The final stage in the strategic planning process, closely linked to implementation, consists of monitoring and adapting plans when actual performance fails to match expectations. Monitoring involves establishing methods of securing feedback about actual performance. Common methods include comparisons of actual sales and market share data with forecasts, information received from supplier and customer surveys, complaints received on the firm's customer hot line, and reports prepared by staff members within production, finance, marketing, and other company departments.

After Daniel P. Burnham took over the CEO post at defense contractor Raytheon, he discovered that the company's projected profits were overly optimistic. As Burnham explained to stock market analysts, senior managers had been reluctant to let go of their original five-year forecasts. Apparently Raytheon had a culture in which management was afraid to change a forecast or admit to problems with it, once it became part of the five-year plan. So, Burnham had to correct the attitudes surrounding his company's planning process, as well as the forecasts themselves.[21]

Ongoing use of such tools as SWOT analysis and forecasting can help management adapt objectives and functional plans as changes occur. An increase in the price of a key product component, for instance, could dramatically affect the firm's ability to maintain planned prices and still earn acceptable profits. An unexpected strike by UPS may disrupt shipments of products to retail and business customers. In each instance, the original plan may require modification to continue to guide the firm toward achievement of its objectives.

MANAGERS AS DECISION MAKERS

In carrying out planning and the other management functions, managers make decisions every day. **Decision making** is the process of recognizing a problem or opportunity and then finding a solution to it. The types of decisions that managers make can be classified as programmed and nonprogrammed decisions.

Programmed and Nonprogrammed Decisions

Programmed and nonprogrammed decisions differ in whether they have unique elements. A **programmed decision** involves simple, common, and frequently occurring problems for which solutions have already been determined. Examples of programmed decisions include choosing the starting salary for a marketing assistant, reordering raw materials needed in the manufacturing process, and selecting the price discounts to offer customers who buy in large amounts. For these types of decisions, organizations develop rules, policies, and detailed procedures that managers apply to achieve consistent, quick, and inexpensive solutions to common problems. Since such solutions eliminate the time-consuming process of identifying and evaluating alternatives and making a new decision each time a situation occurs, they free managers to devote time to the more complex problems associated with nonprogrammed decisions.

A **nonprogrammed decision** involves a complex and unique problem or opportunity with important consequences for the organization. Examples of nonprogrammed decisions include entering a new geographic market, acquiring another company, or introducing a new product. Many nonprogrammed decisions arise in the still-new world of e-commerce. Business strategies are still being tested in cyberspace, so companies do not have a historical basis for predicting the success of their ideas. Blue Mountain Arts has generated heavy traffic from the millions of people who visit its Web site to select and send free online greeting cards. Now the company, which created the site as a way to generate awareness of its printed cards, which cost money, is trying to make the Web site profitable. The company is experimenting with selling advertising on its site and providing links to product offerings related to the subject of a greeting card a person decides to send someone. A person sending a romantic card can click on a link to Blue Mountain's Proflowers.com or Dan's Chocolates' Web site and order flowers or candy for that special person. These enterprises have the advantage of communicating with a huge group of greeting-card senders, but the notion of converting people who received a free service into paying customers is so unusual that Blue Mountain's profitability is difficult to predict.[22]

How Managers Make Decisions

Many executives rely on their intuition, or gut feelings, to decide how to solve problems or take advantage of opportunities. Intuitive decision making serves as a substitute when managers lack enough information to determine the probable outcome of a decision. They rely on their instincts and previous experience to solve problems and take advantage of opportunities. Alain Rossmann, CEO of Phone.com, says management believed programmers would be more productive if the company enabled them to work wherever and whenever they wanted. The company gave every programmer powerful workstations and Internet connections and declared that no one was required to be in the office on Tuesdays, Wednesdays, or Thursdays. However, says Rossmann, this arrangement did not provide for enough interaction among employees: "We had to amend the rules and make it that only the senior guys and power coders could work at home."[23] Although such trial-and-error decision making is common, information gathering and analysis can improve decisions.

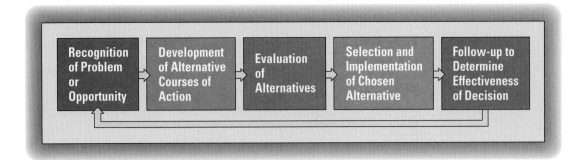

Recognition of Problem or Opportunity → Development of Alternative Courses of Action → Evaluation of Alternatives → Selection and Implementation of Chosen Alternative → Follow-up to Determine Effectiveness of Decision

FIGURE 8.7
Steps in the Decision-Making Process

In a narrow sense, decision making involves choosing among two or more alternatives; the chosen alternative becomes the decision. In a broader sense, decision making involves a systematic, step-by-step process that helps managers make effective choices. This process begins when someone recognizes a problem or opportunity; it proceeds with developing potential courses of action, evaluating the alternatives, selecting and implementing one of them, and assessing the outcome of the decision. The steps in the decision-making process are illustrated in Figure 8.7. This systematic approach can be applied to all decisions, with either programmed or nonprogrammed features.

Managers can follow the steps in this decision-making process as a rational way to reduce the risks associated with the outcomes of decisions. Such a methodical approach is especially beneficial for high-stakes decisions. Siemens, a German high-tech company, has established a system for making complex decisions. It brings together teams of managers to develop ways to earn money or cut costs. Siemens realized that its employees' mobile-phone use in Britain was an expensive mess. A team of six middle managers tackled the problem. They started by announcing that they were developing ways to centralize purchasing of phone services, and they directed Siemens employees worldwide to review detailed bills of their phone usage. Even before the decision group formulated any changes, phone bills shrank as employees saw what wasted phone calls were costing the company. The management team analyzed the data and drew up a plan, then got busy selling it to those who would be affected. They traveled throughout Britain, presenting the savings that would result, and they set up a site on the company's computer network where employees could learn details about the project. Cost-cutting decisions such as these have saved the company more than $11 million in a single year.[24]

Making good decisions is never easy, however, because it involves taking risks that can influence a firm's success or failure. At Procter & Gamble (P&G), managers must make difficult decisions about the company's large mix of consumer products. Focusing on the company's old standbys, like Pampers diapers and Crest toothpaste, keeps risks low but also stifles growth. But developing new products is more expensive and riskier. Under Durk I. Jager, P&G tried launching four or five new products a year, but sales and earnings disappointed investors so much that Jager resigned. His replacement, A. G. Lafley, must decide whether to dump the company's less-profitable products, develop new products in-house, or buy companies with profitable product lines. Such decisions can make a difference of billions of dollars on P&G's bottom line.[25]

MANAGERS AS LEADERS

The most visible component of a manager's responsibilities is **leadership,** directing or inspiring people to attain organizational goals. *Fortune* magazine's survey of the Best Companies to Work for in America has identified an important distinguishing characteristic of these successful companies: a powerful, visionary leader. Leaders such as Continental Airlines' Gordon Bethune, Microsoft's Bill Gates, SAS Institute's Jim Goodnight, and Hewlett-Packard's Carly Fiorina are demanding managers, yet they inspire their employees to reach their full potential.[26] These leaders not only inspire their subordinates to work hard but also motivate others to model their own leadership behavior. Such influence is especially important in companies where technology enables employees to work at remote locations. When employees are in a home office, at the client's site, or wherever they are most inspired, managers cannot attain results by constantly checking on employees. Instead, they depend on leadership to bring out the best in their people.

Because effective leadership is so important to organizational success, a large amount of research has focused on the characteristics of a good leader. Great leaders do not all share the same qualities, but three traits are often mentioned: empathy, which is the ability to imagine oneself in another's position; self-awareness; and objectivity in dealing with others. Many great leaders share other traits, including courage, ability to inspire others, passion, commitment, flexibility, innovation, and willingness to experiment.

Leadership involves the use of influence or power. This influence may come from one or more sources. One source of power is the leader's position in the organization. A marketing manager has the authority to direct the activities of employees in that department. Another source of power comes from a leader's expertise and experience. A first-line supervisor with expert machinist skills will most likely be respected by employees in the machining department. Some leaders derive power from their forceful personalities. Employees may admire a leader because they recognize an exceptionally kind and fair, humorous, energetic, or enthusiastic person.

A well-known example is Herb Kelleher (see photo on page 290), who has gained leadership power partly through his position as cofounder and CEO of Southwest Airlines. But Kelleher's influence in motivating employees to outperform those at rival airlines comes from his dynamic personality, boundless energy, love of fun, and sincere concern for his employees. Kelleher leads by example, modeling the behavior he wants to see in his employees. He's not above pitching in to help serve snacks to passengers and load luggage. Employees, inspired by his example, unload and reload a plane in 20 minutes—one-third of the average for other airlines.

Another inspiring leader is E*Trade Group's chief executive, Christos M. Cotsakos. According to a former E*Trade executive, Cotsakos landed the top job primarily because "he knew how to excite the troops." To enable E*Trade to compete at breathtaking speed and in the high-risk environment of the Internet, Cotsakos inspires his employees to work hard, act fast, and cooperate with one another. When problems arise, he expects everyone to pull together. When E*Trade's chief information officer, Debra Chrapaty, and CEO, Leonard Purkis, became locked in an angry dispute, Cotsakos secretly sent them identical bouquets of roses, each bearing a card saying, "We're a team. Let's work it out." Each thinking the other had sent the flowers, the two executives resumed their efforts at problem solving and developed a fresh view of their interdependence. And when a computer shutdown drove the company's Internet customers to their phones to place trading orders, E*Trade's senior vice president for marketing and everyone on his staff who was licensed to sell stock helped handle the flood of phone calls. Like Chrapaty and Purkis, the marketing executive had bought into Cotsakos's view on leadership, developed during his service as a rifleman during the Vietnam War: "It's about loyalty and trust and who you have in the foxhole with you."[27]

Leadership Styles

The way a leader uses power to lead others determines his or her leadership style. Researchers have identified a continuum of leadership styles based on the amount of employee participation allowed or invited. At one end of the continuum, **autocratic**

leadership is centered on the boss. Autocratic leaders make decisions on their own without consulting employees. They reach decisions, communicate them to subordinates, and expect prompt implementation of instructions. An autocratic sales manager might assign quotas to individual salespeople without consulting them.

Democratic leadership involves subordinates in making decisions. Located in the middle of the continuum, this leadership style centers on employees' contributions. Democratic leaders delegate assignments, ask employees for suggestions, and encourage participation. A democratic sales manager would want sales personnel to participate in setting their own sales quotas.

At the other end of the continuum from autocratic leadership is **free-rein leadership.** Free-rein leaders believe in minimal supervision. They leave most decisions to their subordinates. Free-rein leaders communicate with employees frequently, as the situation warrants. Figure 8.8 summarizes the differences among the three leadership styles.

An important trend that has developed in business during the past decade is the concept of **empowerment,** a practice in which managers lead employees by sharing power, responsibility, and decision making with them. Shared leadership is the style of Doug Merritt, CEO of Icarian, a company that provides online software for managing human resources. Merritt explains his approach to leadership this way: "The way you get superior performance is to get people's passionate loyalty and belief." In an environment where 60-hour workweeks are the norm, Merritt does this by offering flexibility and giving employees the resources they need to do their jobs. Rather than dictating all the details of work schedules and rewards, Icarian offers flexible work arrangements. The company grants time off to business development analyst Adam Nelson, who is training as a shot-putter for the U.S. Olympic Team, and to marketer Debi Memmolo, who leaves early once a week to volunteer with inner-city kids. Each month, the company gives each employee 50 "Icarian bucks" to reward one another with treats like therapeutic massage.[28]

FIGURE 8.8
Comparison of Leadership Styles

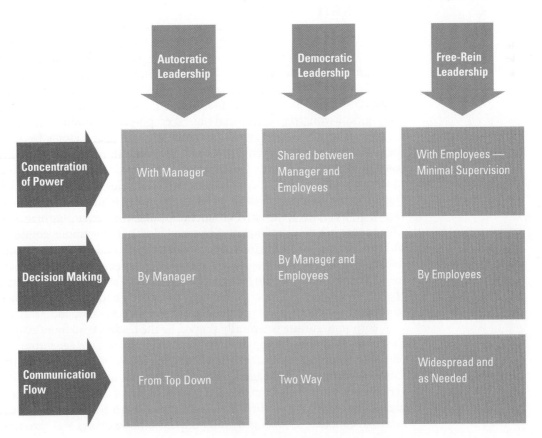

	Autocratic Leadership	Democratic Leadership	Free-Rein Leadership
Concentration of Power	With Manager	Shared between Manager and Employees	With Employees — Minimal Supervision
Decision Making	By Manager	By Manager and Employees	By Employees
Communication Flow	From Top Down	Two Way	Widespread and as Needed

Merritt's view of empowerment is embraced by leaders of many companies, including General Electric, Harley-Davidson, Ford, DaimlerChrysler, and Intel. Chapter 10 discusses many different ways in which organizations are empowering employees.

Which Leadership Style Is Best?

The most appropriate leadership style depends on the function of the leader, the subordinates, and the situation. Some leaders cannot work comfortably with high participation of subordinates in decision making. Some employees lack the ability or the desire to assume responsibility. In addition, the specific situation helps to determine the most effective style of interactions. Sometimes managers must handle problems that require immediate solutions without consulting employees. When time pressure is less acute, participative decision making may work better for the same people.

Democratic leaders often ask for suggestions and advice from their employees but make the final decisions themselves. A manager who prefers the free-rein leadership style may be forced by circumstances to make a particular decision in an autocratic manner. A manager may involve employees in interviewing and hiring decisions but take complete responsibility for firing any employee.

After years of research intended to determine the best types of leaders, experts agree that they cannot identify any single best style of leadership. Instead, they contend that the most effective style depends on the leader's base of power, the difficulty of the tasks involved, and the characteristics of the employees. Both extremely easy and extremely difficult situations are best suited to leaders who emphasize the accomplishment of assigned tasks. Moderately difficult situations are best suited to leaders who emphasize participation and good working relationships with subordinates.

CORPORATE CULTURE

The best leadership style to adopt often depends on the organization's **corporate culture**, its system of principles, beliefs, and values. Managerial philosophies, communications networks, and workplace environments and practices all influence corporate culture. At Home Depot, the corporate culture is based on the belief that employees should fully understand and be enthusiastic about the core business of serving do-it-yourselfers. All newly hired employees, including top managers, must spend their first two weeks working on the sales floor of a Home Depot store. There they are exposed to the company's customers and, the company hopes, will soak up some of their can-do spirit. The company also encourages employees to get involved in service projects, like building houses for Habitat for Humanity, which brings them closer to their community while seeing the stores' products in use. In addition, Home Depot gets employees excited about the business by granting them stock options. This benefit has made millionaires of many Home Depot employees. Stories like that of Franc Gambatse, who started as a sales clerk and less than a decade later was managing a Home Depot store and enjoying prosperity he "never could have imagined," inspire other employees to give their all. The retailer even has a company cheer: "Gimme an H!" and on through the store's name, as the troops reply, ready to support the company's continued growth in stores, sales, and profits.[29]

A corporate culture is typically shaped by the leaders who founded and developed the company and by those who have succeeded them. One generation of employees passes on a corporate culture to newer employees. Sometimes, this transfer is part of formal training. New managers who attend sessions at McDonald's Hamburger University may learn skills in management, but they also acquire the basics of the organization's corporate culture. Employees can absorb corporate culture through informal contacts, as well as by talking with other workers and through their experiences on the job.

Managers use symbols, rituals, and ceremonies to reinforce corporate culture. At Hewlett-Packard, the primary symbol is the simple garage where two engineering students, Bill Hewlett and Dave Packard, tinkered for hours on what became one of the first PCs. When the two young men built their invention into a major company, they helped to transform the way work is done. Today, the company's current CEO, Carly Fiorina, uses that symbol in internal communications and the company's advertising to convey the company's role as an innovator. In this way, she inspires employees to continue innovating. Similarly, Amazon.com's Jeff Bezos started his company in humble surroundings, at a desk he constructed from a door, some angle brackets, and two-by-fours. Today, Amazon.com has plenty of money it could spend on fancy office furniture, but Bezos insists that all employees use similar door-desks. The image reminds employees of the company's roots, making them members of a special group. By association, they become part of an entrepreneurial culture.[30]

Corporate culture can have a big impact on a company's success. In an organization with a strong culture, employees tend to work hard toward the company's goals and to stay with the company longer. In a company with 40,000 employees, reducing turnover by 3 percent can save as much as $36 million in costs to recruit, hire, and train new people, according to Curt Coffman, senior vice president with the Gallup Organization.[31]

SAS Institute, which sells a sophisticated package of statistical analysis software used by 98 of the 100 largest U.S. companies, maintains exceptionally low employee turnover with a culture that places a high value on respecting employees. The company demonstrates trust in employees by offering unlimited sick leave and time off to care for family. Respect also incorporates accountability; product manuals list the names of the people who developed, tested, and updated the software. The company actively seeks feedback from employees through annual surveys. Perhaps most important, SAS creates a healthy working climate. In an industry characterized by 60- or 80-hour workweeks, SAS embraces a seven-hour workday. Promptly at five o'clock, the automated switchboard starts answering phones with the message, "Most of SAS Institute is closed at this time. . . ." The company also provides on-site child care, a beautiful gymnasium with laundry services for workout clothes, and help for setting up elder care for aging parents. The purpose is to make employees want to keep working for SAS. The company's turnover is so low that SAS saves tens of millions of dollars a year compared with the average software company's turnover expenses. And that measure doesn't even count the benefits of highly committed employees. Kathy Passarella, who trains employees in computer skills, says, "You're given the freedom, the flexibility, and the resources to do your job. Because you're treated so well, you treat the company well."[32]

In an organization with a strong culture, everyone knows and supports the same objectives. A company with a weak or constantly shifting culture lacks a clear sense of purpose. To achieve its goals, a business must also provide a framework that defines how employees should accomplish their tasks. This framework is the organization structure, which results from the management function of organizing.

STRUCTURE IN ORGANIZATIONS

The management function of organizing is the process of blending human and material resources through a formal structure of tasks and authority. It involves arranging work, dividing tasks among employees, and coordinating them to ensure implementation of plans and accomplishment of objectives. The result of the organizing process is an **organization**, a structured grouping of people working together to achieve common objectives. An organization features three key elements: human interaction, goal-directed activities, and structure. The organizing

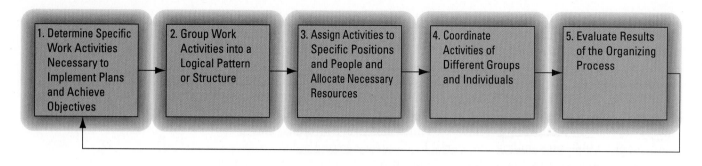

FIGURE 8.9
Steps in the Organizing Process

process should result in an overall structure that permits interactions among individuals and departments needed to achieve company goals.

The steps involved in the organizing process are shown in Figure 8.9. Managers must first determine the specific activities needed to implement plans and achieve goals. Next, they group these work activities into a logical structure. Then they assign work to specific employees and give the employees the resources they need to complete it. Managers must coordinate the work of different groups and employees within the business. Finally, they must evaluate the results of the organizing process to ensure effective and efficient progress toward planned goals. Evaluation often results in changes to the way work is organized.

Many factors influence the results of organizing. The list includes a firm's goals and competitive strategy, the type of goods or services it offers, the way it uses technology to accomplish work, and its size. Small firms typically create very simple structures. The owner of a dry-cleaning business generally is the top manager, who hires several employees to process orders, launder the clothing, and make deliveries. The owner handles the functions of purchasing supplies such as detergents and hangers, hiring and training employees and coordinating their work, preparing advertisements for the local newspaper, and keeping accounting records.

As a company grows, its structure increases in complexity. With increased size comes specialization and growing numbers of employees. A larger firm may employ many salespeople, along with a sales manager to direct and coordinate their work, or organize an accounting department and hire employees to work as cost clerks, payroll clerks, and accountants.

The organizing process should result in a well-defined structure so that employees know what expectations their jobs involve, to whom they report, and how their work contributes to the company's effort to meet its goals. To help employees understand how their work fits within the overall operation of the firm, managers prepare an **organization chart,** which is a visual representation of a firm's structure that illustrates job positions and functions. Figure 8.10 illustrates a sample organization chart. Each box in the chart would show the name of the person who holds the position. An organization chart depicts the division of a firm into departments that meet organizational needs.

Drawing and studying an organizational chart can help management decide whether the company's structure is well designed for the company's strategy. For example, when Conray, Arkansas–based Acxiom Corporation was having difficulty meeting the challenges of fast growth in the early 1990s, management determined that the problem was a structure that had grown out of control like a cancerous tumor. Whenever Acxiom wanted to give an employee a raise, the company created a management position for that employee. The result was a company that had a manager for every 2.7 employees, and some departments had 13 levels of management. Within this structure, people spent all their time seeking approval for decisions, and both customers and employees were dissatisfied. Management decided to start from scratch, eliminating the fancy titles, finding other ways to reward employees, and organizing employees into work teams. Now decisions are made by whichever

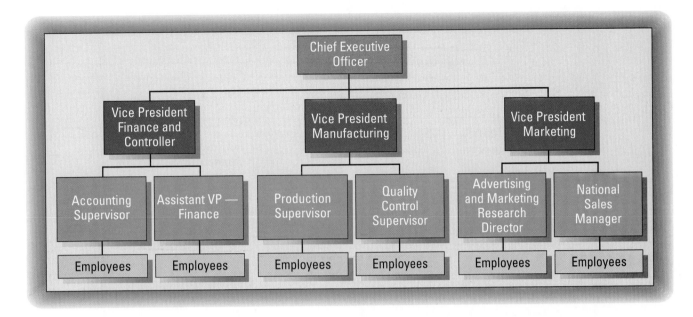

FIGURE 8.10
Sample Organization Chart

employees are closest to the situation, and employees are more preoccupied with pleasing customers than with their place on the organization chart.[33]

Departmentalization

Departmentalization is the process of dividing work activities into units within the organization. This arrangement lets employees specialize in certain jobs to promote efficient performance. A marketing department may be headed by a marketing vice president, who directs the work of salespeople, marketing researchers, and advertising and public relations personnel. A human resources manager may head a department made up of people with special skills in such areas as recruiting and hiring, employee benefits administration, and labor relations. The five major forms of departmentalization subdivide work by product, geographic area, customer, function, and process:

- *Product departmentalization*—This form organizes work units based on the goods and services a company offers. The organization structure of Sony Corp. spans ten separate companies that define its different product groups such as semiconductors, home entertainment, recording media, broadcasting, and image and sound communications products.

- *Geographic departmentalization*—This form organizes units by geographic region within a country or, for a multinational firm, by region throughout the world. Retailers like Dillard's are organized by divisions that serve different parts of the country. Railroads and gas and oil distributors also favor geographic departmentalization.

- *Customer departmentalization*—A firm that offers a variety of goods and services targeted to different types of customers might structure itself based on customer departmentalization. The Boeing Company has defined one operating unit that builds aircraft for commercial customers such as United Airlines and another that builds military airplanes, helicopters, and missile and space systems for government customers.

- *Functional departmentalization*—Some firms organize work units according to business functions such as finance, marketing, human resources,

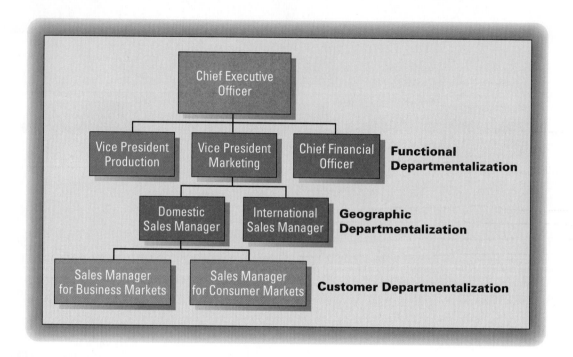

FIGURE 8.11
Different Forms of Departmentalization within One Company

and production. An advertising agency may create departments for creatives such as copywriters, media buyers, and account executives.

- *Process departmentalization*—Some goods and services require multiple work processes to complete their production. A manufacturer may set up separate departments for cutting material, heat-treating it, forming it into its final shape, and painting it.

As Figure 8.11 illustrates, a single company may implement several different departmentalization schemes. The departments initially are organized by functions, then subdivided by geographic areas, which are further organized according to customer types. In deciding on a form of departmentalization, managers take into account the type of good or service they produce, the size of their company, their customer base, and the locations of their customers.

As organizations grow and change, they frequently restructure their operations. The need to act more quickly in the face of growing demand was the inspiration for the changes in Acxiom's structure, described earlier. On a larger scale but for similar reasons, Microsoft recently adopted a new structure. Microsoft had used a product structure, based on two product categories: operating systems and applications software, like word processing and spreadsheets. This broad structure meant that people in the same division were trying to coordinate efforts for the operating systems of everything from palm-top computers to corporate networks. Microsoft's 30,000 employees handling 183 products tried to get things done through five layers of management, and many became frustrated with the slow pace of decision making. When Steven A. Ballmer took on the job of Microsoft president, he decided to rearrange the company into divisions based on customer groups: software developers, consumers buying home PCs and computer games, and corporate leaders and knowledge workers. Says Ballmer, "The new structure puts the customer at the center of everything we do."[34]

Delegating Work Assignments

After grouping activities into departments, managers assign this work to employees. The act of assigning activities to employees is called **delegation**. Managers delegate work to free their own time for planning and decision making. Subordinates to

SOLVING AN ETHICAL CONTROVERSY

The late president Harry S Truman had a plaque on his desk that read, "The buck stops here." We might think that the leader of any large company would follow the same principle. But that's not necessarily true. While management experts struggle to analyze the depth of loyalty and organizational commitment that workers feel toward their employers, CEOs sometimes seem to shuffle among companies as if they were attending a progressive dinner. When the company stumbles, they often get fired. Sometimes they leave of their own accord. In either case, they don't leave the party empty-handed. Take Jill Barad, toy-manufacturer Mattel's CEO for only three years. During her tenure, turnover among managers escalated, and the company's stock plunged from a high of $46 to $12 when she resigned. Yet she left the company with a huge "golden parachute," including $26 million in cash, $12.8 million in retirement benefits, payoff of her very sizable home mortgage, and a country-club membership, among other severance benefits.

Lew Platt, former CEO of Hewlett-Packard, had to return $2.4 million worth of company stock when HP's earnings growth sharply declined so far that the company did not meet certain performance goals. His total compensation dropped about 75 percent that year, but he still cleared $1.8 million, in addition to 200,000 stock options. And Doug Invester, formerly of The Coca-Cola Co., received a severance package worth a reported $25.5 million.

Since top executives are responsible for setting the course for their companies, who should be held accountable when they don't deliver?

When a company stumbles, should its leaders be held financially responsible?

PRO

1. Top managers typically receive bonuses or stock options when a company does well, so they should also be penalized when it does poorly. They also set the overall strategy, so a company's success depends on their abilities.
2. Employees depend on managers to make good strategic decisions, and when they don't, employees can suffer through job loss, wage freezes, and other cost-cutting measures.

3. Shareholders feel the pain through losses in their investments, so top managers should share in the same financial pain of failure.

CON

1. Top managers can set the tone and overall policies, but there are many factors to a company's success or failure that are completely beyond their control, such as the overall economic or political environment.
2. Priorities are constantly shifting in today's new economy, so holding top managers responsible for a company's overall success or failure is unfair and unrealistic.
3. High-level managers lose their jobs when a company doesn't meet or exceed expectations, so they are already paying the ultimate price for failure.

SUMMARY

When a large company stumbles, many people are affected—employees, customers, stockholders. Often, housecleaning—or at least finger-pointing—results at top levels. Some people believe that "the buck stops" with a company's leader, whereas others believe that a single leader cannot be held responsible for the performance of an entire firm in an uncertain environment. At the defense contractor Raytheon, where severe failures in strategic planning and an organizational culture that discouraged lower-level managers from giving bad news to former CEO Dennis Picard, the company's revenues went into a nosedive. Former U.S. Senator Warren Rudman, one of Raytheon's board members, took the diplomatic approach to assigning responsibility. "I don't think anyone is blameless in this," he remarked.

Sources: Dean Foust, "CEO Pay: Nothing Succeeds Like Failure," *Business Week*, September 11, 2000, p. 46; Margaret Loftus, "Golden Parachute Barbie," *U.S. News & World Report*, May 15, 2000; Pamela Sherrid, "Troubles in Barbieland," *U.S. News & World Report*, January 17, 2000; Ram Charan and Geoffrey Colvin, "The Right Fit," *Fortune*, April 17, 2000, pp. 226–238; Geoffrey Smith and Victoria Murphy, "Reality Bites at Raytheon," *Business Week*, November 15, 1999, pp. 78–82; Geoffrey Colvin, "A CEO's Pay Goes Negative," *Fortune*, March 15, 1999, p. 35; Ram Charan and Geoffrey Colvin, "CEOs: The Right Fit," *Fortune*, January 17, 2001, vol. 141, no. 8.

whom managers assign tasks thus receive responsibility, or obligations to perform those tasks. Along with responsibilities, employees also receive authority, or the power to make decisions and to act on them so they can carry out their responsibilities. Delegation of responsibility and authority makes employees accountable to their supervisor or manager. *Accountability* means that employees are responsible for the results of the ways they perform their assignments; they must accept the consequences of their actions. The "Solving an Ethical Controversy" box explores the debate over accountability among top executives who fail to perform well for their companies.

BUSINESS DIRECTORY

➤ **delegation** *act of assigning work activities to subordinates.*

Authority and responsibility tend to move downward in organizations, as managers and supervisors delegate work to subordinates. However, accountability moves upward, as managers assume final accountability for performance by the employees they manage. So, managers carefully delegate tasks to the best-qualified people.

Span of Management   The span of management, or *span of control*, is the number of subordinates a manager can supervise effectively. A top manager usually works within a narrow span of management, directing the work of the firm's top executives. First-line managers have wider spans of management, monitoring the work of many employees. The span of management varies considerably depending on many factors, including the type of work performed and employees' training. In recent years, a growing trend has brought ever wider spans of control, as companies have reduced their layers of management to flatten their organization structures, in the process increasing the decision-making responsibility they give to employees.

Information technology can also broaden the span of management. Firms like Owens-Corning, the building supplies manufacturer, have equipped their salespeople with laptop computers that provide instant access to product and customer information. This automation supports wide spans of control by regional managers, because the information allows salespeople to make decisions on their own.

Centralization and Decentralization   How widely should managers disperse decision-making authority throughout an organization? A company that emphasizes centralization retains decision making at the top of the management hierarchy. A company that emphasizes decentralization locates decision making at lower levels. A trend toward decentralization has pushed decision making down to operating employees in many cases. Firms that have decentralized believe that the change can enhance their flexibility and responsiveness in serving customers. At SAS Institute, decentralization and delegation are logical, given the company's high trust in its talented staff. Employee groups set project deadlines. Because of their input, project timetables and new-product announcements are usually on target.[35]

Types of Organization Structures

Organizations can be classified under four main types according to the nature of their internal authority relationships. The four primary types are line, line-and-staff, committee, and matrix structures. These terms do not specify mutually exclusive categories, though. In fact, most contemporary organizations combine elements of one or more of these structures.

Line Organizations   A line organization, the oldest and simplest organization structure, establishes a direct flow of authority from the chief executive to subordinates. The line organization defines a simple, clear chain of command—the set of relationships that indicates who gives direction to whom and who reports to whom. This arrangement helps to prevent buck passing. Decisions can be made quickly because the manager has authority to control subordinates' actions.

A line organization brings an obvious defect, though. Each manager must accept complete responsibility for a number of activities and cannot possibly be an expert in all of them. This defect is apparent in medium-sized and large firms, where the pure line structure fails to take advantage of the specialized skills that are so vital to modern business. Managers become overburdened with administrative details and paperwork, leaving them little time for planning.

As a result, the line organization is an ineffective model in any but the smallest organizations. Hairstyling salons, so-called mom-and-pop grocery stores, and small law firms can operate effectively with simple line structures. Ford, General Electric, and Boeing cannot.

Line-and-Staff Organizations   A line-and-staff organization combines the direct flow of authority of a line organization with staff departments that serve, advise, and support the line departments. Line departments participate directly in decisions that affect the core operations of the organization. Staff departments lend specialized technical support. Examples of staff departments include labor relations, legal counsel, research and development, accounting, taxes, and information technology. Figure 8.12 illustrates a line-and-staff organization. Accounting, engineering, and human resources are staff departments that support the line authority extending from the plant manager to the production manager and supervisors.

A line manager and a staff manager differ significantly in their authority relationships. A line manager forms a part of the primary line of authority that flows throughout the organization. Line managers interact directly with the functions of production, financing, or marketing—the functions needed to produce and market goods and services. A staff manager provides information, advice, or technical assistance to aid line managers. Staff managers do not have authority to give orders outside their own departments or to compel line managers to take action.

The line-and-staff organization is common in midsized and large organizations. It is an effective structure because it combines the line organization's capabilities for rapid decision making and direct communication with the expert knowledge of staff specialists.

Committee Organizations A committee organization is a structure that places authority and responsibility jointly in the hands of a group of individuals rather than a single manager. This model typically appears as part of a regular line-and-staff structure. Examples of the committee structure emerge throughout organizations. Nordstrom, the department store chain, until recently had an "office of the co-presidency" in which six members of the Nordstrom family shared the top job. SAS Institute uses a committee of employees to meet regularly and evaluate proposals for employee benefits. The committee evaluates ideas in terms of prescribed criteria such as whether the idea fits the company's culture and offers a value that exceeds its cost.

Committees also work in other areas such as new-product development. A new-product committee may include managers from such areas as accounting, engineering, finance, manufacturing, marketing, and research. By including representatives from all areas involved in creating and marketing products, such a committee generally improves planning and employee morale, because decisions reflect diverse perspectives.

Committees tend to act slowly and conservatively, however, and they often make decisions by compromising conflicting interests rather than by choosing the best alternative. The definition of a camel as "a racehorse designed by committee" provides an apt description of some limitations of committee decisions. At Nordstrom, the six-person office of the co-presidency was the object of much ridicule, and five Nordstrom cousins were later reassigned to line management jobs.[36]

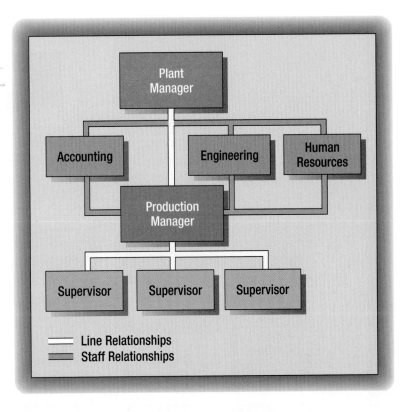

FIGURE 8.12
The Line-and-Staff Organization

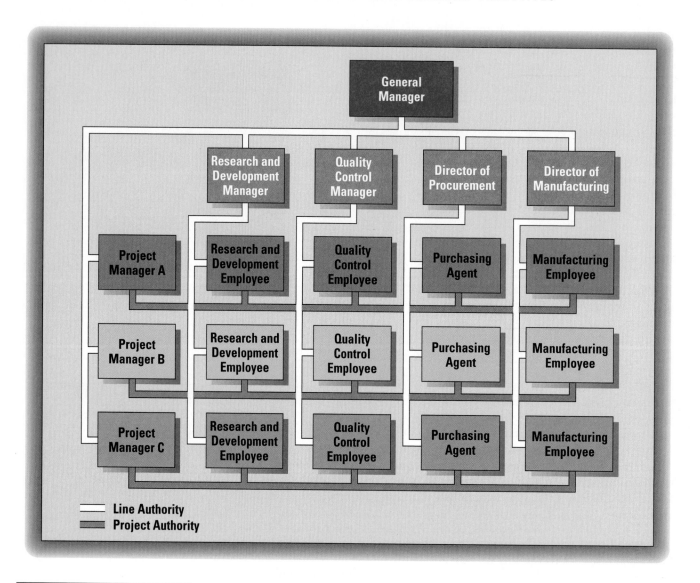

FIGURE 8.13
The Matrix Organization

Matrix Organizations   A growing number of organizations are using the **matrix**, or project management, **structure.** This structure links employees from different parts of the organization to work together on specific projects. Figure 8.13 diagrams a matrix structure. For a specific project, a project manager assembles a group of employees from different functional areas. The employees retain their ties to the line-and-staff structure, as shown in the vertical white lines. As the horizontal gold lines indicate, however, employees are also members of project teams. Upon completion of a project, employees return to their "regular" jobs.

In the matrix structure, each employee reports to two managers—one line manager and one project manager. Employees who are selected to work on a special project, such as development of a new product, receive instructions from the project manager (horizontal authority), but they continue as employees in their permanent functional departments (vertical authority). The term *matrix* comes from the intersecting grid of horizontal and vertical lines of authority.

The matrix structure has become popular at high-technology and multinational corporations, as well as hospitals, consulting firms, and aerospace firms. Dow Chemical, Chase Manhattan Bank, and P&G have all established matrix structures.

Table 8.3	**Comparing the Four Organization Structures**	
Form of Organization	**Advantages**	**Disadvantages**
Line	Simple and easy for both managers and subordinates to understand Clear delegation of authority and responsibility for each area	No specialization Overburdens top executives with administrative details
Line-and-staff	Specialists to advise top managers Employees reporting to one superior	Conflict between line and staff departments without clear relationships Staff managers limited to making recommendations to line managers
Committee	Combines judgment of several executives in diverse areas Improves morale through participation in decision making	Slow decisions Compromises rather than choices of the best alternatives
Matrix	Flexibility Strong focus on specific problems or unique technical issues Allows innovation without disrupting regular organizational structure	Potential problems from accountability to more than one boss Potential difficulty in developing a cohesive team from diverse individuals recruited from various departments Potential for conflict between project managers and other department managers

The National Aeronautics and Space Administration used the matrix structure for its Mercury and Apollo space missions.

The major benefits of the matrix structure come from its flexibility in adapting quickly to rapid changes in the environment and its capability for focusing resources on major problems or products. It also provides an outlet for employees' creativity and initiative, giving them opportunities that their functional jobs may deny them. However, it challenges the project manager to integrate the skills of specialists from many departments into a coordinated team. Another disadvantage is that employees may be confused and frustrated in reporting to two bosses.

Comparing the Four Types of Organization Structures

Table 8.3 summarizes the advantages and disadvantages of each structure. Although most large companies are organized according to line-and-staff structures, the line organization is usually the best form for a small business. The committee form appears in limited applications in major corporations. The matrix approach is increasingly common in both medium-sized firms and large, multiproduct firms that need to focus diverse organizational resources on specific problems or projects.

WHAT'S AHEAD

In the next chapter, we sharpen our focus on the importance of people—the human resource—in shaping the growth and profitability of the organization. We examine how firms recruit, select, train, evaluate, and compensate employees in their attempts to attract, retain, and motivate a high-quality workforce. The concept of motivation is examined and we will discuss how human resource managers apply theories of motivation in attracting, developing, and maintaining employees.

➤ Summary of Learning Goals

1. Define *management* and the three types of skills necessary for managerial success.

Management is the process of achieving organizational objectives through people and other resources. The management hierarchy depicts the levels of management in organizations: top managers provide overall direction for company activities, middle managers implement the strategies of top managers and direct the activities of supervisors, and supervisors interact directly with workers. The three basic managerial skills are technical skills, or the ability to apply the techniques, tools, and knowledge of a specific discipline or department; human skills, which involve working effectively with and through people; and conceptual skills, or the capability to see the "big picture" of the organization and how each part contributes to its overall functioning.

2. Explain the role of vision in business success.

Vision is the ability to perceive the needs of the marketplace and develop methods for satisfying those needs. Vision helps new businesses to pinpoint the actions needed to take advantage of opportunities. In an existing firm, a clear vision of company purpose helps to unify the actions of far-flung divisions, keep customers satisfied, and sustain growth.

3. Summarize the major benefits of planning and distinguish among strategic planning, tactical planning, and operational planning.

The planning process identifies organizational goals and develops a road map of the actions necessary to reach them. Planning helps a company to turn vision into action, take advantage of opportunities, and avoid costly mistakes. Strategic planning is a far-reaching process. It views the world through a wide-angle lens to determine the long-range focus and activities of the organization. Tactical planning focuses on the current and short-range activities required to implement the organization's strategies. Operational planning sets standards and work targets for functional areas such as production, human resources, and marketing.

4. Describe the strategic planning process.

The first step of strategic planning is to translate the firm's vision into a mission statement that explains its overall intentions and aims. Next, planners must assess the firm's current competitive position, using tools like SWOT analysis—which weighs the firm's strengths, weaknesses, opportunities, and threats—and forecasting. Based on this information, managers set specific objectives that elaborate what the organization hopes to accomplish. The next step is to develop strategies for reaching objectives that will differentiate the firm from its competitors. Managers then develop an action plan that outlines the specific methods for implementing the strategy. Finally, the results achieved by the plan are evaluated and the plan is adjusted as needed.

5. Distinguish major types of business decisions and list the steps in the decision-making process.

A programmed decision applies a company rule or policy to solve a frequently occurring problem. A nonprogrammed decision forms a response to a complex and unique problem with important consequences for the organization. The five-step approach to decision making includes recognizing a problem or opportunity, developing alternative courses of action, evaluating the alternatives, selecting and implementing an alternative, and following up the decision to determine its effectiveness.

6. Define *leadership* and compare different leadership styles.

Leadership is the act of motivating others or causing them to perform activities designed to achieve specific objectives. The basic styles are autocratic, democratic, and free-rein leadership. The best leadership style depends on three elements: the leader, the followers, and the situation. In contemporary business, leaders tend increasingly to involve employees in making decisions about their work.

7. Discuss the meaning and importance of corporate culture.

Corporate culture refers to an organization's values, beliefs, and principles. It is typically shaped by a firm's founder and perpetuated through formal programs such as training, rituals, and ceremonies, as well as through informal discussions among employees. Corporate culture can powerfully influence a firm's success by giving it a competitive advantage.

8. Describe the purposes of an organization structure.

Companies need to organize, or create structures through which to implement plans and accomplish objectives. To organize, managers determine the work to be done, then group those activities logically, assign work to specific employees, and allocate the resources they need to accomplish the work. Finally, managers coordinate the work of different groups and evaluate the results of the organizing process.

9. Explain the five major forms of departmentalization and the four main types of organization structures.

The subdivision of work activities into units within the organization is called departmentalization. It may be based on products, geographic locations, customers, functions, or processes. Most firms implement one or more of four structures: line, line-and-staff, committee, and matrix structures. Each structure has advantages and disadvantages.

Business Terms You Need to Know

management 286
planning 290
vision 291
forecasting 301
objectives 301
decision making 304
leadership 305

corporate culture 308
organization 309
departmentalization 311
delegation 312
span of management 314
chain of command 314

Other Important Business Terms

top management 286
glass ceiling 287
middle management 287
supervisory management 287
technical skills 288
human skills 288
conceptual skills 289
organizing 290
directing 290
controlling 291
business plan 293
strategic planning 293

tactical planning 294
operational planning 294
adaptive planning 295
contingency planning 296
mission statement 297
SWOT analysis 298
competitive differentiation 302
programmed decision 304
nonprogrammed decision 304
autocratic leadership 306
democratic leadership 307
free-rein leadership 307

empowerment 307
organization chart 310
centralization 314
decentralization 314
line organization 314
line-and-staff organization 315
line manager 315
staff manager 315
committee organization 315
matrix structure 316

➤ Review Questions

1. What is the management hierarchy? In what ways does it help organizations develop structure? In what ways could it be considered obsolete?

2. What are the three basic types of skills that managers must possess? Which type of skill is most important at each management level? In addition, describe some special skills managers who work abroad may need.

3. Identify and describe the four basic functions of managers.

4. Why is a clear vision particularly important for companies that have numerous operations around the country or around the world? Cite an example.

5. Which type of planning is the most far-reaching? How does this type of planning affect other types of planning?

6. Suppose you planned a large cookout for your friends and classmates, but when you woke up on the morning of the party, it was pouring rain. What type of plan would allow you to cope with this situation? Specifically, what could you do?

7. As a student, you have a mission in school. Write your own mission statement for your college education, including your goals and how you plan to accomplish them.

8. Identify each of the following as a programmed or nonprogrammed decision:

   a. reordering printer ink cartridges

   b. choosing among different types of phone services

   c. picking up your favorite toothpaste and shampoo at the supermarket

   d. selecting a college to attend

   e. filling your car with gasoline

9. Identify the three traits that are most often associated with great leaders. Which trait would be most important in the leader of a large corporation? A small company? Why?

10. Why is a strong corporate culture important to a company's success? Relate your answer to a specific company.

➤ Questions for Critical Thinking

1. Create a management résumé for yourself, identifying your technical skills, human skills, and conceptual skills. Which set of skills do you think is your strongest? Why?

2. Think of a company with which you are familiar—either one you work for or one with whom you conduct business as a customer. Or select your own college or university. Consider ways in which your organization can meet the needs of its marketplace. Then write a sentence or two describing what you think the organization's vision is—or should be.

3. Conduct your own SWOT analysis for an Internet company with which you are familiar. Visit the organization's Web site to learn as much about the company as you can before stating your conclusions. Be as specific as possible in identifying your perceptions of the company's strengths, weaknesses, opportunities, and threats. How might the company's managers use adaptive planning to capitalize on strengths and opportunities?

4. Identify someone whom you think is an effective leader—someone you've worked for, a sports team captain, a politician, or the like. Describe the traits that you think are most important in making this person an effective leader.

5. Your college or university has its own organizational culture. Describe what you perceive to be its characteristics. Is the culture strong or weak? In what ways does the culture affect you as a student?

➤ Experiential Exercise

Background: Effective leaders have special qualities that energize their coworkers. This exercise is designed to help you gather information on people's work experiences with the managers they have had in their careers.

Directions: Identify five people of various ages and work experiences to complete the following survey for you. All the individuals you select should have worked under another person's supervision at one time. After compiling the responses to the survey, analyze the data to determine any common responses. For example, did any leadership traits appear within the top five rankings for everyone you surveyed? For rankings that included totally different qualities, can you identify any possible reasons that might account for the differences, such as age or gender or the type of work the manager was involved in? Be prepared to compare your results with others in your class. What did you learn about leadership as a result of completing this exercise?

Note: Give a blank copy of these five questions to each participant to avoid the possibility of anyone being influenced by another person's rankings.

LEADERSHIP SURVEY
To be completed by five people of varying ages and work experience

1. Identify your gender:
   _____ Male   _____ Female

2. Identify your age range:
   _____ 18–25   _____ 26–35   _____ 36–45
   _____ 46 or older

3. Approximately how many different managers have you had throughout your years of employment?
   _____ 1–2   _____ 3–4   _____ 5–6
   _____ 7 or more

4. Here is an alphabetical list of 15 qualities often associated with effective leaders. Of all the managers you've had, identify your favorite boss. From the following list rank the top five characteristics of that individual. If you've never had a "favorite" boss, then rank the qualities based on the following question: "What five qualities are most important in managers for you to consider them to be good bosses?"
   _____ Ambitious   _____ Flexible
   _____ Caring   _____ Honest
   _____ Competent   _____ Humorous
   _____ Courageous   _____ Innovative
   _____ Dependable   _____ Inspiring
   _____ Empathetic   _____ Kind
   _____ Enthusiastic   _____ Loyal
   _____ Fair

5. In the following space, write the type of business that the manager was involved in:

   _____

   _____

   _____

   _____

   _____

   _____

➤ **Nothing but Net**

1. **Company mission statement.** Southwest Airlines usually ranks high each year in customer service satisfaction surveys and low in the number of complaints filed with the U.S. Department of Transportation. Visit the company's Web site and read its mission statement. Then click on Southwest's customer service policy statement. Read the statement and prepare a brief report for your class. Be sure to answer the following question: How is Southwest's customer service policy related to its mission statement?

   www.southwest.com/about_swa

   (Note: In order to read the entire customer service statement, you must have Adobe Acrobat Reader installed on your computer. You may download it for free by visiting the Adobe Web site: **www.adobe.com/products/readstep.html**.)

2. **Dealing with adversity.** Often one of the true tests of a company's management is how well it responds to a crisis. In the late 1990s, Nike came under severe criticism for labor practices at some of the Asian factories that manufacture its products. Nike responded with a series of actions, including opening a public dialogue on corporate responsibility and establishing a set of minimum working condition standards. Go to the following Nike Web site and review these actions. Write a summary of Nike's actions. Were you favorably or unfavorably impressed? Explain.

   www.nikebiz.com

3. Some management experts believe that charisma is one factor that makes a person a leader. Visit the following Web site and take the interactive quiz. Do you have charisma or are you charismatically impaired?

   www.fortune.com/fortune/careers/tools/quizzes/charismaquiz.html

   Note: Internet Web addresses change frequently. If you do not find the exact sites listed, you may need to access the organization's or company's home page and search from there.

Want to work for the number-two company on *Fortune*'s list of one hundred best companies to work for? Just over 4,000 people already do, and 27,000 applicants each year compete for about 900 open positions. The company is not a dot.com that's trying to make its employees millionaires on paper overnight, and it's not based in Silicon Valley. The firm is SAS Institute, founded in 1976 in Cary, North Carolina. While SAS does engage in e-commerce, it has a decidedly solid base as the largest privately held software company in the world. SAS focuses on producing high-quality e-commerce software and fostering a corporate culture that makes employees want to stay. While employee turnover in the software industry hovers around 20 percent, SAS's rate is a rock-bottom 4 percent. How did it become such a great place to work?

The corporate culture and the vision of SAS leadership are closely linked. "The well-being of our company is linked to the well-being of our employees," explains CEO Jim Goodnight. "Employees determine whether we flourish or fail. If we make the effort and invest resources in our employees' professional welfare, everyone wins—the employee, the customer, and the company." Benefits that SAS workers enjoy include low-cost day care facilities, a cafeteria with high chairs for employees' children, and free access to a 36,000-square foot gym, an indoor pool, a putting green, and stress-relieving massages. "If you treat employees as if they make a difference to the company, they will make a difference to the company," says Goodnight.

Top-notch employees allow SAS managers to engage in long-range strategic planning, including global expansion. Recently, a major tactic toward this goal has been the establishment of its India-based worldwide software services operations. "The focus of SAS Global Services is in providing services such as research and development, applications development, consulting, and train-

ing," announced a company press release. Hari Gupta, general manager of the new endeavor explains the plan this way: "At the end of the day customers are really seeking solutions and I'm looking forward to having my organization repackage and distribute these solutions on a worldwide basis via the respective SAS geographical operations."

Adaptive planning has been an important component of SAS's enduring success. At a time when new data mining software seemed to threaten SAS's more traditional statistical analysis tools, the company didn't fold. Instead, SAS developed its own data mining product called Enterprise Miner and integrated it with the SAS system. The tool was so easy to use that it became an industry leader and a source of profit for SAS.

SAS Institute has won many awards—for performance, innovation, and work environment. SAS cofounder, chairman, and CEO Goodnight is especially proud of those who recognize his company's commitment to a workplace that is "designed to nurture and encourage creativity, innovation, and quality." He understands that there is an essential connection between the corporate culture and his company's overall success. "Employee and customer loyalty continue to drive us," states the company Web site. "We seek out the industry's finest talent to develop our solutions and services. And we retain that talent by providing an award-winning work environment, which fosters a healthy balance between real work and real life."

QUESTIONS
1. Which management skills do you think are most important for managers who work at SAS? Why?
2. Write a mission statement for SAS Institute.

3. How would you describe Jim Goodnight's leadership style? Do you think it is the best style for his company? Why or why not?

4. Pretend you work for SAS and want to update its Web site. Write a brief paragraph describing the company's corporate culture for prospective employees. Would you want to work for SAS Institute? Why or why not?

Sources: "About SAS Institute," company Web site, **www.sas.com,** accessed January 26, 2001; "SAS Establishes Worldwide Software Services Operations to be Based in Pune, India," company press release, November 14, 2000; Sherwood Ross, "Workplace: Can't Find Great Hires? Develop 'Ordinary' Workers," Reuter's Limited, November 6, 2000; Anne Fisher, "Expert Advice on Keeping Workers Happy: Just Do It," *Fortune,* October 30, 2000, **http://northernlight.com;** Nicholas Stein, "Winning the War to Keep Top Talent," *Fortune,* May 29, 2000, **www.fortune.com;** David Stodder, "The Dozen: The 12 Most Influential Companies in IT," *Intelligent Enterprise,* January 1, 2000, **www.intelligententerprise.com.**

CHAPTER 9

Human Resource Management and Motivation

Learning Goals

1. Describe the importance of human resource management and the responsibilities of human resource managers.

2. Explain the role of human resource planning in an organization's competitive strategy.

3. Discuss the ways firms recruit and select employees and the importance of compliance with employment-related legislation.

4. Summarize how firms train and evaluate employees to develop effective workforces.

5. Identify the various pay systems and benefit programs.

6. Discuss employee separation and the impact of downsizing and outsourcing.

7. Explain the concept of motivation in terms of satisfying employee needs.

8. Describe how human resource managers apply theories of motivation in attracting, developing, and maintaining employees.

9. Identify trends that influence the work of human resource managers in the 21st century.

Ryder System Goes the Extra Mile for Employees—and Their Children

You've seen those yellow rental trucks everywhere. Sometimes they're transporting the goods of people moving into a new home or apartment. Small businesses often rent them to ship inventory from one factory or retail store to another. A few years ago, you may even have seen them on television hauling presidential ballots from Miami to Tallahassee. Ryder System is the company that leases trucks and solves transportation problems for individuals and companies worldwide. But you may not know that the company also has 30,000 employees. Like many of today's organizations, Ryder knows the importance of its human resources. "We recognize our employees—our knowledge capital—as our most valuable asset," states the Career Information Center page on the company's Web site. "We're looking for experienced, career-minded individuals who value professionalism, teamwork, innovation, and the highest level of service to clients, both external and internal." To find such talent to help the company grow and maintain its competitive edge, Ryder's human resource professionals search the globe for the best people. You can apply for a job at Ryder anywhere in the world with the click of your computer mouse. In fact, the Web site will even help you build a resume—the company is that serious in its endeavor.

To attract the "best and brightest," as Ryder refers to its employees, the company offers a full range of benefits—everything from competitive salaries and wages to medical and dental benefits, to profit sharing and pension plans. All of these benefits are common among *Fortune* 500 companies, as is subsidized day care. Understanding the needs of working parents, Ryder even opened a day care center right across

the street from its Miami headquarters. But here's a new twist: the company is building an elementary school next door. That way, 300 children of Ryder employees will con-

tinue to go to school near the building where their parents work.

"The school is helping us reinforce the concept that we want to be the employer of choice in south Florida," explains Ryder CEO Anthony Burns. Ryder will spend $5 million of its own money to build the school on property it has already donated for the purpose. The gain? Aside from attracting high-quality employees, Ryder will receive tax breaks and about $4,000 a year per student from the state to cover its costs. Because it's a charter school, Ryder receives public funding, but the company has much greater latitude in establishing a curriculum, setting school rules, and hiring teachers and other employees. The school plans to limit enrollment to 20 students per class, require students to wear uniforms, teach several languages, and be equipped with state-of-the-art computer technology. The school day will run a bit longer than a typi-

cal public school day, and after-school programs will last until 6:30 to accommodate parents' work schedules. The impact of this benefit will be immediate: "with the kids right across the street, I can afford an extra hour at work," says James Green, a claims analyst with two young children.

Ryder isn't the first corporation to build its own school as a way of attracting and keeping employees. American Bankers Insurance Group and Hewlett-Packard, among others, have already done so. But those schools are corporate-sponsored and private. Ryder's will be a chartered public school, which means that it will also be open to students whose parents are not Ryder employees.[1] As you read this chapter, you'll come across a number of organizations that are going the extra distance to help their employees balance work and family responsibilities, which may be one of the greatest changes in the employer–employee relationship over the past 100 years.

CHAPTER OVERVIEW

The importance of people to the success of any organization is stressed in the very definition of *management:* the use of people and other resources to accomplish organizational objectives. Ryder System is just one of the thousands of businesses that have found creative ways to attract the best workers and encourage them to stay with the company.

In this chapter we address the critical issues of human resource management and motivation. We begin with a discussion of the ways organizations attract, develop, and retain employees. Then we describe the concepts behind motivation and the way human resource managers apply them to increase employee satisfaction and organizational effectiveness.

HUMAN RESOURCE MANAGEMENT: A VITAL ORGANIZATIONAL FUNCTION

Most organizations devote considerable attention to human resource management, the function of attracting, developing, and retaining enough qualified employees to perform the activities necessary to accomplish organizational objectives. Human resource managers are responsible for developing specific programs and activities as well as creating a work environment that generates employee satisfaction and efficiency.

Relationships between employers and employees changed enormously during the past century. At the beginning of the 20th century, firms hired employees by posting notices at their sites stating that workers were needed and would be hired the following day. Such a notice might list required skills, such as carpentry or welding, or simply list the number of employees the firm required. People looking for work would line up at the employer's shop or factory the next day—a small number in prosperous times and a larger number in leaner times. Someone in authority made hiring decisions after reviewing these candidates, often based on arbitrary criteria; sometimes the first people in line were hired, sometimes the healthiest and strongest were hired. After being hired, the new employees were expected to work under a precise set of rules, such as the humorous list shown in Figure 9.1.

Today, flexibility and complexity characterize the relationship between employers and employees. In Chapter 1, you learned that developing and sustaining a world-class workforce is essential for a firm to compete effectively. Human resource managers face challenges created by profound changes in the makeup of the labor force, a shortage of qualified job candidates, changes in the structure of the workplace, and employees' desires to balance their work and personal lives. These managers must also develop programs and policies that satisfy an increasingly diverse employee population while monitoring a growing number of employment-related laws that influence how they implement their firms' practices.

Large organizations create human resource departments that systematically handle the tasks of attracting, training, and retaining employees. Some human resource managers are *generalists,* because they are responsible for several tasks. Others are *specialists,* because they focus on individual areas of human resource management such as diversity training or employee benefits.

Entrepreneurs and small-business managers usually assume most of the responsibility for human resource management. However, a growing number of small firms are outsourcing the function of human resource management to **professional employer organizations (PEOs)**. A PEO is a company that helps small and midsized firms with a wide range of human resource services, including hiring and training employees, administering payroll and benefits programs, handling workers' compensation and unemployment insurance, and maintaining compliance with labor

FIGURE 9.1
Rules for Clerks, 1900

1. This store must be opened at sunrise. No mistake. Open at 6:00 A.M. summer and winter. Close about 8:30 or 9 P.M. the year round.

2. Store must be swept and dusted, doors and windows opened, lamps filled and trimmed, chimneys cleaned, counters, base shelves, and showcases dusted, pens made, a pail of water and the coal must be brought in before breakfast, if there is time to do it and attend to all the customers who call.

3. The store is not to be opened on the Sabbath day unless absolutely necessary and then only for a few minutes.

4. Should the store be opened on Sunday the clerks must go in alone and get tobacco for customers in need.

5. Clerks who are in the habit of smoking Spanish cigars, being shaved at the barber's, going to dancing parties and other places of amusement, and being out late at night will assuredly give the employer reason to be overly suspicious of employee integrity and honesty.

6. Clerks are allowed to smoke in the store provided they do not wait on women while smoking a "stogie."

7. Each store clerk must pay not less than $5.00 per year to the church and must attend Sunday school regularly.

8. Men clerks are given one evening a week off for courting and two if they go to the prayer meeting.

9. After the 14 hours in the store, leisure hours should be spent mostly in reading.

laws. PEOs work in partnership with employers in these key decisions. Because the PEO typically negotiates benefits for all its clients, it can shop for better deals. And by handling a firm's human resource activities, a PEO enables a small firm to focus on production, marketing, and finance, as well as on motivating and leading employees. In Fennville, Michigan, West Michigan Flocking & Assembly uses a PEO called ADP TotalSource to provide employee benefits, process payroll, and give advice on human resource issues. West Michigan Flocking, which produces a decorative finish used in automobiles, also wanted to improve workplace safety. ADP's safety manager responded by developing a safety policy, conducting regular inspections, and helping the manufacturer set up a safety committee.[2]

One can view human resource management in two ways. In a narrow sense, it includes the functions performed by human resource professionals. But in a broader sense, it involves the entire organization, even when a staff department assumes those responsibilities or a firm outsources the functions. Supervisors and general managers also participate in hiring, training, evaluating performance, and motivating employees. Since a company's success depends largely on the commitment and talents of its people, a growing number of firms are measuring and rewarding managers' performance in retaining employees and attracting qualified job candidates. Autodesk, American Express, and Hartford Insurance are among the companies at which managers' performance reviews include measures of employee turnover.[3] Similarly, many companies consider workforce diversity to be a source of competitive advantage in serving diverse customer groups and thinking creatively. At these organizations, management goals may also include measures of employee diversity. At Alliant Energy a belief that diversity is a source of competitive advantage has

BUSINESS DIRECTORY

➤ **human resource management** *function of attracting, developing, and retaining sufficient numbers of qualified employees to perform the activities necessary to accomplish organizational goals.*

FIGURE 9.2
Human Resource Management Responsibilities

prompted the company to reward managers for their performance in hiring women and minorities.[4] In addition, some firms ask non-management employees to participate in hiring decisions and evaluating their coworkers' performance.

The core responsibilities of human resource management include planning for staffing needs, recruitment and selection, training and evaluating performance, compensation and benefits, and terminating employees. In accomplishing these five tasks shown in Figure 9.2, human resource managers achieve their objectives of (1) providing qualified, well-trained employees for the organization, (2) maximizing employee effectiveness in the organization, and (3) satisfying individual employee needs through monetary compensation, benefits, opportunities to grow and advance, and job satisfaction.

HUMAN RESOURCE PLANNING

Human resource managers develop staffing plans based on their organization's competitive strategies. They forecast the number of employees their firm will need and determine the types of skills necessary to implement its plans. Human resource managers are responsible for adjusting their company's workforce to meet the requirements of expanding in new markets, reducing costs (which may require laying off employees), or adapting new technology. They formulate both long-term and short-term plans to provide the right number of qualified employees.

Human resource managers also must plan how to attract and keep good employees with the right combination of pay, benefits, and working conditions. At Trilogy Software, this aspect of human resource planning is at the core of the company's strategy. Trilogy develops software that handles information processing related to sales and marketing, an industry in which only fast-moving, highly sophisticated companies can succeed. So, the company has a strategy to continually expand its staff of software developers. Knowing that it is competing for talent with rich software giants like Microsoft and Cisco Systems, Trilogy targets college campuses, recruiting the brightest, most energetic students it can find. As a substitute for work experience, the company sends these young recruits to an intense three-month orientation program called Trilogy University, where they work on Trilogy products as they learn about the software industry and the company culture. The long workdays at Trilogy University, followed by company-sponsored parties, are an early taste of working for the company, which consciously strives to maintain the intense atmosphere of a start-up. When recruiting employees, Trilogy sells that atmosphere as an asset, attracting people who are stimulated by working on challenging projects in a close-knit team of bright and energetic coworkers. It's a strategy that attracts people like Joshua Walsky, who has no complaints about working until late at night: "Trilogy hires people who are smart, talented, interesting, and cool. Those are exactly the sort of people I want to be around."[5]

Like Trilogy, many high-tech businesses set ambitious plans for expanding their human resources, and the market for talent is highly competitive. Some of these companies plan acquisitions of other businesses to meet human resource needs. Kana Communications needed more engineers to meet growth targets for its software firm. So Kana purchased smaller companies, including Net Dialogue and BEI. Similarly, Redback Networks purchased Siara Systems, most of whose employees were engineers. Redback then put its human resource personnel to work meeting with each of those engineers to help them with the transition.[6]

RECRUITMENT AND SELECTION

In recruiting and selecting employees, human resource managers strive to match applicants' skills with those the organization needs. To ensure that potential employees bring the necessary skills or have the capacity to learn them, most firms implement the recruitment and selection process shown in Figure 9.3.

Finding Qualified Candidates

Businesses access both internal and external sources to find qualified candidates for specific jobs. Policies of hiring from within emphasize internal sources, so employers consider their own employees first for job openings. Internal recruiting is less expensive than external methods, and it helps boost employee morale. But if recruiters can find no qualified internal candidates, they must look for people outside the organization. Recruitment from external sources involves advertising in newspapers and trade magazines, placing radio and television ads, and working through employment agencies, college recruiting and internship offices, retiree job banks, job fairs, and state employment agencies. Some firms find creative ways to recruit from external sources, as did TJX in the "Clicks and Mortar" box.

One of the most effective external sources is employee referrals, in which employers ask current employees to recommend applicants, rewarding them with bonuses or prizes for new hires. The demand for employees with high-tech skills is so great that some companies are offering generous rewards to employees who refer qualified candidates. Docent, which provides online learning resources, pays $5,000 to any employee whose referral the company hires. Software firm Adobe Systems also pays $5,000 for referrals, and employees with three referrals get an additional $5,000 toward a vacation. Respond.com awarded an employee a Hawaii trip for two for referring an engineer who joined the company.[7]

Many firms are using the Internet as a recruiting tool. They may post jobs and accept résumés at their own Web sites, as well as list positions at job banks such as Headhunter.net, HotJobs.com, Monster.com, and America's Job Bank (www.ajb.dni.us), sponsored by the U.S. Department of Labor. Internet recruiting is a quick, efficient, inexpensive way to reach a large, global pool of job seekers. According to employers and career counselors, online recruiting is becoming the prevalent method of finding qualified job candidates.

Cisco Systems, which develops and sells Internet connection technology, relies heavily on electronic recruiting to help the company find thousands of new employees every year. To lure job hunters to the recruiting pages of its own Web site, Cisco posts banner ads on a variety of Web sites. The company targets its efforts by placing ads on job search sites like Monster.com, as well as by directing that ads appear on the screens of people with designated Web addresses, such as those of competitors. Other recruiting efforts, from newspaper advertising to booths at public events, also direct interested people to the Cisco Web site. Once there, job hunters find links to job descriptions, which they can search by title, job type, location, and other relevant factors. Links are even provided to Cisco employees who will share information about working there. Job hunters also can provide information about themselves, which helps the company link them to appropriate jobs. With these resources, Cisco receives over two-thirds of candidates' résumés electronically. Once those résumés arrive at Cisco, the company uses software to screen each one for key words that signal the expertise or backgrounds it needs and to match résumés with job openings.[8]

Selecting and Hiring Employees

In selecting and hiring employees, human resource managers must follow the requirements set out by federal and state laws. Chapter 2 describes legislation that

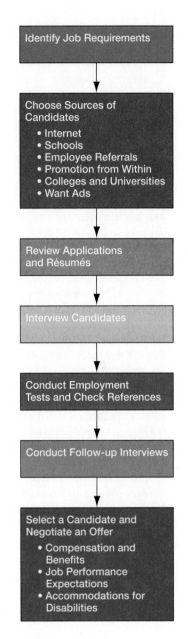

FIGURE 9.3
Steps in the Recruitment and Selection Process

Background. Everyone loves a booming economy; everyone, that is, except managers who are trying to find qualified people to work for them. With the unemployment rate close to below 4 percent, it's hard for many businesses—including TJX Cos., the parent of off-price retailers T.J. Maxx and Marshalls. "The job market is such that you can't go out and hire good people—you have to make them," explains John D'Amico, a T.J. Maxx store manager.

What Happened? When the U.S. government announced its welfare reform policy in the late 1990s, TJX founder Ben Cammarata went to Washington and pledged to hire 5,000 people from the welfare rolls by the year 2000. The only problem was, where would he find them? One strategy was to hire CIC Enterprises to set up and run a job hot line connected to various agencies that help get welfare recipients ready for the world of work. Through the hot line network, a store manager for a T.J. Maxx or Marshalls in any location could call and request potential candidates for a job opening.

The Response. The results of the hot line have been even better than TJX managers had hoped. For every ten calls made to the hot line, eight calls have resulted in a candidate who has been hired. Traditionally, retailers retain only about 43 percent of the people they hire, but TJX claims that 61 percent of the former welfare recipients hired are still with the company after a year. TJX chairman Ted English notes, "The welfare-to-work associates we're hiring are looking for a little bit more stability and a little bit more of a long-term relationship. It's worked out great for us." So, the company has reduced its recruiting and hiring costs in the long run.

Many of these employees do need special training, since they may come to the job without a high school diploma or be unprepared for the daily requirements of work. To that end, TJX started a pilot program called First Step. The program prepares former welfare recipients for work and follows them for at least a year.

Today and Counting. The job hot line has been so successful that TJX has recently expanded it to include searches for older workers, immigrants, and individuals with developmental disabilities as the nation and the workforce continue to change. Although the First Step program does not solve everyone's problems—a number do drop out—it has helped workers like Vicki Glover, a single mom who dropped out of high school 20 years ago. Glover has already received three promotions and is now on an assistant manager's track. She still has trouble paying all her bills on $8.50 an hour, but she's determined to stick with it. TJX vows to continue its programs, helped in part by the tax credits it receives for hiring these candidates. It's a step in the right direction.

QUESTIONS FOR CRITICAL THINKING
1. Would the Internet be an effective recruiting tool for TJX? Why or why not?
2. In what ways must TJX human resource managers be careful to comply with equal employment opportunity legislation?

Sources: "About TJX," TJX company Web site, **www.tjx.com**, accessed February 19, 2001; Ann Harrington, "How Welfare Worked for T.J. Maxx," *Fortune*, November 13, 2000, pp. 453–456; Chris Reidy, "3. TJX Cos.," The Eleventh Annual Globe 100, *The Boston Globe*, **www.boston.com/globe**, May 18, 1999.

influences employers' hiring practices. Title VII of the Civil Rights Act of 1964 prohibits employers from discriminating against applicants based on their race, religion, color, sex, or national origin. The Americans with Disabilities Act of 1990 prohibits employers from discriminating against disabled applicants. The Civil Rights Act created the Equal Employment Opportunity Commission (EEOC) to investigate discrimination complaints. The EEOC also assists employers in setting up affirmative-action programs to increase job opportunities for women, minorities, disabled people, and other protected groups. The Civil Rights Act of 1991 expanded the remedies available to victims of employment discrimination by including the right to a jury trial, punitive damages, and damages for emotional distress.

Failure to comply with equal employment opportunity legislation can expose an employer to such risks as fines and penalties, bad publicity, and poor employee morale. The EEOC files hundreds of cases each year, with damages paid by businesses in the tens of millions annually. At the same time, opponents to such laws have launched initiatives to restrict affirmative-action standards and protect employers against unnecessary litigation. In one instance, California voters passed a proposition that prohibits the state from granting hiring preferences to minorities. Other proposed federal legislation is aimed at protecting employees from discrimination because of their religious beliefs or sexual orientation. In this environment of change coupled with a tight labor market, many companies are trying to broaden their pool of applicants so that they can comply with legal requirements even as they increase the odds of finding talented people. Xerox, for example, develops relationships with colleges, including those with significant enrollments of African American or Hispanic students. The company also supports organizations ranging from the National Society of Black Engineers to the Institute for Women and Technology.[9]

Increases in protected employees and discrimination lawsuits have elevated the importance of human resource managers in the hiring process. To prevent violations, human resource personnel must train managers involved in interviewing to make them knowledgeable about employment law. For example, the law prohibits asking an applicant any questions relating to marital status, number of children, race, nationality, religion, or age. Interviewers also may not ask questions about applicants' criminal records, mental illness histories, or alcohol-related problems. In addition, human resource managers can help organizations establish systems to promote fair employment practices. Home Depot was sued by women who claimed they were more often unfairly steered toward lower-paying jobs than were males with similar qualifications. As part of the settlement, Home Depot began using software called the Job Preference Program, which automates the process of ranking candidates for jobs and promotions. Not only does the software provide store managers with lists of candidates based on legitimate criteria, it also creates lists of questions and criteria for evaluating the answers. Besides creating more opportunities for its female employees, Home Depot's software has helped its managers make better employment decisions.[10] For more information about employment-litigation issues, visit the Web sites of the Society for Human Resource Management and the EEOC.

Employers must also observe various other legal restrictions governing hiring practices. Some firms try to screen out high-risk employees by requiring drug testing for job applicants, particularly in industries where employees are responsible for public safety, such as airlines and other public transportation. Drug testing is controversial, however, due to concerns about privacy. Also, positive test results may not accurately indicate drug use; traces of legal drugs, such as prescribed medications, may chemically resemble traces of illegal substances. Several states have passed laws restricting drug testing by employers.

The law prohibits the use of polygraph (lie detector) tests in almost all prehiring decisions, as well as in random testing of current employees. The only organizations exempt from this law are federal, state, and county governments; firms that do sensitive work under contract to the Defense Department, Federal Bureau of Investigation, or Central Intelligence Agency; pharmaceuticals firms that handle controlled substances; and security guard services.

Recruitment and selection is an expensive process, because a firm incurs costs for advertising job openings, interviewing applicants, and conducting background checks, employment tests, and medical exams. A bad hiring decision is even more expensive, though. A hiring mistake costs a firm in efforts to train and motivate a less than optimal employee, as well as potential costs of poor decisions by that employee. Other costs resulting from a bad hiring decision may include lawsuits, unemployment compensation claims, recruiting and training a replacement, and reductions in productivity and employee morale.

To avoid the costly results of a bad hiring decision, many employers require applicants to complete employment tests. These tests help verify the skills that candidates list on their application forms or résumés to ensure that they meet the performance expectations of the job. A variety of tests are available to gauge applicants' knowledge of mechanical, technical, language, and computer skills. One example is the Basic Skills Tests published by Wonderlic in Libertyville, Illinois, which measure candidates' basic math and verbal skills. These tests are intended to be a more objective and accurate way to measure qualifications than simply asking candidates about their educational background.[11] Capital One Financial established tests through a process that was more complicated but better tailored to the company's specific needs. Capital One had 1,600 of its current employees take skills tests to create a database the company could use as a basis for comparing new job candidates. The database also helps the company analyze who will be the best performers; it learned that applicants referred by existing employees tend to perform better on the tests. Consequently, Capital One has begun to rely more heavily on referrals as part of its recruitment strategy.[12]

Following a hiring decision, a growing number of firms protect themselves from discrimination lawsuits by including explicit employment-at-will policies in their employee manuals. **Employment at will** means that the employment relationship can be started or terminated at any time by either the employee or the employer for any reason. Many people believe that the law prohibits employers from firing employees, but successful lawsuits must cite specific illegal practices such as discrimination in hiring based on sex, race, age, or disability. Although most state laws recognize the principle of employment at will, court decisions in firing disputes sometimes favor employees when their employers have failed to provide written proof of at-will policies and employees' acceptance of the policies. For further protection, some employers are also publishing policies that call for mandatory arbitration of employment disputes and waivers of the right to jury trials in such disputes.

ORIENTATION, TRAINING, AND EVALUATION

FIGURE 9.4
New Horizons: Communicating the Importance of Training

Once hired, employees need information about what is expected of them and how well they are performing. Companies provide this information through orientation, training, and evaluation. A newly hired employee often completes an orientation program administered jointly by the human resource department and the department in which the employee will work. During orientation, employer representatives inform employees about company policies regarding employee rights and benefits. Many organizations give new hires copies of employee manuals that describe benefits programs and working conditions and expectations. They also provide different types of training to ensure that employees get a good start at the company.

Training Programs

Employees are increasing their requests for training so they can build skills and knowledge that will prepare them for new job opportunities. Training is also a good investment from the employer's perspective. As Figure 9.4 reports, untrained employees take six times longer to perform tasks than trained employees, so it is important to help new employees build their skills quickly. In a relatively new industry, such as Internet retailing, companies need to find creative ways to train their employees, as described in the "Business Hits & Misses" box.

A firm should view employee training as an ongoing process throughout each employee's tenure with the company. At Federal Express Corp., training is part of the company's investment in its people, which helps keep employees committed to the firm. Of FedEx's total expenses, 3 percent goes to training. Although the percentage may sound small, it is six times higher than most companies of similar size. Employees attend FedEx's Leadership

Institute, where they learn about the company's operations and culture. As Larry McMahan, vice president for human resources, puts it, "One reason people like to work here is that they just don't come in with a set of skills that stay stagnant. We believe heavily in individual development."[13]

Information technology (IT) employees tend to place a high value on knowledge. For employees like these, training is essential. At accounting firm BDO Seidman, IT employee training develops their ability to apply technology to the company's specific situation, so it is a good investment. The field technicians who staff the company's offices in various locations receive encouragement to train for the accounting firm's higher-level jobs. BDO's director of field operations received such training when he was a field technician, and he now manages 200 employees.[14]

On-the-Job Training   One popular instructional method is **on-the-job training,** which prepares employees for job duties by allowing them to perform the tasks under the guidance of experienced employees. A variation of on-the-job training is apprenticeship training, in which an employee learns a job by serving for a time as an assistant to a trained worker. Patio Enclosures, a construction firm, made its employees more productive and more committed to the company by setting up an apprenticeship program. Employees who manufacture and install sunrooms receive a booklet that details skills and training requirements. As employees meet the requirements for each level of skill, they have the booklet stamped—and receive an increase in pay. Patio Enclosures' executive vice president, Jerry Fox, says the apprenticeship program builds commitment to the company: "If an employee knows he's two or three jobs from the next pay level, why would he want to jump to another place?"[15] Apprenticeship programs are much more common in Europe than in the United States. While American apprenticeships usually focus on blue-collar trades, in Europe many new entrants to white-collar professions complete apprenticeships.

Classroom and Computer-Based Training   Off-the-job training involves some form of classroom instruction such as lectures, conferences, audiovisual aids, programmed instruction, and special machines to teach employees everything from basic math and language skills to complex, highly skilled tasks. Some firms are replacing classroom training with computer-based training programs. These programs can save an employer money by reducing travel costs and employee time away from work. In addition, computer-based training offers consistent presentations, since the training content won't vary with the quality of the instructor. Audio and visual capabilities help these systems to simulate the work environment better than some classroom training could, and employees also benefit from greater control over the learning process. They can learn at their own pace and convenience, and they generally do not have to wait for the company to schedule a class before they can begin adding to their knowledge. Despite these advantages, firms also offer traditional classroom training, because it usually provides more opportunities for employees to interact with the instructor and with one another. Some people learn more readily from human interaction, and some have difficulty disciplining themselves to complete a computer-based learning program on their own.[16]

Today, off-the-job training frequently involves use of the Internet. The Web provides a convenient means of delivering text, audio, and video training materials to employees wherever they are located. Online training programs also can offer interactive learning, such as simulations in which employees see the results of their decisions.

When a firm decides to enter a foreign market, human resource managers must prepare employees who will work in overseas assignments by providing training in language skills, cultural practices, and adapting to the everyday living requirements abroad. Employees may begin an international assignment with the

BUSINESS DIRECTORY

➤ **employment at will**   *practice that allows the employment relationship to begin or end at any time at the decision of either the employee or the employer for any legal reason.*

➤ **on-the-job training**   *training method that teaches an employee to complete new tasks by performing them under the guidance of an experienced employee.*

E-tailers Learn the Value of the Question, "May I Help You?"

You wouldn't automatically think of the Internet as a place for personal assistance from a salesperson. But many e-tailers, stung by customer dissatisfaction with their Internet shopping experiences, have begun to pay closer attention to personal customer service at their Web sites. Datamonitor PLC in London estimates that worldwide, Web sites may lose $3.2 billion in sales because they do not offer personal assistance. According to Forrester Research, two-thirds of all consumers who place goods in an electronic shopping cart during a visit to a site do not complete the sale. That's a lot of business lost, and a growing number of companies are now doing something about it.

A shopper who logs on to www.landsend.com can chat live with a Lands' End operator, asking questions about size, style, and color. "They make you feel incredibly comfortable," says Julia Deputy, who bought a pair of cargo pants for her daughter because the operator's daughter had a pair too. Other e-tailers, such as HometownStores.com, personally "greet" each consumer as he or she enters the site, asking if they can help. Still others are upgrading their sites with Internet-telephone capability so that shoppers who have only one phone line can browse online and talk with a salesperson at the same time.

Staffing for these positions requires human resource managers to look for people who have both technical and people skills. Knowledgeable service representatives may mean the difference between success and failure to some companies. Zany Brainy, an Internet toy retailer, insists that its online customer service staff know as much about the company's merchandise as regular store clerks and trains them to become "certified KIDsultants." In fact, as part of its training program, the company sends the online reps to its bricks-and-mortar stores to familiarize them with the toys. Trainees also take a creativity test to determine whether they can think fast in difficult customer situations. Zany Brainy managers believe that having live reps available to answer questions is vital to the success of their business, which is largely educational toys.

"We're learning a lot in the same way that Zany Brainy stores learned from listening to our customers," says Thomas G. Vellios, Zany Brainy's president.

Not all e-tailers agree with this approach. Instead of training employees in customer service, they are putting more effort into stocking items and improving delivery times. But companies that have spent the time and money to train employees to increase their customer service efforts say they are already seeing a payoff. HometownStores.com, which has a personal greeter service, reports that sales rose 30 percent in the first month of the service's operation. Cameraworld.com says that after it installed a service allowing shoppers to talk with reps by Internet phone, 1 in 4 bought something, compared with only 3 of every 100 of all visitors previously.

Consumers will undoubtedly let Internet retailers know—with their credit cards—whether training for personal service makes the difference between a visit and a purchase. Meanwhile, human resource managers have the same task they've always had: to find the best people for the job, train them for excellence, and keep them.

QUESTIONS FOR CRITICAL THINKING

1. Which type (or combination of types) of training do you think would be most effective for online customer service reps? Why?
2. On what basis might online customer service reps be evaluated?

Sources: Lands' End Web site, **www.landsend.com,** accessed February 19, 2001; "Zany Service," Zany Brainy Web site, **www.zanybrainy.com,** accessed February 19, 2001; Timothy J. Mullaney, "Needed: The Human Touch," *Business Week, E.Biz,* December 13, 1999, pp. EB53–54.

professional skills and job qualifications they need, but most benefit from additional cultural and language training to help them make successful transitions.

Management Development A management development program provides training designed to improve the skills and broaden the knowledge of current and potential executives. This type of training is critical to organizations today, because traditional sources of top talent are not as plentiful as they once were. When companies downsized to become more efficient during the 1980s and 1990s, they often eliminated middle-management jobs that once were a training ground for a company's top executives. Also, the share of the workforce in their mid-20s to mid-30s, who traditionally have been the group developing management skills, is shrinking, and a large share of the workforce is approaching retirement age. Without the luxury of developing executive talent slowly over the years, organizations must instead provide programs that help managers quickly learn how to lead a fast-moving company through turbulent times.[17]

Management training is often conducted off the company premises. The content of management development programs may involve reviews of issues facing the company, as well as benchmarking, or learning the best practices of the best companies so they can serve as performance standards to strive for. The teachers may be the company's own executives. At other times, managers may be encouraged to receive counseling from an outside management coach, who helps them improve interpersonal skills. When Twentieth Century Fox's chief information officer Justin Yaros wanted to give more responsibility to Sharon McCracken, Fox's vice president of information technology, he asked McCracken to receive coaching to develop her leadership skills. McCracken's coach has helped her focus on broad business issues and improve her ability to convey a vision to her employees.[18]

General Electric's management development programs are widely considered to be a major reason why that company has been able to succeed in a number of different industries. Every January, the company's top 500 executives travel to Boca Raton, Florida, for meetings at which they set companywide priorities and trade ideas. Beginning in March, GE holds quarterly meetings of its Corporate Executive Council to foster development among the company's highest executives. Each April, GE's chief executive, human resource vice president, and other executives evaluate management needs and performance, and they discuss plans and expectations with managers who are viewed as capable of filling top jobs in the future. Managers receive additional guidance and coaching in follow-up meetings led by the chief executive in May and November. Also, executives of the company's business units recommend managers to attend management training at company headquarters to groom them for promotion to top leadership positions. GE managers also can participate in development programs where they analyze case studies of actual challenges facing GE, reporting their recommendations to the company's top leaders.[19]

Performance Appraisals

Organizations also help employees improve their performance by providing feedback about their past performance. A **performance appraisal** is an evaluation of an employee's job performance by comparing actual results with desired outcomes. Based on this evaluation, managers make objective decisions about compensation, promotions, additional training needs, transfers, or firings. Rating employees' performance and communicating perceptions of their strengths and weaknesses are important elements in improving a firm's productivity and profits. Performance appraisals are not confined to business. Government agencies, not-for-profit organizations, and academic institutions also conduct them.

Some firms conduct peer reviews, in which employees assess the performance of coworkers, while other firms allow employees to review their supervisors and managers. A fairly recent trend in performance appraisal is the **360-degree performance review,** a process that gathers feedback from a review panel of about 8 to 12 people, including coworkers, supervisors, team members, subordinates, and sometimes customers. The idea is to get as much frank feedback from as many perspectives as possible. However, this approach to performance appraisal tends to generate considerable work for both employees and managers—who may each have to review 20 or more people—and volumes of paperwork. Also, since the evaluations are anonymous, staff members with an ax to grind can use the system to even scores.

Still, the 360-degree system is extremely popular. A recent survey of large U.S. firms found that two-thirds are using the multirater system, up from about 40 percent in 1995. At United Parcel Service (UPS), managers receive 360-degree reviews every six months. The managers' peers, employees, and supervisors rate them on such areas of performance as leadership, customer focus, people skills, and knowledge of financial and business issues. To ensure that the feedback is used constructively, UPS's human resource department first provides employees with training in the purpose of the regular surveys and ways to use them. The training includes instruction in how to give constructive feedback. Then, after each evaluation is complete, the human

BUSINESS DIRECTORY

➤ **management development program** *training designed to improve the skills and broaden the knowledge of current and potential executives.*

➤ **performance appraisal** *method of evaluating an employee's job performance by comparing actual results with desired outcomes.*

resource department analyzes the data and prepares a report comparing the manager's self-rating with the ratings of others. Managers are expected to develop goals for themselves, based on the feedback from the 360-degree reviews. UPS trainer Hope Zoeller Stith believes managers appreciate the information they get from the process: "I think people are hungry for this type of feedback. It's vitally important to us that communication is ongoing."[20]

COMPENSATION

Human resource managers work to develop an equitable compensation system spanning wages and salaries plus benefits. Because human resource costs represent a sizable percentage of any firm's total product costs, excessive wage rates may make its goods and services too expensive to compete effectively in the marketplace. Inadequate wages, however, lead to difficulty in attracting qualified people, high turnover rates, poor morale, and inefficient production.

The terms *wages* and *salary* are often used interchangeably, but they refer to different types of pay systems. **Wages** represent compensation based on an hourly pay rate or the amount of output produced. Firms pay wages to production employees, maintenance workers, and sometimes retail salespeople. **Salaries** represent compensation calculated on a weekly, monthly, or annual basis. Office personnel, executives, and professional employees usually receive salaries.

An effective compensation system should attract well-qualified workers, keep them satisfied in their jobs, and inspire them to succeed. Most firms base their compensation policies on five factors:

1. Salaries and wages paid by other companies that compete for the same people
2. Government legislation, including the federal, state, or local minimum wage
3. The cost of living
4. The firm's ability to pay
5. Worker productivity

On average, earnings of U.S. workers, adjusted for inflation, declined slightly in the 1980s and first half of the 1990s. During the second half of the decade, earnings began to rise as companies enjoyed greater productivity gains and faced increased competition for qualified workers.[21] Some of that increase is driven by increases in pay for entry-level jobs. Random House—a major publisher—recently raised the bottom of its pay scale by 20 percent, and some local governments require a minimum wage above the national standard. Several cities—including Chicago, Detroit, and Los Angeles—have required businesses with city contracts to pay a so-called *living wage* of as much as $10 per hour. In spite of worries that requiring higher wages will increase unemployment, evidence so far suggests that in a tight labor market, companies will reduce their profit margins rather than cut jobs or leave town.[22]

Many employers balance rewarding workers with maintaining profits by linking more of their pay to superior employee performance. They try to motivate employees to excel by offering some type of incentive compensation in addition to salaries or wages. Most implement several types of incentive compensation programs:

- Profit sharing, which awards bonuses based on company profits
- Gain sharing, which awards bonuses based on surpassing predetermined performance goals
- Lump-sum bonuses, which award one-time cash payments based on performance
- Pay for knowledge, which distributes wage or salary increases as employees learn new job tasks

In addition, many large companies award part of employees' compensation in the form of stock options, which reward executives for increases in their firms' stock prices by giving them opportunities to buy stock at preset prices within certain time periods. Today, almost one-tenth of the compensation of salaried workers is some form of variable pay.[23]

Incentive compensation based on profitability and stock performance is especially common among corporate executives. Most top U.S. executives receive salaries plus long-term incentives such as stock options. The compensation paid to top management has accelerated a trend in which the pay of highly paid employees is growing much faster than the pay of those at the bottom of the compensation ladder. Earnings vary dramatically according to the skills offered and risks taken by employees. Twenty years ago, the typical college graduate earned 38 percent more, on average, than a high school graduate, and that difference has almost doubled to 71 percent today.[24]

EMPLOYEE BENEFITS

In addition to wages and salaries, firms provide many benefits to employees and their families as part of the compensation they pay. **Employee benefits** are rewards such as retirement plans, insurance, sick leave, child and elder care, and tuition reimbursement, provided entirely or in part at the company's expense. Some benefits are required by law. Firms are required to make social security contributions and payments to state employment insurance and workers' compensation programs that protect workers in case of job-related injuries or illnesses. The Family and Medical Leave Act of 1993 requires covered employers to offer up to 12 weeks of unpaid, job-protected leave to eligible employees. Firms voluntarily provide other employee benefits, such as child care and health insurance, to help them attract and retain employees. Sometimes companies try to change the way benefits, such as pension plans, are structured, which creates controversy, as in the case of the cash-balance pension plans discussed in the "Solving an Ethical Controversy" box.

Benefits represent a large component of an employee's total compensation. Although wages and salaries account for 72 percent of the typical employee's earnings, benefits make up the other 28 percent. The share of total compensation provided as benefits has grown over the past few decades, especially in the categories of insurance and legally mandated benefits such as Social Security.[25] Figure 9.5 illustrates the breakdown of employer-paid benefits. Perhaps because the cost of noncash benefits is rising, some employers are scaling back. The Department of Labor found that the share of employees with health insurance, life insurance, and paid vacation time declined during the 1990s. However, most employees still receive these benefits, especially at medium-sized and large companies.[26]

A growing number of companies are meeting employee demands for "family-friendly" benefits that help them care for children, aging parents, or other dependents. Such benefits, from child care facilities to paid time off and flexible work hours, assist employees in juggling responsibilities. Almost nine out of ten large U.S. companies currently offer dependent-care spending accounts to help pay for child care, and almost half offer some form of elder-care program.[27] AFLAC, a 2,600-employee insurance company based in Columbus, Georgia, goes further. It has an on-site child-care center for employees' children and grandchildren and offers up to 12 weeks of fully paid leave to employees who need to care for a sick child, parent, or spouse. Such benefits can pay off in terms of improved productivity, greater employee satisfaction, and a chance to recruit the best employees. AFLAC recently received 12,143 applications to fill 546 jobs at the growing company.[28]

BUSINESS DIRECTORY

➤ **employee benefits** *employee rewards such as health insurance and retirement plans that employers give, entirely or in part, at their own expense.*

SOLVING AN ETHICAL CONTROVERSY

One of the challenges a human resource manager faces is determining the best way to distribute benefits to employees. Recently, about 500 large companies, including IBM and AT&T, have switched from traditional pensions to cash-balance pension structures, and they have come under fire for doing so. Under a traditional plan, benefits are calculated based on the number of years an employee has worked and on the average earnings during the last five to ten years of work, which is when earnings are typically highest. The cash-balance plan, on the other hand, bases benefits on a worker's average annual wages over a lifetime. In many situations, older workers would have accumulated more under the traditional plan than under the cash-balance plan, and younger workers, who enter at higher pay rates, will potentially accrue more under the cash-balance plan. And in many situations, workers have not been given a choice about which plan they prefer to adopt.

Are cash-balance pension plans fair to workers?

PRO

1. Unlike traditional plans, cash-balance pensions are portable—workers can transfer them from one company to another when they change jobs—making them potentially more valuable in today's less-permanent work arrangements.
2. Younger and shorter-term workers, who earn fewer benefits under the traditional plans, will do better with the cash-balance plan.
3. Many companies, such as Kodak, give everyone the option to choose which type of plan they want, so those who choose the cash-balance plan do so fairly.

CON

1. Older workers will lose under the cash-balance plan. "Because of the way cash-balance plans are structured," explains AARP senior economic lobbyist David Certner, "hundreds of thousands of midcareer employees may have been stripped of as much as one-half of their expected benefits."
2. Some companies such as IBM have only made choice available to a limited number of employees and will not disclose what the impact of the conversion will be on individual workers.
3. Once the traditional plan has been converted to a cash-balance plan by a company, many older employees actually stop earning any pension benefits at all for several months or even years, a situation known as "wear away" or "pension plateau."

SUMMARY

Not surprisingly, a series of lawsuits have been filed against companies that have made the conversion, particularly those that have not given their employees a choice in the matter. In addition, members of Congress have filed bills to regulate the new plans, and three government agencies—the IRS, Department of Labor, and Equal Employment Opportunity Commission—have begun to review cash-balance pensions.

Sources: Curt Anderson, "Making It Easier to Save," **ABCNEWS.com** September 12, 2000, accessed February 28, 2001, **http://www.abcnew.go.com/ sections/business/dailynews/retirementplans000912.html;** "AARP's Perkins Criticizes Cash Balance Pension Plan Conversions," AARP news release, June 5, 2000. February 28, 2001, **http://www.aarp.org/press/2000/ nr060500a.html;** Robert Lewis, "Objections from Workers, Feds Brake Cash-Balance Bandwagon," *AARP Bulletin,* November 1999, p. 4; Robert F. Hill and William K. Carr, "Are Cash-Balance Pension Plans Good for Older Workers? No: They Conceal Benefit Cutbacks," *AARP Bulletin,* November 1999, p. 29; James M. Delaplane, Jr., "Are Cash-Balance Pension Plans Good for Older Workers? Yes: Workers of All Ages Benefit from New Plans," *AARP Bulletin,* November 1999, p. 29; Stephanie Armour, "Workers Continue Pension Debate," *USA Today,* November 24, 1999, p. B1.

Flexible Benefits

In response to the increased diversity in the workplace, human resource managers are developing creative ways to tailor their benefit plans to the varying needs of employees. One approach sets up **flexible benefit plans,** also called *cafeteria plans.* Such a benefit system offers employees a range of options from which they can choose, including different types of medical insurance coverage, dental and vision plans, life and disability insurance, and extra vacation days. This way, one working spouse may choose his or her firm's generous medical coverage for the entire family and the other spouse can allocate benefit dollars to purchasing other types of coverage. Some plans also offer memberships in health clubs and child-care benefits. Typically, each employee receives a set allowance (called *flex dollars* or *credits*) to pay for purchases from this menu. Xerox Corp. employees receive an allowance to spend on health insurance; if they spend less than the maximum, they can use the balance for benefits such as disability or dental insurance.[29]

Another way of increasing the flexibility of employee benefits involves time off from work. Instead of establishing set numbers of holidays, vacation days, and sick days, some employers give each employee a bank of *paid time off (PTO).* Employees use days from their PTO accounts without having to explain why they need the time.

Flexible Work

Another part of the trend toward responsiveness to employee needs is the option of flexible work plans. **Flexible work plans** are benefits that allow employees to adjust their working hours and places of work to accommodate their personal lives. Flexible work plan options include flextime, compressed workweeks, job sharing, and home-based work. By implementing these benefit programs, employers have reduced employee turnover and absenteeism and boosted productivity and job satisfaction.

Flextime is a scheduling system that allows employees to set their own work hours within constraints specified by the firm. An employer may require employees to be at work between the core hours of 10 A.M. and 3 P.M., rather than the regular workday hours of 9 A.M. to 5 P.M. Outside the core hours, employees can choose when to start and end their workdays, opting either to arrive at work early, say at 7 A.M., and leave early, or to arrive later and work later. Flextime works well in jobs where employees can work relatively independently but not so well when they must work together in teams, such as in manufacturing, or must provide direct customer services. Flextime is common in European countries; an estimated 40 percent of the Swiss workforce and 25 percent of German workers set flextime schedules. Growing numbers of U.S. firms are offering flextime, and increasing numbers of employees are taking advantage of this benefit.

The **compressed workweek** is a scheduling option that allows employees to work the regular number of weekly hours in fewer than the typical five days. Employees might work four ten-hour days and then have three days off each week. Such arrangements not only reduce the number of hours employees spend commuting each week but can stretch out the company's overall workday, providing more availability to customers in other time zones. At Northern Trust in Chicago, one-fourth of the employees have compressed workweeks, as do two-thirds of the employees at insurer USAA.[30]

A **job sharing** program allows two or more employees to divide the tasks of one job. This plan appeals to a growing number of people who prefer to work part-time rather than full-time, such as older workers, students, working parents, and people who want to devote time to personal interests or leisure. Job sharing requires a high degree of cooperation and communication between the partners, but it can permit a company to benefit from the talents of people who do not want to work full-time. Job sharing enabled Sandra Cavanah and Kathleen Layendecker to participate in the exciting but demanding world of Internet start-ups. They had plenty of management experience and a burning desire to be part of the Internet revolution, but they also wanted time with their children. So the two women presented themselves as a team to Mark Jung, CEO of Snowball.com, an Internet media company. Jung was reluctant to accept their proposal to share a position as vice president, but he agreed to try them as joint directors of affiliate services. Each woman spends three days at work, and during their overlapping time, they brief one another and discuss work-related issues. Within a few months, the two women proved themselves and received a promotion to the job they originally wanted. Cavanah believes the job-sharing arrangement offers

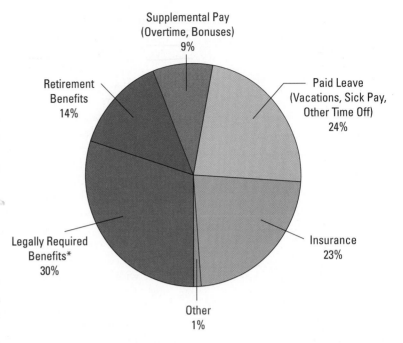

FIGURE 9.5
Types of Employer-Paid Benefits
Note: Percentages do not total 100 due to rounding.
*Social Security, Medicare, unemployment insurance, and workers' compensation

Number of adults using
the internet for business
from home (in millions)

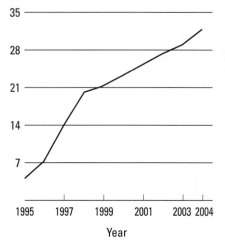

FIGURE 9.6
Workers Using the Internet for
Business from Home

great benefits to workers and company alike: "A job share is intoxicating. You start realizing how much better you are as two, and you want to discuss every issue [with your partner]."[31]

A **home-based work** program allows employees to perform their jobs from home instead of at the workplace. Home-based workers are sometimes called *teleworkers* or *telecommuters,* because many "commute" to work via telephones, e-mail, computers, and fax machines. Working from home has great appeal to disabled workers, elderly people, and parents with small children. Over 16 million teleworkers are currently employed in the United States, and their numbers are growing. About one-fifth of them have supervisors in another state. Although the U.S. is ahead of the European Union in its reliance on telecommuters, three EU countries—Finland, the Netherlands, and Sweden—have a greater share of their workforce engaged in telework, and EU businesses are moving workers home at a faster rate than U.S. businesses.[32]

Because telecommuters work with minimal supervision, they need to be self-disciplined and reliable employees. They also need managers who are comfortable with setting goals and managing from afar. Companies that succeed in their use of telecommuting provide training in how to manage from a remote location by focusing on results and improving communication. At Merrill Lynch, employees and their managers undergo team training that includes opportunities for the employees and managers to discuss their goals and expectations for projects and communications.[33] Under those circumstances, telecommuting can improve productivity. At AT&T, almost three out of ten managers work from home at least one day a week, and many of these teleworking managers work exclusively from home. Since the company began permitting this practice, productivity at AT&T has risen.[34]

The trend toward telework is likely to accelerate because the Internet has provided so many ways to collaborate and share information over great distances. As shown in Figure 9.6, the share of U.S. workers who use the Internet for business from their homes has already surpassed 20 million and is expected to exceed 30 million within two or three years. Often, these workers say they get more done when they are away from workplace distractions.[35]

EMPLOYEE SEPARATION

Either employer or employee can take the initiative to terminate employment. Employees decide to leave firms to start their own businesses, take jobs with other firms, move to another city, or retire. Some firms ask employees who leave voluntarily to participate in **exit interviews** to find out why they decided to leave. These interviews give employers a chance to learn about problems in the workplace, such as unreasonable supervisors or unfair work practices.

Employers sometimes terminate employees due to poor job performance, negative attitudes toward work and coworkers, or misconduct such as dishonesty or sexual harassment. Terminating poor performers is necessary, because they lower productivity and employee morale. Coworkers resent employees who receive the same pay and benefits as themselves without contributing fairly to the company's work. But employers need to document reasons for terminating employees carefully. Complaints of wrongful dismissal are often involved in complaints filed by the EEOC. Besides poor performance, reasons for terminating employees include downsizing and outsourcing.

Downsizing

During the 1980s and 1990s, employers terminated millions of employees, including many middle managers, through downsizing. **Downsizing** is the process of reducing the number of employees within a firm by eliminating jobs. Many downsizing firms have reduced their workforces by offering early retirement plans, voluntary severance programs, and opportunities for internal reassignment to different jobs. Employers who valued their employees helped them to find jobs with other companies and set up job counseling centers.

Companies downsize for many reasons. The two most common objectives of downsizing are to cut overhead costs and streamline the organizational structure. Some firms report improvements in profits, market share, employee productivity, quality, and customer service after downsizing. Others, however, lose so many valuable, high-performing employees that their ability to compete declines. Chevron downsized some years back and ended up losing some of its most experienced managers. For a while, enough talented people remained, but eventually the company had to begin focusing more on developing management expertise. Now the company conducts annual reviews to spot possible human resource shortages before they occur, and it actively encourages retired employees to serve as consultants.[36]

Eliminating jobs through downsizing often has devastating effects on employee morale. Workers who remain after a downsizing worry about job security and become angry when they have to work harder for the same pay. As their feelings of commitment to their jobs wane, many employees may leave the firm voluntarily to seek employment offering greater job security. This situation has contributed to a shift in values away from loyalty to an employer in favor of concern for individual career success.

Recent employee surveys reveal that workers are now more interested in *career security* than in *job security*. Specifically, the typical employee wants opportunities for training to improve the skills needed for the next job. People are willing to work hard at their current jobs, but they also want to share in the success of their companies by receiving pay-for-performance compensation and stock options. For human resource managers, the new employer–employee relationship requires developing continuous training and learning programs for employees.

Outsourcing

In their continuing efforts to remain competitive against domestic and international rivals, a growing number of firms choose to hold down costs by evolving to a *leaner* organization. A number of functions that were performed previously by company employees may be contracted to other firms whose employees will perform them on a contractual basis in a practice called *outsourcing*. Outsourcing began on a small scale, with firms contracting out services such as maintenance, cleaning, and delivery. Services commonly outsourced today include housekeeping; architectural design; grounds, building, utility, and furniture maintenance; food service; security; and relocation services. Today, outsourcing has expanded to include outside contracting of many tasks once considered fundamental internal functions. Early in the chapter we explain how many small firms outsource the entire human resource function by using the services of PEOs. Large firms also outsource certain human resource tasks such as recruiting, training, and compensation. Some companies outsource such functions as information technology management, production of one or more elements of their product lines, accounting and legal services, and warehousing and delivery services. The "Clicks and Mortar" box discusses one company that helps others retain valuable knowledge that could be lost when employees leave for other jobs, a difficult problem in the fast-moving high-tech sector.

Motorola recently arranged to outsource the production of many of the cellular phones, pagers, and switches bearing its name. The company contracted with Flextronics International, a Singapore firm known for building a variety of electronics at plants in China, Brazil, Hungary, and Mexico. Outsourcing production to flexible factories like those of Flextronics enables Motorola to move quickly in introducing new products without the expense of building and staffing new factories. The

BUSINESS DIRECTORY

➤ **downsizing** *process of reducing a firm's workforce to reduce costs and improve efficiency.*

idea of an electronics company not building its own products is relatively new, but it is already a widespread practice. Companies like Flextronics build most computer components, and they are expanding their services to include product design, order taking, and repairs.[37] If Motorola outsources production, what is its role as a business? The core challenge left is for Motorola to find out what customers need and tell them how its products can meet those needs.

Outsourcing complements today's focus on business competitiveness and flexibility. It allows a firm to continue performing the functions it does best, while hiring other companies to do tasks that they can handle more competently and cost-effectively than its own people can. Another benefit of outsourcing is the firm's ability to negotiate the best price among competing bidders and the chance to avoid the long-term resource costs associated with in-house operations. Firms that outsource also gain flexibility to change suppliers at the end of contract periods, if they desire. The key to successful outsourcing is a total commitment by both parties to form a partnership from which each derives benefits.

MOTIVATING EMPLOYEES

As illustrated in Figure 9.7, effective human resource management makes important contributions to employee motivation. This ad for Principal Financial Group says, "Do you look forward to going to work? If you had great benefits, you might."

Flexible benefit programs, flexible work schedules, on-site child care, and bonus pay are all designed to motivate people to join a firm and become satisfied and productive employees. When The Coca-Cola Company decided to lay off over 5,000 employees, it tried to boost morale by improving its benefits and working conditions. The company switched to a compressed workweek in which employees work longer on Monday through Thursday in exchange for Friday afternoons off. It also added a new paid holiday, May 8, which is the anniversary of Coca-Cola's introduction in 1886.[38]

In his book *A Great Place to Work*, author Robert Levering examined 20 top U.S. firms to discover what made them outstanding employers. He identified three factors, which he calls "the three *R*s." The first *R* is expanding workers' *responsibility* for their jobs. The second involves sharing the *rewards* that the firm generates as fairly as possible. The third *R* calls for ensuring that employees have *rights,* including some kind of grievance procedure, access to corporate records, and the right to confront those in authority without fearing reprisals.

Building the three *R*s into an organization should contribute to employee morale. **Morale** is the mental attitude of employees toward their employer and jobs. It involves a sense of common purpose among the members of work groups and throughout the organization as a whole. High morale is a sign of a well-managed organization, because workers' attitudes toward their jobs affect the quality of their work. One of the most obvious signs of poor manager–worker relations is poor morale. It lurks behind absenteeism, employee turnover, and strikes. It shows up in falling productivity and rising employee grievances.

In contrast, high employee morale occurs in organizations where employees feel valued and heard and where they are able to contribute what they do best. This climate reinforces a human tendency—that people perform best when they believe they are capable of succeeding.[39] High morale also results from an organization's understanding of human needs and its success at satisfying those needs in ways that reinforce organizational goals. Each person is motivated to take action designed to satisfy needs. A **need** is simply a lack of some useful benefit. It reflects a gap between an individual's actual state and his or her desired state. A **motive** is an inner state that directs a person toward the goal of satisfying a felt need. Once the need—the gap between where a person is now and where he or she wants to be—becomes important enough, it produces tension. The individual is then moved—the root word for motive—to reduce this tension and return to a condition of equilibrium. Figure 9.8 depicts the principle behind this process. A need produces a motivation, which leads to goal-directed behavior, resulting in need satisfaction.

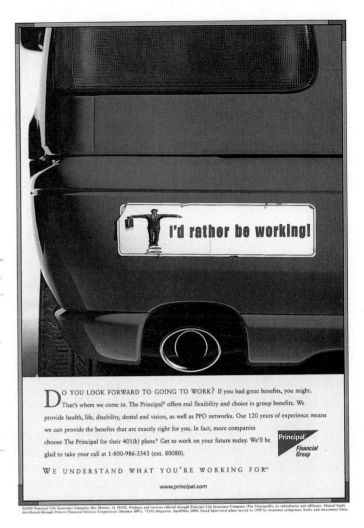

FIGURE 9.7
Principal Financial Group: Recognizing the Importance of Employee Benefits

Maslow's Hierarchy of Needs Theory

The studies of psychologist Abraham H. Maslow have provided an understanding of how employers can motivate employees. Maslow developed a widely accepted list of human needs based on these important assumptions:

- People are wanting animals whose needs depend on what they already possess.

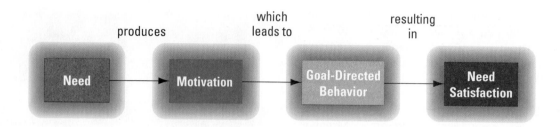

FIGURE 9.8
The Process of Motivation

- A satisfied need is not a motivator; only needs that remain unsatisfied can influence behavior.

- People's needs are arranged in a hierarchy of importance; once they satisfy one need, at least partially, another emerges and demands satisfaction.

In his hierarchy of needs theory, Maslow proposed that all people have basic needs that they must satisfy before they can consider higher-order needs. He identified five types of needs:

1. *Physiological needs.* These most basic human needs include food, shelter, and clothing. In the workplace, employers satisfy these needs by paying salaries and wages and establishing comfortable working environments.
2. *Safety needs.* These needs refer to desires for physical and economic protection. Employers satisfy these needs by providing benefits such as retirement plans, job security, and workplaces that comply with OSHA requirements.
3. *Social (belongingness) needs.* People want to be accepted by family and other individuals and groups. At work, employees want to maintain good relationships with their coworkers and managers and to participate in group activities.
4. *Esteem needs.* People like to receive attention, recognition, and appreciation from others. Employees feel good when they are recognized for good job performance and respected for their contributions.
5. *Self-actualization needs.* These needs drive people to seek fulfillment, realizing their own potential, fully using their talents and capabilities. Employers can satisfy these needs by offering challenging and creative work assignments and opportunities for advancement based on individual merit.

According to Maslow, people must satisfy the lower-order needs in the hierarchy (physiological and safety needs) before they are motivated to satisfy higher-order needs (social, esteem, and self-actualization needs). Table 9.1 elaborates on employers' efforts to motivate employees by satisfying each level of needs.

The diversity of today's workforce challenges employers to satisfy the belongingness needs of people from many different cultures and ethnic backgrounds. The challenge is even greater in organizations where employees telecommute or spend much of their time with clients. At Butler International, a firm providing technical services to business customers, most employees spend their days at client sites, so management consciously seeks ways to reinforce what CEO Ed Kopko calls "a sense of belonging and connectedness to Butler." The firm holds quarterly conference calls with all employees, and employees meet regularly in teams to hear and implement one another's ideas. Butler has also set up its Web site to serve as a "virtual office" for its employees, enabling them to carry out activities employees would normally do in an office setting.[40]

Because most people in industrialized nations can afford to satisfy their lower-order needs, higher-order needs typically play more important roles in motivating employees. Effective managers who understand higher-order needs can design programs to satisfy them. At A. G. Edwards brokerage, management asked its account executives what job title they preferred. They asked to be called "financial consultants," reflecting the service they provide for their clients.[41] Honoring this request was a way for the investment firm to satisfy the consultants' esteem needs. Likewise, a management development program gives an employee the opportunity to grow by

Table 9.1 **Maslow's Hierarchy of Human Needs**

Human Needs	Key Ingredients	Example
1. Physiological needs	Wages and working environment	Granite Rock, an operator of rock, sand, and gravel quarries, pays entry-level employees $15.90 per hour and gives opportunities to move up to a "job owner" or "improvement champion" and earn base pay of $29.50 an hour.
2. Safety needs	Protection from harm, employee benefits	Computer software maker SAS Institute believes that healthy employees make good employees. Two doctors and ten nurses staff its 7,500-square-foot on-site medical center, where employees and their dependents get free consultations, physical exams, emergency care, and many wellness programs.
3. Social (belongingness) needs	Acceptance by other employees	Valassis Communications, which prints coupon inserts for newspapers, sends employees memos introducing new hires. The employees, including the president of the company, then write "welcoming" notes to the new employee. "On your first day on the job, you're so nervous and you feel uncomfortable, and it just really makes a difference and makes you feel comfortable," says one new employee.
4. Esteem needs	Recognition and appreciation from others	Entrepreneur Candace Bryan, chief executive of Kendle, a firm that designs clinical tests for drugs, keeps a photo gallery of her 288 employees posing with their favorite outside activities, from scuba diving to grandparenting. The recognition boosts employee morale and helps to make Bryan an inviting supervisor for prospective employees.
5. Self-actualization needs	Accomplishment, opportunities for advancement, growth, and creativity	Procter and Gamble's promotion-from-within policy gives employees chances to grow. Human resource manager Carol Tuttle has been promoted 7 times in 22 years. She's worked in brand management, advertising, and recruiting and spent 6 years in Venezuela. "It's always challenging, always exciting. I don't think I've ever been bored for 5 minutes," she says.

learning leadership skills. But how do firms satisfy higher-order needs for first-line employees such as factory workers? Some companies are experimenting with ways to add meaning to these workers' jobs through job enlargement and job enrichment.

Motivating Employees through Job Design

In their search for ways to improve employee productivity and morale, a growing number of firms are focusing on the motivation inherent in the job itself. Rather than simplifying the tasks involved in a job, employers are broadening tasks to add meaning and satisfaction to employees' work. Two ways employers are applying motivational theories to restructure jobs are job enlargement and job enrichment.

Job enlargement is a job design change that expands an employee's responsibilities by increasing the number and variety of tasks they entail. Some firms have successfully applied job enlargement by redesigning the production process. A typical approach is to replace assembly lines where each worker repeats the same step on each product with modular work areas in which employees perform several tasks on a single item. Many companies have enlarged administrative assistants' jobs from the traditional tasks of word processing, filing, and answering phones. Those tasks have been largely automated, but especially at companies that have downsized, administrative assistants are taking on a variety of duties related to record keeping and communications. Phyllis Moseley, a senior executive secretary at Dallas-based Central and South West Corp., once spent much of her time with a word processor, but today her duties extend to updating her division's Web site.[42]

Job enrichment is a change in job duties to increase employees' authority in planning their work, deciding how it should be done, and learning new skills that help them grow. Many companies have developed job enrichment programs that empower employees to take responsibility for their work. The concept of worker empowerment is discussed in the next chapter.

Through job enrichment, employers can motivate employees to satisfy higher-level needs. Born Information Services, a consulting firm specializing in

BUSINESS DIRECTORY

➤ **job enrichment** *change in job duties to increase employees' authority, responsibility, and skills.*

Table 9.2	Assumptions of Theory X and Theory Y
Theory X Assumptions	**Theory Y Assumptions**
1. Employees dislike work and will try to avoid it whenever possible.	1. Employees view work as a normal activity as natural as play or rest.
2. Employees must be coerced, controlled, or threatened to achieve organizational goals.	2. Employees will exercise self-direction when they are committed to achieving organizational objectives.
3. Employees try to avoid responsibility and want direction.	3. Employees typically accept and even want to take responsibility for their work.
4. Employees view job security as the most important factor associated with their work.	4. Employees have the intellectual potential to make decisions and find creative solutions to problems.

computer systems, has made interesting work part of its strategy for attracting and keeping talent. When the company was founded a decade ago, big companies relied heavily on mainframe computers, and a business like Born could find a steady stream of clients by writing software for mainframes. However, the work was also routine. Company founder Rick Born concluded, "The really good people want to do new stuff," so he decided to focus on new technologies, beginning with networking and later moving into Internet applications. The company routinely asks employees what new technologies they want to add to their repertoire. The focus on giving employees interesting work has helped Born Information Services exceed its financial goals as well as keep a dedicated staff of talented programmers.[43]

Motivating Employees through Managers' Attitudes

The attitudes that managers display toward employees also influence worker motivation. Managers' traditional view of workers as cogs in the production process—much like lathes, drill presses, and other equipment—led them to believe that money was the best way to motivate employees. Maslow's theory helped managers to understand that employees feel needs beyond those satisfied by monetary rewards.

Psychologist Douglas McGregor, a student of Maslow, studied motivation from the perspective of how managers view employees. After observing managers' interactions with employees, McGregor coined the terms *Theory X* and *Theory Y* as labels for the assumptions that different managers make about worker behavior and how these assumptions affect management styles.[44] Table 9.2 lists these assumptions.

Theory X assumes that employees dislike work and whenever possible try to avoid it. So, managers must coerce or control them or threaten punishment to achieve the organization's goals. Managers who accept this view feel that the average person prefers to receive direction, wishes to avoid responsibility, has relatively little ambition, and can be motivated only by money and job security. Managers who hold these assumptions are likely to keep their subordinates under close and constant observation, holding out the threat of disciplinary action, and demanding that they adhere closely to company policies and procedures.

Theory Y assumes that the typical person likes work and learns, under proper conditions, to accept and seek out responsibilities to fulfill social, esteem, and self-actualization needs. Theory Y managers consider the expenditure of physical and mental effort in work as an ordinary activity, as natural as play or rest. They assume that most people are capable of conceiving creative ways to solve work-related problems but that most organizations do not fully utilize the intelligence that most employees bring to their jobs. Unlike the traditional management philosophy that relies on external control and constant supervision, Theory Y emphasizes self-control and self-direction.

Theory Y requires a different management approach that includes worker participation in decisions that Theory X would reserve for management. If people actually behave in the manner described by Theory X, they may do so because the

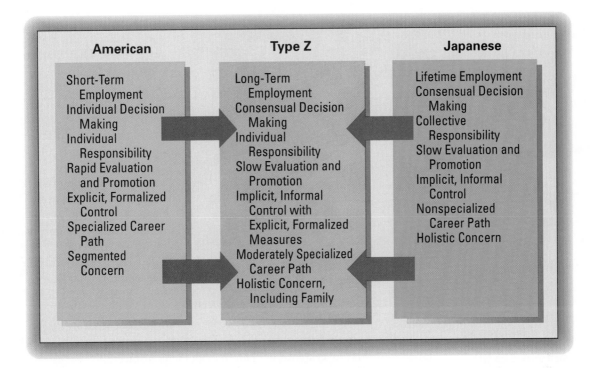

American

Short-Term
    Employment
Individual Decision
    Making
Individual
    Responsibility
Rapid Evaluation
    and Promotion
Explicit, Formalized
    Control
Specialized Career
    Path
Segmented
    Concern

Type Z

Long-Term
    Employment
Consensual Decision
    Making
Individual
    Responsibility
Slow Evaluation and
    Promotion
Implicit, Informal
    Control with
    Explicit, Formalized
    Measures
Moderately Specialized
    Career Path
Holistic Concern,
    Including Family

Japanese

Lifetime Employment
Consensual Decision
    Making
Collective
    Responsibility
Slow Evaluation and
    Promotion
Implicit, Informal
    Control
Nonspecialized
    Career Path
Holistic Concern

FIGURE 9.9
Theory Z Management: A Blend of American and Japanese Methods

organization satisfies only their lower-order needs. If the organization instead designs ways to satisfy their social, esteem, and self-actualization needs as well, employees may be motivated to behave in different ways.

One company that applies Theory Y is Kraft Foods. When Kraft's director of finance for research and development, Kathy McKenna, wanted shorter work hours so that she would have more time for her family, Kraft put her to work on solving the problem—both for herself and other employees. The company appointed her to a task force that studied ways to offer more flexible work arrangements and also encourage women to advance within the organization. McKenna and others on the task force proposed an in-house consulting group: the Financial Resources Group. Qualified employees in finance—men as well as women—could join this group and work part-time on specific projects with specific duties and goals. McKenna, the first to participate, worked four days a week. Others have since joined, and thanks in part to their challenging, visible projects, several have received promotions at Kraft. Ralph Nicoletti, Kraft's vice president of financial planning and analysis, says, "Through the program, we have highly talented people working on important projects—and no one's career is in a holding pattern."[45]

Another perspective on management proposed by UCLA management professor William Ouchi has been labeled **Theory Z**. Organizations structured on Theory Z concepts attempt to blend the best of American and Japanese management practices. Figure 9.9 shows how the strengths of the two approaches are combined. This approach views worker involvement as the key to increased productivity for the company and improved quality of work life for employees. Many U.S. firms have adopted the participative management style used in Japanese firms by asking workers for suggestions to improve their jobs and then giving them the authority to implement proposed changes.

A growing number of U.S. firms are showing concern for employees and their families. Many employers are adjusting the workplace to satisfy the needs of employees. Internet data company digitalNATION offers them buffets, bowling nights, yachting trips, and outings to play paintball. Says digitalNATION's CEO,

A growing number of employers are adjusting the workplace to satisfy the needs of their workforce. If you're working for Kansas City architectural firm Gould Evans Goldman and get tired, you can head for the nap tent. Three separate tents await you. The nap tents are camping tents pitched in a corner of the office and equipped with sleeping bags, pillows, alarm clocks, and soothing music.

Bruce Waldack, "Employees want good salaries, but today, they also want more. They want to like their coworkers and hang out with them." Waldack believes that meeting those needs has helped his company keep most of its employees on board in an industry where employee turnover is the norm.[46] At San Antonio–based Valero Energy, concern for employees extends to the community as well. Valero actively seeks employees who share management's commitment to community involvement. Chief executive Bill Greehey also routinely eats in the employee cafeteria and visits work sites to make himself available to employees. Greehey considers sending a note to employees before surgery a part of letting employees know the company appreciates them. Says Greehey, "[Employees] know when management is sincere."[47]

HUMAN RESOURCE CONCERNS FOR THE 21ST CENTURY

Four kinds of trends—demographic, workforce, economic, and work/life events—are shaping the responsibilities and practices of human resource managers. Managers need to monitor these trends to prepare their organizations for recruiting, training, and retaining workers who are motivated to direct their efforts toward achieving company goals.

Demographic Trends

As discussed in Chapter 1, the percentage of older people in the workforce is growing. This trend poses a number of human resource challenges. One is that a growing share of the workforce will be reaching the age at which employees traditionally retire. Another is that as the population ages, many employees will be juggling the responsibility of caring for aging parents—sometimes along with child-care responsibilities. These challenges require that employers develop more flexibility in creating an environment in which they can attract and keep older workers.

Some companies are responding by structuring jobs to fit the needs and availability of older workers. This accommodation may entail letting workers gradually cut back their hours instead of shifting abruptly from full-time work to retirement. When chemical engineer Jesse B. Krider was approaching retirement at Chevron, the company let him switch to work he found more fulfilling than managing technological operations: he began developing the company's younger executives. Then, when Krider retired as a Chevron employee, the company arranged consulting contracts with him. Explains Chevron vice chairman James N. Sullivan, "He brings 30 to 40 years of detailed technical expertise and experience that we just can't replace right now." At Deloitte Consulting, partners typically retired from their demanding jobs at age 50, when they became eligible for their full pensions. To retain this valuable talent, Deloitte launched its Senior Leaders Program, which gives its top employees the option to redesign their jobs, including the content and hours of their work.

Flexibility at Deloitte kept Daniel G. Gruber with the company. Gruber was worn out from long hours and travel, but instead of leaving, he arranged to work three days a week and says he is doing "the best consulting of [his] life."[48]

Another form of flexibility, discussed earlier, involves flexible benefits. Aging workers rarely need child-care benefits, but they may need time off to help ailing parents. They may also want more health care for themselves or a chance to update their skills for the high-tech economy. Cafeteria plans are attractive in companies with diverse employees, so the use of such plans is likely to accelerate, especially as firms outsource this function.

Flexibility is also necessary in dealing with other aspects of workforce diversity. Because of the rising education level of people with disabilities, more-sophisticated assistive technology, and the influence of the Americans with Disabilities Act, disabled people are entering the workforce in increasing numbers. This trend is just beginning. Of the 15 million Americans of working age who have disabilities, only about one in four is currently employed, but most of the rest would like to have jobs. Among those who are working is Chris Harmon, a customer service representative with Crestar Bank. He cannot use his arms or legs, but voice-activated technology lets him use a computer to resolve customers' problems when they call.

Other technologies that enable disabled workers include software that converts text into synthetic speech, programs that convert the eyes' gazing at points on a computer screen into "typed" commands, and large-type displays on computer screens for workers with visual impairment. Pitney Bowes has introduced an accessible photocopier called the Universal Access Copier System. It features Braille labels, speech recognition software, a large-type graphic-user interface, and buttons that can be operated by mouse, fingers, or pointing stick. The copier is designed to sit low to the ground, so that a user in a wheelchair can operate it. Companies that invest in assistive technology can tap a segment of the workforce that is eager for jobs, as well as keep talented employees who become disabled. When lawyer Joseph Martin began to lose the ability to control his arms and legs because of Lou Gehrig's disease, his employer, Bank of America, outfitted his office with an Eyegaze System by LC Technologies. By directing his gaze to control keys on his computer monitor, Martin uses the system to activate the keys with a laser beam. He uses a voice synthesizer to deliver speeches.[49]

Other sources of diversity involve differences in ethnic and cultural backgrounds. As discussed in Chapters 1 and 2, ethnic minorities are becoming a larger share of all employees. Immigration is an important source of employees in the U.S. Family structures are diverse, too. Increasing numbers of employees will be single people and couples without children. The number of childless couples is expected to grow by almost 50 percent by 2010.

Workforce Trends

The use of contingent workers, already about one-quarter of the workforce, is expected to grow. **Contingent workers** are employees who work part-time, temporarily, or for the length of time involved in fulfilling a specific contract. Hiring contingent workers enables companies to maintain the efficiency of a pared-down workforce while being flexible enough to meet new and changing needs. Traditionally, contingent workers often earned less pay than full-time employees and did not receive benefits or have access to employer-provided pension plans. However, among highly skilled workers, contingent work may be a profitable alternative to traditional employment, as these workers negotiate contracts with generous enough pay to cover self-paid benefits. Figure 9.10 shows a few recent ads for contingent workers. In a survey of workers who consider themselves "free agents," six out of ten respondents said they earn more money as consultants than they did as employees, and over half said their quality of life

BUSINESS DIRECTORY

► **contingent worker** *employee who works part-time, temporarily, or for the length of time involved in fulfilling a specific contract.*

Computer/Info Systems
MS Consulting Services has immediate openings for the following positions:
- UNIX Admin to $ 100K
- VC + + Prog. to $ 100K
- Lotus Admin to $ 75K

Please fax to 630-555-0123 or email: jobs@____.com

DRAFTING
ARCHITECTURAL/STRUCTURAL
DETAILER
Part-Time
Positions Available
Suburban Mfg Co seeking Architectural/Structural Detailer experienced in Autocad Rev 14 or LT97. Must be capable of reading architectural & structural drawings. Working knowledge of miscellaneous steel design with the ability to produce fabrication drawings. Must be able to work within project deadlines. Company paid medical, dental and life insurance - 401K pension plan offered. Pleasant smoke-free environment.
Resumes for Mechanical and Electrical Detailers will not be considered.
Please send resume with salary requirements to:
XYZ Company
ATTN: Drafting Manager
123 Skyline Drive
Suburbia, IL 60446
PH: 815-555-9876
FX: 815-555-0987
EM: ----@----.com

Editorial
ASSOCIATE EDITOR
Loop-based food industry consulting firm seeks part-time Associate Editors for its growing publications staff. Duties/responsibilities include: interviewing, editing, writing copy and managing production for several business-oriented newsletters and reports covering industry trends and financial analysis. 2 to 3 years related experience, word processing/desktop publishing skills and the ability to work independently and under deadlines are required. For consideration, send resume including salary history and 2 writing samples to:
P.O. Box 00000,
Chicago, Il. 60680

ATTORNEYS
Our company provides attorneys and paralegals with permanent and temporary opportunities with law firms and corporate law depts in the Chicago area. We have current permanent openings in the following areas:
Corporate Transactions
Intellectual Property
Commercial Litigation
Commercial Real Estate
Estate Planning
Education
We are also looking for attorneys in all practice areas for various temporary assignments. Please submit your resume for immediate consideration to:
Legal Consultants
312-555-1234
Fax: 312-555-2345
----@----.com

FIGURE 9.10
Current Want-Ads for Contingent Workers

improved after they became consultants. Some people enjoy the variety and flexibility that can accompany contingent work. However, others miss the continuing relationships with coworkers and the predictability of a regular paycheck.[50]

The demand for skilled workers is growing significantly, but employers are concerned about a potential shortage of educated and qualified workers. Adult illiteracy continues to be a problem. Some companies are coping by providing training in basic skills. A growing number of businesses are hiring immigrants, which intensifies the need for expertise in managing a diverse workforce. Human resource professionals are responding with training and advice in this aspect of management.

The wired, globalized marketplace is changing the definition of work hours. Customers and employees are online and on the phone day and night. Although hospital workers and police officers routinely have worked night shifts, night work is becoming part of the lives of new categories of employees. Software engineers are fixing crashed Web sites at midnight, and stockbrokers are tracking stocks on exchanges open halfway around the world. When these workers need toner or light bulbs, they expect to find a store open. An estimated 23 million Americans are currently working nights, evenings, or split or rotating shifts, and their numbers are growing.[51] Not only does this trend pose recruiting challenges, but human resource professionals must find ways to make their own services available to people working when traditional offices are usually closed.

Work teams are expected to be the most important format for high-performance work, with employees from different functions such as marketing, purchasing, service delivery, and human resources collaborating on producing goods and services. Work teams are discussed in detail in the next chapter.

Economic Trends

Changes in the economic environment will create new sets of human resource needs. With a significant portion of economic growth occurring in countries outside the U.S. and Europe, programs and practices of American firms will show a growing influence from conditions and cultures of other countries. Employers will need to recruit global managers and employees with international skills and experience. They also will require human resource plans that address the needs of employees in more than one country. Many will work with benefits providers and professional employer organizations that can help with international operations. For example, Figure 9.11 describes the services of a company that offers insurance and financial benefits in many countries.

With the growing discrepancy between earnings at the top and bottom of America's income distribution, companies will have to consider that some workers will be motivated by relatively basic needs. Job enrichment and similar programs are key trends, but minimum-wage employees may be more concerned about making ends meet. Jen-Cyn, a distributor of galvanized steel, hires workers near its facility in Camden, New Jersey, where wages are low and unemployment is high.

The company helps workers cope with emergencies by making small pay advances when they need help to buy a car or put a security deposit on an apartment. Jen-Cyn also picks up the cost of workers' steel-toed shoes.[52]

Companies will continue to focus on reducing costs, including labor costs. For human resource managers, this trend creates a challenge of finding ways to motivate employees to increase their productivity by making the workplace attractive while reducing employment costs. Employee discontent with executive compensation will grow, and workers will demand an increasing portion of firms' profits. Company shareholders and investors will want stronger voices in determining the employment-related policies that influence a firm's economic performance.

Austin, Texas-based Trilogy Software responds in a creative way to its needs for skilled technical personnel. The firm recruits the best engineers it can hire from college campuses and immediately enrolls them in Trilogy University, a 3-month-long intensive training program where every teacher is a member of the firm's top management. The new-hires learn not only how they can contribute to the company but how they can reshape it. To date, six new companies have been spun off, including an online auto site that sells hundreds of millions of dollars' worth of cars annually. "The same way people look at customers, we look at our jobs," says president Joe Liemandt. "If you don't get the best people into the company, there is no product."

Work/Life Trends

Employer-sponsored benefits and programs for elder care and child care will become increasingly common as employers recognize the need to accommodate aging workers, single parents with children, and two-income families. As a result of improved treatments, some AIDS patients have returned to work. Employers must integrate these workers into their organizations and comply with laws that prohibit discrimination against them.

The physical work environment also has changed. Casual dress policies have become widespread. Even such hallowed institutions of Wall Street as Dean Witter, Goldman Sachs, and J. P. Morgan have permitted their employees to leave their dark suits in the closet—or at least hanging on the office door, in case an important client shows up. HBO and Credit Suisse First Boston each have invited Banana Republic to set up shop in their offices temporarily to help employees define—and find—casual clothing.

Another environmental change is that a growing number of companies are making room for play. Campus Pipeline, which develops Internet software, has an 18-hole indoor golf course installed in its fifth-floor office. At the Los Angeles headquarters of advertising firm TBWA/Chiat/Day, an indoor "Main Street" boasts a basketball court, Tilt-a-Whirl cars, punching bags decorated with executives' faces, and much, much more. Other companies are providing for naps. Technest has furnished a nap room with bunk beds, and Gould Evans Goodman Associates has placed two tents in a quiet corner, along with air mattresses, sleeping bags, and tapes of peaceful music. One company that seems to have all of employees' needs covered is BMC Software. The Houston company stocks its kitchens with free popcorn, fruit, coffee, and soft drinks. A massage therapist works on site, and a pianist plays welcoming music near the entrance each morning. Outside, employees can take a break to enjoy the basketball court, putting green, or beach volleyball court. Also on the premises are a bank, hair stylist, dry cleaner, and other services.[53]

Companies are adding benefits like these to reduce the level of stress that many of today's employees feel, because they are often expected to work ten-hour days or longer. These nonmonetary benefits add convenience to workers' daily lives, and these efforts can make the workplace feel like home. Companies are helping

FIGURE 9.11
CIGNA: Providing Benefits for a Global Workforce

employees resolve work/life dilemmas by deciding that work *is* life. The big question for the 21st century may become "Why go home?" Some people are already wondering. BMC Software provides many ways to get away from work stress, whether in the gym, on a hammock on the grounds, or in BMC's bright cafeterias. The firm's human resource manager, Roy Wilson, says, "It gives you a balanced life without having to leave." In the 21st century, employees will have to sort out whether their company and colleagues are a valid, partial substitute for community, friends, and family. If a firm no longer needs their talents, will it treat them like valued friends or obsolete resources? Will employees grieve the lost relationships or simply find another company to which they can transfer their affections? Employees' answers to these questions will go a long way toward influencing the meaning of work/life balance in the 21st century.

WHAT'S AHEAD

Treating employees well by enriching the work environment will continue to gain importance as a way to recruit and retain a highly motivated workforce. In addition, managers can tap the full potential of their employees by empowering them to make decisions, leading them to work effectively as teams, and fostering clear, positive communication. The next chapter covers these three means of improving performance. By involving employees more fully through empowerment, teamwork, and communication, companies can benefit from the employees' knowledge while the employees enjoy a more meaningful role in the company.

➤ Summary of Learning Goals

1. Describe the importance of human resource management and the responsibilities of human resource managers.

Organizations devote considerable attention to attracting, training, and retaining employees to help maintain their competitiveness. Human resource managers are responsible for recruiting, selecting, training, compensating, terminating, and motivating employees. They accomplish these tasks by developing specific programs and creating a work environment that generates employee satisfaction and efficiency.

2. Explain the role of human resource planning in an organization's competitive strategy.

A human resource plan is designed to implement a firm's competitive strategies by providing the right number of employees, training them to meet job requirements, and motivating them to be productive and satisfied workers.

3. Discuss the ways firms recruit and select employees and the importance of compliance with employment-related legislation.

Firms use internal and external methods to recruit qualified employees. Internal recruiting, or hiring from within the organization, is less expensive than external methods and can boost employee morale. For needs that the company cannot meet with existing employees, the company may find candidates by encouraging employee referrals, advertising, accepting resumes at its Web site, and using job search Web sites. In selecting from among the resulting candidates, human resource managers must follow legal requirements designed to promote equal employment opportunity. Failure to comply with employment laws can result in legal cases and negative publicity.

4. **Summarize how firms train and evaluate employees to develop effective workforces.**

Human resource managers use a variety of training techniques, including on-the-job training, computerized training programs, and classroom methods. In addition, management development programs help managers make decisions and improve interpersonal skills. Companies conduct performance appraisals to assess employees' work, as well as their strengths and weaknesses. With 360-degree performance reviews, companies provide feedback from coworkers, supervisors, employees, and sometimes customers.

5. **Identify the various pay systems and benefit programs.**

Firms compensate employees with wages, salaries, and incentive pay systems such as profit sharing, gain sharing, bonuses, and pay-for-knowledge programs. Benefit programs vary among firms, but most companies offer health care programs, insurance, retirement plans, paid holidays, and sick leave. A growing number of companies are offering flexible work plans such as flextime, compressed workweeks, job sharing, and home-based work.

6. **Discuss employee separation and the impact of downsizing and outsourcing.**

Either an employer or an employee can decide to terminate employment. Downsizing reduces a company's workforce in an effort to improve the firm's competitive position by reducing labor costs. The company may transfer some responsibilities to contractors, a practice called outsourcing. The goals of outsourcing are to reduce costs by giving work to more efficient specialists and to allow the company to focus on the activities it does best.

7. **Explain the concept of motivation in terms of satisfying employee needs.**

All employees feel needs, and these needs differ among employees. Each person is motivated to take actions that satisfy his or her needs. Employers who recognize and understand differences in employee needs can develop programs that satisfy different needs and motivate workers to achieve organizational goals.

8. **Describe how human resource managers apply theories of motivation in attracting, developing, and maintaining employees.**

Human resource managers develop benefits and other policies and programs to satisfy employees' physiological, safety, social, esteem, and self-actualization needs. Some motivational efforts, such as job enlargement and job enrichment, focus on the job duties themselves. Managers' attitudes toward employees also influence workers' motivation. Managers who display positive attitudes toward employees can motivate them by including them in decision making and problem solving.

9. **Identify trends that influence the work of human resource managers in the 21st century.**

Demographic, workforce, economic, and work/life trends will influence the tasks of human resource managers. The workforce is aging and becoming more diverse, trends that require great flexibility in terms of human resource management. Organizations are increasing their use of contingent workers, night workers, and teams, and they are addressing skills shortages by providing training. Economic growth outside the U.S. is creating a need for international human resource strategies, and companies are under pressure to meet human resource needs while keeping costs down. Employers of the 21st century also are expected to help employees manage work/life issues.

Business Terms You Need to Know

human resource management 326
employment at will 332
on-the-job training 333
management development program 334
performance appraisal 335
employee benefits 337
flexible benefit plan 338

flexible work plan 339
downsizing 340
job enrichment 345
Theory X 346
Theory Y 346
Theory Z 347
contingent worker 349

Other Important Business Terms

professional employer organization (PEO) 326

360-degree performance review 335

wages 336

salaries 336

flextime 339

compressed workweek 339

job sharing 339

home-based work 340

exit interview 340

morale 343

need 343

motive 343

job enlargement 345

Review Questions

1. In what ways have relationships between employers and employees changed during the past century?

2. What are the core responsibilities of human resource management? What are the three main objectives of human resource managers?

3. What methods do companies use to find qualified candidates? How has the Internet influenced this process?

4. In what ways does equal employment opportunity legislation restrict or guide recruitment decisions made by human resource managers?

5. What techniques do firms use to train employees? How has the Internet changed training methods?

6. Identify and define four types of incentive compensation programs. Why are they so popular today?

7. Describe four types of flexible work plans. Name an industry that would be well suited to each type of plan and explain why.

8. Why do companies downsize? What are some of the difficulties they may encounter in doing so?

9. What types of needs on Maslow's hierarchy do firms in industrialized nations try to satisfy? What types of needs must they satisfy in developing nations? Explain the difference.

10. Identify the four trends that are shaping the responsibilities and practices of human resource managers. Why is it important for these managers to monitor these trends?

Questions for Critical Thinking

1. In the United States, CEO compensation is currently 475 times greater than that of the average production worker. Do you think this discrepancy is justified in most cases? Why or why not?

2. Would you accept or keep a job you didn't like because the company offered an attractive benefits package? Why or why not? Do you think you will give the same answer ten years from now? Why or why not?

3. Choose one of the following organizations (or select one of your own) and write a memo describing a plan for outsourcing some of the tasks performed by workers in the company. Give reasons for your choices.

   a. A family resort in Florida

   b. A regional high school

   c. A software development firm

   d. A hospital

   e. An Internet retailer

4. Suppose you are a human resource manager and you have determined that your organization, a health maintenance organization, would benefit from hiring some older workers. Write a memo explaining your reasons for this conclusion. Alternatively, select another company or industry that interests you and make the same determination.

5. Many companies are adding more employer-sponsored benefits aimed at enhancing the quality of their employees' lives. Do you think this trend will continue? Why or why not?

Experiential Exercise

Background: A recent survey of more than 1,200 U.S. workers was conducted by Sibson & Co. in partnership with WorldatWork. The so-called Rewards of Work Study examined worker attitudes toward monetary and nonmonetary rewards to determine their impact on employee performance, retention, and satisfaction.

This exercise focuses on the portion of the study that examined the importance of rewards for performance motivation. Of the five reward categories on which this study is based, a majority of the respondents reported that all five types of rewards are "very important" or "extremely important" to them in motivating their best performance.

Directions: To compare what motivates you to perform your best on the job with the results of this research, complete the following steps:

1. Rank the five reward categories presented in the following table according to how important each is to motivating your best performance.

2. Within each category, rate the reward using numbers 1 through 5, with 1 = most important to 5 = least important.

3. After filling in the table, compare your rankings with the two charts that present the results of the Rewards of Work Study.

4. Be prepared to answer this question: "What have you learned about motivation from this exercise?"

Reward Category	Brief Definition	Your Rank
Direct financial	All the monetary rewards you receive	
Indirect financial	Your benefits	
Work content	The satisfaction that comes from the work you do	
Affiliation	The feeling of belonging to an admirable organization that shares your values	
Career	Your long-term opportunities for development and advancement in the organization	

Results of Rewards of Work Study:

**Overall Results
Importance for Motivation**

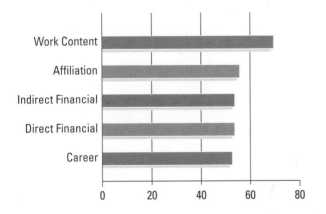

Percent indicating very or extremely important

**Percent of Respondents by Age
Indicating High Importance for
Motivating Performance**

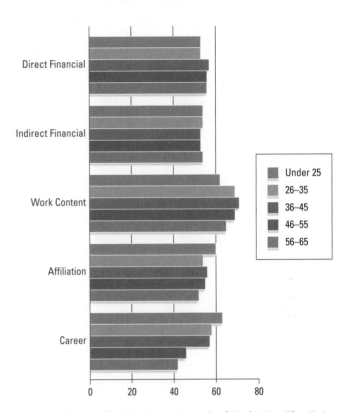

Source: Mulvey, Ledford, LeBlanc, "Rewards of Work: How They Drive Performance, Retention and Satisfaction," *Worldat Work Journal,* Third Quarter 2000, pp. 6–18.

➤ Nothing but Net

1. **Using the Web to find a job.** Many companies advertise open positions on their Web sites. Some will even allow you to submit applications online. Visit the following company Web sites and explore the employment sections. Write a brief summary of the types of positions advertised, the application procedure, and other employment information provided. Based on your visits to the three sites, would you be interested in working for any of these companies? Why or why not?

   www.ey.com/global/gcr.nsf/us

   www.dell.com/dell/careers/index.html

   www.johnsonandjohnson.com/job_posting/career_ops.html

2. **Employee benefits.** The Bureau of Labor Statistics conducts regular surveys on employee benefits. Visit the Bureau's Web site (**stats.bls.gov.ebshome.htm**) and review the results of the most recent survey. Answer the following:

   a. List the benefits offered by the "typical employer."

b. Rank these benefits in terms of importance to you specifically.

c. What percentage of employees enroll in employer health care plans, retirement plans, and flexible spending plans?

d. Are there any differences between the benefits offered by large employers and those offered by small employers?

3. **Outsourcing.** An organization called The Outsourcing Center provides a wide range of information and tools on outsourcing. Visit the Center's Web site and prepare a report on the ten most frequently asked questions concerning outsourcing and the thirteen most common outsourcing mistakes.

www.outsourcing-center.com

Note: Internet Web addresses change frequently. If you do not find the exact sites listed, you may need to access the organization's or company's home page and search from there.

A few years ago, it seemed that every office worker's dream was to go to work in pajamas. Not that they'd actually *go* to work. They'd wake up, get the kids off to school, flick on the coffeemaker, and shuffle off to a corner of the house, where they'd check e-mail messages that had arrived overnight on their home computer. Many employees did try telecommuting, with their companies' sometimes reluctant blessing. But often it didn't work out. People quickly dropped out of the communication loop, had equipment problems, or couldn't establish a work routine—and productivity suffered. Lonely employees drifted back into the office. Companies reeled others in or cut them loose. It seemed as though telecommuting, which was supposed to revolutionize the workforce and the workday, was a flop.

But not at Merrill Lynch, where managers were determined to develop a highly effective workforce and satisfy the needs of employees at the same time. Merrill Lynch concluded that the key to developing a successful group of telecommuters is planning and training. "You can't just give people computers, send them home, and call them telecommuters," explains Camille Manfredonia, a Merrill Lynch vice president in charge of the company's alternative work arrangements group. "There are so many issues. What kind of equipment do you need? How will working from home affect your clients, your manager, your coworkers? How will it affect your career? How do you manage people effectively from a distance?" So Manfredonia and her colleagues set up a rigorous training program for prospective Merrill Lynch telecommuters. First, applicants must submit a detailed proposal for telecommuting; second, they must attend a series of meetings with their own managers and with Manfredonia's group; and third, they spend two weeks simulating a telecommuting situation while still at the office. The program focuses on four principles:

1. Communicate. "Don't expect people to connect with you," says Manfredonia. "You have to stay connected with them."
2. Get organized. "You have to learn to think like a telecommuter," notes Manfredonia. "You have to plan a day ahead, a week ahead."
3. Create new routines and stick with them.
4. Make sure you have the right equipment for the job you plan to do.

Why was developing a strong telecommuting workforce so important to Merrill Lynch? It is part of the company's competitive strategy to satisfy employee needs, create loyalty by doing so, and ultimately increase productivity. When the company started the program, "We didn't care about cutting costs," remarks chief technology officer and senior vice president Howard Sorgen. "Our goal was to promote loyalty and productivity." In addition, Merrill Lynch sought to recruit the best staff from a tight labor market in which there were not enough skilled technical workers. "To become the employer of choice, we had to consider all the things we could be doing above and beyond what we had in place today to give us the edge over the competition," says Sorgen. "One of them was telecommuting." Manfredonia explains further, "We're a technology organization. What do technologists need to be happy [in their work]? . . . You just know that [telecommuting makes] people feel comfortable and productive."

But even though Merrill Lynch developed its telecommuting program methodically and deliberately, there were glitches. For instance, in the beginning the company underestimated the need for technical support for its telecommuters. "If I couldn't get my computer to work, I had to come into the office," recalls Susan Davelman, a systems analyst. So Merrill Lynch organized an information technology support group for its remote workers, available from 7:00 AM to 7:00 PM on weekdays.

Three years after the telecommuting training program was established, an in-house survey showed that employee satisfaction was up 30 percent, particularly among working parents. The magazine *Working Mother* voted Merrill Lynch one of its top 100 places to work, and *Business Week* named the company one of the top family-friendly workplaces. Eileen Keyes, business manager for the alternative work group says that productivity has increased, and turnover among the telecommuting group has decreased. "These people genuinely love their jobs," she says. "There's a lot less stress. Their satisfaction levels are way up." Has the telecommuting program been a successful competitive strategy for Merrill Lynch? Howard Sorgen thinks so. "This is an employee perk to create loyalty to the firm and a happy populace that wants to jump on a grenade for Merrill Lynch," he comments. "It's a tremendous retention tool and a phenomenal recruiting tool."

QUESTIONS

1. How might Merrill Lynch use the telecommuting program to create a more diverse workforce as part of its equal opportunity hiring program?
2. The case discusses ways telecommuters are trained at Merrill Lynch. What steps could the firm take to train in-house managers of those telecommuters?
3. Do you think that telecommuters are motivated by different factors than employees who might be eligible for a telecommuting assignment but choose to continue working at the company?
4. Access Merrill Lynch's Web site at **www.ml.com**. List some ways that the company could use its Web site to assist its telecommuters.

Sources: Company Web site, **www.ml.com**, accessed February 12, 2001; "Merrill Lynch Selects the National Organization on Disability to Receive $50,000 Grant," company press release, November 27, 2000; "Merrill Lynch's Approach to Flexible Workforce Management," *Best Practices*, February 2, 1999, **http://internet8.eapps.com**.

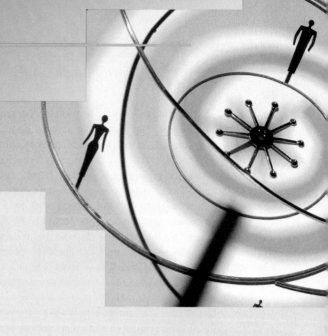

CHAPTER 10

Improving Performance through Empowerment, Teamwork, and Communication

Learning Goals

1. Describe why and how organizations empower employees.

2. Distinguish between the two major types of teams in the workplace.

3. Identify the characteristics of an effective team and the roles played by team members.

4. Summarize the stages of team development.

5. Relate team cohesiveness and norms to effective team performance.

6. Describe the factors that can cause conflict in teams and ways conflict can be resolved.

7. Explain the importance of effective communication skills in business.

8. Compare the different types of communication.

9. Discuss how advances in technology affect business communication.

The Pampered Chef: Performance through Empowerment

Our love affair with food is enduring. People enjoy getting together and sampling treats and sharing techniques for food preparation. One woman decided to take that interest to another level. Two decades ago, Doris Christopher decided to start her own business. She chose a new venture that would let her combine her love of cooking with her need to work out of her home and still have time for her two young daughters. So her husband, Jay, suggested that she host Tupperware-like parties. The difference would be that Doris could do cooking demonstrations for customers, who would then sample the food and buy the utensils needed to make the appetizers, entrées, and desserts. Doris liked the idea. She borrowed $3,000 on her life-insurance policy, bought some basic items for inventory, and set up business in her basement. Her first cooking demonstration was held at a friend's house, where Doris cooked for 15 people. Word of mouth resulted in more demonstrations, and within a year the one-woman operation began to grow. Salespeople were recruited to keep up with demand. Christopher taught her recruits how to do their own demonstrations, and in turn they earned money both from sales and from their own recruits. Today, Christopher's company—The Pampered Chef—employs 1,100 corporate employees in two offices in Illinois. Some 60,000 independent sales consultants sell Pampered Chef products throughout the U.S., Canada, the United Kingdom, and Germany.

Doris Christopher relies on the performance of her independent sales organization for the ultimate success of her business. These people, called Kitchen Consultants, "organize, develop and maintain independent business according to their personal needs," says the company's Web site. "They also determine their own hours, goals, and levels of achievement." Many of them work part time, while others choose

to reap the added rewards of a full-time career. In addition, Kitchen Consultants who wish to advance within the organization can work toward management positions.

For The Pampered Chef to succeed, its consultants and managers must be granted both the opportunity and the authority to make decisions about many aspects of their jobs. In other words, they must be empowered to think and act in ways that they believe will best reach their customers and benefit their business efforts. Although they receive professional training and guidance from company headquarters, they decide which dishes to cook to demonstrate The Pampered Chef's high-quality tools in the best light; they schedule their own demonstrations; they present cooking techniques that will best suit their own customers. In fact, the firm deliberately recruits individuals who enjoy independent decision making—but who also enjoy interacting with other people. "All Consultants enjoy valuable training and incentive programs, sponsored by the Home Office," says the Web site. "We supply the tools and motivation, but the rest is up to them." In addition to conducting in-home demonstrations, Kitchen Consultants are encouraged to attend bridal expos and other

events where potential customers may be located. The idea is for them to create new and different ways to find, entertain, educate, and sell to customers. Their success is

directly linked to their own performance, as well as to the performance of the company as a whole.

Because The Pampered Chef is a direct-selling organization, its products are available only through the Kitchen Consultants or at the company Web site, which increases convenience for consumers. But the cornerstone of the firm's business is the in-home demonstration where the consultants make the products come to life. After all, who wouldn't buy a set of high-quality knives after eating freshly sliced gourmet cheese? And who wouldn't want a pastry stone after sampling some warm, delicious tarts? Of course, this means that Kitchen Consultants must not only be skilled in cooking basics but also be able to present and serve meals attractively. They do—and with zest. It seems that Doris Christopher—and her husband—were right about their recipe for success. Twenty years after the first demonstration, The Pampered Chef is cooking up annual sales of $600 million.[1]

CHAPTER OVERVIEW

In the competitive business environment of the 21st century, The Pampered Chef and thousands of other companies are working diligently to improve their performance. Like Doris Christopher, top managers at most firms recognize that empowerment, teamwork, and communication are essential for encouraging employees to participate in improving organizational performance. Advances in information technology have powerfully influenced the ability of firms to give employees needed resources to make decisions, work in teams, and share information.

Chapter 10 focuses on how organizations are involving employees by applying the concepts of empowerment, teamwork, and communication. We begin by discussing the ways managers are expanding their employees' decision-making authority and responsibility. Then we explain why and how a growing number of firms rely on teams of workers rather than individuals to make decisions. Finally, the chapter discusses how effective communication allows workers to share information that improves decision making.

Three college chums, Adam and Bob Rizika and Scott Brazina (pictured along with CFO Stuart Krentcil), used total quality management (TQM) to found their company, Reflective Technologies. As Brazina recalls, the original mission of the partners was "to find a new technology that would produce high-value benefits for consumers and would be difficult to copy." They planned and created illumiNITE, a highly reflective fabric that would protect runners at night. They worked together to develop the technology, generate market contacts, and convince runners of the product's benefits. Today, Reflective Technologies is a multimillion dollar firm with such major clients as Adidas, Eddie Bauer, Honda, Lands' End, L.L. Bean, Polaris, and the U.S. military.

EMPOWERING EMPLOYEES

Organizations throughout the world are working to supply high-quality goods and services to meet the needs of their buyers and create customer satisfaction. As part of this effort, many firms have adopted an approach to improving quality called **total quality management (TQM)**. This concept envisions a companywide commitment to quality based on achieving world-class performance and customer satisfaction as a crucial strategic objective.

A TQM organization involves all employees in determining what customers require and what they need to do to meet those expectations. Marketers develop products that people want to buy. Engineers design products to work the way customers want to use them. Production workers build quality into every product they make. Salespeople deliver what they promise to customers. Information systems specialists use technology to ensure that the firm fills customer orders correctly and on time. Financial managers help to determine prices that give value to customers.

The teachings of quality advocates such as the late W. Edwards Deming set guidelines for top managers in establishing quality programs. Total quality management pioneers have proposed that effective quality programs begin with the leadership of top managers, who build quality values into their organizations and communicate quality goals and benefits to employees, suppliers, and customers. Top management must also provide training for employees and the tools and resources they need to continuously improve products and work processes.

An important component of quality programs is **empowerment** of employees. Top managers promote this goal by giving employees authority and responsibility to make decisions about their work without traditional managerial approval and control. Empowerment seeks to tap the brainpower of all employees to find improved ways of doing their jobs and executing their ideas. Empowering employees frees managers from hands-on control of subordinates. It also motivates workers by adding challenge to their jobs and giving them a feeling of ownership. Managers empower employees by sharing company information, giving them decision-making authority, and rewarding them based on company performance.

Sharing Information

One of the most effective methods of empowering employees is to keep them informed about the company's financial performance. Companies like Anderson & Associates provide regular reports to their employees on key financial information, such as profit and loss statements. Anderson, an engineering firm that designs roads, water and sewer lines, and water treatment facilities, posts financial statements, training schedules, policy documents, and other information on its intranet. Any employee can visit the site to look up accounts receivable, design standards, and photos of their coworkers in other cities, as well as basic measures of financial performance. Like other companies that practice this strategy of *open-book management,* Anderson also trains its employees in techniques for interpreting financial statements so they can understand how their work contributes to company profits. Anderson's policy is to hire engineers before they have completed their formal education, then help them develop their skills in one of the firm's offices following graduation. Once they have learned all facets of managing a branch office, they are ready to open—and manage—a new branch office. The company's president, Ken Anderson, says, "We believe in training all our employees to help expand the company. To do that they need to understand both the engineering and the financial ends of the business."[2]

In addition to sharing information about the company itself, top management can empower employees by communicating information about the company's business environment. Companies use intranets, meetings, and other tools to keep their employees posted about industry trends, competitive performance, suppliers and customers, and external opportunities and threats. Figure 10.1 shows an example of a company that provides software for maintaining this level of information sharing on a global scale. Communication technology is covered in more detail later in this chapter.

Employee empowerment has benefited from advances in information technology. Firms once needed multiple layers of management to analyze information and communicate it up and down their organizational hierarchies. Now, however, the Internet, internal company networks and databases, and communication tools such as e-mail and videoconferencing allow employees to carry out many activities on their own. Anderson and Associates' first formal method of information sharing involved posting data on a wide-area network of linked office computers. When the Internet provided user-friendly browser technology, the firm switched to an intranet. On the intranet, employees can readily search for historical data, and they know they can find regular updates without having to wait for someone to send e-mail announcements or distribute printed reports.

Using information technology to empower employees does carry some risks. One is that information may leak to competitors. Although this problem was considered by Anderson & Associates, management decided that sharing information was essential to the company's strategy. Also, in evaluating what competitors would do with the information, president Ken Anderson concluded, "We operate so

FIGURE 10.1
Lotus: Software for Sharing Information across Geographic Boundaries

differently from most other companies, our numbers would most likely just confuse them."[3] Another risk of giving employees access to information and information technology is that they might use resources like Internet access for personal matters. Most large U.S. companies record and review employees' communications and Internet usage. Companies that sell software for monitoring keystrokes and mouse clicks are doing a brisk business; some software even sends a signal to human resource personnel when it detects that a company computer is accessing a pornography site on the Internet.

A recent study discovered that at least one-third of lost productivity is caused by employees using the Internet for something other than work. However, some observers argue that employers' anxiety about Internet abuse is misplaced. They point out that U.S. workers are putting in more hours than ever and that companies themselves are blurring the boundaries between work and personal time. Consultant Shel Holtz of Holtz Communication & Technology says employers should appreciate that their employees are hardworking and pressed for time: "How committed am I going to be to an organization that blatantly [by checking up on employees] says, 'I don't trust you'?"[4]

Sharing Decision-Making Authority

As Chapter 9 explains, employees are being given more authority and responsibility in choosing the most appropriate benefits through cafeteria-style plans and in scheduling their workdays through flexible work programs. Going beyond those efforts, companies empower employees in the workplace when they give them broad authority to make decisions that implement a firm's vision and its competitive strategy. Trust and freedom can be expressed in different ways. Bed Bath & Beyond lets individual store managers decide how much of each item to stock. It is assumed that store managers know their customers better than anyone at headquarters can. The results are sometimes unexpected. In Manhattan, the Bed Bath & Beyond store carries electric fans in November. Although the temperature outside may be frigid, Manhattanites often live in stuffy apartments, so demand for fans doesn't end with the change of seasons. Thanks to such knowledge of local conditions, empowerment at Bed Bath & Beyond helps to keep sales per square foot high and turnover among store managers low.[5]

Empowerment ranges from allowing employees to suggest improvements in their work to granting them the authority and resources to turn their ideas into actions. Roles of managers change, too, from inspecting and approving work to enabling employees by providing them with the necessary resources. In leading Walt Disney Co.'s Internet activities, Jake Winebaum views empowerment as essential to seizing new opportunities as they arise. Says Winebaum, "My job as part of a 120,000-person traditional media company is to remove impediments, to give teams every resource they need to respond to opportunities quickly—and to ensure that they have enough capital to create an environment that's going to attract the best talent."[6]

At Pervasive Software, chief executive Ron Harris doesn't just empower people; he treats them as equals. When the company takes on new projects or expands into new regions, Harris finds someone with the leadership ability required to make the new project or new territory successful and appoints that person CEO of the new area. As the CEO of the company's Northern European division, Gilbert van Cutsem is responsible for everything from business plans to acquiring resources. Sandy Rios was CEO in charge of Pervasive's move from its original headquarters into new and larger space. Rios drew up a plan for the move, and the company's board of directors accepted it unhesitatingly. Harris said of her plan, "Because Sandy was the CEO, I don't think I spent five minutes on the plan," indicating that his empowerment is based on trust in employees' ability to make sound business decisions.[7]

Even among nonmanagement employees, empowerment extends to decisions and activities traditionally handled by managers. Employees might be responsible for such tasks as purchasing supplies, making hiring decisions, scheduling production or work hours, overseeing the safety program, and granting pay increases. Often, they make these decisions as part of a team, an arrangement discussed later in this chapter.

Linking Rewards to Company Performance

To provide incentives for excellence, employers should reward their employees for contributing desirable ideas and actions. Compensation plans such as pay for performance, pay for knowledge, and gain sharing give employees a sense of ownership. To tie rewards to company performance, home builder BBL Buildings and Components uses a program it calls "bucket of profits." BBL records its profits on an image of a bucket, which is posted in the company's break room. Each time the company reaches $50,000 in profits, it declares that the bucket is full and pays a bonus to each employee. As employees fill more buckets throughout the year, the size of each bonus grows. BBL's management also makes sure employees understand how their individual actions affect the amount of profits in the bucket. The firm conducts regular meetings to show how employees in each division are performing and how individual jobs contribute to the company's overall performance.[8]

Perhaps the ultimate step in convincing employees of their stake in the continuing prosperity of their firm is worker ownership, which makes employees financial participants in company performance. Two widely used ways that companies provide for worker ownership are employee stock ownership plans and stock options. Table 10.1 compares these two methods of employee ownership.

Employee Stock Ownership Plans By 2002, about 9 million U.S. employees at 11,000 different companies were participating in **employee stock ownership plans (ESOPs)**.[9] These plans benefit employees by giving them ownership stakes in their companies, leading to potential profits as the value of their firm increases. Under ESOPs, the employer buys shares of the company stock on behalf of the employees, as a retirement benefit. The accounts continue to grow in value tax-free, and when employees leave the company, they cash in their stock shares. Employees should be motivated to work harder and smarter than they would without ESOPs, because as part owners, they share in their firm's financial success.

To help employees understand the benefits of their ownership stakes, employers offering ESOPs to their workforce share financial information about company assets, revenues, and expenses. Anderson & Associates, described earlier for its use of open-book management, has an ESOP. Anderson's ESOP is open to any employee who is at least 21 years old and has worked at least 1,000 hours during the previous year. As company president Ken Anderson says, "Our employees are our owners and are entitled to understand the business."[10]

Table 10.1 **Employee Stock Ownership Plans and Stock Options**

ESOP	Stock Options
Company-sponsored trust fund holds shares of stock for employees	Company gives employees the option to buy shares of its stock
Usually covers all full-time employees	Can be granted to one, a few, or all employees
Employer pays for the shares of stock	Employees pay a set price to exercise the option
Employees receive stock shares (or value of stock) upon retiring or leaving the company	Employees receive shares of stock when (and if) they exercise the option, usually during a set period

As retirement plans, ESOPs must comply with government regulations designed to protect pension benefits. Setting up such plans can cost $20,000 or more, even at a small company. So, most companies with ESOPs have at least 15 employees.[11] Large firms with ESOPs include Avis and Publix Supermarkets.

Stock Options   Another popular way for companies to share ownership with their employees is through the use of **stock options,** or rights to buy a specified amount of the company's stock at a given price within a given time period. In contrast to an ESOP, in which the company holds stock for the benefit of the employees, stock options give employees a chance to own the stock themselves, if they exercise their options by completing the stock purchase. Stock options became popular during the 1990s as a way for high-tech start-up companies to recruit and retain employees. In a recent year, between 7 million and 10 million employees were eligible for stock options.[12] Among the companies that grant stock options to employees at all levels are Bristol-Myers Squibb, Ford Motor Co., Motorola, and Aetna.

Stock options have turned about 1,000 Home Depot employees into millionaires. One of them is Rob Gordon, who a decade ago took a job as an assistant manager of a Home Depot store. He worked his way up to the job of general manager at the company's store in Princeton, New Jersey. Along the way, he bought Home Depot stock at prices as low as $15 a share. Later, Gordon realized the shares he had purchased were worth over $1 million. Gordon says the stock options have made him more enthusiastic about his work. His evaluation of stock options as an employee benefit/employer motivator: "the best benefit that anybody could receive."[13]

TEAMWORK

Teamwork is the practice of organizing a group of workers to achieve a common objective. You have most likely experienced teamwork as a member of a sports team, debate team, band, or school project work group. Teamwork is vital in both business and other areas. A team of workers cooperates to perform a certain function, such as developing a motorized scooter or solving a particular problem, such as improving methods of filling customer orders.

Teamwork is widely used in business and in many not-for-profit organizations such as hospitals, museums, military units, police departments, and government agencies. The ability to work effectively as a team member rather than solely as an individual is more important now than ever before, as Figure 10.2 demonstrates. Teamwork is one of the most frequently discussed topics in employee training programs, where individuals often learn team-building skills. Many firms emphasize the importance of teamwork during their hiring processes, asking job applicants about their previous experiences as team members. Companies want to hire people who can work well with other people.

Teamwork is an important consideration in employee recruitment and training, because it encourages employees to pool their talents and ideas to achieve more together than they could achieve working as individuals. Xerox Business Services (XBS) applied teamwork to the complex job of multisite asset management, which involves managing its clients' office equipment needs. At each client facility, XBS identifies the requirements for each piece of equipment, provides supplies, and keeps the equipment maintained. When Xerox's Houston office signed a major contract with Continental Airlines, it formed an XBS team to manage the office equipment at each of the airline's 60 sites. The team included an expert in developing databases, as well as two employees with expertise in service and supplies. Any Continental employee with a question or problem with the office equipment can speak directly to a member of the XBS team. Team members meet weekly to review their work, recognize one another's accomplishments, and build stronger work relationships. Besides providing a high level of customer service, the teamwork has built positive feelings

**FIGURE 10.2
Importance of Teamwork to Accomplish Goals**

among employees. Team members registered perfect scores in morale and satisfaction on a recent performance evaluation questionnaire. Not surprisingly, Xerox has applied the team approach to its other XBS offices.[14]

What Is a Team?

A **team** is a group of people with complementary skills who are committed to a common purpose, approach, and set of performance goals. All team members hold themselves mutually responsible and accountable for accomplishing their objectives.

The trend in U.S. business toward developing teams started in the 1980s, when managers began to address quality concerns via the formation of quality circles, in which workers meet weekly or monthly to discuss ways to improve quality. This concept spread as the teams demonstrated their ability to help companies reduce output of defective products and the time wasted in reworking those units. Eventually, two-thirds of America's 1,000 largest firms operated quality circles. By the mid-1990s, the percentage of major firms implementing quality circles to solve minor quality problems had declined, primarily because their focus on activities with limited scope typically produced only modest increases in productivity.

Companies continued to reduce layers of management through downsizing, as they became increasingly involved in international business. These trends encouraged formation of many different types of teams. As Figure 10.3 shows, the list includes work teams, problem-solving teams, management teams, quality circles, and even virtual teams made up of geographically separated members who interact via computer. The

BUSINESS DIRECTORY

➤ **teamwork**   *practice of organizing groups of people to work together to achieve a common objective.*

➤ **team**   *group of employees who are committed to a common purpose, approach, and set of performance goals.*

FIGURE 10.3
Five Species of Teams

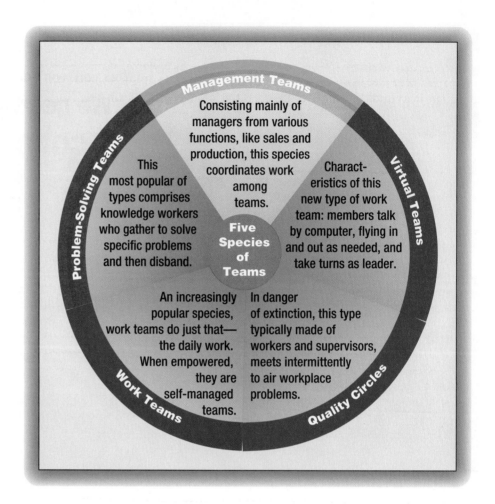

current focus on teamwork centers on two basic types of teams: work teams and problem-solving teams.

Work Teams   About two-thirds of U.S. firms currently use work teams, which are relatively permanent groups of employees. In this approach, small numbers of people with complementary skills perform the day-to-day work of the organization. The earlier example of XBS is a good description of a work team.

When a work team is empowered with authority to make decisions about how the members complete their daily tasks, it is called a *self-managed team*. A self-managed team works most effectively when it combines employees with a range of skills and functions. Members are cross-trained to perform each other's jobs as needed. As part of empowering these teams with the decision-making authority they need to perform their organizational roles, a firm usually must allow them to select fellow team members, spend money, solve problems, evaluate results, and plan future projects. Distributing decision-making authority in this way can free members to concentrate on satisfying customers.

The Whole Foods Market chain of natural-foods stores has a structure based on self-managed work teams. Company managers decided that Whole Foods could be most innovative if employees made decisions themselves. Every Whole Foods employee is part of a team, and each store has about ten teams handling separate functions, such as groceries, seafood, customer service, bakery, and coffee/juice bar. Each team handles responsibilities related to setting goals, hiring and training employees, scheduling team members, and purchasing goods to stock. The teams meet at least monthly to review goals and performance, solve problems, and explore new ideas. Whole Foods awards bonuses based on the teams' performance relative to their goals. This structure extends all the way to the top of the company. The leaders of a store's teams make up a team called the Team Member Advisory Group, which meets regularly to discuss issues related to the store as a whole. Within each of the company's geographic regions, the leaders of each store's Team Member Advisory Group form a regional team. The leaders of the seven regional teams form a national team.[15]

Problem-Solving Teams   In contrast to work teams, a problem-solving team is a temporary combination of workers who gather to solve a specific problem and then disband. Like work teams, special-purpose problem-solving teams typically self-manage their work. They differ from work teams in important ways, though. Whereas work teams are permanent units designed to handle any workplace problem that arises, problem-solving teams pursue specific missions. These missions can be broadly stated—such as finding out why customers aren't satisfied—or narrowly defined—such as solving the overheating problem in Generator 4. Once the team completes its task by solving the problem, it usually disbands.

A current trend is to set up teams to foster intrapreneurship by identifying and selecting worthwhile innovations. DaimlerChrysler uses what it calls "outposts" of teams to come up with new product ideas. In California's Silicon Valley, one of these outposts is helping designers with plans for automobiles that feature Internet connections. At Royal Dutch/Shell Group, teams hold weekly meetings to review ideas submitted by employees. The teams, called GameChangers, have been the source of some of the company's biggest initiatives.[16]

When a team is made up of members from different functions, such as production, marketing, and finance, it is called a *cross-functional team.* Most often cross-functional teams work on specific problems or projects, but they can also serve as permanent work-team arrangements. The value of cross-functional teams comes from their ability to bring many different perspectives to a work effort. General Electric's Bayamón, Puerto Rico, factory uses teams drawn from various departments to evaluate proposed changes. The team members discuss how each change will affect the different departments. This approach has lessened morale problems resulting from rumors about proposed changes and has contributed to improved productivity at the facility.[17]

Certain types of teams work more effectively than others in particular circumstances, depending on their purposes. A cross-functional team can effectively develop an entirely new product. However, a vertical team with members from a single department, such as product engineering, may be a better choice to modify an existing product. Members of a cross-functional team need time to establish their roles and begin working together productively, and such a delay could be costly in a competitive marketplace.

One of the most innovative team approaches in business today involves vendor–client partnerships. In this type of arrangement, representatives from the vendor and client companies work together to identify client problems and outline solutions that the vendor can provide. Turner Corp. uses teams to carry out the activities related to building large structures like sports stadiums and commercial high-rise buildings. Many of those teams include people from outside the company, including architects, designers, and materials suppliers.[18] Often, the use of vendor–client partnerships is a form of customer-driven marketing, discussed in Chapter 13.

TEAM CHARACTERISTICS

Effective teams share a number of characteristics. These include appropriate sizes, an understanding and acceptance of the roles played by members, and diversity among team members.

Team Size

Teams can range in size from as small as 2 people to as large as 150 people. In practice, however, most teams have fewer than 15 members. Although no ideal size limit applies to every team, research on team effectiveness indicates that they achieve maximum results with about 7 members. A group of this size is big enough to benefit from a variety of diverse skills, yet small enough to allow members to communicate easily and feel part of a close-knit group. Two executives who advocate keeping teams as small as possible are Ray Oglethorpe of AOL Time Warner and H. David Aycock of Nucor Corp. Oglethorpe believes the ideal size is fewer than 10 members. "Ideally, your team should have 7 to 9 people. If you have more than 15 or 20, you're dead: The connections between team members are too hard to make."[19]

Certainly, groups smaller or larger than this general ideal size can do effective work, but they can create added challenges for a team leader. Participants in small teams of 2–4 members often show a desire to get along with each other. They tend to favor informal interactions marked by discussions of personal topics, and they make only limited demands on team leaders. A large team with more than 12 members poses a different challenge for team leaders, because decision making may work slowly and participants may feel limited commitments to team goals. Larger teams also tend to foster disagreements, absenteeism, and membership turnover. Subgroups may form, leading to possible conflicts among various factions. As a general rule, a team of more than 20 people should be divided into subteams, each with its own members and goals.

Team Roles

Team members tend to take on certain roles, as shown in Figure 10.4.[20] They can be classified as task specialist and socio-emotional roles. People who assume the **task specialist role** devote time and energy to helping the team accomplish its specific goals. These team members are the ones who actively propose new ideas and solutions to problems, evaluate the suggestions of others, ask for more information, and summarize group discussions.

Team members who play the **socio-emotional role** devote their time and energy to supporting the emotional needs of team members and to maintaining the team as a social unit. They encourage others to contribute ideas, try to reduce tensions that arise among team members, reconcile conflicts, and often change their own opinions in trying to maintain team harmony.

Some team members may assume dual roles by performing both task specialist and socio-emotional activities. Those who can assume dual roles often are chosen as team leaders, because they satisfy both types of needs. At Microsoft, Iain McDonald led the team that developed the Windows 2000 operating system. He describes his responsibility primarily in terms of a task specialist: "It's my job to work out the schedule, and then kick people in the shins and darken their doorways when they don't keep it." However, the laugh that accompanies these words implies that McDonald is being somewhat ironic and also recognizes socio-emotional dimensions to the role of motivating team members.[21]

Finally, some members may fall into a nonparticipative role. These team members contribute little or nothing to accomplishing the task or satisfying social and emotional needs.

Managers work to form balanced teams with members capable of performing both task-oriented and social roles. Both roles are important, but too many members of either type can impair the team's ability to function effectively. A team with too many task specialists may be productive in the short term but create an unsatisfying situation over a longer time period, because team members may become unsupportive of each other. Teams with too many socio-emotional types can be satisfying but unproductive, since participants may hesitate to disagree or to criticize each other.

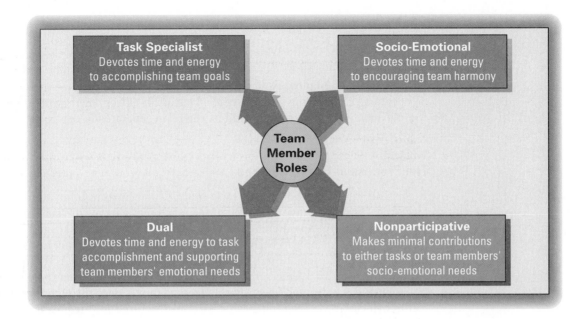

Task Specialist
Devotes time and energy to accomplishing team goals

Socio-Emotional
Devotes time and energy to encouraging team harmony

Team Member Roles

Dual
Devotes time and energy to task accomplishment and supporting team members' emotional needs

Nonparticipative
Makes minimal contributions to either tasks or team members' socio-emotional needs

FIGURE 10.4
Team Member Roles

Team Diversity

Besides playing different roles, team members may bring to the team varied perspectives based on differences in their work experiences and age, gender, and cultural backgrounds. A cross-functional team establishes one type of diversity by bringing together the expertise of members from different functions in the organization.

Many firms are realizing that diverse teams can help them to operate on a global scale. Intel, Maxus Energy, and other companies have set up international work teams to foster exchanges of insights about international markets and dissimilar business cultures. International teamwork can be a challenge, though. People from different countries have to overcome physical distance as well as cultural differences in their expectations about how team members should behave. In cultures like those of Russia and China, people place great importance on hierarchy. Team members expect to listen to managers carefully and extensively. They tend to be slow to express their own opinions. In contrast, team members from Israel and the U.S. tend to place greater value on equality, so each member expects that his or her opinion should be heard and valued. To address cultural and language differences, some international teams have created a position called "cultural liaison." This team member has a primarily socio-emotional role, helping the members communicate with one another. Software teams in India may include an Indian member who has spent a number of years working in the United States and so is able to communicate with U.S. clients and colleagues.[22]

Teamwork in Small Organizations

Like large firms, small companies can benefit from teamwork. Whole Foods, described earlier, set up its team-based structure when the company opened its second store. In fact, small firms themselves may function as teams. If a firm is limited to a small number of employees, say, between 10 and 15, the principles of managing teams may apply to the entire organization. Sometimes, small firms apply teamwork principles to their relationships with outside vendors or consultants.

The owner–manager of a small firm can cultivate the characteristics of successful teams. The manager can direct everyone's efforts toward the team's common purpose, empower team members, and ensure that the team includes a balance of task specialists and members comfortable playing a socio-emotional role. The manager also can recruit team members with diverse backgrounds and encourage everyone to contribute to the team.

The concept of teamwork also applies to entrepreneurs. The key to success in managing the growth of a new venture often rests with the founder's ability to assemble a team of employees who bring complementary skills and experiences to his or her own. Perhaps the greatest challenge for an entrepreneur who wants to encourage teamwork is to sit back and let the team generate ideas.

The Process of Forming Teams

Teams can increase productivity, raise morale, and nurture innovation. However, these benefits result only if the type of team created matches the task to be accomplished. In addition to matching the type of team to the task, managers must select the right types of people to become team members. Although many firms use teams, they often limit participation to certain groups of employees. At AOL Time Warner, a desire for teamwork emerged from managers' observations that new technology development was being slowed by the need to move ideas through the company's hierarchy. The AOL Technologies division restructured into teams. Satellite teams now focus on specific projects and goals. They bring their ideas to the division's "core teams," which have the power to make "go" or "no-go" decisions about new products under consideration. The division's president, Ray Oglethorpe is convinced the team arrangement is "the best thing that we could have done," largely because the teams are empowered to authorize projects.[23]

Since firms invest so much time and money creating and supporting teams, they must form these units carefully with several factors in mind. The first consideration must be the need for a team to accomplish a particular task. People often work more productively as individuals rather than as team members. Before forming a team, managers should analyze the work to be done, decide whether a team approach is preferable, and then select the best type of team. Besides identifying the purpose of forming a team, the organization must clearly communicate that purpose to team members.

Procter & Gamble (P&G) executives saw a clear need for teams focused on innovation. The company decided that teams could bring much-needed change to a company that had not launched a new product line in a decade and a half. P&G set up a team-based division called Corporate New Ventures (CNV) and armed it with $250 million to spend on new ideas. Ideas from company employees are assigned to CNV teams, who study them and identify the ones they consider worth pursuing. The teams are empowered to obtain resources from the rest of the company, such as engineering support to develop product ideas. Within two years, the CNV teams had launched 58 new products. One of them was Swiffer disposable cleaning cloths, developed when CNV's president brought together employees who normally worked separately on the company's paper products and cleaning agents.[24]

Managers can increase the likelihood of forming effective work teams by following the step-by-step approach outlined in Figure 10.5. The process begins by studying other successful teams and ends by designing compensation plans for team members. When a firm's managers decide to form teams, they must accompany the move with a team-based pay plan that rewards members for achieving team goals. This new pay scheme can be difficult, since compensation must motivate individual team members while encouraging them to act together as a team. The most effective pay plans reward both team and individual performance. Procter & Gamble not only funds and rewards the members of its CNV teams but also rewards the employees who provide ideas to the teams. When CNV teams develop employee ideas, the people who submit the ideas receive stock options.

Stages of Team Development

Teams typically progress through five stages of development: forming, storming, norming, performing, and adjourning.[25] These stages are summarized in Figure 10.6.

Stage 1: Forming The first stage, forming, is an orientation period during which team members get to know each other and find out what behaviors are acceptable to the group. Team members begin with curiosity about expectations of them and whether they will fit in with the group. An effective team leader provides time for members to become acquainted.

Stage 2: Storming The personalities of team members begin to emerge at the storming stage as members clarify their roles and expectations. Conflicts may arise, as people disagree over the team's mission and jockey for position and control of the group. Subgroups may form based on common interests or concerns. At this stage, the team leader must encourage everyone to participate, allowing members to work through their uncertainties and conflicts. Teams must move beyond this stage to achieve real productivity.

Stage 3: Norming During the norming stage, members resolve differences between them, accept each other, and reach consensus about the roles of the team leader and other participants. This stage is usually brief in duration, and the team leader should use it to emphasize the team's unity and the importance of its objectives.

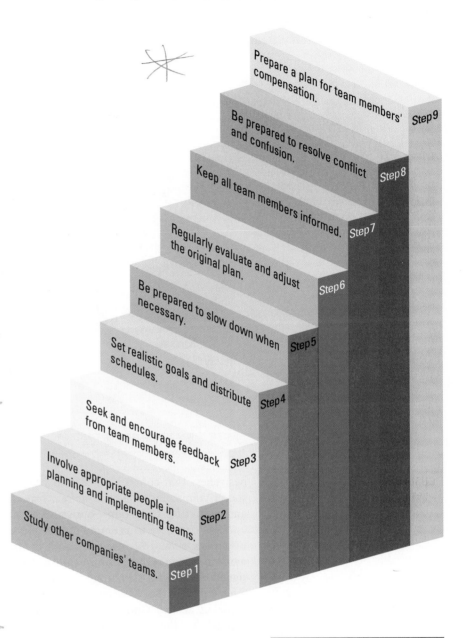

FIGURE 10.5
A Step-by-Step Approach to Forming Effective Teams

Stage 4: Performing Team members focus on solving problems and accomplishing tasks at the performing stage. They interact frequently and handle conflicts in constructive ways. The team leader encourages contributions from all members. In their book *Hot Groups,* Jean Lipman-Blumen and Harold J. Leavitt describe this high level of performance with a comparison to a team of athletes:

> We like Charles Handy's description, comparing a team of Englishmen to a rowing crew, . . . "eight men going backward as fast as they can without talking to each other, steered by the one person who can't row!"
>
> But as an Olympic oarsman once told Handy, "How do you think we could go backward so fast without communicating, steered by this little fellow in the stern, if we didn't know each other very well, didn't have total confidence to do our jobs and a shared commitment—almost a passion—for the same goal? It is the perfect formula for a team."[26]

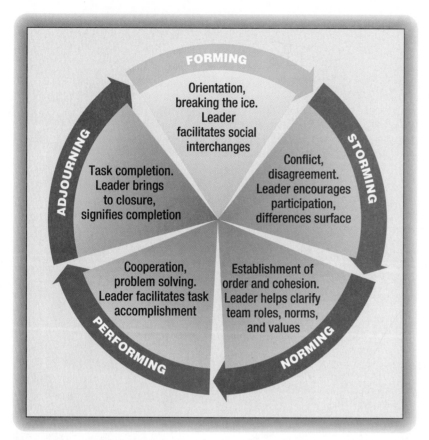

FIGURE 10.6
Stages of Team Development

Figure 10.7 illustrates this level of team performance.

Stage 5: Adjourning The team disbands at the adjourning stage after members have completed their assigned task or solved a problem. During this phase, the focus is on wrapping up and summarizing the team's experiences and accomplishments. The team leader may recognize the team's accomplishments with a celebration, perhaps handing out plaques or awards.

Team Cohesiveness

Teams tend to maximize productivity when they form into highly cohesive units. **Team cohesiveness** is the extent to which team members are attracted to the team and motivated to remain part of it. This cohesiveness typically increases when members interact frequently, share common attitudes and goals, and enjoy being together. When cohesiveness is low, morale suffers. Coach Tony DiCicco attributes the success of the U.S. Women's World Cup championship soccer team and gold medal–winning U.S. Women's Olympic soccer team to the cohesiveness that comes from shared values. DiCicco believes that members of these soccer teams placed high value on "fitness, intensity in training, individual respect, and respect for the group—both on and off the field."[27]

Some firms try to promote interaction among team members through the design of work spaces. To foster teamwork in an office, the firm may have team members work in large rooms without walls dividing them. A production facility may be designed to bring workers together around a single product being assembled. Among the companies that have used open office spaces are Alcoa, Monsanto, Intel, and advertising agency Chiat/Day. However, employees at many companies have complained that they can't think in a busy open office, so organizations are looking for better ways to bring people together. Workplace designer Michael Brill says, "There's this funny idea that openness feeds interaction. Where [interaction really] happens is in the hallways, the coffee bar—exactly where it should happen."[28] As a result, companies have begun blending private offices with attractive and conveniently located common areas that draw team members together naturally, bringing them into frequent contact with one another. In addition, as discussed in Chapter 9, many employers provide opportunities for employees to socialize during and after their workdays.

To promote cohesiveness when team members work in different facilities, companies have to schedule opportunities for them to interact. Teams can schedule "virtual retreats"—Internet discussion groups or chat sessions during which they trade messages about personal as well as project-related matters. However, face-to-face meetings have the greatest potential to build cohesiveness, even though this requires extensive travel for a geographically separated or even international team.[29] As illustrated in Figure 10.8, companies like General Motors build team cohesiveness by scheduling activities in which team members must work together on physical challenges. The photograph shows GM's Excel training course. Besides crossing a tightrope, team members tackle other challenges, such as wall climbing.

"Mind, Muscle, Timing and Teamwork"

At the Port of Savannah our level of competition goes head to head with the very best. Our team is well-trained and dedicated to a single goal: delivering a world class performance so that you come in first every time.

We out perform the competition with superior equipment and know-how that can mean the difference between victory and defeat. From a computerized cargo tracking system to the fastest cranes in the world, our team keeps your cargo moving smoothly to its destination—on time, every time.

Our strategy is to enable you to compete in world trade by consistently delivering the highest level of service of any port, every day. Meeting the challenge of champions isn't our main priority, it's our only one. We give you our personal best!

For additional information contact: Mr. Byron X. Hock, Director of Trade Development, Georgia Ports Authority, P.O. Box 2406, Savannah, GA 31402. Or call toll-free 1-800-342-8012.

Port of Savannah

"We Run Rings Around the Competition"

**FIGURE 10.7
Team Members at the Performing Stage: Pulling Together toward a Common Goal**

Team Norms

A **team norm** is a standard of conduct shared by team members that guides their behavior. Norms are not formal, written guidelines; they are informal standards that identify key values and clarify team members' expectations. In a highly productive team, norms are consistent with working together constructively and accomplishing team goals. One such team is what Lipman-Blumen and Leavitt call a "hot group," a group intensely dedicated to its task. The researchers have found that members of this kind of team "tend to volunteer for extra work, even to make additional work for themselves," not because the company requires it, but out of their passion for the group's work.[30] In other words, a norm of a hot group is to devote oneself to the group's goals.

Team Conflict

Among all of a team leader's skills, none is more important than the ability to manage conflict. **Conflict** is an antagonistic interaction in which one party attempts to thwart the intentions or goals of another. A certain amount of conflict is inevitable in teams, but too much can impair the ability of team members to exchange ideas, cooperate with each other, and produce results.

Conflict can stem from many sources. It frequently results from competition for scarce resources, such as information, money, or supplies. In addition, team members may experience personality clashes or differ in their ideas about what the team should accomplish. Poor communication also can cause

BUSINESS DIRECTORY

➤ **team cohesiveness** *extent to which team members feel attracted to the team and motivated to remain a part of it.*

➤ **team norm** *informal standard of conduct shared by team members that guides their behavior.*

➤ **conflict** *antagonistic interaction in which one party attempts to thwart the intentions or goals of another.*

"If the people who make the car don't fit together, the car won't either."

General Motors.

Welcome to the Excel training course. Before it's over, Saturn's Dennis Bowman will take these General Motors employees on a real adventure. They'll scale walls. Walk across high wires. Plunge backwards into the waiting arms of their coworkers. And take away some valuable lessons about trust, cooperation and seeing things from the other person's point of view. Developed by Saturn, Excel is now used throughout General Motors. It's turning out graduates who know the power of teamwork. Who go a little further to build quality automobiles. And who believe that the right way to treat a customer is the way you'd want to be treated yourself.

FIGURE 10.8
Building the Cohesiveness of a General Motors Team

misunderstandings and resentment. Finally, conflict can result in the absence of clear job responsibilities or team roles. Levi Strauss team members experienced conflict from all of these sources in the events described in the "Clicks and Mortar" box.

Styles of Conflict Resolution

No single resolution method can manage all conflicts. The most effective reaction depends on the particular situation. Conflict resolution styles represent a continuum ranging from assertive to cooperative responses:

- *The competing style.* This decisive, assertive approach might be summarized by the expression "We'll do this task my way." Although it does not build team rapport, the competing style can be useful for unpopular decisions or emergencies. This approach also helps to end conflict that escalates beyond hope of any other form of resolution.

- *The avoiding style.* Neither assertive nor cooperative, avoiding conflict is an effective response when the problem results from some trivial cause or creates a no-win situation, when more information is needed, or when open conflict would cause harm.

- *The compromising style.* This style blends both assertiveness and cooperation. It works well when conflict arises between two opposing and equally important goals, when combatants are equally powerful, or when the situation brings pressure to achieve an immediate solution.

- *The accommodating style.* Marked by active cooperation, this style can help to maintain team harmony. A team member may choose to back down in a disagreement on an issue that seems more important to others in the group than it does to that individual.

Background. In the early 1990s, when many companies were restructuring themselves to incorporate teams of empowered workers, Levi Strauss & Co. found itself facing lower-cost competitors who were sending their manufacturing overseas. Levi's wanted to continue making most of its famous denim jeans in the U.S., but it couldn't unless it could increase productivity in its plants and reduce costs, especially those related to injuries sustained by workers who pushed themselves to meet piecework quotas.

What Happened? The company decided to phase out piecework and implement teamwork. "This change," wrote Max Cowan, Levi's operations vice president almost a decade ago, "will lead to a self-managed work environment that will reduce stress and help employees become more productive." But the ideal work environment did not emerge. Instead, serious conflicts arose. If a team member was absent, less experienced, or slower than the others, the rest of the team had to make up for the weakness. "If one person had a lot of flaws," explained one manager, "that cost everyone their bonuses." Managers and workers received little training in teamwork, and ended up improvising norms, roles, and expectations. Team members began to resent one another rather than work together. The teams "created pressures and tensions and a lot of unhappiness, and some people would rather go back," admitted CEO Robert Haas.

The Response. Conflict among team workers eroded productivity instead of increasing it. "You heard so much shouting, lots of times you didn't even look up from your work," recalled one seamstress. The actual quantity of pants produced per hour plummeted to 77 percent of piecework levels. "We bet the farm with team manufacturing, but the whole system wasn't ready to take advantage of it," said Ralph Pollard, a manufacturing manager who has since retired. A year after the teams were implemented, Levi's hired consulting firm Sibson & Co. to assess its problems and look for solutions to the conflicts. Sibson discovered the root of one problem: Many traditional plant managers were uncomfortable with the idea of employee empowerment through teams. "Some managers don't like having sewing-machine operators challenge their authority," reported Sibson consultant Peter LeBlanc.

Today and Counting. Over the past few years, Levi's has continued to struggle and has been forced to move as much as 45 percent of its production overseas, closing several U.S. plants. Although upper management remains committed to the team strategy, in reality middle managers are abandoning teams in their efforts to increase productivity. "People in the plants are gradually going back to the old way of doing things," said Larry Garland, a Levi's controller. Haas continues to defend Levi's use of teams, arguing that teamwork allows employees to be free from "having to park their brains at the factory gate." He believes that, without the teams, more U.S. plants would have closed—and sooner. Today, productivity has risen to about 93 percent of what it was before the teams were implemented. Haas claims that, unlike other apparel manufacturers, his company is committed to the well-being of its employees. "There are humans involved, and we have the opportunity to be different. We want to exhaust all our options before we throw up our hands and exit."

QUESTIONS FOR CRITICAL THINKING

1. What steps could Levi's have taken early on to avoid or resolve conflicts within teams?
2. Do you think that Levi's should continue with the team strategy? Why or why not?

Sources: "Levi Strauss & Co. Third-Quarter and Nine-Month Financial Results Reflect Ongoing Progress in Business Turnaround," company press release, September 19, 2000; N. Munk, "How Levi's Trashed a Great American Brand," *Fortune*, April 12, 1999, pp. 83–90; Ralph T. King Jr., "Levi's Factory Workers Are Assigned to Teams, and Morale Takes a Hit," *The Wall Street Journal*, May 20, 1998, pp. A1, A6.

- *The collaborating style.* This style combines active assertiveness and cooperation. It can require lengthy, time-consuming negotiations but can achieve a win-win situation. It is useful when consensus from all parties is an important goal, or when the viewpoints of all participants must be merged into a single, mutually acceptable solution.

A team leader can handle conflict by encouraging adversaries to negotiate an agreement between themselves. This method works well if the individuals deal with the situation in a businesslike, unemotional way. A stubborn disagreement may be turned over to a mediator, an outside party who will discuss the situation with both sides and bring the parties to a mutual decision. Ford Motor Co. has socioemotional specialists, called "team-effectiveness coaches," who are available to help teams when they have trouble resolving conflicts on their own. According to Janine Bay, director of vehicle personalization at Ford's Consumer Services Group, the team-effectiveness coaches enable the teams to benefit from members' diversity while overcoming the difficulties that diverse viewpoints can present.[31]

Phone.com's policies specifically forbid conduct that benefits the individual at the expense of the company or the person's colleagues. To discourage such behavior while resolving conflicts, Phone.com's marketing vice president, Ben Linder, directs his team members to be assertive: "Whenever I hear someone in my group saying that . . . a particular person is incompetent, I just say, 'Look, don't tell me. Go tell it to them. . . . Go face it.'"[32]

Perhaps the team leader's most important contribution to conflict resolution is to facilitate good communication. Ongoing, effective communication ensures that team members perceive each other accurately, understand what is expected of them, and obtain the information they need. Improved communication increases the chances of working cooperatively as a team. The remainder of this chapter discusses the importance of effective communication and the development of good communication skills.

THE IMPORTANCE OF EFFECTIVE COMMUNICATION

Communication can be defined as a meaningful exchange of information through messages. Few businesses can succeed without effective communication. Managers spend about 80 percent of their time—six hours and 24 minutes of every eight-hour day—in direct communication with others, whether on the telephone, in meetings, via e-mail, or in individual conversations. The other 20 percent is typically spent on working at their desks, much of which also involves communication in the form of writing and reading.

Communication skills are important throughout an organization—in every department and at all levels. Communication with the marketplace in the form of marketing research helps a company to learn what products people want and what changes they would like in existing offerings. Communication among engineers, marketers, and production employees enables a company to create products that satisfy customers. Communication through advertising and personal sales presentations creates a favorable image for the company and persuades customers to buy.

Well-planned, open communication was essential to the success of the merger between architectural firms Cunningham Group, located in Minneapolis, and Solberg + Lowe Architects, with offices in Los Angeles and Phoenix. As the two firms planned the merger, they allowed plenty of time for their people to communicate on work-related and personal matters. They collaborated on a major current project facing them: the design of two Mississippi hotels. As they worked, staffers resolved differences through dialogue, asking, "Why do you do it this way?" rather than arguing. The managers of the two companies stayed in one another's homes when they traveled back and forth in the months leading up to the merger. Explains Rick Solberg, "We wanted to have time where we turned off the pagers and the phones and talked about what we like to do outside of work." The two firms extended a similar opportunity to their staff members a few months before the companies merged. Cunningham Group hosted a holiday party and flew the Solberg + Lowe staff and their families to Minneapolis. According to John Cunningham, "That [party] probably saved us five or six months in long-distance bonding time."

Since the merger, the firm, which now operates under the name the Cunningham Group, continues to arrange for face-to-face communication with management retreats and frequent travel. Visiting in person seems to be especially important for visually oriented architects. According to Wade Morgan, a project manager who has rotated between projects at the three offices, "Often when we're describing a project, we have to talk with our hands or draw it out. Trying to explain something visually on the phone, or even through videoconferencing, just isn't the same." These efforts have helped the companies develop trust among the members of two firms with different cultural styles.

Besides arranging for plenty of face time, the combined firms have a policy for openness and honesty. With revenues flowing in faster after the merger, management is open to the idea of acquiring other firms. And if they do, they plan to apply the same emphasis on communication. Rick Solberg points out, "You can't hold anything back. Chances are, what you're concealing will be the problem." He adds, "Ultimately, the more you do to confront possible problems up front, the less you're going to get hurt."[33]

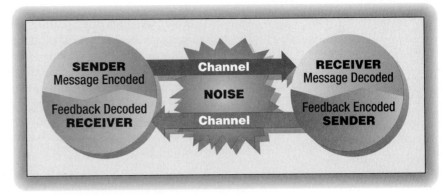

FIGURE 10.9
The Communication Process

The Process of Communication

Every communication follows a step-by-step process that involves interactions among six elements: sender, message, channel, audience, feedback, and context. This process is illustrated in Figure 10.9.

In the first step, the *sender* composes the message and sends it through a communication carrier, or *channel. Encoding* a message means that the sender translates its meaning into understandable terms and a form that allows transmission through a chosen channel. The sender can communicate a particular message through many different channels, including written messages, face-to-face conversations, and electronic mail. A promotional message to the firm's customers may be communicated through such forms as radio and television ads, billboards, magazines, and personal selling messages. The *audience* consists of the person or persons who receive the message. In *decoding,* the receiver of the message interprets its meaning. *Feedback* from the audience—a response to the sender's communication—helps the sender to determine whether the audience has correctly interpreted the intended meaning of the message.

Every communication takes place in some sort of situational and cultural context. The *context* can exert a powerful influence on how well the process works. A conversation between two people in a quiet office, for example, may be a very different experience from the same conversation held in a crowded and noisy restaurant. A request by an American to borrow a flashlight from an Australian friend might only produce confusion; what Americans call *flashlights,* Australians call *torches.*

Senders must pay attention to audience feedback, even solicit it if none is forthcoming, since this response clarifies whether the communication has conveyed the intended message. Feedback can indicate whether the receiver paid attention to a message and was able to decode it accurately. Even when the receiver tries to understand, the communication will fail if the message was poorly encoded with difficult or ambiguous words. Businesspeople sometimes become fond of using fuzzy language like "have a dialogue" for "talk," "facilitate" for "help," or "scaleable" for a vague growth strategy. Feedback can indicate whether the sender's audience succeeded in decoding this jargon—or bothered to try.

Even with the best of intentions, sender and audience can misunderstand each other. Rob Wrubel, CEO of the online information service Ask Jeeves, constantly checks whether the people in his organization understand messages, and he is often surprised by the feedback. When the senior managers first began creating a yearlong plan of operations, Wrubel discovered that participants often interpreted phrases in difference ways. If one person said, "I'll get it done by next week," one listener might decode "by next week" to mean "next Monday," while another might think "next Friday." Also, "get it done" meant "give me your thoughts" to one listener, while another decoded the phrase to mean the speaker would present a fully thought-out plan with a PowerPoint slide presentation.[34]

Noise during the communication process is some type of interference that influences the transmission of messages and feedback. Noise can result from simple physical factors such as poor reception of a cell-phone message or static that drowns out a radio commercial. It can also be caused by more complex differences in people's attitudes and perceptions. A message communicated by a manager may be interpreted differently by coworkers with different ethnic and cultural backgrounds. Following their merger, the partners of Solberg + Lowe and the Cunningham Group found that they had very different communication styles. The midwestern employees of the Cunningham Group were much more careful than the southwestern founders of Solberg + Lowe to avoid direct criticisms. To avoid unnecessary offense, Rick Solberg and Doug Lowe—who are quite frank with one another—learned to express themselves tactfully when speaking to their Minnesota colleagues.

Basic Forms of Communication

People communicate in many different ways. Some obvious methods include calling a meeting of team members or writing a formal mission statement. Other, much less obvious methods include gestures and facial expressions during a conversation or leaning forward when speaking to someone. These subtle variations can significantly influence the reception of the message. As Table 10.2 points out, different communications can assume various forms: oral and written, formal and informal, and verbal and nonverbal communications.

Oral Communication   Managers spend a great deal of their time engaged in oral communication, both in person and on the phone. Some people prefer to communicate this way, believing that oral channels more accurately convey messages. Face-to-face oral communication allows people to combine words with such cues as facial expressions and tones of voice. Oral communication over the telephone lacks visual cues, but it offers some of the advantages of face-to-face oral communication, such as opportunities to hear the tone of voice, and provide immediate feedback by asking questions about anything the receiver doesn't understand or raising new issues related to the message.

In spite of the telephone's limitations, Gale Varma must rely heavily on this medium, because her staff members are scattered among several locations. Varma is vice president of human resources for the Prudential Institutional division of Prudential Insurance Co., which operates units at various sites around the country. Besides traveling to meet with her staff at each location, she schedules regular phone meetings and makes it a policy to return phone and e-mail messages quickly.

Table 10.2   Forms of Communication

Form	Description	Examples
Oral communication	Communication transmitted through speech	Personal conversations, speeches, meetings, voice mail, telephone conversations, videoconferences
Written communication	Communication transmitted through writing	Letters, memos, formal reports, news releases, e-mail, faxes
Formal communication	Communication transmitted through the chain of command within an organization to other members or to people outside the organization	Internal—memos, reports, meetings, written proposals, oral presentations, meeting minutes; External—letters, written proposals, oral presentations, speeches, news releases, press conferences
Informal communication	Communication transmitted outside formal channels without regard for the organization's hierarchy of authority	Rumors spread informally among employees
Verbal communication	Transmission of messages in the form of words	Meetings, telephone calls, voice mail, videoconferences
Nonverbal communication	Communication transmitted through actions and behaviors rather than through words	Gestures, facial expressions, posture, body language, dress, makeup

Recognizing that phone conversations lack visual cues, Varma makes an effort to listen carefully and attend to her own voice tone as well. So that she does not signal impatience, she takes her time and expresses personal interest in employees: "I try not to just say, 'What do you want?' but also 'How are you?'"[35] Another way businesspeople add visual cues for geographically separated listeners is to use videoconferencing, which combines cameras, computers, and sometimes satellite systems to transmit images as well as voice messages. A basic desktop system uses a personal computer to display an image of the person sending the message along with data, charts, and text.

In any medium, a vital component of oral communication is listening—receiving a message and interpreting its genuine meaning by accurately grasping the facts and feelings conveyed. Although listening is the first communication skill that people learn and the one they use most often, it is also the one in which they receive the least formal training.

Listening may seem easy, since the listener makes no obvious effort. This apparent passivity creates a deceptive picture, however. The average person talks at a rate of roughly 150 words per minute, but the brain can handle up to 400 words per minute. This discrepancy can lead to boredom, inattention, and misinterpretation. In fact, immediately after listening to a message, the average person can recall only half of it. After several days, the proportion of a message that a listener can recall falls to 25 percent or less.

Certain types of listening behaviors are common in both business and personal interactions:

- *Cynical listening.* This defensive type of listening occurs when the receiver of a message feels that the sender is trying to gain some advantage from the communication.

- *Offensive listening.* In this type of listening, the receiver tries to catch the speaker in a mistake or contradiction.

- *Polite listening.* In this mechanical type of listening, the receiver listens to be polite rather than to communicate. Polite listeners are usually inattentive and spend their time rehearsing what they want to say when the speaker finishes.

- *Active listening.* This form of listening requires involvement with the information and empathy with the speaker's situation. In both business and personal life, active listening is the basis for effective communication.

Learning how to be an active listener is an especially important goal for business managers, since effective communication is essential to the manager's role.

Written Communication   Channels for written communication include reports, letters, memos, online chat sessions, and e-mail messages. Most of these channels permit only delayed feedback and create a record of the message. So, it is important for the sender of written communication to prepare the message carefully and review it to avoid misunderstandings.

Effective written communication reflects its audience, the channel carrying the message, and the appropriate degree of formality. When writing a formal business document, such as a complex report, a manager must plan in advance and carefully construct the document. The process of writing a formal document involves planning, research, organization, composition and design, and revision. Written communication via e-mail and computer networks may call for a less formal writing style, including short sentences, phrases, and lists. Writers for electronic media often communicate through combinations of words, acronyms, and emoticons, which are symbols constructed with punctuation marks and letters.

E-mail has made written communication simple and fast. Some managers, like security agency manager Winn Schwartau, rely almost exclusively on e-mail to

BUSINESS DIRECTORY

▶ **listening**   *skill of receiving a message and interpreting its intended meaning by grasping the facts and feelings it conveys.*

communicate with employees. Schwartau sees his assistant only about once a week. In addition, he has never met—or spoken to—some of his employees. Schwartau believes that the mere fact that he is willing to rely on e-mail for employee communication is a sign that he considers his employees to be both independent and professional. But relying exclusively on e-mail poses risks since it lacks the emotional content of voice, gestures, and facial expressions, so misunderstandings can arise. Employees or managers who never interact face-to-face may find it easier to avoid delivering bad news. In addition, workers who receive only e-mail may get the feeling the manager doesn't care about them, and that feeling can intensify when messages occasionally go astray.[36]

Because e-mail messages are informal, senders sometimes forget that they create a written record, and senders have at times embarrassed themselves. Once, for example, John Blumenthal sent a message to a partner in which he criticized the team that was helping him develop software for a bank. Somehow, the message was forwarded to the team members, who were offended. In addition, employers and courts can review the contents of e-mail, which is generally saved unless the user employs software designed to electronically "shred" the messages after a set period of time.[37]

Formal Communication A **formal communication channel** carries messages that flow within the chain of command structure defined by an organization. The most familiar channel, downward communication, carries messages from someone who holds a senior position in the organization to subordinates. Managers may communicate downward by sending employees e-mail messages, presiding at department meetings, giving employees policy manuals, posting notices on bulletin boards, and reporting news in company newsletters. To make sure that she and her staff members at Prudential are sharing information, Gale Varma schedules a monthly teleconference with them. Two weeks before each meeting, the participants receive an agenda and a number to call to join the teleconference.[38]

Many firms also define formal channels for upward communications. These channels encourage communication from employees to supervisors and upward to top management levels. Some examples of upward communication channels are employee surveys, suggestion boxes, and systems that allow employees to propose new projects or voice complaints. Companies also create policies for using upward communications. Xerox Palo Alto Research Center scientist Geoffrey Nunberg laments the need to reduce presentations at Xerox to computer-generated slides. "It used to be that you got ten minutes of a CEO's time; now you get three slides to make your pitch."[39]

Informal Communication **Informal communication channels** carry messages outside formally authorized channels within an organization's hierarchy. A familiar example of an informal channel is the **grapevine,** an internal information channel that passes information from unofficial sources. Research shows that many employees cite the grapevine as their most frequent source of information. Grapevines rapidly disseminate information. A message sent through formal channels may take days to reach its audience, but messages that travel via grapevines can arrive within hours. Grapevines also are surprisingly reliable links. They pass on accurate information 75 to 96 percent of the time. However, even a tiny inaccuracy can distort an entire message.

The spontaneity of informal communication may diminish when a company's employees are spread among many locations. Employees who telecommute or travel frequently may miss out on opportunities to build smooth working relationships or exchange ideas. In those situations, communication technology can help firms to promote informal communication. Some companies establish online chat areas for employees, so they can visit each other during breaks. Some also encourage employees to create home pages that describe their interests and hobbies.

Verbal and Nonverbal Communication   So far, this section has considered different forms of verbal communication, or communication that conveys meaning through words. Equally important is **nonverbal communication,** which transmits messages through actions and behaviors. Gestures, posture, eye contact, tone of voice, even clothing choices—all of these nonverbal actions become communication cues. Nonverbal cues can strongly influence oral communication by altering or distorting intended meanings.

Nonverbal cues can have a far greater impact on communications than many people realize. One study divided face-to-face conversations into three sources of communication cues: verbal cues (the actual words spoken), vocal cues (pitch or tone of a person's voice), and facial expressions. The researchers found some surprising relative weights of these factors in message interpretation: verbal cues (7 percent), vocal cues (38 percent), and facial expressions (55 percent).[40] Prudential's Gale Varma has observed that employees may interpret her words as criticism if she talks rapidly or in an impatient-sounding tone. Over the phone, they cannot tell whether she is impatient with them or with something unrelated. Varma tries to counter this effect by giving praise lavishly.[41]

Companies that offer computerized voice technology are applying knowledge about nonverbal cues to make their applications more appealing and effective. Software developer General Magic is creating a service called Virtual Advisor that will deliver information to drivers over a cell phone to be sold with certain General Motors cars. Virtual Advisor uses vocal tones that convey friendliness but efficiency in a female voice. The company also offers a more direct, matter-of-fact voice developed for conveying data such as stock transactions. This data-oriented voice sounds like a male. In research, subjects have rated male-sounding voices as more informative and accurate about technical subjects, even when a female-sounding voice reads the same information.[42] As this research suggests, interpretation of communications tends to be a subjective process.

Even personal space—the physical distance between people who are engaging in communication—can convey powerful messages. Figure 10.10 shows a continuum of personal space and social interaction with four zones: intimate, personal, social, and public zones. In the U.S., most business conversations occur within the social zone, roughly between 4 and 12 feet apart. If one person tries to approach closer than that, the other will likely feel discomfort or even a threat.

Interpreting nonverbal cues can be especially challenging for people with different cultural backgrounds. Concepts of appropriate personal space differ dramatically throughout the world. Latin Americans conduct business discussions in positions that most Americans and northern Europeans find uncomfortably close. Americans often back away to preserve their personal space, a gesture that Latin Americans perceive as a sign of cold and unfriendly relations. To protect themselves from such personal "threats," experienced Americans separate themselves across desks or tables from their Latin American counterparts—at the risk of challenging their colleagues to maneuver around those obstacles in order to reduce the uncomfortable distance.

People send nonverbal messages even when they consciously try to avoid doing so. Sometimes, nonverbal cues convey a person's true attitudes and thoughts, which may differ from spoken meanings. Generally, when verbal and nonverbal cues conflict, receivers of the communication tend to believe the nonverbal content.

COMMUNICATION WITHIN THE ORGANIZATION

Internal communication consists of messages sent through channels within an organization. Examples include memos, meetings, speeches, phone conversations, even a simple chat over lunch. When Carly Fiorina took on

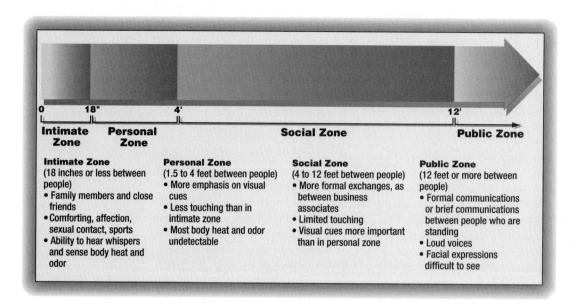

FIGURE 10.10
Influence of Personal Space in Nonverbal Communication

the top job at Hewlett-Packard (HP), she wanted to foster a faster-moving culture, so she launched a leadership campaign emphasizing internal communication. Fiorina had HP buy a corporate jet to make it faster and easier for her to travel to 20 company sites in ten countries, delivering impassioned speeches about the need for change and fielding questions from the audience. To continue this dialogue, she composes a letter to employees for each issue of the company's quarterly magazine, reads thousands of e-mail messages from employees each month, and records occasional voice-mail messages to be broadcast companywide.[43]

Internal communication may be relatively simple in a small organization, since it often takes the form of face-to-face interactions. Unclear interpretations can be remedied by further conversation. Internal communication becomes increasingly difficult as the organization grows and adds employees. Messages, many of them transmitted in writing, often pass through several different layers of management in a typical large organization. The sender of a message must continually make certain that it is both clearly communicated orally or in writing and likely to be interpreted correctly.

To address the challenges of keeping open communication, many organizations plan a variety of formal channels in all directions. Whole Foods supports employee empowerment by keeping employees well informed. It publishes a company newsletter, called *Innerviews,* which employees receive on the first week of each month. Members of the stores' management teams have access to the company's intranet, called the Team Member Network. On the intranet, they can look up information about products, store locations, company history, and plans for the immediate future, as well as send and receive e-mail. Employees are encouraged to share their opinions in the annual Employee Morale Survey and in letters to the company newsletter.[44]

Modern organizations are likely to include people who speak different languages. Under these circumstances, internal communication requires special care. Managers can improve internal communications with employees who have limited English skills by keeping messages simple and straightforward. Supplementing oral communication with written information like meeting agendas and e-mail messages helps employees who can read a foreign language better than they speak it. Encouraging written messages also may help managers understand employees who speak with a heavy foreign accent. Employees can practice speaking and listening to English by attending regular meetings that cover only two or three agenda items. Managers can also create a positive environment for communications by learning and using some phrases of their employees' languages.[45]

Communicating in Teams

Communications among team members can be divided into two broad categories: centralized and decentralized communications. In a **centralized communication network,** team members exchange messages through a single person to solve problems or make decisions. Michael Leinbach, shuttle-launch director at the John F. Kennedy Space Center, fosters centralized communication when he says, "The most critical element of a successful shuttle-launch team is an open channel of communication from each member to the team

leader." Leinbach expects any team member who discovers a problem of any size to report it to him.[46] In a **decentralized communication network,** members communicate freely with other team members and arrive at decisions together. Lipman-Blumen and Leavitt believe that decentralized communication is the norm among the fast-moving, results-oriented teams they call hot groups: "Communication flows freely, up, down, and across these groups. Members treat one another with casual respect, focusing on colleagues' contributions to the task at hand rather than on title or status."[47]

Which type of network supports more effective communications? The answer depends on the nature of the problem or decision facing the team. Research has shown that centralized networks usually solve simple problems more quickly and accurately than decentralized ones. This is an important consideration for life-or-death operations like the launch of a space shuttle. With a centralized network, members simply pass information along to the central decision maker, who acts. However, for complex problems, a decentralized network actually works faster and comes up with more accurate answers. This characteristic is important for task-oriented, creative groups. Team members pool their data, provide wide-ranging input into decisions, and emerge with high-quality solutions.

While most researchers agree that organizations should establish centralized team networks to deal with simple problems, they also believe that these organizations should set up decentralized teams to handle complex issues. Members of decentralized teams should be encouraged to share information with each other and to generate as much input as possible to improve the quality of the final decision.[48]

Decentralized teams work well for the complex process of new-product development. Two important keys to success in this process are allowing all members of the team to voice concerns and working hard to get all of the members involved early in the project.

Using a decentralized communication network, Pat Eichen and his small band of 27 employees launched a rare breed of a new company: an independent—and successful—American toy company, Rokenbok Toy Co. In the photo is the firm's most successful product, a classic construction toy. Eichen is convinced that his firm's decentralized communication structure is at least partly responsible for the creation of this easy-to-understand product. "Coworkers can make suggestions, help solve problems, commiserate . . . and a sense of team can evolve." Such focus has built Rokenbok Toys, a company that is on track to reach $12 million in annual revenues.

COMMUNICATION OUTSIDE THE ORGANIZATION

External communication is a meaningful exchange of information through messages transmitted between an

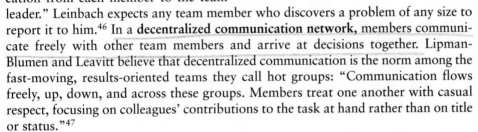

BUSINESS DIRECTORY

➤ **external communication** *meaningful exchange of information through messages transmitted between an organization and its major audiences.*

The Press Release: Information or Misinformation?

Investors are always looking for information that can help them make decisions about companies they may want to sink their money into, and it's not news that stock prices rise and fall based on reports related to everything from interest and unemployment rates to changing weather patterns. Press releases, issued by the companies themselves, have always occupied a middle ground—not as objective as traditional journalism, but at least honest reporting of the facts. Now the Securities and Exchange Commission (SEC), stock analysts, and other experts are concerned that press releases—particularly those posted on the Internet—may not only be having undue influence on investors but also be less than accurate.

Do press releases mislead investors about companies' financial health and business activities?

PRO

1. It has been documented that some companies, such as office products retailer Staples, have issued press releases that presented financial information in a way that made them appear more healthy than they were. Staples buried a fourth-quarter loss of $9.8 million in the fine print of one press release.
2. Companies sometimes use press releases to exaggerate the relationship they have with a larger or more influential organization. "You'd think the two companies are getting married," notes Robert V. Green, an analyst at financial Web site Briefing.com Inc. "But often, just one employee has signed up for a company's service."
3. Companies post press releases almost daily to keep themselves in view of potential investors. "Companies create questionable new divisions, mergers, and products just to stay on investors' radar screens," says Briefing.com's Green. These announcements may or may not have substance.

CON

1. Investors are responsible for their own actions, and they should take responsibility for obtaining accurate news about a company. Instead, says G.S. Schwartz CEO Gerald S. Schwartz, "Investors are increasingly putting as much credence in paid releases posted on the Internet as they do in real journalism."
2. Investors and others often misunderstand a legitimate press release. NeoRx suffered from this type of misunderstanding when investors interpreted one of its press releases to mean that the company had found a cure for cancer—and the stock soared to artificially high prices. Later, CEO Dr. Paul G. Abrams went on financial news channel CNBC to explain that "it was the first step of a multistep process that would involve testing of humans over several years."
3. The press release is simply a communications device and cannot force an investor to buy or sell a stock.

SUMMARY

The language and information presented in releases may or may not be accurate. "While we don't regulate press releases, we are on guard for fraudulent and manipulative statements," says SEC spokesman Chris Ullman. Still, this is a difficult area for the SEC to monitor. So investors might be wise to heed Ullman's advice: "Investors must look beyond press releases and review a company's filings with the SEC, which subscribe to generally accepted accounting principles." In other words: buyer beware.

Sources: Marcia Vickers, "Beware the Press Release," *Business Week*, April 24, 2000, pp. 153–154; Richard E. Rotman, "New Role for Press Release: The Truth about the Company," *BrandEra.com*, January 31, 2000, accessed at **www.brandera.com;** "Who Says Money Isn't Everything," by CEO Judd Spence, PRW Newsletter, Web site accessed March 8, 2001, **www.pressrelease-writing.com.**

organization and its major audiences, such as customers, suppliers, other firms, the general public, and government officials. Businesses use external communication to keep their operations functioning, to maintain their positions in the marketplace, and to build customer relationships by supplying information about topics such as product modifications and price changes. South Carolina real estate broker Elizabeth Gray-Carr uses her Web site to attract buyers and build positive relationships with them. Visitors to her site can look up information about the weather, local schools, mortgage rates, and selling prices, as well as all the homes listed by Gray-Carr's firm. Sellers who list their home or condo with the agency have access to a personal page where they can keep track of their listing, including scheduled advertisements and feedback from people who have viewed the property. The site receives and sends messages, inviting visitors to send e-mail.[49] But sometimes external communication causes problems, as described in the "Solving an Ethical Controversy" box.

FIGURE 10.11
Expectations Created by Technology: Fast Communication and Great Responsiveness

As with internal communications, two-way communication is important. Customers in the 21st century expect to be listened to. Managers are responding to this expectation by visiting online chat sessions and posting their e-mail addresses on Web sites. Continental Airlines routinely assembles groups of travel agents, corporate clients, and frequent fliers to provide feedback about their experiences. Sales executives from Continental also visit the company's hub airport in Newark to visit with people waiting to board flights there.[50] Communicators in today's high-tech environment, like the one pictured in Figure 10.11, also expect messages to travel fast and to get fast responses.

External communications move messages through many different channels, including telephone calls, fax transmissions, e-mail, Web sites, and advertisements. Widespread use of the Internet has contributed to customers' expectations that they should be able to communicate with companies wherever and whenever they want. So organizations that invite customers to send e-mail should be prepared to show they are listening. Employees should be trained to read each message and reply within a day. When employees who usually perform these tasks are on sick leave or away from the office, e-mail and voice-mail systems should be programmed to provide automatic responses explaining the situation.[51] Broker Elizabeth Gray-Carr trained her agents to reply quickly to e-mail, as well as encourage prospects to visit the company's Web site.

Every communication with customers—including sales presentations, order fulfillment documents, and advertisements—should create goodwill and contribute to customer satisfaction. Careless communication can produce doubt among customers, as discussed in the "Business Hits and Misses" box. A *Fortune* reporter who ordered a CD-ROM from Mattel one winter was startled to receive a confirmation e-mail dated 10/19/1919. When she pointed out the error, a company representative worsened the situation by replying with a form e-mail listing replies to eight

Internet Customers Want Personalized Communication

The Internet has opened the door to a flood of potential and actual communication between companies and their customers, but so far most of these participants have been drowned by the flood. Amazon.com pioneered this new field of communication with customers by using technology to create databases of information that included books that customers had previously ordered as well as dates of anniversaries and birthdays. Then marketers would send "personalized" e-mails to customers, to let them know about new books that might interest them or to remind them of an upcoming birthday—and a gift-giving, book-ordering opportunity. Soon other companies followed suit, and customers began to expect more. Eventually, those who didn't offer this kind of communication—or, worse yet, jammed people's in-boxes with irrelevant "junk" mail—began to fall out of favor with consumers.

With the advent of e-mail customer communication, Internet customers also want more personalized and customized products, and they expect companies to meet their demands—or they will shop somewhere else. "Markets will no longer be driven by what manufacturers choose to make and sell but by what consumers want to buy," predicts Steve Larsen, senior vice-president for marketing at Net Perceptions Inc. So the combination of personalized communication and customized goods and services has created a new challenge for companies. "The tail end of this is delivering mass-customized products and services," predicts Bruce E. Kasanoff, CEO of Accelerating1to1, a consulting firm that helps companies personalize their customer relationships. "Without personalization, there's no loyalty; there's no reason for the customer to come back again," he explains.

How are some companies meeting the challenge? International publishing and music giant BOL (Bertelsmann Online) is planning to change the way it produces and markets books. "My vision would be a totally personalized media network, which is different for who-

ever signs into it," says Andrew D. Dorward, director of personalization for the firm's Web site, BOL.com. At the other end of the scale, a tiny company called American Quantum Cycles lets its motorcycle buyers customize their own bikes before they are even made. This process results in a customized bike at a lower factory price. Procter & Gamble used its Internet site and some marketing research that identified customers who were "chatters," those who would most likely tell their friends about a new product, to complete a successful launch of Physique, its new line of haircare products. The campaign generated over 1 million referrals and saved P&G plenty in avoiding wasted television ads.

With the Internet, "companies can now have conversations with hundreds or thousands of customers, all over the world, all of them personal, all of the time," says Greg A. Tucker, CEO of Futurize Now. The key is to conduct these conversations without allowing them to be reduced to useless noise—noise that the consumer shuts off.

QUESTIONS FOR CRITICAL THINKING

1. What steps can companies take to make sure that personalized communications with customers don't become reduced to noise?

2. How can business executives strengthen the bond between personalized communication and resulting customized goods and services? What pitfalls might they encounter?

Sources: "BOL at a Glance," BOL (Bertelsmann Online) Web site, accessed March 2, 2001, at **newsroom.bol.com**; Wendy Zellner, "Hey, Are You Listening to Me?" *Business Week*, August 28, 2000, pp. 138–140; Timothy J. Mullaney, "Needed: The Human Touch," *Business Week E.Biz*, December 13, 1999, pp. EB53–54.

frequently asked questions, none of which pertained to dates on e-mail messages. Two days later, a customer service representative wrote that the reporter's message would be forwarded to the company's technical department, but by then the reporter had written a story about the incident and shared it with the world.[52]

In contrast, Nick's Auto Repair, in Boulder, Colorado, achieves the goals of external communication with its Web site. The information posted on the site conveys an image of an auto-repair firm that is both forthright and trustworthy. Visitors to its Web site can look up details about an automobile's inner workings, receive estimates via e-mail, and study photos and biographical information about the company's employees. The site assures prospective customers that if the shop turns down work, it is due to needed repairs that are beyond the limits of the small company's capacity.[53]

COMMUNICATION TECHNOLOGY

Whether managers are communicating with employees, customers, or suppliers on the other side of the world or across the country, they rely increasingly on the latest technology such as intranets, videoconferencing, fax machines, cellular telephones,

VocalTec Communications Ltd: A Big Revolution from a Small Company

Background. VocalTec Communications embodies its roots quite well: it is a pioneering company based in a pioneering country, Israel. If you've never heard of the firm, you are not alone. But VocalTec's claim to fame is its development of early commercial versions of the hardware and software that allow people to make phone calls on the Internet. Users would download the software from the Web for a fee, install it in any PC containing a speaker and a microphone, and then make free calls to equipped computers anywhere in the world.

What Happened? In the beginning, technological challenges seemed endless. For instance, both users had to be logged on at the same time, and each person had to take turns pushing a "talk" button as if they were communicating through two-way radios. Not surprisingly, the sound quality was terrible—bad enough that no one was particularly interested in further development. But Vocal-Tec kept working on it, and several years later launched a device called a "gateway" that allowed people to make their Internet calls with regular telephones. The gateway connected the Internet and local phone services around the world, allowing users to bypass long-distance carriers. The result? People could make Internet calls anywhere in the world for the price of a local call.

The Response. Start-up phone companies, like Net2Phone, began to buy VocalTec's gateway software and marketing their services worldwide. Acceptance was so widespread that in some countries, like South Korea, Voice-on-the-Net transmissions quickly accounted for 20 percent of all international calls. From there, the technology virtually exploded. Merrill Lynch has installed 6,500 Internet phones, which not only allow employees to have free conference calls over the Net but empower them to exchange instant text messages at the same time. American Express uses the tech-

nology to fight credit card fraud; if the company suspects that a stolen credit card is being used online, an AmEx manager will send a text message to the user and immediately begin a voice transmission over the Internet. If the user can't answer some standard security questions, the transaction will be halted.

Today and Counting. VocalTec's Voice-on-the-Net technology recently accounted for less than 1 percent of global telecommunications activity. Experts expect that number to rise to 17 percent in 2003 and 30 percent by 2005. "I think voice over [the Net] is the inevitable outcome of technology," predicts C. Michael Armstrong, chairman and CEO of AT&T, which is now investing billions of dollars in Internet technology. Because the technology is cheaper than traditional telephone technology and, through digitization, allows many calls to share the same phone line, many experts see the possibilities for innovation as nearly limitless. It looks like VocalTec started a revolution.

QUESTIONS FOR CRITICAL THINKING

1. In what ways might VocalTec's technology enhance teamwork at companies where the Voice-on-the-Net is used?
2. In what ways might Voice-on-the-Net enhance communications between a company and its customers?

Sources: "About VocalTec: History," VocalTec Web site, **www.vocaltec. com,** accessed March 16, 2001; "VocalTec's Surf&Call Network Services Wins Internet Commerce Exposition—ICe—'Best of Show' Award for Customer Service and Support," BusinessWire, September 14, 2000; Steve Rosenbush and Bruce Einhorn, "The Talking Net," *Business Week,* May 1, 2000, pp. 174–188.

and e-mail. The most recent developments provide for richer communication channels by conveying images as well as sound and providing for greater interaction, often in real time.

Voice-on-the-Net technology lets Internet users make phone calls over Internet lines, talking as well as viewing images or words on computer screens, as described in the "Clicks and Mortar" box. At Merrill Lynch, employees can use the Internet to conduct conference calls and transmit instant text messages simultaneously. Compaq Computer lets visitors to its Web site click on an icon to speak with a company representative, and in France, the brokerage firm Capitol.fr staffs a call center with employees who speak live to prospective customers visiting its site.[54]

Yet another technology, project collaboration software, combines a variety of software tools to let employees post and look up documents and conduct online conversations. Software developer Eques Technology Corp. uses software called eRoom to allow cooperation between employees and contract specialists as far away as Ukraine and India. Instead of sending work and schedules back and forth via e-mail, participants in a project simply post them using eRoom, so anyone can see the latest update. Communicating via eRoom is also much less expensive than the long-distance phone calls that once were common at Eques.[55]

Benefits of Communication Technology

Technological developments provide four major benefits for organizations. First, they speed up business operations by letting people exchange information and make decisions much more quickly than they could without the new tools. Second, technologies bypass functional boundaries, so people in different departments can communicate directly rather than through formal channels. Third, they make it easier for people with diverse skills, such as employees in different departments, to work together. Finally, by improving internal processes and easing external communication, they may enhance customer service. Chapters 7 and 17 explain in detail how new technologies are enhancing communications within firms and with customers, vendors, and others outside the firm.

Challenges of Communication Technology

Today's technology often increases the range of communication skills required of each employee. But as Figure 10.12 shows, communication technology presents challenges as well as benefits. With widespread access to word-processing programs and e-mail, employees prepare their own written documents, instead of relying on clerical staff to handle decisions about formatting and grammar. Similarly, instead of using graphic artists to prepare visual aids for presentations, many employees use PowerPoint and other software to create their own illustrations. Effective use of this technology requires employees to be able to communicate clearly through written words and images, not just know the commands that operate the software.

Technological developments—in particular, wireless communications and the Internet—have also revolutionized people's choices about when and with whom they communicate. Cell phones that allow text messaging let a user send a message to any e-mail address at any time, from almost any place. This ability is a benefit for employees who are trying to reach a client while on the road or working parents who want to check on the kids during a long commute home. However, the ease with which people communicate at a distance has also created some challenges for business and society. One challenge is that it is harder to leave work behind when people can get messages and phone calls almost anywhere.

Consider Harriet Donnelly, who runs a marketing firm called Technovative. Her company has no central office; its 100 employees and regular contract workers operate from home offices and, when traveling, hotel rooms. They communicate primarily by telephone and the Internet. Donnelly herself travels almost half the time, visiting clients from St. Louis to San Diego, armed with a briefcase containing a notebook PC, cell phone, and personal digital assistant. Her 80-hour workweeks have bought Donnelly a comfortable life in a large New Jersey home, with a live-in nanny for her young son. Another high-tech communicator, Neil Daswani, gets 250 messages a day on his text pager. Daswani, who leads a team of engineers for an Internet company called Yodlee, has his e-mail forwarded from his computer to the pager, and he immediately taps out replies to each as it arrives.

A recent Pitney Bowes survey found that people who rely heavily on mo-

FIGURE 10.12
Communication Technology:
Benefits and Challenges

Benefits

- Business operations are speeded up as people exchange information and make decisions quicker than before.
- People in different departments can communicate directly rather than through formal channels.
- People with diverse skills can work together more easily.
- Customer service may improve due to improved internal processes and external communication.

Challenges

- Limited access to clerical staff requires communicators to possess the skills needed to prepare polished written documents and prepare their own visual aids using software like PowerPoint.
- People may feel tethered to their work on a 24/7 basis.
- Employees may feel disconnected from their physical environment.
- Managers and operative employees may sacrifice desirable face-to-face interactions because they are overwhelmed with electronic messages.

bile devices like Daswani's pager tend to feel more distracted and overloaded by the volume of messages they receive than do other people. However, Daswani views the technology as a source of convenience. He took his cell phone on a rafting trip, figuring he could afford to be away from the office if people could reach him.[56] Twenty-first-century technology has given people the ability to communicate almost anytime, anywhere. But that ability requires its users to think about when, where, and how they *want* to communicate.

INTERNATIONAL BUSINESS COMMUNICATION

Communication can be a special challenge in the international business arena. An international message's appropriateness depends in part on an accurate translation that conveys the intended nuances of meaning. When PepsiCo marketers wanted to build sales in China, they created a promotional campaign based on the theme "Come Alive with Pepsi." Poor sales surprised them, until they discovered that the direct Chinese translation of their slogan was "Bring your ancestors back from the dead." Managers ordered a hasty rewrite of the theme. As this example shows, businesspeople who want to succeed in the global marketplace must ensure that they send only linguistically and culturally appropriate messages.

Increasingly, business communications take place in English. One reason is that the strength and size of the U.S. economy have spread familiarity with U.S. products and media. Another is that the Internet originated in the U.S., so the English language has dominated Internet usage. Public school children in Japan and Korea take between 9 and 12 years of English. In over 75 nations, English is an official language. However, the English language is constantly expanding by borrowing words and expressions from other languages, so it varies radically from one country to another. The British, for example, call trucks *lorries,* and an elevator is a *lift* to them. In English-speaking Nigeria, a traffic jam is a *go-slow;* Jamaicans refer to highway speed bumps as *sleeping policemen.*[57] So communication snafus occur even among English-speaking countries.

One of every two Internet users has a first language other than English, and research suggests that Web site visitors are much more likely to buy products from sites that use the customers' language. Avis Europe originally set up an English-only Web site offering global car rentals. Avis has since added pages in several other European languages, beginning with German and Spanish, and online reservations have increased as a share of total bookings. Yahoo! sets up portals in any language with enough users to make up a viable market. So far, it operates in more than a dozen languages.[58]

Translating also poses challenges with oral communication. The speaker needs to work with a translator who can quickly capture the nuances of spoken language. For translating telephone messages, communicators might use a service like Language Line. This service, detailed in Figure 10.13, offers customers groups of interpreters who can speak 140 different languages to assist in interpreting telephone messages. For planned, formal communications, like speeches or presentations, speakers can develop a team relationship with a translator. Patricia Fripp, an author, executive speech coach, and professional business speaker, has spoken at seminars in Asia, and she recommends getting acquainted with the translator well in advance and rehearsing the presentation. In preparing for a recent presentation to a group of Asian employees, Fripp and her translator reviewed the signs posted on the walls of the meeting room then wrote down the translation of each. Her notes enabled her to incorporate the company's slogans into her presentation, which signaled knowledge of her audience. Fripp also advises providing written handouts in the audience's language and minimizing the use of jokes, which are difficult to translate in a humorous way.[59]

FIGURE 10.13
Language Line: Translating Oral Communications

Communication also improves when each party understands the cultural contexts that surround and influence every attempt at sending an international message. Translations have to consider not only the meanings of words but the audience's familiarity with elements of nonverbal communication. The mailbox that signals, "You've Got Mail," on America Online is a familiar icon of rural American life, but to Europeans, it looks more like a loaf of bread.[60]

Anthropologists divide cultures by low context and high context. Communication in **low-context cultures** tends to rely on explicit written and verbal messages. Examples include Switzerland, Germany, Australia, and the U.S. In contrast, communication in **high-context cultures**—such as those of Japan, Latin America, and India—depends not only on the message itself but also on the conditions that surround it, including nonverbal cues, past and present experiences, and personal relationships between the parties. Westerners must carefully temper their low-context style to the expectations of colleagues and clients from high-context countries. Although Americans tend to favor direct interactions and want to "get down to business" soon after shaking hands or sitting down to a business dinner, businesspeople in Mexico and Asian and Near Eastern countries prefer to become acquainted before discussing details. When conducting business in these cultures, wise visitors allow time for relaxed meals during which business-related topics are avoided and individuals engage in small talk and discuss their families, countries, and leisure activities. They may get together for several meetings before actually transacting any business.[61]

Workplace differences also influence the process of communication. For example, the open communication style in U.S. firms is foreign to workers in Russia, where employees have long expected specific directions about what to do and where asking questions was an invitation to trouble. Managers of foreign firms operating in Russia often encounter difficulties communicating with Russian employees, who are reluctant to ask for help and avoid giving feedback to messages. Success in this situation requires patience as managers learn to be very specific in directing employees while also encouraging them to express their point of view. In general, learning about the cultures of the countries in which they operate is essential for managers and employees who want to communicate effectively.

WHAT'S AHEAD

Communication is essential for building cooperation and teamwork when people bring different points of view to the job. A significant source of differences involves the positions of managers and nonmanagement employees. Businesses can address these differences constructively through positive labor–management relations, the subject of the next chapter. That chapter explores the role of labor unions in contemporary business, the ways management works with unions, and the nature of employer–employee relationships in nonunion firms.

➤ Summary of Learning Goals

1. Describe why and how organizations empower employees.

By empowering employees, a firm finds better ways to perform jobs, motivates employees by enhancing the challenges and satisfaction in their work, and frees managers from hands-on control so they can focus on other tasks. Employers empower workers by sharing information, distributing decision-making authority and responsibility, and linking rewards to company performance.

2. Distinguish between the two major types of teams in the workplace.

The two major types of teams are work teams and problem-solving teams. Work teams are permanent groups of coworkers who perform the day-to-day tasks necessary to operate the organization. Problem-solving teams are temporary groups of employees who gather to solve specific problems and then disband.

3. Identify the characteristics of an effective team and the roles played by team members.

Three important characteristics of a team are its size, member roles, and diversity. Effective teams typically combine between 5 and 12 members, with about 7 members being the ideal size. Team members can play task specialist, socio-emotional, dual, or nonparticipator roles. Effective teams balance the first three roles. Diverse teams tend to display broader ranges of viewpoints and produce more innovative solutions to problems than do homogeneous teams.

4. Summarize the stages of team development.

A team passes through five stages of development: (1) Forming is an orientation period during which members get to know each other and find out what behaviors are acceptable to the group. (2) Storming is the stage during which individual personalities emerge as members clarify their roles and expectations. (3) Norming is a stage when differences are resolved, members accept each other, and consensus emerges about the roles of the team leader and other participants. (4) Performing is characterized by problem solving and a focus on task accomplishment. (5) Adjourning is the final stage, with a focus on wrapping up and summarizing the team's experiences and accomplishments.

5. Relate team cohesiveness and norms to effective team performance.

Team cohesiveness is the extent to which team members are attracted to the team and motivated to remain in it. Team norms are standards of conduct shared by team members that guide their behavior. Highly cohesive teams whose members share certain standards of conduct tend to be more productive and effective.

6. Describe the factors that can cause conflict in teams and ways conflict can be resolved.

Conflict can stem from many sources: competition for scarce resources, personality clashes, conflicting goals, poor communication, unclear job responsibilities, or team role assignments. Conflict resolution styles range from assertive to cooperative measures. The most effective resolution style varies according to the situation. Resolution styles include the competing style, the avoiding style, the compromising style, the accommodating style, and the collaborating style. A team leader can limit conflict by focusing team members on broad goals, clarifying participants' respective tasks and areas of authority, acting as mediator, and facilitating effective communication.

7. Explain the importance of effective communication skills in business.

Managers and employees spend much of their time exchanging information through messages. Communication helps all employees to understand the company's goals and values and the parts they play in achieving those goals.

8. Compare the different types of communication.

People exchange messages in many ways: oral and written, formal and informal, verbal and nonverbal communication. Although some people prefer oral channels because they accurately convey messages, nonverbal cues can distort meaning. Effective written communication reflects its audience, its channel, and the appropriate degree of formality. Formal communication channels carry messages within the chain of command. Informal communication channels, such as the grapevine, carry messages outside the formal chain of command. Nonverbal communication plays a larger role than most people realize. Generally, when verbal and nonverbal cues conflict, the receiver of a message tends to believe the meaning conveyed by nonverbal elements.

9. Discuss how advances in technology affect business communication.

Information technology tools such as intranets, video-conferencing, and e-mail can improve the efficiency and speed of communications by helping businesspeople to create, organize, and distribute messages among employees in different time zones and geographic locations. The ease of communication can improve collaboration among employees from different functions, improving customer service as well as efficiency. Technology also poses some challenges. Employees may feel tethered to their work around the clock, feel disconnected from their physical environment, and sacrifice desirable face-to-face interactions because they are overwhelmed with electronic messages. Overcoming these challenges requires that communicators make choices about when, where, and how they use technology to communicate.

Business Terms You Need to Know

total quality management (TQM) 360
empowerment 360
teamwork 364
team 365
work team 366
problem-solving team 367
team cohesiveness 372

team norm 373
conflict 373
communication 376
listening 379
grapevine 380
internal communication 381
external communication 383

Other Important Business Terms

employee stock ownership plan
  (ESOP) 363
stock options 364
task specialist role 368
socio-emotional role 368

formal communication channel 380
informal communication channel 380
nonverbal communication 381
centralized communication
  network 383

decentralized communication
  network 383
low-context culture 390
high-context culture 390

➤ Review Questions

1. What is total quality management? How does it affect the way employees function in their jobs?

2. Describe the ways employers can empower their employees, and give a specific example of each.

3. Identify and briefly explain the approaches companies use to provide for worker ownership. What are the main differences between them?

4. What are the two major types of teams? How does each function? In what instances might a company use each type?

5. What are the characteristics of an effective team?

6. Identify and describe briefly the five stages of team development. At what stages might a team get "stuck" and not be able to move forward?

7. Describe the five different styles of conflict resolution. Which style do you think you might be most likely to use? Why?

8. What are the major elements in the communication process? Briefly define each element.

9. What are the two channels for formal communication? Give an example of each.

10. What is the central focus of a company's external communication? List two or three examples of this type of communication.

➤ Questions for Critical Thinking

1. Consider your current job or one you have held in the past. Did your employer practice any kind of empowerment? If so, what? If not, why not? Or think of your family as a company. Did your parents empower their children? If so, in what ways? If not, why not? In either scenario, what do you think were the consequences of empowerment or nonempowerment?

2. As discussed in the chapter, one of the most innovative team approaches in business today involves vendor–client partnerships. Imagine that you have been hired as a consultant for a company and asked to outline a plan for a vendor–client partnership. Choose an industry or company that interests you, and write a memo describing with whom you think your company should partner, and why.

3. Do you consider yourself a good listener? First, identify which listening style you think you practice. Then show the list of listening styles in this chapter to a friend, family member, or classmate and ask that person what type of listening style he or she thinks you practice. Finally, compare the two responses. Do they agree or disagree? *Note:* You can take this exercise a step farther by asking more than one person what type of listening style you practice, then comparing all the responses.

4. The grapevine is one of the strongest communication links in any organization, from large corporation to college classroom to family. Do you rely on information that travels along the grapevine? Why or why not?

5. Take a seat in the library, the dorm lounge, in a mall, in a restaurant, or wherever there is a flow of people whom you can watch unobtrusively. For at least 15 minutes, observe and jot down the nonverbal cues that you see pass between people. Then try to interpret these cues. How would your interpretation affect any actual communication you might have with one of these people?

➤ Experiential Exercise

Background: Customers don't have to look far to see companies using open and direct communications to develop personal relationships with customers. For example, Wal-Mart is well known for its greeters, who provide a cheerful welcome to the stores and help personalize the shopping experience. This practice is being adopted by more retailers, such as Kmart Corp., and many mall-based specialty stores.

In the online world, Amazon.com was a pioneer in establishing personal relationships with its customers by studying the books they purchased and making recommendations based on what they're reading. Dell Computer, which sells PCs built to order, remembers what customers have bought in the past and, with personalized Web pages, makes it easier for its customers to add new equipment, upgrade what they already own, or troubleshoot technical problems.

Directions: Submit to your instructor a one-page paper in which you identify five to ten examples similar to those already given that show how companies are communicating with customers on a one-on-one basis, as opposed to the mass marketing, mass media communication approach. For each example you include, identify the source of the example: a personal experience, library research source (such as the ones listed for this exercise), or a friend or co-worker's experience.

Sources: Leslie Earnest, "Wal-Mart's Greeting Practice Catching on with Other Retailers," *The Morning News,* December 20, 2000, p. 3C; Wendy Zellner, "Hey, Are You Listening to Me?" *Business Week,* August 21, 2000, p. 138.

➤ Nothing but Net

1. ESOPs. The chapter discusses the basics of employee stock option plans (ESOPs) and their growing importance today. Visit the following Web site listed and review the current statistics on ESOPs. How many plans are there today compared with 1974 and 1990? List five other interesting statistics concerning ESOPs today.

www.the-esop.employer.org/pubs/stats.html

2. Communicating using e-mail. According to recent statistics, e-mails exceed all other forms of communication today. Visit the following two Web sites listed and prepare a brief report on the do's and don'ts of communicating using e-mail.

www.salesdoctors.com/keller/kel49.htm

www.iaphc.org/e-dodont.htm

3. Team building. The following Web site listed contains information on team building. Visit the site and prepare an oral report to your class on the characteristics of an effective team member and the five ways to become a more effective member of a team.

www.mapnp.org/library/grp_skll/teams/teams.htm

Note: Internet Web addresses change frequently. If you do not find the exact sites listed, you may need to access the organization's or company's home page and search from there.

When Bill Rosenberg opened the doors of his first doughnut shop in Quincy, Massachusetts, in 1948, he called it "The Open Kettle." Although he sold plenty of coffee and doughnuts from his shop, he thought the name didn't do much to reach out and draw in new customers. So, during a brainstorming session, Rosenberg asked his employees for ideas. One of them quipped, "What do you do with a doughnut? You dunk it!" And the name Dunkin' Donuts was born.

More than 50 years and 8 billion cups of coffee later, Dunkin' Donuts now operates 5,000 shops in 40 countries, making it the largest doughnut chain in the world. Dunkin' Donuts sells about 20 cups of coffee every second and 6 million doughnuts each day, or about 2.3 billion per year. How has Dunkin' Donuts kept its image fresh while so many other doughnut chains have gone stale?

One answer is teamwork—working together with franchisees, employees, suppliers and even the company's advertising agency to maintain high standards. For instance, after years of running ads that featured Fred the Baker—who woke before dawn each morning saying, "It's time to make the doughnuts"—Dunkin' Donuts executives decided it was time to bake up something fresh. They went to the advertising agency of Hill, Holliday, Connors and Cosmopulos looking for a new way to reach doughnut dunkers. They found it in the creative team of Marty Donohue and Tim Foley, who immediately quipped, "We don't take anything seriously."

But Foley and Donohue did some serious work for their new clients. They listened to what Eddie Binder, Dunkin' Donuts vice president of marketing, wanted. Donohue recalls Binder offering his opinion that "a doughnut strategy was an oxymoron. There was no real strategy. We were told to make Dunkin' Donuts fun again." In addition, the company wanted to grow. "They've been a great regional company, but they have expansion plans," notes Donohue.

Foley and Donohue understood what Dunkin' Donuts had communicated to them, and how the company wanted to communicate with its customers. Together they came up with a new ad campaign featuring the slogan, "Loosen up." One commercial features a fake car chase in which both the police car and the fugitive car pull into a Dunkin' Donuts parking lot while the officer and the fugi-

tive run into the shop and run back out again carrying doughnuts and coffee. Both leap into their vehicles and continue the chase. Another ad shows commuters on a crowded bus, where one executive brags about his accomplishments and behaves rudely to others. When the bus lurches to a stop, the woman behind the executive accidentally touches his suit with a Dunkin' bagel. Instead of telling him and apologizing, she deftly paints two cream cheese "eyes" above the crescent left by the bagel and lets him get off the bus bearing a cream cheese "smile" on his suit jacket.

The ads have been so successful that many viewers have forgotten the retired Fred. Donohue and Foley's bosses aren't surprised by the results. "They're an *A* team," says Mike Sheehan, Hill/Holliday's co-president and chief creative officer. "They're young and they do comedy very well." Sheehan believes that Donohue and Foley listen and communicate well—both with clients and with consumers. "They are street savvy. They are the audience," he comments.

Most important, the Foley/Donohue team understands the message that Dunkin' Donuts wants to convey to people. "Basically, we are a wickedly delicious emotional reward for the hassles in life one deals with every day," explains Dunkin' Donuts CEO Jack Shafer. In other words, Dunkin' Donuts wants people to think of a trip to one of their shops as one of life's little sweet rewards.

QUESTIONS

1. What makes Foley and Donohue an effective team?
2. What challenges might Dunkin' Donuts and its advertisers face in communicating with consumers around the globe?
3. In what ways might Dunkin' Donuts empower its employees to help make a visit to their shop a treat for consumers?
4. Access the Dunkin' Donuts Web site at **www.dunkindonuts.com** and then come up with your own idea for an ad for Dunkin' Donuts based on the slogan, "Loosen up."

Sources: Dunkin' Donuts Web site, **www.dunkindonuts.com,** accessed April 16, 2001; Hill/Holliday Web Site, **www.hhcc.com,** accessed April 16, 2001; David Gianatasio, "Dough Boys," *Adweek*, September 4, 2000, pp. 28–29.

CHAPTER 11

Labor–Management Relations

Learning Goals

1. Summarize the history of labor unions and list their primary goals.

2. Describe the structure of organized labor.

3. Identify the major federal laws that affect labor unions and explain the key provisions of each law.

4. Explain the process of forming unions, the way they achieve goals through collective bargaining, and the issues typically addressed in union contracts.

5. Describe the roles played by mediators and arbitrators in labor negotiations.

6. Identify the steps in the union grievance process.

7. Outline the tactics of labor and management in conflicts between them.

8. Describe how unions and employers are developing partner relationships.

9. Discuss employee–employer relationships in nonunion firms.

10. Explain the challenges facing labor unions and strategies currently being used to rebuild union membership.

SAG and AFTRA: Two Strikes against Hollywood

When you watch a television commercial for Bufferin or Tostitos, you probably aren't paying too much attention to the actors themselves, unless they happen to be celebrities. But the typical actor in a commercial is a person who belongs either to the Screen Actors Guild (SAG) or the American Federation of Television and Radio Artists (AFTRA), unions formed to represent their interests. These actors don't get paid the millions movie stars can command. According to their contract, they receive pay-per-play wages for network television commercials and a flat fee for ads on cable television. Although the flat fee is higher, most actors prefer the per-play fee because those spots will earn them more in the long run if the ads are widely replayed. But as the union contract came up for renegotiation in 2000, advertisers wanted to abolish the pay-per-play structure and pay commercial actors a flat fee—regardless of the medium on which the ad appeared. Then there was the gray area of a new medium: the Internet. The industry didn't budge. The actors went on strike.

Six months later—the longest talent strike in the history of Hollywood—SAG and AFTRA reached an agreement with advertisers. Not much changed, but both sides claimed victory. "Our members knew what was at stake in this negotiation and have unflinchingly stood their ground," boasted SAG president William Daniels. The unions won status quo on pay-per-play wages for commercials run on network stations and an increase in the flat fee for cable ads. But the industry was able to retain the flat fee for cable ads and got the unions to accept a three-year-contract. Perhaps most impor-

tant, though, was that the unions were able to establish claims for commercials produced for the Internet. "We always had jurisdiction of our broadcasts that were

moved over to the Internet, but now we'll get jurisdiction over commercials made for the Internet, exclusively," explained union actor Rick Elliott. On the loss side of the settlement, actors believe that historically they have not received a fair share of the money made by companies in cable television and foreign television. Studios and networks argue that the money they make in cable and foreign television barely compensates for what they've lost to declining network television audiences.

Ironically, most television viewers might never have noticed the strike except for the coverage it had on the news. But the strike

is an illustration of how conflicts begin and how they are resolved. In this case, special mediators were called in to help smooth the way toward an agreement. In fact, dis-

sension arose within the unions themselves, and SAG reportedly asked some of its negotiating team to step down because of certain members' "militant style." One of the challenges facing both unions going forward will be actually keeping its members united.[1] In this chapter, you'll read about conflicts that arise between workers and management in many industries and the different ways they can be resolved. Not every problem can be solved, but perhaps a major theme of this chapter could be summed up in a single word: *compromise.*

CHAPTER OVERVIEW

Every society and culture develops some system of industrial relations. The people who head the organizations that provide needed goods and services, the people who do the work, and the government organizations that maintain the society define the various industrial relationships. This chapter focuses on the relationships between labor and management.

We begin the chapter by exploring reasons for the emergence of labor unions and a brief history of their operations in the U.S. Next, the chapter focuses on legislation that affects labor–management relations. The process of collective bargaining is then discussed, along with an examination of union and management weapons. The chapter concludes with a look at the future of labor–management relations.

EMERGENCE OF LABOR UNIONS

Organized labor did not originate in the U.S. For hundreds of years, organizations of craft workers have operated in Europe and Asia. Over the years, they developed into powerful workers' organizations. Today, with the growing interdependence among nations around the world and the increasing number of multinational corporations, an understanding of labor–management relations is critical for business students.

In recent years, private-sector (nongovernment) union membership has declined significantly in many industrial nations, including the U.S., Great Britain, France, and Germany. Reasons include the shift away from traditionally unionized manufacturing jobs, corporate downsizing, outsourcing, and increased employment of temporary and part-time workers, who are less likely to be union members. Union membership also dropped substantially in central and eastern European countries following the end of compulsory unionism.

But union membership has grown considerably in some industrialized and developing nations. Membership more than doubled in South Africa and almost doubled in Spain and Chile recently. And in countries whose governments employ tens of thousands of employees, such as Canada, Japan, and many European countries, union membership is strong because of unionization of these workers.[2] But whether a nation's union membership is rising or falling, the basic underlying purpose of unions—to protect and provide for workers—is a consistent characteristic of every organized labor union throughout the world.

Need for Labor Unions

The industrial revolution improved efficiency through specialization and division of labor. These changes to the factory assembly line system allowed workers to become proficient at some aspect of the production process, converting the jack-of-all-trades into a specialist. Also, businesses brought together in a single location many workers, which permitted greater output than did traditional handicraft methods of production.

This focus on efficiency created some hardships for workers in the 19th and early 20th centuries. Specialization made them dependent on the factory for their livelihoods. In prosperous times, they could count on employment, but periodic depressions threw them out of work, and unemployment insurance was nonexistent. Working conditions were typically exhausting and even dangerous. Work hours lasted from daybreak to dark, all for low wages. By the end of the 19th century, the typical workweek ran to 60 hours, but in some industries, such as steel, 72- or even 84-hour workweeks—the equivalent of seven 12-hour days a week—were common.

Another problem was the reliance on child labor. At the beginning of the 19th century, young children worked for a few pennies a day to help their families. In Boston in 1830, children made up two-fifths of the labor force.

Workers gradually learned that bargaining as a unified group could bring them improvements in job security, wages, and working conditions. The organized efforts of Philadelphia printers in 1786 resulted in the first U.S. minimum wage—$1 a day. After 100 more years, New York City streetcar conductors banded together in successful negotiations that reduced their workday from 17 to 12 hours.

The sweeping changes in labor–management relations over the past century produced profound improvements in wages, hours of work, and working conditions for employees in most industrialized nations. These changes have not eliminated the conditions that first convinced workers of the need to unionize, however. Long hours, dangerous work, and child labor still persist today in many parts of the world. The International Labor Organization (ILO), an agency of the United Nations, estimates that 250 million children between the ages of 5 and 14 years are victims of child labor. Of these, the agency believes tens of millions are engaged in the "worst forms of child labor": slavery, debt bondage, prostitution, pornography, forced recruitment for armed conflicts, drug trafficking or other illegal activities, and dangerous or unhealthful work. To combat these abuses, the ILO has adopted a convention—binding on member nations—that requires nations to prohibit and eliminate these worst forms of child labor.[3] Many countries, including the United States, are making efforts to eradicate other forms of child labor, but the problem persists. The U.S. Customs Service recently banned imports of clothing manufactured at the Chinese-owned Dong Fang Guo Ji factory, where children work as much as 14 hours a day, seven days a week.[4]

Today, attitudes toward unions are mixed. A recent poll sponsored by the AFL–CIO, the largest U.S. union organization, revealed that a slight majority of Americans believe that employees who work in a unionized firm are better off than those without union representation. In addition, a slight majority believe that an increase in union membership would be good for the nation.[5] With regard to compensation, evidence supports the majority. As shown in Figure 11.1, wage rates tend to be higher for union jobs than for nonunion jobs, and benefits are more generous as well. Reasons employees give for not joining unions include objections to paying union dues and fear that unions will make their employers less competitive, potentially putting their jobs at risk. In addition, U.S. culture highly values the individual, which makes it difficult for unions to sell the idea of benefiting workers as a group. In a tight labor market, many employees believe they can get the best deal for themselves by shopping around for the employer who offers them the best job.[6]

As this illustration shows, the industrial revolution increased output, but its view of human resources was little more than a cog in a machine. Unions emerged in response to such attitudes and assisted workers in improving wages, work hours, and working conditions.

History of U.S. Labor Unions

Although the history of U.S. trade unionism began before the Declaration of Independence, early unions were loose-knit, local organizations that served primarily as friendship groups or benevolent societies to help fellow workers in need. Such

FIGURE 11.1
Union and Nonunion Wages and Benefits

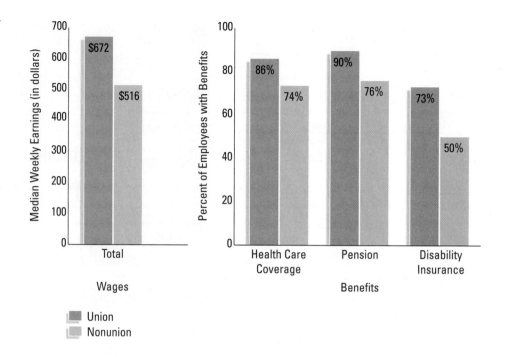

Union
Nonunion

unions were typically short-lived, growing during prosperous times and suffering severely during depressions.

Over time, as workers began to unite, they realized that collectively they often grew strong enough to get results to their demands. This inspired the birth of labor unions. A labor union is a group of workers who have banded together to achieve common goals in the important areas of wages, hours, and working conditions.

These early workers formed two types of unions: craft unions and industrial unions. A *craft union* unites skilled workers in a specific craft or trade, such as carpenters, painters, printers, and heavy-equipment operators. An *industrial union* combines all workers in an industry, regardless of their occupations or skill levels. Industrial unions include the United Steelworkers, the United Auto Workers (UAW), the Amalgamated Clothing Workers, and the United Transportation Union.

The first union to operate on a national scale was the Knights of Labor, founded in 1869. By 1886, its membership exceeded 700,000 workers, but it soon split into factions. One faction promoted revolutionary aims, wanting the government to take over production. The second faction wanted the union to continue focusing on the economic well-being of union members and opposed the socialist tendencies of some members. This faction merged with a group of unaffiliated craft unions in 1886 to form the **American Federation of Labor (AFL)**, uniting these individual craft unions under a common affiliation.

The AFL's first president was Samuel Gompers, a dynamic man who believed that labor unions should operate within the framework of the existing economic system and who vehemently opposed socialism. Gompers's bread-and-butter concept of unionism kept the labor movement focused on the objectives of wages, hours, and working conditions. The AFL grew rapidly, and by 1920, three out of four organized workers were AFL members.

Unions grew slowly between 1920 and 1935, as few nonunion, skilled craft workers remained for the AFL to organize. Several unions in the AFL began to organize workers in the mass-production automobile and steel industries. Successes in organizing the communications, mining, newspaper, steel, rubber, and automobile industries resulted in the formation of a new group, the **Congress of Industrial Organizations (CIO)**—a group of individual industrial unions. The technique of organizing entire industries rather than individual crafts was so successful that the CIO soon rivaled the AFL in size.

THEY SAID IT

"Fairness and decency for American workers means more than simply keeping them alive and safe from injury and disease. It means an effort to make it possible for workers to live, not just as robots or machines, but as men and women who are human beings. Additionally, making the assembly line more human and humane is a large and difficult task, but it is at the heart of everything we mean by social justice in America."

EDWARD M. KENNEDY (B.1932)
U.S. SENATOR

As a percentage of the total work-force, union membership peaked during the 1940s and 1950s. By 1945, total union membership had passed 14 million workers, over one-third of the U.S. labor force. In 1955, the AFL and CIO united under the presidency of George Meany. Today, almost all major U.S. national unions are affiliated with the AFL–CIO. With 68 member unions and 13 million union members, the AFL–CIO represents nearly 80 percent of organized American workers. They include the workers who erected the Millennium Force roller coaster at Cedar Point Amusement Park in Ohio, shown under construction in Figure 11.2. The steel towers and tracks were set up by members of Ironworkers Local 17, using five cranes operated by members of the Operating Engineers union. The world's tallest roller coaster rests on 226 concrete footers built by the Carpenters and Laborers union.[7]

FIGURE 11.2
The World's Tallest Roller Coaster: Union-Made at Cedar Point Amusement Park, Sandusky, Ohio

Union membership as a percentage of the workforce steadily declined during the second half of the past century, except among government employees. Until the late 1970s, the total number of unionized workers continued to rise, but not as fast as the overall workforce. Currently, 16.5 million U.S. workers—13.5 percent of the nation's labor force—belong to labor unions. Although less than 1 in 10 workers in the private sector is unionized, 2 of every 5 workers for federal, state, and local governments belong to unions.[8]

As shown in Figure 11.3, the highest proportions of union membership are in government and the transportation, communication and public utilities, construction, and manufacturing industries. Although blue-collar workers represent the traditional strength of unions, organized labor has gained an increasingly white-collar profile, as the U.S. economy has evolved from a manufacturing base to a service-based system. Union membership is somewhat more common among men than women, but the gap has been shrinking.

In recent years, unions have been most successful in recruiting government workers and employees in service industries such as health care. The largest national union in the U.S. is the Service Employees International Union (SEIU), with 1.4 million members. The membership is made up of a wide range of service workers, including clerical staff, nurses' aides, and janitors. The SEIU has also organized such professionals as nurses, doctors, engineers, and librarians. Today, the SEIU is the nation's largest union of health care workers, with over half its members employed by institutions like nursing homes and hospitals.[9]

LOCAL, NATIONAL, AND INTERNATIONAL UNIONS

Like the formal structure of a large organization, labor unions typically forge links to form a hierarchy. A **national union** joins together many local unions, which make up the entire union organizational structure. The **local union** operates as a branch of a national union, representing union members in a given geographic area. One example is Local 4321, a union that represents postal workers in Salisbury, Maryland. Local 4321 is a branch of a large national union, the American Postal Workers Union.

BUSINESS DIRECTORY

➤ **labor union** *group of workers who have banded together to achieve common goals in the key areas of wages, hours, and working conditions.*

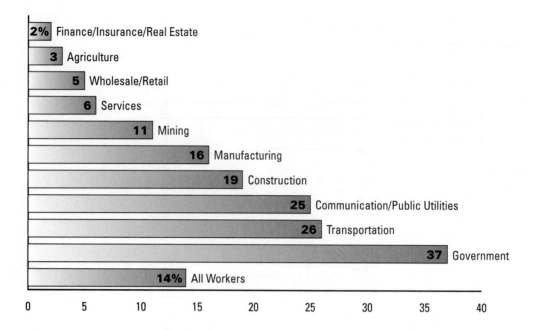

FIGURE 11.3
Percentage of U.S. Workers in Unions, by Industry

Local craft unions represent workers such as carpenters and plumbers in a particular area. The local union receives its charter from the national union and operates under the national union's constitution, bylaws, and rules. Most organized workers identify closely with their local unions and are acquainted with local union officers, even though they seldom attend regular union meetings, except for those that deal with important issues such as contract negotiations, strike votes, or union elections. An estimated 5 to 10 percent of unionized workers typically attend local union meetings.

Large national and international unions in the U.S. include the National Education Association, Teamsters, International Brotherhood of Electrical Workers, International Association of Machinists and Aerospace Workers, United Steelworkers of America, and the American Federation of Teachers. Almost half of U.S. union members belong to one of these giant organizations.

In such industries as automobiles, steel, and electrical products, collective bargaining over major issues occurs at the national level with participation by representatives of various local unions. An **international union** is a union with members outside the U.S., usually in Canada. Some unions choose names to reflect their international status, such as the International Union of Operating Engineers and the Seafarers International Union.

Whereas local unions form the base of the union structure, federations such as the AFL–CIO occupy the top. A **federation** brings together many national and international unions to serve mediation and political functions. Public Services International is an international trade union federation that represents 20 million public-sector workers in 130 countries. A major function of a federation is to mediate disputes between affiliated unions. In addition, it performs a political function, representing organized labor in world affairs and in contacts with unions in other nations. Federation representatives frequently speak before Congress and other branches of government, and they assist in coordinating efforts to organize nonunion workers. However, some unions, such as the National Education Association, do not belong to the major U.S. federation, the AFL–CIO.

Unions may also participate in federations at the international level. The International Confederation of Free Trade Unions (ICFTU) is the world's largest union organization. Based in Brussels, it has over 200 member unions from 148 countries, representing about 155 million workers. Among its most recent members are three Russian unions. Cooperation with Russian unions is a relatively new development

1932
Norris–La Guardia Act

Reduced management's ability to obtain court injunctions to halt union activities. Before this act, employers could easily obtain court decrees forbidding strikes, peaceful picketing, and even membership drives, making these union activities illegal following the injunction.

1935
National Labor Relations Act (Wagner Act)

Legalized collective bargaining and required employers to negotiate with elected representatives of their employees. Established the National Labor Relations Board (NLRB) to supervise union elections and prohibit unfair labor practices such as firing workers for joining unions, refusing to hire union sympathizers, threatening to close if workers unionize, interfering with or dominating the administration of a union, and refusing to bargain with a union.

1938
Fair Labor Standards Act

Set a federal minimum wage (25 cents an hour, with exceptions for farm workers and retail employees) and maximum basic workweek for workers employed in industries engaged in interstate commerce. Outlawed child labor.

1947
Taft–Hartley Act (Labor–Management Relations Act or LMRA)

Limited unions' power by prohibiting such practices as coercing employees to join unions; coercing employers to discriminate against employees who are not union members, except for failure to pay union dues under union shop agreements; discrimination against nonunion employees; picketing or conducting secondary boycotts or strikes for illegal purposes; featherbedding; and excessive initiation fees under union shop agreements.

1959
Landrum–Griffin Act (Labor–Management Reporting and Disclosure Act)

Amended the Taft–Hartley Act to promote honesty and democracy in running unions' internal affairs. Required unions to set up a constitution and bylaws and to hold regularly scheduled elections of union officers by secret ballot. Set forth a bill of rights for members. Required unions to submit certain financial reports to the U.S. Secretary of Labor.

1988
Plant-Closing Notification Act

Required employers with more than 100 employees to give workers and local elected officials 60 days' warning of a shutdown or mass layoff. Created the Worker Readjustment Program to assist displaced workers.

FIGURE 11.4
Federal Labor Laws

for the ICFTU, which traditionally had objected to the Soviet government's strict control of labor unions. The ICFTU requires that its member unions have democratic structures. The federation defends workers' rights by working with member unions and international organizations such as the ILO, the World Bank, and the World Trade Organization. As businesses increasingly operate on an international scale, organizations like the ICFTU are likely to play an important role in influencing policy related to their operations.

LABOR LEGISLATION

Government attitudes toward unions have varied considerably during the past century. These shifting attitudes influenced major pieces of legislation enacted during this period, as summarized in Figure 11.4.

Union Security Provisions

Since unions focus their efforts on improving the incomes and working conditions of all workers, their belief that every employee should join a union should not seem surprising. A **closed shop** is a business with an employment agreement that prohibits management from hiring nonunion workers. To get a job at such a firm, a worker must join the union, and remaining a union member is a condition of continued employment. Unions have considered the closed shop an essential ingredient of security, giving them unquestioned power in demands for wages and working conditions. Unions argue in favor of the closed shop; they claim that because all employees enjoy the benefits of union contracts, all should support the union.

Employers have argued, however, that forcing people to join an organization as a condition of employment violates a fundamental principle of freedom. In addition, if an employer can hire only union members, it might have to pass over the best, most qualified workers. Finally, employers have claimed that a guaranteed membership may make union leaders irresponsible and lead them to deal dishonestly with their members. The U.S. Congress showed its support for these arguments by passing the Taft–Hartley Act, which prohibits the closed shop.

Under a modification of the closed shop, the **union shop**, all current employees must join the union as soon as an election certifies it as their legitimate bargaining agent. New employees must join the union within a specified period, normally 30 days after hiring. The majority of all union contracts specify union shop requirements.

An **agency shop** is a business with an employment agreement that allows it to hire all qualified employees, but nonunion workers must pay the union a fee equal to union dues. This agreement eliminates what the unions have labeled *free riders*, nonmembers who might benefit from union negotiations without financially supporting the union.

The **open shop**, the opposite of the closed shop, makes union membership voluntary for all current and new employees. Individuals who choose not to join a union are not required to pay union dues or fees.

The Taft–Hartley Act permits states to pass **right-to-work laws** that prohibit union shops and outlaw compulsory union membership. Located mainly in the South, West, and Great Plains areas, the 21 right-to-work states are identified in Figure 11.5. In right-to-work states, the percentage of workers who belong to unions is significantly lower than in other states.[10]

Unfair Union Practices

Prior to passage of the Taft–Hartley Act, federal labor legislation had focused mainly on unfair practices on the part of employers. The Taft–Hartley Act shifted this focus by outlawing a number of unfair practices of unions, as well as employers, such as refusal to bargain with the employer, striking without 60 days' notice, most secondary boycotts, and "featherbedding," or demanding pay for workers who do no work. In one classic example, the British civil service created a job in 1803 for a worker to stand on the Cliffs of Dover with a spyglass and ring a bell if Napoleon approached. The job was not eliminated until 1945.

One of a union's most powerful weapons is a **boycott,** an effort to prevent people from purchasing a firm's goods or services. The law identifies two kinds of boycotts: primary and secondary boycotts. In a *primary boycott*, union members urge people not to patronize a firm directly involved in a labor dispute. In contrast, a *secondary boycott* is intended to force an employer to stop dealing with another firm involved in a labor dispute. The union pressures an otherwise uninvolved party to force its real adversary into capitulating. The Taft–Hartley Act outlaws secondary boycotts deemed coercive by the courts.

Taft–Hartley also allows employers to sue unions for breach of contract and to engage in antiunion activities as long as they do not stoop to coercive tactics. Unions

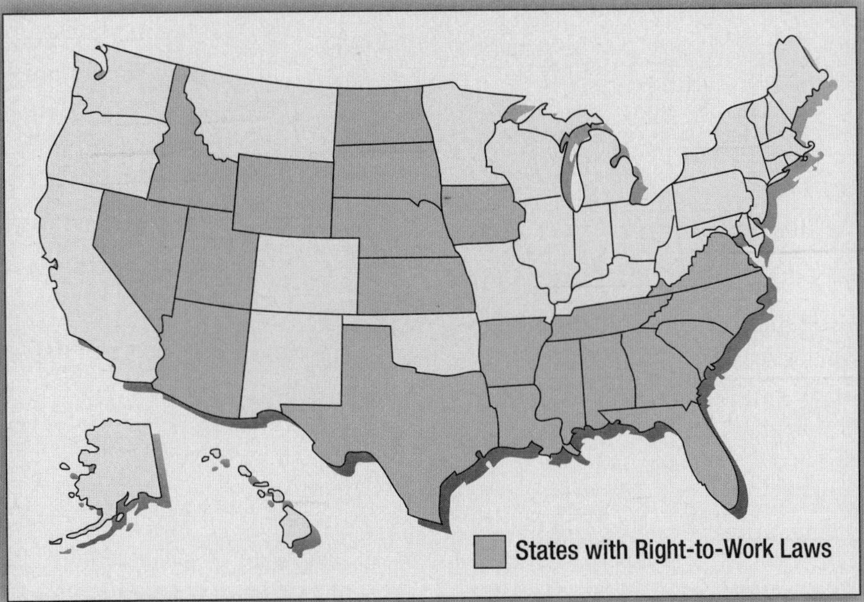

FIGURE 11.5
States with Right-to-Work Laws

States with Right-to-Work Laws

must make financial reports to their members and disclose their officers' salaries. The act also provides for a *cooling-off period*—an 80-day suspension of threatened strikes that the president of the United States and the courts find "imperil the national health and safety." During this period, employees are required to stay on the job. At the end of the 80 days, union members must vote by secret ballot on the latest company offer.

THE COLLECTIVE BARGAINING PROCESS

As its primary objective, a labor union seeks to improve wages, hours, and working conditions for its members. It works to achieve this goal primarily through collective bargaining, a process of negotiation between management and union representatives for the purpose of arriving at mutually acceptable terms for employees' wages and working conditions.

How Employees Form a Union

Before workers can form a union, they must conduct an organizing drive to collect the signatures of at least 30 percent of their fellow employees on special authorization cards. These cards designate the union as the employees' exclusive representative in bargaining with management. If the drive secures the required signatures, the union can then petition the National Labor Relations Board (NLRB) for an election. As Figure 11.6 describes, if more than 50 percent of the employees vote in favor of union representation, the union achieves certification. The "Clicks and Mortar" box describes a recent union organization effort in the high-tech industry.

The process of collecting signatures and campaigning for workers' votes can be long and difficult.

> **THEY SAID IT**
>
> *"Let us never negotiate out of fear. But let us never fear to negotiate."*
>
> JOHN F. KENNEDY (1917–1963)
> 35TH PRESIDENT OF THE
> UNITED STATES

BUSINESS DIRECTORY

➤ **closed shop** *employment policy, illegal in the United States, requiring a firm to hire only current union members.*

➤ **union shop** *employment policy requiring nonunion workers to join a union that represents a firm's workers within a specified period after being hired.*

➤ **agency shop** *employment policy allowing workers to reject union membership but requiring them to pay fees equal to union dues.*

➤ **open shop** *employment policy making union membership and dues voluntary for all workers.*

➤ **collective bargaining** *negotiation between management and union representatives concerning wages and working conditions for an entire group of workers.*

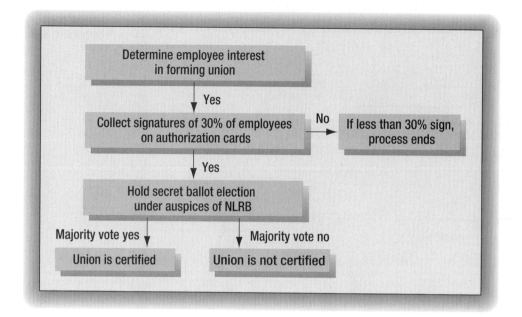

FIGURE 11.6
Steps in Starting a Union

Unions provide literature itemizing their benefits and encourage workers to attend meetings outside the workplace, while businesses usually hold meetings and prepare their own literature warning about the drawbacks of unionization. Over a five-year period, the Transport Workers Union of America conducted a campaign to organize the ramp and cargo workers of Delta Air Lines. During the campaign, Delta arranged to play antiunion videos continuously in the company's break room. In a vote held in 2000, the union resoundingly lost, a loss that was repeated in a second election held later the same year. Many workers were bitter about cutbacks the company had made before the beginning of the union drive. But many also feared that a unionized workforce would give the company an incentive to outsource more jobs and would take away Delta's advantage relative to its mostly unionized competitors.[11]

One of the largest successful organizing efforts in recent years involved over 9,000 workers who provide home health care services for Sacramento County, California. The county workers voted to join Local 250 of the SEIU after a seven-year organizing effort. According to the union, the employees had been earning just minimum wage with no employee benefits package. Of those who voted, 93 percent supported the union.[12]

Once a majority of a firm's workers accept a union as their representative, the NLRB certifies the union, and the firm's management must recognize it as the legal collective bargaining agent for all employees. This move sets the stage for union representatives and management to meet formally at the bargaining table to work out a collective bargaining agreement.

Bargaining Patterns

Bargaining patterns and the number of unions and employers involved vary for different industries and occupational categories. Most collective bargaining involves *single-plant, single-employer agreements*. In contrast, a *multiplant, single-employer agreement* applies to all plants operated by an employer.

Coalition bargaining involves negotiations between a coalition of several unions that represent the employees of one company. Recently, 24 unions negotiated an agreement for 64,000 workers employed by Kaiser Permanente, whose hospitals and clinics serve millions of patients in nearly a dozen states. The employees covered by the contract belong to a wide range of unions, including the Office and Professional

Amazon.com Battles a New Challenger: Organized Labor

Background. The new economy was hailed as a brave new world: boundaryless business transactions, new rules, sometimes no rules at all. But as we watch many of the dot.com companies fold, we are beginning to see some of the old rules of business re-emerge. One of those is that when workers begin to feel nervous about the security of their jobs or the way they may be treated by their employers, they turn to organized labor for help. Recently, the customer service employees of Amazon.com turned to an affiliate of the Communication Workers of America (CWA) for help in organizing a union.

What Happened? Amazon's customer service reps, unhappy with their wages (which start at $10 per hour), pressured to work overtime on short notice, and worried that their jobs might be moved to lower-paying regions of the country—not to mention the company's plan to outsource some of its jobs to India—sought assistance from the CWA. "This campaign should end the myth that high-tech workers in the new economy do not want to seek representation on the job and that unions are irrelevant in the 21st century," said Marcus Courtney, an organizer and cofounder of WashTech, a unit of CWA.

The Response. Amazon management immediately held employee meetings to discuss the unionizing efforts and point out the potential disadvantages of joining a union, particularly the possibility of a strike and the costs of dues and fines. In addition, management downplayed the organizing effort. "It's not the first time they have tried to organize. It's nothing new," said spokesperson Patty Smith. "We don't have unions at Amazon and [we] don't really need them.

Every employer is an owner at Amazon, since they own stock and can exercise their right to raise workplace issues or concerns [at] any time."

Today and Counting. Regardless of whether an organizing effort is successful, it's important to point out that Amazon's financial results could be hurt by unionization because the company—like many Internet companies—operates on extremely narrow margins. In other words, although Amazon might generate over $600 million in revenue in a single three-month period, only about $3 million in profits may be left over after expenses are paid. If a union contract stipulates certain benefits or wage increases, the company might not survive—putting employees out of work. Still, the right of Amazon workers to organize is protected by law, even in this brave new world.

QUESTIONS FOR CRITICAL THINKING
1. Do you think Amazon workers should unionize? Why or why not?
2. What ways might the CWA and Amazon.com work together to create a beneficial relationship for everyone involved?

Sources: "Amazon.com Union Bid," *CNNfn*, November 16, 2000; "Amazon Reacts Swiftly to Union Campaign," *WashTech News*, November 16, 2000, **www.washtech.org**, accessed March 16, 2001; "Amazon.com to Begin Outsourcing Customer Service Operations to India," *WashTech News*, September 7, 2000, **www.washtech.org**, accessed March 16, 2001.

Employees, United Food and Commercial Workers, and Professional and Technical Engineers, as well as health care providers in the SEIU.[13]

In *industrywide bargaining,* a single, national union engages in collective bargaining with several employers in a particular industry. The UAW and Canadian Auto Workers routinely conduct industrywide bargaining with the major U.S. automakers. In 1999 Ford announced plans to sell off its parts-making division, Visteon Automotive Systems. Concerned that the spinoff would leave Visteon employees outside its protection, the UAW removed Ford from the list of automakers included in contract negotiations. Not including Ford in the industrywide bargaining meant that the company would have little say in the terms of the resulting contract.[14]

In general, employers prefer to bargain with individual, local unions rather than dealing with coalitions of several unions. Small, separate unions are likely to exert less influence and power than a coalition would wield.

Bargaining Zone

Issues covered in bargaining agreements include wages, work hours, benefits, union activities and responsibilities, grievance procedures and arbitration, and employee rights and seniority. Unions can be creative in meeting the needs of their constituency. In New York City, Local 32B-J of the SEIU negotiated an agreement that provided employees with low-cost home computers plus training in how to use them. The local, which represents janitors and doormen in apartment buildings, negotiated with building owners for its members to receive vouchers that would enable them to buy computer systems with Internet access for $200. The union described the agreement as a way to close the "digital divide" between the haves and have-nots of the Internet age.[15]

As in all types of negotiations, the collective bargaining process features volleys of demands, proposals, and counterproposals that ultimately result in compromise and agreement. Negotiations begin with lists of initial demands by the union and management. These demands are simply starting points in the negotiations, and they rarely, if ever, become final agreements. Each party also identifies a final offer beyond which it will not bargain. If the union does not accept management's final offer, its members may strike. If management rejects the union's final offer, it may close the plant, move its operations, or bring new employees into its existing facility rather than agree to a settlement that would prevent profitable operation.

Between the union's and management's initial and final offers is the **bargaining zone,** an area within which both parties will likely come to agreement. Sometimes bargaining breaks down, however. The 18,000 engineers and technical workers at Boeing who are represented by the Society of Professional Engineering Employees in Aerospace (SPEEA) recently met resistance to their efforts to negotiate pay and benefit increases. So the members of the SPEEA, an AFL–CIO local, walked off the job. As workers stayed away over the course of several weeks, Boeing began to make concessions. Eventually, the negotiations ended with a three-year contract that met some of each side's demands. The company agreed to increase pay and bonuses and to pay the full cost of health insurance premiums. But the amount of the pay increases was less than what the union had asked for, and over half the bonus is tied to company performance.[16] As in this example, the final agreement depends on the negotiating skills and relative power of management and union representatives.

Union Contracts

A union contract typically covers a two- or three-year period. Such an agreement often represents days and even weeks of discussion, disagreement, compromise, and eventual agreement. Once the negotiators reach agreement, union members must vote to accept or reject the contract. If they reject it, union representatives may resume the bargaining process with management representatives, or the union members may strike to try to fulfill their demands.

Once ratified by the union membership, the contract becomes a legally binding agreement that governs all labor–management relations during the period specified. Union contracts typically cover such areas as wages and benefits, industrial relations, and the methods for settlement of labor–management disputes. Some contracts are only a few pages long, while others run more than 200 pages. Figure 11.7 indicates topics typically included in a standard union contract.

Some industries or occupations call for specific contract provisions. A contract for a local teachers' union included a guarantee of equipment and materials to help teachers include special-needs students in regular classrooms. A United Farm Workers contract for lettuce pickers included a modest housing allowance, formation of a labor–management safety committee, and limitations on the use of pesticides. More recently, the nationwide agreement between two dozen unions and the Kaiser Permanente managed-care organization called for establishment of a joint labor–management structure for making decisions about staffing levels, quality of care, and business planning.[17]

Wage Adjustments in Labor Contracts

In addition to setting wages during contract negotiations, labor and management representatives often agree to provisions for wage adjustments during the life of the contract. In the contract between Boeing and the SPEEA discussed earlier, Boeing agreed to give its engineers at least a 3 percent pay increase each year and to give its technical employees a 4 percent raise after one year and a 3 percent raise in the

FIGURE 11.7
Typical Provisions in a Union Contract

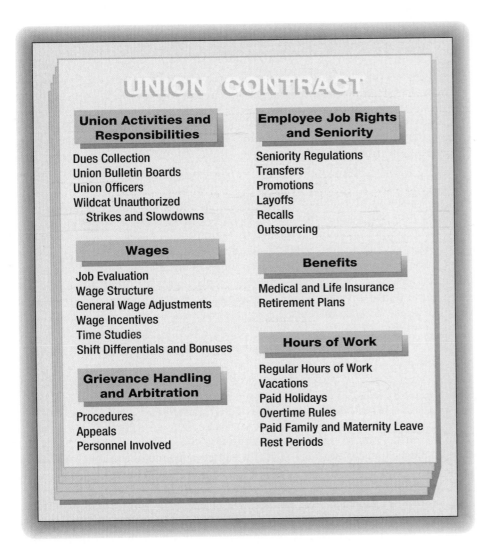

UNION CONTRACT

Union Activities and Responsibilities

Dues Collection
Union Bulletin Boards
Union Officers
Wildcat Unauthorized
    Strikes and Slowdowns

Wages

Job Evaluation
Wage Structure
General Wage Adjustments
Wage Incentives
Time Studies
Shift Differentials and Bonuses

Grievance Handling and Arbitration

Procedures
Appeals
Personnel Involved

Employee Job Rights and Seniority

Seniority Regulations
Transfers
Promotions
Layoffs
Recalls
Outsourcing

Benefits

Medical and Life Insurance
Retirement Plans

Hours of Work

Regular Hours of Work
Vacations
Paid Holidays
Overtime Rules
Paid Family and Maternity Leave
Rest Periods

second and third years. In addition, the company budgeted funds to reward individual employees for special skills or superior performance.[18] Some adjustments, such as cost-of-living adjustments (COLAs) and wage reopeners, can benefit employees; others, such as givebacks, can benefit the employer.

During periods of rising prices, unions attempt to include wage-increase demands during the time period covered by the contract by arguing that cost of living increases without an offsetting wage increase amounts to a cut in real wages and a drop in purchasing power. Consequently, unions and management must agree on an indicator for the cost of living. Usually, they settle on the *Consumer Price Index (CPI)*. The CPI, discussed in Chapter 3, tracks the costs of such expenses as housing, clothing, food, and automobiles. The union and management must negotiate the base period, the starting date, and the CPI configuration most appropriate for the contract's calculations. Management receives nothing in return for this wage increase, since it does not reflect a change in employees' productivity.

Approximately 30 percent of all organized workers are covered by contracts with **cost-of-living-adjustment (COLA)** clauses, also called *escalator clauses*. Such clauses are designed to protect the real incomes of workers during periods of inflation by increasing wages in proportion to increases in the CPI. A low inflation rate during the past few years has diminished the importance of COLA clauses in labor contracts. Still, COLA provisions are becoming more

BUSINESS DIRECTORY

➤ **bargaining zone**   *range of collective bargaining between conditions that induce a union to strike and those that induce management to close the plant.*

common, not only in labor agreements but also outside the collective bargaining arena. Benefits for social security recipients and military and civil service retirees now rise automatically with inflation. Millions of U.S. citizens now have their incomes adjusted by some automatic COLA.

Wage reopener clauses, another method of achieving wage adjustments, allow contract parties to renegotiate wages at a predetermined date during the life of the contract. Reopener clauses are written into almost one in ten labor contracts.

Attention of both union and nonunion employees in recent years has focused sharply on the nation's trade deficit and the ability of U.S. companies to compete in world markets. As one tangible response, unions in many major industries have allowed **givebacks**—wage and benefit concessions to help employers remain competitive and continue to provide jobs for union members. Givebacks may occur in industries fighting off competition from abroad—autos, rubber manufacturing, steel mills, cement, agricultural and construction equipment, and meatpacking. They have also occurred in the airlines, trucking, and telecommunications industries, where deregulation has forced firms to become more cost conscious to remain competitive.

Wage adjustments and givebacks raise controversies in other countries, too. Through the years, Germany's powerful unions have negotiated generous wage increases, making German workers the highest-paid employees in the world. But recently, German workers have made concessions to help improve their employers' productivity and global competitiveness and to stem the tide of job loss to lower-wage countries.

SETTLING UNION–MANAGEMENT DISPUTES

Although strikes make newspaper headlines, more than nine of every ten union–management negotiations result in signed agreements without work stoppages, despite conflicts such as those described in the "Clicks and Mortar" box. The courts are the most visible and familiar vehicles for dispute settlement, but negotiation settles most labor disputes. Both sides feel motivation to make a negotiation work, since so much time, money, and personnel costs are involved on both sides in a court settlement. Other dispute resolution mechanisms such as mediation, factfinding, and arbitration are quicker, cheaper, less complicated options that generate less publicity.

Mediation

When negotiations between union and management representatives break down, they sometimes resort to a voluntary process to settle disputes. This **mediation** process brings in a third party, called a *mediator,* to make recommendations for settling differences.

The Taft–Hartley Act requires union and management representatives to notify each other of desired changes in a union contract 60 days before it expires. They must also notify a special agency, the Federal Mediation and Conciliation Service, within 30 days after that time if workers have not accepted a new contract. The agency's staff of several hundred mediators assists in settling the union–management disagreements that affect interstate commerce. In addition, some states, among them New York, Pennsylvania, and California, operate their own labor mediation agencies. A federal mediator was involved in resolving the contract dispute between Boeing and the SPEEA.

Although the mediator does not serve as a decision maker, he or she can assist union and management representatives in reaching an agreement by offering suggestions and advice and by recommending compromise solutions. Because both sides must give their confidence and trust to the mediator, that person's impartiality is essential to the process. Community, social, or political leaders; attorneys; professors; and distinguished national figures often serve as mediators.

Uniting Workers at United

Background. Several years ago, the International Association of Machinists and Aerospace Workers (IAM) conducted a major drive to organize the 18,000 ticketing agents of United Airlines. United employees were receptive to unionization not only because of promised pay hikes but because they felt shortchanged by the company's Employee Stock Ownership Plan (ESOP), for which they had made concessions in pay.

What Happened? The ticket agents voted to join the union. United's 26,000 mechanics already belonged to the same union. The mechanics were leery that potential pay raises for the new union members would mean that less money would be left over for their own raises. In addition, since employees had been required to take less pay in order to join the ESOP, a change in wages would technically mean a change in the ESOP, which wouldn't expire for another two years. "It's very difficult to change the terms of the ESOP before it expires," noted United's chief operating officer John A. Edwardson.

The Response. The vote to unionize seemed to create conflicting demands on both sides. To renew the ESOP, United's unions would have to buy stock in order to maintain employee ownership in the company. But the employees did not want to make any more concessions—they wanted the money in their paychecks, not on paper. Although United's stock had quadrupled during the past few years, workers were worried about another airline industry slump. "Our members have money invested and can't get their hands on it. They're frustrated," remarked William L. Scheri, vice president of the IAM transportation unit. At the same time, neither the unions nor the workers wanted to give up the control that comes with majority stock ownership.

Today and Counting. Two years after the IAM union vote, the board of directors of the Air Line Pilots Association International (ALPA) voted on a drive to organize all airline pilots in the U.S. and Canada into one union. "This is a watershed event for airline pilots," said Captain Duane Woerth of ALPA. United management and ALPA reached an agreement shortly thereafter. In the meantime, United and IAM conducted negotiations for a new contract covering the company's mechanics. Issues included mandatory overtime during what the company called "operational emergencies." Experts agree that many of the conflicts between unions and management in the airline industry stem from the increase in passenger air travel during conditions in which jobs have been cut and workloads increased. Both sides are worried about a slowdown in the economy—and they want the money in their pockets now.

QUESTIONS FOR CRITICAL THINKING
1. In what ways might a mediator help resolve some of the conflicts at United?
2. Do you think that uniting American and Canadian pilots under one union is a beneficial move for the industry? For the pilots? Why or why not?

Sources: "United–ALPA 2000 Agreement—Summary," United Airlines Web site, **www.ual.com**, accessed January 29, 2001; "ALPA Takes Initiatives to Unite Pilots Under One Union," *PR Newswire*, October 19, 2000; Michael Arndt and Aaron Bernstein, "From Milestone to Millstone," *Business Week*, March 20, 2000, pp. 120–122.

Arbitration

When parties cannot resolve disputes voluntarily through mediation, they begin the process of **arbitration**—bringing in an impartial third party called an *arbitrator* to render a binding decision in the dispute. Both union members and management must approve the impartial third party, and he or she renders a legally enforceable decision. In essence, the arbitrator acts as a judge, making a decision after listening to both sides of the argument. In *voluntary arbitration*, both union and management representatives decide to present their unresolved issues to an impartial third party. Arbitration provisions appear in most union contracts to resolve issues on which union and management representatives fail to agree.

Occasionally, a third party, usually the federal government, will require management and labor to submit to *compulsory arbitration*. Although it remains rare in the U.S., considerable interest focuses on compulsory arbitration as a means of eliminating prolonged strikes in major industries that threaten to disrupt the economy.

GRIEVANCE PROCEDURES

A union contract guides relations between the firm's management and its employees and states the rights of each party. No contract, regardless of how detailed it is, can eliminate the possibility of later disagreement, though. Differences of opinion may

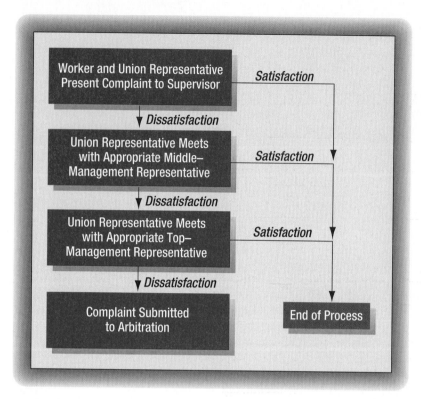

FIGURE 11.8
Steps in the Grievance Procedure

arise on how to interpret a particular clause in the contract, for example. Management could interpret a contract's layoff policy based on seniority for each work shift. The union could see it as based on the seniority of all employees. Over half of the contract disagreements that occur each year involve employee suspensions, transfers, and terminations; seniority; and vacation and work schedules.

Such a difference can generate a **grievance**, a complaint, by a single worker or the entire union, that management is violating some provision of the union contract. Because grievance handling is the primary source of contact between union officials and management during periods between contract negotiations, the resolution of grievances plays a major role in the parties' relationship.

Since grievances are likely to occur over such matters as transfers, work assignments, and seniority, almost all union contracts require that workers submit these complaints to formal grievance procedures. Figure 11.8 shows the five steps in a typical grievance procedure. The employee first submits the grievance to the immediate supervisor through the shop steward, the union's representative in that particular unit of the organization. If the supervisor solves the problem, it goes no further. If this first step does not produce a satisfactory agreement, however, a higher union official may take the grievance to a higher manager. If the highest company officer cannot settle the grievance, an outside arbitrator makes a final, binding decision.

A recent high-profile grievance procedure involved the umpires in Major League Baseball. In a contract dispute with team owners, Richie Phillips, the negotiator for the Major League Umpires Association (MLUA), called on members to protest with a mass resignation. But only 22 umpires resigned, and team owners accepted their resignations and quickly hired 25 replacements. Phillips and the MLUA appealed the action to an arbitrator, saying the umpires had been wrongly terminated in an effort to break the union. After months of testimony by both sides, the umpires eventually called Phillips and the MLUA out for their handling of the negotiations. They held an election and voted in a new union, the World Umpires Association, giving the old union and its 22 members few options.[19]

COMPETITIVE TACTICS OF UNIONS AND MANAGEMENT

Although labor and management settle most differences through the collective bargaining process or through formal grievance procedures, both unions and management occasionally resort to various tactics to make their demands known.

Union Tactics

The chief tactics of unions are strikes, picketing, and boycotts. In a **strike** or *walkout,* one of the most effective tools of the labor union, employees stop work until a dispute has been settled or a contract signed. Since a company does not pay striking workers, the union generally establishes a fund to provide workers' wages, allowing them to continue striking without financial hardship. During the strike by its engineers and technical workers, Boeing was unable to make production and financial targets because it lacked the skilled workers needed to resolve production problems. Able to deliver only a few completed airplanes, the company felt pressured to make concessions during contract talks.

Although the power to strike represents unions' ultimate weapon, they do not wield it lightly. The number of strikes has diminished significantly over recent decades. In 1975, over 3,000 strikes took place. In 1982, the number of major strikes dropped below 100, and that number hasn't been reached since then. The U.S. Department of Labor reported only 17 major work stoppages during 2000, the lowest number since it began keeping track.[20]

Not all union members can resort to strikes or threats of strikes. Even though federal employees have been permitted to join unions and bargain collectively since 1962, they are not allowed to strike. Each federal civilian employee takes a no-strike pledge when hired. In 1981, when the Professional Air Traffic Controllers union went on strike, President Ronald Reagan fired more than 11,000 workers and replaced them with nonunion employees, contending that strikes by public employees are not in the public's best interest. In some instances, laws prohibit strikes by state and municipal employees. In these cases, workers such as police officers and firefighters, sanitation workers, hospital employees, and even prison guards who want to use work stoppages to pressure management to increase pay or other benefits may instead call in sick. Police strikes have come to be known as the *blue flu*.

Picketing—workers marching at the entrances of the employer's plant as a public protest against some management practice—gives unions another effective way to apply pressure. As long as picketing does not involve violence or intimidation, it is protected under the U.S. Constitution as free speech. Picketing may accompany a strike, or it may protest alleged unfair labor practices. When the law firm Jackson & Lewis hosted a seminar titled "How to Stay Union-Free" in Chicago, 300 union members and community activists staged a picket line outside the doors of the facility where the seminar was taking place. The picketing resulted in substantial media coverage and caused seminar participants to exit through the back door.[21]

Because union workers usually refuse to cross picket lines maintained by other union members, the picketed firm may be unable to obtain deliveries and other services. At Boeing, the unionized machinists supported the strike by engineers and other white-collar technical workers. Delivery companies including UPS also operate under union contracts, so it would also be difficult to obtain such services during the course of a strike.

As defined earlier, a boycott is an organized attempt to keep the public from purchasing the goods or services of a firm. Some unions have organized remarkably successful boycotts, and some unions even fine members who defy primary boycotts. The AFL–CIO endorses national boycotts when its member unions initiate them on behalf of a broader effort for their members. The organization's Union Label and Service Trades Department publishes a "Don't Buy" list of the boycotted goods and services and makes the list available at its Union Label Web site (http://unionlabel.org/). One of the most famous boycotts was the United Farm Workers' 16-year boycott of California table grapes, which ended in 2000 after unions persuaded farmers to eliminate or restrict use of five pesticides.[22]

Although the Taft–Hartley Act outlaws coercive secondary boycotts, Supreme Court rulings have significantly expanded the rights of unions to use this weapon. Although unions may not picket a firm to force it to stop dealing with another company involved in a labor dispute, the court protects other forms of expression, such as distributing handbills at the site of the first firm.

Management Tactics

Management has its own tactics for dealing with organized labor. In the past, firms have used the **lockout**— in effect, a management strike to bring pressure on union members by closing the firm. Firms rarely lock

BUSINESS DIRECTORY

➤ **grievance** *employee or union complaint that management is violating some provision of the union contract.*

➤ **strike** *temporary work stoppage by employees until a dispute is settled or a contract signed.*

➤ **picketing** *workers marching at a plant entrance to protest some management practice.*

out workers today unless a union strike has partially shut down a plant. However, Crown Petroleum Corp.'s 1996 decision to lock out more than 250 workers at its Pasadena, Texas, refinery contributed to a standoff that has persisted for several years. In 2000, the Crown Petroleum workers rejected a tentative contract, and the Paper Allied–Industrial Chemical & Energy Workers International Union intensified an effort to boycott Crown.[23]

Managers at organizations ranging from International Paper Co. to Major League Baseball have resorted to replacing striking workers with **strikebreakers,** nonunion workers who cross picket lines to fill the jobs of striking workers. Firms can easily recruit strikebreakers in high-status fields such as professional sports and in high-paying industries located in areas of high unemployment. Yet even in favorable conditions, management frequently encounters difficulties in securing sufficient numbers of replacement workers with required skills. Some employers have resorted to reassigning supervisory personnel and other nonunion employees to continue operations during strikes.

Management sometimes obtains an **injunction**—a court order prohibiting some practice—to prevent excessive picketing or certain unfair union practices. Before passage of the Norris–La Guardia Act, firms frequently used injunctions to prohibit all types of strikes. Since then, court orders have been limited to restraining violence, restricting picketing, and preventing damage to company property.

Some employers have formed **employers' associations** to cooperate in their efforts and present a united front in dealing with labor unions. Employers' associations may even act as negotiators for individual employers who want to reach agreements with labor unions. An industry characterized by many small firms and a single large union may follow an increasing tendency for industrywide bargaining between the union and a single representative of the industry's employers. Building contractors may bargain as a group with construction unions, for example. Although they do not negotiate contracts, the National Association of Manufacturers and the U.S. Chamber of Commerce are examples of employers' associations. Both groups promote the views of their members on key issues.

THE TREND TOWARD UNION–MANAGEMENT COOPERATION

The hostile and antagonistic attitudes that have sometimes characterized labor–management relationships are changing. As described in Chapter 10, companies should treat employees as valuable human resources and adopt policies designed to empower them. Some unions and employers are developing partner relationships based on the belief that when the company prospers, so do its employees. General Motors Corp. takes this viewpoint in Figure 11.9, using the slogan, "From professional grade people come professional grade trucks. We are professional grade."

Cooperation can take various forms. Some local teachers' unions have teamed with school management in an effort to satisfy the public's demands for quality improvements in schools. With a focus on raising academic standards, restructuring schools, and improving quality in education, teachers and administrators are transforming collective bargaining into collaborative negotiations. At Delphi Automotive Systems Corp., workers have abandoned their past reliance on strikes as a bargaining tool to help the company compete with nonunion suppliers. Together, union representatives and management have developed new work arrangements designed to improve productivity. They replaced a system in which workers waited for materials to come to them with an arrangement where workers move from one workstation to another.[24]

Among businesses, one reason for greater cooperation is the trend toward employee ownership, described in Chapter 10. Among the nongovernment workforce, over 15 percent of employees participate in ESOPs or broad-based stock option plans.[25] When employees own a share of the company where they work, their

FIGURE 11.9
GMC: Employees as Valued Resources

employer's success contributes to their own well-being. In addition, workers see that globalization has increased the competitive threats facing their employers. During the 1970s and 1980s, auto workers grew increasingly concerned that Japanese-made automobiles were claiming a growing market share. They knew, too, that unless the firms where they worked became more competitive, they could lose their jobs to the foreign companies. Ford, General Motors, and Chrysler all strengthened that concern by setting up profit-sharing plans to pay bonuses based on company performance. The average hourly worker who has been with Chrysler, now part of DaimlerChrysler, since it set up its plan has earned over $37,000 in profit-sharing payments.[26]

EMPLOYEE–MANAGEMENT RELATIONS IN NONUNION ORGANIZATIONS

Although unionization is an assumption in almost any discussion of labor–management relations, most private-sector employees do not belong to unions. Small businesses often employ nonunion workers. Another nonunionized segment of the U.S. labor force consists of managerial employees. Other nonunion employees work in industries where organized labor has never developed strength. Still other nonunion employees have simply rejected attempts to establish unions in their workplaces.

At nonunion companies, management often chooses to offer a compensation and benefit structure comparable to those of unionized firms in the area. Willingness to offer comparable wages and working conditions coupled with effective communications, emphasis on promotions from within, employee empowerment, and employee

FIGURE 11.10
Grievance Programs for Nonunion Workers

Alternative dispute resolution program

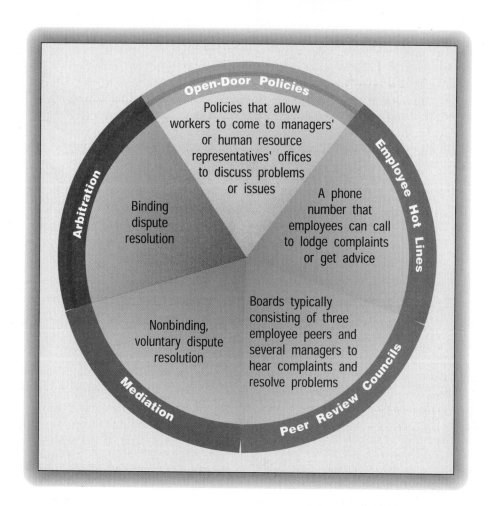

participation in goal setting and grievance handling may help an employer avert unionization. Satisfied workers may conclude that they would receive few additional benefits for the union dues they would have to pay. In fact, many observers argue that the *threat* of joining a union gives nonunion employees an effective tool in securing desired wages, benefits, and working conditions.

Grievance Programs for Nonunion Employees

Even without a union, workers may have formal avenues for resolving grievances. Employees who believe they have suffered discrimination, sexual harassment, dismissal without cause, or inadequate promotion opportunities can file lawsuits against their firms or file charges with the U.S. Equal Employment Opportunity Commission or a state human rights commission. These actions, however, can lead to expensive and lengthy proceedings.

The need for worker protection provided by labor unions diminishes considerably in firms that encourage employees to communicate their complaints through programs designed to resolve grievances. A growing number of businesses and not-for-profits have instituted **alternative dispute resolution programs.** As Figure 11.10 points out, these programs vary but usually include open-door policies, employee hot lines, peer-review councils, mediation, and arbitration. An *open-door policy* assures employees that they can discuss issues with supervisors or other managers or the human resource department. An *employee hot line* gives employees the opportunity to call a phone number and air a complaint or get advice on how to file a formal complaint. Some firms provide employees with a phone number so they can talk confidentially to someone outside the firm about the grievance process. *Mediation* and *arbitration* work in much the same way as they do in unionized organizations, with mediation resulting in a nonbinding solution and arbitration in a binding solution. **Peer-review boards** typically consist of three employee peers and several management representatives. Peer review can build an open, trusting atmosphere that deters union organizing and, perhaps most importantly, stems costly legal claims for wrongful discharge, discrimination, and harassment.

An effective grievance procedure generally includes the following elements:

- The grievance procedure should follow written policies and procedures, and every employee should receive a copy.

- Grievances should be settled at the lowest possible organizational level, preferably between the dissatisfied employee and the supervisor.

- The grievance procedure should follow a series of distinct steps; each stage should exhaust all possible solutions before progressing to the next step.

Job Security in Nonunion Companies

Job security has always been a primary motivation for workers to form or join labor unions. Today, however, not even unions can guarantee their members lifetime job security.

Recognizing that job security is a major concern, firms needing to reduce staffing levels may try to provide alternatives to layoffs. Some companies offer incentives for early retirement and resignation. These workforce reductions have separated hundreds of thousands of workers over the past few years, allowing companies to cut staff without resorting to layoffs. Although such a program may cost the employer some of its most highly qualified and experienced workers, the change often replaces older workers with younger employees who are likely to receive lower wages. At the same time, rewarding senior employees with early retirement bonuses is likely to enhance overall employee morale, in contrast to the destructive effects of a decision to lay off workers.

CHALLENGES FACING ORGANIZED LABOR

Throughout the world, unions are representing a declining share of the workforce. The reasons for the decline vary from country to country, but several factors are significant in industrialized nations: downsizing by large, unionized firms to improve global competitiveness; a shift in favor of free-market ideologies; and the growth of the information economy.

With global competition forcing companies to improve their efficiency and productivity, many union jobs have been replaced by technology such as automated production facilities. Employers are also trying to minimize their labor costs by hiring temporary, part-time, and contract workers, who tend not to be union members, and by outsourcing work to nonunion suppliers. Membership in the UAW has declined as the industry shifts from a model in which automobile companies owned the parts-making operations into one in which they outsource more activities. In recent years, auto assembly plants, largely unionized, have lost 90,000 jobs, while parts producers—generally nonunion companies—have added 40,000 jobs. In addition, foreign-owned auto plants located in the U.S. tend not to be unionized.[27]

At Wal-Mart's Jacksonville, Texas, store, meat cutter Maurice Miller led an organizing campaign after the store did not enroll him in a management-training program. The United Food and Commercial Workers Union won the vote, but a week later, Wal-Mart announced that it would begin purchasing prepackaged meat from a meatpacker, IBP Inc. Wal-Mart said the decision had to do with new technology, not the union activity, and that meatpackers were welcome to keep working at the store, where their jobs would primarily involve putting meat on the shelves.[28]

These challenges are especially great because of the political trend in favor of worldwide free trade. Free-trade policies make it easier for companies to cut costs by arranging to have work performed by suppliers or employees in countries with lower wages and limited employee benefits. Unions have a weaker bargaining position because they know that a company can shift operations overseas rather than meet the union's demands. The current trend toward moving and restructuring operations to improve productivity has created a climate in which a sizable share of American workers express insecurity about their future. Companies are more likely to threaten to move or shut down operations where unions are trying to organize, and workers tend to believe those threats. A Cornell University study found that unions were much less likely to win an election if the employer threatened plant closings. Directly making such a threat is against U.S. labor laws, but the researchers identified instances in which companies merely hinted at the possibility of plant closings, say, by describing other facilities that had shut down following unionization.[29]

Today's workplace is very different from the workplaces in which early unions emerged. Unions grew by giving industrial workers a voice in decisions about their wages and working conditions. As the U.S., Western Europe, and Japan have shifted from a manufacturing economy to an information and service economy, the makeup of the workforce has become less favorable for unions. Although unions have retained their strength in manufacturing industries such as automotive, steel, and aerospace, they have been slow to organize employees in fast-growing, high-tech industries such as computers and electronics and in service industries such as financial services. Employees in these industries often think of themselves as professionals with unique skill sets they can take elsewhere if they are not satisfied with what their employer offers. Today, many employers value their employees as their most important assets, train them to boost productivity, involve them in decision making, and motivate them with highly competitive wages, benefits, and flexible work hours.

INITIATIVES TO REBUILD UNIONS

Despite the challenges facing unions, union leaders cite favorable public opinion to make a case that there is a future role for organized labor. Polls commissioned by the AFL–CIO have found that although Americans' attitudes toward unions are mixed, the share of people who have positive attitudes toward unions is growing. Also, the percentage of respondents reporting negative attitudes has shrunk from one in three Americans in the mid-1980s to just one in four today. In addition, when asked if they would vote for a union if an election were held at their workplace, the share of nonunion workers who say they would vote in favor of a union has been rising, recently reaching 43 percent.[30]

A few years ago, AFL–CIO president John Sweeney called on the organization's member unions to spend 30 percent of their budget on organizing. So far, most of the unions have not met the challenge, but some, including the Hotel Employees and Restaurant Employees International and United Steelworkers of America, have made progress. The United Brotherhood of Carpenters has begun spending half its budget on organizing.[31] Organizing efforts can take years, but the AFL–CIO sees hope in the fact that at the start of the 21st century the union enjoyed its largest annual increase in members in two decades. In a single year, over 150,000 workers joined the SEIU. Almost 50,000 workers joined the International Brotherhood of Electrical Workers, and the same number joined the UAW.[32] The UAW's membership is broader than its name suggests. UAW workers include those who assemble the Selmer and Bach band instruments shown in Figure 11.11.[33] Just as the global economy provides opportunities as well as challenges to businesses, it provides jobs for workers.

The AFL–CIO has backed its organizing efforts with advertising designed to create a more appealing image of unions than the traditional pictures of striking factory workers.[34] The federation also has formed a separate department for organizing workers and has established programs to involve students and retired workers in organizing activities.

Another of the AFL–CIO's strategies to strengthen labor unions is coordinating multiunion membership drives. In the past, individual unions have organized their own campaigns. Today, different unions are joining forces to stage recruitment drives targeted at workers in specific cities or industries. In addition, they are encouraging members to align with the union that can best present a unified front in a particular industry. The SEIU and the Hotel Employees and Restaurant Employees (HERE) unions are cooperating, with HERE focusing on hotel workers and gaming employees, while SEIU is organizing building services and health care workers. Recently, 2,000 Disney World employees switched from an SEIU local to HERE in keeping with this strategy. The switch put them into locals with about 13,000 members who work in Orlando-area theme parks, hotels, and restaurants. The unions hope to gain strength from collaborating rather than competing for members.[35]

To increase their membership, unions are focusing their organizing efforts on unskilled, low-wage service workers in the health care and lodging industries and on agricultural workers. Instead of simply passing out organizing literature, they visit workers at their homes and in the fields to discuss forming unions. Organizers are also targeting professionals such as doctors and the growing number of skilled contingency workers. The CWA has been conducting organizing efforts among part-time employees of Microsoft, and it helped IBM employees fend off changes in that company's pension plan, as described in the "Business Hits and Misses" box. The Graduate Student Employee Action Coalition organized teaching assistants at the University of Washington.

On yet another front, unions are using so-called *corporate campaigns* to pressure employers to accept unions. In such a campaign, a union contacts an employer's suppliers, customers, creditors, stockholders, and board members to rally support for its cause. Through their pension fund investments, unions are stockholders in many corporations. The AFL–CIO formed an investments department to monitor union assets, giving unions the opportunity to suggest corporate board members and prepare shareholder resolutions that benefit their members.

U.S. unions are also developing a role in the world economy. The AFL–CIO has taken actions to improve the conditions facing workers outside the U.S. Its lobbyists have pressed for debt relief in the underdeveloped nations, and it is cooperating with the ILO in its efforts to eradicate child labor. Presumably, as working conditions improve in other countries, businesses will have less incentive to find cheap labor by moving work overseas, as discussed in the "Solving an Ethical Controversy" box. In addition, the AFL–CIO has supported amnesty for millions of undocumented immigrant workers. The organization had formerly taken the stance that immigrants

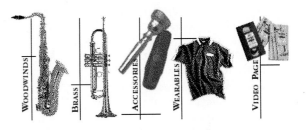

FIGURE 11.11
Selmer Woodwinds/Bach Brass Instrument Assemblers: UAW Members in Unlikely Places

IBM has stumbled before and recovered its balance. But recently it stumbled again, this time in its effort to convert employees to the controversial cash-balance pension plan, which many experts say leaves older workers at a distinct disadvantage when it comes time to collect their pensions. But the pension plan actually created a bigger headache for Big Blue: a serious effort by the CWA to organize IBM employees. For decades, no union was able to crack the IBM organization, perhaps because the company was successful at keeping employees happy, despite massive layoffs and corporate downsizing during the 1990s. But now IBM's 140,000 workers had a cause: their retirement savings. And the CWA cited other potential grievances: a growing workforce of "permanent" temporary workers who did not receive benefits, a reduction in medical benefits, the core of employees who annually receive pay raises regardless of performance, and elimination of double time for working Sundays.

The CWA initially set up worker committees in ten locations around the country in order to recruit potential union members. Eventually, these activists formed a nationally affiliated organization "to address workplace concerns at IBM and to organize for eventual union recognition and bargaining rights at the technology giant." Although IBM insisted that union organizing activity was not widespread throughout the company, within several months management had restored some pension options to some workers. CWA President Morton Bahr remarked at a press conference, "We're convinced that the protests, the meetings, the increased communications among IBM employees nationwide, and the growing talk of a need for a union at IBM are exactly what caused the company to announce it was reversing course."

The battle lines were clearly drawn. Management at IBM insisted that it must continue with its benefits overhaul to remain competitive in an industry where it is not uncommon for employers to offer either less expensive 401(k) retirement plans or no pension. In fact, IBM employees had become accustomed to pension benefits that many similar companies don't provide at all. Yet the reduction of these benefits seemed to many to be an attack on their rights as employees, and any trust they had in their employer was destroyed in one fell swoop. "I have always been against unions," said Calvin Aranson, a 25-year veteran at IBM's Global Services unit in Portland, Oregon. "[But] like a lot of IBM employees, I have come to the conclusion that, when dealing with IBM, a union is the only solution."

Similarly, IBM worker Garrett Lanzy noted: "It's obvious that the only way to get IBM executives to truly listen to employees is through a legally binding contract that is negotiated through collective bargaining. It's clearer than ever that a union is the only way to attain this goal."

QUESTIONS FOR CRITICAL THINKING

1. What type of union shop do you think would be most effective—for both sides—at IBM? Why?
2. If an organizing drive is successful, what two or three steps might IBM management take to rebuild a positive relationship with its employees?

Sources: "Alliance at IBM," IBM Employees' Union/Communication Workers of America Web site, **www.allianceibm.org,** accessed March 11, 2001; Ira Sager and Aaron Bernstein, "Look for the Union Label—At IBM?" *Business Week,* October 11, 1999, p. 48; "IBM Employees and CWA Launch Alliance@IBM," *CWA News,* October 1999.

would drive down U.S. workers' wages, but its new policy recognizes that many of its own members are immigrants.[36] This policy accompanies an effort to target immigrant populations in union organizing campaigns. From Mexican construction workers in the Northwest to Haitian cab drivers in the Northeast, some of the largest growth in the ranks of laborers is among immigrants. Organizing these workers requires the ability to cross language and cultural barriers, including fears that some workers bring from their experiences in their countries of origin. In Los Angeles, however, the SEIU recently won a campaign to represent 75,000 home health care workers; half of them are immigrants to the United States.[37]

WHAT'S AHEAD

Most union members are employees who perform the basic work of producing and delivering goods and services. In today's marketplace, customers expect these goods and services to be of the highest value for the price. Companies ensure this value by developing efficient systems for producing goods and services, as well as for maintaining high quality. The next chapter covers the ways in which businesses produce world-class goods and services.

SOLVING AN ETHICAL CONTROVERSY

By definition, American unions and the global economy seem to be completely at odds with each other. On the one hand, organized labor has historically opposed free trade in an effort to protect the jobs of American workers. On the other, the global economy encourages boundaryless business transactions, with much freer trade than anyone had imagined even a few decades ago. Still, in order to survive, organized labor believes it must find a way to function in this new world while still protecting its workers.

Can organized labor participate in the global economy and still oppose free trade?

PRO

1. Union leaders assert that they don't oppose free trade itself, just policies that exploit low-cost labor overseas at the expense of American workers. "There's no turning back the clock on the global economy," notes Terry Shea, assistant to AFL–CIO president John Sweeney. "But we don't see any reason why you can't create a rules-based global economy."
2. The AFL–CIO has already voted to revise its tough policies against illegal immigrants working in the U.S. and their employers. The union called for blanket amnesty for an estimated 5 million such workers.
3. American unions are now working together with the ILO to remove underage children from garment factories and coffee fields.

CON

1. "As long as they [unions] are marching to oppose free trade, it kind of stretches credibility for them to talk about freedom for foreign workers," argues U.S. Chamber of Commerce spokesman Frank Coleman.
2. AFL–CIO president John Sweeney admits that foreign governments do not trust the motives of American organized labor. "It became clear to me that there was a lack of trust, and that we had to do something about it," he notes.
3. As the U.S. attempts to establish normal trade relations with some of the world's poorest countries such as those in Africa, organized labor continues to object.

SUMMARY

The global economy illustrates how small the world is—and how large and complex it is. Some experts believe that American organized labor has no place in the new economy; others believe that unions must simply find a way to adapt. Michael Baroody, senior vice president at the National Association of Manufacturers, maintains that the problem lies in labor's view of its own membership. "It starts from a premise that our workers can't compete with workers around the world," he explains. And he argues that this premise is "wrong."

Sources: Daniel T. Griswold, "Free Trade Empowers Americans to Better Their Lives," Cato Institute's Center for Trade Policy Studies, **www. freetrade.org/pubs,** accessed March 10, 2001; Glenn Burkins, "Labor Reaches Out to Global Economy," *The Wall Street Journal,* April 11, 2000, pp. A2, A6; "Trade, Labor, and the Environment: Preview of the IMF/World Bank Meetings," April 11, 2000, accessed at the Brookings Institution Web site, **www.brook.edu.**

➤ Summary of Learning Goals

1. Summarize the history of labor unions and list their primary goals.

Attempts to form labor unions began in the 19th century when workers united to improve their pay and working conditions. Two types of unions emerged: Craft unions joined skilled workers in crafts or trades; industrial unions joined workers from different occupations in the same industry. Unions grew slowly until 1935. From 1935 to 1955, they experienced their greatest period of growth. Since then union membership has steadily declined.

2. Describe the structure of organized labor.

Unions have a hierarchical structure. At the base is the local union that operates in a given geographic area. Many local unions constitute a national union. An international union joins members from multiple countries. At the top of the hierarchy is the federation, an association such as the AFL–CIO, which consists of many national and international unions.

3. Identify the major federal laws that affect labor unions and explain the key provisions of each law.

The Norris–La Guardia Act of 1932 protects unions by reducing management's ability to stop union activities. The National Labor Relations Act (Wagner Act) of 1935 requires management to bargain collectively with elected employee representatives and outlaws a number of unfair management practices. The Fair Labor Standards Act of 1938 set a federal minimum wage and outlawed child labor. In efforts to balance power between labor and management, the Taft–Hartley Act of 1947 and the Landrum–Griffin Act of 1959 were passed to outlaw a number of unfair labor practices of unions and employers. The Plant-Closing Notification Act of 1988 requires any employer with more than 100 employees to give

60 days' notice before a plant shutdown or mass layoff.

4. **Explain the process of forming unions, the way they achieve goals through collective bargaining, and the issues typically addressed in union contracts.**

Employees form a union by initiating an organizing drive, collecting signatures of 30 percent or more of their fellow workers, and petitioning the National Labor Relations Board for an election. The union is certified if it receives votes from more than 50 percent of the employees. Union representatives and employers negotiate their demands during collective bargaining sessions. The agreement they reach is set forth in a contract that is accepted or rejected by a vote of union members. Contracts cover wages and benefits, working conditions, grievance handling and arbitration, union activities and responsibilities, and employee rights and seniority.

5. **Describe the roles played by mediators and arbitrators in labor negotiations.**

Mediators and arbitrators assist negotiations. A mediator offers advice and makes recommendations. An arbitrator listens to both sides and then makes a decision that becomes binding for both parties.

6. **Identify the steps in the union grievance process.**

An employee with a complaint and a union representative (the shop steward) present the grievance to a supervisor. If this contact fails to resolve the dispute, union representatives meet with higher-level managers. If no satisfactory agreement is reached, the grievance is submitted to an arbitrator.

7. **Outline the tactics of labor and management in conflicts between them.**

Although most differences between labor and management are settled through the collective bargaining or grievance processes, both unions and management have other ways to make their demands known. The chief tactics of unions are the strike, picketing, and the boycott. Management's weapons are hiring strikebreakers, petitioning courts for injunctions, locking out workers, and forming employers' associations.

8. **Describe how unions and employers are developing partner relationships.**

Some unions and employers are teaming up to develop cooperative partnerships such as training programs and committees to help make companies more competitive in the global economy. These partnerships improve workers' job security and employers' competitiveness. Increasing employee ownership contributes to employees' desire to participate in such partnerships.

9. **Discuss employee–employer relationships in non-union firms.**

Employees in many small firms and many occupational groups, including managers, are not union members. Employers in nonunion settings try to prevent unionization by satisfying employees with competitive wages and benefits. Employers help employees to resolve grievances through a number of resolution practices including open-door policies, employee hot lines, peer-review boards, mediation, and arbitration. Some employers establish no-layoff guarantees. Some employers that reduce their workforces offer employees incentives for early retirement and resignation, rather than using involuntary layoffs.

10. **Explain the challenges facing labor unions and strategies currently being used to rebuild union membership.**

A number of factors have contributed to the decline in union membership, including the loss of traditionally unionized jobs in the manufacturing sector, greater international competition, and employers' increasing use of temporary and contract workers. Unions' growth strategies include changing the structure of unions to improve their efficiency and empower local union members, committing more financial resources to organizing, cooperating in organizing activities, and forming alliances with different organizations. Unions are trying to rebuild their membership base by organizing both professional and unskilled workers in service industries, as well as immigrant workers.

Business Terms You Need to Know

labor union 400
closed shop 404
union shop 404
agency shop 404
open shop 404

collective bargaining 405
bargaining zone 408
grievance 412
strike 412
picketing 413

Other Important Business Terms

American Federation of Labor (AFL) 400	federation 402	lockout 413
Congress of Industrial Organizations (CIO) 400	right-to-work law 404	strikebreaker 414
	boycott 404	injunction 414
national union 401	cost-of-living adjustment (COLA) 409	employers' association 414
local union 401	giveback 410	alternative dispute resolution program 416
international union 402	mediation 410	peer-review board 417
	arbitration 411	

➤ Review Questions

1. What is a labor union? Define and describe briefly the two different types of labor unions.

2. According to the chapter discussion and Figure 11.3, who belongs to unions today?

3. Define and describe briefly the four types of union "shops." How do state right-to-work laws, under the Taft–Hartley Act, affect the establishment of these shops?

4. How is a union formed?

5. What role does a mediator play in negotiations between union and management representatives? How is this role different from that of an arbitrator?

6. What are the chief tactics unions use against management? Are these usually effective? Why or why not?

7. What are the chief tactics management uses against organized labor? Are these usually effective? Why or why not?

8. What are some ways in which union and management cooperate with each other?

9. In what ways are employee–management relations in nonunion organizations similar to those in unionized organizations? In what ways might they be different?

10. What major challenges are unions facing in their efforts to rebuild their membership? Which union strategies do you think will be most effective in gaining new members?

➤ Questions for Critical Thinking

1. What was your view of unions before reading and studying this chapter? What is it now? Has it changed at all? Why or why not?

2. Access the Web site of one of the large national or international unions such as the National Education Association, Teamsters, or International Association of Machinists and Aerospace Workers. At the site, learn what you can about the union's mission and write a brief summary of it.

3. Do you agree with workers such as teachers and airline pilots who strike? Why or why not?

4. Do you agree with the AFL–CIO's Union Label and Service Trades Department's practice of publishing a "Don't Buy" list of boycotted goods and services? Why or why not?

5. Are you optimistic about the trend toward union–employer partnerships? Why or why not?

➤ Experiential Exercise

Background: Every new year begins with professional baseball players filing for salary arbitration, followed by arbitration hearings during the first three weeks in February. The data indicate that the very act of filing for arbitration speeds up the salary negotiation process between the individual players and their clubs. From 1988 to 2000 only 13 percent of the players who filed for arbitration went through the entire arbitration process, while the remaining 87 percent settled their salary differences with their clubs without the use of arbitration hearings.

Among the 63 players who exchanged arbitration figures with their clubs in early 2001 was Yankee shortstop Derek Jeter, with Jeter asking for $18.5 million and the Yankees offering $14.25 million. Jeter's case for the higher salary figure was greatly bolstered by two earlier free-agent signings by players of similar caliber. All-Star shortstop Alex Rodriguez signed a record ten-year, $252 million contract with the Texas Rangers, and slugging outfielder Manny Ramirez became a Boston Red Sox for an eight-year contract that paid him $20 million annually.

Directions: To learn more about the arbitration process, conduct research on a recent baseball arbitration case and report those findings in a three-minute oral presentation *or* a two-page paper, based on your instructor's instructions. Your example should be of a case in which the parties went through the entire arbitration process.

Sources: Murray Chass, "Jeter Seeks Record $18.5 Million," *The New York Times,* January 19, 2001, online edition **www.nytimes.com/2001/01/19sports/19BASE.html**; Murray Chass, "Jeter and Rivera File for Salary Arbitration," *The New York Times,* January 16, 2001, online edition **www.nytimes.com/2001/01/16sports/16BASE.html**.

➤ Nothing but Net

1. **Airline employees.** One industry with a history of contentious relations between companies and unions is the airline industry. Many of the most recent disputes involve the various pilots' unions. Visit the Web site for one of the pilots' unions and then the Web sites of several of the airlines whose pilots are represented by that union. Prepare an oral report to your class outlining the major issues from the perspective of both the union and the airline.

   www.alpa.org

   www.americanair.com

   www.delta.com

   www.nwa.com

   www.ual.com

2. **Union membership statistics.** The Bureau of Labor Statistics (BLS) publishes an annual report on the characteristics of workers who belong to labor unions. Visit the BLS Web site (**http://stats.bls.gov/news. release/union2.toc.htm**) and review the most recent report. Answer the following questions:

   a. Which worker age groups have the highest and lowest concentrations of union members?

   b. Which industries and occupations have the highest and lowest concentrations of union members?

   c. Workers belonging to which union have the highest median wages?

3. **Worker friendly companies.** Each year the AFL–CIO hands out awards to companies for exemplary labor relations. Two of the past winners are Harley-Davidson and Kellogg's. Visit the AFL–CIO Web site and make a list of other companies that have recently won the AFL–CIO labor relations award. Pick one of the winners and visit its Web site. Why do you think the company won the AFL–CIO award?

   www.aflcio.org

   www.workingfamilies.com

   Note: Internet Web addresses change frequently. If you do not find the exact sites listed, you may need to access the organization's or company's home page and search from there.

Writers Guild of America versus the Alliance of Motion Picture & Television Producers

When the credits roll for a movie and you see the words "A film by . . . ," do you notice the name that follows? If the name is the director's, does the credit make you think that the director wrote the screenplay? This confusion is one of the issues that screenwriters—the 12,500 members of the Writers Guild of America (WGA)—have been debating with the movie producers who are their employers. In contrast, for TV shows, writers are given more clout and recognition than their counterparts in film. "There certainly has been a snowballing notion of the director being the author of the movie," notes Steve Harrigan, a Texas-based screenwriter. "It's just a perception that has been allowed to creep in."

Other issues have also spurred this labor dispute. Once a film begins shooting, the writers say they are basically shut out of the process. Anyone can tinker with their scripts, and they are not allowed to watch "dailies"—scenes that are shot each day. Writers are not invited to meetings or readings in which the script is discussed, nor are they invited to screenings when a movie is completed. One writer puts the situation bluntly: "We are basically treated like dirt," says Michael Mahern, a long-time screenwriter who is a member of the WGA's contract negotiating committee. "Over the past 15 years, the situation has gotten substantially worse."

Then there is the issue of money. Although top writers may sell scripts for $2 million, or get paid $150,000 a week to add action or humor to a script, many earn only a few thousand dollars a year for their scripts. The formula by which writers are paid for cable and foreign TV rights, as well as Internet ventures, video, and DVD sales, is up for grabs. Current pay formulas have been in use since the late 1980s, and writers claim that they are outdated, particularly with new-technology media such as the Internet and DVD. A strike looms on the horizon if the issues can't be resolved. "The [potential] strike is not, as much as it will be portrayed in the media, about rich millionaires wanting more," explains actor Tim Robbins. "It's about the rank and file [who] are working-class people, with average incomes of about $5,000 per year."

Directors, producers, and film industry executives disagree with the writers' demands and their perceptions of how they are treated. "I'm a collaborative person; I always work with the writer," argues director Brett Ratner. "But the only person in the process who is on the film from the very beginning to the very end is the director. The writer delivers the script and his work kind of ends." Jack Shea, president of the Directors Guild of America, wrote to his 12,000 members that the writers' proposals would "seriously impact a director's ability to deliver a product on time, on budget, and within his or her creative vision." A statement on the Web site of the Alliance of Motion Picture and Television Producers (AMPTP) cited the erosion of movie audiences, decline in some markets, and uncertainty about future technology as reasons for the writers to avoid disrupting the process further with demands for change and more money. In addition, statistics from the AMPTP cited that the average working writer makes more than $200,000 each year in salary, residual payments, and benefits—not the few thousand claimed by Robbins and others.

In 2001, talks between the two sides broke down, and the 135,000 members of the Screen Actors Guild threatened to support the writers with a strike of their own, despite their long strike of the year before. As in labor-management disputes in other industries, little common ground seemed to exist between the two sides—except perhaps a love of movie making, which in the end might prove to be the point on which the entire argument turns.

QUESTIONS

1. Imagine that you were asked to be a mediator in this disagreement. What kind of advice and recommendations might you make to each side in order to settle the immediate dispute?
2. Identify what you see as the alternatives each side in this dispute could use if talks fail.
3. What steps might the WGA and the AMPTP take to build better cooperation in the future?
4. Go to the Web sites for both sides—the Writers Guild of America at **www.wgaeast.org** or **www.wgawest.org** and the Alliance of Motion Picture and Television Producers at **www.amptp.org**—to learn the outcome of this disagreement. Write a brief summary of where the debate currently stands and what issues have been resolved or remain unresolved.

Sources: Writers Guild of America East Web site, **www.wgaest.org**, accessed April 23, 2001; Writers Guild of America West Web site, **www.wgawest.org**, accessed April 23, 2001; Alliance of Motion Picture and Television Producers Web site, **www.amptp.org**, accessed April 23, 2001; Daniel B. Wood, "High Drama in Hollywood: Strikes Ahead?" *Christian Science Monitor*, February 1, 2001, **www.csmonitor.com**; Paul Pringle, "Screenwriters Just Want a Little Respect—Or Else," *The Dallas Morning News*, January 18, 2001, **www.dallasnews.com**; Bernard Weinraub, "Entertainment Writers Weigh Strike," *The New York Times*, January 16, 2001, **www.nytimes.com**.

CHAPTER 12

Creating and Producing World-Class Goods and Services

Pella Corp. Focuses on Bright Future through Team Manufacturing

Unless you are currently building your own home, you'd probably assume—like most people—that all windows, and all window manufacturing companies, are alike. Pella Corp., based in Pella, Iowa, disagrees. This family-owned business has been manufacturing quality windows and doors on the same Iowa site since 1925. But when national retailers like Home Depot and Lowe's, and another family-owned window manufacturer, Andersen, began to chip away at Pella's market share during the early 1990s, Pella executives took a hard look at their production process, hoping to find ways to put the company back on top. With the help of Time Based Management Consulting Group (TBM) of Durham, North Carolina, Pella dove into a quality-enhancement process that originated in Japan. The process is called *continuous improvement*.

Pella managers and TBM looked at every square inch of the production process, from the location of the company's factories and the way they were laid out, to inventory levels and the firm's relationships with suppliers. In fact, Pella even found a way to acquire a new customer, one who buys its byproducts—but more on that later.

Pella is a small Midwestern town of 10,000 residents. The 1.6 million-square-foot Pella factory has been operating outside the town for over 75 years, employing locals and treating its employees well. The company recently ranked 21st on *Fortune* magazine's list of the 100 Best Companies to Work For in America. Throughout its history, the outside of the factory has changed little, but what goes on inside has changed—a lot. Before the implementation of continuous improvement, production of double-hung windows took up a huge amount of floor space. Now the production line takes only half its previous space, and the windows are produced by teams of workers. Instead of ordering necessary parts from a distant location within the large plant, team members make them right there, at the location where they are assembling the windows. The result is, in TBM vice president Mark Oakeson's words, "a focused factory—that is, a largely self-sufficient mini-factory within a factory."

When windows are being manufactured, mounds of leftover wood chips, shavings, and sawdust are piled on the factory floor. In the past, these by-products of

the production process were simply considered waste and were discarded. Then Pella managers found a way to convert this waste into a salable by-product. Today, this scrap is simply blown through a pipe directly to a new customer located next door—American Wood Fiber, a business that processes wood chips and shavings into pet and horse bedding.

Pella has also radically changed the way it buys supplies. The company has reduced the number of lumber suppliers it deals with as well as the amount of inventory it maintains as raw materials and components. Pella used to hold 6.9 million board feet of wood in inventory; this amount has been reduced to less than 2 million. Getting vendors to cooperate with this new system wasn't easy, but one relationship that has succeeded is the one with Cardinal IG, which has a plant in nearby Greenfield, Iowa. Cardinal makes the insulated glass

that Pella uses in its windows. With help from Cardinal, the lead time has been cut to about six hours from order placement to its receipt.

Recently, Pella made one of its biggest production moves yet: it ventured outside Iowa. Determining that the company could benefit from expanding production to other locations, Pella broke ground on a new factory in Gettysburg, Pennsylvania. The philosophy of continuous improvement has taught Pella managers the value of not standing still or resting on the laurels of success. Since the implementation of many of these changes, annual sales have tripled to more than $600 million. The new plant in Gettysburg, along with other proposed improvements, is just one more window of opportunity for a company that believes in continuously evaluating and improving the way it makes its products.[1]

CHAPTER OVERVIEW

Society allows businesses to operate only as long as they contribute to the public well-being. By producing and marketing desired goods and services, businesses satisfy this commitment. They create what economists call *utility*—the want-satisfying power of a good or service. Businesses can create or enhance four basic kinds of utility: time, place, ownership, and form utility. A firm's marketing operation generates time, place, and ownership utility by offering goods and services to customers when they want to buy at convenient locations where ownership of the products can be transferred.

Production creates form utility by converting raw materials and other inputs into finished products. Nautica converts fabric, thread, zippers, and other materials and components into teenage apparel. **Production** applies resources such as people and machinery to convert materials into finished goods or services. The task of **production and operations management** is to manage the application of people and machinery in converting materials and resources into finished goods and services. Figure 12.1 illustrates the production process.

People sometimes use the terms *production* and *manufacturing* interchangeably, but they ignore an important difference when they do so. *Production* is a broader term that spans both manufacturing and nonmanufacturing industries. For instance, companies in extractive industries such as fishing, lumber, and mining engage in production, and so do creators of services. Services are intangible outputs of production systems. They include outputs as diverse as trash hauling, education, haircuts, tax accounting, dental care, mail delivery, transportation, and lodging. Figure 12.2 lists five examples of production systems for a variety of goods and services.

Whether the production process results in a tangible good or an intangible service, it always converts inputs into outputs. This conversion process may make major changes in raw materials or simply combine already finished parts into a new product. A butcher performs a production function by reducing a side of beef to ground beef, steaks, and roasts. A subway system combines rails, trains, and employees to create its output: passenger transportation services. Both of these processes create form utility.

This chapter describes the process of producing goods and services. It looks at the importance of production and operations management to a business and discusses new technologies that are transforming the production function. It then discusses the tasks of the production and operations manager, the importance of quality, and the methods businesses use to ensure high quality.

STRATEGIC IMPORTANCE OF THE PRODUCTION FUNCTION

Along with marketing, finance, and human resource management, production is a vital business activity. In fact, without production, none of the other functions would operate. Without a good or service to sell, a company cannot generate money to pay its employees, lenders, and stockholders. Without profits, the firm quickly fails. The production process is just as crucial in a not-for-profit organization, since the good or service it offers justifies the organization's existence. In short, the production function adds value to a company's inputs by converting them into marketable outputs. This added value comes from features of the outputs for which customers will pay money.

Clearly, effective production and operations management can lower a firm's costs of production, boost the quality of its goods and services, and allow it to respond dependably to customer demands. Skillful

FIGURE 12.1
The Production Process: Converting Inputs to Outputs

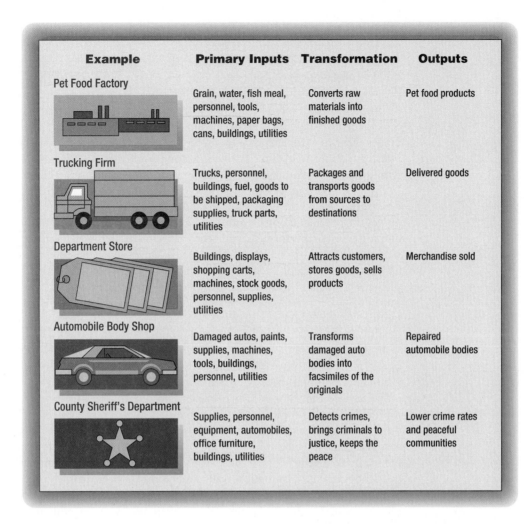

Example	Primary Inputs	Transformation	Outputs
Pet Food Factory	Grain, water, fish meal, personnel, tools, machines, paper bags, cans, buildings, utilities	Converts raw materials into finished goods	Pet food products
Trucking Firm	Trucks, personnel, buildings, fuel, goods to be shipped, packaging supplies, truck parts, utilities	Packages and transports goods from sources to destinations	Delivered goods
Department Store	Buildings, displays, shopping carts, machines, stock goods, personnel, supplies, utilities	Attracts customers, stores goods, sells products	Merchandise sold
Automobile Body Shop	Damaged autos, paints, supplies, machines, tools, buildings, personnel, utilities	Transforms damaged auto bodies into facsimiles of the originals	Repaired automobile bodies
County Sheriff's Department	Supplies, personnel, equipment, automobiles, office furniture, buildings, utilities	Detects crimes, brings criminals to justice, keeps the peace	Lower crime rates and peaceful communities

FIGURE 12.2
Typical Production Systems

management of production can also promote flexibility, so a company can respond quickly when customer demands change. Advances in production technology can enable a company to renew itself by providing new items for sale.

Consider some examples of how production allows businesses to gain these advantages. The Ritz-Carlton hotel chain uses computer networks and databases to provide employees with information about customers' likes and dislikes, so employees can cater to the individual tastes of its guests. The U.S. textile industry has used production technology to remain competitive amid worldwide cost cutting. According to the Textile Manufacturers Association, manufacturing advances have reduced the time required to make enough cloth for one shirt from 13 minutes to 3. Greater automation has reduced the number of jobs in the industry, but measured in terms of the fiber used, U.S. textile mills are producing more than ever.[2]

Mass Production

From its beginnings as a colonial supplier of raw materials to Europe, the U.S. evolved into an industrial giant. Much of this remarkable change resulted from **mass production,** a system for manufacturing products in large amounts through effective combinations of employees with specialized skills, mechanization, and standardization. Mass production makes outputs available in large quantities at lower prices than individually crafted items would cost.

BUSINESS DIRECTORY

➤ **production** *application of resources such as people and machinery to convert materials into finished goods or services.*

➤ **production and operations management** *managing people and machinery in converting materials and resources into finished goods and services.*

Mass production begins with specialization of labor, dividing work into its simplest components so that each worker can concentrate on performing one task. By separating jobs into small tasks, managers create conditions for high productivity through mechanization, in which machines perform much of the work previously done by people. Standardization, the third element of mass production, involves producing uniform, interchangeable goods and parts. Standardized parts simplify the replacement of defective or worn-out components. If your car's windshield wiper blades wear out, for instance, you can buy replacements at a local auto-parts store like AutoZone. Just think how long you would wait—and how much more you would spend—if you had to hire someone to individually craft the replacements!

A logical extension of these principles of specialization, mechanization, and standardization led to development of the **assembly line.** This manufacturing technique moves the product along a conveyor belt past a number of workstations, where production workers perform specialized tasks such as welding, painting, installing individual parts, and tightening bolts. Henry Ford generated phenomenal results by applying this concept and, in the process, revolutionized auto assembly. Before implementing the assembly line, Ford's workers assembled Model T cars at the rate of one per worker for each 12-hour workday. The assembly-line technique slashed the number of work hours per car to 1.5. Not surprisingly, dozens of other industries quickly adopted the assembly-line technique.

In the 21st century, businesses continue to advance the ways they apply these principles. General Motors (GM) has led automobile manufacturers in developing the use of common platforms—the basic structures on which cars are built. Several GM models share the same platform design, so manufacturing the different models is more efficient. The company has expanded this practice to its partnerships with other car makers, including Isuzu Motors, which is half owned by GM. General Motors and Isuzu have been negotiating plans to develop a common platform for possible future GM vehicles and Isuzu's Rodeo and Trooper sport-utility vehicles (SUVs).[3]

Although mass production brings advantages for a firm, it imposes limitations, too. It is highly efficient for producing large numbers of similar products. However, mass production loses its efficiency advantage when production requires small batches of different items. The trade-off tempts some companies to focus on efficient production methods rather than on making what customers really want. In addition, specialization can lead to boring jobs, since each worker must repeat the same task all day. To improve their competitive capabilities, many firms are adopting increasingly flexible production systems, such as flexible production, customer-driven production, and the team concept. These techniques may not replace mass production altogether but may simply improve a company's use of mass production.

Flexible Production

While mass production efficiently creates large batches of similar items, flexible production can cost-effectively produce smaller batches. Flexible production can take many forms, but it generally involves using information technology to share the details of customer orders, programmable equipment to fulfill the orders, and skilled people to carry out whatever tasks are needed to fill a particular order. This arrangement is efficient when combined with *lean* production methods that use automation and information technology to reduce requirements for workers and inventory. Flexible production also requires a high degree of cooperation and communication among customers and employees throughout the organization.

Print-on-demand technology is bringing flexible production to the publishing industry. With print-on-demand, a book's contents are stored electronically and can be downloaded as an e-book or printed out to fill orders as small as a single copy. Xerox's DocuTech Book Factory provides all the equipment needed to print, perforate, bind, and finish paperback books. Publishers that have already spent the half million dollars required to buy the Book Factory include Random House and

Germany's Bertelsmann. Retail bookstore chain Barnes & Noble has purchased a similar system from IBM Printing Solutions. Barnes & Noble installed IBM Infoprint in a distribution warehouse. Customers can order a print-on-demand title from a Barnes & Noble store, and it will be printed and shipped to the customer the same day. Barnes & Noble also offers e-books online at its Web site and at kiosks in its stores.[4]

Customer-Driven Production

A customer-driven production system evaluates customer demands in order to link what a manufacturer makes with what customers want to buy. Many firms have implemented this approach with great success. One method is to establish computer links between factories and retailers' systems, using data about sales as the basis for creating short-term forecasts and designing production schedules to meet those forecasts.

Some companies make products to order. Paccar Inc. builds powerful Kenworth trucks, customized according to buyers' specifications. The trucks, which range in price from $80,000 to $350,000, are a major investment for their customers, who expect them to run for 1.5 million miles or more. Production begins shortly after a customer visits a dealership and selects from more than 100 options, from different choices of seats and dashboards to the comforts in the sleeping cabins of long-haul truckers. The order data travel electronically to the company's factory in Renton, Washington, where engineers review the order to make sure it fits the customer's needs. Then the order goes out over Paccar's computer network so suppliers can see what components are needed. Suppliers make deliveries several times a week, filling specifications precisely, down to the predrilled holes in the metal rails used to form a chassis. Workers assemble each chassis and send it to a booth for painting. As it dries, other workers assemble the cab. Computers and printed work orders provide access to assembly instructions, and plant supervisors carry portable radios to help them keep the work flowing smoothly. The company fills a typical order within three weeks, compared with the industry standard of six to eight weeks. By bringing the rest of its records onto its computer network, Paccar hopes to improve the time to just two weeks.[5]

This type of customer-driven production is especially appropriate for expensive, highly profitable products like Kenworth trucks, as well as for many kinds of services. But as we discuss later in the chapter and in Chapter 13, advances in information technology are enabling companies to customize many kinds of products profitably.

Team Concept

Some production methods challenge mass production's emphasis on specialized workers performing repetitive tasks. The team concept combines employees from various departments and functions such as design, manufacturing, finance, and maintenance to work together in designing and building products. Work teams may also include members from outside the firm, such as suppliers and customers. This kind of teamwork may include *concurrent engineering*, in which product development brings together engineers, designers, production staff, marketing personnel, and employees from other functions.

Honda used the team concept to launch its redesigned 2001 Civic. The company set up a New Model Center in Tochigi, Japan, where its research and development facilities are located. Honda sent representatives from its five global regions to the New Model Center, where they collaborated on the Civic's tooling, production processes, equipment, and manufacturing methods. They compiled changes sent in by employees from all of Honda's Civic factories

BUSINESS DIRECTORY

➤ **assembly line** *manufacturing technique that carries the product on a conveyor system past several workstations, where workers perform specialized tasks.*

into a database and used the data to modify the automobile's design. The information the team shared during production planning enabled the company to operate more efficiently. Honda's past strategy had been to launch the model in Japan, then move it to other facilities, making changes to accommodate differences in equipment and production methods.[6]

PRODUCTION PROCESSES

The methods by which firms produce goods and services differ according to their means of operating and time requirements involved. The means of operating may involve either an analytic or a synthetic system, and time requirements call for either a continuous or an intermittent process.

An analytic production system reduces a raw material to its component parts in order to extract one or more marketable products. Petroleum refining breaks down crude oil into gasoline, wax, fuel oil, kerosene, tar, and other products. A meat-packing plant slaughters cattle to produce various cuts of meat, glue from the horns and hooves, and leather from the hides.

A synthetic production system reverses the method of an analytic system. It combines a number of raw materials or parts, or transforms raw materials to produce finished products. A Gateway assembly line produces a personal computer (PC) by assembling the components ordered by each customer. As shown in Figure 12.3, a Chrysler assembly line uses a variety of metal components to produce automobiles. Other synthetic production systems make drugs, chemicals, computer chips, and canned soup.

A continuous production process generates finished products over a period of days, months, or even years in long production runs. The steel industry provides a classic example. Its blast furnaces never completely shut down except for malfunctions. Petroleum refineries, chemical plants, and nuclear power facilities also practice continuous production. A shutdown can ruin such equipment, with extremely costly results.

An intermittent production process generates products in short production runs, shutting down machines frequently or changing their configurations to produce different products. Most services result from intermittent production systems. Accountants, plumbers, electricians, and dentists traditionally have not attempted to standardize their services, because each service provider confronts different problems that require individual approaches or production systems. Some companies, including Jiffy Lube auto service, Terminix pest control services, and home-cleaning services such as Merry Maids, offer standardized services as part of a strategy to operate efficiently and compete with low prices. In contrast, McDonald's recently moved toward a more intermittent production model. The fast-food chain invested millions in new cooking equipment to set up kitchens for preparing sandwiches quickly to order, rather than producing large batches ahead of time and keeping them warm under heat lamps.[7]

TECHNOLOGY AND THE PRODUCTION PROCESS

Like other business functions, production has changed dramatically as computers and related technologies have developed. At Square D's facility in Lincoln, Nebraska, a fully automated production line makes 100,000 circuit breakers a day. Instead of 250 workers assembling these products the traditional way, the production line requires just 37 operators, who earn almost $20 an hour for their highly skilled work. The efficiency of automation allows the company to produce so many parts so fast that distributors can keep a lower stock on hand and place more frequent orders. This frees up funds so they can order a wider range of different Square D

In the right hands, iron, steel and aluminum   can be transformed into precious metals.

At Chrysler, we have one simple philosophy: to create great cars. It's about sculpting innovative, influential designs and the quest for engineering excellence. It's about taking the basic elements and crafting something dynamic, unique and extraordinary. For more information, just call 1.800.CHRYSLER or you can visit our Web site at www.chryslercars.com.

ENGINEERED TO BE GREAT CARS **CHRYSLER**

FIGURE 12.3
Example of a Synthetic Production System

products. The factory is so efficient that the company is moving some production to Lincoln from Mexico. And although Square D needs fewer assemblers for its automated Lincoln facility, meeting the strong demand requires more skilled workers such as mold makers.[8]

In addition to boosting efficiency in the production process, automation and information technology allow companies to redesign their current methods to enhance flexibility. These changes allow a company to design and create new products faster, modify them more rapidly, and meet customers' changing needs more effectively than it could achieve with traditional methods. However, employers need to keep in mind how these changes affect the health and safety of their employees, as discussed in the "Solving an Ethical Controversy" box. Important production technologies today include robots, computer-aided design and manufacturing, flexible manufacturing systems, and computer-integrated manufacturing.

Robots

A growing number of manufacturers have freed people from boring, sometimes dangerous assignments by replacing many of their blue-collar workers with steel-collar workers: robots. A **robot** is a reprogrammable machine capable of performing a variety of tasks that require manipulations of materials and tools. Robots can repeat the same tasks many times without varying their movements. In manufacturing the Civic, Honda uses robots to handle, move, and weld parts. Robots move pieces of sheet metal into fixtures and move parts around the end of the gun that sprays on a coating of sealant. A single general welder using 20 programmable electric robots to make about 130 welds attaches the floor, sides, and roof of each automobile.

BUSINESS DIRECTORY
➤ **robot** *reprogrammable machine capable of performing numerous tasks that require manipulations of materials and tools.*

SOLVING AN ETHICAL CONTROVERSY

According to the Occupational Safety and Health Administration (OSHA), more than half a million people each year miss work because of injuries related to repetitive movements required by their jobs—stretching, bending, lifting, even word processing. These aren't the types of work-related injuries you can see—no broken bones or lacerations. But OSHA says they are just as important, and that employers are responsible for taking action to prevent the injuries. So in 2000, the federal agency issued regulations detailing standards for employers to follow in order to prevent and reduce repetitive-stress injuries, including everything from how many pounds an employee should lift in a workday to how long a worker should spend working at a keyboard. Not surprisingly, the regulations had their critics, and Congress voted to rescind them in 2001.

Were the proposed OSHA regulations regarding prevention of repetitive-motion injuries fair to both employers and employees?

PRO

1. According to some estimates, companies would have saved $9.1 billion a year in medical and worker's compensation claims by preventing workplace injuries.
2. The Bureau of Labor Statistics reports that about 40 percent of the affected workforce are employed at large companies that have already taken measures to reduce these injuries. So the regulations would not have cost them any more time or effort than they already spent.
3. According to OSHA, 102 million workers would have been protected, and 4.6 million injuries would have been prevented in the first ten years, which ultimately benefits employers as well.

CON

1. The National Association of Manufacturers and other trade organizations argued that OSHA has actually stepped outside its designated role by issuing these regulations.

2. The same groups believed that OSHA had tremendously underestimated the costs involved to refit workstations or redesign jobs to meet the new regulations. These costs would hurt small and midsize businesses more than large companies.
3. Similar groups questioned the premise of these regulations, arguing that many companies have already taken voluntary steps to reduce repetitive-stress injuries and that regulation is not necessary. "Regulation is for when the market fails," says Ronald Bird, chief economist at the Employment Policy Foundation, a nonprofit group. Instead, Bird asserts, sales of furniture, workstations, and tools that promote the correct movement of the body are "soaring."

SUMMARY

No one argues that repetitive-stress injuries in the workplace present a problem that must be addressed. Plenty of disagreement exists, however, over whether steps for preventing these injuries should be subject to regulation by OSHA. This federal agency and others claim that businesses will actually save money in insurance claims, reduced productivity, and employee turnover in the long run. But detractors say that small and midsize companies that are forced to comply with the regulations would be forced to absorb costs that jeopardize their survival in the marketplace. They are appealing to the Bush administration to push Congress to overturn the new regulations.

Sources: Stephanie Armour, "Young Tech Workers Face Crippling Injuries," *USA Today,* February 9, 2001, **www.usatoday.com;** Diane Rezendes Khirallah, "IT Industry Opposes Impending Ergonomics Rules," Planet IT, **www.planetit.com,** January 25, 2001; Charles Haddad, "OSHA's New Regs Will Ease the Pain—for Everybody," *Business Week,* December 4, 2000, p. 90; Michael Rosenwald, "New Rules Aim at Eradicating Repetitive-Stress Injury," *The Boston Globe,* November 14, 2000, **www.bostonglobe.com.**

Not only are robots more efficient for these activities, they are more consistent than a human, who would grow tired after hours of lifting.[9]

Initially, robots were most common in automotive and electronics production, but growing numbers of industries are adding them to production lines, as improvements in technology bring progressively less expensive and more flexible alternatives. Firms operate many different types of robots. The simplest kind, a pick-and-place robot, moves in only two or three directions as it picks up something from one spot and places it in another. So-called *field robots* assist human workers in nonmanufacturing, often hazardous, environments such as nuclear power plants, space stations, and even battlefields.

A recent development called *nanotechnology* is enabling the use of production techniques that operate at the level of molecules. IBM researchers have developed a process by which DNA powers a robot with fingers one-fiftieth the breadth of a single human hair. More sophisticated versions of this robot may be useful for destroying cancer cells. Nanotechnology is already being used to build "read heads" for computer disk drives and to create tiny particles used to make extremely hard eyeglass lenses and car and floor waxes.[10]

Computer-Aided Design and Computer-Aided Manufacturing

A process called computer-aided design (CAD) enables engineers to design parts and buildings on computer screens faster and with fewer mistakes than they could achieve working with traditional drafting systems. Using an electronic pen, an engineer can sketch 3-D designs on an electronic drafting board or directly on the screen. The computer then provides tools to make major and minor design changes and to analyze the design for certain characteristics or problems. Engineers can put a new car design through a simulated road test to project its real-world performance. If they find a problem with weight distribution, for example, they can make the necessary changes on a computer terminal. Only when they satisfy themselves with all of the structural characteristics of their design will they manufacture an actual car model.

The process of computer-aided manufacturing (CAM) picks up where the CAD system leaves off. Computer tools enable a manufacturer to analyze the steps that a machine must take to produce a needed product or part. Electronic signals transmitted to processing equipment provide instructions for performing the appropriate production steps in the correct order. Both CAD and CAM technologies are now used together at most modern production facilities.

Flexible Manufacturing Systems

A flexible manufacturing system (FMS) is a production facility that workers can quickly modify to manufacture different products. The typical system consists of computer-controlled machining centers to produce metal parts, robots to handle the parts, and remote-controlled carts to deliver materials. All components are linked by electronic controls that dictate activities at each stage of the manufacturing sequence, even automatically replacing broken or worn-out drill bits and other implements.

Flexible manufacturing is entering a new, more user-friendly generation with the development of software called OpenCNC. This software runs on a PC and directs the activities of computer numerical control (CNC) machine tools from a variety of makers. Operators can reprogram machine tools using the same program, so a company can move operators from one tool to another without retraining them in each machine's hardware controls. In addition, OpenCNC can reprogram machine tools even while they are running, and it can be hooked up to the Internet to receive updates or to control machine tools at other sites. Cessna uses OpenCNC to control three massive routers that cut out 30,000 different aircraft parts from aluminum. With the new software, the routers are more productive, partly because operators don't have to shut them down to load new programs for making different parts. In addition, since the OpenCNC software resides on the company's computer network, engineers can use it to diagnose production problems anytime, from anywhere they can access the network.[11]

Another technological development that is taking flexibility to new heights is a process called Virtual Engineered Composites (VEC), which uses digital commands to drive the manufacturing process. The process operates in a box, which can be as small as a mop bucket or as large as a freight container, depending on the product's size. A chemical reaction hardens skins of a composite material around a foam model of the product to create a mold. It is then used to manufacture the product by filling the mold with a composite material

FIGURE 12.4
Example of Computer-Integrated Manufacturing

and using a chemical process to cause the material to harden. These self-contained production units can be used to set up a manufacturing operation virtually anywhere, and the type of product can be switched in the hour it takes to insert a different mold. The entire process can be carried out by three people with a link to the software that runs the system. A pioneer in applying VEC is Genmar Holdings, which makes boats for recreational use. The traditional production methods involve applying fiberglass to each hull, an unpleasant and unhealthful eight-hour task. In contrast, with VEC, Genmar can turn out a hull every 35 minutes without the noise, styrene fumes, and itchy glass fibers of the traditional process. Also, the VEC hulls are stronger than the fiberglass hulls, so Genmar has begun replacing its five-year warranty with a lifetime warranty. With these results, Genmar announced plans to set up a fully automated boat factory—the world's first.[12]

Computer-Integrated Manufacturing

Companies integrate robots, CAD/CAM, FMS, computers, and other technologies to implement computer-integrated manufacturing (CIM), a production system in which computers help workers to design products, control machines, handle materials, and control the production function in an integrated fashion. This type of manufacturing does not necessarily imply more automation and fewer people than other alternatives. It does involve a new type of automation organized around the computer. The key to CIM is a centralized computer system that integrates and controls separate processes and functions. Circuit-CAM, the CIM system described in Figure 12.4, programs computer-controlled machinery, designs efficient production layouts, manages changes required when a process is revised, reports quality and cost performance, and prepares production-related documents.

The Internet is advancing the integration of manufacturing and linking it to marketing and other activities. In Holland, Michigan, Herman Miller uses the Internet to fill orders for its office furniture within two weeks, a fraction of the usual delivery time. Herman Miller set up a system called SQA (for "simple, quick, and affordable") to link selling, manufacturing, and delivery for fast turnaround. Salespeople are equipped with laptop computers and can show their customers 3-D layouts of the options available in Herman Miller's SQA line, configuring the choices to the customer's floor plan. When customers make a selection, the software creates an order listing all the necessary parts, then transmits it to the manufacturing floor, schedules the work, and reserves space on a delivery truck. Another software program lets vendors check in to see what the factory will need to fill the orders. When Herman Miller's inventory of materials drops below about a day's worth, the supplier replenishes the inventory. Workers use those materials to assemble desks, cubicle partitions, and other furniture according to schedule. With the information sharing, SQA has improved efficiency, speeded up order fulfillment, and cut errors in order entry almost to zero.[13]

Background. Can you order your McDonald's Big Mac with fries over the Internet? Well, not exactly—but McDonald's Corp. has decided to grow in several directions, including expansion onto the Internet via an alliance with Kraft Foods and Blockbuster in which the three marketers sunk $80 million into Food.com.

What Happened? McDonald's realized that it could no longer grow by simply opening more McDonald's franchises, many of which had already started to cannibalize each other—"eat" each other's customers—because the stores were located so close to one another. So the company, under newly appointed chief executive officer Jack M. Greenberg, embarked on a new strategy for growth that would locate its facilities in a variety of creative ways, including its investment in the Internet. First, McDonald's acquired different types of restaurants, including 148 Donatos Pizza outlets that are spread from Michigan to Georgia, along with 23 coffee bars in London called Aroma Cafe. The company now also controls the 56 Chipotle Mexican Grill shops and has acquired 859 Boston Market shops, which specialize in fresh chicken dinners. Instead of competing with McDonald's restaurants, these new acquisitions will complement them. Says Richard Adams, president of a San Diego group of McDonald's franchise restaurants, "McDonald's is lunch. Pizza is dinner." In other words, even if some of the new restaurants are located right next door to McDonald's, they won't take a bite out of each other.

How does Food.com fit the expansion plan? Donatos already uses the site for advertising as well as taking pizza orders. McDonald's executives hope to build on this simple idea by developing a way for customers to order takeout Happy Meals and burritos with the click of a mouse.

The Response. Though it has already sunk millions into its new ventures, McDonald's claims that the company is moving slowly. "We're going to be particularly disciplined about not opening up hundreds of restaurants before we've figured out that these concepts are franchisable and profitable," claims Greenberg. Figuring out how to franchise Internet transactions may be more difficult than those of traditional stores. And financial experts are watching. "McDonald's went from being a company not objective about itself to one that is more open and willing to acknowledge its shortcomings," observes Paul Wayne, research director at Kayne, Anderson Investment Management, which owns two million shares of McDonald's stock.

Today and Counting. While executives and analysts pore over the opportunities on the Internet, kitchen crews at McDonald's restaurants are churning out the burgers on new cooking equipment that allows them to make sandwiches to order rather than slapping together hundreds of Big Macs that sit for minutes under heat lamps. "In my 24 years, the core business is in the best shape it's ever been in," says Marilyn Wright, a franchisee who owns six restaurants in the Chicago area. Given the volatility of Internet businesses, it's probably a good thing that McDonald's hasn't lost sight of how its bread—or hamburger buns—is buttered. That's with extra ketchup and pickles, please.

QUESTIONS FOR CRITICAL THINKING

1. In addition to allowing consumers to order meals online, in what ways might the Internet affect the way McDonald's could improve its methods of production? How might the purchasing process and inventory decisions be affected?

2. How many McDonald's restaurants are located within a ten-mile radius of where you live? Do you think there are too many McDonald's near you, too few, or the right amount? Explain why.

Sources: Bob Burgdorfer, "McDonald's New Menu Seen Eyeing Economy," Reuters Ltd., January 18, 2001; Michael Arndt, "Did Somebody Say McBurrito?" *Business Week*, April 10, 2000, pp. 166, 170; "McDonald's Buys Donatos Chain," *Business First*, May 5, 1999, **www.bizjournals.com/columbus.**

THE LOCATION DECISION

One of a firm's major decisions is choosing the right place to set up a production facility, as described in the "Clicks and Mortar" box on McDonald's. As Table 12.1 shows, the best locations provide advantages in three categories: transportation, physical, and human factors.

Transportation factors include proximity to markets and raw materials, along with availability of alternative modes for transporting both inputs and outputs. If transporting raw materials is expensive or difficult, the facility should be near those materials. And a company that relies heavily on human resources should be easy for employees to reach. Other companies, especially services businesses, may benefit from locating near their customers. The VEC manufacturing system, described earlier, makes production facilities so portable that companies using it can place more importance on locating production near customers. Also, if the VEC

> **BUSINESS DIRECTORY**
>
> ➤ **computer-integrated manufacturing (CIM)** *production system that integrates computer tools and human workers to design products, handle materials, and control production.*

Table 12.1   **Factors in the Location Decision**

Location Factor	Examples of Affected Businesses
Transportation	
Proximity to markets	Baking companies and manufacturers of other perishable products, dry cleaners, hotels, other services
Proximity to raw materials	Mining companies
Availability of transportation alternatives	Brick manufacturers, retail stores
Human Factors	
Labor supply	Auto manufacturers, software developers
Local regulations	Explosives manufacturers, welding shops
Community living conditions	All businesses
Physical Factors	
Water supply	Paper mills
Energy	Aluminum, chemical, and fertilizer manufacturers
Hazardous wastes	All businesses

system is hooked up to the Internet, the controls can be operated from anywhere with Internet access.[14]

Physical variables involve such issues as water supplies, available energy, and options for disposing of hazardous wastes. A firm that wants to locate near a community often must prepare an **environmental impact study** that analyzes how a proposed plant would affect the quality of life in the surrounding area. Regulatory agencies typically require such studies to cover topics like the impact on transportation facilities; energy requirements; water and sewage treatment needs; natural plant life and wildlife; and water, air, and noise pollution.

Human factors include an area's labor supply, local regulations, and living conditions. Management considers local labor costs, as well as the availability of workers with needed qualifications. Some labor-intensive industries have located plants in rural areas with readily available labor pools and limited high-wage alternatives. Some firms with headquarters in the U.S. and other industrialized economies have moved production offshore in search of low wages.

In the United States, this trend, coupled with automation, has shrunk manufacturing's share of the nation's gross domestic product. However, manufacturing continues to be an important segment of the U.S. economy, with total output greater than it ever has been. During the previous decade, U.S. manufacturing output grew faster than the nation's economy as a whole, and the number of people employed by manufacturing companies has held steady. One reason that some companies locate facilities in the United States is that creative use of technology has made U.S. workers extremely productive. Output per hour worked is much higher in the U.S. than in Canada, the United Kingdom, or Japan.[15]

For companies that produce either goods or services, availability of qualified employees is a key factor in many location decisions. Software makers and other high-tech firms concentrate in areas with the technical talent they need, including Silicon

Service providers like Disney locate theme parks in warmer regions where visitors can combine a family vacation with the visit. Disney sites include Anaheim's Disneyland, Walt Disney World in Florida, Paris Disneyland, and Tokyo Disneyland. The newest edition, Disney's California Adventure, is also located near the original Disneyland and is intended to attract more visitors by updating the park, adding rides, and converting Disneyland from a one-day visit to a multiday family trip.

PRODUCTION MANAGEMENT TASKS

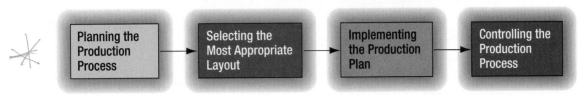

| Planning the Production Process | → | Selecting the Most Appropriate Layout | → | Implementing the Production Plan | → | Controlling the Production Process |

Valley in and around San Jose, California; Seattle; Boston; Portland, Oregon; Austin, Texas; and North Carolina's Research Triangle.

FIGURE 12.5
Tasks of Production Managers

TASKS OF PRODUCTION MANAGERS

Production and operations managers oversee the work of people and machinery to convert inputs (materials and resources) into finished goods and services. As Figure 12.5 shows, these managers perform four major tasks. First, they plan the overall production process. Next, they determine the best layout for the firm's production facilities and implement the production plan. Finally, they control the production process to maintain the highest possible quality. Part of the control process involves continuous evaluation of results. If problems occur, managers return to the first step and adjust the process.

Planning the Production Process

A firm's production planning begins with its choice of the goods or services to offer its customers. This decision is the essence of every company's reason for operating. Other decisions such as machinery purchases, pricing decisions, and selection of retail outlets all grow out of product planning.

Marketing research studies elicit consumer reactions to proposed products, test prototypes of new items, and estimate their potential sales and profitability levels. The production department concerns itself primarily with (1) converting original product concepts into final specifications and (2) designing the most efficient facilities to produce the new product. The new good or service must not only win acceptance from customers but also achieve economical production to ensure an acceptable return on company funds invested in the project.

At Chrysler and other U.S. auto companies, the traditional approach to production planning has been to build enough cars to meet marketing projections. Under this method, called *production push,* the company relies on dealers to find buyers for all the vehicles. If sales are disappointing, the supplier has to offer discounts to move cars out of inventory. After Chrysler's merger with Daimler, it began losing money, and Daimler's management called for a shift to its own practice of *production pull,* in which production schedules are based on actual orders from customers. Production pull requires greater flexibility and faster response, especially in the U.S., where customers are not used to waiting for the factory to build their new car.[16]

Besides planning to meet demand, production planners try to keep costs low. This streamlining requires building only enough capacity and carrying only enough parts and materials to meet demand. Unused capacity and shelves full of materials cost the company, but on the opposite end of the scale, a company without the necessary resources cannot fill all its orders on time. During the cost cutting of the 1980s, many businesses adopted lean production methods and shed unused resources. These changes helped them meet global competition, but as the economy expanded throughout the 1990s, some companies had trouble keeping up. Manco, which makes duct tape in Avon, Ohio, began running its machinery 23 hours a day, delaying preventive maintenance and paying its workers overtime. Similarly, Intermet, which makes auto parts for SUVs and light trucks, also has been operating around the clock. Scrambling to meet demand, the company had to put off maintenance on equipment and paid premium rates to ship out products at the last minute.[17]

Production planning can benefit from the insights of suppliers and product engineers. When Square D planned its advanced production line to make circuit breakers in Lincoln, Nebraska, manufacturing engineers collaborated with other employees to create a high-quality, efficient process. They reviewed the design of the circuit breakers, modifying it so that machines could assemble the product flawlessly. They spent months on a part called the toggle spring, which pulls the breaker's trip lever, interrupting an overloaded circuit. The spring had to meet precise specifications for size, force requirements, and endurance. Production team members also visited their machine tool suppliers in New Jersey, helping them redesign their machinery to reduce downtime. And they learned techniques for welding "alloys nobody had welded before," in the words of Jim Fixemer, the engineering manager in charge of the plans. Besides designing the production process itself, the manufacturing engineers also set up tests for the completed circuit breakers.[18]

Determining the Facility Layout

Once managers have established the activities needed in their firm's production process, they can determine the best layout for the facility. This decision requires them to consider all phases of production and the necessary inputs at each step. Figure 12.6 shows three common layout designs: process, product, and fixed-position layouts. It also shows a customer-oriented layout typical of service providers' production systems.

A process layout groups machinery and equipment according to their functions. The work in process moves around the plant to reach different workstations. A process layout often facilitates production of a variety of nonstandard items in relatively small batches. Honda also uses a version of a process layout to build its Civic. The company organizes into several workstations, or "zones," grouping together activities related to the interior, chassis, and wiring and tubing. At the end of each zone, workers perform an inspection before sending the car to the next zone. Nonstandard activities, such as preparing tanks for natural gas-powered vehicles, take place in a subassembly area.[19]

A product layout sets up production equipment along a product-flow line, and the work in process moves along this line past workstations. This type of layout efficiently produces large numbers of similar products, but it may prove inflexible and able to accommodate only a few product variations. Although product layouts date back at least to the Model T assembly line, companies are refining this approach with modern touches. In Saarlouis, Germany, the Ford Focus assembly plant uses a conveyor belt to move workers along the assembly line, rather than expecting them to trudge from car to car. The resulting productivity increase allowed the company to transfer two workers off the assembly line to other jobs. Based on the success of this idea in Saarlouis, Ford has since installed similar conveyor belts in other factories.[20]

A fixed-position layout places the product in one spot, and workers, materials, and equipment come to it. This approach suits production of a very large, bulky, heavy, or fragile product. Examples include building a bridge or assembling an airplane.

Service organizations also must decide on appropriate layouts for their production processes. A service firm should arrange its facilities to enhance the interactions between customers and its services. A hospital, for instance, arranges various departments, each specializing in a different function such as radiology, intensive care, and surgery. Patients move to different departments depending on their needs. If you

FIGURE 12.6 Basic Facility Layouts

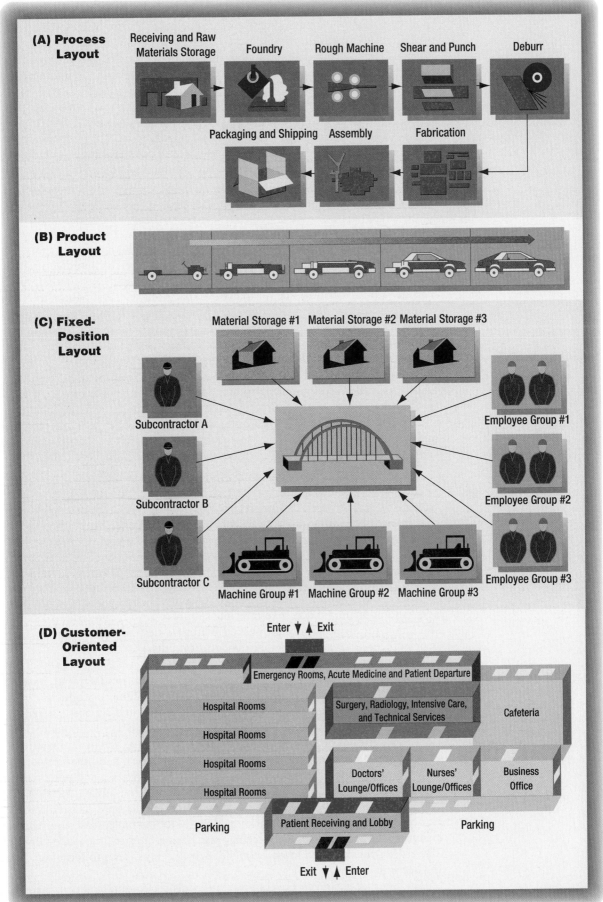

(A) Process Layout

Receiving and Raw Materials Storage — Foundry — Rough Machine — Shear and Punch — Deburr

Packaging and Shipping — Assembly — Fabrication

(B) Product Layout

(C) Fixed-Position Layout

Material Storage #1   Material Storage #2   Material Storage #3

Subcontractor A

Subcontractor B

Subcontractor C

Machine Group #1   Machine Group #2   Machine Group #3

Employee Group #1

Employee Group #2

Employee Group #3

(D) Customer-Oriented Layout

Enter ▼ ▲ Exit

Emergency Rooms, Acute Medicine and Patient Departure

Hospital Rooms

Hospital Rooms

Hospital Rooms

Hospital Rooms

Surgery, Radiology, Intensive Care, and Technical Services

Cafeteria

Doctors' Lounge/Offices

Nurses' Lounge/Offices

Business Office

Parking

Patient Receiving and Lobby

Parking

Exit ▼ ▲ Enter

think of patients as inputs, the hospital implements a form of the process layout. In other service organizations, direct contact with the recipient of services is a less significant part of production. For example, much of a law or accounting firm's work might take place away from clients. Access to colleagues and the Internet, as well as a quiet environment, might be more important for such processes.

Implementing the Production Plan

After planning the production process and determining the best layout, a firm's production managers begin to implement the production plan. This activity involves (1) deciding whether to make, buy, or lease components; (2) selecting the best suppliers for materials; and (3) controlling inventory to keep enough, but not too much, on hand.

Make, Buy, or Lease Decision   One of the fundamental issues facing every producer is the **make, buy, or lease decision**—choosing whether to manufacture a needed product or component in house, purchase it from an outside supplier, or lease it. This decision is a critical one for many organizations. General Motors recently tried to outsource more of its assembly work in an arrangement that called for suppliers to assemble modules such as doors, dashboards, and chassis and suspension systems. Traditionally, GM has assembled these sections in its own factories. The United Auto Workers objected to this change, which would move union assembly jobs to nonunion suppliers, and GM has continued doing its own assembly work. However, DaimlerChrysler uses modular production of pickup trucks in Brazil. At its factory in Curitiba, Brazil, Dana Corp. builds a fully assembled chassis, including tires, springs, shock absorbers, brakes, and other components, then ships it two miles to another DaimlerChrysler facility. Dana itself orders modular components from its suppliers, allowing it, like DaimlerChrysler, to operate a smaller factory.[21]

Several factors affect the make, buy, or lease decision, including the costs of leasing or purchasing parts from outside suppliers compared with the costs of producing them in-house. The decision sometimes hinges on the availability of outside suppliers that can dependably meet standards for quality and quantity. The need for confidentiality sometimes affects the decision, as does the short- or long-term duration of the firm's need for supplies. Because airlines often experience equipment shortages, they may arrange for short-term leases of engines and other aircraft components to meet immediate operating needs.

Even when the firm decides to purchase from outside suppliers, production managers should maintain access to multiple supply sources. An alternative supplier ensures that the firm can obtain needed materials despite strikes, quality assurance problems, or other situations that may affect inputs.

Selection of Suppliers   Once a company decides what inputs to purchase, it must choose the best vendors for its needs. To make this choice, production managers compare the quality, prices, dependability of delivery, and services offered by competing companies. Different suppliers may offer virtually identical quality levels and prices, so the final decision often rests on factors such as the firm's experience with each supplier, speed of delivery, warranties on purchases, and other services.

For a major purchase, negotiations between the purchaser and potential vendors may stretch over several weeks or even months, and the buying decision may rest with a number of colleagues who must say yes before the final decision is made. The choice of a supplier for an industrial drill press, for example, may require a joint decision by the production, engineering, purchasing, and maintenance departments. These departments often must reconcile their different views to settle on a purchasing decision.

The Internet has given buyers powerful tools for finding and comparing suppliers. Buyers can log on to business exchanges to compare specifications, prices, and availability. As illustrated in Figure 12.7, Free Trade Zone lets customers search a database of over 12 million parts from thousands of manufacturers, comparing prices and features of items that meet the buyer's specifications. Suppliers that provide easy ordering and up-to-the-minute information have an edge in the competition for business customers. Aeroquip, for example, lets customers check the availability of parts online. Aeroquip's customers, including Caterpillar, John Deere, and Navistar, can select from among almost 200,000 customized products and request that they be shipped the same day.[22]

Firms often purchase raw materials and component parts on long-term contracts. If a manufacturer requires a continuous supply of materials, a one-year or two-year contract with a supplier helps to ensure availability.

Today, many firms are building long-term relationships with vendors and slashing the number of suppliers with whom they do business. At the same time, they call on vendors to expand their roles in the production process. The previous example of Dana making chassis for DaimlerChrysler is a case in point. Chrysler relies on Dana for timely delivery of a major segment of DaimlerChrysler's pickup trucks, as well as for the quality of those components. To meet the strict demands of today's production managers, suppliers must raise their own quality standards. Part of this task involves ensuring that parts meet manufacturers' specifications before they leave a supplier's factory.

Inventory Control   Production managers' responsibility for **inventory control** requires them to balance the need to keep stocks on hand to meet demand against the costs of carrying the inventory, as described in the "Clicks and Mortar" box about Cessna. Among the expenses involved in storing inventory are warehousing costs, taxes, insurance, and maintenance. A firm wastes money if it holds more inventory than it needs, but a shortage of raw materials, parts, or goods for sale often results in delays and unhappy customers. Firms lose business when they consistently miss promised delivery dates or turn away orders. Production managers must balance this threat against the cost of holding inventory to set acceptable stocking levels.

Effective inventory control can save a great deal of money. In one common technique, many firms maintain **perpetual inventory** systems to continuously monitor the amounts and locations of their stocks. Such inventory control systems typically rely on computers, and many automatically generate orders and print necessary documents at the appropriate times. Many supermarkets link their scanning devices to perpetual inventory systems that reorder needed merchandise without human interaction. As the system records a shopper's purchase, it reduces an inventory count stored in the computer. Once inventory on hand drops to a predetermined level, the system automatically reorders the merchandise.

Some companies go further and hand over their inventory control functions to suppliers. This concept is known as **vendor-managed inventory.** Audio equipment maker Bose Corp. has made arrangements with some of its vendors that effectively transfer control of its inventory to the sellers. An on-site representative is responsible for monitoring Bose's inventory and placing orders when needed without Bose's

FIGURE 12.7
Free Trade Zone: Internet Tools for Selecting Suppliers

Cessna Gets Independent

Background. A few years ago, several airplane executives at Cessna were championing their ideas for promoting new sales growth. Most of them are pilots, and they still love to fly. But Cessna no longer made the plane they really wanted to fly, the one that Cessna had originally built its name on: the small, single engine, piston-powered plane. So they decided to take another run at it.

What Happened? When Cessna surveyed customers who already owned late-model aircraft, they learned that these customers felt much the same as the Cessna executives: they wanted a small plane that mirrored the old Cessna. The tools and machines for making these planes were still in storage, but there the easy part ended. They had to build a new plant to manufacture the new planes. Decisions had to be made regarding where to locate the plant and what type of production process to use in assembling the planes. Where would they get the parts? Since forecasting sales for a new product is a difficult undertaking, how much inventory would they keep on hand in case sales were much greater—or much lower—than they expected?

Cessna preferred to assemble the new plane in its headquarters city of Wichita, Kansas. But its current plants were filled with other business, mostly jets. They could add on to the current plants, but, as technician Pat Boyarski explained, proponents of the new project were afraid that doing so would mean "absorbing the jet mentality: low volume, high customization, slow move rates on the line." So they settled on a location 120 miles away but still in Kansas: a town called Independence.

Once the plant was built, Cessna had to staff it. But skilled aircraft workers were in short supply in Independence. And the company had already made a commitment to the team approach to production. So Cessna decided to recruit workers who seemed to have potential to be good team members even though their technical qualifications would require further development in-house.

Finally, production managers for the Independence plant turned to company-owned facilities for parts, such as a sheet metal plant in Georgia that builds rudders, elevators, and flaps. Other parts were outsourced, as the firm attempted to push inventories further back in the supply chain and rely on just-in-time, just-in-place deliveries.

The Response. Cessna managers set a goal of churning out 1,000 planes during the first year, but the actual number built was 360. Immediately, the problem with the team approach was evident. "What

we did was kick off the team concept with a whole new workforce," explains one employee. Other companies that implement teams do so with workers who are already skilled and experienced. So the Independence plant decided to scrap the team effort for a while to train the workers and get the planes built. Meanwhile, materials manager H.D. Cartwright asked a local investor to open a warehouse in a hangar close to the Independence assembly lines. Then Cartwright persuaded about 20 of his suppliers to move their inventory to the new warehouse. "Initially, some dragged their feet, but now most seem to like it." The new warehouse—called Supplier City—now stocks a week's worth of inventory at a time. Soon it plans to be able to take and make daily deliveries.

Today and Counting. The new Cessna single-engine planes—the Skyhawk, Skylane, and Stationair—are now rolling out of the factory faster, at about 900 per year. With the help of trainers experienced in team development, the Independence teams are back in place and are now skilled enough to move across the assembly lines and work on different plane models, as needed. And Supplier City now plays an enhanced role, mounting both tires and wheels. The purchased parts inventory has been reduced $4 million. Managers continue to look for ways to tighten the waiting time between an order and delivery of a finished plane, which would satisfy customers and even give them less time to change their minds about an order. The code phrase at the Independence plant is "lean manufacturing." The focus, says chief operating officer Charlie Johnson, is "building our business to a business where we have operating excellence."

QUESTIONS FOR CRITICAL THINKING

1. Do you think that the new Cessna plant would have been more successful immediately if it had been located outside Kansas? Why or why not?
2. In what ways could Supplier City be expanded to perform more roles? Do you think this would be a good idea? Why or why not?

Sources: "Our Aircraft" and "Cessna Story," Cessna Web site, **www.cessna.com,** accessed February 12, 2001; Gene Bylinsky, "Better Brains for the Behemoths of Metal Cutting," *Fortune,* June 26, 2000, **www.fortune.com;** Philip Siekman, "Cessna Tackles Lean Manufacturing," *Fortune,* May 1, 2000, pp. I222b–I222z, **www.bizjournals.com/wichita.**

approval. Some firms—such as Wal-Mart—have modified vendor-managed inventory to an approach called CPFAR (collaborative planning, forecasting, and replenishment). CPFAR is a planning and forecasting technique involving collaborative efforts by both purchasers and vendors. Figure 12.8 describes how TTI provides a similar service for electronic parts with its Auto Replenishment Program.

Just-in-Time Systems A **just-in-time (JIT) system** implements a broad management philosophy that reaches beyond the narrow activity of inventory control to influence the entire system of production and operations management. A JIT system seeks to eliminate all sources of waste—anything that does not add value—in operations activities by providing the right part at the right place at the right time. Compared with traditional production, this program reduces inventory and costs as it improves the quality of goods and services.

The inventory control function in a JIT system supplies parts to a production line or an entire company as they are needed. This action lowers factory inventory levels and inventory carrying costs. The JIT system also lets firms respond quickly to changes in the market, retaining only the most essential personnel to maintain inventory. Ford recently tested a program to let customers order customized Mustang models over the Internet and pick them up at dealerships in its Tulsa, Oklahoma, test market. Customers selected options for style, color, engine, and other features, and the order data traveled to the Mustang factory, which operates with a JIT system. From the factory, an electronic link to suppliers automatically ordered the parts needed for producing the cars. Within a month, Ford delivered every car ordered to a Tulsa dealership to await the customer. Not only does this system give customers exactly what they want, it lets Ford and its suppliers capture data about customer preferences, data that can be used in product and production planning.[23]

Production using JIT shifts much of the responsibility for carrying inventory to vendors, which operate on forecasts and keep stocks on hand to respond to manufacturers' needs. Suppliers who cannot keep enough high-quality parts on hand often lose customers to suppliers who can. Another risk of JIT became evident during the 1990s. Strong demand began to overtax JIT systems, as suppliers and their customers struggled to keep up with orders with no cushion of inventory to tide them over.

Producers address the risks of JIT by building long-term relationships with suppliers who demonstrate their ability to meet high standards. Facing a backlog of hundreds of locomotive orders, General Electric Transportation Systems was confident it could meet its production schedule because it uses certified parts from suppliers that it carefully monitors.[24] And Paccar, whose assembly of customized trucks was described earlier in the chapter, has fine-tuned its use of JIT systems by working closely with suppliers. Not only are schedules so precise that components are often delivered directly to the Kenworth assembly line, but specifications are exacting in order to speed up assembly. For example, orders for the rails used to construct a chassis specify that suppliers drill holes as needed for each chassis. Assembly workers at Kenworth can attach cross-linking bars to the rails and quickly create the frame needed to fill each order.[25]

Suppliers can also take the initiative to build these close customer relationships. In Louisville, Kentucky, Badgett Constructors set up an extranet to communicate with Ford, for which Badgett manages construction projects. Ford employees can use the extranet to look up cost estimates, invoices, project status, and other data, as well as provide information for estimating jobs. Not only does the extranet save Ford from copying and distributing paper documents, it helps both supplier and customer communicate with fewer misunderstandings. The extranet was so successful that Badgett now offers the system as a separate

Now you see it.   Now you don't.   Now you see it.

Auto Replenishment from TTI.

Getting the passive components you need can be easier, faster, and more cost-efficient than ever with a customized Auto Replenishment program from TTI. Especially when managing your passive component inventory is costing you more than the components themselves are worth.

If some of the cheapest components you buy end up costing you the most, Auto Replenishment may be just what you need, with product on the shelf even before you know you need it. And, the lower

the price of the component, the more TTI can help you save.

When you're buying passive components, you shouldn't be paying much more than a penny for a penny's worth of product. The sooner you start Auto Replenishment with TTI, the sooner you begin to reduce those acquisition costs. To find out more about a customized Auto Replenishment program for your inventory, call TTI Strategic Program Management at (817) 740-9000.

ALWAYS DELIVERING MORE
RESISTORS CAPACITORS CONNECTORS
1 - 8 0 0 - C A L L - T T I
www.ttiinc.com

FIGURE 12.8
Automatic Reordering of Electronic Components

business called the Internet Contracting, Estimating and Accounting System (ICEAS).[26]

Reengineering Reducing cycle times has become a major goal of production and operations management. *Cycle time* is the time required to complete a work process or activity from beginning to end. At Paccar, the company's advantages over competitors include the Kenworth factory's ability to fill orders within two or three weeks, compared with the industry norm of six to eight weeks. It can also measure the time it takes to design a conveyor system, handle a customer inquiry, or create an employee training video. Cycle time reductions accomplish two important objectives:

- Reducing the time required to bring new products to the marketplace
- Permitting the firm to produce and deliver customer orders more quickly

Many firms are reengineering their processes to accomplish these objectives. **Reengineering** is the process of mapping out delivery-chain processes in detail to identify potential ways of reducing cycle times or process errors by applying technology to each step in a process. When a company reengineers a process, it carefully evaluates and then modifies management systems, job designs, and work flows in an effort to improve efficiency and reduce cycle time. Paccar improved its processes by incorporating workers' suggestions into its production plans. The company rearranged the placement of parts, cutting the amount of walking to retrieve parts from 3,213 feet per shift to just 500 feet.[27]

Materials Requirement Planning Besides efficiency, effective inventory control requires careful planning to make sure the firm has all the inputs it needs to make its products. How do production and operations managers coordinate all of this information? They rely on **materials requirement planning (MRP)**, a computer-based production planning system that lets a firm ensure that it has all the parts and materials it needs to produce its goods and services at the right time and place and in the right amounts.

Production managers use MRP programs to create schedules that identify the specific parts and materials required to produce an item. These schedules specify the exact quantities required of each and the dates on which to release orders to suppliers so deliveries will support the best timing within the production cycle. A small company might get by without an MRP system. If a firm makes a simple product with few components, a telephone call may ensure overnight delivery of crucial parts. For a complex product, however, such as a car or an F-15 fighter jet, MRP becomes an invaluable tool.

Controlling the Production Process

After planning, determining plant layout, and implementing the production plan comes the final task of production and operations managers, and perhaps the most important one of all: controlling the production process to maintain the highest possible quality. **Production control** creates a well-defined set of procedures for coordinating people, materials, and machinery to provide maximum production efficiency. Suppose that a watch factory must produce 80,000 watches during October. Production-control executives break down this total into a daily production assignment of 4,000 watches for each of the month's 20 working days. Next, they determine the number of workers, raw materials, parts, and machines the plant needs to meet the production schedule. Similarly, a manager in a service business such as a restaurant must estimate how many meals the outlet will serve each day and then determine how many people are needed to prepare and serve the food, as well as what food to purchase.

| Planning | → | Routing | → | Scheduling | → | Dispatching | → | Follow-up |

FIGURE 12.9
Steps in Production Control

Figure 12.9 illustrates production control as a five-step process composed of planning, routing, scheduling, dispatching, and follow-up. These steps are part of the firm's overall emphasis on total quality management.

Production Planning   The phase of production control called **production planning** determines the amount of resources (including raw materials and other components) a firm needs to produce a certain output. The production planning process develops a bill of materials that lists all needed parts and materials. By comparing information about needed parts and materials with the firm's perpetual inventory data, purchasing personnel can identify necessary purchases. Employees or automated systems establish delivery schedules to ensure that needed parts and materials arrive as required during the production process. Production planning also ensures the availability of needed machines and workers. Although material inputs contribute to service-production systems, production planning for services tends to emphasize human resources more than materials.

Routing   Another phase of production control, called **routing,** determines the sequence of work throughout the facility and specifies who will perform each aspect of production at what location. Routing choices depend on two factors: the nature of the good or service and the facility layouts discussed earlier in the chapter—product, process, fixed-position, or customer-oriented layouts.

Observing production activities can improve routing decisions. At the Fenton, Michigan, factory of TRW Chassis Systems, a team of employees charged with improving work processes on an assembly line discovered that one worker's job consisted of simply moving parts from the end of a conveyor line to a test stand. The team moved the test stand, placing it next to the end of the assembly line so that the tester could unload the items. The unnecessary worker moved to another—probably more gratifying—job in a different part of the plant.[28]

Scheduling   In the **scheduling** phase of production control, production managers develop timetables that specify how long each operation in the production process takes and when workers should perform it. Efficient scheduling ensures that production will meet delivery schedules and make efficient use of resources.

Scheduling is an extremely important activity for a manufacturer of a complex product with many parts or production stages. Think of all the component parts needed to make a CT or MRI scanner or other hospital equipment. Scheduling must make each one available in the right place, at the right time, and in the right amounts to ensure a smooth production process.

Scheduling practices vary considerably in service-related organizations. Local delivery companies or doctors' offices may use relatively unsophisticated scheduling systems, resorting to such devices as "first come, first served" rules, appointment schedules, or take-a-number systems. They may call in part-time workers and use standby equipment to handle demand fluctuations. On the other hand, hospitals typically implement sophisticated scheduling systems similar to those of manufacturers.

Production managers use a number of analytical methods for scheduling. One of the oldest methods, the *Gantt chart*, tracks projected and actual work progress over time. Gantt charts like the one in Figure 12.10 remain popular because they show at a glance the status of a particular project. However, they are most effective for scheduling relatively simple projects.

BUSINESS DIRECTORY

▶ **materials requirement planning (MRP)**   *computer-based production planning system by which a firm can ensure that it has needed parts and materials available at the right time and place in the correct amounts.*

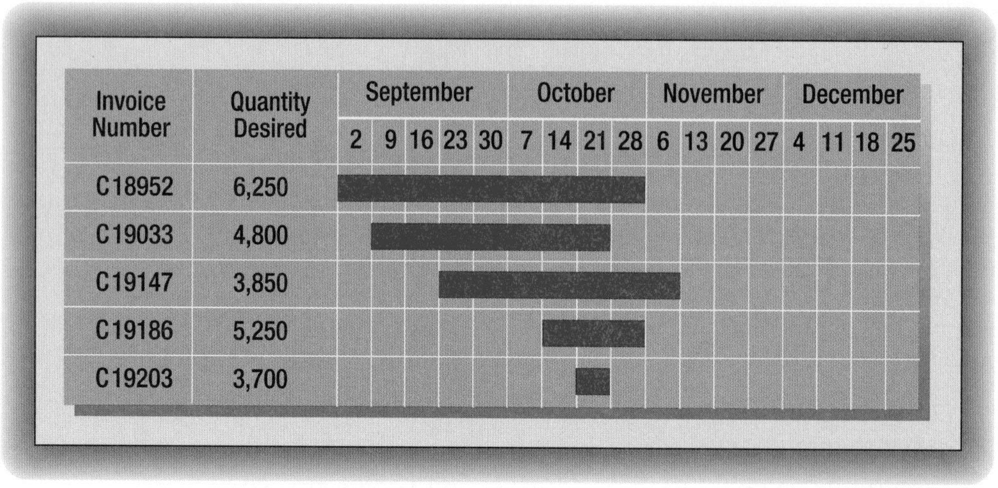

Invoice Number	Quantity Desired	September					October				November				December			
		2	9	16	23	30	7	14	21	28	6	13	20	27	4	11	18	25
C18952	6,250																	
C19033	4,800																	
C19147	3,850																	
C19186	5,250																	
C19203	3,700																	

FIGURE 12.10
Sample Gantt Chart

A complex project might require a **PERT (Program Evaluation and Review Technique)** chart, which seeks to minimize delays by coordinating all aspects of the production process. First developed for the military, PERT has been modified for industry. The simplified PERT diagram in Figure 12.11 summarizes the schedule for construction of a house in a subdivision developed by a national home builder. The red line indicates the **critical path**—the sequence of operations that requires the longest time for completion. Operations outside the critical path allow some slack time and can be performed earlier or delayed until later in the production process. Large-scale builders can assign some workers and machinery to critical-path tasks early in the process and then reassign them to noncritical operations as needed.

In practice, a PERT network may consist of thousands of events and cover months of time. Complex computer programs help production managers to develop such a network and find the critical path among the maze of events and activities.

Dispatching   The phase of production control in which the manager instructs each department on what work to do and the time allowed for its completion is called **dispatching**. The dispatcher authorizes performance, provides instructions, and lists job priorities. Dispatching may be the responsibility of a manager or a self-managed work team.

Follow-Up   Because even the best plans sometimes go awry, production managers need to be aware of problems that arise. **Follow-up** is the phase of production control in which employees and their supervisors spot problems in the production process and determine needed adjustments. Problems take many forms: machinery malfunctions, delayed shipments, and employee absenteeism can all affect production. The production-control system must detect and report these delays to managers or work teams so they can adjust schedules and correct the underlying problems.

Even when production is meeting schedules, follow-up can detect opportunities to improve processes. As described earlier, TRW assigned teams at its Fenton, Michigan, plant to study operations and identify areas for improvement. One team measured cycle times for every activity on an assembly line. Based on the company's existing data, the team expected to find a bottleneck at the final test station. But after taking careful measurements along the assembly line, the team discovered that production was actually slowing down at a bar-code scanner. The team members studied the problem and determined that the scanner had stopped working properly when the assembly line changed over to making a different product. An employee rewired the scanner, and the assembly line's cycle time improved.[29]

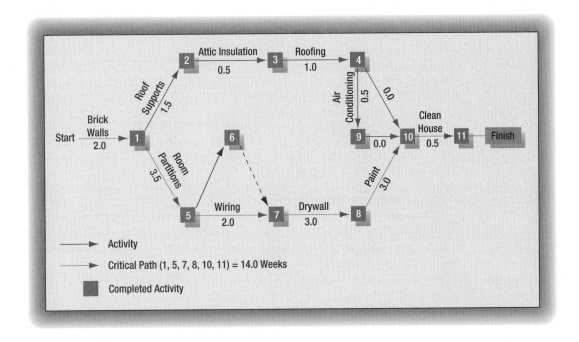

FIGURE 12.11
PERT Diagram for Building a House

Manufacturing Resource Planning

While an MRP system controls inventory, production and operations managers can use a more advanced computer-based system to manage all of a firm's production resources. Called **manufacturing resource planning (MRP II)**, the system integrates planning data from individual departments—marketing, production, engineering, and finance—to produce a master business plan for the entire organization. MRP II then translates the business plan into various forecasts, setting requirements for inventory, materials handling, human resources, and the production schedule. All managers have access to this information. MRP II automatically responds to a change in a sales forecast by adjusting production scheduling. Some MRP II software can even advise managers on solutions to manufacturing and other production problems.

IMPORTANCE OF QUALITY

As discussed throughout the text, quality is vital in all areas of business, including the product development and production functions, which the "Business Hits and Misses" box explores. Many companies realize that they can build high-quality products most effectively by incorporating quality into product designs from the very beginning. In contrast, problems can be costly and sometimes even deadly. Evidence now suggests that the relatively frequent rollovers of SUVs result partly from such design faults as a high center of gravity and a wheelbase that is too narrow to provide enough stability.[30]

Investing money up front in quality design and development ultimately decreases the cost of quality, measured by costs that result from failure to make the good or service right the first time. These costs average at least 20 percent of sales revenue for most companies. Some typical costs of poor quality include downtime, repair costs, rework, and employee turnover. Production and operations managers must set up systems to track and reduce such costs. If managers concentrate on making a high-quality product that satisfies the needs of customers, they will reduce costs of quality as a by-product. Figure 12.12 conveys a company's focus on quality and customer satisfaction.

BUSINESS DIRECTORY

➤ **manufacturing resource planning (MRP II)** *production-control system that integrates planning data from individual departments to produce a master business plan.*

To every driver with a poor sense of direction, it sounds like a great idea: push a button and you'll be connected to a friendly voice who will tell you where to turn left or right as you navigate toward that new restaurant. Or if you've locked yourself out of your car as you leave the restaurant, you can head straight back inside, make a phone call, and the car will be unlocked by remote control. This technology already exists—not on the drawing board, but in reality. We're describing OnStar, a division of General Motors that uses the satellites and wireless communication of the Global Positioning System (GPS) to assist drivers in trouble.

The idea itself is fairly simple. When drivers push the OnStar buttons in their cars, they are instantly connected to human beings located in a call center who are trained to help them. But "smart car" technology is complicated and doesn't always work. Because the technology is new, complicated, and sometimes confusing, it is not surprising that quality problems have created bumps in the road for users as well as producers. For instance, although OnStar's assistants are personable and well trained, they might be based many miles from the driver's call and so not be quick enough at giving directions in an unfamiliar city. Several auto manufacturers plan to introduce an automated form of OnStar, which will instruct autos to read aloud everything from local weather to stock quotes. However, the limitations of voice recognition and slow cellular connections will probably prohibit two-way communications, and customers will have to complete lengthy questionnaires that will be fed into a personal Web page on a PC, which will then be sent to the car. Ford and Yahoo! plan to team up to offer this service, and OnStar will launch its own news portal. Clarion's AutoPC is a voice-activated service that runs on Windows CE, displayed on a tiny screen that fits into a car's dashboard. The problem is that the screen is too small to be read easily by many drivers, and the system has trouble recognizing the higher-pitched voices of women. All of this "smart" technology is not free to consumers, either. The OnStar service runs about $400 per year, and the AutoPC will cost around $2,000, not including installation or monthly fees.

Auto companies are well aware of the quality problems that accompany the new technology. OnStar maintains that it is working hard to alleviate them and that their device is an important tool for drivers, not just a frivolous option. "Whatever we put in the cars needs to be completely intuitive and to work, period," asserts OnStar's general manager, Chet Huber. "We're not trying to demonstrate what's possible technologically." While they work out the bugs, most auto manufacturers are holding off on installing smart devices in regular production vehicles. Instead, they will continue to focus on the higher-end, luxury cars. Even so, GM is about to begin trying out a new system from Visteon called ICES, which is similar to AutoPC but has a larger screen and better voice-recognition technology. And many of the cars that come equipped with GPS devices will also be able to report real-time traffic information and road conditions. Soon you'll be able to find your way to the best steakhouse, avoid a traffic tie-up, and even book airline or concert tickets from the comfort of your car. And all this may cost less than the rent on your first apartment.

QUESTIONS FOR CRITICAL THINKING

1. What criteria might production managers use to set quality standards for "smart car" technology?
2. How might production managers use MRP II to improve the quality of "smart car" technology?

Sources: "About OnStar: Introduction," OnStar Web site, **www.onstar.com**, accessed February 13, 2001; Susan Gregory Thomas, "Smart Cars," *U.S. News & World Report,* February 14, 2000, pp. 62–63; Jeff Rothfeder, "Know It Alls," *Excellence Edge,* August/September 1999, pp. 39–43; "Clarion Launches Vetronix Corporation's Carport for the AutoPC," Clarion press release, December 28, 1999.

Quality Control

Quality control involves measuring goods and services against established quality standards. Firms need such checks to spot defective products and to avoid delivering inferior shipments to customers. Standards should be set high enough to meet customer expectations. A 90 or 95 percent success rate might sound like a good number, but consider what your phone service or ATM network would be like if it operated for that share of time. Every year it would be out of service for 438 hours (5 percent of the year) to 875 hours (10 percent). Even companies whose service has been down for just a few hours during a year—as has happened to eBay and E*Trade—have received volumes of negative publicity.[31] Ways to monitor quality levels of a firm's output include visual inspections, electronic sensors, robots, and X-rays. Customer surveys can provide quality-control information for service businesses. Negative feedback or a high rejection rate on a product or component sends a danger signal that production is not achieving quality standards.

Of course, a company cannot rely solely on inspections to achieve its quality goals. A typical American factory spends up to half its operating budget identifying and fixing mistakes, a costly and time-consuming process. Instead, quality-driven production managers identify all processes involved in producing goods and services and work to maximize their efficiency. The causes of problems in the processes must be found and eliminated. If a company concentrates its efforts on improving processes, a high-quality product will result.

General Electric and Motorola are just two of the growing number of major manufacturers using the so-called *Six Sigma* concept to achieve these goals. Six Sigma means a company tries to make error-free products 99.9997 percent of the time—a tiny 3.4 errors per million opportunities. At GE, the goal is to eliminate virtually all defects in its products, processes, and transactions. Just three years after implementing the concept, GE reported that it was saving the company more than $2 billion a year. GE's Web site states: "Six Sigma has changed the DNA of GE. It is now the way we work on everything we do and is in every product we design."[32]

ISO Standards

For many goods, an important measure of quality is to meet standards of the **International Organization for Standardization,** known as **ISO** for short—not an acronym but a shorter name derived from the Greek word *isos,* meaning "equal." The organization uses ISO as an alternative to different acronyms for every member's language. Established in Europe in 1947, ISO includes representatives from about 130 nations. Its mission is to promote the development of standardized products to facilitate trade and cooperation across national borders. ISO standards govern everything from camera film speeds to the thickness of credit cards and even the terminology of international measurement units and the symbols for automobile controls. The U.S. member body of ISO is the American National Standards Institute.

During the 1980s and 1990s, ISO developed standards not just for products themselves but for systems of management. The ISO 9000 series of standards (www.iso.ch) sets requirements for quality processes; these standards define how a company should ensure that its products meet customers' requirements. The ISO 14000 series sets standards for operations that minimize harm to the environment. ISO accredits organizations in member countries to evaluate performance against these standards. To receive ISO 9000 certification, a company must undergo an on-site audit. The audit ensures that documented quality procedures are in place and that all employees understand and follow these procedures. Production managers meet these requirements through an ongoing process involving periodic recertification.[33]

Over 300,000 companies in 150 countries have received certification in the ISO 9000 family of standards. Their numbers are growing rapidly, with the fastest growth in Australia and the U.S.[34] Over half the certificates have been awarded in Europe. In fact, ISO 9000 certification has become a condition of doing business with many major European firms, as well as with a significant number of corporations worldwide.

FIGURE 12.12
Importance of Quality Control to Customers

WHAT'S AHEAD

Maintaining high quality is an important element of satisfying customers. Product quality and customer satisfaction are also objectives of the business function of marketing. The next part consists of four chapters that explore the many activities involved in customer-driven marketing. These activities include product development, pricing, distribution of products to customers, and promotion.

➤ Summary of Learning Goals

1. Outline the importance of production and operations management.

Like marketing, accounting, and human resource management, production and operations management is a vital business function. Without a marketable good or service, a company cannot create profits, and it soon fails. The production process is also crucial in a not-for-profit organization, since the good or service it produces justifies the organization's existence. Production and operations management plays an important strategic role by lowering the costs of production, boosting output quality, and allowing the firm to respond flexibly and dependably to customers' demands.

2. Explain the roles of computers and related technologies in production.

Computer-driven automation allows companies to design, create, and modify products rapidly and produce them in ways that effectively meet customers' changing needs. Important design and production technologies include robots, computer-aided design (CAD), computer-aided manufacturing (CAM), and computer-integrated manufacturing (CIM).

3. Identify the factors involved in a plant location decision.

Criteria for choosing the best site for a production facility fall into three categories: transportation, human, and physical factors. Transportation factors include proximity to markets and raw materials, along with availability of transportation alternatives. Physical variables involve such issues as water supply, available energy, and options for disposing of hazardous wastes. Human factors include the area's labor supply, local regulations, and living conditions.

4. Identify and briefly explain the major tasks of production and operations managers.

Production and operations managers use people and machinery to convert inputs (materials and resources) into finished goods and services. Four major tasks are involved. First, the managers must plan the overall production process. Next, they must pick the best layout for production facilities and implement their production plans. Finally, they are responsible for controlling the production process and evaluating results to maintain the highest possible quality.

5. Compare alternative layouts for production facilities.

Process layouts effectively produce nonstandard products in relatively small batches. Product layouts facilitate production of designs with limited variations in relatively large quantities. Fixed-position layouts are common when production involves very large, heavy, or fragile products. Customer-oriented layouts are typical for service facilities where success depends on interaction between customers and service facilities.

6. List the steps in the purchasing process.

In the make, buy, or lease decision, production and operations managers determine whether to manufacture needed inputs in-house, purchase them, or lease them from an outside supplier. Managers responsible for purchasing determine the correct materials to purchase, select appropriate suppliers, and develop an efficient ordering system. The objective is to buy the right materials in the right amounts at the right time and in the right place.

7. Compare the advantages and disadvantages of maintaining large inventories.

The task of inventory control is to balance the need to maintain adequate supplies against the need to minimize funds invested in inventory. Excessive inventory results in unnecessary expenditures for warehousing, taxes, insurance, and maintenance. Inadequate inventory may mean production delays, lost sales, and inefficient operations.

8. Identify the steps in the production-control process.

The production-control process consists of five steps: planning, routing, scheduling, dispatching, and follow-up. Quality control is an important consideration throughout this process. Coordination of each of these phases should result in high production efficiency and low production costs.

9. Explain the benefits of quality control.

Quality control involves evaluating goods and services against established quality standards. Such checks are necessary to spot defective products and to see that they are not shipped to customers. Devices for monitoring quality levels of the firm's output include visual inspection, electronic sensors, robots, and X-rays. Quality is just as vital in product development; investing money up front in quality design and development ultimately decreases the costs of quality.

Business Terms You Need to Know

production 428
production and operations management 428
assembly line 430
robot 433
computer-aided design (CAD) 435

computer-aided manufacturing (CAM) 435
computer-integrated manufacturing (CIM) 436
just-in-time (JIT) system 444
materials requirement planning (MRP) 446
manufacturing resource planning (MRP II) 449

Other Important Business Terms

mass production 429
flexible manufacturing system
    (FMS) 435
environmental impact study 438
make, buy, or lease decision 442
inventory control 443
perpetual inventory 443

vendor-managed inventory (VMI) 443
reengineering 446
production control 446
production planning 447
routing 447
scheduling 447
PERT (Program Evaluation and Review
    Technique) 448

critical path 448
dispatching 448
follow-up 448
quality control 450
International Organization for
    Standardization (ISO) 451

➤ Review Questions

1. What is *utility?* Define and describe briefly the four different types of utility.

2. Distinguish between production and manufacturing. In what ways does each of the following perform a production function?

   a. a delicatessen

   b. a hair stylist

   c. an air traffic control system

3. Why is production such an important business activity? In what ways does it create value for the company and its customers?

4. How does mass production work? What are its benefits and limitations? Describe a good or service that would lend itself well to mass production and one that would not lend itself well to mass production.

5. Describe briefly the four different production systems and give an example of a good or service that is produced by each.

6. Distinguish between computer-aided design (CAD) and computer-aided manufacturing (CAM).

7. In what ways is the Internet advancing the integration of manufacturing and linking it to marketing and other activities?

8. What are the three categories that provide advantages for the best locations for companies? How does each function provide its advantage?

9. What would be the best type of facility layout for each of the following?

   a. a retail gift shop

   b. a chain of economy motels

   c. a car wash

   d. a dentist's office

   e. a shoe repair shop

10. Identify and describe briefly the five steps involved in the process of production control.

➤ Questions for Critical Thinking

1. As discussed in the chapter text, most U.S. auto companies—except DaimlerChrysler—use the production push method in their production planning. How do you think the auto industry would change if auto companies began to shift more toward production pull?

2. Imagine that you have been hired as a management consultant for one of the following types of service organizations to decide on an appropriate layout for its facility. Select one, and sketch or describe the layout that you think would be best.

   a. a chain of dry-cleaning outlets

   b. a doctor's office

   c. a small, elegant Chicago restaurant

   d. a resort hotel located on the U.S. Gulf Coast

   e. a coffee house

3. Imagine that you have been hired as production manager for a snowboard manufacturer (or choose another type of manufacturer that interests you). What

type of inventory control would you recommend for your company? Write a brief memo explaining why.

4. As production manager for the company in Question 3, evaluate your community or its surrounding area as a prospective site for one of your company's facilities. What are the area's strengths and weaknesses? Would you recommend it as a site for your company? Why or why not?

5. Suggest two or three ways in which each of the following firms could practice effective quality control:

   a. a pharmaceuticals manufacturer

   b. a miniature golf course

   c. an Internet florist

➤ Experiential Exercise

Background: As discussed in this chapter and throughout the text, quality is vital in all areas of business. One measure of a product's quality is the feedback a company receives from its customers.

Directions: Complete the following items to learn how companies solicit customer feedback about their products.

1. Randomly select five food or personal care products you've recently purchased and complete the following chart. If no feedback options are provided on the packaging, list "none" in the second column. The first one is provided as an example.

Item No.	Product Name	Customer Feedback Option(s)
Example	Kraft Macaroni & Cheese	www.thecheesiest.com 1-800-847-1997
1.		
2.		
3.		
4.		
5.		

2. Select one product from those you've listed that provides a toll-free telephone number and call the customer service representative. Tell the person handling your call that you're doing research for a college business class where you're studying the topic "Creating and Producing World-Class Goods and Services" and that you'd appreciate the answers to a few questions.

   a. What kinds of calls do you handle most frequently: compliments, complaints, or suggestions for improving your product?

   b. When a customer calls with a complaint about one of your products, what kind of information about the complaint are you required to find out?

   c. What are you authorized to do to satisfy a disgruntled customer?

   d. What do you do with the information you've collected?

   e. What does your company do with the information?

3. Be prepared to share your feelings in a class discussion.

➤ Nothing but Net

1. **Six Sigma.** As mentioned in the chapter, several large manufacturers use a technique called Six Sigma to improve product and service quality. Visit the following Web sites listed and prepare a brief oral report on the Six Sigma technique. Include a brief description of how it works and its overall objective. Cite several examples of where it has been successfully implemented.

   www.sixsigmasystems.com

   www.admssixgima.com

   www.bus.miami.edu/dept/execed/sigma.html

2. **Improving manufacturing processes.** Recently the Boeing Co. has undertaken two initiatives designed to improve the efficiency and effectiveness of its commercial aircraft manufacturing process. Visit Boeing's Web site and write a report on these two initiatives. Answer the following questions:

   a. What are the names of the two initiatives?

   b. What is the overall goal of each initiative?

   c. What are the key elements?

   d. How has each been implemented?

   www.boeing.com/commercial/initiatives

3. **CAD software.** The chapter describes the use of computer-aided design (CAD) software in the design and manufacturing of various products. Some CAD programs are proprietary, and others are commercially available. Some CAD programs run on PCs, and others require more sophisticated computer systems. Visit the ZDNet Web site and search for reviews of CAD software programs that can be used on PCs. Read reviews of these programs. What can these programs do? What are their limitations? How much computing power do they require? How much do they cost? Summarize your findings and write a brief description of the kind of business that would benefit from using a CAD-based software program.

   www.zdnet.com

Note: Internet Web addresses change frequently. If you do not find the exact sites listed, you may need to access the organization's or company's home page and search from there.

By the time Keith Clinkscales began his graduate studies in business, he was already a magazine publisher. After college, while working at Chemical Bank in New York, Clinkscales noticed a trend in journalism that he didn't like: a lack of attention to African Americans. So the 24-year-old decided to start his own magazine. With money borrowed from friends, Clinkscales put together his first issue of *Urban Profile,* which immediately became popular—almost unheard of in the publishing industry. Within a few years, *Urban Profile* was up and running.

Meanwhile, music legend Quincy Jones was feeling much the same way about the music industry that Clinkscales was. So he teamed up with Time Warner to launch a magazine that would cover traditionally African American music genres that were often overlooked by *Rolling Stone,* which had been in circulation for 25 years with a readership of 1.2 million. *Urban Profile* came to the attention of Jones and Time Warner, and Clinkscales was offered the chance to head up a new publication called *Vibe.* Clinkscales was ambitious from the start. "We wanted to be *Rolling Stone,* only with different music. For me to even utter in a meeting that we were going to challenge *Rolling Stone* sounded crazy," recalls Clinkscales, "but I knew that if I didn't lay out the vision, it would not happen."

Today *Vibe,* along with its sister publications *Spin* and *Blaze,* reaches 1.5 million readers seeking news and stories on the alternative rock scene, hip-hop, and other popular music trends. Production of these publications is now much more sophisticated than it was a decade ago—the computer and digital technology have revolutionized what once was a time- and labor-intensive business. Vibe/Spin Ventures, now a subsidiary of the Miller Publishing Group, recently contracted with high-tech printing giant R.R. Donnelly to print the three magazines. Although the initial production work like design and page layout is done in-house with Macintosh computers and the desktop publishing program Quark Xpress, Donnelly has become the supplier for the final printed product. *Vibe* staffers transmit digital files to Donnelly via WAMNET—a high-powered e-mail system—or via Federal Express, depending on content and time constraints. If a piece of art or photograph for an advertisement doesn't arrive in time to be included in the page files, page designers save a "window" in the file for the missing image, which they later send via FedEx. The WAMNET service costs about $8,000 a month, but it lets *Vibe* transmit larger page document files than a standard e-mail system would allow—and do so instantaneously. According to Cara Donatto of *Vibe,* the digital technology used in-house is quite costly, but it does tighten production time and bypasses the older, traditional generation of film for printing processes. Now, digital data files can link to the prepress equipment at Donnelly's printing plant to produce the plates from which the magazine pages will be printed. However, the whole system requires skilled workers, and only saves time—and related costs—if it runs smoothly.

With the move to Donnelly, *Vibe* managers decided to make changes in the look of the magazine as well. Shifting from the larger tabloid size, *Vibe* and *Spin* are now printed on standard-sized magazine pages. According to Donnelly, the new page dimensions "allow for improved paper and print quality, more advertising design flexibility and reduced postage costs," all of which create enhanced value for advertisers and readers.

The choice of Donnelly as print supplier was based on a variety of factors. "We chose R.R. Donnelly in no small part because of their manufacturing acumen, paper management expertise, distribution strengths, and ability to identify cost savings while enhancing the quality of our magazines," notes Ryan Jones, group production director of Vibe/Spin Ventures. "Donnelly found a way to help us improve our publications."

"Shifting to the standard-sized page format will benefit readers, advertisers, and Miller Publishing alike, and is an example of how printers can manage resources to great effect," agrees Robert Pyzdrowski, president of R.R. Donnelly Magazine Publishing Services. "We approached Miller with a new way to look at how they produce and distribute their magazines, and in doing so, we helped them find more value in the printing process. This is the consultative role printers must play to maximize the printing process for their publishing customers."

Former *Vibe* chief Keith Clinkscales has since moved on to launch and head up Vanguarde Media, which publishes other magazines, but *Vibe* is clearly thriving. "Many media companies have had great concepts, but ultimately failed because they could not execute well once in the market." In partnership with strategic suppliers like Donnelly, *Vibe* is executing its production function just fine.

QUESTIONS

1. In what ways does *Vibe* create utility?
2. In what ways does *Vibe* maintain quality control during its production process?
3. Describe or draw the layout that you think would be most efficient for the staffers who work at *Vibe.*
4. Visit the Vibe Web site at **www.vibe.com** or purchase a copy of *Vibe* or *Spin,* and note the layout and overall look of the magazine. What do you like about it? What do you dislike? Write a brief "review" outlining your opinions.

Sources: Company Web site, **www.vibe.com,** accessed April 4, 2001; "Vibe Time," Apple Computer Web site, **www.apple.com,** accessed April 6, 2001; Gregory Pal, "Keith Clinkscales: Chairman and CEO of Vanguarde Media, Inc.," Vanguarde Web site, **www.vanguaredemedia.com,** April 10, 2000; "R.R. Donnelly Inks Multi-Year Contract to Produce *Vibe, Spin,* and *Blaze,*" Donnelly Web site, **www.rrdonnelly.com.** January 4, 2000.

PART IV

Marketing Management

CHAPTER 13

Customer-Driven Marketing

Learning Goals

1. Summarize the ways in which marketing creates utility.

2. Explain the marketing concept and relate how customer satisfaction contributes to added value.

3. Describe the components of a market and distinguish between B2B and B2C marketing.

4. Outline the basic steps in developing a marketing strategy.

5. Describe the marketing research function.

6. Identify each of the methods available for segmenting consumer and business markets.

7. Distinguish between buyer behavior and consumer behavior.

8. Discuss relationship marketing, including its importance in strategic planning.

WWF: "We're Not Afraid of Anything"

Even if you're not a fan, you've heard of them. Names like Stone Cold Steve Austin and Hulk Hogan are familiar to many Americans. They are part of the WWF—the World Wrestling Federation—which sounds like an international athletic association, but it's not. The WWF is in the entertainment business. It was founded by third-generation wrestling promoter Vince McMahon, who still owns 78 percent of the company's stock and controls 97 percent of its voting shares. Although the organization is now an entertainment giant, it is definitely a family-run operation. At the WWF's $15 million headquarters, where Vince is chairman, his wife Linda is company chief executive officer; their son Shane heads the company Web site, wwf.com; and Shane's wife Marissa is WWF's publicity director. Sister Stephanie is part of the creative writing team. What do they do, and for whom?

The WWF stages 200 live professional wrestling shows a year around the country, featuring stars with names like Lethal Weapon and The Rock. These matches allow performers, usually attired in costumes and wild makeup, to slam dunk each other in a variety of creative ways. In addition to the live shows, the company's entertainment delivery system includes television programs, most of which are taped at the live performances; the Web site; plenty of merchandising tie-ins, including action figures for children; and the McMahons' newest venture, a professional football league called the XFL.

Who watches these performances? A lot of people. Wrestlemania 2000, the WWF's headline show, was the highest grossing nonboxing pay-per-view program of all time. Fans pack the live arenas, large and small. And the audience is usually booing and cheering at near hysteria pitch. "It's one thing to hear about us selling out the arena," comments chief operating officer (COO) Stuart Snyder, but "it's another thing to see us blow the roof off." The specific definition of the WWF target audience consists of males between the ages of 12 and 34 years, but the actual market is much broader. About 50 million fans worldwide tune in to the WWF's cable television program, *Raw Is War,* making it the most popular regularly scheduled cable television program, even among young women. More young men in the target market watch the

WWF program than *Monday Night Football.* And more people attend the live shows than go to music concerts. Even books by WWF stars like The Rock and Mankind hit number one on the *New York Times* bestseller list. Several years ago, when Vince McMahon saw his four-year-old son Shane playing with GI Joe figures, he decided that WWF action figures would be just as popular among the younger set. So he struck a licensing deal with Hasbro. Then there's Jim Johnston, a self-taught musician who writes, produces, and performs the music that accompanies all of WWF's shows. Two CDs of the music have gone platinum, leading the WWF to start its own record label called Smackdown Records.

Many marketing experts agree that the McMahon family has successfully identified what consumers crave and given it to them. "I think it's a totally spectacular business, one of the best consumer businesses I've ever seen," says Larry Haverty, an analyst who also happens to be a WWF shareholder. However, the WWF has its critics.

Parents worry about the influence that the staged violence may have on their children and about the message that the performances send to kids in the audience. A Los Angeles–based group called the Parents' Television Council has been influential in persuading some large companies like The Coca-Cola Company and AT&T to pull their advertising from WWF events and publications. Linda McMahon argues that "there's no portrayal of murder, rape, or robbery" in the WWF shows. "There's no use of guns or knives." But there certainly is violence, so it's not surprising that plenty of journalists and parents question the impact of WWF performances. Still, the WWF retains major advertisers whose goods and services are geared to young people, such as Nestlé, Burger King, and Nintendo. And the cable networks that air WWF shows seem undaunted. Vince McMahon simply views the criticism as a challenge, one he intends to win. His goal is to create a sports-entertainment empire that overshadows Disney, and he's already begun to extend it through the XFL football league that debuted in 2001. "We're not afraid of anything," he likes to say. No one would doubt that he means it.[1]

CHAPTER OVERVIEW

Business success in the 21st century is directly tied to a company's ability to identify and serve its target markets. In fact, all organizations—profit-oriented and not-for-profit, manufacturing and retailing—*must* serve customer needs to succeed. Marketing is the link between the organization and the people who buy and use its products. It is the way organizations determine buyer needs and inform potential customers that their firms can meet those needs by supplying a quality product at a reasonable price.

Although final consumers who purchase for their own use and enjoyment or business purchasers seeking products to use in the operation of their firms may seem to be massive, formless markets, marketers see different wants and needs for each group. To understand buyers, from huge manufacturers to Web surfers to shoppers in the grocery aisles, companies are gathering mountains of data on every aspect of lifestyles and buying behaviors. Marketers use the data to understand the needs and wants of both final customers and business buyers so that they can satisfy them.

This chapter begins with an examination of the marketing concept and the way businesspeople develop a marketing strategy. We then turn to marketing research techniques, leading to an explanation of how businesses apply marketing research data to market segmentation and understanding customer behavior. The chapter closes with a detailed look at the important role played by customer relationships in today's highly competitive business world.

WHAT IS MARKETING?

All organizations—profit-oriented and not-for-profit—must serve customer needs to succeed. Perhaps J. C. Penney best expressed this priority when he told his store managers, "Either you or your replacement will greet the customer within the first 60 seconds."

Marketing is the process of determining customer wants and needs and then providing the goods and services that meet or exceed expectations. In addition to selling goods and services, marketing techniques also help people to advocate ideas or viewpoints and to educate others. The American Diabetes Association mails out questionnaires that ask, "Are you at risk for diabetes?" The documents help educate the general public about this widespread disease by listing its risk factors and common symptoms and describing the work of the association.

Department store founder Marshall Field explained marketing quite clearly when he advised one employee to "give the lady what she wants." The phrase became the company motto, and it remains a business truism that reflects the importance of a customer orientation to an organization. This orientation may permit marketers to respond to customer wants that the customers themselves have not yet identified. Moretti Polegato, founder of an Italian shoe company called Geox, identified a need for shoes that increase comfort by keeping feet dry. He developed a sole made of perforated rubber that allows air to circulate, combined with a membrane inside the sole to keep water out. Geox shoes, which combine this modern technology with sophisticated Italian design, are available at shops in Europe, North and South America, Asia, Australia, and South Africa. Geox informs customers about its products with a message that emphasizes the shoes' high-tech soles, as shown at the company's Web site in Figure 13.1.[2]

As the Geox example illustrates, marketing is more than just selling. It is a process that begins with discovering unmet customer needs and continues with researching the potential market; producing a good or service capable of satisfying the targeted customers; and promoting, pricing, and distributing that good or service. Throughout the entire marketing process, a successful organization focuses on building customer relationships.

When two or more parties benefit from trading things of value, they have entered into an **exchange process.** Consider a hypothetical island society consisting of two groups, each producing its own food and clothing. One group is particularly skilled in textiles and pottery; the other group consists of farmers and ranchers. The exchange process allows each group to concentrate on what it does best and then trading excess goods for scarce ones. This specialization and division of work increases the island's total production and raises the standards of living of both groups. The exchange process could not occur, however, if each group did not market its products. This example shows that marketing is a prime determinant of society's overall standard of living.

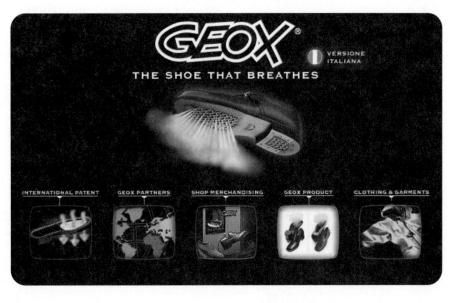

FIGURE 13.1
Marketing at Geox: Determining and Meeting Wants and Needs

How Marketing Creates Utility

Marketing is a complex activity that affects many aspects of an organization and its dealings with customers. The ability of a good or service to satisfy the wants and needs of customers is called **utility.** A company's production function creates *form utility* by converting raw materials, component parts, and other inputs into finished goods and services. But the marketing function creates time, place, and ownership utility. *Time utility* is created by making a good or service available when customers want to purchase it. *Place utility* is created by making a product available in a location convenient for customers. *Ownership utility* refers to an orderly transfer of goods and services from the seller to the buyer. In the case of the Big n' Tasty burger, McDonald's creates time, place, and ownership utility by preparing its new hamburger for sale at competitive prices in more than 10,000 U.S. retail outlets and thousands more in dozens of other nations. Promotions like the one shown in Figure 13.2 featuring spokesperson Kobe Bryant are designed to inform, persuade, and remind customers to make trial purchases so they can experience the superiority of the new entry in the McDonald's product line.

Like the Geox example described earlier, another shoe company that creates these types of utility is Nike. A recent Nike innovation is a service called NikeID, available at the company's Web site. Visitors to Nike.com can sign up with NikeID and provide information about their shoe size and their style and color preferences. They can even request a name they want to have stitched on the shoes. Customers place orders at their computers; then the shoes are manufactured in Asia and shipped directly to the customers, with delivery promised within three weeks. Nike offers a high level of place and ownership utility by enabling customers to complete transactions simply by visiting the Web site and waiting for the product to be delivered to them. Time utility takes the form of a customized product delivered quickly.[3]

EVOLUTION OF THE MARKETING CONCEPT

Marketing has always been a part of business, from the earliest village traders to large 21st century organizations producing and selling complex goods and

KOBE BRYANT CAME INTO THIS SEASON WITH A HUNGER.

WHICH WE FIXED.

INTRODUCING THE BIG N' TASTY.™

THE NEXT BIG THING FROM McDONALD'S.®

we love to see you smile™

At participating McDonald's. ©2001 McDonald's Corp.
©2001 NBA Properties, Inc. All rights reserved. Kobe Photo: Andrew D. Bernstein.

FIGURE 13.2
The McDonald's Big n' Tasty:
Providing Customer Satisfaction by
Creating Time, Place, and
Ownership Utility

services. Over time, however, marketing activities evolved through the four eras shown in Figure 13.3: the production, sales, and marketing eras, and now the relationship era.

For centuries, organizations of the *production era* stressed efficiency in producing quality products. They shared an attitude toward marketing summed up in a paraphrase of the story line to the award-winning motion picture *Field of Dreams:* "If you build it, they will come." Although this production orientation continued into the 20th century, it gradually gave way to a *sales orientation,* in which businesses assumed that consumers would buy only as a result of energetic sales efforts. Organizations didn't fully recognize the importance of their customers until the *marketing era* of the 1950s, when they began to adopt a consumer orientation. This focus has intensified in recent years, leading to the emergence of the *relationship era* in the 1990s. This era's emphasis on customer satisfaction is discussed in detail later in the chapter.

Emergence of the Marketing Concept

The term marketing concept refers to a companywide customer orientation with the objective of achieving long-run success. The basic idea of the marketing concept is that marketplace success begins with the customer. In other words, a firm should analyze each customer's needs and then work backward to make products that fulfill them. The emergence of the marketing concept can be explained best by the shift from a *seller's market*—one with a shortage of goods and services—to a *buyer's market*—one with an abundance of goods and services. During the 1950s, the U.S. became a strong buyer's market, forcing companies to satisfy customers rather than just producing and selling goods and services.

Delivering Added Value through Customer Satisfaction and Quality

What is the most important sale for a company? Some assume that it's the first, but many marketers argue that the second sale is the most important one, since repeat purchases are concrete evidence of customer satisfaction. The concept of a good or service pleasing buyers because it has met or exceeded their needs and expectations is crucial to an organization's continued operation. A company that fails to match the customer satisfaction that its competitors provide will not stay in business for very long. In contrast, increasing customer loyalty by just 5 percent translates into significant increases in lifetime profits per customer.

The best way to keep a customer is to offer more than just products. Customers today want *value,* their perception that the quality of goods or services is in balance with the prices charged. When a company exceeds value expectations by adding features, lowering its price, enhancing customer service, or making other improvements that increase customer satisfaction, it provides a **value-added** good or service. As long as customers believe they have received value—good quality for a fair price—they are likely to remain satisfied with the company and continue their relationships. Providing superior customer service can generate long-term success.

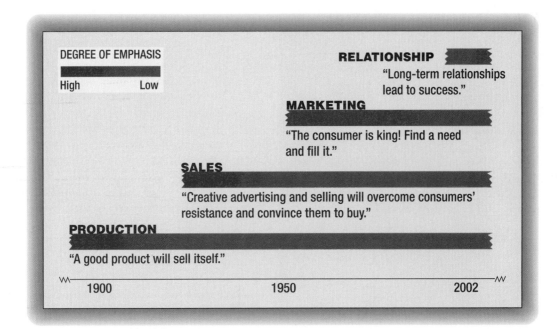

FIGURE 13.3
Four Eras in the History of Marketing

The emergence of the relationship era has changed the way salespeople view customers. They have modified the attitude "I'm here to sell you" to emphasize a mind-set of "I'm here to serve you." Firms build relationships with customers by listening to them and responding to their special needs and wants. In today's high-tech environment, customer service is often the factor that gives a firm a competitive advantage.

Quality—the degree of excellence or superiority of an organization's goods and services—is another way firms enhance customer satisfaction. Quality can encompass both the tangible and intangible characteristics of a good or service. *Inc.* magazine editor Leigh Buchanan found quality at a store called Duck Soup in Sudbury, Massachusetts. Buchanan was shopping for imported jam, but when she entered the store, she also found an irresistible atmosphere:

> The shop was always crowded, with knots of people loitering near the counter where the Ducks set out plates of creamy, pungent cheeses and thick slices of crusty bread. There was always conversation. Often there was laughter.[4]

No wonder that when the store burned down, there was an outpouring of support among loyal customers. As Duck Soup rebuilt, the owners developed a Web site (www.quackquackquack.com) serving up articles emphasizing the bonds that had been forged among customers and employees, rather than product offerings. When the store reopened, its attention to the intangibles of quality had preserved a loyal customer base, and its Web site provided a new means to maintain ties with customers who had moved away from the area.

While quality relates to physical product traits, such as durability and reliability, it also includes customer service. A Boston-headquartered concierge service called Circles seeks to provide a level of service that makes the company indispensable, whether customers need help making restaurant reservations or, in one case, hunting for a circular staircase to fit a dollhouse. After receiving permission from its customers, Circles gathers as much data about its frequent purchasers as it can, from the types of car they drive to the food they eat for dinner. When a customer calls, employees can look up the data to help them tailor their services to individual tastes.[5]
A contrasting dimension of quality is to appeal to

BUSINESS DIRECTORY

➤ **marketing concept**   *companywide consumer orientation to promote long-run success.*
➤ **customer satisfaction**   *result of a good or service meeting or exceeding the buyer's needs and expectations.*

Do you know me?*

Probably not. In my daily life I like to be recognized, but when I'm shopping online I prefer a little privacy. With Private Payments℠ from American Express, I get the security of a unique number created for each purchase I make. It's a safer way to shop because my actual Card number isn't sent out over the Internet. And soon when I'm surfing the Net I'll be able to choose the amount of personal information I reveal about myself, even if it's nothing. So whenever I travel the World Wide Web, I'll be able to travel incognito.

Introducing anonymity online from American Express
Don't leave homepages without it℠ Enroll at www.americanexpress.com

©2000 American Express

FIGURE 13.4
American Express: Providing Quality by Meeting the Desire for Privacy

consumer desires to protect their online privacy, as American Express highlights in Figure 13.4.

Achieving customer satisfaction sometimes requires marketers to redefine quality. This requirement posed a challenge at Polaroid recently, when customers were no longer wowed by Polaroid's former leadership in camera technology. The firm's engineers were appalled at plans to introduce a small instant camera to be targeted at teenagers. But embarrassment quickly turned to excitement when the I-Zone pocket camera became the top-selling model in the U.S.

Half of the new cameras were purchased by teenage girls. Although they sell for just $25 each, the I-Zones accounted for over one-fourth of Polaroid's revenues from new products. Samuel H. Liggero, a Polaroid vice president, had initially disagreed with the decision to make a low-tech camera. After its successful launch, he admitted the camera "doesn't involve the great inventions, but what I failed to appreciate was, it was good enough" for teenagers who just want to play with thumbnail photos of one another.[6]

Importance of Customer Satisfaction

Successful companies share an important characteristic: they make every effort to ensure the satisfaction of their customers. Customer satisfaction is critical for building long-lasting relationships. In the realm of e-commerce, surveys found that over 9 of every 10 customers who were satisfied with their online shopping experiences said they would return to the same sites in the future. Almost as many said they would recommend the site to others. In contrast, 1 of every 12 Web visitors abandon online shopping carts before making a purchase. The lost business is worth billions of dollars every year.[7]

The fundamental premise of the marketing concept is to focus all organizational efforts on providing superior customer service to retain existing customers and attract new ones. The following section discusses the increased use of customer feedback.

Obtaining Customer Feedback One of the best ways to find out how buyers perceive a company or its products is to obtain *customer feedback* through toll-free telephone hot lines, customer satisfaction surveys, Web site message boards, or written correspondence. Some firms find out how well they have satisfied their customers by calling them or making personal visits to their businesses or residences. Pillsbury invites customer feedback by publishing a toll-free phone number on the package of its products. As thousands of calls stream into the company each day, representatives enter their comments into a database. Employees can sort the data by product or other topics to spot problems and better target their offerings to customer tastes. A few years ago, thousands of customers called to ask why Pillsbury didn't offer a chocolate version of its Toaster Strudel, so the company added the flavor. Eventually, Pillsbury hopes the database will be available to its salespeople so they can use it to serve the customers who buy products to resell to their customers. Perhaps a store's buyer wonders whether a particular flavor or package size will appeal to her customers; with the database, the salesperson could find the marketing data on the spot.[8]

Customer complaints are excellent sources of customer feedback, since they present companies with an opportunity to overcome problems and improve their services. Customers often feel greater loyalty after a conflict has been resolved than if they had never complained at all. Complaints can also allow firms to gather innovative ideas for improvement.

Some Of Our Plant Neighbors Have Gotten A Little Wild.

Today, for a quarry or chemical facility to be a good neighbor, operators have to be sensitive to an increasing number of environmental concerns both inside and outside the plant gates. At Vulcan, we're striving to be a good neighbor by maintaining a strong commitment to environmental stewardship.

In the early 1970s, Vulcan's quarry beautification efforts led to the creation of an industry wide awards program that encourages landscaping and other beautification measures in and around quarries.

Most recently, Vulcan instituted a wildlife habitat enhancement program. In 1990, our Sanders, Virginia, quarry became the first site in the nation to be certified by the Wildlife Habitat Council as a sanctioned, enhanced habitat for indigenous wildlife. Currently, 32 of our sites have been certified by the Wildlife Habitat Council.

Vulcan is proud to be among America's companies that have taken a leadership position in establishing innovative and environmentally sound corporate land management practices. Because of these efforts, there's a good chance that our "wild" neighbors will stay that way.

Vulcan
Materials Company

The nation's leading producer of construction aggregates and a significant producer of basic industrial and specialty chemicals.

Quarries like those operated by Vulcan Materials Co. can produce a devastating impact on the surrounding environment. Thirty years ago, Vulcan launched quarry beautification efforts at 32 sites, each of which has received Wildlife Habitat Council certification as sanction, enhanced habitat for indigenous wildlife. The firm uses surveys to obtain feedback from both customers and residents of areas surrounding its quarries to measure improvements in attitudes about its operations.

EXPANDING MARKETING'S TRADITIONAL BOUNDARIES

The marketing concept has traditionally been associated with products of profit-seeking organizations. Today, however, it is also being applied to not-for-profit sectors and other nontraditional areas ranging from religious organizations to political campaigns. This section examines the evolution of nontraditional marketing applications.

Not-for-Profit Marketing

Not-for-profit organizations ranging from national research foundations to state parks and recreation departments to local museums are benefiting by applying many of the strategies and business concepts used by profit-seeking firms. An example is the Hunger Site, a Web site operated by GreaterGood.com (www.thehungersite.com).

THEY SAID IT

"We view a customer who is complaining as a real blessing in disguise. He or she is someone we can resell."

LOUIS CARBONE (B.1905)
VICE PRESIDENT, NATIONAL
CAR RENTAL

FIGURE 13.5
Categories of Nontraditional Marketing

The Hunger Site provides information about the problem of world hunger, including a world map that indicates for each country how often someone there dies of starvation. The site also includes a button labeled Donate Free Food. By clicking on the button, visitors to the site increase the amount of food donations paid for by the advertisers that post their messages on the Web site. The United Nations World Food Program handles distribution of the donated food.[9] GreaterGood.com and other not-for-profits market tangible or intangible goods, services, or both.

Not-for-profit organizations operate in both public and private sectors. Public groups include federal, state, and local government units as well as agencies that receive tax funding. A state's department of natural resources, for instance, regulates land conservation and environmental programs; the local animal-control officer enforces ordinances protecting people and animals; a city's public health board ensures safe drinking water for its citizens.

The private not-for-profit sector comprises many different types of organizations, including labor unions, hospitals, Pensacola Junior College's basketball team, art museums, and local youth organizations. Although some private not-for-profits generate surplus revenue, their primary goals are not earning profits. If they earn funds beyond their expenses, they invest the excess in their organizational missions.

Many not-for-profits apply marketing tools to reach their audiences, secure funding, improve their images, and accomplish their overall missions. Marketing activities such as advertising and public relations are part of operating the American Museum of Natural History, YMCAs, the Audubon Zoo in New Orleans, and art museums like New York's Museum of Modern Art. Besides promoting specific classes and exhibitions, these organizations may sell memberships and operate gift shops to raise operating funds.

In some cases, not-for-profit organizations form a partnership with a profit-seeking company to promote the firm's message or distribute its goods and services. The 2002 Salt Lake City Winter Olympics received millions of dollars by selling Olympic sponsorships to corporations, which benefited from associating their products with the world's best-known not-for-profit sports organization. More than one-third of the revenues flowing into the International Olympic Committee came from corporate sponsorships.[10] The U.S. Postal Service has negotiated with Federal Express to couple the Postal Service's door-to-door delivery with FedEx's network of air routes. This arrangement gives the postal service access to FedEx's air transportation and its advanced information technology, which enables the company to keep tabs on delivery status.[11]

Nontraditional Marketing

Growth in the number of not-for-profit organizations has forced their executives to adopt businesslike strategies and tactics to reach diverse audiences and successfully compete with other nontraditional organizations. Figure 13.5 summarizes the five major categories of nontraditional marketing. Although most involve not-for-profit organizations, profit-seeking organizations conduct special events like FanFests linked with major sporting events and person marketing involving celebrities.

Person Marketing Efforts designed to attract the attention, interest, and preference of a target market toward a person are called **person marketing.** Campaign managers for a political candidate like Israel's prime minister Ariel Sharon conduct

FIGURE 13.6
Place Marketing and
Cause Marketing

marketing research, identify groups of voters and financial supporters, and then design advertising campaigns, fund-raising events, and political rallies to reach them. Celebrities ranging from high-priced Texas Rangers shortstop Alex Rodriguez to Grammy-winning rapper Eminem also engage in person marketing to expand their audiences; improve sales of tickets to games and concerts, books, licensed merchandise and CDs; and enhance their images among fans.

Many careful job seekers apply the tools of person marketing. They research the wants and needs of prospective employers, and they identify ways they can meet them. They seek out employers through a variety of channels, sending messages that emphasize how they can benefit the employer.

Place Marketing   As the term suggests, **place marketing** attempts to attract people to a particular area, such as a city, state, or nation. It may involve appealing to consumers as a tourist destination or to businesses as a desirable business location. A strategy for place marketing often includes advertising. In Figure 13.6, Puerto Rico advertises its tropical reefs to lure scuba divers and other vacationers to its beauty and warm climate. In the small print, the figure includes an address, telephone number, and Web site where interested tourists can go for information about planning a trip.

In the Southern Finger Lakes region of New York, the Steuben, Chemung, and Schuyler county governments recently participated in a public–private venture aimed at increasing the number of visitors to the tri-county area during a single 30-day period. The marketing effort included a promotion in Chemung County's Arnot Mall, where shoppers received cards listing prize packages and activities required to win the packages. A card might direct the recipient to answer trivia questions or complete a scavenger hunt to win prizes like a bed-and-breakfast stay plus tickets to a local museum. As project leader Stephanie Watts explains, "People won't generally come to the area for just one museum or one lake day, but they will come for several attractions"—attractions that ranged from winery tours to the National Warplane Museum and the Corning Museum of Glass.[12]

Cause Marketing Marketing that promotes a cause or social issue, such as the prevention of child abuse, antilittering efforts, and antismoking campaigns, is **cause marketing.** The promotional message of the Partnership for a Drug-Free America encouraging parents to discuss the risks of marijuana with their children shown in Figure 13.6 is a well-known example.

Special fund-raising programs for charities and causes range from the annual Jerry Lewis Labor Day Telethon for the Muscular Dystrophy Association to the American Red Cross's "Fit for Life" relay races. Noting that the most common form of cancer among Hispanic women is breast cancer, the Cancer Research Foundation of America and other organizations are distributing Spanish-language videos about early detection to churches, community organizations, and medical centers. They are also providing public-service announcements to Spanish-language radio stations.[13]

Profit-seeking companies attempting to enhance their public images often join forces with charities and causes, providing financial, marketing, and human resources. The National Football League builds goodwill by airing advertisements for United Way during its broadcasts and by encouraging its teams to support causes in their local communities. The San Diego Chargers have adopted Children's Hospital as the focus of their community. They also sponsor a blood drive considered to be the nation's largest. Similarly, well-known entertainers and individual athletes in various professional sports volunteer as banquet speakers and play in celebrity golf tournaments. In the words of Paul Anderson, assistant director of Marquette University's National Sports Law Institute, "If a charity in Milwaukee can get Brett Favre to come to a luncheon to raise money, they are going to sell out, make a lot of money, and help their members."[14]

The classic approach to a cause-related promotion ties a donation to a consumer purchase, such as a company's promise to donate $1 for each item it sells. An Oakland, California, office-products company called Give Something Back distinguishes itself from big rivals like Office Depot and Staples by donating a portion of its profits to charity. The firm's marketing strategy emphasizes such practical benefits as free next-day delivery, but sales reps describe the policy of giving away profits to explain the meaning of the company's name. Give Something Back lets customers decide where to send 40 percent of the company's donations, employees vote on 30 percent of the total, and the company's founders decide where to send the rest. The strategy has enabled the company to find a niche in a competitive market by attracting loyal employees who appreciate the chance to do good in their community.[15]

Sometimes, though, two causes collide, as illustrated in the "Solving an Ethical Controversy" box. Advocates for each side in the debate over the content of movies and television programs must work to present their cause in the best light, in the hope that the general public will agree.

Event Marketing Marketing or sponsoring short-term events such as athletic competitions and cultural and charitable performances is known as **event marketing.** Like cause marketing, event marketing often forges partnerships between not-for-profit and profit-seeking organizations. Many businesses sponsor fund-raising events like 10K runs to raise funds for health-related charities. These events require a marketing effort to plan the event and attract participants and sponsors. Fund-raising concerts, including singer Willie Nelson's annual Farm Aid concert, are another example of event marketing.

Organization Marketing Finally, **organization marketing** influences consumers to accept the goals of, receive the services of, or contribute in some way to an organi-

SOLVING AN ETHICAL CONTROVERSY

Which is more important—freedom of speech or responsibility toward children? Both causes are caught up in the same issue that has the entertainment industry and two federal agencies—the Federal Trade Commission (FTC) and the Federal Communications Commission (FCC)—locked in an argument, and neither seems willing to budge. Politicians, parents, and civic groups have long been lobbying the entertainment industry to accept more responsibility for curbing the amount of sex and violence portrayed on television, in movies, and by video games. Following the release of a report on this subject by the FTC, former FCC chairman William Kennard added his agreement. "Broadcast standards have coarsened. There is indisputably more inappropriate content—more questionable language, sex, and violence in today's prime time [programming]." Spokespeople for the entertainment industry, such as Motion Picture Association of America president Jack Valenti, took up the cause for free speech, pointing out that if viewers did not like the content of a certain film or television program, all they need to do is "stay away, keep your children away, and tell your friends as well."

Should the entertainment industry be required by law to take more responsibility for providing better quality, more educational, and less violent content to audiences that might include children?

PRO

1. Former FCC chairman William Kennard says that television networks "have failed the educational needs of children and have increased the amount of sex and violence in prime time." This failure comes despite an FCC ruling several years ago requiring broadcasters to air at least three hours of educational and informational programming for children each week.
2. A recent Kaiser Family Foundation study shows that more than half of television shows contain sexual themes. During prime time, when families are watching, two of every three shows include at least some sexual content. These shows are not appropriate for young children, and they represent irresponsibility on the part of programmers.
3. The FTC has found that despite the rating system in place since 1968, many R-rated movies—those not intended for viewers under age 17 unless accompanied by a parent—are actually marketed directly to 10- and 11-year-olds.

CON

1. "Saddling stations with additional regulation cannot be justified, given the billions that broadcasters provide annually in public service," argues Dennis Wharton, a spokesperson for the National Association of Broadcasters.
2. The constitutional right of free speech is at stake, according to Jack Valenti. "The central, indisputable fact is that the creative artistry of the American film industry, with all its warts and all its splendor, is part of America's global glory."
3. Deciding what children may view is the responsibility of parents, not the entertainment industry, argues Valenti. "Building that shield is mainly the duty of parents, with help from school and church."

SUMMARY

Taken at face value, each cause has a legitimate basis. Most Americans would agree that the protection of free speech—even if that speech is offensive to some—is vital to the freedoms that they enjoy. However, many of these same people would also argue that responsible speech is important, especially when it comes to children. Perhaps everyone would benefit if marketers for both sides could find a way to come together in a compromise.

Sources: Brooks Boliek, "Senate to Studios: Big Brother Is Watching," *The Hollywood Reporter Online,* Yahoo! News, October 23, 2000, **http://dailynews.yahoo.com;** Christopher Stern, "FCC Chief Chastises TV Networks," *Washington Post,* October 17, 2000, **www.washingtonpost.com;** Jack Valenti, "Lawmakers' Goal Is Content Control," *Variety,* October 16, 2000, **www.msnbc.com;** James M. Wall, "Film Ratings Under Fire," *Chicago Tribune,* October 1, 2000, sec. 1, p. 23.

zation. Many groups employ this practice, including mutual-benefit organizations like political groups, churches, and labor unions; service organizations such as community colleges, museums, and hospitals; and government organizations like police and fire departments, military services, and the U.S. National Park Service. Many charitable organizations mail greeting cards with donation requests enclosed to raise awareness of their groups and explain their objectives.

DEVELOPING A MARKETING STRATEGY

Decision makers in any successful organization, for-profit or not-for-profit, follow a two-step process to develop a *marketing strategy:* First, they study and analyze potential target markets and then choose among them. Second, they create a marketing mix to satisfy the chosen market. Figure 13.7 shows the relationship among the target market, the marketing mix variables, and the marketing environment.

FIGURE 13.7
Target Market and Marketing Mix within the Marketing Environment

Later discussions will refer back to this figure as they cover each topic. This section describes the development of a marketing strategy.

Earlier chapters introduce many of the environmental factors that impact the success or failure of a firm's business strategy. Chapter 1 begins with an overview of today's rapidly changing and highly competitive world of business. This competitive environment is influenced by a vast array of social-cultural factors, as discussed in Chapter 2, and economic factors, the subject of Chapter 3. Political and legal factors, such as those presented in Chapter 4, also define what marketers can and cannot do in certain situations. In Chapter 7 and throughout the text, examples highlight technological innovations like the Internet on every aspect of business, showing how it can assist firms in trading goods, services, and information. Chapter 17 again focuses on the Internet and other information technology components as they support business decisions in all areas, including marketing. Although these external forces frequently operate outside managers' control, marketers must still consider the impact of environmental factors on their decisions.

A written marketing plan often becomes a key component of a firm's overall business plan. The marketing plan outlines its marketing strategy and includes information about the target market, sales and revenue goals, the marketing budget, and the timing for implementing the elements of the marketing mix.

Selecting a Target Market

The expression "find a need and fill it" is perhaps the simplest explanation of the two elements of a marketing strategy. A firm's marketers find a need through careful and continuing study of the individuals and business decision makers in its potential market. A *market* consists of people with purchasing power, willingness to buy, and authority to make purchase decisions.

Markets can be classified by type of product. **Consumer products**—often known as business-to-consumer (B2C) products—are goods and services purchased by end users, such as DVDs, shampoo, and dental care. **Business products**—or business-to-business (B2B) products—are goods and services purchased to be used, either directly or indirectly, in the production of other goods for resale. Some products can fit in either classification, depending on who buys them and why. A computer or checking account, for example, can be either a consumer or business product.

An organization's **target market** is the group of potential customers toward whom it directs its marketing efforts. Customer needs and wants vary considerably, and no single organization has the resources to satisfy everyone. Foot Locker is a chain of stores specializing in the needs of active people looking for shoes and other sportswear. The chain's management determined that the stores were more appealing to men than women, so the company created a separate line of stores, called Lady Foot

Locker, with active women in mind. Lady Foot Locker defines its target market as active women age 20 years and older. This target market buys athletic shoes for participation in sports, not just to trudge between commuter train and office, so the company displays many brands of shoes, organized by the sport for which they are designed. And it provides its salespeople with extensive training so they can help customers with well-informed recommendations.[16]

Developing a Marketing Mix

Decisions about marketing involve strategies for four areas of marketing activity: product, pricing, distribution, and promotion. A firm's marketing mix blends the four strategies to fit the needs and preferences of a specific target market. Marketing success depends, not on the four individual strategies, but on their unique combination.

Product strategy involves more than just designing a good or service with needed attributes. It also includes decisions about package design, a brand name, trademarks, warranties, product image, new-product development, and customer service. Think, for instance, about your favorite fruit drink. Do you like it for its taste alone, or do other attributes, such as clever ads, attractive packaging, and overall image, also contribute to your brand preference? Many of the decisions related to product strategy are analyzed in Chapter 14.

One of the most difficult areas of marketing decision making, *pricing strategy,* deals with the methods of setting profitable and justifiable prices. Such actions are subject to government regulation and considerable public scrutiny. Research shows that consumer perceptions of product quality relate closely to price: a high price correlates to high perceived quality. Most marketers believe that this perceived price–quality relationship spans a relatively wide range of prices, although extreme prices may contribute to an overly expensive or cheap image. Chapter 14 discusses pricing in depth.

Distribution strategy ensures that customers receive their purchases in the proper quantities at the right times and locations. Chapter 15 focuses on the various modes of transportation and the roles retailers and wholesalers play in distribution channels.

Promotional strategy, the final marketing mix element, involves informing, persuading, and influencing purchase decisions. Chapter 16 examines the many aspects of promotion, including personal selling, advertising, sales promotion, and public relations.

Consider how the elements of the marketing mix allow one California firm to reach its target market. Mrs. Beasley's is a bakery business whose marketing strategy includes premium quality and prices to match, coupled with highly targeted promotion and convenient distribution. Mrs. Beasley's started as a two sisters' home-based business in Tarzana, California. The women chose the name to sound homey, and they set high quality standards, insisting on top ingredients and plenty of human touches, like placing M&Ms on cookies by hand. Even though they built the business into a chain of stores with $2 million in sales, they were unable to turn a profit, so they sold it to another company. The new management then modified several elements to convert Mrs. Beasley's into a profitable marketing operation.

Mrs. Beasley's continues offering top quality at top prices—$30 to $200 for a basket of goodies. Instead of relying on advertising to reach consumers, marketers now focus on building relationships with big customers, particularly corporate buyers who order gift baskets for their clients. Mrs. Beasley's places links to its Web site at sites such as 1-800-Flowers.com and Staples.com, where corporate buyers often are already making purchases. These sites provide the links in exchange for a share of Mrs. Beasley's sales generated through the

BUSINESS DIRECTORY

➤ **target market** *group of people toward whom an organization markets its goods, services, or ideas with a strategy designed to satisfy their specific needs and preferences.*

➤ **marketing mix** *blending the four elements of marketing strategy— product, price, place, and promotion—to satisfy chosen customer segments.*

This is a cucumber

Chinese   Korean   Japanese

Not all Asians like it the same way...

Reaching a diverse group of 3 billion Asians is no easy task. **Click2Asia, Inc.** is the leading Asian internet media company providing integrated advertising and marketing solutions. Doing business in Asia now has one flavor - no matter how you slice it. Please call **(888)333-2839** or visit www.click2asia.com for more information

The Global Asian Internet Media Company

www.click2asia.com

FIGURE 13.8
Cultural Differences: Sound Reason for an Adaptation Strategy

links. The company also arranges links to its site from corporate intranets, offering discounts to employees at companies including AOL Time Warner and Barnes & Noble. Similar arrangements with auto clubs and other associations involve discounts to members rather than paid advertising.

The Mrsbeasleys.com site emphasizes convenient ordering, focusing on the needs of large corporate customers. The site lets customers place multiple orders; they can choose from among 200 selections and send orders to as many as 500 recipients. To back up the site, Mrs. Beasley's operates a call center located at its factory and uses an automated order-processing system to fill orders accurately and get them out the door on schedule. With this strategy, Mrs. Beasley's has pushed sales past the $10 million mark and, at least as important, has begun generating profits.[17]

Developing a Marketing Mix for International Markets

Marketing a good or service in foreign markets means deciding whether to offer the same marketing mix in every market—*standardization*—or to develop a unique mix to fit each market—*adaptation*. The advantages of standardizing the marketing mix include reliable marketing performance and low costs. This approach works best with business goods, such as steel, chemicals, and aircraft, with little sensitivity to a nation's culture.

Adaptation, on the other hand, lets marketers vary their marketing mix to suit local competitive conditions, consumer preferences, and government regulations. As Figure 13.8 illustrates, consumer tastes are often shaped by local cultures. Because consumer products generally tend to be more culture dependent than business products, they more often require adaptation. Dunkin' Donuts adapts its marketing strategy outside the United States. U.S. donut buyers generally are rushed when they stop at a Dunkin' Donuts outlet; they want to grab a bagful of pastries and go. But in most of the company's international markets, people want to sit down and relax with their food.

The chain's largest outlet, which seats 130, is in Thailand. There, business is stronger in the afternoon and evening, as customers gather with family members to spend time together. Local Dunkin' Donuts marketers position the company as caring for society and families. One promotion, called "Longest Love Message to Moms," coincided with the birthday of Thailand's queen mother, which is also Thailand's Mother's Day. During the five-week promotion, Dunkin' Donuts invited Thai customers to visit the stores, where they could write notes to their mothers on a vinyl banner displayed at each store. The company launched the campaign with popular Thai actors signing a banner at a Dunkin' Donuts store in Bangkok, generating plenty of media coverage. The public enthusiastically joined in the project, and the company upped its efforts, arranging for the prime minister to sign a banner and for 2,000 banners to be sewn together into a mile-long display, which employees carried in the national parade on the queen's birthday. The effort boosted the donut chain's share of the Thai fast-food market and solidified its image as a company that, although foreign, cares about the Thai people.[18]

Increasingly, marketers are trying to build adaptability into the designs of standardized goods and services for international and domestic markets. *Mass customization* allows a firm to mass-produce goods and services while adding unique features to individual orders. This technique seeks to retain enough flexibility to satisfy a wide segment of the population without losing a product's identity and brand awareness. Oshkosh Truck Corp. applies mass customization to the business of making and marketing its trucks. Buyers of fire trucks can choose from among 19,000 options such as compartments, ladders, and foam systems for hard-to-extinguish fires. Buyers of concrete mixers can select options like the placement of the discharge chute from which the concrete pours. By catering to customer needs, Oshkosh has tripled sales at a time when the industry as a whole has been slowing.[19]

MARKETING RESEARCH FOR IMPROVED MARKETING DECISIONS

Marketing research involves more than just collecting data. Researchers must decide how to collect the data, interpret the results, convert the data into decision-oriented information, and communicate those results to managers for use in decision making. **Marketing research** is the process of collecting and evaluating information to help marketers make effective decisions. It links marketing decision makers to the marketplace by providing data about potential target markets that help them design effective marketing mixes. Marketers conduct research for five basic reasons:

LeatherClassic.

The amusing ad is typical of the new Reebok strategy formulated as a result of marketing research and intended to gain the attention and interest of male sport shoe purchasers.

1. To identify marketing problems and opportunities
2. To analyze competitors' strategies
3. To evaluate and predict customer behavior
4. To gauge the performance of existing products and package designs, and assess the potential of new ones
5. To develop price, promotion, and distribution plans

British-based shoe marketer Reebok ranks first in the U.S. in the sale of women's sport shoes. However, it lags far behind rival Nike in the considerably larger men's sport shoe market. Marketing research focusing on qualities desired by male purchasers formed the basis of Reebok's new attempt to generate added sales of its Classic Marathon Racer shoe line to men. Humor was a major part of the new Reebok promotional strategy.

Obtaining Marketing Research Data

Marketing researchers are concerned with both internal and external data. They generate *internal data* within their organizations. Financial records provide a tremendous amount of useful information, such as changes in unpaid bills, inventory levels, sales generated by different categories of customers or product lines, profitability of particular divisions, or comparisons of sales by territories, salespeople, customers, or product lines.

> **BUSINESS DIRECTORY**
>
> ➤ **marketing research** *collection and use of information to support marketing decision making.*

Researchers gather *external data* from sources outside their firms, including previously published data. Trade associations publish reports on activities in particular industries. Advertising agencies collect information on the audiences reached by various media. National marketing research firms offer information through subscription services.

Low cost and quick, easy access prompt marketing researchers to begin searching for needed information by exhausting all possible sources of previously collected *secondary data* before investing the time and money required to collect firsthand data. Federal, state, and local government publications are among the marketing researcher's most important data sources. The most frequently used government statistics include census data, containing such population characteristics as age, gender, ethnic backgrounds, education level, household size and composition, occupation, employment status, and income. Such information helps marketers assess the buying behavior of certain segments of the population, anticipate changes in the marketplace, and identify markets with above-average growth potential. Most government data can now be accessed over the Internet. Chapter 5 identifies a number of Web addresses where business owners can surf for needed data.

Even though secondary data represent a quick and inexpensive resource, marketing researchers often discover that previously published information gives insufficient insight into some marketing problems. In some cases, the secondary data may be too old for current purposes. The Census Bureau is still analyzing data collected in 2000, but much of the data available for fast-growing areas like Las Vegas and Orlando quickly become obsolete. Previously collected data may also be in an inappropriate format for a current marketing research investigation. For example, a researcher may need data divided by city blocks but might only find data for the city as a whole. Other data—particularly data about consumer attitudes or intentions—may be impossible to find. Facing these obstacles, researchers may conclude they must collect *primary data*—data collected for the first time through observation or surveys.

Marketing researchers commonly collect primary data through *observational studies,* in which they view the actions of selected subjects, either directly or through mechanical devices. Traffic counts and visual inspections help in making decisions about location, hours of operation, or usage patterns. Envirosell is a research firm that specializes in using such observational techniques as hidden cameras to measure shopper behavior in stores. The firm's research uncovered the tendency of U.S. shoppers to head to the right when they enter a store. By contrast, shoppers in Britain and Australia—because of their century-old practice of driving on the left—will usually veer left.[20] Internet sites measure traffic, typically by counting the number of unique visitors to a Web site during a given period. Web-based data collection can also track what links each visitor clicks on while at a Web site, as well as what a visitor orders and how much money the visitor spends.

Simply observing customers cannot provide some types of information. When researchers need information about attitudes, opinions, and motives, they must ask questions by conducting *surveys.* Survey methods include telephone interviews; mail, fax, and online questionnaires; personal interviews; and focus groups. A focus group brings together 8–12 people in a room or over the Internet to discuss a particular topic. Ideas generated during focus group interviews can be especially helpful to marketers in developing new products, improving existing products, and creating effective advertising campaigns.

Applying Marketing Research Data

As the accuracy of information collected by researchers increases, so does the effectiveness of resulting marketing strategies. Consider how the Internet is providing more precise data about which advertisements are effective. SmarterKids.com, which sells educational products, hired a research firm called AdKnowledge to keep track of which of its ads Web users were most likely to click on and which of the clicks resulted in sales to SmarterKids. The data showed that among all the sites on which the educational products marketer was placing online ads, most of the traffic was being generated by three or four sites. SmarterKids marketers responded with more advertising at those Web sites, and the move quickly increased the firm's Internet-generated business.[21]

Heinz applied research data when it was looking for ways to expand sales of its ketchup, which already is the best-selling brand in a mature product category. The company talked to mothers and learned that many are reluctant to let their children handle bottles of ketchup, for fear of a big, red mess. So Heinz researchers watched children wield bottles of ketchup, and they agreed that the traditional plastic bottles were difficult for small hands to manipulate. The company launched new kid-friendly packaging called EZ Squirt. That bottle is designed to be easy to hold with two little hands and offers a nozzle to aim either the company's basic red ketchup or its Blastin' Green alternative, the same flavor but dyed bright green.[22]

Sometimes marketing research can become the focal point of a firm's marketing efforts. When Starwood Hotels & Resorts Worldwide decided to launch its Preferred Guest program, it looked for ways to provide guests with superior service. The hotel chain, which includes Westin and Sheraton hotels, asked active members of its frequent-guest programs—those who had stayed in at least one of the company's hotels within the previous year—what they liked and disliked. They learned that guests most often requested improvement in check-in procedures. So Starwood focused training efforts on this area and gave all the hotels access to a database of member preferences. When these frequent guests arrive, Starwood employees use the database to see that guests get their preferred bed type, newspaper, and other comforts.[23]

Research also is central to media, which typically generate most of their revenues, not from subscriber or viewer purchases but by selling ads. Media ranging from television and radio stations to magazines and Web portals gather data about their audiences to convince would-be advertisers that they can target their ads to match consumer ages, geographic locations, gender, ethnicity, marital status, and product interests.

Computer-Based Marketing Research Systems

Computer technology helps many businesses create a strategic advantage in collecting and analyzing research data. Companies can gather detailed data with the *universal product code (UPC)* symbols that appear on most packaging. After scanning the information carried in the fine lines of the bar code, a computer identifies the product, its manufacturer, and its price. Managers use the data to schedule inventory, ordering, and delivery; track sales; and test the effectiveness of promotions and new-product introductions.

Marketing research firms, such as AC Nielsen and Data General, store consumer data in commercially available databases. The AC Nielsen promotional message shown in Figure 13.9 describes its global reach—the

FIGURE 13.9
AC Nielsen: Marketing Research with Global Reach

We've got our

on the ground
in over 100 countries worldwide

Successful multi-country customised research requires intimate understanding of regional issues, cultural factors and local market situations.

The global leader in market research, information and analysis
ACNielsen International Research
New York
Contact: Travyn Rhall (Travyn.Rhall@ACNielsen.com)
Manjima Khandelwal (Manjima.Khandelwal@ACNielsen.com)
Wendy Jenkins (Wendy.Jenkins@ACNielsen.com)
Sylvia Coman (Sylvia.Coman@ACNielsen.com)
Tel (914) 769-4444   Fax (914) 769-7760
Chicago
Contact Arleen Macaraeg-Denque (ADenque@ACNielsen.com)
Tel (847) 605-5772   Fax (847) 605-2581

company operates in more than 100 countries worldwide. Businesses subscribe to these databases to obtain data on sales and promotions of their products. Subscribing to the databases typically is more efficient than doing similar research in-house. Using information from the databases, consulting firms such as Inter-Act Systems, Retail Systems Consulting, and Stratmar Systems work with firms to develop programs that reward their best customers. An important aspect of this process is a technique called data mining.

Data Mining

Using a computer to search through massive amounts of customer data to detect patterns and relationships is referred to as **data mining**. These patterns may suggest predictive models of real-world business activities. Accurate data mining can help researchers forecast recessions, weed out credit-card fraud, and pinpoint sales prospects.

Data mining uses **data warehouses,** which are sophisticated customer databases that allow managers to combine data from several different organizational functions. Wal-Mart's data warehouse, considered the largest in the private sector, contains over 100 terabytes (trillions of characters) of data. The retail giant uses data mining to assess local preferences for merchandise so that it can tailor the inventory of each store to the tastes of its neighborhood. The number of data warehouses containing at least a terabyte of data is only in the hundreds, but many companies are applying data-mining tools on a smaller scale.[24]

By identifying patterns and connections, marketers can increase the accuracy of their predictions about the effectiveness of their strategy options. A company interested in the music industry found that among buyers of rap recordings, a significant share were older than 62, not the usual age segment associated with this type of music. Further investigation showed that these customers tended to be grandparents buying presents for their younger relatives. The company used this information to create a promotional effort focusing on low price.[25]

MARKET SEGMENTATION

The information collected by marketing researchers is valuable only when it helps managers make better decisions. Improving the accuracy of information being collected also increases the effectiveness of resulting marketing strategies. Marketing research can cover a broad range, perhaps an entire industry or nation, or it can focus on highly specific details, such as individual purchase patterns. Identifying the characteristics of a target market is a crucial step toward creating a successful marketing strategy. **Market segmentation** is the process of dividing a total market into several relatively homogeneous groups. Both profit-seeking and not-for-profit organizations use market segmentation to help them reach desirable target markets.

The broadcast industry provides an excellent example of market segmentation. During the 1960s, most American viewers watched programming from the major television networks—ABC, CBS, and NBC—and few tuned in to the UHF stations. During the 1970s, however, the fledgling cable industry added such drawing cards as HBO and Turner Broadcasting's TBS superstation. Then came new cable networks like CNN and MTV during the 1980s, coupled with the introduction of the VCR, which let viewers watch recorded programs whenever they wanted. The direct-broadcast satellites of the 1990s made the notion of narrowcasting a reality, giving viewers access to hundreds of channels, each specializing in topics from golf to gardening to food—all vying for an audience. Eventually digital broadcasting services and Internet channels are expected to offer more than 1,000 channels, or "content windows."

Table 13.1   Criteria for Market Segmentation

Criterion	Example
A segment must be a measurable group.	Disposable income data are available for such segments as senior citizens, teens, and gays.
A segment must be accessible for communications.	The growing Hispanic American market can be reached through Spanish-language television stations, hundreds of radio stations, and at least 1,000 print publications.
A segment must be large enough to offer profit potential.	Some retail stores specialize in products designed especially for left-handed consumers. Although dwarfs represent a market for small autos and other products, their numbers are insufficient to attract firms willing to specialize in these products.

Market segmentation attempts to isolate the traits that distinguish a certain group of customers from the overall market. However, segmentation does not always promote marketing success. Table 13.1 lists several criteria that marketers should consider. The effectiveness of a segmentation strategy depends on how well the market meets these criteria. Once marketers identify a market segment to target, they can create an appropriate marketing strategy.

How Market Segmentation Works

An initial distinction separates consumer (B2C) and business (B2B) markets based on the types of products and their uses. Depending on whether their firms offer consumer or business products, marketers segment their target markets differently. Four common bases for segmenting consumer markets are geographic segmentation, demographic segmentation, psychographic segmentation, and product-related segmentation. Business markets are segmented on only three criteria: customer-based segmentation, end-use segmentation, and geographic segmentation. Figure 13.10 illustrates the segmentation methods for these two types of markets.

Segmenting Consumer Markets

Market segmentation has been practiced since people first produced surpluses and resold the unneeded products to others. Garment producers made some items for men and others for women. Some specialized in producing shoes or clothing for children. A millennium ago, Europeans fell in love with exotic spices and luxurious silk fabrics. Merchants began to serve this untapped market by bringing these precious items thousands of miles by land and sea from production sites in Asia and the Pacific islands to a waiting market in Europe. In addition to demographic and geographic segmentation, today's marketers also define customer groups based on psychographic criteria as well as product-related distinctions.

Geographic Segmentation   Perhaps the oldest segmentation method is **geographic segmentation**—dividing an overall market into homogeneous groups on the basis of population locations. While geographic location does not ensure that consumers in a particular area will make the same kinds of buying decisions, this segmentation approach is useful when consumer preferences and purchase patterns for a good or service differ between regions. Suburbanites predictably purchase more lawn-care products than do their urban counterparts. Also, residents of northern states purchase snowblowers and car windshield ice scrapers and spray-on de-icers, products considered oddities in warmer climates.

Besides looking at patterns of product use, marketers may base geographic segmentation on other regional differences. General Mills recently developed

BUSINESS DIRECTORY

➤ **data mining**   *using a computer to search through massive amounts of customer data to detect patterns and relationships.*

➤ **market segmentation**   *process of dividing a total market into several relatively homogeneous groups.*

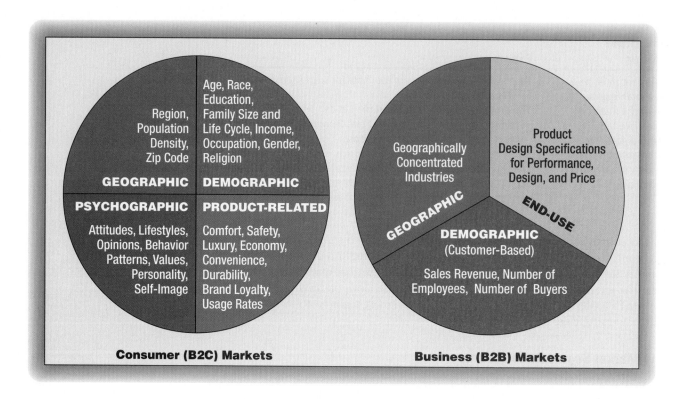

FIGURE 13.10
Methods of Segmenting Consumer and Business Markets

mixes for two traditional Mexican desserts, rice pudding and flan, a caramel custard. The company introduced the products, under the Betty Crocker brand, in 13 geographic markets, including New York, Miami, Los Angeles, Houston, and San Antonio. The company selected these cities because they have large Hispanic populations.[26]

Population size, a common geographic segmentation factor, helps define target markets as urban, suburban, and rural markets. However, businesses also need to consider a wide variety of other variables, such as job growth and migration patterns, before deciding to expand into new areas. Some businesses may decide to combine areas or even entire countries that share similar population and product-use patterns instead of treating each as an independent segment.

Demographic Segmentation By far the most common method of market segmentation, **demographic segmentation** distinguishes markets on the basis of various demographic or socioeconomic characteristics. Common demographic measures include income, age, occupation, household size, stage in the family life cycle, education, ethnic group, and gender. The U.S. Census Bureau is one of the best sources of demographic information for the domestic market. The "Clicks and Mortar" box describes a book that was initially intended for one demographic market—children—but crossed over into others.

Gender has traditionally been a simple way to define markets for certain products—perfume and cosmetics for women and hammers and drills for men. However, many products have spread beyond such gender stereotypes. Men no longer dominate purchases of sporting goods, exercise equipment, or automobiles. Women's participation in weight lifting—they represent more than four out of every ten users of free weights—has made that fitness activity America's most popular.[27] Automobile manufacturers know that over half of all auto purchase decisions are made by women. But rather than eliminating gender segmentation, they often develop different marketing mixes for their male and female customers. Women tend to place heavier emphasis on a car's safety features and comfort, so advertisements targeting

Harry Potter: A New Hero for Kids—and Marketers—Everywhere

Background. A few years ago, J.K. Rowling was a divorced, nearly destitute mom with a young son to feed. She also had a story to tell. So she took a chance and wrote the story down. Today, Jo Rowling is a millionaire, and her character, Harry Potter, is a hero to thousands of children and adults. Naturally, Harry has attracted the attention of marketers as well.

What Happened? *Harry Potter and the Sorcerer's Stone* was first published in Britain—after many rejection slips—then made its way to American children's hands via publisher Scholastic Inc. From there, the book seemed to take on a life of its own. Older children read it and then told their friends about it. Parents read the book to younger children and fell in love with it themselves. In the story, Harry Potter, a young British orphan, is sent to a school where he will eventually learn to be a sorcerer. Rowling created not only a cast of colorful—and sometimes scary—characters with names like Snape and Dumbledore, she conjured up an entire world that both children and adults could completely believe in. But Rowling didn't stop with one book about Harry. By the time the fourth book was released in the U.S., Harry Potter fans were lining up in front of their local bookstores waiting for their copies.

The Response. Even before the release of the fourth book, *Harry Potter and the Goblet of Fire,* anxious readers had already reserved over 1 million copies. Scholastic printed 6.8 million copies of the book, and required bookstores to sign agreements that they would not put the books on their shelves until after midnight of the release date. Talk about Midnight Madness. Children and parents stormed the stores, some wearing replicas of Harry's trademark black glasses. AOL Time Warner and Mattel had already made merchandising and entertainment agreements with Rowling for action figures and a movie based on the first book. That Halloween, lots of Harry Potter look-alikes went trick-or-treating in neighborhoods across the country. Also, it became clear that although the target market for Harry Potter books and merchandise items consisted of children ages 8 to 12 years, the appeal of Harry extended through college-age students—who were also devouring the books—as well as to parents of small children.

Today and Counting. While J.K. Rowling continues to pen her series of books, AOL Time Warner, Mattel, and now Hasbro are churning out the related goods. Rowling maintains a strong degree of control over the spin-offs. She is also candid with her audience about them. In an interview for *60 Minutes,* she said, "I can only say now to all the parents out there, if the action figures are horrible, just tell the kids that I said don't buy them." There is no question among Rowling's fans that the world of Harry Potter is here to stay, long after the movie and action figures are gone. Rowling clearly understands and respects her readers, regardless of their age, and is adept at giving them what they want—a good story. She has accomplished a feat that every writer would love to achieve: she has created a classic.

QUESTIONS FOR CRITICAL THINKING

1. Using demographic segmentation, create a portrait of an "average" Harry Potter reader.
2. Why do you think the Harry Potter series is popular worldwide, among readers of different cultures and backgrounds?

Sources: Elizabeth Weise, "'Potter' Fans Put Hex of a Boycott on Warner Bros.," *USA Today,* February 22, 2001, p. D1; "The Wizard of Marketing," *Business Week,* July 24, 2000, pp. 85–87; David Lieberman, "Marketers Count on Potter Film for Golden Touch," *USA Today,* July 18, 2000, pp. B1–B2.

---

women emphasize those features. Ford has set up a team of employees to focus on products and marketing for female customers. Feedback from customers has led Ford to develop and promote such features as adjustable pedals and seats, as well as tailgates that are easy to open.[28]

Age is perhaps the most volatile factor in demographic segmentation in the U.S., with our rapidly aging population. By 2020, one of every three Americans will be over 50 years old, and companies are increasingly focusing attention on reaching this growing part of the market. For many products, however, the bulk of purchasers are younger, so marketers must also devise strategies to meet the smaller age groups. Toyota's median customer is 46 years old, and the company is trying to attract younger buyers so that sales do not fall off when its loyal customers retire and, presumably, start cutting back on new-car purchases. Toyota recently hired a team of young marketers and charged them with developing and selling three cars aimed at consumers in their 30s: the Echo subcompact, a two-door Celica, and a convertible called the MR2 Spyder. Toyota's advertising tries to appeal to younger consumers by using real-life scenarios laced with humor. In addition, these ads are more likely to run on the Web or cable channels than on network television. The company also is establishing a presence with youthful buyers by sponsoring the Gravity Games and pricing the models below competitors' offerings.[29]

Be yourself. Race. Ethnicity. Religion. Nationality. Gender. In the end, there's just one variety of human being. The individual. All six billion of us. **Be bullish.**

ml.com

As incomes of different ethnic groups rise steadily, investment firms like Merrill Lynch are creating strategies aimed at attracting more diverse groups as clients. Promotional messages directed to these ethnic groups are increasingly common.

U.S. ethnic minority groups hold combined purchasing power of more than $1 trillion a year, an amount that marketers must not overlook. The three largest minority groups in the United States—African Americans, Hispanic Americans, and Asian Americans—represent almost three out of ten U.S. residents. Because of rapid growth from immigration and births, the Hispanic-American segment is expected to become the nation's largest ethnic group by 2005. In terms of spending on advertising, U.S. marketers are only beginning to reach ethnic minorities. Less than 2 percent of U.S. advertising budgets is devoted to ads in minority-focused media like the Spanish-language Univision television network or *Black Enterprise* magazine, even though research suggests that such targeted advertising can be profitable.

Consider Hispanic Americans, whose U.S. population of more than 33 million exceeds the entire population of Canada. Although Hispanic Americans typically speak English as a first or second language, many view the Spanish language as part of their cultural identity. A study of Hispanic teens found that most of them watch English-language television programs with their friends but Spanish-language programs at home in the evening with their families. Advertisers that want to reach Hispanic teens during prime time would need to place ads on networks like Univision and Telemundo. So far, however, ad spending on Spanish-language television is only about one-fourth the level it would be if it were in proportion to the size of the Hispanic population.[30]

But some companies are highly successful in reaching ethnic target markets. AsianAvenue is an English-language Web site targeting young Asian Americans, a group for which Internet use is high. The company places representatives on campuses with large Asian-American enrollments; they communicate to students about the Web site and alert the company to campus activities likely to draw many Asian students, so AsianAvenue can conduct promotions there.[31] Procter & Gamble (P&G) set up a multicultural market development organization, which is responsible for building sales and brand loyalty among ethnic target markets. The organization's initial efforts are focused on Hispanics, and P&G has significantly increased spending on Spanish-language advertising. It launched a series of promotions designed to convince Hispanic women that its Secret stick deodorants are more effective than the roll-ons they typically use.[32]

Parry Singh established a series of Web sites to cater to the demand for ethnic foods. The first site, Namaste.com, came in response to his sister-in-law's frustration in her search for Indian groceries. About eight out of ten Indian immigrants in the U.S. have personal computers (PCs), and many use them to stay connected to their relatives via the Internet. Namaste.com caters to their needs by providing them with a means of purchasing not only groceries but also Indian movies, music, and jewelry, as well as sending gifts to India. With revenues growing rapidly, Singh has since gone online with Gongshee.com, a bilingual site that offers Chinese products; QueRico.com, whose Spanish- and English-language versions offer food, music, and other items from Mexico, Cuba, and South America; and EthnicGrocer.com, an English-language site that educates visitors about 15 international cuisines and offers recipes plus the capability to order the necessary ingredients.[33]

Demographic segmentation is somewhat more difficult in foreign markets than in domestic ones. Many countries do not regularly conduct census studies of their populations, and others, such as Great Britain, Japan, Spain, France, and Italy, do not collect income data. One online source of global demographic information is the International Programs Center (IPC), part of the Census Bureau's Population Division. The IPC provides a searchable database of population statistics for many countries. A link appears on the Census Bureau's Web site (www.census.gov/ipc/www/).

Psychographic Segmentation   In recent years, marketing researchers have tried to formulate lifelike portraits of consumers. This effort has led to another strategy for segmenting target markets, **psychographic segmentation,** which divides consumer markets into groups with similar psychological characteristics, values, and lifestyles. *Lifestyle* is the summation of a person's needs, preferences, motives, attitudes, social habits, and cultural background.

Psychographic studies have evaluated motivations for purchases of hundreds of goods and services, ranging from soft drinks to health care services. Using the resulting data, marketers tailor their marketing strategies to carefully chosen market segments. A frequently used method of developing psychographic profits involves the use of *AIO* statements—verbal descriptions of various activities, interests, and opinions. Researchers survey a sample of consumers, asking them whether they agree or disagree with each statement. The answers are then tabulated and analyzed for use in identifying various lifestyle categories.

Procter & Gamble used a combination of psychographic and demographic data to identify consumers it calls "chatterers," shoppers who exert considerable influence on the purchase decisions of other people. To launch its Physique line of hair-care products, P&G targeted this segment, sending them samples and inviting them to a Web site that encouraged visitors to tell others about the product line. Within months, the effort had generated a million referrals to the Physique Web site.[34]

Although demographic classifications like age, gender, or income are relatively easy to identify and measure, researchers need to define psychographic categories. Often, marketing research firms conduct extensive studies of consumers, then share their psychographic data with marketers who sign up as clients. The marketing research firm Yankelovich periodically conducts a study called Monitor MindBase to classify consumers according to such measures as their attitudes and values. A recent Monitor MindBase study developed eight categories of consumers with 32 subcategories. The subcategories ranged from New Visionaries, who think of themselves as innovative and are very concerned about getting ahead, to Complacent Seniors, who feel overwhelmed by information and are reluctant to embrace technological developments.[35]

Product-Related Segmentation   Using **product-related segmentation,** marketers can divide a consumer market into groups based on buyers' relationships to the good or service. The three most popular approaches to product-related segmentation are based on benefits sought, usage rates, and brand loyalty levels.

Segmenting by *benefits sought* focuses on the attributes that people seek in a good or service and the benefits they expect to receive from it. Reel.com, which sells movies online, uses software to track the buying behavior of its customers. With the data, Reel.com segments customers according to how much they respond to price discounts. The company also identifies other preferences, such as the tendency of consumers who buy more than three movies or choose titles that are several years old.[36]

Differences in benefits sought can also shape the products a customer selects or how customers use a given product. KeyCorp, which offers financial services, uses the Web to identify individual customers in product segments. The company's computers combine data about customers with information about where they are clicking on its Web site, then customize the offers displayed to each customer. If a customer looks up information about college loans, KeyCorp's Web site will display offers relevant to a person with that interest.[37] Even if a business offers only one product line, marketers must remember to consider product benefits. Two people may buy the same product for very different reasons. A can of WD40 lubricant may help users to quiet a squeaking door hinge, clean an electrical contact point, or loosen a bolt on a lawn-mower engine.

A consumer market can also be segmented according to the amounts of a product that different consumers buy and use. Segmentation by *product usage rate* usually defines such categories as heavy users, medium users, and light users. The *80/20 principle* states that roughly 80 percent of a product's revenues come from only 20 percent of its buyers. Companies can now pinpoint which of their customers are the heaviest user—and even the most profitable customers—and to direct their heaviest marketing efforts to those customers. Charles Schwab Corp. segments customers who have at least $100,000 invested with Schwab or make at least 12 securities purchases and sales a year as "Signature clients." These clients have a customer-service number with a wait time of 15 seconds or less, compared with at least a ten-minute wait for other Schwab customers. The company can afford the higher level of service for Signature clients because they are more profitable. Similarly, First Union classifies holders of its credit cards according to product usage. When customers call for assistance, a color-coded square pops up on the computer screen of the customer service representative: green for profitable customers, red for the unprofitable ones, and yellow for everyone in between. Service decisions, such as rates to offer, depend partly on the codes.[38]

The third technique for product-related segmentation divides customers *by brand loyalty*—described in the next chapter as the degree to which consumers recognize, prefer, and insist on a particular brand. Marketers define groups of consumers with similar degrees of brand loyalty. They then attempt to tie loyal customers to a good or service by giving away logo-emblazoned premiums, such as T-shirts, nylon sports bags, or foam-rubber drink holders.

Segmenting Business Markets

In many ways, the segmentation process for business markets resembles that for consumer markets. However, some specific methods differ. Marketers divide business markets through geographic segmentation; demographic, or customer-based, segmentation; and end-use segmentation.

Geographic segmentation methods for business markets resemble those for consumer markets. Many B2B marketers target geographically concentrated industries, such as aircraft manufacturing, automobiles, and oil-field equipment. Especially on an international scale, customer needs, languages, and other variables may require differences in the marketing mix from one location to another.

Demographic, or *customer-based, segmentation* begins with a good or service design intended to suit a specific organizational market. Gulfstream aircraft, shown in Figure 13.11, serve a number of business segments: the business aircraft market, government markets in 30 different countries, and as transportation for military and scientific missions around the world. Online exchanges like DirectAg.com, Rooster.com, XSAg.com, and Farmbid.com specialize in linking suppliers with farmers. They serve this industry segment by offering products such as seeds, fertilizer, livestock, and farm machinery such as tractors.

To simplify the process of focusing on a particular type of business customer, the federal government recently established a new system called the *North American Industry Classification System (NAICS)* for classifying businesses. The six-digit NAICS codes reflect changes in business such as new technology, as well as new kinds of businesses, from HMO medical centers to warehouse clubs. In addition, NAICS codes are an effort to apply a common classification system to data generated by the

U.S., Canada, and Mexico. The first five digits are set for the three NAFTA member countries. The final digit can vary according to the specific data needs of each trading partner.

Another way to group firms by their demographics is to segment them by size based on their sales revenues or numbers of employees. Consolidated Freightways collects data from visitors to its Web site and uses the data to segment customers by size. Customers who look up rates or routing guides see a pop-up window where they can click for online help. Those who request help provide data about themselves, and Consolidated targets the smaller companies—which, on average, have bigger profit margins—in later marketing efforts. Modern information processing enables companies to segment business markets based on how much they buy, not just how big they are. Government Computer Sales Inc. (GCSI), which provides computer hardware and software for government agencies, gathers data about each agency with which it interacts. It identifies customers with high purchase rates and focuses selling efforts on those customers. The targeted effort has significantly boosted GCSI's profits.[39]

End-use segmentation focuses on the precise way a B2B purchaser will use a product. Resembling benefits-sought segmentation for consumer markets, this method helps small and medium-sized companies to target specific end-user markets rather than competing directly with large firms for wider customer groups. A marketer might also craft a marketing mix based on certain criteria for making a purchase. A company whose owners are members of ethnic minorities might list its product on M-Xchange, an Internet exchange specializing in minority-owned companies. Participating in M-Xchange could support a strategy to target business customers who promote diversity among their suppliers. Other decision criteria that a marketer might target include companies that choose suppliers based on low price or ability to support just-in-time inventory management.

THE LEADER SHIP

For forty-two years, Gulfstream has served nearly half of all FORTUNE 500® companies, more than 30 world governments, a host of prominent individuals and countless military and scientific missions around the world. In that time, we have come to understand and appreciate the rigors of leadership – its challenges and its requirements. If you are a business leader or a player on the world stage, only a Gulfstream can provide you with legendary safety, reliability, comfort and performance. Perhaps now is the best time to experience The Leader Ship. Gulfstream – the aircraft of choice for business and world leaders since 1958.

To learn more, call Joe Walker, Senior Vice President, Worldwide Sales, at (912) 965-5555 (joe.walker@gulfaero.com) or visit us at www.gulfstream.com.

THE WORLD STANDARD.™
Gulfstream
A GENERAL DYNAMICS COMPANY

FIGURE 13.11
Using Demographics and Geography to Segment Business Markets

BUYER BEHAVIOR: DETERMINING WHAT CUSTOMERS WANT

A fundamental marketing task is to find out why people buy one product and not another. The answer requires an understanding of **buyer behavior,** the series of decision processes by individual consumers who buy products for their own use and organizational buyers who purchase business products to be used directly or indirectly in the sale of other items. In contrast, **consumer behavior** refers more specifically to the actions of ultimate consumers directly involved in obtaining, consuming, and disposing of products, and the decision processes that precede and follow these actions. Determining what customers want is an inexact science, as illustrated by the "Business Hits and Misses" box.

Determinants of Consumer Behavior

By studying people's purchasing behavior, marketers can identify consumers' attitudes toward and uses of

One of the most challenging tasks for a marketer is to figure out why customers buy what they buy. Another great challenge is to figure out *how* both consumers and businesses prefer to make their purchases. Over the past decade, the whole concept of shopping on the Internet has taken shape. Online retailers have emerged with great fanfare, only to disappear within a few months. Businesses engaged in e-commerce must be able to understand buyer behavior in order to survive and grow.

One idea that has experienced both success and failure is online group buying. Simply put, the more people who commit to buying a good or service, the more the seller cuts the price. On the face of it, this seems like a win-win situation. "I'd always rather sell ten [items] at a time than one," explains Leora Schacter, marketing director at Sundial, a site that offers group-buying situations for wireless devices. MobShop, a site that caters to B2B transactions as well as consumers, describes the group-buying experience as a "river of orders" compared with "a single drop." People like to be associated with groups, particularly groups of winners. They also like to feel as though they are the winners in any deal. So the thought of teaming up with other likeminded consumers is appealing to many buyers. If you convince five friends to buy a certain PC at MobShop, you might see the price drop by as much as $500. Or suppose your ten-year-old is begging for a Razor scooter—pop onto CoShopper and you're bound to find other parents who want the scooter as well, for less. And your "friends"—co-shoppers—can be located anywhere in the world.

Perhaps this type of deal sounds too good to be true; in some ways it is. For one thing, a group price at a particular site might not be the lowest you could find anywhere on the Internet. You have to be willing to shop around, which is something the group sites would rather you didn't do. "There are so many sources of goods out there, it's hard to be sure anyone is giving you the lowest price," notes Steve Salter, project director for the Better Business Bureau's Online Reliability Program. For another, selection isn't always comprehensive. Click on the Swedish or Danish section of LetsBuyIt, and you might see a kitchen knife and one or two electronic doodads for sale. Click on the British or Irish section of the site, and you may be told that the site has no products for sale and is closed. Finally, not all sites allow you to back out of an offer once you've made it. So if you find a better price on the item elsewhere, you may be out of luck.

Consumers may like the concept of group buying, but the actual experience must be lacking, because some sites have already shut down. As mentioned, only some of LetsBuyIt's locations are operational. Marketers may have to go back to the drawing board to come up with a more attractive picture of group buying for the average consumer.

QUESTIONS FOR CRITICAL THINKING
1. In what ways might studying the steps of group buying behavior process help marketers revamp their sites to make the experience more attractive?
2. How might marketers for group buying sites build stronger relationships with customers?

Sources: CoShopper Web site, **www.coshopper.com**, accessed April 21, 2001; Women's Consumer Network, accessed April 21, 2001; LetsBuyIt.com, **www.letsbuyit.com**, accessed April 21, 2001; Joellen Perry, "Bulk Buying on the Web Rewards Togetherness," *U.S. News & World Report*, August 21, 2000, p. 62.

their products. This investigation also helps to improve the effectiveness of marketing strategies for reaching these target markets. Both personal and interpersonal factors influence the behavior of an ultimate consumer. Personal influences on consumer behavior include individual needs and motives, perceptions, attitudes, learned experiences, and their self-concepts. Marketers frequently apply psychological techniques to understand what motivates people to buy and to study consumers' emotional reactions to goods and services.

The interpersonal determinants of consumer behavior include cultural, social, and family influences. Retailers of ethnically oriented lines of clothing have found that carrying these goods enhances the loyalty of customers from the appropriate groups. Such factors, however, vary in different countries—even countries with a common language, such as Great Britain and Ireland.

Determinants of Business Buying Behavior

Because a number of people can influence purchases of B2B products, business buyers face a variety of organizational influences in addition to their own preferences. A design engineer may help to set the specifications that potential vendors must satisfy. A procurement manager may invite selected companies to bid on a purchase. A production supervisor may evaluate the operational aspects of the proposals that the firm receives, and the vice president of manufacturing may head a committee making the final decision.

Steps in the Consumer Behavior Process

Consumer decision making follows the sequential process outlined in Figure 13.12, with interpersonal and personal influences affecting every step. The process begins when the consumer recognizes a problem or opportunity. If someone needs a new pair of shoes, that need becomes a problem to solve. If someone receives a promotion and a $5-an-hour raise, that change may also become a purchase opportunity.

To solve the problem or take advantage of the opportunity, the consumer seeks out information about the intended purchase and evaluates alternatives, such as available brands. The goal of this activity is to find the best response to the perceived problem or opportunity.

Eventually, the consumer reaches a decision and completes the transaction—the purchase act. Later, he or she evaluates the experience with the purchase—postpurchase evaluation. Feelings about the experience serve as feedback that will influence future purchase decisions. The various steps in the sequence are affected by both interpersonal and personal factors.

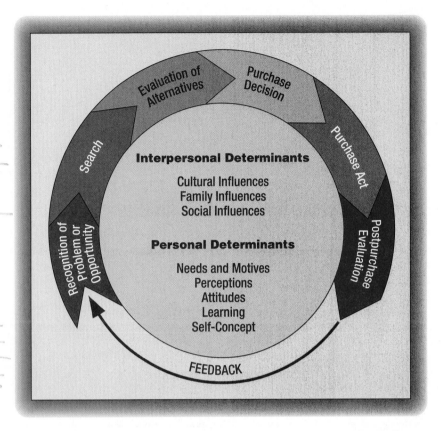

FIGURE 13.12
Steps in the Consumer Behavior Process

CREATING, MAINTAINING, AND STRENGTHENING MARKETING RELATIONSHIPS

The past decade has brought rapid change to most industries, as customers have become better informed and more demanding purchasers through closely comparing competing goods and services. They expect, even demand, new benefits from the companies that supply them, making it harder for firms to gain competitive advantage based on product features alone. Meanwhile, most businesses have traditionally focused on **transaction marketing,** characterized by buyer and seller exchanges with limited communications and little or no ongoing relationships between the parties. In transaction management, the goal is simple: negotiate hard with suppliers to secure the least expensive raw materials and components, then build products and find customers to buy them at prices high enough to cover costs and still earn a profit.

In today's hypercompetitive era, however, businesses need to find new ways of relating to customers if they hope to maintain long-term success. Instead of keeping customers at arm's length, businesses are developing strategies and tactics that draw them into a tighter connection with their customers. Such webs may expand to include stronger bonds with suppliers, employees, and even, in some cases, competitors. As a result, many firms are turning their attention away from managing transactions to the broader issues of **relationship marketing**. Relationship marketing goes beyond an effort for making the sale to a drive for making the sale again and again. To keep particular customers coming back,

BUSINESS DIRECTORY

➤ **relationship marketing**   *developing and maintaining long-term, cost-effective exchange relationships with individual customers, suppliers, employees, and other partners for mutual benefit.*

FIGURE 13.13
GE Plastics: Transforming Buyer–Seller Transactions into a Partnership

firms must exceed customers' needs and wants so they will make repeat purchases. As its ultimate goal, relationship marketing seeks to achieve customer satisfaction.

Managing relationships instead of simply completing transactions often leads to creative partnerships. As Figure 13.13 illustrates, customers enter into relationships with marketing organizations only if they are assured that the relationship will be rewarding. As the intensity of commitment increases, so does the likelihood of a business continuing a long-term relationship with its customers. The following list reviews a few of the ways businesses are using relationships to reach corporate goals:

- *Partnering with customers*—Inspired by the popular novel *The Hitchhiker's Guide to the Galaxy,* in which galactic travelers contribute reviews to an electronic guide, an Internet company called h2g2 is creating a collaborative guide to the travels of earthlings. Volunteer researchers are building the guide, which provides advice ranging from how to navigate Beijing's subway system to where to get the best curry dishes in Britain. The information is available on the Internet, so travelers can use laptops or Web-enabled cell phones to get information about the location they are visiting. The company is developing the capability to use global positioning technology to tailor information to the location from which a person is calling. The appeal of h2g2 lies in the offbeat nature of some recommendations and users' personal involvement in creating the guide. Traditional travel publishers like Thomas Cook agree. Thomas Cook's head of mobile commerce, Richard Roberts, says, "The principle of getting feedback, engaging in conversations and the creation of community interest is exactly the right thing we should be facilitating."[40]

- *Partnering with suppliers*—Scott Paint buys ingredients for its paint from Gulf Coast Chemical. Gulf Coast won the contract by offering to do much more than ship products to Scott's factory. Gulf Coast provides Scott with just-in-time inventory management. It tracks Scott's needs, brings in raw materials from several suppliers, and consolidates them into four monthly shipments. For Scott, partnering with Gulf Coast means lower inventory costs, better prices for consolidated orders, and the ability to focus on paint production, rather than inventory.

- *Partnering with other businesses*—Cisco Systems is a leader in computer networking. Rather than tackling many new technologies on its own, the company often supports high-tech start-ups in areas of interest to Cisco. If the start-ups create viable goods and services, Cisco may then offer to purchase these companies. In another industry, many of the largest pharmaceutical companies collaborate with small research firms that have expertise in a particular field, such as biotechnology. Such arrangements give the pharmaceutical giants access to innovation without requiring them to be leaders in every kind of research.[41]

Benefits of Relationship Marketing

Relationship marketing helps all parties involved. In addition to mutual protection against competitors, businesses that forge solid links with suppliers and customers are often rewarded with lower costs and higher profits than they would generate on their own. Long-term agreements with a few high-quality suppliers frequently reduce a firm's production costs. Unlike one-time sales, these ongoing relationships encourage suppliers to offer customers preferential treatment, quickly adjusting shipments to accommodate changes in orders and correcting any quality problems that might arise.

Good relationships with customers can be vital strategic weapons for a firm. By identifying current purchasers and maintaining positive relationships with them, organizations can efficiently target their best customers. Studying current customers' buying habits and preferences can help marketers identify potential new customers and establish ongoing contact with them. Attracting a new customer can cost as much as five times more than keeping an existing one. Not only do marketing costs go down, but long-term customers usually buy more, require less service, refer other customers, and provide valuable feedback. Together, these elements contribute to a higher **lifetime value of a customer**—the revenues and intangible benefits (referrals and customer feedback) from the customer over the life of the relationship, minus the amount the company must spend to acquire and serve that customer.

Businesses also benefit from strong relationships with other companies. Purchasers who repeatedly buy from one business may find that they save time and gain service quality as the business learns their specific needs. Some relationship-oriented companies also customize goods and services based on customer preferences. Because many businesses reward loyal customers with discounts or bonuses, some customers may even find that they save money by developing long-term relationships. Alliances with other firms to serve the same customers also can be rewarding. The alliance partners combine their capabilities and resources to accomplish goals that they could not reach on their own. In addition, alliances with other firms may help businesses develop the skills and experience they need to successfully enter new markets or improve service to current customers.

Tools for Nurturing Customer Relationships

Although relationship marketing has important benefits for both customers and business, most relationship-oriented businesses quickly discover that not all customers justify equal treatment. Some customers generate more profitable business than others. If, as noted earlier, 20 percent of a firm's customers account for 80 percent of its sales and profits, a customer in this category undoubtedly has a higher lifetime value than a customer who buys only sporadically or in small amounts.

While businesses shouldn't ignore any customer, of course, their objectives and tactics for managing relationships with individual customers often reflect the overall value to the firm of the resulting business. A firm may choose to custom-manufacture goods or services for high-value customers while working to increase repeat sales of stock products to less-valuable customers. An important task in developing relationship strategies is to differentiate between customer groups when seeking ways to pull each one closer to an intense commitment to the firm. The firm can then choose the particular tactics that suit each customer group.

Popular techniques through which firms try to build and protect customer relationships include frequent-buyer and frequent-user programs. Such a marketing initiative, commonly known as a **frequency marketing** program, rewards purchasers with cash, rebates, merchandise, or other premiums. Bass Hotels and Resorts has a frequency marketing program called Priority Club Worldwide. Frequent guests are offered points that can be used for redeeming items from the club's catalog. Redeeming points for room upgrades or in-room movies is common for frequent hotel guests, but Priority Club even offers a personal shopper who will help guests convert points into whatever they want. One Priority Club guest who worked as a firefighter arranged to convert his points into a Resuscitation Annie—a lifelike rubber dummy used to teach mouth-to-mouth resuscitation—for his firehouse.[42]

Affinity programs are another tool for building emotional links with customers. An **affinity program** is a marketing effort sponsored by an organization that solicits involvement by individuals who share common interests and activities. Affinity programs are common in the credit-card industry. Under such a program, a person can sign up for a credit card emblazoned with the logo of a favorite charity, sports or entertainment celebrity, or photograph of his or her college. The arrangement typically calls for the company to donate a percentage of the person's charges to the organization displayed on the credit card.

Many businesses also use co-marketing and co-branding. In a **co-marketing** deal, two businesses jointly market each other's products. Many PC manufacturers use co-marketing to promote the Intel Pentium processors in their machines. The PC makers gain credibility through their association with the high-quality, cutting-edge reputation of Intel Corp., and Intel benefits by having its name appear in more places and more often than it could achieve on its own. Ford is engaged in a co-marketing project with the Yahoo! Web portal. Ford invites owners of its vehicles to sign up at Yahoo's "Autos" Web page, where they can look up owner guides, recall notices, and service reminders, as well as information about Ford Credit, road conditions, and other resources for planning trips. Ford and Yahoo! have also collaborated on a sweepstakes promotion in which the top prize is a Ford Focus painted in Yahoo's purple and yellow graphics.[43]

When two or more businesses team up to closely link their names for a single product, **co-branding** occurs. Some fast-food restaurants have joined forces to house more than one restaurant choice under one roof so customers can stop by for, say, Great American Bagels in the morning and Caffe Luna for a smoothie in the afternoon. Kolcraft Enterprises recently began offering a new line of baby strollers bearing the Jeep brand. The Jeep strollers, like their sport-utility vehicle counterparts, have all-terrain tires and cater to upscale families. Parents who wheel around in the top-of-the-line Grand Cherokee model cement their relationship with Jeep while baby plays with the toy steering wheel, key, and push-button radio mounted in front.[44]

Recent technological advances have enabled businesses to develop new capabilities for managing customer relationships. The ability to customize and rapidly deliver goods and services has become increasingly dependent on investments in technology like computer-aided design and manufacturing. The Internet offers a way for businesses to connect with customers in a much more intimate manner than was previously available. Not only can companies take orders for customized products, but they can also gather data about customer characteristics and buying histories and then use the data to make predictions about what additional goods or services a given customer might want. Web sites or salespeople can tailor their messages based on those predictions. As long as customers are willing to share this information about themselves, the marketing possibilities are endless.

Computer databases provide strong support for effective relationship marketing. Marketers can maintain databases on current customers' tastes, price-range preferences, and lifestyles, and they can quickly obtain names and other information about good prospects. Managers can then use the information in data warehouses to create a centralized, accurate profile of each customer's relationship with the firm as an aid to decision making. The Internet, with its capabilities for interactive electronic commerce, creates additional opportunities for firms to build close customer relationships.

Service industries, such as the airlines, have been in the forefront of relationship marketing, since their employees often personally meet and interact with customers. However, manufacturing businesses also can apply this technology. In the earlier example of Ford, that company has established a presence on Yahoo's Web site, where Ford offers a variety of ways for customers to interact with the company throughout the time they own their car. At the same time, Ford can gather data about what kinds of information its customers look for at the Web page, as well as track service data that customers enter while on the site. If the company also gathers data about what customers want in their next car—perhaps learning that customers are becoming more interested in gas mileage or adding new family members—it can better position itself as the customers' next choice.

The owners of the National Basketball Association's Portland Trail Blazers used Web-based customer relationship management to identify and respond to interest in a women's team, the Portland Fire. The Blazers used special software called Front Office to build a customer database. Whenever the team sold tickets, it entered sales and demographic data about the customer. Sales reps used the data to target customers that might be interested in the Fire. During the Fire's first season, they quickly surpassed their sales objectives. The teams continue to use the database to find other marketing opportunities. As an example, Tony Cesarano, database marketing manager, says, "If a customer takes his son to 'Boy Scout Night' at a Harlem Globetrotters game, we'll cross-market his interest in a Boy Scout theme night at a Blazers game." In addition, the company is developing the capability to send e-mail announcements to customers who have expressed interest in particular kinds of events.[45]

Whatever the technology, the success of relationship marketing depends not on the type of software or the size of the database but on how well the company uses data to meet customer needs. The Internet can offer the same type of interaction to a worldwide customer base, as Williams-Sonoma found, as explained in the "Clicks and Mortar" box. On any scale, marketing's goal is to focus the interaction on customer satisfaction.

WHAT'S AHEAD

The following three chapters examine each of the elements of the marketing mix by which firms satisfy selected target markets. The first two mix elements—product and price—are the subject of Chapter 14. Chapter 15 focuses on distribution and examines channel design and logistics. The final chapter in this section covers promotion and the various methods marketers use to communicate with their target customers.

Williams-Sonoma Cooks Up Relationship Marketing on the Web

Background. Relationship marketing is one of those buzzwords that sounds great in theory—but does it really work? More specifically, can it work on the Web? California-based cookware retailer Williams-Sonoma decided to put this concept to the test, on the premise that even customers who shop the Internet like the feeling that they're returning to a small shop where the proprietor always knows their names and their needs. Industry experts agreed that the move made sense for a company as strong as Williams-Sonoma. "The company has a long established history in direct-to-customer marketing through its catalogs," notes Barbara E. Miller of Goldman Sachs. "It has the data necessary to communicate effectively with customers and a strong direct-to-customer infrastructure and management team in place."

What Happened? A few years ago, Williams-Sonoma launched its first Web effort with a bridal registry at www.wsbridal.com. The registry maintained an alliance with the portal WeddingChannel.com. Five months later, the Williams-Sonoma brand itself went online with www.williams-sonoma.com. In less than a year, Williams-Sonoma was using every available Web tool to collect data on customers and develop relationships with them. The company's objectives were to establish a business with two primary factors: a profitable and sustainable business model implementation of relationship marketing through creation of the ultimate consumer experience across all business channels—the Web, its stores, and its catalogs.

The Response. During the first six months online, the Web site outperformed expectations in several ways, from total sales to the percentage of customers who actually made a purchase after visiting the site—a real barrier for most Web sites. Williams-Sonoma was both surprised and pleased to learn that 34 percent of its Internet buyers were actually new to the company, rather than people who had made previous purchases through its catalog or in one of the company's retail stores. This gave Williams-Sonoma marketers important information for building relationships with these new customers.

Today and Counting. Williams-Sonoma marketers are now looking for ways to extend relationship marketing concepts and connect Web customers to their brick-and-mortar stores and vice versa. "The Williams-Sonoma stores frequently have chefs on hand who offer cooking exhibitions," says chief marketing officer Pat Connolly. Connolly envisions using the Internet to identify customers who might like to attend one of these demonstrations in their area and inviting them via e-mail. Williams-Sonoma also plans to place Internet-linked kiosks in its stores that would let customers search for items and get more information about them. One industry analyst says that the future of relationship marketing and its integrated application by retail stores, Web sites, and Williams-Sonoma catalogs look bright. "The pluses for Williams-Sonoma are that the company has a consistent brand with a strong and consistent message to customers. It also offers quality products with reliable, store-based customer service."

QUESTIONS FOR CRITICAL THINKING

1. In addition to those mentioned, describe two other ways that Williams-Sonoma could use relationship marketing to connect customers from the Web to its retail stores, or vice versa. How might each of these customer-contact locations aid in strengthening the customer-marketer bond?

2. Describe an instance in which Williams-Sonoma might use co-marketing or co-branding with another organization via the Internet.

Sources: "Corporate Overview" and "Chuck Williams's Story," Williams-Sonoma Web site, **www.williams-sonomainc.com**, accessed April 21, 2001; "Williams-Sonoma, Inc., Selects Exel for National Home Delivery Services; Partnership Covers Traditional, Catalog, and E-commerce Fulfillment," *Business Wire*, December 11, 2000.

➤ Summary of Learning Goals

1. Summarize the ways in which marketing creates utility.

Through an exchange, two or more parties give something of value to one another to satisfy felt needs. Marketing is closely linked with the exchange process. It creates utility—the want-satisfying power of a good or service—by making the product available when and where consumers want to buy and by arranging for orderly transfers of ownership. In other words, while production creates form utility, marketing creates time, place, and ownership utility.

2. Explain the marketing concept and relate how customer satisfaction contributes to added value.

The marketing concept refers to a companywide customer orientation with the objective of achieving long-run success. This concept is essential in today's marketplace, which is primarily a buyer's market, meaning buyers can choose from an abundance of goods and services. Customers seek more than just a fair price; they want added value. A good or service provides added value by delivering more than buyers expect in the form of added features, reduced prices, enhanced customer service, a strengthened warranty, or other marketing mix improvements that increase customer satisfaction.

3. Describe the components of a market and distinguish between B2B and B2C marketing.

A market consists of people with purchasing power and willingness and authority to buy. Markets can be classified by the types of products they handle. Consumer (or B2C) products are goods and services purchased by ultimate users. Business (or B2B) products are goods and services purchased to be used, directly or indirectly, in the production of other products for resale.

4. Outline the basic steps in developing a marketing strategy.

All organizations, profit-oriented and not-for-profit, need to develop marketing strategies to effectively reach customers. This process involves analyzing the overall market, selecting a target market, and developing a marketing mix that blends decision elements related to product, price, distribution, and promotional decisions. Often, company marketers develop a marketing plan that expresses their marketing strategy.

5. Describe the marketing research function.

Marketing research is the information-gathering function that links marketers to the marketplace. It provides the information about potential target markets that planners need as they construct effective marketing mixes. Marketers conduct research in order to identify marketing problems and opportunities, analyze competitors' strategies, evaluate and predict customer behavior, gauge the performance of existing products and package designs and assess the potential of new ones, and develop plans for pricing, promotion, and distribution. Besides collecting information, marketing research includes planning how to collect the information, as well as interpreting and communicating the results.

6. Identify each of the methods available for segmenting consumer and business markets.

Consumer markets can be divided according to demographic characteristics, such as age and family size; geographic factors; psychographic variables, which involve behavioral and lifestyle profiles; and product-related variables, such as the benefits consumers seek when buying a product or the degree of brand loyalty they feel toward it. Business markets are segmented according to three criteria: geographic characteristics, customer-based specifications for products, and end-user applications.

7. Distinguish between buyer behavior and consumer behavior.

Buyer behavior refers to the purchase processes of both individual consumers who buy goods and services for their own use and organizational buyers who purchase business products. Consumer behavior refers to the actions of ultimate consumers with direct effects on obtaining, consuming, and disposing of products, as well as the decision processes that precede and follow these actions. Personal influences on consumer behavior include an individual's needs and motives, perceptions, attitudes, learned experiences, and self-concept. The interpersonal determinants include cultural influences, social influences, and family influences. A number of people may participate in business purchase decisions, so business buyers encounter a variety of organizational influences in addition to their own preferences.

8. Discuss relationship marketing, including its importance in strategic planning.

Relationship marketing is an organization's attempt to develop long-term, cost-effective links with individual customers for mutual benefit. Good relationships with customers can be a vital strategic weapon for a firm. By identifying current purchasers and maintaining a positive relationship with them, an organization can efficiently target its best customers. Information technologies, such as computers, databases, and the Internet, support effective relationship marketing.

Business Terms You Need to Know

marketing 460
utility 461
marketing concept 462
customer satisfaction 462
target market 470
marketing mix 471

marketing research 473
data mining 476
market segmentation 476
buyer behavior 483
relationship marketing 485

Other Important Business Terms

exchange process 461

value-added 462

person marketing 466

place marketing 467

cause marketing 468

event marketing 468

organization marketing 468

consumer (B2C) product 470

business (B2B) product 470

data warehouse 476

geographic segmentation 477

demographic segmentation 478

psychographic segmentation 481

product-related segmentation 481

end-use segmentation 483

consumer behavior 483

transaction marketing 485

lifetime value of a customer 487

frequency marketing 488

affinity program 488

co-marketing 488

co-branding 488

➤ Review Questions

1. Define and distinguish among the four different types of utility. Explain how marketing contributes to the creation of utility.

2. What might be some good ways for a large food manufacturer like General Mills to obtain customer feedback?

3. What constitutes a market? Distinguish between the B2C market and the B2B market.

4. Identify five types of nontraditional marketing, and give an example of each.

5. Identify each of the following as a consumer product or a business product, or classify it as both:

   a. carton of orange juice

   b. computer

   c. scooter

   d. bank account

   e. sweater

6. Explain each of the basic steps in developing a marketing strategy. What is a target market? Why is target market selection the first step performed in marketing strategy development?

7. What are the five basic reasons that marketers conduct research? Identify the basic methods used in collecting research data.

8. Explain each of the bases used to segment consumer and business markets.

9. Describe two ways that businesses use relationships to reach corporate goals.

10. What are the benefits—to all parties—of relationship marketing?

➤ Questions for Critical Thinking

1. Consider a hypothetical society in which three distinct groups are self-sufficient but have particular strengths. One group grows fruit trees and cotton. Another is skilled at fishing and producing lumber. The third raises beef cattle and dairy cows in addition to farming grains. In what ways might these three groups create exchange processes to increase the total production and raise the standard of living for all three?

2. Choose one of the following businesses and describe ways in which the owner might add value to the goods or services offered:

   a. a tanning salon

   b. a for-profit career placement service

   c. an online clothing retailer

   d. a supermarket

3. This chapter describes an example in which Polaroid introduced a low-tech camera called I-Zone, which became popular among teenage girls. Do you think the product would have been as successful with this market if Polaroid had increased both the quality and the price of the camera? Why or why not? Can you identify any other target markets in which the camera might be successful?

4. Think of two situations in which you have been a customer: one in which you have been satisfied with the goods or services you received and one in which you have not. Make a list of the reasons why you were satisfied in the first case and another list of the reasons why you were not satisfied in the second case. Would you say that the failure was the result of marketers not understanding your needs?

5. As noted in the chapter, many products have now spread beyond certain stereotypes in demographic or psychographic segmentation. For instance, many men now have pierced ears and many women buy motorcycles. Identify three such goods or services and describe how you might adjust parts of the marketing strategy to accommodate the crossover.

➤ Experiential Exercise

Background: You learned in this chapter the various ways businesses segment their consumer markets: geographic segmentation, demographic segmentation, psychographic segmentation, and product-related segmentation. This exercise will help you apply what you've learned about demographic segmentation.

Directions: Select two popular television programs, each with an audience representing two different generations. Mostly teens/young adults should view the first program you select, and mostly the parents of teens/young adults should view the second.

1. Videotape both programs this week—each on separate videotapes—and view the commercials aired throughout the program.
2. Select one commercial from each program that you think did the best job of appealing to its dominant audience.
3. In the following chart, list the characteristics of the commercial you identified as appealing to the age demographic. In addition, if any other demographic categories were targeted in the commercial, such as occupation, stage of family life cycle, education, or ethnic group, be sure to list those characteristics as well.
4. Introduce the first commercial to your class, alerting them to watch for the characteristics you listed in your chart and then play the videotaped commercial for them to view and discuss. Repeat the procedure for the second commercial.
5. Reminder: Before you come to class, be sure to queue up the commercial on each videotape so that you don't waste class time trying to locate the commercial.

Age Group	Name of TV Program	Commercial Selected	Characteristics Appealing to Age Demographic	Examples of Other Demographic Categories
Teens/Young Adults				
The Parents of Teens/Young Adults				

➤ **Nothing but Net**

1. **Online customer privacy.** One of the more contentious issues today in marketing is that of online customer privacy. Online retailers collect and store a variety of information on their customers. Some argue that retailers may store too much information and provide some of it to others without the customer's knowledge. Others worry about the security of personal information stored on the Internet. Visit the Web sites of at least four online retailers (some suggested online retailers are listed below) and review each retailer's privacy policy. Prepare a report comparing and contrasting the privacy policies of online retailers. Did your review make you more or less likely to shop online?

   www.landsend.com

   www.amazon.com

   www.eddiebauer.com

   www.levenger.com

2. **Marketing colleges.** Virtually all colleges have Web sites. Most use their Web sites to market their schools to prospective students. Visit your college's Web site and the Web sites of at least two others. Identify and evaluate the impact on you personally (positive, neutral, or negative) of the Web site marketing strategies used by each college. What elements of the site made you react the way you did?

3. **Customer feedback.** Many companies use their Web sites as a means of obtaining feedback from customers. Visit the two Web sites listed following—or those of other companies in which you have some interest—and review the companies' customer feedback section. Summarize the reaction actual customers might have to this means of obtaining customer input. What are some of the pluses and minuses for companies who use the Internet to obtain customer input?

   www.marriott.com/suggest/suggest.asp? path=mdot.com

   www.honda2001.com/owners/customer_relations.html

   Note: Internet Web addresses change frequently. If you don't find the exact sites listed, you may need to access the organization's home page and search from there.

Everyone has a favorite radio station, whether it's rock, folk, urban, or news. Just like other businesses, radio stations use strategies for segmenting markets and target those who are most likely to listen to their format. But unlike some other businesses, radio stations must engage in marketing both to consumers—listeners—and businesses—potential advertisers. WBRU is no exception. Based in Providence, Rhode Island, WBRU serves a mainly college-educated audience spread throughout Rhode Island and southeastern Massachusetts.

WBRU presents what it calls a "modern rock format" with nine commercial breaks each hour. Calling itself "music interactive," WBRU concentrates on hot new music groups, boasting that its programming contains "no endless morning talk, no off-color or offensive humor. . . . We only feature targeted lifestyle programs and promotions . . . with the most dynamic, exciting playlists in the business."

Local advertisers and listeners meet on the common ground of WBRU's radio waves. According to the station's most recent demographic survey, 29 percent of WBRU's listeners are employed full time; 28 percent have a home mortgage; 13 percent own a computer; 11 percent drive a Lexus, BMW, or Saab; and 10 percent work in executive or managerial positions. During a recent 12-month period, WBRU listeners spent $21 million on furniture, $17 million on appliances, $26 million on clothing, $9 million on TV sets, and $9 million on jewelry. WBRU attracts its advertisers by providing them with this listener profile information. Through the years, such corporate heavyweights as Blockbuster Video, Dunkin' Donuts, New England Sports Network, and Tweeter Home Entertainment have signed on for commercials at the station—to gain its listeners' ears.

Segmenting the market is important for attracting advertisers, but it is even more important for attracting listeners. If WBRU knows who its listeners are, it can fine-tune its programming to offer selections they want to hear. To get such information, the station conducts an online survey at its Web site—listeners can answer questions about other stations they like, what they do in their free time, what consumer items they purchase, and who their favorite recording artists are. In one market segment, the station targets African Americans by offering gospel music on Sundays by its DJ Brother Don, followed by DJs Cas Casino and Commish, who specialize in hip-hop and rhythm and blues. Other programming slots include "Retro Lunch" and jazz at 2 AM. Each of those time slots is targeted to a specific listening market.

Listeners can get music news and win free CDs and other prizes at the WBRU Web site, as well as look up future programming schedules. They can browse through the BRU Store, view the message board and photo gallery, and download interviews with the likes of Dave Matthews. All of these opportunities to interact with the station help WBRU sharpen its understanding of its listeners. If you want to go see Big Dumb Face at Lupo's on Friday, you can find out about it at WBRU. If you prefer Papa Roach or Alien Ant Farm, keep listening to the station for your chance to win free tickets. And if you're not sure whether you want to plunk down your cash for the new Buckcherry CD, check out the review first on WBRU. Falling asleep while pulling an all-nighter? Tune into WBRU LOUD at 10 PM on Thursday nights, and you're guaranteed to stay awake. If all of this sounds good to you, you're probably the perfect WBRU listener, even if you don't own a Lexus or your own company—yet.

QUESTIONS

1. In what ways does WBRU attempt to add value to its basic service?
2. In addition to providing businesses with demographic information about listeners, what types of marketing efforts might WBRU make to attract businesses to advertise on its airwaves and Web site?
3. Describe a typical WBRU listener from what you have read in the case.
4. Go to the WBRU Web site at **www.wbru.com** and look for ways that the station conducts research about its listeners, either directly or indirectly.

Source: WBRU Web site, **www.wbru.com,** accessed April 5, 2001.

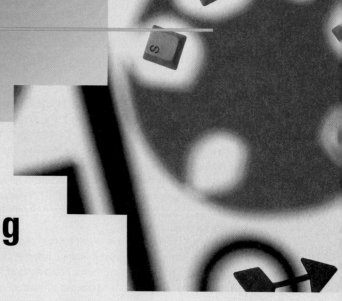

CHAPTER 14

Developing and Pricing Goods and Services

Learning Goals

1. Define *product* and list the elements of a product strategy.

2. Describe the classifications of consumer goods, business goods, and services.

3. Distinguish between the product mix and product lines.

4. Describe the four stages of the product life cycle.

5. List the stages of new-product development.

6. Explain how firms identify their products.

7. Outline the different types of pricing objectives and discuss how firms set prices in the marketplace.

8. Explain how to use breakeven analysis in pricing strategy.

9. Differentiate between skimming and penetration pricing strategies.

Razor: A New Generation of Scooters

"Everything old is new again." "What goes around comes around." You've heard these clichés before, but never are they more applicable in the business world than when a new generation breathes life back into a product that had been considered extinct. Ask your parents, and they'll tell you they remember having big, clunky metal scooters—or maybe they fashioned their own from wood and roller-skate wheels. But scooters faded from the scene decades ago, until the president of J.D. Corp., a bicycle-parts factory in Taiwan, came up with a new way to get around his factory quickly and efficiently—on a streamlined scooter with in-line skate wheels. The design was so simple it was perfect: a lightweight, folding scooter that just about anyone could operate. When representatives from upscale gadget retailer Sharper Image saw him scooting around trade shows, they begged him to produce scooters for sale. The new product, called the Razor scooter, quickly caught on among U.S. teenagers, as well as commuters in Japan and Europe. In fact, by the time the Razor actually hit the marketplace, J.D. Corp. was struggling to keep up with demand, and it soon set up a U.S. office to coordinate domestic distribution.

Within months, competitors were churning out their own brand of scooters. Established names like Ohio-based bike manufacturer Huffy and newcomers such as Zappy all introduced their own versions of the new scooter in an attempt to cash in on the trend. Ironically, in order to enter the market, Huffy licensed its Micro scooters from J.D. Corp. The Micro, whose platform is designed for the larger American foot, is built at the same factory as the Razor. But Razor continues to hang on to the top spot for now, simply because it was first to the marketplace. When people think of the term *scooter,* they think of the brand name Razor at the same time, which is perhaps the most valuable association a company

can build for a new product. In fact, when the Razor was the topic of a question on the hit television show *Who Wants to Be a Millionaire* and the contestant had to poll

the audience for help with the answer, "54 percent [of the audience] said the Razor was a scooter," recalls Carlton Calvin, J.D. Corp.'s head of U.S. operations. "That's pretty amazing when you consider we were unknown just a year ago."

Razor marketers know that the company will have to roll fast to keep ahead of the competition over the long haul. So to keep the brand name visible, they are considering alliances with fast-food outlets, video game and clothing companies, as well as deals with movie companies in which Razor scooters will make appearances. Right now, everyone wants to sign up. "It's a good position to be in," admits Calvin. "We get to choose who we want to partner with." Another good position to be in is manufacturing a good that consumers across the board seem to want. "The college student and the urban hipster [are] key [demographics] for us," says Calvin. But

school-age children and adult commuters are jumping on their scooters as well. "In overcrowded Tokyo, commuters use them to get from the subway to work," explains Maria Vrachnos, general manager of the *Lreport* in Del Mar, California. "From Tokyo they migrated to the West Coast among the 19- to 24-year-olds, but then came the rise in gas prices and some older people picked up on it for commuting." Younger kids who can't quite manage skateboards love the scooters, too, because they are much easier to handle.

One early bump in the road that Razor hit, however, was price. When J.D. Corp. and Sharper Image first teamed up to sell the scooters, "we started with the Razor priced at $119," notes Lou Soucie of Sharper Image. The scooters sold pretty well, but then J.D. Corp. dropped the price to $99. "At that point it just exploded," says Soucie. "We had found the price point. It's now the number-one selling product in our line."[1] And with no gas tank to fill or expensive maintenance and repairs to make, the $99 price tag looks like a very good deal.

CHAPTER OVERVIEW

To prepare a successful plan for satisfying a firm's target market, managers must design a unique marketing mix. In essence, creating products designed to fill customer needs is the reason for a firm's existence. Society permits businesses to operate as long as they serve its members by providing want-satisfying products at competitive prices. Pricing strategy is a second major determinant of consumer acceptance and a critical factor in ensuring that a profit-seeking firm earns adequate profits and that a not-for-profit organization generates sufficient revenues to meet its expenses. Pricing strategies are being increasingly scrutinized in the interconnected world of cyber-shopping and e-commerce. Businesses have to adjust to consumers' newfound power in exchanges.

This chapter begins by describing the classifications of goods and services, the product mix, and the product life cycle. We then discuss how firms develop, identify, and package products. Next, we examine pricing strategies for those products and how firms determine the most appropriate prices for their goods and services. We conclude with a look at consumer perceptions of prices.

WHAT IS A PRODUCT?

Engineers and other production specialists tend to think of products as collections of physical characteristics. A Honda automobile is a combination of tires, plastic components, sheet metal panels, glass windows, an engine, and seats. By contrast, the marketing definition describes a **product** as a bundle of physical, service, and symbolic attributes designed to provide customer satisfaction. Included in this broader definition are considerations of package design, brand names, warranties, and product image.

Focusing on Benefits

The chief executive officer (CEO) of a major tool manufacturer once startled his stockholders with this statement: "Last year our customers bought over 1 million quarter-inch drill bits, and none of them wanted to buy the product. They all wanted quarter-inch holes." Successful marketers recognize the need to focus their firm's product design, packaging, and promotional decisions on giving customers the bundle of benefits they seek from the product.

Coca-Cola is the best-selling soft drink in part because of its formula, a well-kept secret for over a century. Along with the caramel color and corn syrup found in other colas, Coke contains a special blend of oils called 7X. The secrecy surrounding the flavorings—known only to three employees, according to company legend—only adds to the product's appeal. However, the value of Coke extends beyond the 17 or 18 ingredients in its secret formula. Consumers enjoy the taste, of course, but they also respond to the familiarity of the brand, its ads, global availability, and its bright red packaging.[2]

Likewise, the almost 100 companies that make the 1,800 or so varieties of golf balls currently offered for sale know that the product is more than the sum of its parts. Each ball must conform to the specifications set out by the Royal & Ancient Golf Club of St. Andrews, Scotland, and the U.S. Golf Association in Far Hills, New Jersey. These rules specify the balls' weight and size, as well as how far they travel when hit by a mechanical driver. Besides simply meeting specifications, marketers of the balls offer their customers confidence. Golfers can buy balls that famous players like Tiger Woods use to win competitions, and they can gain hope from slogans like Bridgestone Sports's "muscle-fiber core technology" in its Precept brand or Wilson Golf's promise that its Smart-Core is "a golf ball so smart that it reacts to your game."[3]

The need to focus on buyer solutions and product benefits is illustrated by the example shown in Figure 14.1. Eveready Battery Co. describes its Energizer e^2 battery in terms of the "outrageous" power it provides. Comparing a battery to a rock star leaping in the air gives the impression that a consumer who wants a powerful energy supply will find it in Energizer e^2 batteries. Eveready reinforces this impression with its slogan, "Take power to the next level." In contrast, the batteries' physical characteristics receive only minor attention in the small print: "the battery with a heart of titanium."

Services Are Products, Too

A big portion of the average personal budget pays for products with no tangible features. A haircut, an oil change, a cell phone message, and a weekend at the beach are all included in a broad category of products called *services*. Businesses buy such services as training programs, marketing research, package delivery, building maintenance, and security. **Services** are intangible tasks that satisfy needs of final consumers or business users.

Most products combine both tangible goods and intangible services. People who go out for a special dinner in a good restaurant expect excellent food coupled with attentive service. Someone who purchases a new set of tires may receive services such as mounting, balancing, and periodic rotation as part of the package. Business customers expect technical support services, not just a do-it-yourself set of instructional CDs and a manual, when they buy computer software.

Without services, people could not receive mail, cash checks, attend college, or even watch a movie. The service sector is becoming an increasingly significant force in the 21st century, as satellite broadcasting and Internet usage continue to grow in economic importance. The growth in sales of Web-enabled cell phones and personal digital assistants is driving a variety of services. Among them are cellular Internet service providers like AT&T and Vodafone, search engines like Google, Internet portals like Yahoo! and Terra Lycos, and content providers like Sony and AOL Time Warner. These and other companies are fighting to dominate the market for Internet services on phones and other pocket devices.[4]

FIGURE 14.1
Emphasizing Benefits for Titanium Batteries

Customer Service as a Product

Every organization—be it profit-seeking or not-for-profit, large corporation or sole proprietorship, manufacturer or service provider—must recognize the importance of customer service and include it as a key ingredient in all product offerings. Every employee must demonstrate a commitment to making customers happy. Paying attention to every detail in the process of delivering satisfaction is the key to success in contemporary business. Organizations with such a focus want to give buyers experiences that exceed any they have had with competitors.

In the mundane world of dry cleaners, Zoots stands out because of its emphasis on making it easy for customers to drop off and pick up clothes. Customers can place orders online, and the company offers a pickup and delivery service. Those who head for one of the several dozen Zoots stores can use a drive-through window. Even customers who want to pick up clothes after regular business hours have an option: they can use a credit card to unlock the door to the vestibule, where they can find their clothes hanging in lockers accessible with a personal identification number.[5]

Warranties Are Important, Too

A warranty or guarantee is an added benefit that accompanies a tangible good or service. A **warranty** is a legal guarantee that a good or service will serve the purpose for which it is intended. Warranties contribute to customer service by protecting consumers from dissatisfaction. Even when a company states no such protections, certain rights are always guaranteed to consumers by law. In addition to these implied rights, sellers may offer explicit product warranties or guarantees. A major factor in the high-quality image of Cross pens is the lifetime warranty provided with the product. No proof of purchase is needed; simply return a defective pen to the manufacturer, and it will be repaired or replaced free of charge.

Cable television marketers have also offered warranties to set their services apart in this increasingly competitive industry. In recent years, cable companies have faced erosion of their earlier monopoly positions as well as new competitors like satellite dish communications and wireless microwave services. To combat these rivals and to counter widespread perceptions of inadequate concern for customer service, a number of major cable television suppliers have agreed to service guarantees. A customer typically receives a month of free service if the company fails to fulfill its service pledges.

CLASSIFYING CONSUMER AND BUSINESS PRODUCTS

Following the distinction between consumer markets and business markets, products can be broadly categorized as either consumer products or business products, depending on who purchases them for what reasons. A sweater purchased by a woman who wants to add to her personal wardrobe is a consumer product. A group of sweaters purchased by a clothing buyer at Dillard's department stores will be resold to shoppers. Both categories can be further subdivided. By determining the category into which each product falls, marketers gain extensive information regarding the appropriate distribution, promotion, and pricing strategies to use in marketing it.

Categories of Consumer Products

Marketers focus on consumer buying habits to classify consumer products (also known as *B2C products*). They seek answers to several questions regarding purchases: Who? What? When? Where? How? The answers place a purchase in one of three categories—convenience, shopping, or specialty products.

Convenience products are items that consumers purchase frequently, immediately, and with little effort. Vending machines, Circle K stores, and local magazine stands usually stock convenience products. Examples include newspapers, chewing gum, magazines, milk, bread, and snack foods.

Shopping products are typically purchased only after comparisons between products in competing stores to evaluate such characteristics as price, quality, style, and color. Someone looking for new carpeting may visit several retail showrooms, examine dozens of patterns and colors, and spend days making the final decision.

Specialty products are those items that purchasers are willing to make special efforts to obtain. Purchasers of specialty products are already familiar with the items and see no reasonable substitutes for them. Specialty products tend to carry expensive price tags and well-known brand names. Often, they are distributed through limited numbers of exclusive dealers. Examples include Louis Vuitton luggage, Porsche autos, designer clothing, and all-inclusive surfing vacations in Australia.

Remember that the good or service itself does not determine its classification. Instead, classification depends on predominant purchasing patterns. A convenience item for one person may be a shopping good for someone else, but if the product is purchased most often on the basis of convenience, then it will be classified that way. Inexpensive watches are widely available in discount stores and supermarkets. More expensive timepieces, like the Rolex Swiss Chronometer shown in Figure 14.2, are specialty products. Similarly, Bartlett or Anjou pears on sale for 99 cents a pound in supermarkets are considered a convenience or shopping product. But a pound of Royal Riviera pears from Harry and David, lovingly packed in a handsome basket and delivered to the recipient's door, costs about five times as much and qualifies as a specialty product. This variety of fruit is easily damaged, but the pears are huge and beautiful, and the mail-order business handles them with exquisite care to prevent bruising. Customers are willing to pay extra because they are buying lovely gifts, not just food for the lunch table.[6]

Categories of Business Goods and Services

Business products (also known as *B2B products*) fall into five main categories: installations, accessory equipment, component parts and materials, raw materials, and supplies. While marketers classify consumer products according to buying patterns, business product classifications are based on how customers use them as well as their basic characteristics. Long-lived and expensive products whose sales usually involve large sums of money are called *capital items*. Less costly products that are consumed within a year are referred to as *expense items*.

Installations are pieces or collections of major capital equipment such as new factory systems, heavy machinery, and custom-made equipment. B2B buyers use installations in producing goods and services for sale to their own customers. New locomotives represent installations for the Burlington Northern Railroad. The transmission stations that companies like Ericsson, Nokia, and Fujitsu are building for wireless telecommunications are installations for service providers.

Accessory equipment includes capital items that are usually less expensive and shorter-lived than installations. Examples are hand tools, scanners, and fax machines. Buyers use some accessory equipment, such as portable drills, to produce other goods and services. Other equipment, such as personal computers, helps them to perform important administrative and operating functions.

Component parts and materials are business products that are included as part of other firms' final products. Some components become visible in finished goods, such as tires in trucks and automobiles. Other parts—like the microchips that Texas Instruments makes for cell phones—are less visible.

Raw materials are similar to component parts and materials, because they become inputs in the production of other firms' final products. The list includes farm products such as cotton, wheat, fertilizer, cattle, and milk, as well as natural materials

**WORLD RENOWNED SAILOR
GARY JOBSON
PUTS HIS TRUST IN
CLASSICS.**

Having competed successfully in a variety of boats, Gary Jobson's choice for himself is a classic Herreshoff 28-footer whose graceful design will never go out of style. The same aesthetic is reflected in his timepiece.

ROLEX

Rolex Submariner Officially Certified Swiss Chronometer.
For the name and location of an Official Rolex Jeweler near you, please call 1-800-36ROLEX. Rolex, ®, Oyster Perpetual and Submariner are trademarks.

**FIGURE 14.2
Advertising a Specialty Product**

like iron ore, turquoise, lumber, and coal. Standardized grading assures buyers of most raw materials that they receive products of uniform quality.

Supplies are expense items that are used in a firm's daily operations and do not become part of final products. They can include paper, pens, paper clips, light bulbs, and cleaning supplies.

Categories of Services

Both ultimate consumers and business purchasers represent markets for services. Child-care centers and shoe-repair shops provide services for consumers. And both Manpower's temporary personnel and the business consulting of Big Five accounting firm Ernst & Young represent business services. Like tangible goods, services can be distinguished on the basis of their buyers and the ways they use the products. When Terminix sprays a home to eradicate pests, it is performing a consumer service. When it performs a similar service for an office complex, Terminix is producing and marketing a business service.

Like tangible goods, services can also be convenience, shopping, or specialty products, depending on the buying patterns of customers. However, six characteristics distinguish them from goods:

- Services, unlike goods, are intangible.
- From a buyer's perspective, the service provider *is* the service; the two are inseparable in the buyer's mind.
- Services are perishable, because firms cannot stockpile them in inventory.
- Services are difficult to standardize, since they must meet individual customers' needs.
- The customer often plays a major role in marketing, producing, and distributing a service.
- Service quality shows wide variations, some of them tied directly to price.

Because of these distinguishing characteristics, marketers of services play up the tangible benefits of these products. Northwest Airlines became the first airline to offer flight check-in via the Internet. To explain this service, the airline ran ads saying, "Hit the snooze button. You've already checked in for the flight." The ads described the convenience of online check-in by noting the comfort of sleeping in on the morning of a flight, rather than rushing to the gate an hour earlier.

Marketing Strategy Implications for Consumer and Business Products

A method for classifying consumer and business products is a useful tool in developing marketing strategies. After classifying an item as a shopping product, marketers gain an immediate idea of its promotion, pricing, and distribution needs. Figure 14.3 details the impact of the consumer product classifications on various aspects of a marketing strategy.

B2B products require different marketing strategies. Because manufacturers sell most installations and many component parts directly to relatively small numbers of business buyers, their promotional efforts emphasize personal selling rather than advertising. By contrast, marketers of supplies and accessory equipment rely more heavily on advertising, since they distribute their products through intermediaries, such as the wholesalers we discuss in Chapter 15. In addition, producers of installations and component parts may involve their customers in new-product development, especially for custom-made items. Finally, firms that market supplies and accessory equipment emphasize competitive pricing strategies more than do other B2B firms, which tend to focus more on product quality and service.

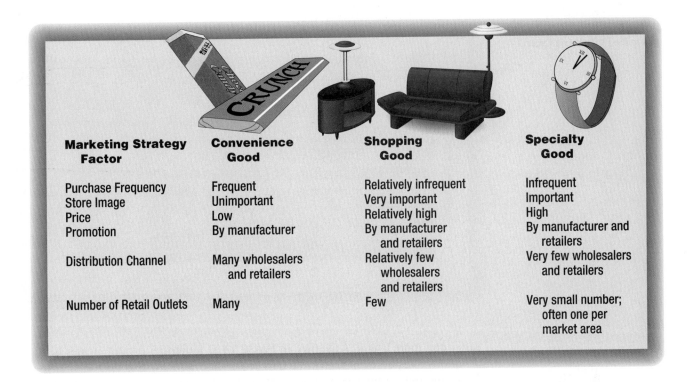

Marketing Strategy Factor	Convenience Good	Shopping Good	Specialty Good
Purchase Frequency	Frequent	Relatively infrequent	Infrequent
Store Image	Unimportant	Very important	Important
Price	Low	Relatively high	High
Promotion	By manufacturer	By manufacturer and retailers	By manufacturer and retailers
Distribution Channel	Many wholesalers and retailers	Relatively few wholesalers and retailers	Very few wholesalers and retailers
Number of Retail Outlets	Many	Few	Very small number; often one per market area

FIGURE 14.3
Marketing Impacts of Consumer Product Classifications

THE PRODUCT LIFE CYCLE

Successful products pass through several stages from initial introduction to ultimate sales decline and removal from the marketplace. The **product life cycle** spans four stages: introduction, growth, maturity, and decline. Figure 14.4 shows typical industry sales and profits over a product's life cycle, giving examples of items currently in each life cycle stage.

Products take widely varying amounts of time to pass through each life cycle stage. A fad item may have a total life span of 2 or 3 years or even less, with an introductory stage of only 90 days. By contrast, refrigerators have been in the maturity stage for over 50 years. Increasing competition and rapid improvements in technology compress the life cycles of many products and force products like audiocassettes and computer floppy disks from the market.

Promotional emphasis shifts from providing product information in the early stages to heavy brand promotion in the highly competitive later ones. Profits assume a similarly predictable pattern through the stages. Understanding the characteristics of all four stages of the product life cycle helps marketers adapt their marketing strategies to fit each stage.

Introduction

In the early stages of the product life cycle, the firm attempts to build demand for its new offering. Because neither customers nor distributors may be aware of the product, promotional programs may concentrate on informing the market about the item and explaining its features, uses, and benefits. An example is the wireless technology known as Bluetooth, which provides radio links among electronic devices, including mobile phones, notebook computers, and digital cameras, so that they can be connected without cables. This technology provides opportunities for engineers to add features to their products and many applications that make mobile computing and telecommunications

FIGURE 14.4
Stages in the Product Life Cycle

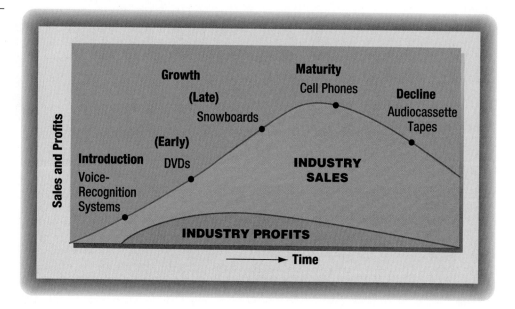

easier and more useful. As shown in Figure 14.5, Bluetooth communicates new applications to build demand for the new technology and wireless devices that use it. This communication requires educating prospective customers—both product-design engineers and product users—about the possible uses of wireless devices.[7]

Firms typically incur financial losses during the introduction stage of the life cycle due to low initial sales, expenses involved in developing the new product, and the promotional outlays needed to inform prospective buyers about it. Although a firm like Procter & Gamble (P&G) or Lever Bros. may spend over $20 million launching a new detergent, such expenditures are necessary to reach the profits possible in later life cycle stages.

Growth

Sales climb quickly during a product's growth stage, as new customers join the early users, who are now repurchasing the item. Personal referrals and continued promotion by the firm induce others to make trial purchases. The higher sales volume begins to generate profits.

During the early part of the growth stage, marketing efforts continue to focus on establishing a product in the market and building brand awareness. Sensing opportunities for high profits, competitors begin to enter the field with similar offerings. As described at the beginning of the chapter, push scooters were at this stage in 2000, when competitors like Huffy entered the market with their own brand of scooter through toy and discount stores, and even cheaper options showed up in unlikely places like supermarkets. U.S. sales of the product numbered in the tens of thousands in 1999 but by 2001 soared over 4 million.[8]

Later in the growth stage, the strategy shifts to building loyalty among consumers and intermediaries. Industry sales continue to grow, but at a slowing rate, since most potential buyers have already purchased the product. Failure to cement customer loyalty can hasten a move into product maturity and decline, as beer importer Gambrinus discovered the hard way. The company enjoyed quick success when it began importing Corona beer from Mexico. Serving Corona became trendy in the 1980s, and the company's managers were so excited that they forgot to develop customer relationships. Gambrinus failed to notice that although many consumers were trying the beer, only a modest share became repeat customers. Within a few years, growth slowed, then declined, in part because of competition from domestic beers in clear bottles similar to Corona. The company switched to a low-price strategy, allowing it

to survive, but it had missed a significant business opportunity during the growth stage.[9]

To expand its share of a growing market, a firm may begin to change styles, target specific segments with different versions, and lower prices. These efforts help stimulate additional sales. As Internet use became widespread at the end of the 1990s, growth was strongest in certain market segments. In particular, Internet usage among African Americans, who earlier had lagged behind other market segments, was beginning to outpace the market as a whole.[10] So, a company selling computers or Internet services could remain in the growth stage by targeting this group. Similarly, easier-to-use versions of a product can stimulate sales. When automobiles first came into general use, they commanded high prices, and you just about had to be a mechanic to operate one. Now many American households have two or three cars parked in the garage or driveway each night.

Maturity

Industry sales continue growing early in the maturity stage, but eventually they reach a saturation level that limits further expansion. Companies emphasize market segmentation during this time, frequently adding new product variations aimed at different customer groups. Often, this activity results in an oversupply of the product in an already saturated marketplace. Competition intensifies, as firms realize that market share growth usually requires them to take sales away from competitors. Some marketers reduce prices to enhance their own products' appeal.

Personal computers (PCs) are at the maturity stage in the U.S., since most interested consumers already own one. Today's computers can perform virtually all the tasks consumers bought them for, so there is little incentive to replace them. As Stephen Baker, an analyst with PC Data Corp., puts it, "The PC is the TV or the refrigerator in the average home right now, where you replace it only if it's broken." Consequently, many sellers are offering discounts to move their computer inventory off the shelves.[11]

During the maturity stage, firms spend heavily on promotion to protect their market shares and to distinguish their products from competitors'. They also try hard to extend the product life cycle. Marketers use several methods to promote continued growth, including encouraging buyers to use the product more frequently, seeking new customers and untapped market segments, finding new product uses, and changing package sizes, labels, and product designs. Service companies focus on improving or adding new service features and promoting guarantees of satisfaction. Aurora Foods specializes in buying brands at risk of decline and extending their life cycle through intensified marketing. Aurora bought Duncan Hines baking mixes and reintroduced them with updated packaging and a new advertising campaign that focused on the good feelings that arise from baking a treat for a loved one. The company also raised the price of the mixes to match the competition so that consumers would perceive the mixes as a high-quality product. Even with the higher prices, market share for Duncan Hines rose following this effort.[12]

Most companies also try to add new products regularly so that their offerings occupy all stages of the product life cycle. Nintendo and its licensees have masterfully used new products to extend the life of their Pokémon entertainment series. Along with the trading cards and Game Boy software, Pokémon releases have included movies; a cartoon series on television and videocassette; a variety of toys, puzzles, and games; a series of activity books; clothing imprinted with the "pocket monsters"; and a Burger King promotion featuring toys that quickly helped the fast-food giant "shatter every sales record ever set." Although kid-fueled fads like Pokémon generally burn out within a couple of years, the Pokémon series has outlasted that average in Japan, where it originated. Marketers hope product line extensions will give the series a similarly long life in the U.S.[13]

Decline

Industry sales fall steadily during the decline stage, as changing consumer preferences or the introduction of a significant product innovation causes purchasing patterns to shift toward new alternatives. Floppy disks have been battered by competition from larger-capacity Iomega Zip Disks, Imation SuperDisks, and rewritable CDs. With the development of software that makes CDs more flexible, allowing them to be recorded and erased, computer makers are equipping PCs with the necessary CD-R and -RW drives, and that technology is expected to eclipse the floppy disk.[14]

Among consumer goods, as buyers have replaced soft drinks with bottled water, tea, and other noncarbonated beverages, sales of Coca-Cola have slowed, and Diet Coke sales have actually fallen—along with companywide profits. Retailers once treated Coke as the king of the soft-drink aisle, but now they occasionally push the company's beverages aside in favor of items in the growth stage, such as SoBe drinks, bottled water, and Arizona Iced Tea. The global king of carbonated beverages recently broadened its product line into four groups: carbonated soft drinks, juices, ready-to-drink coffees and teas, and sports drinks. The juice group has been moved into a venture with P&G. A similar venture with Nestlé features teas and coffees.[15]

Although the industry as a whole does not generate profits during the decline stage, some businesses can prosper as a growing number of their competitors exit the industry. Prices tend to hold steady if a loyal market segment continues to buy the product. Because they expect a continuing sales decline, marketers are reluctant to invest in significant changes in a product's style, design, or other features during this stage. Sometimes being true to the past provides exactly what consumers want. New Dana Corp. specializes in packaging and selling old standards of the perfume world, including Canoe and Tabu, popular decades ago but retired by their original makers. On the Internet, Longlostperfume.com offers almost two dozen old perfume brands, including My Sin and Tuxedo. The scents tend to be stronger than today's popular fragrances, but that makes them perfect for older consumers, whose sense of smell may be weakened by age. Because these companies are selling to consumers who are already loyal, they can skip most of the usual advertising, focus their marketing on letting buyers know where they can be contacted, and enjoy comfortable profits.[16]

Marketing Strategies for Stages in the Product Life Cycle

The product life cycle concept is an invaluable management tool for designing a marketing strategy flexible enough to match the varying marketplace characteristics at different life-cycle stages. Table 14.1 shows appropriate adaptations to marketing strategies to match the characteristics of each stage. Each element of the marketing mix may require adjustment as the product moves from one stage to the next.

Marketers know, for instance, that advertising emphasis will change from informative to persuasive messages as the product faces new competitors during the growth stage. This knowledge helps them anticipate competitors' actions and make adjustments. Competitive moves may include product and package variations and changes in pricing and distribution.

One example of *product variation* is technology upgrades to computers so that newer models can perform more applications or are easier to use. In the toy industry, Barbie doll sales have declined as girls lose interest in them at younger and

Table 14.1   Marketing Strategies for Stages in the Product Life Cycle

Objective	Competition	Product	Price	Distribution	Promotion
Introduction					
Build consumer awareness Encourage trial purchases	Few direct competitors	Highly standardized product Few variations in features	Either skimming (high price) or penetration (low price)	Set up a distribution network	Heavy expenditures on informative promotion and advertising
Growth					
Build brand loyalty and market share Practice market segmentation	Competition intensifies as high profits attract new entries	Differentiated products for different market segments	Different prices for different segments	Expand distribution coverage	Focus on building demand and strengthening brand preference
Maturity					
Seek new product uses—and users Encourage increasing purchase frequency	Intense competition as marketers practice market segmentation	Emphasis on quality and cost reductions	Pricing to maintain market share and meet competition	Emphasize relationship marketing to build dealer loyalty	Promotion to wholesalers and retailers Consumer promotions focus on persuasive and reminder advertising
Decline					
Consider leaving the industry if declining sales result in losses	Competitors begin to leave the industry	Few changes in product features	Stable prices Resistance to price cutting	Begin to phase out marginal dealers	Minimal promotion

younger ages. Mattel has sought to extend the brand's appeal to older girls by varying Barbie products. The company introduced dolls with street-fashion clothing and rhinestone-studded hair, as well as products designed to carry the Barbie name over to girls who are too old for dolls: books, activity sets, kits for mixing makeup, and trendy clothes with the Barbie logo. Even the doll's unbelievable and distinctive physique has been modified—the new Barbie is a bit more natural and athletic looking.[17]

Package variations can support product variations or stand on their own as part of a marketing strategy. With Barbie dolls, part of the strategy for appealing to older girls was to redesign the company's logo and shocking-pink packaging. The products targeted to girls over six years old now replace the bright pink packaging with a combination of metallic mauve, orange, and yellow. The old frilly Barbie logo was also replaced with a script "Barbie" that resembles a teenager's handwriting.[18]

Price changes force industrywide adaptation. When e-commerce was in the introduction stage, many online retailers convinced customers to try this new mode of shopping by offering low prices, steep discounts, and free shipping. More recently, in e-commerce's growth stage, online retailers have begun to seek profitability by raising prices. Tavolo.com, which sells cookware, and Beauty.com, which offers cosmetics, have both ended their offers of free shipping. The Kozmo.com home-delivery service kept its free delivery but began requiring a minimum purchase, which helps the company cover the cost of delivery.[19]

Finally, *changes in distribution* contribute to marketing efforts for many firms responding to new opportunities or facing fierce competition. Krispy Kreme Doughnut Corp. has moved into a stage of rapid growth by expanding from a regional to a national marketplace. The chain of doughnut shops became a legend in the Southeast by displaying its baking operations behind big windows, showcasing its trademark soft and gooey glazed doughnuts, and hanging bright red neon signs announcing, "Hot Doughnuts Now." From that solid base, Krispy Kreme is expanding into a number of major cities in other parts of the U.S. and Canada by selling franchises.[20]

PRODUCT LINES AND THE PRODUCT MIX

The product life cycle concept is a helpful tool for making product decisions. However, companies usually sell more than just a single product. They typically offer several different, complementary products or develop new products to replace those finishing out their life cycles. A company's **product line** is a group of related products marked by physical similarities or intended for a similar market. Figure 14.6 shows various product lines that make up Church & Dwight's **product mix,** the assortment of product lines and individual goods and services that a firm offers to consumers and business users. Under the Arm & Hammer name, Church & Dwight's product mix has several product lines, including detergents, toothpastes, baking soda, and deodorant. Within the toothpaste product line are such varieties as gel, tartar control, and baking soda and peroxide. Within the detergent product line, the consumer's choices include powder or liquid detergent, available with or without bleach.

Service providers also use the product line and product mix terminology. The product mix for AOL Time Warner combines goods and services. Among its Internet services are America Online, CompuServe, Netscape Navigator, and MapQuest. Its television stations include CNN, the Cartoon Network, HBO, TBC, and WB. Its content providers include Warner Bros., Electra, and the television shows *Friends* and *ER*. The company also publishes a line of magazines that includes *Time, People,* and *Sports Illustrated*.

Marketers must continually assess their firm's product mix to ensure company growth, satisfy changing customer needs and wants, and respond to competing offerings. Successful product mixes and product lines undergo constant change. To remain competitive, marketers look for gaps in their firm's assortment and fill them

What's the most important ingredient in all these products?

© 1994 Church & Dwight Co., Inc.

This.

THE STANDARD OF PURITY

Once the ARM & HAMMER® name goes on a product, that product is improved. And not just because of the baking soda in it.

Of all the trademarks in the United States, ARM & HAMMER® is one of the ten most recognized*. What this means for you is power...brand power that translates into selling power.

Put some power on <u>your</u> shelves, with ARM & HAMMER®.

ARM & HAMMER® BRAND POWER.

*Source: Equitrend® Consumer Survey, 1993

FIGURE 14.6
Product Mix for Church & Dwight

with new products or modified versions of current ones. Hershey Foods Corp. has added to its spring chocolate sales by developing products specially packaged for Easter. To its Easter staple, Cadbury Creme Eggs, the company has added versions with chocolate creme and caramel fillings. Hershey has also extended its usual lines of chocolate products with small chocolate eggs, and pastel-wrapped Reese's peanut-butter cups, and Mounds and Almond Joy candy bars.[21]

A firm may also gain by canceling a product line that is not meeting business objectives. DaimlerChrysler cut back on its product mix by ending production of cars bearing the Plymouth name. Plymouth sales had been declining, and the company decided it would be more efficient to sell all its minivans as Chryslers and consolidate the almost-identical Plymouth Breeze and Chrysler Cirrus. With this change, the automaker no longer needs separate promotional efforts for its Chrysler and Plymouth lines. A year later, General Motors made a similar decision in discontinuing its century-old Oldsmobile product line.[22]

NEW-PRODUCT DEVELOPMENT

New products are the lifeblood of any organization. A firm must periodically add new ones to assure continued prosperity. In a mature consumer market like the U.S., the result is a multitude of choices. In 1970, there were 5 basic choices of women's hosiery; 90 were offered for sale at the beginning of this decade. During the same period, the

FIGURE 14.7
Levi Strauss Product Development
Strategy

variations on Pop-Tarts more than doubled—from 15 to 31.[23] Some new products may result from major technological breakthroughs; others simply extend current product lines.

At each stage of new-product development, the potential for failure increases. In fact, estimates suggest that firms work on 50 new-product ideas for every product that finally reaches the marketplace. Of the tens of thousands of household, grocery, and drugstore items introduced in a typical year, only one in ten ever makes it to retailers' shelves.

Product Development Strategies

A firm's product development strategy depends on its existing product mix, the match between current offerings and overall marketing objectives, and the current market positions of products early in their life cycles. Four alternative product development strategies exist: market development, product development, market penetration, and market development.

A *market development strategy* concentrates on finding new markets for current products. McDonald's has responded to slowing sales in the mature U.S. fast-food market by expanding overseas. More than nine out of ten new McDonald's restaurants open in countries other than the U.S. The chain builds demand by varying products to meet local tastes—for example, Chicken McKrispy, a bone-in fried-chicken sandwich, in Singapore and Taiwan, and a teriyaki burger in Japan.[24]

By contrast, *product development strategy* seeks to introduce new products into identifiable or established markets. Firms often try to increase market share by introducing new products into markets where they already have established positions. As sales for jeans slowed during the past ten years, Levi Strauss began to offer new colors and patterns in an attempt to offset the decline. Figure 14.7 shows an example of one of the new designs.

Celestial Seasonings has tried various products to expand its sales to established markets. The company's efforts to market salad dressings and herbal shampoo failed, but it has seen more success from sales of cough drops and extensions of the tea line to include green teas and supplement-enriched "wellness" teas.[25] Gerber Products is trying to increase sales to parents of babies by expanding from baby food into products for baby hygiene—baby oil, shampoo, and ointment to soothe diaper rash.[26]

A third approach, the *market penetration strategy,* seeks to increase sales of current products in familiar markets. Firms using this strategy may modify products, improve quality, or promote new uses and benefits. Besides developing foreign markets, McDonald's has tried to increase sales to domestic customers by setting up its Made-For-You production system to deliver hotter food. Eagle Family Foods has attempted to counteract flagging sales of its condensed milk by educating consumers in ways they can use the product. It prepared a recipe booklet, featuring easy-to-prepare foods, and published it as an advertising insert in *Better Homes and Gardens* magazine. Eagle also distributes recipes on the Internet and in a larger cookbook sold in supermarkets.[27]

The fourth alternative, a *product diversification strategy,* focuses on developing entirely new products for new markets. Some firms look for new target markets that complement their existing markets; others look in completely new directions. Ralph Lauren built on its success in designer clothes by launching a line of house paints. The products are vastly different, but both trade on the brand's association with impeccable taste. In contrast, Calvin Klein's move from upscale apparel to underwear initially boosted sales, but when discount stores started carrying Calvin Klein undershirts and briefs, the name lost much of its prestige.[28]

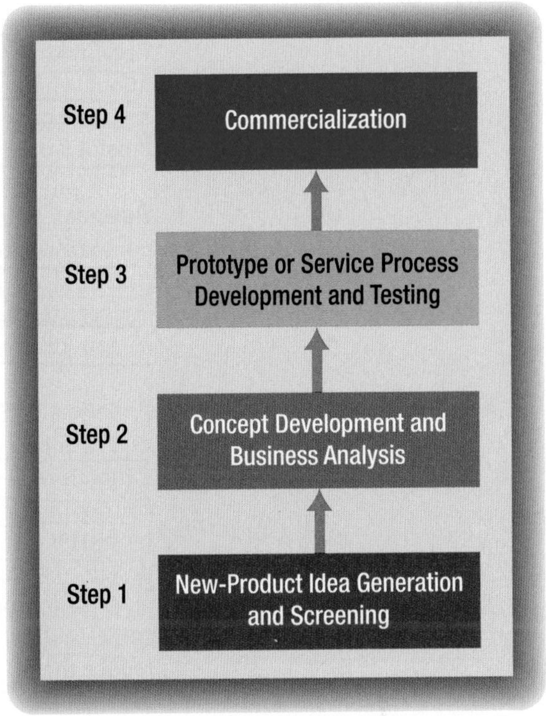

FIGURE 14.8
Process for Developing New Goods and Services

Stages in New-Product Development

The most successful new products are significant innovations that deliver unique benefits. Getting a new product to market involves an orderly process of overlapping steps. Teamwork among experts across divisional boundaries throughout this effort allows a firm to strengthen its new-product development process. Figure 14.8 shows the path that new-product development follows. Each of these steps is discussed in the following sections.

Generating New-Product Ideas   The process starts by generating ideas for new offerings. Ideas come from many sources, including customers, suppliers, employees, research scientists, marketing researchers, inventors outside the firm, and competing products. The most successful ideas work directly to satisfy customer needs or resolve customer complaints.

Two centuries ago, a Scottish chemist named Charles Macintosh discovered a means to help people stay dry on rainy days. Macintosh was studying naphtha, a by-product of coal tar. He discovered that naphtha causes rubber to liquefy, and he came up with the idea of spreading the liquid rubber between layers of cloth. The waterproof, layered fabric was used to produce raincoats. Much more recently, Ricoh Co. charged engineer Yousuke Yamada with creating a digital product that would engage all of the user's senses. After much research and thought—some while riding Tokyo's commuter trains—Yamada came up with an idea for a digital camera with a touch-sensitive screen, wireless Internet connectivity, and the ability to record voice messages. The resulting RDC-i700 camera lets users take photos and transmit them to Web pages for display on the Internet. Now competitors like Kodak and Polaroid are using the camera as inspiration for their own new products.[29]

Screening In screening ideas, marketers evaluate their commercial potential. Some organizations maintain checklists of development standards that guide judgments about whether an idea should be abandoned or pursued. The screening stage often involves representatives of different functional areas in an organization in open discussions of new-product ideas.

Business Analysis Once an idea is screened, it is evaluated to see if it fits with the company's product, distribution, and promotional resources. Marketers also assess potential sales, profits, growth rate, and competitive strengths. This stage includes concept testing, or marketing research designed to solicit initial consumer reactions to new-product ideas before proceeding with product development.

Prototype or Service Process Development Financial outlays increase substantially as a firm first converts a product idea into a physical product. At this stage, it creates a functioning prototype or a detailed description of the services to be provided. The conversion process is the joint responsibility of the firm's development engineers and its marketers, who provide feedback on consumer reactions to the proposed product design, package, color, and other physical features.

A prototype may go through many modifications before the original mock-up becomes a final product. Many firms implement computer-aided design systems to reduce the number of prototypes that developers must build. Tests measure the product's actual features and benefits as well as consumer perceptions of it. Inadequate testing during this stage can doom a product introduction, and even a company, to failure. W. L. Gore & Associates develops synthetic fabrics for a variety of uses, including sneakers. To test Gore-Tex fabrics, the company shoots several pounds of water at fabric samples, then rams them with steel rods and subjects them to other tortures, including applications with DEET, an insect repellent. Nike and other companies that use Gore-Tex in their shoes send samples to Gore labs, where technicians place them on mechanical feet that move in a water-filled trough. If sensors on the mechanical feet detect water, the shoe or boot is removed for analysis. Finally, shoe prototypes are tested on human subjects, who march on a treadmill while sensors measure foot temperature and humidity. Afterward, the subjects rate the comfort of the shoes.[30]

Test Marketing To gauge customer acceptance of a product, many firms test-market their new offerings. Up to this point, the product development team has obtained customer feedback by submitting free products to customers, who then give their reactions. Test marketing is the first stage at which the product must perform in an actual business environment.

Test marketing introduces a trial version of a new product, supported by a complete marketing campaign, to a selected city or media coverage area with a population reasonably similar to that of the expected market for the product. Test market results help managers determine the product's likely performance in a full-scale introduction.

Some firms choose to skip test marketing and move directly from product development to commercialization. These companies cite four main problems with test marketing:

1. Test marketing is an expensive project.
2. Competitors who learn about a test-marketing project may try to skew results by lowering their prices, distributing coupons, or running special promotions in the area.
3. Long-lived durable goods (like refrigerators and televisions) are seldom test-marketed due to the major financial investments required to develop and launch them.
4. Test marketing can alert competitors to plans prior to full-scale introduction.

Table 14.2   The Five Worst Cars of the Millennium

Rank	Auto	Typical Owner Comment
1	Yugo	"At least it had heated rear windows—so your hands would stay warm while you pushed."
2	Chevy Vega	"Burned so much oil, it was singlehandedly responsible for the formation of OPEC."
3	Ford Pinto	"The car would do 75 mph in 2nd gear, shaking apart and sounding like a bat out of hell. In 4th gear, the top speed was 70 mph. What's wrong with this picture? You do the math."
4	AMC Gremlin	"Calling it a pregnant roller skate would be kind."
5	Chevy Chevette	"If I got on the Interstate without being run over, the car would creep towards 55. About an hour later, I'd reach it. Then the shaking would begin."

Just missing the top five were, in order, the Renault Le Car, the Dodge Aspen/Plymouth Volare, Cadillac Cimarron, Renault Dauphine, and the Volkswagen Bus, which one owner described as having "no heat, a tendency to blow over in the wind, and used the driver's legs as its first line of defense in an accident."

Test marketing for Oil of Olay cosmetics lasted about four years.[31] During that time, P&G was missing out on the revenue from a nationwide rollout of the product line, and it was vulnerable to competitors who moved quickly.

But in general, marketers should omit test marketing only for a product that is highly likely to succeed. Companies that do skip test marketing can choose several other options to predict market acceptance. A firm may simulate a test marketing campaign through computer modeling software. A second approach is actually a compromise between a small-scale test market and a full-scale product launch. Marketers using this approach may offer the item in a single geographic region and use feedback from this partial launch to adjust prices, vary options or warranty terms, change promotional appeals, or modify channels for distributing the product. Another option is to limit a product's introduction to just one retail chain, which allows marketers to control and evaluate promotions and results. In still another method, a firm may try out a new product in another country before marketing it in the U.S. or globally.

Commercialization   In the commercialization stage, sometimes referred to as a *product launch*, the firm offers its new product in the general marketplace. A company might invest considerable time and money devising pricing, distribution, and promotion strategies to support the new product offering, but, as Table 14.2 illustrates, success is not guaranteed until it achieves customer acceptance. General Motors witnessed this principle when the company launched its much-ridiculed Aztek sport-utility vehicle. The design had started out as a smaller vehicle, like a tall station wagon meant to appeal to young drivers. But for cost considerations, the design was adapted to fit the company's minivan platform, then further modified to fit Pontiac's aggressive image. In testing, markets were divided in their opinion, but GM delivered a crushing blow to its own product by pricing the vehicle at the high end of what its younger target market could afford. Following the product launch, instead of taking to the back roads, Azteks sat quietly in dealers' lots.[32]

For commercialization, a firm must establish marketing programs, fund production facilities, and acquaint its sales force, marketing intermediaries, and potential customers with the new product. A firm today can expect to spend $20 million to $50 million to complete a successful new product launch.

PRODUCT IDENTIFICATION

Organizations identify their products in several ways, including distinctive brands, packages, and labels. This section's discussion of product identification begins with a look at brands, brand names, and trademarks.

Almost every product design incorporates some way for consumers to distinguish it from others. A brand is a name, term, sign, symbol, design, or some combination of these elements that helps to identify a firm's products and differentiate them from competitors' offerings. Diet Coke, Fruitopia, and Nestea are all made by The Coca-Cola Company, but a unique combination of name, symbol, and package design distinguishes each brand from the others.

A **brand name** is the part of a brand consisting of words or letters that form a name that identifies and distinguishes an offering from those of competitors. A brand name is the part of a brand that can be vocalized; a *brand mark* is a symbol or pictorial design that cannot be vocalized. Many brand names, such as McDonald's, Ford, American Express, and IBM, are famous around the world. Likewise, the "golden arches" brand mark of McDonald's also is widely recognized.

Brands are important elements of product images. If consumers are aware of a particular brand, its appearance anywhere becomes advertising for the firm. Nike's "swoosh" brand mark, for example, provides instant advertising to anyone who sees it. Successful branding also helps a firm to escape some price competition, since well-known brands often sell at a premium over their competitors.

A **trademark** is a brand with legal protection against another company's use, not only of the brand name but also of pictorial designs, slogans, packaging elements, and product features such as color and shape. The U.S. Patent and Trademark Office issues regulations and processes the paperwork for registering a trademark in the United States. When Warner Brothers purchased the rights to make a movie of the book *Harry Potter and the Sorcerer's Stone,* it acquired trademarks for the characters' names and for made-up words such as "quidditch," a game played by characters on broomsticks. The company swiftly moved to prevent unauthorized use of the trademarks. Its lawyers wrote to fans who started such Web sites as www.harry potterguide.co.uk and www.harrypotternetwork.net, asking them to remove trademarked names and images from their sites.[33]

Brand Categories

Some firms market their goods and services without branding them. Such items are called **generic products** or *generic brands.* They are characterized by plain packaging, minimal labeling, and little or no advertising. Generic brands typically meet only minimal quality standards but are usually priced considerably lower than comparable manufacturers' and private brands.

Most products carry distinctive brand names. Even standardized grocery items like fruit, vegetables, and prepared salads carry small labels identifying them as Dole grapes, Sunkist lemons, or Chiquita bananas. Brands may be classified in several ways: family brands, individual brands, manufacturer's (national) brands, and private (store) brands. In making branding decisions, marketers must weigh the benefits and shortcomings of each type of brand.

Family and Individual Brands   A **family brand** is a single brand name that identifies several related products. Spalding initially sold sporting goods. As Figure 14.9 shows, the company has built on its leading role in sports by recently offering a line of clothing using the Spalding brand. The Arm & Hammer family brand, shown earlier in Figure 14.6, ties together a number of household products with the image of freshness and purity. When a firm that practices family branding introduces a new product, both customers and retailers recognize the familiar brand name—even though they may have never purchased the item before. Promoting individual products in the line benefits all products within the family brand.

Other firms create **individual brands** by giving a different brand name to each product within a line. Lever Bros. markets its different bath soaps (Caress, Dove, Lifebuoy, and Lux) and toothpastes (Aim, Close Up, and Pepsodent) under individual brand names. Each brand targets a unique market segment. Lever Bros. hopes that toothpaste purchasers who dislike Pepsodent will buy another of its own brands, like Close Up, instead of a competitor's brand. Individual branding builds competition within a firm and enables the company to increase overall sales.

Manufacturer's Brands Versus Private Brands   A brand offered and promoted by a manufacturer or producer is known as a **manufacturer's (or national) brand.** Examples include Chanel, Swatch, Bic, Crest, and Dr Pepper. Among prescription drugs, manufacturer's brands tend to be priced much higher than generic equivalents. Lanoxin, a drug for heart conditions, costs about $28 for 100 pills, compared with a generic equivalent at around $11. Some generics offer even steeper discounts. When a drug company's patent expires, the company knows it will be competing with lower-priced generics, so it will sometimes raise the price in order to reap profits from the share of customers who remain loyal to the brand.[34]

Not all brand names belong to producers. Some are the property of wholesalers or retailers. A **private (or store) brand** identifies a product that is not linked to the manufacturer, but instead carries the label of a retailer or wholesaler. Kmart's Martha Stewart line of towels and other household items is a well-known private brand. Private-label products control 25 percent of the apparel industry. JCPenney's Arizona label and Sears's Canyon River Blues line of jeans are private brands. Sears has been a leader in private brands for years with its Diehard batteries, Craftsman tools, and Kenmore appliances.

FIGURE 14.9
Promoting a Family Brand

The growth of private brands parallels that of chain stores in the U.S. These retailers define their own brands to maintain control over the images, quality levels, and prices of products they sell. In addition, private brands usually carry lower prices, sometimes up to 35 percent less, than manufacturer's brands. Many manufacturers boost their business with retail giants by producing merchandise to their specifications and adding the retailers' private brand names. To these producers, private brands represent additional sales. By contrast, other producers mount aggressive responses to threats from private brands in the belief that such low-priced offerings siphon off sales of their own brands.

Characteristics of an Effective Brand Name

Brand names promote buyer awareness of the nature and quality of competing products. To accomplish this goal, they should communicate appropriate product images to consumers. One effective technique is to create a name that links the product with its positioning concept. The name *Dial* reinforces the concept of 24-hour protection, *DieHard* batteries give an impression of dependability, and *Taster's Choice* instant coffee supports the promotional claim "Tastes and smells like ground roast coffee."

An effective brand name must be easy to pronounce, recognize, and remember. Short names such as *Sony* and *Tide* meet this requirement, as do *Bud* and *Coke*. Effective brand names must also attract attention. Top brand names

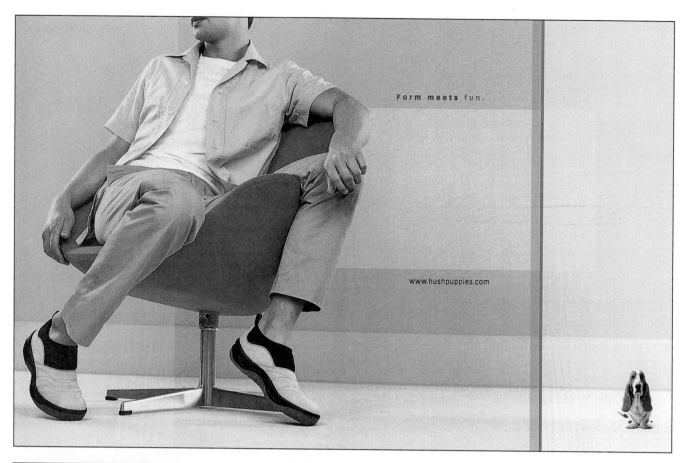

Form meets fun.

www.hushpuppies.com

For decades, the suede Hushpuppies casual shoe—and the photo of the basset hound with its floppy brown ears—has been one of America's most recognizable brands. The firm is currently attempting to expand sales into other shoe products by capitalizing on the Hushpuppies name.

for attention-getting value are Intensive Care lotion, Cheerios, and "I Can't Believe It's Not Butter" margarine.

Some brand names identify products too effectively for the producers' own good. When a class of products becomes generally known by the original brand name of a specific offering, the brand name may legally become a *generic name*. In such cases, the original owner loses exclusive claim to the brand name. Generic names that once were brand names include *nylon, aspirin, escalator, cola, kerosene,* and *zipper.*

Typically, companies take precautions to protect their brand names. No organization can claim exclusive use of generic words—words that describe types of products. Some companies have tried to define themselves as e-commerce experts by using generic words plus an Internet-related prefix like *i-, e-,* or *cyber-* or a suffix like *-.com.* However, the Patent and Trademark Office is rethinking the use of such prefixes with descriptive words.

Marketers are increasingly hard-pressed to coin effective brand names, as multitudes of competitors rush to stake out identities for their own products. Companies that use familiar words as trademarks risk choosing the same name as someone with a different product. Wrigley chose "Eclipse" as a name for its gum, while P&G began using the same name for a fruit drink, and R. J. Reynolds Tobacco put the name on a new brand of cigarettes.[35] To find effective names, some firms rely on computer software or databases that spew out options. Others prefer brainstorming. Executives at Arthur Andersen selected the widely disparaged name *Accenture* as a replacement for Andersen Consulting Group and then launched a $40 million advertising campaign to teach the marketplace about its origin, meaning, and the services the firm performed.

Besides adding to the sheer volume of trademark registrations, the Internet also presents challenges to marketers searching for effective brand names by making any Web site a worldwide presence. An excellent brand name in one country may prove disastrous in another. Sometimes, a brand name must accommodate universal promotions or those in specific countries or regions. One helpful tool in selecting a name is to remember that every language has short *a*, long *o*, and *k* sounds, so Coca-Cola and Kodak work as effective brand names in any country.

BUILDING BRAND LOYALTY AND BRAND EQUITY

Brands achieve varying consumer familiarity and acceptance. The marketer's task is to generate the maximum consumer loyalty for a brand. While a racing enthusiast may insist on a Callaway Speedster when buying a car, a purchase of a loaf of bread might involve little preference for any one brand. Increasing consumer loyalty to a brand augments the value of that brand to the firm. So, brand loyalty is at the heart of brand equity.

For years, brand-building strategies remained limited to the consumer realm—products sold to retail customers rather than to business purchasers. Not many B2B brands have become famous, although the short list includes Intel, Xerox, and IBM, along with service providers such as Manpower and ServiceMaster. The focus on building brand equity for business brands has increased in recent years.

Brand Loyalty

Marketers measure brand loyalty in three stages: brand recognition, brand preference, and brand insistence. **Brand recognition** is brand acceptance strong enough that the consumer is aware of a brand, but not enough to cause a preference over competing brands. Advertising and distributing free samples are the most common ways to increase brand recognition. Once consumers have used a product, seen it advertised, or noticed it in stores, it moves from the unknown to the known category, increasing the probability that they will purchase it. Other strategies include offering discount coupons for purchases.

Building brand recognition is a particular challenge for e-commerce businesses. Potential customers do not run across the brand while browsing through a store or driving down the street, as they do with Wrigley's gum or Starbucks coffee. As a result, Internet-only businesses have spent heavily for advertising to build brand recognition. A few, such as Monster.com and HotJobs.com, developed Super Bowl campaigns at rates as high as $2.5 million for each 30-second spot, but the rest had to resort to less expensive, more targeted methods for communicating their brand.[36]

More likely than not, a consumer who is satisfied with a purchase will buy that brand again. **Brand preference** occurs when a consumer chooses one firm's brand, when it is available, over a competitor's. At this stage, consumers rely on previous experience when selecting a product. Automobiles and apparel fall into this category. DaimlerChysler reports that eight out of ten owners of a Mercedes-Benz choose that brand again when they buy a new car.[37]

Brand insistence is the ultimate degree of brand loyalty, in which the consumer will accept no substitute for a preferred brand. If the desired product is not readily available, the consumer will look for another outlet, special order it from a dealer, or turn to mail-order or Internet buying. A product at this stage has achieved a monopoly position with its consumers. Few firms can achieve brand insistence for their products. Cosmetics are one example of a product that might inspire this degree of brand loyalty. And, as described in the "Clicks and Mortar" box, Sony is hoping for this degree of brand loyalty with its PlayStation products.

Sony Isn't Playing Games

Background. Sony's launch of its PlayStation 2 was serious business. When the company's Web site began taking advance orders a month before the game's launch, it was so overrun that the site crashed. Six months later, it was a lucky parent who could find PlayStation 2 to put under the Christmas tree. The Sony PlayStation brand is already strong, but company executives have been conjuring up ways to convert consumers' brand loyalty to brand insistence—and not just for its video games. "We want to build a new entertainment platform for the home," says Ken Kutaragi, CEO of Sony Computer Entertainment, the video game division of Sony Corp.

What Happened? As it became clear that the demand for PlayStation 2 might outstrip supply, Sony Entertainment executives were already planning for the PlayStation brand to play a larger role in consumers' lives. They reached agreements with several music companies and Hollywood studios to construct new Internet services and interactive entertainment designed for the PlayStation. This move was not just a simple extension of a brand the way a bath-soap manufacturer might introduce laundry detergent and floor cleaner under the same brand. Instead, the plan was designed so the PlayStation brand would dominate a "new wave of Internet gadgets and services" in the way that Dell and Gateway have recently ruled the mail-order, customized PC business. PlayStation already ranked number one in the global video game market, but Sony wanted more. In addition to the deals struck with other companies, Sony introduced graphics-processing power comparable to that used by scientists and engineers. In one game the light shimmered on a lake and a character's hair ruffled in the breeze. A DVD player and hard drives that store music and video downloaded from PlayStation 2 Web sites were also designed to attract a broader audience.

The Response. Consumers had no doubt about the added value of PlayStation 2, particularly those who placed advance orders based on their brand loyalty to previous PlayStation products. But convincing colleagues that PlayStation could represent more than a video game was Ken Kutaragi's challenge. Convince them he has, partly because of his previous successes with PlayStation. "The PlayStation 2 is a new *dohyou*," predicts Sony senior executive vice president Masayoshi Morimoto. *Dohyou* is the Japanese word for the sumo wrestlers' arena. Even Kutaragi's competitors are taking note. "The world is changing—the PC will remain as one of the strong powers, but other devices will emerge as communications vehicles for the Internet," remarks Taizo Nishimuro, CEO of Toshiba Corp. "One very strong candidate, naturally, is Kutaragi-san's PlayStation 2."

Today and Counting. Square Co., the maker of PlayStation 2's Final Fantasy game, plans to open Internet service where PlayStation 2 users can meet and chat online, listen to music, and check baseball scores, all while playing Final Fantasy with each other. Sony will face tough competition from the likes of Sega, and the PC will not disappear, despite Kutaragi dismissing it as "a very nice calculator." But if Kutaragi plays the game right, his PlayStation will be a strong brand for decades to come.

QUESTIONS FOR CRITICAL THINKING

1. Do you think that Sony will be able to generate brand insistence with its PlayStation products, considering its competitive environment? Why or why not?
2. What steps might Sony take to enhance and protect PlayStation's brand equity?

Sources: "Newly Formed Organization PlayStation.com (America) Inc. Transforms Web Site into Complete Online Entertainment Destination," Sony Computer Entertainment America press release, January 25, 2001, **www.scea.com**; Robert A. Guth, "Inside Sony's Trojan Horse," *The Wall Street Journal,* February 25, 2000, pp. B1, B4; Martyn Williams, "Sony's PlayStation 2 Hopes Are High," *PC World,* March 30, 2000, **www.pcworld.com**.

Brand Equity

Brand equity refers to the added value that a widely respected, highly successful name gives to a product in the marketplace. This value results from a combination of factors including awareness, loyalty, and perceived quality, as well as any feelings or images the customer associates with the brand. *Brand awareness* means that the product is the first one that comes to mind when a product category is mentioned. *Brand association* is a link between a brand and other favorable images. Marketers create brand awareness and association with tie-ins to other product users or by featuring a popular celebrity.

High brand equity offers financial advantages to a firm, since the product commands a comparatively large market share. Because brand loyalty often reduces the price sensitivity of consumers, high-equity brands generate higher profits. Measuring brand equity in terms of the brand's sales, market capitalization, and earnings potential, the world's ten most valuable brands include Coca-Cola, Microsoft Windows, IBM, Intel, Nokia, GE, Ford, Disney, McDonald's, and AT&T.[38]

Starwood Hopes to Make Westin Brand New

Background. High brand equity is something that every organization covets. Who wouldn't want their brand name to equal that of Coca-Cola, Nike, Disney, or McDonald's? But high brand equity isn't easy to achieve, as Starwood Hotels & Resorts, owners of the Westin chain of hotels, has learned.

What Happened? The Westin brand of hotels has burdened itself with the reputation of inconsistent quality around the world as well as low consumer awareness of the brand itself, especially in Europe. Although Westin is intended to be an upscale brand, a recent survey discovered that many European travelers confuse Westin with the lower-budget, lower-scale Best Western brand hotels that are scattered around Europe. "We just died [when we saw the results of the survey]," says K.C. Kavanagh, a Starwood spokesperson.

The Response. The misperception about its brand was a bitter lesson, but it kicked Starwood marketers and executives into action, in a major attempt to develop improved brand awareness for the Westin brand. First, the organization announced that it would convert nine of its Ciga brand luxury hotels to the Westin name—a huge marketing step. The former Ciga hotels, which Starwood acquired from ITT when it purchased the firm's Sheraton hotels, include the Excelsior in Rome, the Palace in Madrid, and the Hotel Alfonso XIII in Florence. The converted Ciga hotels "will definitely elevate the brand," says Sue Brush, Westin's brand manager. Starwood hopes to draw consumer attention to the Westin name and link it to the perception of luxury. Second, Starwood is rolling out a new advertising campaign with slogans such as "Imagine sleeping in a Westin tonight," and "We now have the luxury of 16 Westins in Europe." Third, Starwood has spent as much as $400 million renovating Westin hotels around the world, changes that will command higher room rates. Ultimately, the company hopes that travelers will perceive a stay at a Westin as a luxury.

Today and Counting. Starwood continues revamping not only the Westin brand but also the five other hotel brands that it now owns, including Sheraton, St. Regis, Luxury Collection, Four Points, and a "boutique" hotel brand called *W*. Yet, one problem in the process has been the frequency with which some of the actual hotels have switched brands. In Philadelphia, a Ritz Carlton became a St. Regis and then a Westin, all in about a year and a half. But as things settle down, marketers hope that when people think of any of the Starwood brands, they will think in terms of quality. "That a Ritz is becoming a Westin tells you a little about what we think of Westin," notes Barry Sternlicht, chairman and CEO of Starwood. Perhaps the next challenge for Starwood is to figure out how to differentiate among their own brands.

QUESTIONS FOR CRITICAL THINKING

1. Do you think that Starwood is taking effective measures to build brand equity for its Westin hotels? Why or why not? What additional steps might marketers take?

2. Should all Starwood-owned hotels carry the Starwood name? Why or why not?

Sources: "Starwood Hotels & Resorts Worldwide, Inc.," Starwood Web site, **www.starwoodhotels.com**, accessed April 9, 2001; Christina Binkley, "Starwood Puts New Face on Westin Brand," *The Wall Street Journal,* February 29, 2000, p. B19; Christina Binkley, "Artful Lodges Woo Frequent Travelers in an Effort to 'De-Commodify' Industry," *The Wall Street Journal,* June 20, 2000, p. B1.

Building favorable brand equity can be difficult, especially if a company has previously suffered from low brand equity as Westin Hotels did in the situation described in the "Clicks and Mortar" box.

Managing Brand Equity A typical large company assigns the task of managing a brand's marketing strategies to a *brand manager* (who may be called a *product manager* at some firms). This marketing professional plans and implements the balance of promotional, pricing, distribution, and product arrangements that leads to strong brand equity. Procter & Gamble first implemented the brand manager system over 70 years ago.

Recently, however, P&G has begun exploring ways to make brand management faster and more responsive, in keeping with today's business environment. To manage the launch of the Reflect.com Web site, which sells customized cosmetics, P&G set up a four-person team. As the project progressed, the team added members from various functions within the company, and the team made product decisions as a unit. Following the launch, some team members retained responsibility for Reflect.com, while others moved on to teams launching different products. In contrast to static jobs, this flexible team approach is intended to help P&G respond to opportunities much faster. With

FIGURE 14.10
Packaging to Distinguish a Product

marketing specialists contributing to a team as needed, the result is a marketing organization in which everyone plays a role in brand management.[39]

PACKAGES AND LABELS

The original purpose of packaging was to protect products against damage, spoilage, and theft. Labels functioned primarily to identify products and communicate usage information. Over the years, however, packaging has played an increasingly important role in product strategy. Besides protecting goods and identifying package contents, packaging and labeling support branding strategies and contribute to advertising efforts.

Packaging

A product's package can powerfully influence buyers' purchase decisions. It serves several objectives that fit loosely under three general goals:

1. Protection against damage, spoilage, and pilferage
2. Assistance in marketing the product
3. Cost-effectiveness

In addition to protecting products, many manufacturers upgrade packages to improve product usage, and still others to reduce waste. Customers can use the packaging for Hewlett-Packard's laser printer ink cartridges to ship used cartridges to a recycling center. Packaging also offers marketers a means for differentiating their product from competitors. They may design packages to convey high-quality images. Innovative packaging plays a key role in the success of global brands like Coca-Cola, Absolut vodka, and Perrier. Beautiful packaging also distinguishes fragrances, such as the ones shown in Figure 14.10.

Packaging represents one of the biggest cost elements for many consumer products. Although it performs a number of functions for the producer, marketers, and consumers, it must do so at a reasonable cost. Some changes can make packages both cheaper and safer for the environment. Others can encourage consumer use. Balancing such benefits against costs has so far been difficult for CD packaging, which must not only protect the recordings and provide information but also discourage theft. The top spine labels seal the lids of the "jewel box" design together and let consumers read basic information without pulling CDs from store bins. They carry bar codes that speed up counting for inventory. The fact that the labels are hard to peel off is not necessarily a problem, at least from a security standpoint. And why is the plastic wrapper so hard to unpeel? Earlier attempts to use pull strips for easy removal caused an outcry from artists that the pull strips covered part of the label. As for the breakable plastic of the jewel box itself, well, a stronger box would simply be too expensive, according to the recording companies.

Choosing the right package is an especially crucial decision in international marketing, since worldwide sales introduce many variables. Color is an important issue in packaging. Package size also varies according to each country's purchasing patterns and market conditions. In Japan, Europe, and Latin America, consumers have less storage or refrigerator space and prefer to buy smaller packages than U.S.

buyers do. Beverages are typically sold by individual containers instead of in six-packs. Package weight is another important issue, since shipping costs are usually based on weight.

Labeling

The **label** is the descriptive part of a product's package that lists the brand name or symbol, name and address of the manufacturer or distributor, product composition and size, nutritional information for food products, and recommended uses. It also plays an important role in attracting consumer attention and encouraging a purchase at this critical point. Effective labeling serves several functions:

- Attracts the buyer's attention
- Describes the package contents
- Conveys the benefits of the product inside
- Provides information on warranties, warnings, and other consumer matters
- Gives an indication of price, value, and uses

An effective label gives customers information that is important to them, helps them make purchase decisions, and entices them to buy the product. Manischewitz recently updated the labels on its kosher foods to make them more attractive to consumers who might not recognize the products or know how to use them. According to brand manager Dan Berkowitz, "Over 56 percent of non-Jews have eaten Manischewitz products, and over 90 percent of them think favorably about the quality and the brand. Now we have to change people's perceptions and make [the products] more inviting." To do this, the new packaging features larger and more attractive images of the foods, in contrast to the old package, which was dominated by the brand name.[40]

PRICE IN THE MARKETING MIX

Every successful product offers some utility, or want-satisfying power. However, individual preferences determine how much *value* a particular consumer associates with a good or service. One person may value leisure-time pursuits while another assigns a higher priority to acquiring property and automobiles. But all consumers have limited amounts of money and a variety of possible uses for it. So, the **price**—the exchange value of a good or service—becomes a major factor in consumer buying decisions.

As Chapter 3 discusses, prices also help to direct activities throughout the overall economic system. A firm uses various factors of production, such as natural resources, labor, and capital, based on their relative prices. High wage rates may cause a firm to install labor-saving machinery, just as high interest rates may lead management to postpone a new capital expenditure. Prices and volumes sold determine the revenue and profits a firm receives.

Marketers attempt to accomplish certain objectives through their pricing decisions. Research has shown that pricing objectives vary from firm to firm, and that many companies pursue multiple pricing objectives. Some try to improve profits by setting high prices; others set low prices to attract new business. As Figure 14.11 shows, the four basic categories of pricing objectives are (1) profitability, (2) volume, (3) meeting competition, and (4) prestige.

Profitability Objectives

Profitability objectives are perhaps the most commonly used objectives in firms' pricing strategies. Marketers

THEY SAID IT

"Free is good—but read the fine print."

ANONYMOUS

BUSINESS DIRECTORY

➤ **price** *exchange value of a good or service.*

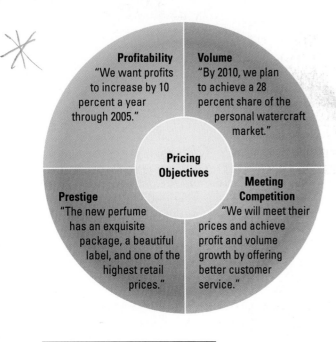

Profitability
"We want profits to increase by 10 percent a year through 2005."

Volume
"By 2010, we plan to achieve a 28 percent share of the personal watercraft market."

Pricing Objectives

Prestige
"The new perfume has an exquisite package, a beautiful label, and one of the highest retail prices."

Meeting Competition
"We will meet their prices and achieve profit and volume growth by offering better customer service."

FIGURE 14.11
Alternative Pricing Objectives

know that profits are the amount of money the company brings in (its revenues) minus its expenses. Usually, there is a big difference between revenue and profit. In the case of a typical pop or rock band tour, selling out a 20,000-seat amphitheater with $30 tickets would bring in revenues of $600,000. Of that, the band gets about $400,000, and the rest goes to the venue. The band then has to pay for sound, lights, transportation, and the salaries of dozens of staff members—from technicians to accountants. Another 30 percent goes to the band's agent and managers. That leaves the band about $200,000 to split up among its members, still a sizable amount of money. An extremely popular band like 'N Sync averages over a million dollars in revenues for each concert.[41]

Some firms try to maximize profits by by reducing costs rather than through price changes. Companies can maintain prices and increase profitability by operating more efficiently or by modifying the product to make it less costly to produce. While maintaining a steady price, Frito-Lay has recently reduced the package weights for Tostitos and Cracker Jack snack foods, and Nestlé has done the same with its Poland Spring and Calistoga bottled waters.[42]

Volume Objectives

A second approach to pricing strategy—called volume objectives—bases pricing decisions on **market share**—the percentage of a market controlled by a certain company or product. One firm may seek to achieve a 25 percent market share in a certain industry, and another may want to maintain or expand its market share for particular products or product lines.

Ford Motor Co. has combined the advantages of pricing based on market share with profit goals in a pricing strategy that emphasizes gaining market share for the most profitable vehicles in its product mix. To develop this strategy, Ford conducted research to determine which features buyers were willing to pay for and then used this information to determine which packages of options would be most profitable. It created bigger options packages for its Windstar minivan, and it standardized many features that had been options. By making it easier to find vehicles with desirable options, Ford hopes to encourage more customers to choose the high-profit models. Already this approach has more than doubled the share of customers who opt for the SuperCab versions of the Ranger pickup.[43]

Pricing to Meet Competition

A third set of pricing objectives seeks simply to meet competitors' prices. In many lines of business, firms set their own prices to match those of established industry price leaders. But companies may not legally work together to agree on prices or force retailers to sell at a set price, as discussed in the "Solving an Ethical Controversy" box. Recently, the Federal Trade Commission determined that music companies must end their practice of paying promotional fees to retailers in exchange for the stores' agreement not to offer compact disks below the suggested retail price. That decision opens the way for stores to price CDs below the amounts charged by their competitors.[44]

These types of objectives deemphasize the price element of the marketing mix and focus competitive efforts on nonprice variables. Price is a highly visible component of a firm's marketing mix and an easily used and effective tool for obtaining an advantage over competitors. The ability of competitors to match a price cut leads many

The Business of Auctioning Art Falls from Its Lofty Lair

Sotheby's and Christie's have long been venerable names in the auction world both in the U.S. and abroad. Until 2000, both houses had enjoyed impeccable reputations for bringing together the wealthiest and most distinguished buyers and sellers to exchange the finest goods. But later that year, several news articles revealed that Christie's had agreed to cooperate with the Department of Justice's antitrust investigation into possible price-fixing practices by both houses, in exchange for conditional amnesty. Shortly after that, Christie's announced a major change in the way it does business: it would increase the premiums it charges to buyers and decrease the premiums it charges to sellers. In other words, someone who bought a painting at auction for $50,000 would now pay Christie's $8,750 for handling the sale, as opposed to the previous premium of $7,500. But a seller's premium would be reduced on a sliding scale, depending on the amount of the sale. Not surprisingly, people in the fine art field questioned the company's motives for making this move.

Should companies be allowed to charge both buyers and sellers unregulated premiums on the same sale?

PRO

1. This type of pricing structure will not affect the way high-end buyers and sellers do business. "Do you think that the consignor of an important work of art is going to decide which house to give it to based on one or two percentage points?" questions one private dealer. "I don't think so. It's nice for the press to write about, but it's not going to make up a seller's mind where to consign."
2. The structure will actually benefit the buyer in the long run. "This structure allows us to benefit buyers for the first time," explains Edward J. Dolman, Christie's current CEO. "Aggregating their purchases allows us to reduce their commissions when they are selling with us. We believe the new mix of charges allows us the flexibility to do that."
3. A buyer's premium provides some stability to an auction house that depends on the availability of disposable income in a very small population of wealthy clients. If goods are scarce, an auc-

tion house can cut the seller's commission in order to increase the number of items for auction, undermine the competition, and still make a profit on the buyer's premium. If goods are abundant, the house can rake in the profits and either issue larger stockholder dividends or reinvest the money.

CON

1. This type of pricing structure discriminates against the buyer. "I find it strange that Christie's has raised the buyer's commission," notes one annoyed New York dealer. "It's an insult that I take personally—that they decide to make the prices higher, not lower."
2. Charging premiums to both sides allows the house to play both sides against each other, even if unintentionally. The house collects no matter how high or low the final price of an item is.
3. The premiums do not coincide with any additional services or enhanced value provided by the auction house, and they can be raised or lowered at will, which puts both buyers and sellers at a disadvantage.

SUMMARY

Before 1975, the buyer's premium did not exist—instead, auction houses had different methods for ensuring good prices and profits. When Christie's announced the first buyer's premium, it did so without warning to the dealers with which the house had done business for generations. When it increased the buyer's premium a quarter of a century later—without warning—many dealers were equally incensed. Since the announcement came on the heels of the company's grant of conditional amnesty in a price-fixing investigation, lawyers and dealers speculated that the move had little to do with benefiting customers and a lot to do with possible conditions of the amnesty and an attempt to distance Christie's from the practices of rival Sotheby's. When the hammer comes down on the dispute over buyer's and seller's premiums, however, it will be customers who decide whether they are fair. After all, they can always take their business somewhere else.

Sources: "Judge Accepts Sotheby's Plea Bargain," *Art & Auction,* March 2001, p. 27. Judd Tully, "What Price Collusion?" *Art & Auction,* March 1, 2000, pp. 60–62; Judd Tully, "To Sell Is Cheaper, To Buy More Expensive," *Art & Auction,* March 1, 2000, p. 63.

marketers to try to avoid price wars by favoring nonprice strategies, such as adding value, improving quality, educating consumers, and establishing relationships.

Widespread use of the Internet and development of new Web applications is expected to increase the necessity of pricing to meet competition, as described in the "Business Hits and Misses" box. Customers can easily compare prices and features online, and a variety of services are helping them choose the best deals. Web services like Decide.com and eSpoke.com let users compare what they are paying for long-distance phone service with the best deals in the Decide.com and eSpoke.com databases. Other sites provide similar comparisons of prices for wireless service. In the

How Much Is a Phone Call Worth?

Business Hits and Misses

Today's telecommunications industry is mired in a swamp of pricing problems. First is the issue of fixed charges that are either outdated or considered unethical by consumers and others. Many consumers can't figure out what determines fixed charges on their phone bills. Consider the 3 percent federal excise charge that appears on every phone bill. That tax was instituted by President Teddy Roosevelt in 1897, when the federal government needed a temporary tax to fund the Spanish American War. The war ended a century ago and Roosevelt died in 1919—but the tax won't go away. It has yet to be repealed by Congress because the money goes directly to the U.S. Treasury.

Then there is the issue of monthly charges levied on consumers who don't make many long-distance calls. The 1996 Telecommunications Act was designed to stimulate greater competition in the phone market, but companies were deadlocked until a group of carriers including AT&T, the Bells, Sprint, and GTE drew up a plan intended to offer monthly savings of $3 to $4 to consumers who make few long-distance calls. Under the plan, AT&T would eliminate its $3 monthly minimum charge for at least five years; Sprint would continue offering its no-minimum plan for the same time period. The plan would also reduce per-minute charges to the long-distance carriers by the local Bells, who promise to pass those savings on to their customers. However, after the five-year period, fees could go up.

Finally, there is the specter of enormous change hovering over the entire phone industry. The monthly charges and excise taxes aside, some experts predict that free phone calls will be within consumers' reach very soon, and the $70 billion long-distance industry may collapse. Fiber-optic capacity has slashed the wholesale cost of carrying a call as much as 40 percent per year. Regulators are going after artificially high charges, as mentioned already. Mobile carriers are gobbling up the long-distance market by offering nationwide calling plans. And Web-based companies such as Dialpad.com are now offering free calls using Internet networks that circumvent the phone network altogether. In addition to free calling, these firms seek to offer special calling features such as using e-mail addresses in place of old-style phone numbers.

With this system, a consumer could log on to a PC, phone, or computer kiosk and enter an e-mail address. The Internet would automatically know which device to connect to. If that sounds like a complicated change, consider this: Internet companies such as AOL Time Warner, Yahoo!, and Hotmail, which already have millions of e-mail addresses on file, would have immediate access to long-distance customers.

While some marketers such as AT&T's John Petrillo believe that consumers will be slow to give up the old pay-per-minute charge, others expect that technological changes will rock the industry sooner rather than later. Tom Evslin, a former AT&T executive who now runs ITXC, which routes voice traffic over Internet networks, says, "We're moving toward a Web model. You don't pay extra for sending e-mail, you don't pay extra for browsing a Web site, and you won't pay extra for making a long-distance phone call." Instead, predicts Evslin, consumers will quickly get used to being billed for long distance much the way they are billed for Internet access.

QUESTIONS FOR CRITICAL THINKING

1. Take a look at your own phone bill, or the one your parents received this past month. Can you figure out what all the charges are? Do you think they reflect the quality of service you receive? Why or why not?
2. Pricing is going to be a critical element in the marketing mix for telecommunications companies in the next few years. What type of strategy do you think will work best for traditional companies such as AT&T? What type of alternative pricing strategy might work best for Web-based companies?

Sources: Catherine Bremer, "Mobile Phone Show Brings Industry Back to Earth," Reuters Limited, February 23, 2001; Scott Woolley, "Meltdown," *Forbes*, July 3, 2000, pp. 70–71; Rebecca Blumenstein, "The Fees that Ate My Phone Bill!" *The Wall Street Journal*, March 6, 2000, pp. B1, B4; Kathy Chen, "Phone Companies Set to Drop Monthly Charges," *The Wall Street Journal*, February 28, 2000, p. B8.

---

auto industry, *Consumer Reports* recently began selling consumers publications showing current wholesale prices of new cars, along with the advice that when consumers negotiate with dealers, they should start with that price and work upward. In this environment, businesses have to offer something extra or keep prices low.[45]

Prestige Objectives

The final category of objectives, unrelated to either profitability or sales volume, encompasses the effect of prices on prestige. Prestige pricing establishes a relatively high price to develop and maintain an image of quality and exclusiveness. Marketers set such objectives because they recognize the role of price in communicating an overall image for the firm and its products. For many people, experiencing a Cirque du Soleil live performance is worth the $40 to $60 ticket price. Likewise, they will pay more for a pen by Michel Perchin, a car by Rolls Royce, or a belt by Gucci. A high price reinforces the value of these items and enables the seller to provide the high level of product quality and customer service that add value to owning them. Figure 14.12 is an example of a product priced to meet prestige objectives.

HOW PRICES ARE DETERMINED

While pricing is usually regarded as a function of marketing, it also requires considerable input from other areas of the company. Accounting and financial managers have always played major roles in pricing by providing sales and cost data necessary for sound decision making. Production and industrial engineering personnel play similarly important roles, and systems analysts ensure that the firm's information system provides access to current data for pricing. Managers at all levels must realize the importance of pricing and the contributions of different departments in choosing the right price.

Prices are determined in two basic ways—by applying the theoretical concepts of supply and demand and by completing cost analyses. Economic theory, as discussed in Chapter 3, assumes that a market price will be set at the point where the amount of a product desired at a given price equals the amount that suppliers will offer for sale at that price. In other words, this price occurs at the point where the amount demanded and the amount supplied are in equilibrium.

A popular current demand-and-supply approach to price setting is to buy and sell through auctions. During the Industrial Age, auctions became impractical as a way to sell in volume. However, the one-on-one possibilities of the Internet are resurrecting the use of auctions. The most popular consumer auction site is eBay. A variant of this strategy for business customers are B2B exchanges. Industrial giants like General Motors, Raytheon, and Quaker Oats buy goods and services at open auctions on an Internet service called FreeMarkets. Sellers can also use the Internet to collect specific data about what price customers will pay and then tailor future pricing decisions accordingly. For example, a customer who is willing to pay the full list price for a camera on a Web site may never receive offers of discounts at that site.[46]

Price Determination in Practice

Although economic theory leads to optimal decisions regarding the overall market for a product, marketers must set the prices of individual brands based on limited information about supply and demand. Anticipating how much of a product they will sell at a certain price requires difficult analysis, so businesses tend to adopt **cost-based pricing** formulas. Those formulas calculate base-cost figures per unit and then add markups to cover overhead costs and generate profits.

Cost-based pricing is simpler and easier to use than economic theory, but marketers must apply it flexibly in particular situations. Cost-based pricing totals all costs associated with offering a product in the market, including production, transportation, and marketing expenses. An added amount, the markup, then covers any unexpected or overlooked expenses and ensures a profit. The total becomes the price. Wholesalers and retailers typically practice markup pricing. As shown in Figure 14.13, the wholesaler of a hardcover book typically adds a markup of about 20 percent to cover costs of distributing a book through bookstores and online retailers and to generate a profit. The retailer adds a similar markup for its profit and

Inspired By The Treasures Of The Tsar

Not since the turn of the century has one been able to own a writing instrument so finely designed that it rivals the beauty of the Fabergé Eggs. Introducing the Blue and Gold Ribbed.

Michel Perchin

314 ◆ 692 ◆ 0505

London   ◆   Paris   ◆   Saint Louis   ◆   New York

FIGURE 14.12
Product Priced to Achieve Prestige Objectives

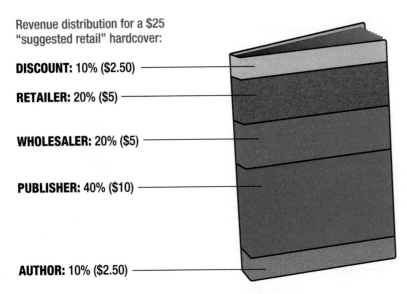

Revenue distribution for a $25 "suggested retail" hardcover:

DISCOUNT: 10% ($2.50)

RETAILER: 20% ($5)

WHOLESALER: 20% ($5)

PUBLISHER: 40% ($10)

AUTHOR: 10% ($2.50)

FIGURE 14.13
The Markup Chain for a Hardcover Book
Book Value: If books by the byte ever do take off, publishers could save significant dollars: Printing, warehousing and distribution charges can eat up 25% of a book's list price, or more than half the publisher's cut, says CIBC Oppenheimer publishing analyst Rudolf Hokanson. But they are unlikely to keep these dollars for themselves—consumers will demand cheaper books, and authors will demand steeper royalties.

expenses of running a store or mail-order business. Most consumers today expect a discount, so a book marked $25 would typically sell for about $22.50.

Breakeven Analysis

Marketers often conduct a **breakeven analysis** to determine the minimum sales volume a product must generate at a certain price level to cover all costs. This method involves a consideration of various costs and total revenues. Total cost is the sum of total variable costs and total fixed costs. *Variable costs* change with the level of production, as labor and raw materials do, while *fixed costs* like insurance premiums and minimum utility rates remain stable regardless of the production level. Total revenue is determined by multiplying price by the number of units sold.

Finding the Breakeven Point The level of sales that will generate enough revenue to cover all of the company's fixed and variable costs is called the *breakeven point*. It is the point at which total revenue just equals total costs. Sales beyond the breakeven point will generate profits; sales volume below the breakeven point will result in losses. The following formulas give the breakeven point in units and dollars:

$$\text{Breakeven point (in units)} = \frac{\text{Total Fixed Costs}}{\text{Contribution to Fixed Costs Per Unit}}$$

$$\text{Breakeven point (in dollars)} = \frac{\text{Total Fixed Costs}}{1 - \text{Variable Cost Per Unit/Price}}$$

A product selling for $20 with a variable cost of $14 per unit produces a $6 per-unit contribution to fixed costs. If the firm has total fixed costs of $42,000, then it must sell 7,000 units to break even on the product. The calculation of the breakeven point in units and dollars is as follows:

$$\text{Breakeven point (in units)} = \frac{\$42,000}{\$20 - \$14} = \frac{\$42,000}{\$6} = 7,000 \text{ units}$$

$$\text{Breakeven point (in dollars)} = \frac{\$42,000}{1 - \$14/\$20} = \frac{\$42,000}{1 - .7} = \frac{\$42,000}{.3} = \$140,000$$

Figure 14.14 illustrates this breakeven point in graphic form.

Marketers use breakeven analysis to determine the profits or losses that would result from several different proposed prices. Since different prices produce different breakeven points, marketers could compare their calculations of required sales to break even with sales estimates from marketing research studies. This comparison can identify the best price, one that would attract enough customers to exceed the breakeven point and earn profits for the firm.

Most firms add demand—determining whether enough customers will buy the number of units the firm must sell at a particular price to break even—by developing estimates of consumer demand through surveys of likely customers, interviews with retailers that would be handling the product, and assessments of prices charged by competitors. Then the breakeven points for several possible prices are calculated and compared with sales estimates for each price. This practice is referred to as *modified breakeven analysis*. Marketers reduce the price alternatives under consideration until they identify only those that appear capable of achieving at least breakeven sales.

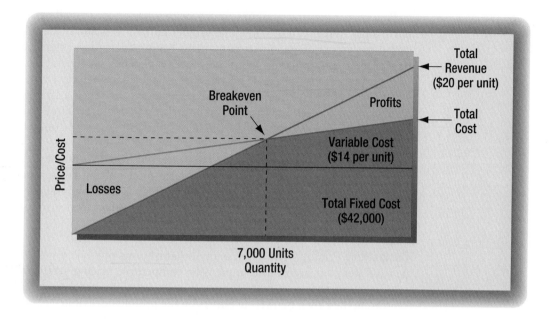

**FIGURE 14.14
Breakeven Analysis**

Alternative Pricing Strategies

The specific strategies that firms use to price their goods and services grow out of the marketing strategies they formulate to accomplish overall organizational objectives. One firm's marketers may price products to attract customers across a wide range; another group of marketers may set prices to appeal to a small segment of a larger market; still another group may simply try to match competitors' price tags. In general, firms can choose from three alternative pricing strategies: skimming, penetration, and competitive pricing.

Skimming Pricing Strategy   A **skimming pricing strategy** sets an intentionally high price relative to the prices of competing products. The name comes from the expression "skimming the cream." This pricing strategy often works for introduction of a distinctive good or service with little or no competition, although it can be used throughout most stages of the product life cycle. A skimming strategy helps marketers to set a price that distinguishes a firm's high-end product from those of competitors.

A skimming strategy also allows a manufacturer to quickly recover its development costs, and it lets a firm maximize revenue from a new product before competitors enter the field. Marketers often use skimming strategies to segment a product's overall market by price. Another advantage is that it permits marketers to control demand in the introductory stages of a product's life cycle and then adjust production to match demand. The one big problem with a skimming strategy is that it attracts competition.

Exclusive perfumes typically employ skimming pricing strategies. The costs of the perfume ingredients are almost insignificant when compared with the retail price; in fact, the most expensive component of such a product is typically a unique container.

Penetration Pricing   By contrast, a **penetration pricing strategy** sets a low price as a major marketing weapon. Marketers often price new products noticeably lower than competing offerings when they enter new industries characterized by dozens of competing brands. Once the new product achieves some market recognition through consumer trial purchases stimulated by its low price, marketers may increase the price to the level of competing products.

BUSINESS DIRECTORY

➤ **breakeven analysis** *pricing technique that determines the sales volume that a firm must achieve at a specified price in order to generate enough revenue to cover its total costs.*

Penetration pricing assumes that a below-market price will attract buyers and move a brand from an unknown newcomer at least to brand recognition or even the brand preference stage. Since many firms begin penetration pricing with the intention of increasing prices in the future, success depends on generating large numbers of consumer trial purchases. This strategy is particularly effective when introduction of a new product will likely attract strong competition. Such a strategy may allow a new product to reach the mass market quickly and capture a large share prior to entry by competitors. Research shows that about 25 percent of companies frequently use penetration pricing strategies.

Everyday low pricing (EDLP) is a strategy devoted to maintaining continuous low prices rather than relying on short-term price-cutting tactics such as cents-off coupons, rebates, and special sales. This strategy is used by retailers like Wal-Mart to consistently offer low prices to consumers; manufacturers also use EDLP to set stable prices for retailers.

Competitive Pricing   Although many organizations rely heavily on price as a competitive weapon, even more implement **competitive pricing strategies**. They try to reduce the emphasis on price competition by matching other firms' prices and concentrating their own marketing efforts on the product, distribution, and promotional elements of the marketing mix. In fact, in industries with relatively homogeneous products, competitors must match one another's price reductions to maintain market share and remain competitive. By pricing their products at the general levels of competing offerings, marketers largely negate the price variable in their marketing strategies.

Competitive pricing is part of the marketing strategy for New London Pharmacy in New York City. Within blocks of New London are two competitors with more-familiar names—Rite Aid and CVS. When they moved into the neighborhood and advertised low prices, the independent store responded by cutting its own prices to comparable levels. New London also has tried to differentiate itself from the big-name competitors by offering attentive service, heavily promoting special deals, and stocking unique products, such as its early introduction of herbal remedies ahead of competitors. These efforts are important, but the store's owners note that when the big competitors make price cuts, their pharmacy sales fall until they match the lower prices. As a result, competitive pricing remains an indispensable part of their overall marketing strategy.[47]

CONSUMER PERCEPTIONS OF PRICES

In addition to costs and competitors, marketers must also consider how consumers perceive prices. If large numbers of potential buyers consider a price too high or too low, the marketer must correct the situation. Price–quality relationships and psychological pricing are important considerations.

Price–Quality Relationships

Research shows that a consumer's perception of product quality is closely related to an item's price. In the previous example of Duncan Hines cake mixes, a high price raised perceptions of quality. Most marketers believe that this perceived price–quality relationship holds over a relatively wide range of prices, although consumers may view extreme prices as either too expensive or too cheap to consider paying. Marketing managers need to study and experiment with prices, because the price–quality relationship can critically affect a firm's pricing strategy.

Some consumers will, for instance, pay extra for organic produce, even in stores where conventionally grown fruits and vegetables are available at a lower price in a nearby aisle. Although there is little support for the belief that organic produce is more nutritious than conventionally grown produce, consumers who buy organic see

Car.   Great American road trip.

The power of a color copier for the price of black and white.   Introducing the Hewlett-Packard desktop color copiers.

Visit us at www.hp.com/info/colorcopiers2 or call 1-800-761-8999, ext. 2371. *Estimated U.S. retail price.

FIGURE 14.15
Establishing Price–Quality Relationships for Printers

other dimensions of quality. They may feel safer eating produce without pesticide residues, or they may feel good about buying from farmers who choose not to spray chemicals on their crops.[48]

In other cases, marketers establish price–quality relationships with comparisons that demonstrate a product's value at the established price. In Figure 14.15, Hewlett-Packard offers a line of color printers that deliver "the power of a color copier for the price of black and white." This message recognizes that getting good value for their money is an important consideration for most buyers of office equipment. Similarly, in advertising diamond engagement rings, De Beers asks, "How can you make two months' salary last forever?" The message does not dispute that a diamond ring is expensive, but it points out that the product is an enduring treasure.

Psychological Pricing

Have you ever wondered why retailers set prices like $39.95, $19.98, or $9.99 instead of $40, $20, or $10? Before the age of cash registers and sales taxes, retailers reportedly followed this practice of *odd pricing* to force clerks to make correct change as part of cash control efforts. It is now a commonly used retail practice because many retailers believe that consumers favor uneven amounts. In Figure 14.15, the "estimated U.S. retail prices" for the three copiers shown are $699, $999, and $1,299. To avoid the look of more common prices like $5.95, $10.98, and $19.99, though, some sellers use prices ending in 1, 2, 3, 4, 6, or 7. However, research has shown that odd pricing has little effect on consumer purchases with the possible exception of amounts under $25.

WHAT'S AHEAD

This chapter introduces the key marketing tasks of developing, marketing, packaging, and pricing want-satisfying goods and services. The next chapter focuses on three major components of an organization's distribution strategy: the design of efficient distribution channels; wholesalers and retailers who make up many distribution channels; and logistics and physical distribution.

➤ Summary of Learning Goals

1. Define *product* and list the elements of a product strategy.

A product is a bundle of physical, service, and symbolic attributes designed to satisfy consumer wants. The marketing conception of a product includes the brand, product image, warranty, service attributes, packaging, and labeling, in addition to the physical or functional characteristics of the good or service.

2. Describe the classifications of consumer goods, business goods, and services.

Goods and services can be classified as consumer (B2C) or business (B2B) products. Consumer products are those purchased by ultimate consumers for their own use. They can be convenience products, shopping products, or specialty products, depending on consumer habits in buying them. Business products are those purchased for use either directly or indirectly in the production of other goods and services for resale. They can be classified as installations, accessory equipment, component parts and materials, raw materials, and supplies. This classification is based on how the items are used and product characteristics. Services can be classified as either consumer or business services.

3. Distinguish between the product mix and product lines.

A firm's product mix is the assortment of goods and services a firm offers to individual consumers and B2B users. A product line is a series of related products.

4. Describe the four stages of the product life cycle.

All products pass through four stages in their product life cycles: introduction, growth, maturity, and decline. In the introduction stage, the firm attempts to elicit demand for the new product. In the product's growth stage, sales climb, and the company earns its initial profits. In the maturity stage, sales reach a saturation level. In the decline stage, both sales and profits decline. Marketers sometimes employ strategies to extend the product life cycle, including increasing frequency of use, adding new users, finding new uses for the product, and changing package size, labeling, or product quality.

5. List the stages of new-product development.

The stages of the new-product development process are idea generation, screening, business analysis, prototype or service process development, test marketing, and commercialization. At each stage, marketers must decide whether to continue to the next stage, modify the new product, or discontinue the development process.

6. Explain how firms identify their products.

Products are identified by brands, brand names, and trademarks, which are important elements of product images. Effective brand names are easy to pronounce, recognize, and remember, and they project the right images to buyers. Brand names cannot contain generic words. Under certain circumstances, companies lose exclusive rights to their brand names if common use makes them generic terms for product categories. Some brand names belong to retailers or distributors rather than to manufacturers. Some retailers offer a third option: no-brand generic products. Brand loyalty is measured in three degrees: brand recognition, brand preference, and brand insistence. Some marketers use family brands to identify several related items in a product line. Others employ individual branding strategies by giving each product within a line a different brand name.

7. Outline the different types of pricing objectives and discuss how firms set prices in the marketplace.

Pricing objectives can be classified as profitability, volume, meeting competition, and prestige objectives. Profitability objectives seek profit maximization and include target-return goals in the form of rates of return on either investment or sales. Volume objectives typically consist of market-share goals, which are specified as percentages of certain markets. Some prices are set simply to meet competitors' prices in the marketplace. Prestige pricing maintains a high price to create an image of exclusivity for a product.

Price determination can be viewed from two perspectives. Economists explain prices by describing the interaction of demand and supply. A more practical, less theoretical approach to price strategy, called cost-based pricing, totals fixed and variable costs and then adds an amount to cover any unexpected or unconsidered expenses and ensure a profit.

8. Explain how to use breakeven analysis in pricing strategy.

Breakeven analysis supports pricing decisions by comparing total costs and total revenues to determine a breakeven point in units. It does this by dividing total fixed costs by the per-unit contribution to fixed costs. Sales beyond the breakeven point result in profits. Breakeven points can be calculated for various prices. The resulting breakeven volumes can then be compared with marketing research estimates of likely sales volume in determining a final price based on both consumer demand and the firm's need to recover its costs and generate a satisfactory return on investment.

9. Differentiate between skimming and penetration pricing strategies.

A skimming strategy sets a relatively high price compared with similar products and then gradually lowers it. Penetration pricing sets a price lower than similar products and eventually raises it after the product gains wide market acceptance.

Business Terms You Need to Know

product 498
service 499
product life cycle 503
product line 508
product mix 508

test marketing 512
brand 514
brand equity 518
price 521
breakeven analysis 526

Other Important Business Terms

warranty 500
brand name 514
trademark 514
generic product 514
family brand 514
individual brand 514

manufacturer's (national) brand 515
private (store) brand 515
brand recognition 517
brand preference 517
brand insistence 517
label 521

market share 522
cost-based pricing 525
skimming pricing strategy 527
penetration pricing strategy 527
competitive pricing strategy 528

➤ Review Questions

1. How do marketers define the term *product?* What is the difference between a good and a service?

2. Classify each of the following consumer products according to type—convenience, shopping, or specialty:

a. *Time* or *Newsweek* magazine

b. Godiva chocolates

c. living room carpet

d. Rolex watch

e. Whirlpool washing machine and dryer

f. carton of milk

3. Classify each of the following business goods and services as installations, accessory equipment, component parts and materials, raw materials, or supplies:

a. photocopying paper

b. lumber

c. notebook computer

d. telecommunications system

e. microchips

4. Identify and describe briefly the four stages of the product life cycle.

5. What is a product line? Go to the supermarket or access the Web site of a manufacturer and make a list of items in one company's product lines.

6. Identify and describe briefly the six stages of new-product development.

7. Name a brand to which you are loyal as a consumer. Why are you loyal to this brand? What conditions might make you shift your loyalty to another brand?

8. Name a product that you think enjoys high brand equity. What factors do you think contribute to this brand equity?

9. What are the objectives of a product's package? Describe a package you've seen that meets these objectives. Describe a package that does not meet these objectives.

10. Define the term *breakeven point*. Calculate the break-even point for a baseball cap embroidered with a team logo, which sells for $16 with a variable cost of $12 per unit, and produces a $4 per-unit contribution to fixed costs. The company that makes the cap has a total fixed cost of $36,000. What is the breakeven point in units? In dollars?

➤ Questions for Critical Thinking

1. Describe an instance in which you received good customer service. Then describe an instance in which you received poor customer service. Did either of these experiences influence whether you returned to buy additional products? Why or why not?

2. As the Razor scooter moves through the various stages in the product life cycle, what adjustments might its marketers make in the strategies they choose for the scooter?

3. Suggest an appropriate brand name for each of the following goods. Defend your choices.
   a. laundry detergent
   b. sports car or sport-utility vehicle
   c. scooter
   d. jeans
   e. outdoor boots
   f. pizza
   g. fresh-fruit drink

4. As a marketer, what steps would you take to build brand loyalty to three of the products you selected in Question 3?

5. Assume you are the marketing manager for a new National Basketball Association developmental league basketball franchise. Your team will be using an arena with 3,000 first-class seats, 5,000 regular seats, and 2,000 seats directly behind the two goals. How will you go about setting ticket prices?

➤ Experiential Exercise

Background: You learned in this chapter the importance of packaging and labeling. This exercise will help you apply what you've learned about the characteristics of effective labeling.

Directions: Select two product labels—one you think is a highly effective label and a second that you regard as less effective.

1. Use the following chart to analyze your two labels based on the five functions of effective labeling.

2. In columns 2 and 3 of the chart, identify what was effective or ineffective for each of the functions.

3. Your second label does not have to be ineffective in every function of effective labeling, but it should be lacking in at least one of the functions.

4. Bring your two labels to class and be prepared to present your analysis during small-group discussions.

Functions of Effective Labeling	Label 1: Effective Labeling	Label 2: Ineffective Labeling
1. Attracts buyer's attention		
2. Describes package contents		
3. Conveys benefits of the product inside		
4. Provides information on warranties, warnings, and other consumer matters		
5. Gives an indication of price, value, and uses		

> ## Nothing but Net

1. **Product standards.** As mentioned in the chapter, both the U.S. Golf Association and the Royal and Ancient Golf Club in St. Andrews, Scotland, have a set of specifications to which golf balls must adhere. Visit the following Web sites and review the current standards for golf balls. What other golf equipment must also meet U.S. Golf Association standards? How do these standards affect manufacturers of golf equipment?

   www.usga.org/rules

   www.randa.org

2. **Product pricing.** Merrill Lynch recently began offering a new service to its customers. The service, called Unlimited Advantage, lets investors pay a flat annual fee rather than the traditional fee assessed for each purchase or sale. Visit the Merrill Lynch Web site listed here and prepare a brief report on how the brokerage firm has applied the pricing concepts you learned about in this chapter.

   http://askmerrill.ml.com

3. **Trademarks.** Visit the Web site for the U.S. Patent and Trademark Office. Review the procedure for registering a trademark and prepare a brief report. Note how much it costs to register a trademark and the benefits of trademark registration. How long is a trademark registration valid?

   www.uspto.gov

Note: Internet Web addresses change frequently. If you do not find the exact sites listed, you may need to access the organization's or company's home page and search from there.

Did you have a favorite pair of shoes when you were a kid? Were they sneakers or shiny patent leather? Maybe you had a pair of Stride Rites—the company has been making shoes for little feet since 1918. Check the feet of your younger brothers, sisters, nieces, or nephews, and there's a good chance they are sporting Stride Rite or Keds shoes, another popular brand that Stride Rite purchased in the early 1970s. Maybe you picked up an adult-sized pair of platform Keds for yourself recently or a pair of Sperry Top-Siders or Tommy Hilfiger shoes. And perhaps your mom likes Grasshoppers—the kind she wears on her feet. All of these brands belong to Stride Rite Corp.—with the exception of Tommy Hilfiger, which Stride Rite sells under an exclusive licensing agreement.

Why so many names under one roof? Stride Rite CFO John Kelliher explains that the brands Stride Rite sells are the keys to the company's success, and a wise choice of product lines has helped balance the company over its long history. Since the footwear market tends to grow slowly—a lot more slowly than, say, the market for computer software—a company like Stride Rite must select and develop its goods carefully. Stride Rite deals "exclusively in quality footwear," says Kelliher. Ideas for new shoes come from everywhere inside and outside the company—from retailers, sales representatives, financial people, and division presidents—in addition to the employees whose job is to develop and design footwear. And although footwear is a consumer product, Kelliher stresses that, in order to develop it successfully, "you have to run your business with the eye of a retailer." In other words, shoes are designed and developed with a strong link to the retailers who will be marketing them to consumers. Recently there has been more interest in different styles of Sperry shoes, so Stride Rite is working to develop a wider assortment for that product line.

Partnerships such as those with Tommy Hilfiger are another important part of the picture in developing products and extending lines. Through a licensing partnership with manufacturer S. Goldberg & Co., Stride Rite is developing and marketing an exclusive line of children's slippers "We're thrilled about this perfect partnership because S. Goldberg is a leader in the children's slipper industry, just as Stride Rite is the dominant brand in the children's shoe business," notes Jerry Silverman, president of the Stride Rite Children's Group. "This is a tactical next step in regard to our brand extension licensing strategy, which is to develop new strategic partnerships with companies that excel in their trade."

CFO Kelliher's statement that Stride Rite deals in quality footwear means that the company's prices are neither rock bottom nor high end. Stride Rite tries hard to give customers the best possible shoe for the best possible price. Since the company buys all of its products from independent manufacturers around the world, production costs vary. So if a shoe is going to cost $35 at retail, then manufacturers will use materials and construction methods to match that price. If a shoe is going to sell for $18, different materials and construction will be used. Stride Rite's price startegy is competitive pricing. If a shoe is too expensive or too inexpensive compared with competitors' shoes, it is unlikely to sell as well. So the company tries to make sure that its prices are in line with similar shoes.

Shoes have a product life cycle, and they are also subject to seasonal changes. For instance, more people buy Sperry boat shoes during the spring and summer months than in the dead of winter. Pink sneakers usually sell better in June than in November, at least in most parts of the U.S. So Stride Rite needs to be in close contact with retailers to know when to take price cuts to move inventory out the door. "We have to know exactly what is happening at retail," says Kelliher. "We must be linked with them." Stride Rite's electronic links to retail stores let it obtain and share information instantly with its retailers and suppliers.

In all aspects of its business, Stride Rite strives to focus on the needs of the customer, whether that person is an infant or a senior citizen. To that end, the company emphasizes the quality of its brands. "Product is king," says Kelliher. Like other Stride Rite employees, he doesn't just talk the talk; he also walks the walk—he can usually be seen sporting a pair of Sperry Top-Siders or Tommy Hilfiger footwear.

QUESTIONS

1. How would you classify Stride Rite shoes in terms of type of consumer product? Why?
2. Stride Rite shoes enjoy brand equity. What factors do you think contribute to this brand equity?
3. Go to the Stride Rite Web site at **www.strideritecorp.com** to learn more about the company's product lines. Write a brief memo describing the features and characteristics of one of the lines.

4. Stride Rite has been in business since 1918, so many of its shoe brands have experienced at least three stages of the product life cycle. Describe a strategy that Stride Rite might use to extend the life cycle of the product line you discussed in question #3.

Sources: Company Web site, **www.strideritecorp.com,** accessed April 9, 2001; "Stride Rite Launches New Munchkin Product Line," Business Wire, January 9, 2001; "Stride Rite Signs Licensing Deal with S. Goldberg," Business Wire, January 18, 2001; The Stride Rite Corporation Annual Report, 1999.

CHAPTER 15

Distributing Goods and Services

Learning Goals

1. Summarize the ways distribution creates value for customers and competitive advantage for businesses.

2. Identify the various categories of distribution channels and the factors that influence channel selection.

3. Discuss the roles marketing intermediaries play in distribution channels.

4. Explain how retailers effectively use pricing, promotion, location, and merchandise selection to compete.

5. Identify and briefly describe each of the major components of an effective distribution strategy.

6. List the different types of conflict that can occur in a distribution channel and the methods firms use to reduce channel conflict.

7. Describe the importance of logistics in controlling the supply chain.

8. Explain how the components of a physical distribution system work together to reduce costs and meet customer service standards.

9. Compare the alternative transportation modes on the bases of flexibility, dependability, and cost.

A fashion force is sweeping across the Atlantic from Spain and hoping to leave its mark on New York and the rest of the U.S.: its name is Zara. Zara, a Spanish fashion boutique with thousands of 20-something fans across Europe, wants to take on the likes of The Gap. With 6 stores already open in the U.S., the company hopes to increase that number to 30 within the next few years. That's still a lot smaller than The Gap, but the chief executive officer (CEO) of Zara's parent company Inditex, José Maria Castellano, remains undaunted. "Even though Gap is more casual, both of us share the goal of becoming global retailers."

What makes Zara think its fashions will also succeed in the U.S. market? First, the company has a high-speed production schedule—it can get current fashion designs produced and to its stores faster than anyone else. With more than 200 designers, Zara creates 12,000 different fashion items each year. The fabric is cut in a Zara factory, then sent to local workshops for sewing. Even though European wages are higher than those in Asia or South America, where many of the world's larger clothing designers have their goods manufactured, Zara keeps inventory to a minimum and does not hold sales, so higher wage costs are offset by low spending elsewhere. "If anything, Zara is nimbler and faster to the market than Gap," notes retail analyst Keith Willis of Goldman, Sachs & Co. in London. "That will be important as fashion trends globalize." In fact, being able to get the goods to market faster than anyone else can be critical to maintaining a competitive edge in the fashion industry, particularly when the target market consists of young buyers who want the latest trends—and are willing to spend on them. Zara can take a new fashion from runway to store shelf in as little as two weeks—at The Gap it takes about a year. Although The Gap operates on a much larger scale, speed has its rewards. When Zara brought out a men's pink

dress shirt during one recent season, customers indicated that they'd rather have purple shirts. So Zara's manufacturing people sped back to the sewing machines. "We

were able to get the new shirt into the stores within two weeks," boasts José Toledo, director of Zara Homme, the men's division. The Gap is not ignoring Zara, either. "Gap is quite aware of Zara and knows that it must focus on reducing its time to market," says Marcia Aaron, a retail analyst at Deutsche Bank.

The shopping experience in a Zara store adds to its styles. Elegantly decorated shop windows attract customers to an interior that may have a marble-like floor and special lighting. "You feel like you're in a classy European boutique," gushes Dyann Klein, owner of her own Manhattan-based theater-props company. She touches a pair of black stretch pants—the New York uniform—that go for $33 at Zara. "This would cost $350 at Prada," she marvels. Another shopper browses through a Zara boutique in New York wearing a Gap T-shirt. "I like Gap for casual clothes, but this is much sexier," she explains. So Zara not only produces the latest fashions quickly, it sells them for a reasonable price in stores whose atmosphere makes shoppers feel good—about themselves and the clothes they are buying.

Castellano admits that if the company grows, its manufacturing facilities will have to grow as well, which may affect the control it has over production and distribution.

"If we had a bigger American network, we would have to open a factory in Mexico," he says. Still, Zara could maintain its unique connection between the salespeople who work in the boutiques and the factory. Each salesperson carries a Casio wireless organizer to log in trends, comments from customers, and orders. All of this data go directly to Zara's headquarters. So, if an item isn't selling well in most of the shops, it can be pulled quickly and replaced with new items. Conversely, if customers express a desire for something that isn't on the shelves, the information can be communicated quickly to the factory, and production can begin immediately. That's how Zara got those purple shirts to the stores so fast. Transportation options between Mexico and Zara's U.S. stores might differ from those in Europe, but it's likely that Zara would find the fastest, most reliable way.[1] As you read this chapter, you'll learn how companies fit the final pieces of the business puzzle together—getting their goods and services to the people who want to buy them.

CHAPTER OVERVIEW

As previous chapters discuss, business involves an exchange between producers and customers. High-quality products and creative promotion may convince customers that they want to buy a firm's goods and services, but if those would-be purchasers cannot actually buy the product, the exchange cannot be completed. The items that people wish to buy are often manufactured thousands of miles away, even in other countries. Yet buyers still want to complete quick, convenient transactions that require minimal effort. To meet these expectations, firms must strategically manage distribution.

Distribution—the element of the marketing mix responsible for moving goods and services from producers to buyers—is a vital marketing concern. The marketing functions and specialized intermediaries in a distribution channel build a bridge that links buyers with the organizations that create the products they want. In fact, distribution contributes to three of the four types of utility—time, place, and ownership utility. This activity adds value to a product by getting it to the right place at the time when the customer wants to buy it.

This chapter examines the basic distribution strategies and marketing intermediaries that help to move goods and services from producers to buyers. It discusses criteria for making decisions about where to offer products for sale and the contributions of successful distribution strategies to a firm's competitiveness. Finally, we examine logistics, the process of physically moving information, goods, and services.

DISTRIBUTION STRATEGY

With tens of thousands of new consumer products entering the market every year, getting the attention of retailers and wholesalers—to say nothing of convincing them to carry a new product—can challenge even the most creative inventor. Brad Young thought up a way for skiers and snowboarders like himself to enjoy music along with sports: a headband containing earphones hooked to a portable cassette player. For six years he waited for someone to start making his "obvious" idea. When no one did, he started his company, Outdoor Dynamics, and developed the product, HeadBANdZ. Young assumed he would sell HeadBANdZ in ski shops, where the logical customers would be found, but the stores were reluctant to add the relatively low-cost product to their more profitable mix of merchandise.

Young had to develop a more creative distribution strategy. He started visiting trade shows, looking for partners who would appreciate an innovative product. There he met representatives from two catalog retailers, Herrington and Early Winters, that were willing to include HeadBANdZ in their lineups. He also found one specialized chain store—Walking Co., which sells products for mall walkers—that decided to carry HeadBANdZ. Those initial successes attracted the interest of a distributor, Mountain States Specialties. The distributor's salespeople offer merchandise to ski shops and customers that Outdoor Dynamics had not considered as target markets—makers of advertising specialties such as giveaways bearing a company's logo. As the company expanded its distribution, HeadBANdZ sales doubled every year.[2]

As shown in the HeadBANdZ example, the importance of distribution strategy to a firm's marketing efforts is hard to overstate. Marketers must carefully choose how and where their goods will reach their target markets by selecting the right distribution channels. Distribution channels are the paths through which products—and legal ownership of them—flow from producer to consumers or business buyers. Ideally, the choice of a distribution channel should support a firm's overall marketing strategy by providing ultimate customers with convenient ways to obtain the goods and services they desire.

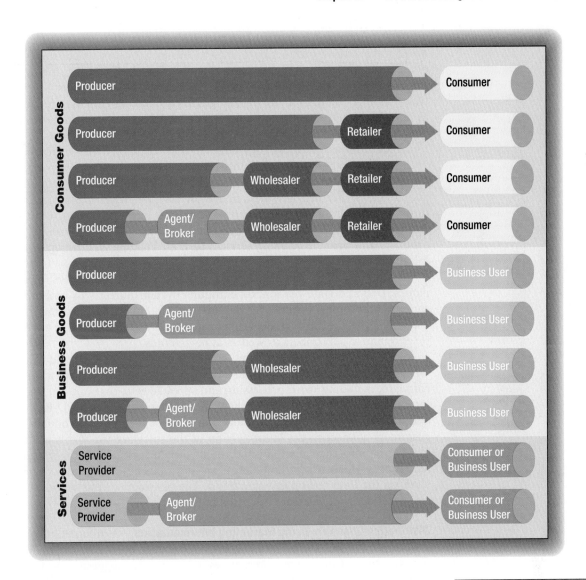

FIGURE 15.1
Alternative Distribution Channels

Types of Distribution Channels

The distribution channel selection process begins by deciding which type (or types) of channel will best meet both the marketing objectives of the firm and the needs of its customers. As shown in Figure 15.1, marketers can choose either a **direct distribution channel,** which carries goods directly from producer to consumer or business user, or distribution channels that involve several different marketing intermediaries. A **marketing intermediary,** or *middleman,* is a business firm that moves goods between producers and consumers or business users. Retailers and wholesalers are both marketing intermediaries.

No one channel suits every product. The best choice depends on the circumstances of the market and on customer needs. The choice of a distribution channel may also change over time as new opportunities arise and marketers strive to maintain their competitiveness. This section takes a closer look at how both direct and indirect distribution channels can support marketing strategies.

Direct Distribution   The shortest and simplest means of connecting producers and customers is a direct

BUSINESS DIRECTORY

➤ **distribution**   *process of moving goods and services from the producer to buyers.*

➤ **distribution channel**   *path through which products—and legal ownership of them—flow from producer to the final customer.*

➤ **direct distribution channel**   *distribution channel that moves goods directly from producer to ultimate user.*

➤ **marketing intermediary**   *channel member, either wholesaler or retailer, that moves goods between producer and consumer or business user.*

channel. Goods and services that travel through direct distribution channels move directly from their production points to business buyers or consumers. This approach is most common in the business-to-business (B2B) market. It also serves consumers who buy fresh fruits and vegetables at rural roadside stands. Services ranging from banking and ten-minute oil changes to ear-piercing employ direct distribution, as does Mary Kay Cosmetics, which sends company sales associates to customers' homes or apartments.

Direct distribution offers advantages in marketing relatively expensive, complex products that might require demonstrations. These strengths are especially valuable in the B2B market. Most major industrial installations, accessory equipment, component parts, business services, and even raw materials are typically marketed through direct contacts between producers and business buyers. For this reason, marketers of business products depend on highly trained sales personnel to sell their products and provide ongoing services to their customers, dealing with any post-sales problems their clients may encounter.

The Internet is making direct distribution an attractive option for many companies. Dell and Gateway market computer systems directly to both ultimate consumers and business buyers over the Internet. Clinique sells its cosmetics at its own Web site as well as through department stores. *The Wall Street Journal* offers its articles online to subscribers as well as at newsstands.

Like *Wall Street Journal* articles, some products can be delivered as well as sold on the Internet. The Star Division of Sun Microsystems markets a suite of office software, including word processing and spreadsheets, that can run on several different operating systems. Rather than distributing software on CD-ROMs in stores and to computer makers, Sun wants Star to be a Web-based product. This means customers connect to the latest version of the software via Web sites, rather than loading it onto their computers through disk drives.[3] Although competing with Microsoft's widely used Office suite is an enormous hurdle, the idea of offering software via the Internet is a growing trend. The providers of this service, called *application service providers,* are discussed in Chapter 17.

Distribution Channels Using Marketing Intermediaries Although direct channels allow simple and straightforward connections between producers and their customers, the extensive list of channel alternatives in Figure 15.1 suggests that direct distribution is not the best choice in every instance. Some products sell in small quantities for relatively low prices to thousands of widely scattered consumers. Producers of such items cannot cost-effectively contact each of these customers directly, so they distribute their products through specialized intermediaries called *retailers.*

Retailers are marketing intermediaries that sell goods and services to final consumers. Since people frequently come in contact with retailers, the "last three feet of the distribution channel," they are much more familiar with retailers than with wholesaling intermediaries. Consumers purchase food, clothing, furniture, appliances, and a host of other products from retailers. Retailers need not operate from physical storefronts. Some, like J. Crew, sell merchandise through catalogs; others, like Amazon.com, sell goods and services over the Internet.

Along with or in place of retailers, many distribution channels include wholesaling intermediaries. These marketing organizations consist of individuals or firms that sell to retailers, other wholesalers, and business buyers ranging from manufacturers to government agencies and not-for-profit organizations. Unlike retailers, wholesalers do not sell directly to ultimate consumers. Instead, they function as pipelines for goods moving from producers to retail stores, business users, or other wholesaling intermediaries.

Fleming Cos., a leading wholesaler of food, health, and beauty products, operates 33 warehouses across the United States. The warehouses are stocked with thousands of products that Fleming purchases from many different U.S. and foreign manufacturers. Fleming then resells these goods to independent grocery stores, convenience stores, drugstores, supermarket chains, and Internet food retailers. In other words, Fleming acts as an intermediary between these retailers and food producers. In addition, Fleming's customers serve as marketing intermediaries between hundreds of manufacturers and millions of consumers.[4]

As with direct channels, the Internet is opening new indirect channels to consumers and businesses. Online retailers include such popular Web sites as Amazon.com, E*Trade, and Buy.com. Wholesalers like W. W. Grainger and services intermediaries like the Sabre airline reservations company have set up Web sites to link their suppliers and customers. An important trend in B2B e-commerce is the use of exchanges. Hundreds of B2B sites specialize in particular industries, such as e-Steel.com and Material-Net.com in the steel industry, and Gofish.com and FoodUSA.com in the perishable foods industry. Buyers visiting an exchange can specify the products they need, the prices they will pay, and the delivery schedules they require. Interested sellers can respond with bids. Buyers that receive multiple bids can select their supplier and finish negotiating a contract. Typically, the seller pays the exchange a transaction fee, and the exchange handles credit checks and collections.[5] Intermediaries that bring together business customers and suppliers are increasingly important as the Internet gives customers access to a worldwide marketplace. Business customers can find tens of thousands of Asian-made products, for instance, through Global Sources, a Hong Kong–based site that lists the products and contact information for the producers.[6]

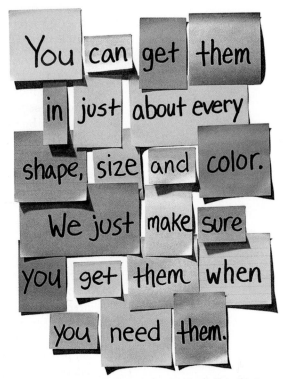

FIGURE 15.2
Quill.com: An Online Wholesaling Intermediary

Until very recently, many observers expected that e-commerce would favor short channels of distribution—direct channels or channels from producers through retailers to consumers. However, Web site operators quickly discovered the expense and complexity of obtaining and delivering products accurately and on time. As a result, they often turn to wholesalers for help. One wholesaler that is strengthening its position in this environment is Ingram Micro, the nation's leading distributor of computer hardware and software. Ingram's traditional customers are stores, but the company boosted its capability for distributing single product units. Ingram can fulfill online retailers' orders by sending products directly to their consumers, with customized packing slips that look like they came from the retailer.[7] Another online wholesaler is Quill, which sells office products through its catalog and Web site. Rather than trying to provide every business user with its Post-It notes, 3M sells through intermediaries like Quill. As shown in Figure 15.2, Quill offers fast delivery and e-mail reminders to reorder routine purchases. The use of e-commerce in retailing strategy is discussed in more detail later in the chapter.

Moving Goods through Marketing Intermediaries Producers can move goods through a distribution channel over many paths, most of which involve one or more marketing intermediaries. The following distribution channels are the most common ones using intermediaries:

- *Producer to retailer to consumer:* Some manufacturers distribute their products directly to retailers. In the clothing industry, many producers employ salespeople who call on retailers.

- *Producer to wholesaler to retailer to consumer:* Thousands of manufacturers rely on this traditional channel to distribute consumer goods. They can often distribute more efficiently through wholesalers than by selling directly to thousands of separate retailers. Many large food-product manufacturers do not want the burden of having to keep small grocery stores stocked with their goods. They prefer to deal directly with larger buyers, such as Fleming Cos. By selling in bulk to Fleming, suppliers avoid hiring a large sales force, yet they still get their products into stores nationwide.

- *Producer to wholesaler to wholesaler to retailer to consumer:* In some industries, distribution channels include multiple wholesaling intermediaries. Two such industries are agricultural products such as canned and frozen foods and petroleum products like gasoline and heating oil. In these industries, two separate levels of wholesaling intermediaries are used to divide, sort, and distribute bulky items.

- *Producer to wholesaler to business user:* Some B2B products flow through indirect channels from producer to wholesaler to user. A producer that finds a business customer through an Internet business exchange is following this channel. In the marketplace for filtration goods and services, manufacturers can provide information to a service called eFiltration, which links buyers and sellers of these products. Rather than scheduling an appointment with each manufacturer's sales representative, customers can look up information online and then choose a supplier through this Web-based service.[8]

Later sections of this chapter take a closer look at the roles that wholesalers and retailers play in the distribution chain. The next section discusses reasons why producers choose to involve marketing intermediaries in their distribution networks.

Functions of Marketing Intermediaries

If a producer of goods or services could work through the shortest and simplest distribution channel by selling directly to consumers or business users, why would its managers involve marketing intermediaries? You might think that adding intermediaries to the distribution process must add to the final cost of products, but more often than not, this choice actually lowers consumer prices. Most intermediaries perform functions essential to efficient marketing. Without them, many of the products people want and need would never reach end users. Marketing intermediaries like wholesalers and retailers often add significant value to a good or service as it moves through the distribution channel. They do so by creating utility, providing services, and reducing costs.

Creating Utility   Marketing intermediaries add utility to the distribution chain by smoothing the distribution process. They help ensure that products are available for sale when and where customers want to purchase them. They also simplify exchanges of ownership required to complete transactions.

If you want something warm to eat on a cold winter night, you don't call up the Campbell Soup Co. and ask them to sell you a can of chicken noodle soup. Instead, you go to the nearest grocery store, where you find not only chicken noodle soup, but also the ingredients for tomorrow's meals, plus paper goods and toiletries. The grocery store has created utility for you in several ways. First, it makes the food you want available in a convenient location. Second, it saves you from having to personally contact and pay the manufacturer for each product you need. Finally, the store gives you a choice of paying with cash, check, credit card, or debit card.

Another way that intermediaries offer buyers utility is by providing information. They organize products on store shelves, in catalogs, or Web pages so customers can compare competing brands or varieties. They may provide access to other information as well. Stores that sell music often provide kiosks at which shoppers can scan a bar code from a CD to listen to clips from the recording. At the more sophisticated end of this technology, the Star Navigator lets the customer scan the CD, watch videos of the artist, and look for special offers on the artist's music.[9] In the automobile industry, the National Automobile Dealers Association has developed a Web site that not only provides links to participating auto dealers but also offers inventory information, invoice prices for new cars, and links to information about trade-in values. By providing valuable information and links to dealers, the site hopes to compete with alternatives like AutoNation, which also links consumers and car dealers.[10]

Providing Services   Marketing intermediaries often specialize in certain functions, so they can perform these activities more efficiently than producers or the final customers could on their own. As Figure 15.3 shows, intermediaries provide services such as buying, selling, storing, and transporting products.

UPS is widely known for its package delivery via its familiar brown trucks. However, the company provides many other services as well. The UPS Web site offers information, including the ability to track the delivery status of parcels. The company

FIGURE 15.3
Services Performed by Marketing Intermediaries

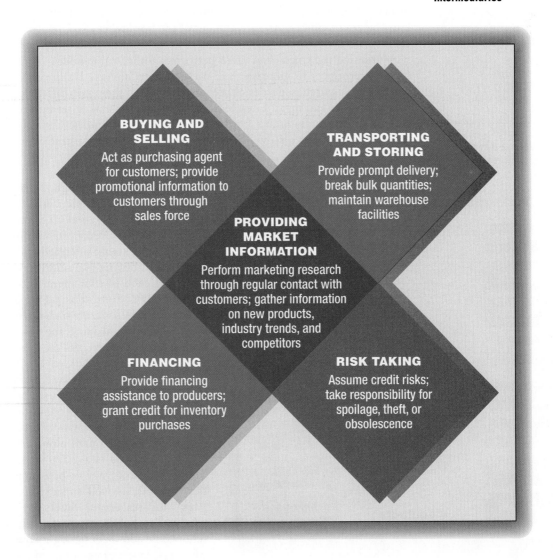

BUYING AND SELLING
Act as purchasing agent for customers; provide promotional information to customers through sales force

TRANSPORTING AND STORING
Provide prompt delivery; break bulk quantities; maintain warehouse facilities

PROVIDING MARKET INFORMATION
Perform marketing research through regular contact with customers; gather information on new products, industry trends, and competitors

FINANCING
Provide financing assistance to producers; grant credit for inventory purchases

RISK TAKING
Assume credit risks; take responsibility for spoilage, theft, or obsolescence

also provides air transportation, as well as the services of its UPS Logistics Group and UPS Capital Corp. UPS Logistics sets up systems for computerized route planning, operates fleets of trucks to deliver a customer's goods, and even handles warehousing and order fulfillment, delivering products just as the customer needs them. The UPS Logistics schedule for delivering materials to Papa John's Pizza stores even takes into account the amount the pizza dough rises while in the truck. For Nike, UPS Logistics maintains inventory and fills orders from the Nike Web site. UPS Capital handles inventory financing. For Gateway, UPS collects payments from the PC maker's customers and deposits the payments into Gateway's bank account. This service enables Gateway to fill cash-on-delivery orders.[11]

Similarly, most of the small, independent grocery stores that buy inventory from wholesalers like Fleming Cos. cannot afford to own and operate their own warehouses. However, their survival depends on having the right items on their shelves. Fleming performs an important function for its customers by handling their transportation and storage needs.

Marketing intermediaries also provide useful information to other channel members. Since wholesalers typically cover large geographic areas, they can supply retail customers with information regarding consumer acceptance of new products, successful promotions by retailers in other cities, and details about new-product introductions. Supermarkets routinely gather data from frequent-shopper cards and checkout scanners, and they may make the data available to suppliers and marketing research firms. When AutoNation sends a lead to one of its dealers, it tells the dealer all the brands of cars the customer has explored. This arms the dealers with knowledge to point out the advantages of the brands they sell, relative to competing cars.[12]

Marketing intermediaries often perform another value-added function by transforming products to increase their usefulness to buyers. Traditionally, retail meat markets have purchased sides of beef and converted them into different cuts of steak, roasts, and ground meat. Intermediaries also often install or set up products. Furniture retailers usually attach hardware such as door handles. Circuit City not only sells car stereos but also will install them and then demonstrate how to use their features.

FIGURE 15.4
Reducing Transactions through Marketing Intermediaries

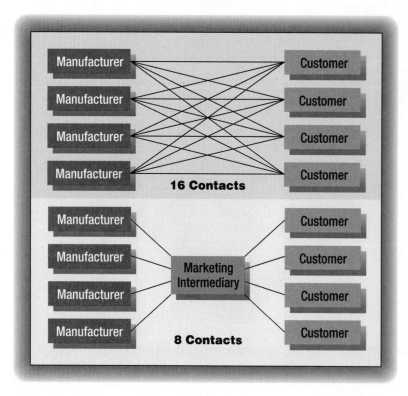

Reducing Costs   Although the costs that marketing intermediaries incur may seem likely to add to the cost of a final product, the opposite often results. By representing numerous producers, a marketing intermediary actually cuts the costs of buying and selling. As Figure 15.4 shows, if each of four manufacturers were to sell directly to four consumers, it would have to complete 16 separate transactions. Adding a marketing intermediary, such as a retailer, to the exchange process cuts the number of necessary transactions to 8.

Often, marketing intermediaries reduce the costs of items that their customers buy from them. If they buy in large quantities, intermediaries may qualify for quantity discounts, which can allow them to pass along cost savings to customers. Sysco is a giant wholesaler to the food-service industry. It buys massive quantities of food, as well as supplies like "doggy bags" for restaurant diners, and sells these products to hotels, restaurants, hospitals, and schools. Besides negotiating low prices from its suppliers, Sysco offers a line of foods under its own private brand. Customers enjoy a share in the savings that come from skipping the advertising needed to support a big consumer brand.[13]

In the health care industry, intermediaries are developing Web-based services to deliver similar efficiencies. Traditionally, hospital purchasing has been high on bureaucracy and low on efficiency. Materials management departments receive requisitions from employees and pore through various suppliers' catalogs, looking for the best price. Services such as Broadlane and empactHealth.com have been setting up extranets so that hospitals can consolidate orders, transmit them electronically, and get the supplier's best price. These intermediaries hope the data they gather from their clients will enable them to help hospitals establish more efficient purchasing schedules and select the products that offer the best value.[14]

WHOLESALING

As many of the preceding examples show, wholesalers play crucial roles in the distribution channels for many goods, particularly consumer goods. As defined earlier, wholesalers are marketing intermediaries that sell to retailers, business purchasers, and other wholesalers—but not directly to ultimate consumers. This section of the chapter focuses on the different types of wholesaling intermediaries and their role in moving goods from producer to consumer.

Wholesaling intermediaries can be classified on the basis of ownership. *Ownership* refers to the person or company that owns and operates the wholesaling function. Manufacturers own or operate some wholesaling operations, retailers own others, and still others operate as independent organizations. Figure 15.5 outlines the various ownership categories of wholesaling intermediaries.

Manufacturer-Owned Wholesaling Intermediaries

A manufacturer's marketing manager may decide to distribute goods directly through company-owned facilities to maintain control of distribution or customer service. Firms operate two main types of manufacturer-owned wholesaling intermediaries: sales branches and sales offices.

Sales branches stock the products they distribute and fill orders from their inventories. In addition to carrying inventory, sales branches provide offices for sales representatives. Sales branches are common in the chemical, petroleum products, motor vehicle, and machine and equipment industries. Snap-on Tools uses a mobile version of the sales branch. Its franchise owners drive white trucks stocked with the firm's premium tools, selling out of the back of the truck to auto dealers, service stations, and other businesses where mechanics work.[15]

A *sales office* is exactly what the name implies, an office for a producer's salespeople, who represent its products in a particular territory. Manufacturers set up sales offices in various regions to support local selling efforts and improve customer service. Some kitchen and bath fixture manufacturers maintain showrooms to display their products. Builders and decorators can visit these showrooms to see how the items would look in place. Unlike sales branches, however, sales offices

FIGURE 15.5
Categories of Wholesaling Intermediaries

do not store or warehouse any inventory. When a customer orders a product at a showroom or other sales office, the merchandise is delivered from a separate warehouse.

Independent Wholesaling Intermediaries

An independent wholesaling intermediary is a profit-seeking business that represents a number of different manufacturers and makes sales calls to retailers, manufacturers, and other business accounts. These intermediaries account for about two-thirds of all wholesale trade. Independent wholesalers are classified as either merchant wholesalers or agents and brokers, depending on whether they take title to the products they handle.

Merchant wholesalers are independently owned wholesaling intermediaries that take title to the goods they handle. Within this category, a *full-function merchant wholesaler* provides a complete assortment of services for retailers or industrial buyers. At one time, as the buying power of giant specialty stores like Staples and Toys 'R' Us was rapidly growing, it looked as if retailers no longer would need merchant wholesalers. However, United Stationers is proving that prediction wrong—at least in the office-supplies market. The company has helped small retailers maintain their presence in the market by stocking its warehouses with 35,000 products. United Stationers will ship products ranging from computer keyboards to colored pencils to a store the same day the order comes in. For customers in a hurry, a store can also request United Stationers to package items and ship them directly to the customer with the store's label attached. In addition, because the big chains like Staples and Office Depot keep costs down by carrying a limited product mix, United Stationers helps them fill orders for less-common items. About 10 percent of the superstores' sales—and 60 percent of their items—come from United Stationers. The company also sells to online retailers of office products.[16]

A subtype of full-function merchant wholesaler is a *rack jobber*. A rack jobber stocks, displays, and services particular retail products, such as paperback books or greeting cards in a drugstore or supermarket. Usually the retailer receives a commission based on actual sales as payment for providing merchandise space to a rack jobber.

A *limited-function merchant wholesaler* also takes legal title to the products it handles, but it provides fewer services to the retailers to which it sells. Some limited-function merchant wholesalers only warehouse products but do not offer delivery service. Others warehouse and deliver products but provide no financing.

One example of a limited-function merchant wholesaler is a *drop shipper*. Drop shippers operate in such industries as coal and lumber, characterized by bulky products for which no single producer can provide a complete assortment. They give access to many related goods by contacting numerous producers and negotiating the best possible prices. Due to the burden of shipping and handling such products, cost considerations call for producers to ship them directly to the drop shipper's customers.

Along with these categories of merchant wholesalers, a second group of independent wholesaling intermediaries consists of *agents* and *brokers*. They may or may not take possession of the goods they handle, but they never take title. They normally perform fewer services than merchant wholesalers offer, working mainly to bring buyers and sellers together. Two similar intermediaries familiar to many people are stockbrokers and real estate agents. Since they represent ultimate consumers, both are considered retailers. However, they perform functions similar to those of agents and brokers at the wholesale level, since they do not take possession or title to sellers' property. They create time and ownership utility for both buyer and seller by helping to carry out transactions.

Manufacturers' agents are another important type of wholesaling intermediary. Also known as *manufacturers' reps* or *independent reps,* they act as independent sales forces by representing manufacturers of related, but noncompeting, products.

They receive commissions based on percentages of the sales they make.

Other agent wholesaling intermediaries include sales agents, which typically represent larger territories than those of manufacturers' agents, and commission merchants, which sell agricultural products for farmers. A final type, auction houses, allow potential buyers to inspect merchandise prior to bidding on it. Art galleries and antique dealers place bids on items of interest, and the auction company earns compensation based on the sales prices.

Retailer-Owned Cooperatives and Buying Offices

Retailers sometimes band together to form their own wholesaling organizations. Such an organization can take the form of either a buying group or a cooperative. The participating retailers set up the new operation to reduce costs or to provide some special service that is not readily available in the marketplace. To achieve cost savings through quantity purchases, independent retailers may form a buying group that negotiates bulk sales with manufacturers. In a cooperative, an independent group of retailers may decide to band together to share functions like shipping or warehousing.

Each of the 10,500 True Value hardware stores is an independent retailer. To compete against such corporate giants as Home Depot and Lowe's, these small retailers have banded together under the name *True Value* and formed a cooperative buying group, TruServ. By combining their orders from hardware manufacturers, the True Value owners can negotiate better prices than they would pay individually, which in turn helps them offer competitive prices to consumers. In addition, TruServ operates distribution and warehousing centers that support the True Value stores, providing additional savings.[17]

ewolfs.com
Online Auctioneers
www.ewolfs.com 800-526-1991 216-575-9653

Some auctioneers combine cost reduction with the ability to reach a large, geographically separated market by operating online. ewolfs.com can avoid the expense of a major showroom by conducting auctions on its Web site. Should successful bids be made by wealthy private collectors, the transaction would be considered a retail sale. Purchases by retail art dealers and museums represent wholesale transactions.

RETAILING

Retailers are the final elements of the distribution channel. Almost $3 trillion worth of goods are sold through retailers in the United States each year. Each of the five largest U.S.-based retailers—Wal-Mart, Kroger, Sears, Home Depot, and Albertson's—generates over $35 billion in sales every year.[18] Since retailers are often the only channel members that deal directly with consumers, they must remain constantly alert to consumer needs. They must also keep pace with the developments in the fast-changing business environment. As Chapter 4 explains, some retailers are also expanding internationally, opening vast new opportunities beyond this nation's borders. This section takes a closer look at retailing and the critical roles that retailers play in the distribution channel.

THEY SAID IT

"I never knew an auctioneer to lie, unless it was absolutely necessary."

JOSH BILLINGS (1818–1885)
AMERICAN HUMORIST

Wheel of Retailing

Retailers never operate in a static environment. Over time, competitive strategies change, new types of retailers emerge, and marketing institutions unable or unwilling to respond to changing markets and new customer expectations go out of

The World Bids Goodbye to Montgomery Ward

In the first decade of the 21st century, we take it for granted. We can pick up a phone and order just about anything we want and have it delivered to our door. We can log on to our computer and do the same. But 100 years ago, no one thought of making a purchase without actually setting foot in a store. That is, until a salesman named Aaron Montgomery Ward came up with a novel idea: ordering from a mail-order catalog. Households across rural America loved the fact that they did not have to travel difficult miles to make their purchases, and a new trend was born.

For its first half century, Montgomery Ward conducted its business exclusively through its catalog. But in the 1920s, the Chicago-based company began to build retail stores around the Chicago area. For the next 80 years, customers enjoyed the selection of general merchandise offered by Ward's through its catalog and its 250 stores. But then the environment began to change. Competitors on both ends of the price scale began to eat away at Ward's market. The company went through a reorganization and remodeled many of its stores, updating lighting and other atmospherics, as well as the merchandise itself. But disappointing sales during one final Christmas season spelled the end of an era. Montgomery Ward could no longer hold on, and in 2001 the country's first mail-order business began the sad process of closing its pages—and doors—forever.

Response to Ward's closing was mixed from shoppers to employees to suppliers. "It's terrible," said one shopper. "A lot of employees will lose their jobs. This hurts the economy." Twenty-eight thousand people lost jobs in the closing. "I think it's great," said Bruce Provo, general manager of a retail plaza in which a Montgomery Ward store was located. "There's a wonderful opportunity for someone [else to take over the space]. We just hope it's the right people. We hope it's Kohl's or Target." Appliance supplier Maytag didn't seem worried at all about lost business. "Other retailers will pick up that business," remarked Maytag spokesperson James Powell. "It will have no significant impact on our business."

Although Montgomery Ward is gone, the company has left a legacy that affects almost every retailer in business today. If Aaron Montgomery Ward hadn't been able to convince consumers that buying products by mail was a safe, convenient way to make purchases, Amazon.com might not be in existence today. Although the next generation of consumers may not even recognize the name Montgomery Ward, "it's a name many people are still in love with because of memories of Ward's in their childhood," says George Rosenbaum, chief executive of a Chicago consumer research firm. "The only good thing about [the closing] is that it happened after Christmas."

QUESTIONS FOR CRITICAL THINKING

1. Using Figure 15.6, describe the history of Montgomery Ward in terms of the wheel of retailing.
2. Do you think that adding an online component to its retailing strategy might have saved Montgomery Ward? Why or why not?

Sources: "An Open Letter to Wards Customers," Wards corporate Web site, **www.wards.com,** accessed March 7, 2001; Susan Chandler, "28,000 to Lose Jobs as Wards Gives Up," *Chicago Tribune,* December 29, 2000, pp. 1, 11; Karen Mellen and Maura Kelly, "Wards' End Brings Little Grief to Area Business, Civic Leaders," *Chicago Tribune,* December 29, 2000, pp. B1, B4.

business—as illustrated by the recent demise of Montgomery Ward described in the "Business Hits and Misses" box. The wheel of retailing is a theory intended to explain how and why these changes occur. According to this theory, new types of retailers enter the market and gain a competitive foothold by offering low prices and limited services. Once they become established, these companies gradually add more services, forcing them to raise prices and making them vulnerable to newer retailing models with appeals based on low prices.

As Figure 15.6 shows, most major retailing developments appear to fit the wheel pattern. The low-price/limited-service position characterized early department stores, catalog retailers, supermarkets, discount stores, and—most recently—Internet retailers and giant "big-box stores," such as PetsMart, Barnes & Noble, and Staples. Most of these retailers have raised price levels gradually as they added new services. Corner grocery stores gave way to supermarkets, then to warehouse clubs like Costco or discount supermarkets like Cub Foods. Department stores lost market share to discount clothing retailers like Target and T. J. Maxx.

For a recent example, consider how bookselling has changed since the 1980s. First, independent bookstores lost business to giant chains like Barnes & Noble, Books-A-Million, and Borders Books. These chains generated sales volumes that allowed them to buy in bulk and offer discounts to customers. Initially, they lacked many of the personalized services that small, local bookstores provided. But eventually, they began to compete by adding services like comfortable reading areas, designer coffees, poetry-reading sessions, and book signings by authors.

Then Amazon.com entered the market in a totally new way, selling books on the Internet at cut-rate prices. Amazon.com minimized costs by relying on book wholesalers to fill its orders. Soon, bricks-and-mortar retailers like Barnes & Noble set up their own Web sites to sell books. To remain competitive, Amazon.com increased its inventory to stretch the selection it offered. This change increased the expenses involved in cataloging, promoting, and shipping the extra selections on its Web site, and Amazon.com's prices have crept upward. Even with these increases, Amazon.com has so far generated losses, not profits. Among booksellers, the wheel of retailing may turn again, forcing Amazon.com to raise prices or look for more innovative ways to meet competition. One possibility is greater customer service, like the real-time customer assistance already available in chat rooms at the sites of Lands' End and Eddie Bauer.

Another type of retailer for which the wheel of retailing has been turning lately consists of stores known as *category killers.* These big specialty retailers use a strategy that involves buying a specialized product mix, such as office supplies or shoes, in such large volume that they can compete with low prices. A decade ago, the category-killer strategy looked invincible. Inspired by Wal-Mart's success in negotiating low prices from suppliers, retailers moved into selling low-priced toys (Toys 'R' Us), home improvement products (Home Depot and Lowe's), shoes (Foot Locker and Athlete's Foot), electronics (Best-Buy and Circuit City), and many other specialties. Recently, however, the strategy has come into question. Shoppers began finding better prices at warehouse clubs and on the Internet, and fewer consumers were willing to drive to a store where they could find just one category of goods. At Toys 'R' Us, market share has fallen below that of Wal-Mart, even as the company struggles to improve customer service and build toy-buyer traffic to its Web site.

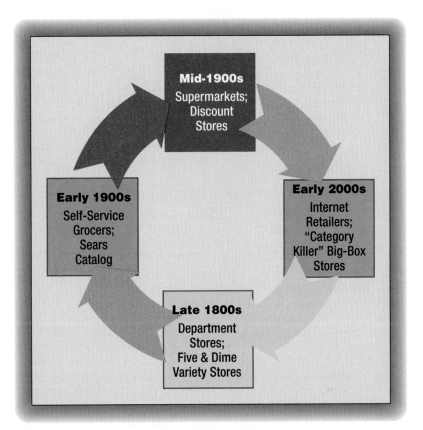

FIGURE 15.6
The Wheel of Retailing

Types of Retailers

The wheel of retailing suggests many different types of retailers. One way to look at retailers is to group them into two broad categories: nonstore retailers and store retailers. Nonstore retailers do not sell through physical storefronts; instead, they contact customers and resell goods through other methods. Examples include catalog houses and Internet retailers. Store retailers maintain traditional, physical storefronts. This category includes convenience stores, department stores, factory outlets, and warehouse clubs. Today, however, many retailers span both categories. JCPenney sells merchandise in its stores, through its catalog, and over its Internet site. Some manufacturers also are retailers. Levi Strauss has operated its own retail outlets in addition to selling through independent outlets.

Nonstore Retailers

Although most retail transactions occur in stores, nonstore retailing serves as an important marketing outlet

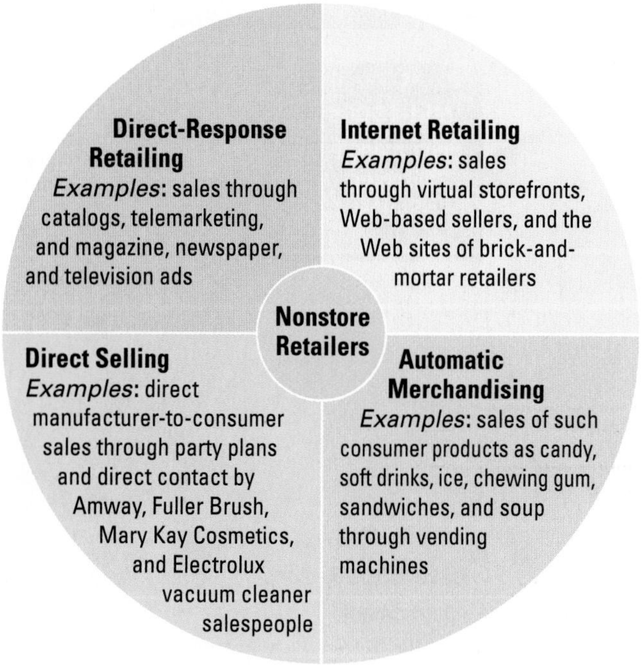

Direct-Response Retailing
Examples: sales through catalogs, telemarketing, and magazine, newspaper, and television ads

Internet Retailing
Examples: sales through virtual storefronts, Web-based sellers, and the Web sites of brick-and-mortar retailers

Nonstore Retailers

Direct Selling
Examples: direct manufacturer-to-consumer sales through party plans and direct contact by Amway, Fuller Brush, Mary Kay Cosmetics, and Electrolux vacuum cleaner salespeople

Automatic Merchandising
Examples: sales of such consumer products as candy, soft drinks, ice, chewing gum, sandwiches, and soup through vending machines

FIGURE 15.7
Types of Nonstore Retailing

for many products. In fact, nonstore retailers currently account for almost $80 billion in sales, and that number is expected to continue to grow.[19] As Figure 15.7 shows, nonstore retailing includes direct-response retailing, Internet retailing, automatic merchandising, and direct selling.

Direct-Response Retailing   Direct-response retailing takes many forms. Retailers reach prospective customers through catalogs, telemarketing, and even magazine, newspaper, and television ads. Every year, billions of catalogs are mailed to consumers and businesses, and almost 200 million adults spend more than $50 billion on merchandise sold through these outlets.[20] The biggest categories of products sold through catalogs are clothing and home furnishings. Another direct-selling vehicle is sales through home-shopping networks.

Direct-response customers can order merchandise by mail, telephone, computer, and fax machine, as well as by visiting the mail-order desk in a retail store. After the customer places an order, the retailer ships the merchandise to the customer's home or to a local store for pickup.

One of the most important reasons customers choose direct-response retailers is convenience. Ordering goods from catalogs can save time and avoid the hassles associated with traveling to retail stores and waiting in line to complete a purchase. Another important motivation for shoppers to buy through direct-response retailers is superior customer service. These retailers may provide toll-free numbers and liberal return policies to satisfy customer expectations.

Internet Retailing   A growing number of Internet-based retailers sell directly to customers via sites on the World Wide Web and online services such as the Shop@AOL section of America Online. Many of these firms operate from virtual storefronts, maintaining little or no inventory. Instead, they order directly from vendors to fill customer orders received via electronic communications.

As discussed in Chapter 7, Internet retailing has grown rapidly. Tens of thousands of retailers have set up shop online, with total sales surpassing $20 billion a year. Despite income shortfalls that led to the widely publicized demise of several large dot.coms, Internet sales to consumers are forecasted to exceed $140 billion within the next few years. The number of online shoppers is growing, too. The newest customers are slower to adopt computer technology, and serving this broader consumer segment challenges Internet retailers to make their Web sites easier to use. Early adopters of the Internet might have been willing to accept slow downloads and some mistakes and confusion in order processing, but mainstream consumers are less forgiving.[21]

Direct-response retailers such as Lands' End, Harry & David, and Lillian Vernon have expanded from printed catalogs to Web sites. As with stores, these companies offer consumers trusted brand names and experience in providing customer service. In contrast, pure-play dot.coms spend so much to create name recognition and brand loyalty that the cost of acquiring each new customer may far exceed what that customer spends.

The Internet's usefulness for sharing information simplifies the work of making price comparisons and buying at the lowest available price. Search engines can provide lists of product information, including many sites offering the same product. The more powerful *shopping bots* are software packages that consumers can use to search the Internet to make price comparisons for a specified product. Consumers who use shopping bots can quickly find the lowest-price retailer from a global set of

If the Shoe Fits, Nordstrom Will Deliver It to Your Door

Clicks and Mortar

Background. Need a new pair of shoes? Forget about need—just want a new pair of shoes? You don't have to hoof it to your nearest shoe store. Instead, Nordstrom wants you to cozy up to your computer and click onto its Web site, which it now bills as "the world's biggest shoe store."

What Happened? In the final months of the 20th century, suffering from nearly flat growth—the company earned only 7 percent more than it had earned five years earlier—Nordstrom knew it had to do something to step up business. The retail chain was competing not only with specialty stores but also with mainstream giants such as Macy's and Target. In addition, marketers discovered that Nordstrom's core customers were older women who tend to spend more on jewelry and other items than on the clothes that had become Nordstrom's main focus. So the retailer decided on a new path: shoes. Led by Daniel Nordstrom, great-grandson of the company's founder, Nordstrom launched a $17 million advertising campaign to promote its Web site as "the world's biggest shoe store." The online channel for selling wasn't without precedent. Nordstrom already had a Web site for online shoppers, in addition to its successful catalog. And consumers had already proved that mail order had become the "fastest-growing channel of shoe distribution," according to one business writer.

The Response. Nordstrom made a huge commitment to its online channel, and consumers seem to like the results. Selection is a major feature of the site. Shoppers can choose from 20 million pairs of shoes from more than 60 manufacturers. Log on, and you'll find brands ranging from Aerosoles to Andre Assous, Skechers to Steve Madden, Vaneli to Via Spiga. You can shop by size, ranging from AAAA to EEEE. Or you can shop by style—boots, pumps, loafers, slides, slippers, or sandals. But Nordstrom doesn't hold all this inventory in its Iowa warehouse. Instead, it relies on other members of the distribution channel—mainly the manufacturers themselves—to fill many of the orders. In this way the company controls its costs.

Nordstrom had already been successfully selling shoes through its catalog for several years when it launched the new online shoe campaign. In fact, shoes have represented a higher percentage of sales through the catalog—and now the Web site—than they had in the Nordstrom stores. Nordstrom makes it easy for customers to combine shopping methods by allowing store clerks to click onto the Web site to find a certain shoe brand or size if the store doesn't have it and ship it to a customer at home. And customers can return any shoes bought over the Internet to one of the bricks-and-mortar stores, even selecting a new pair at the store if they choose to. Although shipping charges tend to be a bit high—$14.95 a pair—Nordstrom encloses a self-addressed, prepaid envelope with each order for returns. All of these services, which help get the shoes to and from customers, help create a positive shopping experience.

Today and Counting. Nordstrom wants to leave the biggest footprint in the online shopping industry. "If we don't do this, somebody will do it for us," says Daniel Nordstrom. To maintain success, the company will have to manage its relationships with channel members efficiently, particularly the shoe manufacturers. If they can do so, they can maintain lower costs and pass those savings on to customers. "We'll have the lowest prices out there," says Dan Nordstrom. It looks like they'll have the highest heels, too.

QUESTIONS FOR CRITICAL THINKING
1. Describe one or two additional steps that Nordstrom could take to combine its online and off-line selling efforts in order to strengthen its position as "the biggest shoe store in the world."
2. What steps can Nordstrom take to ensure cooperation among its channel members, particularly the shoe manufacturers?

Sources: Nordstrom Web site, **www.nordstrom.com**, accessed March 26, 2001; Beth Miller, "Nordstrom Unveils $15M Campaign for Online Shoes," Media Central, **www.mediacentral.com**, October 29, 2000.

---

retailers. In this environment, many Internet retailers have sacrificed profits in order to build market share—and some have gone out of business as a result.

In spite of the dot.com shakeout, four out of ten Internet retailers are recording profits.[22] Adding a large product mix to a Web site is less costly than making room on a store's shelves. Kmart's BlueLight.com product mix includes more items, including large-screen televisions, than Kmart carries in its stores. The Gap recently added maternity clothing to its Web site, giving consumers access to a line of clothes that many had requested, while maintaining the stores' emphasis on teens and young adults. For many kinds of retailers, online sales transactions can be more efficient than other kinds of order processing. American Airlines spends $12 to generate each paper ticket but just 10 cents to generate an e-ticket.[23]

Companies deciding to merge the best of the online and off-line worlds need to ensure that the channels cooperate. Nordstrom currently faces this challenge with its online shoe store, as described in the "Clicks and Mortar" box. When Toys 'R' Us was new to e-commerce, it didn't set up an arrangement for Internet shoppers to take returns to local stores. The company may have seen the Internet and store operations as separate, but consumers saw only the Toys 'R' Us name, and they were furious. The company quickly built connections between the customer service operations for the two channels. In contrast, Tupperware Corp. planned from the beginning for the relationship between direct selling and its Web site. The site asks shoppers to name the salesperson who referred them, so that it can direct commission payments to that salesperson. For customers who found the site without a salesperson, the company divides the commissions among all its distributors. In this way, Tupperware gains sales support for the Web site while the Web site contributes to company sales—and to salespeople's earnings.[24]

Automatic Merchandising   Another retailing method for some consumer goods is automatic merchandising through vending machines. Candy, soft drinks, ice, chewing gum, sandwiches, and soup are typical vending-machine items. Food and beverages account for 85 percent of all vending-machine sales. More than $1 out of every $10 spent on soft drinks goes into vending machines.[25] Automatic merchandising is especially appropriate for convenience products like snacks, newspapers, and postage stamps. They make these products available around the clock in convenient locations.

The ability of vending machines to accept payment in the form of paper currency or credit cards has greatly expanded automatic merchandising sales. Some movie theaters now place vending machines selling movie-inspired CDs in their lobbies. Paul Griff, president of Media Express, one of the companies that sells these machines, says, "We're courting the classic impulse buyer." So, too, is Joe Boxer Corp., which has introduced an Underwear to Go vending machine to sell its whimsical boxer shorts, cleverly packaged in aluminum cans.[26] Triton Systems offers an automated teller machine (ATM) for use in convenience stores that comes with an attachment for selling money orders, prepaid phone cards, or ski-lift tickets.

Direct Selling   In the final type of nonstore retailing, some manufacturers have salespeople offer their products directly to consumers, bypassing independent wholesalers and retailers. Well-known firms using the direct-selling approach include Kirby and Electrolux vacuum cleaners, Avon cosmetics, and Amway household products. Party-plan selling methods of companies like Tupperware, Mary Kay Cosmetics, and Home Interior also are forms of direct selling.

Store Retailers

Although nonstore retailing methods—especially direct-response retailing and Internet selling—are rapidly growing, more than 95 percent of all retail sales take place in retail stores. Store retailers range in size from tiny newsstands to multistory department stores. As Table 15.1 shows, they compete by varying the product lines they carry and the services they offer to their customers.

Wal-Mart not only is a corporate giant but operates giant stores. Along with its original discount stores, Wal-Mart operates hundreds of superstores, which bring groceries and general merchandise together in 180,000 square feet under one roof.

In contrast, specialty retailers like Stambaugh Hardware Co. offer thousands of products to hardware customers who don't want the athletic challenge of hiking past cabbages and toilet paper in a superstore to find a screwdriver or gallon of paint. Stambaugh's 18,000 products are far fewer even than Home Depot's mix, but the hardware specialist also has a special-product ordering computer kiosk set up in the store. Shoppers can select from many available items that are not on the shelves and then pick up the orders at their local store or have them delivered.[27]

Another retail competitive strategy involves developing unique bundles of services desired by target customers. Full-service retailers such as Bloomingdale's and Nordstrom have built global reputations for outstanding service. By contrast,

Table 15.1	Types of Retail Stores	
Store Type	**Description**	**Example**
Specialty store	Offers complete selection in a narrow line of merchandise	Shoe stores, jewelry stores, camera shops
Convenience store	Offers staple convenience goods, easily accessible locations, long store hours, and rapid checkouts	7-Eleven, Circle K, gasoline stations
Discount store	Offers wide selection of merchandise at low prices; off-price discounters offer designer or brand-name merchandise	Kmart, Target, Wal-Mart, T. J. Maxx, Marshall's
Warehouse club	Large, warehouse-style store selling food and general merchandise at discount prices to membership cardholders	Costco, Sam's Club, BJ's
Factory outlet	Manufacturer-owned store selling seconds, production overruns, or discontinued lines	Nike, Reebok, Dooney & Bourke, Liz Claiborne, Eddie Bauer
Supermarket	Large, self-service retailer offering a wide selection of food and nonfood merchandise	Safeway, Winn-Dixie, Kroger, Albertson's
Supercenter	Giant store offering food and general merchandise at discount prices	Super Kmart
Department store	Offers a wide variety of merchandise selections (furniture, cosmetics, housewares, clothing) and many customer services	Bloomingdale's, Dillard's, Marshall Field's, JCPenney, Sears

limited-service retailers such as supermarkets, discount houses, and off-price retailers charge lower prices by eliminating the costs of such traditional services as credit, extensive salesperson assistance, and delivery.

How Retailers Compete

Retailers compete with each other in many ways. Nonstore retailers focus on making the shopping experience as convenient as possible for consumers. Shoppers at the Nature Company enjoy maximum atmosphere in the form of soothing background music and hands-on access to such environmentally oriented products as telescopes, globes, and books.

Like manufacturers, every retailer must develop a marketing strategy based on solid goals and strategic plans. Successful retailers convey images that alert consumers to the stores' identities and the shopping experiences they provide. Convenience stores like 7-Eleven have established a retail image very different from that of Family Dollar. The 7-Eleven stores are small and conveniently located, and they offer customers an easy way to buy a cup of coffee, batteries, gasoline, or other items consumers frequently run out of. Deep-discount stores like Family Dollar, in contrast, appeal to shoppers looking for cheap merchandise. These customers will accept little or no service in exchange for prices below what other stores charge.

To create the desired retail image, all components of a retailer's strategy must complement each other. After identifying their target markets, retailers must choose merchandising, customer service, pricing, and location strategies that will attract customers in those market segments. Family Dollar stores keep prices down by locating in low-rent shopping centers and cramming as much merchandise as they can into limited space. They draw in customers by featuring brand-name basics like detergent and breakfast cereal at rock-bottom prices. The stores make money on their displays of low-priced but higher-margin extras, from greeting cards to holiday decorations to toys.[28]

Identifying a Target Market   The first step in developing a competitive retailing strategy is to select a target market. This choice requires careful evaluation of the size and profit potential of the chosen market segment and the current level of competition for the segment's business. In the previous example, Family Dollar targets consumers who are extremely price conscious, and convenience stores target consumers who want an easy way to repurchase items they buy frequently. Williams-Sonoma's stores, catalog, and Web site target consumers for whom cooking and entertaining are an important source of pleasure. All three channels feature beautiful displays or images coupled with information about how to use the products. The stores group merchandise by themes, and the Web site uses photographs to present comparable images, giving consumers entertainment ideas as well as products.

Target marketing plays a major role at Gap Inc., which operates Gap, Old Navy, and Banana Republic stores. Customer research conducted by the retailer revealed that a substantial percentage of the chain's regular customers had children and sufficient purchasing power to dress them in fashionable, high-quality garments. Separate sections within Gap outlets were created to feature babyGap and Gap Kids clothing lines.[29] Figure 15.8 shows a sample of the babyGap product line.

Product Strategy After identifying a target market, the retailer must develop a product strategy to determine the best mix of merchandise to carry to satisfy that market. Retail strategists must decide on the general product categories, product lines, and variety to offer. A retailer's product strategy should be a major component of a consistent choice of pricing, promotional, and customer service strategies to attract and retain target customers.

At Home Depot, customer demand is at the heart of product strategy. In fact, seven out of ten products carried in its stores were suggested by customers. Based on marketing research, the retailer stocks the product lines and brands that are most popular. Home Depot asked consumers which brands of water heaters they owned,

FIGURE 15.8
Clothing for the babyGap
Target Market

chunky cardigan $29.50

babyGap is warmth.

baby
GAP

Available at babygap.com (in the US only) and at any babyGap store. Call 1.800.GAPSTYLE for the nearest location.

and their number-three response was General Electric (GE). Undaunted by the fact that GE does not actually produce water heaters, the home-improvement products retailer arranged for the Rheem division of Paloma Industries to make water heaters bearing the GE name—GE receives royalty payments for use of its name. Home Depot carries the exclusive line, and consumers are able to find a brand they expect.[30]

Many retailers try to increase sales by diversifying their product lines, a practice known as **scrambled merchandising.** Originally, drugstores just sold medicines. Then they added soda fountains and newspapers. Today, their shelves are stocked with cameras, small appliances, greeting cards, cosmetics, toys, and even clothing. Supermarkets are changing as well, offering varied goods and services beyond traditional grocery products. On-site delicatessens and bakeries are now commonplace, as are ATMs and sales of postage stamps. Kroger supermarkets have perfume counters, and Fred Meyer stores sell jewelry and apparel in addition to food. Moving from general merchandise to include groceries, Target has begun opening SuperTarget superstores that carry groceries ranging from canned goods and dairy products to prepared meals for takeout. Apparently concerned that consumers do not associate the Target name with fresh food, the company is building separate entrances to the grocery sections and naming each of them Archer Farms Market. The expansion into scrambled merchandising does, however, trade on the company's reputation for introducing fashion into the realm of discount stores. Rather than emphasize low prices, SuperTarget's strategy is to provide high-quality merchandise like gourmet brands, natural foods, and takeout items prepared to order.[31]

In contrast to scrambled merchandising, other product strategies provide different benefits. A retailer can minimize prices by offering a limited selection. Another alternative is to offer great variety and expertise in a single product category. This has been the strategy of the so-called category killers, discussed earlier. On the Internet, many of the earliest businesses, such as Reel.com, offered narrow but deep product lines. In contrast, Amazon.com expanded quickly to carry a multitude of products. E-commerce is still too young for anyone to know whether enough consumers will support both product strategies at profitable price levels.

Customer Service Strategy   A retailer's customer service strategy focuses on attracting and retaining target customers to maximize sales and profits. Some stores offer customers a wide variety of services, such as gift wrapping, alterations, return privileges, interior design services, and delivery. Less obvious forms of customer service include ways to make shopping easy, fast, and convenient. Other stores offer only bare-bones customer service, stressing low prices instead. This range of strategies applies to sales of groceries. Consumers looking for convenience can order online through a service like WebVan or Peapod, which handles product selection, packing, and delivery. Or they can visit a supermarket, walking through the store and making their own selection. Shoppers looking for the lowest price can visit a discount supermarket like Cub Foods, where they not only assemble their orders but also bag their own groceries at the checkout counter.

Some retailers distinguish themselves by the level of service they provide. Customer service is an essential part of the strategy for upscale stores like Nordstrom and Marshall Field's. Harry & David, the catalog retailer mentioned earlier, also offers premium customer service to complement its premium fruit. The company's Web site may not be the flashiest, but it is designed to be helpful. Back in 1998, when most Web sites were bare bones, the Harry & David Web site provided real-time information on whether items were in stock. Linking inventory information with order placement was an important service for preventing disappointments. In addition, a *Fortune* columnist reported that a year after ordering Christmas gifts from Harry & David, he received a catalog with a list of the gifts he had ordered the year before, identifying each recipient. He checked the Web site, and there was the same list, along with boxes to click if he wanted to send the same orders again. The site made repeat ordering easier than shopping anywhere else.[32]

Pricing Strategy   Retailers are the channel members that determine the prices consumers pay for goods and services. They base their pricing decisions on the costs of purchasing products from other channel members and offering services to customers. Discount retailers, for example, usually provide limited services and buy in large volumes so they can offer merchandise at low prices.

Pricing can play a major role in consumers' perceptions of a retailer. So, a retailer's pricing strategy must support its overall marketing objectives and policies. During the first half of the 1990s, Pier 1 grew sales and profits by polishing its image. The company once had a reputation for selling a jumble of low-quality imports, but as Pier 1 raised the quality of its product mix, it became a more attractive source for household goods. Along with the revised product strategy came higher prices. However, consumers shopping in the higher price range became more interested in buying from specialty stores like Crate & Barrel and Pottery Barn. Consumers looking for bargains could find better deals at Cost Plus and other discount stores. As a result, Pier 1's sales suffered in the latter half of the 1990s. Pier 1 responded with price cuts and an advertising campaign reemphasizing the affordability of its merchandise.[33]

Location Strategy   A good location often makes the difference between success and failure in retailing. The location decision depends on the retailer's size, financial resources, product offerings, competition, and, of course, its target market. In addition to deciding whether to locate in a downtown business district, an outlying area, or a neighborhood shopping center, a retailer must also consider factors like the side of the street to choose to take advantage of traffic patterns. The visibility of a store's signage, parking availability, and complementary stores located nearby should also influence the choice of a retail location.

Retail stores quickly followed the country's shifting population from urban to suburban areas beginning in the 1950s. Department stores began to augment their traditional downtown sites by opening branches in suburban shopping centers. Other retailers focused exclusively on suburbanites for their business. A **planned shopping center** is a group of retail stores planned, coordinated, and marketed as a unit to shoppers in a geographic trade area. By providing single, convenient locations with free parking facilities, shopping centers have largely replaced downtown shopping in many urban areas. Each year, U.S. consumers spend over $1 trillion at the nation's 43,000 shopping centers. About 3 out of 5 shopping centers currently operating in the U.S. contain less than 100,000 square feet each.[34]

Planned shopping centers have evolved to meet changing consumer tastes. During the 1980s, consumers flocked to superregional malls larger than 800,000 square feet. The largest of these malls in North America is the West Edmonton Mall in Alberta, Canada, which boasts 5.5 million square feet. Besides shopping, these giants offer movie theaters, restaurants, and other forms of entertainment. More recently, the popularity of category killers gave rise to the development of *power centers,* which bring together category killer stores, usually near a regional or superregional mall. Also, consumers' desire for value inspired the building of hundreds of factory outlet centers, which include manufacturer-owned outlet stores and other discount stores.[35]

Today's time-pressed consumers are less inclined to spend a day at the mall. They increasingly look for more efficient ways to shop, including catalogs, Internet retailers, and one-stop shopping at large, free-standing stores like Wal-Mart. To lure more customers, shopping centers are recasting themselves as entertainment destinations. They offer shoppers art displays, carousel rides, and musical entertainment. Some industry leaders have taken entertainment to a higher level. One of the best known is the giant Mall of America in Bloomington, Minnesota, which features a seven-acre amusement park and an aquarium with viewing tunnels. Other shopping centers specifically look for tenants that offer exciting experiences. Outside Los Angeles at the Ontario Mills Mall, sporting goods retailer Vans operates a skate park and a track for off-road bicycling. Laurence C. Siegel, chief executive of the mall's developer, explains, "There are no Macy's at our centers. We want to create destination retail." Other stores favored by Mills include Guitar Showcase, where shoppers can watch instruments being built, and Bass Pro Shops, where customers can stroll past waterfalls and take classes in outdoor sports.[36]

As shopping centers and their retail clients scramble to become more exciting, others are concluding that any artificially manufactured theme will become stale eventually. They point to another future for retailing: a return to the old Main Streets of the city's center. The appeal of Main Street retailing is that a city can offer a unique sense of history and place that distinguishes it in consumers' minds. In addition, Main Street offers shoppers the ability to see neighbors and enjoy the area's cultural attractions. Cities from Newark, New Jersey, to San Diego, California, have been developing new cultural institutions in city centers to draw people back to the heart of the city.[37]

Promotional Strategy   A retailer designs advertisements and develops other promotions both to stimulate demand and to provide information, such as the store's location, merchandise offerings, prices, and hours. Nonstore retailers identify phone numbers and Web site addresses. Store retailers also set up in-store displays to attract shoppers' attention to featured merchandise. Store personnel also play a key role in a retailer's promotional strategy. Retail salespeople communicate the store's image and persuade shoppers to buy. They serve as sources of information about the store's goods and services. Many retailers have intensified their efforts to train and motivate salespeople to keep customers satisfied and increase the likelihood of repeat purchases.

In the introductory stage of e-commerce, promotional strategy was at the heart of Internet retailers' marketing efforts, as they raced each other to establish brand equity. Start-ups poured money into advertising aimed at building consumer recognition of their names and product mixes. As the industry entered its growth phase, promotional strategies for online retailing became more modest and better targeted. Online retailers scaled back big advertising campaigns and worked to build traffic through word of mouth and clever promotions. Some small specialty retailers discovered that they could find buyers by participating in Web auctions such as eBay.

Store Atmosphere   A successful retailer closely aligns its merchandising, pricing, and promotion strategies with *store atmospherics,* the physical characteristics of a store and its amenities, to influence consumer perceptions. Atmospherics begin with the store's exterior, which should help to draw customers inside. Many retailers use eye-catching architectural designs to gain customer attention and interest. Interior atmospheric elements include store layout, merchandise presentation, lighting, color, sounds, and cleanliness. These elements should support overall strategy by complementing the retailer's image, responding to customer interests, and encouraging shoppers to buy. Some retailers, including Hard Rock Cafe and the Seattle-based REI sporting-goods company, are widely known for using atmospherics to create an entertaining retail environment.

High-fashion—and highly priced—specialty retailer Van Cleef & Arpels uses eye-catching advertisements to remind high-income shoppers of the well-known chain's distinctive product offerings. In addition to its flagship store on New York's Fifth Avenue, shoppers can also visit Van Cleef & Arpels outlets in Beverly Hills and in two high-income Florida cities: Palm Beach and Bal Harbour.

J'Amy Owens and her company, the Retail Group, specialize in helping retail clients improve their businesses by overhauling their layout and atmospherics. Owens worked with Trient Partners, which operates a chain of Blockbuster video and DVD rental stores in the Pacific Northwest, when the company became concerned that one out of five shoppers left without renting a movie. Owens toured the stores and concluded that they were unfriendly, to say the least. Bright fluorescent lights unintentionally signaled that store management wanted to keep an eye on customers, and entering the blazing environment at the end of a long day was unpleasant.

Owens imagined the thoughts of the typical weary customer: "All I want is to find a video and go home and veg out. And they're putting me under these lights that show how old and tired I am and asking me to browse." Owens redesigned the Trient-owned stores to draw in customers with softer lighting, more subdued colors, and videos arranged into smaller sections. Video monitors on the walls play customized clips from classic films. Following their redesign, the Blockbuster stores enjoyed higher sales.[38]

Global Retailing

Fiercely competitive retailing in the U.S. has resulted in saturated markets that limit opportunities to increase sales and market share. This competitive environment has spurred an increasing number of retailers to look abroad for new markets. Toys 'R' Us, Wal-Mart, Pier 1 Imports, and Bath & Body Works are among the thousands of retailers opening outlets in Asia and Europe. U.S. catalog retailers are also going global for new business. Europe's relatively affluent, well-developed markets have attracted such catalogers as Eddie Bauer, Lillian Vernon, and L.L. Bean.

Foreign retailers are also joining the competitive battles in the U.S. market. Benetton, Food Lion, and IKEA are all foreign companies with U.S. outlets. The world's second-largest retailer, behind Wal-Mart, is Carrefour, a French supermarket and supercenter operator. Wal-Mart dominates North America; it has over 3,000 U.S. stores and a few hundred more in Canada and Mexico. But although Carrefour operates no stores north of the U.S.–Mexico border, its stores far outnumber Wal-Mart's in Europe, Asia, and Brazil. Most of the growth potential for retailers lies outside Wal-Mart's territory, posing a huge competitive challenge as the U.S. retailer expands overseas. Wal-Mart hopes to win with American-style friendliness and services such as acceptance of credit cards. Carrefour, for its part, sees its advantage in its international culture.[39]

Global retailing offers growing opportunities, but it also presents challenges. While many products travel easily among different countries and cultures, others require significant modifications to their original marketing strategies to attract and meet the needs and wants of international shoppers. Distribution channels themselves may differ from one country or region to another. In Japan, retailers exert strong control in their channels, often forcing concessions from manufacturers. Retailers selling personal computers have persuaded Japanese manufacturers to charge higher prices for computers sold through their Web sites than those sold through stores. This arrangement gives an advantage to non-Japanese direct sellers, like Dell and Gateway, which offer their best prices on the Web.[40]

DISTRIBUTION STRATEGY DECISIONS

Every firm faces several strategic decisions when choosing how to distribute its goods and services. The most basic are the selection of a specific distribution channel and the level of distribution intensity. Also, businesses need to pinpoint strategies to successfully manage their distribution channels and limit conflict between channel members.

Selecting a Distribution Channel

Firms can distribute goods and services through a wide variety of channels. In deciding which distribution channel is most efficient, business managers need to consider the factors shown in Figure 15.9: the market, the product, the producer, and the competition. These factors are often interrelated and may change over time.

Market Factors   A firm's most important consideration in choosing a distribution channel is the market segment it will serve. Ideally, a channel decision should reflect the needs and desires of the company's target customers. Who are the company's customers and where are they located? How often will they need to purchase the firm's products? To reach a target market with a small number of buyers or buyers concentrated in a geographic area, the most feasible alternative may be a direct channel. In contrast, if the firm must reach customers who are dispersed or who make frequent, small purchases, then the channel may need to incorporate marketing intermediaries to make goods available when and where customers want them.

MARKET FACTORS Market Size Business Buyers or Ultimate Consumers Order Size Frequency	**PRODUCT FACTORS** Perishability Product Complexity Product Costs Product-Service Purchase Requirements
PRODUCER FACTORS Management, Financial, and Marketing Resources Size of Current Product Line Need for Channel Control	**COMPETITIVE FACTORS** Availability of Independent Intermediaries with ability and willingness to perform required marketing functions

FIGURE 15.9
Factors Affecting Channel Choice

Product Factors   Product characteristics also affect a distribution channel strategy. In general, complex, expensive, custom-made, or perishable products require short distribution channels involving few intermediaries. On the other hand, standardized merchandise or products with low unit values usually pass through relatively long distribution channels. Levi's tried selling its regular lines of jeans through its Web site but quickly realized it was impractical to fill orders for a single pair of pants. In the words of a company spokesperson, "We decided that our retail partners, Macy's and JCPenney, were in a better position to sell our products to consumers." Now, the Levi's Web site concentrates on the sale of higher-priced custom-created jeans designed to fit the precise measurements of the online shopper.[41]

Product factors also influence choices of intermediaries in the distribution channels. Household furniture is awkward and expensive to transport to consumers. A piece of furniture often requires finishing touches like attachment of handles, and it is often heavy and must be handled carefully. To provide this level of service, most furniture producers prefer to work through retail stores. In contrast, Web site retailers have yet to establish their ability to provide a comparable level of service, and selling directly is inefficient for producers, who know it is not cost-effective to ship one couch here and one table there. Working through retail stores also permits the manufacturers to build relationships with the retailers and develop confidence that consumers will be satisfied with their purchases.[42]

Producer Factors   A firm's management, financial, and marketing resources also influence its choice of distribution channels. Financially strong manufacturers with broad product lines typically have their own sales representatives, warehouses, and credit departments to serve both retailers and consumers. Small firms usually depend on marketing intermediaries to perform these functions. Businesses without adequate financial resources may also have difficulty satisfying bulk orders from large wholesalers or retailers.

Despite these obstacles, start-up manufacturers sometimes use direct channels because they have difficulty persuading intermediaries to carry their products. Direct Focus launched production of an exercise bench called Bowflex, designed to be easier to store and use than competing products. Stores were not interested in the product, so the company's owners decided to offer it directly to consumers with television informercials featuring product benefits and stressing the company's toll-free telephone number. Anyone who inquires about the product but doesn't purchase one receives plenty of follow-up by mail, e-mail, and phone calls. With this distribution and promotion strategy, Bowflex sales skyrocketed from $5 million to $138 million over just five years. Knowing that fitness products tend to be fads, the company's strategy emphasizes new-product development coupled with its expertise in using direct channels.[43]

Competitive Factors Competitive performance is a key consideration when choosing a distribution channel. A producer loses customers when an intermediary fails to achieve effective promotion or delivery of its products. Levi's, as mentioned earlier, selected Macy's and JCPenney as channels for its products. So, the apparel company's success hinges in part on the success of Macy's and Penney's stores and Web sites.

Competitors' distribution channels also can influence decisions. E*Trade initially attracted a flood of investors to its online brokerage. However, deep-discount brokers like Ameritrade have cut into the company's business from price-conscious investors, and established brick-and-mortar brokerages have drawn away business from investors who decide they want more service. To compete, E*Trade has adapted its Internet-only nonstore strategy to include offices and ATMs. The company's first offices included one located in a SuperTarget store near Atlanta and another in a three-story building in New York City. The offices allow the company to offer confidence-building face-to-face advice, while the ATMs add an extra level of convenience for busy customers.[44]

Selecting Distribution Intensity

Another important strategic distribution decision sets the level of distribution intensity. *Distribution intensity* refers to the number of intermediaries or outlets through which a manufacturer distributes its goods. Only one Mercedes-Benz dealership may be operating in your immediate area, but you can find Coca-Cola sold everywhere—in supermarkets, convenience stores, gas stations, vending machines, and restaurants. Mercedes-Benz has chosen a different level of distribution intensity than used for Coca-Cola. In general, market coverage varies along a continuum with three different intensity levels:

1. **Intensive distribution** involves placing a firm's products in nearly every available outlet. Generally, intensive distribution suits low-priced, convenience goods such as chewing gum, newspapers, and soft drinks. This kind of market saturation requires cooperation by many intermediaries, including wholesalers and retailers, to achieve maximum market coverage.
2. **Selective distribution** is a strategy in which a manufacturer selects only a limited number of retailers to distribute its product lines. Selective distribution can reduce total marketing costs and establish strong working relationships within the distribution channel. Godiva ice cream, as shown in Figure 15.10, uses selective distribution. The bottom of the ad says, "Available wherever premium ice cream is sold."
3. **Exclusive distribution,** at the opposite end of the continuum from intensive distribution, involves limited market coverage by a single retailer or wholesaler in a specific geographic territory. The approach suits relatively expensive specialty products. Retailers are carefully selected to enhance the product's image in the market and to make certain that well-trained sales and service personnel will contribute to customer satisfaction. Although manufacturers may sacrifice some market coverage by granting an exclusive territory to a single intermediary, the decision usually pays off in developing and maintaining an image of quality and prestige.

Distribution intensity can affect a company's performance. Calvin Klein started out as a prestigious designer brand, but as the designer's product mix grew, its distribution became more intensive, and the brand lost its exclusive image. The company licensed to a manufacturer called Warnaco the rights to sell underwear and jeans under the Calvin Klein label. Initially, Warnaco distributed the products through upscale department stores, but it eventually built up revenues by moving unsold merchandise into warehouse clubs like Costco and BJ's. Warnaco also arranged to sell Calvin Klein products through JCPenney. Concerned that Penney's did not have the desired image, Calvin Klein claimed that Warnaco had reduced the brand's value. The designer is not alone. Other designer labels, including Gucci and Dior, have ended licensing deals and moved toward selling through their own boutiques—an exclusive strategy—rather than through department stores. To sell off slow-moving items without hurting their exclusive image, they operate their own factory-outlet stores as well.[45]

Managing Distribution Channels

After selecting the most appropriate distribution strategy and the degree of intensity, attention then turns to channel management. Manufacturers must develop and maintain relationships with wholesalers and retailers in their distribution channels to ensure that these intermediaries devote sufficient time and resources to selling and marketing their products. Several concerns arise in the course of distribution channel management. First, producers must carefully identify incentives to induce channel members to promote their products. Decisions about pricing, training, packaging, and other product support must complement a firm's overall distribution strategy to build positive relationships with channel members.

Not all channel members exert equal influence in the distribution chain. The **channel captain** is the dominant channel member, that is, the producer, wholesaler, or retailer with the most power in the distribution channel. The channel captain often controls many operations decisions throughout the channel and the role each channel member plays in the distribution process. Traditionally, channel captains have been producers of the products distributed by other firms or wholesalers with power over small manufacturers and tiny, localized retailers. While these relationships are common in some distribution networks, the growth of large retailers like Wal-Mart and Home Depot has increasingly moved power away from producers and wholesalers. In food retailing, mergers and acquisitions have consolidated the industry into about a dozen supermarket chains. So one chain's purchasing and promotional decisions have a huge impact on its suppliers.[46]

Consider also the power wielded by Costco. With more than $24 billion in annual sales through its warehouse stores and Web site, the company has enormous buying power. Costco carries far less variety than a supermarket, but it stocks an enormous quantity of each item. Producers wanting to place products on Costco shelves must meet the retailer's high standards for quality, as well as its packaging and pricing objectives. Costco had Crystal Geyser produce 32-bottle packs of its mineral water, bringing the unit cost down to a minimal 19 cents per bottle. Intensifying the pressure, Costco arranges for production of popular items

FOR PRECIOUS MOMENTS.
LIKE RIGHT AFTER DINNER.

GODIVA
Ice Cream
Chocolate Raspberry Truffle

SIX INDULGENT ICE CREAM FLAVORS
*White Chocolate Macadamia Toffee • Chocolate Hazelnut Truffle • Pecan Caramel Truffle
Belgian Dark Chocolate • Chocolate Raspberry Truffle • White Chocolate Raspberry
Available wherever premium ice cream is sold.*

FIGURE 15.10
Selective Distribution of Godiva Ice Cream

Picasso
Ceramic editions

Big plaid vase
1956
Large vase. 37.5 x 46.5 cm
White earthenware clay
25 numbered copies produced

Galerie Madoura

06220 Vallauris, France
Telephone: 04 93 64 66 39 - Fax: 04 93 64 93 14
www.madoura.com

The collector possessing the financial means and desire to own one of the 25 numbered copies of this Picasso vase is not going to be discouraged that it cannot be purchased anywhere in the U.S. In fact, buying this product will require a trip to Galerie Madoura in Vallauris, France. After all, it's a specialty good, and such products typically use a strategy featuring exclusive distribution.

THEY SAID IT

"There are no problems we cannot solve together, and very few we can solve by ourselves."

LYNDON B. JOHNSON (1908–1973)
36TH PRESIDENT OF THE U.S.

under its Kirkland private brand. Alongside six-packs of Kodak film, shoppers can find Kirkland film at one-third the price. This pressures national brands to keep their own prices down.[47]

Channel Conflict A distribution network functions smoothly only when all members cooperate in a well-organized effort to achieve maximum operating efficiencies. Because of the imbalance of power within many distribution channels, however, conflict often occurs between channel members, as described in the "Solving an Ethical Controversy" box. Finding ways to resolve channel conflict is an important distribution management task, one that usually falls to the channel captain.

Horizontal or vertical conflict can interfere with a distribution channel's effectiveness. In **horizontal channel conflict,** disagreements erupt among members at the same level in the distribution chain. Deere & Co. dealers became upset when Home Depot began carrying lawn mowers made by Deere, even though the mowers are sold under the brand name Scotts. Formerly, Deere sold its mowers and other lawn and farm equipment exclusively through its dealers.[48] Scrambled merchandising and the diversity of channels for groceries have generated horizontal conflict among supermarkets, discount stores, warehouse clubs, online retailers, and even drugstores. Participants in these channels compete to offer the lowest prices or the most services. Internet retailers offer home delivery and save money by not operating stores, but they must bear the extra cost of processing orders.[49]

Vertical channel conflict occurs between members at different levels in the distribution chain. Such problems may arise if retailers develop their own private brands to compete with producers' brands, or if producers establish their own retail stores or create mail-order operations that compete with retailers. Today's powerful retailers often have the advantage in such conflicts. Wal-Mart, for example, has introduced a variety of store brands. Recently, it began stocking Sam's American Choice laundry detergent, making the retailing giant a direct competitor with Procter & Gamble (P&G), one of its major suppliers. The Wal-Mart detergent package also uses a similar color to Tide's packaging, and it sells for a fraction of the price. Laundry detergent is an important product category because consumers buy it often, and they will make a trip to the store even if it is the only product they need. The conflict is also significant for P&G, because Tide is one of the household-products giant's most important revenue generators. With private labels controlling a growing share of the market, producers like P&G are pressured to keep costs down and innovate to keep ahead of the private-label competition.

Preventing vertical conflict is an even trickier challenge in the age of e-commerce. American Leather produces custom leather furniture and distributes it exclusively through dealers. Each dealer has a contract making it the exclusive retailer of a collection within a geographic area. American Leather refused to sell furniture over its own Web site to avoid alienating its network of dealers. This arrangement preserved harmony among dealers until some began setting up Web sites, giving them access to customers from other areas. American Leather discovered the problem when dealers

Do Slotting Fees Have a Place in the Private Enterprise System?

Imagine that you're an entrepreneur who has come up with a tasty new snack chip or a fruit drink with a can't-miss flavor. You've found a manufacturer for your new food, tested it with groups of consumers, and come up with a marketing plan. But when you take your product to the local supermarket chain, you hit a wall: the buyer wants to charge you a huge fee for placing your chip or drink on the shelf. This is called a *slotting fee,* and the charge has been around for a long time. Large manufacturers don't complain much because they have deeper pockets and their well-established goods give them bargaining power with stores. But smaller producers often have a tough time affording the fees, which can be as much as $25,000 per item, per store. Recently, the Federal Trade Commission (FTC) has begun to examine the practice of charging slotting fees.

Should supermarkets be allowed to charge slotting fees to food manufacturers?

PRO

1. Slotting fees actually transfer the cost of experimenting with a new food product from the retailer—the grocery store—to the manufacturer. The store shouldn't have to cover the costs associated with the risks of launching a new product.
2. Slotting fees help cover the cost of restocking the store shelves to accommodate new products.
3. If a product that is already on the shelves fails to sell, it is taking up costly space and does not generate revenue for the store. Slotting fees help cover this cost.

CON

1. Slotting fees discourage innovation because small food manufacturers cannot afford to take risks on new food products. They have already spent time and money to develop products, so they shouldn't be charged huge fees just to put them on the store shelves.
2. Slotting fees discourage competition. The FTC has investigated McCormick & Co., which produces 40 percent of the spices currently stocked on U.S. grocery store shelves, because the company may have offered to pay high slotting fees just to keep the spices of smaller competitors from reaching store shelves.
3. Some slotting fees are paid in cash, "under the table." Industry critics maintain that slotting fees for these products could be considered a form of bribery.

SUMMARY

Slotting fees can help spread out the costs associated with bringing food products to market, but they certainly cause channel conflict and can discourage small food manufacturers from entering the marketplace. When owners of small businesses become afraid to speak on the record for fear of retribution from large grocery chains—their bread and butter—it's time for the FTC to step forward and take a closer look at the practice.

Sources: "Suffering from Slotting Fees," *Sales & Marketing News,* Small Business Depot, **www.smallbusinessdepot.com,** accessed March 26, 2001; "Western Growers Association Testimony to U.S. Senate on Slotting Fees," Statement of David Moore, President, **www.wga.com,** accessed March 26, 2001; Chana R. Schoenberger, "Ca-Ching!" *Forbes,* June 12, 2000, pp. 84–85.

started complaining about online offers that promised price breaks to customers outside a dealer's region. Dealers were furious with American Leather, believing the manufacturer played a role in this new competition. American Leather responded by increasing its own Internet presence. It redesigned its Web site to provide more information about products, along with a service linking Web site visitors to the American Leather dealer nearest them. To support this effort, American Leather conducted advertising to draw consumers to its Web site, so that they would start there and go to the dealer in their region, rather than to the site of a dealer who might be in another part of the country. The company has also considered setting up the site to take orders, which would be processed through and credited to the customer's local dealer.[50]

LOGISTICS AND PHYSICAL DISTRIBUTION

A firm's choice of distribution channels creates the final link in the supply chain, the complete sequence of suppliers that contribute to creating and delivering a good or service to business users and final consumers. The supply chain begins when the raw materials used in

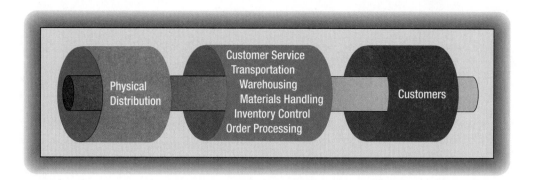

FIGURE 15.11
Elements of a Physical Distribution System

production are delivered to the manufacturer and continues with the actual production activities that create finished goods. Finally, the finished goods move through the producer's distribution channels to the end users.

Caterpillar, the world's biggest maker of construction equipment, produces both full-size and compact lines of equipment. A full-size bulldozer or backhoe might be used by a highway crew, while the smaller equipment serves the needs of landscapers and home contractors. The compact equipment is produced in factories in England and North Carolina. One of them, the skid-steer loader, is available with 52 interchangeable work tools, such as hammers, buckets, and pallet forks, produced in factories in the U.S., Britain, Finland, Hungary, and Mexico. To meet the demands of contractors, who may need equipment on short notice, the distribution system and the product design must be flexible. Caterpillar has more than 200 dealers in 90 countries. The company set up a system to move the equipment and tools from the factories to these dealers through its almost two dozen parts distribution centers (PDCs). Caterpillar turned to a team from a local university, which designed a computer model of the company's supply chain. The complex program established a plan for achieving optimum efficiency by sending tools from the factories to the company's PDCs in Illinois and Belgium. From there, based on estimates of demand, items are shipped to several other PDCs. Merchandise may travel by ship or by truck. This arrangement brings inventory close enough to the ultimate customers that the company only rarely has to use air freight for rapid delivery.[51]

The process of actually coordinating the flow of goods, services, and information among members of the supply chain is called **logistics.** Although the term originally referred to strategic movements of military troops and supplies, today it describes all of the business activities involved in actually managing movements through the supply chain with the ultimate goal of getting finished goods to customers. For some companies, such as the firm discussed in the "Clicks and Mortar" box, logistics is the very basis of their entire business.

Businesses spend billions every year on logistics management, looking for ways to add value throughout their supply chains. Logistics and supply chain management also gain importance as increasing numbers of firms enter global markets, expanding the need for efficient movement of goods, not just across the country, but around the world.

Physical Distribution

A major focus of logistics management is **physical distribution,** the activities aimed at efficiently moving finished goods from the production line to the consumer. Although some marketers use the terms *physical distribution* and *transportation* interchangeably, their meanings differ. As Figure 15.11 shows, physical distribution is a broader concept that includes transportation and numerous other elements that help to link buyers and sellers. An effectively managed physical distribution system can

How E-tailers Get the Goods to You—Fast

Background. In the real estate business there's a saying that all value is derived from "location, location, location." But in the delivery business, it's logistics, logistics, logistics. At the dawn of the previous century, homemakers ordered their groceries to be delivered daily from the local market. Bread, milk, and fresh vegetables came to the door via delivery boy. Today's Internet customers—businesses and individual consumers—want the same kind of service. They want to click on an item on their computer screen and have it delivered to their door within hours. Impossible? Not if an e-tailer has the right software, a fleet of delivery vehicles, and employees who are good at making quick decisions.

What Happened? Sameday.com does exactly what its name suggests: deliver goods the same day they are ordered, provided the orders are placed by 2 P.M. and are to be delivered within a certain metropolitan radius around Los Angeles, San Francisco, Chicago, or New York. If so, they will be delivered before 8 P.M. Sameday.com maintains a warehouse that stores client companies' toys, books, compact discs, clothing, software, household items, and gifts. Sameday.com CEO Alex Nesbitt says that consumers still want "the almost instant satisfaction they get by buying goods in person," even if they don't shop in person.

The Result. Sameday.com employees use two types of software to figure out which delivery trucks should follow which routes to deliver the most packages with the greatest efficiency. The first is Cheetah Software. As its name implies, the software determines the fastest, most efficient way to get the job done. A Cheetah wireless Internet tracking program stores each day's orders on a Net server to which drivers have constant access. ArcLogistics Route, a software program developed by ESRI, generates the actual itineraries that drivers follow, including figuring out exactly where a customer's home or business is located. But the Sameday.com dispatcher makes the final decision about where a driver should go. If a truck is stuck in rush-hour traffic, for instance, the dispatcher can choose to send a second truck to meet the first one at an off-ramp or cross street and transfer some of the merchandise.

Today and Counting. Are Sameday.com's clients happy with the distribution service they receive? Its revenues have been growing 200 percent a month, says Nesbitt. And the online grocer was recently named one of the 25 fastest growing technology companies of 2000 by the *Los Angeles Business Journal*. Apparently, technology and logistics make great partners in the e-commerce supply chain.

QUESTIONS FOR CRITICAL THINKING

1. Customer service is the basis on which Sameday.com has built not only its physical distribution system but its entire business. As competitors enter its market, what steps might the company take to ensure that it maintains its competitive edge?
2. Do you think that Sameday.com will be able to maintain its level of service as it expands both geographically and in terms of the types of goods it delivers? Why or why not? What specific challenges might it face?

Sources: "Sameday and US&T Launch First Fully Integrated Nationwide Rapid-Response Network," company press release, January 16, 2001; "Sameday Named One of the 25 Fastest Growing Technology Companies of 2000," company press release, October, 25, 2000; Stuart F. Brown, "How E-tailers Deliver within Hours," *Fortune*, May 29, 2000, pp. T210C–10M.

---

increase customer satisfaction by ensuring reliable movements of products through the supply chain.

A firm's physical distribution system begins by establishing guidelines for customer service. **Customer service standards** are the quantitative guidelines set by a firm to specify the quality of service it intends to provide for its customers. A firm's managers may decide that all customer orders will be processed within 24 hours after receipt in the company's telemarketing center.

Thomson Multimedia, the top U.S. maker of television sets, upgraded its customer service standards when retailers complained that it was underperforming in terms of keeping orders filled. Compared with competitors, Thomson was less likely to fill orders fully, accurately, and on time. Retailers had even begun the expensive practice of keeping a sizable "safety stock" on hand, in case Thomson failed to deliver. So the company invested in software that modeled its entire supply chain from suppliers through retailers and their customers. The supply chain software helped Thomson negotiate shorter lead times from suppliers and forecast consumer demand, so the manufacturer is now more flexible in responding to changes in demand. The software also helps Thomson plan deliveries so that its retail customers no longer run out of stock.[52]

BUSINESS DIRECTORY

➤ **logistics** *all business activities involved in managing movements of goods through the supply chain.*

Table 15.2 **Comparison of Transportation Modes**

Type of Carrier	Total Transportation Expenditures	Domestic Intercity Volume	Factor				
			Speed	Dependability in Meeting Schedules	Frequency of Shipments	Availability in Different Locations	Cost
Truck	74%	28%	Fast	High	High	Very high	High
Rail	13	37	Average	Average	Low	High	Medium
Water	6	15	Very slow	Average	Very low	Low	Very low
Air	4	<1	Very fast	High	Average	Average	Very high
Pipeline	3	19	Slow	High	High	Very low	Low

After setting customer service standards, managers continue to assemble and coordinate the other five elements of physical distribution in ways that achieve these service goals at the lowest possible cost. Considerations include transportation, warehousing, materials handling, inventory control, and order processing.

Transporting Goods The choice of which transportation option to ship products is best depends on several factors. Some products, such as perishable items, require relatively quick transportation to ensure satisfactory customer service. Cost is another important consideration, as transportation expenses can account for half of all distribution costs.

Physical distribution managers can choose among several different types of transportation modes. The five major alternatives are railroads, trucking carriers, water carriers, air freight carriers, and pipelines. Table 15.2 compares them according to the criteria of speed, reliability, shipment frequency, availability, and cost.

Railroads—The Nation's Transportation Backbone Although trucks overshadow all other transport modes based on dollar expenditures by users, railroads carry the heaviest burden as measured by ton-miles. A ton-mile indicates the shipping activity required to move 1 ton of freight 1 mile. Railroads carry over 1.3 trillion ton-miles of freight a year, in part because they offer the most efficient way to move bulky commodities over long distances. Industries that rely heavily on this transportation mode include manufacturers of coal, chemicals, grain, and wood products. Freight railroads carry 70 percent of domestically produced cars and trucks, and almost two-thirds of the coal transported in the U.S.[53]

A recent industry trend has brought extensive consolidation through mergers and acquisitions. These mergers have combined large railroad companies such as Burlington Northern and the Santa Fe line. Most recently, as shown in Figure 15.12, government-operated Conrail was acquired by Norfolk Southern.

Motor Carriers—The Flexible Giant The trucking industry has grown dramatically in recent decades. Today, three-quarters of the nation's transportation expenditures pay to move freight over the highway system. Trucking offers a relatively fast method of shipment and consistent service for both large and small volumes. Another significant advantage is flexibility. A truck carrier can operate over tens of thousands of miles of roads, whereas trains depend on rails, and planes require airports. Although a number of transcontinental highway carriers move goods from coast to coast, motor carriers are most efficient for shorter distances of 300 to 400 miles. Products most often transported by truck include clothing, furniture, fixtures, food, leather products, and machinery.

Air Freight—Fast but Expensive Air carriers are handling a small but significant volume of freight, as shippers seek to satisfy increased customer demand for fast delivery. The growth of international business operations has also contributed to the use of air transport. The cost of air transportation usually limits it to perishable and

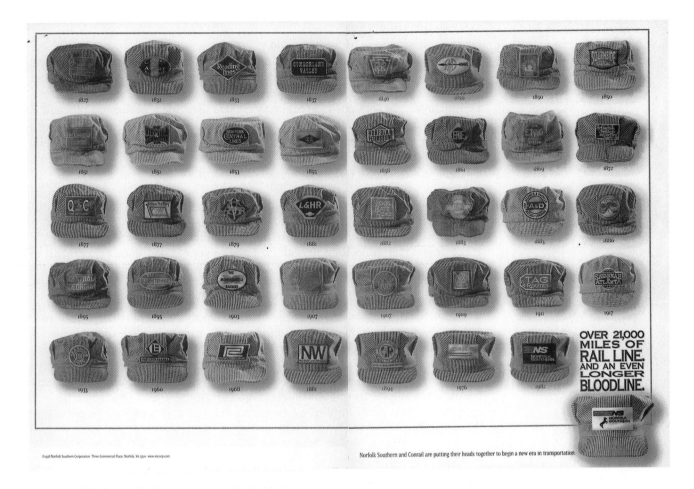

Norfolk Southern and Conrail are putting their heads together to begin a new era in transportation.

Copyright Norfolk Southern Corporation. Three Commercial Place, Norfolk, VA 23510. www.nscorp.com.

FIGURE 15.12
Mergers in the Railroad Industry

valuable products, such as flowers and furs, as well as time-critical shipments of industrial equipment components. In addition, more sophisticated supply chain management software permits companies to forecast demand and plan logistics to use lower-cost modes for most shipments.

Most U.S. airlines also operate as common carriers and handle air freight. Some of them engage in charter work, a form of contract carriage. Other air carriers, known as *supplemental carriers,* may operate air fleets specifically for cargo transport. Some business organizations own or lease their own aircraft to transport freight.

Water Carriers—Cheap but Slow   Water transportation, although slow, is one of the least expensive modes of transportation. Loading freight into standardized, modular shipping containers maximizes the savings of water transportation by limiting costs for loading, unloading, and other handling of goods. Water transportation lends itself mainly to hauling bulk commodities like fuel, petroleum products, coal, chemicals, minerals, and farm products.

Water carriers may operate on inland waterways or across oceans. *Inland water carriers* move cargo on rivers such as the Mississippi, Arkansas, Ohio, and the Tennessee-Tombigbee waterways. Much of this freight travels on barges pushed by mammoth tugs. Large freighters operate on the Great Lakes, between U.S. port cities, and in international commerce. Technology is expected to lead to new ship designs for ocean-going vessels that will expedite shipping times.

Pipelines—Specialized Conveyance   More than 400,000 miles of pipelines crisscross the U.S., forming an extremely efficient network for transporting natural gas, crude oil, and petroleum products. Pipelines represent a small share of companies'

U.S. transportation expenditures, but for suitable products, they provide the cheapest and fastest mode of transportation.

Intermodal Transportation   Increasingly, shippers are choosing to combine transportation methods to move products. Intermodal transportation allows shippers to gain the service and cost advantages of various transportation modes. For instance, a company might ship goods in highway trailers that ride part way on railroad flatcars. Trucking offers the benefits of door-to-door service, but shipping some of the distance by train is more economical. The use of intermodal trailers and containers has almost tripled in recent decades.[54] Other intermodal methods combine train and truck modes with water or air modes of transportation.

Warehousing   The physical distribution element of **warehousing** involves storing products as they move through the distribution channel. Goods flow through two types of warehouses: storage and distribution warehouses. *Storage warehouses* hold goods for moderate to long periods to balance supply and demand between producers and purchasers. *Distribution warehouses* are temporary storage facilities, often holding goods for 24 hours or less, that collect shipments and redistribute goods to other channel members.

Internet retailers that originally planned to skip this element of physical distribution by sending products directly from producers to buyers have since learned that most producers are not set up to process individual orders. Dot.coms like Amazon have resorted to building their own distribution warehouses, and store retailers accustomed to buying in quantity to stock their shelves are revamping their systems to handle small shipments to their online customers. Others, as discussed earlier in the chapter, are turning to fulfillment experts to take care of Web-based customers on their behalf.

Materials Handling   **Materials handling** is the physical distribution activity that moves items within plants, warehouses, transportation terminals, and stores. Firms handle goods with equipment such as forklifts, conveyor belts, and trucks. Costs rise every time an item is handled during its flow through the supply chain. It is critical to eliminate steps that do not add value for final customers.

Two techniques that help firms accomplish this goal are unitization and containerization. *Unitization* involves combining as many packages as possible into one load to be handled by a single truck or forklift. *Containerization* collects packages, usually from several unitized loads, into a compact form that is relatively easy to transfer. Both containerization and unitization have significantly reduced transportation costs for many products by cutting materials handling time, theft, insurance costs, damage, and scheduling problems.

Another way companies improve the efficiency of materials handling is to keep track of products by labeling them with electronically readable codes. Universal product codes (UPCs), or bar codes, have become a common method for tracking shipments. More recently, some companies have begun testing the use of radiofrequency identification tags. The tags contain memory chips that use radio waves to transmit information about products. Not only do they contain much more information than a bar code, but materials handlers can update the information.

Inventory Control   A firm's *inventory* is the amount of finished goods the company has ready for distribution. It is also an expensive resource. Holding $1,000 worth of inventory for just a year can cost a company hundreds of dollars for storage, insurance, taxes, and handling. At the same time, however, businesses need to keep enough inventory on hand to meet customer demand. **Inventory control** involves balancing the priority of limiting costs of holding stocks with that of meeting customer demand through a variety of management methods.

Thanks to advanced computer processing, large retailers are moving beyond inventory management to management of the entire supply chain, and beyond replenishment to inventory control based on demand forecasting. A case in point is Longs Drug Stores. The drugstore chain has begun using software for supply chain management based on sophisticated analysis of consumer buying patterns. For each product, the system uses a model that analyzes over 150 variables to forecast customer demand over a three-month period. Based on the forecasts, Longs places frequent orders for just the amount of product it expects to use. Although it spends more on shipping, the extra expense is more than offset by lower inventory costs. The Longs distribution warehouse in Ontario, California, has managed to cut its inventory by more than half. Many shipments go immediately from the distribution center to stores, without spending any time on warehouse shelves. In addition, pharmacists receive twice-monthly reports indicating how much they can save the company by returning medicines that are selling below anticipated levels. Not only does Longs spend less to carry its original product mix, but it gains room to increase sales by offering a greater variety of products. Initially, managers were worried about the risks and costs of carrying a small inventory and ordering several times a week, but the savings quickly overcame their fears.[55]

Order Processing   The final element of physical distribution, **order processing**—sometimes called fulfillment—includes all of the tasks required to prepare customer orders for shipment. It also includes the steps involved in receiving shipments when they arrive. Like the other components of physical distribution, order processing directly affects a firm's ability to meet its customer-service standards. Inefficient order-processing procedures also add to costs. To satisfy customers, firms may have to compensate for order-processing inefficiencies by shipping products via costly transportation modes or by maintaining large inventories.

In distribution channels where retailers are the channel captains, stores are pushing more of the order-processing responsibility back to manufacturers in a process called *vendor-managed inventory*. Costco has arranged for Kimberly-Clark to ship its Huggies diapers to Costco stores as needed, rather than waiting for the stores to place orders. Costco provides Kimberly-Clark with detailed data about Huggies sales in each store, and a data analyst at Kimberly-Clark reviews the sales data each morning. Knowing that it takes Kimberly-Clark about a week to fill an order after it is entered on the computer, the analyst determines how many packages of diapers to send to each store. The analyst's goal is to meet Costco's objective of carrying a two-week supply. Any more, and Costco's inventory costs begin to interfere with the retailer's low-price strategy. Along with order placement, Kimberly-Clark assigns employees to arrange transportation and to field questions and complaints from Costco. Kimberly-Clark is also taking advantage of supply chain management by asking its own suppliers to adopt similar practices. One supplier is Velcro USA, with which the company shares production data so it can receive just-in-time deliveries of Velcro tabs for its diapers.[56]

WHAT'S AHEAD

This chapter discusses how businesses ensure that customers receive the right products at the right times and places. Of course, we assume that customers want the goods and services being offered. It also describes the major types of retailers and wholesaling intermediaries and the process of designing an efficient, customer-responsive distribution channel. The next chapter looks at how businesses use advertising, selling, and other promotional methods to inform, persuade, and remind customers to buy their product offerings.

➤ Summary of Learning Goals

1. Summarize the ways distribution creates value for customers and competitive advantage for businesses.

Distribution creates value by providing place, time, and ownership utility. It helps customers to purchase goods conveniently, quickly, and with a minimum of effort. By strategically managing distribution, firms can gain a competitive advantage. Not only does effective distribution support the demand created by superior product design and promotion, but it also satisfies customer expectations. A well-chosen distribution strategy also helps to cut costs and boost profits by eliminating unnecessary steps in the supply chain.

2. Identify the various categories of distribution channels and the factors that influence channel selection.

Marketers can choose either a direct distribution channel, which moves goods directly from the producer to the consumer, or indirect distribution channels, which involve marketing intermediaries in the paths through which products—and legal ownership of them—flow from producer to the final customer. Ideally, the choice of a distribution channel should support a firm's overall marketing strategy by providing customers with convenient ways to obtain the goods and services they desire. The distribution channel should support a firm's overall marketing strategy. Before selecting distribution channels, firms must consider their target markets, the type of good being distributed, their own internal systems and concerns, and competitive factors.

3. Discuss the roles marketing intermediaries play in distribution channels.

Marketing intermediaries, or middlemen, include wholesalers and retailers. They help to smooth the distribution paths for goods by creating utility, performing marketing functions, and cutting costs. They save producers from dealing directly with large numbers of end users. Instead, marketing intermediaries handle these tasks. They often specialize in certain functions and can perform these activities more efficiently than producers can. By representing numerous producers, marketing intermediaries cut the costs of buying and selling. Because they can consolidate orders, they may also negotiate better prices than individual buyers could obtain.

4. Explain how retailers effectively use pricing, promotion, location, and merchandise selection to compete.

After identifying a target market, a retailer must adopt effective and coordinated pricing, promotion, product,

and location strategies. These activities help to create a retail image that sets the store apart from its competitors. In developing a product strategy, retailers must decide on the general product categories, product lines, and selections to offer. Pricing can play a major role in consumers' perceptions of a retailer. Retailers are the channel members that determine the prices consumers pay for goods and services, and they base their prices on the costs of their own purchases from vendors and the services they offer customers. Their location decisions depend on size, financial resources, product offerings, and the target market. Retailers use promotion to project an image that will attract targeted customers. Promotional activities also provide information about a store's location, prices, and merchandise to entice consumers. Store atmospherics, the physical characteristics of a retail outlet and its amenities, also encourage customers to shop there.

5. Identify and briefly describe each of the major components of an effective distribution strategy.

A firm must consider whether to move products through direct or indirect distribution. Once the decision is made, the company needs to identify the types of marketing intermediaries, if any, through which it will distribute its goods and services. Another component is distribution intensity. The business must decide on the amount of market coverage—intensive, selective, or exclusive—needed to achieve its marketing strategies. Finally, attention must be paid to managing the distribution channel. It is vital to minimize conflict between channel members.

6. List the different types of conflict that can occur in a distribution channel and the methods firms use to reduce channel conflict.

Power is not distributed evenly in most distribution channels. Imbalances often lead to conflicts between channel members. Conflict can be either horizontal, involving disagreements between channel members at the same level in the distribution chain, or vertical, occurring between channel members at different levels.

7. Describe the importance of logistics in controlling the supply chain.

A firm's choice of distribution channels creates the final link in its supply chain, the complete sequence of suppliers that contribute to creating and delivering its good or service. The process of coordinating the flow of goods, services, and information among members of the supply chain is called *logistics*. Ideally, value is added to goods along each step of the supply chain through activities like superior product design, quality manufacturing, customer service, and efficient delivery. A major focus of logistics is physical distribution, the activities aimed at physically moving finished goods from the production line to the consumer. Effective management of physical distribution can increase customer satisfaction by ensuring reliable, cost-efficient movement of goods through the supply chain.

8. **Explain how the components of a physical distribution system work together to reduce costs and meet customer service standards.**

A firm's physical distribution system begins by establishing guidelines for customer service. The firm must also identify the most cost-effective and reliable methods of transporting goods through the distribution channel. Other components of a physical distribution system include warehousing, materials handling, inventory control, and order processing. Each of these components also contributes to the firm's ability to get goods to consumers on time and in a reliable, cost-efficient manner.

9. **Compare the alternative transportation modes on the bases of flexibility, dependability, and cost.**

Rail transportation is the most efficient way to move bulk shipments over long distances. Rail is a relatively dependable and cost-effective option, but it is not always a flexible one. Trucking offers a fast way to ship and consistent service for both large and small shippers. Trucking is a very flexible alternative, because trucks can go everywhere. Air carriers are the fastest way to move shipments, but air transport is more expensive than other transportation modes. Water transportation, although slow, is one of the least expensive modes of transportation. It lends itself mainly to hauling bulk commodities that are easily containerized. Pipelines form an extremely efficient, rapid, and inexpensive transportation network for natural gas and petroleum. Many shippers combine transportation methods in a technique called *intermodal transportation* to move shipments as needed. This approach allows shippers to gain the service and cost advantages of various transportation modes.

Business Terms You Need to Know

distribution 538
distribution channel 538
direct distribution channel 539
marketing intermediary 539
retailer 540

wholesaling intermediary 540
wheel of retailing 548
channel captain 561
supply chain 563
logistics 564

Other Important Business Terms

scrambled merchandising 555
planned shopping center 556
intensive distribution 560
selective distribution 560
exclusive distribution 560

horizontal channel conflict 562
vertical channel conflict 562
physical distribution 564
customer service standards 565
warehousing 568

materials handling 568
inventory control 568
order processing 569

➤ Review Questions

1. What are the advantages of direct distribution? When is direct distribution most often used by companies?

2. Identify and describe briefly the four distribution channels most likely to use intermediaries. What are the major benefits to companies that use intermediaries?

3. What is the wheel of retailing? How has the Internet affected the wheel of retailing?

4. Identify and describe the major types of nonstore retailers. Then give an example of at least one type of

good or service that would be suited to each type of nonstore retailer.

5. Describe briefly the seven steps a retailer must take to develop a competitive strategy. Cite an illustration of each step.

6. Identify and describe each of the four factors that help determine the distribution channel or channels that a company is most likely to select for its goods and services.

7. Explain each of the three levels of distribution intensity. Give an example of two products for each level.

8. In what ways has the Internet created conflict among distribution channels?

9. Explain the concept of supply chain management and the role of logistics in a firm's distribution strategy.

10. Describe the strengths and weaknesses of each of the major modes of transportation and explain how companies can improve their competitiveness through effective physical distribution.

➤ Questions for Critical Thinking

1. How has the Internet changed both direct and indirect distribution? The chapter describes how *The Wall Street Journal* both sells and delivers articles via the Internet. What other types of products could be sold and delivered this way?

2. Which type of distribution intensity would best suit the following products?

   a. Ferrari sports cars

   b. Microsoft Windows 2000 software

   c. tissue paper

   d. bulldozers and other large earth-moving equipment

   e. Tommy Hilfiger apparel

3. As described in the chapter, more than 200 Internet enterprises shut down in the first two years of the 21st century, three quarters of which were retail businesses. Discuss steps that you think the surviving Internet retailers should take to thrive and grow beyond the "dot.com shakeout."

4. Think of your favorite store. If it is near where you live or go to school, stop by for a visit. If not, rely on your memory. Describe the store in terms of its atmospherics. What features contribute to your positive experiences and feelings about the store?

5. Suggest the best method for transporting each of the following goods. Explain your choices.

   a. heating oil

   b. dried pasta

   c. oranges and grapefruit

   d. teak furniture from Thailand

   e. cherry lumber from Pennsylvania

   f. industrial machine parts

➤ Experiential Exercise

Background: Honda Motor Co., in an effort to reduce its 120-day time lag between when a vehicle is manufactured and when a new owner drives it off the lot, implemented its Market Oriented Vehicle Environment (MOVE) project. The goal of MOVE was to build a network that would allow everyone involved in the flow from production to buyer purchase—including headquarters to assembly plants to dealers—to collaborate to improve the flow.

With the new system, all 1,300 American Honda dealerships are able to place their orders directly with Honda headquarters and get regular updates on order-shipment status. The up-to-the-minute market data received from the dealerships lets Honda generate production orders and send them to seven plants, with MOVE software calculating the most efficient way to make the production assignments among the assembly plants. In addition to reducing lead time from 120 days to 60—and sometimes even 30—days, Honda executives claim that the new automated ordering system has slashed unsold inventories at factories and dealerships by 50 percent.

According to American Honda spokesperson Stephen Keeney, "For any company selling 100,000 or more vehicles per month, 50 percent reductions in wholesale and retail inventories result in substantial cost savings in areas ranging from storage fees to finance costs. Plus, the increased efficiency of being able to distribute particular vehicles to the points where the greatest demand exists for those models provides a definite competitive advantage."

Source: Deborah Gage, "American Honda: Turbo-Charged Supply Chain Drastically Cuts Automaker's Lead Time and Inventory," *Ecompany Now,* April 2001, p. 125.

Part 1 Directions: Based on this description of Honda's distribution strategy, answer the following questions:

1. What type of distribution strategy does Honda have?

   a. direct distribution channel

   b. marketing intermediary

2. Which of the following distribution channels does American Honda use?

   a. producer to wholesaler to business user

   b. producer to wholesaler to retailer to consumer

   c. producer to wholesaler to wholesaler to retailer to consumer

   d. producer to retailer to consumer

3. Which marketing functions do the Honda dealers perform?

   a. creating utility

   b. providing services

   c. reducing costs

4. What type of distribution intensity does American Honda use?

   a. intensive distribution

   b. selective distribution

   c. exclusive distribution

Part 2 Directions: Complete this part of the exercise only if one of the 1,300 Honda dealerships is within what you or your instructor would consider a reasonable driving distance from your campus.

Analyze the Honda dealership you visit based on the following factors discussed in more detail in the section "How Retailers Compete."

1. What market segment does Honda target?

2. What is Honda's product strategy?

3. Does Honda try to distinguish itself from other auto dealers by the level of service it provides? If yes, how?

4. Where is the Honda dealer you visited located? Are other dealers nearby?

5. Describe the visibility of the dealer's signage, parking availability, and the businesses located nearby.

6. Describe the following interior atmospheric elements:
   a. layout
   b. merchandise presentation
   c. lighting
   d. color
   e. sounds
   f. cleanliness

Part 1 answers: 1 (b); 2 (d); 3 (a and b); 4 (c).

➤ **Nothing but Net**

1. **Transportation modes.** As noted in the chapter, two of the major transportation modes are railroads and trucks. The *Commodity Flow Survey* is a regular publication of the Bureau of Transportation Statistics and the U.S. Census Bureau, and provides detailed information on transportation of goods. Visit the following Web site and access the most recent *Commodity Flow Survey* you can find. Review the *Survey* and answer the following questions:

   a. Which of the two transportation modes is growing faster?

   b. What types of goods are most commonly transported by rail? By truck?

   c. What is the average distance of goods shipped by rail? By truck?

   d. What is the average cost-per-mile for goods shipped by rail? By truck?

   e. Are your answers to the previous questions consistent with Table 15.2? Explain.

   www.bts.gov/ntda/cfs

2. **Distribution channels.** One of the world's largest personal computer (PC) manufacturers is Dell Computer. Dell uses a direct approach to the distribution of its products to consumers and business purchasers. Visit the following Web site and prepare a brief report on the distribution approach used by Dell. How does it differ from the approaches used by other PC makers, including Compaq, Gateway, and Hewlett-Packard? What are the advantages and disadvantages of the direct approach to product distribution? Does a mall in your area share any of these three factors?

   www.dell.com/us/en/gen/corporate/factpack_000.htm

3. **Location strategy.** Alberta's West Edmonton Mall promotes itself as the largest enclosed shopping center in the world. Visit the mall's Web site and list three factors that make this mall's location a desirable one. Does a mall in your area share any of these three factors?

   www.wesedmall.com

   Note: Internet Web addresses change frequently. If you do not find the exact sites listed, you may need to acces the organization's or company's home page and search from there.

When you go to a restaurant, perhaps you order seafood—fresh scallops, lobster, shrimp, clams. If you do, your dinner could have come from the cold waters of the Atlantic Ocean off the coast of Maine or the warmer waters of Chesapeake Bay in Maryland. Either way, there's a good chance that your dinner arrived fresh at the restaurant courtesy of Ipswich Shellfish.

Ipswich Shellfish was founded in the coastal Massachusetts town of Ipswich by George Pappas and Joe Sikora in 1935, when much of the country was deep in the Great Depression. Back then, a bucket of clams could feed a family of four for 80 cents. The two young entrepreneurs decided to dig and shuck clams in small shacks and then sell them by the bucket. "They didn't have any regulations in those days," recalls Pappas, who is still at the helm of the company. (Sikora eventually moved on to other pursuits.) "We used to shuck clams in little shacks and sell them out of our car in open buckets. It was a huge attraction. Wherever we parked, people would come up and look and ask questions. It was the best advertisement I could have had." Then the two men decided to try selling their seafood to restaurants. "I used to drive up to the restaurant without an order and just open the door of the truck and show the cook what I had—that's how I got business," says Pappas. This improvised system is how one of the largest wholesalers, retailers, and distributors in the seafood industry was born.

Today, the Ipswich Shellfish Group employees more than 400 people at five facilities, from Maine to Maryland. The company makes direct delivery to restaurants and supermarkets, flies daily air freight across the country, ships luxury seafood gifts directly to consumers, and operates a gourmet seafood takeout shop in Ipswich.

At the largest seafood plant, located in Ipswich, more than 100 people process seafood, including native Ipswich clams—which locals claim to be the sweetest in the world—local lobster, scallops, and shrimp. The seafood is packed and shipped either fresh or frozen, depending on customer needs, to states as far away as Florida and California. Figuring out how to hold an inventory of perishable seafood is a tricky business, but Ipswich Shellfish manages. For example, it has one of the largest state-of-the-art lobster pools in the nation. "When lobsters arrive here, they're stressed," says Kevin O'Donnell, administrative director of the lobster division. "We call this the lobster spa—you need to rejuvenate them before they ship out." The lobster tank can hold 100,000 pounds of lobster. "We sometimes ship as many as 50,000 pounds a day," remarks O'Donnell.

Choosing a mode of transportation is critical in the seafood business. Any delay or fluctuation in temperature can ruin an entire shipment—and possibly relationships with customers as well. When Pappas started out, he bought a couple of refrigerator trucks to haul his clams, scallops, and lobsters. Today, Ipswich Shellfish maintains vital relationships with several major airlines, FedEx, and Common Carrier Refrigerated and Freezer Trucks. The company offers service from Boston's Logan Airport three times a day Monday through Friday. "Orders are packed in special insulated boxes with poly-bag liners and leak-proof gel ice to insure that your product arrives in top condition and at the proper temperature," explains the company Web site. Customers then have the option to pick up the order themselves at the destination airport or have Ipswich Shellfish arrange for a courier service.

Although Ipswich Shellfish's main customers over the last 70 years have been restaurants, recently George's daughter Chrissi Pappas decided to take a risk and launch a retail business in her hometown of Ipswich. Now a thriving gourmet takeout shop and catering business, the Ipswich Shellfish Market offers specially selected shellfish and fish, as well as prepared meals for busy, working consumers who still want fresh meals without taking the time to prepare them at home. The market also offers side dishes such as Mediterranean specialty foods, fresh breads, imported cheeses, and rich desserts.

Ipswich Shellfish has grown from a tiny business started in the midst of the Great Depression to a large company that engages in various types of distribution nationwide. Despite its size, the company maintains close relationships with its customers. "We've grown up together," says Marie Christine Sullivan, vice president of the Back Bay Restaurant Group, which owns five restaurants in Boston and several others around New England. "We deal with a number of seafood suppliers, but they're the best by far."

QUESTIONS

1. Do you think it makes more sense for Ipswich Shellfish to own its own facilities, such as the lobster tank, or to rely on other suppliers for this function? Why?
2. Discuss some of the challenges that Ipswich Shellfish faces in managing supply-chain logistics because of the nature of its products.
3. Imagine that you are in charge of selecting modes of transportation for Ipswich Shellfish. Put together a plan for delivering a shipment of live lobsters from the plant to an exclusive restaurant in Los Angeles.
4. Visit the company Web site at **www.ipswichshellfish.com** to learn more about some of Ipswich Shellfish's other operations, such as its corporate gift program and its online catalog. In what ways does the company have to handle physical distribution for these programs differently from that of wholesale orders for restaurants?

Sources: "Company Profile" and information on company divisions and distribution methods from the Ipswich Shellfish Web site, **www.ipswichshellfish.com,** accessed April 5, 2001; Tonia Noell Molinski, "Ipswich Shellfish Keeps It Fresh," *Pulse 2001,* Essex County Newspapers, **www.northshoreonline.com,** accessed April 6, 2001.

CHAPTER 16

Promoting Goods and Services Using Integrated Marketing Communications

Learning Goals

1. Relate the concept of integrated marketing communications to the development of a firm's promotional strategy.

2. Explain the concept of a promotional mix and list the objectives of promotion.

3. Summarize the different types of advertising and advertising media.

4. Describe the role of sales promotion in promotional strategy.

5. Identify the various personal selling tasks and the steps in the sales process.

6. Explain how public relations supports other elements of the promotional mix.

7. Identify the factors that influence the selection of a promotional mix.

8. Contrast pushing and pulling promotional strategies.

9. Discuss major ethical issues involved in promotion.

Since the beginning of time, humans have adorned themselves—with clothing, jewelry, hairstyles, and face paint. Today's cosmetics industry is much more complicated than those early beauty efforts, but French company L'Oréal has learned to thrive among the competition and become a stunning presence. Founded in 1907 when French chemist Eugène Schueller came up with one of the first stable synthetic hair dyes, L'Oréal is now proud parent to numerous smaller companies—and their products—around the world. The company acquired American firms Soft Sheen and Carson Products, which produce hair care items for an urban ethnic market. It also scooped up Maybelline, the U.S. mass-market makeup brand, and revived its U.S. and international sales. L'Oréal dominates several markets, from hair color to eye makeup, beating out such giants as Clairol and Revlon in market share.

Accomplishing such success requires savvy product promotion, which starts with understanding the market you are trying to reach. L'Oréal is skilled at both. "L'Oréal has a Ninja mentality," says Terri Gardner, president of the company's new Soft Sheen/Carson division, "very focused, very strategic, no wasted effort." L'Oréal believes that promoting a product begins with its development. In the mid-1990s, L'Oréal marketers decided that they needed a natural fruit juice shampoo to target to Europe's teenagers. Through research, the company's scientists found that fructose—natural sugar—is loosely related to hair growth. Voilà! The company had a nearly foolproof basis on which to promote the shampoo. The success of Fructis, the fruit juice shampoo, is one reason why L'Oréal now has captured 28 percent of the European shampoo market.

Another reason for the firm's success is that it is generous in promoting its innovative products. It uses all major media—television, print, outdoor advertising, sales promotion, and event marketing—to spread the word about its products. Although L'Oréal does not publish its advertising and

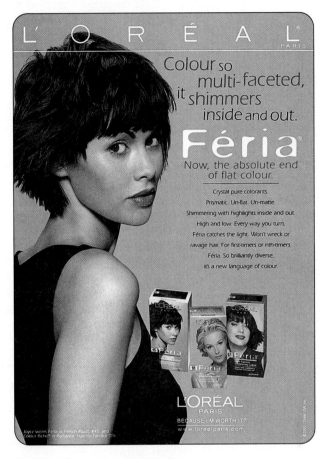

promotional expenditures, experts estimate this spending now approaches 47 percent of sales for the company. L'Oréal's global advertising budget is estimated to be about $1.25 billion per year—almost as much as global colossus The Coca-Cola Company spends.

Since personal selling—face-to-face interaction with customers—is an important part of the promotional mix for many of L'Oréal's product lines, the company has embraced new ways to communicate with and train some of its salespeople. Recently, the firm launched a program through

which its 120,000 Lancôme beauty consultants worldwide can receive training online at its Web site. Lancome-pro.com was introduced in four pilot countries—France, Italy, Sweden, and the U.S.—to teach beauty advisers how to sell and apply the Lancôme line of makeup and build relationships with customers.

Today, L'Oreal chairman and chief executive officer (CEO) Lindsay Owen-Jones spends his days focusing on the business of beauty and finding ways for his company to stay at the top of its industry. "We just love the business a little bit more than our competition," he says. He has every intention of keeping it that way.[1]

CHAPTER OVERVIEW

L'Oréal illustrates how one company can use different promotional strategies to capture markets around the world. This chapter completes our discussion of marketing strategy by focusing on the different types of promotional activities. In the process, it introduces the concept of integrated marketing communications.

Promotion is the function of informing, persuading, and influencing a purchase decision. This activity is as important to not-for-profit organizations such as the YMCA and Boston's Brigham & Women's Hospital as it is to profit-seeking companies like Palm and the Oakland Athletics.

Some promotional strategies try to develop *primary demand,* or consumer desire for a general product category. The objective of such a campaign is to stimulate sales for an entire industry, so that individual firms benefit from this market growth. A popular example is the dairy industry's "Got Milk?" campaign. Print and television messages about the nutritional benefits of milk show music, sports, and fashion celebrities, including the Dixie Chicks, Brett Favre, and tennis stars Venus and Serena Williams, each wearing a milk moustache. For Hispanic consumers in California, the advertisements were modified, not simply translated. Hispanic women felt insulted by the implication they would run out of milk, and the slogan does not translate directly anyway. (It means "Are you lactating?") Also, young Hispanics in America were familiar with and liked the English slogan. So, the promotional strategy for Hispanics couples was to combine Spanish-language messages about sharing milk-based recipes in families with the English "Got Milk?" slogan. Besides advertising, the promotional strategy has included sponsoring a tour by Britney Spears and offering retailers large stickers with the "Got Milk?" slogan printed over chocolaty cupcake treats in white icing. Stores can place the stickers on the floor near dairy cases to spur sales of milk among consumers who might not otherwise think of it.[2] Figure 16.1 shows two advertisements in this campaign.

Most promotional strategies, in contrast, seek to stimulate *selective demand*—desire for a specific brand. By promoting Tiger Woods's endorsement of its company's golf apparel, Nike marketers want to encourage customers to purchase its clothes, not some other brand. Sales promotions that distribute cents-off coupons also encourage shoppers to purchase specific brands.

Marketers choose among many promotional options to communicate with potential customers. Each marketing message a buyer receives—through a television or magazine ad, Web site, direct-mail ad, or sales call—reflects on the product, place, person, cause, or organization promoted in the content. In a process of **integrated marketing communications (IMC),** marketers coordinate all promotional activities—advertising, sales promotion, personal sales presentations, and public relations—to execute a unified, customer-focused promotional strategy. This coordination avoids confusing the consumer and focuses positive attention on the promotional message.

This chapter begins by explaining the role of IMC, then discusses the objectives of promotion and the importance of promotional planning. Next, it examines the components of the promotional mix—advertising, sales promotion, personal selling, and public relations—and demonstrates how marketers incorporate several elements into an IMC plan. Then the chapter examines promotional strategies and techniques for selecting a promotional mix and measuring effectiveness. It concludes with a brief discussion of ethical issues related to promotion.

INTEGRATED MARKETING COMMUNICATIONS

An integrated marketing communications strategy focuses on customer needs to create a unified promotional message. To gain a competitive advantage, marketers who implement IMC need a broad view of promotion. Media options continue to multiply, and marketers cannot simply rely on traditional broadcast and print media and

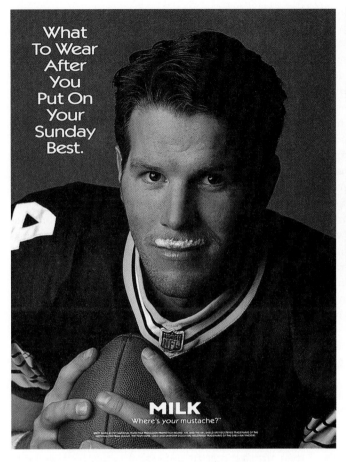

FIGURE 16.1
Promotional Campaign to Stimulate Primary Demand

direct mail. Plans must include all forms of customer contact. Packaging, store displays, sales promotions, sales presentations, and online and interactive media also communicate information about a brand or organization. Unless marketers develop an integrated approach and present a consistent message from all sources, they may confuse consumers with conflicting messages. With IMC, marketers create a unified personality for the good, brand, or service they promote. Coordinated activities also enhance the effectiveness of reaching and serving target markets.

Designing Effective Integrated Marketing Communications Programs

Today's complex marketing environment presents both opportunities and challenges from multiple markets and expanding media options. A good IMC program provides a unifying framework within which an organization can develop promotional strategies to reach many different market segments.

Marketing managers set the goals and objectives for the firm's promotional strategy with overall organizational objectives and marketing goals in mind. Based on these objectives, marketers weave the various elements of the strategy—personal selling, advertising, sales promotion, publicity, and public relations—into an integrated communications plan. This document becomes a central part of the firm's total marketing strategy to reach its selected target market. Feedback, including marketing research and field reports, completes the system by identifying any deviations from the plan and suggesting improvements.

In General Motors' Pontiac-GMC division, the Web's capabilities for one-to-one customer interaction was key in linking online and off-line integrated marketing communications efforts. The division's relationship-marketing manager, Joyce Fierens, starts by asking who is in the division's target market, as well as whether and how they will use the Internet. From there, she considers how various communications channels can work together to tell customers what they want to know. With more and more consumers gathering information online, all of the division's advertising—in print, on television, and on the Internet—encourages consumers to visit the Web site.

Pontiac-GMC's original Web presence had primarily consisted of pictures accompanied by lists of features. Although this presented the desired brand image, Fierens determined that many customers weren't interested in learning about the brand; they wanted details about the cars. So the company improved the ease with which consumers can use the site to gather information. The Web-based information presented conforms with the brand image. The Pontiac Web page leads off with the slogan "Driving Excitement" and invites consumers to look up cars with such attributes as "solid excitement" or "wide-track luxury," which—not coincidentally—are themes Pontiac ads associate with its vehicles. Because Web sites can provide many product details, the division's strategy for offline advertising attempts to interest consumers in visiting its Web site. In the words of Fierens, "All of Pontiac's print, television, and promotional material encourages prospective customers to visit the Web site, where the message is then followed through in greater detail."[3]

THE PROMOTIONAL MIX

Just as every organization creates a marketing mix combining product, pricing, distribution, and promotional strategies, each also requires a similar mix to blend the many facets of promotion into a cohesive plan. The **promotional mix** consists of two components—personal selling and nonpersonal selling activities—that marketers combine to meet the needs of their firm's target customers and effectively and efficiently communicate its message to them. *Personal selling* is the most basic form of promotion: a direct person-to-person promotional presentation to a potential buyer. The buyer–seller communication can occur during a face-to-face meeting or via telephone, videoconference, or interactive computer link.

Nonpersonal selling consists of advertising, sales promotion, direct marketing, and public relations. Although advertising is the best-known form of nonpersonal selling, sales promotion accounts for about one-half of marketing expenditures in this category.

Each component in the promotional mix offers its own advantages and disadvantages, as Table 16.1 demonstrates. By selecting the appropriate combination of promotional mix elements, marketers attempt to achieve their firm's promotional objectives. Allocations of funds within the promotional mix vary by industry. Manufacturers of business-to-business (B2B) products typically spend more on personal selling than on advertising, while consumer-goods marketers may focus more on advertising. Later sections of this chapter discuss how the individual parts of the mix contribute to an effective promotional strategy.

Objectives of Promotional Strategy

Promotional strategy objectives vary among organizations. Some use promotion to expand their markets, others to defend their current positions. As Figure 16.2 illustrates, common objectives include providing information, differentiating a product, increasing sales, stabilizing sales, and accentuating a product's value.

Marketers often pursue multiple promotional objectives at the same time. To promote children's clothing, marketers typically want to convince kids that the clothes and brand are fashionable and to persuade parents that the clothes are a good value. Among parents of children age nine and younger, almost three of every

Table 16.1   **Comparing the Components of the Promotional Mix**

Component	Advantages	Disadvantages
Advertising	Reaches large consumer audience at low cost per contact Allows strong control of the message Message can be modified to match different audiences	Difficult to measure effectiveness Limited value for closing sales
Personal selling	Message can be tailored for each customer Produces immediate buyer response Effectiveness is easily measured	High cost per contact High expense and difficulty of attracting and retaining effective salespeople
Sales promotion	Attracts attention and creates awareness Effectiveness is easily measured Produces short-term sales increases	Difficult to differentiate from similar programs of competitors Nonpersonal appeal
Public relations	Enhances product or company credibility Creates a positive attitude about the product or company	Difficult to measure effectiveness Often devoted to nonmarketing activities

four respondents told researchers that their children influence purchases of clothing; but only one in three said they are influenced by advertising. The Nautica Girls line of clothing was introduced with a joint promotion cosponsored by *Girls' Life* magazine. The promotion included a mall tour featuring concerts, gifts, and a fashion show. Eddie Bauer introduced its line of children's clothing with advertising and promotions in *Disney* magazine, *Family PC, Family Fun,* and *Working Mother,* as well as catalog and online advertising and a joint promotion with KB Kids. These placements for promotional messages are designed to reach more than one generation.[4]

Providing Information   A major portion of U.S. advertising is information oriented. Large sections in Wednesday and Thursday editions of daily newspapers consist of ads and inserts that tell shoppers about featured specials at grocery stores and other local retail outlets. Advertisements in Friday or Sunday newspaper supplements provide schedules and ticket information about plays, movies, and concerts. Field salespeople keep buyers aware of the latest technological advances in a particular field.

Information is an essential part of advertisements for prescription and over-the-counter drugs. Pharmaceutical companies provide information about the kinds of conditions their products are designed to treat. In the U.S., ads for allergy medication Claritin and stomach-acid treatment Prilosec have spurred an increase in doctor visits for these conditions—and an increase in sales for the drugs. Insurers complain that when patients get their information from advertisements for these high-priced remedies, they may miss the chance to be treated with less costly alternatives. In Europe, pharmaceutical marketers are prohibited from using such advertising. European advertisements for prescription drugs are limited to simply providing

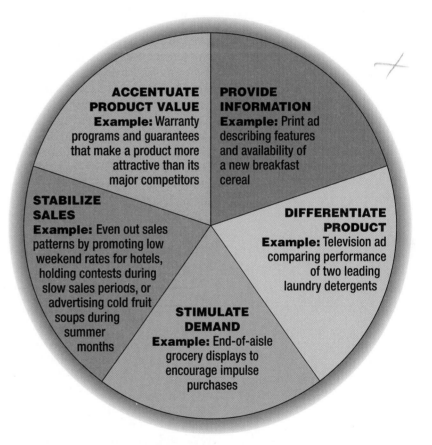

FIGURE 16.2
Five Major Promotional Objectives

BUSINESS DIRECTORY

➤ **promotional mix**   *combination of personal and nonpersonal selling techniques designed to achieve promotional objectives.*

information about medical conditions, along with encouragement to seek a doctor's advice. European consumer advertising for Viagra explains the symptoms of erectile dysfunction. The drug's maker, Pfizer, then promotes Viagra to doctors, so that they will prescribe it when patients seek help.[5]

Differentiating a Product Promotion can also be used to differentiate a firm's goods and services from the competition. Applying a concept called positioning, marketers attempt to establish their own places in the minds of customers. The idea is to communicate to prospective purchasers meaningful distinctions about the attributes, price, quality, or use of a good or service, as in the following examples:

- **Attributes:** Procter & Gamble says Scope mouthwash tastes better than Listerine.
- **Price/quality:** Burger King says the Whopper tastes better and costs less than the Big Mac.
- **Use:** Yoplait markets Gogurt yogurt in squeezable tubes with images of kids who are too active to sit down and eat their yogurt with a spoon.

In the crowded marketplace for soft drinks, PepsiCo has experimented with ways to differentiate its Pepsi One cola. Recognizing that many consumers dislike the taste of diet sodas, PepsiCo developed Pepsi One with a new sweetener, sold under the name Ace-K, that it says produces a better-tasting drink. Then it tried to develop a message stating that Pepsi One tastes better than diet soft drinks, without implying that the company's Diet Pepsi tastes bad. The nation's second-leading cola bottler used ads with exciting images and the slogan "Only one has it all," but these ads failed to provide enough information to explain the new product. Then PepsiCo changed the slogan to "True cola taste. One calorie," but this slogan did not differentiate Pepsi One from Diet Pepsi. As a result, the new drink achieved dismal results, gaining less than a 1 percent share of the U.S. market for carbonated beverages.

Pepsi has since developed new advertising to more clearly differentiate Pepsi One. Because the company wants to clarify that Pepsi One's taste is unlike other diet soft drinks, the revised advertising avoids the word *diet*. However, the advertising identifies a product attribute, the use of Ace-K to sweeten the drink. To demonstrate Pepsi One's taste, television ads show preoccupied commuters unknowingly taking alternating sips of Pepsi One and Coca-Cola Classic without noticing the difference. The phrase "Too good to be one calorie . . . but it is" communicates the product's low-calorie attribute. And to persuade people to learn about Pepsi One's taste firsthand, the company increased its use of sampling. Marketers have offered samples of the drink at locations such as college campuses, movie theaters, and company cafeterias.[6]

Increasing Sales Increasing sales volume is the most common objective of a promotional strategy. Naturalizer has employed a promotional strategy designed to increase shoe sales by broadening the appeal of its brand to a larger target market. Naturalizer became the third-largest seller of women's dress shoes by appealing to Baby Boomers. But as these women have grown older, they have been buying fewer pairs of shoes each year. To attract younger, freer-spending women, the company developed a new line of fashionable shoes along with a promotional strategy that positions Naturalizer shoes as stylish and even sexy.

The effort includes magazine ads featuring young women in beach attire and Naturalizer shoes, placing them in situations that convey sex appeal. The ad copy says, "More than comfortable. Naturalizer." The placement of these ads is another part of Naturalizer's strategy for increasing sales. While past campaigns to reach Baby Boomers included ads in magazines like *Better Homes and Gardens* and *Good Housekeeping,* the newer advertising has run in fashion magazines like *Elle,*

Harper's Bazaar, and *Marie Claire.* The company also developed displays to carry the updated image to shoppers in stores. The initial response to this promotional strategy was a substantial increase in Naturalizer's sales through department stores.[7]

Stabilizing Sales   Sales stabilization is another goal of promotional strategy. Firms often use sales contests during slack periods, motivating salespeople by offering prizes such as vacation trips, television sets, cell phones, and cash to those who meet certain goals. Companies distribute sales promotion materials—such as calendars, pens, and note pads—to customers to stimulate sales during off-seasons. A stable sales pattern brings several advantages. It evens out the production cycle, reduces some management and production costs, and simplifies financial, purchasing, and marketing planning. An effective promotional strategy can contribute to these goals.

Advertising supports other promotional efforts to stabilize sales. A common problem in the hotel industry occurs when hotels crowded on weekdays with business travelers sit nearly empty on weekends. These hotels often advertise weekend packages to attract tourists, offering low rates and, occasionally, free meals or tickets to local attractions. Similarly, airlines may advertise special low airfares during off-peak periods. These deals often require travelers to stay through a Saturday night, when business travelers are most likely to be home.

Accentuating the Product's Value   Some promotional strategies enhance product values by explaining often unrecognized ownership benefits. Car makers offer long-term warranty programs and promote the excellence of their repair services. Other promotional efforts focus on low-price aspects of value. Teenage entrepreneur Kevin Mbithe was struggling to stimulate sales of his unusual invention, which has the descriptive name Toilet-Seat Light and was priced at $6.99. Jerry Fisher, an advertising copywriter, advised using a promotional message that offers a lot for a low price: "Pay just $11.99 for one Toilet-Seat Light and get a second one FREE!" Although the stated price is higher, the ad suggests buyers will get a lot for their money.[8]

The creation of brand equity, as discussed in Chapter 14, also enhances a product's image and increases its desirability. Advertising with luxurious images supports the reputation of premium brands like Jaguar, Tiffany, and Rolex. Other promotional messages associate brands with desirable qualities such as fun, youthfulness, or even spirituality.

Promotional Planning

Today's marketers can promote their products in many ways, and the lines between the different elements of the promotional mix are blurring. A growing number of marketers pay placement fees to have their products showcased in movies and television shows. Bebe Stores went from a struggling mall retailer to a fashion trendsetter by giving away clothing for stars to wear on television shows. Calista Flockhart has appeared in Bebe fashions on *Ally McBeal,* and Sarah Michelle Gellar has worn

Game sales, even games as popular as Trivial Pursuit, tend to be concentrated during the Christmas gift-giving season and during the summer when families decide to take vacations involving many hours in the automobile. Trivial Pursuit marketers are attempting to supply information about the various game editions and persuade people to make purchases.

Bebe on *Buffy the Vampire Slayer*. A star's appearance in a stunning outfit has more than once sent fashion-conscious consumers flocking to Bebe Stores.

The increasing complexity and sophistication of marketing communications requires careful promotional planning to coordinate IMC strategies. In the United Kingdom, Cadbury wanted to increase sales of its Cadbury Creme Egg. The company sells the candy each year from January through Easter, and it had been promoting the product with television ads containing the slogan "How Will You Eat Yours?" Cadbury's research showed that although its Eggs were the most popular brand of filled, egg-shaped chocolates, competing products such as the Rolo Egg were becoming a threat. Still Cadbury's promotional message remained popular with consumers.

Cadbury turned to Triangle Communications to create a promotion to get consumers more involved with its brand. Triangle created a contest in which consumers were invited to answer the "How Will You Eat Yours?" question. Cadbury's ads and in-store displays invited consumers to call a toll-free phone number and describe their egg-eating method. Everyone who called received two premiums: a plastic cap resembling a bald head—a "Creme EggHead"—imprinted with the "How Will You Eat Yours?" slogan, and a letter from the television personality who starred in the Cadbury ads. Cadbury selected the 50 most creative ideas and invited the callers to participate in a weekend competition at the Cadbury World exhibition area at the company's factory. During the weekend, the company selected 12 winners to appear in a series of television ads. The resulting ads were among the most-recalled by consumers in research conducted during the following weeks. Even more importantly, sales of Creme Eggs were up over previous levels.

From this overview of the promotional mix, we now turn to discussions of each of its elements. The following sections detail the major components of advertising, sales promotion, personal selling, and public relations.

ADVERTISING

Of the elements of the promotional mix, advertising is the most visible form of nonpersonal promotion—and the most effective for many firms. **Advertising** refers to paid, nonpersonal communications usually targeted at large numbers of potential buyers. Although U.S. citizens often think of advertising as a typically American function, it is a global activity. In fact, of the world's top ten advertisers, half are headquartered outside the U.S. Each of these companies spends billions of dollars a year for advertising. Figure 16.3 lists the top ten worldwide advertisers and their annual expenditures.

Advertising expenditures can vary considerably from industry to industry, from company to company, and from one advertising medium to another. For television, the top advertising spenders are manufacturers of cars and light trucks; automobile dealers spend the most on newspaper ads. On the radio, the leading industry is telecommunications, followed, ironically, by advertising for broadcast and cable television.[9] Among individual companies, giants like Ford and McDonald's buy million-dollar ad time on television. In contrast, small companies may be able to achieve their promotional

FIGURE 16.3
Top Ten Worldwide Advertisers

Company and Headquarters

Company	Headquarters	Spending
Procter & Gamble	U.S.	$4.74*
Unilever	U.K.	$3.42
General Motors	U.S.	$3.19
Ford Motor Co.	U.S.	$2.23
Philip Morris	U.S.	$1.98
Nestlé	Switzerland	$1.83
Toyota Motor Corp.	Japan	$1.69
Sony Corp.	Japan	$1.34
The Coca-Cola Company	U.S.	$1.33
Volkswagen	Germany	$1.32

*Worldwide ad spending in U.S. $billions

objectives by spending a few thousand dollars on carefully targeted ads in local newspapers or coupon packages mailed to consumers.

Types of Advertising

The two basic types of ads are product and institutional advertisements. **Product advertising** consists of messages designed to sell a particular good or service. Advertisements for the *Harry Potter* movie, an American Airlines vacation package, or shopping at Abercrombie & Fitch are examples of product advertising. **Institutional advertising** involves messages that promote concepts, ideas, philosophies, or goodwill for industries, companies, organizations, or government entities. G&G Advertising created institutional ads when it advertised to Native Americans the advantages of being included in the Census Bureau's year 2000 count. The advertising message to most U.S. population groups was that being counted enabled groups to receive a larger share of government benefits, such as federal assistance and representation in Congress. However, G&G downplayed the government connection, determining that Native Americans have little trust of the government. Instead, the campaign defined Census 2000 as an opportunity for individuals and groups to be heard.[10]

A form of institutional advertising that is growing in importance, **advocacy advertising,** promotes a specific viewpoint on a public issue as a way to influence public opinion and the legislative process. Both not-for-profit organizations and businesses use advocacy advertising, sometimes called *cause advertising*. Chapters 1, 2, and 13 give examples, including the advertising campaign by the Partnership for a Drug-Free America, which encourages parents to talk to their children about drugs. Figure 16.4 provides another example, part of the "Picture Them Home" campaign to locate missing children.

FIGURE 16.4
Advocacy Advertising

Advertising and the Product Life Cycle

Both product and institutional advertising fall into one of three categories, based on whether the ads are intended to inform, persuade, or remind. A firm uses *informative advertising* to build initial demand for a product in the introductory phase of the product life cycle. L'Oréal strengthened its presence in the Japanese cosmetics market with Maybelline Wonder Curl mascara. Ads on television, in magazines, and on billboards describe the mascara's ability to curl as well as color eyelashes. Japanese women loved the new look, and before long, sales of Wonder Curl—at 50,000 units a day—exceeded L'Oréal's most optimistic expectations.[11]

Persuasive advertising attempts to improve the competitive status of a product, institution, or concept, usually in the growth and maturity stages of the product life cycle. When the U.S. economy is strong, the military struggles to maintain its recruiting targets, so it uses persuasive advertising. Ads like the one shown in Figure 16.5 for the U.S. Army seek to entice young men and women to their local recruiting office by demonstrating the excitement of a military

I was called up for the peacekeeping mission, and we were on alert for six months. I never fired my weapons. I didn't need to. But I know my presence made a difference. **I AM AN ARMY OF ONE.** And you can see my strength.

AN ARMY OF ONE

U.S. ARMY
RESERVE

FIGURE 16.5
Use of Persuasive Advertising by the U.S. Army

life. The ad also features the new theme "An Army of One" to convey the importance of the individual—even in this huge organization. The Marines appeal to adventure-loving young people with ads in music and teen magazines. One shows a woman climbing a rope beneath a headline that says, "Every day you have to test yourself. If not, it's a wasted day."[12]

One of the most popular types of persuasive product advertising, **comparative advertising,** compares products directly with their competitors. Clorox used an advertising campaign to say that Clorox disinfectant spray cleans certain types of bacteria from surfaces for 24 hours, but a competing Lysol product does not. Lysol's maker, Reckitt & Colman, countered with print advertising claiming that Clorox spray fails to work for 24 hours against some viruses. However, too much comparative advertising can create confusion when consumers remember only the advertising criticisms, but not which brand is supposedly best. Third-place Ray-O-Vac concluded that comparative advertising campaigns between the leading battery brands, Duracell and Energizer, had begun to leave consumers wondering what to believe. So Ray-O-Vac simply offered to give consumers their money back if they noticed their Ray-O-Vac batteries differed significantly from the competition.[13]

Reminder-oriented advertising often appears in the late maturity or decline stages of the product life cycle to maintain awareness of the importance and usefulness of a product, concept, or institution. To counter declining sales of its consumer products, such as toys and videos, Disney launched an advertising campaign to revive the appeal of Mickey Mouse and other Disney characters. The black-and-white television ads bring Disney cartoons to a younger generation by featuring modern stars giving testimonials. In one ad, rap star Coolio says Mickey is a "black role model," and in another, singer Christina Aguilera says she has a Mickey Mouse tattoo.[14]

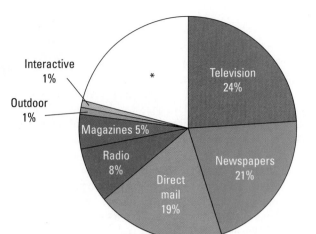

FIGURE 16.6
Carving Up the Advertising
Media Pie

*An additional 21% is spent on such miscellaneous media as Yellow Pages listings, business papers, transit displays, cinema advertising, and farm papers.

Advertising Media

Marketers must choose how to allocate their advertising budgets among various media. All media offer advantages and disadvantages. Cost is an important consideration in media selection, but marketers must also choose the media best suited for communicating their message. As Figure 16.6 indicates, television and newspaper advertising represent the two leading media, in large part because of their flexibility. Online (interactive) advertising receives only about 1 percent of total advertising spending—and was not even measured a few years ago. Still, advertising on the Internet is expected to grow far faster than the other media over the next four years. Other media expected to enjoy strong growth are cable television and outdoor advertising.[15]

Newspapers   Daily and weekly newspapers continue to dominate local advertising. Marketers can easily tailor newspaper advertising for local tastes and preferences. Advertisers can also coordinate their newspaper messages with other promotional efforts. In fact, readers rank advertising as the third most useful feature in newspapers, after national and local news. A disadvantage comes from the relatively short life span; people usually discard their papers after reading.

The sheer volume of advertising in a typical newspaper produces intense competition for reader attention. Successful newspaper advertisers make newsworthy announcements in their ads, such as sales, the opening of new stores, or the launch of new products. Retailers and automobile dealers rank first among newspaper advertisers.

Newspaper publishers once worried that the Web would erode their traditional role of providing news, advertising, and entertainment guides, but they have experienced the opposite result. Most newspapers now maintain Web sites to complement their print editions, some of which offer separate material and features.

Television   Television is America's leading national advertising medium. Television advertising can be classified as network, national, local, and cable ads. The major national networks—ABC, CBS, NBC, Fox, Warner Brothers, and United Paramount Network—represent about 28 percent of all television ads. Despite a decline in audience share and growing competition from cable, network television remains the easiest way for advertisers to reach large numbers of viewers—10 million to 20 million with a single commercial. Among the heavy users of network television advertising are auto manufacturers, financial services companies, and fast-food chains. The "Clicks and Mortar" box discusses one fast-food outlet that has had tremendous success with television ads.

Dave Thomas Cooks Up Successful Commercials

Background. He's not glamorous. He's not young. But by now, his face is unforgettable. In his television commercials, he has worn a hockey uniform and a cowboy costume. He has been seen meditating on a mountaintop. And of course, he has been seen serving burgers. He is Dave Thomas, founder of Wendy's International, and according to the Guinness record keepers, he has starred in the longest-running advertising campaign featuring a company founder.

What Happened? When Thomas appeared in his first Wendy's commercial, no one—including Thomas himself—thought he had a career ahead of him as a television star. *Advertising Age* panned the commercial, saying that Thomas had the "screen presence of a side of beef." Jim McKennan, the copywriter who wrote the ad recalls, "He was bad." Art director Paul Basile says, "We . . . thought our careers were over." But the professionals hadn't counted on the American public's response to Thomas's closing line in the commercial, "Our hamburgers are the best in the business, or I wouldn't have named the place after my daughter."

The Response. To nearly everyone's surprise, people loved the down-home, no-nonsense Thomas. So he did more commercials. He appeared in punk-rock clothes and strummed an electric guitar. He perched a French beret atop his head and pedaled a bike. He shared the spotlight with figure skater Kristi Yamaguchi and National Hockey League goalie Mike Richter. He began to develop an on-camera signature style, including rolling his eyes as he delivered funny lines. "He becomes the punch line to a joke," says Paul Basile. "He's like a period at the end of a sentence." Wendy's executive vice president, Charlie Rath, says that all this exposure "has given Thomas a 90-plus [percent] recognition factor, up with Michael Jordan." That recognition "opens doors," notes Thomas,

which not only sells more burgers but also gives him a platform to promote a social cause that is close to his heart: adoption. He has traveled to the White House, written to *Fortune* 1000 CEOs, and weighed in for new adoption legislation in his efforts to find homes for kids. His recognizable name and face have made it easier for him to get through to people.

Today and Counting. Thomas doesn't plan to stop making his commercials anytime soon—they're just too popular. Wendy's has already spent $1.5 billion on the Thomas-based campaign since 1989 because they attract consumers to Wendy's restaurants. "We see it in the daily readings," says Thomas. But maybe that is because Thomas still comes across as a regular guy. "I think the good thing about Dave is that he hasn't gotten too good at [doing commercials], because that's part of the charm," explains Jim McKennan. "Because he's not an actor, he's a hamburger cook. He's still who he is, and that's why the commercials are so successful."

QUESTIONS FOR CRITICAL THINKING

1. Do you think other media would be as successful for the Wendy's campaign featuring Dave Thomas as television has been? Why or why not?
2. At some point, Dave Thomas and his executives will probably be thinking ahead to a new television ad campaign that does not feature Thomas. Can you think of some possible scenarios for a commercial? Describe one or two.

Sources: "The Ads," Wendy's Web site, **www.wendys.com**, accessed March 21, 2001; "Biography: Dave Thomas," Wendy's High School Heisman Program Web site, **wendyshighschoolheisman.com**, accessed March 21, 2001; John Grossman, "Dave Thomas's Recipe for Success," *Sky*, November 2000, pp. 103–107.

Cable services continue to make inroads into the television sector, with ad revenues expected to grow about seven times faster than those of traditional broadcast television. Drawn to the dozens or even hundreds of channels available through cable or satellite services, many viewers have switched away from network programming. Today, only about half the television audience during prime time is watching network shows. As cable modems and satellite services broaden their offerings to Internet and interactive programming, their audience is expected to continue growing. The variety of channels on cable and satellite networks lets advertisers target specialized markets and reach selected demographic groups, often very small ones. This capability is drawing more and more ad dollars to cable, making it the second-fastest-growing advertising medium after the Internet.[16]

The tremendous growth in television advertising is easy to understand. Television combines sound with dynamic visuals of products and their associated images. One ad that took advantage of this strength was a memorable 30-second spot run by the Gap during a recent Oscar presentation. Women wearing capri pants from the Gap danced to the song "America" from the musical *West Side Story*. Television ads can also simulate one-on-one sales presentations by demonstrating product usage and benefits. Mass coverage, repetition, flexibility, and prestige are other positive features. In addition, marketers can now beam their television commercials to grocery store checkout lines, health clubs, and even schools.

On the other hand, television is an expensive advertising medium. The price to air a 30-second ad during weeknight prime time on network television generally ranges from $100,000 to more than $500,000 for the most popular shows. Because of the high cost, advertisers demand guarantees of audience size and receive compensation if a show fails to deliver the promised number of viewers. Recently, when many viewers ignored the television debut of XFL football, NBC had to compensate advertisers with free air time to use for running ads on other network programs.

Radio   The average U.S. household owns five radios, a market penetration that makes radio an important advertising medium. Advertisers like the captive audience of listeners as they commute to and from work. As a result, morning and evening drive time shows command top ad rates. In major markets, many stations serve different demographic groups with targeted programming. The potential of the Internet to deliver radio programming also offers opportunities for yet more focused targeting. Satellite transmission technology may soon let consumers subscribe to a service like 100-channel Sirius Satellite Radio or XM Satellite Radio.[17]

Magazines   Magazines include consumer publications and trade journals that serve as B2B links. *Time, GQ,* and *Sports Illustrated* are consumer magazines, and *Advertising Age, HR Focus, Biotech Business,* and the *Journal of Environmental Health* fall into the trade category.

While you may agree with Bruce Springsteen's song "57 Channels and There's Nothing On," market segmentation is alive and well on cable television. Dozens of channels engage in a practice called *narrowcasting* to compete for viewers seeking specific types of entertainment. One of the more popular new cable channels is Animal Planet, created by the Discovery Channel.

Magazines often can customize their publications and target advertising messages to different regions of the country. One method places local advertising in regional editions of the magazine. *Sunset* magazine, which specializes in coverage of Western living, includes articles about gardening and other topics tailored to individual regions. An advertiser wanting to reach San Diego readers can place ads in that edition. Other magazines attach wraparounds—half-size covers on top of full-size covers—to highlight articles inside that relate to particular areas; different wraparounds appear in different parts of the country.

Magazines are a natural choice for targeted advertising. Media buyers study demographics of subscribers and select magazines that attract the desired readers. A company with a product geared to young women would advertise in *Glamour* and *Cosmopolitan;* one with a product that appeals to entrepreneurs might choose *Inc., Success,* or *Entrepreneur.*

Direct Mail   The average American household receives about 550 pieces of direct mail each year, including 100 catalogs. The huge growth in the variety of direct-mail offerings combined with the convenience they offer to today's busy, time-pressed shoppers has made direct-mail advertising a $44 billion business.[18]

One media-effectiveness study showed that every dollar spent on direct-mail advertising generates $10 in sales, over twice the effectiveness of television advertising. In a recent year, Lands' End tried cutting back on its catalog mailings, substituting television advertising to drive shoppers to the company's Web site. Although Internet sales increased, they did not offset the significant decline in catalog sales, so Lands'

FIGURE 16.7
Using Telephone and Internet Access to Support the Lands' End Catalog

End determined that catalogs remain essential to the company's promotional mix. The following year, it restored most of the catalog mailings.[19] Figure 16.7 shows a recent Lands' End ad that demonstrates how the firm supports its catalog through easy access via toll-free telephone access or by ordering online.

Although the cost per person reached via direct mail is high, a small business may be able to spend less on a limited direct-mail campaign than on a television or radio ad. For businesses with a small advertising budget, a carefully targeted direct-mail effort with a message that interests recipients can be highly effective. In New York City, Carol Konop uses direct mail to promote her small business, the Shirt Store. Konop built a mailing list from personal contacts and referrals and sends mailings containing handwritten greetings. She also mails everyone on her list a monthly newsletter featuring articles about customers and fashion events. The direct mail has helped the Shirt Store, which sells custom- and ready-made shirts, to build 20,000 customer relationships and increase sales every year since the store opened.[20]

Another way to minimize costs while maximizing the targeting of direct mail is to use e-mail, which bypasses the printing and postage costs. Marketers can target the most interested Internet users by offering Web site visitors an option to register to receive e-mail. They can gather names through their own Web site, as well as sites like Yesmail.com, which invite consumers looking for special offers to register to receive e-mail on subjects of interest to them. Marketers can then buy lists of names from Yesmail.com. One study found that generating a sale through such an opt-in campaign costs an average of just $2 per sale.[21]

For both e-mail and postal campaigns, address lists are at the heart of direct-mail advertising. Using data-mining techniques to develop models for market segmentation, direct-mail marketers develop customer profiles that show the traits of consumers who are likely to buy their products or donate to their organizations. Catalog retailers sometimes experiment by mailing direct-mail pieces randomly to people who subscribe to particular magazines. Next, they analyze the orders received from the mailings and develop profiles of purchasers. Finally, they rent additional subscriber names that match the profiles they have developed.

The National Consumers League surveyed consumers about a number of business practices, including telemarketing, computerized phone systems, fees for using automated teller machines (ATMs), and small print on bills. Respondents rated "junk mail" as more annoying than any of these practices.[22] Among Internet users, another pet peeve is *spam,* or unsolicited e-mail containing sales messages. Many states have outlawed such practices as sending e-mail promotions without legitimate return addresses. The Direct Marketing Association (DMA; www.the-dma.org) helps marketers combat negative attitudes by offering its members guidelines on ethical business practices. The DMA also provides consumer information at its Web site, as well as services that enable consumers to opt out of receiving unsolicited offers by mail, phone, or e-mail.

Outdoor Advertising Outdoor advertising, like billboards and illuminated or animated signs or displays, accounts for a little more than 1 percent of total advertising expenditures, but its share is growing. The majority of spending on outdoor advertising is for billboards, but spending for other types of outdoor advertising, such as signs in transit stations, stores, airports, and sports stadiums, is growing faster. Advertisers are exploring new forms of outdoor media, many of which involve technology: computerized paintings, video billboards, trivision that displays three revolving images on a single billboard, and moving billboards mounted on trucks. Other innovations include putting ads under clear plastic covers on airport baggage carousels and displaying ads on the Goodyear blimp, using an electronic system that offers animation and video.[23]

Outdoor advertising suffers from several disadvantages, however. The medium requires brief messages, and mounting concern for aesthetic and environmental issues is raising opposition. The Highway Beautification Act of 1965 regulates placement of outdoor advertising near interstate highways. And debates still rage about whether billboards should be allowed at all, as discussed in the "Solving an Ethical Controversy" box.

The leading outdoor advertisers include travel and tourism, retailers, clothing, services, and cars. Companies wanting to convey a gritty, urban image also turn to outdoor advertising, but they may look instead for brick walls to paint. Lipton Brisk iced tea uses graffiti on walls as outdoor advertising that doubles as a backdrop for television advertising. The company obtained permission for graffiti artist Lady Pink to spray-paint "Yo, Yo, Yo. That's Brisk, baby" on a lumber yard's wall. The advertising agency then filmed a commercial using a puppet figure of rap artist Coolio. The images also appeared in the print ads for Lipton Brisk.[24]

Interactive Media   Ranging from Web sites and compact discs (CDs) to information kiosks in malls and financial institutions, interactive media are changing the nature of advertising. Although it currently commands only a tiny portion of media spending, interactive advertising is the fastest-growing media segment.

Online advertising has changed dramatically in just a few years. Companies first began experimenting with advertising on this medium in the mid-1990s. At that time, the Web was a novelty for most users. They were exploring what was available, and it was common for two out of five people who saw a *banner ad* to click on it. But within a short time, the novelty wore off. In the words of G. M. O'Connell, one of the pioneers of Internet advertising, "Nobody surfs the Web anymore. . . . People used to do hyperlinking. Now it is utility oriented. . . . We go on the Web to research something specific."[25] Today, successful interactive advertising adds value by offering the audience more than just product-related information. In a campaign for Liberty Mutual insurance, Web ads offered information that would be useful in making insurance decisions. One banner asked, "Is your home properly insured?" Consumers could fill in blanks with how many years ago they purchased their home and the price they paid. When they clicked "submit," they went to a "home evaluator" tool on Liberty Mutual's Web site, where they could learn more about an appropriate level of insurance, as well as Liberty Mutual's products.[26]

In addition to the Internet, technological advances are enabling other forms of interactive advertising. After years of hype, interactive television is making inroads into households and presenting new advertising opportunities. NBC has added interactive features to its broadcasts, such as merchandise offers related to its programs. Someone watching "The Tonight Show with Jay Leno" can use WebTV to order a CD by a musician he or she saw on the show or request more information from one of the show's advertisers.[27] Other marketers are combining direct mail and interactive advertising by sending prospective customers computer disks or DVDs containing marketing messages with opportunities to respond. Unlike a simple brochure, a CD—like a mail-out videotape—is frequently perceived as representing a significant value, so recipients are more likely to investigate its content.

Sponsorships   One of the hottest trends in promotion offers marketers the ability to integrate several elements of the promotional mix. **Sponsorship** involves providing

Billboards: Are They Art or an Eyesore?

Billboards are deeply ingrained in American culture. From the post–World War II Burma Shave signs to huge, flickering billboards that fill Times Square in New York, these outdoor advertisements have been the poster child for American marketing for decades. Although American outdoor advertising accounts for only about 1 percent of every dollar spent on advertising in the U.S., spending is now on the rise. Some experts believe that billboards have a negative impact as a contributor to visual pollution. Others believe that a good billboard is a work of art.

Should billboards be strictly limited or eliminated?

PRO

1. Opponents argue that billboards are not good for tourism and not good for communities. They represent only 1 percent of all advertising—but their impact on visual pollution is many times more severe. The late humorist Ogden Nash paraphrased the well-known Joyce Kilmer poem *Trees* to state his opinion of billboards:

   > I think that I shall never see a billboard lovely as a tree.
   > Perhaps unless the billboards fall, I'll never see a tree at all.

   It's little wonder that communities throughout the nation are gaining the courage to say, "Enough is enough."

2. Over 1,000 communities and several states, including Alaska, Hawaii, Oregon, and Vermont, have already voted to prohibit billboards. Vermont actually uses its billboard-free status as a tourist attraction. "In Vermont, you won't see any billboards," reads one tourism brochure.

3. Billboards can be seen by everyone, including children. Since they may contain content that is inappropriate for children, such as sexually suggestive images or information about alcoholic beverages, they should not be allowed in public places.

CON

1. Billboard advertisers argue that their services actually promote and improve business and tourism.

2. Private industry should not be so strictly regulated. "We don't want to put billboards in scenic places," says Nancy Fletcher, president of the Outdoor Advertisers Association of America. "We never have. But [they do] belong in the commercial areas."

3. Outdoor advertising can be—and has been—an effective medium for public service announcements and information, so it should not be eliminated. In addition, billboards are a positive contribution to the local business community.

SUMMARY

The controversy over billboards is heating up. New technology has allowed an explosion of creativity among billboard manufacturers. Disney's huge re-creation of an asteroid strike on a building tied up traffic for hours, and billboards are now bigger than ever. Figures move, eyes blink, sometimes the entire board rotates. But community activists don't see these as positive developments. "More people are starting to speak up and say they just won't take it anymore," observes Mary Houser.

Sources: "Fighting Billboard Blight," Scenic America Web site, **www.scenic.org**, accessed March 21, 2001; Angelas Rozas, "Billboard Battles Continue in U.S.," *Mobile Register,* November 8, 2000, p. 14A; Ellen Neuborne and Ronnie Weil, "Road Show," *Business Week,* May 8, 2000, pp. 75–90.

funds for a sporting or cultural event in exchange for a direct association with the event. Sports sponsorships attract two-thirds of total sponsorship dollars in this $9 billion annual business in the U.S. alone. The "Business Hits and Misses" box discusses one huge sports sponsorship, NASCAR, and its difficulties in dealing with a star's tragic death. Entertainment, festivals, causes, and the arts divide up the remaining third of sponsorship dollars.

Sponsors receive two primary benefits: exposure to the event's audience and association with the image of the activity. Sponsors typically gain the rights to use the name of the person or event in their promotions, to advertise during media coverage of the event, to post promotional signs at the venue, to set up sales promotions, and to engage in personal selling to clients invited to attend the event. Event sponsors frequently set up hospitality tents where they entertain channel members and potential customers. Sponsorships play an important role in relationship marketing, bringing together the event, its participants, and the sponsoring firms, and allowing marketers to reach a narrow but highly desirable audience.

Other Media Options As consumers filter out familiar advertising messages, marketers look for novel ways to catch their attention. In addition to the major media, firms promote through many other vehicles such as infomercials and specialized

No one expected it, perhaps least of all the driver himself. But when veteran NASCAR driver Dale Earnhardt was killed during the last lap of the 2001 Daytona 500 race, his death affected a wide circle of family, friends, fans, and even marketers. That's because the NASCAR industry relies heavily on sponsorships both for funding and for publicity. And while the base of NASCAR fans has been growing steadily, the death of the 49-year-old star forced some marketers to think twice about their relationship with a sport that is inherently dangerous. "There is a reevaluation of NASCAR sponsorships going on in some circles," noted Mike Bartelli, vice president of Millsport Motorsports, a sports marketing agency.

Only a few months before the tragedy, NASCAR inked a six-year Internet rights deal with America Online for $100 million, in which AOL's Turner Sports would operate the Nascar.com Web site and the two organizations would share promotional and marketing rights. NASCAR executives were betting that the agreement with AOL would make NASCAR the top sports site on the Web. "We'll double our traffic and eventually become the No. 1 sports site over the next 18 months," predicted NASCAR vice president of broadcasting, Bray Cary. "As digital space continues to grow geometrically, the critical importance of sports and entertainment properties as a link between the Internet and traditional broadcasting and cable will continue to grow," explained Ed Desser, president of NBA New Media and TV Ventures. "The value and attraction of sports content, where there is a real sense of a community and passion, is *the* evolving story between the two media."

And there is a real sense of community among NASCAR fans, as the outpouring of grief over Earnhardt's accident and sentiment toward his family illustrated. The new Web site posted a tribute to Earnhardt, including statements made by his wife and son, as well as NASCAR drivers and officials. But this tragedy didn't force the web site to shut down. Instead, it continued providing race results, schedules of events, and stories about drivers, and offering games and other promotions for fans, along with a list of sponsors and products that reads like a Who's Who of American industry: Bud-

weiser, Chevrolet, Circuit City, The Coca-Cola Company, Craftsman Tools, Eastman Kodak, Home Depot, Kellogg's, Motorola, Nabisco, UPS, and Visa, to name a few.

Most of the sponsors reacted to the tragedy with sensitivity as well as practicality. "From a marketing standpoint, this is a sensitive time for us and the sport. We have withdrawn some billboard, TV and print ads for an indeterminate amount of time," noted Dave Elshoff of DaimlerChrysler. "We've had a number of sponsors call and tell us of their support," reported George Pyne of NASCAR. "Our conversations with our partners have been very positive and very supportive."

It makes sense for companies to take a close look at their sponsorship of a dangerous sport, regardless of how popular it is. It also makes sense for sponsors to treat a tragedy with grace and respect for all those involved. But in the end, it is very likely that, at NASCAR, life will go on as it always has, perhaps with the addition of new safety equipment or rules. Matt Pye, group product manager for a candy company that promotes NASCAR racing, said, "NASCAR has a huge fan base. They will probably latch on to another driver and stay with racing." And as long as there is NASCAR racing, there will be NASCAR sponsors, from the track to television to the Web.

QUESTIONS FOR CRITICAL THINKING

1. Do you think NASCAR's sponsors made the right decision in continuing their relationship with the sport? Why or why not?
2. In what ways can sponsors benefit from a successful NASCAR Web site?

Sources: "Tribute to a Legend," NASCAR Web site, **www.nascar.com,** accessed March 22, 2001; Ushma Patel, "Such Intimidating Prices on eBay," *Business Week,* March 12, 2001, p. 14; Hilary Cassidy, "On-Track Tragedy May Create Hazard for Future NASCAR Sponsorships," *Brandweek,* February 26, 2001, p. 8; "Start the Engines," *Brandweek,* October 9, 2000, pp. 1, 7.

media. **Infomercials** are a form of broadcast direct marketing. These 30-minute programs resemble regular television programs, but they are devoted to selling goods or services. The long format allows an advertiser to thoroughly present product benefits, increase awareness, and make an impact on consumers. Advertisers also receive immediate responses in the form of sales or inquiries, because most infomercials feature toll-free phone numbers. DAPTV Associates used infomercials to promote its dance instruction videotape with the promise, "If you can walk, you can dance." The small company had not generated a single response with Web advertising, but the infomercials brought in a steady stream of customers.[28]

Other specialized media used for product promotions include advertising in movie theaters and on airline movie screens. Movie theaters show commercials for soft drinks like Coca-Cola, Pepsi, and Dr Pepper before beginning feature presentations. Ads appear in printed programs of live-theater productions, and firms such as PepsiCo and DaimlerChrysler advertise on videocassettes of popular movies. Advertisers also place messages on subway tickets in New York City and toll receipts on the Massachusetts turnpike. A more recent development is the use of ATMs for advertising. Some ATMs can play 15-second commercials on their screens, and many can print advertising messages on receipts. An ATM screen has a captive audience because the user must watch the screen to complete a transaction.

Directory advertising includes the familiar Yellow Pages listings in telephone books and thousands of other types of directories, most presenting business-related promotions. About 6 percent of total advertising revenue goes to Yellow Pages ads. Besides local and regional directories, publishers also have produced versions of the Yellow Pages that target ethnic groups. In the Chicago area, Ameritech has distributed Yellow Pages geared to African Americans and Hispanics, featuring listings of cultural festivals. Ameritech's parent company, SBC Communications, has also distributed a directory targeting Arabic people in Detroit, as well as eight ethnically targeted products in Southern California. In Florida, BellSouth publishes targeted directories for Caribbean- and Latin Americans, Greek Americans, and gay residents. Advertising agency TMP Worldwide tested the usefulness of such targeted directories by placing ads in several ethnic directories for companies offering wireless services. Each ad gave a different phone number, to test the response rates. The ads generated sales from one of every ten callers, considered an excellent return on the cost of the ads.[29] A major advantage of Yellow Pages advertising is that most people who look in the Yellow Pages have already decided they want to locate a convenient restaurant, a nearby store carrying a needed product, or a service provider, and are ready to make a purchase.

SALES PROMOTION

Traditionally viewed as a supplement to a firm's sales or advertising efforts, sales promotion has emerged as an integral part of the promotional mix. Promotion now accounts for close to half as many marketing dollars as are spent on advertising, and promotion spending is rising faster than ad spending. **Sales promotion** consists of forms of promotion such as coupons, product samples, and rebates that support advertising and personal selling.

Both retailers and manufacturers use sales promotions to offer consumers extra incentives to buy. Beyond the short-term advantage of increased sales, sales promotions can also help marketers to build brand equity and enhance customer relationships. Examples include samples, coupons, contests, displays, trade shows, and dealer incentives.

Consumer-Oriented Promotions

The goal of a consumer-oriented sales promotion is to get new and existing customers to try or buy products. In addition, marketers want to encourage repeat purchases by rewarding current users, increase sales of complementary products, and boost impulse purchases. Figure 16.8 shows how marketers to consumers allocate their spending among six major categories of promotions.

Coupons, Rebates, Samples, and Premiums The most widely used sales promotion techniques are coupons, advertising clippings, and cards included in packages. Customers redeem coupons for small price discounts when they purchase the promoted products. Such offers may persuade a customer to try a new or different product. Some retailers, including southern supermarket giant Winn-Dixie and West Coast competitors Ralph's and Von's, double the face values of manufacturers' coupons.

Of the 250 billion coupons distributed annually, consumers typically redeem less than 2 percent.[30] Coupons have the disadvantage of focusing customers on price, rather than brand loyalty, and major consumer-products companies like Procter & Gamble tried to cut back on couponing during the previous decade. However, discount stores like Wal-Mart have made that

FIGURE 16.8
Spending on Consumer-Oriented Promotions

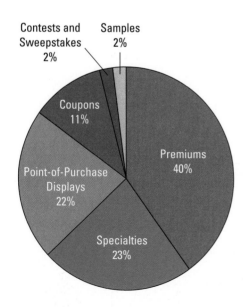

Contests and Sweepstakes 2%
Samples 2%
Coupons 11%
Point-of-Purchase Displays 22%
Premiums 40%
Specialties 23%

strategy difficult. Wal-Mart lures price-conscious shoppers with its own brands. Procter & Gamble has recently begun to offer more coupons for products like detergent and diapers to counter the everyday low pricing and national brands of discount retailers.[31]

Rebates offer cash back to consumers who mail in required proofs of purchase. Rebates help packaged-goods manufacturers increase purchase rates, promote multiple purchases, and reward product users. Other types of companies also offer rebates, especially for electronics, computers and their accessories, and automobiles. Processing rebates gives marketers a way to collect data about their customers.

A sample is a gift of a product distributed by mail, door-to-door, in a demonstration, or inside packages of another product. America Online has widely distributed CDs providing free trials of its Internet service. After the sample period, users have the option to continue the service for a monthly fee. Although sampling is an expensive form of sales promotion, it generates a higher response rate than most other techniques. About three-quarters of consumers who receive samples try them. Malt-O-Meal, which sells lower-priced breakfast cereals, used sampling to persuade grocery shoppers that its cereals were just as good as better-known competitors like Fruit Loops and Cheerios. To drive home the similarity of the brands, the company recruited identical twins to work in supermarkets. The twins invited shoppers with competing brands of cereal in their carts to take a taste test. Among those who agreed, about eight out of ten replaced the cereal in their cart with Malt-O-Meal's comparable product.[32]

A premium is an item given free or at a reduced price with the purchase of another product. Cosmetics companies like Estée Lauder and Clinique offer gifts with purchases of special cosmetics and perfume sets. Fast-food restaurants also are big users of premiums. One of McDonald's most successful promotions involved giveaways of Teenie Beanie Babies with Happy Meals. Consumers also like in-pack items like stickers, trading cards, and other small collectibles. Phone cards are also gaining popularity as premiums. Whenever possible, marketers should choose a premium that is likely to get consumers thinking about and caring about the brand and the product. The premiums given by Estée Lauder and Clinique, for example, are usually samples of new makeup products and related accessories such as mirrors or makeup bags.

Contests and Sweepstakes   Contests, sweepstakes, and games offer cash, merchandise, or travel as prizes to participating winners. Firms often sponsor these activities to introduce new goods and services and to attract additional customers. Contests require entrants to solve problems or write essays, sometimes with proofs of purchase. Sweepstakes choose winners by chance and require no product purchase. Consumers typically prefer them since contests require more effort. Companies like sweepstakes, too, because they are inexpensive to run and determine the number of winners from the beginning. With contests, the company cannot predict the number of people who will correctly complete a puzzle or gather the right number of symbols from scratch-off cards. Sweepstakes and contests can reinforce a company's image and advertising message, but consumer attention may focus on the promotion rather than the product.

In recent years, court rulings and legal restrictions have limited the use of contests. Companies must proceed carefully in advertising their contests and prizes. Marketers must indicate the chances of winning and avoid false promises such as implying that a person has already won.

Specialty Advertising   Take a look around your home. Do you have any pens, T-shirts, calendars, or calculators imprinted with a business name? These offers are examples of **specialty advertising,** in which a company gives away useful merchandise carrying its name, logo, or business slogan. Because those products are useful and sometimes personalized with recipients' names, people tend to keep and use them, giving advertisers repeated exposure. Originally designed to identify and create goodwill for advertisers, specialty advertising now generates sales leads and develops traffic for stores and trade show exhibitors. Like premiums, specialties should reinforce the brand's image and its relationship with the recipient. Over the years, the publishers of your textbook—*Contemporary Business*—have used specialty advertising ranging from fortune cookies and T-shirts to message cubes and tote bags to create awareness and interest in new editions.

Trade-Oriented Promotions

Sales promotion techniques can also contribute to campaigns directed to retailers and wholesalers. *Trade promotion* is sales promotion geared to marketing intermediaries rather than to consumers. Marketers use trade promotion to encourage retailers to stock new products, continue carrying existing ones, and promote both new and existing products effectively to consumers. Successful trade promotions offer financial incentives. They require careful timing, attention to costs, and easy implementation for intermediaries. These promotions should bring quick results and improve retail sales. Major trade promotions include point-of-purchase advertising and trade shows.

Point-of-purchase (POP) advertising consists of displays or demonstrations that promote products when and where consumers buy them, such as in retail stores. Kellogg created a point-of-purchase display for an entire cereal aisle. The display, called Breakfastland, included overhanging signs featuring characters from Kellogg's cereals, labels for a "New Releases" section of the aisle, and interactive features such as a Tony the Tiger paw with a recording that roared "They're grrreat!" when someone pressed it.[33] A high-tech version of POP advertising is the use of kiosks that display product information and promotional offers. Target has installed kiosks with messages about Hasbro toys. The kiosks provide exciting graphics to attract youthful shoppers, as well as up-to-date price information to help parents make decisions. Whether cardboard or electronic, POP advertising takes advantage of many shoppers' tendencies to make purchase decisions in the store.

Also, POP ads can effectively continue a theme developed by some other aspect of the firm's promotional strategy. Rolling Rock beer used POP advertising as part of its promotional strategy in Belgium's bars. Desiring to capitalize on Belgian beer drinkers' growing interest in American-style lagers, Rolling Rock used a promotion based on themes from American history. Bars and discos catering to young adults were invited to display POP ads featuring black-and-white images like the First Millionaire of Las Vegas, the end of Prohibition, and the first moon landing. Establishments that participated in the promotion purchased at least 100 bottles of Rolling Rock for each theme in the promotion, agreed to offer the brand at a discount during the campaign, and participated in the various contests and events accompanying each theme. During the First Vegas Millionaire promotion, servers hung dice on each bottleneck, which patrons could roll to win a free bottle of Rolling Rock. The 12-event campaign was so successful that every bar targeted by Rolling Rock agreed to participate, and many that had not been invited asked to participate.[34]

Manufacturers and importers often host or exhibit at **trade shows** to promote goods or services to members of their distribution channels. These shows are often organized by industry trade associations, typically during annual meetings or conventions. Each year, thousands of trade shows attract millions of exhibitors and hundreds of millions of attendees. Such shows are particularly important in fast-changing industries like those for computers, toys, furniture, and fashions. The annual electronic show, which is held in Las Vegas and attracts hundreds of thousands of visitors, is the nation's largest. These shows are especially effective for introducing new products and generating sales leads.

PERSONAL SELLING

Many companies consider **personal selling**—a person-to-person promotional presentation to a potential buyer—as the key to marketing effectiveness. Unless a seller matches a firm's goods or services to the needs of a particular client or customer, none of the firm's other activities produces any benefits. Today, sales and sales-related jobs employ about 16 million Americans. Businesses often spend five to ten times as much on personal selling as on advertising. A recent survey found that the average cost of a U.S. sales call is $170.[35] Given the significant cost, businesses are very concerned with the effectiveness of their personal selling.

How do marketers decide whether to make personal selling the primary component of their firm's marketing mix? In general, firms are likely to emphasize personal selling rather than advertising or sales promotion under four conditions:

1. *Customers* are relatively few in number and geographically concentrated.
2. The *product* is technically complex, involves trade-ins, and requires special handling.
3. The product carries a relatively high *price*.
4. It moves through *direct-distribution channels*.

The sales functions of most companies are experiencing rapid change. Some changes have been only cosmetic, such as changing the job title from salesperson to account representative or associate, while maintaining the duties. But many firms are making more significant changes in their sales forces—expanding duties and sometimes changing the job itself. Today's salespeople are more concerned with establishing long-term buyer–seller relationships and acting as consultants to their customers than in the past. Like the salesperson shown in Figure 16.9, they focus not just on closing sales but on helping customers decide what they need and working with them to ensure efficient product use.

Personal selling can occur in several environments, each of which can involve B2B or business-to-consumer selling. Sales representatives who make sales calls on prospective customers at their homes or businesses are involved in *field selling*. Companies that sell major industrial equipment typically rely heavily on field selling. *Over-the-counter selling* describes sales activities in retailing and some wholesale locations, where customers visit the seller's facility to purchase items. *Telemarketing* sales representatives make their presentations over the phone. A later section reviews telemarketing in more detail.

Sales Tasks

All sales activities involve assisting customers in some manner. Although a salesperson's work can vary significantly from one company or situation to another, it usually includes a mix of three basic tasks: order processing, creative selling, and missionary selling.

Order Processing   Although both field selling and telemarketing involve this activity, **order processing** is most often related to over-the-counter selling in retail and wholesale firms. The salesperson identifies customer needs, points out merchandise to meet them, and processes the order. Efficient and accurate order handling is critical to satisfying customers' needs. Good salespeople check the quality of the products their customers receive, know their customers' markets, and ensure that their firms can supply products when needed.

Route sales personnel process orders for such consumer goods as bread, milk, soft drinks, and snack foods. They check each store's stock, report inventory

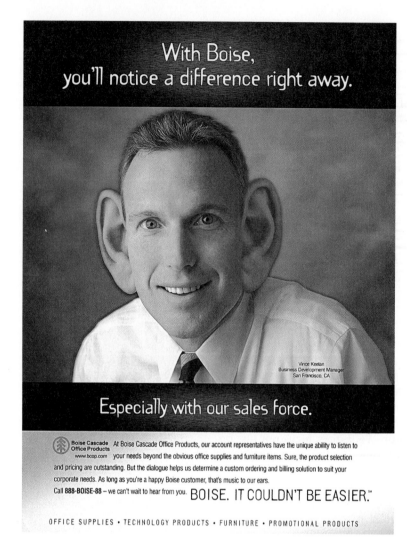

With Boise,
you'll notice a difference right away.

Vince Keelan
Business Development Manager
San Francisco, CA

Especially with our sales force.

Boise Cascade Office Products   At Boise Cascade Office Products, our account representatives have the unique ability to listen to
www.bcop.com   your needs beyond the obvious office supplies and furniture items. Sure, the product selection
and pricing are outstanding. But the dialogue helps us determine a custom ordering and billing solution to suit your
corporate needs. As long as you're a happy Boise customer, that's music to our ears.
Call **888-BOISE-88** – we can't wait to hear from you.   BOISE. IT COULDN'T BE EASIER.™

OFFICE SUPPLIES • TECHNOLOGY PRODUCTS • FURNITURE • PROMOTIONAL PRODUCTS

FIGURE 16.9
Listening is at the Core of Personal Selling

needs to the store manager, and complete the sale. Most of these jobs include at least minor order-processing functions. These activities become the primary duty in cases where customers can readily identify and acknowledge their needs. A later section discusses sales force automation, showing how companies now use technology to simplify order processing.

Creative Selling   Sales representatives for most business products and some consumer items perform creative selling, a persuasive type of promotional presentation. Creative selling promotes a good or service whose benefits are not readily apparent or whose purchase decision requires a careful analysis of alternatives. Sales of intangible products such as insurance rely heavily on creative selling.

Some store salespeople primarily process orders, but a department store's cosmetics department relies heavily on creative selling. Stores like Lord & Taylor, Macy's, and Marshall Field's hire salespeople known as *beauty advisers,* who receive training, supervision, and part of their compensation from the cosmetics company whose products they sell. Training programs prepare beauty advisers to listen to their customers sympathetically, suggest not only the products they ask about but related items, and respond to objections positively. At the Macy's store in Manhattan, beauty adviser Muffie Ferrel greets shoppers with a smile and "How are you today?" She doesn't say, "May I help you?" because it is too easy to answer with "No, thanks." When a mother and daughter ask for guidance on foundation for the mother, Ferrel helps the older woman select the right Estée Lauder product for her skin type. Along the way, she also counsels the daughter on how to use lip liner so that lipstick will not look "too red." Before long, Ferrel has turned a question into an $82 transaction. She also keeps records of her top customers, so she can follow up with holiday greetings or news of product introductions. Estée Lauder's president attributes much of the difference among stores' sales figures to the skills of the company's beauty advisers.[36]

Missionary Selling   Sales work also includes an indirect form of selling in which the representative promotes goodwill for a company or provides technical or operational assistance to the customer; this practice is called missionary selling. Many businesses that sell technical equipment, such as IBM and Xerox, provide systems specialists who act as consultants to customers. These salespeople work to solve problems and sometimes to help their clients with questions not directly related to their employers' products. Other industries also use missionary selling techniques. Pharmaceutical company representatives—called *detailers*—visit physicians to describe the firm's latest products. The actual sales, however, are handled through wholesalers, which sell to pharmacies, which fill the prescriptions.

The Sales Process

The sales process typically follows the seven-step sequence shown in Figure 16.10: prospecting and qualifying, the approach, the presentation, the demonstration,

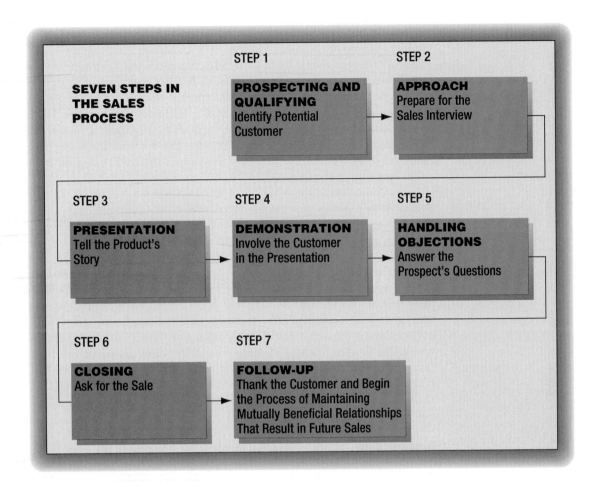

SEVEN STEPS IN THE SALES PROCESS

STEP 1
PROSPECTING AND QUALIFYING
Identify Potential Customer

STEP 2
APPROACH
Prepare for the Sales Interview

STEP 3
PRESENTATION
Tell the Product's Story

STEP 4
DEMONSTRATION
Involve the Customer in the Presentation

STEP 5
HANDLING OBJECTIONS
Answer the Prospect's Questions

STEP 6
CLOSING
Ask for the Sale

STEP 7
FOLLOW-UP
Thank the Customer and Begin the Process of Maintaining Mutually Beneficial Relationships That Result in Future Sales

FIGURE 16.10
Seven Steps in the Sales Process

handling objections, the closing, and the follow-up. Remember the importance of flexibility, though; a good salesperson is not afraid to vary the sales process based on a customer's responses and needs. The process of selling to a potential customer who is unfamiliar with a company's products differs from the process of serving a long-time customer.

Prospecting and Qualifying   At the prospecting stage, salespeople identify potential customers. They may seek leads for prospective sales from such sources as previous customers, friends, business associates, neighbors, other sales personnel, and other employees in the firm. The qualifying process identifies potential customers who have the financial ability and authority to buy. Those who lack the financial resources or who cannot make purchase decisions are not qualified prospects.

Companies use different tactics to identify and qualify prospects. Some companies rely on business development teams to do this legwork. They send direct mail and use the responses to provide leads to sales reps. Other companies believe in the paramount importance of personal visits from sales representatives. Galileo International, which markets its computerized reservation system to travel agencies, uses dozens of salespeople to travel from city to city, calling on travel agents. The product is complex and represents a large investment for customers, who are often less than eager to try something new. So skillful and patient sales effort is essential, even at the prospecting stage.[37]

Approach   Successful salespeople make careful preparations, analyzing available data about a prospective customer's product lines and other pertinent information before making the initial contact. They realize the importance of a first impression in influencing a customer's future attitudes toward the selling company and its products.

Successful salespeople learn to "read" customers and determine their needs. John James rose through the ranks of selling to become chief executive of Tom Cat USA, the American division of a company that makes staging and lighting equipment used in concert tours. Despite his managerial role, James still handles 50 customer accounts. When he visits a concert scene, he takes time to size up the activities and note which suppliers' equipment the tour is using besides Tom Cat's. He also chats with members of the road crew as they scurry about their work to find out details that could help him in the future.[38]

Presentation   At the presentation stage, salespeople communicate promotional messages. Usually they describe the major features of their products, highlight the advantages, and cite examples of satisfied consumers. John James knows that when he visits the crew preparing for a concert tour, no one will have time to listen to a long sales presentation. So he takes every opportunity to convey his products' benefits. While visiting a crew at work on a Ricky Martin tour, James met the tour's manager after an hour on the set. As manager Joyce Fleming watched crew members hang spotlights, James commented, "You guys have the tough job," then told them about a Tom Cat product that could be set up faster than a competing product the tour was using. Within minutes Fleming was off on other business, but before the concert began, James heard that Fleming was interested in buying the equipment he had described. James understands that his busy customers want to focus on product benefits: "She doesn't have time for me unless I have something really good— and I do."[39]

Demonstration   A demonstration involves the prospect in the sales presentation, reinforcing the message that the salesperson has been communicating—a critical step in the sales process. Paper manufacturers produce elaborate booklets to help their salespeople demonstrate different types of paper, finishes, and graphic techniques. Such demonstrations allow salespeople to show printed samples to art directors, designers, printers, and other potential customers. While selling Estée Lauder cosmetics at Macy's Manhattan store, Muffie Ferrel demonstrates lipstick colors by marking several different shades on the back of her hand. Next, she demonstrates the use of a lip pencil by drawing an outline on her other hand, then filling it in with lipstick. She holds out both hands so the customer can compare the two techniques. She started the demonstration by using her own hands because Estée Lauder recommends this less invasive approach instead of touching the customer.[40]

Some products are too large to carry to prospective buyers or require special installation to demonstrate. Using laptop computers and multimedia presentations, sales representatives can demonstrate these products for customers.

Handling Objections   Some salespeople fear prospects' objections because they view the questions as criticism. Instead, salespeople should try to view objections as opportunities to extend presentations and answer questions. Proper handling of objections allows sales personnel to remove obstacles and complete sales. This step can become a positive stage of the sales process by allowing the salesperson to present additional information and offer a unique solution as a way to clarify a point. Estée Lauder trains its salespeople to respond to objections about high price by restating the product's benefits to the user. As a general rule, the key is to sell benefits, not features: How will this product help the customer?

Closing   The critical point in a selling relationship—the time at which the salesperson actually asks the prospect to buy—is the closing. If the presentation effectively matches product features to customer needs, the closing should be a natural conclusion.

Salespeople use a variety of closing techniques. Some of the more popular ones include the following:

- The technique, "If I can show you . . ." first identifies the prospect's major concern in purchasing the good or service and then offers convincing evidence of the offering's ability to resolve it. ("If I can show you how the new heating system will reduce your energy costs by 25 percent, would you be willing to let us install it?")

- The alternative-decision technique poses choices for the prospect, either of which favors the seller. ("Do you prefer this sweater or the other one?")

- In the SRO (standing room only) technique, the seller warns the prospect to conclude a sales agreement immediately because the product may not be available later, or an important feature, such as its price, will soon change.

- A seller can use silence as a closing technique, since discontinuing the sales presentation forces the prospect to take some type of action, making either a positive or negative decision.

- An extra-inducement close offers special incentives designed to motivate a favorable buyer response. Extra inducements may include quantity discounts, special servicing arrangements, or layaway options.

The term *close* actually portrays an inaccurate picture. The sales process should emphasize relationship management, not special closing techniques. When a sale closes, the customer and company should be at the beginning, not the end, of a relationship.

Follow-up   A salesperson's actions after the sale continue the relationship and may well determine whether the customer will make another purchase. After closing, the seller should process the order quickly and efficiently, and reassure the customer about the purchase decision. Follow-up is a vital activity for building a long-term relationship with customers to ensure that products satisfy them and to deliver needed service. By calling soon after a purchase, the salesperson provides psychological reinforcement for the customer's decision to buy. It also gives the seller a chance to correct any problems.

Follow-up strengthens the bond between salespeople and customers. Car dealers implement extensive follow-up programs, including calls soon after purchase decisions, thank-you notes from salespeople, customer satisfaction surveys from both dealerships and car manufacturers, and calls from service managers inviting customers to use the dealer's service department. Quest Diagnostics, which sells diagnostic testing services, conducts annual customer surveys to measure satisfaction with the company's products, as well as its sales and other services. Quest learned that some of its biggest customers were unhappy with how well company representatives listened when problems arose. Armed with this knowledge, Quest improved its process for handling complaints, which in turn improved customer satisfaction. Follow-up strengthened Quest's relationships with its major customers by identifying a way to make them happier.[41]

Proper follow-up is a logical part of the sales process. It involves not only continuing contact with customers but also a review of the sales process. Salespeople should ask themselves, "Why did I lose or close that sale? What could I have done differently to improve the outcome?"

Recent Trends in Personal Selling

As noted earlier, personal selling requires different strategies in today's competitive business environment than salespeople used in the past. Rather than making face-to-face presentations to potential customers, firms may rely on telemarketing to solicit business or to fill orders placed directly by buyers. Especially in B2B situations involving technical products, customers expect sales reps to answer technical questions, understand technical jargon, and communicate using sophisticated technological tools—or they must bring along someone who can. Patience is also required, because the sales cycle, from initial contact to closing, may take months or even years, especially for large, expensive equipment. To address these concerns, companies are turning to relationship selling, consultative selling, team selling, and sales force automation—major personal selling trends that are changing the sales forces of companies of all sizes.

Telemarketing   Telemarketing, personal selling conducted entirely by telephone, provides a firm's marketers with a high return on their expenditures, an immediate response, and an opportunity for personalized, two-way conversation. Many firms use telemarketing because expense or other obstacles prevent salespeople from meeting all potential customers in person. Telemarketers can use databases to target prospects based on demographic data.

Telemarketing takes two forms. A sales representative who calls you at your place of business is practicing *outbound telemarketing. Inbound telemarketing* occurs when the customer calls a toll-free phone number to get information or place an order. Print ads for catalog companies like Lands' End and The Sharper Image encourage customers to call and request catalogs or place orders.

Outbound telemarketers must abide by the Federal Trade Commission's 1996 Telemarketing Sales Rule. Telemarketers must disclose that they are selling something and on whose behalf they call before they make their presentations. The rule also limits calls to between 8 A.M. and 9 P.M., requires sellers to disclose details on exchange policies, and requires them to keep lists of people who do not want to receive calls.

Relationship Selling and Consultative Selling

As competitive pressures mount, a widening universe of firms are emphasizing **relationship selling**, in which a salesperson builds a mutually beneficial relationship with a customer through regular contacts over an extended period. To create strong, lasting relationships with customers, salespeople must meet buyers' expectations. Such buyer–seller bonds become increasingly important as companies reduce the number of suppliers from which they buy and look for companies that provide excellent customer service and satisfaction. Salespeople must also find ways to distinguish themselves from others offering similar products. Previous examples illustrate relationship selling: John James visiting his customers to help them find ways to set up stages more smoothly and efficiently, and Quest Diagnostics' efforts to retain customers by providing better customer service.

Businesses often carry out relationship marketing by using consultative selling, which shifts the emphasis of the sales process from the product to the customer. **Consultative selling** means meeting customers' needs by listening to them, understanding and caring about their problems, paying attention to details, suggesting solutions, and following through after the sale. Consultative selling is not cheap. A company may invest more than $100,000 in sales calls, demonstrations, and research to close a sale.[42] With such an investment, companies that

The biggest flower delivery day of the year is Mother's Day—and leading online foes FTD and 1-800-flowers.com couldn't be more aware of it. To make sure that their telephone lines and Web sites stay busy, both firms spend millions on traditional cable and network television ads, direct mail, and online advertising. FTD, with 16,000 stores off-line, will spend $40 million this year on ads such as this one, featuring a mom holding a "Touch of Spring" bouquet.

use consultative selling are determined to stand out from the competition. Salespeople are expected to educate themselves so well that they deliver value in every sales call, and companies invest in the information technology that will enable their salespeople to answer questions on the spot. IBM demonstrated success in consultative selling by using its research laboratory to help Monsanto—now part of global pharmaceutical giant Pharmacia—solve problems related to its work in genetic engineering. This valuable service gave IBM the advantage when Monsanto awarded a billion-dollar contract for maintaining desktop computers.[43]

Team Selling   Team selling joins salespeople with specialists from other functional areas of the firm to complete the selling process. In this way, it complements relationship and consultative selling strategies. Teams can be formally assigned units or assembled for specific, temporary selling situations. Hewlett-Packard (HP) uses team selling to assess the needs of its biggest customers. In a change from the past practice of having individual salespeople sell particular product lines, the company brings together teams of employees representing its different products and assigns them to study each customer. The teams identify customer needs and the solutions that would be most profitable to HP. Through the team approach, HP has substantially increased sales to its largest customers.[44]

In sales situations involving new, complex, and ever-changing technologies, team selling has enhanced many companies' abilities to meet customers' needs. Many customers prefer the team approach, making them feel like they receive exceptional service. Another advantage is the formation of relationships between companies rather than individuals.

Sales Force Automation   Recent advances in communications and information technology have many applications to the sales process. Together, these applications have produced a trend called **sales force automation (SFA)**. This trend incorporates a broad range of tools, from e-mail, telecommunications devices like pagers and cell phones, and notebook computers to increasingly sophisticated software systems that automate the sales process. These SFA software packages help sales managers develop account territories, plan sales campaigns, perform detailed analyses of sales trends, and forecast future sales. Sales personnel can use the system to analyze customer databases to develop leads, schedule sales campaigns, automatically file orders and expense reports, and tap into company databases for instant updates on prices and product availability.

Among its many benefits, SFA improves the consistency of the sales approach, speeds response times, and reduces the sales cycle. Salespeople can design product packages and close deals on the spot, instead of collecting information from customers and returning to their offices to prepare proposals.

PUBLIC RELATIONS

A final element of the promotional mix, public relations (PR)—accompanied by its subsidiary element publicity—supports advertising, personal selling, and sales promotion, usually by pursuing broader objectives. Through PR, companies attempt to improve their prestige and image with the public by distributing specific messages or ideas to target audiences. Cause-related promotional activities are often supported by PR and publicity campaigns. As such, PR is an important part of a company's promotional plan.

Public relations refers to an organization's nonpaid communications with its various public audiences, such as customers, vendors, news media, employees, stockholders, the government, and the general public. Many of these communication efforts serve marketing purposes. Public relations is an efficient, indirect

BUSINESS DIRECTORY

➤ **public relations**   *organization's nonpaid communications and relationships with its various audiences.*

communications channel for promoting products. It can publicize products and help to create and maintain a positive image of the company.

The PR department links a firm with the media. It provides the media with news releases and video and audio clips, as well as holding news conferences to announce new products, formation of strategic alliances, management changes, financial results, and similar developments. Publications issued by the PR department include newsletters, brochures, and reports.

Publicity

The type of public relations that most closely approaches promoting a company's products is **publicity**, nonpersonal stimulation of demand for a good, service, place, idea, event, person, or organization by unpaid placement of information in print or broadcast media. Businesses generate publicity by engaging in unusual or significant activities. Web portal Yahoo! received extensive media coverage when it posed "the world's laziest shopper" in a storefront of Rockefeller Center in New York. For a month, this person laid back in a La-Z-Boy recliner and shopped online from merchants listed in Yahoo! Shopping. Thousands of passersby stopped to watch and shop.[45] Utility.com, which sells energy and telecommunications services, received thank-yous and customer orders when it paid the tolls of commuters passing through the Allston-Brighton toll plaza west of Boston for a day. The publicity effort was a successful way to target consumers geographically.[46]

PROMOTIONAL STRATEGIES

Many of this chapter's examples demonstrate the considerable overlap existing among the elements of the promotional mix. Clear boundaries no longer distinguish advertising from sales promotion. The Internet and other interactive media also change how marketers promote products. By blending advertising, sales promotion, personal selling, and public relations, marketers create an integrated promotional mix that reflects the market, product type, stage in the product life cycle, price, and promotional budget. Then they implement one of two promotional alternatives: pulling or pushing strategies. Finally, marketers must measure the effectiveness of their promotional strategies.

Selecting a Promotional Mix

Choosing the most appropriate promotional mix is one of the toughest tasks confronting a company's marketers. The following questions provide some general guidelines for allocating promotional efforts and expenditures among personal selling and advertising:

- **What is your target market?** A drill-press manufacturer that markets to business buyers is likely to emphasize personal selling in its promotional mix. By contrast, sportswear marketers such as Nike depend more on reaching a broad audience through effective advertising campaigns featuring people using their products. The ad in Figure 16.11 shows a person well protected by Nike clothing and says that his teeth aren't chattering—because he is "neither cold, nor wet, nor a pathetic sniveling wuss."

- **What is the value of the product?** Most companies cannot afford to market low-priced goods like toothpaste, soft drinks, and candy through personal selling, so they choose advertising instead. High-priced products in both business and consumer markets, however, require promotional mixes based on personal selling. Examples include time-share vacation condominiums on Maui and Boeing aircraft.

If your teeth still chatter, it's fear.

The Storm-F.I.T.™ full-zip waterproof jacket is part of the NIKE F.I.T.™ line of apparel, a layering system that keeps you warm when you need to be warm, dry when you need to be dry. David Bryson's teeth do not chatter because he is neither cold, nor wet, nor a pathetic sniveling wuss.

APPAREL

FIGURE 16.11
Advertising Used in Nike's Promotional Mix

- **What time frame is involved?** Marketers usually advertise sales before the actual event. An effective and consistent advertising theme may favorably influence a person's reaction to an approaching salesperson, and except for self-service situations, a salesperson is typically involved in completing a transaction. Marketers often expose customers to advertising again after a sale to assure them that they made the right choices and to condition them for repeat purchases.

Pushing and Pulling Strategies

Marketers can choose between two general promotional strategies: a pushing strategy or a pulling strategy. A **pushing strategy** relies on personal selling to market a product to wholesalers and retailers in a company's distribution channels. So marketers promote the product to members of the marketing channel, not end users. Sales personnel explain to marketing intermediaries why they should carry a particular item, usually supported by offers of special discounts and promotional materials. Marketers also provide **cooperative advertising** allowances, in which they share the cost of local advertising of their firm's product or line with channel partners. All of these strategies are designed to motivate wholesalers and retailers to push the good or service to their own customers.

A **pulling strategy** attempts to promote a product by generating consumer demand for it, primarily through

---

BUSINESS DIRECTORY

➤ **publicity** *stimulation of demand for a good, service, place, idea, person, or organization by disseminating news or obtaining favorable media presentations not paid for by the sponsor.*

➤ **pushing strategy** *promotional effort by a seller to members of the distribution channel intended to stimulate sales of the good or service.*

➤ **pulling strategy** *promotional effort by a seller to stimulate demand among final users.*

Sega's Dreamcast Has Pull with Consumers

Background. Several years ago, Sega Enterprises came up with a new video game system. That was the easy part. The hard part was finding a way to reach consumers—gamers—with a message letting them know that the new product, Dreamcast, was a must-have. So Sega marketers created the ultimate pulling strategy, generating consumer demand every way they knew how.

What Happened? The popularity of Sega products had waned somewhat, falling behind PlayStation and other blockbuster games. But Sega marketers thought that if they could get the system into the hands of players, it would sell itself. "The consumer has to experience the product [to generate] a sense of anticipation," explains Peter Moore, Sega America's senior vice president of marketing. So Sega came up with a promotional mix that involved everything from joint promotions with MTV to publicity. Sega conducted trial rentals through the Hollywood Video chain, a partnership with IGN.com (a popular Web site for gamers), and a Dreamcast Mobile Assault Tour led by distinctive vehicles. Then the company found out that MTV was going to hold its annual music awards around the same time as the actual product launch, and signed on early as a sponsor. The awards show became the launch's key event. Sega bought television commercial space on the show and conducted an online contest at its Web site, which gave away a trip to New York to attend the show and celebrate the Dreamcast launch. "We received e-mail submissions in the six figures," recalls Peter Moore. Sega also gave Dreamcast systems to all the show's featured presenters.

The Response. A week after the promotion began, over 300,000 consumers had paid the $25 pre-order fee at retail outlets, reserving their own Dreamcast. Nearly $100 million in Dreamcast systems and related software were sold within 24 hours following the product's launch. So, the promotion seemed to be a success. But after the initial rush, sales proved disappointing. As Sony and Nintendo prepared to release their new systems, interest in Dreamcast faded. Finally, in 2001 Sega pulled the plug on its hardware console business. The game was over for Dreamcast.

Today and Counting. To recoup some of its losses, Sega slashed prices in half on its remaining console inventory of 2 million units. Meanwhile, the company plans to supply video games to run on systems manufactured by Sony, Nintendo, and Microsoft. It also may further develop its online gaming strategy. Time will tell whether the new moves are successful.

QUESTIONS FOR CRITICAL THINKING
1. Why do you think a pulling strategy was not ultimately successful in the case of the Dreamcast launch? Do you think a pushing strategy would have worked better? Why or why not?
2. What steps might Sega take to ensure its competitive position as online gaming becomes more popular?

Sources: "Events," Sega Web site, **www.sega.com,** accessed March 20, 2001; Alexandra Hainey, "Sega to Halve Prices," *Financial Times,* **news.ft.com,** February 5, 2001; Alexandra Hainey, "Game over for Dreamcast," *Financial Times,* **news.ft.com,** January 31, 2001; David Vaczek, "Dream Weavers," *Promo,* October 1999, pp. 75–78.

advertising and sales promotion appeals. Potential buyers will then request that their suppliers (retailers or local distributors) carry the product, thereby "pulling" it through the distribution channel. Although pulling strategies can be tremendously effective, they don't always work, as the "Clicks and Mortar" box describes.

Most marketing situations require combinations of pushing and pulling strategies, although the primary emphasis can vary. Consumer products usually depend more heavily on pulling strategies than do B2B products, which favor pushing strategies. In the earlier example of Pepsi One, PepsiCo has relied heavily on advertising to build product familiarity. However, getting consumers to try the product requires that they notice it while shopping. Following the product's launch. PepsiCo noticed that though Pepsi products were well-represented by end-aisle displays, few of these displays included Pepsi One. So, the marketing campaign broadened to place more emphasis on the push strategy of persuading bottlers to feature Pepsi One in end-aisle displays.[47]

ETHICS IN PROMOTION

Of all of the elements in a 21st century business organization, promotion ranks high among those raising the most ethical questions. Many people view advertising negatively, labeling it as propaganda rather than information. They criticize its influence on consumers, its potential for creating unnecessary needs and wants, its overemphasis on sex and beauty, and its delivery of inappropriate messages to children. The National Institute for Health Care Management Foundation reports that 41 percent of the market for prescription drugs is held by 25 heavily promoted drugs. Consumers often take a heavily promoted and expensive medication without ever having tried less-expensive, less-advertised alternatives that can work as well. Some observers conclude that promotional strategies of pharmaceutical companies are supporting high prices, to the detriment of patients and the public and private insurance plans that subsidize their health care.[48]

This section examines three controversial issues related to the promotion element of the firm's marketing mix: puffery and deception, promotion to children and teens, and promotion in public schools and on college campuses.

Puffery and Deception

Legally as well as ethically, there are limits on the claims a marketer may make. A statement such as "The most advanced system ever developed" is an example of *puffery,* exaggerated claims of a product's superiority or use of doubtful, subjective, or vague statements. Puffery is usually considered unbelievable and so is legal. But although consumers may accept some puffery to distinguish a product without tricking them, puffery raises ethical questions. Where is the line between claims that attract attention and those that imply a guarantee? To what degree are advertisers deliberately making misleading statements?

The Uniform Commercial Code, which standardizes laws for business practices throughout the U.S., distinguishes puffery from specific or quantifiable statements about product quality or performance. Those statements amount to an "express warranty," for which the company must stand behind its claim. General boasts of product superiority and vague claims are considered puffery, not warranties. A marketer's quantifiable statement, on the other hand, implies a certain level of performance. Tests can establish the validity of a claim that one brand of batteries outlasts a rival brand.

Although puffery and other incorrect statements are usually associated with advertising, other promotional elements can also involve deception. Sales promotions may tempt unscrupulous companies to deceive consumers by inaccurately stating the odds of winning sweepstakes or contests. Salespeople have deceived customers with misleading information or deceived their employers by using company cars for personal purposes, shipping unordered merchandise to win sales contests, or padding expense reports. Bribing customers with large gifts or cash kickbacks to increase sales is another example of unethical conduct. Many firms have adopted company codes of ethics to promote ethical awareness and prevent lapses.

Promotion to Children and Teens

The risk of deception is especially great with promotional messages targeted to children and teens. Although today's children are certainly accustomed to promotional messages, they are not sophisticated at analyzing them. In addition, to woo young consumers, advertisers often make ads as unadlike as possible—designing messages that resemble entertainment. With modern media companies owning a variety of broadcast, print, Internet, and other outlets, children watching Saturday-morning cartoons are exposed to an integrated marketing effort that combines advertising for related videos, books, and video games, as well as licensed merchandise from toys to backpacks to T-shirts. And they often see advertisements for foods that most parents would prefer they eat only occasionally, as a treat. By contrast, in Sweden, broadcasters may not direct advertising to children under 12.

As children grow older and become more sophisticated, so does the marketing effort. The U.S. teen population is larger than it ever has been, and marketers are working harder than ever to learn about them. MTV even borrowed the techniques

THE NEW WRX DOESN'T JUST HUG CURVES. IT THROWS THEM IN A HEADLOCK AND GIVES THEM A NOOGIE.

The humorous claims of unforgettable performance of the Subaru WRX are intended to support the visual image of the car in motion on a winding stretch of highway and attract attention from potential purchasers.

of anthropology to visit teens and observe their lives firsthand. With their activities under a microscope, teen music habits are quickly absorbed by companies in the industry; even the extremes of rage rock quickly became big business.

Promotion in Public Schools and on College Campuses

A related ethical issue is the placement of promotional messages in schools, from kindergartens through university campuses. The idea of school as a haven where kids and young adults are exposed only to messages tailored to their mental development seems quaint in light of the promotional book covers, posters, and even curriculum materials provided to today's schools. Some schools are bringing in income by signing contracts that give certain brands exclusive access to their students. Last year, Wheeler High School in Marietta, Georgia, used some of the $50,000 it received in annual vending machine revenues to refinish the gym floor, install a new high-jump pit, and pay $7,000 for two buses. At De Anza College in Cupertino, California, the administration arranged for a student identification in the form of a smart card that combines a First USA credit card, a Citibank ATM card, a Z-Line phone card, and a debit card that operates Coca-Cola vending machines. Besides the implied endorsement of certain brands and the limitations on consumer choice, such a program raises other ethical concerns—for example, does a first-year college student even need a credit card? Shoe marketers and sports apparel firms like adidas, Nike, Reebok, and Russell Athletic compete for exclusive rights to provide shoes and sports attire for intercollegiate athletic teams. Around the country, The Coca-Cola Company also signed exclusive deals to market its drinks in schools and at athletic events through vending machines and eating facilities. The arrangement provides the schools with extra income while linking the sponsor's product to the institution.

In-school promotions are beginning to generate a backlash, however. San Francisco's school board has banned textbooks that use brand names inappropriately, following complaints about a math book that included computations with brand-name snack foods. Criticism also helped The Coca-Cola Company decide to revise its in-school marketing. The company announced that it would begin including healthier products—bottled water, juice, and other beverages—in school vending machines. In addition, the company said it would replace corporate logos on the machines with images of students exercising and playing. The timing seems to be good marketing strategy. Soft-drink companies had been receiving negative publicity linked with a medical journal article that reported greater obesity rates in children who drank at least one soft drink a day. Also, although most U.S. children drink sweetened beverages every day, they have been switching from soda pop to other beverages.[49] Associating its name with healthy drinks may be the best strategy for selling Coke.

WHAT'S AHEAD

As the four chapters in Part IV demonstrate, information systems are playing an increasingly important role in marketing strategy. Marketers can gather and analyze data that enable them to tailor their products, prices, distribution, and promotional messages to individual customers, as well as to build long-term business relationships with them. Along with marketing, other areas of business operations, from accounting and finance to human resource management and production, use information systems to improve efficiency and increase profitability. Chapter 17 discusses how information systems, including the Internet, and other forms of technology change the business environment and help businesses succeed.

➤ Summary of Learning Goals

1. Relate the concept of integrated marketing communications to the development of a firm's promotional strategy.

In practicing integrated marketing communications, a firm coordinates all promotional activities to produce a unified, customer-focused message. IMC begins by identifying consumer needs and then moves backward to show how a company's products meet those needs. Then marketers select the promotional media that best target and reach customers. Teamwork and careful promotional planning to coordinate IMC strategy components are important elements of these programs. Increasing complexity and sophistication in marketing communications require careful promotional planning to coordinate IMC strategies.

2. Explain the concept of a promotional mix and list the objectives of promotion.

A company's promotional mix integrates two components: personal selling and nonpersonal selling, which includes advertising, sales promotion, and public relations. By selecting the appropriate combination of promotional mix elements, marketers attempt to achieve the firm's five major promotional objectives: provide information, differentiate a product, increase demand, stabilize sales, and accentuate the product's value.

3. Summarize the different types of advertising and advertising media.

Advertising, the most visible form of nonpersonal promotion, is designed to inform, persuade, or remind. Product advertising promotes a good or service, while institutional advertising promotes a concept, idea, organization, or philosophy. Newspapers and television represent the largest advertising media categories. Other media include magazines, radio, direct mail, and outdoor advertising. Interactive media such as the World Wide Web represent the fastest-growing type of advertising. Interactive advertising directly involves the viewer, who controls the flow of information.

4. Describe the role of sales promotion in promotional strategy.

Although less well known as a promotional element, sales promotion accounts for greater expenditures than does advertising. Consumer-oriented sales promotions like coupons, rebates, samples, premiums, contests, sweepstakes, and specialty advertising offer an extra incentive to buy a product. Point-of-purchase advertising displays and trade shows are sales promotions directed to the trade markets.

5. **Identify the various personal selling tasks and the steps in the sales process.**

Personal selling involves face-to-face interactions between seller and buyer. The primary sales tasks are order processing, creative selling, and missionary selling. The seven-step sales process includes prospecting and qualifying, approach, presentation, demonstration, handling objections, closing, and follow-up.

6. **Explain how public relations supports other elements of the promotional mix.**

Public relations is an indirect promotional alternative to advertising, sales promotion, and personal selling. It improves a company's prestige and image with the public. Public relations uses a variety of marketing communications such as media releases, news conferences, and article placements and story ideas in other media to generate publicity for a company.

7. **Identify the factors that influence the selection of a promotional mix.**

Marketers begin by focusing on their company's target market, product value, time frame, and budget. By analyzing these factors, they develop a promotional mix and allocate resources and expenditures among personal selling, advertising, sales promotion, and public relations.

8. **Contrast pushing and pulling promotional strategies.**

With pushing strategies, marketers use personal selling to promote their company's product to retailers and wholesalers, not end users. Practices include special incentives such as discounts, promotional materials, and cooperative advertising. Advertising and sales promotions are part of pulling strategies, which build consumer awareness so that consumers will ask retailers to carry the product. The strategies are not exclusive choices; in fact, most companies combine them to increase promotional effectiveness.

9. **Discuss the major ethical issues involved in promotion.**

Promotion is the element of the marketing mix that raises the most ethical questions. Many consumers believe that advertising exerts too much influence on buyers and that it deceives customers by exaggerating product claims and consciously blurring the line between promotion and entertainment. Contests that don't disclose the odds of winning and bribes to customer representatives to increase sales are other examples of unethical behavior. Many consumers question the appropriateness of marketing to children and through schools.

Business Terms You Need to Know

promotion 578
integrated marketing communications (IMC) 578
promotional mix 580
advertising 584
sales promotion 594
personal selling 597
order processing 597

creative selling 598
missionary selling 598
public relations 603
publicity 604
pushing strategy 605
pulling strategy 605

Other Important Business Terms

positioning 582
product advertising 585
institutional advertising 585
advocacy advertising 585
comparative advertising 586
sponsorship 591

infomercial 593
specialty advertising 595
point-of-purchase (POP) advertising 596
trade show 596
telemarketing 602

relationship selling 602
consultative selling 602
team selling 603
sales force automation (SFA) 603
cooperative advertising 605

➤ Review Questions

1. Explain the integrated marketing communications process. Why do marketers use this process to develop their companies' promotional strategies?

2. What are the two major components of the promotional mix? What promotional mix might be appropriate for each of the following?

   a. a new energy candy bar

   b. wireless phone service

   c. specialty auto parts sold to car manufacturers

   d. a honeymoon resort

3. Identify and define the two basic types of advertising. Give an example of each. Then identify and define the three categories that each of these basic types falls into.

4. Identify the two leading advertising media. What are the benefits and drawbacks of each?

5. Distinguish between advertising and sales promotion.

6. Under what conditions is a firm most likely to emphasize personal selling rather than advertising or sales promotion?

7. Identify and describe briefly each of the seven steps in the sales process.

8. Relate the concepts of sales force automation and team selling.

9. Describe some of the recent trends in sales strategies. What are the pros and cons of each?

10. Differentiate between pushing and pulling strategies. Under what conditions should each be employed?

➤ Questions for Critical Thinking

1. Choose a product that you purchased recently. Identify the various media that were used to promote the product and analyze the promotional mix. Do you agree with the company's marketing strategy, or would you recommend changes to the mix? Why?

2. Create your own print ad for the product in question 1, using any strategies or knowledge you have learned in this course so far.

3. As a consumer, what is your typical response to some of the closing techniques described in the chapter?

Which is (or are) the most successful with you? Which is (or are) the least? Why?

4. What type of sales promotion techniques would you recommend for the following businesses, and why?

   a. a Subaru dealership located in upstate New York

   b. an Oregon-based chain of retail stores that sells skis and snowboards in the winter, bicycles and skateboards in the summer

   c. a Thai restaurant located in Denver

   d. a luxury health spa in Arizona

5. School Markets Associates develops advertiser-supported lunch fliers for school cafeterias. A recent example was a school lunch menu with a scene from a Fox animated feature movie. The company encourages school food-service directors to create menu items using character names that relate directly to its clients' entertainment products. Some school-lunch program managers say that the colorful menus encourage kids to eat more nutritious foods. But many parents and educators criticize such promotional efforts, saying that marketing messages don't belong on the school sites and may imply endorsement from teachers. Do you think this type of brand-oriented promotion to schoolchildren is ethical? Why or why not? Do you think this type of promotion (adjusted for age appropriateness, of course) would be ethical on a college campus? Why or why not? If your answers are different for each age group, explain why.

➤ Experiential Exercise

Background: You have learned in this chapter how to promote goods and services using integrated marketing communications. This exercise, which may be done either as an individual or a group project, will help you apply many of the chapter concepts to the promotion of a new product.

Directions: Develop the concept for a new product in a familiar category to compete with any product you currently use.

1. Use the following table to record the specifics of your promotional strategy.

2. Be prepared to present the results of this exercise during a class discussion.

Product Description
Product Name

On what basis is your product differentiated? • Attributes • Price/quality • Use	Explain the differentiation.

Describe your target market

In launching the advertising campaign for your new product, describe the content of your informative advertising.

Select three media you believe would be best for carrying your advertising message and explain why you selected each medium:
• Newspapers
• Television
• Radio
• Magazines
• Direct Mail
• Outdoor Advertising
• Interactive Media
• Infomercial
• Yellow Pages
• Other specialized media _____

Will you use coupons, rebates, samples, or premiums? If yes, which ones, and why?

Indicate whether any of the following would be appropriate in promoting your product, and explain why you would or would not use each option:
• Contests or sweepstakes
• Specialty advertising
• Point-of-purchase advertising

Include any other aspects of your promotional strategy not provided for in the preceding sections.

> ## Nothing but Net

1. **Professional certification.** An organization called Sales and Marketing Executives International offers several certifications for sales and marketing professionals. Visit the organization's Web site (**www.smei.org**) and read about these certifications. Prepare a report answering the following questions:

   a. What professional certifications are available?

   b. What are the objectives of professional certification?

   c. What are the benefits?

2. **Promotional Products and Specialty Advertising.** The use of promotional products and specialty advertising is another form of marketing communication. Visit the Web sites listed at the end of this question to answer the following questions:

   a. What are promotional products?

   b. Which ones are the most popular?

   c. What are the advantages of using promotional products?

   www.ppa.org

   www.ssac.net

   www.saagny.org

3. **Advertising Standards of Practice.** The American Association of Advertising Agencies (AAAA) is a professional organization whose members include many of the nation's largest agencies. Visit the Association's Web site and prepare an oral report to your class, citing the Association's mission, its standards of practice, and its creative code. Find an ad in a recent newspaper or magazine that you believe adheres to the Association's creative code.

   www.aaaa.org

   Note: Internet Web addresses change frequently. If you don't find the exact sites listed, you may need to access the organization's home page and search from there.

On a recent Super Bowl Sunday, among the multimillion dollar dot.com commercials, one commercial was aimed directly at women. Set in the newborn nursery at a hospital, a nurse carefully placed a pink knitted cap on the head of a baby girl. Within seconds, the cap was on the floor. Within a few more seconds, several caps were on the floor, along with pink booties flying out of other bassinets in the nursery. "A new voice," declared a caption. "For women, by women."

The commercial advertised a new 24-hour cable network and Web site, Oxygen Media, whose target audience is women. The Super Bowl ad was produced by Massachusetts-based Mullen Advertising, which counts among its customers such diverse organizations as Swiss Army and General Motors. The placement of the Oxygen commercial surprised some viewers. Women and football? "Advertising in this venue says Oxygen thinks women can mix it up with men," explains Alan Johnson of Mullen. "We partly did it because it's a completely unexpected place to be," acknowledges Tricia Melton, marketing vice president of Oxygen Media. "[But] it's the best place to reach women en masse." After all, millions of women do watch the Super Bowl. "It's a tremendous opportunity," said Linda Ong, Oxygen's senior vice president for marketing. "It's the largest viewing audience of women on television. Women have been there all along, watching with families, friends, boyfriends, husbands."

The commercial, part of a larger campaign to launch the channel and Web site, required teamwork among Mullen employees and with Oxygen founders. Mullen has always included teamwork in its integrated marketing communications planning. "When you work with each other for a long time, you end up knowing each other really well, you trust one another, you share objectives, you know each other's strengths and weaknesses, you're not lobbying or jockeying for position, and you're not trying to take each other's jobs," explains Edward Boches, executive creative director for Mullen.

The launch of Oxygen Media itself was preceded by plenty of publicity, partly because of its association with celebrities such as Oprah Winfrey, an Oxygen co-founder who promised a 12-week series to the network in its first year and Candice Bergen, who was slated to host a late-night talk show called *Exhale.* Co-founder Geraldine Laybourne, a high-profile executive who had already turned a little station called Nickelodeon into an empire of its own, enjoyed plenty of press as well as financial support from giants such as AT&T, AOL Time Warner, and Paul Allen, a co-founder of Microsoft. "It's a creation of media and hype," quipped Peter Kreisky of New York's Mercer Management Consulting, "which now has to prove itself."

Although the cable network began in a small number of urban and suburban markets, the Web site was immediately available to anyone who logged on to **www.oxygen.com.** Advertising and promotional efforts on the Web site have been interactive since the beginning. Through the use of multimedia technology, customers—Web site visitors as well as consumers who use goods and services advertised on the site—tell their personal stories as they relate to the products. "By listening and sharing with your customers, you're essentially having them co-write your brand," remarks Kit Laybourne, chief of Oxygen's digital storytelling unit and Geraldine Laybourne's husband. "And they're doing it for nothing, or next to nothing." Bob Johanson, chief director for the Internet think tank Institute for the Future, agrees that this new method of advertising has merit. "Stories are both ads and content for Web sites," he says.

From the beginning, Oxygen Media entered into cross-promotional arrangements with other companies. Starbucks agreed to sell its coffee products through the Oxygen Web site as the two organizations looked for ways to build a community and cross-promote their Web sites. "It gives us the opportunity to lower the cost of customer acquisition by fully leveraging the convergence that is now occurring with the Internet, cable, and other media channels," noted Howard Schultz, chairman and CEO of Starbucks. "We have 10 million customers who visit our locations weekly, and with 70 percent of these customers already online, we have an extremely loyal and Internet-savvy customer base."

Meanwhile, back at Mullen Advertising, taglines and slogans continued to fly. In one advertisement, "First in lifeboats" and "No back hair" were followed by the tagline "Another great reason to be a woman." Eventually, an ad tagline might be bold enough to say, "Another great reason to breathe Oxygen."

QUESTIONS

1. Why is it important for Mullen to use integrated marketing communications in its development of a promotional strategy for Oxygen?
2. In addition to Starbucks, name another company that you think might be a good partner in a cross-promotional effort with Oxygen Media, and explain why.
3. Imagine that you work for Mullen Advertising. Sketch a one-page print advertisement for Oxygen Media with a tagline.
4. Visit the Oxygen Media Web site at **www.oxygen.com** to learn more about it. Describe as many tactics as you can that Oxygen uses to promote itself on the site.

Sources: "The Lowe Group Merges Mullen and Long Haymes Carr," January 17, 2001, **http://lhcadv.com;** Marcia Stepanek, "Tell Me a Digital Story," *Business Week Online,* May 15, 2000, **www.businessweek.com;** Michael Johns, "Oxygen Media an Ambitious Effort," *Media Central,* March 16, 2000, **www.mediacentral.com;** Marci McDonald, "A Network of Her Own," *U.S. News Online,* January 31, 2000, **www.usnews.com;** James Poniewozik, "Will Women Take a Breath of Oxygen?" *Time,* January 31, 2000, pp. 62–66; Katie Makal, "Tackling Super Bowl Ads," *Post Industry,* January 29, 2000, **www.postindustry.com.**

PART V

Managing Technology and Information

CHAPTER 17

Using Technology to Manage Information

Learning Goals

1. Distinguish between data and information.

2. Explain the role of management information systems in business.

3. Identify and briefly describe each of the different types of information system programs.

4. Describe the major types of computer hardware and software.

5. Articulate how specific types of software, such as word processing and desktop publishing, can help businesspeople.

6. Indicate the importance of special network technologies.

7. Discuss ways that companies can protect themselves from computer crimes.

8. Explain steps that companies can take toward disaster recovery and backup.

Roger Ham: The LAPD's First CIO

If you have to dial 911 in Los Angeles, you can thank Roger Ham that the call goes through and your emergency is answered. Ham, an electrical engineer, is the Los Angeles Police Department's (LAPD's) first chief information officer, or CIO, in charge of computer systems and communications. His job is much like that of a CIO in the corporate world.

For a large, urban police department to run effectively, rapid, smooth flows of information are critical—from officers on the street to headquarters, through databases of convicted criminals and missing persons, and between the police and fire departments. Technology has improved that flow of information tremendously during the past decade, but Ham's challenge was to integrate the department's different systems—in effect, to create order from chaos. When he arrived, no single, organized information technology system or plan existed. Instead, information technology resources were spread out among the different branches, with one branch directing communications projects and another in charge of desktop computers. Ham's predecessor, Troy Hart, recalls the bad old days of fragmented information flow from two separate in-house systems: "We were married in intent, but divorced in paths of delivery." For instance, both of the previous information groups agreed that police on the streets needed better information systems to keep them informed and safe. But one division lobbied for notebook computers, while the other advocated upgrading mobile data terminals (MDTs) in squad cars. Under Ham's direction, both projects were implemented, and they now work together.

The first six months of Ham's career as CIO of the department were spent working six days a week, 12 hours a day. "It was like a major fire drill," he recalls. "There were stacks of paperwork, projects, contracts being sent out." He had three major goals to fulfill: (1) merge the department's resources; (2) mend fences with the public, which had funded the construction of new police dispatch centers while politicians fought over where they should be located; and (3) fulfill staffing needs, including not only hiring new staff but also finding dependable outside contractors, when they were needed.

Ham achieved those goals and more. By the beginning of his second year on the job, 700 new MDTs had been installed in patrol cars, as the first step toward increasing the amount of crime-related information readily available to officers. They can now enter crime data and write reports in the field, instead of having to return to their stations. "We have 9,600 police officers on the streets," observes Ham, "and if I can improve their efficiency just 10 percent, then I've effectively put 1,000 additional officers on the streets."

Ham has also endured the kinds of crises that inevitably plague a large police department like the LAPD. When a fire broke out in the building that contained the city's central 911 system, Ham got to the scene to discover that the system had been damaged not only by fire but also by the water used to extinguish it. He stayed on the job to oversee a huge data and systems recovery effort that some people feared would take up to four days. Under Ham's direction, the task was completed in only 13 hours. "And we never lost a single 911 call," he recalls with pride. So, if you are one of the 6,000 callers who dial the LAPD 911 number each day, Ham is the kind of guy you want in charge.[1]

CHAPTER OVERVIEW

Information is the final frontier for organizations seeking to gain and maintain an edge over their competitors. In the past, managers focused on producing quality goods and services, hiring and training the best workers, and finding ways to create value for their customers. As competition gets tougher and tougher, particularly in the global marketplace, businesses must look for opportunities to provide the quality goods and services that customers want and need but do it faster, better, and with greater customization than anyone else. To accomplish this feat, they need information and technology.

This chapter explores how businesses successfully manage information as a resource, particularly how they use technology to do so. It looks at ways they use information systems to organize and use information, including databases and information system programs. Because computers drive information systems, the chapter also discusses computer types and their applications in business settings. Today specialized networks make information access and transmission function smoothly, so the chapter examines new types of networks to see how businesses are applying them for competitive advantage. Finally, the chapter explores the importance of protecting valuable information and recovering from disasters.

MANAGEMENT INFORMATION SYSTEMS

Every day, businesspeople ask themselves questions such as the following:

- How well is our brand selling in Sacramento compared with Miami? How well is it doing in London or Beijing?
- If we raise the price for our product by 2 percent, how will the change affect sales in each city? In each country?
- If we make our employee benefits systems available to employees through networks, will it streamline our costs?
- What are the per-unit storage costs for our flagship model?

An effective information system can help answer these and many other questions. *Data* consist of raw facts and figures that may or may not be relevant to a business decision. *Information* is the knowledge gained from processing those facts and figures. So, while businesspeople need to gather data about the demographics of a target market or the specifications of a certain product, the data are useless unless they are transformed into relevant information that can be used to make a competitive decision. Technology has advanced so quickly in the past few years that even small businesses now have access to data and information that can make them competitive in a global arena. Figure 17.1 shows the increasingly rapid pace at which the U.S. adopts new technology.

A management information system (MIS) is an organized method for providing past, present, and projected information on internal operations as well as external intelligence to support decision making. A large organization typically assigns responsibility for directing its MIS and related computer operations to an executive called the chief information officer (CIO). Generally, the CIO reports directly to the firm's chief executive officer (CEO). But small companies rely just as much on an MIS as do large ones, even if they do not employ a manager assigned to this area on a full-time basis. The role of CIO is both expanding and changing as the technology to manage information continues to develop. An effective CIO is someone who is capable of understanding and harnessing technology in such a way that the company can communicate internally and externally in one seamless operation. Cisco Systems CEO John T. Chambers feels that the role of the top information executive in a company "has been elevated to that of a strategic partner with the CEO and CFO."[2]

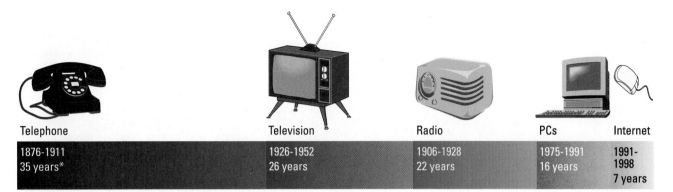

Telephone	Television	Radio	PCs	Internet
1876-1911 35 years*	1926-1952 26 years	1906-1928 22 years	1975-1991 16 years	1991-1998 7 years

*Number of years for new technology to be adopted by one-fourth of U.S. households.

FIGURE 17.1
Increasing Speed of Technology Acceptance

Information systems can be tailored to assist many business functions and departments—providing reports for everything from human resource management, to manufacturing, to finance and accounting. A **marketing information system** can help marketing researchers manage an overwhelming flood of information by organizing data in a logical and accessible manner. Through the system, a company can monitor its marketing strategies and identify problems and opportunities. A marketing information system gathers data from inside and outside the organization; it then processes that data to produce information that is relevant to marketing issues and supports the marketing function. Processing steps could involve storing data for later use, classifying and analyzing it, and retrieving it easily when needed.

Many companies use a combination of high-tech and low-tech solutions to manage the flow of information. Information can make the difference between staying in business and going broke. Keeping on top of changing consumer demands, competitors' actions, and the latest government regulations will help a firm fine-tune existing products, develop new winners, and maintain effective marketing. Great American Events, a $3 million events-marketing firm in Scottsdale, Arizona, relies on everything from Internet access to Microsoft Outlook communications software and Palm wireless devices to share files on projects and engage in group scheduling. But when company president Eric Schecter wants to get a message out quickly, he posts a note on a whiteboard in the company conference room where workers eat lunch. "We want the secretary, or the warehouse guy, who doesn't get on the computer all the time, to see it every day," explains Schecter. Word spreads like wildfire.[3] The "Clicks and Mortar" box focuses on another company that relies on centralizing information to achieve success.

Databases

The heart of a management information system is its **database,** a centralized integrated collection of data resources. A company designs its databases to meet particular information processing and retrieval requirements that its decision makers encounter. A database serves as an electronic filing cabinet, capable of storing massive amounts of data and retrieving it within seconds. A database should be continually updated; otherwise, a firm may find itself with outdated, useless data. One problem with databases is that they can contribute to **information overload**—too much data for people to absorb, or data that are not relevant to decision making, as Figure 17.2 illustrates. Since computer processing speed has doubled every two years for the past 30 years and data are more abundant, businesspeople need to be careful that their databases contain only the facts that they need, so they do not waste time wading through unnecessary data.[4]

Background. During the recession of the early 1990s, Duncan Highsmith's company suffered the same sluggish sales experienced by most other companies. Highsmith Inc. supplies equipment like book displays, audio-video tools, and educational software to schools and libraries, so when funding for schools began to dry up, so did the company's revenues. But CEO Highsmith took a different view of the situation than most other executives at the time. He blamed his company's decline on his own lack of foresight in not seeing how much his company was going to be affected by the tax-cut trends that had started nearly a decade earlier. In other words, he felt some of the sales-decline problems resulted from his inability to look for relevant information in seemingly unorthodox places.

What Happened? Highsmith put aside his spreadsheets and sales reports for a while and began to follow his own instincts to identify information that he believed "could become a compelling factor in the future of the business beyond a one- to three-year horizon." He came up with a plan for developing such knowledge that he called "Life, the Universe, and Everything." (Highsmith did admit borrowing the name from pop culture author Douglas Adams's *The Hitchhiker's Guide to the Galaxy*.) He believed that the kind of information his managers needed was nonquantitative, nonobvious tidbits floating around in different locations—and that different managers needed different information that required packaging into a format suitable for each of them. But Highsmith couldn't manage this knowledge quest himself; he needed a partner. He found her down the hall in the corporate library. Lisa Carreno was a five-year veteran at Highsmith, and she understood the nature of information—where to find it and what to do with it. "Over the years it became clear to me that Lisa had the kinds of skills and insights that would make this project possible," notes Highsmith. So he gave her a $185,000 annual budget and placed the library dead center in the corporate headquarters, so that all hallways would lead to information.

The Response. At first Carreno was apprehensive about her new responsibility, but she hired two assistants and tackled the job. She familiarized herself with all the different aspects of the company and learned how to customize information for certain managers, proving that people skills do count in gathering information. As a result, she's a hit with Highsmith executives. "She knows from conversations we've had that I'm a very touchy-feely person and that I prefer working with people to numbers," says Patty Schnert, team coordinator for customer service. "She works with finance and human resources, so she knows the financial ratios and what kind of turnover we have—she's got a global understanding of the company," notes John Kiley, director of marketing.

Today and Counting. Carreno and her staff continue to take on increasingly complex projects for Highsmith managers. Usually they start with in-depth interviews to get an idea of what a manager wants and needs. Recently, she conducted research to find out whether nursing homes would be a potential new market for Highsmith. Carreno came back to top management with information on market size, competitors, public and private institutions, ownership, products purchased, and vendors used. "Lisa just thinks like a marketer," says John Kiley. "It's not just providing a torrent of materials, it's also her interpretation of it. I take her opinions into account a lot."

QUESTIONS FOR CRITICAL THINKING
1. What types of sources do you think Carreno and her staff might find useful in their research? Use your imagination.
2. Other than the school funding issue mentioned previously, describe one trend that you think might affect Highsmith in the next few years. Explain why and where you got your information.

Sources: "About Us," Highsmith Web site, **www.highsmith.com**, accessed April 22, 2001; Joanne M. Haas, "Demand for Educational Products on the Upswing," *Madison Business First* (Wisconsin) Special Report, January 18, 2000, **www.business-first.net**; Leigh Buchanan, "The Smartest Little Company in America," *Inc.*, January 1999, pp. 43–54.

Businesses create databases in a variety of ways. They can hire a staff person to build them on site, hire an outside source to do so, or buy database programs that are readily available. One of the largest databases is owned by the U.S. Census Bureau; findings from the most recent installment began to be released in 2001. The census, conducted by the bureau every ten years, attempts to collect data on 120 million households across the country. Participants fill out forms containing questions about marital status, place of birth, ethnic background, citizenship, place of work, commute time, income, occupation, type of housing, number of telephones and vehicles, even grandparents as caregivers. Households receiving the most recent census questionnaire could respond in English, Spanish, Chinese, Tagalog, Vietnamese, or Korean. Assistance was provided for other languages as well. Not surprisingly, sifting through all the collected data takes time. Although there are certain restrictions on how marketers can access and use specific census data, the general public may access the data via the American Fact Finder on the Census Bureau's Web site (www.census.gov), as well as at state data centers and public libraries.[5]

FIGURE 17.2
Information Overload

80% of information filed but never used

40% of workers say their duties are interrupted more than 6 times an hour

Executives spend 42% of their time annually just reading

190 messages sent and received daily by the average *Fortune 1,000* office worker

2.8 million tons of paper used in offices from mid 1980s to beginning of 21st century

Business decision makers can also look up online data. Online systems give access to enormous amounts of government data, such as the census and agency regulations. Another source of free information is company Web sites. Managers can visit home pages to look for information about customers, suppliers, and competitors. Trade associations and universities also maintain Web sites with information on topics of interest.

Companies also subscribe to commercial online services that provide fee-for-service databases on particular topics. In addition to broad-based online databases available through such services as Prodigy, CompuServe, and AOL, firms can access specialized databases geared to particular industries and functions. Many professional groups have set up bulletin board systems on the Internet where experts trade information. Businesspeople who gather data online should try to verify the reliability of their sources, however.

Once a company has built a database, its managers need to be able to analyze the data in it. *Data mining,* described in Chapter 13, is the task of using sophisticated technology to retrieve and evaluate data in a database to identify useful trends. Some consulting firms, such as Data Miners Inc., specialize in mining data for their clients. According to Gordon S. Linoff of Data Miners, businesses must look for patterns within the data they have collected to make sense of it. As Linoff explains, "The process is like playing a game of 20 questions—ask a bunch of questions, arrive at a

FIGURE 17.3
Information Systems: Turning Data into a Clear Picture

conclusion."[6] Successful data mining can help a business discover patterns in the sale of certain goods and services, find new customers, track customer complaints and requests, and evaluate the cost of materials.

Information Systems for Decision Making

So much data clogs the Internet and other sources that the challenge for businesses has shifted from acquiring data to sorting through it to find the most useful elements, which can then be turned into valuable information. As shown in Figure 17.3, the keys to a useful information system are the programs that link users to data and help them analyze it.

New types of information system programs are being developed all the time. These range from general tools that help users look up data by letting them type in topics, to specialized systems that track costs, sales, inventory levels, and other data. Businesses can develop and implement their own systems or hire someone else to do so. They can even hire an outside service to manage the data for them.

Decision Support Systems A **decision support system (DSS)** is an information system that quickly provides relevant data to help businesspeople make decisions and choose courses of action. It includes software tools that help decision makers generate the information they need. These DSS tools may vary from company to company, but they typically include retrieval features that help users obtain needed information from a database, simulation elements that let decision makers create computer models to evaluate future company performance under different conditions, and presentation tools that help them create graphs and charts.

An *information interface* is a program that sits between the user and the underlying information system. Advances in information interfaces have simplified and synthesized data into useful information for a variety of users. Chefs at several college campuses can access their systems through an easy-to-use interface to find out what combinations of food students prefer and develop menus accordingly. Instead of having to scroll through hundreds of written comments on a survey, a chef can click on a particular school or region, the specific food he or she is considering preparing, and find out what students would like to eat along with that food. If the chef clicks on grilled chicken, he or she could find out whether students prefer mashed potatoes or rice with the chicken.[7] Such sophisticated interfaces make information retrieval more efficient.

Executive Information Systems   Although the trend is increasingly toward employee empowerment and decision making at all levels of an organization, sometimes companies do need to create specialized information systems to address the needs of executives. An **executive information system (EIS)** allows top managers to access the firm's primary databases, often by touching the computer screen, pointing with a mouse, or even via voice recognition. This software typically produces easy-to-read, full-color graphics and charts. A typical EIS allows users to choose between many kinds of data, such as the firm's financial statements and sales figures as well as stock market trends for the company and for the industry as a whole. If they wish to, managers can start by looking at summaries and then proceed toward more detailed information.

Top executives at Kmart can retrieve detailed, daily information on sales of any of the 100,000 items carried at the company's stores, thanks to the firm's Retail Automation System. Satellite dishes mounted on all Kmart stores transmit daily sales reports to a mainframe computer at company headquarters. If a Kmart manager wants to determine yesterday's sales of the popular Timex Indiglo watch, the information is available within a matter of seconds. Want to compare per-store sales of the watch in Oregon with those in Georgia? A simple query will display the data in a full-color chart on the screen.

Expert Systems   An **expert system** is a computer program that imitates human thinking through complicated sets of "if . . . then" rules. The system applies human knowledge in a specific subject area in order to solve the problem.

Figure 17.4 illustrates an expert system based on relevant facts and information regarding misfiring in an auto engine. If you take your car to a repair shop with such a complaint, the mechanic will generally follow certain rules to diagnose the problem. The process usually begins by starting up and listening to the engine. If the mechanic detects misfiring, the process continues by checking the spark plug wires, distributor, and spark plugs one by one. The step-by-step expert system approach solves problems based on "if x, then y" relationships developed from a knowledge base accumulated over years of experience, classes, reports from other mechanics, and books and repair manuals.

Expert systems are used for a variety of business purposes: determining credit limits for credit card applicants, diagnosing medical problems, monitoring machinery in a plant to predict potential problems or breakdowns, making mortgage loans, or determining optimal plant layouts. They are typically developed by capturing the knowledge of recognized experts in a field, whether within a business itself or outside it.

Trends in Information Systems

As technology advances, new types of information systems are being developed all the time. Today's computer networks help businesspeople to obtain and

FIGURE 17.4
Partial Expert System for Auto Engine Repair

IF the engine is misfiring **AND**
IF the plug wires are worn,

THEN turn off the engine, replace the plug wires, turn on the engine, listen again for misfiring cylinders.

IF the engine fires properly, **QUIT.**

IF the engine is misfiring **AND**
IF the distributor cap is cracked,

THEN turn off the engine, replace the distributor cap, turn on the engine, listen again for misfiring cylinders.

IF the engine fires properly, **QUIT.**

IF the engine is misfiring **AND**
IF any spark plug tests faulty,

THEN turn off the engine, replace all spark plugs, turn on the engine, listen again for misfiring cylinders.

IF the engine fires properly, **QUIT.**

IF the engine is misfiring **AND**
IF the fuel filter is clogged,

THEN turn off the engine, replace the filter element, turn on the engine, listen again for misfiring cylinders.

IF the engine fires properly, **QUIT.**

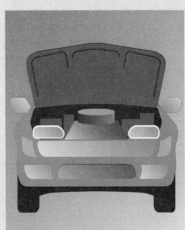

share information, even to collaborate in real time, across departments, across the country, and around the world.

Local Area Networks and Wide Area Networks   Many companies already connect their offices and buildings by creating **local area networks (LANs),** computer networks that connect machines within limited areas, such as one building or several buildings near each other. LANs are useful tools because they link personal computers and allow them to share printers, documents, and information.

Wide area networks (WANs) tie larger geographic regions together by using telephone lines and microwave and satellite transmission. One familiar WAN is long-distance telephone service, and Worldcom and AT&T are telecommunication companies that provide WAN services to the general public. Firms also use WANs to conduct their own operations. Typically, companies own their own network systems at their operations sites and link to outside data communications equipment and services for transmission across long distances. Later in the chapter, we cover other specialized networking systems.

Enterprise Resource Planning   As information systems developed in organizations, they were at first contained within functional departments. Soon, managers noticed that the data being collected about customers during order processing were being reentered by inventory control and shipping. The same duplication was found in human resource management systems and finance and accounting. To avoid such rework, eliminate mistakes or inconsistencies in data, and streamline processes, businesses began to demand a system to unify these separate systems. An **enterprise resource planning (ERP)** system is a set of integrated programs designed to collect, process, and provide information about all business operations. Organizations use ERP systems to manage vital business operations as part of an overall strategy of *knowledge management*. Because of their huge initial cost, large, multisite global organizations were the first to implement ERP systems. Firms such as Baan and SAP offer enterprise software programs to help companies run factories, keep track of accounting, and assist in marketing efforts. The "Clicks and Mortar" box discusses another software company that has been transformed by offering ERP systems.

One company that offers ERP software designed to help firms organize their marketing data is Indianapolis-based Aprimo. With Aprimo software, users can log in key variables such as names of suppliers, material costs, design layouts, deadlines, and names of project managers and come up with clean, easy-to-read templates that are customized for particular marketing campaigns. "We took on the marketing process itself," explains Aprimo cofounder Robert McLaughlin. With its high-quality offerings and strikingly low prices, Aprimo, which charges far less for its services than its rivals—$5,000 as opposed to the typical $100,000 or more—is growing rapidly.[8]

Application Service Providers Because of the increasing cost and complexity of obtaining and maintaining

BUSINESS DIRECTORY

➤ **enterprise resource planning (ERP)** *information system that collects, processes, and provides information about an organization's entire enterprise.*

The meteoric rise and fall of many dot.coms is legendary. Experts will be picking through the debris for years to come. But lessons can be learned by examining the fate of one such company that had such promise, yet filed for bankruptcy less than a year after its initial public offering (IPO) of stock. Some blame for the company's downfall can be tied to its decision to outsource its information systems.

eToys was one of the many brainchildren of Bill Gross, founder and CEO of Idealab, the think-tank "incubator" company that spun out ideas for companies such as Goto.com, cooking.com, FreePC, Tickets.com, and CarsDirect. "When we get an idea and start working on it, and then make a company out of it, that's just the most awesome thing." Hindsight makes his enthusiasm seem a little naive and the way he started companies a little chaotic, but at the time eToys was born, the Internet seemed to be exploding with possibilities.

The toy business accounts for about $22 billion of spending each year, which makes it an attractive market. Bill Gross and Toby Lenk, a former Disney manager, got the idea for eToys during a hectic holiday shopping season. "I saw long lines and screaming kids, and I figured there had to be a better way," says Lenk. A company that would allow busy, frazzled parents to order toys at their convenience on home computers seemed like a sure bet. And in fact, during its first full year of operation, eToys's sales topped $15 million, with competitors like Toys 'R' Us scrambling to catch up. Shoppers supported the idea, plunking down $71 million total on toys and hobbies purchased online.

But attracting customers is just part of running a business. Delivering the goods, backed by customer service, is another. For that, a company needs effective information systems. Most likely in an effort to streamline its business, eToys initially outsourced its order fulfillment—a move that proved to be a disaster. By early 2000, the company decided to "bring fulfillment in-house because of the poor performance of its fulfillment outsourcing partner last holiday season," explained analysts at Goldman Sachs. But with a poor holiday season behind them, eToys couldn't generate enough revenue to cover the cost of setting up in-house systems. Then the stock market began to tumble, and a year later eToys was in bankruptcy.

The issue of its information systems is only one piece of the eToys puzzle, but it illustrates the importance of managers' keeping close tabs on the flow of information—whether it involves timely delivery of ordered goods or response to customer complaints and questions—for their companies to succeed. Neither the parent company of eToys nor founder Bill Gross has disappeared. In fact, Idealab continues to churn out ideas for new companies. But in the future, executives at these new companies might do well to learn a lesson from eToys: managing information is not child's play.

QUESTIONS FOR CRITICAL THINKING

1. Outsourcing information systems is not always a poor decision. What steps could eToys managers have taken to avoid problems before they got out of hand?
2. What types of in-house information systems might eToys managers have benefited from using? In what ways might they have been used?

Sources: "eToys Files for Bankruptcy," Associated Press, March 14, 2001; "eToys Makes Chapter 11 Filing," *Reuters Business News,* March 7, 2001; Joseph Nocera, "Bill Gross Blew through $800 Million in 8 Months," *Fortune,* March 5, 2001, pp. 71–82; Lee Gomes, "P-to-P, B-to-B—R.I.P.?" *The Wall Street Journal,* April 4, 2001, p. B1.

information systems, a firm may choose to engage an **application service provider (ASP)**, an outside supplier that provides both the computers and the application support for managing an information system. An ASP can simplify complex software for its customers so it is easier for them to manage and use. When an ASP relationship is successful, the buyer can then devote more time and resources to its core business instead of struggling to manage its information systems. Other benefits include stretching the technology dollar farther and giving smaller companies the kind of information power that, in the past, has only been available to much larger organizations. Paul Rudolph, CEO of Agilera, a Colorado-based ASP, believes that business is entering the "knowledge-value revolution." According to Rudolph, "For the first time, we have the ability—at the enterprise level—to develop knowledge about customers that enables us to create one-on-one relationships with them. Through those relationships, businesses can create value that is uniquely meaningful to the individual customer."[9]

Companies that decide to use ASPs should check the backgrounds and references for these firms before hiring them to manage critical systems, as noted in the "Business Hits and Misses" box. "If you're going to outsource any business-critical data, you should go see the facility and make sure it's not in someone's garage," advises Joseph Fuccillo, a senior vice-president for Xand Corp., which provides hosting hardware and services to ASPs themselves.[10] While it seems that the reason for hiring an ASP is that data can be stored and accessed anywhere, many business owners

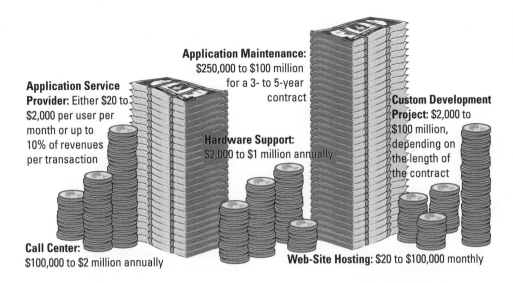

FIGURE 17.5
Costs of Outsourcing Information
Systems

Application Service Provider: Either $20 to $2,000 per user per month or up to 10% of revenues per transaction

Application Maintenance: $250,000 to $100 million for a 3- to 5-year contract

Hardware Support: $2,000 to $1 million annually

Custom Development Project: $2,000 to $100 million, depending on the length of the contract

Call Center: $100,000 to $2 million annually

Web-Site Hosting: $20 to $100,000 monthly

prefer to be within an easy drive of the data center, which coincides with Fuccillo's advice. In addition, customers should try to ensure that the service provider has taken appropriate measures to block computer hackers or other unauthorized access to data and that its data centers are up and running consistently. Figure 17.5 shows some of the costs associated with hiring an ASP as well as outsourcing other elements of information technology.

Although information systems can help a company run smoothly and efficiently, the firm must carefully plan and organize them. Otherwise, it can lose control of a critical function—and tremendous amounts of time and money. Issues of privacy and security also arise. Should everyone in the company be able to access all of the company's data? What about confidential human resource files or the corporation's payroll system? A later section of the chapter examines several of these issues.

COMPUTER HARDWARE AND SOFTWARE

Computers are programmable, electronic devices that can store, retrieve, and process data. Just a few decades ago, computers were considered exotic curiosities, used only by scientists and the military. Today, they have become indispensable not only to businesses but to households as well. Who can imagine daily life without sending e-mails to friends, booking airline tickets over the Internet, preparing reports with a word processing program, and speed-dialing your home number on the phone?

Types of Computer Hardware

Hardware consists of all the tangible elements of a computer system—the input devices, the machines that store and process data and perform required calculations, and output devices that present the results to information users. Input devices allow users to enter data and commands for processing, storage, and output. Common input devices include the keyboard, mouse, scanner, modem, microphone, and touch screen. Storage and processing components consist of the hard drive and CD-ROM drive. The newer CD-RW drives can write disks as well as read them. Output devices are the hardware elements that transmit or display documents and other results of a computer system's work. Examples include the monitor screen, printer, fax machine, modem, and audio system. Notice that some devices, such as the screen and modem, can serve both input and output functions. And keep in mind that the screen, once reserved for text and still graphics display, now commonly displays video.

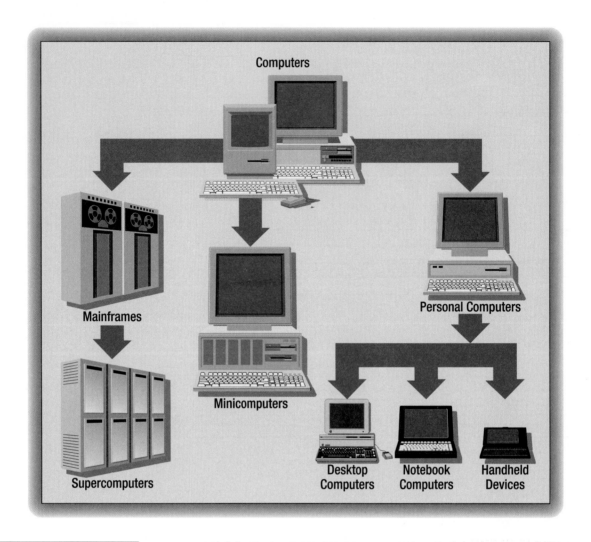

FIGURE 17.6
Types of Computers

Computer processing units incorporate widely varying memory capacities and processing speeds. As shown in Figure 17.6, these differences define three broad classifications: mainframes, minicomputers, and personal computers. A **mainframe** computer is the largest type of computer system with the most extensive storage capacity and the fastest processing speeds. Especially powerful mainframes called **supercomputers** can handle extremely rapid, complex calculations involving thousands of variables. They are most commonly found in scientific research settings. A **minicomputer** is an intermediate-sized computer—more compact and less expensive than a mainframe but also slower and with less memory. These intermediate computers often toil in universities, factories, and research labs. Minicomputers also appeal to many small businesses that need more power than personal computers can offer to handle specialized tasks.

Personal computers (PCs) are everywhere today—in homes, schools, businesses, nonprofit organizations, and government agencies. They have earned increasing popularity due to their ever-expanding capability to handle many of the functions that cumbersome mainframes performed only a few decades ago. These advances were made possible by the development of powerful chips—thin silicon wafers that carry integrated circuits (networks of transistors and electronic circuits). A microprocessor is a fingernail-size chip that contains the PC's entire central processing unit. Intelligent functions of today's new cars, toys, watches, and other household items also rely on microprocessors. Additional chips provide instruction and memory to convert a microprocessor into a PC.

FIGURE 17.7
Wireless Handheld Device for E-Mail, Voice, and Data Communications

As technology continues to advance, computers have diminished in size. **Desktop computers** are the standard PCs that you see in offices and homes everywhere. **Notebook computers** are small enough to slip into a briefcase, yet more powerful than many two- or three-year-old desktop computers. Many notebook models accept CD-ROMs and have "docking" capabilities that allow them to plug into a desktop PC to share data. **Handheld devices**—made by companies like Palm and Handspring—are even smaller. They fit in a shirt pocket and run on ordinary batteries. Handhelds can run common applications like word processing and database software, as well as store documents and graphics created on a desktop computer. Many models have color screens and can link up through wireless modems to stationary systems as well as the Internet.

The future will bring even smaller PCs that can perform even more functions. Industry technologists have been developing a credit-card sized computer for storing and retrieving information such as phone numbers and appointments. And voice and data communications systems are merging. A recent batch of wireless telephones can be used as PCs. Sprint PCS Group recently began offering data capability on its national network. Businesspeople can now use a PCS phone to browse the Internet and send and receive e-mail messages from their phones.[11] This capability is especially helpful for those who are traveling, calling on customers, or working at remote sites. Figure 17.7 demonstrates the e-mail capabilities of a wireless handheld device.

Types of Software

Software refers to the sets of instructions that tell the computer hardware what to do. These instructions, written in various computer languages, may take the form of custom-designed packages uniquely created to fulfill a business's specialized needs or off-the-shelf, commercial packages that provide commonly desired capabilities.

The software that controls the basic workings of a computer system is its **operating system.** Today, most business PCs use a version of Microsoft's popular Windows operating system. Other widely used operating systems include UNIX, developed by AT&T; Solaris, developed by Sun Microsystems; Linux, available in the public domain; and the Mac Operating System, developed by Apple Computers.

Operating-system designers have faced important challenges as businesses have shifted from stand-alone computers to networks, since computers running different operating systems may have difficulty sharing data. This problem is losing significance, however, thanks to a programming language called *Java.* Programs written in Java can run on any type of computer or operating system, so businesses are increasingly snapping up Java applications to develop their databases and computer networks. Sabre Group's airline reservations unit even rewrote its popular reservations system in Java.[12]

A program that performs the specific tasks that the user wants to carry out—like writing a letter or looking up data—is called **applications software.** Leading off-the-shelf software include Microsoft Word, Lotus Notes, and Netscape Navigator. Myers Industries, a parts-manufacturing company, uses an applications software program called BizWorks from interBiz Solutions to "make sense of all the data gathered by factory sensors." The software predicts when one of Myers's large injection-molding machines are about to spit out a defective product. And when BizWorks spots a problem, it automatically identifies the customer who ordered the product. If the problem indicates a possible delay, the sales and customer-service managers get a pager alert so they can personally contact customers if necessary. "It can really create new business opportunities by putting management back on top of the technology horse," says Myers CIO Andrew J. Weiner. "We'll be able to decide what information we want and tailor BizWorks to provide it, instead of tailoring management to the software."[13] The next section discusses the major categories of applications used by businesses.

HOW COMPUTERS HELP BUSINESSPEOPLE

Computers and their related technologies continue to revolutionize the methods by which businesses manage information. These technologies affect contemporary business in three important ways. First, the enhanced speed and quantity of information now available improve the speed and effectiveness of decision making. Second, computers make accurate, unbiased data available to all interested parties. Third, their information-sharing capabilities support team decision making at low levels of an organization's hierarchy. Every industry has felt at least some impact as computers and information systems have spread.

Consider the Great Harvest Bread Co., headquartered in Dillon, Montana, which operates 137 franchised bakeries. Unlike other franchise operations, Great Harvest believes that its franchise operators should be free—after a one-year apprenticeship—to run their stores as they see fit. They aren't required to use the same bread recipe or paint their storefronts the same color. But they are required to share information with each other, which they do via computers. The Great Harvest internal Web site, called the Breadboard, contains announcements of equipment for sale, ongoing electronic chats among franchisees, new recipes, tips for maintaining certain ovens, and archives of other information. "Right now the marketing area gets by far the most hits," says chief operating officer (COO) Tom McMakin. "People love the clip art and other materials for making posters and flyers to support a product or campaign."[14] Computers help people manage information in an industry that has historically been considered low tech.

Some of the most widely used business applications of computers include word processing, desktop publishing, spreadsheets, electronic mail, presentation graphics, multimedia and interactive media, and groupware. Users once acquired applications such as these as individual software packages. Today, however, they normally buy **integrated software,** or **software suites,** which combine several applications into a single package that can share modules for data handling and processing. Great Harvest uses software that includes network applications through which franchisees share information and software that conducts financial analyses of various franchises. Microsoft's popular Office software suite brings together word processing, presentation graphics, database management, spreadsheets, and an information manager, all on a PC. Some integrated software packages are designed to help businesses handle a specific task, such as developing and writing a business plan. Business Plan Pro, Planwrite Expert Edition, and Guerilla Business are three examples. These programs contain such features as ready-made formatting and spreadsheets, graphing, and the capability to evaluate a company's competitiveness in the marketplace.[15] Besides such off-the-shelf packages, businesses also may buy integrated software tailored to their specific needs, such as SageMaker, a software system that automatically rakes in data from up to 4,300 sources and gives users only the information they need, based on criteria they have previously defined.[16]

Despite all the advantages of computers, it is important to keep in mind that they do have their limitations and should be used to serve the mission of the organization, not just for their own sake. Many businesses have found that their use of computers is actually enhanced by maintaining a human touch—or adding it—to the process. Although Performance Personnel, a $10 million staffing company in California, uses e-mail and other computer software to share information, CEO Shari Franney has discovered that old-fashioned, regular staff meetings contribute to knowledge management and a feeling of camaraderie among her sales staff. "This industry is tough," she explains. "You get pounded by everyone. It's good for people to know they're not in this alone."[17]

Finally, recognizing the limitations of computers, such as people's struggle with keyboards, some companies have come up with answers. Speech recognition programs have been around for a while—and filled with glitches—but recent versions are much more accurate and easier to use. Such technology allows users to navigate through other software such as Microsoft's Office by voice. Users can speak at a rate of up to 140 words per minute and create a three-page document in about seven minutes.[18] Examples of these speech recognition programs include Dragon System's Naturally Speaking Preferred and Lernout & Hauspie's Voice Xpress Professional. Currently, Dragon's software accepts only one user voice, whereas Voice Xpress allows users to create multiple-voice profiles, which means that several people can use the same computer to dictate copy.[19]

Word Processing

One of the most popular business applications, word processing, uses computers to type, store, retrieve, edit, and print various types of documents. With word processing, users can revise sentences, check spelling, correct mistakes, and move copy around quickly and cleanly.

Word processing helps a company to handle huge volumes of correspondence, process numerous documents, and personalize form letters. Although some firms use special-purpose computers called *dedicated word processors* that are designed exclusively for this purpose, most use general-purpose computers running such word-processing software packages as Microsoft Word and WordPerfect. The newest versions of these programs enable users to include graphics and spreadsheets from other programs in their documents and to create Web sites by translating documents into hypertext markup language (HTML), the language of the World Wide Web.

As word-processing capabilities have grown, a number of businesspeople have tried to create "paperless offices." They want to set achievable goals for electronically creating, transmitting, storing, and retrieving documents, eliminating

THEY SAID IT

"A computer does not substitute for judgment any more than a pencil substitutes for literacy. But writing without a pencil is no particular advantage."

ROBERT MCNAMARA (B.1916)
U.S. SECRETARY OF DEFENSE DURING THE KENNEDY AND JOHNSON ADMINISTRATIONS

BUSINESS DIRECTORY

► **word processing**   *software that uses a computer to type, store, retrieve, edit, and print various types of documents.*

any need to print them. Although the idea appeals to both efficiency and environmentalist priorities, it is not always practical, and people are naturally resistant to change. When Great Harvest first launched its Breadboard site, some of its franchisees were reluctant to use it. "For a while we suspended the hard-copy newsletter of the Breadboard so that people would break old habits and start going online," says COO Tom McMakin. But people wanted to see and touch the newsletter, or take it home to read. So the paper newsletter was reinstated as a complement to the online version.[20]

Desktop Publishing

Many business systems extend word processing capabilities to create sophisticated documents. **Desktop publishing** employs computer technology to allow users to design and produce attractively formatted printed material themselves rather than hiring professionals. Desktop publishing software combines high-quality type, graphics, and layout tools to create output that can look as attractive as documents produced by professional publishers and printers. Advanced equipment can scan photos and drawings and duplicate them on the printed page.

Many firms use desktop publishing systems to print newsletters, reports, and form letters. Advertising and graphic arts departments often use desktop publishing systems to create brochures and marketing materials. A good desktop publishing system can save a company money by allowing staff members to produce such documents, whether they are for internal or external use. Freelance graphic artist Merin Tougas uses Microsoft Word and Quark Xpress as a cost-efficient way to produce magazine ads, brochures, mailers, business cards, stationery, and Web pages for her customers. "Desktop publishing in general not only streamlines the creative process for me but allows for greater and more precise communication between my clients and me." With desktop publishing software, Tougas can produce professional-looking documents from her home.[21]

Entrepreneur Ron Bienvenu has launched several businesses that involve using desktop publishing to distribute information to various industries. One publication was called *ThriftWatch,* which he developed while employed at SNL Securities. Bienvenu took daily bank filings from the Securities and Exchange Commission and put them into a newsletter that SNL sold to bank analysts for a $2,500 annual subscription fee. Now Bienvenu is head of *SageMaker,* a sophisticated electronic newsletter that is delivered over the Internet to computers inside energy companies.[22]

Spreadsheets

An electronic **spreadsheet** is the computerized equivalent of an accountant's worksheet. This software program permits businesspeople to manipulate decision variables and determine their impacts on such outcomes as profits or sales. With a spreadsheet, a manager can have an accurate answer to a question in seconds and can often glance at the whole financial picture of a company on a single page. Popular spreadsheet software packages include Lotus 1-2-3, Excel, and Quattro Pro. Spreadsheets are also bundled in packages designed to create business plans and compute taxes. Spreadsheets may seem daunting at first, but good spreadsheet programs are clear, even for the first-time user. When evaluating business software programs, reviewers often say how easy the spreadsheets are to navigate.

Figure 17.8 demonstrates how a manager uses a spreadsheet to set a price for a proposed product. Note that the manager can analyze alternative decisions using a spreadsheet. A more complex spreadsheet may stretch across many more columns, but the software still makes new calculations as fast as the manager can change the variables.

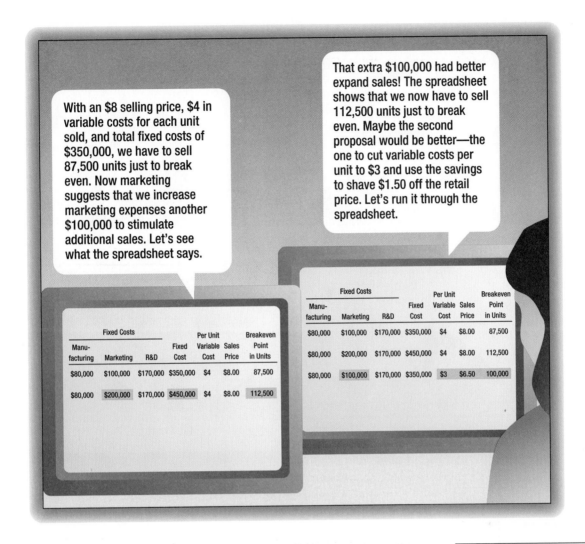

FIGURE 17.8
How a Spreadsheet Works

Electronic Mail

Businesspeople need to communicate directly with company colleagues as well as customers, suppliers, and others outside their organization. Increasingly, they turn to their computers for this function, replacing much of their regular mailings (the so-called *snail* mail) by sending messages via *e-mail*. As discussed in Chapter 7, e-mail and its more recent adaptation, *instant messaging*, are rapid ways to communicate both inside and outside the organization. As a means of internal communication, e-mail is especially useful in organizations with employees located in different parts of the country or in different countries altogether. For the cost of dialing a local access number, employees can send and receive messages around the world, each logging on at whatever time suits his or her schedule.

Certainly, e-mail can help companies reduce paperwork, time wasted in playing telephone tag, and similar inefficiencies. But e-mail does have its limitations. It works best for short, unemotional messages. Long documents are best sent as attachments to e-mail or via fax. And e-mail users should be aware that messages are not private; employers may be monitoring messages, so employees should refrain from sending personal messages or jokes to each other. Finally, some messages, such as those containing potentially emotional news, or that may need an explanation, are best transmitted by telephone or in person.

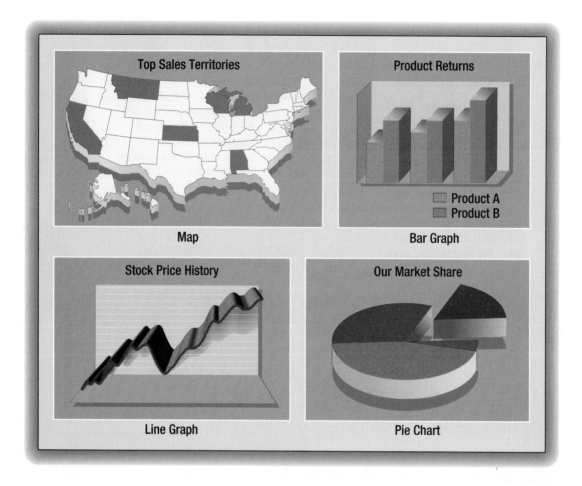

FIGURE 17.9
Examples of Visuals Created with
Presentation Software

Presentation Graphics

Analyzing columns of numbers can be a tedious task. But when people see data displayed as charts or graphs, they can often identify patterns and relationships that raw data do not reveal. Such tools can improve knowledge management and, ultimately, decision making. Businesspeople once had to labor to create charts and graphs, or send the data or rough sketches to professional artists and then wait for the results. Those practices have changed with the widespread availability of **presentation software** such as Microsoft's PowerPoint and Corel's Presentations. Such a program includes graphics and tools for manipulating them to create a variety of charts, graphs, and pictures, like those shown in Figure 17.9. By combining these elements in ways that are easy to read, a user can prepare slide shows, handouts, or transparency masters for effective reports and proposals. To persuade management to fund a new project, an employee might create a series of graphs to illustrate how the project will benefit the organization over time.

Multimedia and Interactive Media

Today's computers have leaped beyond numbers, text, and graphs to encompass multimedia and interactive media capabilities. **Multimedia computing** refers to technologies that integrate two or more types of media, such as text, voice, sound, full-motion video, still video, graphics, and/or animation into computer-based applications. Many multimedia applications are stored on CD-ROMs or DVDs, because their storage patterns and huge capacities effectively support retrieval of continuous blocks of data, such as converted music or animation sequences.

One of the growing business applications for multimedia computing is employee business presentations and conferences. And the Internet has made transmission of these meetings widely available. Many companies routinely provide multimedia Webcasts of their annual meetings and offer them for viewing on their Web sites. Salespeople can make presentations on their notebook computers to customers in their offices.

Many applications of multimedia computing use **interactive media**—programs that allow users to interact with computer displays. Home Depot's Expo Design Centers use interactive software to allow customers to plan and design home remodeling and building projects. Customers and a Home Depot salesperson can view a variety of 3-D products, enter their room dimensions, create orders, and track the installation of their projects on a computer screen. The new systems have streamlined Home Depot's system—avoiding cumbersome paper orders and samples—while providing better customer service.[23]

Designers and engineers also use interactive programs to aid in developing products. One program from Play Inc., called Amorphium, allows product designers to "build" 3-D models of possible products, rotate them on the screen, move the light source, even stretch and bend them.[24] **Virtual reality** programs take interactive media a step farther. Hewlett-Packard has developed a system called Visualize Center, which lets industrial designers immerse themselves in an environment so they can "walk" through a life-size vehicle, aircraft, or building before constructing a physical prototype. Visualize Center is intended to free designers from the restrictions of conventional desktop monitors, explains Vern Rhead, product manager for Visualize. "It allows teams of engineers to get together to review these very complex designs in real-time at a human scale." Of course, virtual reality programs require specialized, powerful computers. But they can save a manufacturer both time and money in the long run. "You can't afford to fly a couple hundred engineers across the pond just for a review meeting," says Jim Garden, director of technical services for Technology Business Research in Hampton, New Hampshire. "Now they can just pass the file and review it at each end or simultaneously." Ian Graham, director of engineering operations for Computer Sciences Corp, agrees that virtual reality programs will continue to save organizations money in the future. "[They] will actually enable users to completely eliminate the costly prototyping stage that many organizations still go through to hone their design."[25]

Groupware

An especially useful interactive medium is groupware, computer software that combines information sharing through a common database with communication via e-mail. Using groupware, employees can work together on a single document at the same time, viewing one another's changes. They can also discuss ideas and check one another's calendars to schedule meetings or group efforts. Popular groupware packages include Lotus Notes and Domino, Exchange, GroupWise, CollabraShare, and GroupSystems.

Intranets, Virtual Private Networks, and Broadband Technology

A previous section discusses the use of LANs and WANs to allow businesses to communicate, transmit and print documents, and share data. Those networks require businesses to install special equipment and connections between office sites. But Internet technology has also been applied to internal company communications and business tasks, tapping a ready-made network. Among these new Internet-based applications are intranets, virtual private networks (VPNs), and

BUSINESS DIRECTORY

➤ **multimedia computing** *technologies that integrate two or more types of media, such as text, voice, sound, video, graphics, and/or animation into computer-based applications.*

➤ **groupware** *software that combines information sharing through a common database with communication via e-mail so that employees can collaborate on projects.*

FIGURE 17.10
Early Perceptions of Intranets

broadband technologies. Each has contributed to the effectiveness and speed of business processes.

Intranets A broad approach to sharing information in an organization is to establish a company network patterned after the Internet. Such a network, called an intranet, links employees through Internet tools like e-mail, hypertext links, and searches using Web browsers. Intranets are similar to the extranets discussed in Chapter 7, but they limit access only to employees or other authorized users. Figure 17.10's advertisement for Sun Microsystems' intranet pokes fun at early perceptions of intranets. An intranet blocks outsiders without valid passwords from entering its network by incorporating software known as a firewall. Firewalls are available as off-the-shelf packages such as Firewall/Plus, On Guard, and SmartWall. They limit data transfers to certain locations and log system use so managers can identify attempts to log on with invalid passwords and other threats to system security. Highly sophisticated packages will immediately alert system administrators about suspicious activities and permit authorized personnel to use smart cards to log on from remote terminals. NASA has been working with Veridian Trident Data Systems to develop a firewall for its space communications with shuttles.[26]

Intranets offer important advantages over more familiar, and now somewhat dated, computer networks. Perhaps most importantly, they solve problems of linking different types of computers. Like the Internet, intranets can integrate computers running all kinds of operating systems. In addition, intranets are relatively easy and inexpensive to set up because most businesses already have some of the required tools, such as PCs and Web browser software. Intranets also support teamwork among employees who travel or work from home. Any intranet member with the right identification, a PC, and a modem can dial up the intranet and gain access to group calendars, document managers, online conferencing rooms, bulletin boards, package tracing, and instant messaging.

WorldExperience.com uses its intranet to securely connect staff members and choose and distribute products around the world. Market development manager Rohan Barnett says that his company has benefited greatly from its intranet service HotOffice. "Apart from e-mail, we have a shared library of documents, like our product and price database, photos of products, address books, and travel information," notes Barnett.[27]

Kid Cardona, founder of The Infamous Cartoon Posse, a Texas-based caricature-entertainment company, uses an intranet from Intranets.com. The intranet offers continuous instant messaging, discussion groups, document sharing, calendars, hosted e-mail, and personal vendor services. Organizations can also sign up for custom news delivery and stock updates. "The calendar is by far the most-used aspect of Intranets.com that has made my life easier," says Cardona. "The calendar allows the artists to log on and see what jobs are coming up, and if they will be working that event or not." Before signing up for the intranet, Cardona wasted a lot of time and money on long-distance phone calls to find cartoonists to fill his company's assignments.[28]

Virtual Private Networks   To gain increased security for Internet communications, companies are now turning to **virtual private networks (VPNs)**, secure connections between two points on the Internet. These VPNs use firewalls and programs that encapsulate data to make them more secure during transit. Loosely defined, a VPN can include a range of networking technologies, from secure Internet connections to private networks from service providers like IBM and Sprint. A VPN is cheaper for a company to use than several leased phone lines, because users only make a local call to the nearest access-point of a service provider, which can save thousands of dollars if employees must make many overseas calls. Also, a VPN is cheaper to install than a WAN, which requires companies to invest in special networking equipment and personnel. In most cases a VPN location can be added in a day. Because users can dial through the Internet from multiple locations, some CIOs have begun to set up VPN technology in their companies to share information between partners and suppliers. "Imagine trying to connect 10,000 third parties," explains Dan Merriman, vice president at Giga Information Group in Cambridge, Massachusetts. "That would be a nightmare with private lines. With the Internet, all you do is ship out your IP address and you're off and running."[29]

At the Tokyo office of 20th Century-Fox Film Corp., executive director for client computing services Nader Karimi makes good use of the company's VPN. His office is paying $350 a month to a local Internet service provider, compared with the $9,000 a month that a leased phone line would cost. Karimi estimates that the VPN saves Fox at least $600,000 a year in e-mail transmissions and file-sharing costs from 21 sites, despite the $6,000 to $8,000 it costs to install the equipment at each site. However, he still maintains one leased line through which critical financial data can be transmitted because of possible security concerns.[30]

Broadband Technology   To maintain their competitive edge, companies want to be able to share larger chunks of information among employees and partners faster than ever before. To do so, they have turned to **broadband technology**—digital, fiber-optic, and wireless network technologies that compress data and transmit them at blinding speeds. Table 17.1 shows the different types of broadband technologies currently available. Broadband technology can be thought of as similar to a multilane communications highway, compared with the single-lane country road represented by traditional phone transmission. With the digital data compression and bigger "lanes" of broadband technology, the same amount of information can travel faster from one destination to another.

Optical networks are one of the newest broadband technologies. They convert information into tiny bits of light that are transmitted over fiber-optic cables made of glass. Long-distance phone carriers are in the process of rapidly installing optical networks to increase the number of transmissions and the speed at which they travel. Optical networks have a million times the capacity that traditional phone networks have because light particles are lighter than electrical impulses, they can be separated into different colors to create separate channels, and glass allows more rapid travel than copper.[31] Since optical networks are expensive, businesses with operations in several different locations often combine them with less-expensive coaxial cable networks to serve parts of their system. However, optical equipment manufacturers like Qtera and Corvis are working to find ways to reduce their product prices.[32] Garry Betty, CEO of Earthlink, believes that broadband technology will change the way businesses use the Internet. "When you have an instant-on, high-speed connection, you use the Internet much more as a reference tool. Instead of dialing 411, I'll use InfoSpace to find a

BUSINESS DIRECTORY

➤ **intranet**   company network that links employees via Internet tools like e-mail, hypertext links, and database searches using Web browsers limiting access to organization members.

➤ **broadband technology**   digital, fiber-optic, and wireless network technology that compresses data and transmits them at blinding speeds.

Table 17.1	Types of Broadband Technologies
Technology	**Transmission Method**
Digital subscriber lines (DSL)	Standard copper-wire phone lines
Cable modems	Coaxial cable (as used in cable television)
Fiber-optic network	Optical cables
Wireless network	Microwave or satellite transmission
Integrated services digital network (ISDN)	Standard copper-wire phone lines and other media
T1 and T3 lines	Special dedicated phone connections

phone number. Instead of asking my assistant when I need directions to go somewhere, I'll use MapQuest."[33]

PROTECTING INFORMATION SYSTEMS

As information systems become increasingly important business assets, they also become progressively harder to replace. When computers are connected to a network, a problem at any location can affect the entire network. Although many computer security issues go beyond the scope of *Contemporary Business,* this section discusses three important security threats: computer crime, viruses, and natural disasters that may damage information systems.

Computer Crime

Computers provide efficient ways for employees to share information. But they may also allow people with more malicious intentions to access information. Or they may allow pranksters—who have no motive other than to see whether they can hack into a system—to gain access to classified information. Common computer crimes involve stealing or altering data in several ways:

- Employees or outsiders may change or invent data to produce inaccurate or misleading information.

- Employees or outsiders may modify computer programs to create false information or illegal transactions, or to insert viruses.

- Unauthorized people can access computer systems for their own illicit benefit or knowledge, or just to see if they can get in.

Computer crime is on the rise. Figure 17.11 shows the number of violations of Internet security as reported to the Computer Emergency Response Team Coordination Center, located on the Web at www.cert.org. In 1988, six incidents were reported. During the first year of the 21st century, the number of incidents had soared to 21,756. Of course, the statistics don't include the number of incidents that were not reported, so the actual total is probably much higher.

Individuals, businesses, and government agencies are all vulnerable to computer crime. Figure 17.12 shows the home page of the Federal Computer Incident Response Capability (FedCIRC), which assists government agencies with computer security issues. Hackers—unauthorized users—sometimes work alone and sometimes in groups. In Singapore, a group of Internet hackers calling themselves the Sm0ked Crew accessed the Web sites of AltaVista, Compaq Computer, Gateway, Hewlett-Packard, and Intel. The group defaced several sites and left messages such as "Admin, You just got Sm0ked. This site was hacked by Sm0ked Crew." The message went on to list the nicknames of the individual hackers.[34]

Microsoft recently reported that a hacker had been able to view some of the company's classified source code. The hacker gained access because an employee forgot

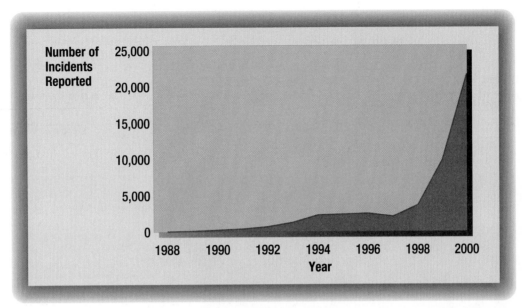

Total incidents reported (1988–2000): 47,711

FIGURE 17.11
Growth in the Number of Computer Security Crimes: 1988–2000

to create a password while configuring a network computer server, leaving the password security blank. So the hacker was able to make up a valid password.[35] In Stockholm, another hacker gained access to classified U.S. computer system codes for guiding space ships, rockets, and satellites. The hacker was identified only by the user name "LEEIF" and was able to hide his or her true identity by breaking into a genuine account.[36]

System administrators implement two basic protections against computer crime: They try to prevent access to their systems by unauthorized users and viewing of data by unauthorized system users. To prevent access, the simplest method requires authorized users to enter passwords. The company may also install firewalls, described earlier. To prevent system users from reading sensitive information, the company may use encryption software, which encodes, or scrambles, messages. To read encrypted messages, users must use a key to convert them to regular text. But as fast as software developers invent new and more elaborate protective measures, hackers seem to break through their defenses. So security is an ongoing battle.

FIGURE 17.12
The Federal Computer Incident Response Center: Fighting Computer Crime

Another form of computer theft is as old as crime itself: theft of equipment. As the size of computer hardware diminishes, it becomes increasingly vulnerable to theft. Notebook computers are big enough to be easily visible to thieves, yet small enough for them to pick up quickly and disappear. Handheld devices can vanish with a pickpocket or purse snatcher. And since these machines may contain all kinds of important information for a business, employees need to be especially careful not to leave them unattended or out of reach. For example, in an airport, travelers should wait until the last possible moment to put equipment on the x-ray conveyor

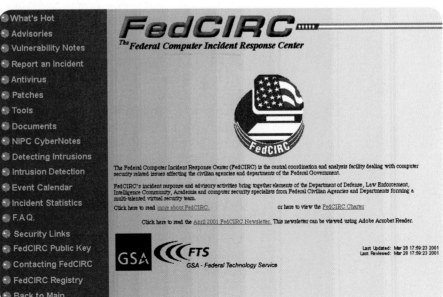

FIGURE 17.13
Effects of Computer Viruses

belt along with any other metal items so someone cannot grab their computer while they wait for possessions to pass through the machine. Or they should ask if they can hand their computer directly to the security agent.

Computer Viruses

Rather than directly tampering with a company's data or computers, computer criminals may create viruses to infect computers at random. **Computer viruses** are programs that secretly attach themselves to other programs or files and change them or destroy data. Figure 17.13 illustrates the devastating effects viruses can have. Viruses can be programmed to remain dormant for a long time, after which the infections suddenly activate themselves and cause problems. One such notorious virus was the Michelangelo virus, which erased data in computers that were used on March 6, the Italian artist's birthday. During a single year, one major U.S. corporation in six reported infections by this virus. It also infected computers in Austria, England, the Netherlands, and South Africa.

A virus can reproduce by copying itself onto other programs stored in the same drive. It spreads as users install infected software on their systems or exchange files with others, usually by e-mail electronic bulletin boards, trading disks, or downloading programs or data from unknown sources on the Internet. With widespread data sharing in networks, including intranets and the Internet, viruses can do more damage today than ever before. A 2001 survey revealed that almost 19 of every 20 computer security specialists at U.S corporations, government agencies, financial institutions, medical institutions, and universities have detected computer viruses in their networks.[37]

SOLVING AN ETHICAL CONTROVERSY

In 2001, a 15-year-old was charged with hacking into at least three NASA computer systems and altering their Web sites. Although the teenager was too young to have his name published in the media, he was charged with a felony—punishable by up to five years in prison. In another incident, a 20-year-old was arrested for unleashing a virus that arrived in people's e-mail in-boxes disguised as a picture of glamorous tennis pro Anna Kournikova. When asked why he had done so he answered, "I didn't do it for fun." Instead, he said he wanted to chastise computer users for not having learned the lessons taught by previous viruses, such as "Melissa" and "I Love You."

Should computer hacking be treated as a serious crime?

PRO

1. Computer hacking can damage a company's or government agency's sensitive files or software systems, causing a breach in security and significant financial losses.
2. Some computer hacking can be considered a type of corporate espionage, in which information is stolen from a company or destroyed.
3. Destroying computer systems and causing losses is similar to outright destruction of property and should be treated accordingly.

CON

1. Today's computer users are much more savvy about viruses and hacking attacks than they were even a few years ago, and they know how to protect themselves. "I think the world has become a lot more aware of these things" and taken precautionary measures, says Vincent P. Gullotto, head of Avert virus labs.
2. Today's computer viruses are less threatening than those of a few years ago were, comments the director of the antivirus research center at Symantec Corp. "They spread very quickly, but they're not that difficult to eradicate and stop."
3. Hackers may just be curious young people who enjoy the challenge of gaining access where they are not supposed to go. Age of the hackers and the damage they do should be considered in evaluating the seriousness of the crime.

SUMMARY

Computer crime is unlikely to disappear, regardless of precautionary measures taken by software companies and users themselves. Neither is the debate over how to handle computer crime itself and the consequences meted out to those convicted. Certainly, it should be treated more seriously than a prank; but whether a 15-year-old should be sent to prison for five years is a question not so easily answered.

Sources: Nedra Pickler, "Teen Accused of Hacking into NASA," *Associated Press,* March 15, 2001; John Schwartz, "Arrest Is Made in Virus Case," *The New York Times,* February 15, 2001, **www.nytimes.com;** Jim Kerstetter, "How Many 'Love Bug' Attacks Will It Take?" *Business Week,* May 22, 2000, p. 50.

Some viruses, as with hacking incidents, result from pranks that get out of hand. But many—including the Michelangelo virus—involve outright vandalism or crime. Another widespread virus labeled the Love Bug, which arrived in people's e-mail in-boxes with the message "I Love You," destroyed music and image files. The "Solving an Ethical Controversy" box discusses the issue of computer crime in more detail.

As viruses become more complex, the technology to fight them must increase in sophistication as well. The simplest way to protect against computer viruses is to install one or more of the many available virus-protection software packages, including Norton Anti-Virus for Windows and Macintosh, Quarterdeck Utility Pack for Windows, and Network Associates' Virex for Macintosh. These programs, costing up to a few hundred dollars, continuously monitor systems for viruses and automatically eliminate any they spot. Users can regularly update them by going online to download the latest virus descriptions.

But management must begin to emphasize security at a deeper level: in software design, corporate servers, Web gateways, and Internet service providers. Because 90 percent of the world's PCs run on Microsoft operating systems, a single virus can spread quickly among them. For example, the Love Bug was launched through Microsoft programs. In addition, although 90 percent of companies use antivirus software on their PCs, few of them install these programs on their computer servers. Managers may be reluctant to install more security because it tends to

BUSINESS DIRECTORY

➤ **computer virus** *program that secretly attaches itself to other computer programs or files and changes them or destroys data.*

slow down the flow of information. But protecting a company's electronic "post office" is much quicker and easier than trying to pinpoint problem mail when it is in transit.

Individual computer users should carefully choose the files they load into their systems, run utility programs often and update them routinely, scan all disks before opening them, install software only from known sources, and avoid viewing e-mail messages from unknown sources.

Disaster Recovery and Backup

Natural disasters, power failures, equipment malfunctions, software glitches, and human error can disrupt even the most sophisticated systems. In one instance, a computer system called the Traffic Collision Avoidance system malfunctioned, apparently placing jets from two different airlines on a collision course southwest of Albany, New York. In another, computers in New York State mistakenly terminated Medicaid coverage for hundreds of valid recipients. In still another, a glitch in Hershey's enterprise software caused shipment delays of Halloween candy during the busiest season of the year.[38]

Sometimes the sheer volume of users attempting to get online can cause a disaster. As approximately 7.5 million U.S. investors have switched to online brokerages, the Securities and Exchange Commission has received more than 20,000 investor complaints of power outages, errors, fund-transfer delays, and other problems.[39] Jim Johnson, president of The Standish Group, a marketing research agency, estimates that software-glitch disasters alone cost American businesses $85 billion in a single year. The U.S. auto industry loses about $1 billion each year because its software systems are not compatible, and an overhaul of the Internal Revenue Service's computer system recently cost taxpayers about $4 billion.[40] That figure doesn't account for disasters related to earthquakes, floods, or power outages.

Disaster recovery planning—deciding how to prevent system failures and continue operations if computer systems fail—is a critical function of all organizations. Disaster prevention programs can avoid some of these costly problems. The most basic precaution is routinely backing up software and data—at an organizational and individual level. Companies can now back up data at online storage services such as Iron Mountain or Network Associates. Technology planners may decide to respond to the possibility of a natural disaster such as an earthquake or flood by paying for extra hardware installation in a secure location, which can be accessed during an emergency. Advanced solutions include using integrated enterprise software from suppliers such as SAP and PeopleSoft, which tie a company's operations together in a single, thoroughly tested suite. Another is for software manufacturers to reduce the complexity of programs.

Sometimes organizations have to prepare for potential global disaster, as in the case of Y2K, a widely forecasted catastrophe that was to have occurred when the calendar shifted from one millennium to the next. Fearful that computer systems would be unable to make the change from the year '99 to '00 without mistakenly reverting to the year 1900—and causing a complete crash—managers spent up to two years evaluating their systems and preparing for what they feared could be a global computer meltdown. Rumors that everything from ATMs to the military would automatically shut down spread. But as the clock struck midnight first in New Zealand and progressively around the world, and as television screens showed elaborate fireworks displays from many countries, nothing much happened. The computers kept humming. And in the end, that's exactly what everyone wished for.

WHAT'S AHEAD

This is the first of two chapters devoted to managing technology and information. Chapter 18, "Understanding Accounting and Financial Statements," focuses on the functions of accounting, steps in the accounting process, functions and components of financial statements, and the role of budgets in a business.

➤ Summary of Learning Goals

1. Distinguish between data and information.

It is important for businesspeople to know the difference between data and information. Data are raw facts and figures that may or may not be relevant to a business decision. Information is the knowledge gained from processing those facts and figures.

2. Explain the role of management information systems in business.

An effective information system can help answer many business questions. A management information system (MIS) is an organized method for providing past, present, and projected information on internal operations as well as external intelligence to support decision making. The heart of an MIS is its database, which serves as an electronic filing cabinet for facts and figures.

3. Identify and briefly describe each of the different types of information system programs.

The key to a useful information system is the program that links users to data. Different types of information system programs include decision support systems (DSSs), which provide relevant data to help businesspeople make decisions and choose courses of action; executive information systems (EISs), which allow top managers to access the firm's primary databases; and expert systems, which imitate human thinking. Trends in information systems include local area and wide area networks (LANs and WANs); enterprise resource planning (ERP) systems that integrate all computer systems within a business; and application service providers (ASPs), outside firms that provide both computers and application support for managing an information system.

4. Describe the major types of computer hardware and software.

Hardware consists of all the tangible elements of a computer system, including input and output devices. Major categories of computers include mainframes, supercomputers, minicomputers, and personal computers (PCs). Newer developments in PCs include notebooks and handheld devices. Computer software provides the instructions that tell the hardware what to do. The software that controls the basic workings of the computer is its operating system. Other programs, called *application software*, perform specific tasks that users want to complete.

5. Articulate how specific types of software, such as word processing and desktop publishing can help businesspeople.

Individual types of software can help businesses in a variety of ways. Word processing helps a company handle huge volumes of correspondence, reports, and other documents. Desktop publishing allows users to design and produce attractively formatted printed material. Spreadsheets calculate and present information clearly. Electronic mail allows businesspeople to communicate rapidly anywhere in the world. Presentation graphics provide graphs and charts that help businesspeople see patterns in data. Multimedia integrates two or more types of media. Interactive media are programs that allow users to interact with computer displays. Integrated software combines several applications into a single package that can share modules for data handling and processing. Groupware lets businesspeople work together on a single project anywhere in the world.

6. Indicate the importance of special network technologies.

Intranets allow employees to share information on a ready-made company network. Virtual private networks (VPNs) help save companies money by providing a secure Internet connection. Broadband technology allows a greater amount of information to flow through a network more quickly.

7. Discuss ways that companies can protect themselves from computer crimes.

Companies can protect themselves from computer crime by requiring users to enter passwords, installing firewalls or encryption software, and keeping up-to-date on new security methods. Managers can also advise employees to be especially careful not to leave their notebook computers and handheld devices unattended or out of reach when they are commuting or traveling. In addition, managers may consider installing antivirus security programs for their corporate networks and checking the security of their Internet service providers.

8. Explain steps that companies can take toward disaster recovery and backup.

Businesses can avoid the results of disaster by routinely backing up software and data, both at an organizational level and at an individual level. They can back up data at online storage services or pay for extra hardware installation in a secure location. They may also want to invest in extra hardware and software sites, which can be accessed during emergencies.

Business Terms You Need to Know

management information system (MIS) 618
chief information officer (CIO) 618
database 619
decision support system (DSS) 622
executive information system (EIS) 623
expert system 623
enterprise resource planning (ERP) 625
application service provider (ASP) 626

word processing 631
spreadsheet 632
multimedia computing 634
groupware 635
intranet 636
broadband technology 637
computer virus 640

Other Business Terms

marketing information system 619
information overload 619
local area network (LAN) 624
wide area network (WAN) 624
hardware 627
mainframe 628
supercomputer 628
minicomputer 628
personal computer (PC) 628

desktop computer 629
notebook computer 629
handheld devices 629
software 629
operating system 630
applications software 630
integrated software (software suites) 631
desktop publishing 632

presentation software 634
interactive media 635
virtual reality 635
firewall 636
virtual private network (VPN) 637
encryption 639
disaster recovery planning 642

➤ Review Questions

1. Explain the difference between data and information. Why is the distinction important to businesspeople in their management of information?

2. Describe three of the different types of information system programs, and give an example of how each might help a particular business.

3. Explain how computer hardware and software work together. Cite some examples.

4. How might a hotel chain use desktop publishing to manage its marketing program?

5. What is enterprise resource planning? How has it streamlined business processes?

6. What is an intranet? Give three specific examples of benefits that result for firms that set up their own intranets.

7. Define broadband technology and describe three different broadband technologies currently in use.

8. What steps can organizations and individuals take to prevent computer crime?

9. How does a computer virus work? What can individuals and organizational computer users do to reduce the likelihood of a computer virus?

10. Why is disaster recovery important for businesses? Relate your answer to an actual disaster.

➤ Questions for Critical Thinking

1. Do you believe that information overload is a serious problem in your life? What steps do you (or can you) take to reduce this overload so that you can function more effectively in all areas of your life?

2. Suppose you were chief information officer for Great Harvest Bread Co. Describe the different parts of an integrated software package (in addition to the intranet described in the chapter) that would help your company manage its flow of information. Give an

example of how each application you choose would help the company.

3. Debate the following statement:
   "Decision support systems are taking over the critical human functions in businesses."

4. Do you think that computer hacking is a serious crime? Defend your answer.

5. Do you think that businesses went too far in their preparations for Y2K? Why or why not? What lessons might companies learn from such an experience?

➤ Experiential Exercise

Background: You learned in this chapter that the U.S. Census Bureau has one of the largest databases in the world. This exercise tests your knowledge about the U.S. population and points you to some interesting information available at the U.S. Census Bureau's Web site database.

Directions: Answer the following questions:

1. In Census 2000, _____ million people were counted in the U.S. (The 1990 census population was 248.7 million.)

2. Which region of the country experienced the highest population growth in the 1990s?
   a. Midwest
   b. South
   c. West
   d. Northeast

3. Which of the following states was *not* among the top five largest population-gaining states?
   a. New York
   b. California
   c. Texas
   d. Florida
   e. Georgia
   f. Arizona

4. True/False. The ten most populous states contained 54 percent of the population in 2000, and the ten least populous states accounted for only 3 percent of the total population.

5. Every state's population grew in the 1990s. _____ _____ had the highest growth rate of 66 percent, and North Dakota had the lowest growth rate of 0.5 percent. This decade was the only one in the 20th century in which all states gained population.

6. Following is an alphabetical listing of the ten largest cities in 2000. See if you can rank them from largest to smallest in the last column:

Alphabetical Order	Population Ranking
Chicago	
Dallas	
Detroit	
Houston	
Los Angeles	
New York	
Philadelphia	
Phoenix	
San Antonio	
San Diego	1

7. If you didn't see or fill out a 2000 Census questionnaire, go to www.census.gov/dmd/www/infoquest.html and look at both the long- and short-form questionnaires used by the Census Bureau to collect the data for the 2000 census.

8. Go to www.census.gov/population/www/cen2000/briefs.html and print out a census brief other than the one used in the source line for this exercise. These census briefs will give you an idea how the Census Bureau is turning the raw data from the questionnaires into useful information about our population.

9. Highlight five useful, interesting, or important pieces of information you found in your census brief.

10. Be prepared to share one or two of your highlighted sections with your class and explain why you believe the information is useful, interesting, or important.

Source: Data from Marc C. Perry and Paul J. Mackun, "Census 2000 Brief: Population Change and Distribution, 1990 to 2000," Economics and Statistics Administration of the U.S. Department of Commerce, issued April 2001.

➤ Answers

1. 281.4; **2.** c. 19.7 percent; **3.** a. New York; **4.** True; **5.** Nevada; **6.** From largest to smallest, the ten largest cities are New York, Los Angeles, Chicago, Houston, Philadelphia, Phoenix, San Diego, Dallas, San Antonio, Detroit.

➤ Nothing but Net

1. **Computer viruses.** Viruses can pose a major problem for business computer users and systems. Software publishers constantly scramble to update their antivirus software programs in response to newly discovered viruses. Visit these two Web sites and answer the following questions:

   www.symantec.com/avcenter

   http://vil.nai.com/vil.default.asp

   a. Approximately how many different computer viruses have been discovered?

   b. How many new viruses are discovered each month?

   c. What is the best way to protect a computer from viruses?

   d. Define the following virus-related terms: bug, hoax, joke, Trojan horse, wild, and worm.

2. **Computer operating systems.** Two of the most talked-about computer operating systems are Linux and Palm. Visit the two Web sites listed following and prepare a brief report on the Linux and Palm operating systems. Record at least three interesting facts about each operating system.

   www.linux.org/info/index.html

   www.palmos.com

3. **Computer shopping.** Assume you have been given the responsibility of buying new computers for your company. Your manager wants you to consider desktop computers, notebook computers, and handheld computers. Visit the two Web sites listed here. Write a brief report on the pros and cons of each type of computer. Which type would you recommend and why? Compare the five top-ranked systems in all three categories on the basis of price and features.

   www.zdnet.cm/computershopper/edit/howtobuy/

   http://computers.cnet.com

   Note: Internet addresses change frequently. If you do not find the exact sites listed, you may need to access the organization's or company's home page and search from there.

"I used to do a lot of work trying to help companies understand who their best customers were," says Susan Jain, marketing executive for IBM Global Resources. In past years, in order for companies to understand who their customers were, they had to pull together information from many places instead of a single cohesive source. Today, enterprise resource planning (ERP) systems like those developed by IBM help companies operate more efficiently by combining data in useful forms. "One of the real wonders of ERP is in bringing that all together, and when it's done well, it's like music," enthuses Jain.

ERP assists firms in "back-office" functions such as accounting and human resources; "front office" functions such as managing relationships with customers; throughout the supply chain; in manufacturing operations; and in various aspects of e-business. The big difference between old data systems and ERP is that the old systems just couldn't relate one piece of information to another. There might be many unrelated databases on one mainframe computer that churned out paper filled with data. But the relationships among those data had to be interpreted manually. ERP, on the other hand, develops relational databases that not only improve efficiency, but also accuracy by pulling information together in one place. "It's really a very organic, integrated system," comments Jain. "In an ERP world, you can instantaneously see if something is in stock. In the old world, you had to take an order first," then find out whether the item was in stock. ERP can link data on manufacturing, scheduling, inventory, accounting and invoicing, human resources, and many other functions. In manufacturing, ERP enables companies to practice just-in-time manufacturing, in which a firm orders exactly the right parts at the right time to fill an order. "We have one customer that builds made-to-order cars. Think about the impact that could have on the auto industry," says Jain.

IBM is one of the largest providers of hardware, software, and consulting services for ERP business solutions. IBM helps companies of all sizes put ERP into place. One such company is Chesapeake Display & Packaging. "When I joined Chesapeake Display & Packaging, we had creative teams scattered across Europe and North America collaborating to produce high-impact consumer displays," recalls Gary Cheimis, vice president of operations at CD&P. "The problem was that they were doing it using phone tag and faxes: there was no messaging system, no groupware, no companywide transactional system . . . not even a shared database. It amazed me that we were able to accomplish what we did without the benefit of an IT infrastructure." Cheimis went to IBM, which was able to assist him in creating an integrated system that

tied together all the elements his company needed to function more smoothly. "The new collaborative solution has had a powerful impact," says Cheimis. "We've seen a big boost in productivity, which is easiest to measure—entering data once instead of three times, for example. That affects quality, too. If you get it right the first time, it stays right as it goes through the system." One of the most important goals that ERP helps firms achieve is a reduction in the time it takes to bring a product to market, or directly to the customer. That's the case at Chesapeake Display & Packaging, so IBM paid particular attention to this element of the ERP system. "In our industry, cycle time is the most critical benefit," remarks Cheimis. "If we can quickly enter everything once and have it travel automatically everywhere it needs to go, we cut days off our cycle time—and that's the real key."

ERP doesn't come cheap. "It's not a thousand dollars," says Susan Jain with a smile. In fact, the software for a medium-sized company will cost upwards of $1 million, with another $2 to $3 million for implementation. Then a company has to factor in the hardware required and expenses for training employees on how to use the system. But Jain makes the crucial point that ERP can become the enabler for a small company to grow larger. And, she explains, if the system isn't in place from the beginning, it is much harder to retrofit it later, when the company's growth has gotten out of control. So, in today's business environment, ERP makes good sense—and IBM intends to be there to provide systems to companies of all sizes.

QUESTIONS

1. What do you see as a CIO's role in obtaining the right ERP for his or her company?
2. Do you think an ERP system runs the risk of creating information overload for those who use it? Why or why not?
3. Does your college or university have an ERP system? Describe ways in which you think your school might benefit from an ERP.
4. Go to the IBM Web site at **www.ibm.com** to learn more about the company's ERP systems and other business solutions. Describe how one of IBM's ERP solutions might benefit any of the other companies described in video cases throughout this book.

Sources: IBM Web site, **www.ibm.com**, accessed April 2, 2001; Gary Cheimis, "Four-Way Integration Boosts Competitiveness at Chesapeake," *Spotlight on Customers*, IBM Web site, accessed April 2, 2001; *IBM Annual Report*, 1999.

CHAPTER 18

Understanding Accounting and Financial Statements

Learning Goals

1. Explain the functions of accounting and its importance to the firm's management, investors, creditors, and government agencies.

2. Identify the three basic activities involving accounting.

3. Describe the roles played by public, management, government, and not-for-profit accountants.

4. Outline the steps in the accounting process.

5. Explain the functions and major components of the three principal financial statements: the balance sheet, the income statement, and the statement of cash flows.

6. Discuss how financial ratios are used to analyze a firm's financial strengths and weaknesses.

7. Describe the role of budgets in a business.

8. Explain how exchange rates influence international accounting practices and the importance of uniform financial statements for global business.

New Accounting Rules for the New Economy?

The year 2000 may be remembered as the year of the great technology stock crash. Internet retailer Priceline.com, for example, plunged from $104 per share to $3 per share in less than a year. On paper, Priceline.com shareholders lost over $17 billion. What caused the meltdown in tech stocks? Part of the cause was simply a recognition on the part of many investors that the bull market of the late 1990s had left many tech stocks substantially overvalued. Yet accounting may have also played a role in the debacle.

Any firm whose stock is publicly traded is required by federal law to prepare and publish a regular set of financial statements. These statements must be prepared in accordance with a set of accounting rules and are required to be regularly examined by independent auditors. Financial statements are an important source of information to investors, and their release can often have a dramatic impact on stock prices. Although accounting rules give firms some latitude in the preparation of financial statements, there is evidence that several tech firms may have stretched the rules.

Consider, for example, the case of MicroStrategy, a Virginia-based Internet software company. In early 2000 MicroStrategy reported revenues of $205 million and profits of $12.8 million, both impressive increases from the prior year. By early March 2000, the company's stock had soared to over $300 a share, an 80-fold increase since the stock first began trading in 1998. The bottom fell out of the stock on March 20, 2000. Under pressure from the Securities and Exchange Commission (SEC)—the government's chief stock market watchdog—the company's independent auditors required MicroStrategy to restate its 1999 results. Revenues were shaved by

$54 million and its reported $12.8 million profit turned into a $33 million loss. The stock price dropped by 62 percent on the day of the announcement. MicroStrategy

had apparently booked revenues for long-term software contracts too quickly, before work was completed and the company was actually paid. According to the auditors and regulators, MicroStrategy should have deferred recognizing the revenue until each contract was actually completed. MicroStrategy eventually settled the resulting civil suit, without admitting or denying any wrongdoing.

MicroStrategy wasn't the only tech company that recognized revenues too soon. According to reports, at least 50 other tech companies have restated or will have to restate their financial results for the past few years. Also, the SEC has directed the nation's independent accounting rule maker, the Financial Accounting Standards Board (FASB), to review a wide range of other accounting practices that can improperly boost revenues or reduce costs.

The whole issue of the accounting practices at tech firms raises a bigger question: Do the accounting rules, many of which were formulated decades ago, need to be modified to reflect the new information economy? Many argue they should. Critics argue that many accounting rules are archaic and can even hinder the growth of firms in the new economy. They point out that today's backward-looking financial statements and accounting rules don't begin to capture the value of critical assets—such as the intellectual firepower of employees, customer service quality, and patents. Cisco Systems' chief executive officer (CEO) John Chambers puts it this way, "When people ask, 'Do you expect to have different rules than General Motors?' we say 'Yes!' They led the industrial revolution, but we're leading the information revolution." Even accounting expert Howard Schilit, a vocal critic of many of the accounting practices of tech companies, believes that the FASB needs to come up with new rules for the new economy.[1]

CHAPTER OVERVIEW

Accounting professionals are responsible for preparing the financial information that organizations present in their annual reports. Whether you begin your career by working for a company or by starting your own firm, you need to understand what accountants do and why their work is so important in contemporary business.

Accounting is the process of measuring, interpreting, and communicating financial information to enable people inside and outside the firm to make informed decisions. Like statistics, accounting is a language of business. Accountants gather, record, report, and interpret financial information in a way that describes the status and operation of an organization and aids in decision making.

Millions of men and women throughout the world describe their occupations as accountant. In the U.S. alone, more than 1 million accountants, more than half of which are women, carry out these critical tasks. The availability of jobs and relatively high starting salaries for talented graduates—starting salaries for accounting graduates average around $35,000 per year—have made accounting one of the most popular business majors on college campuses.[2]

This chapter begins by describing who uses accounting information. It also discusses the three basic categories of business activities in which all organizations participate or by which they are influenced: financing, investing, and operating. It explains the accounting process and then discusses the development of accounting statements from information about financial transactions. It presents the methods of interpreting these statements and examines the role of budgets in planning and controlling for a business.

Accountants working for Deloitte & Touche, a major international accounting firm, supply large businesses with accounting advice, tax services, and, in Alan Alpert's department, expert advice on mergers and acquisitions.

"Financial buyers demand fast action. Like when one client called and said, 'We need to put a deal team together ASAP.' Within 48 hours our team of 35 partners and managers hit the ground running — a team with every aspect of the deal covered."

— Ken Wexel, M&A Services

For M&A services
the answer is the people of Deloitte & Touche

Deloitte & Touche Assurance & advisory, tax services and consulting

www.us.deloitte.com/m&a

©2001 Deloitte & Touche LLP. Deloitte & Touche refers to Deloitte & Touche LLP and related entities.

USERS OF ACCOUNTING INFORMATION

People both inside and outside an organization rely on accounting information to help them make business decisions. Figure 18.1 lists the users of accounting information and the applications they find for it.

Managers within a business, government agency, or not-for-profit organization are the major users of accounting information, since it helps them to plan and control daily and long-range operations. Business owners and boards of trustees of not-for-profit groups also rely on accounting data to determine how well managers are operating the businesses or organizations. Union officials use accounting data in contract negotiations, and employees refer to it as they monitor their firms' productivity and profitability performance.

To help employees understand how their work affects the bottom line, many companies share sensitive financial information with their employees and teach them how to understand and use financial statements. For example, Anderson & Associates, an engineering firm headquartered in Blacksburg, Virginia, puts all of its financial information, including salaries, on its company intranet for all to see. Ken Anderson, the company's president, believes this

FIGURE 18.1
Users of Accounting Information

openness is part of a general policy of employee empowerment and has helped his company grow and prosper. According to Anderson, employees can see the financial implications of each decision they make. Reviewing financial information helps employees better understand that "they've got to make the pie bigger if they're going to get a bigger pie."[3] Not all companies, however, like the idea of sharing financial data with employees.

Outside the firm, potential investors evaluate accounting information to help them decide whether to buy its securities. Bankers and other lenders use accounting information to evaluate a potential borrower's financial soundness. The Internal Revenue Service (IRS) and state tax officials use it to evaluate a company's tax payments for the year. Citizens' groups and government agencies use such information in assessing the efficiency of operations like a charitable organization, a local school system, or a city museum or zoo.

ACCOUNTING AND THE ENVIRONMENTS OF BUSINESS

Accountants play fundamental roles in not only business but also other aspects of society. Their work influences each of the business environments discussed earlier in this book. They clearly contribute important information to help managers deal with the competitive and economic environments. Less obvious contributions help others to understand, predict, and react to the technological, regulatory, and social and cultural environments.

> **BUSINESS DIRECTORY**
>
> ➤ **accounting** *practice of measuring, interpreting, and communicating financial information to support internal and external business decision making.*

For example, Karen Stevenson Brown, a certified public accountant, provides accounting services to a variety of health care providers. Brown also contributes to the understanding of a significant social concern: the care of the elderly. She has combined her interest in computers and her concern for the welfare of older people in a Web site for those who need information related to elder care. Recognizing that eldercare is growing in importance as the U.S. population ages, Brown designed ElderWeb, an online resource directory of articles and links to useful information that covers all aspects of the subject. Brown's site offers guidance to the elderly, their families, and caregivers on a wide variety of subjects, including financial, legal, medical, and spiritual. The site has won numerous awards from a variety of organizations.[4]

BUSINESS ACTIVITIES INVOLVING ACCOUNTING

The natural progression of a business begins with financing. Subsequent steps, including investing, lead to operating the business. All organizations, profit oriented and not-for-profit, perform these three basic activities, and accounting plays a key role in each one:

1. Financing activities provide necessary funds to start a business and to expand it after it begins operating.
2. Investing activities provide valuable assets required to run a business.
3. Operating activities focus on selling goods and services, but they also consider expenses as important elements of sound financial management.

Dan Weinfurter performed these three activities during the start-up and growth of Parson Group LLC, a consulting firm specializing in accounting, finance, and corporate risk management. He financed his new company with $7.2 million in venture capital along with $800,000 of his own money. Weinfurter invested these funds in computer systems and other office equipment. His operating activities involved hiring professional and clerical staff and promoting the company's services to a variety of clients. The role of accounting has increased considerably since Parson Group began operating in 1995, driven by the firm's rapid growth. Since 1995, it has been the fastest growing private company in the U.S., according to *Inc.* magazine. Annual revenues have increased from $200,000 to more than $56 million, and the number of employees has risen from 5 to almost 1,000.[5]

ACCOUNTING PROFESSIONALS

Accounting professionals work in a variety of areas in and for business firms, government agencies, and not-for-profit organizations. They can be classified as public, management, government, and not-for-profit accountants.

Public Accountants

A **public accountant** provides accounting services to individuals or business firms for a fee. Most public accounting firms provide three basic services to clients: (1) auditing, or examining, financial records; (2) tax preparation, planning, and related services; and (3) management consulting. Since they are not employees of a client firm, public accountants are in a position to provide unbiased advice about the firm's financial condition.

The five largest U.S. public accounting firms, the so-called "Big Five," are Arthur Andersen, Deloitte & Touche, Ernst & Young, KPMG Peat Marwick, and PricewaterhouseCoopers. Together, the Big Five collect about half of the $70 billion revenue paid to accounting firms in the U.S. each year. An increasing proportion of Big Five revenues comes from management consulting services. In fact, consulting contributes over half of Big Five revenues, and this revenue source is growing three times faster than revenue from their basic auditing business.[6] The Ernst & Young ad in Figure 18.2 suggests some of the ways the firm can help clients to improve operations and profitability. The ad promotes the accounting firm's tax expertise and how it can help improve a company's bottom line.

The fact that many accounting firms play a dual role for firms—both as consultant and auditor—has raised a number of issues. Recently, the SEC adopted a rule that restricts the consulting services an accounting firm can provide a company for which it is also the company's auditor. The process leading up to the SEC's rule provoked strong comments, both pro and con, from a variety of interested parties. The "Solving an Ethical Controversy" box debates the dual role many accounting firms play.

Management Accountants

An accountant employed by a business other than a public accounting firm is called a **management accountant.** Such a person is responsible for collecting and recording financial transactions and preparing financial statements used by the firm's managers in decision making. Management accountants provide timely, relevant, accurate, and concise information that managers can use to operate their firms more effectively and more profitably than they could without this input. In addition to preparing financial statements, a management accountant plays a major role in interpreting them. In presenting financial information to managers, a management accountant should provide answers to many important questions: Where

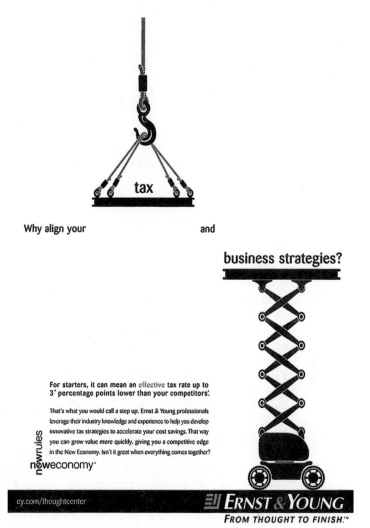

FIGURE 18.2
Accounting Firms Do More than Just Prepare Financial Statements

is the company going? What opportunities await it? Do certain situations expose the company to excessive risk? Does the firm's information system provide detailed and timely information to all levels of management? **Certified public accountants (CPAs)** demonstrate their accounting knowledge by meeting state requirements for education and experience and successfully completing a number of rigorous tests in accounting theory and practice, auditing, law, and taxes. Other accountants who meet specified educational and experience requirements and pass certification exams carry the titles certified management accountant or certified internal auditor.

Management accountants frequently specialize in different aspects of accounting. A cost accountant, for example, determines the cost of goods and services and helps to set their prices. A tax accountant works to minimize a firm's tax bill and assumes responsibility for its federal, state, county, and city tax returns. An internal auditor examines the firm's financial practices to ensure that records include accurate data and that its operations comply with federal, state, and local laws and regulations.

Government and Not-for-Profit Accountants

Federal, state, and local governments also require accounting services. **Government accountants** and those who work for not-for-profit organizations perform professional services similar to those of management accountants. Instead of the business firm's reporting emphasis on measuring profit or loss, however, accountants in these sectors concern themselves with determining how efficiently the organizations accomplish their objectives. Among the many government agencies that employ accountants are the Environmental Protection Agency, the Federal Bureau of

SOLVING AN ETHICAL CONTROVERSY

2. Allowing accounting firms to consult for audit clients undermines confidence in the quality of financial statements.

3. If the reliability of financial statements is questioned, investor confidence in the financial markets will be diminished.

CON

1. There is no hard evidence that allowing accounting firms to also consult for audit clients compromises auditor independence.

2. Consulting actually improves the quality of audits by allowing the accounting firm to better understand the business.

3. Barring accounting firms from also offering consulting services will make it more difficult for accounting firms to hire and retain key people.

SUMMARY

By the time the SEC issued its final rule in November 2000, it had backed off its initial hard line somewhat. The final rule, which became effective on February 5, 2001, puts restrictions on the consulting services accounting firms can provide to audit clients, but it didn't ban them outright. The final rule also requires that firms disclose the range and types of consulting services their auditors have provided to them. The final rule was a compromise, something both sides seem content to live with, at least for the time being. This issue, however, is far from settled.

On June 27, 2000, the SEC proposed a rule that would bar accounting firms from providing a range of consulting services to the companies they also audit. The SEC, especially then-Chairman Arthur Levitt, argued that accounting firms were becoming too cozy with clients, and as a result, they were losing their independence. The quality of financial statements, he suggested, was declining and with it investor confidence. According to Levitt, "When the public loses confidence in our markets, or when the reliability of the [accounting] numbers is diminished, the whole system is jeopardized. The sanctity of the numbers and of their reliability must be there."

The reaction from many public accountants was swift and negative. The SEC, they argued, proposed a severe rule based on nothing more than sketchy anecdotal evidence that consulting compromises auditors' independence. In addition, the accounting firms argued, the rule would effectively cripple their consulting businesses and might actually degrade the quality of their audits. Accounting firms insisted that there was no way they could effectively audit companies—especially technology companies—without talented computer and management professionals. Accounting firms were already having trouble recruiting and retaining these specialists. The proposed rule, they contended, would make the matter even worse.

The SEC held a series of public hearings and collected thousands of comments, both pro and con. Corporations were split—some testified in favor of the rule, others testified against it. Congress even got involved in the controversy. Some members questioned whether the SEC was overstepping its regulatory authority.

Should accounting firms be prohibited from advising firms they also audit?

PRO

1. The practice of accounting firms consulting for audit clients violates the principle that auditors should be truly independent and creates an inherent conflict of interest.

Sources: "Final Rule: Revision of the Commission's Auditor Independence Requirements," Securities and Exchange Commission, November 25, 2000, downloaded from **www.sec.gov** on January 22, 2001; "Fact Sheet: The Commission's Proposal to Modernize the Rules Governing the Independence of the Accounting Profession," Securities and Exchange Commission, November 15, 2000, downloaded from **www.sec.gov** on January 22, 2000; "Proposed Federal Regulation Threatens CPA Profession," American Institute of CPAs, August 10, 2000, downloaded from **www.aicpa.org** on January 22, 2001; "Accounting Wars," *Business Week,* September 25, 2000, pp. 157–166.

Investigation, the IRS, the Commonwealth of Pennsylvania, and the City of Fresno, California. Not-for-profit organizations, such as churches, labor unions, political parties, charities, schools, hospitals, and universities, also hire accountants. In fact, the not-for-profit sector is one of the fastest-growing segments of accounting practice. An increasing number of not-for-profits are publishing financial information, because contributors want to know how the groups spend the money that they donate.

THE ACCOUNTING PROCESS

Accounting deals with financial transactions between a firm and its employees, customers, suppliers, owners, bankers, and various government agencies. For example, weekly payroll checks result in cash outflows to compensate employees. A payment to a vendor results in receipt of needed materials for the production process. Cash, check, and credit purchases by customers generate funds to cover the costs of operations and to earn a profit. Prompt payment of bills preserves the firm's credit rating and its future ability to obtain loans. The procedural cycle in which accountants convert data about individual transactions to financial statements is called the accounting process. Figure 18.3 illustrates the activities involved in the accounting process: recording, classifying, and summarizing transactions in order to produce financial statements for the firm's management and other interested parties. *page 656*

The Impact of Computers and the Internet on the Accounting Process

For hundreds of years, bookkeepers have recorded, or posted, accounting transactions through manual entries in journals. They then transferred the information, or posted it, to individual accounts listed in ledgers. The computer revolution has simplified the process, making it faster and easier than the manual method. As point-of-sale terminals replace cash registers, computer systems perform a number of functions each time they record sales. These terminals not only recall prices from computer system memory and maintain constant inventory counts of individual items in stock but also automatically perform accounting data-entry functions.

Accounting software programs are used widely in both large and small businesses today. They allow a do-it-once approach, in which a single input leads to automatic conversion of a sale into a journal entry, which then is stored until needed. Up-to-date financial statements and financial ratios then can be requested when needed by decision makers. Improvements in accounting software continue to make the process even faster and easier than it is now. Another benefit of automated accounting systems is their ability to produce financial reports that convert numbers into easily understood graphs and charts.

Because the accounting needs of entrepreneurs and small businesses differ from those of larger firms, accounting software makers have designed programs that meet specific user needs. Some examples of accounting software programs designed for entrepreneurs and small businesses include M.Y.O.B. Accounting, Quick Books Pro, and Peachtree Complete Accounting. Software programs designed for larger firms include products from Computer Associates, Oracle, and SAP.

For firms that conduct business worldwide, software producers have introduced new accounting programs that handle all of a company's accounting information for every country in which it operates. This change represents an improvement over systems that require different programs for individual countries. The software handles different languages and currencies as well as the financial, legal, and tax requirements of each nation in which the firm conducts business.

A CPA CAN SEE MORE IN NUMBERS THAN JUST NUMBERS. (APPARENTLY, THE EYE IS THE WINDOW TO MORE THAN JUST THE SOUL.)

In every number, there is a question. Is your retirement plan the best it could be? What will be the impact of your company's merger with another? Where will you find the capital you need? But without the vision to see the true meaning within the numbers, the answers can remain frustratingly obscured. A CPA can provide the financial insights so crucial to everything from retirement planning to evaluating prospective mergers and ferreting out re-engineering opportunities.

You see numbers. We see opportunities.

THE CPA. NEVER UNDERESTIMATE THE VALUE.

American Institute of Certified Public Accountants

Certified public accountants (CPAs) are accounting professionals who have met education and experience requirements and have passed a comprehensive examination.

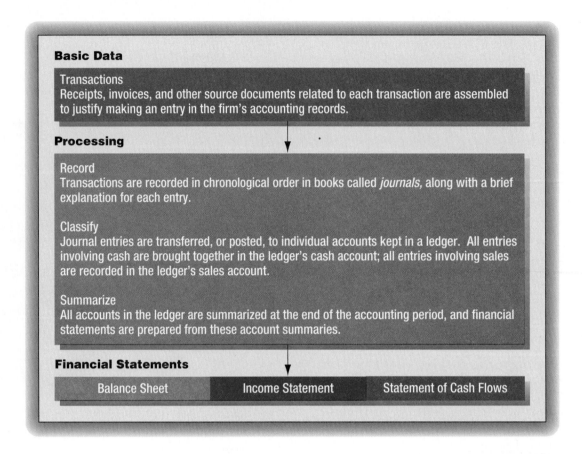

Basic Data

Transactions
Receipts, invoices, and other source documents related to each transaction are assembled to justify making an entry in the firm's accounting records.

Processing

Record
Transactions are recorded in chronological order in books called *journals,* along with a brief explanation for each entry.

Classify
Journal entries are transferred, or posted, to individual accounts kept in a ledger. All entries involving cash are brought together in the ledger's cash account; all entries involving sales are recorded in the ledger's sales account.

Summarize
All accounts in the ledger are summarized at the end of the accounting period, and financial statements are prepared from these account summaries.

Financial Statements

| Balance Sheet | Income Statement | Statement of Cash Flows |

FIGURE 18.3
The Accounting Process

FIGURE 18.4
Web-Based Accounting Services

The Internet is also influencing the accounting process. Several software producers offer Web-based accounting products designed for small business. One company, Virtual Growth, has gone one step further. It provides outsourced Web-based bookkeeping and accounting services to fast-growing small and medium-sized businesses. Virtual Growth clients are companies that have outgrown off-the-shelf small business accounting programs and need more sophisticated financial reports and accounting services.[7] An example of the services offered by Virtual Growth is shown in Figure 18.4.

The Internet has also given firms new options for presenting their financial information. Financial information and annual reports for many companies can be downloaded from their respective Web sites. The "Clicks and Mortar" box describes how companies and others use the Internet to present financial information.

THE FOUNDATION OF THE ACCOUNTING SYSTEM

To provide reliable, consistent, and unbiased information to decision makers, accountants follow guidelines, or standards, known as generally accepted accounting principles (GAAP). These principles encompass the conventions, rules, and procedures for determining acceptable accounting practices at a particular time. In the U.S., the FASB is primarily responsible for evaluating, setting, or modifying GAAP. Accountants adhere to GAAP to create uniform financial statements for comparison between firms. Using GAAP ensures a solid basis for sound business decision making.

Two financial statements form the foundation of the accounting system: the balance sheet and the income statement. The information found in these statements is calculated using the accounting equation and the double-entry bookkeeping system. A third statement, the statement of cash flows, is also prepared to focus specifically on the sources and uses of cash for a firm from its operating, investing, and financing activities.

The Accounting Equation

Three fundamental terms appear in the accounting equation: assets, liabilities, and owners' equity. An **asset** is anything of value owned or leased by a business. Assets include land, buildings, supplies, cash, accounts receivable and notes receivable (amounts owed to the business as payment for credit sales), and marketable securities.

Although most assets are tangible objects such as equipment, buildings, and inventories, intangible possessions such as patents and trademarks are often some of a firm's most important assets. This kind of asset is especially essential for many companies

BUSINESS DIRECTORY

➤ **asset** *anything of value owned or leased by a business.*

POLO RALPH LAUREN

THE CORDOVAN TASSEL LOAFER

Trademarks and patents are valuable property. The instantly recognized polo player trademark of Polo Ralph Lauren identifies its products and distinguishes them from competitive offerings.

including computer software firms and biotechnology companies. Merck, for example, has intangible assets of over $7.5 billion, much of which consist of the value of the firm's drug patents.[8]

There are two claimants to the assets of a firm: creditors and owners. A **liability** of a business is anything owed to creditors—that is, the claims of the firm's creditors. When the firm borrows money to purchase inventory, land, or machinery, the claims of creditors are shown as accounts payable, notes payable, or long-term debt. Wages and salaries owed to employees also represent liabilities (known as wages payable).

Owners' equity represents the owners' initial investment in the business plus retained earnings that were not paid out over time in dividends. A strong owners' equity position often is used as evidence of a firm's financial strength and stability.

The basic **accounting equation** states that assets equal liabilities plus owners' equity. This equation reflects the financial position of a firm at any point in time:

$$\text{Assets} = \text{Liabilities} + \text{Owner's Equity}$$

Since financing comes from either creditors or owners, the right side of the accounting equation also represents the business's financial structure.

The relationship expressed by the accounting equation underlies development of the balance sheet and the income statement. These two statements reflect the firm's current financial position and the most recent analysis of its income, expenses, and profits for interested parties inside and outside the firm. They provide a fundamental basis for planning activities and help companies to attract new investors, secure borrowed funds, and complete tax returns.

FINANCIAL STATEMENTS

Financial statements provide managers with essential information they need to evaluate the liquidity position of an organization—its ability to meet current obligations and needs by converting assets into cash; the firm's profitability; and its overall financial health. The balance sheet, income statement, and statement of cash flows provide a foundation on which managers can base their decisions. By interpreting the data provided in these financial statements, the appropriate information can be communicated to internal decision makers and to interested parties outside the organization.

The Balance Sheet

A firm's **balance sheet** shows its financial position on a particular date. It is similar to a photograph of the firm's assets together with its liabilities and owners' equity at a specific moment in time. Balance sheets must be prepared at regular intervals, since a firm's managers and other internal parties often request this information every day, week, or at least every month. On the other hand, external users, such as stockholders or industry analysts, may use this information less frequently, perhaps every quarter or once a year.

The balance sheet follows the accounting equation. On the left side of the balance sheet are the firm's assets—what it owns. These assets, shown in descending order of liquidity (in other words, convertibility to cash), represent the uses that management has made of available funds. On the right side of the equation are the claims against the firm's assets. Liabilities and owners' equity indicate the sources of the firm's assets and are listed in the order in which they are due. Liabilities reflect the claims of creditors—financial institutions or bondholders that have loaned the firm money, suppliers that have provided goods and services on credit, and others to be paid, such as federal, state, and local tax authorities. Owners' equity represents the owners' claims (those of stockholders, in the case of a corporation) against the firm's assets. It also amounts to the excess of all assets over liabilities.

Figure 18.5 shows the balance sheet for Sierra Pasta Company, a California-based gourmet food retailer. The basic accounting equation is illustrated by the three classifications of assets, liabilities, and owners' equity on the company's balance sheet. Total assets must equal the total of liabilities and owners' equity.

The Income Statement

Whereas the balance sheet reflects a firm's financial situation at a specific point in time, the income statement represents the flow of resources that reveals the performance of the organization over a specific time period. Resembling a video rather than a photograph, the **income statement** is a financial record summarizing a firm's financial performance in terms of revenues, expenses, and profits over a given time period.

In addition to reporting the firm's profit or loss results, the income statement helps decision makers to focus on overall revenues and the costs involved in generating these revenues. Managers of a not-for-profit organization use this statement to determine whether its revenues from contributions and other sources will cover its operating costs. Finally, the income statement provides much of the basic data needed to calculate the financial ratios managers use in planning and controlling activities. Figure 18.6 shows an income statement for Sierra Pasta Company.

BUSINESS DIRECTORY

➤ **liability** *claim against a firm's assets by a creditor.*

➤ **owners' equity** *all claims of the proprietor, partners, or stockholders against the assets of a firm, equal to the excess of assets over liabilities.*

➤ **accounting equation** *basic relationship that states that assets equal liabilities plus owners' equity.*

➤ **balance sheet** *statement of a firm's financial position—what it owns and the claims against its assets—at a particular point in time.*

➤ **income statement** *financial record of a company's revenues, expenses, and profits over a period of time.*

① Current Assets
Cash and other liquid assets that can or will be converted to cash or used within one year.

② Fixed Assets
Plant, property, equipment, and other assets expected to last for more than one year. Accumulated depreciation represents the cumulative value of fixed assets that have been expensed, or depreciated.

③ Current Liabilities
Claims of creditors that are to be repaid within one year.

④ Long-Term Debt
Debts that come due one year or longer after the date on the balance sheet.

⑤ Owners' (Shareholders') Equity
Claims of the proprietor, partners, or stockholders against the assets of the firm; the excess of assets over liabilities.

SIERRA PASTA COMPANY
Balance Sheet
Year Ending January 31

ASSETS

	2002	2001
① Current Assets		(000s)
Cash and Equivalents	$ 5,000	$ 4,500
Accounts Receivable	4,800	4,600
Inventory	14,500	12,500
Total Current Assets	24,300	21,600
② Gross Fixed Assets	45,000	32,500
(Accumulated Depreciation)	(22,500)	(16,000)
Net Fixed Assets	22,500	16,500
Total Assets	$ 46,800	$ 38,100

LIABILITIES AND EQUITY

	2002	2001
③ Current Liabilities		
Notes Payable	$ 4,000	$ 5,500
Accounts Payable	3,750	3,500
Accrued Expenses	3,000	2,600
Total Current Liabilities	10,750	11,600
④ Long-Term Debt	2,050	500
Total Liabilities	12,800	12,100
⑤ Shareholders' Equity		
Common stock (2,000 Shares Outstanding)	10,000	10,000
Retained Earnings	24,000	16,000
Total Shareholders' Equity	34,000	26,000
Total Liabilities and Equity	$ 46,800	$ 38,100

FIGURE 18.5
Balance Sheet for Sierra Pasta Company

An income statement (sometimes called a profit and loss, or P&L, statement) begins with total sales or revenues generated during a year, quarter, or month. Subsequent lines then deduct all of the costs related to producing the revenues. Typical categories of costs include administrative and marketing expenses, costs involved in producing the firm's good or service, interest, and taxes. After all of them have been subtracted, the remaining net income may be distributed to the firm's owners (stockholders, proprietors, or partners) or reinvested in the company as retained earnings.

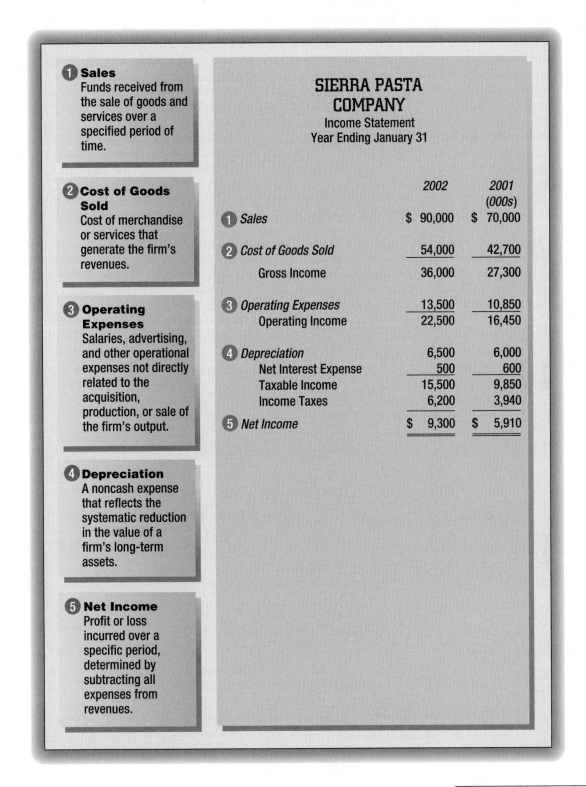

① Sales
Funds received from the sale of goods and services over a specified period of time.

② Cost of Goods Sold
Cost of merchandise or services that generate the firm's revenues.

③ Operating Expenses
Salaries, advertising, and other operational expenses not directly related to the acquisition, production, or sale of the firm's output.

④ Depreciation
A noncash expense that reflects the systematic reduction in the value of a firm's long-term assets.

⑤ Net Income
Profit or loss incurred over a specific period, determined by subtracting all expenses from revenues.

SIERRA PASTA COMPANY
Income Statement
Year Ending January 31

	2002	2001
		(000s)
① Sales	$ 90,000	$ 70,000
② Cost of Goods Sold	54,000	42,700
Gross Income	36,000	27,300
③ Operating Expenses	13,500	10,850
Operating Income	22,500	16,450
④ Depreciation	6,500	6,000
Net Interest Expense	500	600
Taxable Income	15,500	9,850
Income Taxes	6,200	3,940
⑤ Net Income	$　9,300	$　5,910

FIGURE 18.6
Income Statement for Sierra Pasta Company

The final figure on the income statement—net income after taxes—is the well-known **bottom line.**

Keeping costs under control is an important part of running a business. After all, reducing expenses by, say, 10 percent has the same impact on profits as a 10 percent increase in revenue. Too often, however, companies concentrate more on increasing revenue than controlling costs. The "Business Hits and Misses" box outlines examples of firms that failed to adequately control costs.

It's been said that the ads run during the Super Bowl are often more memorable than the game itself. Because the Super Bowl attracts such a large audience, many companies take the opportunity to put out creative, innovative, and occasionally controversial ads—ads people will remember long after the game is over. The ads run during the 2000 Super Bowl were memorable for another reason. Out of the 36 ads that ran during the 2000 Super Bowl, 17 were for dot.com companies. Each advertiser paid over $2 million to run a 30-second spot.

One of the dot.com companies that ran an ad during Super Bowl XXXIV was Pets.com, an online retailer of pet supplies. The ad featured the company's "spokes puppet"—actually a sock—and won rave reviews. Unfortunately, things went downhill for Pets.com after the Super Bowl. The company began running out of cash during the summer of 2000, and after failing to obtain additional financing or find a merger partner, it soon shut down operations. Over 250 people lost their jobs, and the company's investors lost millions of dollars.

Pets.com was certainly not alone. According to *The Wall Street Journal*, 210 dot.com companies folded that year, and many of those that managed to stay in business are in precarious financial condition. One of the main causes of the collapse of many dot.com companies was their inability or unwillingness to control costs. Many aspiring dot.com tycoons simply didn't realize how expensive it can be to start and grow a business.

Out of control expenses certainly helped do in Pets.com. Here are two examples:

- *Negative gross profit margin.* A negative gross profit margin means that a company actually loses money on each item it sells—even before it pays other expenses, such as wages. During its short history, Pets.com never had a positive gross profit margin.
- *Too much spending on advertising, marketing, salaries, and other operating expenses.* Pets.com, for example, spent over $60 million on advertising and marketing during one nine-month period. Yet during the same period the company had sales of only $26 million. Not only did Pets.com, and other Internet firms, spend lavish amounts of money on marketing—witness the Super Bowl ads—the effectiveness of these expenditures is questionable. Commenting on Pets.com's Super Bowl ad, one analyst said, "It was very entertaining, very cute, but it doesn't tell me why I should go to Pets.com instead of buying food from my veterinarian."

According to Steve Johnson, codirector of e-commerce for Accenture—formerly Andersen Consulting—many dot.com entrepreneurs, and the venture capitalists who financed them, lost sight of one of the fundamental rules of starting a business: Entrepreneurs need to have a sound business plan, a defined market, and a clear path to making money. In the new economy, as in the old, the bottom line matters.

QUESTIONS FOR CRITICAL THINKING

1. Many dot.com executives thought that if they could just grow revenues at a rapid enough pace, the other things—such as profitability and positive cash flow—would take care of themselves. In retrospect, what's wrong with only focusing on revenue growth?

2. In your opinion, what is the current outlook for Internet companies? Do you think they've learned their lesson about the importance of controlling costs?

Sources: "Dot-Com Layoffs and Shutdowns," *The Wall Street Journal*, downloaded from **http://interactive.wsj.com** on January 19, 2001; Ruth Shalit, "Super Bowl Ads: Winners and Losers," *Salon Magazine*, downloaded from **www.salonmag.com** on January 19, 2001; "Pets.com at Its Tail End," CNNfn, downloaded from **www.cnnfn.com** on January 19, 2001; "Dot-coms Fumble with Ads," CNNfn, downloaded from **www.cnnfn.com** on January 19, 2001; Matt Krantz, "Dot-coms without Plans Die, Many Thought They Could Skip Old Economy Step," *USA Today*, downloaded from **www.cnetinvestor.com** on January 19, 2001.

The Statement of Cash Flows

In addition to the income statement and the balance sheet, many firms prepare a third accounting statement—the statement of cash flows. Public companies are required to prepare and publish a statement of cash flows. In addition, commercial lenders often require a borrower to submit a statement of cash flows. The statement of cash flows provides investors and creditors with relevant information about a firm's cash receipts and cash payments for its operations, investments, and financing during an accounting period. Figure 18.7 shows the statement of cash flows for Sierra Pasta Company.

Companies often prepare a statement of cash flows due to the widespread use of accrual accounting. Accrual accounting recognizes revenues and costs when they occur, not when actual cash changes hands. As a result, there can be differences between what is reported as sales, expenses, and profits, and the amount of cash that actually flows in and out of the business during a period of time. An example is depreciation. Companies depreciate fixed assets—such as machinery and buildings—over a specified period of time, meaning that they systematically reduce the value of the asset. Depreciation is reported as an expense on the firm's income statement—see

① Operating Activities
The nuts-and-bolts, day-to-day activities of a company carrying on its regular business; in financially healthy firms, net cash flow from operating activities should be positive.

② Investing Activities
Transactions to accumulate or use cash in ways that will affect operating activities in the future; often a use of cash.

③ Financing Activities
Ways to transfer cash to/from outsiders and/or owners; can be either negative or positive.

④ Net Cash Flow
A reconcilement of cash from the beginning to the end of the account period.

SIERRA PASTA COMPANY
Statement of Cash Flows
Year Ending January 31

	2002 (000s)
① Cash Flow from Operating Activities	
Net Income	$ 9,300
Depreciation	6,500
Cash provided (used) by changes	
in Accounts Receivable	(200)
Inventory	(2,000)
Accounts Payable	250
Accruals	400
Net Cash Flow from Operating Activities	14,250
② Cash Flow from Investing Activities	
Capital Investments	(12,500)
Net Cash Flow from Investing Activities	(12,500)
③ Cash Flow from Financing Activities	
Repayment of Short-Term Notes	(1,500)
Sale of Long-Term Debt	1,550
Cash Dividends to Shareholders	(1,300)
Net Cash Flow from Financing Activities	(1,250)
④ Net Cash Flow	500
Cash and Equivalents (beginning of year)	4,500
Cash and Equivalents (end of year)	$ 5,000

FIGURE 18.7
Statement of Cash Flows for Sierra Pasta Company

Figure 18.6—but does not involve any cash. The fact that depreciation is a noncash expense means that what a firm reports as net income (profits after tax) for a particular period actually understates the amount of cash the firm took in, less expenses, during that period of time. Consequently, depreciation is added back to net income to obtain **cash flow.**

The fact that cash flow is the lifeblood of every organization is evidenced by the business failure rate. Many owners of firms that fail put the blame on inadequate cash flow. Proponents of the statement of cash flows hope that its preparation and scrutiny by affected parties will prevent financial disaster for

BUSINESS DIRECTORY

➤ **statement of cash flows** *statement of a firm's cash receipts and cash payments that presents information on its sources and uses of cash.*

➤ **accrual accounting** *accounting method that records revenue and expenses when they occur, not necessarily when cash actually changes hands.*

Slow-paying clients generate major cash-flow problems for most firms—both large and small. But these gaps between the time a product has been delivered or a service performed and when the payment arrives can be devastating for smaller, cash-starved businesses.

otherwise profitable firms, too many of which are forced into bankruptcy due to a lack of funds needed to continue day-to-day operations.

Even for firms for which bankruptcy is not an issue, the statement of cash flows can provide investors and other interested parties with vital information. For example, when Motorola announced on October 11, 2000, that sales and earnings would not meet Wall Street's expectations, some investors were surprised, but others were not caught off guard. These investors had seen the signs of impending problems at Motorola by examining the company's cash flow statement that it released on July 31, 2000. The statement showed that sales were rising slower than inventories—often a signal that demand for a company's products is softening.[9]

FINANCIAL RATIO ANALYSIS

Accounting professionals fulfill important responsibilities beyond preparing financial statements. In a more critical role, they help managers to interpret the statements by comparing data about the firm's current activities to that for previous periods and to results posted by other companies in the industry. **Ratio analysis** is one of the most commonly used tools for measuring the firm's liquidity, profitability, and reliance on debt financing, as well as the effectiveness of management's resource use. This analysis also allows comparisons with other firms and with the firm's own past performance.

Ratios assist managers by interpreting actual performance and making comparisons with what should have happened. Comparisons with ratios of similar companies help managers to understand their firm's performance relative to competitors' results. These industry standards serve as important yardsticks and help to pinpoint problem areas as well as areas of excellence. Ratios for the current accounting period also may be compared with similar calculations for previous periods to spot developing trends. Ratios can be classified according to their specific purposes. The four major categories of financial ratios are summarized in Table 18.1.

Liquidity Ratios

A firm's ability to meet its short-term obligations when they must be paid is measured by **liquidity ratios.** Increasing liquidity reduces the likelihood that a firm will face emergencies caused by the need to raise funds to repay loans. On the other hand, firms with low liquidity may be forced to choose between default or borrowing from high-cost lending sources to meet their maturing obligations.

Two commonly used liquidity ratios are the current ratio and the acid-test ratio. The current ratio compares current assets to current liabilities, giving managers information about the firm's ability to pay its current debts as they mature. The current ratio of Sierra Pasta Company can be computed as follows:

Current ratio = $24.30 million/$10.75 million = 2.26

Table 18.1   Financial Ratios and What They Measure

Ratio	What It Measures	Sierra Pasta Company's Ratio
Liquidity Ratio	The firm's ability to meet its short-term obligations	
Current ratio		2.26
Acid-test ratio		0.91
Profitability Ratios	The firm's ability to generate revenues in excess of expenses and earn an adequate rate of return	
Gross profit margin		40.0%
Net profit margin		10.3%
Earnings per share		$4.65
Return on assets		19.9%
Return on equity		27.4%
Leverage Ratios	The extent to which the firm relies on debt financing	
Total liabilities to total assets		27.4%
Activity Ratios	The effectiveness of the firm's resources use	
Inventory turnover		3.72
Total asset turnover		1.92

In other words, Sierra Pasta Company has $2.26 of current assets for every $1.00 of current liabilities. In general, a current ratio of 2 to 1 is considered to indicate satisfactory financial conditions. This rule of thumb must be considered along with other factors, such as the nature of the business, the season, and the quality of the company's management. Sierra Pasta Company management and other interested parties are likely to evaluate this ratio of 2.26 to 1 by comparing it with ratios for previous operating periods and with industry averages.

The acid-test (or quick) ratio measures the ability of a firm to meet its debt payments on short notice. This ratio compares quick assets—the most liquid current assets—against current liabilities. Quick assets generally consist of cash and marketable securities, and accounts receivable.

Sierra Pasta Company's current balance sheet lists the following quick assets: cash and marketable securities ($5.0 million) and accounts receivable ($4.8 million). The firm's acid-test ratio is computed as follows:

$$\text{Acid-test ratio} = \$9.80 \text{ million}/\$10.75 \text{ million} = 0.92$$

Because the traditional rule of thumb for an adequate acid-test ratio is around 1 to 1, Sierra Pasta Company appears to be have a reasonable level of liquidity. However, the same cautions apply here as for the current ratio. The ratio should be compared with industry averages and data from previous operating periods in determining whether it is adequate for the firm.

Profitability Ratios

Some ratios measure the organization's overall financial performance by evaluating its ability to generate revenues in excess of operating costs and other expenses. These measures are called **profitability ratios**. To compute these ratios, accountants compare the firm's earnings with total sales or investments. Over a period of time, profitability ratios may reveal the effectiveness of management in operating the business.

Five important profitability ratios are gross profit margin, net profit margin, earnings per share, return on assets, and return on equity:

Gross profit margin = \$36.0 million/\$90.0 million = 40.0%
Net profit margin = \$9.3 million/\$90.0 million = 10.3%
Earnings per share = \$9.3 million/2.0 million = \$4.65
Return on assets = \$9.3 million/\$46.8 million = 19.9%
Return on equity = \$9.3 million/\$34.0 million = 27.4%

All of these ratios support positive evaluations of the current operations of Sierra Pasta Company. For example, the net profit margin indicates that the firm realizes a profit of about 10.3 cents on each dollar of products it sells. Although this ratio varies widely among business firms, Sierra Pasta Company compares favorably with retailers in general, which have an average net profit margin of around 5 percent. However, this ratio, like the other profitability ratios, should be evaluated in relation to profit forecasts, past performance, or more specific industry averages to enhance the interpretation of results. Similarly, while the firm's return on equity of more than 27 percent appears to reflect excellent performance, the degree of risk in the industry also must be considered.

Profitability ratios are widely used indicators of business success. For example, over a five-year period the earnings per share of retail giant Home Depot more than quadrupled. During that same five-year period, the price of Home Depot's stock rose by more than fivefold.[10]

Leverage Ratios

Leverage ratios measure the extent to which a firm relies on debt financing. They provide particularly interesting information to potential investors and lenders. If management has assumed too much debt in financing the firm's operations, problems may arise in meeting future interest payments and repaying outstanding loans. Relying too heavily on debt financing can lead to bankruptcy. More generally, both investors and lenders may prefer to deal with firms whose owners have invested enough of their own money in their companies to avoid overreliance on borrowing. The total liabilities to total assets ratio helps analysts to evaluate these concerns:

Total liabilities to total assets = \$12.8 million/\$46.8 million = 27.4%

A total liabilities to total assets ratio greater than 50 percent indicates that a firm is relying more on borrowed money than owners' equity. Since Sierra Pasta Company's total liabilities to total assets ratio is 27.4 percent, the firm's owners have invested considerably more than the total amount of liabilities shown on the firm's balance sheet.

Activity Ratios

Activity ratios measure the effectiveness of management's use of the firm's resources. One of the most frequently used activity ratios, the inventory turnover ratio, indicates the number of times merchandise moves through a business:

Inventory turnover = \$54.0 million/\$13.5 million = 4.0

Average inventory for Sierra Pasta Company is determined by adding the January 1, 2002, beginning inventory of \$12.5 million and the December 31, 2002, ending inventory of \$14.5 million and dividing by 2.

Comparing the 4.0 inventory turnover ratio with industry standards gives a measure of efficiency. Furniture and jewelry retailers average an annual turnover of 1.5 times. A supermarket's annual inventory turnover can be as high as 30 times.

Another measure of efficiency is total asset turnover. It measures how much in sales each dollar in assets generates:

Total asset turnover = \$90.00 million/\$42.45 million = 2.19

Average total assets for Sierra Pasta Company equals total assets at the beginning of 2002 ($38.1 million) plus total assets at the end of the period ($46.8 million) divided by 2.

Sierra Pasta Company generates about $2.19 in sales for each dollar invested in assets. Although a higher ratio generally indicates that a firm is operating more efficiently, care must be taken when comparing firms that operate in different industries. For example, Southwest Airlines has a total asset turnover of around .92, low in comparison with some firms but high in comparison with other airlines.

The four categories of financial ratios relate balance sheet and income statement data to one another and assist management in pinpointing a firm's strengths and weaknesses. Large, multiproduct firms that operate in diverse markets use their information systems to update their financial ratios every day or even every hour. Each company's management must decide on an appropriate review schedule to avoid the costly and time-consuming mistake of overmonitoring.

BUDGETING

Although the financial statements discussed in this chapter focus on past business activities, they also provide the basis for planning in the future. A **budget** is a planning and controlling tool that reflects the firm's expected sales revenues, operating expenses, and cash receipts and outlays. It quantifies the firm's plans for a specified future period. Since it reflects management estimates of expected sales, cash inflows and outflows, and costs, the budget serves as a financial blueprint and can be thought of as a short-term financial plan. It becomes the standard for comparison against actual performance.

Budget preparation is frequently a time-consuming task that involves many people from various departments within the firm. The complexity of the budgeting process varies with the size and complexity of the organization. Large corporations such as Alcoa, Johnson & Johnson, and Nokia maintain complex and sophisticated budgeting systems. Their budgets help managers to integrate their numerous divisions in addition to serving as planning and controlling tools. But budgeting in both large and small firms is similar to household budgeting in its purpose: to match income and expenses in a way that accomplishes objectives and correctly times cash inflows and outflows.

Since the accounting department is an organization's financial nerve center, it provides much of the data for budget development. The overall master, or operating, budget is actually a composite of many individual budgets for separate units of the firm. These individual budgets typically include the production budget, cash budget, capital expenditures budget, advertising budget, and sales budget.

At the HON Company, a maker of office furniture in the U.S. and Canada, accountants develop a master budget as a composite of its functional budgets such as the sales budget. The sales budget, in turn, is composed of data from a territory budget and a marketing budget. Budgets are usually

SIERRA PASTA COMPANY
P.O. Box 2646
Pueblo, Colorado

Three-Month Cash Budget
April–June

Cash Inflows	April	May	June
			(000s)
Cash Sales	3,000	4,500	6,000
Collections of Receivables	1,500	2,250	3,375
Other Cash Inflows	500	0	0
Total Cash Inflows	5,000	6,750	9,375
Cash Outflows			
Cash Purchases	2,025	2,700	2,700
Payment of Credit Purchases	1,000	1,519	2,030
Cash Operating Expenses	1,125	1,125	1,125
Other Cash Outflows	1,500	1,500	0
Total Cash Outflows	5,650	6,844	5,855
Net Cash Flow	(650)	(94)	3,520
Beginning Cash Balance	2,000	2,000	2,000
Net Cash Flow	(650)	(94)	3,520
Ending Cash Balance	1,350	1,906	5,520
Target Cash Balance	2,000	2,000	2,000
Cash Surplus (deficit)	(650)	(94)	3,520
Cumulative Surplus (deficit)	(650)	(744)	2,776

FIGURE 18.8
Three-Month Cash Budget for Sierra Pasta Company

prepared annually, but some firms prepare them monthly or quarterly for control purposes. HON managers, for example, prepare budgets four times a year, because the office furniture industry is highly cyclical and its variations generally reflect the state of the economy as a whole. Department managers work together to produce an updated four-quarter budget at the start of each quarter. This continuous updating helps managers to react quickly to unexpected changes in the industry and economy. HON has won several awards from professional organizations and business publications for its budgeting and cash management practices.[11]

Figure 18.8 illustrates a sample cash budget for Sierra Pasta Company. Management has set a $2 million target cash balance. The cash budget indicates months in which the firm will need temporary loans (April and May in the case of Sierra Pasta

Company). The document also indicates months in which the firm can invest excess funds in marketable securities to earn interest rather than leaving them idle in a bank account (June in the case of Sierra Pasta Company). Finally, the cash budget produces a tangible standard against which to compare actual cash inflows and outflows.

A budget is also an important tool for managing an individual's or household's finances. The "Clicks and Mortar" box lists some suggestions on how to prepare and stick to a personal budget.

INTERNATIONAL ACCOUNTING

Today, accounting procedures and practices must be adapted to accommodate an international business environment. The Coca-Cola Company and McDonald's both generate over half their annual revenues from sales outside the U.S. Nestlé, the giant chocolate and food products multinational, operates throughout the world. It derives 98 percent of its revenues from outside Switzerland, its home country. International accounting practices for global firms must reliably translate the financial statements of the firm's international affiliates, branches, and subsidiaries and convert data about foreign-currency transactions to dollars. Also, the euro, Europe's new single currency, will influence the accounting and financial reporting processes of firms operating in some European countries.

STRONG CASH FLOW. A LITTLE KNOWN BY-PRODUCT OF OUR INTEGRATED MANUFACTURING PROCESS.

BASF. A COMPANY THAT'S RETURN-FOCUSED AND GLOBALLY POSITIONED. WHETHER IT'S IN CHEMICALS, HEALTH AND NUTRITION, OR OIL AND GAS, BASF ISN'T JUST POSITIONED FOR LONG-TERM GROWTH, BUT FOR PROFITABLE GROWTH AS WELL. GIVEN OUR STRONG CASH FLOW, WE CAN MOVE QUICKLY TO SEIZE STRATEGIC OPPORTUNITIES AND FUND INTERNAL INVESTMENT AROUND THE WORLD. ALL OF WHICH MAKES BASF AN INVESTMENT OF GLOBAL PROPORTIONS. MAKING PRODUCTS BETTER.

BASF

Exchange Rates

As defined in Chapter 4, an exchange rate is the ratio at which a country's currency can be exchanged for other currencies. Currencies can be treated as goods to be bought and sold. Like the price of any good or service, currency prices change daily according to supply and demand. So, exchange rate fluctuations complicate accounting entries and accounting practices.

Accountants who deal with international transactions must appropriately record their firms' foreign sales and purchases. Today's sophisticated accounting software helps firms to handle all of their international transactions within a single program. An international firm's consolidated financial statements must reflect any gains or losses due to changes in exchange rates during specific periods of time. Financial statements that cover operations in two or more countries also need to treat fluctuations consistently to allow for comparison.

German-based BASF is a diversified multinational with billions in revenues from such broad product categories as chemicals, health and nutrition products, as well as oil and gas. Since it operates in dozens of countries on most of the world's continents, BASF's accounting systems must be capable of dealing with exchange rate variations as well as country-by-country differences in accounting practices.

International Accounting Standards

The International Accounting Standards Committee (IASC) was established in 1973 to promote worldwide consistency in financial reporting practices. The IASC is recognized worldwide as the body with sole responsibility and authority to issue pronouncements on international accounting standards. The International Federation of Accountants supports the work of the IASC and develops international guidelines for auditing, ethics, education, and management accounting. Every five years, an international congress is held to judge progress in achieving consistency in standards

Preparing a Personal Budget for Anita Martinez

Background. The cash budget is an important planning tool for companies. But a budget is also an important financial planning tool for individuals like Anita Martinez. Her budget is designed to monitor and control expenditures so that her short- and longer-term financial goals can be achieved. Budgets permit people like Anita to track past and current expenditures, and plan new ones.

What Happened. Anita decides to prepare her personal budget on a monthly basis. Most of her bills—such as her rent, Visa bill, utilities, and car payment—are due once a month. She is also paid once a month. The balance in her checking account always seems to get pretty low by the end of the month. She's hoping the monthly budget will help her better monitor and control her expenses.

The Response. Like a company's cash budget, Anita's personal budget is divided into two components: income (or cash inflows) and expenses (or cash outflows). She divides her expenses into two additional categories: fixed expenses (those that vary little from month to month) and variable expenses (those that vary from month to month). Examples of fixed expenses include her apartment rent, the car payment on her Honda Civic, insurance payments, and contributions to a Vanguard mutual fund. Variable expenses include Anita's food, electricity, and phone expenses. Her cash flow is simply the difference between cash inflows and outflows. The difference between her actual cash flows and estimated cash flows is referred to as variance.

Today and Counting. Anita once took a personal finance course at American River College in Sacramento. She knows that you should keep your budget as simple as possible. Anita limits the number of categories and rounds off to the nearest dollar. She also budgets some "personal spending money" each month. Anita is planning to get married within the next year. She and her fiancé, Al, have already discussed how they will budget their household income and expenses. They both know that arguments over money are a leading cause of divorce. Neither has any intention of getting caught in that financial trap.

QUESTIONS FOR CRITICAL THINKING

1. Now it is your turn to design a budget like Anita does. Fill out the worksheet shown here.
2. How difficult will it be for you to stick to your budget? Do you think it is realistic?

	Estimate	Actual	Variance
Cash Inflows			
Salary (take-home)			
Other cash inflows			
Total cash inflows			
Cash Outflows			
Fixed expenses			
Rent			
Auto loan			
Student loan			
Auto insurance premium			
Transfer to savings			
Variable expenses			
Utilities			
Food			
Medical & dental			
Clothing & personal care			
Entertainment			
Transportation expenses			
Gifts and contributions			
Personal spending money			
Total cash outflows			
Net cash flow			

Source: Adapted from Louis E. Boone, David L. Kurtz, and Douglas Hearth, *Planning Your Financial Future*, 2nd ed. (Ft. Worth, TX: Harcourt College Publishing, 2000), pp. 75–79.

and works toward increasing comparability among nations' financial data and currencies.

The formation of a single European market and adoption of NAFTA in North America have led to widespread recognition of the necessity for comparability and uniformity of international accounting standards. An increasing number of investors are buying shares in foreign multinational corporations. In response to global investors' needs, more and more firms are beginning to report their financial information according to International Accounting Standards. This practice helps investors compare the financial results of firms in different countries.

WHAT'S AHEAD

This chapter describes the role of accounting in an organization. Accounting is the process of measuring, interpreting, and communicating financial information to interested parties both inside and outside the firm. The next chapter introduces the finance function of an organization. Finance deals with planning, obtaining, and managing the organization's funds to accomplish its objectives in the most efficient and effective manner possible.

➤ Summary of Learning Goals

1. **Explain the functions of accounting and its importance to the firm's management, investors, creditors, and government agencies.**

   Accountants measure, interpret, and communicate financial information to parties inside and outside the firm to support improved decision making. Accountants are responsible for gathering, recording, and interpreting financial information to management. They also provide financial information on the status and operations of the firm for evaluation by such outside parties as government agencies, stockholders, potential investors, and lenders.

2. **Identify the three basic business activities involving accounting.**

   Accounting plays key roles in financing activities, which help to start and expand an organization; investing activities, which provide the assets it needs to continue operating; and operating activities, which focus on selling goods and services and paying expenses incurred in regular operations.

3. **Describe the roles played by public, management, government, and not-for-profit accountants.**

   Public accountants are providers of accounting services to other firms or individuals for a fee. They are involved in such activities as tax statement preparation, management consulting, and accounting system design. Management accountants are responsible for collecting and recording financial transactions, preparing financial statements, and interpreting them for managers in their own firms. Government and not-for-profit accountants perform many of the same func-

   tions as management accountants, but their analysis emphasizes how effectively the organization or agency is operating rather than its profits and losses.

4. **Outline the steps in the accounting process.**

   The accounting process involves recording, classifying, and summarizing data about transactions and then using this information to produce financial statements for the firm's managers and other interested parties. Transactions are recorded chronologically in journals, posted in ledgers, and then summarized in accounting statements.

5. **Explain the functions and major components of the three principal financial statements: the balance sheet, the income statement, and the statement of cash flows.**

   The balance sheet shows the financial position of a company on a particular date. The three major classifications of balance sheet data represent the components of the accounting equation: assets, liabilities, and owners' equity. The income statement shows the results of a firm's operations over a specific period. It focuses on the firm's activities—its revenues and expenditures—and the resulting profit or loss during the period. The major components of the income statement are revenues, cost of goods sold, expenses, and profit or loss. The statement of cash flows indicates a firm's cash receipts and cash payments during an accounting period. It shows the sources and uses of cash in the basic business activities of financing, investing, and operating.

6. Discuss how financial ratios are used to analyze a firm's financial strengths and weaknesses.

Liquidity ratios measure a firm's ability to meet short-term obligations. Examples are the current ratio and acid-test ratio. Profitability ratios assess the overall financial performance of the business. The gross profit margin, net profit margin, return on assets, and return on owners' equity are examples. Leverage ratios, such as the total liabilities to total assets ratio, measure the extent to which the firm relies on debt to finance its operations. Activity ratios, such as the inventory turnover ratio and total asset turnover ratio, measure how effectively a firm uses its resources. Financial ratios assist managers and outside evaluators in comparing a firm's current financial information with that of previous years and with results for other firms in the same industry.

7. Describe the role of budgets in a business.

Budgets are financial guidelines for future periods reflecting expected sales revenues, operating expenses, and/or cash receipts and outlays. They represent management expectations for future occurrences based on plans that have been made. Budgets serve as important planning and controlling tools by providing standards against which actual performance can be measured.

8. Explain how exchange rates influence international accounting practices and the importance of uniform financial statements for global business.

An exchange rate is the ratio at which a country's currency can be exchanged for other currencies. Daily changes in exchange rates affect the accounting entries for sales and purchases of firms involved in international markets. These fluctuations create either losses or gains for particular companies. Data about international financial transactions must be translated into the currency of the country in which the parent company resides. The International Accounting Standards Committee was established to provide worldwide consistency in financial reporting practices and comparability and uniformity of international accounting standards.

Business Terms You Need to Know

accounting 650
accounting process 655
asset 657
liability 658
owners' equity 658

accounting equation 658
balance sheet 659
income statement 659
statement of cash flows 662
accrual accounting 662

Other Important Business Terms

public accountant 652
management accountant 653
certified public accountant (CPA) 653
government accountant 653

bottom line 661
cash flow 663
ratio analysis 664
liquidity ratios 664

profitability ratios 665
leverage ratios 666
activity ratios 666
budget 667

➤ Review Questions

1. Define *accounting*. Who are the major users of accounting information?

2. What role does accounting play in the larger business environment? List the three major business activities where accountants play a major role.

3. How does a public accountant differ from a management accountant? What is a certified public accountant?

4. Explain the steps involved in the accounting process. How have computers and the Internet influenced the accounting process?

5. What is the basic accounting equation? List the three principal financial statements.

6. Explain the difference between current assets and fixed assets; between current liabilities and long-term liabilities; and between liabilities and owners' equity. Why is cash typically the first asset listed on the balance sheet?

7. Define *accrual accounting*. Give an example of how accrual accounting affects a firm's financial statements.

8. What are the four categories of financial ratios? Give an example in each category and explain what it means.

9. What is a budget? Why do firms and other organizations prepare budgets?

10. What financial statements are affected by exchange rates for firms with global operations? What are the benefits of uniform international accounting standards?

➤ Questions for Critical Thinking

1. Your grandmother sends you a large check for your birthday, asking that you use the money to buy shares of stock in a company. She recommends that you review the company's financial statements before investing. What can a company's financial statements tell you about the investment potential of its stock?

2. Suppose you work for a U.S. firm that has extensive European operations and owns several European businesses. You need to restate data from the various European currencies in U.S. dollars in order to prepare your firm's financial statements. Which financial statements and which components of these statements will be affected? Has the adoption of the euro made your job easier or more difficult?

3. Why does contemporary accounting involve much more than recording numbers and preparing financial statements? Put yourself in the role of an entrepreneur. How could accountants help you plan and grow your business?

4. Suppose you are offered a job with a small, private company. Since the company isn't required to publish its financial information—as public companies are—you ask the owner if you could review the financial statements prior to accepting the job. The owner refuses and says that only the firm's accountant and banker are allowed to see the statements. What could you say that might convince the company's owner to share financial information with employees?

5. You've been appointed treasurer of a local not-for-profit organization. You would like to improve the quality of the organization's financial reporting to existing and potential donors. Describe the kinds of financial statements you would like to see the organization's accountant prepare. Why do you think better quality financial statements might help to reassure donors?

➤ Experiential Exercise

Adapting the format of Figure 18.8, Three-Month Cash Budget for Sierra Pasta Company, prepare on a separate sheet of paper your personal one-month cash budget for next month. Keep in mind the following suggestions as you prepare your budget.

1. **Cash Inflows.** Your sources of cash would include your salary/wages, gifts, scholarship monies, tax refunds, dividends and interest, and income from self-employment.

2. **Cash Outflows.** When estimating next month's cash outflows, include any of the following that may apply to your situation:

   a. Household expenses (mortgage/rent, utilities, maintenance, home furnishings, telephone/cell phone, cable TV, household supplies, groceries)

   b. Education (tuition, fees, textbooks, supplies)

   c. Work (transportation, meals)

   d. Clothing (purchases, cleaning, laundry)

   e. Automobile (auto payments, fuel, repairs)

   f. Insurance (life, auto, homeowner's, renter's, health and dental)

   g. Taxes (income, property, social security)

   h. Savings and Investments

   i. Entertainment/Recreation (health club, vacation/travel, dining, movies)

   j. Debt (credit cards, installment loans)

   k. Miscellaneous (charitable contributions, child care, gifts, medical expenses)

3. **Beginning Cash Balance.** This amount could be based on a minimum cash balance you keep in your checking account and should include only the cash available for your use; therefore, money, such as that invested in a 401(k) retirement plan should not be included.

➤ Nothing but Net

1. **Finding financial information.** Pick a public company in which you have some interest. Visit the company's Web site, one of the following investment-oriented Web sites, and download the company's financial statements for the most recent year you can find. Calculate the financial ratios listed in the text. Briefly assess the financial strength and investment potential of the firm.

   http://investor.msn.com

   www.morningstar.com

   www.quicken.com

   www.sec.gov/edgar

2. **The Financial Accounting Standards Board (FASB).** The chapter briefly describes the FASB, the nation's chief accounting rule maker. Visit the following Web site and prepare a brief report on the FASB. Make sure you answer the following questions: When and why was FASB established? What is its mission? Who appoints members of its board?

   www.rutgers.edu/accounting/raw/fasb

3. **Accounting as a career.** As noted in the chapter, accounting is one of the most popular undergraduate business majors. Ernst & Young—one of the Big Five public accounting firms—has an extensive section on accounting careers on its Web site. Visit the firm's Web site and review the material on "Career Paths." Prepare an oral report for your class on the various career paths taken by actual Ernst & Young employees. Take an informal poll, before and after your presentation, asking your classmates how many are interested in accounting careers. Based on what you learned, do you think you'd be interested in a career in public accounting? Why or why not?

   www.ey.com/global/grc.nsf/US/Paths_-_Campus_-_Careers_-_Ernst_&_Young

Note: Internet Web addresses change frequently. If you don't find the exact sites listed, you may need to access the organization's home page and search from there.

If your mouth is watering by the time you finish reading this, that's okay with Craig Miller, CFO of Uno Restaurant Corp., parent company of the many Pizzeria Uno Chicago Bar & Grill restaurants around the country. Now located in 29 states and several foreign countries, Pizzeria Uno started in downtown Chicago in 1943 when Ike Sewall opened his first pizza restaurant. Sewall believed that customers would flock to a place where traditional Chicago-style deep-dish pizza was served in a cozy, casual atmosphere—and he was right. In 1978, Sewall and partner Aaron Spencer made a deal to begin expanding the business, and the following year the first Pizzeria Uno opened in Boston, which would eventually become company headquarters.

Today, if you visit one of the 150 Pizzeria Uno restaurants located around the country, you can order a deep-dish pizza with your choice of fresh toppings. Or you can select from a number of other favorites: gourmet thin-crust pizza, fresh salad, chicken, fajitas, a hamburger, pasta, ribs, and even steak. Costs associated with all of this food have to be managed carefully, from supplier to your table, in order for the company to stay in business and turn a profit. Here's how Uno's does it.

"Margins in the restaurant business average three to four cents out of the dollar," says CFO Craig Miller. "When you are managing pennies, you need to account for them." Cost management of food items, labor, and maintenance is important because it all adds up. So, accounting professionals play a role in just about everything Pizzeria Uno does, from general financial management to menu planning. According to Miller, accounting starts at the store level. Recently, Pizzeria Uno installed computerized NCR point-of-sale systems in every restaurant to record daily data on types of meals customers bought, sales totals, number of employees on duty, amount of inventory in stock, and other operating details. Each night, that data is fed back to a computer system at company headquarters, where accounting employees analyze and interpret the information. The software program also provides information on what food *should* cost compared with what it *does* cost, which helps each store—and the company as a whole—establish food cost controls.

In another effort to improve its profit margins, Pizzeria Uno recently reviewed the design of its restaurants as well as the content of its menus. "Uno has been developing a new prototype," notes analyst Mathew McKay, "experimenting a lot with the look of the restaurant, new menu items, and expanding the menu away from deep dish and into other areas." Many of the restaurants have been remodeled to evoke the company's roots in the Chicago industrial scene, with black and white tile mixed with brick and open ceilings. "They're trying to get the same fun feeling but doing so by reinvesting less capital into each unit, thereby improving the return on investment," explains McKay.

Pizzeria Uno accountants use financial ratios to decide whether to borrow money, invest in "futures" such as milk, or buy the land on which they plan to build a new restaurant. The company also relies on working capital. "The restaurant business is a cash business," comments Miller. He explains that if a restaurant buys a shipment of cheese, uses it in its cooking, and sells it the next day, the restaurant still has 30 days to use the money it received on the sale before it has to pay the supplier from which it bought the cheese. Pizzeria Uno also uses debt to build equity value for the company. "The average Pizzeria Uno requires $1.7 million to build and open," says Miller. The company can borrow money at 7 percent interest, build the restaurant, and enjoy the 30 percent return that the restaurant generates. Whenever possible, Pizzeria Uno tries to buy the land on which the restaurant will be built, even if it involves a mortgage loan. "By buying land, we control our destiny and our future," explains Miller, because in general the value of real estate increases.

Because a tiny shift in costs can throw profits in the trash can along with uneaten pizza crusts, Pizzeria Uno takes a conservative approach to its finances. "We take all the money we can and reinvest it in the business," comments Miller. That's sound financial practice for any business that plans to survive the ups and downs of an economy, not to mention the changing tastes of consumers who want to eat deep-dish pizza with the works on one day, and thin crust pizza with a salad the next.

QUESTIONS

1. Why is the accounting function so important to a company like Pizzeria Uno?
2. How might activity ratios help accountants at Pizzeria Uno assess their company's performance?
3. Describe how the steps in the accounting process would be put into play by accounting staff who use the point-of-sale system at Pizzeria Uno.
4. Go to the Pizzeria Uno Web site at **www.pizzeriauno.com** to look for ways that the accounting function influences different aspects of the business. Write a brief memo describing the role that accounting would play in a particular aspect that interests you—say, building a new restaurant, setting up a franchise, or adding a new food item to the menu.

Sources: "Uno Restaurant Corporation," *Hoover's Online*, **www.hshbn.com.**, accessed January 12, 2001; "Profile: Uno Restaurant Corp.," *Yahoo! Market Guide*, **http://biz.yahoo.com**, accessed January 11, 2001; "Uno Restaurant Corp. to Install NCR Point-of-Sale System," *Bizjournals.com*, April 13, 2000, **www.bizjournals.com.**

PART VI

Managing Financial Resources

CHAPTER 19

Financial Management and Institutions

Learning Goals

1. Identify the functions performed by a firm's financial managers.

2. Describe the characteristics a form of money should have, and list the functions of money.

3. Identify the various measures of the money supply.

4. Explain how a firm uses funds.

5. Compare the two major sources of funds for a business.

6. Identify likely sources of short- and long-term funds.

7. Describe the financial system and the major financial institutions.

8. Explain the functions of the Federal Reserve System and the tools it uses to control the money supply.

9. Describe the global financial environment.

Financing the New Economy

Have you ever heard of a company named Benchmark Capital? Perhaps not, but if you were an aspiring Silicon Valley entrepreneur, looking to start a high-tech company, you probably would not only have heard of Benchmark Capital, but may have met with them as well. Benchmark Capital—based in Menlo Park, California—is one of the best known technology-oriented venture capital firms in the world. It has provided financing for dozens of new technology start-ups including Palm Computing, Red Hat Software Ariba, Handspring, Juniper Networks, Matrix Semiconductor, and Shasta Networks, just to name a few.

Venture capital firms provide critical financing to start-up companies in exchange for an ownership share in the business. These companies are struggling to develop and market innovative goods or services and need the capital in order to continue operating. If the company succeeds and is able to go public (sell stock to the investing public), or is acquired by a larger firm, the venture capitalists often sell their ownership stake, earning large returns on their investment. In a recent year, venture capitalists invested over $100 billion in close to 5,500 firms.

Of the thousands of venture capital firms in the U.S., Benchmark Capital is a relative newcomer—it was founded in 1995. This is unusual in an industry where long-term relationships and a lengthy track record are considered to be the coin of the realm. But what really sets Benchmark Capital apart is its investment track record. Although a few of the firm's investments have flopped, most have returned many times their original investment. Benchmark's most spectacular investment success has been eBay—the online auction company. In 1997, the firm invested $5 million in return for a 22 percent stake in eBay. Today that investment is worth over $3 billion. Each of Benchmark's partners—average age of around 40 years—is worth

hundreds of millions of dollars. The firm's success has enabled it to raise money for its investments from such notable individuals as Michael Dell and Bill Gates. Some

predict that Benchmark will eventually outshine many of the more established venture capital firms in Silicon Valley, some of whom have been around for 25 or more years. Benchmark recently raised over $350 million for new investments and formed a subsidiary in Israel to fund promising technology start-ups in that country.

Benchmark Capital's investment philosophy is fairly straightforward. The firm seeks to be the first investor in technology companies that are creating new markets. Andy Rachleff, one of the firm's founding partners, puts it this way: "Typically what we look for are companies that are addressing a very large market that is hopefully very small today. We want to back market creators or market leaders. The other thing

we're looking for is a visionary." Benchmark is very selective when making investments. The firm meets with almost 800 companies a year but invests in only 15 to 20. Benchmark typically invests $3 million to $5 million initially and up to around $15 million over the life of the investment. While some entrepreneurs complain that venture capitalists meddle too much in the day-to-day operations of their businesses, Benchmark takes more of a hands-off approach. The firm has a reputation of being constructive and cooperative, not heavy handed. Bob Howe, president and chief executive officer (CEO) of Scient, summarizes his opinion of Benchmark this way: "They are absolutely one of the best partners we could ever have in our business." Adds Meg Whitman, CEO of eBay, "They are there when you need them, and they are not there when you don't need them."[1]

CHAPTER OVERVIEW

Previous chapters discuss two essential functions that a business must perform. First, the firm must produce a good or service, or contract with suppliers to produce it. Second, the firm must market its good or service to prospective customers. This chapter introduces a third, equally important function: a company's managers must ensure that it has enough money to perform its other tasks successfully, in both the present and the future. Adequate funds must be available to buy materials and equipment, pay bills, purchase additional facilities, and compensate employees. This third business function is **finance**—planning, obtaining, and managing the company's funds in order to accomplish its objectives effectively and efficiently.

An organization's financial objectives include not only meeting expenses but also maximizing its overall value, often determined by the value of the firm's common stock. Financial managers are responsible for both meeting expenses and increasing profits for shareholders.

This chapter focuses on the role of financial managers, why businesses need funds, and the various types and sources of funds for businesses. It discusses the role of money and measures of the money supply. The chapter explains the purpose and structure of the financial system, the operations of financial institutions, and how the Federal Reserve System functions. A discussion of the role of the financial system in the global business environment concludes the chapter.

THE ROLE OF THE FINANCIAL MANAGER

Organizations are placing greater emphasis on measuring and reducing the costs of conducting business as well as increasing revenues and profits. As a result, **financial managers**—executives responsible for developing and implementing their firm's financial plan and for determining the most appropriate sources and uses of funds— are among the most vital people on the corporate payroll.

The finance organization of a typical company might look like the structure shown in Figure 19.1. At the top is the chief financial officer (CFO). The CFO usually reports directly to the company's CEO. In many companies, the CFO is also a member of the board of directors. Reporting directly to the CFO are three senior managers. While titles can vary, these three executives are commonly called the **vice**

FIGURE 19.1
Organizational Structure of the Finance Function

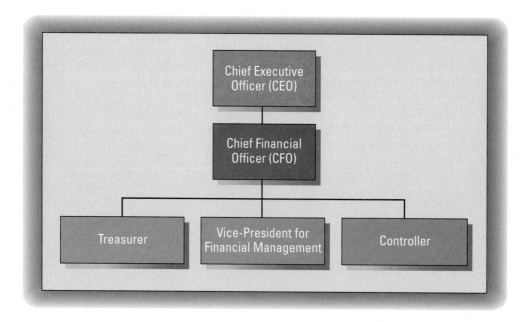

president for financial management, the treasurer, and the controller. The controller is the chief accounting manager. The controller's functions include keeping the company's books, preparing financial statements, and conducting internal audits. The treasurer is responsible for all of the company's financing activities, including managing cash, the tax department, and shareholder relations. The treasurer also works on the sale of new security issues to investors. The vice president for financial management is responsible for preparing financial forecasts and analyzing major investment decisions. Major investment decisions include new products, new production facilities, and acquisitions.

The growing importance of financial professionals is reflected in an expanding number of CEOs promoted from financial positions. An example is Alan J. Lacy, the chairman and CEO of Sears. Prior to being named CEO, Lacy was the company's executive vice president and CFO. Previously, he held a number of other finance positions with Sears and other companies. The importance of finance professionals is also reflected in how much CFOs earn today. According to one survey, the median pay for CFOs is around $1.1 million per year, double what it was five years ago.[2]

In performing their jobs, financial professionals continually seek to balance risks with expected financial returns. Risk is the uncertainty of gain or loss; return is the gain or loss that results from an investment over a specified period of time. Financial managers strive to maximize the wealth of their firm's shareholders by striking the optimal balance between risk and return. This balance is called the **risk–return trade-off.** For example, a heavy reliance on borrowed funds may increase the return to shareholders; but at the same time, the more money a firm borrows, the greater the risks to shareholders. An increase in a firm's cash on hand reduces the risk of meeting unexpected cash needs. However, because cash does not earn any return, failure to invest surplus funds in an income earning asset—such as in marketable securities—reduces a firm's potential return or profitability.

Every financial manager must perform this risk–return balancing act. For example, in the late 1980s, Boeing was wrestling with a major decision: whether to begin development of the 777 jetliner. The development costs were estimated to be over $5 billion. Before committing to such a huge investment, financial managers had to weigh the potential profits of the 777—the jetliner was expected to produce profits in excess of $50 billion over a 25-year period—with the risk that the profits would not materialize. With its future on the line, Boeing decided to go ahead with the development of the 777. The decision has turned out favorably for Boeing. Careful financial management helped to keep development costs well below the estimates, and sales have exceeded the original forecasts. At the present time, Boeing has delivered almost 350 of the 777 jetliners and has orders for another 300.[3]

The Financial Plan

Financial managers develop their organization's **financial plan,** a document that specifies the funds needed by a firm for a period of time, the timing of inflows and outflows, and the most appropriate sources and uses of funds. The financial plan is based on forecasts of production costs, purchasing needs, and expected sales activities for the period covered. Financial managers use forecasts to determine the specific amounts and timing of expenditures and receipts. They build a financial plan based on the answers to three questions:

1. What funds will the firm require during the appropriate period of operations?
2. How will it obtain the necessary funds?
3. When will it need more funds?

Some funds flow into the firm when it sells its goods or services, but funding needs vary. The financial plan must reflect both the amounts and timing of inflows and outflows of funds. Even a profitable firm may well face a financial squeeze as a result of its need for funds when sales lag, when the volume of its credit sales increases, or when customers are slow in making payments.

The cash inflows and outflows of a business are similar to those of a household. The members of a household may depend on weekly or monthly paychecks for funds, but their expenditures vary greatly from one pay period to the next. The financial plan should indicate when the flows of funds entering and leaving the organization will occur and in what amounts.

Belinda Young, owner of a small public relations firm in Seattle, understands the importance of careful financial planning. As with most small business owners, she has little excess cash laying around. Her customers are often slow to pay, and her creditors and vendors expect to be paid promptly. Consequently, Young must carefully and constantly monitor her cash inflows and outflows, as well as the balance in her business bank account. Young uses her personal computer (PC) and a financial management program to track cash flows. She learned the hard way what can happen if cash flow is not watched closely. Young once racked up almost $100 in bounced check fees because a deposit was recorded late by her bank. Bouncing checks, she learned, not only is expensive but also hurts her professional image with clients.[4]

A good financial plan also involves financial control, a process of checking actual revenues, costs, and expenses and comparing them against forecasts. If this process reveals significant differences between projected and actual figures, it is important to discover them early in order to take timely corrective action.

At Cisco Systems, effective financial planning has given the company another competitive edge. Cisco's CFO, Larry Carter, is credited with helping to develop a "virtual close," a system that generates updates of revenues, costs, profit margins, and other financial data every hour, comparing them with budgeted amounts. Cisco credits the real-time financial information with allowing the company to rapidly enter the Japanese market at what turned out to be a very opportune time.[5]

CHARACTERISTICS AND FUNCTIONS OF MONEY

Playwright George Bernard Shaw once said that the lack of money is the root of all evil. Added comedian Woody Allen, "Money is better than poverty, if only for financial reasons." Many businesspeople would agree, because money is the lubricant of contemporary business.

Characteristics of Money

Money is anything generally accepted as payment for goods and services. Most early forms of money imposed a number of serious disadvantages on users. For example, a cow is a poor form of money for an owner who wants only a loaf of bread and some cheese. Exchanges based on money permit economic specialization and provide a general basis for purchasing power provided that the form of money used has certain characteristics. It must be divisible, portable, durable, and difficult to counterfeit, and it should have a stable value.

Divisibility A U.S. dollar is divided into cents, nickels, dimes, and quarters. The Canadian dollar is divided similarly, except that Canada has a 20-cent coin and no quarter. Mexico's nuevo peso is broken down into centavos (100 centavos equals one nuevo peso). A British pound is divided into 100 pence. People can easily exchange these forms of money for products ranging from chewing gum to automobiles. Today, most economic activity involves making and spending money.

Getting Americans to Use Dollar Coins

In January 2000 the U.S. Mint launched its newest dollar coin, the golden Sacagawea, with much fanfare. The Mint commenced a glitzy advertising campaign featuring a hip George Washington telling people to use the new coin. The Mint enlisted the assistance of giant retailer Wal-Mart, shipping 100 million coins to the company's stores for distribution. The idea was to quickly get the new coin in the hands of the public and encourage other businesses to request the coins from their banks. Unlike the failed Susan B. Anthony dollar—which many complained was too easily confused with a quarter—introduced 20 years earlier, the Mint thought it finally had a winner. Although dollar coins are three times more expensive to manufacture, compared with paper bills, they last 20 times longer. The Mint estimated that it could save the government hundreds of millions of dollars if the public would switch from paper bills to dollar coins.

It hasn't happened yet. According to surveys, over 90 percent of Americans have heard of the Sacagawea—thanks in part to the Mint's $40 million ad campaign—but far less claim to have ever seen one, much less use them regularly. Interest has been so low that many banks no longer stock them. Heather Tollybauer of Citizens Bank of Connecticut comments, "We don't have it as part of our normal coin within the branches. If a customer were to ask for it specifically, we could order it from the Federal Reserve." Even Wal-Mart has stopped pushing the coin. Thomas Williams of Wal-Mart notes that stores are no longer requesting any Sacagawea coins from their banks. He adds, "I think the common denominator is there are a few that are used in tender, but we just don't see a lot of them." Even when the coins do appear, the public's reaction is less than enthusiastic. For example, when employees at a suburban Maryland Burger King try to give Sacagawea coins out as change, people often give them back, asking for paper bills instead. One resident of Washington, D.C., said flatly, "I've never used it. It would be a nuisance."

Why is the Sacagawea having such a difficult time catching on with the public? For one thing, dollar coins weigh much more than paper bills and are less convenient to carry. For another, many vending machines still don't accept dollar coins, and cash registers often don't have room for another coin. People also get most of their cash from ATMs today, and they don't dispense coins.

The real problem, though, may be the fact that Americans are simply reluctant to give up the dollar bill—the greenback is one of the great icons of American culture. Those who advocate greater coin usage point out that when Congress authorized the new dollar coin in 1997 it specifically prohibited the Treasury from eliminating the paper dollar bill. By contrast, when Canada introduced dollar and two dollar coins—nicknamed the "loonie" and "toonie"—it phased out its dollar and two-dollar paper bills. Britain and other countries did likewise. Notes Pierre Morin of the Royal Canadian Mint, "If we hadn't removed the paper money, the coin would not have the success it's had."

QUESTIONS FOR CRITICAL THINKING

1. Have you ever seen a Sacagawea dollar coin? If so, have you ever used one to pay for a purchase?
2. Some felt that the Mint shouldn't have spent taxpayer money promoting the Sacagawea. Do you agree or disagree? What other steps do you think the Mint could have taken to increase public acceptance of a dollar coin?

Sources: Kathleen Day, "Sacagawea Comes Up Tails," *Washington Post*, January 26, 2001, p. A1; Christine Woodside, "Dollars and Cents," *New York Times*, January 21, 2001, p. WC14; "Seeking Sacagawea," *The Times-Picayune*, January 9, 2001, money section p. 1.

Portability   The light weight of modern paper currency facilitates the exchange process. Portability is an important characteristic, since a typical dollar bill changes hands around 400 times during its lifetime, staying in the average person's pocket or purse fewer than two days.

Durability   U.S. dollar bills survive an average of 12 to 18 months, and they can survive folding some 4,000 times without tearing. Coins, on the other hand, can last 30 years, or longer. The greater durability of coins has led to efforts to persuade Americans to use dollar coins instead of dollar bills. The "Business Hits and Misses" box describes the latest attempt to get us to switch from dollar bills to dollar coins.

Difficulty in Counterfeiting   Widespread distribution of counterfeit money could undermine a nation's monetary system and economy by ruining the value of legitimate money. For this reason, governments consider counterfeiting a serious crime and take elaborate steps to prevent it. Among counterfeiters, U.S. currency is the most popular. To increase the difficulty of counterfeiting U.S. currency in this age of sophisticated

BUSINESS DIRECTORY

> **money**   *anything generally accepted as payment for goods and services.*

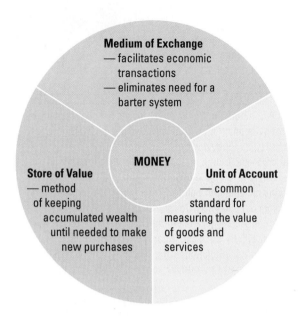

FIGURE 19.2
The Functions of Money

FIGURE 19.3
M1 Components

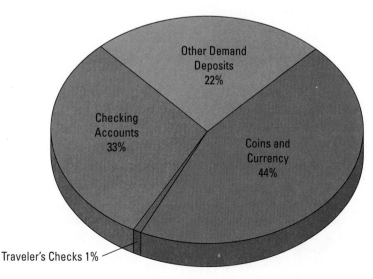

computers and color printers, the U.S. Treasury has recently redesigned paper bills. The new currency adds a letter to each bill's serial number along with the seal of the Federal Reserve, larger portraits that are off-centered, and polymer threads that run vertically through the bills and glow under ultraviolet light.

Stability A good form of money should maintain a relatively stable value. If the value of money fluctuates too much, people hesitate to use it. They begin to abandon it and look for safer means of storing their wealth. Businesses start to demand that bills be paid in other more stable currencies.

The Asian economic crisis of the late 1990s was caused, in part, by a sharp decline in the value of many Asian currencies. Because of concern about these countries' economic and political stability, the value of many Asian currencies, relative to more stable currencies such as the U.S. dollar, began falling. As the crisis took hold, millions of South Koreans, Indonesians, and Thais scrambled to convert their won, babts, and rupiah into dollars, and the value of these Asian currencies collapsed. Over one seven-month period, the value of the Indonesian rupiah lost over 80 percent of its value relative to the U.S. dollar.

Functions of Money

Money performs three basic functions as shown in Figure 19.2. First, it serves primarily as a medium of exchange—a means of facilitating economic transactions and eliminating the need for a barter system. Second, it functions as a unit of account—a common standard for measuring the value of goods and services. Third, money acts as a temporary store of value—a way of keeping accumulated wealth until the owner needs it to make new purchases. Money offers one big advantage as a store of value: its high liquidity allows people to obtain it and dispose of it in quick and easy transactions. Money is immediately available for purchasing products or paying debts.

THE MONEY SUPPLY

Ask someone on the street to define the money supply, and he or she might answer that the money supply is the total value of all currency and coins in circulation. That answer, however, is only half right. One measure of the U.S. money supply consists of coins and currency as well as financial assets that also serve as a medium of exchange: traveler's checks, bank checking accounts, and other so-called **demand deposit accounts** (such as NOW accounts and credit union share draft accounts). Government reports and business publications use the term **M1** to refer to the total value of coins and currency, traveler's checks, bank checking account balances, and the balances in other demand deposit accounts. The current breakdown of M1 is shown in Figure 19.3.

Another broader definition of the money supply is also widely used. Called **M2**, this measure of the money supply includes M1 plus a number of other financial assets that are almost as liquid as cash but do not serve directly as a medium of exchange. These assets include various savings accounts, certificates of deposit, and money market mutual funds. Users must complete some sort of transaction before these assets can fulfill the functions of money.

In recent years, the use of credit cards—often referred to as plastic money—has significantly increased. Over the past 20 years the amount of outstanding credit card debt has increased by more than five times. Americans carry over 1 billion credit cards. MasterCard and Visa, so-called bank credit cards, dominate the credit card market, though the Discover Card—owned by Morgan Stanley—has made some inroads into the credit card market. The ad in Figure 19.4 from the Discover Card stresses to potential customers that it's becoming more widely accepted each day. American Express is another source of credit cards. However, its flagship American Express card is not a credit card but rather a charge card; that is, balances must be paid in full each month. Customers do not have the option of carrying a balance from month to month.

Many entrepreneurs rely on plastic money, as mentioned in Chapter 6, to provide seed capital in financing their new ventures. Director Spike Lee, for example, reportedly used his American Express card to finance his first film.

Although credit cards are convenient and easy to use, they are a very expensive source of business or consumer credit, with annual interest rates averaging around 16 percent. Another problem with credit cards is fraud. Online purchases are especially vulnerable to fraud and cost credit card issuers and merchants billions of dollars each year. Consequently, several credit card issuers are starting to experiment with so-called "smart" credit cards. These cards contain a small microprocessor chip that stores information about the user, including the account number. The information is electronically scrambled when sent over the Internet. The "Clicks and Mortar" box describes the new American Express Blue Card, the firm's first smart credit card.

The Discover Card is accepted at 1000 new locations every day including *Hard Rock* CAFE

FIGURE 19.4
The Discover Card: Third in Market Acceptance Behind Visa and MasterCard, but Growing in Market Share

WHY ORGANIZATIONS NEED FUNDS

Organizations require funds for many reasons. They need money to run day-to-day operations, compensate employees and hire new ones, pay for inventory, make interest payments on loans, pay dividends to shareholders, and purchase property, facilities, and equipment. A firm's financial plan identifies the amount and time of its specific cash needs.

By comparing these needs with expenditures and expected cash receipts (from sales, payments made by credit purchasers, and other sources), financial managers determine precisely what additional funds they must obtain at any given time. If inflows exceed cash needs, financial managers invest the surplus to earn interest. On the other hand, if inflows do not meet cash needs, they seek additional sources of funds. Figure 19.5 illustrates this process.

American Express Goes Blue

Background. Smart cards look like ordinary credit cards except that they contain a small microprocessor. In addition to credit and debit functions, the chip can be programmed to carry a variety of information on the user, including account balances, secure identification, and club or frequent-flyer memberships. Though popular in Europe and some parts of Asia, smart cards have been slow to catch on in the U.S., where the norm has been magnetic strip cards. Merchants have recoiled at the expense of the hardware necessary to read smart cards. However, as online shopping has grown, so has online fraud. Some estimate that Internet-based credit card fraud is ten times higher than it is in the bricks-and-mortar world. Because smart cards have extra layers of security, they are safer to use online than ordinary credit cards.

What Happened? In the late 1990s, American Express began to recognize the potential benefits of smart credit cards. The company was also growing alarmed about the health of its credit card business. American Express was a distant third to the two bank credit cards, Visa and MasterCard, with less than 15 percent of the credit card market. What's more, its market share was noticeably shrinking. So, American Express introduced a new credit card it called Blue. Blue has an embedded computer chip that provides added security for shopping on the Web by containing a unique digital certificate that acts much like a key. Those who want extra security when shopping online can swipe their cards through a special reader attached to their PCs. (American Express gave away the card readers for the first year. Now the company charges about $20 for a reader.) After the cardholder enters his or her personal identification number (PIN), the certificate is read, and the necessary information to complete the purchase is transmitted securely. Blue also contains a magnetic strip so it can be used like an ordinary credit card.

The Response. Consumer reaction to Blue has been positive. Since its introduction, American Express has issued over 5 million Blue cards to customers. Some contend, however, that customers are drawn to Blue more by its other features—such as no annual fee and the fact that customers can carry a balance from month to month—than by its smart technology. Nevertheless, it appears American Express has a winner on its hands. So much so that the banks have begun issuing their versions of Blue. Providian Financial Corporation, Fleet Boston Financial, and First USA, three of the nation's largest issuers of Visas and Master-Cards, have all recently rolled out smart credit cards. Most other issuers of Visas and MasterCards are expected to follow along within the next couple of years.

Today and Counting. The demand for smart cards shows no signs of slowing. Most believe that smart cards will only get "smarter," allowing for other services such as electronic ticketing. More and more bricks-and-mortar merchants are installing the hardware necessary to take full advantage of smart card technology. At the same time, American Express and other credit card issuers are exploring other ways of improving the security of online transactions. Recently, American Express announced plans to offer a service to all of its credit card holders under which card holders will be able to obtain single-use credit card numbers.

QUESTIONS FOR CRITICAL THINKING

1. In your opinion, is security a major issue when it comes to shopping online? Do you avoid online shopping because you worry about security?
2. Some privacy advocates worry that, in an attempt to make shopping safer and more convenient, too much personal financial information will be stored on smart card chips. Do you agree or disagree?

Sources: Ross Kerber, "Banks Push Smart Credit Cards as Key to Shopping Online Securely," *Boston Globe,* downloaded from **www.northernlight.com** on February 9, 2001; Ellen Messmer, "Visa, MasterCard Plan Anti-Fraud Initiatives," *Network World,* downloaded from **www.nwfusion.com** on February 9, 2001; Maria Trombly, "American Express Offers Disposable Credit Card Numbers for Online Shopping," *Computerworld,* downloaded from **www.computerworld.com** on February 9, 2001; Maria Trombly, "Banks Announce Release of Visa 'Smart' Cards," *Computerworld,* downloaded from **www.cnn.com** on February 9, 2001; "American Express Introduces Internet Charge Card," Bloomberg News, downloaded from **www.cnet.com** on February 9, 2001; "American Express Launches Blue," Press release, American Express Corporation, downloaded from **www.americanexpress.com** on February 9, 2001.

Generating Funds from Excess Cash

Many financial managers choose to invest the majority of their firms' excess cash balances in marketable securities. These financial instruments are very close to cash because they are, by definition, marketable and easy to convert into cash. Four of the most popular marketable securities are U.S. Treasury bills, commercial paper, repurchase agreements, and certificates of deposit (CDs).

Treasury bills are short-term securities issued by the U.S. Treasury and backed by the full faith and credit of the U.S. government. Treasury bills are sold with a maturity of either 91 or 180 days, and have a minimum denomination of $10,000. They are considered to be virtually risk-free and easy to resell. Commercial paper consists of securities sold by corporations, maturing anywhere from 1 to 270 days

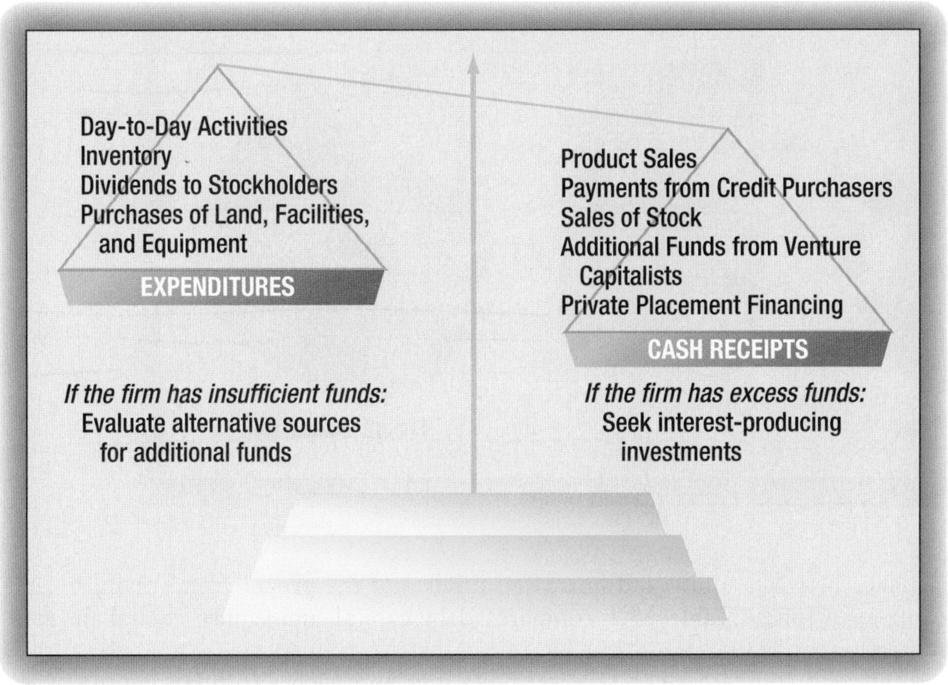

FIGURE 19.5
The Financial Planning Process

Day-to-Day Activities
Inventory
Dividends to Stockholders
Purchases of Land, Facilities,
 and Equipment
EXPENDITURES

Product Sales
Payments from Credit Purchasers
Sales of Stock
Additional Funds from Venture
 Capitalists
Private Placement Financing
CASH RECEIPTS

If the firm has insufficient funds:
Evaluate alternative sources
 for additional funds

If the firm has excess funds:
Seek interest-producing
 investments

from the date of issue. Though slightly riskier than Treasury bills, commercial paper is generally still considered to be a low-risk security. Repurchase agreements, or repos, are arrangements whereby one party sells a package of U.S. government securities to another party, agreeing to buy back, or repurchase, the securities at a higher price on a later date. Repos are also considered to be low-risk securities.

A CD is a time deposit at a financial institution, such as a commercial bank, savings bank, or credit union. The sizes and maturity dates of CDs vary considerably and can often be tailored to meet the needs of purchasers. All CDs with denominations of $100,000 or less are federally insured. CDs with larger denominations are not federally insured but can be sold more easily prior to maturity.

SOURCES OF FUNDS

To this point, the discussion has focused on half of the definition of finance—the reasons why organizations need funds and how they use them. A firm's financial plan must give equal importance, however, to the choice of the best sources of needed funds. Sources of funds fall into two categories: debt capital and equity capital.

Debt capital represents funds obtained through borrowing (referred to as debt financing in Chapter 6). **Equity capital** consists of funds provided by the firm's owners when they reinvest earnings, make additional contributions, liquidate assets, issue stock to the general public, or raise capital from venture capitalists and other investors (referred to as equity financing in Chapter 6). A firm also obtains equity capital whenever it makes a profit. These sources are shown in Figure 19.6.

A company's cash needs vary from one time period to the next, and even an established firm may not generate sufficient funds from operations to cover all costs of a major expansion or a significant investment in new equipment. In these instances, financial managers must evaluate the potential benefits and drawbacks of seeking funds by borrowing. As an alternative to borrowing, the firm may raise new equity capital. A financial manager's job includes determining the most cost-effective

BUSINESS DIRECTORY
➤ **debt capital** *funds obtained through borrowing.*
➤ **equity capital** *funds provided by the firm's owners when they reinvest earnings, make additional contributions, or issue stock to investors.*

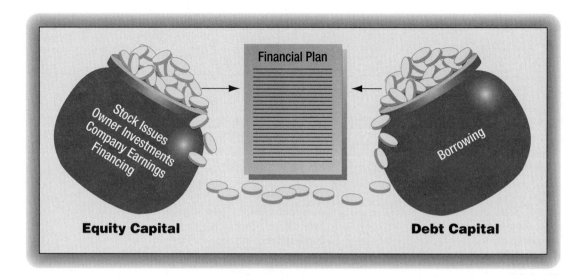

FIGURE 19.6
Debt and Equity Capital: Two Basic Sources of Funds

balance between equity and borrowed funds and the proper blend of short- and long-term funds. Table 19.1 compares debt capital and equity capital on four criteria.

Different companies can take very different approaches to financing major investments. For example, both American Home Products and Johnson & Johnson have made a series of major investments in recent years. These include new products, joint ventures with other firms, and even acquiring other companies. Johnson & Johnson relies more on equity financing and internal funds to finance its large investments. Johnson & Johnson recently acquired biotech company Centocor for $5 billion, using cash and stock to pay for the acquisition. On the other hand, American Home Products has tended to rely more heavily on debt financing. When it acquired American Cyanamid, for instance, American Home Products borrowed around $9 billion.

Short-Term Sources of Funds

Many times throughout a year, an organization may discover that its cash needs exceed its available funds. For example, retailers generate surplus cash for most of the year, but they need to build up inventory during the late summer and fall to get ready for the holiday shopping season. Consequently, they often need funds to finance merchandise purchases until holiday sales generate revenue. Then retailers use the incoming funds to repay the borrowed funds. In these instances, financial managers evaluate short-term sources of funds. By definition, short-term sources of funds are repaid within one year.

There are three major sources of short-term funds: trade credit, short-term loans, and commercial paper. Trade credit is extended by suppliers when a firm receives goods or services, agreeing to pay for them at a later date. Short-term loans can be either unsecured—meaning the firm does not pledge any assets as collateral—or secured—meaning that specific assets such as inventory are pledged as collateral. A major source of short-term loans is commercial banks. Commercial paper is briefly described in an earlier section. The interest cost on commercial paper is typically 1 or 2 percent lower than the rate on short-term bank loans. However, only large firms with unquestioned financial strength and stability are able to sell commercial paper.

Long-Term Sources of Funds

Funds from short-term sources can help a firm to meet current needs for cash or inventory. A larger need, however, such as acquiring another company or making a

Table 19.1	**Comparison of Debt and Equity Capital**	
Criterion	**Debt**	**Equity**
Maturity	A contract specifies a date by which the borrower must repay the loan.	Securities specify no maturity dates.
Claim on assets	Lenders have prior claims on assets.	Stockholders have claims only after the firm satisfies the claims of lenders.
Claim on income	Lenders have prior claims on fixed interest payments, which must be paid before dividends can be paid to stockholders. Interest payments are a contractual obligation of the borrowing firm.	Stockholders have a residual claim after all creditors have been paid. Dividends are paid at the discretion of the board of directors; they are not a contractual obligation of the firm.
Right to a voice in management	Lenders are creditors, not owners. They have no voice in company affairs unless they do not receive interest payments.	Stockholders are the owners of the company, and most can voice preferences for its operation.

major investment in property or equipment, often requires funds for a much longer period of time. Unlike short-term sources, long-term sources are repaid over many years.

Organizations acquire funds from three sources. One is long-term loans obtained from financial institutions such as commercial banks, life insurance companies, and pension funds. A second source is **bonds**—certificates of indebtedness sold to raise long-term funds for corporations and governments. A third source is equity financing acquired by selling stock in the company or reinvesting company earnings.

Public Sale of Stocks and Bonds Sales of stocks and bonds represent a major source of funds for corporations. Such sales provide cash inflows for the issuing firm and either a share in its ownership (for a stock purchaser) or a specified rate of interest and repayment at a stated time (for a bond purchaser). Because stock and bond issues of many corporations are traded in the securities markets, stockholders and bondholders can easily sell these assets. The decision of whether to issue stock or bonds to finance a corporation's plans is an important decision discussed in more detail in Chapter 20.

Private Placements Some new stock or bond issues may not be sold publicly but rather only to a small select group of large investors such as pension funds and life insurance companies. These sales are referred to as **private placements.** Most private placements involve corporate debt issues. In a typical year, about one-third of all new corporate debt issues are privately placed. It is often cheaper for a company to sell a security privately than publicly, and there is less government regulation with which to contend. Institutions buy private placements because they typically carry slightly higher yields than publicly issued bonds. In addition, the terms of the issue can be tailored to meet the specific needs of both the issuer and the institutional investor. Of course, the institutional investor gives up liquidity. Privately placed securities do not trade in securities markets.

Venture Capitalists In the opening vignette to the chapter one of the more successful venture capital firms is profiled. Venture capitalists are an important source of long-term financing, especially to new companies. **Venture capitalists** raise money from wealthy individuals and institutional investors, and invest these funds in promising firms. Venture capitalists provide management consulting advice as well as funds. In exchange for their investment, venture capitalists become part owners of the business. Should the business succeed, venture capitalists can earn substantial profits. (Recall how profitable Benchmark Capital's investment in eBay became.)

BUSINESS DIRECTORY

➤ **bond**   *certificate of indebtedness sold to raise long-term funds for a corporation or government agency.*

➤ **venture capitalist**   *organization that provides long-term financing in exchange for an ownership share of firms needing additional capital.*

Table 19.2	How Leverage Works

Leverage Corporation		Equity Corporation	
Common stock	$ 10,000	Common stock	$100,000
Bonds (at 10% interest)	90,000	Bonds	0
	100,000		100,000
Earnings	30,000	Earnings	30,000
Less bond interest	9,000	Less bond interest	0
Net income/profit	21,000	Net income/profit	30,000
Return to stockholders	21,000 = 210%	Return to stockholders	30,000 = 30%
	$ 10,000		$100,000

Leverage Raising needed cash by borrowing allows a firm to benefit from the principle of **leverage,** a technique of increasing the rate of return on funds invested through the use of borrowed funds. The key to managing leverage is ensuring that a company's earnings remain larger than its interest payments, which increases the leverage on the rate of return on shareholders' investment. Of course, if the company earns less than its interest payments, shareholders lose money on their original investments.

Table 19.2 shows two identical firms that choose to raise funds in different ways. Leverage Corporation obtains 90 percent of its funds from lenders who purchase company bonds. Equity Corporation raises all of its funds through sales of company stock. Each company earns $30,000. Leverage Corporation pays $9,000 in interest to bondholders and earns a 210 percent return for its owners' $10,000 investment. Equity Corporation provides only a 30 percent return on its shareholders' investment of $100,000.

As long as earnings exceed interest payments on borrowed funds, financial leverage allows a firm to increase the rate of return on its shareholders' investment. However, leverage also works in reverse. If, for example, Equity Corporation's earnings drop to $5,000, shareholders earn a 5 percent return on investment. Because Leverage Corporation must pay its bondholders $9,000 in interest, however, shareholders end up with a $4,000 loss. Another problem with borrowing money is that an over-reliance on borrowed funds reduces management's flexibility in future financing decisions.

THE FINANCIAL SYSTEM AND FINANCIAL INSTITUTIONS

Households, businesses, government, financial institutions, and financial markets together form what is known as the financial system. The **financial system** is the process by which money flows from savers to users. A simple diagram of the financial system is shown in Figure 19.7.

On the left are savers—those with excess funds. For a variety of reasons, savers choose not to spend all of their current income so they have a surplus of funds. Users are the opposite of savers: their spending needs exceed their current income so they have a deficit. They need to obtain additional funds to make up the difference. Savings are provided by households, businesses, and government. At the same time, borrowers also consist of households, businesses, and government. Households need money to buy automobiles or homes. Businesses need money to purchase inventory or build new production facilities. Governments need money to build highways, new schools, or to fund budget deficits.

Generally, in the U.S., households are net savers—meaning that in the aggregate they save more funds than they use—whereas businesses and governments are net users—meaning that they use more funds than they save. The fact that most of the net savings in the U.S. financial system are provided by households may be a bit of a surprise initially since Americans do not have the reputation of being very thrifty.

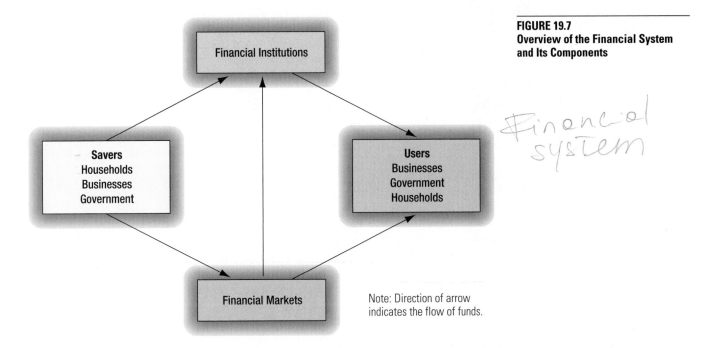

Note: Direction of arrow indicates the flow of funds.

Yet, even though the savings rate of American households is low compared with that of other countries, American households still save hundreds of billions of dollars each year.

There are two ways in which funds can be transferred between savers and users. One is through the financial markets. Whenever, for example, a company sells stocks or bonds publicly or privately, funds are being transferred between savers and users. Savers expect to receive some sort of return from the company for the use of their money. The role and functioning of the financial markets is described in more depth in Chapter 20.

The other way in which funds can be transferred is through financial institutions, such as commercial banks. For instance, whenever a consumer or business deposits money into a bank account, money is being transferred indirectly to users. The bank pools customer deposits and uses the funds to make loans to businesses and consumers. These borrowers pay the bank interest, and it in turn pays depositors interest for the use of their money.

Financial institutions greatly increase the efficiency and effectiveness of the transfer of funds between savers and users. Because of financial institutions, savers earn more, and users pay less, than they would without financial institutions. Indeed, it is difficult to imagine how any modern economy could function without well-developed financial institutions. Think about how difficult it would be for a businessperson to obtain inventory financing, or a consumer to purchase a new home, without financial institutions. Prospective borrowers would have to identify and negotiate with each saver individually.

Traditionally, financial institutions have been classified into **depository institutions**—institutions that accept deposits that customers can withdraw on demand—and nondepository institutions. Examples of depository institutions include commercial banks, savings banks, and credit unions. Nondepository institutions include life insurance companies and pension funds.

Commercial Banks

Commercial banks are the largest and probably the most important financial institutions in the United States, and in most other countries as well. In the U.S., the approximately 8,300 commercial banks have total

Should Bank Mergers Be Restricted?

Every year there are fewer and fewer commercial banks, as banks buy other banks. In 1985, for example, there were over 18,000 commercial banks; today, there are less than half that number. Fifteen years ago, the average bank had assets of $151 million. Today the average bank has more than $700 million in assets. In one recent year, over 700 banks—with almost $630 billion in assets—were acquired by other banks. Some predict that within the next ten years, more than half of the banks that exist today will be acquired. Although all bank mergers are subject to federal regulatory approval, the government has generally gone along with the trend toward fewer and larger banks.

Should the government restrict bank mergers?

PRO

1. Larger banks have a record of charging higher fees to customers. More bank mergers mean that customers will end up paying higher and higher fees.
2. Larger banks have a record of being less responsive to the loan needs of small businesses. As bank mergers increase, small business lending activity declines, negatively affecting the economic health of local communities.
3. Larger banks could put more strain on the FDIC insurance fund. One large bank failure could wipe out the FDIC's insurance fund reserves.

CON

1. Only larger banks have the financial resources to effectively compete globally against foreign banks.

2. Larger banks are financially stronger and more efficient. Only larger banks can offer enhanced services to customers as well as afford the expensive technologies needed to provide the conveniences customers expect today.
3. Bank mergers have created a niche for small, community banks to differentiate themselves. This segment of the banking industry has never been healthier financially and has been expanding.

SUMMARY

The banking industry strongly disputes the notion that larger banks mean higher banking fees. A comprehensive study by the Federal Reserve found that while bank fees for some services—most notably ATMs—have risen sharply as banks have merged, fees for other services have actually declined somewhat. The banking industry also points out that even with all the bank mergers, there are thousands of financial institutions, including savings banks and credit unions, competing with banks today. Consumer and small business groups, however, argue the opposite. They point to studies that suggest that larger banks lend a smaller percentage of their assets to farmers, small businesses, and consumers than do larger banks. While still keeping a generally "hands-off" approach to bank mergers, government regulators have promised Congress that they will keep a careful eye on bank mergers and their impact.

Sources: Federal Deposit Insurance Corporation Web site **www.fdic.gov**, accessed on February 9, 2001; Stephen Rhoades, "Bank Mergers and Banking Structure in the United States: 1980–1998," Federal Reserve Board Staff Study, downloaded from **www.federalreserve.gov** on February 9, 2001; American Banking Association Web site, accessed on February 8, 2001; "Marrying Money," *The News Hour with Jim Lehrer* transcript, downloaded from **www.pbs.org** on January 29, 2001.

assets that exceed $6 trillion. Commercial banks also offer the most services of any financial institution. These services include a wide range of checking and savings deposit accounts, consumer loans, credit cards, home mortgage loans, business loans, and trust services. Commercial banks were recently given permission to offer other products, including securities and insurance.

Although 8,300 may sound like a lot of banks, the number of banks has actually declined dramatically in recent years. At the same time, banks have gotten larger: today, the typical commercial bank is about five times larger than it was ten years ago. Both changes can be explained by the fact that larger banks are buying smaller banks. In one recent year, almost 700 banks were acquired by other banks. As bank mergers have become more and more common in recent years, a growing number of critics contend that consumers and businesses are being hurt by consolidation in the banking industry. The "Solving an Ethical Controversy" box debates the pros and cons of bank consolidation.

How Banks Operate   Banks raise funds by offering a variety of checking and savings deposit options to customers. The banks then pool these deposits and lend most of them out in the form of a variety of consumer and business loans. At the end of a recent year, banks held over $4 trillion in deposits and had almost $3.8 trillion in loans outstanding. The distribution of outstanding loans is shown in Figure 19.8. As the figure shows, banks lend a great deal of money to both households and businesses, for a variety of purposes. Commercial banks are an especially important source of funds for small businesses. The ad shown in Figure 19.9 illustrates the importance one large bank places on loans to small businesses.

Banks make money primarily because the interest rate they charge borrowers is higher than the rate of interest they pay depositors. In one recent year, banks collected approximately $367 billion in interest from loans and other investments and paid out $197 billion to depositors. Banks also make money from other sources, such as fees charged customers for checking accounts and using automated teller machines (ATMs). In fact, the fees banks collect have risen sharply in recent years. Fees account for approximately 30 percent of bank profits today, up from less than 10 percent five years ago.

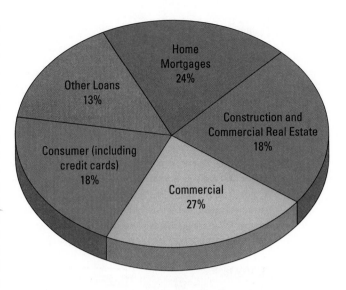

FIGURE 19.8
Distribution of Outstanding Bank Loans

Electronic Banking   More and more funds each year move through **electronic funds transfer systems (EFTSs),** computerized systems for conducting financial transactions over electronic links. Millions of businesses and consumers now pay bills and receive payments electronically. Most employers, for example, directly deposit employee paychecks in their bank accounts, rather than issuing employees paper checks. Today nearly all Social Security checks and other federal payments made each year arrive as electronic data rather than paper documents.

One of the original forms of electronic banking, the ATM continues to grow in popularity. The ATM allows customers to make banking transactions 24 hours a day, seven days a week by inserting an electronic card into the machine and entering a personal identification number. Networked systems enable ATM users to access their bank accounts in distant states and even throughout the world. In the U.S. alone, there are close to 200,000 ATMs, which process over 11 billion transactions annually.[6]

Most banks now offer customers debit cards—also called check cards—which allow customers to make purchases directly from their checking or savings account. A debit card looks like a credit card but acts like a check and replaces the customer's ATM card. Several large retailers—including Home Depot, Wal-Mart, and Walgreen's—have installed special terminals that allow customers to use their ATM or debit cards to make purchases. Customers are required to enter their personal identification numbers and can often get cash back. Consumers enjoy the convenience of this feature; at the same time, it eliminates the problem of bad checks for retailers.

Online Banking   Today, many consumers do some or all of their banking on the Internet. According to one survey, regular online bank users now exceed 20 million, and that number is projected to triple within the next five years. Bank of America recently reported that it had 3 million online customers and was adding new customers at a rate of over 130,000 per month.[7] There are two types of online banks: Internet-only banks (such as E*Trade Bank and SFBN) and traditional bricks-and-mortar banks with Web sites (such as Bank of America). The "Clicks and Mortar" box describes E*Trade's decision to enter online banking.

According to surveys, a major reason people are attracted to online banking is convenience. Customers can transfer money, check account balances, and pay bills, 24 hours a day, seven days a week on their PCs. According to Anthony Felderhoff, online banking is the most convenient way for him to handle his sometimes complicated financial transactions. He comments, "My wife and I own several properties,

Small Business Services

Do we really care about your small business?

We're large, admittedly. We're also more committed to small business than you ever thought possible. We now have more people dedicated solely to small business than some banks have people. The tangible tools you need, like Business Credit Express, payroll services, dedicated small business branches and a small business phone center. As well as the intangibles, like resources, brains, and an unabashed desire to help you succeed. To learn more, call 1-800-CALL-FLEET, visit any Fleet branch, or log on to fleet.com.

Forward. Thinking.℠ **Fleet**

FIGURE 19.9
Commercial Banks: Important Source of Funds for Small Business

and on any day, we have as much as $5,000 coming and going out of our accounts, so it was a major task to write checks each month."[8] Even nonbanks are getting into the act. The ad in Figure 19.10 touts the convenience of paying monthly bills using Yahoo's bill-paying service.

Another advantage of online banking is cost. Scott Pattern and Michael Reardon, owners of Boston's popular North East Brewing Company, took their microbrewery's banking online and saved 80 percent on payroll services alone. The benefits did not stop there, however. According to Reardon, "We've signed up for bill-pay services, too. It used to take two people half a day to pay all our bills. Now, I can do it online in one hour."[9]

Bank Regulation

Banks are among the nation's most heavily regulated businesses. The main purpose of bank regulation is to ensure public confidence in the safety and security of the banking system. Banks are critical to the overall functioning of the economy, and a collapse of the banking system can have disastrous results. Many believe that one of the causes of the Great Depression was the collapse of the banking system starting in the late 1920s.

Who Regulates Banks? All banks are either state or federally chartered. The majority of banks are state chartered; however, federally chartered banks control over 60 percent of banking assets. State-chartered banks are regulated by the appropriate state banking authorities, and federally chartered banks are regulated by the Federal Reserve, the Federal Deposit Insurance Corporation (FDIC), and the Comptroller of the Currency. In addition, state banks that are federally insured—and virtually all are—are also subject to FDIC regulation.

Banks are subject to periodic examination by state and/or federal regulators. Examinations are designed to ensure that the bank is following safe and sound banking practices, and is complying with all applicable regulations. Bank examinations include the review of detailed reports on the bank's operating and financial condition, as well as on-site inspections.

Federal Deposit Insurance A cornerstone of bank regulation is deposit insurance. Deposits of up to a set amount—currently $100,000—are insured by the FDIC. Deposit insurance means that, in the event the bank fails, depositors are paid in full by the FDIC, up to $100,000. Federal deposit insurance was enacted by the Banking Act of 1933 as one of the measures designed to restore public confidence in the banking system. Before deposit insurance, so-called "runs" were common as people rushed to withdraw their money from a bank, often just on a rumor that the bank was in precarious financial condition. At some point, the bank was unable to meet withdrawal demands and closed its doors. Remaining depositors often lost most of the money they had in the bank. Deposit insurance shifts the risk of bank failures from individual depositors to the FDIC.

E*Trade Moves into Online Banking

Background. Online banking continues to grow rapidly. The number of customers performing such banking functions as checking account balances, transferring money, and paying bills is expected to triple over the next five years. Hundreds of banks offer online banking services today, including both Internet-only banks as well as traditional bricks-and-mortar banks. At the same time, changes in banking laws have allowed banks to enter new businesses, such as investments and insurance. Conversely, investment firms and insurance companies can now offer banking services.

What Happened? E*Trade was founded in 1996 and was one of the first Internet-only brokerage firms. E*Trade offered individual investors access to relevant information and market news 24 hours a day, seven days a week from the convenience of their PCs. E*Trade also charged much less to buy and sell securities than traditional bricks-and-mortar brokerage firms. E*Trade's business surged, and today it is the second largest online brokerage firm in the country. However, along with success has come increased competition from established brokerage firms such as Charles Schwab and Merrill Lynch. E*Trade's growth rate slowed, and its profitability declined. Management decided it was time to diversify into other financial services. But where to start?

The Response. The opportunity presented itself in early 2000. E*Trade purchased struggling Internet Bank Telebanc Financial Corporation for $1.6 billion. All of a sudden, E*Trade could offer its customers not only brokerage services but also a full range of banking services. Without the expense of bricks-and-mortar branches, E*Trade Bank, as it became known, could offer customers lower fees and higher rates on deposits. A few mouse clicks and customers could complete virtually all of their banking transactions 24 hours a day, seven days a week.

Initially, however, there was one major stumbling block: E*Trade Bank didn't have any ATMs of its own. Its customers could still use other banks' ATMs, but they usually ended up having to pay a fee. E*Trade overcame that problem when it purchased the nation's third-largest ATM network. Now E*Trade Bank customers have access to over 9,600 no-fee ATMs located throughout the country. The company's Web site provides a guide to ATM locations and proclaims, "Find an E*Trade ATM near you and never pay an ATM fee again!" Today, E*Trade Bank has roughly 350,000 accounts and over $5 billion in deposits.

Today and Counting. E*Trade appears on track toward its goal of becoming the nation's first Internet-based financial services company. The company recently acquired a large stake in E-Loan, Inc., an online mortgage lender. While the services offered at E*Trade Bank's ATMs are currently limited—they don't accept deposits, for example—plans are in the works to turn them into financial services kiosks where customers can check stock prices, apply for loans, and access other services. The company is also expanding its wireless services. At some point, customers will be able to use their handheld devices or cell phones to conduct a wide range of financial transactions. Although the future looks bright for E*Trade Bank, don't count out the traditional bricks-and-mortar banks just yet. Fleet Financial Bank of Massachusetts, for example, is in the process of aggressively expanding its ATM network and online services, and has taken specific aim at the online banks. The bricks-and-mortar banks also have one major advantage over online banks: actual people customers can talk to. Many bank experts believe that online banks such as E*Trade Bank will eventually have to offer human help. One expert puts it this way: "Every once in a while, you need to talk to someone."

QUESTIONS FOR CRITICAL THINKING

1. Do you currently conduct any of your banking business online? If so, what kinds of banking transactions do you perform online? If not, why not?
2. Do you agree or disagree with the observation that eventually the online banks will have to offer the level of personal service and contacts that bricks-and-mortar banks offer customers? What factors did you consider when choosing your current bank?

Sources: E*Trade Bank Web site **www.etradebank.com,** accessed on February 9, 2001; Beth Healy, "Reinventing ATMs: Online Brokerage Challenges Banks with Hip Brand, New Services," *Boston Globe,* December 23, 2000, p. G1; "E*Trade Merger Creates Full Service Financial Site," *Chicago Sun-Times,* June 2, 1999, p. 66.

Recent Changes in Banking Laws   In addition to establishing the FDIC, Depression-era banking legislation also put restrictions on the kinds of activities in which banks could engage, including restricting their role in the securities markets. Believing that some of these restrictions were outdated, Congress recently passed a law that allows banks to enter the securities and insurance businesses. In return, other financial services firms are now allowed to offer banking services. It is still too early to tell what the ultimate outcome of this law will be.

Savings Banks and Credit Unions

Although commercial banks are by far the largest depository financial institutions in the U.S., savings banks and credit unions are also important financial institutions. Today, savings banks and credit unions offer many of the same services that commercial banks do.

Yes. All my bills were paid on time.

Honesty,
integrity and Yahoo! Bill Pay.
These things will keep you
out of trouble.
Get online bills, monthly reminders
and automatic payments
on recurring bills. Then you'll
be primed for success.
Oh yeah, be a nice person, too.
finance.yahoo.com

Yahoo! Bill Pay

Do You YAHOO!?

FIGURE 19.10
Convenience of Online Bill Payments

Savings banks used to be called savings and loan associations, or thrift institutions. They were originally established in the early 1800s to make home mortgage loans. Savings and loans raised funds by accepting only savings deposits and then lent these funds to consumers to buy homes. Deposits at thrift institutions became federally insured during the 1930s, and the industry generally prospered until the 1970s.

Several factors contributed to a series of crises in the savings and loan industry during the 1970s and 1980s. Hundreds of savings and loans were forced to merge with financially stronger institutions. Today there are around 1,700 savings banks with total assets of just over $1 trillion. Although the typical savings bank offers many of the same services as a commercial bank, including checking accounts, savings banks are not major lenders to businesses. Over 70 percent of their outstanding loans are still home mortgage loans. Deposits in savings banks are now FDIC insured, and savings banks are regulated in much the same way as commercial banks.

Credit unions are unique financial institutions. They are cooperative financial institutions that are owned by their depositors, all of whom are members. Over 70 million Americans belong to one of the nation's 11,000 credit unions. Combined credit unions have around $350 billion in assets. By law, credit union members must share similar occupations, employers, or membership in certain organizations. This law effectively caps the size of credit unions. Over 80 percent of members belong to occupational or employer-based credit unions. The Navy Federal Credit Union is the largest credit union in the country, with over 700,000 members.

Credit unions are designed to serve consumers, not businesses. Credit unions raise funds by offering members a number of demand and saving deposits—checking accounts at credit unions are referred to as share draft accounts. They then lend these funds to members. Because credit unions are not-for-profit institutions, they often pay savers higher rates of interest, charge lower rates of interest on loans, and have fewer fees than other financial institutions. Credit unions can have either state or federal charters, and deposits are insured by a federal agency.

Nondepository Financial Institutions

Nondepository financial institutions accept funds from businesses and households, much of which they then invest. Generally these institutions do not offer checking accounts or other types of demand deposits. Three examples of nondepository financial institutions are insurance companies, pension funds, and finance companies.

Insurance Companies Households and businesses buy insurance to transfer risk from themselves to the insurance company. The insurance company accepts the risk in return for a series of payments, called premiums. **Underwriting** is the process used by insurance companies to determine whom to insure and what to charge. During a typical year, insurance companies collect more in premiums than they pay in claims. After paying operating expenses, this difference is invested. Insurance companies are a major source of short- and long-term financing for businesses. Life insurance companies alone have total assets exceeding $2.3 trillion.

Pension Funds Pension funds provide retirement benefits to workers and their families. They are set up by employers and are fueled by regular contributions made by employers and employees. Because pension funds have predictable long-term cash inflows and very predictable cash outflows, they invest heavily in long-term assets, such as common stocks. By some estimates, over 25 percent of all common stocks are owned by pension funds. In total, pension funds have over $7 trillion in assets.

Finance Companies Consumer and commercial finance companies offer short-term loans to borrowers. A commercial finance company supplies short-term funds to businesses that pledge tangible assets such as inventory, accounts receivable, machinery, or property as collateral for the loan. A consumer finance company plays a similar role for consumers. Finance companies raise funds by selling securities or borrowing funds from commercial banks. Though there are exceptions, loans from finance companies tend to carry higher interest rates than loans from banks.

THE FEDERAL RESERVE SYSTEM

Created in 1913, the **Federal Reserve System,** or Fed, is the central bank of the U.S. and is an important part of the nation's financial system. The Fed has four basic responsibilities: regulating commercial banks, performing banking-related activities for the U.S. Treasury, servicing member banks, and setting monetary policy. Not all banks belong to the Fed. Banks with federal charters are required to belong to the Fed, but membership is optional for state-chartered banks. Because the largest banks in the country are all federally chartered, the bulk of banking assets are controlled by Fed members. The Fed acts as the banker's bank for members. It provides wire transfer facilities, clears checks, replaces worn-out currency, and even lends banks money.

Organization of the Federal Reserve System

The nation is divided into 12 federal reserve districts, each with its own federal reserve bank. Each district bank supplies banks within its district with currency and facilitates the clearing of checks. District banks are run by a nine-member board of directors, headed by a president.

The governing body of the Fed is the Board of Governors. The Board consists of seven members, including a chair and vice-chair, appointed by the president and confirmed by the Senate. The chair of the Board of Governors is a very important position. Some have commented, only half jokingly, that the Fed chair is the second most powerful person in the nation.

The Fed is designed to be politically independent. Fed governors are appointed to 14-year terms that are staggered in such a way that a president could not appoint a majority of members during a single term. The Fed also has its own sources of revenue and does not depend on congressional appropriations.

An important part of the Fed is the Federal Open Markets Committee (FOMC). The FOMC is responsible for setting most policies regarding monetary policy and interest rates. It consists of 12 members—the seven Fed governors plus five representatives of the district banks who serve on a rotating basis. The Fed chair is also chair of the FOMC.

Check Clearing and the Fed

As mentioned earlier, one of the Fed's responsibilities is to help facilitate the clearing of checks. Even in this

1. Sea View Apartments in Jacksonville, Florida, purchases a $300 carpet cleaner from Home Depot by writing a check.

2. Home Depot deposits the check in its account in an Atlanta bank.

3. The Atlanta bank deposits the check for credit in its account at the Federal Reserve Bank of Atlanta.

4. The Federal Reserve Bank of Atlanta forwards the check to the First National Bank of Jacksonville, which deducts $300 from Sea View Apartment's account.

5. The First National Bank authorizes the Atlanta Federal Reserve Bank to deduct $300 from its deposit account with the district bank.

6. The Federal Reserve Bank of Atlanta credits the Atlanta bank's account. The Atlanta bank adds $300 to Home Depot's bank account.

7. Sea View Apartments receives the canceled check at the end of the month from First National Bank of Jacksonville.

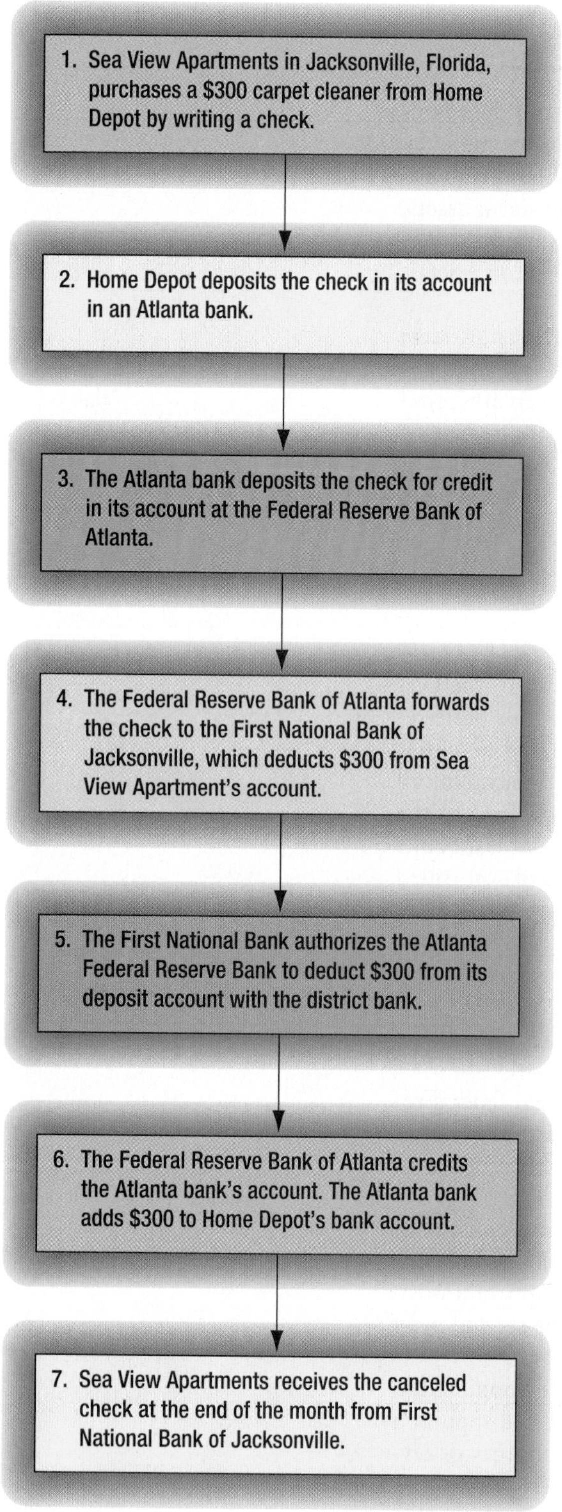

FIGURE 19.11
A Check's Journey through the Federal Reserve System

age of electronic and online banking, Americans still write billions of paper checks each year. **Check clearing** is the process by which funds are transferred from the check writer to the recipient.

Assume the owner of Sea View Apartments in Jacksonville, Florida, buys a $300 carpet cleaner from the local Home Depot and writes a check. If Home Depot has an account at the same bank as Sea View, the bank will clear the check in-house. It will decrease the balance in the owner's account by $300 and increase the balance in Home Depot's account by $300. If Home Depot has an account at another bank in Jacksonville, the two banks may still clear the check directly with one another. This process is cumbersome, however, so it is more likely that the banks will use the services of a local check clearinghouse.

On the other hand, if Home Depot has its account with a bank in another state—perhaps in Atlanta, Georgia, where Home Depot is based—the check will likely be cleared through the Federal Reserve System. Home Depot will deposit the check in its Atlanta bank account. Its bank, in turn, will deposit the check in the Federal Reserve Bank of Atlanta. The Atlanta Federal Reserve bank will present the check to Sea View's bank for payment, which pays the check by deducting $300 from Sea View's account. The journey of a check through the Federal Reserve System is shown in Figure 19.11. Regardless of the method used, it is Fed policy that all checks should clear within two business days.

Monetary Policy

The Fed's most important function is controlling the supply of money and credit, or **monetary policy**. The Fed's job is to make sure that the money supply grows at an appropriate rate, allowing the economy to expand and inflation to remain in check. If the money supply grows too slowly, economic growth will slow, unemployment will increase, and the risk of a recession will increase. If the money supply grows too rapidly, inflationary pressures will build. The Fed uses its policy tools to push interest rates up or down. If the Fed pushes interest rates up, the growth rate in the money supply will slow, economic growth will slow, and inflationary pressures will ease. If the Fed pushes interest rates down, the growth rate in the money supply will increase, economic growth will pick up, and unemployment will fall. The Fed has three major policy tools: changes in the reserve requirements of banks, discount rate changes, and open market operations. In addition, it can use selective credit controls like increasing or decreasing margin requirements on the purchase of stock.

The Fed requires that banks maintain reserves—defined as cash in their vaults plus deposits at district Federal Reserve banks—equal to some percentage of what the banks hold in deposits. For example, if the Fed sets the reserve requirement at 10 percent, a bank that receives a $500 deposit must reserve $50, so it has only $450 to invest or lend out. By changing the reserve requirement, the Fed can affect the amount of money available for making loans. The higher the reserve requirement, the less banks can lend out to consumers and businesses. The lower the reserve requirement, the more banks can lend out. Because any change in the reserve requirement can have a sudden and dramatic impact on the money supply, the Fed rarely uses this tool. In fact, the Fed has not changed reserve requirements in over ten years.

Another policy tool is the so-called **discount rate**, the interest rate at which Federal Reserve banks make short-term loans to member banks. A bank might need a

Table 19.3   Federal Reserve Tools

General Tool	Action	Effect on Money Supply	Short-Term Effect on the Economy
Reserve requirement change	Increase reserve requirements	Reduces money supply	Boosts interest rates and slows economic activity
	Decrease reserve requirements	Increases money supply	Reduces interest rates and accelerates economic activity
Discount rate change	Increase discount rate	Reduces money supply	Boosts interest rates and slows economic activity
	Decrease discount rate	Increases money supply	Reduces interest rates and accelerates economic activity
Open market operation	Buy government securities	Increases money supply	Reduces interest rates and accelerates economic activity
	Sell government securities	Reduces money supply	Boosts interest rates and slows economic activity
Selective Credit Controls			
Margin requirement change	Increase margin requirements		Reduces credit purchases of securities with a negative impact on prices and trading activity on securities exchanges
	Reduce margin requirements		Increases credit purchases of securities with a positive impact on prices and trading activity on securities exchanges

short-term loan if transactions leave it short of reserves. If the Fed wants to slow the growth rate in the money supply, it will increase the discount rate. This increase will make it more expensive for banks to borrow funds. Banks will, in turn, raise the interest rates they charge on loans to consumers and businesses. The end result will be a slowdown in economic activity. Lowering the discount rate will have the opposite effect.

The third policy tool, and the one most often used, is **open market operations,** the technique of controlling the money supply growth rate by buying or selling U.S. Treasury securities. If the Fed buys Treasury securities, the money it pays enters circulation, increasing the money supply and lowering interest rates. When the Fed sells Treasury securities, money is taken out of circulation and interest rates rise. When the Fed uses open market operations it employs the so-called federal funds rate—the rate at which banks lend money to one another over night—as its benchmark. Table 19.3 illustrates how the tools of the Federal Reserve stimulate or slow the economy.

The Federal Reserve also has the authority to exercise selective credit controls when its members feel the economy is growing too rapidly or too slowly. These credit controls include the power to set margin requirements—the percentage of the purchase price of a security that an investor must pay in cash on credit purchases of stocks or bonds.

Transactions in international markets also affect the U.S. money supply. On the foreign exchange market, purchases and sales exchange one nation's currency for that of another country. Billions of U.S. dollars are traded this way every day. The Fed can lower the exchange value of the dollar by selling dollars and buying foreign currencies, and it can raise the dollar's exchange value by doing the opposite— buying dollars and selling foreign currencies. When the Fed buys foreign currencies, the effect is the same as buying securities because it increases the U.S. banking system's reserves. Selling foreign currencies, on the other hand, is like selling securities, in that it reduces bank reserves.

U.S. FINANCIAL INSTITUTIONS: A GLOBAL PERSPECTIVE

Financial institutions have become a global industry and any review should consider U.S. financial

BUSINESS DIRECTORY

➤ **check clearing** *process by which funds are transferred from the check writer to the recipient.*

➤ **monetary policy** *managing of the growth rate in the supply of money and credit, usually through the use of interest rates.*

institutions in their international context. Major U.S. banks—such as J.P. Morgan Chase—have extensive international operations. They have offices, lend money, and accept deposits from customers throughout the world. According to recent statistics, U.S. banks have around $200 billion in outstanding loans to international customers.[10]

Although most Americans recognize large U.S. banks such as Bank America and Citibank among the global financial giants, only 3 of the 20 largest banks in the world (measured by total assets) are U.S. institutions—Bank America, Citibank, and J.P. Morgan Chase. The other 17 are based in France, Germany, Holland, Japan, Switzerland, and the United Kingdom. These international banks also operate worldwide, including in the U.S.

Virtually all nations have some sort of a central bank, similar to the U.S. Federal Reserve. Canada's central bank, for example, is the Bank of Canada. Germany's central bank is the Bundesbank. These central banks play roles much like the Fed, such as controlling the money supply. Policy makers at other nations' central banks often respond to changes in the U.S. financial system by making similar changes in their own systems. For example, if the Fed pushes U.S. interest rates lower, central banks in Japan and Europe may also push their interest rates lower. These changes can influence events in countries around the world. Lower U.S. and European interest rates not only decrease the cost of borrowing for U.S. and European firms, but also increase the amount of money available for loans to borrowers in Africa and South America.

International banks and other providers of financial services play important roles in global business. They help to transfer purchasing power from buyers to sellers and from lenders to borrowers. They also provide credit to importers and reduce the risk associated with changes in exchange rates.

WHAT'S AHEAD

This chapter introduces the finance function of contemporary business. Finance deals with the planning, obtaining, and managing of the company's funds in order to accomplish its objectives effectively and efficiently. The chapter also describes the role of money, where and how firms obtain funds, and the financial system. The next chapter explores how securities—stocks and bonds—are bought and sold. It also describes the investment characteristics of stocks and bonds, and how investors choose specific securities. It also outlines how securities market regulations protect investors.

➤ Summary of Learning Goals

1. Identify the functions performed by a firm's financial managers.

The major responsibility of financial managers is to develop and implement a financial plan for their organization. The firm's financial plan is based on forecasts of expenditures and receipts for a specified period and reflects the timing of cash inflows and outflows. The financial managers systematically determine their company's need for funds during the period and the most appropriate sources from which it can obtain them. In short, the financial manager is responsible for both raising and spending money.

2. Describe the characteristics a form of money should have, and list the functions of money.

Money should be divisible, portable, durable, stable in value, and difficult to counterfeit. Money in countries with modern economies have all of these characteristics.

3. Identify the various measures of the money supply.

The two most commonly used measures of the money supply are M1 and M2. M1 is defined as anything generally accepted as payment for goods and services, such as coins, paper money, and checks. M2 consists of M1 plus other assets that are almost as liquid as money but that do not function directly as a medium of exchange, such as savings deposits and money market mutual funds.

4. Explain how a firm uses funds.

Organizations use funds to run their day-to-day operations, pay for inventories, make interest payments on loans, pay dividends to shareholders, and purchase land, facilities, and equipment. If a firm finds itself with a surplus of cash, most financial managers choose to invest that excess cash in marketable securities.

5. Compare the two major sources of funds for a business.

Debt capital and equity capital are the two major sources from which businesses acquire funds. Debt capital represents funds obtained through borrowing. Equity capital comes from several sources, including the sale of stock, additional investments by the firm's owners, and previous earnings reinvested in the firm.

6. Identify likely sources of short- and long-term funds.

Sources of short-term funds include trade credit (generally automatically through open-account purchases from suppliers), unsecured loans, secured loans (for which the firm must pledge collateral), and sales of commercial paper by large, financially sound firms. Sources of long-term funds include long-term loans repaid over one year or longer, bonds, equity funds (ownership obtained from selling stock, accumulating additional contributions from owners, or reinvesting earnings in the firm).

7. Describe the financial system and the major financial institutions.

The financial system is the process by which funds are transferred between savers and users of funds. Funds can be transferred either through the financial markets or through financial institutions. Depository institutions—commercial banks, savings banks, and credit unions—accept deposits from customers that can be redeemed on demand. Depository institutions are closely regulated by state and federal authorities. Nondepository institutions include pension funds and insurance companies. Nondepository institutions invest a large portion of their funds in stocks, bonds, and real estate.

8. Explain the functions of the Federal Reserve System and the tools it uses to control the money supply.

The Federal Reserve System is the central bank of the United States. The Federal Reserve regulates banks, performs banking functions for the U.S. Treasury, and acts as the banker's bank (clearing checks, lending money to banks, and replacing worn-out currency). It controls the supply of credit and money in the economy in order to promote growth and control inflation. The Federal Reserve's tools include reserve requirements, the discount rate, and open market operations. Selective credit controls and purchases and sales of foreign currencies also help the Federal Reserve manage the economy.

9. Describe global financial environment.

Large U.S. banks and other financial institutions have a global presence. They accept deposits, make loans, and have branches throughout the world. Foreign banks also operate throughout the world, including in the U.S. The average European or Japanese bank is much larger than the average American bank. Virtually all nations have central banks that perform the same roles as the U.S. Federal Reserve System. Central bankers often act together raising and lowering interest rates as economic conditions warrant.

Business Terms You Need to Know

finance 680
financial manager 680
financial plan 681
money 682
debt capital 687
equity capital 687
bonds 689

venture capitalist 689
leverage 690
financial system 690
depository institutions 691
Federal Reserve System 697
check clearing 698
monetary policy 698

Other Important Business Terms

vice president for financial
    management 681

treasurer 681
controller 681

risk–return trade-off 681
demand deposit accounts 684

➤ Review Questions

1. Define *finance*. Briefly explain the risk–return trade-off in finance.

2. What is a financial plan? When building a financial plan, what are the three questions that have to be answered?

3. What characteristics should money have? List the three functions of money.

4. Explain the difference between M1 and M2. What is a demand deposit?

5. What are some of the reasons organizations need funds? What do many companies do if they find themselves with excess cash?

6. What is the difference between debt capital and equity capital? List several examples of each.

7. What is the financial system? By what two ways are funds transferred between savers and users?

8. Explain the difference between a depository and a nondepository financial institution. Give several examples of each type of financial institution.

9. Briefly outline how a commercial bank operates. Why is deposit insurance so important?

10. How is the Federal Reserve System organized? What are the three policy tools the Fed can use to control the supply of money and credit?

➤ Questions for Critical Thinking

1. Assume you would like to start a business. Put together a rough financial plan that addresses the three financial planning questions listed in the text.

2. Your business has really taken off; now it needs a huge infusion of capital. A venture capital firm has agreed to invest the money you need. In return, the venture capital firm will own 75 percent of the business. You will be replaced as board chairperson, though retain the title of company founder and president, and the venture capital firm will provide a new CFO. Would you be willing to take the money but lose control of your business?

3. The owner of your company is trying to decide how to raise an additional $1.5 million, and she has asked for your advice about whether the firm should use debt capital or equity capital. Prepare a brief memo to the owner outlining the advantages and disadvantages of both debt capital and equity capital. Be sure to explain the concept of leverage. Assume your company can borrow $1.5 million at an annual interest rate of 10 percent. It currently has $1.5 million in equity and no debt.

4. Compared with most businesses, explain why a bank is more vulnerable to failure. Why does federal deposit insurance help protect the soundness of the banking system?

5. As noted in the chapter, the U.S. Federal Reserve System is politically independent. How is the Fed politically independent? Do you think it should remain so?

➤ Experiential Exercise

Background: You learned in this chapter and in the previous one about investors, creditors, accountants, the accounting process, financial statements, budgeting, and other aspects of what's involved in a company's management of its financial assets. This chapter's exercise will test how much you know about the common denominator in all of these topics: money.

Matching: In the answer column, write the letter for the individual pictured on the front of each denomination of currency listed.

Number	Answer	Denomination of Currency
1.	_____	$1
2.	_____	$2
3.	_____	$5
4.	_____	$10
5.	_____	$20
6.	_____	$50
7.	_____	$100

Letter	Picture
A.	Ulysses S. Grant (18th U.S. President)
B.	George Washington (1st U.S. President)
C.	Benjamin Franklin
D.	Abraham Lincoln (16th U.S. President)
E.	Thomas Jefferson (3rd U.S. President)
F.	Alexander Hamilton (1st U.S. Treasury Secretary)
G.	Andrew Jackson (7th U.S. President)

Multiple Choice: Circle the letter for the correct answer for each of the following questions:

8. The $500, $1000, $5000, and $10,000 bills have not been printed since
   a. 1901
   b. 1929
   c. 1946
   d. 1972
   e. 2000

9. The Bureau of Engraving and Printing (BEP), located in Washington, D.C., is responsible for designing and printing our paper currency. There is also a satellite production facility located in Fort Worth, Texas, which began operation in January 1991. Every day, the BEP prints approximately _____ worth of currency in denominations ranging from $1 to $100.
   a. $500,000
   b. $1.8 million
   c. $10.7 million
   d. $22.5 million
   e. $37.3 million

Fill in the Blank:

10. The $100 bill was redesigned in _____, the $50 in 1997, and the $20 in 1998. The $10 and $5 bills made their debut in a ceremony at the Lincoln Memorial in Washington, D.C., and in 30 major cities across the U.S. on May 24, _____.

Complete the Following Task:

11. Locate one of the new $10 or $5 bills and find two of the new security features that you were able to identify:
    - A larger portrait has been moved off center and to the left to create more space for the watermark. The watermark to the right of the portrait depicts the same historical figure as the portrait, which can only be seen when held up to a light.
    - A security thread is embedded to the right of the portrait on the $10 that glows orange in ultraviolet light, and a security thread is embedded to the left of the portrait on the $5 that glows blue in ultraviolet light. The words "USA FIVE" and a flag and "USA TEN" and a flag are printed on the threads of the $5 and $10, respectively, and can be seen from both sides of the notes when held up to a bright light.
    - Color-shifting ink in the numeral on the lower right corner of the $10 bill looks green when viewed straight on but appears black when viewed at an angle. There is no color shifting ink on the $5.
    - On the front of the $10, "TEN" is printed in the lower left-hand corner, and "The United States of America" is repeated above Hamilton's name. On the front of the $5, "FIVE DOLLARS" is continually printed on both side borders, and "The United States of America" appears on the lower edge of the portrait's oval frame.

Sources: "United States Treasury Currency Information," downloaded from **www.ustreas.gov/currency**; "Frequently Asked Questions about United States Paper Currency," downloaded from **www.ustreas.gov/opc/opc0034.html**; "U.S. Treasury and Federal Reserve Issue New $10 and $5 Bills," May 24, 2000, downloaded from **www.treas.gov/press/releases/ps650.htm** on February 12, 2001.

➤ **Answer Key**

1. B; **2.** E; **3.** D; **4.** F; **5.** G; **6.** A; **7.** C; **8.** C; **9.** D; **10.** 1996; 2000; **11.** Security features selected will vary.

➤ **Nothing but Net**

1. **Venture capital.** Visit the Venture Economics Web site. Review the most recent set of data on venture capital activity. Prepare a brief report for your class summarizing venture capital investment activity.

www.ventureeconmics.com

2. **Banking statistics.** Visit the FDIC's Web site and access the latest data you can find on commercial banks, **www.fdic.gov/statistics.** Answer the following questions:

   a. How many commercial banks are there? Has the number increased or decreased during the past year?

   b. Which state has the most commercial banks?

   c. What are the total assets of commercial banks?

   d. How many banks have state charters and how many have federal charters? What are the total assets of state and federally chartered banks?

   e. How much do banks hold in deposits? How much do they hold in reserves? How much money have banks lent out and to whom?

3. **Central banks.** As noted in the chapter, virtually all nations have a central bank. In the U.S. the central bank is the Federal Reserve System. Visit the Federal Reserve's Web site and the Web site of Canada's central bank, the Bank of Canada. Prepare a written report comparing and contrasting the organization and functions of the Bank of Canada and the Federal Reserve System.

   www.federalreserve.gov

   www.bank-banque-canada.ca

   Note: Internet Web addresses change frequently. If you don't find the exact sites listed, you may need to access the organization's home page and search from there.

When asked what your favorite style of music is, you might answer rock, country, folk, urban, or jazz. You can also name your favorite musical groups, composers, or performers—almost without thinking. Chances are, you also have a sound system. Joe McGuire, CFO of Tweeter Home Entertainment Group, hopes it was bought at one of his stores. But even if it wasn't, he is happy if you've heard of his company.

Tweeter Home Entertainment is a retail chain that concentrates on selling mid- to high-priced audio and video equipment. In fact, McGuire isn't worried about selling younger consumers their first stereo or television. Those lower-priced items simply fail to generate the kind of revenue that Tweeter thrives on. Gross margin—the difference between a sound system's sales price and its purchase price—is the name of the game when it comes to making money, and high-end equipment generates a gross margin of about 28 percent for Tweeter. By contrast, gross margins for entry-level TV sets and stereos are only in the mid-teens. In other words, a 20-inch television that most electronics stores sell for around $300 generates less profit overall than a high-end big-screen TV that sells for $3,000, even though a store is likely to sell many more of the smaller, less expensive sets.

McGuire explains that the most important task of his company is "managing the pace of growth." Tweeter is a publicly held corporation whose shareholders expect regular growth in profits. McGuire and his fellow executives must look for creative yet financially sound ways to help the company grow. Making wise use of the funds that Tweeter generates not only from the sales of home entertainment equipment but also from investors is critical to the company's continued growth. Recently, the retail chain has been using funds to make strategic acquisitions of smaller firms—companies that complement its business, such as Bryn Mawr Stereo & Video stores in the mid-Atlantic states and Douglas TV and United Audio Centers, both located around Chicago. Tweeter doesn't just plunk down the cash for any store that's available. McGuire explains that, to be considered, a store "has to have a similar product mix." Stores that Tweeter acquires are usually privately owned and might not be profitable, but McGuire and his fellow executives must be able to see ways that the firm can be turned around. Acquiring another company naturally affects Tweeter's own earnings during the first year or two, but as in the case of the United Audio purchase, "We expect this acquisition to contribute to earnings per share growth as we further develop the greater Chicago market where United Audio currently operates," notes McGuire. Most of these transactions involve more complicated funding than the act of writing a big check. They are typically funded by taking on some debt and an exchange of stock, if the company is already publicly held.

Of course, another way for Tweeter to grow is simply to open more stores. But that decision must also be carefully managed. For instance, if Tweeter has recently expanded an existing store in an area, grabbing an empty building simply to launch another store in a nearby town may not benefit the company in the long run—no matter how good an opportunity it may seem to be at the time. "Anything faster than 20 percent to 30 percent storefront growth in a year is dangerous," warns McGuire. "You can mess up what has been successful." The reason for such caution is that Tweeter has to make the investments required to support growth—such as training new employees and managing benefits.

Finally, McGuire bases many of his company's financial decisions on the niche that Tweeter has been so successful at filling. "We are a specialty retailer," he notes. Tweeter sells audio and video equipment only—no computers or telecommunications devices. And Tweeter operates relatively small stores—10,000 to 12,000 square feet—compared with the 30,000 to 50,000 square feet occupied by big discounters such as BestBuy and Circuit City.

Then there's the matter of store sales—or rather the lack of them. Tweeter doesn't hold promotional sales. Instead, it uses an everyday competitive pricing strategy that assures shoppers that they will find not only quality items in an intimate environment but also competitive prices that aren't going to change tomorrow.

Tweeter has come a long way from its 1970s beginnings as a tiny shop selling mostly speakers on Harvard Square in Cambridge, Massachusetts. The company now has more than 2,000 employees working in 95 stores nationwide. Joe McGuire believes that this is because founder and chairman Sandy Bloomberg has never lost sight of the company's identity. That identity is supported by good financial decisions. "In order to be successful, it's very important that the back end of the house is in order," says McGuire in reference to the importance of finance. In the final analysis, he says, "the only thing that counts is how much money did you make." Those words are music to the ears of Tweeter shareholders.

QUESTIONS

1. Identify two ways that Tweeter could raise more cash if the company decided it was needed.
2. Based on what you've read in this chapter, write a brief job description for Joe McGuire.
3. Go to Tweeter's Web site at **www.tweeter.com**. What is the company's current financial status?

Sources: "Company Profile," Tweeter Home Entertainment Group Web site, **www.tweeter.com,** accessed May 5, 2001; "Tweeter Home Entertainment Group Sales," *Business Wire,* January 4, 2001; "Tweeter Home Entertainment Group Announces That It has Completed the Acquisition of Douglas TV, the Big Screen Store," company press release, October 2, 2000.

CHAPTER 20

Financing and Investing through Securities Markets

Learning Goals

1. Distinguish between the primary market for securities and the secondary market.

2. Compare money market instruments, bonds, and common stock, and explain why particular investors might prefer each type of security.

3. Identify the five basic objectives of investors and the types of securities most likely to help them reach each objective.

4. Explain the process of buying or selling a security listed on an organized securities exchange.

5. Describe the information included in stock, bond, and mutual fund quotations.

6. Explain the role of mutual funds in securities markets.

7. Evaluate the major features of regulations designed to protect investors.

Virtual Stock Markets

One of the hottest new developments in securities markets is the emergence of so-called **electronic communication networks (ECNs).** These networks link investors, usually over the Internet, allowing them to buy or sell stocks directly with one another. When a trade is executed on a traditional stock exchange, such as the New York Stock Exchange (NYSE) or the Nasdaq stock market, the order often goes through an intermediary called a market maker, whose task is to bring together buyers and sellers who agree on a market price. By contrast, when an order is executed on an ECN, the buyer trades directly with the seller. This offers investors a number of advantages—including faster order execution and often better prices—since no intermediary is involved. ECNs have grown rapidly in the past few years and, according to some estimates, one of every four shares of stock traded on a typical day is executed through ECNs.

One of the largest ECNs is Island.com, a unit of Datek Online Holdings. It was founded in 1997 by three entrepreneurs with a vision of a truly open, competitive market. During one recent 12-month period, over 53 billion shares—collectively worth more than $3 trillion—were traded on Island.com. Island also became one of the first U.S. stock markets to quote prices in decimals, rather than fractions, well before the NYSE and Nasdaq stock market switched from fractions to dollars and cents.

Island's network creates a virtual securities market in which investors meet directly. Assume an order to buy Cisco Systems at a given price is received. Island's system is instantaneously scanned to determine whether a matching sell order—an order to sell Cisco Systems at that price—exists. If a matching order exists, the buy order is executed immediately. If no matching sell order exists at the time, the buy order is displayed on Book Viewer—Island's real-time order book—until a matching sell order is entered or the buy order is canceled. Anyone with a Web connection can access Book Viewer free of charge and see the current prices quoted to buy or sell stocks.

Island's mission is to permit investors to make purchases and sales in a transparent and open marketplace. Everyone sees the same information at the same time. With a

few mouse clicks, investors anywhere in the world can get a better picture of the current market for a particular stock and can thus make better informed decisions. In traditional markets, intermediaries often have access to the most current information, and investors must obtain this information from them. With Island's system, all investors have simultaneous access to the most complete, most current information available.

Island is also amazingly fast. While traditional markets can often take several seconds to complete a trade, especially if an intermediary is involved, Island claims that it can complete an order in 3/100ths of a second. Buyers and sellers pay only three-fourths of a cent per share on each transaction, compared with the usual 5 to 6 cents per share. Further, Island offers extended

trading hours. Traditional markets are open between 9:30 A.M. and 4 P.M. (Eastern time). Island's network is available from 7 A.M. to 8 P.M. (Eastern time). Extended trading hours are important because market-moving news—such as mergers, employee layoffs, and earnings announcements—often are made after the NYSE and Nasdaq close. Finally, investors who use Island remain anonymous. Only the price and number of shares are displayed. Island provides no clues as to the investor's identity.

So, are ECNs like Island.com the stock markets of the future? Answering that question is difficult, but there is little doubt that ECNs will continue to grow in importance. They are already closely integrated into the Nasdaq stock market. Recently, the venerable NYSE announced closer links with one ECN, Archipelago LLC. It is now easier for investors to get price information and execute orders for NYSE-listed stocks on Archipelago. More formal links between the NYSE and other ECNs will likely follow.[1]

CHAPTER OVERVIEW

The previous chapter discusses two sources of funding for long-term financial needs: debt capital and equity capital. Long-term debt capital takes the form of U.S. government bonds, municipal bonds, and corporate bonds. Equity capital takes the form of common and preferred stock—ownership shares in corporations. Stocks and bonds are commonly called **securities**, because both represent obligations on the part of issuers to provide purchasers with expected or stated returns on the funds invested or loaned.

This chapter examines how securities are bought and sold in two markets—the primary market and the secondary market. We describe the characteristics of stocks, bonds, and money market instruments (short-term debt securities), and how investors choose the specific securities that best help them to meet their investment objectives. We also examine the role of organized securities exchanges in the financial sector and outline the information included in reports of securities transactions. Finally, we review the laws that regulate the securities markets and protect investors.

THE PRIMARY MARKET

FIGURE 20.1
Example of a Tombstone Ad

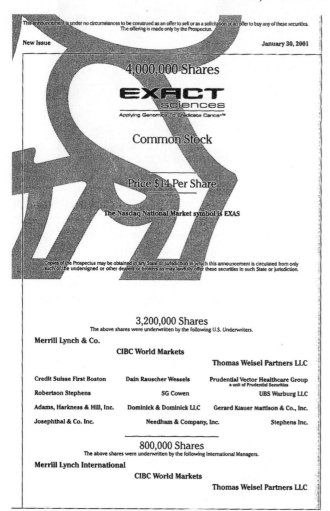

In the **primary market,** firms and governments issue securities and sell them initially to the public. When a company needs capital to purchase inventory, expand a plant, make major investments to develop new products, acquire another firm, or pursue other business goals, it may make a bond or stock offering to the investing public. For example, recently the Federal National Mortgage Association (or Fannie Mae) sold bonds to raise funds to purchase home mortgages. Similarly, when Ohio needs capital to build a new highway or a new community college, or to fulfill other public needs, its leaders may also decide to sell government bonds.

A stock offering gives investors the opportunity to purchase ownership shares in a firm like well-known drug maker Amgen and to participate in its future growth, in exchange for providing current capital. When a company offers stock for sale to the general public for the first time, it is called an **initial public offering (IPO)**. During a recent 12-month period, over 700 IPOs were made—a huge increase over previous years. These IPOs raised a combined total amount of over $144 billion.[2] The "Clicks and Mortar" box shows how IPOs work by describing the IPO of common stock by software maker Embarcadero Technologies.

Both profit-seeking corporations and government agencies also rely on primary markets to raise funds by issuing bonds. For example, the federal government sells Treasury bonds to finance parts of federal outlays such as interest on outstanding federal debt. State and local governments sell bonds to finance capital projects such as the construction of sewer systems, streets, and fire stations.

Announcements of stock and bond offerings appear daily in business publications such as *The Wall Street Journal*. These announcements are in the form of a simple, black-and-white ad called a *tombstone*. The tombstone ad in Figure 20.1 informs the public that Exact Sciences is offering 4 million shares of common stock at $14 per share.

Embarcadero Technologies Goes Public

Background. An IPO is the process whereby a company first sells its stock to the investing public. The IPO is also referred to as *going public*. The stock is sold in the primary market and begins trading almost immediately in a secondary market. Many IPOs turn out to be spectacular investments. A $1,000 investment in the 1990 Cisco Systems IPO would be worth in excess of $450,000 today. Other IPOs, however, turn out to be flops. Companies go public primarily because they need additional funds to finance their growth and private sources of capital are no longer adequate. Further, venture capitalists and others who provide early financing to a company profit only when the company goes public. When a company accepts financing from venture capitalists, the agreement often specifies a time frame for the company going public.

What Happened? Embarcadero Technologies was founded in San Francisco in 1993 by a small group of individuals. The company develops a variety of software products that enable businesses to build and manage their e-business applications and databases. Embarcadero was funded initially by a combination of personal resources from the firm's founders, venture capital investments, bank loans, and leases. Embarcadero shipped its first software products in 1993. Other products soon followed, and the firm's products earned numerous awards and honors. The company's revenues soared, doubling almost every year. It even earned a small profit, a major accomplishment for a start-up firm.

The Response. As Embarcadero continued to grow, it needed more and more financing. As the 20th century moved to an end, the company realized that its growth would be severely limited without significant additional financing. So, Embarcadero decided to parlay its success into a public offering of its stock. The company selected a lead investment banking firm—Donaldson, Lufkin, and Jenrette (DLJ)—and began the task of designing the IPO. In 2000, Embarcadero announced the company's intention to go public and filed the necessary Securities and Exchange Commission (SEC) registration documents. The company offered 4.2 million shares of common stock for sale at $10 per share. After the underwriting

commission, Embarcadero would receive slightly more than $39 million. According to the registration statement, the company would use the proceeds "for working capital and other general corporate purposes." After the public sale, Embarcadero would have around 26 million shares of common stock outstanding, the bulk of which would still be held by the company's founders and venture capitalists. DLJ formed a syndicate consisting of itself and 31 other investment banking firms that would be responsible for selling the issue. Each firm underwrote between 25,000 shares to slightly over 1.5 million shares.

Today and Counting. Embarcadero completed its IPO on April 20, 2000. The issue was well received by investors and quickly sold out. Even though 2000 was a difficult year for technology stocks in general, and IPOs in particular, Embarcadero did very well. The stock traded as high as $66.50 per share after going public and closed the year at $45 per share. It was the best-performing IPO that year. The company reported record sales and profits and filed for a secondary offering of an additional 4.6 million shares of common stock during the following year.

QUESTIONS FOR CRITICAL THINKING

1. Why do venture capitalists eventually want a company to go public? Are venture capitalists likely to insist on a firm timetable for going public as a condition for making an investment in a firm?

2. Why does the popularity of IPOs tend to run in cycles? What is the relationship between stock prices and the level of IPO activity?

Sources: Embarcadero Technologies Prospectus, downloaded from **www.freeedgar.com** on April 28, 2001; "Embarcadero Technologies Files Registration Statement for Follow-Up Public Offering," Embarcadero Technologies press release, February 23, 2001; "Embarcadero Technologies Announces Record Fourth-Quarter and Fiscal Year 2000 Results," *Business Wire*, January 29, 2001.

There are two ways in which securities are sold to the investment public: in open auctions and through investment bankers. Virtually all securities sold through open auctions consist of U.S. Treasury securities. A week prior to an upcoming auction, the Treasury announces the type and number of securities it will be auctioning. Treasury bills are auctioned weekly, whereas longer-term Treasury securities are auctioned once a month or once a quarter. Prospective buyers submit bids to the Treasury specifying how much they wish to purchase and the price they are willing to pay. The higher the price specified, the lower the return to the investor, and the lower the cost to the Treasury. The Treasury typically accepts about half of the bids submitted. Any investor may submit a bid to the Treasury.

The IPOs of most corporate and municipal securities are sold through financial specialists called **investment**

Once again, clients named Deutsche Bank the world's #1 investment bank

"For the second year in succession, Deutsche Bank ranks number one in Euromoney's annual survey of the world's biggest and best providers of financial services...Deutsche Bank dominates... by a wide margin."

Euromoney, January 2001

PERFORMANCE
leading to results™†

We've always believed that if our clients came first, so would we. Another reason why Deutsche Bank is leading to results.

Deutsche Bank

FIGURE 20.2
An Example of the Services Provided by Investment Bankers

bankers. Lehman Brothers and CS First Boston are examples of well-known investment banking firms. An investment banker is a financial intermediary that purchases the issue from the firm or government and then resells the issue to investors. This process is known as **underwriting.** Some of the investment bankers that underwrote the new security issue shown in Figure 20.1 are listed at the bottom of the tombstone. As a way of attracting new business, investment banking firms often advertise the number of new security issues that they have underwritten recently. The ad shown in Figure 20.2 from Deutsche Bank Alex. Brown highlights the fact that the firm has underwritten more new security issues than any other investment bank in recent years.

Investment bankers underwrite stock and bond issues at a discount, meaning that they pay the issuing firm or government less than the price the investment banker charges investors. This discount is compensation for services rendered, including the risk investment bankers incur whenever they underwrite a new security issue. Although the size of the discount is often negotiable, they usually range between 4 and 8 percent of the public offering price. The size of the underwriting discount is generally higher for stock issues than it is for bond issues.

Corporations and federal, state, and local governments are willing to pay for the services provided by investment bankers because they are financial market experts. In addition to locating buyers for the issue, the underwriter typically advises the issuer on such details as the general characteristics of the issue, its pricing, and the timing of the offering. Several investment bankers commonly participate in the underwriting process. The issuer selects a lead, or primary, investment banker, which in turn forms a syndicate consisting of other investment banking firms. Each member of the syndicate purchases a portion of the security issue, which it resells to investors. For the Exact Sciences stock issue shown in Figure 20.1, Merrill Lynch was selected as the lead underwriter. Other members of the syndicate—such as CIBC World Markets and Thomas Weisel—purchased and resold lesser amounts of the stock issue.

THE SECONDARY MARKET

Daily news reports of stock and bond trading are most likely to refer to trading in the **secondary market,** a collection of financial markets where previously issued securities are traded among investors. The corporations that originally issued the securities being traded are not directly involved in the secondary market. They neither make any payments when securities are sold nor receive any of the proceeds when securities are purchased. The NYSE and the Nasdaq stock market are both secondary markets. In terms of the dollar value of securities bought and sold, the secondary market is about four times larger than the primary market. Around $40 billion worth of stock is traded daily on the NYSE alone. The various elements of the secondary market are discussed later in the chapter.

SECURITIES

Securities can be classified into three categories: money market instruments, bonds, and stock. Money market instruments and bonds are both debt securities, and stocks are units of ownership in corporations like AOL Time Warner, Nike, and Sun Microsystems.

Money Market Instruments

Money market instruments are short-term debt securities issued by governments, financial institutions, and corporations. By definition, all short-term debt—money market instruments—matures within one year from the date of issue. Investors are paid interest by the issuer for the use of their funds. Money market instruments are generally low-risk securities and are purchased by investors when they have surplus cash. As noted in Chapter 19, financial managers often choose to invest surplus cash in money market instruments because they are low-risk and easily convertible into cash. Recently, Microsoft carried almost $10 billion in money market securities as a current asset on its balance sheet. Examples of money market instruments include U.S. Treasury bills, commercial paper, repurchase agreements, and bank certificates of deposit (CDs). Each of these securities is described in the previous chapter.

Bonds

Bondholders are creditors of a corporation. By selling bonds, a firm obtains long-term debt capital. Federal, state, and local governments also acquire funds in this way. Bonds are issued in various denominations (face values), usually between $1,000 and $25,000. Each issue indicates a rate of interest to be paid to the bondholder—stated as a percentage of the bond's face value—as well as a maturity date on which the bondholder is paid the bond's face value. Because bondholders are creditors, they have a claim on the firm's assets that must be satisfied before any claims of stockholders in the event of the firm's dissolution. In the case of the first bankruptcy of TWA, bondholders received roughly three-fourths of the face value of their bonds.

Types of Bonds

A prospective bond investor can choose among a variety of bonds. Eight major types of bonds are summarized in Figure 20.3. A secured bond is backed by a specific pledge of company assets. For example, mortgage bonds are backed by real and personal property owned by the firm, such as machinery or furniture, and collateral trust bonds are backed by stocks and bonds of other companies owned by the firm. In the event of default, bondholders may receive the proceeds from selling these assets.

Because bond purchasers want to balance their financial returns with their risks, bonds backed by pledges of specific assets are less risky than those without such collateral. Consequently, a firm can issue secured bonds at lower interest rates that it would have to pay for comparable unsecured bonds. However, many firms do issue unsecured bonds, called debentures. These bonds are backed only by the financial reputation of the issuing corporation.

Government bonds are bonds issued by the U.S. Treasury. Because government bonds are backed by the full faith and credit of the U.S. government, they are considered the least risky of all bonds. **Municipal**

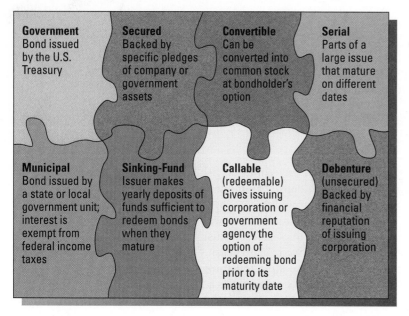

Government Bond issued by the U.S. Treasury	**Secured** Backed by specific pledges of company or government assets	**Convertible** Can be converted into common stock at bondholder's option	**Serial** Parts of a large issue that mature on different dates
Municipal Bond issued by a state or local government unit; interest is exempt from federal income taxes	**Sinking-Fund** Issuer makes yearly deposits of funds sufficient to redeem bonds when they mature	**Callable** (redeemable) Gives issuing corporation or government agency the option of redeeming bond prior to its maturity date	**Debenture** (unsecured) Backed by financial reputation of issuing corporation

FIGURE 20.3
Types of Bonds and the Significant Features of Each

bonds are bonds issued by state or local governments. There are two types of municipal bonds. A revenue bond is a bond issue whose proceeds are to be used to pay for a project that will produce revenue—such as a toll road or bridge. The Oklahoma Turnpike Authority has issued such bonds. A general obligation bond is a bond whose proceeds are to be used to pay for a project that will not produce any revenue—such as a new police station. General obligation bonds can be only sold by state governments like Arizona or local governmental units like Des Moines, Iowa, or Fairfax County, Virginia, that have the power to levy taxes. An important feature of municipal bonds is that their interest payments are exempt from federal income tax. Because of this, municipal bonds generally carry lower interest rates than either corporate or government bonds.

Quality Ratings for Bonds

Two factors determine the price of a bond: its risk and its interest rate. Bonds vary considerably in terms of risk. One tool used by bond investors to assess the riskiness of a bond is its so-called **bond rating.** Two investment firms—Standard & Poor's (S&P) and Moody's—rate corporate and municipal bonds. The bonds with the least amount of risk are assigned a rating of either AAA (S&P) or Aaa (Moody's). The ratings descend as risk increases. Table 20.1 lists the S&P and Moody's bond ratings. Bonds with ratings below BBB (S&P) or Baa (Moody's) are classified as speculative, or so-called *junk bonds.* Junk bonds attract investors by offering high interest rates in exchange for elevated risk. Today, junk bonds pay between 3 and 5 percent higher interest rates than AAA bonds.

The second factor affecting the price of a bond is its interest rate. Other things being equal, the higher the interest rate, the higher the price of a bond. However, everything else usually is not equal; the bonds may not be equally risky, or one may have a longer maturity. Investors must evaluate the trade-offs involved.

Another important influence on bond prices is the market interest rate. Because bonds pay fixed rates of interest, as market interest rates rise, bond prices fall, and vice versa. In this way, bonds paying a specified interest rate can be adjusted to current market conditions when the purchaser buys them for less—or more—than the actual denomination printed on the bond. For example, during the final year of the 20th century, interest rates rose. As they did, bond prices fell. The market price of long-term Treasury bonds fell by around 10 percent. On the other hand, as interest rates started to decline during the first two years of the 21st century, bond prices rose. Long-term Treasury bond prices rose by almost 15 percent during this period.

Retiring Bonds

Because bonds in an issue mature on a specific date, corporate borrowers such as Bed Bath & Beyond or a governmental unit like Harris County, Texas, must have the necessary funds available to repay the principal at that time. In some instances, this can create a cash flow problem. To ease the repayment problem, some borrowers issue serial bonds. A serial bond issue consists of several bonds that mature on different dates. For example, assume a corporation issues $20 million in serial bonds for a 30-year period. None of the bonds mature during the first 20 years. However,

Table 20.1	**Moody's and Standard & Poor's Bond Ratings**		
Moody's	**Interpretation**	**Standard & Poor's**	**Interpretation**
Aaa	Prime quality	AAA	Bank investment quality
Aa	High grade	AA	
A	Upper medium grade	A	
Baa	Medium grade	BBB	
		BB	
Ba	Lower medium grade or speculative	B	Speculative
B	Speculative	CCC	
		CC	
Caa	From very speculative to near or in default	C	
Ca			
C		DDD	In default (with a rating based on the issuer's relative salvage value)
		DD	
		D	

beginning in the 21st year, $2 million in bonds mature each year until all the bonds are repaid at the end of the 30 years.

A variation of the concept of serial bonds is the *sinking-fund bond*. Under a sinking fund, an issuer like Fannie Mae makes annual deposits to accumulate funds for use in redeeming the bonds when they mature. These deposits are made to the bond's trustee—usually a large bank—which is responsible for representing bondholders. The deposits must be large enough that their total, plus accrued interest, will be sufficient to redeem the bonds at maturity.

Most corporate and municipal bonds—and some government bonds—are callable. A **call provision** allows the issuer to redeem the bond prior to its maturity at a prespecified price. Not surprisingly, issuers tend to call bonds when market interest rates are declining. Assume, for example, that retailing giant Nordstrom has $50 million in bonds outstanding that pay a 9 percent annual interest rate. If interest rates decline to 7 percent, Nordstrom may decide to call the 9 percent bonds, repaying the principal from the proceeds of newly issued 7 percent bonds. Calling the 9 percent bonds and issuing 7 percent bonds would save the firm $200,000 a year in interest payments. The savings in annual interest expense should more than offset the cost of retiring the old bonds and issuing new ones.

Stock

The basic form of corporate ownership is embodied in **common stock.** Purchasers of common stock are the true owners of a corporation. They are entitled to vote on major company decisions, such as purchasing another company or electing a board of directors. In return for the money they invest, they expect to benefit from increasing stock values as the firm prospers and, in some cases, to receive payments in the form of dividends. For example, stockholders of Johnson & Johnson have recently received a 2 percent annual dividend.

Stockholders benefit from company success, and they risk the loss of their investments if the company fails. Should a firm experience financial failure, claims of creditors must be satisfied before stockholders will receive anything. Because creditors have a senior claim to assets, holders of common stock are said to have a residual claim on company assets.

Sometimes confusion arises over the difference between book value and market value. Book value is determined by subtracting the company's liabilities from its assets and then dividing this net figure by the number of shares of common stock outstanding. Recently, Capstone Turbine had a book value of around $3.50 per share.

BUSINESS DIRECTORY

➤ **common stock** *share of ownership in a company.*

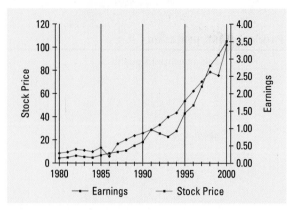

FIGURE 20.4
Relationship between Earnings and Stock Prices for Johnson & Johnson

The market value of a stock is the price at which the stock is currently selling. It is easily found by referring to the financial section of daily newspapers or on the Internet and may be more, or less, than the book value. What determines market value, however, is more complicated. Although a number of variables cause stock prices to fluctuate up and down in the short term, in the long run stock prices tend to follow a company's profits. Figure 20.4 shows the relationship between the earnings per share and stock price for Johnson & Johnson over a recent 20-year period. Notice that as the company's earnings rose, so, too, did its stock price.

Preferred Stock In addition to common stock, described earlier, a few companies also issue preferred stock—ownership shares whose holders receive preference in the payment of dividends. American Electric Power is such a firm. Also, if a company is dissolved, holders of preferred stock have prior claims on the firm's assets below those of bondholders but ahead of the claims of common stockholders. However, preferred stockholders rarely have any voting rights, and the dividend they are paid is fixed, regardless of how profitable the firm becomes. Therefore, although preferred stock is an equity position in the corporation, many investors consider it to be more like a bond than common stock.

Convertible Securities Corporations may decide to issue bonds or preferred stock containing a conversion feature. This feature gives the bondholder or preferred stockholder the right to exchange the bond or preferred stock for a fixed number of shares of common stock. For example, Starbucks Corp. has a convertible bond outstanding that its holder can exchange for 43 shares of Starbucks' common stock. The value of the conversion feature depends on the current price of Starbucks' common stock. If the company's stock price is less than $23.25 per share, the conversion feature has little value. On the other hand, if the stock price is $50 per share, the conversion feature is worth over $1,000. Convertible bonds pay lower interest rates than those lacking conversion features, helping reduce the interest expense of the issuing firms. Investors are willing to accept these lower interest rates since they value the potential for additional gains should the firm's stock price increase.

SECURITIES PURCHASERS

Two general types of investors buy securities: institutions and individuals. An **institutional investor** is an organization that invests its own funds or those it holds in trust for others. Institutional investors include insurance companies like New York Life, pension funds like Calpers, Janus mutual funds, and not-for-profit organizations such as the Nature Conservancy. Many institutional investors are huge. Pension funds, for example, have over $8 trillion in assets, and the total assets of life insurance companies currently exceed $3 trillion.[3]

Institutional investors buy and sell large quantities of securities, often in blocks of 10,000 or more shares per transaction. Such block trading represents well over half of the total daily volume on major securities exchanges, and institutional investors account for around two-thirds of all trading volume. The number of investors who own shares through mutual funds or their employer's retirement plans is steadily rising, and the firms that manage their funds now control more than half of all U.S. equities.

Institutional investors have become the most important force in today's securities markets. In fact, mutual funds such as T. Rowe Price and Vanguard now provide most of the new money that goes into stocks. Despite the importance of institutional investors, however, individual investors still play a vital role. Well over half of all

Table 20.2	Primary Investment Objectives by Type of Security		
	Type of Security		
Investment Objective	**Money Market Instruments**	**Bonds**	**Common Stock**
Potential growth in capital	None	Little or none	Highest
Stability of principal	Highest	Good	Lowest
Liquidity	Highest	Good	Lowest
Current income	Variable	Highest	Good
Growth in income	Variable	Lowest	Highest

Americans now own stocks, either directly or by investing in stock mutual funds. By contrast, 30 years ago, less than one-third of American households owned any stocks at all.[4]

Investment Motivations

Why do individuals and institutions invest? What are their motivations for investing? In general, individuals and institutions have five primary motivations for investing: growth in capital, stability of principal, liquidity, current income, and income growth. All investors must rank each motivation in terms of importance; all investments involve trade-offs. For example, an investment that has the potential for substantial growth in capital may provide no current income. By contrast, an investment that has very stable principal may have little potential for capital growth. The bottom line is this: some investments are more appropriate for certain investors than for others. Table 20.2 provides a useful guide for evaluating money market instruments, bonds, and stocks.

Growth in Capital   When it comes to potential growth in capital over time, especially over long periods of time, common stocks are the clear winner. For example, $1,000 invested in common stocks over a recent 25-year period would have grown to over $217,000. A similar investment in bonds, made during the same period, would have grown to only a little over $90,000. This is not to imply, however, that the prices of all common stocks go up all the time, nor do they go up by the same amount. There is considerable variation in the performance of stocks. For instance, the market value of Home Depot's common stock increased tenfold during the past decade. By contrast, during the same period, General Motors' stock price grew slightly less than 50 percent.

Stability of Principal   Treasury bills and other money market instruments are the clear winners when it comes to stability of principal. The odds that the price of a money market investment will fall below the price the investor originally paid are virtually zero. Further, when an investor buys a Treasury bill or other money market instrument, he or she can be pretty sure the original investment will be returned. With stocks, there is no such guarantee.

Liquidity   Because the prices of stocks—and, to a lesser extent, bonds—can vary widely, investors cannot count on making profits whenever they decide or need to sell. Liquidity is a measure of the speed at which assets can be converted into cash. Since money market instruments such as a CD issued by Washington Mutual Savings Bank have short maturities and stable prices, they offer investors the highest amount of liquidity.

Current Income   Historically bonds have provided the highest current income of any security. Interest rates

BUSINESS DIRECTORY

➤ **preferred stock**   *stock whose holders receive preference in the payment of dividends.*

---

on bonds are usually higher than money market interest rates or the dividends paid on common stocks. For instance, Fannie Mae issued an 8 percent bond at the same time it was paying a common stock dividend of only around 2 percent. Further, money market interest rates experience up and down swings in response to economic conditions, while the interest rate on a bond remains constant. Investors who seek high current income should invest a large portion of their funds in bonds.

Growth in Income   When you buy a bond, the interest you receive is fixed for the life of the bond. Interest rates on money market instruments can increase over time—but can decrease as well. In contrast, common stock dividends have historically risen at a rate that exceeds that of inflation. Over the past 20 years, for instance, Johnson & Johnson's common stock dividend has risen at an average annual rate of around 14 percent. There is, however, no guarantee that a company's common stock dividend will *always* increase. AT&T, for example, recently cut its common stock dividend for the first time in the company's history.

Taxes and Investing

Interest received from government and corporate bonds is considered ordinary income and is taxed at the investor's marginal tax rate. The same rule applies to dividends received from common and preferred stock investments. Further, investors who sell securities they have owned for over a year at a profit pay capital gains taxes on the difference between the purchase price and the selling price. For individual investors, capital gains are taxed at a lower rate than ordinary income, gains on stocks held for less than one year, as well as interest and dividend income.

Taxes can influence investment decisions in a number of ways. For example, investors with high marginal tax rates may wish to avoid stocks that pay high dividends in favor of those paying little or no dividends but offering more potential for price appreciation. Investors may also elect not to sell securities at the end of the year to delay paying capital gains taxes for that year.

SECURITIES EXCHANGES

Securities exchanges are centralized marketplaces where stocks and bonds are traded. Most of the largest and best known securities exchanges are commonly called **stock exchanges,** or *stock markets,* since the vast majority of securities traded are common stock issues. Stock exchanges are secondary markets. The securities have already been issued by firms, which received the proceeds from the issue when it was sold in the primary market. Sales in a securities exchange occur between individual and institutional investors.

The New York Stock Exchange

The New York Stock Exchange—sometimes referred to as the *Big Board*—is the largest, and probably most famous, stock market in the world. It is also one of the oldest, having been founded in 1792. Today, more than 2,600 common and preferred stock issues are traded on the NYSE. These stocks represent most of the largest, best-known companies in the U.S. with a total market value in excess of $5 trillion. In order for a company's stock to be traded on the NYSE, the firm must apply to the exchange for listing. Corporate bonds are also traded on the NYSE, but bond trading makes up less than one percent of the total value of securities traded there during a typical year.

Trading on the NYSE takes place face-to-face on a trading floor. Buy and sell orders are transmitted to one of 42 posts—each stock is assigned a post—on the floor of the exchange. Buyers and sellers then bid against one another in an open auction. Only investment firms that are members of the NYSE are allowed to trade, meaning the firm owns at least one of 1,366 "seats." Seats are occasionally bought and sold. Currently, the asking price for a NYSE seat is around $1.3 million.[5]

Each NYSE stock is assigned to one of 42 specialist firms. Specialists are unique investment firms that are responsible for maintaining an orderly and liquid market in the stocks assigned to them. Specialists must be willing to buy when there are no other buyers and sell when there are no other sellers. Specialists also act as auctioneers and catalysts, bringing buyers and sellers together.

A number of observers portray the NYSE and its trading practices as old-fashioned, especially in this technological age. Even though the NYSE still retains a trading floor, the exchange has become highly automated in recent years. Its computer systems automatically match and route most orders, which are typically filled in less than one minute. In recent years, the NYSE has also moved aggressively to attract more firms and showcase its technological advances.

The Nasdaq Stock Market

The second largest stock market in the U.S. is the Nasdaq Stock Market. It is a very different market than the NYSE. Nasdaq—which stands for National Association of Securities Dealers Automated Quotation System—is actually a computerized communications network that links member investment firms. All trading on Nasdaq takes place through its network, rather than on a trading floor. Buy and sell orders are entered into the network and executed electronically. All Nasdaq-listed stocks

BUSINESS DIRECTORY

➤ **stock exchange** *centralized marketplace where primarily common stocks are traded.*

have two or more market makers—investment firms that perform essentially the same functions as NYSE specialists.

Almost 5,000 stock issues trade on the Nasdaq Stock Market. Compared with firms listed on the NYSE, Nasdaq-listed corporations tend to be smaller, less-well-known firms. Some are relatively new businesses and cannot currently meet NYSE listing requirements. It is not uncommon for firms eventually to move the trading of their stocks from Nasdaq to the NYSE. Some notable examples in recent years include Gateway Computer and Qwest Communications. However, there are dozens of companies currently trading on Nasdaq—including Amgen, Cisco Systems, Dell Computer, Intel, and Microsoft—that would easily meet NYSE listing requirements. For a variety of reasons, these firms have decided to stay on Nasdaq for the time being.

Other U.S. Securities Markets

In addition the NYSE and Nasdaq Stock Market, there are several other U.S. securities exchanges currently operating. The American Stock Exchange, or AMEX, is also located in New York. It focuses on the stocks of smaller firms as well as other financial instruments (such as options). In comparison with the NYSE and Nasdaq, the AMEX is tiny. Daily trading volume is only around 25 million shares compared with 1 billion-plus shares on each of the two larger exchanges.

Several regional stock exchanges also operate throughout the U.S. These include the Chicago, Pacific (San Francisco), Boston, Cincinnati, and Philadelphia exchanges. Originally established to trade the shares of small, regional companies, the regional exchanges now list securities of many large corporations as well. In fact, over half of the companies listed on the NYSE are also listed on one or more regional exchanges. The largest regional exchange, the Chicago, handles around 10 percent of all trades in NYSE-listed stocks.[6]

Foreign Stock Exchanges

Securities exchanges exist throughout the world. Virtually all developed, and many developing, countries have stock exchanges. Examples include Bombay, Helsinki, Hong Kong, Mexico City, and Toronto. The collapse of communism in Central Europe has led to the emergence or reemergence of stock markets in many former Warsaw-Pact countries. In Poland, for example, the Warsaw stock exchange reopened recently—after being closed more than 50 years—in the same building that once housed the central committee of the Polish communist party.

The largest stock exchange outside the U.S. is the London Stock Exchange. Founded in the early 17th century, the London Stock Exchange lists approximately 2,900 stock and bond issues, more than 500 of which are shares of companies located outside the United Kingdom and Ireland. Trading on the London Stock Exchange takes place using a Nasdaq-type computerized communications network.

The London Stock Exchange is very much an international market. Around two-thirds of all cross-border trading (for example, the trading of stocks of U.S. companies outside the United States) takes place in London. It is not uncommon for institutional investors in the U.S. to trade NYSE- or Nasdaq-listed stocks in London. These investors claim they often get better prices and faster order execution in London than they do in the United States.

The Fourth Market and Electronic Communication Networks

For years a so-called fourth market has existed: the direct trading of exchange-listed stocks off the floor of the NYSE, or outside the network, in the case of Nasdaq-listed stocks. Trading in the fourth market has traditionally been limited to institutional investors buying or selling large blocks of stock.

Recently, the fourth market has begun to open up to smaller, individual investors. As the opening vignette of this chapter describes, ECNs (electronic communications networks), such as Island.com and Instinet, have become quite visible in recent years. ECNs are part of the fourth market. Buyers and sellers meet in a virtual stock market where they trade directly with one another. No specialist or market maker is involved.

BUYING AND SELLING SECURITIES

Unless investors are members of one of the stock exchanges, they must use the services of a brokerage firm that is a member of one or more stock exchanges. A **brokerage firm** is a financial intermediary that buys and sells securities for individual and institutional investors. Examples include A.G. Edwards, Morgan Stanley, Prudential, Quick and Reilly, and Solomon Smith Barney. Choosing a brokerage firm, and a specific stockbroker, is one of the most important decisions investors make.

Placing an Order

An investor who wants to purchase shares of a stock would typically initiate the transaction by contacting his or her brokerage firm. The firm would transmit the order to the appropriate market, complete the transaction, and confirm the transaction with the investor, all within a few minutes.

An investor's request to buy or sell stock at the current market price is called a market order. A **market order** instructs a brokerage firm like Paine Webber to obtain the highest price—if the investor is selling—or the lowest price—if the investor is buying—possible. By contrast, a **limit order** instructs the brokerage firm not to pay more than a specified price for a stock if the investor is buying, or not to accept less than a specified price if the investor is selling. If Paine Webber is unable to fill a limit order immediately, it is left with either a NYSE specialist or Nasdaq market maker. If the price reaches the specified amount, the order is carried out. Limit orders are often recommended during periods of extreme price volatility.

Stock trading is normally conducted in quantities of 100 shares, called round lots. Investors can buy or sell fewer than 100 shares, called odd lots, though these trades involve a surcharge and may take a little longer to carry out.

Costs of Trading

When investors buy or sell securities through a brokerage firm, they pay a fee for the related services. Today, these costs vary widely among brokerage firms. A trade that costs less than $20 using E*Trade might cost more than $50 when handled by Merrill Lynch. Often the cost depends on what type of brokerage firm the investor uses. A full-service firm—such as Merrill Lynch or A.G. Edwards—provides a large number of services, offers considerable investment advice, and charges higher fees. Account executives at full-service firms make recommendations and provide general advice to investors.

The bigger the crowd, the better the performance.

You're a major player in the securities markets worldwide, so when it comes to trading, you know what you need. Liquidity.

A world of buyers and sellers — ready to trade. And when you're trading electronically, you know the place to come for global liquidity. Instinet.

We give you electronic access to some of the broadest, deepest — most liquid — trading opportunities around the world.

What's more, we don't have our own portfolio so we never compete with your trades or take a position against you.

Our only goal is to help you get the fastest trade at the best price — and we handle the follow-up automatically.

All of which can add up to better performance.

If that's what you're looking for, by all means call toll free 1-877-INSTINET or visit www.instinet.com

Instinet
A REUTERS Company

Nothing comes between you and the best price.

> Instinet is one of the leaders in the growing ECN market that is open during hours that extend beyond the trading day of the traditional securities exchanges. Instinet allows securities purchasers and sellers to trade directly with one another with no intermediaries. As the Instinet slogan puts it, "Nothing comes between you and the best price."

THEY SAID IT

"Spend at least as much time researching a stock as you would choosing a refrigerator."

PETER LYNCH (B.1944)
AMERICAN INVESTMENT GURU AND
VICE CHAIRMAN, FIDELITY
MANAGEMENT

BUSINESS DIRECTORY

➤ **brokerage firm**   *financial intermediary who buys and sells securities for individual and institutional investors.*

Sarah Ferguson
Schwab Investor

SARAH FERGUSON would be the first to tell you
that financial security doesn't have to be a fairytale.
It's about knowing. And planning.
And making smart decisions.
Charles Schwab Stock Explorer.™
It's an approach that helps you carefully screen stocks.
For potential investment ideas. Online or off.
The featured strategies can be used
as a starting point to select stocks.
So you can explore the potential of your portfolio.
And start planning for your own happily ever after.
To sample the new Stock Explorer, visit schwab.com
and click on 'welcome' or call 1-800-745-2670.

stock explorer

call
1-800-745-2670

click
www.schwab.com
welcome ▶

visit
384 locations nationwide

CharlesSchwab
creating a world of smarter investors™

FIGURE 20.5
Investment Services Provided by
Discount Broker Charles Schwab

By contrast, a discount firm—such as Charles Schwab or National Discount Brokers—charges lower fees but offers less advice and fewer services. However, even discount firms provide research tools to customers to help them make better decisions. The ad in Figure 20.5 highlights one of the investment tools Charles Schwab offers its customers. All investors need to weigh the appropriate trade-off between cost, advice, and services when choosing a brokerage firm.

Online brokerage firms—such as Ameritrade and Datek Online—charge some of the lowest fees of all brokerage firms. Investors enter buy and sell orders on their computers or personal digital assistants. Most online firms also give customers access to a wide range of investment information, though they do not directly provide advice to investors. Over 1 of every 10 stock trades are conducted online today. In response to this growth, most discount and full-service brokerage firms have begun offering online trading services. The "Clicks and Mortar" box describes Merrill Lynch's move into online trading.

Direct Investing

A growing number of corporations—including Walt Disney, Exxon Mobil, Hewlett-Packard, and Ford—offer investors a direct way of purchasing stock. Hundreds of dividend reinvestment plans (DRIPs) are available today. When an investor enrolls in a DRIP, the company uses the dividends paid on shares owned by the investor to buy additional shares of the company's stock. The investor ends up with more shares while avoiding brokerage fees. Another form of direct investing is the stock purchase program. Over 100 companies allow first-time investors to buy shares directly from the company, again avoiding brokerage fees. Firms like direct investing programs because it gives them another source of long-term capital.

Companies offering direct investment programs charge one-time enrollment fees and perhaps a small fee on individual transactions. Most firms set a minimum purchase requirement starting as low as $50. To buy a stock directly, investors simply call the company and ask for an enrollment form. Information on direct investing is also available on most company Web sites. The Netstock Direct Web site (www.netstockdirect.com) lists firms offering direct investing and information on minimum purchase requirements and fees.

Reading the Financial News

At least four or five pages of most daily newspapers are devoted to reporting current financial news. This information is also available on countless Web sites. Much of the financial news coverage focuses on the previous day's securities transactions. Stocks and bonds traded on the various securities markets are listed alphabetically in the newspaper, with separate sections for each of the major markets. Information is provided on the volume of sales and the price of each security.

The U.S. stock markets have abandoned the traditional practice of quoting stock prices in fractions. In other words, a trade price 38⅛ translated into $38.125 per share—a practice the NYSE had used since its founding in 1792. Today, all major

Background. Online trading has been around for many years, but it really took off during the final months of the 20th century. Faster computers, improved communication technology, and the emergence of well-financed online brokerage firms like Ameritrade and E*Trade all contributed to the growth in online trading. By the beginning of the 21st century, online brokers were handling around 10 percent of all trades. Customers flocked to online brokers because of the speed and convenience of trading online, as well as the startling savings for transactions handled by online brokerage firms compared with fees at most brick-and-mortar brokerage firms.

What Happened? At first, brick-and-mortar brokerage firms dismissed online trading as a fad. Only computer geeks would invest online, they thought. The vast majority of investors would still want to trade using the services of a real broker, not a virtual one. However, as online trading volume rose, attitudes at some of the brick-and-mortar firms began to shift about online trading. The discount brokerage houses, such as Charles Schwab and Fidelity Investments, were among the first brick-and-mortar firms to launch ambitious online investing services. Full-service firms, including Merrill Lynch, the world's largest brokerage firm, hesitated. But after watching online competitors add investor accounts, the full-service firms decided that online trading wasn't merely a passing fad and that they had to get into the online game. For Merrill Lynch's executives, the final straw was apparently this: during the first nine months of 1999, Charles Schwab brought in over $73 billion in new investor money, most of which was from new online accounts, or almost three times as much as Merrill Lynch brought in during the same period.

The Response. Merrill Lynch chief executive officer David Komansky issued an edict: the firm would offer online services. The dilemma for the brokerage giant was how to offer investors the speed, convenience, and lower fees to compete with online brokers, while preserving the company's full-service approach to investing. Merrill Lynch had to do more than execute trades for customers; it had to continue to provide the advice and expertise investors had come to expect. This was especially important to the company's almost 16,000 brokers (called account executives), who earn most of their income from commissions and are expected to establish long-term relationships with clients. In response, Merrill Lynch rolled out its Unlimited Advantage account.

Unlimited Advantage gives investors unlimited online trades, along with advice and other services, for a flat annual fee (1 percent of assets, with a $1,500 minimum). Customers can even get personalized financial plans from Merrill Lynch account executives. In essence, Unlimited Advantage was designed to offer the best of both online and full-service accounts. A few months later, Merrill Lynch unveiled ML Direct. Customers pay $29.95 per trade, and although they can obtain free research from Merrill Lynch, they can't consult a broker for recommendations or an investment plan.

Today and Counting. So far the record for Merrill Lynch's move into online trading could best be described as somewhat mixed. ML Direct has been slow to catch on, partly because at $29.95 per trade it is still more expensive than essentially the same service at most other online brokerage firms. On the other hand, Unlimited Advantage appears to be a qualified success. It has attracted around $85 billion from investors, but over 60 percent of that money has come from other Merrill Lynch accounts. Nevertheless, many believe that ML Direct and Unlimited Advantage have helped stem the erosion of Merrill Lynch's market share, while also attracting a significant number of new customers. Around 40 percent of the money flowing into Unlimited Advantage accounts is from new clients, up from less than 20 percent when the service was first launched.

QUESTIONS FOR CRITICAL THINKING

1. From an investor's perspective, what are the advantages and disadvantages of an Unlimited Advantage account compared with a traditional brokerage account?
2. Some believe that full-service firms, such as Merrill Lynch, are poised to dominate the next phase of the online brokerage business because of the services they can offer. Do you agree or disagree with this comment?

Sources: Merrill Lynch Web site (**www.ml.com**), accessed on April 27, 2001; Geoffrey Smith, "On the Web—but with a Broker on Standby," *Business Week,* May 22, 2000, pp. 150–152; Charles Gasparino, "Heard on the Street: Merrill's Online Trading Plan Lures Big Bucks, But Most of the Inflow is from Its Own Clients," *The Wall Street Journal,* January 25, 2000, p. C4.

stock markets throughout the world quote prices in decimals. In the U.S., this means that stock prices are now quoted in dollars and cents per share.

Stock Quotations

To understand how to read the stock tables found in newspapers, you need to understand how to interpret the symbols in the various columns. As Figure 20.6 explains, the symbol in Column 1 is the 52-week indicator. An arrow pointing up means that a stock hit its 52-week high during the day, and an arrow pointing down means that a stock hit its 52-week low. Column 2 gives the stock's highest and lowest trading prices during the past 52 weeks. Column 3 contains the abbreviation for

1	2		3		4	5	6	7	8		9	10
	52-Weeks High	52-Weeks Low	Stock	Sym	Div	Yld %	PE	Vol. (100s)	High	Low	Close	Net Chg
↑	50^{70}	29^{45}	AAAComp	AAC	1.00	2.00	20	15800	50^{70}	49^{50}	50^{00}	$+\ ^{50}$
	30^{00}	14^{00}	AAElec	AAE		...	26	510	22^{00}	19^{45}	21^{06}	-1^{34}
↓	78^{23}	65^{00}	AaronInc.	AAI	.25	.38	17	890	66^{56}	65^{00}	65^{00}	-1^{78}
	51^{55}	48^{00}	AaronInc. pf.		3.50	7.00	...	54	50^{10}	49^{75}	50^{00}	$+\ ^{05}$

1. **52-Week Indicators:** ↑ = Hit 52-week high during the day. ↓ = Hit 52-week low.
2. **52-Week High/Low:** Highest and lowest per share trading prices in the past 52 weeks, adjusted for splits (dollars and cents—$78.^{23}$ means $78.23 per share).
3. **Stock, Symbol, and Footnotes:** The company's name abbreviated. A capital letter usually means a new word. AAAComp, for example, is AAA Computer. The stock ticker symbol is expressed in capital letters. For AAA Computer, it is AAC. Stock footnotes include the following: **n**—new issue, **pf**—preferred stock, **rt**—rights, **s**—stock split within the past 52 weeks, **wi**—when issued, **wt**—warrant, **x**—ex-dividend.
4. **Dividends:** Dividends are usually annual payments based on the most recent quarterly declaration. AAA Computer, for instance, declared a dividend of $0.25 per share in the most recent quarter.
5. **Yield:** Percentage return from a dividend based on the stock's closing price.
6. **PE:** Price-to-earnings ratio, calculated by taking the last closing price of the stock and dividing it by the earnings per share for the past fiscal year.
7. **Volume:** Trading volume in 100-share lots. A listing of 510 means that 51,000 traded during the day. A number preceded by a "z" is the actual number of shares traded.
8. **High/Low:** The high and low for the day (dollars and cents).
9. **Close:** Closing price (dollars and cents).
10. **Net Chg:** Change in price from the close of the previous trading day.

FIGURE 20.6
How to Read Stock Quote Tables

the company's name, footnotes that provide information about the stock (pf, for instance, refers to preferred stock), and the stock's ticker symbol. Column 4 lists the dividend, usually an annual payment based on the last quarterly declaration. Column 5 presents the yield, the annual dividend divided by the stock's closing price.

Column 6 lists the stock's **price-earnings (P/E) ratio,** the current market price divided by the annual earnings per share. The stock's trading volume in 100 share lots is in Column 7, and its highest and lowest prices for the day appear in Column 8. Column 9 gives the closing price for the day, and Column 10 summarizes the stock's net change in price from the close of the previous trading day.

THEY SAID IT

"The P/E ratio doesn't mean anything when there is no E."

RAYMOND ROSE (B.1946)
CHAIRMAN, OLIVER ROSE SECURITIES

Bond Quotations

To learn how to read corporate bond quotations, pick a bond listed in Figure 20.7 and examine the adjacent columns of information. Most corporate bonds are issued in denominations of $1,000; thus, bond prices must be read a little differently from stock prices. The closing price of the first AAA bond reads $104\frac{3}{4}$, but this does not mean $104.75. Because bond prices are quoted as a percentage of the $1,000 price stated on the face of the bond, the $104\frac{3}{4}$ means $1,047.50.

The notation following the bond name—such as 6.5s10 in the case of AB Gas and Electric—indicates the annual interest rate stated on the bond certificate, 6.5 percent, and the maturity date of 2010. The *s* means that the bonds pays half of its annual interest every six months so the investor would receive $32.50 every six months. The current yield for the AB Gas and Electric bond is 6.6 percent, slightly more than the 6.5 percent interest rate because the bond is selling for slightly less than $1,000. The price of a bond rises and falls to keep the current yield in line with market interest rates. The cv notation means that the bond is convertible.

FIGURE 20.7
How to Read Bond Quote Tables

1. **Bond:** Abbreviation of company name.
2. **Annual Interest Rate:** Annual percentage rate of interest specified on the bond certificate.
3. **Maturity Date:** Year in which the bond matures and the issuer repays the face value of each bond.
4. **Current Yield:** Annual interest payment divided by current price; **cv** means a convertible bond.
5. **Volume:** Number of bonds traded during the day.

			Cur Yld	Vol	Close	Net Chg
①	②	③	④	⑤	⑥	⑦
Bonds						
AAA 9s20			7.8	15	104 3/4	−1 1/8
ABGasElec 6.5s10			6.6	10	98 1/2	+3/4
AlbertoPharm 5s15			cv	20	109 1/2	+1/2

6. **Close:** Closing price.
7. **Net Change:** Change in the price from the close of the previous trading day.

The next column indicates the total trading volume for the day. The volume of 20 listed for the AAA bond means that $20,000 worth of bonds were traded. The closing bond price is listed next, followed by the change in price since the previous day's closing price.

STOCK INDEXES

A feature of most daily financial news media is the report of current stock indexes or averages. The most familiar is the Dow Jones Average (or *Dow*). Two other widely reported indexes on U.S. stocks are the S&P 500 and Nasdaq Composite indexes. In addition, there are numerous indexes on foreign stocks, including the DAX (Germany); the FT-100, or "Footsie" (London); and the Nikkei (Tokyo). All of these indexes have been developed to reflect the general activity of the stock market.

Although there are several Dow Jones indexes, the most widely followed is the so-called Dow Jones Industrial Average, consisting of 30 stocks of large, well-known companies. The S&P 500 is made up of 500 stocks, including industrial, financial, utility, and transportation stocks, and is considered to be a broader measure of overall stock market activity than the Dow. The Nasdaq Composite is an index made up of all the 5,000-plus stocks that trade on the Nasdaq Stock Market. Because technology companies—such as Cisco, Intel, and Oracle—make up a substantial portion of the Nasdaq Stock Market, the Nasdaq Composite is considered to be a bellwether of the "tech" sector of the economy.

The Dow Jones Industrial Average has served as a general measure of changes in overall stock prices and a reflection of the U.S. economy since it was developed by Charles Dow, the original editor of *The Wall Street Journal,* in 1884. The term *industrial* is somewhat of a misnomer today, because the index now combines industrial corporations such as Alcoa, General Motors, and United Technologies with such nonindustrial firms as American Express, Citigroup, and Walt Disney.

Periodic changes in the Dow reflect changes in the U.S. economy. In fact, General Electric is the only original member of the Dow that remains in the index today. Recent changes have involved adding Home Depot, Intel, Microsoft, and SBC Communications to the Dow and dropping Chevron, Goodyear, Sears, and Union Carbide. These changes were made to increase the representation of firms in communications, specialized retailing, and technology industries so that the index better reflects the overall stock market and U.S. economy.[7]

FIGURE 20.8
Mutual Funds—Active Participants in Firms in Which They Invest

MUTUAL FUNDS

Instead of purchasing relatively small numbers of shares in a few corporatons and hoping for price increases, many investors choose to diversify their holdings by investing in **mutual funds,** financial institutions that pool money from purchasers of their shares and use it to acquire diversified portfolios of securities consistent with their investment objectives. Investors who buy shares of a mutual fund become part owners of a large number of securities, thereby lessening their individual risk. Mutual funds also allow investors to purchase part of a diversified portfolio of securities for a relatively small investment—$250 to $3,000 in most cases. Mutual funds are managed by experienced investment professionals whose careers are based on success in analyzing the securities markets and choosing the right mix of securities for their funds. Mutual fund ads often stress performance or highlight the fund's investment philosophy. The ad shown in Figure 20.8 highlights the investment approach taken by Franklin Templeton mutual funds. Most mutual funds are part of mutual families, a number of different funds with different objectives—such as growth, income, global, and technology orientation—but sponsored by the same organization. The largest mutual fund families in the U.S. include Dreyfus, Fidelity, Janus, T. Rowe Price, and Vanguard.

Mutual funds have become extremely popular in recent years. Today their assets exceed $7 trillion. The number of Americans owning mutual fund shares has increased from less than 5 million in 1980 to over 50 million today. Mutual funds are not limited to the United States either. Mutual funds currently operating outside the U.S. have over $12 billion in assets.

Today's mutual fund investors choose among more than 8,000 U.S.-based mutual funds. Some limit their investments to stocks, some invest only in bonds, and still others invest in money market instruments. The approximate breakdown of mutual fund assets by stock, bond, and money market funds is shown in Figure 20.9. Most funds pursue more specific goals within these broad categories. Some stock funds concentrate on small companies, while others concentrate more on the shares of larger firms. Some bond funds limit their investments to municipal bonds, while other bond funds invest in only junk corporate bonds.

A number of mutual funds have been developed for investors who want their religious or personal philosophies reflected in the management of the fund. Socially responsible funds, for example, limit their investments to companies that have good records in areas such as employee relations, community involvement, environmental awareness, and the treatment of women and minorities. The "Business Hits and Misses" box discusses the pros and cons of socially responsible investing.

Reading mutual fund tables is a relatively simple task. The first two columns in Figure 20.10 list the organization issuing and managing the fund, the different types of funds offered for investors, and footnotes. The "NAV" column lists the fund's net asset value (the market value of fund assets divided by the number of outstanding shares)—the price at which investors can buy shares if the fund is a no-load fund. Purchasers of shares of load funds pay a fee called a *load charge* on top of the NAV.

The "Net Change" column shows gains or losses in the NAV from the previous day's close. The figures in the last column, the "Year-to-Date Percentage Return," indicate each fund's total return from the beginning of the year.

LEGAL AND ETHICAL ISSUES IN SECURITIES TRADING

As the number of Americans owning securities has increased, so too have concerns about illegal and unethical trading practices. Examples of unethical trading practices include brokers urging investors to buy high-risk investments and "churning" accounts (excessive trading) just to generate higher commissions. Examples of illegal trading practices include broker theft from a client's portfolio and giving false or misleading information to investors. Even Internet chat rooms have come under increased scrutiny. The Internet is full of investment-oriented chat rooms where participants discuss various investment topics daily. Recently, the Securities and Exchange Commission (SEC) settled a case against Jonathan Lebed, a 15-year-old high school student. The SEC accused Lebed of stock market fraud because he had used his computer to hype stocks he had just bought. Using "multiple fictitious names," the SEC alleged, Lebed posted hundreds of messages on electronic bulletin boards recommending his stocks. When the prices of the stocks jumped, he quickly sold his shares. In the process, he earned profits of over $250,000.[8]

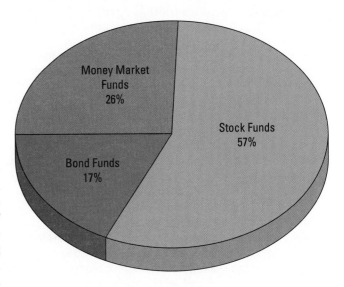

FIGURE 20.9
Breakdown of Mutual Fund Assets by Type

Government Regulation of the Securities Markets

Regulation of U.S. securities markets is primarily a function of the federal government, though states also regulate the securities markets. Federal regulation grew out of various trading abuses during the 1920s. During the Great Depression, in an attempt to restore confidence and stability in the financial markets after the 1929 stock market crash, Congress passed a series of landmark legislative acts that have formed the basis of federal securities regulation ever since.

As noted earlier, the SEC, created in 1934, is the principal U.S. federal regulatory overseer of the securities markets. The SEC's mission is to administer securities laws and protect investors in public securities transactions. The SEC is a quasijudicial agency with broad enforcement power. It has the power to take civil action against individuals and corporations. Actions requiring criminal proceedings are referred to the U.S. Department of Justice.

The SEC requires that virtually all new public issues of corporate securities be registered. Before offering securities for sale, an issuer must file a registration statement with the SEC. As part of the registration process for a new security issue, the issuer must prepare a **prospectus**. The typical prospectus gives a detailed description of the company issuing the securities, including financial data, products, research and development projects, and pending litigation. It also describes the stock or bond issue and underwriting agreement in detail. The registration process is intended to guarantee **full and fair disclosure.** The SEC does not rule on the investment merits of a registered security. It is concerned only that an issuer gives investors enough information to make their own informed decisions.

Besides primary market registration requirements, SEC regulation extends to the secondary markets as well, keeping tabs on trading activity to make sure it is fair to all participants. Every securities exchange, including Nasdaq, must, by law, follow a set of trading

BUSINESS DIRECTORY

➤ **mutual fund** *financial institution that pools investment money from purchasers of its shares and uses it to acquire diversified portfolios of securities consistent with its investment objectives.*

➤ **full and fair disclosure** *regulatory philosophy that investors should be told all relevant information so they can make informed decisions.*

For many years, John Rempel had a problem when it came to investing. The Mennonite minister struggled to find investments that didn't conflict with his religious beliefs. Once he discovered a company whose stock he owned had close business ties with a South American dictator. When Rempel questioned his broker about the company, the broker replied, "You can't be in stocks if you're going to ask moral questions." Rempel was grateful, therefore, when he discovered a family of mutual funds designed by Mennonites specifically for Mennonites. These funds avoided owning stocks of firms such as casino operators, tobacco companies, and military contractors. Mennonites aren't the only religious group to have funds specifically designed for them. There are funds for, among others, Catholics, conservative Christians, Lutherans, and Muslims. All attempt to follow investment philosophies that don't conflict with their religious teachings. Some Muslim funds, for example, do not invest in banks because banks charge interest, and that is contrary to Islamic teachings.

These types of mutual funds are part of what is often called socially responsible investing. Socially responsible investing has been around for a long time and isn't limited to faith-based mutual funds. There are funds designed to appeal to supporters of animal rights, environmentalists, and labor-rights activists, to name just a few. The Humane Equity Fund, for example, avoids companies that conduct animal testing, use animals as an end product (such as meat packers), or make products adverse to the humane treatment of animals.

Other socially responsible funds take a broader approach. The Domini Social Equity Fund, for instance, invests in the 400 companies that make up the Domini Social Equity Index. The companies selected have positive records in community involvement, environmental issues, employee relations, and hiring practices. Companies that generate significant revenues from alcohol, tobacco, gambling, and military weapons are excluded. Social goals are important, but so are financial ones. Domini argues that socially responsible companies make the best investments in the long run.

In recent years, socially responsible mutual funds have grown in terms of size, number, and diversity. The number of funds that screen stocks based on some set of social or religious criteria has more than doubled in the past five years, and their net assets have almost tripled. Three of the largest socially responsible funds—Domini, Dreyfus Third Century, and Pax World Fund—each have over $1 billion in assets. The nation's second-largest mutual fund family—Vanguard Group—has also launched a socially responsible fund.

So, as interest in socially responsible investing continues to grow, the question becomes this: Does socially responsible investing come at the cost of poorer performance? The performance track record of socially responsible funds is mixed. For example, the Timothy Plan Small Cap Value fund—a fund designed to cater to conservative Christians—has ranked near the bottom of its category for several years. On the other hand, both the Dreyfus Third Century fund and the Domini Social Equity fund rank toward the top of their respective categories. The Domini Social Equity fund has actually outperformed the overall stock market in recent years.

QUESTIONS FOR CRITICAL THINKING

1. Do you agree with the concept of socially responsible investing? Why or why not? If so, what social goals are most important to you personally?
2. Some argue that socially responsible investing violates the important investment principal of diversification (spreading your investment dollars among many different investments). Do you agree?

Sources: Danny Hakim, "Rising Numbers of Investors Make Social Goals a Priority," *New York Times*, February 10, 2001, downloaded from **www.nytimes.com**; Jeanne Sahadi, "Sniffing for a Pet-Friendly Fund," CNNfn, downloaded from **www.cnnfn.com** on February 12, 2001; Martine Costello, "A Fund for Earth Lovers," CNNfn, downloaded from **www.cnnfn.com**, on February 12, 2001.

rules that have been approved by the SEC. In response to the 1987 market break, Congress passed the Market Reform Act of 1990, giving the SEC emergency authority to halt trading and restrict practices such as program trading (the controversial practice in which computer systems are programmed to buy or sell securities if certain conditions arise) during periods of extreme volatility.

One area to which the SEC pays particular attention is insider trading. Insider trading is defined as the use of material nonpublic information about a company to make investment profits. Examples of material nonpublic information include a pending merger or a major oil discovery. The SEC's definition of insider trading goes beyond corporate insiders—people such as the company's officers and directors. It also includes lawyers, accountants, investment bankers, and even reporters—anyone who uses nonpublic information to profit in the stock market at the expense of ordinary investors.

Recently, the SEC instituted a new regulation, called Regulation FD, that requires that firms share information with all investors at the same time. Regulation FD is designed to prohibit selective disclosure of information by companies to favored investment firms. Clients of these firms often received the information sooner than

FIGURE 20.10
How to Read Mutual Fund Tables

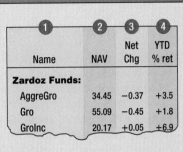

	①		②	③	④
				Net	YTD
	Name		NAV	Chg	% ret
Zardoz Funds:					
	AggreGro		34.45	−0.37	+3.5
	Gro		55.09	−0.45	+1.8
	GroInc		20.17	+0.05	+6.9

① **Issuer:** Financial organization issuing and managing the mutual fund. Under the Zardoz family of funds are the different funds developed for investors with different objectives.

② **NAV:** Net asset value. Market value of fund's assets divided by the number of outstanding shares. Also the purchase price for no-load funds. (Load funds assess a sales charge on top of the NAV.)

③ **Net Change:** The change in NAV from the previous day's close.

④ **Year-to-Date Percentage Return:** The fund's total return for the year to date, from December 31 of the previous year. The percentage return assumes that all cash distributions were reinvested.

other investors. Regulation FD, however, is very controversial. The "Solving an Ethical Controversy" box debates whether Regulation FD really helps investors.

Securities laws also require every public corporation to file several reports each year with the SEC; the contents of these reports become public information. The best known, of course, is the annual report. Public corporations prepare annual reports for their shareholders, and they file another report containing essentially the same information, Form 10-K, with the SEC. The SEC requires additional reports each time certain company officers and directors buy or sell a company's stock for their own accounts (Form 4) or any time an investor accumulates more than 5 percent of a company's outstanding stock (Form 13-d). All of these reports are available for viewing and download at the FreeEDGAR Web site (www.freeEDGAR.com).

Industry Self-Regulation

The securities markets are also heavily self-regulated by professional associations and the major financial markets. The securities industry recognizes that rules and regulations designed to ensure fair and orderly markets will promote investor confidence to the benefit of all participants. Two examples of self-regulation are the rules of conduct established by the various professional organizations and the market surveillance techniques used by the major securities markets.

Professional Rules of Conduct   Prodded initially by federal legislation, the National Association of Securities Dealers (NASD) established, and periodically updates, rules of conduct for members (both individuals and firms). These rules are meant to ensure that brokers perform their basic functions honestly and fairly, under constant supervision. Failure to adhere to rules of conduct can result in a variety of disciplinary actions. The NASD also established a formal arbitration procedure through which investors can attempt to resolve disputes with brokers without litigation.

Market Surveillance   All securities markets use a variety of market surveillance techniques to spot possible

BUSINESS DIRECTORY

➤ **insider trading**   *use of material nonpublic information to make an investment profit.*

Is Regulation FD Needed?

The SEC now uses Regulation FD—for "fair disclosure"—to combat what it sees as a growing problem with companies' selective disclosure of material nonpublic information to certain persons and institutions. These investors, including securities analysts and institutional investors, would often receive information on sales, earnings, or other vital company data before the general public. According to the SEC, one glaring example occurred when clothier Abercrombie & Fitch tipped off an analyst at a brokerage firm about the company's sluggish sales, about a week before the news was revealed to the public. The analyst allegedly put out a quiet sell recommendation to a handful of his clients. When the news was made public, the price of the popular clothier's stock dropped sharply. Regulation FD explicitly prohibits companies such as Abercrombie & Fitch from selectively disclosing vital information. The information now must be disclosed to everyone at the same time. According to then–SEC chairman Arthur Levitt, "High-quality and timely information is the lifeblood of strong, vibrant markets. It is at the very core of investor confidence."

Is Regulation FD needed?

PRO

1. Analysts will become more hard-nosed and objective about the companies they follow. Before Regulation FD, analysts rarely said anything negative about the companies they followed for fear that the companies would cut them out of the information loop.
2. Regulation FD levels the playing field for all investors. Selective disclosure violates the fundamental principles of integrity and fairness, undermining investor confidence and faith in the U.S. financial markets.
3. Regulation FD will lead companies to disclose more information, more often. This will help all investors make better informed decisions.

CON

1. Far from increasing the amount of information companies disclose, Regulation FD will cause companies to clam up. The easiest way to comply with Regulation FD is to say nothing at all.
2. Because of fear that they are violating Regulation FD, companies will provide less guidance to analysts. Earnings forecasts will be less accurate and earnings surprises more frequent. The result will be increased market volatility.
3. Regulation FD simply isn't needed. Existing laws and regulations regarding insider trading are more than adequate to deal with the most serious cases of selective disclosure.

SUMMARY

Since Regulation FD went into effect, there is some evidence that companies are disclosing more information through press releases, Web casts, conference calls, and SEC filings. According to one survey, more than 80 percent of all companies have made policy and procedural changes to the way in which they disclose information in light of Regulation FD. Further, the number and severity of earnings surprises hasn't changed significantly since Regulation FD went into effect. On the other hand, there is also evidence that companies are no longer giving earnings guidance between quarterly announcements. (Guidance, simply put, is informing the investing public of whether the firm is likely to achieve its sales and profit forecasts for the coming quarter.) One survey respondent—an anonymous corporate officer—put it this way: "The most significant change is that we are no longer answering questions about how the quarter is going or whether or not we are tracking to guidance." Said another, "We have discontinued quarterly previews. Each quarterly conference call includes earnings guidance for the next quarter and for the current year, and no earnings guidance is given between conference calls."

Sources: "Fact Sheet: Regulation Fair Disclosure and New Insider Trading Rules," Securities and Exchange Commission, downloaded from **www.sec.gov** on April 23, 2001; Judith Burns, "Impact of SEC Fair Disclosure Rule Still Debated," *Dow-Jones News Service,* January 25, 2001, downloaded from **www.ccbn.com**; Neal Lipschutz, "Disclosure Rule's Early Mixed Report Card," *Dow-Jones News Service,* January 19, 2001, downloaded from **www.ccbn.com**.

violations of trading rules or securities laws. For example, the NYSE continuously monitors trading activity throughout the trading day. A key technical tool used by the NYSE is called Stock Watch, an electronic monitoring system that flags unusual price and volume activity. Personnel then investigate to seek explanations for unusual activity from the member firms and companies involved. In addition, all market participants must keep detailed records of every aspect of every trade (called an audit trail). The NYSE's enforcement division may impose a variety of penalties on members for rule violations. Further, the exchange turns over evidence to the SEC for further action if NYSE personnel believe that violations of federal securities laws may have occurred.

WHAT'S AHEAD

Following the written case materials for the end-of-part continuing case, *Contemporary Business* concludes with two appendixes. Appendix A examines risk management and insurance. It discusses the concept of risk, the alternative ways of dealing with it, and the various kinds of insurance available for businesses and individuals. Finally, Appendix B offers a comprehensive summary of the legal environment of business. It also outlines the key points of business law, including contract law, the uniform commercial code, and the law of agency.

➤ Summary of Learning Goals

1. Distinguish between the primary market for securities and the secondary market.

The primary market for securities serves businesses and governments that want to sell new security issues to raise funds. The secondary market handles transactions of previously issued securities between investors. The business or government that issued the security is not directly involved in secondary market transactions. It is estimated that around 80 percent of the value of all transactions that take place in the securities markets do so in the secondary market.

2. Compare money market instruments, bonds, and common stock, and explain why particular investors might prefer each type of security.

Money market instruments and bonds are debt instruments. Money market instruments are short-term debt securities and tend to be low-risk securities. Bonds are longer-term debt securities and pay a fixed amount of interest each year. Bonds are sold by the U.S. Treasury (government bonds), state and local governments (municipal bonds), and corporations. Most municipal and corporate bonds have risk-based ratings. Common stock represents ownership in corporations. Common stockholders have voting rights and the residual claim on the firm's assets.

3. Identify the five basic objectives of investors and the types of securities most likely to help them reach each objective.

The five basic objectives are growth in capital, stability of principal, liquidity, current income, and growth in income. Common stocks are the most likely to meet the objectives of growth in capital and growth in income. Historically, common stock investments have had far higher returns on average than either bonds or money market instruments. Common stock dividends have also generally risen over time. Money market instruments are the most stable in price and rarely ever lose value. Money market instruments are also the most liquid security. Bonds tend to provide the highest current income of any security.

4. Explain the process of buying or selling a security listed on an organized securities exchange.

Investors use the services of a brokerage firm that is a member of one of the stock exchanges. After a broker receives a customer's order, it is conveyed electronically to the appropriate stock exchange for execution. A market order instructs the broker to obtain the best possible price, and a limit order places a limit on the transaction price. Full-service brokers provide the most advice but charge the highest fees. Customers at discount firms have to make their own decisions but are charged lower fees. Online brokerage firms are popular today, and many full service and discount firms have begun offering online trading services.

5. Describe the information included in stock, bond, and mutual fund quotations.

Information in a stock quote includes the 52-week indicator, the highest and lowest trading prices during the previous 52 weeks, the dividend, dividend yield, price-earnings ratio, trading volume, the stock's highest and lowest prices for the day, the closing price for that day, and the stock price's change from the close of the previous trading day. A bond quotation includes the maturity date and interest rate, the current yield, trading volume, and a comparison of the day's closing price with that of the previous day. Tables of mutual funds list each fund's general investment objective, net asset value (NAV), the change in NAV from the previous day, and the year-to-date total return.

6. Explain the role of mutual funds in the securities markets.

Mutual funds are professionally managed investment companies that own securities consistent with their overall investment objective. Investors purchase shares of a mutual fund, which make them part owners of a diversified investment portfolio. Investors can purchase shares of mutual funds for relatively small amounts. Mutual funds have become extremely popular in recent years. Over half of all American households own mutual fund shares.

7. Evaluate the major features of regulations designed to protect investors.

In the U.S. financial markets are regulated at both the federal and state levels. Markets are also heavily self-regulated by the financial markets and professional organizations. The chief regulatory body is the federal Securities and Exchange Commission. It sets forth a number of requirements for both primary and secondary market activity, prohibiting a number of practices including insider trading. The SEC also requires that public companies disclose financial information regularly.

Business Terms You Need to Know

security 708
primary market 708
secondary market 710
money market instrument 711
secured bond 711
debenture 711
common stock 713

preferred stock 714
stock exchange (stock market) 717
brokerage firm 719
mutual fund 724
full and fair disclosure 725
insider trading 726

Other Important Business Terms

electronic communications network (ECN) 707
initial public offering (IPO) 708
investment banker 709
underwriting 710

government bond 711
municipal bond 711
bond rating 712
call provision 713
institutional investor 714

market order 719
limit order 719
price-earnings (P/E) ratio 722
prospectus 725

➤ Review Questions

1. Distinguish between a primary market and a secondary market. What two ways are securities sold in the primary market?

2. Outline the underwriting process. Why do corporations and state and local governments use investment bankers?

3. What are the major characteristics of money market instruments? How do money market instruments differ from bonds?

4. Distinguish between a government bond and a municipal bond. Explain the purpose of bond ratings.

5. What is common stock and how does it differ from preferred stock? Over the long run, what seems to be the major factor in explaining changes in a company's stock price?

6. What are the primary investment motivations or objectives? Which security best meets each of these objectives?

7. Distinguish between a market order and a limit order. What are the major differences between full-service, discount, and online brokerage firms?

8. How does the New York Stock Exchange operate? Compare the operations of the NYSE with those of the Nasdaq stock market.

9. Explain how a mutual fund operates. What are the benefits of investing in mutual funds?

10. Define *insider trading* and give an example. List some ways in which the securities industry is self-regulated.

➤ Questions for Critical Thinking

1. Assume that you're a physician and one of your patients tells you of an impending takeover of the company he works for. This information is not yet public. You act on the information by buying stock in the company. Based on the definition of insider trading, would you be guilty? What if you were about to run a 10k race and heard the same information from two runners behind you and then invested? Would you be crossing the legal line?

2. Assume you just inherited $50,000 from your uncle, and his will stipulates that you must invest all the money until you complete your education. Prepare an investment plan. What is (are) your primary

investment objective(s)? How much would you invest in each of the following: money market instruments, bonds, and common stocks?

3. Would you feel comfortable investing the $50,000 you inherited in Question 2 using an online broker, or would you use a full-service firm? Explain your choice.

4. Many believe that conventional markets, such as the NYSE, are fast becoming relics, and eventually all securities markets will resemble Island.com. Do you agree with this assessment? Why or why not?

5. Assume you are considering buying shares of Merck. Describe how you would go about analyzing the stock and deciding whether now is a good time to buy it.

➤ Experiential Exercise

Background: You have been learning about financial management, financial institutions, and financing and investing through securities markets. Perhaps you are thinking about whether you are suited to a career in the financial services industry. This quiz, while highly unscientific, will give you some insight to answer that question.

Directions:

1. Circle the answer that best describes you for each of the 15 questions in the financial services quiz.

2. Complete the "Scoring Directions" section.

3. Use the "Score Interpretation" section to find out whether and where you might fit best into the financial services industry.

Where Do You Belong in Financial Services? A Quiz

1. Which of the following best matches your life philosophy?
   a. Party time! Excellent!
   b. I work to live, not live to work.
   c. All work and no play makes Jack a dull boy.
   d. He who dies with the most toys, wins.

2. Which of the following television shows do you like best?
   a. The Jerry Springer Show
   b. Ally McBeal
   c. anything on CNBC
   d. I'm too busy to watch television.

3. How important is vacation time in your career decision?
   a. I need my summers free to work on my tan.
   b. I can go to the tanning salon after work, but I still want four weeks off.
   c. The standard two weeks' vacation is fine by me.

d. Doesn't matter to me; I'm going to be working too hard to take much time off.

4. What's your favorite restaurant?
   a. Taco Bell
   b. Red Lobster
   c. That tasty ethnic place downtown
   d. That hip new fusion restaurant with the excellent wine list

5. What kind of car do you think fits you best?
   a. Pickup truck with shotgun rack.
   b. BMW 300 series
   c. BMW 500 series
   d. BMW 700 series

6. Which of the following best describes your academic performance?
   a. Is abysmal a real word? I missed that day in class.
   b. Decent grades, decent school.
   c. Excellent grades, decent school, or vice versa (decent grades, excellent school).
   d. Top grades, top school.

7. Which of the following books would you consider the most enjoyable reading?
   a. *Babbitt,* by Sinclair Lewis
   b. *The Firm,* by John Grisham
   c. *The 7 Habits of Highly Effective People,* by Stephen Covey
   d. Why waste valuable time reading when you can just rent the movie?

8. Which of the following people do you most admire?
   a. Ru Paul. No, Karl Marx.
   b. Michael Jordan
   c. Warren Buffett
   d. Mario Andretti. No, Michael Milken.

9. Which of the following do you consider a reasonable workweek?
   a. I think those French are onto something; 35 hours per week.
   b. The standard 40-hour workweek.
   c. I have no problem working long workweeks occasionally, just as long as it's not a consistent thing.
   d. I'll set up a cot so I can sleep in the office if I have to.

10. Many big financial services companies face an ongoing battle with bureaucracy. Which of the following statements best describes your attitude toward bureaucracy?

a. The heck with financial services companies. I'm going to interview for jobs at nimble start-up Internet companies.

b. I enjoy repetitive tasks, like filling out forms in triplicate. Besides, three's my lucky number.

c. I can't stand bureaucracy, though I do understand that it can be a fact of life in big companies.

d. I'm going to be making my company enough money that they'll keep me from getting bogged down in bureaucratic hassles.

11. What kind of career path do you envision for yourself?

a. I'm too busy working on my Mortal Kombat skills to worry about my career path.

b. Same kind my dad had: I'll put in my time and move up the ranks.

c. If I work hard and have a little luck, I think I can make it to top management.

d. I don't care about career paths; I'll follow any career path as long as it means I live in Greenwich and get to sit on the boards of my favorite charities.

12. How closely do you follow financial and economic news?

a. I dated someone who took a couple of economics classes in college.

b. I read the business section regularly.

c. I read the business section regularly and have a diversified portfolio of investments.

d. I read SEC filings on vacation.

13. Which of the following would you consider a dream vacation?

a. Making it through a weekend in Tijuana without getting arrested

b. A week in Orlando

c. A week on the beach in Cozumel

d. BASE jumping in the Chilean Andes

14. What kind of work/family-life balance are you looking for in your career?

a. I'd like to homeschool my kids.

b. I plan on being home to eat dinner with my kids every night.

c. I'll have to work through dinner occasionally, but I want to be there to help my kids with their homework every night.

d. I'm going to be working too hard to see much of my kids during the week, but I'll be making enough to take them on some killer vacations.

15. What are your compensation goals?

a. I just need to make enough to keep getting piercings and tattoos.

b. I want to make a decent living, enough to buy a house and a nice car someday.

c. I plan on making enough to send my kids to good private schools.

d. I'm going to make enough money to buy a racehorse. And stables to put it in. And a track to race it on.

Scoring Directions

Give yourself one point for every time you answered "A," two points for every time you answered "B," three points for every time you answered "C," and four points for every time you answered "D." Total your score and then see where you fall in the Score Interpretation descriptions.

Score Interpretation

15 to 24 points: Sorry, but financial services probably isn't the right place for you. Go to www.WetFeet.com to get information on other career opportunities that you might be better suited to do.

25 to 39 points: If you really think you want to make a career in financial services, there's probably a place in the industry for you. There are plenty of relatively stable jobs that pay well in financial services, which, rather than requiring you to give up your firstborn to get ahead, reward hard work and loyalty with regular raises and promotions. Possibilities include insurance, accounting, and jobs on the retail side of banking.

40 to 49 points: You're willing to work hard for real rewards. You're willing to take on some risk to get ahead, but you're not about to bet the farm on any one game. You probably have the right mind-set to get ahead in commercial banking, mutual funds and brokerage, or asset management.

50 to 60 points: You're a hard-charger to whom money and prestigious hobbies are a means of measuring success. In other words, you were born to be in investment banking, or, failing that, venture capital investing.

Source: Quiz by Eric Wilinski, posted 02/01/2000 at **WetFeet.com**, 2 March 2001.

➤ Nothing but Net

1. **Buying U.S. Treasury securities.** As noted in the chapter, anyone may bid on Treasury securities when they are auctioned. Visit the Bureau of Public Debt Web site and review the procedures for bidding on a Treasury security. Prepare a report outlining the bidding procedure, what the buyer must specify, and how the Treasury decides which bids to accept. If you were going to

make a bid, would you have to go through a brokerage firm or a bank?

www.publicdebt.treas.gov

2. **IPO information.** Visit Hoover's Online's IPO central (www.hoovers.com/ipo) and pick a recent IPO. Find out as much as you can about the company and the offering (such as the amount of money raised, the lead underwriter, and the company's products or services). How has the stock performed since the IPO? The following Web sites are other good sources of information about the IPO you selected:

www.freeedgar.com

http://investor.msn.com

www.morningstar.com

3. **Online Trading.** Visit the Web site of a brokerage firm that offers online trading (such as Datek Online—www.datek.com—or National Discount Brokerage—www.ndb.com) to learn more about online trading. Most online brokerage firms also offer a trading demonstration. Use the demonstration to see how you obtain price information, company news, place buy or sell orders, and check account balances. Write a brief report summarizing your experience. Did the experience make you more or less likely to actually use an online broker?

Note: Internet Web addresses change frequently. If you don't find the exact sites listed, you may need to access the organization's home page and search from there.

Whether or not they have money invested in the securities market, people seem fascinated by the bulls and bears who make and lose fortunes. They enjoy a thrill when the market is riding high, and they hold their breath when the market takes a plunge. Investment firms like Morgan Stanley want their business customers to feel confident that their money is safely invested with them—and will gain them a handsome return over the long run. Regardless of an individual business's or consumer's investment objectives, from growth in capital to growth in income, Morgan Stanley seeks to help its customers meet their financial goals.

Morgan Stanley is a global financial services company that holds significant market positions in three business segments: securities, asset management, and credit services, including credit cards and real-estate loans. Morgan Stanley offers a variety of investment instruments and services, from bond trading 24 hours a day, 5 days a week, to customized programs like NetWorth, in which a customer can gain access to all of his or her online account information on one secure Web page. With its wireless trading service called TradeRunner, customers can trade anytime, anywhere. The company even has a service called the Blue Chip Basket, in which a customer can buy ten stocks for a trading fee of $49.95. On the Web site alone, customers are offered free delayed quotes and graphs, a look at the 5,600 mutual funds located in the Mutual Fund Center, and access to historical analyses modeling that describes interesting market activity. All of these services have one aim in mind—convenience and value for customers, whatever their needs.

Because it is vital for investors to understand the information presented in stock, bond, and mutual fund quotations, the Morgan Stanley Web site offers an Investment Basics section to newcomers. The section offers a variety of information, including a glossary of terms such as *maturity, price-earnings ratio,* and *interest rates,* so customers can learn more about financial markets. Such additional assistance helps new investors understand the information that is being provided to them when they look at their investment statements.

As the Internet continues to offer opportunities for financial services, Morgan Stanley is expanding its global online reach. The company launched a huge Web procurement project in 2000, in which it sought to place a total of 10,000 employees in 500 U.S. locations, with a launch in Europe and Asia shortly thereafter. "We'll be the benchmark for online buying in financial services," predicts Gerry Fitzmaurice, director of national purchasing for Morgan Stanley. However, the slowdown in the stock market in 2001 brought caution to financial services companies—Morgan Stanley included. In early 2001, Morgan Stanley's chief economist Stephen Roach addressed executives and warned of a possible recession. "The idea of recession wasn't even in the realm of possibility for our clients then," says Richard Berner, Morgan Stanley's chief U.S. economist. But within a few months, Roach's foresight proved correct: most of Wall Street, from economists to brokers, was murmuring about the stock market slowdown. Predicting such a downturn can help investment professionals protect their clients. Morgan Stanley wisely cut its growth forecast in anticipation of the uncertainty in the national and global economy. And the expertise of its advisors became all the more important for its clients' financial well-being as the swings in the market continued. Trust is crucial in any ongoing relationship, but it is particularly important in investments.

No one can truly predict what will happen to an economy in the future. It's like trying to pinpoint where a tornado will touch down or how many inches of rain will fall to feed bumper crops. The rises and falls of the stock market can seem as fickle as the weather. But economists at companies like Morgan Stanley need to act like meteorologists, using their knowledge, experience, financial tools, and the information they have at hand to help their customers make the best investment decisions possible. "We believe in educated customers," says one slogan on the firm's Web site. But the statement is more than a mere slogan; it is part of Morgan Stanley's goal to create enhanced value for its customers by teaching them what they need to know in order to become investment partners and make sound decisions and, ultimately, decisions about their future.

QUESTIONS

1. How important is it for Morgan Stanley's customers to identify their investing objectives? In what ways might the firm help customers make this determination?

2. Based on your chapter reading, describe the major features of regulations that affect Morgan Stanley's business activities.

3. Would you feel comfortable making investments online? Why or why not?

4. Access the company's investment Web site at **www.online. msdw.com** and take the "demo test drive" to see how its online investing service works. Did you find the experience to be positive? Why or why not?

Sources: Morgan Stanley corporate Web site, **www.morganstanley.com,** accessed April 11, 2001; Morgan Stanley Online investment services Web site, **www.online.msdw.com,** accessed April 11, 2001; Anna Bernasek, "Papa Bear," *Fortune,* January 8, 2001, **www.fortune.com.**

Part II

"Hi, I'm from the Geek Squad. Just the fax, Ma'am, the Data, Eudora File, and Internet"

Recall the video case in Part I. The Geek Squad is a real business. It is growing and enjoying phenomenal success! Here's more of the story.

When Special Agent 66, a.k.a. Robert Stephens, founded the Geek Squad, he was looking for a way to augment his income from the computer tech job he was holding at the University of Minnesota. Stephens felt that he was underpaid for the job, and that there was more to computer support than met the eye. He decided to look into starting his own business in the field of information technology. His idea was to create a fun computer support business that combines the glamour of rock stardom with the technical support provided by the best of the computer support world. Using $200 as start-up capital, Stephens started the Geek Squad, an innovative consulting business. Currently, the company has more than 50 employees; 25 Geek Squad cars; locations in Minneapolis and Los Angeles; a loyal following of consumers, business leaders, actors, and rock stars; and several million dollars in annual sales. The business has grown from a sole proprietorship to a corporation. Stephens receives inquiries from people who want to buy his business, but he says he isn't interested in selling. For him, the offers are simply evidence that he has done a wonderful job creating an image for the Geek Squad and following that through with superior marketing and customer service.

The Geek Squad solves computer problems. It prepares small businesses for an Internet presence. It also provides computer advice to all sorts of people from suburban home-dwellers and home-based businesses, to entertainment superstars and actors. According to Stephens, "Rock stars are the ultimate telecommuters! They need computers to stay in touch with their families, producers, backers, and record labels." Geek Squad clients include performers like The Rolling Stones, Ozzy Osbourne, Ice Cube, Jonny Lang, and the Artist formerly known as Prince. The Rolling Stones were so impressed with the Geek Squad's services they invited the special agents to tour with them on their "Bridges to Babylon" and "No Security" tours. Unfortunately, the Geek Squad turned down the touring offer because it was too busy to dedicate the time to a major concert tour. Instead, the Stones and other bands mail in their computers. The Geek Squad sends the computers back to a future tour destination. Serving rock superstars does have its benefits. Stephens says, "We're like a legal Mafia! We keep their teleprompters and computers running, and we got the best seats in the house! We also get referrals to bands like Dr. Dre, Eminem, Snoop Doggy Dog, KISS, and Black Sabbath. We get great tables in restaurants!"

As an entrepreneurial venture, the Geek Squad is a business concept that utilizes the fertile imagination of its members. Everyone has fun with the geek concept and plays the role to the hilt. Members of the Geek Squad wear white button-down shirts, pocket protectors, too-short black pants, black shoes, and black clip-on neckties. Sometimes, they may even wear masking tape on their eyeglasses! While this dress is natural for some members of the Geek Squad, it does have the effect of entertaining customers and gaining their trust. To add more fun to the mix, the Geek Squad combines its "geektitude" with a James Bond/Get Smart/Dragnet-type secret agent demeanor. Each Geek Squad special agent has a number, like "Special Agent 66" or "Special Agent 33." Everyone carries a badge, a black tool kit, and drives a special black and white car emblazoned with the Geek Squad emblem. Tied with the cars is the concept "James Bond *meets* Ghost Busters *meets* Maxwell Smart *meets* Computer Geeks capable of fixing hardware or software problems *while* making you smile." This is one reason the Geek Squad has such a loyal following.

Robert Stephens had a very simple vision in starting this business: it was to be a consulting business for people who need on-site help with their computer problems. He got the idea one day while standing in the supermarket checkout line and overhearing two suburban homemakers discussing their options for upgrading computer memory and storage capabilities. His appraisal of the situation was unique! He felt that if suburban homemakers were discussing issues like this in the checkout line, computers must have hit the mainstream! Upon doing a little investigation, he discovered there were no help facilities for consumers or small businesses apart from computer technical support provided by computer companies. These services had long waiting times and charged by the hour for technical support. They didn't provide any personal assistance, provided little follow-up, and may not have solved consumers' problems at all! Stephens's idea was different: he would offer computer assistance to consumers in person, speaking normal language, and charging by the job, not the hour. Geek Squad was a very creative solution. So far it has provided employment, created a decent lifestyle for Stephens, his family, and his employees, and has fostered the quality of life that many people can only imagine.

Soon, the one-person consulting business became a multi-consultant operation, complete with dispatchers, financial officers, special agents, and a walk-in service that Geek Squad cleverly calls "counter intelligence." From there, the business grew to include small business clients who can't afford full-time computer technicians, and a traveling geek show that has offered services for people around the globe.

Stephens calls his secret to entrepreneurial success "creativity in the absence of capital." This vision, creating the concept of the "special agent" who shows up at "crime scenes," has "case files," and drives "Geekmobiles," blends humor with plain-language computer support. It is designed to create ecstatic customers who will call again and again, and who will look forward to the next visit. Stephens hopes customers will also tell their friends. Word of mouth for additional clients travels fast. Most Geek Squad customers come from referrals.

So how does the Geek Squad get paid? The special agent in charge of each crime scene estimates an up-front cost. When services are performed and completed, the special agent presents an invoice containing the words, "Pay Up Sucka!" At that time, the agent uses an Internet connection to clear a credit card or bank debit. They also take cash and checks. The company is then paid before the agent leaves the crime scene.

DISCUSSION QUESTIONS

1. Look at your chapter on Entrepreneurship. What opportunities did Stephens see that the Geek Squad met? Do you think those opportunities would exist anywhere? Why?

2. What would be the best strategy for the Geek Squad from this point? Should it grow to other cities? Should it franchise? Should it license the concept? Why?

3. What personal elements of entrepreneurial success does Stephens show? Are these necessary for his success? Are they sufficient? How is Stephens like the entrepreneurs described in your readings? How is he different?

4. Why do other businesses want to acquire Geek Squad? What is it about Geek Squad's success that prompts this sort of behavior?

Part III — Management and Motivation at the Geek Squad: Everyone Wants to Drive a Geekmobile

Recall what you know about the Geek Squad. The business has been doing very well. In fact, it has grown to a second location in the Los Angeles area. Here's more of the story.

As you know, when Special Agent 66 (a.k.a Robert Stephens), founded the Geek Squad, he was looking for a business opportunity that provided a unique blend of rock stardom with computer technical support. The Geek Squad proved to be an excellent business concept, generating customer loyalty, income, and growth. The concept was to play on the geek image of computer people, while providing personal technical support on a flat-fee basis. Growth has not been without its problems, but generally, things have gone well for the Geek Squad. The chief problems have been related to management of the business. Growing a business is one thing; planning, leading, organizing and controlling performance is quite another. Promoting fun is one thing; turning that into a stable corporate culture is also quite another. Stephens professes his desire to find a natural balance between growth and predictability that ensures the stability and preserves the fun the Geek Squad enjoys.

The business has grown from a sole proprietorship to a corporate business with more than 50 employees. Now, there is a support staff for the special agents. The staff consists of in-house technical support, walk-in services for clients, dispatchers, support for the fleet of cars, and a full-time financial officer who keeps track of revenues and income, and who allocates money for projects that are necessary to business growth. Generally, Robert Stephens's role has gone from being a technical support person to being a figurehead and chief spokesman for the Geek Squad.

Motivation at the Geek Squad has always been good. While there have been complaints from inside technical support people that they too need a Geekmobile, Stephens has been able to answer the complaint by allowing people to take Geek cars home, as long as they "promise to drive them around a lot." There have also been noises from the special agents that they don't have everything they need to fully serve Geek Squad clients.

On a positive note, the culture at Geek Squad is still fun and flexible. Geek Squad special agents drive cool cars, wear weird clothes, and play the part of computer geeks dispensing clear advice, for flat fees, to customers who are both entertained and educated by the demeanor and advice at each crime scene. If a consultant were to categorize the Geek Squad, that person might call it a "line organization with support staff." Nothing is more important than the service provided to customers of Geek Squad.

According to Stephens, the heart and soul of the company belongs to the special agents who serve customers. One surprising fact is that none of the special agents are certified computer technicians. Stephens says, "I look for people with the right attitude and a passion to pick up the knowledge they need." He believes, "the typical job description requires impeccable verbal communications skills; general familiarity with PC systems, software, and hardware is necessary."

While the culture at Geek Squad is fun and flexible, there are things that motivate some, but not all. According to Mike Kannenberg, Special Agent 42, "the hardest part of the job is not knowing what kind of problem I'll have to solve before I arrive at a customer's premises . . . once I understand the problem, the next task is finding the best path to solving it." Another tough part of the job, according to Kannenberg, is "having to ask lots of questions to find problems. Some people get defensive because they think they did something wrong or they think they'll get burned and be billed for unnecessary work." Kannenberg finds the challenge to be fun, but not everyone shares that interest.

Special agents have the flexibility to decide how to solve problems. Stephens "used to think money was the Number 1 motivator." He changed his mind and now believes it is the "self esteem that comes from being passionate about what a person does." Stephens calls his secret to motivating people, "giving people the opportunity to do a great job and then paying them well for their efforts."

Beyond customer service and house calls, special agents also have the opportunity to write for a regular column in ComputerUser.com. Questions may be simple, but the exposure is tremendous for the agent who can answer questions in a normal tone and in a limited space. In addition, Special Agents at the Geek Squad also have the opportunity to contribute to editions of a book published by Simon and Schuster called *Geek Squad Guide to Solving Any Computer Glitch*.

Beyond this, work at the Geek Squad is unpredictable. When asked about unusual occurrences, Robert Stephens likes to tell several stories. The first is about a call from a writer who had spilled a soda on his keyboard. What should he do to make it work again? Stephens told him to unplug the keyboard and put it in the dishwasher, while turning off the heat dry. The hot water alone would dissolve the sugar that was making the keys stick. It worked. Another story relates to a fashion magazine having a local shoot. According to Stephens, the magazine was having trouble sending photos back to New York and Los Angeles. Its computer crashed. Who would the magazine call? The Geek Squad! Shortly after, an employee came into Stephens's office, indicating that "there's a photo shoot with models on line 4. Who should we send out there?" Stephens's question was, "Who's been good this week?" Imagine a bunch of beautiful models sitting around, waiting to get to work. Then, here comes a computer geek with a clip-on tie to work on the computers and spend time there during the photo shoot. It's a geek's dream come true.

DISCUSSION QUESTIONS

1. Look at your chapter on management. What are some of the problems that Robert Stephens might face in planning work, organizing activities, leading people, and controlling their performances?
2. In start-up companies, decisions are frequently made on an "as needed" basis. Are there any costs or benefits you can see to this practice?
3. Look at the job description example in your text. It's in the chapter on Human Resource Management and Motivation. If you were to write a job description for a special agent, what would it look like?
4. From your reading of the chapter on Motivation, how would you describe the motivation of employees at the Geek Squad? Create your own theory that predicts what would motivate Special Agents in this business.

Part IV   Everything is Advertising

Once again, recall what you know about the Geek Squad so far. Management and market niche are fundamental areas it seems to have under control. One thing that separates Geek Squad from the rest of the New Economy companies is a visionary and efficient marketing management strategy. As recognition for this, Robert Stephens was given high praise by the Minnesota Entrepreneur's Association for his genius at marketing and in gathering media attention to his business. Here's more of the story.

For Robert Stephens, Special Agent 66, the Geek Squad could have been a small consulting opportunity designed to generate only enough income for him to finish his degree. Stephens had bigger plans for it. He wanted to compete with IBM in terms of customer service. Not having the deep pockets or history of IBM, he decided he could compete through implementing an efficient manipulation of the marketing mix. How did he do this? He adopted the attitude that "everything is advertising," including service, finance, auto pool, and billing. Call it Disney *meets* Hollywood *meets* relentless impression management. There's no money to waste in a small business. The Geek Squad therefore engineered everything to generate great products, unique pricing, personal service delivery, and image creation.

Marketers use the marketing concept to deliver goods and services to consumers and clients. Of primary importance in the marketing concept is a consumer need. Stephens recognized a need for personal computer support services on the local level. This filled a unique niche that IBM, Dell, Gateway, Micron, and Hewlett Packard wouldn't want to fill. All these companies are happy to offer tech support over the telephone, but to actually put someone on East Lake Street in Minneapolis or at Gate 22 of the Minneapolis/St. Paul International Airport would be a burden to any of those corporations. For a business like the Geek Squad, however, that sort of support is exactly what it does. This recognition of a need can come from anywhere. Once the need is recognized, it's up to the marketer to deliver the product at a place the consumer desires, at a price the consumer is willing to pay, while generating information so that consumers know the service is available. This is exactly what Stephens did.

The Geek Squad provides on-site computer support with style. This is the product. It's a perishable product that begins when the special agent geek enters a crime scene, and ends when the agent leaves. Computer support, bits, baud, RAM, ROM, modems, and drives are not very exciting concepts to most people. In fact, most people think that technical support for their computers is beyond their immediate grasp. Technical support, for most people, comes over the telephone, billed at per hour (or per minute) rate, and given to them by people who speak unintelligible tech language. The Geek Squad has a different product concept. While many people think computer experts are nerds, the Geek Squad knows they are actually geeks. What's the difference? According to Stephens, a nerd doesn't know he is a nerd. A geek knows it and can take advantage of the perception! Thus, the Geek Squad shows up at a customer's door, dressed to play a role, and solve computer problems. The drama is what brings people back. Geek Squad agents speak English. They're personable and communicative. And of course, they wear clip-on ties and pocket protectors. For the Geek Squad, the product is simultaneously fun and informative! This makes the customer smile. Not only do customers get their computers fixed but they also have fun and get caught up in the special agent drama. This has people coming back for more.

To price the business services, Stephens chooses to bill by the job and not by the hour (or even the minute, like some tech support lines bill). Price lists are provided up front. Binding estimates are provided before the Special Agent arrives. There's no guessing and no uncertainty when it comes to price. There's no room for overcharging. There's no provision for ineffective service. If the client isn't happy, the Geek Squad does the job again. In short, what the Geek Squad does is provide effective computer support at a dependable price! Stephens has it set up so Special Agents get paid by the job; it's to their advantage to be effective.

Distribution is important to the Geek Squad. It does a great deal to make its services available to consumers. Rather than offering only call-in customer support, the Geek Squad offers choices to the customer. The first is "on-site." In this case, a Geek Squad special agent drives a geekmobile to the client's address and spends as much time as it takes to fix the problems. The second, is the drive-up type of support. Consumers can bring their computers to Geek Squad headquarters and speak with support staff there. The Geek Squad calls these special agents, "counter intelligence" (this rate is lower than the on-site rate). The third type of computer support is "mail-in" support. In this case, consumers have the option of packing up their computers and shipping them to Geek Squad headquarters. The Geek Squad will fix the computer and ship it back, along with a Geek Squad T-shirt. To date, people have mailed in their computers from all over the world, had them fixed, and gotten them back, complete with the T-shirt.

Finally, promotion is *everything* to the Geek Squad! Everything it does, from dress to drive, is specifically designed to attract attention and brand awareness. Geek Squad cars are specially painted Volkswagen Beetles, or other classic cars, designed to attract attention. When Stephens started the business with one car, he drove it around constantly to give his business name recognition. When the opera ended in St. Paul, Minnesota, Stephens would be there, driving around the block so people would see the car. When Special Agents stop for coffee, the main requirement is for them to park on the street. In this way, they get attention even when they're not working. If an agent wants to take a car home, he or she needs to drive it around a lot to generate exposure. If there's a local movie or TV shoot, the Geek Squad drives around the area, hoping to get into a camera shot and generate a product placement. Every customer gets a T-shirt. Everyone gets business cards. Everyone is asked to recommend Geek Squad to their friends if they are happy. If they're not, the Geek Squad makes it right. Stephens's promotional philosophy in this case is telling: to the Geek Squad, everything is advertising! If it's good, it's advertising! If it's bad, it's advertising, and it's made right. If it's there, it's advertising. It's relentless and efficient.

All these strategies work well for the Geek Squad. It truly uses its product, price, distribution, and promotional strategies to reinforce under the simple phrase, "Everything is advertising." It gets brand awareness, recognition, brand loyalty, and equity. It's created a recognizable logo and significant worldwide recognition of its trademarks. What it has is the ultimate in integrated marketing. What it has is a strategy that works.

DISCUSSION QUESTIONS

1. Recall the section on Customer Satisfaction in your book. What is the importance of customer satisfaction with the Geek Squad? How does the Geek Squad create, maintain, and strengthen marketing relationships?

2. Look at your chapter on Product Pricing. How does the Geek Squad's pricing strategy feed brand loyalty, equity, and repeat business?
3. Recall the product life cycle figure in your book. Where would you say the Geek Squad was in its product lifecycle?
4. Recall the chapter on Distribution. What type of distribution channel is the Geek Squad using? What are some of the problems you may see in the future regarding physical distribution of the Geek Squad's product?
5. Look at the chapter on Promoting Goods and Services. Why is everything the Geek Squad does considered to be advertising? Is this a good strategy? Why or why not?

Part V   Dr. No Practices Flexible Fiscal Responsibility

The Geek Squad has been a financially successful business venture. Enjoying such quick success, there is the temptation to reap rewards early by paying big salaries, buying big cars, selling stock, and buying unnecessary toys.

The Geek Squad has been growing, hiring more people, buying more cars, and considering expanding its horizons to include new cities in addition to Minneapolis and Los Angeles. The goal, according to Robert Stephens, is "5 cities in 10 years." This is a growth strategy that will require major funding. A very important thing to remember is that growth doesn't provide capital. Growth consumes cash. A business on a growth track has to watch its finances carefully to make sure there is enough capital available to provide fuel to the fire. This is where the chief financial officer (CFO) plays an important role.

At the Geek Squad, employees have lovingly given the title "Dr. No" to their CFO, Terry McIntyre. Why the title "Dr. No"? She says "no" to almost everything! Here's more of the story.

Given good growth prospects, Geek Squad founder Robert Stephens hired a CFO to oversee the handling of finances at company headquarters. For Dr. No, it seems that her job is to say "no" to most every request that comes along. She has a tough job, for she is charged with the task of disciplining the enthusiasm of creative geeks who would like computer-support toys and special equipment that would make James Bond jealous. Not every request can be granted. In fact, in most cases, requests are not granted. Should there be raises for everyone? No! Can Geek Squad cars be issued to the internal support people? No! The cars are mobile billboards for outside sales and service people. Internal people shouldn't be out driving around. Should there be more toys for the Special Agents? No! Can the company get a dog? No. A cat? No. A ferret? Eek! No!

While this doesn't make her the most popular of Special Agents, it is her professional responsibility to monitor the financial health of the Geek Squad. The CFO must keep liquidity, profitability, leverage, and activity ratios at healthy levels. Dr. No must keep enough cash to pay the short-term and long-term obligations of the firm and make sure there is enough inventory, but not too much, to keep the agents stocked. She must also make sure that any excess cash is invested so that the money can grow and make the company's growth prospects even better. Money, is what fuels future growth in the business. For her, the concept of "flexible financial responsibility" is more than three little words. It is what preserves the growth potential of the Geek Squad, ensures that salaries and commissions are paid, pools the funds to pay for health coverage, and pays the taxes that the business owes. Having enough money to buy equipment and supplies is critical to the growth of the company, but it isn't the only activity the company has to perform. The best-case scenario is when the company can do all these things with existing capital. If the company has to borrow to meet its obligations, that would slow the growth potential and future income growth of the company. Dr. No makes sure that doesn't happen.

Part of a CFO's responsibility is to make sure there is cash flow. This cash flow is what keeps the company healthy. It ensures the company's ability to deal with reality and to have flexibility to pay for unexpected situations.

Dr. No requires Special Agents to be paid by clients before they leave the crime scene. Geek Squad agents accept most major credit cards. They can log on to the Internet and receive approval on the spot! They also take checks and cash. At the end of the job, the special agent presents an invoice to the client that says, "Pay Up Sucka."

Dr. No has a motto and a goal. Her motto is "to stay Dr. No, no matter what!" Her goal is to keep the company healthy and make sure it gets what it needs, not necessarily what it wants. With this in mind, the Geek Squad should be around a long time!

DISCUSSION QUESTIONS

1. Why is it that CFOs can be unpopular?
2. What's wrong with the following statement: A growing business generates cash and that cash should be used to make sure everyone is happy?
3. Review the section on financial ratio analysis in the Accounting chapter. Given what you know about the Geek Squad, what do you think would be reasonable liquidity, profitability, and inventory levels? Why?
4. Should the Geek Squad sell stock? Why or why not? What do you think that would do to its culture?

Risk Management and Insurance

Based in Mayfield Village, Ohio, Progressive Corp. has been selling auto insurance throughout the U.S. since 1937. Today it is the nation's fourth largest auto insurer, with annual revenues in excess of $6 billion. But what separates Progressive from the hundreds of other auto insurers is the enthusiasm with which and degree to which the firm has embraced the Internet. No other insurance company offers a more extensive menu of online services for customers than Progressive. By clicking on its Web site, progressive.com, auto-insurance shoppers can quickly obtain price quotes, buy policies, change their coverage, check the status of claims, and even pay bills online. Progressive.com's Web traffic surpasses that of all other insurance-oriented Web sites combined. Recently, Progressive.com was named Best Site for Auto Insurance Buyers by the leading e-commerce authority Gomez.com.

Progressive has a long history of innovation. It was one of the first auto insurers to offer time-premium payment plans and mobile claims services. It was also one of the first companies to sell auto insurance directly to consumers, bypassing traditional agents. Progressive also became the first auto insurer to provide customers with a comparison rate shopping service. Customers could contact Progressive and obtain insurance rates from Progressive as well as several other companies. In 1994, the company became one of the first insurance companies with a presence on the World Wide Web. And in 1997, Progressive became the insurance industry's pioneer—the first firm to offer real-time online sale of auto insurance.

Progressive's embrace of the Internet is based on a simple notion: shopping for auto insurance isn't too many people's idea of fun. Phil Conley, the vice president of a commercial-property insurance company, puts it this way: "Insurance is something you have to have but don't want, and I don't want to spend a lot of time on it."[1] Yet, Mr. Conley, along with thousands of other drivers, has found that devoting time to comparison shopping can have a big payoff. By comparing rates and coverage offered by a variety of insurers, he was able to increase his coverage and lower his annual premium. The Internet is the perfect vehicle for making comparison shopping for auto insurance easier and faster. Robert Sanchez of San Luis Obispo, California, thought he was paying too much for his car insurance. Calling around to different insurance agents was slow and frustrating, and often resulted in weeks of follow-up calls from insurance agents, so he went online. Ten minutes later, he had whittled down his annual premium from $880 to $286.[2]

By offering such a wide array of services on its Web site, Progressive is in an ideal position to appeal to the growing number of online comparison shoppers and to take advantage of another benefit of direct selling on the Internet: Selling insurance directly to consumers online is a cheaper method of operating.

Progressive's e-strategy appears to be working. During a recent five-year period, the firm's premium income increased at a compound annual rate of 20 percent, compared with less than 5 percent for the auto insurance industry as a whole. *Underwriting profits*—the difference between what the company collects in premiums and its operating expenses and what it pays out in claims—has averaged about 6 percent for the past five years. Over this same period, the industry as a whole experienced average underwriting losses of 1.2 percent.

Other auto insurance companies are also aggressively moving into cyberspace. GEICO, another large direct seller of auto insurance, is an especially strong competitor. GEICO's Web site has dramatically expanded the number of services it offers. The nation's two largest auto insurers, State Farm and Allstate, have also expanded their presence on the Internet.

In addition to company Web sites, a number of online insurance brokers are competing online by offering insurance from dozens of different companies. Quotesmith.com, one of the largest of the online insurance brokers, can offer customers insurance price quotations from over 300 different insurers. And it's not just auto insurance. Individual consumers and business buyers can now shop online for most other types of insurance online. The sleepy old insurance industry is certainly changing.

OVERVIEW

Risk is a daily fact of life for both individuals and businesses. Sometimes it appears in the form of a serious illness. In other instances, it takes the form of properly loss, such as the extensive damage to homes in Los Alamos, New Mexico, as a result of devastating fires in the early years of the 21st century. Risk can also occur as the result of the actions of others—such as a driver running a red light and striking another vehicle. In still other cases, risk may occur as a result of our own actions—we talk on a cell phone while driving or decline an extended service warranty on a new computer.

Businesspeople must understand the types of risk they face and develop methods for dealing with them. One important method of dealing with risk is to shift it to specialized firms called *insurance companies*. This appendix discusses the concept of insurance in a business setting. It begins with a definition of risk.

CONCEPT OF RISK

Risk is uncertainty about loss or injury. Consider the risks faced by a typical business. A factory or warehouse faces the risk of fire, burglary, water damage, and physical deterioration. Accidents, judgments due to lawsuits, and customers failing to pay bills are other risks faced by businesses. Risks can be divided into two major categories: speculative risk and pure risk.

Speculative risk gives the firm or individual the chance of either a profit or a loss. Purchasing shares of stock on the basis of the latest hot tip from a day trader can result in profits or losses. Expanding operations into a new market may result in higher profits or the loss of invested funds.

Pure risk, on the other hand, involves only the chance of loss. Motorists, for example, always face the risk of accidents. Should they occur, both financial and

Businesses—both large and small—often turn to insurance companies to shift pure risks. In return for a relatively small premium, they purchase protection against the risk of a much larger cost.

physical losses may result. If they do not occur, however, drivers do not profit. Insurance often helps individuals and businesses protect against financial loss resulting from pure risk.

RISK MANAGEMENT

Since risk is an unavoidable part of business, managers must find ways of dealing with it. The first step in any risk management plan is to recognize what's at risk and why it's at risk. After that, the manager must decide how to handle the risk. In general, businesses have four alternatives in handling risk: avoid it, minimize it, assume it, or transfer it.

Executives must consider many factors when evaluating the risk of conducting business, both at home and abroad. These factors include a nation's economic stability; social and cultural factors, such as language; available technologies; distribution systems; and government regulations. International businesses are typically exposed to less risk in countries with stable economic, social/cultural, technological, and political/legal environments.

Avoiding Risk

Some of the risks facing individuals can be avoided by taking a conservative approach to life. Abstaining from smoking, regular exercise and staying physically fit, and not driving during blizzards and other hazardous conditions are three ways of avoiding risk. By the same token, businesses can also avoid some of the risks they face. For example, a manufacturer can locate a new production facility away from a flood-prone area.

Some firms are willing to take high risks for potentially high rewards; others are less willing to risk the potential losses involved in developing new and untried products. Although avoiding all risks may ensure profitability, it stifles innovation. As a result, most industry-leading companies are willing to take prudent amounts of risk.

Reducing Risk

Managers can reduce or even eliminate many types of risk by removing hazards or taking preventive measures. Many companies develop safety programs to educate employees about potential hazards and the proper methods of performing certain dangerous tasks. For instance, any employee who works at a hazardous waste site is required to have training and medical monitoring that meet the federal Office of Health and Safety (OSHA) standards. The training and monitoring not only reduces risk, it pays off on the bottom line. Aside from the human tragedy, accidents cost companies time and money.

Although many actions can reduce the risk involved in business operations, they cannot eliminate risk entirely. Most major business insurers assist their clients in avoiding or minimizing risk by offering the services of loss-prevention experts to conduct thorough reviews of their operations. These health and safety professionals evaluate customers' work environments and recommend procedures and equipment to help firms minimize worker injuries and property losses.

Self-Insuring Against Risk

Instead of purchasing insurance against certain types of pure risk, some companies accumulate funds to cover potential losses. Such a **self-insurance fund** is a special fund created by periodically setting aside cash reserves that the firm can draw upon in the event of a financial loss resulting from a

> **THEY SAID IT**
>
> *"If the lion didn't bite the tamer every once in a while, it wouldn't be exciting."*
>
> DARRELL WALTRIP (B.1947)
> AMERICAN RACE-CAR DRIVER

BUSINESS DIRECTORY

➤ **risk** *uncertainty about loss or injury.*

➤ **self-insurance fund** *special fund created by setting aside cash reserves periodically that can be drawn upon in the event of a loss.*

pure risk. The firm makes regular payments to the fund, and it charges losses to the fund. Such a fund typically accompanies a risk-reduction program aimed at minimizing losses. Self-insurance is most useful in cases in which a company faces similar risks and the risks are spread over a broad geographic area.

One of the most common forms of self-insurance is in the area of employee health insurance. Most companies provide health insurance coverage to employees as a component of their benefit program. Many firms, especially large ones, find it more economical to create a self-insurance fund covering employee health care expenses, as opposed to purchasing a health insurance policy from an insurance provider.

Shifting Risk to an Insurance Company

Although a business or not-for-profit organization can take steps to avoid or reduce risk, the most common method of dealing with it is to shift it to others in the form of **insurance**—the process by which a firm (the insurance company), for a fee, agrees to pay another firm or individual a sum of money stated in a written contract should a loss occur. The insured party's fee to the insurance company for coverage against losses is called a **premium.** Insurance substitutes a small, known loss—the insurance premium—for a larger, unknown loss that may or may not occur. In the case of life insurance, the loss—death—is a certainty; the main uncertainty is the date when it will occur.

It is important for the insurer to understand the customer's business, risk exposure, and insurance needs. Firms that engage in production and marketing activities in several countries usually choose to do business with insurance companies that maintain global networks of offices.

BASIC INSURANCE CONCEPTS

Figure A.1 illustrates how an insurance company operates. The insurer collects premiums from policyholders in exchange for insurance coverage. The insurance company takes some of these funds and uses them to pay current claims and operating expenses. What's left over is held in the form of reserves, which are in turn invested. Reserves can be used to pay for unexpected losses. The returns from insurance company reserves may allow the insurer to reduce premiums, generate profits, or both. By investing reserves, the insurance industry represents a major source of long-term financing for other businesses.

An insurance company is a professional risk taker. For a fee, it accepts risks of loss or damage to businesses and individuals. Three basic principles underlie insurance: the concept of insurable interest, the concept of insurable risks, and the law of large numbers.

Insurable Interest

To purchase insurance, an applicant must demonstrate an **insurable interest** in the property or life of the insured. The policyholder must stand to suffer a loss, financial or otherwise, due to fire, storm damage, accident, theft, illness, death, or lawsuit. A home owner, for

FIGURE A.1
How an Insurance Company Operates

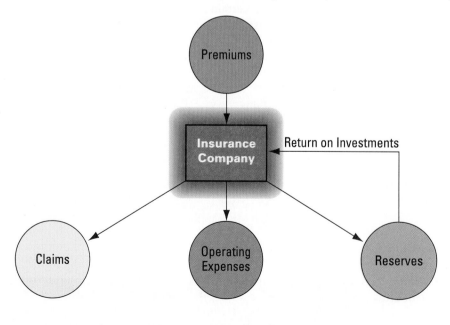

example, has an insurable interest in his or her home and its contents. In the case of life insurance coverage purchase for the head or co-head of the household, the policyholder's spouse and minor children have a clear insurable interest.

A firm can purchase property and liability insurance on physical assets—such as offices and factories—to cover losses due to such hazards as fire and theft because the company can demonstrate an obvious insurable interest. Similarly, because top managers are important assets to a company, the firm can purchase key executive insurance on their lives. By contrast, a businessperson cannot collect on insurance to cover damage to property of competitors because that person cannot demonstrate an insurable interest.

Insurable Risk

Insurable risk refers to the requirements that a risk must meet in order for the insurer to provide protection. Only some pure risks, and no speculative ones, are insurable. Insurance companies impose five basic requirements for a pure risk to be considered an insurable risk:

1. The likelihood of loss should be reasonably predictable.
2. The loss should be financially measurable.
3. The loss should be accidental.
4. The risk should be spread over a wide geographic area.
5. The insurance company has the right to set standards for accepting risk.

Law of Large Numbers

Insurance is based on the law of averages, or statistical probability. Insurance companies have studied the chances of occurrences of deaths, injuries, property damage, lawsuits, and other types of hazards. Table A.1 is an example of the kind of data insurance companies examine. It shows the number of automobile accidents, by the age of the driver, for a recent year. From their investigations, insurance companies have developed **actuarial tables,** which predict the number of fires, automobile accidents, or deaths that will occur in a given year. Premiums charged for insurance coverage are based on these tables. Actuarial tables are based on the **law of large numbers.** In essence, the law of large numbers states that seemingly random events will follow a predictable pattern if enough events are observed.

An example can demonstrate how insurers use the law of large numbers to calculate premiums. Previously collected statistical data on a small city with 50,000 homes indicates that the city will experience an average of 500 fires a year, with damages averaging

Lincoln Financial Group is one of a large number of insurance companies offering business succession insurance designed to increase the likelihood of transferring the business to the owner's successors. The two daughters shown in this photograph can demonstrate a clear insurable interest.

BUSINESS DIRECTORY

➤ **insurance**   *process by which a firm (the insurance company), for a fee (the premium), agrees to pay another firm or individual a sum of money stated in a written contract (the insurance policy) should a loss occur.*

➤ **insurable interest**   *demonstration that a direct financial loss will result if some event occurs.*

➤ **insurable risk**   *requirement that a pure risk must meet for the insurer to agree to provide protection.*

➤ **actuarial table**   *probability calculation of the number of specific events—such as deaths, injuries, fire or windstorm losses—expected to occur within a given year.*

➤ **law of large numbers**   *concept that seemingly random events will follow a predictable pattern if enough events are observed.*

Table A.1	Age of Driver and Number of Motor Vehicle Accidents	
Age Group	Number of Licensed Drivers	Accidents per 100 Licensed Drivers
19 and under	8,919,000	30
20 to 24	15,262,000	19
25 to 34	37,781,000	12
35 to 44	40,415,000	10
45 to 54	30,928,000	8
55 to 64	19,345,000	6
65 to 74	15,648,000	5
75 and older	9,522,000	6

$30,000 per occurrence. What is the minimum annual premium an insurance company would charge to insure a house against fire?

To simplify the calculations, assume that the premiums would not produce profits or cover any of the insurance company's operating expenses—they would just produce enough income to pay policyholders for their losses. In total, fires in the city would generate claims of $15 million (500 homes damaged × $30,000). If these losses were spread over all 50,000 homes, each homeowner would be charged an annual premium of $300 ($15 million divided by 50,000 homes). In reality, though, the insurance company would set the premium at a higher figure to cover operating expenses, build reserves, and earn a reasonable profit.

Some losses are easier for insurance companies to predict than others. Life insurance companies, for example, can pretty accurately predict the number of policyholders who will die within a specified period of time. Losses from such hazards as automobile accidents and weather events are much more difficult to predict. For instance, damage from 1992's Hurricane Andrew resulted in insured losses of almost $30 billion, the largest amount in history. However, had the hurricane struck the Florida coast only a few miles further north, near the heart of Miami, insurance industry experts believe that insured losses from storm damage might have approached $70 billion.

SOURCES OF INSURANCE COVERAGE

The insurance industry includes both private companies, such as Prudential, State Farm, and GEICO, and a number of public agencies that provide insurance coverage for business firms, not-for-profit organizations, and individuals. Let's look at the primary features of this array of insurers.

Public Insurance Agencies

A **public insurance agency** is a state or federal government unit established to provide specialized insurance protection for individuals and organizations. It provides protection in such areas as job loss (unemployment insurance), work-related injuries (workers' compensation), and retirement (Social Security). Public insurance agencies also sponsor specialized programs, such as deposit, flood, and crop insurance.

Unemployment Insurance Every state has an **unemployment insurance** program that assists unemployed workers by providing financial benefits, job counseling, and placement services. Compensation amounts vary depending on workers' previous incomes and the states in which they file claims. For example, Delaware's maximum weekly unemployment benefit for unemployed workers is $315, while unemployed workers in Georgia receive a maximum weekly benefit of $284. These insurance programs are funded by payroll taxes paid by employers.

Workers' Compensation Under state laws, employers must provide **workers' compensation insurance** to guarantee payment of wages and salaries, medical care costs, and such rehabilitation services as retraining, job placement, and vocational rehabilitation to employees who are injured on the job. In addition, workers' compensation provides benefits in the form of weekly payments or single, lump-sum payments to survivors of workers who die as a result of work-related injuries. Premiums are based on the company's payroll, the on-the-job hazards to which it exposes workers, and its safety record.

Social Security The federal government is the nation's largest insurer. The Social Security program, established in 1935, provides retirement, survivor, and disability benefits to millions of Americans. **Medicare** was added to the Social Security program in 1965 to provide health insurance for persons 65 years or older and certain other Social Security recipients. More than nine out of ten workers in the U.S. and their dependents are eligible for Social Security program benefits. The program is funded through a payroll tax, half of which is paid by employers and the other half paid by workers.

Private Insurance Companies

Much of the insurance in force is provided by private firms. These organizations provide protection in exchange for the payment of premiums. Some private insurance companies are stockholder owned, and therefore are run like any other business, and others are so-called mutual associations. Most, though not all, mutual insurance companies specialize in life insurance. Technically, mutual insurance companies are owned by their policyholders, who may receive premium rebates in the form of dividends. In spite of this, however, there is no evidence that an insurance policy from a mutual company costs any less than a comparable policy from a stockholder-owned insurer. In recent years a number of mutual insurance companies have reorganized as stockholder-owned companies, including Prudential Insurance Co., one of the nation's largest insurers.

Since losses from floods and mud slides can amount to hundreds of millions of dollars within a narrow geographic area, they fail to meet one of the basic requirements of insurable interest. So coverage is provided by a public agency, the National Flood Insurance Program and administered by FEMA—the Federal Emergency Management Agency.

TYPES OF INSURANCE

Individuals and businesses spend hundreds of billions of dollars each year on insurance coverage. All too often, however, both business firms and individual households make poor decisions when buying insurance. Several commonsense tips for buying insurance are offered in Table A.2. Although insurers offer hundreds of different policies, they all fall into three broad categories: property and liability insurance, health and disability insurance, and life insurance.

Table A.2	**Some Commonsense Tips for Buying Insurance**

- *Insure against big losses, not little ones.* Buy insurance to protect against big potential losses, but don't buy insurance to protect against small losses. A good example of this tip in action is to select the highest deductible you can afford on your property and liability insurance policies.
- *Buy insurance with broad coverage, not narrow coverage.* For example, it is much more cost-effective to buy a comprehensive health insurance policy, one that covers a wide range of illnesses and accidents, rather than several policies that cover only specific illnesses and accidents. It is extremely expensive to buy insurance coverage one disease at a time.
- *Shop around.* Insurance premiums for the same coverage can vary substantially. Insurance premiums also change frequently, so make sure to compare rates before renewing a policy.
- *Buy insurance only from financially strong companies.* Insurance companies occasionally go bankrupt. If this happens, you'll be left with no coverage and little chance of getting your premiums back. Several organizations—such as A.M. Best and Standard & Poor's—rate the financial strength of insurance companies.

Property and Liability Insurance

Insurance that protects against fire, accident, theft, or other destructive events is called **property and liability insurance**. Examples of this insurance category include home owners' insurance, auto insurance, business or commercial insurance, and liability insurance.

Home Owners' Insurance   Home owners' insurance protects home owners from damage to their homes due to various perils. If a home is destroyed by fire, for example, the home owners' policy will pay to replace the home and its contents. Although standard policies cover a wide range of perils, most do not cover damage from widespread catastrophes such as floods and earthquakes. The federal government, through the National Flood Insurance Program, offers flood insurance as a supplement to a standard home owners' policy. At an average cost of around $350 a year, flood insurance is often a wise purchase.

Home owners in earthquake-prone areas can purchase earthquake insurance from a private insurer as an add-on to their home owners' policy. However, earthquake coverage is expensive—the annual premium can exceed $1,000—and few home owners have it—even in California. Following the 2001 quake in Seattle that produced property damage topping the $2 billion mark, a number of additional states are studying the possibility of coverage. The industry is working closely with several states to make earthquake insurance more affordable.

Auto Insurance   With more than $120 billion in annual premiums, automobile insurance is the country's largest single type of property and liability insurance. Automobile insurance policies cover losses due to automobile accidents, including personal and property claims that result from accidents, fire, or theft. Virtually all states require drivers to have a minimum amount of auto insurance.

Commercial and Business Insurance   Commercial and business insurance protects firms from financial losses resulting from the interruption of business operations or physical damage to property as a result of fires, accidents, thefts, or other destructive events. Commercial and business insurance policies may also protect employers from employee dishonesty or against losses resulting from the nonperformance of contracts.

Liability Insurance   **Liability insurance** protects an individual or business against financial losses to others for which the individual or business was responsible. If a driver runs a red light and hits another car, his or her liability insurance would pay to repair the damage to the other car. If a business sells a defective product, the firm's liability insurance would pay for financial losses sustained by customers. A standard amount of liability coverage is usually attached to auto, home owners', and commercial insurance policies. Additional amounts of liability insurance can be purchased if needed. Adequate liability insurance is critically important today. Wal-Mart Stores, for example, requires all of its suppliers to have a minimum of $2 million in liability coverage.

Health and Disability Insurance

Each of us faces the risk of getting sick or being injured in some way. Even a relatively minor illness can result in thousands of dollars in health care bills. To guard against this risk, most Americans have some form of **health insurance**—insurance that provides coverage for losses due to sickness or accidents. With soaring costs in health care, this type of insurance has become an important consideration for both businesses and individuals.

Sources of health insurance include private individual policies, private group policies, and the federal government, through Medicare and Medicaid (health insurance for the poor). Sixty-four percent of Americans, over 180 million, are covered by private group health insurance provided by their employer as an employee benefit. Four of every five U.S. employees work for businesses and not-for-profits that offer some form of group health insurance. Group policies resemble individual health insurance policies but are offered at lower premiums. Individual health insurance policies are simply too expensive for most people. Of every ten dollars spent by employers on employee compensation (wages, salaries, and employee benefits), almost one dollar goes to cover the cost of health insurance. One large company, General Motors, spends over $4.5 billion a year on employee health care.

Private health insurance plans fall into one of two general categories: fee-for-service plans and managed-care plans. In a **fee-for-service plan,** the insured picks his or her doctor, pays the doctor, and then is reimbursed by the insurance company. Fee-for-service plans charge an annual deductible and copayments. By contrast, a **managed-care plan** pays most of the insured's health care bills. In return, the program has a great deal of say over the conditions of health care provided for the insured. Most managed-care plans, for example, place restrictions on the use of specialists and may specify which hospitals and pharmacies can be used. Some employers offer employees a choice between a fee-for-service and a managed-care plan. (Some may even offer multiple managed-care plans.) Table A.3 compares the pros and cons of both types of health care plans.

Managed-care plans have become extremely popular in recent years. An estimated 150 million Americans are currently enrolled in some form of managed-care plan. A primary reason is simply cost: managed-care plans generally cost employers and employees less than fee-for-service plans. Managed care, however, is not without its critics. The effort to control costs has caused a backlash because of restrictions placed on doctors and patients. Managed care has now become a major public policy debate in the U.S.

Types of Managed Care Plans   Two types of managed care plans can be found in the U.S.: health maintenance organizations and preferred provider organizations. Although both manage health care, important differences exist between the two.

Health maintenance organizations (HMOs) do not provide health insurance, they provide health care. An HMO supplies all of the individual's health care needs, including prescription drugs and hospitalization. The individual must use the HMO's own doctors and approved treatment facilities in order to receive benefits. Doctors and other health care professionals are actually employees of the HMO. Individuals are assigned a

THEY SAID IT

"He was eating things we wouldn't even go swimming with in Alabama."

CHARLEY HANNAH (B.1955) AMERICAN PROFESSIONAL FOOTBALL PLAYER (ON DINING WITH TEAMMATE ABE GIBRON)

BUSINESS DIRECTORY

➤ **property and liability insurance**   *general category of insurance that provides protection against financial losses due to a number of perils.*

➤ **health insurance**   *insurance designed to provide coverage for losses due to sickness or accidents.*

Table A.3   **Comparing a Fee-for-Service Plan with a Managed-Care Plan**

	Fee-for-Service Plan	Managed-Care Plan
Pros	• Almost unlimited choice of health care providers • Easy access to medical specialists • Fewer limits on tests and diagnostic procedures	• Little paperwork • Lower out-of-pocket expenses • No wait in getting reimbursed • Pays for routine physicals and immunizations
Cons	• Higher out-of-pocket expenses (deductible and copayment) • More paperwork and delays in getting reimbursed • Potentially more disputes with insurance company over charges • Often will not pay for routine physicals and immunizations	• Choice of health-care providers limited • More difficult to change doctors • Access to specialists restricted • Limits on tests and diagnostic procedures

primary care physician and cannot see a specialist without a referral. An HMO charges no deductibles and only a low, fixed-dollar copayment.

The second type of managed care plan is the **preferred provider organization** (**PPO**). While PPOs may get less publicity than HMOs, they actually cover more people. A PPO is an arrangement in which an employer negotiates a contract between local health-care providers (physicians, hospitals, and pharmacies) to provide medical care to its employees at a discount. These plans do not charge deductibles and have low, fixed-dollar copayments. They are generally much more flexible than HMOs. Members can choose their primary care physician from a list of doctors. If a referral is given, or hospitalization required, the member again chooses from a list of approved health care providers. A member who obtains treatment from a health care provider outside the PPO network will likely still be reimbursed for some of the cost.

Disability Income Insurance   Not only is disability income insurance one of the most overlooked forms of insurance, but many workers don't have enough coverage. The odds of a person developing a disability are considerably higher than most people realize. Take a group of five randomly selected 45-year-olds. There is approximately a 95 percent chance that one of the five will become disabled during the next 20 years. Disability income insurance is designed to replace lost income when a wage earner cannot work due to an accident or illness.

Two sources of disability income insurance exist: Social Security and private disability insurance policies. Social Security disability benefits are available to virtually all workers, but they have very strict requirements. Private disability insurance is available on either an individual or group basis. As with health insurance, a group policy is much cheaper than an individual policy. Many employers provide at least some disability coverage as a fully or partially paid employee benefit. Employees often have the option of obtaining additional coverage by paying more.

Life Insurance

Life insurance protects people against the financial losses that occur with premature death. Three of every four Americans own some form of life insurance. The main reason people buy life insurance is to provide financial security for their families in the event of their death. With assets totaling around $2.5 trillion, life insurance is one of the nation's largest businesses.

Types of Life Insurance   As with health and disability insurance, both individual and group life insurance policies are available. Many employers offer life insurance to employees as a component of the firm's benefit program. However, unlike health and disability insurance, an individual life insurance policy is often cheaper than a group policy for people under age 50.

THEY SAID IT

"Insurance is death on the installment plan."

PHILIP SLATER (B.1927)
AMERICAN AUTHOR

The different types of life insurance fall neatly into two categories: term policies and so-called cash value policies. **Term policies** provide a death benefit if the policyholder dies within a specified period of time. It has no value at the end of that period. **Cash value policies** combine life insurance protection with a savings feature. A cash surrender policy represents the savings portion of the policy. While there are arguments in favor of cash value policies, many experts believe that term insurance is a better choice for most consumers. For one thing, a term policy is much cheaper than a cash value policy, especially for younger people.

How Much Life Insurance Should You Have?   People can purchase life insurance policies for almost any amount. Life insurance purchases are limited only by the amount of premiums people can afford and their ability to meet medical qualifications. The amount of life insurance a person needs, however, is a very personal decision. The general rule of thumb is that a person needs life insurance if he or she has family members who financially depend on that person. A young parent with three small children could easily need $500,000 or more of life insurance. A single person with no dependents would reasonably see little or no need for a life insurance policy.

Businesses, as well as individuals, buy life insurance. The death of a sole proprietor, partner, or a key executive is likely to result in financial losses to an organization. **Key executive insurance** is life insurance designed to reimburse the organization for the loss of the services of an essential senior manager and to cover the executive search expenses needed to find a replacement. In addition, life insurance policies may be purchased for each member of a partnership to be able to repay the deceased partner's survivors for his or her share of the firm and permit the business to continue.

BUSINESS DIRECTORY

➤ **disability income insurance**   *insurance that replaces lost income when a wage earner cannot work due to an accident or illness.*

➤ **life insurance**   *insurance that protects people against the financial losses that occur with premature death.*

Business Terms You Need to Know

Other Important Business Terms

➤ **Assignments**

1. As noted earlier, many companies currently sell insurance online. Go to the insurance section of Quicken.com (**www.quicken.com/insurance**) for a list of these companies. Choose two or three from the list and visit their respective Web sites. Write a brief report on your experience. Would you consider buying

insurance online? What are the advantages and disadvantages?

2. For many people one frustrating aspect of insurance is deciphering insurance terminology. A Web site exists that provides a lexicon of insurance terms: **www.insweb.com/learningcenter/glossary.** Visit the Web site and look up the following terms:

act of God

fortuitous

housekeeping

earned premium

tickler

3. Several insurance-oriented Web sites have interactive worksheets to help you determine whether you need life insurance and, if so, how much you need. Visit the Money Central Web site (**http://moneycentral.msn. com/insure/home.asp**). Complete the interactive worksheet. If you need life insurance, what kind of policy should you buy? How much will it cost?

4. The American Association of Retired Persons (AARP) has an excellent Web site (**www.aarp.org**). One of the issues covered in great depth on its Web site is managed care. Visit the site and prepare a report on what AARP indicates are the relevant questions to ask, and issues to consider, when selecting a managed care health plan.

5. Assume you're the owner of a small manufacturing facility. Make a list of some of the major risks you face. How should each risk be handled (avoided, reduced, assumed, or transferred)? What types of insurance will you likely have to have, including those required by law?

The Legal Framework for Business

THE LEGAL FIRESTORM ENCIRCLING MICKEY MOUSE

Walt Disney never dreamed of the empire he would build from his little exercise in animated filmmaking. He assembled his team of writers and animators and put them to work on *Steamboat Willy*. The 1928 film contained a number of firsts: first full-length "talking" cartoon and first appearance of the film's star—a soon to be world-famous rodent by the name of Mickey Mouse.

Steamboat Willy was followed by success after success. Cartoon shorts, comic books, and unforgettable films like *Snow White and the Seven Dwarfs, Fantasia, Lady and the Tramp,* and *The Lion King*. A highly successful prime-time network television series launched during the 1950s continues into the 21st century. By 2002, Disney had become the nation's number two media company.

Then Walt got another idea: theme parks. Disneyland, which opened in Southern California during the 1950s, was the first of a globe-spanning chain of parks. They include Florida's Walt Disney World, and DisneylandParis and Tokyo Disneyland international parks. Along the way, new characters—Donald Duck, Pluto, Snow White, Goofy, and Dumbo—were created and added to the Disney cast. But then came a bogeyman more threatening than Snow White's Evil Queen. And the Disney empire was under siege.

The problem facing Walt's successors was the nation's federal copyright law. The act, which had been in effect for nearly a century, placed a 75-year limit on copyrights held by companies—and a company named Walt Disney Enterprises holds all of the Disney copyrights. In 2004, Disney would begin losing protection on its copyrights. This would mean that the familiar mouse character and his friends could be used by anyone who chose to attach their likenesses on T-shirts, caps, or skateboards or to feature them in films, plays, and other forms of entertainment.

What could the Disney executives do? Rather than do nothing but cry about the hand fate had dealt them, they decided to try to change the legal environment of business. Disney pressed Congress to change the copyright law—and it succeeded. The Copyright Term Extension Act of 1998 extends by 20 years the previous 75-year limit, equaling the copyright protection adopted in the European Union.

Also elated was Jack Valenti, president of the Motion Picture Association of America. As he expressed it, the new law "confirms that our nation's creators and copyright owners are deserving of the same level of protection enjoyed by their counterparts in the European Union."

Although Disney executives breathed a sigh of relief, it is not a permanent solution. After all, Mickey and his friends' protection under the new law begins to run out in 2024.[1]

OVERVIEW

The preceding chapters of *Contemporary Business* show that businesspeople must keep abreast of the legal framework within which their firms operate. An overview of the legal environment is presented in Chapter 2. Legislation affecting international business operations is discussed in Chapter 4. Chapter 5 covers laws designed to assist small businesses. Laws related to human resource management are examined in Chapter 8 and those affecting the formation and operation of labor unions are described in Chapter 11. Laws affecting business operations, such as environmental regulations and product safety, are one of the topics in Chapter 12, and marketing-related legislation is examined in Chapter 14. Finally, legislation pertaining to banking and the securities markets is discussed in Chapters 19 and 20. In this appendix, we provide an overall perspective of legislation at the federal, state, and local levels and point out that, while business executives may not be legal experts, they do need to be knowledgeable in their specific area of responsibility. A good dose of common sense also helps to avoid potential legal problems.

Despite business's best efforts, legal cases do arise in all aspects of business: contractual relationships, employment law, the environment, and other areas. The United States is clearly the world's most litigious society. Take, for example, the experience of just one major U.S. firm: At any one time, Wal-Mart is involved in approximately 10,000 legal cases.

This appendix looks at the general nature of business law, the court system, basic legal concepts, and finally, the changing regulatory environment for U.S. business. Let's start with some initial definitions and related examples.

LAW

Law consists of the standards set by government and society in the form of either legislation or custom. This broad body of principles, regulations, rules, and customs that govern the actions of all members of society, including businesspeople, is derived from several sources. **Common law** refers to the body of law arising out of judicial decisions, some of which can be traced back to early England.

Statutory law, or written law, includes state and federal constitutions, legislative enactments, treaties of the federal government, and ordinances of local governments. Statutes must be drawn precisely and reasonably to be constitutional (and thus enforceable). Still, courts must frequently interpret their intentions and meanings.

With the growth of the global economy, a knowledge of international law becomes crucial. **International law** refers to the numerous regulations that govern international commerce. Companies must be aware of the domestic laws of trading partners, trade agreements such as NAFTA, and the rulings of such organizations as the World Trade Organization. For example, UPS recently brought a case against the Canadian postal service, contending that Canada is violating NAFTA by subsidizing the parcel delivery service of its post office.

In a broad sense, all law is business law because all firms are subject to the entire body of law, just as individuals are. In a narrower sense, however, **business law** consists of those aspects of law that most directly influence and regulate the management of various types of business activity. Specific laws vary widely in their intent from business to business and from industry to industry. The legal interests of Internet firms, for example, differ from those of hotel chains.

State and local statutes also have varying applications. Some state laws affect all businesses that operate in a particular state. Workers' compensation laws, which govern payments to workers for injuries incurred on the job, are an example. Other state laws apply only to certain firms or business activities. For example, states have specific licensing requirements for businesses like law firms, funeral directors, and hair salons. Many local ordinances also deal with specific business activities. Local regulations on the sizes and types of business signs are commonplace.

THE COURT SYSTEM

The judiciary, or court system, is the branch of government charged with deciding disputes among parties by applying laws. The judiciary consists of several types or levels of courts, each with a specific jurisdiction. Court systems are organized at the federal, state, and local levels. Administrative agencies also perform some limited judicial functions, but these agencies are more properly regarded as belonging to the executive or legislative branches of government.

Trial Courts

At both the federal and state levels, **trial courts**—courts of general jurisdiction—hear a wide range of cases. Unless a case is assigned by law to another court or to an administrative agency, a court of general jurisdiction will hear it. The majority of cases, both criminal and civil, pass through these courts. Within the federal system, trial courts are known as *U.S. district courts,* and at least one such court operates in each state. In the state court systems, the general jurisdiction courts are often called *circuit courts,* and states typically provide one for each county. Other names for general jurisdiction courts are *superior courts, common pleas courts,* or *district courts.*

State judiciary systems also include numerous courts with lower, or more specific, jurisdictions. These courts have limited jurisdictions in that they hear only certain sizes or types of cases. In most states, parties can appeal the decisions of these lower courts to the general jurisdiction courts. Examples of lower courts are probate courts (which settle the estates of deceased persons) and small-claims courts (where people can represent themselves in suits involving limited amounts of money).

Appellate Courts

Appeals of decisions made at the general trial court level are heard by **appellate courts.** Both the federal and state systems have appellate courts. An appeal usually is filed when the losing party feels that the case was wrongly decided by the judge or jury. The appeals process allows a higher court to review the case and correct any lower court error indicated by the appellant, the party making the appeal. Consider the recent case involving Napster, an Internet site that allowed users to swap copyrighted music. (The details of copyrights are discussed later in the appendix.) A federal judge in San Francisco issued a preliminary injunction essentially shutting the Web site down. The judge ruled that Napster would likely lose at trial. An appeals court stayed the injunction temporarily, but in 2001 the court ruled that copyright violations were occurring and ordered Napster not to download any copyrighted music.[2]

The federal court's appeals system, together with those of most states, consists of two tiers of courts. The federal courts at the intermediate level, called *U.S. circuit courts of appeal,* hear appeals of decisions from the U.S. district courts. The intermediate level of a state's appellate courts, if it exists, is known as the *court of appeals* or the *district court of appeals* in most states.

Appeals from decisions of the U.S. circuit courts of appeals can go all the way to the nation's highest court, the U.S. Supreme Court. Appeals from state courts of appeal are heard by the highest court in each state, usually called the *state supreme court.* In a state without intermediate appellate courts, the state supreme court hears appeals directly from the trial

BUSINESS DIRECTORY

➤ **law**   *standards set by government and society in the form of either legislation or custom.*

➤ **business law**   *aspects of law that most directly influence and regulate the management of business activity.*

➤ **judiciary**   *branch of the government charged with deciding disputes among parties through the application of laws.*

The nation's nine top jurors handle some of the United States's most pressing legal issues at the U.S. Supreme Court. The Court's Web site provides a wealth of information about the court and its activities.

courts. Parties not satisfied by the verdict of a state supreme court can appeal to the U.S. Supreme Court and may be granted a hearing if they can cite grounds for such an appeal and if the Supreme Court considers the case significant enough to be heard. It is unusual for a case to go all the way to the U.S. Supreme Court. In a typical year, the court hears roughly 100 of the 7,000 cases filed with it.

Specialized Courts

While the great majority of cases are resolved by the system of courts described here, certain highly specialized cases require particular expertise. Such cases are assigned to special courts by constitutional provisions or statutes. Examples of specialized federal courts are the U.S. Tax Court (for tax cases) and the U.S. Court of Claims (which hears claims against the U.S. government itself). Similar specialized courts operate at the state level.

Delaware's Chancery Court is a 200-year-old institution specializing in corporate governance. In a recent year, the court issued 130 opinions. This tiny court, located in Wilmington's Rodney Square, is important because almost 50 percent of the companies listed on the New York Stock Exchange are incorporated in Delaware. As early as 1913, many firms, attracted by Delaware's low corporate taxes, began relocating from New Jersey. As another draw, Delaware updates its corporate laws regularly. A Corporate Law Council, made up of members drawn from many of the state's largest law firms, periodically reviews trends in corporate law and recommends changes.

Administrative Agencies

Administrative agencies, also known as *bureaus, commissions,* or *boards,* decide a variety of cases at all levels of government. They usually derive their powers and responsibilities from state or federal statutes. In limited instances, their authority is constitutionally based. Technically, they conduct hearings or inquiries rather than trials. The parties are often represented by attorneys, evidence and testimony are included, and the agency issues legally binding decisions based on government regulations.

Examples of federal administrative agencies are the Federal Trade Commission (FTC), the National Labor Relations Board, and the Federal Energy Regulatory Commission. Examples at the state level include public utility commissions and boards that govern the licensing of various trades and professions. Zoning boards, planning commissions, and boards of appeal operate at the city or county level.

The FTC has the broadest power of any of the federal regulatory agencies. It enforces laws regulating unfair business practices, and it can stop false and deceptive advertising practices. Mergers of companies that result in large conglomerates have drawn much of the FTC's recent attention. For example, the FTC and its European counterpart effectively stopped WorldCom's acquisition of Sprint.

BASIC CONCEPTS OF THE LEGAL SYSTEM FOR BUSINESS

The cornerstones of U.S. business law consist of contract law; the Uniform Commercial Code; sales law; negotiable instruments law; property law; the law of bailment; agency law; tort law; bankruptcy law; trademark, patent, and copyright law; and tax law. The sections that follow set out the key provisions of each of these legal concepts.

Contract Law

Contract law is important because it is the legal foundation on which business dealings are conducted. A **contract** is a legally enforceable agreement between two or more parties regarding a specified act or thing.

Contract Requirements As Figure B.1 points out, the four elements of an enforceable contract are agreement, consideration, legal and serious purpose, and capacity. The parties must reach agreement about the act or thing specified. For such an agreement, or contract, to be valid and legally enforceable, each party must furnish consideration—the value or benefit that a party provides to the others with whom the contract is made. Assume, for example, that a builder hires an electrical contractor to wire a new house. The wiring job and the resulting payment are the considerations in this instance. In addition to consideration, an enforceable contract must involve a legal and serious purpose. Agreements made in a joking manner, related purely to social matters, or involving the commission of crimes are not enforceable as legal contracts. An agreement between two competitors to fix the prices for their products is not enforceable as a contract because the subject matter is illegal.

The last element of a legally enforceable contract is capacity, the legal ability of a party to enter into agreements. The law does not permit certain persons, such as those judged to be insane, to enter into legally enforceable contracts.

Contracts govern almost all types of business activities. Examples of valid contracts are purchase agreements with suppliers, labor contracts, franchise agreements, and sales contracts.

Breach of Contract A violation of a valid contract is called a **breach of contract**. The injured party can go to court to enforce the contract provisions and, in some cases, collect **damages**—financial payments to compensate for a loss and related suffering.

An oral contract Mike Tyson once made with his trainer cost the former heavyweight boxing champion an estimated $4.4 million. Tyson allegedly promised to employ the trainer as long as he fought professionally. The Second U.S. Court of Appeals ruled that a contract existed in this instance.[3]

Uniform Commercial Code

Most U.S. business law is based on the Uniform Commercial Code—usually referred to simply as the UCC. The UCC covers topics like sales law, warranties, and negotiable investments. With the exception of Louisiana, which continues to use the Napoleonic code, all the states have adopted the UCC. Even Louisiana has adopted some provisions of the UCC.

Sales law governs sales of goods or services for money or on credit. Article 2 of the UCC specifies the circumstances under which a buyer and a seller enter into a sales contract. Such agreements are based on the express conduct of the parties. The UCC generally requires written agreements for enforceable sales contracts for products worth more than $500. The formation of a sales contract is quite flexible because certain missing terms in a written contract or other ambiguities do not prevent the contract from being legally enforceable. A court will look to past dealings, commercial customs, and other standards of reasonableness to evaluate whether a legal contract exists.

FIGURE B.1
Four Elements of an Enforceable Contract

BUSINESS DIRECTORY

➤ **contract** *legally enforceable agreement between two or more parties regarding a specified act or thing.*
➤ **sales law** *law governing the sale of goods or services for money or on credit.*

Courts will also consider these variables when either the buyer or the seller seeks to enforce his or her rights in cases in which the other party fails to perform as specified in the contract, performs only partially, or performs in a defective or unsatisfactory way. The UCC's remedies in such cases consist largely of monetary damages awarded to injured parties. The UCC defines the rights of the parties to have the contract performed, to have it terminated, and to reclaim the goods or place a lien—a legal claim—against them.

Warranties   Article 2 of the UCC also sets forth the law of warranties for sales transactions. Products carry two basic types of warranties: an express warranty is a specific representation made by the seller regarding the product, and an implied warranty is only legally imposed on the seller. Generally, unless implied warranties are disclaimed by the seller in writing, they are automatically in effect. Other provisions govern the rights of acceptance, rejection, and inspection of products by the buyer; the rights of the parties during manufacture, shipment, delivery, and passing of title to products; the legal significance of sales documents; and the placement of the risk of loss in the event of destruction or damage to the products during manufacture, shipment, or delivery.

Negotiable Instruments

The term **negotiable instrument** refers to commercial paper that is transferable among individuals and businesses. The most common example of a negotiable instrument is a check. Drafts, certificates of deposit, and notes are also sometimes considered negotiable instruments.

Article 3 of the UCC specifies that a negotiable instrument must be written and must meet the following conditions:

1. It must be signed by the maker or drawer.
2. It must contain an unconditional promise or order to pay a certain sum of money.
3. It must be payable on demand or at a definite time.
4. It must be payable to order or to bearer.

Checks and other forms of commercial paper are transferred when the payee signs the back of the instrument, a procedure known as *endorsement*. Figure B.2 lists the four kinds of endorsement:

FIGURE B.2
Four Kinds of Endorsements

1. A *blank endorsement* consists only of the name of the payee. To make a blank endorsement, the payee need only sign the back of the instrument, which makes the check payable to the bearer. A blank endorsement should not be used for an instrument that moves through the mail.
2. A *special endorsement* specifies the person to whom the instrument is payable. With this kind of endorsement, only the person whose name appears after "Pay to the order of . . ." can benefit from the instrument.
3. A *qualified endorsement* contains words stating that the

endorser is not guaranteeing payment of the instrument. The qualified endorsement of "Without Recourse (signed)" limits the endorser's liability if the instrument is not backed by sufficient funds.

4. A *restrictive endorsement* limits the negotiability of the instrument. One of the most common restrictive endorsements, "For Deposit Only," is useful if an instrument (usually a check) is lost or stolen, because the instrument can only be deposited to the indicated account; it cannot be cashed.

Property Law

Property law is a key feature of the private enterprise system. Property is something for which a person or firm has the unrestricted right of possession or use. Property rights are guaranteed and protected by the U.S. Constitution.

As Figure B.3 shows, property can be divided into three basic categories. *Tangible personal property* consists of physical items such as equipment, supplies, and delivery vehicles. *Intangible personal property* is nonphysical property like mortgages, stocks, and checks that are most often represented by a document or other written instrument, although it may be as vague and remote as a computer entry. Students probably are familiar with certain types of intangible personal property such as checks and money orders. Other lesser known examples are important to the businesses or individuals that own and use them: bonds, notes, letters of credit, and warehouse receipts.

A third category of property is *real property*, or real estate. All firms have some concern with real estate law because of the need to buy or lease the space in which to operate. Some companies are created to serve these real estate needs. Real estate developers, builders, contractors, brokers, appraisers, mortgage companies, escrow companies, title companies, and architects all deal with various aspects of real property law.

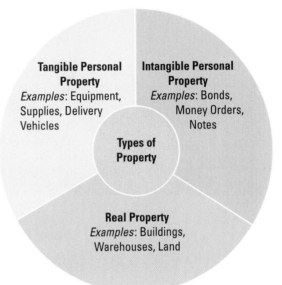

FIGURE B.3
Three Basic Types of Property

Law of Bailment

The law of bailment deals with the surrender of personal property by one person to another when the property is to be returned at a later date. The person delivering the property is known as the *bailor*, and the person receiving the property is the *bailee*. Some bailments benefit bailees, others benefit bailors, and still others provide mutual benefits. Most courts now require that all parties practice reasonable care in all bailment situations. The degree of benefit received from the bailment is a factor in court decisions about whether parties have met the reasonable care standards.[4]

Bailment disputes are most likely to arise in business settings such as hotels, restaurants, banks, and parking lots. A series of rules have been established to govern settlement of such disputes. The law focuses on actual delivery of an item. For example, the proprietor of a restaurant is not liable for theft or damage to a coat a patron decides to hang on a hook or on the back of a chair. The reason: the patron has made no actual delivery to the restaurant's proprietor. On the other hand, if the restaurant has a coat-checking room and the patron receives a claim check, the coat has been delivered and the proprietor is liable for theft or damage to the coat.

Law of Agency

An **agency** relationship exists when one party, called a *principal*, appoints another party, called the *agent*, to enter into contracts with third parties on the principal's behalf. All types of firms conduct business affairs through a variety of agents, such as partners, directors, corporate officers, and sales personnel.

The law of agency is based on common law principles and case law decisions of state and federal courts. Relatively little agency law has been enacted into statute. The law of agency is important because the principal is generally bound by the actions of the agent.

The legal basis for holding the principal liable for acts of the agent is the Latin maxim *respondent superior* ("let the master answer"). In a case involving agency law, the court must decide the rights and obligations of the various parties. Generally, the principal is held liable if an agency relationship exists and the agent has some type of authority to do the wrongful act. The agent in such cases is liable to the principal for any damages.

Law of Torts

A **tort** (French for "wrong") refers to a civil wrong inflicted on another person or the person's property. The law of torts is closely related to the law of agency because a business entity, or principal, can be held liable for torts committed by its agents in the course of business dealings. Tort law differs from both criminal and contract law. While criminal law is concerned with crimes against the state or society, tort law deals with compensation for injured persons who are the victims of noncriminal wrongs.

Tort cases are often extremely complex and frequently result in considerable judgments. A few years ago, Alamo Rent-A-Car was found liable for not warning a Dutch couple of a high crime area in Miami. The foreign tourists had rented the car in Tampa and were planning to drop it off in Miami on the other side of the state. When the wife was killed in a botched holdup, the family sued Alamo. A Florida jury awarded the family $5.2 million in damages, a verdict appealed by the car-rental company.[5]

Types of Torts   A tort may be intentional, or it may be caused by negligence. Assault, slander, libel, and fraud are all examples of intentional torts. Businesses can become involved in such cases through the actions of both owners and employees. A security guard who uses excessive force to apprehend an alleged shoplifter may have committed a tort. Under agency law, the guard's employers, such as a shopping mall or individual retailer, can be also held liable for any damages or injury caused by the security guard.

The other major group of torts result from negligence. This type of tort is based on carelessness rather than intentional behavior that causes injury to another person. Under agency law, businesses can also be held liable for the negligence of their employees or agents. The delivery truck driver who kills a pedestrian while delivering goods creates a tort liability for his or her employer if the accident results from negligence.

Product Liability   An area of tort law known as **product liability** has been developed by both statutory and case law to hold businesses liable for negligence in the design, manufacture, sale, or use of products. Some states have extended the theory of tort law to cover injuries caused by products, regardless of whether the manufacturer is proven negligent. This legal concept is known as strict product liability.

The business response to product liability has been mixed. To avoid lawsuits and fines, some recall defective products voluntarily; others decide to fight recall mandates if they feel the recall is not justified. Upon receiving reports of four infants falling through the leg openings of its backpack baby carriers, Huffco-Delaware responsibly recalled the 111,000 units sold to date. It also provided consumers with replacement kits with smaller leg openings.

Bankruptcy Law

Bankruptcy, the legal nonpayment of financial obligations, is a common occurrence in contemporary society. The term *bankruptcy* is derived from *banca rotta,* or "broken bench," referring to the medieval Italian practice of creditors breaking up the benches of merchants who did not pay their bills.

Federal legislation passed in 1918 and revised several times since then provides a system for handling bankruptcies. Congress is now considering further revisions to the bankruptcy code. Bankruptcy has two purposes. One is to protect creditors by providing a way to seize and distribute debtors' assets. The second goal, which is almost unique to the U.S., is to also protect debtors, allowing them to get a fresh start.

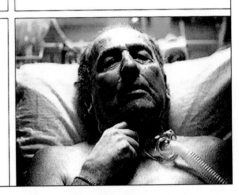

The tobacco industry's huge settlement with the nation's state attorneys general included funds to be used to inform the American public of the risks of smoking and to discourage the 3,000 kids who become regular smokers every day. A powerful television ad, "Electrolarynx," has appeared in programs as widely watched as a recent Super Bowl broadcast. The ad uses the voice of a former smoker to remind viewers that what hasn't changed is the tobacco industry's deadly and addictive product—and the consequences of using it.

Federal law recognizes two types of bankruptcy. Under *voluntary bankruptcy,* a person or firm asks to be judged bankrupt because of inability to repay creditors. Under *involuntary bankruptcy,* creditors may request that a party be judged bankrupt.

Personal Bankruptcies   Personal bankruptcy law has recently been revised to encourage more individuals to repay their debts rather than have them erased. Bankruptcy law offers individuals two primary options: Chapter 13 bankruptcy or Chapter 7 bankruptcy. Chapter 13 of the bankruptcy law—the wage earner plan—allows a person to set up a five-year debt repayment plan. Debtors often end up repaying only a portion of what they owe under Chapter 13. The court considers the bankrupt party's current income in determining the repayment schedule.

Chapter 7 sets out a liquidation plan under which a trustee sells the bankrupt person's assets and divides the proceeds among creditors. Changes to bankruptcy law in 2001 made it more difficult for individuals to file for Chapter 7 bankruptcy.[6] Debtors must generally participate in credit-counseling programs before they file for bankruptcy protection. In addition, bankruptcy judges use a complex formula to decide whether an individual's debts can be eliminated. Both of these provisions are expected to reduce the number of people qualifying for Chapter 7 bankruptcy.

Chapter 7 exempts limited amounts of selected property from the claims of creditors. These exemptions include retirement accounts, pensions, and limited levels of household furnishings, clothes, books, tools of one's trade, and prescribed health needs. Previous exemptions from full repayment of auto loans have been removed, and the amount of home equity that can be shielded from creditors has been greatly reduced.

Business Bankruptcies   Businesses can also go bankrupt. The specific provision under which they do this, Chapter 11, allows a firm to reorganize and develop a plan to repay its debts. Chapter 11 also permits prepackaged bankruptcies, in which companies enter bankruptcy proceedings after obtaining approval of most—but not necessarily all—of their creditors. Often companies can emerge from prepackaged bankruptcies sooner than those that opt for conventional Chapter 11 bankruptcy proceedings.

THEY SAID IT

"If it isn't the sheriff, it's the finance company. I've got more attachments on me than a vacuum cleaner."

JOHN BARRYMORE (1882–1942)
AMERICAN ACTOR

BUSINESS DIRECTORY

➤ **bankruptcy**   *legal nonpayment of financial obligations.*

Financially strapped firms sometimes seek out a merger with another firm. Given the potential liabilities, potential acquirers often require that the troubled company file under Chapter 11. This action is intended to avoid further litigation. Examples of this type of Chapter 11 filings include Washington Construction Group's takeover of Morrison-Knudsen and Mattel's acquisition of Purple Moon Media.[7]

Trademarks, Patents, and Copyrights

Trademarks, patents, and copyrights provide legal protection for key business assets by giving a firm the exclusive right to use those assets. A **trademark** consists of words, symbols, or other designations used by firms to identify their offerings. The Lanham Act (1946) provides for federal registration of trademarks. Trademarks are a valuable commercial property. For instance, Coca-Cola is considered to be the world's most widely recognized trademark.

If a product becomes too well known, this notoriety can create problems. Once a trademark becomes a part of everyday usage, it loses its protection as a legal trademark. Consider the fate of the terms *aspirin, cola, nylon, kerosene, linoleum,* and *milk of magnesia.* All of these products were once the exclusive property of their manufacturers; but they have passed into common language, and now anyone can use them. Companies often attempt to counter this threat by advertising that a term is actually a registered trademark. Xerox takes this approach to protecting its brand name with ads that point out that "Xerox" should never be used as a verb.

A **patent** guarantees an inventor exclusive rights to an invention for 17 years. Copyrights and patents have a constitutional basis; the U.S. Constitution specifies that the federal government has the power "to promote the progress of science and useful arts, by securing for limited times to authors and inventors the exclusive rights to their respective writings or discoveries." Patent owners often license others to use their patents for negotiated fees.

A **copyright** protects written material such as this textbook, designs, cartoon illustrations, photos, computer software, and so on. This class of business property is referred to as *intellectual property.* The Napster case mentioned earlier involved copyrighted intellectual property. Copyrights are filed with the Library of Congress. An author or his or her heirs hold exclusive rights to published works for the author's lifetime, plus 50 years. Works for hire and works whose authors use pseudonyms or write them anonymously receive copyright protection for a period of 75 years from publication or 100 years from creation, whichever is shorter.

Tax Law

A branch of law that affects every business, employee, and consumer in the U.S is tax law. A **tax** is an assessment by which government produces revenue. Federal, state, and local governments and special taxing authorities all levy taxes.

How Taxes Are Assessed

Some taxes are paid by individuals and some by businesses. Both have a decided impact on contemporary business. Business taxes reduce profits, and personal taxes cut the disposable incomes that individuals can spend on the products of industry. Governments spend their revenue from taxes to buy goods and services produced by businesses. Governments also act as transfer agents, moving tax revenue to other consumers and transferring Social Security taxes from the working population to retired or disabled persons.

Governments can levy taxes on several different bases: income, sales, business receipts, property, and assets. The type of tax varies from one taxing authority to the other. The individual income tax is the biggest source of revenue for the federal government. Many states rely heavily on revenue generated from sales taxes. In addition to sales taxes, some cities collect taxes on earnings. Finally, many community college districts get the bulk of their revenue from real estate or property taxes.

STAGES OF BUSINESS REGULATION

The emphasis in government regulation of business has changed over time. In fact, five specific regulatory eras can be identified: antitrust, protection of competition, consumer and employee protection, deregulation, and now cyberspace. Let's look at each of these eras and the legislation that characterized them.

Antitrust Era

John D. Rockefeller's Standard Oil monopoly precipitated the antitrust era. Breaking up monopolies and restraints of trade was a popular issue in the late 1800s and early 1900s. In fact, President Theodore Roosevelt always promoted himself as a "trust-buster." The highly publicized Microsoft case is a recent example of antitrust litigation.

The major federal legislation of the era includes the following:

Law	What It Did
Sherman Act (1890)	Set a competitive business system as a national policy goal. The act specifically banned monopolies and restraints of trade.
Clayton Act (1914)	Put restrictions on price discrimination, exclusive dealing, tying contracts, and interlocking boards of directors that lessened competition or might lead to a monopoly.
Federal Trade Commission Act (1914)	Established the FTC with the authority to investigate business practices. The act also prohibited unfair methods of competition.

Competitive Protection Laws

The 1930s saw the passage of several laws designed to protect the competitive environment for business. Actually, the rationale for many of these laws was protecting employment. Remember the world was in the midst of the Great Depression during the 1930s. So, government was very much concerned about keeping its citizens employed. Here are some specific examples of the state and federal laws passed during this era:

Law	What It Did
Robinson-Patman Act (1936)	Outlawed price discrimination in sales to wholesalers, retailers, or other producers. The act also banned pricing designed to eliminate competition.
Wheeler-Lea Act (1938)	Banned deceptive advertising. The act gave the FTC jurisdiction in such cases.
Fair Trade Laws (1930s)	Allowed manufacturers to stipulate retail prices (enacted at state level).
Unfair Trade Laws (1930s)	Set price floors for products (enacted at state level).

The IRS web site reflects the service's enhanced efforts at being taxpayer friendly.

Consumer and Employee Protection Era

The consumer and employee protection era is impossible to date since so many laws have been passed in this area. Although we cite just the major federal laws, it is important to note that much of this legislation was passed on the state and local levels. For instance, states like Oregon, Maine, and Michigan have bottle deposit laws. But, so does the city of Columbia, Missouri. Similarly, New Jersey mandates recycling, but so do many municipalities across the country.

The major federal laws of this era include the following:

Law	What It Did
Federal Food and Drug Act (1906)	Banned adulteration and misbranding of foods and drugs involved in interstate commerce.
Consumer Credit Protection Act (1968)	Required disclosure of annual interest rates on loans and credit purchases.
National Environmental Policy Act (1970)	Set up the Environmental Protection Agency to monitor various types of pollution and organizations that create pollution.
Public Health Cigarette Smoking Act (1970)	Prohibited tobacco advertising on radio and television.
Consumer Product Safety Act (1972)	Established the Consumer Product Safety Commission with authority to specify safety standards for most products.
Nutrition Labeling and Education Act (1990)	Stipulated detailed information on the labeling of most foods.
Americans with Disabilities Act (1991)	Banned discrimination against the disabled in public accommodations, transportation, and telecommunications.

Growing concerns about the environment coupled with a series of laws aimed at environmental protection have led thousands of businesses to move environmental protection to the top of the lists of corporate objectives. Major companies such as Chevron invest tens of millions of dollars in improving the habitats of both humans and threatened animal populations.

Coming In For A Safe Landing.

Their wings may span six feet. Bringing bald eagles grace and majesty, but also danger. And that's because the place an eagle decides to land might be a high-voltage power line. So people working in Wyoming built special platforms on top of power poles. Helping this threatened species land safely. And soar to new heights.

Chevron
People Do.
www.peopledo.com

Deregulation Era

Deregulation was a child of the 1970s. Many formerly regulated industries were freed to pick the markets they wanted to serve. The deregulated industries were also allowed to price their products without the guidance of federal regulations. For the most part, deregulation led to lower consumer prices. In some cases, it also led to a loss of service, as many smaller cities currently complaining about inadequate commercial air carrier service can attest.

Law	What It Did
Airline Deregulation Act (1978)	Allowed airlines to set fares and pick their routes.
Motor Carrier Act and Staggers Rail Act (1980)	Permitted the trucking and railroad industries to negotiate rates and services.
Telecommunications Act (1996)	Cut barriers to competition in local and long-distance phone, cable, and television markets.

The Era of Cyberspace

The Napster case demonstrates how the Internet is creating a whole new arena of regulatory decisions. Some cases like Microsoft's antitrust case are based on laws on the books for years. Other Internet-related regulation is based on more contemporary legislation. Just a few laws will suffice to illustrate this new regulatory era:

Law	What It Did
Children's Online Privacy Protection Act (1998)	Authorized the FTC to set rules regarding how and when firms must obtain parental permission before asking children marketing research questions.
Anticybersquatting Consumer Protection Act (1999)	Prohibited people from registering Internet domain names similar to company or celebrity names and then offering them for sale to these same parties.

Business Terms You Need to Know

law A-14
business law A-14
judiciary A-15
contract A-17
sales law A-17

negotiable instrument A-18
agency A-19
bankruptcy A-21
tax A-22

Other Important Business Terms

common law A-14
statutory law A-14
international law A-14
trial courts A-15

appellate courts A-15
breach of contract A-17
damages A-17
tort A-20

product liability A-20
trademark A-22
patent A-22
copyright A-22

➤ Assignments

1. Appendix B notes that many firms incorporate in Delaware. Such choices are at least partially because

Delaware regularly updates its corporate laws. A recent update permits the roughly 500,000 corporations registered in Delaware to hold electronic annual meetings. Delaware also allows annual meetings to be held via Web, e-mail, or fax. What is your opinion of the First State's novel approach to corporate governance? What advantages and disadvantages occur to you?

2. U.S. companies have long had to comply with the Sherman and Clayton Acts' provisions about restraint of trade, price discrimination, and monopolies. The United Kingdom has now adopted similar, but even stronger, rules. The Competition Act sets up the Office of Fair Trading (OFT) and grants it the power to investigate industrial cartels, price fixing, restrictions on customers or markets, no-compete agreements, and exclusive purchasing arrangements. The OFT also has the power to seize documents without notice and to levy hefty fines. While often compared with the U.S.'s Sherman Act, the new UK law is really closer to the European Union's competition law. How might the Competition Act benefit UK businesses and consumers? What, if any, downside do you see?

3. Use the Internet to select and research a state or federal business-related law enacted during the past year.

Why was this legislation passed? What were the arguments for and against it? How do you think the new law will affect businesses? Consumers? Society in general?

4. In lieu of professional fees—typically billed on an hourly basis—some attorneys accept cases on a contingency basis. The attorney earns nothing if he or she loses the case. If the case results in an award, the attorney collects a contingency fee, which is typically 30 percent of the total award. Use the Internet to research the arguments for and against contingency fees.

5. A Florida jury awarded the state's cigarette smokers over $140 billion in damages from the tobacco companies. Ignoring the arguments of both the plaintiffs and the defense in this case, what is your opinion of a damage award of this magnitude? What are the economic and legal implications of such an award? Discuss.

NOTES

PROLOGUE

1. Alex Salkever, "A Better Way to Float Your Résumé," *Business Week*, October 9, 2000, p. 202.
2. Patricia Kitchen, "Quality of Internet Job-Hunting Sites Can Make a Big Difference to Users," *Mobile Register*, April 17, 2000, p. D1.
3. Daniel Lyons, "'A' for Effort," *Forbes*, March 6, 2000, p. 140.
4. "Job Misplacement," *Forbes*, November 13, 2000, p. 44.
5. Career Center Online, accessed April 11, 2001, at www. jobweb.org.
6. Reported in Louis E. Boone, *Quotable Business*, 2nd Ed. New York: Random House, 1999, p. 103.

CHAPTER 1

1. Nantucket Nectars Web site, www.juiceguys.com, accessed August 26, 2000; "Two Men and a Bottle," *Inc., The State of Small Business 1998 (special issue)*, pp. 60–63.
2. Jodie T. Allen, "These Are the Good Old Days," *U.S. News & World Report*, January 31, 2000, pp. 36–38; Lee Walczak, Richard S. Dunham, and Howard Gleckman, "The Politics of Prosperity," *Business Week*, August 7, 2000, 96–100+; James C. Cooper and Kathleen Madigan, "The Great Jobs Machine Starts to Downshift," *Business Week*, July 24, 2000, pp. 27-28; Joseph Weber, "Tight Labor? Tech to the Rescue," *Business Week*, March 20, 2000, pp. 36–37; Mike Mandel, "The Case against Greenspan's Tougher Tactics," *Business Week*, March 20, 2000, pp. 38+.
3. Ronald Grover, "Meade Instruments: Back from a Black Hole," *Business Week*, May 29, 2000, p. 186.
4. J. William Gurley, "If iWon Wins, Do Portals Lose?" *Fortune*, February 7, 2000; Katie Motta, "Dot-Com Flop Tracker," *The Industry Standard*, July 18, 2000, downloaded from the Standard Web site, www.thestandard.com, August 14, 2000.
5. Beth Negus, "Where Everybody Knows Your Name," *1 to 1*, February 2000, pp. 34, 38; Beth Negus, "Personalized Broadcasting Systems," *1 to 1*, February 2000, pp. 33, 35.
6. Diane Brady, "When Nonprofits Go after Profits," *Business Week*, June 26, 2000, pp. 173–174, 178.
7. George Hager, "Sawmill Illustrates the Buzz about Productivity," *USA Today*, March 21, 2000, pp. 1B–2B.
8. Ibid.
9. Kathleen Kerwin, "Workers of the World, Log On," *Business Week*, February 21, 2000, p. 52.
10. Edward O. Welles, "The Greenhouse Effect," *Inc.*, State of Small Business 2000 issue, May 16, 2000, pp. 126–128, 131.
11. Adrian Slywotzky, "How Digital Is Your Company?" *Fast Company*, February–March 1999, pp. 94–96+.
12. Zoltan Acs, "The New American Evolution: The Role and Impact of Small Firms," Small Business Administration white paper, June 1998, downloaded from the SBA Web site, www.sba.gov, August 16, 2000; "Statistics about Small Business and Large Business from the U.S. Census Bureau," downloaded from the Census Bureau Web site, www.census.gov, August 14, 2000.
13. Don Debelak, "Music for the Masses," *Business Start-Ups*, December 1999, pp. 78, 80.
14. Quentin Hardy, "All Carly All the Time," *Forbes*, December 13, 1999, pp. 138–144.
15. Nancy K. Austin, "Rock through the Ages," *Inc.*, State of Small Business 2000 issue, May 16, 2000, pp. 68–70, 73–74, 76.
16. Daniel Gross, *Forbes' Greatest Business Stories of All Time* (New York: John Wiley & Sons, 1996), pp. 23–38 and 41–57.
17. Austin, "Rock through the Ages," pp. 70, 73.
18. Austin, "Rock through the Ages," p. 74.
19. Graniterock Web site, www.graniterock.com, downloaded August 17, 2000.
20. Geoffrey Colvin, "America's Most Admired Companies," *Fortune*, February 21, 2000, pp.108–111+; Daniel Lyons, "Make the Little Guys Feel Big," *Forbes*, April 17, 2000, pp. 210–211; Eryn Brown, "Selling to Businesses: Dell Computer," *Fortune*, May 24, 1999, p. 114.
21. U.S. Department of Commerce, "The Emerging Digital Economy II," June 1999, quoted in *Fast Company*, March 2000, p. 217.
22. "Computers Are in Half of U.S. Households," *USA Today*, October 17, 2000, p. B1; and Andy Reinhardt, "The Good Old Telephone Becomes a Hot New Web Tool," *Business Week*, April 24, 2000, p. 62.
23. "The World's Online Populations," June 8, 2000, downloaded from the CyberAtlas Web site, http://cyberatlas. internet.com, June 28, 2000.
24. "B-to-B," *Marketing News*, July 3, 2000, p. 19; Kathryn Kranhold, "Web Sites Toot Their Horns Amidst Advertising Chill," *The Wall Street Journal*, June 27, 2000, Interactive Edition downloaded at http://interactive.wsj.com.
25. George Hager, "Internet Industry Surges 'Startling' 62%," *USA Today*, June 6, 2000, downloaded from the USA Today Web site, www.usatoday.com.
26. Hager, "Internet Industry Surges"; Cliff Edwards, "Digital Economy: Internet-Related Jobs Double," *Mobile Register*, June 6, 2000, Business section, p. 1.

27. Liz Sly, "Mongolia's Nomads Roam World on Internet," *Chicago Tribune,* July 16, 2000, section 1, pp. 1, 10.

28. Albert F. Case Jr. and Kevin Murphy, "The Net Effect," *Executive Edge,* April/May 2000, pp. 27–31.

29. Robert McGarvey, "Connect the Dots," *Entrepreneur,* March 2000, pp. 78–80+.

30. "It's You, Virtually," *Direct,* November 15, 1999, p. 6.

31. Colvin, "America's Most Admired Companies," p. 110.

32. Peter A. Buxbaum, "Web of Collaboration," *Executive Edge,* April/May 2000, pp. 40–45.

33. Robert McGarvey, "Find Your Partner," *Entrepreneur,* February 2000, pp. 72–79.

34. Jim Collins, "Best Beats First," *Inc.,* August 2000, pp. 48–51.

35. Maryanne Murray Buechner, "How'd They Do?" *Time,* January 24, 2000, pp. B1–B4.

36. World Trade Organization, "Statistics: World Trade Overview," downloaded from the WTO Web site, www.wto.org, August 21, 2000.

37. World Trade Organization, "Statistics: Leading Exporters and Importers," downloaded from the WTO Web site, www.wto.org, August 21, 2000.

38. U.S. Census Bureau, "Top Ten Countries with which the U.S. Trades," downloaded from the Census Bureau Web site at www.census.gov/foreign-trade/www/balance.html, August 21, 2000.

39. Marc Ballon, "Upstarts: NAFTA," *Inc.,* February 1999, downloaded from the Inc. Web site, www.inc.com/magazine, August 22, 2000.

40. Welles, "The Greenhouse Effect," p. 131.

41. Ray Moseley, "Europe's Vacation Season Only a Dream for Americans," *Chicago Tribune,* August 7, 2000, downloaded from the Tribune Web site, www.chicago.tribune.com; "If Europeans Worked More . . . ," *Business Week,* July 14, 1997, p. 18.

42. Michael J. Mandel, "How Fast Can This Hot-Rod Go?" *Business Week,* November 29, 1999, pp. 40–42; David Wessel, "Report Says Technological Progress, Innovations Are Keys in New Economy," *The Wall Street Journal,* June 21, 2000, downloaded from the Interactive Edition, http://interactive.wsj.com.

43. Population Reference Bureau, "World Population Writers Forum: Quickfacts by Topic," downloaded from the PRB Web site, www.prb.org, August 22, 2000.

44. Courtney Rubin, "Consult a Kid," *USA Weekend,* December 10–12, 1999, p. 6.

45. Stephanie Armour, "As Workers Grow Older, Age-Bias Lawsuits Decline," *USA Today,* June 26, 1998, sec. B, p. 1.

46. U.S. Department of Labor, "Futurework: Trends and Challenges for Work in the 21st Century," Labor Day 1999, downloaded from the Labor Department Web site, www.dol.gov, July 24, 2000.

47. Population Reference Bureau, "World Population Writers Forum."

48. Wendy Zellner, "Keeping the Hive Humming," *Business Week,* April 24, 2000, pp. 50–52.

49. U.S. Department of Labor, "Futurework."

50. Mike Hofman, "Lost in the Translation," *Inc.,* May 2000, pp. 161–162.

51. Jenny C. McCune, "Telecommuting Revisited," *Management Review,* February 1998, pp. 10–16.

52. Anne Stuart, "Nailing It," *Inc. Technology,* March 14, 2000, pp. 111–112+.

53. U.S. Department of Labor, "Futurework."

54. Jerald Hyche, "Revolving Door Plagues Employers," *Mobile Register,* September 3, 2000, p. F1.

55. Christopher Caggiano, "The Appeasement Trap," *Inc.,* September 2000, pp. 46, 48–49.

56. Hemisphere Inc., "Diversity: The Bottom Line—Part III: Leveraging Diversity," *Forbes,* special advertising section, November 1, 1999.

57. "Making Diversity Work," *Business Week,* June 19, 2000, p. 16.

58. Norm Brodsky, "The View from Brooklyn," *Inc.,* State of Small Business 2000 issue, May 16, 2000, pp. 21–22.

59. Wes George, "Steve Jobs: We Want to Stand at the Intersection of Computers and Humanism," *The Mac Observer,* July 24, 2000, accessed at www.macobserver.com; Michael Krantz, "Steve Jobs at 44," *Time,* October 18, 1999, accessed at www.time.com.

60. Samuel Fromartz, "Creation Theory," *Inc.,* March 2000, pp. 97–98, 100, 103.

61. Nick D'Alto, "Think Big," *Business Start-Ups,* January 2000, pp. 61–65.

62. Mindy Blodgett, "Fast Forward," *CIO,* August 15, 1999, pp. 46–48+.

63. Blodgett, "Fast Forward," pp. 50, 54.

64. Blodgett, "Fast Forward," p. 56.

CHAPTER 2

1. Patagonia Web site, www.patagonia.com, accessed September 11, 2000; Roger Rosenblatt, "The Root of All Good," Time, October 18, 1999, pp. 88–91.

2. Joseph Weber, "3M's Big Cleanup," *Business Week,* June 5, 2000, pp. 96–98.

3. Weber, "3M's Big Cleanup," p. 98.

4. Susan J. Wells, "Turn Employees into Saints?" *HR Magazine,* December 1999, downloaded from the Society for Human Resource Management Web site, www.shrm.org, August 31, 2000; Karyn-Siobhan Robinson, "Employees Engaging in Deceptive Behaviors at Alarming Rates," HR News Online, July 21, 2000, downloaded from the Society for Human Resource Management Web site, www.shrm.org, August 31, 2000.

5. Polly Schneider, "Protecting What's Yours," *CIO,* February 15, 1999, sec. 1, p. 24; Daniel Eisenberg, "Eyeing the Competition," *Time,* March 22, 1999, pp. 58–60.

6. Ronald Grover, "The Perils of Teeing Off Online," *Business Week,* March 13, 2000, p. 44.

7. Paul Raeburn, "Drug Safety Needs a Second Opinion," *Business Week,* September 20, 1999, pp. 72, 74.

8. Jim Collins, "Built to ~~Last~~ Flip," *Fast Company,* March 2000, pp. 131–132+.

9. Melanie Warner, "Friends and Family," *Fortune,* March 20, 2000, pp. 102–104.

10. Peter Elkind, "Cendant Case Scorecard: Government 3; Book-Cookers 0," *Fortune,* July 10, 2000, p. 42.

11. Kenneth Labich, "No More Crude at Texaco," *Fortune,* September 6, 1999, pp. 205–206, 208, 210.

12. Dawn Marie Driscoll and W. Michael Hoffman, "Spot the Red Flags in Your Organization," *Workforce,* June 1997, pp. 135–136.

13. Society for Human Resource Management, "Businesses Paying More Attention to Ethics; Management Support Essential, Report Says," HR News Online, June 14, 2000, downloaded from the SHRM Web site, www.shrm.org, August 31, 2000.

14. Web pages from the Corporate Information section of the Nortel Networks Web site, www.nortelnetworks.com, downloaded August 30, 2000.

15. Michael J. McCarthy, "How One Firm Tracks Ethics Electronically," The Wall Street Journal, October 21, 1999, pp. B1, B4.

16. Wells, "Turn Employees into Saints?"

17. Jerry Useem, "New Ethics . . . or No Ethics?" Fortune, March 20, 2000, pp. 82–86.

18. SHRM, "Businesses Paying More Attention to Ethics."

19. Wells, "Turn Employees into Saints?"

20. Nortel Networks, "Ethical Business Practices," downloaded from the Nortel Networks Web site, www.nortelnetworks.com, August 30, 2000.

21. Amie Smith, "Canada Goes Green," Promo, July 1999, p. 67.

22. Shawn Young and Thor Valdmanis, "Justice Pulls Plug on Merger," USA Today, June 28, 2000, pp. 1B–2B.

23. Toys "R" Us v. Federal Trade Commission, No. 98–4107 (7th Cir. 2000), downloaded from the Federal Trade Commission Web site, www.ftc.gov, August 28, 2000.

24. "Federal Trade Commission Issues Interim Report on Midwest Gas Price Investigation," news release, July 28, 2000, downloaded from the FTC Web site, www.ftc.gov, August 28, 2000; Dan Carney, "The New Math of Antitrust," Business Week, February 28, 2000, [no page number]; Susan Warren, "The Outlook," The Wall Street Journal, July 3, 2000, downloaded from the Interactive Edition at http://interactive.wsj.com; Federal Trade Commission.

25. Federal Trade Commission, "Now Consumers Can Tell It to the FTC—Toll-Free," alert on the FTC Web site, July 1999, downloaded from the FTC Web site, www.ftc.gov, August 28, 2000.

26. "San Diego Utility Deregulation Causes Increased Bills, Ratepayer Revolt," The Electricity Forum, August 2000, accessed at www.electricityforum.com/news; Derek Slater, "High Wire Act," CIO, September 1, 1999, sec. 1, pp. 57–59, 61.

27. Deborah Kong, "Internet Auction Fraud Increases," USA Today, June 23, 2000, downloaded from the USA Today Web site, www.usatoday.com; Kara Swisher, "Seller Beware," The Wall Street Journal, December 7, 1998, p. R22; Glenn R. Simpson, "As FTC Rides Herd on the Web, Marketers Begin to Circle the Wagons," The Wall Street Journal, February 29, 2000, pp. B1, B4.

28. Heather Green, "Privacy: Outrage on the Web," Business Week, February 14, 2000, pp. 38–40; Amy Borrus, "The Privacy War of Richard Smith," Business Week, February 14, 2000, p. 40; Simpson, "As FTC Rides Herd on the Web"; Fred Vogelstein, "The Internet's Busybody," U.S. News & World Report, March 6, 2000, pp. 39–40; Fred Vogelstein, "Minding One's Business," U.S. News & World Report, March 13, 2000, p. 45; Wendy Melillo, "Getting Personal," Adweek, March 27, 2000, pp. 26–28; Marcia Stepanek, "None of Your Business," Business Week, June 26, 2000, pp. 78, 80; Art Jahnke, "Uninformed Consent,"

CIO Web Business, sec. 2, November 1, 1999, p. 22; Michael Moss, "A Web CEO's Elusive Goal: Privacy," The Wall Street Journal, February 7, 2000, pp. B1, B6; Jathon Sapsford, "That's Progress," Chicago Tribune, August 30, 2000, sec. 6, pp. 1, 7.

29. "Appeals Court Strikes Net Porn Law," Reuters Limited, June 23, 2000, accessed at www.zdnet.com; James Heckman, "COPPA to Bring No Surprises, Hefty Violation Fines in April," Marketing News, January 31, 2000, p. 6.

30. Anheuser-Busch Consumer Awareness and Education Web site, www.beeresponsible.com, downloaded August 30, 2000.

31. AT&T Foundation Web pages, downloaded from the AT&T Web site, www.att.com, August 30, 2000.

32. Procter & Gamble, "P&G Community Activity," downloaded from the P&G Web site, www.pg.com, August 30, 2000.

33. Jeffrey Kluger, "Watchdogs Who Bite," Time, February 7, 2000, p. 67.

34. Patricia Odell, "Blacklist," Direct, June 2000, pp. 1, 67–69.

35. Ellen Simon, "Philip Morris: Tobacco Giant Wants to Show its Good Side," Mobile Register, July 16, 2000, pp. 1F, 3F.

36. Harris Collingwood, "It Isn't Easy Being Green," Worth, July/August 2000, p. 22.

37. Ivan Amato, "Green Chemistry Proves It Pays," Fortune, July 24, 2000, pp. 270U–270JJ.

38. Sara Shay, "What a Waste" (interview with Peter Senge), CIO, February 1, 2000, pp. 42, 46.

39. Shay, "What a Waste," p. 46.

40. Daniel Wetzel, "McDonald's Seeks to Curtail Cruelty to Hens," Chicago Tribune, August 24, 2000, sec. 3, pp. 1, 4; David Greising, "McDonald's Gets a Leg Up with Bigger Hen Pens," Chicago Tribune, August 25, 2000, sec. 3, p. 1.

41. James R. Healey, "Toyota to Sell Prius Hybrid Only on Net," USA Today, April 19, 2000, p. 3B; Jeff Green, "Attention Techies and Assorted Geniuses: Toyota Prius Wants You," Brandweek, May 8, 2000, p. 113.

42. David Stipp, "Is Monsanto's Biotech Worth Less than a Hill of Beans?" Fortune, February 21, 2000, pp. 157–158, 160; David Stipp, "The Voice of Reason in the Global Food Fight" (interview with Gordon Conway), Fortune, February 21, 2000, pp. 164+; Helene Cooper and Scott Kilman, "Trade Rules on Biocrops Benign to U.S.," The Wall Street Journal, January 31, 2000, p. A3.

43. U.S. Department of Labor, "Futurework: Trends and Challenges for Work in the 21st Century," Labor Day 1999, downloaded from the Labor Department Web site, www.dol.gov, July 24, 2000.

44. David H. Freedman, "Restoration Software," Inc., May 2000, pp. 95–98+.

45. Labich, "No More Crude at Texaco."

46. Nortel Networks, "Community Involvement," downloaded from the Nortel Networks Web site, www.nortelnetworks.com, August 30, 2000.

47. "Campbell Recalling Soup after Consumers Found Aluminum Bits," The Wall Street Journal, February 28, 2000, p. A32.

48. Jennifer Brown, "Crayola Counters Charges," downloaded from the ABC News Web site, www.abcnews.go.com, May 25, 2000.

49. Dean Foust, "Easy Money," *Business Week,* April 24, 2000, pp. 107–110+.

50. Federal Trade Commission, "Business Opportunity Telemarketer Agrees to Pay $100,000 to Settle FTC Fraud Charges," news release, August 3, 2000, downloaded from the FTC Web site, www.ftc.gov, August 28, 2000.

51. Chris Adams, "Splitting Hairs on Supplement Claims," *The Wall Street Journal,* February 22, 2000, pp. B1, B4.

52. Steven C. Bahls and Jane Easter Bahls, "Risky Adventures," *Entrepreneur,* February 2000, pp. 128–130.

53. Christine Dugas, "Credit Card Fees on Increase, but Are Often Hard to Spot," *USA Today,* June 27, 2000, p. 1B.

54. Kong, "Internet Auction Fraud Increases."

55. Occupational Safety and Health Administration, "1998 OSHA Summary Estimates: Supplementary Charts," December 16, 1999, downloaded from the OSHA Web site, www.osha.gov, August 28, 2000.

56. Kathleen Furore, "Keeping Teens Safe on the Job," *Chicago Tribune,* August 27, 2000, sec. 6, pp. 1, 7.

57. Susan Chandler and Karen Mellen, "Shopper Concern about Sweatshop Labor Carries Uncertain Price Tag for Retailers," *Chicago Tribune,* August 24, 2000, sec. 3, pp. 1, 4; Aaron Bernstein, "Sweatshops: No More Excuses," *Business Week,* November 8, 1999, pp. 104, 106.

58. U.S. Department of Labor, "Futurework."

59. Jon G. Auerbach, "For Sycamore, Pressure Takes Its Toll in the Race to Build a Fiber-Optic Switch," *The Wall Street Journal,* July 19, 2000, downloaded from the Interactive Edition, http://interactive.wsj.com.

60. U.S. Department of Labor, Employment and Training Administration, "Birth and Adoption Unemployment Compensation; Final Rule," Federal Register Online, vol. 65, no. 114, June 13, 2000, pp. 37, 209–37, 227, downloaded at the Employment and Training Administration Web site, www.doleta.gov, August 28, 2000.

61. Robert McNatt, "Up Front: Gender-Neutral Benefits," *Business Week,* May 15, 2000, p. 14.

62. Equal Employment Opportunity Commisstion, "Policy Guidance on Executive Order 13145: To Protect Discrimination in Federal Employment Based on Genetic Information," EEOC notice, July 26, 2000, downloaded from the EEOC Web site, www.eeoc.gov, August 28, 2000.

63. Equal Employment Opportunity Commission, "EEOC Settles Egregious Racial Harassment Lawsuit against Louisiana Car Dealership," news release, August 16, 2000, downloaded from the EEOC Web site, www.eeoc.gov, August 28, 2000.

64. Stephanie N. Mehta, "What Minority Employees Really Want," *Fortune,* July 10, 2000, pp. 181–184, 186.

65. Joann Muller, "Ford: The High Cost of Harassment," *Business Week,* November 15, 1999, pp. 94, 96.

66. "Women Still Paid Far Less than Men," CBS MarketWatch, May 26, 2000, downloaded from the CBS MarketWatch Web site, http://cbs.marketwatch.com; Matthew Barakat, "Women Narrow Pay Gap," *Mobile Register,* July 4, 2000, p. 8B.

67. Nick Pachetti, "Tempest in a Coke Can," *Worth,* October 1999, pp. 51–56; Vern E. Smith, "Things Are Going Better with Coke," *Newsweek,* January 17, 2000, p. 52.

68. Securities and Exchange Commission, "Chairman Arthur Levitt Hails Leveling of Information Playing Field," news release, August 10, 2000, downloaded from the SEC Web site, www.sec.gov, August 28, 2000.

69. Peter Elkind, "The New Role of Directors," *Fortune,* March 20, 2000, pp. 116, 118.

70. Marc Ballon, "Yankee Pulled South by Mexican Magnet," *Inc.,* February 1999, downloaded from the Inc. Web site, www.inc.com.

71. Council on Economic Priorities Accreditation Agency Web site, www.cepaa.org, downloaded September 7, 2000.

72. Julie Schmit, "Nike's Image Problem," *USA Today,* October 4, 1999, pp. 1B–2B.

CHAPTER 3

1. U.S. Sports Camps Web site, www.esportcamps.com, accessed February 28, 2001; Lynn Woods, "Mom, Please Send Rocket Fuel," *Kiplinger's Magazine,* February 2000, accessed at www.kiplinger.com; Leigh Buchanan, "Pitching Camp," in "The Best of the Small Business Web," *Inc. Tech 1999,* no. 4, pp. 74–75.

2. John W. Schoen, "Analysts: It's a Banner Year for PC Sales," MSNBC, May 31, 2000, downloaded from the ZD-Net Web site, www.zdnet.com, September 13, 2000; "Surprise: PC Prices Increase," *The Wall Street Journal,* January 13, 2000, downloaded from the Interactive Edition at the ZDNet Web site, www.zdnet.com, September 13, 2000; Peter Burrows, "The Vise Trapping PC Makers," *Business Week,* October 25, 1999, pp. 40–41; Reuters News Service, "Lower-Income Web Users on the Rise," August 22, 2000, downloaded from the ZDNet Web site, www.zdnet.com, September 13, 2000.

3. Jeff Glasser and Marianne Lavelle, "Pump and Circumstance," *U.S. News & World Report,* July 3, 2000, pp. 16–18.

4. Ron Stodghill II, "Pump Up the Volume," *Time,* July 3, 2000, pp. 34–35.

5. Stodghill, "Pump Up the Volume"; Glasser and Lavelle, "Pump and Circumstance"; Christopher Palmeri and Stephanie Anderson Forest, "Who's to Blame?" *Business Week,* July 3, 2000, pp. 36–38.

6. Palmeri and Forest, "Who's to Blame?"

7. Jerry Edgerton, "A Trio of Hot Wheels," *Money,* August 2000, pp. 133–134.

8. "Heat Expected to Give Some Crop Prices a Lift," *Chicago Tribune,* September 13, 2000, sec. 3, p. 3. See also Joseph Weber, "Will Agribusiness Plow Under the Family Farm?" *Business Week,* October 23, 2000, pp. 50–52.

9. Arlene Weintraub, "For Online Pet Stores, It's Dog-Eat-Dog," *Business Week,* March 6, 2000, pp. 78, 80.

10. Christopher Palmeri, "Psst! Let's Raise Prices!" *Forbes,* October 4, 1999, pp. 60, 62.

11. Chana R. Schoenberger, "Go to Jail," *Forbes,* May 29, 2000, p. 62.

12. Romesh Ratnesar, "A Gem of a New Strategy," *Time,* September 25, 2000, p. B18.

13. Emily Barker, "Energy Deregulation: A Shock to the System," *Inc.,* November 2000, pp. 27–29; Dana James, "Deregulation Growing by Fits and Starts," *Marketing News,* June 5, 2000, pp. 10–11.

14. Central Intelligence Agency, "The World Factbook 2001—China," downloaded from the CIA Web site, www.cia.gov, February 11, 2001.

15. Shawn Tully, "Water, Water Everywhere," *Fortune,* May 15, 2000, pp. 343–344+.

16. Nick Pachetti, "The Decade of New Riches," *Money,* August 2000, p. 105; Nick Pachetti, "A Million Doesn't Buy What It Used To," *Money,* August 2000, p. 109.

17. Bureau of Labor Statistics, "Consumer Price Indexes: Frequently Asked Questions," April 18, 2000, downloaded from the BLS Web site, http://stats.bls.gov, February 11, 2001.

18. The Fraser Institute, "Canada Ranks Number Seven," news release, January 11, 2000, downloaded from the Fraser Institute Web site, www.fraserinstitute.ca, September 11, 2000; The Fraser Institute, "Hong Kong Recognized as the Most Economically Free Jurisdiction in the World," news release, January 11, 2000, downloaded from the Fraser Institute Web site, www.fraserinstitute.ca, February 28, 2001.

19. Reuters, "Warning: PCs May Be a Danger to Kids," news release, September 12, 2000, downloaded from the ZDNet News Web site, www.zdnet.com/zdnn/.

20. Geri Smith, "Tax Reform: Fox Is Pushing the Case," *Business Week,* July 24, 2000, pp. 52, 54.

21. "National Debt Clock Stops, Despite Trillions of Dollars of Red Ink," CNN.com, September 7, 2000, downloaded from the CNN.com Web site, www.cnn.com; Bureau of the Public Debt, "The Public Debt to the Penny," September 15, 2000, downloaded from the Bureau of the Public Debt Web site, www.publicdebt.treas.gov, September 18, 2000.

22. William Neikirk, "Debt-Free U.S. Might Be Too Rich to Stomach," *Chicago Tribune,* September 3, 2000, sec. 1, pp. 1, 19; Robert Kuttner, "What's Wrong with Paying Off the National Debt," *Business Week,* May 15, 2000, p. 35.

23. Rich Miller, Laura Cohn, Howard Gleckman, and Paula Dwyer, "How Prosperity Is Reshaping the American Economy," *Business Week,* February 14, 2000, pp. 100–104+.

24. Chana Schoenberger, "Campus Connection," *Forbes,* September 6, 1999, pp. 128, 130, 132.

25. Data from the Bureau of Labor Statistics Web site, http://stats.bls.gov, downloaded September 11–15, 2000.

26. Miller, Cohn, Gleckman, and Dwyer, "How Prosperity Is Reshaping the American Economy," p. 101.

27. Gene Koretz, "Retail's Wage-Price Squeeze," *Business Week,* September 20, 1999, p. 26.

28. U.S. Department of Labor, "Futurework: Trends and Challenges for Work in the 21st Century," Labor Day 1999, downloaded from the Labor Department Web site, www.dol.gov, July 24, 2000; Michael J. Mandel, "The Prosperity Gap," *Business Week,* September 27, 1999, pp. 90–92+.

29. Patrick Barta, "In This Expansion, as Business Booms, So Do the Layoffs," *The Wall Street Journal,* March 13, 2000, pp. A1, A16.

30. Miller, Cohn, Gleckman, and Dwyer, "How Prosperity Is Reshaping the American Economy," p. 103.

31. Gene Koretz, "The Hot New U.S. Labor Market," *Business Week,* September 20, 1999, p. 26.

32. Barta, "In This Expansion, as Business Booms, So Do the Layoffs," p. A1.

33. Scott Thurm, "Silicon Valley Economy Refuses to Join the Slump," *The Wall Street Journal,* July 18, 2000, downloaded from the Interactive Edition, http://interactive.wsj.com.

34. Howard Gleckman, "The Surplus: Now You See It . . . ," *Business Week,* February 14, 2000, p. 44; Associated Press, "Clinton Sees Much Higher Surplus: Over 10 Years, $1.87 Trillion in Black Ink," June 26, 2000, downloaded from the CBS MarketWatch Web site, cbs.marketwatch.com; Steven Butler, "The Trouble with the Soaring Surplus," *U.S. News & World Report,* June 26, 2000, p. 23; Jodie T. Allen, "First, Assume a Windfall," *U.S. News & World Report,* July 12, 2000, pp. 40–41.

35. Michael J. Mandel, "The Risk That Boom Will Turn to Bust," *Business Week,* February 14, 2000, pp. 120–122; George J. Church, "And the Beat Slows Down," *Time,* June 19, 2000, pp. B2–B3, B6.

36. Steven Butler and Jodie T. Allen, "The Economy Downshifts," *U.S. News & World Report,* June 19, 2000, pp. 38–40.

37. Miller, Cohn, Gleckman, and Dwyer, "How Prosperity Is Reshaping the American Economy," p. 106; Brian Bremner and Moon Ihlwan, "Edging towards the Information Age," *Business Week,* January 31, 2000, pp. 90–91; Scott Thurm, "Technology Spurs Economic Expansion," *The Wall Street Journal,* January 31, 2000, pp. A2, A13.

38. U.S. Department of Commerce, "The Emerging Digital Economy II," June 1999, quoted in *Fast Company,* March 2000, p. 217.

39. Jill Hecht Maxwell, "Fire Up the Handhelds," *Inc. Technology,* September 15, 2000, p. 26.

40. Church, "And the Beat Slows Down," p. B6; George J. Church, "The Economy of the Future?" *Time,* October 4, 1999.

41. Debra Aho Williamson, "The Net Effect," *Advertising Age,* Interactive Future special issue, 2000, pp. 64, 68+.

42. David Fairlamb and Gail Edmondson, "Work in Progress," *Business Week,* January 31, 2000, pp. 80–81, 84, 87.

43. Bremner and Ihlwan, "Edging towards the Information Age," p. 91.

44. Michael J. Mandel, "The New Economy," *Business Week,* January 31, 2000, pp. 73–77.

45. Population estimates and projections from the Census Bureau Web site, www.census.gov, downloaded September 18, 2000.

46. Gary S. Becker, "Longer Life Was the Century's Greatest Gift," *Business Week,* January 31, 2000, p. 32.

47. Gene Koretz, "Medical Costs of the 'Old Old,'" *Business Week,* January 31, 2000, p. 34.

48. U.S. Department of Labor, "Labor Day 2000: 10 Workforce Facts," September 2000, downloaded from the Labor Department Web site, www.dol.gov, September 11, 2000.

49. Koretz, "The Hot New U.S. Labor Market."

50. U.S. Department of Labor, "Labor Day 2000: 10 Workforce Facts."

51. George Hager, "Computers Complicate Productivity," *USA Today,* April 12, 2000, p. 3B.

52. Timothy J. Mullaney, "Needed: The Human Touch," *Business Week e.Biz,* December 13, 1999, pp. EB 53–EB 54.

53. Jim Sterne, "People Who Need People," *Inc. Technology,* September 15, 2000, pp. 131–132.

54. Yochi J. Dreazen, "Raleigh, N.C., Shows a Tight Labor Market Can Spur Productivity," *The Wall Street Journal,* February 7, 2000, pp. A1, A6.

55. U.S. Department of Labor, "Labor Day 2000: 10 Workforce Facts."

56. Ibid.

57. Robert Kuttner, "Ireland's Miracle: The Market Didn't Do It Alone," *Business Week,* July 10, 2000, p. 33.

58. Burrows, "The Vise Trapping PC Makers."

59. Justin Doebele, "The Big Tuna," *Forbes,* November 1, 1999, p. 386.

CHAPTER 4

1. "Asiacontent.com and MTV Launch MTVIndia.com," PR Newswire, October 13, 2000; Brett Pulley and Andrew Tanzer, "Sumner's Gemstone," *Forbes,* February 2000, pp. 107–111; MTV Web site, www.mtv.com, accessed October 10, 2000.

2. Central Intelligence Agency, "United States," *The World Factbook 2000,* downloaded at www.odci.gov/cia/ publications, August 21, 2000; Table 1, "U.S. International Trade in Goods and Services: Balance of Payments (BOP) Basis," June 20, 2000, downloaded from the International Trade Administration Web site, www.ita.doc.gov, September 22, 2000.

3. William Echikson, "American E-tailers Take Europe by Storm," *Business Week,* August 7, 2000, pp. 54–55.

4. Michael J. Mandel, "The New Economy," *Business Week,* January 31, 2000, pp. 73–77; John Rossant, "Old World, New Mandate," *Business Week,* January 31, 2000, p. 92.

5. David Fairlamb and Gail Edmondson, "Work in Progress," *Business Week,* January 31, 2000, pp. 80–81, 84, 87.

6. Rossant, "Old World, New Mandate."

7. Jeanette Borzo, "Russian Internet Companies Are Seeking Western Expertise," *The Wall Street Journal,* June 6, 2000, downloaded from the Interactive Edition at http:// interactive.wsj.com.

8. Mandel, "The New Economy," p. 73–74; Fairlamb and Edmondson, "Work in Progress," p. 84; Brian Bremner and Moon Ihlwan, "Edging toward the Information Age," *Business Week,* January 31, 2000, pp. 90–91.

9. Population Division of the Department of Economic and Social Affairs of the United Nations Secretariat, "Box 1, The World at Six Billion: Highlights," in *The World at Six Billion,* October 12, 1999, downloaded from the UN Population Division Web site, www.popin.org.

10. Dawn Thorndike Pysarchik, Jae-Eun Chung, and Linda Fernandes Plank, "Western-Style Prepared Foods Blaze Trail in Indian Market," *Marketing News,* August 16, 1999, p. 14.

11. Asia Recovery Information Center of the Asian Development Bank, "Regional Overview," September 18, 2000, downloaded from the ARIC Web site, www.aric.adb.org.

12. Central Intelligence Agency, "India," *The World Factbook 2000,* downloaded from the CIA Web site at www.odci.gov/ cia/publications/factbook/, September 26, 2000.

13. Pamela Druckerman, "Brazil Is a Free Internet-Access Test Site," *The Wall Street Journal,* February 7, 2000, p. A28.

14. Population data from the Global Statistics Web site, www.xist.org, downloaded September 22, 2000; GDP data from the World Bank, "Table 12, Structure of Output," *World Development Report 1999/2000,* downloaded from the World Bank Web site, www.worldbank.org, September 22, 2000.

15. Central Intelligence Agency, "Canada," *The World Factbook 2000,* downloaded from the CIA Web site at www.odci.gov/cia/publications/factbook/, September 26, 2000.

16. "U.S. Direct Investment Abroad in Selected Countries and Territories," *The World Almanac and Book of Facts 2000* (Mahwah, NJ: Primedia, 1999), p. 125.

17. Stephen Baker, "High-Tech Hibernia," *Business Week,* November 8, 1999, p. 78; Rob Norton, "The Luck of the Irish," *Fortune,* October 25, 1999, pp. 194–196+.

18. James Cox, "House to Back China Trade," *USA Today,* May 24, 2000, pp. A1–A2.

19. Gary Strauss, "China in WTO 'Is a Great Deal,'" *USA Today,* November 17, 1999, p. 3B.

20. Erik Guyot, "Reined In," *The Wall Street Journal,* September 27, 1999.

21. Matt Moffett, "Latin America Supplants Asia on Direct Investment," *The Wall Street Journal,* February 22, 2000, p. A24.

22. Jonathan Friedland, "The Have-Nots," *The Wall Street Journal,* September 27, 1999.

23. "FYEye: Mr. Mustard," *Forbes FYI,* Fall 2000, p. 31.

24. "Canon: A New Age of the Image," *Fortune* special advertising section, July 24, 2000, p. S4.

25. Data from the U.S. Department of Commerce, "Table 1, U.S. International Trade in Goods and Services: Balance of Payments (BOP) Basis," June 20, 2000, downloaded from the International Trade Administration Web site, www.ita.doc.gov.

26. Lorraine Woellert, "Deficit Noshing," *Business Week,* March 20, 2000, p. 8.

27. Mark Frankel, "Now Hong Kong Is a Magic Kingdom," *Business Week,* November 15, 1999, p. 54.

28. Nancy Coltun Webster, "El Sitio USA Pitches Image in Bilingual Ads," *Advertising Age,* May 22, 2000, p. 30.

29. Data from the International Trade Administration, "Table 7, U.S. Total Imports from Individual Countries, 1991–99," downloaded from the ITA Web site, www.ita.doc.gov, September 22, 2000.

30. "Falling Euro," *Mobile Register,* July 14, 1999, p. 10A; "Euro Jumps against Dollar after Concerted Intervention," *The Wall Street Journal,* September 22, 2000, downloaded from the Interactive Edition at http:// interactive.wsj.com.

31. Moffett, "Latin America Supplants Asia on Direct Investment."

32. Justin Fox, "The Euro Is a Raging Success—*Really* It Is," *Fortune,* October 30, 2000, p. 50.

33. Ameet Sachdev, "Singing the Currency Blues," *Chicago Tribune,* September 22, 2000, sec. 3, pp. 1, 10; Christopher Rhoads, "Policy Makers Choose to Take Little Action on Weak Euro," *The Wall Street Journal,* January 31, 2000, pp. A21, A26.

34. "The 50 Most Widely Spoken Languages in the World," based on data from Barbara F. Grimes, ed., *Ethnologue,* 13th ed. (Summer Institute of Linguistics, 1996), downloaded from the Information Please Web site, www. infoplease.com, August 11, 2000. Some of the languages listed are technically dialects, listed separately because they are different enough that speakers of other dialects cannot understand them.

35. Sally McGrane, "Cultural Web Faux Pas," *Forbes ASAP,* February 21, 2000, p. 28.

36. Kate Murphy, "Gifts without Gaffes for Global Clients," *Business Week,* December 6, 1999, p. 153.

37. Ray Moseley, "Europe's Vacation Season Only a Dream for Americans," *Chicago Tribune,* August 22, 2000, sec. 1, downloaded from the Tribune Web site, http://archive. chicago.tribune.com.

38. Normandy Madden, "Asia Online: Business Growing Despite Barriers," *Advertising Age International,* May 2000, pp. 23, 25; Juliana Koranteng, "Dial 'M' for E-Commerce," *Advertising Age International,* May 2000, pp. 1, 24.

39. "The International Beat: 'We're Number, uh, Whatever,'" *Inc. Technology,* September 15, 2000, p. 28.

40. Ken Belson, "Net Shopping: Why Japan Won't Take the Plunge," *Business Week,* July 31, 2000, p. 64.

41. Elisabeth Malkin, "Can This Man Crack Open the Mexican Markets?" *Business Week,* September 20, 1999, p. 56.

42. Paul Starobin and Sabrina Tavernise, "Russia: Can Putin Squash Dissent and Free the Economy?" *Business Week,* May 29, 2000, p. 73; Paul Starobin, "Will Putin Crack Down?" *Business Week,* April 3, 2000, pp. 54–56.

43. Organization for Economic Cooperation and Development, "Membership," September 19, 2000, downloaded from the OECD Web site, www.oecd.org; Frédéric Wehrlé, "Enforcing the Convention," *OECD Observer,* May 19, 2000, downloaded from the OECD Web site at www. oecdobserver.org; Martine Milliet-Einbinder, "Writing Off Tax Deductibility," *OECD Observer,* May 26, 2000, downloaded from the OECD Web site at www.oecdobserver.org; Transparency International, "The Transparency International Bribe Payers Survey," January 20, 2000, downloaded from the Transparency International Web site, www. transparency.de.

44. Transparency International, "The Transparency International Bribe Payers Survey"; Transparency International, "Transparency International Releases the Year 2000 Corruption Perceptions Index," news release, September 13, 2000, downloaded from the Transparency International Web site, www.transparency.de.

45. Helene Cooper and David Rogers, "Senate Passes Bill to Normalize U.S. Trade Relations with China," *The Wall Street Journal,* September 20, 2000, downloaded from the Interactive Edition at http://interactive.wsj.com; Dexter Roberts and Paul Magnusson, "Welcome to the Club," *Business Week,* November 29, 1999, pp. 34–36.

46. Michael Plogell and Felix Hofer, "No-Nos in Europe," *Promo,* April 2000, pp. 23, 24, 26.

47. Neal E. Boudette, "In Europe, Surfing a Web of Red Tape," *The Wall Street Journal,* October 29, 1999, pp. B1, B4.

48. Julian Nundy, "French Stage Big Mac Attack," *USA Today,* July 29, 1999, p. 3B.

49. Michael Doyle, "U.S. Pistachio Growers Ponder Competition from Iran," *Nando Times,* March 19, 2000, downloaded from the Nando Times Web site, www.nandotimes.com.

50. Margot Hornblower, "The Battle in Seattle," *Time,* November 29, 1999, pp. 40–42, 44; Aaron Bernstein, "Backlash: Behind the Anxiety over Globalization," *Business Week,* April 24, 2000, pp. 38–42, 44.

51. Dina Temple-Raston, "Protesters vs. Globalization, Part 2," *USA Today,* April 13, 2000, p. 3B.

52. Rich Miller, "Does Anybody Love the IMF or World Bank?" *Business Week,* April 24, 2000, pp. 46–47.

53. Laura Cohn and David Fairlamb, "Will the IMF Get a Dose of Its Own Medicine?" *Business Week,* October 4, 2000, pp. 36–37.

54. Miller, "Does Anybody Love the IMF or World Bank?"

55. Adam Zagorin, "Seattle Sequel," *Time,* April 17, 2000, pp. 57–58.

56. Geri Smith, "Mexico Pulls Off Another Trade Coup," *Business Week,* February 7, 2000, p. 56.

57. Michelle Mittelstadt, "Impact of NAFTA Eyed after 5 Years," Associated Press, January 28, 1999, downloaded from the Hartford Web Publishing site, www. hartford-hwp.com.

58. Smith, "Mexico Pulls Off Another Trade Coup;" "The Nonsense About NAFTA," *Fortune,* October 2, 2000, p. 244.

59. Stephen Baker, "The Future Goes Cellular," *Business Week,* November 8, 1999, p. 74.

60. David Fairlamb, "How Far, How Fast?" *Business Week,* November 8, 1999, pp. 64–66.

61. J. William Gurley, "Like It or Not, Every Startup Is Now Global," *Fortune,* June 26, 2000, p. 324.

62. "In a Foreign Market? Watch Out for the Bank," *Inc.,* September 1999, p. 10.

63. Cheryl Rosen, "HoJo Heads to Europe," *Business Travel News,* July 19, 1999, p. 12.

64. Thomas K. Grose, "Brand New Goods," *Time,* November 1, 1999.

65. Gene Bylinsky, "For Sale: Japanese Plants in the U.S.," *Fortune,* February 21, 2000, pp. 240C–240D+.

66. Brian Zajac, "Global Giants," *Forbes,* July 24, 2000, p. 335.

67. Alexandra Kirkman, "Demolition Racer," *Forbes,* November 1, 1999, p. 388.

68. Robert L. Simison, Gregory L. White, and Deborah Ball, "GM's Linkup with Fiat Opens Final Act of Consolidation Drama for Industry," *The Wall Street Journal,* March 14, 2000, pp. A3, A8.

69. Erika Rasmusson, "Global Sales on the Line," *Sales & Marketing Management,* March 2000, pp. 76, 78, 80–82.

70. Normandy Madden, "Nike Sells $25 Shoe Line in Recession-Hit Region," *Advertising Age International,* November 1999, p. 17.

71. Bradford W. Ketchum Jr., "Going Global," *Inc. Technology* special advertising section, November 16, 1999.

72. Zach Coleman, "Asian Airlines Aim to Rival U.S. with a New Joint Internet Site," *The Wall Street Journal,* June 7, 2000, downloaded from the Interactive Edition, http:// interactive.wsj.com.

73. Bernard Wysocki Jr., "The Outlook," *The Wall Street Journal,* June 12, 2000, downloaded from the Interactive Edition, http://interactive.wsj.com.

74. Jean Halliday, "Toyota Leads in Hispanic Niche," *Advertising Age,* July 3, 2000, p. 16.

75. Peter Malbin, "Chrysler Shifts into New Gear," *Advertising Age International,* February 2000, pp. 17–18.

76. Ian Johnson, "Herbal Remedies Aimed at East and West," *The Wall Street Journal,* January 31, 2000, p. A26.

77. Erika Rasmusson, "E-Commerce around the World," *Sales & Marketing Management,* February 2000, p. 94.

78. Margaret McKegney, "Dell Adapts Well to Online Sales," *Advertising Age International,* May 2000, p. 26.

79. David Osterhout, "Maytag Name Missing in China Ad Effort," *Advertising Age International,* May 2000, pp. 2, 11.

CHAPTER 5

1. "Mission" and "Products," Ritz Foods Web site, accessed January 8, 2001, at www.ritzfoods.com; "The Snack Chip with a Twist: Newly Introduced Yuca Chip 40% Less Fat and More Flavorful than Potato Chips," press release of the Pennsylvania Food Merchants Association, February 9, 2000, www.pfma.org; John Grossman, "The World's Oldest Start-up," *Inc.,* March 1999, pp. 59–69.

2. U.S. Census Bureau, "Statistics about Small Business and Large Business from the U.S. Census Bureau," downloaded from the Census Bureau Web site, www.census.gov, October 6, 2000.

3. Office of Advocacy, U.S. Small Business Administration, "The Facts about Small Business, 1999," p. 1, downloaded from the SBA Web site, www.sba.gov/advo.

4. Office of Advocacy, U.S. Small Business Administration, "Minorities in Business," 1999, p. 27, downloaded from the SBA Web site, www.sba.gov.

5. Small Business Administration, "SBA Size Standards: Frequently Asked Questions," downloaded from the SBA Web site at www.sba.gov/size, October 9, 2000.

6. D. M. Osborne, "Taking on Procter & Gamble," *Inc.,* October 2000, pp. 67–68, 70–71.

7. Roger O. Crockett, "Diamond Technology: Attack of the Killer Apps," *Business Week,* May 29, 2000, p. 188.

8. Adam L. Penenberg, "Crossing Amazon," *Forbes,* April 17, 2000, pp. 168, 170.

9. U.S. Department of Agriculture, *Agriculture Fact Book 1999,* July 2000, pp. 20, 23, downloaded from the USDA Web site, www.usda.gov.

10. Bureau of the Census, "Increase in At-Home Workers Reverses Earlier Trend," *Census Brief,* No. CENBR/98-2, March 1998, downloaded from the Census Bureau Web site, www.census.gov.

11. Millicent Lownes-Jackson and Gerda Gallop-Goodman, "Flying Solo: How to Build a Profitable Enterprise," *Black Enterprise,* January 2000, pp. 73–74+.

12. John Hechinger, "A Tiny Bank Has Cast Its Spell on the Internet," *The Wall Street Journal,* July 20, 2000, downloaded from the Interactive Edition, http://interactive.wsj.com.

13. SBA, "The Facts about Small Business, 1999," p. 1.

14. SBA, "The Facts about Small Business, 1999," p. 2.

15. SBA, "The Facts about Small Business, 1999," p. 1.

16. Emily Barker, "The Company They Keep," *Inc.,* May 2000, pp. 85–86, 88, 91.

17. Christopher Caggiano, "The New Urban Chic," *Inc.,* May 1999, pp. 59–62.

18. Stephen Barlas, "Inner-City Innovation," *Entrepreneur,* February 2000, pp. 136–137.

19. Leigh Buchanan, "Send in the Clowns," *Inc.,* September 2000, pp. 90–94.

20. John Carey, "Albany Molecular Research: All R&D, All the Time," *Business Week,* May 29, 2000, p. 192.

21. SBA, "The Facts about Small Business, 1999," p. 5.

22. Jim Carlton, "EBay Diversifies to Meet Needs of Small Firms," *The Wall Street Journal,* March 16, 2000, p. B12.

23. D. M. Osborne, "Start-Ups for Start-Ups," *Inc.,* February 2000, pp. 23–24, 26.

24. Maudlyne Ihejirika, "Untapped Workforce," *Chicago Tribune,* August 27, 2000, sec. 6, p. 3.

25. Christopher Cooper and Erik Portanger, "Flashy Clothing Site Had Good Ideas, but Financial Controls Were Lacking," *The Wall Street Journal,* June 27, 2000, downloaded from the Interactive Edition at http://interactive.wsj.com.

26. SBA, "The Facts about Small Business, 1999," p. 9.

27. Julie Carrick Dalton, "Start-Up's Epitaph: One Product Beats Three," *Inc.,* February 2000, p. 28.

28. Jonathan Kaufman, "Instead of Making Him Rich, a Dot-Com Gives Mr. Carter the Boot," *The Wall Street Journal,* January 4, 2000, pp. A1, A6.

29. Dale D. Buss, "Issue of the Decade," *The Wall Street Journal,* May 24, 1999, p. R28.

30. Mike Hofman, "Stifled Growth," *Inc.,* September 2000, pp. 107–108.

31. Mary Kwak, "Name That Business Plan," *Inc. Technology,* September 15, 2000, p. 23.

32. C. J. Prince, "The Ultimate Business Plan," *Success,* January 2000, pp. 44–49.

33. Prince, "The Ultimate Business Plan."

34. National Business Incubator Association Web site, www.nbia.org, downloaded March 16, 2000.

35. James Lardner, "Ideas on the Assembly Line," *U.S. News & World Report,* March 20, 2000, pp. 48–50.

36. Amy Barrett, "Incubators Are Feeling the Chill," *Business Week,* May 8, 2000, p. 113.

37. Rachael King, "Joe's Dot-Com Garage," *Inc. Technology,* September 15, 2000, pp. 125–126, 128.

38. Janet Rae-Dupree, "A Real Shot in the Arm for a Virtual Pharmacy," *Business Week,* March 8, 1999, p. 40.

39. William M. Bulkeley, Joseph Pereira, and Bruce Orwall, "Toysmart, Disney Deal Hit Snags in a Web of Conflicting Goals," *The Wall Street Journal,* June 7, 2000, downloaded from the Interactive Edition at http://interactive.wsj.com.

40. National Foundation for Women Business Owners, "Key Facts," downloaded from the NFWBO Web site, www.nfwbo.org, March 16, 2000.

41. NFWBO, "Key Facts."

42. Don Debelak, "Let's Make a Deal," *Entrepreneur,* December 1999, pp. 170–171.

43. SBA, "The Facts about Small Business, 1999," pp. 3–5; SBA, "Minorities in Business," pp. iii, 1.

44. SBA, "Minorities in Business," pp. 14–15.

45. Doug Levy, "Colorblind Commerce?" *USA Today,* August 17, 1999, pp. 1B–2B.

46. Michelle Prather, "Heat of the Moment," *Entrepreneur,* January 2000, pp. 157–161.

47. SBA, "Minorities in Business," pp. 4, 26.

48. Andrew A. Caffey, "Analyze This," *Entrepreneur,* January 2000, pp. 163–167.

49. "Be Your Own Boss: 112 Top Franchises for 2000," *Black Enterprise,* April 2000, pp. 169–171.

50. Bernadette Adams Davis, "Fabulous Frozen Fruit Operation," *Black Enterprise,* September 1999, p. 42.

51. David M. Fritz, "Franchising Has Its Limitations," *Marketing News*, March 13, 2000, p. 16.

52. Sonya Kimble-Ellis, "10 Franchises You Can Afford," *Black Enterprise*, September 2000, pp. 113–114+.

53. Caffey, "Analyze This."

54. SBA, "Minorities in Business," p. 26. The data exclude C corporations (generally the larger businesses) and businesses with less than $500 in receipts.

55. SBA, "The Facts about Small Business, 1999," p. 5.

56. Andrea Petersen, "StarMedia Is Set to Boost Reach in Spain Market," *The Wall Street Journal*, June 22, 1999, p. B9.

57. Jim Kerstetter, "Serena Software: Keeping All Systems Go," *Business Week*, May 29, 2000, p. 194.

58. "*Fortune* 1000 List," downloaded from the *Fortune* Web site, www.fortune.com, January 8, 2001.

59. Gail Edmondson, "See the World, Erase Its Borders," *Business Week*, August 28, 2000, pp. 113–114.

60. Carol Vinzant, "Why *Do* Corporations Love Delaware So Much?" *Fortune*, February 1, 1999, p. 32.

61. Bo Burlingham, "The Boom in Employee Ownership," *Inc.*, August 2000, pp. 106–108, 110, 112 (interview with Corey Rosen).

62. National Center for Charitable Statistics, Center on Nonprofits and Philanthropy, Urban Institute, "Number of Nonprofit Entities in the United States, 1989–1997," table downloaded from the NCCS Web site, http://nccs.urban.org, October 13, 2000.

63. Data and examples are from "Let's Make a Deal: Mergers, Acquisitions Set Record," *Providence Journal*, December 31, 1999, downloaded from the Northern Light Web site, http://library.northernlight.com; Lori Pugh, "Acquisition Faucet Continues Steady Flow," *Indianapolis Business Journal*, January 24, 2000, downloaded from the Northern Light Web site, http://library.northernlight.com; David R. Francis, "How Global Wave of Mergers Hits Candidates, Customers," *Christian Science Monitor*, September 25, 2000, downloaded from the Northern Light Web site, http://library.northernlight.com; Charles P. Wallace, "A Vodacious Deal," *Time*, February 14, 2000, p. 63; Karl Taro Greenfeld, "A Media Giant," *Time*, September 20, 1999, pp. 48–54.

64. Eleena de Lisser, "Banking on Mergers," *The Wall Street Journal*, May 24, 1999, p. R25.

65. William J. Holstein and Fred Vogelstein, "You've Got a Deal!" *U.S. News & World Report*, January 24, 2000, pp. 34–40.

66. Jim Carlton, "Webvan Will Acquire HomeGrocer for $1.09 Billion as Market Heats Up," *The Wall Street Journal*, June 27, 2000, downloaded from the Interactive Edition at http://interactive.wsj.com.

67. Sean Donahue, "Pipe Dreams," *Business 2.0*, January 2000, pp. 90, 93, 95.

CHAPTER 6

1. Richie Whitt, "The Challenger: After Years in the NBA Wasteland, the Mavericks Hope to Show They're Ready for Prime Time, *Fort Worth Star-Telegram*, November 10, 2000, accessed at dailynews.yahoo.com; Dwain Price, "Cuban Sets Sights on Smith," *Fort Worth Star-Telegram*, November 10, 2000, accessed at dailynews.yahoo.com; Richard Hoffer, "Dallas Maverick," *Sports Illustrated*, November 6, 2000, pp. 88–93.

2. Martha E. Mangelsdorf, "Follow the Numbers," *Inc.*, October 17, 2000, pp. 67–68; "Data Mine," *Inc.*, October 17, 2000, pp. 57–61, 64–65.

3. Steven Berglas, "<u>G</u> Is for *Guts*," *Inc.*, May 2000, pp. 45, 46, 48.

4. Deidra-Ann Parrish, "Cooking Up Profits," *Black Enterprise*, January 2000, p. 42.

5. Telephone interview with Marianne Sullivan, Administrative Director, Center for Entrepreneurial Leadership, June 1, 1995.

6. Silvia Sansoni, "A Man in a Hurry," *Forbes*, October 4, 1999, pp. 78, 80.

7. Stephen D. Solomon, "Bear Feat," *Inc.*, October 17, 2000, pp. 167–168.

8. Parrish, "Cooking Up Profits."

9. "The Phoenix 500," *Success*, July 1998, pp. 37–38+.

10. Kauffman Center for Entrepreneurial Leadership, "Entrepreneurship QuickFacts," downloaded from the EntreWorld Web site, www.entreworld.org, October 24, 2000.

11. Paulette Thomas, "Rewriting the Rules," *The Wall Street Journal*, May 22, 2000, downloaded from the Interactive Edition at http://interactive.wsj.com.

12. Stephanie Armour, "Net Firms Soar on Campus," *USA Today*, April 12, 2000, pp. 1B–2B.

13. Thomas, "Rewriting the Rules."

14. Nancy J. Lyons, "Moonlight over Indiana," *Inc.*, January 2000, pp. 71, 73–74.

15. Gayle Sato Stodder, "The Insiders," *Business Start-Ups*, February 2000, pp. 54–59.

16. Ron MacLean, "My Start-Up, Myself," *Inc.*, October 17, 2000, pp. 210–211.

17. "Data Mine," *Inc.*, October 17, 2000, pp. 57–61, 64–65.

18. Michael Maiello, "Hot Dogs," *Forbes*, April 3, 2000, p. 32.

19. Sara Callard, "'Supersize Those Fries!'" *Inc.*, October 17, 2000, p. 124.

20. Kavin G. Salwen, "Thinking about Tomorrow," *The Wall Street Journal*, May 24, 1999, pp. R30–R31 (interview with David L. Birch).

21. Office of Advocacy, U.S. Small Business Administration, "The Facts about Small Business, 1999," downloaded from the SBA Web site at www.sba.gov/advo.

22. Edward O. Welles, "Flexible Flyers," *Inc.*, October 17, 2000, pp. 172–173, 175.

23. Eleena de Lisser, "Start-Up Attracts Staff with a Ban on Midnight Oil," *The Wall Street Journal*, August 23, 2000, pp. B1, B6.

24. Leigh Buchanan, "Mother Is the Necessity of Invention," *Inc.*, January 2000, pp. 49, 51–52.

25. Marci McDonald, "A Start-Up of Her Own," *U.S. News & World Report*, May 15, 2000, pp. 34–38+.

26. Thaddeus Wawro, "Hero Worship," *Entrepreneur*, March 2000, pp. 114–121.

27. Stodder, "The Insiders," p. 59.

28. Thomas, "Rewriting the Rules."

29. Thomas, "Rewriting the Rules."

30. "Data Mine," p. 61.

31. Moira Allen, "East Meets World," *Entrepreneur*, April 2000, p. 60.

32. Robert Horn, "Thailand's Big Cheese," *Time,* September 25, 2000, p. B13.
33. Sharpe, "Teen Moguls," p. 114.
34. Emily Barker, "The VC in My Dorm Room," *Inc.,* October 2000, pp. 42–45, 48.
35. Michael Warshaw, "Top Gun for Start-Ups," *Inc.,* October 2000, pp. 53–54.
36. Armour, "Net Firms Soar on Campus," p. 2B
37. Joan O'C. Hamilton, "*Survivor* for Student Startups," *Business Week E.Biz,* July 24, 2000, pp. EB 99–EB 102+.
38. Marc Ballon, "What Level Playing Field?" *Inc.,* May 1999, pp. 34–36+.
39. Mangelsdorf, "Follow the Numbers."
40. Lee Rainie, "MomandPop.com," *The Standard,* February 28, 2000, downloaded from The Standard Web site, www.thestandard.com.
41. Susan Hansen, "Discount Club Throws Bone to Pet Owners," *Inc.,* September 1999, pp. 23–24.
42. Ewing Marion Kauffman Foundation, "Global Study on Entrepreneurship Reveals Direct Link between Rate of New Business Start-Ups and Economic Growth," news release, June 21, 1999, downloaded from the Kauffman Foundation Web site, www.emkf.org.
43. Carleen Hawn, "Juggling Act," *Forbes,* November 1, 1999, pp. 242, 244.
44. William Boston, "Berlin's 'Cool' Lifestyle Becomes a Magnet for Internet Start-Up," *The Wall Street Journal,* February 29, 2000, pp. A17, A19.
45. National Commission on Entrepreneurship, "Fast Facts," downloaded from the Policy Makers Toolkit of the NCOE Web site, www.ncoe.org, October 24, 2000.
46. George Gendron, "The Origin of the Entrepreneurial Species," *Inc.,* February 2000, pp. 105–106+ (interview with Amar V. Bhidé).
47. Megan Santosus, "RSVP," *CIO Web Business,* December 1, 1999, sec. 2, p. 18.
48. "Fill 'Er Up—Anytime," *Success,* February 1999, p. 66.
49. Kauffman Center, "Entrepreneurship QuickFacts"; NCOE, "Fast Facts." For more background on gazelles, see also the Cognetics Web site, www.cogonline.com.
50. Sean M. Lyden, "Pass It On," *Business Start-Ups,* February 2000, p. 62.
51. Christopher Caggiano, "Insider Training," *Inc.,* May 1999, pp. 63–64.
52. Kauffman Center for Entrepreneurial Leadership, "Does Gender Matter?" October 2000, downloaded from the EntreWorld Web site, www.entreworld.org.
53. Sharon Nelton, "Who's the Boss?" *Success,* June 2000, pp. 76–79.
54. This discussion is based on Donald F. Kuratko and Richard M. Hodgetts, *Entrepreneurship: A Contemporary Approach,* 4th ed. (Fort Worth, Tex.: Dryden Press, 1998), pp. 101–106.
55. National Public Radio, "Leadership in America: Jeff Bezos," *Morning Edition,* October 3, 2000, downloaded from the NPR Web site, www.npr.org.
56. Gendron, "The Origin of the Entrepreneurial Species," p. 106.
57. "Crunching the Numbers," *Success,* February 1999, p. 70.
58. Thea Singer, "The Power of Balance," *Inc.,* October 17, 2000, pp. 105–108, 110.
59. Gendron, "The Origin of the Entrepreneurial Species," p. 110.
60. Michelle Prather, "Gettin' Jiggly with It," *Entrepreneur,* January 2000, pp. 143–145.
61. Alex Purugganan, "No Bull," *Entrepreneur's Start-Ups,* November 2000, downloaded from the Entrepreneur.com Web site, www.entrepreneur.com.
62. Anne Marie Borrego, "Start-Up Springboards," *Inc.,* October 17, 2000, pp. 202, 204.
63. Gerda D. Gallop, "At the Top of Their Game," *Black Enterprise,* November 1998, pp. 115–116+.
64. Cynthia E. Griffin, "Look a Little Closer . . . ," *Entrepreneur,* February 2000, p. 44.
65. Gendron, "The Origin of the Entrepreneurial Species," pp. 109–110.
66. Purugganan, "No Bull."
67. Thomas Melville, "Throwing a Tea Party," *Success,* September 2000, pp. 38–39.
68. Emily Barker, "When Creating Companies Is Habit-Forming," *Inc.,* October 17, 2000, p. 19.
69. Wendy Beech, "Look before You Leap," *Black Enterprise,* September 1999, pp. 95–96+. [at p. 96]
70. MacLean, "My Start-Up, Myself," p. 210.
71. Jeffrey L. Seglin, "Superman in Recovery," *Inc.,* October 1999, pp. 66–68, 71.
72. Gendron, "The Origin of the Entrepreneurial Species," p. 110.
73. Salwen, "Thinking about Tomorrow," p. R31.
74. Emily Barker, "Red-Tape Brainstorms," *Inc.,* October 17, 2000, pp. 17–18; "*Inc.* 500: The List," *Inc.,* pp. 121, 123+.
75. Robert Johnson, "This Pair's Shoes Are Soles of Indiscretion; That's a Selling Point," *The Wall Street Journal,* February 25, 2000, pp. A1, A4.
76. Jill Andresky Fraser, "Seven Entrepreneurs in Search of a Deal," *Inc.,* April 2000, pp. 116–118, 120.
77. Frieda Rapoport Caplan, "The Kiwi Queen Plays Songs of Love," October 2000, downloaded from the EntreWorld Web site, www.entreworld.org.
78. "*Inc.* 500: The List," p. 145; "Data Mine," p. 65.
79. Millicent Lownes-Jackson and Gerda Gallop-Goodman, "Flying Solo: How to Build a Profitable Enterprise," *Black Enterprise,* January 2000, pp. 73–74+.
80. Michelle Prather, "Street Smarts," *Entrepreneur,* February 2000, p. 24.
81. Fraser, "Seven Entrepreneurs in Search of a Deal," p. 118.
82. McDonald, "A Start-Up of Her Own," p. 38.
83. Jill Andresky Fraser, "How to Finance Anything," *Inc.,* March 1999, pp. 32–37+. [at p. 39].
84. Emily Barker, "Bust-Up's Outcome: More Start-Ups," *Inc.,* October 17, 2000, p. 19.
85. "Grassroots Venture Capital," *Inc.,* September 2000, p. 51; Mangelsdorf, "Follow the Numbers."
86. "Let Your People Go," *Inc.,* September 2000, pp. 78–79 (interview with Gary Hamel).
87. Anne Marie Borrego, "Inside Play," *Inc.,* September 2000, pp. 74–76, 78–80; Elite.com Web site, http://elite.com, downloaded February 12, 2001.

CHAPTER 7

1. "Razorfish Named One of New York's Fastest-Growing Technology Companies in Deloitte & Touche's Fast 50,"

Business Wire, September 7, 2000; "Sharp Unveils New Consumer Intuitive Web Site, Razorfish Work Breaks New Ground in Ease of Navigation," *Business Wire,* September 7, 2000; "Razorfish Gains an Edge," *BBC News,* April 4, 2000, http://news.bbc.com.uk; Megan Doscher, "Decisions, Decisions," *The Wall Street Journal,* November 22, 1999, p. R54.

2. "The World's Online Populations," June 8, 2000, accessed at the CyberAtlas Web site, http://cyberatlas.internet.com, June 28, 2000; "Two-Thirds of Americans Online," May 10, 2000, accessed at the CyberAtlas Web site, http://cyberatlas.internet.com, June 15, 2000.

3. NetNames, "DomainStats.com," June 29, 2000, downloaded at www.domainstats.com, June 29, 2000.

4. George Anders, "Better, Faster, Prettier," *The Wall Street Journal,* November 22, 1999, p. R6.

5. "If You Lived in Finland," *Forbes,* May 22, 2000, p. 24.

6. Robyn Meredith, "Digital Drive," *Forbes,* May 29, 2000, pp. 128–134.

7. "The World's Online Populations," June 8, 2000, accessed at the CyberAtlas Web site, http://cyberatlas.internet.com, June 28, 2000.

8. Liza Roberts, "Women on the Web," CBS MarketWatch, Internet Daily Europe, August 9, 2000, www.cbs.marketwatch.com; "European Internet Use Still behind the U.S.," May 1, 2000, accessed at the CyberAtlas Web site, http://cyberatlas.internet.com, June 15, 2000.

9. The Internet Economy Indicators, "Facts and Figures," accessed at the Internet Indicators Web site, www.internetindicators.com, June 15, 2000.

10. Bevolyn Williams-Harold, "Across the Great Divide," *Black Enterprise,* March 2000, p. 30.

11. "Baby Boomers and Seniors Fastest Growing Web Groups," April 4, 2000, accessed at the CyberAtlas Web site, http://cyberatlas.internet.com, June 29, 2000.

12. "Two-Thirds of Americans Online."

13. Joellen Perry, "Only the Cyberlonely," *U.S. News & World Report,* February 28, 2000, p. 62.

14. "More Small Businesses Going Online," May 31, 2000, accessed at the CyberAtlas Web site, http://cyberatlas.internet.com, June 15, 2000.

15. Michael Warshaw, "The Thing That Would Not Die," *Inc. Technology,* March 14, 2000, pp. 89–90+.

16. "Why Consumers Value the Internet," *Sales & Marketing Management,* March 2000, p. 90.

17. Alessandra Bianchi, "E Is for E-School," *Inc.,* July 2000, pp. 29–30, 32.

18. "The Top 50 Sites of May 2000," June 13, 2000, accessed at the CyberAtlas Web site, http://cyberatlas.internet.com, June 15, 2000.

19. Gwendolyn Mariano, "Stock Fraud Spurs Regulators to Look Online," CNet News.com, June 21, 2000.

20. "40 Percent of America's Kids Online," and "TV Viewers, Gamers Catch Internet Bug," June 8, 2000, accessed at the CyberAtlas Web site, http://cyberatlas.internet.com, June 15, 2000.

21. Kenneth Hein, "Stephen King Scares Up Interest in E-Books," *iMarketing News,* March 20, 2000, accessed at the Northern Light Web site, http://library.northernlight.com, July 11, 2000.

22. Arlene Weintraub, "A Ticket to Dot.Com Heaven?" *Business Week,* April 10, 2000, pp. 87–88.

23. Leigh Buchanan, "The Best of the Small Business Web," *Inc. Technology,* no. 4 1999, pp. 62–64+.

24. The Internet Economy Indicators, "Facts and Figures," accessed at the Internet Indicators Web site, www.internetindicators.com, June 15, 2000.

25. Ira Sager, "Inside IBM: Internet Business Machines," *Business Week E.Biz,* December 13, 1999, pp. EB 20–EB 23+.

26. Don Tapscott, "Startups in the Game to Trim Bureaucracy," *Forbes ASAP,* May 29, 2000, p. 70.

27. Anne Stuart, "B-to-Bs Bring in the Bucks," *CIO Web Business,* November 1, 1999, sec. 2, p. 24.

28. Bob Tedeschi, "Catalog Retailers Fly to Success on the Web," July 3, 2000, sec. 4, pp. 1–2.

29. "The State of Small Business: This Moment in Numbers," *Inc.,* State of Small Business 2000 issue, p. 98; "$6 Trillion in B2B Trade by 2005," June 26, 2000, accessed at the CyberAtlas Web site, http://cyberatlas.internet.com, June 28, 2000.

30. Elise Ackerman, "To B2B or Not to B2B?" *U.S. News & World Report,* February 7, 2000, p. 36.

31. Ackerman, "To B2B or Not to B2B?"

32. "Company Profile," Covisint Web site, www.covisint.com, accessed September 5, 2000; David Welch, "Oh, What a Feeling: B2B," *Business Week,* May 15, 2000, p. 14; Alex Taylor III, "Detroit Goes Digital," *Fortune,* April 17, 2000, pp. 170–172, 174; Lauren Gibbons Paul, "The Biggest Gamble Yet," *CIO,* April 15, 2000, pp. 144–150+.

33. Robert Guy Matthews, "Web Sites Made of Steel," *The Wall Street Journal,* September 16, 1999, pp. B1, B4.

34. Calmetta Y. Coleman and Ernest Beck, "Big Retailers in U.S., Europe Form Exchange," *The Wall Street Journal,* April 3, 2000, p. B19.

35. Sari Kalin, "High-Flying Extranet," *CIO Web Business,* December 1, 1999, sec. 2, p.70.

36. Bruce Bond, "Dial C for C-Commerce," *Executive Edge,* April/May 2000, pp. 13, 16–17.

37. Steve Konicki, "Exchanges Go Private," *InformationWeek,* June 12, 2000, accessed at the InformationWeek Online Web site, www.informationweek.com, June 16, 2000.

38. "U.S. Internet Sales Grow 5.3% in Q2," *USA Today* online, August 31, 2000.

39. "Maybe the End Can Wait," April 18, 2000, accessed at the CyberAtlas Web site, http://cyberatlas.internet.com, July 5, 2000.

40. Richard B. Schmitt, "Online Venture Invites Law Firms to Bid for Work," *The Wall Street Journal,* April 12, 2000, pp. B1, B4.

41. "Top E-tailers of April 2000," May 9, 2000, accessed at the CyberAtlas Web site, http://cyberatlas.internet.com, June 15, 2000.

42. "Cyberconsumption," *Inc.,* January 2000, p. 23.

43. Sreenath Sreenivasan, "Clicking for Cash," *Time Digital,* July 2000, p. 70.

44. Marcia Stepanek, "None of Your Business," *Business Week,* June 26, 2000, pp. 78, 80.

45. "President Signs E-signature Bill," *USA Today* online, June 30, 2000, www.usatoday.com.

46. Susan Headden, "A New John Hancock," *U.S. News & World Report,* June 26, 2000, p. 10; Juliet Eilperin and John Schwartz, "Electronic Signatures Bill Passes the House," *Washington Post,* June 15, 2000, accessed at the

Washington Post Web site, www.washingtonpost.com, June 15, 2000.

47. Stepanek, "None of Your Business."

48. "Amazon Modifies Privacy Policy," *Reuters Limited,* August 27, 2000; Nick Wingfield, "Amazon Clarifies Customer Info Policy," *The Wall Street Journal,* September 1, 2000, Interactive Edition, accessed at www.zdnet.com.

49. Tim Jones, "FTC Asks Court to Halt Toysmart's Biggest Sale Yet: Customer Data Lists," *Chicago Tribune,* July 11, 2000, sec. 3, pp.1, 4; Nick Wingfield, "Amazon Clarifies Customer Info Policy," *The Wall Street Journal,* September 1, 2000, Interactive Edition, accessed at www.zdnet.com.

50. Tom Weber, "Protecting Consumers' Privacy May Start to Pay Off on Internet," *The Wall Street Journal,* June 12, 2000, Interactive Edition, accessed at http://interactive.wsj.com.

51. Mary Kwak, "Fair Play?" *Inc. Technology,* March 14, 2000, p. 24.

52. Mike Hofman, "Software to Watch over Me," *Inc.,* July 2000, pp. 49, 51–52.

53. Scott McCartney, "Security System Breach Stirs Up Airline Rivalry," *The Wall Street Journal,* June 27, 2000, Interactive Edition, accessed at http://interactive.wsj.com.

54. Noelle, Knox, "Online Auctions Top List of Internet Fraud," *USA Today,* August 28, 2000, www.usatoday.com.

55. Anne Kates Smith, "The Web's Dark Side: The Cybersmear," *U.S. News & World Report,* August 28, 2000, p. 40.

56. William Symonds, "Akamai Figured Out How to Make a Faster I-Way," *Business Week,* April 3, 2000, accessed at the Northern Light Web site, http://library.northernlight.com, July 8, 2000.

57. Silvia Sansoni, "Santa Flaws," *Forbes,* December 27, 1999, pp. 282–284.

58. Marci McDonald, "You Haven't Got Mail," *U.S. News & World Report,* February 28, 2000, p. 62.

59. "Upstarts: Internet Convenience Services," *Inc.* September 2000, p. 26.

60. Katrina Brooker, "The Nightmare before Christmas," *Fortune,* January 24, 2000, pp. 24–25.

61. Jenny Price, "Lands' End Sews Up Online Sales with Top Service," *Indianapolis Star,* December 27, 1999, p. B3.

62. Lisa Bannon, "With Christmas Closing In Fast, Mattel's Web Site Is Sidelined by Snarls," *The Wall Street Journal,* December 2, 1999, pp. B1, B4.

63. Bob Duncan, "First Do No Harm," *Inc. Technology,* March 14, 2000, pp. 29–30.

64. Anna Wilde Mathews, " Concerned Father Makes Transition to Media Pirate," *The Wall Street Journal,* June 30, 2000, Interactive Edition, accessed at http://interactive.wsj.com.

65. Andrew G. McCormick and Laura N. Mankin, "The Death of Cybersquatting?" *CIO,* April 15, 2000, pp. 60–64.

66. Fara Warner, Jeffrey Ball, and George Anders, "Can the Big Guys Rule the Web? Ask Ford or Dunkin' Donuts," *The Wall Street Journal,* August 30, 1999, pp. A1, A10.

67. Emily Barker, Anne Marie Borrego, and Mike Hofman, "I Was Seduced by the Web Economy," *Inc.,* February 2000, pp. 48–51+ (quoting Tod Johnson on page 51).

68. Megan Doscher, "Decisions, Decisions," *The Wall Street Journal,* November 22, 1999, p. R54.

69. Nick Wingfield, "The Game of the Name," *The Wall Street Journal,* November 22, 1999, p. R14.

70. Alessandra Bianchi, "What's Cooking On-Line?" *Inc.,* January 2000, pp. 23–24.

71. Melissa Campanelli, "E-Business Busters," *Entrepreneur,* January 2000, pp. 46, 50.

72. Marc Ballon, "What Level Playing Field?" *Inc.,* May 1999, pp. 34–36+.

73. Jill Hecht Maxwell, "Almost Free E-Commerce," *Inc. Technology,* March 14, 2000, pp. 80–83.

74. Keith Ferrell, "What Does EC Stand For? Today, Easy Commerce," *Success,* February 1999, pp. 73–75.

75. Kathryn Kranhold, "Web Sites Toot Their Horns Amidst Advertising Chill," *The Wall Street Journal,* June 27, 2000, Interactive Edition, accessed at http://interactive.wsj.com; Charlie Morris, "Banner Advertising Statistics," *Web Developer's Journal,* June 28, 2000, accessed at http://WebDevelopersJournal.com, June 29, 2000.

76. J. William Gurley, "The One Internet Metric That Really Matters," *Fortune,* March 6, 2000, p. 392.

77. "Maybe the End Can Wait," April 18, 2000, accessed at the CyberAtlas Web site, http://cyberatlas.internet.com, July 5, 2000.

78. Barker, Borrego, and Hofman, "I Was Seduced by the Web Economy," p. 64.

79. "Worldwide E-Commerce" and "World's Online Population," figures in *Marketing News,* July 3, 2000, p. 15.

80. Lee Gomes, "(Not) Made in America," *The Wall Street Journal,* November 22, 1999, p. R66.

81. "The Multilingual Net," *CIO Web Business,* sec. 2, December 1, 1999, p. 18.

82. "Latin America Still Trails in Internet Race," June 13, 2000, accessed at the CyberAtlas Web site, http://cyberatlas.internet.com, June 15, 2000.

83. Katarzyna Moreno, "Global Pains," *Forbes,* March 20, 2000, pp. 286, 288.

84. Neal E. Boudette, "In Europe, Surfing a Web of Red Tape," *The Wall Street Journal,* October 29, 1999, pp. B1, B4.

CHAPTER 8

1. "Nokia History," Nokia Web site, www.nokia.com, accessed April 14, 2001; Nokia Corporation, Business and Financial Summaries, Yahoo Finance, biz.yahoo.com, April 10, 2001; Justin Fox, "Nokia's Secret Code," *Fortune,* May 1, 2000, pp. 160–174.

2. Amy Barrett, "Can Bonsignore Get the New Honeywell Humming?" *Business Week,* April 10, 2000, p. 171.

3. Jay Greene, "If at First You Don't Succeed," *Business Week,* April 24, 2000, pp. 120–121+.

4. Michelle Conlin, "Tough Love for Techie Souls," *Business Week,* November 29, 1999, pp. 164, 166+.

5. Michael Moeller, "Remaking Microsoft," *Business Week,* May 17, 1999, pp. 106–112+; Greene, "If at First You Don't Succeed."

6. Adam Bryant, "Up Top from Down Under," *Newsweek,* January 17, 2000, p. 52.

7. Emily Thornton, "Remaking Nissan," *Business Week,* November 15, 1999, pp. 70–72+.

8. Polly Labarre, "Unit of One: Leaders.com," *Fast Company,* June 1999, pp. 95–98+.

9. Diane Brady, "WWF: One Rock-'Em, Sock-'Em Company," *Business Week,* May 29, 2000, p. 182.

10. John A. Byrne, "PepsiCo's New Formula," *Business Week,* April 10, 2000, pp. 172–174+.

11. Mark Henricks, "Change of Face," *Entrepreneur,* April 2000, pp. 125, 127.

12. Henricks, "Change of Face," p. 125.

13. Byrne, "PepsiCo's New Formula," p. 172.

14. Labarre, "Unit of One," p. 108.

15. Jeff Schlegel, "Something Brewin'," *Individual Investor,* February 2000, pp. 60–61.

16. Ibid.

17. Anne Marie Borrego, "Stop Worrying and Love eBay," *Inc.,* State of Small Business 2000 issue, May 16, 2000, pp. 33–34, 39–40.

18. Brian O'Reilly, "The Mechanic Who Fixed Continental," *Fortune,* December 20, 1999, pp. 176–178+.

19. Jonathan Eig, "General Mills to Reshape Doughboy in Its Own, User-Friendly Image," *The Wall Street Journal,* July 18, 2000, downloaded from the Interactive Edition, http://interactive.wsj.com.

20. Chandrani Ghosh, "Station Roundup," *Forbes,* July 3, 2000, pp. 122–124.

21. Geoffrey Smith, "Reality Bites at Raytheon," *Business Week,* November 15, 1999, pp. 78, 80, 82.

22. Stephen D. Colomon, "Go Sell It on the Mountain," *Inc.,* December 1999, pp. 48–50+.

23. "Stop the Politics," *Forbes ASAP,* April 3, 2000, p. 126.

24. Jack Ewing, "Siemens: Building a 'B-School' in Its Own Backyard," *Business Week,* November 15, 1999, pp. 281–282.

25. Emily Nelson and Nikhil Deogun, "New Chief of Procter & Gamble Faces Tough Strategic Choices," *The Wall Street Journal,* June 12, 2000, downloaded from the Interactive Edition, http://interactive.wsj.com.

26. For these and other current examples, see "100 Best Companies to Work For," at *Fortune*'s Web site, www.fortune.com.

27. Louise Lee, "Tricks of E*Trade," *Business Week E.Biz,* February 7, 2000, pp. EB 18–EB 22+.

28. Joan Hamilton, "Net Work," *Business Week E.Biz,* April 3, 2000, pp. EB 116–EB 118+.

29. Constance Gustke, "Hammer Time," *Worth,* July/August 2000, pp. 61–62, 64; Daintry Duffy, "Cultural Evolution," *CIO Enterprise,* January 15, 1999, pp. 44–46+.

30. Marc Burckhardt, "The Sacred and the Mundane," *Inc.,* State of Small Business 2000 issue, May 16, 2000, pp. 160–162, 164, 167.

31. Duffy, "Cultural Evolution," p. 46.

32. Charles Fishman, "Sanity Inc.," *Fast Company,* January 1999, pp. 85–89, 92–94, 96.

33. Duffy, "Cultural Evolution," pp. 48, 50.

34. Moeller, "Remaking Microsoft."

35. Fishman, "Sanity Inc.," p. 94.

36. Louise Lee, "Nordstrom Cleans Out Its Closets," *Business Week,* May 22, 2000, pp. 105–106, 108.

CHAPTER 9

1. "Corporate Information," Ryder System Web site, www.corporate-ir.net/ireye, accessed February 21, 2001; "Ryder Opens the Nation's First Charter School-in-the-Workplace," company press release, August 19, 1999; Susan Adams, "Build It and They Will Come," *Forbes,* April 5, 1999, pp. 66–67.

2. Phaedra Brotherton, "HR Efficiency without the Hassles," *Black Enterprise,* September 2000, pp. 49–50.

3. Stephanie Armour, "Bosses Held Liable for Keeping Workers," *USA Today,* April 12, 2000, p. 1B.

4. Susan DeGrane, "Davis Champions Diversity," *Chicago GSB* (University of Chicago Graduate School of Business), Summer 2000, pp. 12–13.

5. Chuck Salter, "Insanity Inc.," *Fast Company,* January 1999, pp. 101–108.

6. Karen Southwick, "To Survive: Hire Up," *Forbes ASAP,* April 3, 2000, pp. 117–118.

7. Erika Brown, "Have Friends, Will Hire," *Forbes,* October 30, 2000, p. 62.

8. Adrian Slywotzky, "How Digital Is Your Company?" *Fast Company,* February/March 1999, pp. 94–96+; John Byrne, "The Search for the Young and Gifted," *Business Week,* October 4, 1999, pp. 108–110+.

9. Hemisphere Inc., "Diversity: The Bottom Line, Part I: Building a Competitive Workforce," *Forbes,* special advertising section, May 31, 1999, pp. 2–6.

10. Cora Daniels, "To Hire a Lumber Expert, Click Here," *Fortune,* April 3, 2000, pp. 267–268, 270.

11. Ellen Paris, "SATs at Work," *Entrepreneur,* March 2000, p. 32.

12. Nicholas Stein, "Winning the War to Keep Top Talent," *Fortune,* May 29, 2000, pp. 132–134+.

13. Byrne, "The Search for the Young and Gifted," p. 116.

14. "While Supplies Last," *HR Magazine,* June 2000, downloaded from the Society for Human Resource Management Web site, www.shrm.org.

15. Christopher Caggiano, "The Appeasement Trap," *Inc.,* September 2000, pp. 39–40+.

16. Charlotte Garvey, "Human, Tech Factors Affect Web Training," *HR News Online,* January 6, 2000, downloaded from the Society for Human Resource Management Web site, www.shrm.org.

17. Robert J. Grossman, "Heirs Unapparent," *HR Magazine,* February 2001, downloaded from the Society for Human Resource Management Web site, www.shrm.org.

18. Rochelle Garner, "Coach Works," *CIO,* February 1, 2000, pp. 114–122.

19. Stein, "Winning the War to Keep Top Talent," p. 134; Ram Charan, "GE's Ten-Step Talent Plan," *Fortune,* April 17, 2000, p. 232.

20. "Travelling beyond 360-Degree Evaluations," *HR Magazine,* September 1999, downloaded from the Society for Human Resource Management Web site, www.shrm.org; Carol Hymowitz, "Do '360' Job Reviews By Colleagues Promote Honesty or Insults?" *The Wall Street Journal,* December 12, 2000, p. B1.

21. Bureau of Labor Statistics, "National Employment, Hours, and Earnings," downloaded from the BLS Web site, www.bls.gov, November 9, 2000; Dean Foust, "Wooing the Worker," *Business Week,* May 22, 2000, pp. 44–46; R. C. Longworth, "Middle-Wage Earners Lagging," *Chicago Tribune,* September 6, 1999, sec. 1.

22. Steven V. Brull, "What's So Bad about a Living Wage?" *Business Week,* September 4, 2000, pp. 68, 70.

23. Michelle Conlin and Peter Coy, "The Wild New Workforce," *Business Week,* December 6, 1999, pp. 39–42+.

24. U.S. Department of Labor, "Futurework: Trends and Challenges for Work in the 21st Century," Labor Day 1999, downloaded from the Labor Department Web site, www.dol.gov.

25. William J. Wiatrowski, "Tracking Changes in Benefit Costs," *Compensation and Working Conditions* (U.S. Department of Labor), Spring 1999, pp. 32–37.

26. U.S. Department of Labor, "Current Labor Statistics: Compensation & Industrial Relations," *Monthly Labor Review,* July 2000, p. 70.

27. Hewitt Associates, "More Employers Offer Work/Life Benefits to Gain Edge in Tight Labor Market," news release, May 4, 2000, downloaded from the Hewitt Associates Web site, http://was.hewitt.com.

28. Robert Levering and Milton Moskowitz, "The 100 Best Companies to Work For," *Fortune,* January 10, 2000, pp. 84+.

29. Ron Winslow and Carol Gentry, "Health-Benefits Trend: Give Workers Money, Let Them Buy a Plan," *The Wall Street Journal,* February 8, 2000, pp. A1, A12.

30. Levering and Moskowitz, "The 100 Best Companies to Work For," pp. 98, 110.

31. Patricia Nakache, "One VP, Two Brains," *Fortune,* December 20, 1999, pp. 327–328, 330.

32. International Telework Association & Council, "Telework America (TWA) 2000: Research Results," downloaded from the ITAC Web site, www.telecommute.org, November 7, 2000.

33. Lin Grensing-Pophal, "Training Supervisors to Manage Workers," *HR Magazine,* January 1999, downloaded from the Society for Human Resource Management Web site, www.shrm.org.

34. Carol Hymowitz, "Remote Managers Find Ways to Narrow the Distance Gap," *The Wall Street Journal,* April 6, 1999, p. B1.

35. Bret Begun, "USA: The Way We'll Live Then," *Newsweek,* January 1, 2000, pp. 34–35; Sue Shellenbarger, "Sailboats and Showers: Home Offices Look Weirder All the Time," *The Wall Street Journal,* March 29, 2000, p. B1.

36. Jennifer Reingold, "Brain Drain," *Business Week,* September 20, 1999, pp. 112–126.

37. Gary McWilliams, "Motorola Becomes Latest Member of Technology-Outsourcing Wave," *The Wall Street Journal,* June 1, 2000, downloaded from the Interactive Edition Web site, http://interactive.wsj.com; Pete Engardio, "The Barons of Outsourcing," *Business Week,* August 28, 2000, pp. 177–178.

38. Del Jones, "Coke Cooks Up Some Perks to Refresh Workers," *USA Today,* May 4, 2000, p. 1B.

39. See, for example, Alexander D. Stajkovic and Fred Luthans, "Social Cognitive Theory and Self-Efficacy: Going beyond Traditional Motivational and Behavioral Approaches," *Organizational Dynamics,* Spring 1998, pp. 62–74.

40. "Motivating and Retaining Employees," *Fortune,* Arthur Andersen Best Practices Awards special advertising section, March 6, 2000.

41. Levering and Moskowitz, "The 100 Best Companies to Work For," p. 92.

42. Charlene Oldham, "Goodbye Secretary, Hello Administrative Professional," *Mobile Register,* May 28, 2000, p. 4F.

43. Donna Fenn, "Redesign Work," *Inc.,* June 1999, pp. 75–76+.

44. Douglas McGregor, *The Human Side of Enterprise* (New York: McGraw-Hill, 1960), pp. 33–48.

45. Carol Kleiman, "Flex Hours a Dream for Kraft Finance Workers," *Chicago Tribune,* November 14, 2000, sec. 3, p. 1.

46. Robert McGarvey, "Fun and Games," *Entrepreneur,* April 1999, pp. 82–84.

47. Stein, "Winning the War to Keep Top Talent," p. 133.

48. Reingold, "Brain Drain."

49. Michelle Conlin, "The New Workforce," *Business Week,* March 20, 2000, pp. 64–66, 68; John Williams, "Enabling Technologies," *Business Week,* March 20, 2000, pp. 68, 70.

50. Michelle Conlin, "And Now, the Just-in-Time Employee," *Business Week,* August 28, 2000, pp. 169–170.

51. Laura Bird, "The New 24/7 Work Cycle: Logging Time on the Night Shift," *The Wall Street Journal,* September 20, 2000, downloaded from the Interactive Edition at http://interactive.wsj.com.

52. Emily Barker, "The Company They Keep," *Inc.,* May 2000, pp. 85–86+.

53. Jerry Useem, "Welcome to the New Company," *Fortune,* January 10, 2000, pp. 62–66+; Reshma Memon Yaqub, "The Play's the Thing," *Worth,* pp. 116–123.

CHAPTER 10

1. Francine Knowles, "21st Century Company: Pampered Chef," *Chicago Sun-Times,* October 23, 2000, accessed at www.suntimes.com; Pamela Margoshes, "Queen of Hearths," in "Secrets of a Start-up," *Success,* September 1998; George Mannes, "Taking on Tupperware," *ABCNEWScom* from *TheStreet.com,* March 16, 1998, accessed at www.abcnews.go.com; "Our Company," Pampered Chef Web site, www.pamperedchef.com, accessed January 8, 2001.

2. Ken Anderson, "By the (Open) Book," *Inc. Technology,* 1999, no. 3, pp. 33–34.

3. Anderson, "By the (Open) Book," p. 34.

4. Michelle Conlin, "Workers, Surf at Your Own Risk," *Business Week,* June 12, 2000, pp. 105–106.

5. Luisa Kroll, "Bed Bath & Beyond: Happy Together," *Forbes,* January 10, 2000, pp. 156–157.

6. Polly LaBarre, "Leaders.com," *Fast Company,* June 1999, pp. 95–98+.

7. Anne Marie Borrego, "Everyone's a CEO," *Inc.,* June 2000, pp. 123–124.

8. Cathy Ivancic, "Growing an Ownership Culture," National Center for Employee Ownership Web site, www.nceo.org, April 2000.

9. National Center for Employee Ownership, "A Short History of the ESOP," NCEO Web site, www.nceo.org, November 17, 2000.

10. Anderson, "By the (Open) Book," p. 33.

11. National Center for Employee Ownership, "A Short History of the ESOP"; Scott Rodrick, "A Tale of Two Acronyms: An 'Employee Stock Option Plan' Is Not an ESOP!" National Center for Employee Ownership Web site, www.nceo.org, August 1997.

12. National Center for Employee Ownership, "A Growing Number of U.S. Employees Receive Stock Options: New Estimates from the NCEO," NCEO Web site, www.nceo.org, February 2000.
13. "Workers Take Stock in Firms," *Mobile Register,* April 11, 1999, pp. 1F–2F.
14. Tim Gilbert, "Great Teamwork Pays Off for Xerox," *Journal for Quality and Participation,* July 1, 1999, downloaded from the Northern Light Web site, http://library. northernlight.com.
15. Ed Carberry, "Hypergrowth Strategy: Create an Ownership Culture," Inc.com case study, December 1, 1999, downloaded from www.inc.com.
16. Marcia Stepanek, "Using the Net for Brainstorming," *Business Week e.Biz,* December 13, 1999, pp. EB 55–EB 57.
17. Bob Nelson, "Energizing Teams of Hourly Workers," *Bob Nelson's Rewarding Employees* (newsletter), May 1, 1999, downloaded from the Inc.com Web site, www. inc.com.
18. "What Makes Teams Work?" *Fast Company,* November 1, 2000, downloaded from the Dow Jones Interactive Publications Library at http://nrstg1p.djnr.com.
19. "What Makes Teams Work?"
20. Adapted from Richard L. Daft, *Management,* 5th ed. (Fort Worth, Tex.: Dryden Press, 2000), pp. 607–609.
21. Gabriel Allan, "Rocking McDonald," *e-directions,* Winter 2000, p. 37.
22. Rochelle Garner, "Round-the-World Teamwork," *Computerworld,* May 24, 1999, downloaded from the Northern Light Web site at http://library.northernlight.com.
23. "What Makes Teams Work?"
24. Stepanek, "Using the Net for Brainstorming," p. EB 57.
25. Adapted from Daft, *Management,* pp. 609–610.
26. Jean Lipman-Blumen and Harold J. Leavitt, *Hot Groups: Seeding Them, Feeding Them & Using Them to Ignite Your Organization* (Oxford University Press, 1999), excerpted in Jean Lipman-Blumen and Harold J. Leavitt, "Jammin'," *CIO,* sec. 1, November 1, 1999, pp. 73–74+.
27. "What Makes Teams Work?"
28. Leigh Gallagher, "Get Out of My Face," *Forbes,* October 18, 1999, pp. 105–106.
29. Garner, "Round-the-World Teamwork."
30. Lipman-Blumen and Leavitt, "Jammin'," p. 80.
31. "What Makes Teams Work?"
32. Rodes Fishburne, "More Survival Advice," *Forbes ASAP,* April 3, 2000, pp. 120+.
33. Christopher Caggiano, "Merge Now, Pay Later," *Inc.,* April 2000, pp. 86–90+.
34. Fishburne, "More Survival Advice," p. 120.
35. Carol Hymowitz, "Remote Managers Find Ways to Narrow the Distance Gap," *The Wall Street Journal,* April 6, 1999, p. B1.
36. Mark Gibbs, "Managing by Messaging," downloaded from the Web site of Gil Gordon Associates, www.gilgordon. com, November 7, 2000.
37. Neil Gross, "E-Mail that Won't Come Back to Haunt You," *Business Week,* November 15, 1999, p. 136.
38. Hymowitz, "Remote Managers Find Ways."
39. Geoffrey Nunberg, "The Trouble with PowerPoint," *Fortune,* December 20, 1999, downloaded from the Northern Light Web site at http://library.northernlight.com.

40. Albert Mehrabian, *Silent Messages* (Belmont, Calif.: Wadsworth, 1971); and Albert Mehrabian, "Communicating without Words," *Psychology Today,* September 1968, pp. 53–55.
41. Hymowitz, "Remote Managers Find Ways."
42. Anne Eisenberg, "Mars and Venus in Cyberspace," *Chicago Tribune,* October 18, 2000, sec. 8, p. 7.
43. Quentin Hardy, "All Carly, All the Time," *Forbes,* December 13, 1999, pp. 138–144.
44. Carberry, "Hypergrowth Strategy."
45. Mike Hofman, "Your Basic *Que Pasa?" Inc.,* May 2000, p. 161; Gibbs, "Managing by Messaging."
46. "What Makes Teams Work?"
47. Lipman-Blumen and Leavitt, "Jammin'," p. 78.
48. Based on Daft, *Management,* pp. 584–585.
49. Lauren Gibbons Paul, "The Site Next Door," *Inc. Technology,* November 14, 2000, p. 63.
50. Wendy Zellner, "Hey, Are You Listening to Me?" *Business Week,* August 28, 2000, pp. 138–140.
51. Gwen Moran, "Priority Mail," *Entrepreneur,* January 2000, p. 38.
52. Carol Loomis, "Would You Buy This Stock?" *Fortune,* March 6, 2000, p. 70.
53. Jim Sterne, "At Your Service," *Inc. Technology,* November 14, 2000, pp. 130–131.
54. Steve Rosenbush, "The Talking Internet," *Business Week,* May 1, 2000, pp. 174–176+; Stephen Baker, "Europe Swoons for Voice-on-the-Net," *Business Week,* May 1, 2000, p. 192.
55. Amy Helen Johnson, "Teamwork Made Simple," *CIO,* November 1, 1999, pp. 86–90, 92.
56. Charles Piller, "Erasing Our Sense of Place," *Chicago Tribune,* November 13, 2000, sec. 4, pp. 1, 8.
57. Ted Anthony, "Former Overlord's Language Becomes the Glue That Holds a Nation Together," *Indianapolis Star,* April 30, 2000, sec. D, pp. 1, 5; Ted Anthony, "English Expansion Is a Foreign Affair," *Indianapolis Star,* April 30, 2000, sec. D, p. 5; Ted Anthony, "English Invasion," April 30, 2000, sec. D, pp. 1, 5.
58. Ben Vickers, "E-tailers Find Global Web Sites Need to Learn Local Languages," *The Wall Street Journal,* November 16, 2000, downloaded from the Interactive Edition at http://interactive.wsj.com.
59. Patricia Fripp, "Speaking Their Language Even When You Don't," downloaded from the Inc.com Web site, www. inc.com, November 22, 2000.
60. Sally McGrane, "Cultural Web Faux Pas," *Forbes ASAP,* February 21, 2000, p. 28.
61. See, for example, Garner, "Round-the-World Teamwork."

CHAPTER 11

1. John Dempsey and Dave McNary, "Actors Celebrate Ad Lib Day," *Yahoo! News,* October 24, 2000, http:// dailynews.yahoo.com; Gary Dretzka, Lauren Comander, and Diana Strzalka, "Entertainers' Peace May Be Brief," *Chicago Tribune,* October 24, 2000, http://chicagotribune. com; "A Lesson for Hollywood," *Los Angeles Times,* October 24, 2000, www.latimes.com; James Bates, "Actors, Ad Firms Reach Tentative Deal to End Strike," *Los Angeles Times,* October 23, 2000, www.latimes.com; David Lipin, "Union Faction Complicates Strike Talks," *Adweek Online,* October 20, 2000, http://dailynews.yahoo.com.

2. Dan Seligman, "Driving the AFL–CIO Crazy," *Forbes*, November 1, 1999, pp. 102, 106, 108.

3. International Labor Organization, "ILO Worst Forms of Child Labour Convention Comes into Force," news release, November 17, 2000, downloaded from the ILO Web site, www.ilo.org.

4. AFL–CIO, "Clothing Barred," *Work in Progress*, December 4, 2000, downloaded from the AFL–CIO Web site, www.aflcio.org.

5. AFL–CIO, "Americans' Attitudes toward Unions," downloaded from the AFL–CIO Web site, www.aflcio.org, March 5, 2001.

6. Seligman, "Driving the AFL–CIO Crazy"; AFL–CIO, "The Union Difference," downloaded from the AFL–CIO Web site, www.aflcio.org, March 5, 2001.

7. "The Millennium Force—World's Tallest Roller Coaster—Is Union-Made," downloaded from the AFL–CIO's Union Label and Service Trade Department's Web site, http://unionlabel.org, March 7, 2001; "Vital Statistics," Cedar Point Web site, www.cedarpoint.com, March 7, 2001.

8. Yochi J. Dreazen, "Percentage of U.S. Workers in a Union Sank to Record Low of 13.5% Last Year," *The Wall Street Journal*, January 19, 2001.

9. Service Employees International Union Web site, www.seiu.org, March 7, 2001.

10. AFL–CIO, "The Union Difference."

11. Martha Brannigan, "Delta Faces First Major Union Vote in Three Decades," *The Wall Street Journal*, January 31, 2000; Martha Brannigan, "Mediation Board Orders New Election for Some Union Employees at Delta," *The Wall Street Journal*, August 1, 2000, p. A4; "Delta Ramp Workers Reject Representation by Transport Union," *The Wall Street Journal*, October 3, 2000, p. A6.

12. Service Employees International Union, "Home Care Workers Win Largest Union Victory in 2000," news release, December 7, 2000, downloaded from the SEIU Web site, www.seiu.org.

13. AFL–CIO, "Unions, Kaiser Permanente Agree on Greater Voice at Work," news release, September 25, 2000, downloaded from the AFL–CIO Web site, www.aflcio.org.

14. Joann Muller, "It Looks Like a Big Payday for Auto Workers," *Business Week*, September 20, 1999, p. 42.

15. Service Workers International Union, "55,000 SEIU Apartment Building Workers in New York City Win Home Computers," news release, April 26, 2000, downloaded from the SEIU Web site, www.seiu.org.

16. Jeff Cole, "Labor Says a White-Collar Walkout at Boeing Boosts Chance for Organizing," *The Wall Street Journal*, February 28, 2000, p. A28; Paul Nyhan, "Boeing Strike Ends," *Seattle Post-Intelligencer*, March 20, 2000, downloaded from the Northern Light Web site at http://library.northernlight.com.

17. AFL–CIO, "Unions, Kaiser Permanente Agree on Greater Voice at Work."

18. Nyhan, "Boeing Strike Ends."

19. Ronald Blum, "NLRB Rules against Phillips," AP Online, January 22, 2000, downloaded from the Northern Light Web site at http://library.northernlight.com; "Baseball Notes; Wait Likely for Umpires," *Washington Post*, August 31, 2000, downloaded from the Northern Light Web site at http://library.northernlight.com.

20. Jeffrey Ball, Glenn Burkins, and Gregory L. White, "Why Labor Unions Have Grown Reluctant to Use the 'S' Word," *The Wall Street Journal*, December 16, 1999, pp. A1, A8; Bureau of Labor Statistics, "Work Stoppages Summary," news release, February 2, 2000, downloaded from the BLS Web site, www.bls.gov.

21. AFL–CIO, "Toddle Out of Chicago," *Work in Progress*, November 27, 2000, downloaded from the AFL–CIO Web site, www.aflcio.org.

22. AFL–CIO, "Thanksgiving Message: UFW Gives Thanks for Recent Gains as It Calls Off Table Grape Boycott," news release, November 21, 2000, downloaded from the AFL–CIO's Union Label and Service Trades Department Web site, http://unionlabel.org.

23. AFL–CIO, "Boycott Grows," *Work in Progress*, December 4, 2000, downloaded from the AFL–CIO Web site, www.aflcio.org.

24. Ball, Burkins, and White, "Why Labor Unions Have Grown Reluctant to Use the 'S' Word."

25. Bo Burlingham, "The Boom in Employee Ownership," *Inc.*, August 2000, pp. 106–108, 110, 112.

26. Ball, Burkins, and White, "Why Labor Unions Have Grown Reluctant to Use the 'S' Word."

27. Ibid, p. A8.

28. Ann Zimmerman, "Pro-Union Butchers at Wal-Mart Win a Battle, Lose War," *The Wall Street Journal*, April 11, 2000, pp. A1, A14.

29. Kate Bronfenbrenner, *Uneasy Terrain: The Impact of Capital Mobility on Workers, Wages, and Union Organizing*, September 6, 2000, U.S. Trade Deficit Review Commission Web site, www.ustdrc.gov.

30. AFL–CIO, "Americans' Attitudes toward Unions."

31. Aaron Bernstein, "Tough Love for Labor," *Business Week*, October 16, 2000, pp. 118, 120.

32. AFL–CIO, "More Workers Are Choosing a Voice at Work," downloaded from the AFL–CIO Web site, www.aflcio.org, March 5, 2001.

33. "Making Music," downloaded from the AFL–CIO's Union Label and Service Trades Department Web site, http://unionlabel.org, March 7, 2001.

34. Ball, Burkins, and White, "Why Labor Unions Have Grown Reluctant to Use the 'S' Word," p. A8.

35. Service Employees International Union, "Disney World Workers Gain Strength by Realigning Union Affiliation," news release, December 7, 2000, downloaded from the SEIU Web site, www.seiu.org.

36. Glenn Burkins, "Labor Reaches Out to Global Economy," *The Wall Street Journal*, April 11, 2000, pp. A2, A6.

37. Marjorie Valbrun, "To Reverse Declines, Unions Are Targeting Immigrant Workers," *The Wall Street Journal*, May 27, 1999, pp. A1, A10.

CHAPTER 12

1. "Pella Corporation: Celebrating 75 Years of Innovation," Pella Corp. Web site, www.pella.com, accessed March 22, 2001; Philip Siekman, "Glass Act: How a Window Maker Rebuilt Itself," *Fortune*, November 13, 2000, www.fortune.com; "Pella Corporation Climbs Listing in *Fortune*'s Annual '100 Best Companies to Work For,'" *PR Newswire*, December 21, 2000.

2. Philip Siekman, "The Big Myth about U.S. Manufacturing," *Fortune*, October 2, 2000, pp. 244BB–244DD+.

3. Norihiko Shirouzu, "GM, Isuzu Discuss a Common Platform for New SUVs," *The Wall Street Journal*, February 25, 2000, p. A12.

4. Francis Hamit, "Changing the Printing Model: Digital Imaging Now Driving Book Business," *Advanced Imaging*, November 2000, pp. 34, 36, 37.

5. Gene Bylinsky, "America's Elite Factories," *Fortune*, August 14, 2000, pp. 232C–232D+.

6. Gary S. Vasilash, "Honda's Hat Trick," *Automotive Manufacturing & Production*, October 2000, pp. 56–61.

7. Michael Arndt, "Did Somebody Say McBurrito?" *Business Week*, April 10, 2000, pp. 166, 170.

8. Bylinsky, "America's Elite Factories," pp. 232H, 232J, 232N.

9. Vasilash, "Honda's Hat Trick," pp. 58–59.

10. Phillip J. Longman, "The Next Big Thing Is Small," *U.S. News & World Report*, July 3, 2000, pp. 30–33.

11. Gene Bylinsky, "Hot New Technologies for American Factories," *Fortune*, June 26, 2000, pp. 288A–288K.

12. Frank Gibney Jr., "The Revolution in a Box," *Time*, July 31, 2000, pp. 30–32.

13. David Rocks, "Reinventing Herman Miller," *Business Week E.Biz*, April 3, 2000, pp. EB 88–EB 90, EB 94, EB 96.

14. Gibney, "The Revolution in a Box."

15. Siekman, "The Big Myth about U.S. Manufacturing."

16. Micheline Maynard, "Amid the Turmoil, a Rare Success at DaimlerChrysler," *Fortune*, January 22, 2001, pp. 112(c)–112(p); Jeffrey Ball and Scott Miller, "Zetsche to Cut Chrysler Incentives and Revamp Car Assembly Lines," *The Wall Street Journal*, December 8, 2000, downloaded from the Interactive Edition at http://interactive.wsj.com.

17. Peter Galuszka, "Just-in-Time Manufacturing Is Working Overtime," *Business Week*, November 8, 1999, pp. 36–37.

18. Bylinsky, "America's Elite Factories," pp. 232J, 232L, 232N.

19. Vasilash, "Honda's Hat Trick," p. 59.

20. Jeff Rothfeder, "Know-It-Alls," *Executive Edge*, August/September 1999, pp. 39–43.

21. Terril Yue Jones, "Body Block," *Forbes*, April 3, 2000, p. 90.

22. William J. Holstein, "Rewiring the 'Old Economy,'" *U.S. News & World Report*, April 10, 2000, pp. 38–40.

23. Rothfeder, "Know-It-Alls," p. 41.

24. Galuszka, "Just-in-Time Manufacturing Is Working Overtime."

25. Bylinsky, "America's Elite Factories," pp. 232D, 232F.

26. Jill Hecht Maxwell, "Automating an Automaker," *Inc. Technology*, November 14, 2000, p. 86.

27. Bylinsky, "America's Elite Factories," p. 232D.

28. Jeff Sabatini, "Turning Japanese," *Automotive Manufacturing & Production*, October 2000, pp. 66–69.

29. Ibid., p. 67.

30. Joann Muller and David Welch, "Making Safer SUVs: It's Not Rocket Science," *Business Week*, October 16, 2000, p. 51.

31. Andrew Freiburghouse, "Keeping It Up," *Forbes ASAP*, February 21, 2000, p. 26.

32. General Electric Web site, accessed March 8, 2001. For a different perspective, see Lee Clifford, "Why You Can Safely Ignore Six Sigma," *Fortune*, January 22, 2001, p. 140.

33. International Organization for Standardization, "The Magical Demystifying Tour," downloaded from the ISO Web site, www.iso.ch, February 26, 2001; William Lankford, "ISO 9000: Understanding the Basics," *Review of Business*, Spring 2000, pp. 7–10; International Organization for Standardization, "Introduction to ISO," January 8, 1999, downloaded from the ISO Web site, www.iso.ch.

34. International Organization for Standardization, "The ISO Survey of ISO 9000 and ISO 14000 Certificates, Ninth Cycle, Up to and Including December 31, 1999," downloaded from the ISO Web site, www.iso.ch, February 26, 2001.

CHAPTER 13

1. "Company Overview," World Wrestling Federation Entertainment Web site, www.wwfecorpbiz.com, accessed February 6, 2001; Bethany McLeon, "Inside the World's Weirdest Family Business," *Fortune*, October 16, 2000, pp. 292–312; "NBC Purchases Minority Stake in World Wrestling Federation Entertainment, Inc.," company press release, June 13, 2000.

2. Geox Web site, www.geox.com, downloaded January 4, 2001; Mercedes M. Cardona, "Italian Shoemaker Moving into U.S.," *Advertising Age*, April 24, 2000, p. 20.

3. Tom Content, "Nike Lets You Be a Shoemaker," *USA Today*, November 22, 1999, p. 14B; Nike Web site, www.nike.com, downloaded January 4, 2001.

4. Leigh Buchanan, "Make Way for Duck Links," *Inc. Technology*, 1999, No. 4, pp. 13–14.

5. "The (Electronic) Personal Touch," *Fortune*, March 20, 2000, p. 214.

6. Alec Klein, "Low-Tech Camera Huge Polaroid Boost," *Birmingham News*, May 7, 2000, pp. 1D, 5D.

7. Jeanette Brown, "Service, Please," *Business Week E.Biz*, October 23, 2000, pp. EB 48, EB 50.

8. Roger O. Crockett, "A Digital Doughboy," *Business Week E.Biz*, April 3, 2000, pp. EB 79, EB 82, EB 86.

9. "Fighting Hunger Couldn't Be Easier," *CIO*, April 1, 2000, p. 34.

10. Paula Lyon Andruss, "Marketing Revs Up Down Under," *Marketing News*, September 11, 2000, pp. 9–10.

11. Timothy Roche, "Who's Got Mail?" *Time*, October 16, 2000, pp. 86, 88.

12. Kathleen V. Schmidt, "Promotions of Place," *Marketing News*, September 13, 1999, p. 9.

13. "Groups Push Latina Breast Cancer Awareness," *Marketing to Women* (EPM Communications), October 1999, p. 8.

14. Rusty Cawley, "Giving: More than Just a Game," *Sports-Business Journal*, January 4–10, 1999, pp. 19, 24–25.

15. Nathan Vardi, "The Profit Givers," *Forbes*, November 13, 2000, pp. 133–134.

16. Michael Eagleson, "For Women Only," *Sports Trend*, July 2000.

17. Anne Stuart, "Sweet Deals," *Inc. Technology*, November 14, 2000, pp. 98–100+.

18. Paula Lyon Andruss, "Thais Sweet on Mom, 'Love' Campaign," *Marketing News*, September 11, 2000, p. 6.

19. Mark Tatge, "Red Bodies, Black Ink," *Forbes*, September 18, 2000, pp. 114–115.

20. Kenneth Labich, "This Man Is Watching You," *Fortune,* July 19, 1999, pp. 131–132, 134.
21. Heather Green, "The Information Gold Mine," *Business Week E.Biz,* July 26, 1999, pp. EB 17–EB20+.
22. Greg Farrell, "What's Green, Easy to Squirt? Ketchup," *USA Today,* July 10, 2000, p. 2B.
23. "Starwood Goes to War," *Colloquy* (Freqency Marketing, Inc.), vol. 7, no. 3, 1999, pp. 7, 15.
24. Todd Wasserman, Gerry Khermouch, and Jeff Green, "Mining Everyone's Business," *Brandweek,* February 28, 2000, pp. 32–34+.
25. Wasserman, Khermouch, and Green, "Mining Everyone's Business."
26. Sonia Reyes, "Betty Crocker Says *Hola!* in TV Ads, Twin Entries, Seeking 'Authenticity,'" *Brandweek,* May 22, 2000, p. 4.
27. "Weighty Proposition," *Promo,* August 1999, pp. 38–39.
28. "Marketing Automobiles to Women Starts with Designing Cars that Meet Their Needs," *Marketing to Women* (EPM Communications), October 1999, pp. 1–2+; "Women Seek Safety and Comfort When Buying a Car," *Marketing to Women,* October 1999, p. 3.
29. Terril Yue Jones, "Not Your Father's Camry," *Forbes,* November 29, 1999, pp. 71, 74; Larry Armstrong, "Toyota: Chasing Boomers' Babies," *Business Week,* December 6, 1999, pp. 67, 70.
30. Frank Solis, "The Next Big Market," *Success,* October 2000, pp. 36, 38; Nancy Coltun Webster, "Teens under Watchful Eye," *Advertising Age,* September 18, 2000, p. 23; Eduardo Porter, "Hispanic TV Takes Off in the U.S.," *The Wall Street Journal,* September 7, 2000, p. B1; Dwight Cunningham, "One Size Does Not Fit All," *Adweek,* Special Report, November 15, 1999, pp. 4–6; Anita Santiago, "Talk the Talk," *Adweek,* Special Report, November 15, 1999, pp. 10, 12; Brook Larmer, "Latino America," *Newsweek,* July 12, 1999, pp. 47–51.
31. Laurie Freeman, "AsianAvenue Goes to School," *Advertising Age,* November 29, 1999, p. S13.
32. Eduardo Porter and Emily Nelson, "P&G Reaches Out to Hispanics," *The Wall Street Journal,* October 12, 2000, pp. B1, B4.
33. EthnicGrocer.com Web site, www.ethnicgrocer.com, downloaded January 3, 2001; Namaste.com Web site, www.namaste.com, downloaded January 3, 2001; GongShee.com Web site, www.gongshee.com, downloaded January 3, 2001; QueRico.com Web site, www.querico.com, downloaded January 3, 2001; "Ethnic E-tailer Builds Expertise in Untappped Market," *Marketing News,* October 9, 2000, p. 24; Jeffery D. Zbar, "The Web Goes Multicultural," *Advertising Age,* November 29, 1999, pp. S1, S4.
34. Wendy Zellner, "Hey, Are You Listening to Me?" *Business Week,* August 28, 2000, pp. 138–140.
35. Michael McCarthy, "Label-Crazy Marketers Have Got You Pegged," *USA Today,* August 1, 2000, pp. 1B–2B.
36. Carol Pickering, "They're Watching You," *Business 2.0,* February 2000, pp. 135–136.
37. Heather Green, "The Information Gold Mine," *Business Week E.Biz,* July 26, 1999, pp. EB 17–EB 20.
38. Diane Brady, "Why Service Stinks," *Business Week,* October 23, 2000, pp. 118–122+.
39. Green, "The Information Gold Mine," p. EB20.
40. Jennifer L. Schenker, "Where Sci-Fi Meets the Net," *Time,* September 25, 2000, pp. B21–B22.
41. John A. Byrne, "Management by Web," *Business Week,* August 28, 2000, pp. 84–88+.
42. "Do Frequent Guest Programs Need a Wake Up Call?" *Colloquy* (Frequency Marketing, Inc.), vol. 7, no. 3, 1999, pp. 1, 4–6.
43. Patricia Riedman and Jean Halliday, "Ford Is Driven to Strengthen Customer Hold," *Advertising Age,* January 10, 2000, pp. 30, 32.
44. Wendy Cole, "SUV Strollers," Time, January 29, 2001, p. 12.
45. Russ Banham, "CRM in the Zone," *Executive Edge,* August/September 2000, pp. 26–30.

CHAPTER 14

1. "About Us," Razor scooter Web site, www.razor-scooter.com, accessed April 23, 2001; Bob Francis, "A Helluva Kick-Start," *Brandweek,* September 4, 2000, pp. 33–36; Brent Hannon, "Riding High on Little Wheels," *Business Week,* September 4, 2000, p. 123.
2. Reed Tucker, "How Has Coke's Formula Stayed a Secret?" *Fortune,* August 14, 2000, p. 42.
3. James P. Sterba, "The Real Revolution in Golf Balls: Marketing," *The Wall Street Journal,* June 15, 2000, downloaded from the Interactive Edition at http://interactive.wsj.com.
4. Stephen Baker, Neil Gross, and Irene M. Kunii, "The Wireless Internet," *Business Week,* May 29, 2000, pp. 136–140, 144.
5. Mike Hofman, "An Opportunity to Clean Up," *Inc.,* January 2001, pp. 21–23.
6. Bruce Horovitz, "Selling Pears at $5 a Pound," *USA Today,* December 3, 1999, pp. B1–B2.
7. Royal Philips Electronics, "What Is the Bluetooth Wireless Technology?" downloaded from the Philips Web site at www.semiconductors.philips.com/Bluetooth, April 18, 2001; "Bluetooth in Brief," downloaded from the HandyTEL.com Web site at www.handytel.com/technology/bluetooth01.htm, April 18, 2001.
8. Francis, "A Helluva Kick-Start," pp. 34–35+; Hannon, "Riding High on Little Wheels."
9. Carlos Alvarez with Mike Hofman, "My Biggest Mistake," *Inc.,* January 2001, p. 102.
10. "The Web Goes Multicultural," *Advertising Age,* November 29, 1999, pp. S1, S4.
11. Cliff Edwards, "Are PC Makers Looking at a Price War?" *Business Week,* December 25, 2000, p. 58.
12. Dana James, "Rejuvenating Mature Brands Can Be Stimulating Exercise," *Marketing News,* August 16, 1999, pp. 16–17.
13. Peter Breen, "Monster Marketing," *Promo,* January 2000, pp. 57–58.
14. Stephen H. Wildstrom, "Kiss the Floppy Good-Bye," *Business Week,* June 12, 2000, p. 34.
15. Theresa Howard, "Coca-Cola Hopes Taking New Path Leads to Success," *USA Today,* March 6, 2001, p. 6B.
16. Robert Johnson, "Fragrances of Yesteryear Are Back, in Supermarkets and on the Web," *The Wall Street Journal,* November 2, 2000, downloaded from the Interactive Edition at http://interactive.wsj.com.

17. Lisa Bannon, "Let's Play Makeover Barbie," *The Wall Street Journal,* February 17, 2000, pp. B1, B4.

18. Bannon, "Let's Play Makeover Barbie," p. B4.

19. Rebecca Quick, "Shoppers Find Blowout Sale on Web Has Come to an End," *The Wall Street Journal,* June 21, 2000, downloaded from the Interactive Edition at http://interactive.wsj.com; Andrea Petersen, "Kozmo.com Breaks Down, Will Require Minimum Order," *The Wall Street Journal,* June 22, 2000, downloaded from the Interactive Edition at http://interactive.wsj.com.

20. James R. Hagerty, "Krispy Kreme at a Krossroads," *The Wall Street Journal,* February 24, 2000, pp. B1, B4.

21. Brian Steinberg and Cathleeen Egan, "Hershey, Nestlé Set Scramble for Piece of Easter Season's Candy-Egg Market," *The Wall Street Journal,* March 13, 2000, p. A9A.

22. James R. Healey and Earle Eldridge, "Curtain Falls on Plymouth," *USA Today,* November 4, 1999.

23. Peter Brimelow, "The Economics of Panty Hose," *Forbes,* August 23, 1999, p. 70.

24. Bruce Upbin, "Beyond Burgers," *Forbes,* November 1, 1999, pp. 218–223; Bruce Horovitz, "Did Somebody Say Better Fast Food?" *USA Today,* May 18, 2000, p. 3B.

25. Christopher Palmeri, "It's in the Tea Leaves," *Forbes,* September 6, 1999, p. 146.

26. Christine Bittar, "Gerber Starts Crawl into Hygiene Aisle," *Brandweek,* January 24, 2000, p. 6.

27. James, "Rejuvenating Mature Brands Can Be Stimulating Exercise."

28. Luisa Kroll, "Ballpoint Perfume," *Forbes,* July 3, 2000, pp. 154–155; Teri Agins and Rebecca Quick, "Calvin Klein's Court Fight with Warnaco Seeks to Burnish Discount-Frayed Brand," *The Wall Street Journal,* June 1, 2000, downloaded from the Interactive Edition at http://interactive.wsj.com.

29. James Burke, "Inventors & Inventions," *Time,* December 4, 2000, pp. 65–66; Anita Hamilton, "Take a Picture that Can Fly," *Time,* December 4, 2000, pp. 69–70.

30. Rebecca Quick, "Walk a Mile in Suede Shoes and You'll Have Sweaty Feet," *The Wall Street Journal,* July 18, 2000, downloaded from the Interactive Edition at http://interactive.wsj.com.

31. Jack Neff, "The New Brand Management," *Advertising Age,* November 8, 1999, pp. S2, S18.

32. David Welch, "Born to Be a Little Too Wild," *Business Week,* December 18, 2000, pp. 69–70.

33. Stephanie Gruner and John Lippman, " 'Harry Potter' Fan Web Sites Can't Shake Off Warner Bros.," *The Wall Street Journal,* December 21, 2000, downloaded from the Interactive Edition at http://interactive.wsj.com.

34. Michael Fumento, "Prescription for Trouble," *Forbes,* May 29, 2000, p. 66.

35. Janet Ginsburg, "The Darkness that Sells," *Business Week,* May 22, 2000, p. 14.

36. Michael McCarthy, "Big Marketers Line Up Again for Super Bowl," *USA Today,* October 5, 2000, p. B1.

37. DaimlerChrysler, letter to shareholders, December 2000.

38. William J. Holstein, "Guarding the Brand Is Job 1," *U.S. News & World Report,* September 11, 2000, pp. 64, 66.

39. Neff, "The New Brand Management."

40. Jessica Shaw, "Manischewitz Leavens Its Image," *Fortune,* November 8, 1999, p. 48.

41. Fred Goodman, "Tour Allure: For Many Young Artists, the Money Is in Concerts, Not Recordings," *Rolling Stone,* August 17, 2000, p. 87.

42. Becky Ebenkamp, "Awards for Our Sponsors," *Brandweek,* January 8, 2001, pp. 19+.

43. "The Power of Smart Pricing," *Business Week,* April 10, 2000, pp. 160, 162, 164; Robert L. Simison, "Ford Pricing Move Aims to Attract Buyers to Higher-End Vehicles," *The Wall Street Journal,* June 23, 2000, downloaded from the Interactive Edition at http://interactive.wsj.com.

44. Anne Newman, "CD Buyers Catch a Break," *Business Week,* May 22, 2000, p. 62.

45. Rachael King, "Cheap Talk," *Inc. Technology,* March 14, 2000, p. 77; Earle Eldridge and Jayne O'Donnell, " 'Consumer Reports' Tells Auto Dealers' Secrets," *USA Today,* March 16, 2000, p. 1B; Debra Aho Williamson, "The Net Effect," *Advertising Age,* Interactive Future special issue 2000, pp. 64+.

46. Williamson, "The Net Effect"; Shawn Tully, "The B2B Tool That Really *Is* Changing the World," *Fortune,* March 20, 2000, pp. 132–134+.

47. Laura Johannes, "Feisty Mom-and-Pops of Gotham Strike Back at Drugstore Chains," *The Wall Street Journal,* March 20, 2000, pp. A1, A6.

48. John Stossel, "How Good Is Organic Food?" ABCNews.com, February 4, 2000, downloaded at http://abcnews.go.com.

CHAPTER 15

1. William Echikson, "The Mark of Zara," *Business Week,* May 29, 2000, pp. 98, 100; "European Retailers Continue to Grow into International Operations," WoolXchange Web site, www.melpub.wool.com, October 16, 2000; Kathy Rebello, "Finding the Nifty Fifty," *Business Week E.Biz,* September 18, 2000, www.businessweek.com.

2. Don Debelak, "Better with Age," *Entrepreneur,* February 2000, pp. 171–172.

3. Peter Burrows, "Free Software from Anywhere?" *Business Week,* September 13, 1999, pp. 37–38.

4. Fleming Companies Web site, www.fleming.com, downloaded March 21, 2001.

5. Robert D. Hof, "E-Malls for Business," *Business Week,* March 13, 2000, pp. 32–34; "Making the Move to e-Commerce," *U.S. News & World Report,* special advertising section, March 27, 2000.

6. Jon Swartz, "Internet's Future Is Screwed on Tight," *USA Today,* December 28, 2000, downloaded from the USA Today Web site, www.usatoday.com.

7. J. William Gurley, "Why Online Distributors—Once Written Off—May Thrive," *Fortune,* September 6, 1999, pp. 270, 272.

8. Erika Rasmusson, "Watch This Channel," *Sales & Marketing Management,* June 2000, pp. 80–82+.

9. Elizabeth Weinstein, "Listening Kiosks Allow Shoppers to Preview Music before Buying," *The Wall Street Journal,* November 2, 2000, downloaded from the Interactive Edition at http://interactive.wsj.com.

10. Joseph B. White, "Auto Dealers Group to Launch Web Site," *The Wall Street Journal,* March 16, 2000, p. A4; Fara Warner, "AutoNation Goes Back to Basics with an Internet Twist," *The Wall Street Journal,* February 25, 2000, p. B4.

11. Philip Siekman, "New Victories in the Supply-Chain Revolution," *Fortune,* October 30, 2000, pp. T208[C]–T208[D]+; Brian O'Reilly, "They've Got Mail!" *Fortune,* February 7, 2000, pp. 101–104+; Kelly Barron, "Logistics in Brown," *Forbes,* January 10, 2000, pp. 78–83.

12. Warner, "AutoNation Goes Back to Basics."

13. Erika Brown, "The Forbes Platinum List: Food Distributors," *Forbes,* January 10, 2000, pp. 132, 134.

14. Rhonda L. Rundle, "E-Commerce Coming to Health-Care Industry," *The Wall Street Journal,* February 28, 2000, p. B4.

15. Steven Wheeler and Evan Hirsh, *Channel Champions: How Leading Companies Build New Strategies to Serve Customers* (San Francisco: Jossey-Bass, 1999).

16. Ashlea Ebeling, "Paper Tiger," *Forbes,* February 21, 2000, pp. 71, 74.

17. TruServ Corp.Web site, www.truserv.com, downloaded March 21, 2001.

18. "*Fortune* 500 2000," downloaded from www.fortune.com, March 26, 2001.

19. U.S. Census Bureau, *Statistical Abstract of the United States: 2000,* p. 772.

20. Ibid., pp. 772, 776.

21. Wendy Zellner, "Wooing the Newbies," *Business Week E.Biz,* May 15, 2000, pp. EB 116, EB 118, EB 120; Heather Green, "Shakeout E-tailers," *Business Week E.Biz,* May 15, 2000, EB 102–EB 104+; William M. Bulkeley and Jim Carlton, "E-Tail Gets Derailed: How Web Upstarts Misjudged the Game," *The Wall Street Journal,* April 5, 2000, pp. A1, A6.

22. Green, "Shakeout E-tailers," p. EB 104.

23. Zellner, "Wooing the Newbies;" Swartz, "Internet's Future Is Screwed On Tight;" "Gap Web Site Begins Selling Pregnant Women's Apparel," *The Wall Street Journal,* March 27, 2000, p. B8.

24. Melinda Ligos, "Clicks & Misses," *Sales & Marketing Management,* June 2000, pp. 69–70+.

25. Rodney Ho, "Vending Machines Make Change," *The Wall Street Journal,* July 7, 1999, pp. B1, B4; "A Case of Supply and Demand," *Marketing News,* November 22, 1999, p. 3.

26. Ho, "Vending Machines Make Change."

27. Joshua Macht, "Mortar Combat," *Inc. Technology,* 1999, no. 3, pp. 102–104+.

28. Chad Terhune, "In Modest Times, 'Dollar' Stores Remain Upbeat," *The Wall Street Journal,* December 22, 2000, pp. B1, B4.

29. Louise Lee, "Why Gap Isn't Galloping Anymore," *Business Week,* November 8, 1999, p. 136; Louise Lee, "A Savvy Captain for Old Navy," *Business Week,* November 8, 1999, pp. 132, 134.

30. Bruce Upbin, "Profit in a Big Orange Box," *Forbes,* January 24, 2000, pp. 122–127.

31. Calmetta Y. Coleman, "Target's Aim: 'Bring Fashion to Food' on a National Scale," *The Wall Street Journal,* March 1, 2000, p. 4.

32. Stewart Alsop, "My Love Affair with Harry & David," *Fortune,* January 24, 2000, pp. 143–144.

33. Sandra Dolbow, "Pier 1 Makes Over," *Brandweek,* March 5, 2001, pp. 1, 10.

34. U.S. Census Bureau, *Statistical Abstract of the United States: 2000,* p. 777.

35. International Council of Shopping Centers, "A Brief History of Shopping Centers," June 2000, downloaded from the ICSC Web site, www.icsc.org, March 21, 2001.

36. Ibid.; Ginsburg, "Xtreme Retailing."

37. Joel Kotkin, *The New Geography: How the Digital Revolution Is Reshaping the American Landscape* (New York: Random House, 2000), excerpted in Joel Kotkin, "It Takes a Village," *Inc.,* November 2000, pp. 73, 75, 77.

38. Edward O. Welles, "The Diva of Retail," *Inc.,* October 1999, pp. 36–38+.

39. Richard Tomlinson, "Who's Afraid of Wal-Mart?" *Fortune,* June 26, 2000, pp. 186–188+; Steven Komarow, "Wal-Mart Takes Slow Road in Germany," *USA Today,* May 9, 2000, p. 3B.

40. "Toshiba Cautious in Internet Sales," *Ad Age International,* November 1999, p. 48.

41. Ligos, "Clicks & Misses," p. 72.

42. Janet Ginsburg, "Selling Sofas Online Is No Snap," *Business Week,* April 3, 2000, pp. 96, 98.

43. Christopher Palmeri, "Flexing Its Marketing Muscle," *Business Week,* May 29, 2000, p. 184.

44. Louise Lee, "Not Just Clicks Anymore," *Business Week,* August 28, 2000, pp. 226–227.

45. Teri Agins and Rebecca Quick, "Calvin Klein's Court Fight with Warnaco Seeks to Burnish Discount-Frayed Brand," *The Wall Street Journal,* June 1, 2000, downloaded from the Interactive Edition at http://interactive.wsj.com, March 21, 2001.

46. Richard Sale, "Change in Store," *Promo,* June 1999, pp. 39–42.

47. Shelly Branch, "Inside the Cult of Costco," *Fortune,* September 6, 1999, pp. 184–186+.

48. Upbin, "Profit in a Big Orange Box," p. 125; Brandon Copple, "Plowed Under," *Forbes,* February 21, 2000, p. 56.

49. Kevin Murphy, "Second Mouse Gets the Cheese," *Executive Edge,* June/July 1999, pp. 41–44.

50. Bob Duncan, "First Do No Harm," *Inc. Technology,* 2000, no. 1, pp. 29–30.

51. Siekman, "New Victories in the Supply-Chain Revolution," pp. T208[D]+; Pete Engardio, "Why the Supply Chain Broke Down," *Business Week,* March 19, 2001, p. 41.

52. Ned Raynolds, "Prime Time," *Executive Edge,* August/September 1999, pp. 50–53.

53. Association of American Railroads, "Economic Impact of U.S. Freight Railroads," downloaded from the AAR Web site, www.aar.org, March 21, 2001.

54. Association of American Railroads, "Intermodal Transport: The Fastest Growing Segment of the Railroad Industry," downloaded from the AAR Web site, www.aar.org, February 21, 2001.

55. Amy Doan, "Vitamin Efficiency," *Forbes,* November 1, 1999, pp. 176, 180+.

56. Emily Nelson and Ann Zimmerman, "Kimberly-Clark Keeps Costco in Diapers, Absorbing Costs Itself," *The Wall Street Journal,* September 7, 2000, pp. A1, A12.

CHAPTER 16

1. Company Web site, www.loreal.com, accessed March 20, 2001; Richard C. Morais, "The Color of Beauty," *Forbes,* November 27, 2000, pp. 170–176; Christine Bittar, "L'Oréal Paints $50M on 'Open' Hair Dye As It Looks

to Reclaim No. 1 Spot," *Brandweek,* March 26, 2001, p. 4.

2. Stephanie Thompson, "Milk Producers Back Britney Spears Tour," *Advertising Age,* March 8, 2000, p. 68; Erika Rasmusson, "Marketing en Español," *Sales & Marketing Management,* September 1999, p. 16; Betsy Cummings, "Star Power," *Sales & Marketing Management,* April 2001, pp. 52–56.

3. Steve Kindel, "Brand-New World," *Critical Mass,* Fall 1999, pp. 50, 52, 54.

4. Mercedes M. Cardona and Alice Z. Cuneo, "Retailers Reaching Out to Capture Kids' Clout," *Advertising Age,* October 9, 2000, p. 16.

5. Pamela L. Moore, "An Overdose of Drug Advertising?" *Business Week,* May 22, 2000, p. 52; Sarah Ellison, "Viagra Europe Ads to Focus on Symptoms," *The Wall Street Journal,* March 22, 2000, p. B10.

6. Betsy McKay, "PepsiCo Tries to Clarify Pepsi One's Image," *The Wall Street Journal,* February 25, 2000, p. B7.

7. "Naturalizer Shoes Are on a Sexy-Ad Kick," *The Wall Street Journal,* March 15, 2000, p. B2.

8. Jerry Fisher, "ADworkshop: Make a Splash," *Entrepreneur,* April 2000, p. 156.

9. "Media," *Marketing News,* July 3, 2000, p. 13.

10. Lou Belmont, "Agency Tunes Message for Native Americans," *Marketing News,* November 22, 1999, p. 29.

11. Normandy Madden, "L'Oréal Mascara Stirs Curling Craze in Japan," *Advertising Age International,* February 1, 2000, p. 13.

12. Diane Brady, "Uncle Sam Wants You . . . to Have Fun!" *Business Week,* February 21, 2000, pp. 98, 101.

13. Jack Neff, "Household Brands Counterpunch," *Advertising Age,* November 1, 1999, p. 26.

14. Keith L. Alexander, "Disney Ads Mad about the Mouse," *USA Today,* January 31, 2000, p. 6B.

15. Jack Myers, "Media Engine Gathers Head of Steam," *Advertising Age,* February 14, 2000, pp. S2, S18; "Media," p. 13.

16. Bob Igiel, "TV Structure Braces for Streamlining," *Advertising Age,* February 14, 2000, pp. S4, S16; Joe Mandese, "Networks Facing a Most Uncertain Fate," *Advertising Age,* February 14, 2000, pp. S4, S16; Myers, "Media Engine Gathers Head of Steam," p. S2.

17. Amanda Beeler, "What's That Noise?" *Advertising Age,* February 14, 2000, p. S8.

18. "Getting Labeled," *Promo,* Industry Report supplement, May 2000, p. A8.

19. Stephanie Miles, "Lands' End Learns Lessons from Christmas Past, Catalogs Still Key," *The Wall Street Journal,* December 20, 2000, downloaded from the Interactive Edition at http://interactive.wsj.com.

20. Erin Strout, "Success Secrets: Customer Loyalty Helps Build a Brand," *Sales & Marketing Management,* February 2000, p. 102.

21. Jim Sterne, "In Praise of E-Mail," *Inc. Technology,* March 14, 2000, pp. 149–150, 152.

22. "No. 1 Nuisance: Junk Mail," *Direct,* December 1999, p. 6.

23. Sandra Block, "Look, Up in the Sky, It's a New Blimp," *USA Today,* March 16, 2000, p. 3B; Rodney Ho, "Baggage Carousel Ad Business's Circuitous Launch," *The Wall Street Journal,* February 15, 2000, p. B2.

24. Beth Snyder Bulik, "Lipton Brisk Iced Tea Effort Adds Graffiti to Music Mix," *Advertising Age,* March 17, 2000, p. 3.

25. Gene Koprowski, "A Brief History of Web Advertising," *Critical Mass,* Fall 1999, pp. 8–9+.

26. Lynn Woods, "Banners by Design," *Critical Mass,* Fall 1999, pp. 62, 64, 66.

27. Direct Marketing Association, "Here Comes 'T-Commerce': Interactive TV's Rosy Future," January 31, 2001, news release, downloaded from the DMA Web site, www.the-dma.org.

28. Neil Weinberg, "Net Losses," *Forbes,* January 10, 2000, pp. 176, 180.

29. Marilyn Halter, "The New Age of Ethnic Marketing," *Brandweek,* March 19, 2001, pp. 24–28; Eugenia C. Daniels, "Critical Shift in Direction," *Advertising Age,* February 14, 2000, p. S12.

30. "Back to Basics," *Promo,* Industry Report supplement, May 2000, pp. A20, A22.

31. Jack Neff, "Trade Promotion Rises," *Advertising Age,* April 3, 2000, p. 24.

32. "These Are the Champions," *Promo,* November 1999, p. 53.

33. Stephanie Thompson, "Kellogg Concept Turns Aisles into Breakfastland," *Advertising Age,* July 3, 2000, pp. 3, 32.

34. "These Are the Champions," pp. 52–53.

35. Michele Marchetti, "What a Sales Call Costs," *Sales & Marketing Management,* September 2000, downloaded from the Sales & Marketing Management Web site, www.salesandmarketing.com.

36. Emily Nelson, "The Art of the Sale," *The Wall Street Journal,* January 11, 2001, pp. B1, B6.

37. Peter Kafka, "Life of a Salesman," *Forbes,* December 11, 2000, pp. 92, 94, 96.

38. Chad Kaydo, "Spotlighting a Sales Success," *Sales & Marketing Management,* February 2000, p. 27.

39. Kaydo, "Spotlighting a Sales Success."

40. Nelson, "The Art of the Sale," p. B6.

41. Erika Rasmusson, "Complaints Can Build Relationships," *Sales & Marketing Management,* September 1999, p. 89.

42. Marchetti, "What a Sales Call Costs"; Neil Rackham, "The Other Revolution in Sales," *Sales & Marketing Management,* March 2000, pp. 34, 36.

43. Rackham, "The Other Revolution in Sales," p. 36.

44. Peter Burrows, "The Radical," *Business Week,* February 19, 2001, pp. 70–74+.

45. Kate Fitzgerald, "Fewer Sponsor Wanna-Bes Given Chance to Yell Yahoo!" *Advertising Age,* August 7, 2000, p. S46.

46. Mary Kwak, "Driving Energy," *Inc. Technology,* no. 3, 2000, p. 23.

47. McKay, "PepsiCo Tries to Clarify Pepsi One's Image."

48. Pamela Sherrid, "Prescription Drug Pushers," *U.S. News & World Report,* October 30, 2000, pp. 40–42.

49. Mary Lord, "School without Soda?" *U.S. News & World Report,* March 26, 2001, p. 54; Kate Zernike, "Coke to Dilute Push in Schools for Its Products," *New York Times,* March 14, 2001, downloaded from the AOL Web site at http://partners.nytimes.com; Paul Simao, "Coke Changes Controversial Drink Strategy," *Reuters News Service,*

March 14, 2001, downloaded from the Yahoo! Web site at http://dailynews.yahoo.com.

CHAPTER 17

1. "Mr. Roger W. Ham." chief information officer biography, Los Angeles Police Department, www.lapdonline.org, accessed April 30, 2001; Tom Field, "L.A. Law," *CIO*, November 1, 1999, pp. 34–42; "CIO Perspectives Conference Series: Anatomy of IT Partnerships," October 3–6, 1999, www2.cio.com/conferences.
2. Andy Reinhardt, "From Gearhead to Grand High Pooh-Bah," *Business Week*, August 28, 2000, pp. 129–130.
3. Christopher Caggiano, "Low-Tech Smarts," *Inc.*, January 1999, pp. 79–80.
4. David Shenk, "Why You Feel the Way You Do," *Inc.*, January 1999, p. 58.
5. Al Urbanski, "Count Countdown," *Promo*, November 1999, pp. 19–20.
6. Gwen Moran, "Cover Your Bases," *Entrepreneur*, February 2000, p. 114.
7. Ellen Mowbray and Chet Zalesky, "Interfaces Simplify Data for Users," *Marketing News*, July 17, 2000, p. 2.
8. Brett Nelson, "Junk Mail Bytes It," *Forbes*, April 3, 2000, p. 150.
9. Greg Holden, "Outsmarting the Outsourcers," *Forbes*, May 21, 2001, pp. 52–53; "Guide to ASPs," *Inc.Tech 2000*, No. 4.
10. Jill Hecht Maxwell, "Healthy Skepticism for ASPs," *Inc.Tech 2000*, No. 4, p. 27.
11. Stephen H. Wildstrom, "Web Phones: Now You're Talking," *Business Week*, October 4, 1999, p. 18.
12. "JSAPI for Java," Sabre Web site, www.sabre.com, accessed April 10, 2001; Michael Helft, "Java's New Reality," *San Jose Mercury News*, February 9, 1998, pp. 1E, 4E.
13. Otis Port, "Plant Manager in a Box," *Business Week*, August 7, 2000, p. 82.
14. Michael Hopkins, "Zen and the Art of the Self-Managing Company," *Inc.*, November 2000, p. 63.
15. Dan Scheraga, "The Plug-In Plan," *Success*, p. 49.
16. Joshua Macht, "Confessions of an Information Sinner," *Inc.*, January 1999, p. 74.
17. Caggiano, "Low-Tech Smarts," p. 79.
18. David Carnoy, "Talk the Type," *Success*, April 1999, p. 34.
19. Ibid.
20. Hopkins, "Zen and the Art of the Self-Managing Company."
21. Interview with graphic artist Merin Tougas, March 23, 2001.
22. Macht, "Confessions of an Information Sinner," pp. 73–75.
23. Bryan Larsen, "Home Depot Strives for IT Simplicity," *Enterprise Development*, March 2000, pp. 10–19; Craig Stedman, "Java Fuels Home Depot Expansion," *Computerworld*, August, 23, 1999, p. 34; Chad Terhune, "Home Depot's Home Improvement," *The Wall Street Journal*, March 8, 2001, p. B1.
24. "Play for Work," *CIO*, April 1, 1999, p. 68.
25. John Edwards, "Design of the Future," *CIO*, April 1, 1999, p. 64.
26. Michale Dornheim, "Firewall in Space," *Aviation Week & Space Technology*, December 13, 1999, p. 29.
27. Michael S. Foley, "Get Hooked on an Intranet," *Success*, July/August 2000, p. 56.
28. Foley, "Get Hooked."
29. Polly Schneider, "A Bargain Hunter's Guide to Global Networking," *CIO*, April 1, 1999, p. 51.
30. Schneider, "A Bargain Hunter's Guide."
31. "Charge of the Light Brigade," *Business Week*, January 31, 2000, p. 62.
32. Eric Nee, "The Upstarts Rocking Telecom," *Fortune*, January 24, 2000, p. 106.
33. Michael Peltz, "What's Driving the Revolution in Broadband Internet Access?" *Worth*, July/August 2000, p. 32.
34. CNET News.com Staff, "Hackers Attack HP, Compaq, Others," CNET News.com, February 15, 2001, http://news.cnet.com.
35. Brier Dudley, "Microsoft Exec Tells How Hacker Got In," *Seattle Times*, February 23, 2001, http://seattletimes.nwsource.com.
36. "Hacker Gets Hold of Top Secret U.S. Space Codes," Yahoo! News, March 2, 2001, http://dailynews.yahoo.com.
37. "2001 Computer Crime and Security Survey," Computer Security Institute, March 12, 2001, www.gocsi.com.
38. Special Report, *Business Week*, December 6, 1999, pp. 106–107.
39. Special Report, pp. 106–107.
40. Special Report, p. 110.

CHAPTER 18

1. David Hilzenrath, "A Matter of Minutes—and Millions," *The Washington Post*, downloaded from www.cfraonline.com, January 12, 2001; Floyd Norris, "SEC Accuses MicroStrategy Executive of Fraud," *The New York Times*, downloaded from www.cfraonline.com, January 12, 2001; Christopher Schmitt and Paula Dwyer, "Did the Auditors Cross the Line?" *Business Week*, September 25, 2000, pp. 168–169; "Micro Panic," *Forbes*, April 17, 2000, pp. 60–61; Mike McNamee, "Techdom's New Bean Counting Battle," *Business Week*, April 17, 2000; Catherine Yang, "Earth to Dot-Com Accountants," *Business Week*, April 3, 2000, pp. 40–41.
2. Bureau of Labor Statistics, accessed from the BLS Web site, stats.bls.gov, on January 15, 2001.
3. Company information, downloaded from Anderson and Associate's Web site, www.andassoc.com on January 13, 2001; "By the (Open) Book," *Inc. Tech*, March 1999, pp. 33–34.
4. "About ElderWeb" downloaded from www.elderweb.com on January 13, 2001; "Cyber Granny, Best of Web," *Forbes*, downloaded from www.forbes.com on January 13, 2001.
5. Francine Knowles, "21st Century Company: Parson Group," *Chicago Sun-Times*, October 30, 2000, downloaded from www.suntimes.com on January 25, 2001; Susan Hansen, "Ready, Set, Grow," *Inc. Magazine*, October 25, 2000, downloaded from www.inc.com on January 25, 2001; "Company Profile," downloaded from www.parsongroup.com on January 25, 2001.
6. "Accounting Wars," *Business Week*, September 25, 2000, p. 157.

7. Virtual Growth Company Information, downloaded from company's Web site, www.virtualgrowth.com, on January 16, 2001.
8. MSN Investor, downloaded from http://investor.msn.com on January 18, 2001.
9. Anne Tergesen, "The Ins and Outs of Cash Flow," *Business Week,* January 22, 2001, p. 102; "Street Talk: Wireless Woes," CNNfn, downloaded from http://cnnfn.com on January 19, 2001; "Analyst Reports," CNET, downloaded from www.cnet.com on January 19, 2001.
10. MSN Investor, downloaded from http://investor.msn.com on January 18, 2001.
11. "About HON," downloaded from company's Web site, www.honcompany.com, on January 17, 2001; "100 Best-Managed Companies," *Industry Week Magazine,* downloaded from www.honi.com/investor on January 17, 2001; Ralph Ortina, "Continuous Budgeting at the HON Company," *Management Accounting,* January 1996, p. 20.

CHAPTER 19

1. Benchmark Capital, "Our Strategy," downloaded from www.benchmark.com on January 31, 2001; Linda Himelstein, "Benchmark's Venture Capitalists Take the Valley by Storm," *Business Week Online,* downloaded from www.businessweek.com on January 31, 2001; Lawrence Aragon, "The Smart VC from Benchmark," Redherring.com, downloaded from www.redherring.com on January 31, 2001; "Venture Capital Investments Achieve Record Levels in 2000," Press release, Venture Economics and National Venture Capital Association, downloaded from www.ventureeconomics.com on January 31, 2001.
2. Marcia Vickers, "Up from Bean Counter," *Business Week,* August 28, 2000, p. 120.
3. Boeing Company Web site www.boeing.com, accessed on February 9, 2001; Robert Brunner, et al., *The Boeing 777,* Case #UVA-F-1017, Charlottesville, Virginia: Darden Graduate School of Business, 1997.
4. Mike Hogan, "Online Banking," *Computer User,* downloaded from www.computeruser.com on January 31, 2001.
5. Marcia Vickers, "Up from Bean Counter," *Business Week,* August 28, 2000, p. 120.
6. Federal Reserve statistics, downloaded from www.federalreserve.gov on February 5, 2001.
7. Tania Padgett, "Interest High in Online Banking," *Los Angeles Times,* downloaded from www.latimes.com on February 5, 2001.
8. Padgett, "Interest High in Online Banking."
9. Juan Hovey, "Bank on It," *Entrepreneur,* April 2001, pp. 103–104.
10. FDIC, *Statistics on Banking,* downloaded from www.fdic.gov on February 5, 2001.

CHAPTER 20

1. About Island" and "How Island Works," downloaded from www.island.com on April 19, 2001; Gaston F. Ceron, "How Technology Has Changed the Way We Invest," *The Wall Street Journal,* November 13, 2000, p. R32; "NYSE Trading Widens via Link to Archipelago," *The Wall Street Journal,* August 8, 2000, p. C17; Matthew Andersen, "Manager's Journal: Don't Clobber ECNs," *The Wall Street Journal,* March 27, 2000, p. A48.
2. Hoover's Online, downloaded from www.hoovers.com/ipo on April 19, 2001.
3. Insurance Information Institute, downloaded from www.financialservicesfacts.org on April 19, 2001.
4. "Survey of Consumer Finances," downloaded from www.federalreserve.gov on April 19, 2001.
5. New York Stock Exchange, downloaded from www.nyse.com on April 19, 2001.
6. "Chicago Stock Exchange Statistics," downloaded from www.chicagostockex.com on April 19, 2001.
7. "About the Dow Jones Averages," downloaded from http://averages.dowjones.com on April 19, 2001.
8. Michael Lewis, "Jonathan Lebed: Stock Manipulator, SEC Nemesis—and 15 Years Old," *New York Times,* downloaded from www.nytimes.com on April 20, 2001.

APPENDIX A

1. Sean O'Neill, "Getting Down," *Kiplinger's Personal Finance Magazine,* December 1999, p. 94.
2. Diane Brady, "Insurers Step Gingerly into Cyberspace," *Business Week Online,* November 22, 1999.

APPENDIX B

1. "Disney Has Mickey until 2024," *The Arizona Republic,* February 7, 2001, p. D1.
2. Ron Harris, "Napster Looks to the Future," and "Timeline of Events in Napster Case," Associated Press stories downloaded from http://dailynews.yahoo.com/h/ap/, February 13, 2001.
3. "Appeals Court Reinstates Jury Award for Mike Tyson's Trainer," *Northwest Arkansas Times,* July 18, 1998.
4. John Allison and Robert A. Prentice, *Business Law: Text and Cases in the Legal Environment* (Fort Worth, TX: Harcourt, Inc., 1994), pp. 301–302.
5. Bill Rankin, "Alamo's Costly Failure to Warn," *The National Law Journal,* May 29, 2000, p. A17.
6. Kathleen Day, "Senate Votes to Toughen Bankruptcy," *Washington Post,* March 16, 2001, p. A1, www.washingtonpost.com; Tom Hamburger, "Senate Approves Bankruptcy Legislation," *The Wall Street Journal,* March 16, 2001, pp. A3, A4; "Bankruptcy Legislation Glance," The Associated Press, March 16, 2001.
7. Dean Foust, "Chapter 11 Never Looked So Good," *Business Week,* March 20, 2000, p. 44.

GLOSSARY

accounting (p. 650) the practice of measuring, interpreting, and communicating financial information to support internal and external business decision making.

accounting equation (p. 658) the basic relationship that states that assets equal liabilities plus owners' equity.

accounting process (p. 655) the set of activities involved in converting information about individual transactions into financial statements.

accrual accounting (p. 662) the accounting method that records revenue and expenses when they occur, not necessarily when cash actually changes hands.

acquisition (p. 201) procedure in which one firm purchases the property and assumes the obligations of another.

activity ratios (p. 666) measures of the effectiveness of management's use of the firm's resources.

actuarial table (p. A–5) probability calculation of the number of specific events—such as deaths, injuries, fire or windstorm losses—expected to occur within a given year.

adaptive planning (p. 295) develops courses of action that are fluid and forward-looking enough to adapt to changes in the business environment; emphasizes focus and flexibility in plans.

advertising (p. 584) paid, nonpersonal communication delivered through various media and designed to inform or persuade members of a particular audience.

advocacy (cause) advertising (p. 585) a form of institutional advertising that promotes a specific viewpoint on a public issue as a way to influence public opinion and the legislative process.

affinity program (p. 488) a marketing effort sponsored by an organization that solicits involvement by individuals who share common interests and activities.

after tax cash flow (p. 663) a firm's profits with depreciation added back into net income.

agency (p. A–19) legal relationship whereby one party, called a principal, appoints another party, called the agent, to enter into contracts with third parties on the principal's behalf.

agency shop (p. 404) employment policy allowing workers to reject union membership but requiring them to pay fees equal to union dues.

alien corporation (p. 197) a firm incorporated in one nation that operates in another nation.

alternative dispute resolution (ADR) program (p. 416) employers give employees other options for resolving their grievances through open-door policies, employee hot lines, peer review councils, mediation, and arbitration.

American Federation of Labor (p. 400) (AFL) a national union of affiliated, individual craft unions.

angel investors (p. 240) wealthy individuals who invest directly in a new venture in exchange for an ownership share.

application service provider (ASP) (p. 626) a company that provides both the computers and the application support for managing an information system.

applications software (p. 630) computer program that performs the specific tasks that the user wants to carry out—like writing a letter or looking up data.

arbitration (p. 411) bringing in an impartial third party called an arbitrator to render a binding decision in the dispute.

assembly line (p. 430) manufacturing technique that carries the product on a conveyor system past several workstations, where workers perform specialized tasks.

asset (p. 657) anything of value owned or leased by a business.

autocratic leadership (p. 306) leaders make decisions on their own without consulting employees.

balance of payments (p. 130) difference in money flows into or out of a country.

balance of trade (p. 130) difference between a nation's exports and imports.

balance sheet (p. 659) a statement of a firm's financial position—what it owns and the claims against its assets—at a particular point in time.

balanced budget (p. 106) the total revenues raised by taxes equal total proposed spending for the year.

bankruptcy (p. A–21) legal nonpayment of financial obligations.

bargaining zone (p. 408) range of collective bargaining between conditions that induce a union to strike and those that induce management to close the plant.

board of directors (p. 199) elected governing body of a corporation.

bond (p. 689) a certificate of indebtedness sold to raise long-term funds for a corporation or government agency.

bond rating (p. 712) One tool used by bond investors to assess the riskiness of a bond.

bottom line (p. 661) the overall profit or loss earned by a firm over a period of time.

boycott (p. 404) an attempt to prevent people from purchasing a firm's goods or services.

brand (p. 514) name, term, sign, symbol, design, or some combination thereof that identifies the products of a firm.

brand equity (p. 518) added value that a certain brand name gives to a product.

brand insistence (p. 517) the ultimate degree of brand loyalty, in which the consumer will accept no substitute for a preferred brand.

brand name (p. 514) the part of a brand consisting of words or letters that form a name that identifies and distinguishes an offering from those of competitors.

brand preference (p. 517) a consumer chooses one firm's brand, when it is available, over a competitor's.

brand recognition (p. 517) brand acceptance strong enough that the consumer is aware of a brand, but not enough to cause a preference over competing brands.

branding (p. 18) the process of creating an identity in consumers' minds for a good, service, or company; one tool used by marketing oriented companies.

breakeven analysis (p. 526) pricing technique that determines the sales volume that a firm must achieve at a specified price in order to generate enough revenue to cover its total cost.

broadband technology (p. 637) digital, fiber-optic, and wireless network technologies that compress data and transmit them at blazing speeds.

brokerage firm (p. 719) financial intermediary who buys and sells securities for individual and institutional investors.

budget (p. 667) A planning and controlling tool that reflects the firm's expected sales revenues, operating expenses, and cash receipts and outlays.

budget deficit (p. 105) funding shortfall that results when the government spends more than the amount of money it raises through taxes and fees.

business (p. 8) profit-seeking activities of those engaged in purchasing or selling goods and services to satisfy society's needs and wants.

business (B2B) product (p. 470) goods and services purchased to be used, either directly or indirectly, in the production of other goods for resale.

business ethics (pp. 37, 46) standards of conduct and moral values involving right and wrong actions arising in the work environment.

business incubator (p. 185) organization that provides low-cost, shared facilities to small, start-up ventures.

business law (p. A–14) aspects of law that most directly influence and regulate the management of business activity.

business plan (pp. 181, 293) written document that provides an orderly statement of a company's goals, the methods by which it intends to achieve those goals, and the standards by which it will measure achievements.

business-to-business (B2B) e-commerce (p. 258) electronic business transactions between organizations using the Internet.

business-to-consumer (B2C) e-commerce (p. 261) selling directly to consumers over the Internet.

buyer behavior (p. 483) series of decision processes by individual consumers who buy products for their own use and organizational buyers who purchase business products to be used directly or indirectly in the sale of other items.

call provision (p. 713) allows the issuer to redeem the bond prior to its maturity at a prespecified price.

capital (p. 11) assets including technology, tools, information, and physical facilities.

cause marketing (p. 468) marketing that promotes a cause or social issue, such as the prevention of child abuse, anti-littering efforts, and antismoking campaigns.

centralization (p. 314) a company retains decision making at the top of the management hierarchy.

centralized communication network (p. 383) team members exchange messages through a single person to solve problems or make decisions.

certified public accountant (CPA) (p. 653) an accountant who has demonstrated his or her knowledge by meeting state requirements for education and experience and successfully completing a number of rigorous tests in accounting theory and practice, auditing, law, and taxes.

chain of command (p. 314) set of relationships that indicates who directs which activities and who reports to whom.

change agent (p. 215) manager who tries to revitalize an established firm to keep it competitive.

channel captain (p. 561) dominant company that exerts the most power in a distribution channel.

chief information officer (p. 618) company executive who is responsible for directing the firm's MIS and related computer operations.

Children's Online Privacy Protection Act (p. 265) (COPPA) requires that Web sites targeting children younger than 13 obtain "verifiable parental consent" before collecting any data that could be used to identify or contact individual users, including names and e-mail addresses.

classic entrepreneur (p. 214) person who identifies a business opportunity and allocates available resources to tap that market.

clearing of a check (p. 698) the process by which funds are transferred from the check writer to the recipient.

click-through rate (p. 274) the percentage of people presented with a Web banner ad who click on it.

client (p. 250) another computer or device that relies on the resources of one or more servers for help with its own processing.

closed shop (p. 404) employment policy, illegal in the United States, requiring a firm to hire only current union members.

co-branding (p. 488) a deal in which two or more businesses team up to closely link their names for a single product.

code of conduct (p. 52) formal statement that defines how the organization expects and requires employees to resolve ethical questions.

collective bargaining (p. 405) negotiation between management and union representatives concerning wages and working conditions for an entire group of workers.

co-marketing (p. 488) a deal in which two businesses jointly market each other's products.

committee organization (p. 315) a structure that places authority and responsibility jointly in the hands of a group of individuals rather than a single manager.

common stock (p. 713) share of ownership in a company.

communication (p. 376) meaningful exchange of information through messages.

communism (p. 96) planned economic system in which private property is eliminated, goods are owned in common, and factors of production and production decisions are controlled by the state.

comparative advertising (p. 586) persuasive product advertising that compares products directly with their competitors.

competition (p. 13) battle among businesses vying for consumer acceptance.

competitive differentiation (pp. 13, 302) the unique combination of organizational abilities and approaches that sets a company apart from competitors in the minds of customers.

competitive pricing strategy (p. 528) a strategy that tries to reduce the emphasis on price competition by matching other firms' prices and concentrating their own marketing efforts on the product, distribution, and promotional elements of the marketing mix.

compressed work week (p. 339) a scheduling option that allows employees to work the regular number of hours in fewer that the typical 5 days.

computer virus (p. 640) program that secretly attaches itself to other computer programs or files and changes them or destroys data.

computer-aided design (CAD) (p. 435) system for interactions between a designer and a computer to design a product, facility, or part that meets predetermined specifications.

computer-aided manufacturing (CAM) (p. 435) electronic tools to analyze CAD output and determine necessary steps to implement the design, followed by electronic transmission of instructions to guide the activities of production equipment.

computer-integrated manufacturing (CIM) (p. 436) production system that integrates computer tools and human workers to design products, handle materials, and control production.

conceptual skills (p. 289) determine a manager's ability to see the organization as a unified whole and to understand how each part of the overall organization interacts with other parts.

conflict (p. 373) antagonistic interaction in which one party attempts to thwart the intentions or goals of another.

conflict of interest (p. 49) situation in which a business decision may be influenced by the potential for personal gain.

conglomerate merger (p. 202) combines unrelated firms, usually with the goals of diversification, spurring sales growth, or spending a cash surplus that might otherwise make a firm a tempting target for a takeover effort.

Congress of Industrial Organizations (p. 400) (CIO) a national union of affiliated, individual industrial unions.

consultative selling (p. 602) meeting customers' needs by listening to them, understanding and caring about their problems, paying attention to details, suggesting solutions, and following through after the sale.

consumer (B2C) product (p. 470) Goods and services purchased by end users, such as DVDs, shampoo, and dental care.

consumer behavior (p. 483) the actions of ultimate consumers directly involved in obtaining, consuming, and disposing of

products, and the decision processes that precede and follow these actions.

consumer orientation (p. 18) a process of marketing that determines what consumers want and need, and then designing products to satisfy those needs.

Consumer Price Index (p. 101) (CPI) measures the monthy average change in prices of goods and services.

consumerism (p. 67) the public demand that a business consider the wants and needs of its customers in making decisions.

contingency planning (p. 296) allows a firm to resume operations as quickly and as smoothly as possible after a crisis while openly communicating with the public about what happened.

contingent worker (p. 349) employee who works part-time, temporarily, or for the length of time involved in fulfilling a specific contract.

contract (p. A–17) legally enforceable agreement between two or more parties regarding a specified act or thing.

controller (p. 681) the chief accounting manager; the person who keeps the company's books, prepares financial statements, and conducts internal audits.

controlling (p. 291) the function of evaluating an organization's performance to determine whether it is accomplishing its objectives.

conversion rate (p. 274) the percentage of visitors to a Web site who make a purchase.

cooperative (p. 203) (co-op) an organization whose owners join forces to collectively operate all or part of the functions in their industry.

cooperative advertising (p. 605) allowances provided by marketers in which they share the cost of local advertising of their firm's product or line with channel partners.

corporate charter (p. 198) a legal document that formally establishes a corporation.

corporate culture (p. 308) organization's system of values, principles, and beliefs.

corporate philanthropy (p. 66) act of an organization giving something back to the communities in which it earns profits.

corporation (p. 196) business that stands as a legal entity with assets and liabilities separate from those of its owner(s).

cost-based pricing (p. 525) formulas that calculate base-cost figures per unit and then add markups to cover overhead costs and generate profits.

cost-of-living adjustment (COLA) clause (p. 409) escalator clause; designed to protect the real incomes of workers during periods of inflation by increasing wages in proportion to increases in the CPI.

countertrade (p. 147) a bartering agreement in which international trade involves payments made in the form of local products, not currency.

creative selling (p. 598) personal selling involving situations in which a considerable degree of analytical decision making on the buyer's part results in the need for skillful proposals of solutions for the customer's needs.

creativity (p. 35) the capacity to develop novel solutions to perceived organizational problems.

critical path (p. 448) the sequence of operations that requires the longest time for completion.

critical thinking (p. 35) the ability to analyze and asses information in order to pinpoint problems or opportunities.

customer satisfaction (p. 26) ability of a good or service to meet or exceed buyer needs and expectations.

customer satisfaction (p. 462) result of a good or service meeting or exceeding the buyer's needs and expectations.

customer service standards (p. 565) the quantitative guidelines set by a firm to specify the quality of service it intends to provide for its customers.

data mining (p. 476) using a computer to search through massive amounts of customer data to detect patterns and relationships.

data warehouse (p. 476) a sophisticated customer database that allows managers to combine data from several different organizational functions.

database (p. 619) centralized integrated collection of data resources.

debenture (p. 711) bond backed only by the reputation of the issuer rather than by a specific pledge of a company's assets.

debt capital (p. 687) funds obtained through borrowing.

debt financing (p. 237) borrowed funds that entrepreneurs must repay.

decentralization (p. 314) a company locates decision making at lower levels.

decentralized communication network (p. 383) members communicate freely with other team members and arrive at decisions together.

decision making (p. 304) process of recognizing a problem or opportunity, evaluating alternative solutions, selecting and implementing an alternative, and assessing the results.

decision support system (DSS) (p. 622) information system that quickly provides relevant data to help businesspeople make decisions and choose courses of action.

delegation (p. 312) act of assigning work activities to subordinates.

demand (p. 85) willingness and ability of buyers to purchase goods and services.

demand curve (p. 86) a graph of the amount of a product that buyers will purchase at different prices; generally slope downward, reflecting the fact that lower and lower prices typically attract larger and larger purchases.

demand deposits (p. 684) NOW accounts and credit union share draft accounts.

democratic leadership (p. 306) leaders delegate assignments, ask employees for suggestions, and encourage participation.

demographic segmentation (p. 478) dividing markets on the basis of various demographic or socioeconomic characteristics; age, income, occupation, household size, stage in family life cycle, education, ethnic group, or gender.

departmentalization (p. 311) process of dividing work activities into units within the organization.

depository institutions (p. 691) financial institutions that accept deposits that can be converted into cash on demand.

deregulation (p. 58) regulatory trend toward elimination of legal restraints on competition.

desktop publishing (p. 632) employs computer technology to allow users to design and produce attractively formatted printed material themselves rather than hiring professionals.

devaluation (p. 132) a fall in a currency's value relative to other currencies or to a fixed standard.

digital subscriber line (p. 249) (DSL) broadband technology; a cable modem, or a satellite link to the Internet.

direct distribution channel (p. 539) distribution channel that moves goods directly from producer to ultimate user.

direct investment (p. 155) occurs when a firm buys an existing company or establishes a factory, retail outlets, or other facilities in a foreign country.

directing (p. 290) guiding and motivating employees to accomplish organizational objectives.

disability income insurance (p. A–10) insurance that replaces lost income when a wage earner cannot work due to an accident or illness.

disaster recovery planning (p. 642) deciding how to prevent system failures and continue operations if computer systems fail.

discount rate (p. 698) the interest rate at which Federal Reserve banks make short-term loans to member banks.

dispatching (p. 448) the phase of production control in which the manager instructs each department on what work to do and the time allowed for its completion

distribution (p. 538) process of moving goods and services from the producer to buyers.

distribution channel (p. 538) path through which products—and legal ownership of them—flow from producer to the final customer.

diversity (p. 33) blending individuals of different genders, ethnic backgrounds, cultures, religions, ages, and physical and mental abilities, in order to enrich a firm's chances of success.

domain name (p. 248) a Web site address.

domestic corporation (p. 198) a firm is considered thus in the state where it is incorporated.

downsizing (p. 340) process of reducing a firm's workforce to reduce costs and improve efficiency.

dumping (p. 140) a practice that developed during the 1980s that can include a company selling its products abroad at prices below their costs of production, or a company exporting a large quantity of a product at a lower price than the same product in the home market and driving down the price of the domestic product.

economic systems (p. 84) the combination of policies and choices a nation makes to allocate resources among its citizens.

economics (p. 84) social science that analyzes the choices made by people and governments in allocating scarce resources.

electronic cash (p. 263) buyers register with a bank and pay for purchases our of their accounts using digital certificates that verify their identities.

electronic commerce (e-commerce) (p. 256) process for online marketing of goods

and services—including product information; ordering, invoicing, and payment processes; and customer service.

electronic communications network (ECN) (p. 707) buyers and sellers meet in a virtual stock market where they trade directly with one another.

electronic data interchange (EDI) (p. 258) computer-to-computer exchanges of invoices, purchase orders, price quotations, and other business documents between buyers and sellers.

electronic exchange (p. 259) online marketplaces that cater to a specific industry's needs.

electronic funds transfer systems (p. 693) computerized systems for conducting financial transactions over electronic links.

electronic shopping cart (p. 262) a file which holds items that the consumer has chosen to buy.

electronic signatures (p. 264) a way to enter into legal contracts such as home mortgages and insurance policies online; the individual obtains a kind of electronic identification and installs it in his or her Web browser.

electronic storefronts (p. 262) Web sites where major retailers offer items for sale to consumers.

electronic wallets (p. 263) a computer data file at an e-commerce site's checkout counter that contains not only electronic cash but credit card information, owner identification, and address.

e-mail (p. 22) the electronic delivery of messages via Internet links.

embargo (p. 141) imposes a total ban on importing a designated product of a total halt to trading with a particular country.

employee benefits (p. 337) employee rewards such as health insurance and retirement plans that employers give, entirely or in part, at their own expense.

employee stock ownership plan (p. 363) (ESOP) plans that benefit employees by giving them ownership stakes in the companies for which they work.

employers' association (p. 414) employers cooperate in their efforts and present a united front in dealing with labor unions.

employment at will (p. 332) practice that allows the employment relationship to begin or end at any time at the decision of either the employee or the employer for any legal reason.

empowerment (pp. 307, 360) giving employees authority and responsibility to make decisions about their work without traditional managerial approval and control.

encryption (pp. 263, 639) the process of encoding data for security purposes; software that encodes, or scrambles, messages.

end-use segmentation (p. 483) a marketing strategy that focuses on the precise way a B2B purchaser will use a product.

enterprise resource planning (ERP) (p. 625) information system that collects, processes, and provides information about an organization's entire enterprise.

entrepreneur (pp. 14, 213) risk taker in the private enterprise system; person who seeks a profitable opportunity and takes the necessary risks to set up and operate a business.

entrepreneurship (p. 12) the willingness to take risks to create and operate a business.

environmental impact study (p. 438) a study that analyzes how a proposed plant would affect the quality of life in the surrounding area.

Equal Employment Opportunity Commission (p. 73) (EEOC) created to increase job opportunities for women and minorities and to help end discrimination based on race, color, religion, disability, sex, or national origin in any personnel action.

equilibrium price (p. 90) the prevailing market price at which you can buy an item.

equity capital (p. 687) funds provided by the firm's owners when they reinvest earnings, make additional contributions, or issue stock to investors.

equity financing (p. 239) funds invested in new ventures in exchange for part ownership.

European Union (EU) (p. 144) 15-nation European economic alliance.

event marketing (p. 468) marketing or sponsoring short-term events such as athletic competitions and cultural and charitable performances.

exchange control (p. 141) administrative trade restriction that sets terms for currency transactions related to international product purchases and sales.

exchange process (p. 461) the ability of two or more parties to benefit from trading things of value.

exchange rate (p. 132) value of one nation's currency relative to the currencies of other countries.

exclusive distribution (p. 560) distribution strategies involving limited market coverage by a single retailer or wholesaler in a specific geographic territory.

executive information system (EIS) (p. 623) system that allows top managers to access a firm's primary databases.

exit interview (p. 340) allows employers to find out why employees who voluntarily leave the company decide to do so.

expert system (p. 623) computer program that imitates human thinking through complicated sets of "if . . . then" rules.

exports (p. 122) domestically produced goods and services sold in other countries.

external communication (p. 383) meaningful exchange of information through messages transmitted between an organization and its major audiences.

extranet (pp. 23, 260) secure networks accessible from outside a firm, but only by trusted third parties such as familiar customers or suppliers; secure network accessible through a Web site by external customers or organizations for electronic commerce. It provides more customer-specific information than a public site.

factors of production (pp. 11, 89) basic inputs into the private enterprise system, including natural resources, human resources, capital, and entrepreneurship.

family brand (p. 514) a single brand name that identifies several related products.

family leave (p. 70) up to 12 weeks of unpaid leave provided annually for an employee who has a child or is adopting a child; who is becoming a foster parent; caring for a seriously ill relative or spouse; or who is seriously ill.

Federal Reserve System (p. 697) U.S. central bank whose board of governors are responsible for regulating commercial banks, performing banking-related activities for the U.S. Treasury, serving member banks, and developing and implementing monetary policies.

federation (p. 402) brings together many national and international unions to serve mediation and political functions.

finance (p. 680) business function of planning, obtaining, and managing a company's funds in order to accomplish its objectives in the most effective possible way.

financial manager (p. 680) an organization's staff member responsible for developing and implementing the firm's financial plan and for determining the most appropriate sources and uses of funds.

financial plan (p. 681) a document that specifies the funds a firm will need for a period of time, the timing of inflows and outflows, and the most appropriate sources and uses of funds; a guide to help a person reach desired goals.

financial system (p. 690) the system by which funds are transferred from savers to users.

firewall (pp. 266, 636) an electronic barrier between a company's internal network and the Internet that limits access into and out of the network; software that limits data transfers to certain locations and log system use so managers can identify attempts to log on with invalid passwords and other threats to system security.

fiscal policy (p. 104) government spending and taxation decisions designed to control inflation, reduce unemployment, improve the general welfare of citizens, and encourage economic growth.

flexible benefit plan (p. 339) benefit system that offers employees a range of options from which they may choose the types of benefits they receive.

flexible manufacturing system (FMS) (p. 435) a facility that workers can quickly modify to manufacture different products.

flexible work plan (p. 339) employment that allows personnel to adjust their working hours and places of work to accommodate their personal lives.

flextime (p. 339) a scheduling system that allows employees to set their own work hours within constraints specified by the firm.

follow-up (p. 448) the phase of production control in which employees and their supervisors spot problems in the production process and determine needed adjustments.

forecasting (p. 301) process of estimating or predicting a company's future sales or income.

foreign corporation (p. 198) a firm that does business in states other than the one where it has filed incorporation papers.

foreign licensing agreement (p. 148) one firm allows another to produce or sell its product, or use its trademark, patent, or manufacturing processes in a specific geographic area in return for royalties or other compensation.

formal communication channel (p. 380) carries messages that flow within the chain of command defined by an organization.

franchise (p. 148) a contractual agreement in which a wholesaler or retailer (the franchisee) gains the right to sell the franchisor's products under that company's brand name if it agrees to the related operating requirements.

franchising (p. 190) contractual agreement that specifies the methods by which a dealer (franchisee) can produce and market a supplier's (franchisor's) good or service.

free-reign leadership (p. 307) leaders believe in minimal supervision and leave most decisions to their subordinates.

frequency marketing (p. 488) a marketing initiative that rewards frequent purchases with cash, rebates, merchandise, or other premiums.

full and fair disclosure (p. 725) regulatory philosophy that investors should be told all relevant information so they can make informed decisions.

gazelles (p. 225) fast-growing start-up companies that have become the primary job creators in the U.S.

General Agreement on Tariffs and Trade (p. 141) (GATT) an international trade accord that substantially reduced worldwide tariffs and other barriers.

generic product (p. 514) goods and services that are marketed without being brand; they are characterized by plain packaging, minimal labeling, and little or no advertising.

genetic engineering (p. 64) a type of biotechnology that involves altering crops or other living things by inserting genes that provide them with a desirable characteristic, such as nutritional value or resistance to pesticides.

geographic segmentation (p. 477) the act of dividing an overall market into homogeneous groups on the basis of population locations.

giveback (p. 410) wage and benefit concessions to help employers remain competitive and continue to provide jobs for union members.

glass ceiling (p. 287) an invisible barrier that resists the efforts of women in moving up the corporate hierarchy beyond a certain point.

global business strategy (p. 155) offering a standardized, worldwide product and

selling it in essentially the same manner throughout a firm's domestic and foreign markets.

government accountant (p. 653) an accountant who performs professional services similar to those of management accountants and determines how efficiently the organizations accomplish their objectives.

government bond (p. 711) the bonds issued by the U.S. Treasury; they are backed by the full faith and credit of the U.S. government.

grapevine (p. 380) internal information channel that passes information from unofficial sources.

green marketing (p. 64) a marketing strategy that promotes an environmentally safe product.

grievance (p. 412) employee or union complaint that management is violating some provision of the union contract.

gross domestic product (GDP) (pp. 28, 100) the sum of all goods and services produced within a country's boundaries; based on the per-capita output of a country.

groupware (p. 635) software that combines information sharing through a common database with communication via e-mail so that employees can collaborate on projects.

hardware (p. 627) all the tangible elements of a computer system—the input devices, the machines that store and process data and perform required calculations, and output devices that present the results to information users.

health insurance (p. A–9) insurance designed to provide coverage for losses due to sickness or accidents.

high-context culture (p. 390) communication depends not only on the message itself but also on the conditions that surround it, including nonverbal cues, past and present experiences, and personal relationships between the parties; Japan, Latin America, and India.

home-based business (p. 171) operated from the residence of the business owner.

home-based work (p. 340) allows employees to perform their jobs from home instead of the workplace.

horizontal channel conflict (p. 562) disagreements that erupt among members at the same level in the distribution chain.

horizontal merger (p. 202) joins firms in the same industry that wish to diversify, increase their customer bases, cut costs, or offer expanded product lines.

human resource management (p. 326) function of attracting, developing, and retaining sufficient numbers of qualified employees to perform the activities necessary to accomplish organizational goals.

human resource (p. 12) anyone who works, including both the physical labor and the intellectual inputs contributed by workers.

human skills (p. 288) interpersonal skills that enable a manager to work effectively with and through people; the ability to communicate with, motivate, and lead employees to accomplish assigned activities.

hyperinflation (p. 100) an economic situation characterized by soaring prices.

imports (p. 122) foreign goods and services purchased by domestic customers.

income statement (p. 659) a financial record of a company's revenues, expenses and profits over a period of time.

independent agent (p. 152) marketing intermediaries that serve as independent sales forces in foreign markets, earning commissions on sales they book.

individual brand (p. 514) a firm gives a different brand name to each product within a line.

inflation (p. 100) rising prices caused by some combination of excess consumer demand and increases in the costs of raw materials, component parts, human resources, and other factors of production.

infomercial (p. 593) a form of broadcast direct marketing; 30-minute programs resemble regular TV programs, but they are devoted to selling goods or services.

informal communication channel (p. 380) carries messages outside formally authorized channels within an organization's hierarchy.

information overload (p. 619) a problem with databases; too much data for people to absorb, or data that are not relevant to decision making.

infrastructure (p. 136) basic systems of communication (television, radio, print media, telecommunications), transportation (roads and highways, railroads, airports), and energy facilities (power plants, gas and electrical utilities).

initial public offering (IPO) (p. 708) the transaction where a company first sells its stock to the investing public.

injunction (p. 414) a court order prohibiting some practice; prevents excessive picketing or certain unfair union practices.

insider trading (p. 726) use of material nonpublic information to make an investment profit.

instant messaging (p. 252) a recent adaptation of e-mail; when someone sends a message, it is immediately displayed on the recipient's computer screen; they can communicate in real time.

institutional advertising (p. 585) messages that promote concepts, ideas, philosophies, or goodwill for industries, companies, organizations, or government entities.

institutional investor (p. 714) an organization that invests its own funds or those it holds in trust for others.

insurable interest (p. A–4) demonstration that a direct financial loss will result if some event occurs.

insurable risk (p. A–5) requirement that a pure risk must meet in order for the insurer to agree to provide protection.

insurance (p. A–4) process by which a firm (the insurance company), for a fee (the premium), agrees to pay another firm or individual a sum of money stated in a written contract (the insurance policy) should a loss occur.

integrated marketing communications (IMC) (p. 578) coordination of all promotional activities—media advertising, direct mail, personal selling, sales promotion, and public relations—to produce a unified customer-focused message.

integrated software, or software suites (p. 631) software packages that combine several applications into a single package that can share modules for data handling and processing.

integrity (p. 49) adhering to deeply felt ethical principles in business situations.

intensive distribution (p. 560) a distribution strategy that involves placing a firm's products in nearly every available outlet.

internal communication (p. 381) system that sends messages through channels within an organization.

International Monetary Fund (IMF) (p. 142) established 1 year after the World Bank to promote trade through financial cooperation, in the process eliminating barriers; makes short-term loans to member nations that are unable to meet their budgetary expenses.

International Organization for Standardization (ISO) (p. 451) an organization established in Europe in 1947 that includes representatives from about 130 nations; its mission is to promote the development of standardized products to facilitate trade and cooperation across national borders.

international union (p. 402) a union with members outside the United States, usually in Canada.

Internet (or Net) (pp. 21, 248) worldwide network of interconnected computers that lets anyone with access to a personal computer send and receive images and data anywhere.

Internet service provider (ISP) (p. 249) organization that provides access to the Internet, usually via the public telephone network.

intranet (pp. 23, 636) closed network system using Internet standards that allow for information sharing among employees, divisions, and geographically diverse locations; a network that links employees through Internet tools like e-mail, hypertext links, and searches using Web browsers; they limit access only to employees or other authorized users.

intrapreneur (p. 214) entrepreneurially oriented person who develops innovations within the context of a large organization.

intrapreneurship (p. 240) process of promoting innovation within the structure of an existing organization.

inventory control (pp. 443, 568) production managers' responsibility to balance the need to keep stocks on hand to meet demand against the costs of carrying the inventory; balancing the priority of limiting costs of holding stocks with that of meeting customer demand through a variety of management methods.

investment banker (p. 709) a financial intermediary who purchases the issue from the firm or government and then resells the issue to investors.

job enlargement (p. 345) a job design change that expands an employee's responsibilities by increasing the number and variety of tasks they entail.

job enrichment (p. 345) change in job duties to increase employees' authority, responsibility, and skills.

job sharing (p. 339) allows two or more employees to divide the tasks of one job.

joint venture (pp. 150, 202) in international business allows companies to share risks, costs, profits, and management responsibilities with one or more host

country nationals; a partnership between companies formed for a specific undertaking.

judiciary (p. A–15) branch of the government charged with deciding disputes among parties through the application of laws.

just-in-time (JIT) system (p. 444) management philosophy aimed at improving profits and return on investment by minimizing costs and eliminating waste through minimizing inventory on hand.

knowledge management (p. 625) enterprise software programs that help companies run factories, keep track of accounting, and assist in marketing strategies.

label (p. 521) the descriptive part of a product's package that lists the brand name or symbol, name and address of the manufacturer or distributor, product composition and size, nutritional information for food products, and recommended uses.

labor union (p. 400) group of workers who have banded together to achieve common goals in the key areas of wages, hours, and working conditions.

law of large numbers (p. A–5) concept that seemingly random events will follow a predictable pattern if enough events are observed.

law (p. A–14) standards set by government and society in the form of either legislation or custom.

leadership (p. 305) ability to direct or inspire people to attain organizational goals.

leverage (p. 689) the technique of increasing the rate of return on an investment by financing it with borrowed funds.

leverage ratios (p. 666) A measure of the extent to which a firm relies on debt financing.

liability (p. 658) a claim against a firm's assets by a creditor.

life insurance (p. A–10) insurance that protects people against the financial losses that occur with premature death.

lifetime value of a customer (p. 487) the revenues and intangible benefits (referrals and customer feedback) from the customer over the life of the relationship, minus the amount the company must spend to acquire and serve that customer.

limit order (p. 719) the instructions that the brokerage firm is not to pay more than a specified price for a stock if the investor is buying, or not to accept less than a specified price if the investor is selling.

limited liability company (LLC) (p. 197) allow business owners to secure the corporate advantage of limited liability while avoiding the double taxation characteristic of corporations.

line manager (p. 315) forms a part of the primary line of authority that flows throughout the organization; interacts directly with the functions of production, financing, or marketing.

line organization (p. 314) the oldest and simplest organizational structure; establishes a direct flow of authority from the chief executive to subordinates.

line-and-staff organization (p. 315) combines the direct flow of authority of a line organization with staff departments that serve, advise, and support the line departments.

liquidity ratios (p. 664) financial ratios measuring a firm's ability to meet its short-term obligations when they must be paid.

listening (p. 379) skill of receiving a message and interpreting its intended meaning by grasping the facts and feelings it conveys.

local area networks (LANs) (p. 624) computer networks that connect machines within limited areas, such as one building or several buildings near each other; allow personal computers to share printers, documents, and information.

local union (p. 401) operates as a branch of a national union, representing union members in a given geographic area.

lockout (p. 413) a management strike to bring pressure on union members by closing the firm.

logistics (p. 564) all business activities involved in managing movements of goods through the supply chain.

low-context culture (p. 390) communication tends to rely on explicit written and verbal messages; Switzerland, Germany, Australia, and the U.S.

M1 (p. 684) the total value of coins, currency, traveler's checks, bank checking account balances, and the balances in other demand deposit accounts.

M2 (p. 684) the measure of the money supply including M1 plus a number of other financial assets that are almost as liquid as cash but do not serve directly as a medium of exchange.

macroeconomics (p. 85) the study of a country's overall economic issues, such as how an economy maintains and allocates resources and how government policies affect people's standards of living.

mainframe (p. 628) the largest type of computer system with the most extensive storage capacity and the fastest processing speeds.

make, buy, or lease decision (p. 442) choosing whether to manufacture a needed product or component in house, purchase it from an outside supplier, or lease it.

management (p. 286) process of achieving organizational objectives through people and other resources.

management accountant (p. 653) an accountant employed by a business other than a public accounting firm, and who is responsible for collecting and recording financial transactions and preparing financial statements used by the firm's managers in decision making.

management development program (p. 334) training designed to improve the skills and broaden the knowledge of current and potential executives.

management information system (MIS) (p. 618) organized method for providing past, present, and projected information on internal operations as well as external intelligence to support decision making.

manufacturer's (national) brand (p. 515) a brand offered and promoted by a manufacturer or producer; they are sometimes priced much higher than generic brands.

manufacturing resource planning (MRP II) (p. 449) production-control system that integrates planning data from individual departments to produce a master business plan.

maquiladora (p. 127) foreign-owned manufacturing plants that produce products for export.

market order (p. 719) an investor's request to buy or sell stock at the current market price.

market segmentation (p. 476) process of dividing a total market into several relatively homogeneous groups.

market share (p. 522) the percentage of a market controlled by a certain company or product.

marketing (p. 460) process of planning and executing the conception, pricing, promotion, and distribution of ideas, goods, services, organizations, and events to create and maintain relationships that satisfy individual and organizational objectives.

marketing concept (p. 462) companywide consumer orientation to promote long-run success.

marketing information system (p. 619) a system that can help marketing researchers manage an overwhelming flood of information by organizing data in a logical and accessible manner.

marketing intermediary (pp. 539, 589) the *middleman*, or business firm that moves goods between producers and consumers or business users; channel member, either wholesaler or retailer, that moves goods between producer and consumer or business user.

marketing mix (p. 471) blending the four elements of marketing strategy—product, price, distribution, and promotion—to satisfy chosen customer segments.

marketing research (p. 473) collection and use of information to support marketing decision making.

mass production (p. 429) a system for manufacturing products in large amounts through effective combinations of specialized labor, mechanization, and standardization.

materials handling (p. 568) the physical distribution activity that moves items within plants, warehouses, transportation terminals, and stores.

materials requirement planning (MRP) (p. 446) computer-based production planning system by which a firm can ensure that it has needed parts and materials available at the right time and place in the correct amounts.

matrix structure (p. 316) (project management structure) links employees from different parts of the organization to work together on specific projects.

mediation (p. 410) brings in a third party, called a mediator, to make recommendations for settling union–management differences.

merger (p. 201) combination of two or more firms to form one company.

microeconomics (p. 85) the study of small economic units, such as individual consumers, families, and businesses.

middle management (p. 287) the second tier in the management pyramid; includes positions such as general managers, plant managers, division managers, and branch managers; focus on specific operation within the organizations.

minicomputer (p. 628) an intermediate-sized computer—more compact and less expensive than a mainframe but also slower and with less memory.

mission statement (p. 297)   a written explanation of an organization's business intentions and aims.

missionary selling (p. 598)   indirect type of selling in which specialized salespeople promote the firm's goodwill among indirect customers, often by assisting customers in product use.

mixed market economy (p. 97)   economic system that combines characteristics of both planned and market economies in varying degrees, including the presence of both government ownership and private enterprise.

monetary policy (pp. 104, 698)   government action to increase or decrease the money supply and change banking requirements and interest rates to influence bankers' willingness to make loans; the managing of the growth rate in the supply of money and credit, usually through the use of interest rates.

money (p. 682)   anything generally accepted as payment for goods and services.

money market instrument (p. 711)   short-term debt security issued by corporations, financial institutions, and governments.

monopolistic competition (p. 93)   a market structure, like that for retailing, in which large numbers of buyers and sellers exchange relatively well-differentiated (heterogeneous) products, so each participant has some control over price.

monopoly (p. 94)   a market structure in which a single seller dominates trade in a good or service for which buyers can find no close substitute.

morale (p. 343)   the mental attitude of employees toward their employer and jobs.

motive (p. 343)   an inner state that directs a person toward the goal of satisfying a felt need.

multidomestic business strategy (p. 156)   developing and marketing products to serve different needs and tastes of separate national markets.

multimedia computing (p. 634)   technologies that integrate two or more types of media, such as text, voice, sound, video, graphics, and/or animation into computer-based applications.

multinational corporation (MNC) (p. 151)   firm with significant operations and marketing activities outside its home country.

municipal bond (p. 711)   credit instrument issued by state or local governments; they can be either revenue bonds or general obligation bonds.

mutual fund (p. 724)   financial institution that pools investment money from purchasers of its shares and uses it to acquire diversified portfolios of securities consistent with its investment objectives.

national debt (p. 105)   occurs when a nation's government borrows money by offering Treasury bills, Treasury notes, and Treasury bonds for sale to investors.

national union (p. 401)   joins together many local unions, which make up the entire union organizational structure.

natural resources (p. 11)   all productive inputs that are useful in their natural states, including agricultural land, building sites, forests, and mineral deposits.

need (p. 343)   a felt lack of some useful benefit.

negotiable instrument (p. A–18)   commercial paper that is transferable among individuals and businesses.

newsgroup (p. 253)   provides a forum for online participants to share information on selected topics.

nonprogrammed decision (p. 304)   a complex and unique problem or opportunity with important consequences for the organization.

nonverbal communication (p. 381)   transmits messages through actions and behaviors.

North American Free Trade Agreement (NAFTA) (p. 143)   1994 agreement among the U.S., Canada, and Mexico to break down tariffs and trade restrictions

notebook computer (p. 629)   a computer that is small enough to slip into a briefcase, yet more powerful than many desktop computers that are two or three years old.

not-for-profit organization (p. 8)   a business-like establishment that has primary objectives, such as public service, other than returning profits to its owners.

objectives (p. 301)   guideposts by which managers define the organization's desired performance in such areas as profitability, customer service, growth, and employee satisfaction.

oligopoly (p. 93)   a market situation, like those in the steel and airline industries, in which relatively few sellers compete, and where high start-up costs form barriers to keep out new competitors.

online community (p. 252)   chat rooms; provide a forum in which a group of people can share messages.

on-the-job training (p. 333)   training method that teaches an employee to complete new tasks by performing them under the guidance of an experienced employee.

open market operations (p. 699)   the technique of controlling the money supply growth rate by buying or selling U.S. Treasury securities.

open shop (p. 404)   employment policy making union membership and dues voluntary for all workers.

operating system (p. 630)   the software that controls the basic workings of a computer's system.

operational planning (p. 294)   creates the detailed standards that guide implementation of tactical plans.

order processing (pp. 569, 597)   all of the tasks required to prepare customer orders for shipment, and the steps involved in receiving shipments when they arrive; selling, mostly at the wholesale and retail levels, that involves identifying customer needs, pointing them out to customers, and completing orders.

organization (p. 309)   structured grouping of people working together to achieve common goals.

organization chart (p. 310)   a visual representation of a firm's structure that illustrates job positions and functions.

organization marketing (p. 468)   a marketing strategy that influences consumers to accept the goals of, receive the services of, or contribute in some way to an organization.

organizing (p. 290)   the process of blending human and material resources through a formal structure of tasks and authority; arranging work, dividing tasks among employees, and coordinating them to ensure implementation of plans and accomplishment of objectives.

outsourcing (p. 31)   contracting with another business to perform tasks or functions previously handled by internal staff members.

owners' equity (p. 568)   all claims of the proprietor, partners, or stockholders against the assets of a firm, equal to the excess of assets over liabilities.

partnership (pp. 25, 195)   an affiliation of two or more companies with the shared goal of assisting each other in the achievement of common goals; form of business ownership in which the company is operated by two or more people who are co-owners by voluntary legal agreement.

peer-review board (p. 417) committee of peer workers and management representatives with the power to make binding decisions to resolve disputes over promotion decisions, dismissals, and other disciplinary actions.

penetration pricing strategy (p. 527) a strategy that sets a low price as a major marketing weapon.

performance appraisal (p. 335) method of evaluating an employee's job performance by comparing actual results with desired outcomes.

perpetual inventory (p. 443) a system that continuously monitors the amounts and locations of a company's stocks.

person marketing (p. 466) the use of efforts designed to attract the attention, interest, and preference of a target market toward a person.

personal computer (PC) (p. 628) desktop computer used in homes, schools, businesses, nonprofit organizations, and government agencies; uses silicon chips to handle functions that used to be done only by cumbersome mainframes.

personal selling (p. 597) interpersonal promotional process involving a seller's face-to-face presentation to a prospective buyer.

PERT (Program Evaluation and Review Technique) (p. 448) a chart that seeks to minimize delays by coordinating all aspects of the production process.

physical distribution (p. 564) the transportation and numerous other elements that help to link buyers and sellers.

picketing (p. 413) workers marching at a plant entrance to protest some management practice.

place marketing (p. 467) an attempt to attract people to a particular area, such as a city, state, or nation.

planned economy (p. 96) strict government controls determine business ownership, profits, and resource allocation to accomplish government goals rather than those set by individual businesses.

planned shopping center (p. 556) a group of retail stores planned, coordinated, and marketed as a unit to shoppers in a geographic trade area.

planning (p. 290) process of anticipating future events and conditions and determining courses of action for achieving organizational objectives.

point-of-purchase (POP) advertising (p. 596) displays or demonstrations that promote products when and where consumers buy them, such as in retail stores.

pollution (p. 60) environmental damage caused by a company's products or operating processes; an important economic, legal, and social issue.

portal (p. 253) site designed to be a user's starting place when entering the World Wide Web.

positioning (p. 582) a concept in which marketers attempt to establish their own places in the minds of customers by communicating to prospective purchasers meaningful distinctions about the attributes, price, quality, or use of a good or service

preferred stock (p. 714) stock whose holders receive preference in the payment of dividends.

presentation software (p. 634) a program that includes graphics and tools for manipulating them to create a variety of charts, graphs, and pictures.

price (pp. 521, 525) exchange value of a good or service.

price-earnings ratio (P/E) (p. 722) the current market price divided by the annual earnings per share.

primary market (p. 708) market where new securities issues are first sold to investors; the issuer receives the proceeds from the sale.

private (store) brand (p. 515) a product that is not linked to the manufacturer, but instead carries the label of a retailer or wholesaler.

private enterprise system (pp. 13, 92) economic system that rewards firms based on how well they match and counter the offerings of competitors to serve the needs and demands of customers; economic system in which business success or failure depends on how well firms match and counter the offerings of competitors; also known as capitalism or a market economy.

private exchange (p. 261) a secure Web site at which a company and its suppliers share all types of data related to e-commerce, from product design through delivery of orders.

private placements (p. 689) a new stock or bond issues that may not be sold publicly but only to a small select group of large investors such as pension funds and life insurance companies.

private property (p. 14) the most basic freedom under the private enterprise

system; encompasses land, buildings, machinery, equipment, inventions, and various intangible kinds of property, and the right to own, use, buy, sell, and bequeath these things.

privatization (p. 98) converting government-owned enterprises into privately held firms in order to improve the economy.

problem-solving team (p. 367) temporary combination of workers who gather to solve a specific problem and then disband.

product (p. 498) bundle of physical, service, and symbolic attributes designed to enhance buyers' want satisfaction.

product advertising (p. 585) messages designed to sell a particular good or service.

product liability (p. 67) the responsibility of manufacturers for injuries and damages caused by their products.

product life cycle (p. 503) four basic stages through which a successful product progresses—introduction, growth, maturity, and decline.

product line (p. 508) group of related products that are physically similar or are intended for a similar market.

product mix (p. 508) company's assortment of product lines and individual offerings.

production (p. 428) application of resources such as people and machinery to convert materials into finished goods or services.

production and operations management (p. 428) managing people and machinery in converting materials and resources into finished goods and services.

production control (p. 446) a process that creates a well-defined set of procedures for coordinating people, materials, and machinery to provide maximum production efficiency.

production planning (p. 447) the phase of production control that determines the amount of resources (including raw materials and other components) a firm needs to produce a certain output.

productivity (pp. 28, 100) the relationship between the goods and services produced in a nation each year and the human work and other production inputs necessary to produce them.

product-related segmentation (p. 481) the act of dividing a consumer market into groups based on benefits sought by buyers and usage rates.

professional employer organization (PEO) (p. 326) a company that helps small and mid-sized firms with a wide range of human resources services that include hiring and training employees, administering payroll and benefits programs, handling workers' compensation and unemployment insurance, and maintaining compliance with labor laws.

profitability ratios (p. 665) ratios used to measure the organization's overall financial performance by evaluating its ability to generate revenues in excess of operating costs and other expenses.

profits (p. 8) financial rewards received by a businessperson for taking the risks involved in creating and marketing want-satisfying goods and services.

programmed decision (p. 304) simple, common, and frequently occurring problem for which a solution has already been determined.

promotion (p. 578) function of informing, persuading, and influencing a purchase decision.

Promotional mix (p. 580) combination of personal and nonpersonal selling techniques designed to achieve promotional objectives.

property and liability insurance (p. A–8) general category of insurance that provides protection against financial losses due to a number of perils.

psychographic segmentation (p. 481) divides consumer markets into groups with similar psychological characteristics, values, and lifestyles.

public accountant (p. 652) provides accounting services to individuals or business firms for a fee.

public ownership (p. 203) a unit or agency of government owns and operates an organization.

public relations (p. 603) organization's nonpaid communications and relationships with public audiences.

publicity (p. 604) stimulation of demand for a good, service, place, idea, person, or organization by disseminating news or obtaining favorable media presentations not paid for by the sponsor.

pulling strategy (p. 605) promotional effort by a seller to stimulate demand among final users, who will then exert pressure on the distribution channel to carry the good or service, pulling it through the distribution channel.

pure competition (p. 92) a market structure, like that of small-scale agriculture, in which large numbers of buyers and sellers exchange homogeneous products so no single participant has a significant influence on price.

pushing strategy (p. 605) promotional effort by a seller to members of the distribution channel intended to stimulate personal selling of the good or service, thereby pushing it through the channel.

quality (p. 25) the degree of excellence or superiority of a firm's goods and services.

quality control (p. 450) the act of measuring goods and services against established quality standards.

quota (p. 140) limits the amounts of particular products that countries can import during specified time periods.

ratio analysis (p. 664) commonly used tools for measuring the firm's liquidity, profitability, and reliance on debt financing, as well as the effectiveness of management's use of its resources, compared to other firms and with the firm's own past performance.

recycling (p. 63) reprocessing of used materials for reuse.

reengineering (p. 446) the process of mapping out delivery-chain processes in detail to identify potential ways of reducing cycle times or process errors by applying technology to each step in a process.

regulated industry (p. 57) industry in which competition is either limited or eliminated, and government monitoring substitutes for market controls.

relationship management (p. 24) the collection of activities that build and maintain ongoing, mutually beneficial ties with customers and other parties.

relationship marketing (p. 485) developing and maintaining long-term, cost-effective exchange relationships with individual customers, suppliers, employees, and other partners for mutual benefit.

relationship selling (p. 602) a salesperson builds a mutually beneficial relationship with a customer through regular service over an extended period.

retailer (p. 540) the marketing intermediaries that sell goods and services to final consumers; channel member that sells goods and services to individuals for their own use rather than for resale.

right-to-work law (p. 404) prohibits union shops and outlaw compulsory union membership.

risk (p. A–2) uncertainty about loss or injury.

risk-return tradeoff (p. 681) the optimal balance between risk and return.

robot (p. 433) reprogrammable machine capable of performing numerous tasks that require manipulations of materials and tools.

routing (p. 447) the phase of production control that determines the sequence of work throughout the facility and specifies who will perform each aspect of production at what location.

salaries (p. 336) compensation calculated on a weekly, monthly, or annual basis.

sales force automation (p. 603) incorporates a broad range of tools, from e-mail, telecommunications devices like pagers and cell phones, and laptop computers to increasingly sophisticated software systems that automate the sales process.

sales law (p. A–17) law governing the sale of goods or services for money or on credit.

sales promotion (p. 594) nonpersonal marketing activities other than advertising and public relations that stimulate consumer purchasing and dealer effectiveness; includes displays, trade shows, demonstrations, and various nonrecurrent selling efforts.

scheduling (p. 447) the phase of production control in which production managers develop timetables that specify how long each operation in the production process takes and when workers should perform it.

scrambled merchandising (p. 555) the act of retailers trying to increase sales by diversifying their product lines.

secondary market (p. 710) collection of financial markets where previously issued securities are traded among investors.

secured bond (p. 711) bond backed by a specific pledge of a company's assets.

security (p. 708) stock, bond, or money market instrument that represents an obligation of the issuer to provide the purchaser an expected or stated return on the investment.

seed capital (p. 237) initial funding needed to launch a new venture.

selective distribution (p. 560) a strategy in which a manufacturer selects only a limited number of retailers to distribute its product lines.

server (p. 250) a larger, special computer that holds information, then provides it to clients on request.

service (p. 499) intangible task that satisfies consumer or business user needs.

set-aside program (p. 184) specifies that certain government contracts (or portions of those contracts) are restricted to small businesses.

sexism (p. 74) discrimination against members of either sex, but primarily affecting women.

sexual harassment (p. 73) inappropriate actions of a sexual nature in the workplace.

skimming pricing strategy (p. 527) a strategy that sets an intentionally high price relative to the prices of competing products.

skunkworks (p. 240) a project initiated by an employee who conceives the idea and then recruits resources from within the firm to turn it into a commercial project.

small business (p. 168) firm that is independently owned and operated, not dominant in its field, and meets industry-specific size standards for income or number of employees.

Small Business Administration (SBA) (p. 184) federal agency that assists small businesses by providing management training and consulting, financial advice, and support in securing government contracts.

Small Business Investment Company (p. 184) (SBIC) licensed by the Small Business Administration to offer loans to small businesses.

smart cards (p. 263) plastic cards that store encrypted information on embedded computer chips rather than magnetic strips; among the most popular methods of Internet payment.

social audit (p. 60) formal procedure that identifies and evaluates all company activities that relate to social issues such as conservation, employment practices, environmental protection, and philanthropy.

social responsibility (pp. 38, 60) management philosophy that highlights the social and economic effects of managerial decisions; management's acceptance of the obligation to consider profit, consumer satisfaction, and societal well-being of equal value in evaluating the firm's performance.

socialism (p. A–3) planned economic system characterized by government ownership and operation of all major industries.

socio-emotional role (p. 368) devoting time and energy to supporting the emotional needs of team members and to maintaining the team as a social unit.

software (p. 629) the sets of instructions that tell the computer hardware what to do.

sole proprietorship (p. 194) form of business ownership in which the company is owned by one person.

span of management (p. 314) number of subordinates a manager can supervise effectively.

specialty advertising (p. 595) a company gives away useful merchandise carrying its name, logo, or business slogan.

sponsorship (p. 592) providing funds for a sporting or cultural event in exchange for a direct association with the event.

spreadsheet (p. 632) the computerized equivalent of an accountant's worksheet; software package that creates the computerized equivalent of an accountant's worksheet, allowing the user to manipulate variables and see the impact of alternative decisions on operating results.

staff manager (p. 315) provides information, advice, or technical assistance to aid line managers; does not have the authority to give orders, outside his/her own department or to compel line managers to take action.

statement of cash flows (p. 662) a statement of a firm's cash receipts and cash payments that presents information on its sources and uses of cash.

stock exchange (p. 717) centralized marketplace where primarily common stocks are traded.

stock options (p. 364) rights to buy a specified amount of the company's stock at a given price within a given time period.

stockholder (p. 199) person who owns shares of stock in a corporation and is entitled to a portion of its profits.

strategic alliance (pp. 25, 154) a partnership formed to create competitive advantage for the businesses involved; an international business strategy in which a company finds a partner in the country where it wants to do business.

strategic planning (p. 293) the process of determining the primary objectives of an organization and then adopting courses of action and allocating resources to achieve those objectives.

strike (p. 412) temporary work stoppage by employees until a dispute is settled or a contract signed.

strikebreaker (p. 414) nonunion workers who cross picket lines to fill the jobs of striking workers.

subcontracting (p. 148) involves hiring local companies to produce, distribute, or sell goods or services.

supercomputer (p. 628) a powerful mainframe that can handle extremely rapid, complex calculations involving thousands of variables, most commonly in scientific research settings.

supervisory management (p. 287) first-line management; includes positions such as supervisor, line manager, and group leader; responsible for assigning non-managerial employees to specific jobs and evaluating their performance every day.

supply (p. 85) willingness and ability of sellers to provide goods and services for sale.

supply chain (p. 563) complete sequence of suppliers that contribute to creating and delivering a good or service.

supply curve (p. 89) graphically shows the relationship between different prices and the quantities that sellers will offer for sale, regardless of demand; generally slope upward, reflecting that as prices rise, the quantities sellers are willing to supply decreases.

SWOT analysis (p. 298) an organized method of assessing a company's internal strengths and weaknesses and its external opportunities and threats.

tactical planning (p. 294) involves implementing the activities specified by strategic plans.

target market (p. 470) group of people toward whom an organization markets its goods, services, or ideas with a strategy designed to satisfy their specific needs and preferences.

tariff (p. 140) tax imposed on imported goods.

task-specialist role (p. 368) devoting time and energy to helping the team accomplish its specific goals.

tax (p. A–22) assessment used to produce income for government.

team (p. 365) group of employees who are committed to a common purpose, approach, and set of performance goals.

team cohesiveness (p. 372) extent to which team members feel attracted to the team and motivated to remain a part of it.

team norm (p. 373) informal standard of conduct shared by team members that guides their behavior.

team selling (p. 603) joins salespeople with specialists from other functional areas of the firm to complete the selling process.

teamwork (p. 364) practice of organizing groups of people to work together to achieve a common objective.

technical skills (p. 288) the manager's ability to understand and use techniques, knowledge, and tools and equipment of a specific discipline or department.

technology (p. 20) business applications of knowledge based on scientific discoveries, inventions, and innovations.

telemarketing (p. 602) personal selling conducted entirely by telephone, which provides a firm's marketers with a high return on their expenditures, an immediate response, and an opportunity for personalized, two-way conversation.

test marketing (p. 512) trial introduction of a new product, supported by a complete marketing campaign, to a selected area with a population typical of the total market.

Theory X (p. 346) assumption that employees dislike work and will try to avoid it.

Theory Y (p. 346) assumption that employees enjoy work and seek social, esteem, and self-actualization fulfillment.

Theory Z (p. 347) assumption that employee involvement is key to productivity and quality of work life.

360-degree performance review (p. 335) a process that gathers feedback from a review panel of several people, including co-workers, supervisors, managers, and sometimes customers.

top management (p. 286) managers at the highest level of the management pyramid; chief executive officer, chief operating officer, and executive vice president; devote most of their time developing long-range plans for their organizations.

total quality management (TQM) (p. 360) companywide program for improving the quality of goods and services by achieving world-class performance and customer satisfaction.

trade show (p. 596) shows that are often organized by industry trade associations, typically during annual meetings or conventions; manufacturers and importers often host or exhibit at them to promote goods or services to members of their distribution channels.

trademark (p. 514) a brand with legal protection against another company's use, not only of the brand name but also of pictorial designs, slogans, packaging elements, and product features such as color and shape.

transaction management (p. 24) concentration on building and promoting products in hopes that enough customers will buy them to cover costs and earn acceptable profits.

transaction marketing (p. 485) marketing that is characterized by buyer and seller exchanges with limited communications and little or no ongoing relationships between the parties.

treasurer (p. 681) the person who is responsible for all of the company's financing activities, including managing cash, the tax department, and shareholder relations.

underwriting (pp. 696, 710) the process used by insurance companies to determine who to insure and what to charge; the process of purchasing an issue from a firm or government and then reselling it to investors.

unemployment rate (p. 103) an indicator of a nation's economic health, usually expressed as a percentage of the total work force.

union shop (p. 404) employment policy requiring nonunion workers to join a union that represents a firm's workers within a specified period after being hired.

utility (p. 461) want-satisfying power of a good or service.

value (p. 25) the customer's perception of the balance between the positive traits of a good or service and its price.

value-added (p. 462) a good or service that exceeds value expectation because the company has added features, lowered its price, enhanced customer service, or made other improvements that increase customer satisfaction.

vendor-managed inventory (p. 443) a company's decision to hand over their inventory control functions to suppliers.

venture capitalist (pp. 239, 689) organization that provides long-term financing in exchange for an ownership share of firms needing additional capital; business firms or groups of individuals who invest in new and growing firms; raise money from wealthy individuals and institutional investors and invest these funds in promising firms.

vertical channel conflict (p. 562) conflict that occurs between members at different levels in the distribution chain.

vertical merger (p. 201) combines firms operating at different levels in the production and marketing process.

vice-president for financial management (p. 681) the person who is responsible for preparing financial forecasts and analyzing major investment decisions.

virtual private network (VPN) (p. 637) secure connections between two points on the Internet.

virtual reality (p. 635) a program that takes interactive media a step further; lets designers "walk" through a life-size model product before building a physical prototype.

vision (pp. 33, 291) perception of marketplace needs and methods an organization can use to satisfy them.

wages (p. 336) compensation based on an hourly pay rate or the amount of output produced.

warehousing (p. 568) the physical distribution element involves storing products as they move through the distribution channel.

warranty (p. 500) a legal guarantee that a good or service will serve the purpose for which it is intended.

Web host (p. 273) a Web site that allows commercial Web sites a spot on its server for a certain price per month.

Web site (p. 248) integrated document composed of electronic pages that integrate text, graphics, audio, and video elements, as well as hypertext links to other documents.

wheel of retailing (p. 548) theory explaining changes in retailing as a process in which new retailers gain a competitive foothold by offering low prices and limited services, then add services and raise prices, creating opportunities for new low-price competitors.

whistle-blowing (p. 51) employee's disclosure to the media or government authorities of illegal, immoral, or unethical practices of the organization.

wholesaling intermediary (p. 540) channel member that sells goods primarily to retailers, other wholesalers, or business users.

wide area networks (WANs) (p. 624) computer networks that tie larger geographic regions together by using telephone lines and microwave and satellite transmission.

word processing (p. 631) software that uses a computer to type, store, retrieve, edit, and print various types of documents.

work team (p. 366) relatively permanent group of employees with complementary skills who perform the day-to-day work of organizations.

World Bank (p. 142) organization established by industrialized nations to lend money to less-developed and developing countries.

World Trade Organization (WTO) (p. 141) 135-member international institution that monitors GATT agreements and mediates international trade disputes.

World Wide Web (Web or WWW) (pp. 22, 248) collection of resources on the Internet that offers easy access to text, graphics, sound, and other multimedia resources.

CREDITS

FIGURE CREDITS

Figure 1.5 Data from "The Big Picture—Geographics: The World's Online Populations," **cyberatlas.internet.com,** accessed October 25, 2000; Liz Sly, "Mongolia's Nomads Roam World on Internet," *Chicago Tribune*, July 16, 2000, sec. 1, pp. 1, 10.

Figure 1.6 Data from U.S. Census Bureau, "Top Ten Countries with Which the U.S. Trades," accessed at the Census Bureau Web site, **www.census.gov/foreign-trade/www/balance.htm,** August 21, 2000.

Figure 1.7 Data from James Cox, "U.S. Success Draws Envy, Protests," *USA Today*, August 3, 2000, pp. 1B–2B, quoting data from Interbrand.

Figure 1.8 Data from *The World Almanac and Book of Facts 2000* (Mahwah, NJ: World Almanac Books, 1999), p. 113, citing data from the CIA World Factbook.

Figure 2.12 Data from Bureau of Labor Statistics, U.S. Department of Labor, December 1999.

Figure 3.9 Data from Bureau of Labor Statistics, "Consumer Price Indexes: Frequently Asked Questions," April 18, 2000, accessed at the BLS Web site, **http://stats.bls.gov,** September 11, 2000.

Figure 3.11 Adapted from Office of Management and Budget, "A Citizen's Guide to the Federal Budget," Fiscal Year 2001, accessed from the Government Printing Office Web site, **www.access.gpo.gov,** September 11, 2000.

Figure 4.4 Data from Bureau of the Census Foreign Trade Division, "Report FT900 (CB-01-12)," November 2000, downloaded from the Bureau of the Census Web site, **www.census.gov,** January 29, 2001.

Figure 4.7 Data from Transparency International, "Transparency International Releases the Year 2000 Corruption Perception Index," news release, September 13, 2000, accessed at the Transparency International Web site, **www.transparency.de.**

Figure 4.11 Data from *The World Almanac and Book of Facts 2000* (Mahwah NJ: Printmedia, 1999), p. 125.

Figure 5.2 Data from Office of Advocacy, U. S. Small Business Administration, "1999 Small Business Profile: United States," March 8, 2000, accessed from the SBA Web site, **www.sba.gov/advo/stats.**

Figure 5.5 Data from Office of Advocacy, U. S. Small Business Administration, "The Facts about Small Business, 1999," p. 9, accessed from the SBA Web site, **www.sba.gov/advo.**

Figure 5.7 Data from Office of Advocacy, U.S. Small Business Administration, "Minorities in Business," 1999, p. 27, accessed at the SBA Web site, **www.sba.gov/advo.**

Figure 5.8 Data from U.S. Census Bureau, "Statistics about Small Business and Large Business from the U.S. Census Bureau," accessed from the Census Bureau Web site, **www.census.gov/epcd/www/smallbus.html,** October 6, 2000.

Figure 5.12 Courtesy of Alfredo Bencomo.

Figure 6.2 Reprinted with permission of *The Wall Street Journal* from "Rewriting the Rules," by Paulette Thomas, May 22, 2000, Interactive Edition, copyright 2000; permission conveyed through Copyright Clearance Center, Inc.

Figure 6.6 Data from Ewing Marion Kauffman Foundation, "Global Study on Entrepreneurship Reveals Direct Link between Rate of New Business Start-Ups and Economic Growth," new release, June 21, 1999, accessed from the Kauffman Foundation Web site, **www.emkf.org.**

Figure 6.11 Copyright Northwestern Mutual Insurance Company. Reprinted with permission.

Figure 6.13 Data from PricewaterhouseCoopers, "MoneyTree U.S. Report: Full Year & Q4 1999 Results," accessed from the PricewaterhouseCoopers Web site at **www.pwcmoneytree.com,** October 30, 2000.

Figure 7.2 Data from "The World's Online Populations," June 8, 2000, accessed at **http://cyberatlas.internet.com,** June 28, 2000.

Figure 7.7 Data from Lauren Gibbons Paul, "The Biggest Gamble Yet," *CIO*, April 15, 2000, pp. 144–148+, citing data from Gary Lapidus's *E-Automotive Report* and Goldman Sachs Investment Research.

Figure 7.11 Courtesy of TRUSTe, **www.truste.org.**

Figure 7.12 Data from "Where Are You on the Web?" *Fast Company*, October 1999, pp. 300–302+.

Figure 9.5 Data from William J. Wiatrowski, "Tracking Changes in Benefit Costs," *Compensation and Working Conditions* (U.S. Department of Labor), Spring 1999, pp. 32–37.

Figure 9.6 Bret Begun, "USA: The Way We'll Live Then," *Newsweek*, January 1, 2000, pp. 34–35.

Figure 11.1 U.S. Department of Labor, "Employment and Earnings," January 2000; Bureau of Labor Statistics, "Employee Benefits in Medium and Large Private Establishments," Bulletin 2517; graphs prepared by the AFL–CIO and published at "The Union Difference," AFL–CIO Web site, **www.aflcio.org,** accessed March 10, 2001.

Figure 11.2 Courtesy of Cedar Point. Photographed by Dan Feicht, Cedar Point.

Figure 11.3 U.S. Department of Labor, "Employment and Earnings," January 2000.

Figure 11.11 Courtesy of The Selmer Company, Inc.

Figure 13.1 Courtesy of Geox-Nottingham Italia.

Figure 14.13 Data from Association of American Publishers and Accenture (formerly Andersen Consulting). Reprinted from *Forbes*, August 21, 2000, p. 134. Reprinted by permission of Forbes Magazine ©2001 Forbes Inc.

Figure 16.3 Data from *Advertising Age International* Global Media Map 2000, special pull-out advertising supplement.

Figure 16.6 Percentages based on data in "Media" *Marketing News,* July 3, 2000, p.13.

Figure 16.8 Data from Peter Breen, "Seeds of Change," *Promo,* Industry Report supplement, May 2000, pp. A3–A6, A25.

Figure 17.1 Federal Reserve System data, reported in "Coming Soon to a Plug Near You," *U.S. News & World Report,* November 13, 2000, p. 16.

Figure 17.2 Data from "Why You Feel the Way You Do," *Inc.,* January 1999, p. 70.

Figure 17.5 Data from Ian S. Hayes, President, Clarity Consulting Inc., Hamilton, Massachusetts, in Jane Salodof MacNeil, "Tracking Tech Time," *Inc. Technology,* no. 4, 2000, page 29.

Figure 17.11 Data from Computer Emergency Response Team, "CERT/CC Statistics: Number of Incidents Reported, 1988–2000," **www.cert.org,** accessed March 30, 2001.

Figure 18.4 Courtesy of Virtual Growth, Incorporated

Figure 20.4 Data from Johnson and Johnson, downloaded from **www.jnj.com** on March 4, 2001.

Figure 20.9 Data from Investment Company Institute, downloaded from **www.ici.org** on March 4, 2001.

TABLE CREDITS

Table 4.1 Data from Borgna Brunner, ed., *The Time Almanac 2000* (Boston: Information Please, 1999), pp. 154–155.

Table 4.2 Data from *The World Almanac and Book of Facts 2000* (Mahwah NJ: Printmedia, 1999), p. 711.

Table 4.3 Data from "Foreign Exchange Rates," *The Wall Street Journal,* accessed from the Interactive Edition, **http://interactive.wsj.com.**

Table 4.6 Data from "Global 500: The World's Largest Corporations," *Fortune,* July 24, 2000, p. F1.

Table 10.1 Based on "ESOPs or Stock Options: Which will Work for Your Company?" accessed at the National Center for Employee Ownership Web site, **www.nceo.org,** March 20, 2001; and Scott Rodrick, "A Tale of Two Acronyms: An 'Employee Stock Option Plan' Is Not an ESOP!" National Center for Employee Ownership Web site, **www.nceo.org,** August 1997.

Table 14.2 Reported in "Car Talk," downloaded from **http://cartalk.cars.com/About/Worts-Cars,** March 4, 2001.

Table 15.2 Data on transportation expenditures from U.S. Census Bureau, *Statistical Abstract of the United States: 1999,* pp. 654, 656, 658, 661, 669.

Table A.1 U.S. Census Bureau, *Statistical Abstract of the United States: 2000* (Washington, DC: U.S. Government Printing Office, 2001), p. 649.

Table A.2 Adapted from Louis E. Boone, David L. Kurtz, and Douglas Hearth, *Planning Your Financial Future,* 2nd ed. (Fort Worth, TX: Harcourt, Inc., 2000), p. 297.

Table A.3 Adapted from Louis E. Boone, David L. Kurtz, and Douglas Hearth, *Planning Your Financial Future,* 2nd ed. (Fort Worth, TX: Harcourt, Inc., 2000), p. 354.

EXPERIENTIAL EXERCISE CREDITS

Chapter 2 Lockheed Martin Corporation's, *The Ethics Challenge.* Reprinted with permission.

Chapter 9 Mulvey, Ledford, LeBlanc, "Rewards of Work: How They Drive Performance, Retention and Satisfaction," *WorldatWork Journal,* Third Quarter 2000, pp. 6–18. Used with permission.

Chapter 15 eCompany Now, Inc., a wholly owned subsidiary of Time, Inc. Principal Office: 1 California Street, San Francisco, CA 94111.

Chapter 20 This article was written by WetFeet.com, Inc., a provider of independent research and information about companies, industries and careers, and has been reprinted with permission. Copyright ©2001, WetFeet.com, Inc. For further information about this or other career-related topics, please visit **www.wetfeet.com,** call (800) 926-4562, or send an e-mail to **info@wetfeet.com.** Reprinted with permission.

PHOTO CREDITS

Page 5 ©Marnie Crawford Samuelson.

Page 45 ©Chuck Savage/The Stock Market.

Page 54 ©AP/WideWorld Photos.

Page 83 Courtesy of U.S. Sports Camps.

Page 121 ©Chuck Savage/The Stock Market.

Page 167 Courtesy of Ritz Foods International, Inc.

Page 170 Courtesy of Powells.com.

Page 171 ©Hosea Johnson.

Page 175 ©Sam Holden.

Page 178 ©Bil Zelman.

Page 211 ©Ed Bock/The Stock Market.

Page 214 Courtesy of Jamaican Jerk Hut.

Page 215 ©Alan Jakubek.

Page 218 Kingston Technology Company, Inc.

Page 221 ©Bob Berg.

Page 227 ©Michael Romanos.

Page 235 Courtesy of Clown Shoes and Props, Inc.

Page 247 Courtesy of Razorfish, Inc.

Page 288 ©Mark Asnin/SABA.

Page 290 ©Mark Peterson—SABA.

Page 325 ©2001 Brian Smith.

Page 348 ©Robert Wright.

Page 351 ©Phillippe Diederich.

Page 359 ©Mug Shots/The Stock Market.

Page 360 ©Jay Reed.

Page 383 ©Michael Grecco.

Page 397 ©AP Photo/Nick Ut.

Page 427 ©Steve Ahlgren.

Page 438 ©Macduff Everton.

Page 459 ©AP Photo/Dan Loh.

NAME INDEX

INTERNATIONAL INDEX

Instructor's Resources
at www.contemporarybusiness.com

MONTHLY NEWSLETTER
Be sure to visit the *Contemporary Business* Web site and register to receive your monthly e-newsletter that will keep you up-to-date on the latest examples to be used with the text.

"GIMME AN A" TESTING SERVICE
Gimme an A gives instructors and students access to a huge database of questions that enables them to create quizzes or be quizzed based on the topic they choose.

"CLASS ACT" COURSE MANAGEMENT SYSTEM
Available for qualified adopters, this system includes a Syllabus Generator function, a Gradebook function, a Class Messaging function, and a Quizzing function. Choose the features you want to import into your current system or opt to use the entire class management system.

BULLETIN BOARD
Visit the Bulletin Board to share ideas and suggestions about the exciting world of *Contemporary Business.*

ADDITIONAL INSTRUCTOR MATERIALS
Supplementary materials to accompany *Contemporary Business* are now available for download.